Lecture Notes in Computer Science 14342

The series Lecture Notes in Computer Science (LNCS), including its subseries Lecture Notes in Artificial Intelligence (LNAI) and Lecture Notes in Bioinformatics (LNBI), has established itself as a medium for the publication of new developments in computer science and information technology research, teaching, and education.

LNCS enjoys close cooperation with the computer science R & D community, the series counts many renowned academics among its volume editors and paper authors, and collaborates with prestigious societies. Its mission is to serve this international community by providing an invaluable service, mainly focused on the publication of conference and workshop proceedings and postproceedings. LNCS commenced publication in 1973.

Jing Deng · Vladimir Kolesnikov ·
Alexander A. Schwarzmann
Editors

Cryptology and Network Security

22nd International Conference, CANS 2023
Augusta, GA, USA, October 31 – November 2, 2023
Proceedings

Springer

Editors
Jing Deng
University of North Carolina
Greensboro, NC, USA

Vladimir Kolesnikov
Georgia Institute of Technology
Atlanta, GA, USA

Alexander A. Schwarzmann
Augusta University
Augusta, GA, USA

ISSN 0302-9743 ISSN 1611-3349 (electronic)
Lecture Notes in Computer Science
ISBN 978-981-99-7562-4 ISBN 978-981-99-7563-1 (eBook)
https://doi.org/10.1007/978-981-99-7563-1

This Springer imprint is published by the registered company Springer Nature Singapore Pte Ltd.
The registered company address is: 152 Beach Road, #21-01/04 Gateway East, Singapore 189721, Singapore

Paper in this product is recyclable.

Preface

The International Conference on Cryptology and Network Security (CANS) is a premier forum for presenting research in the field of cryptology and network security. The conference includes in its scope original contributions from academic, industry, and government institutions on all theoretical and practical cryptology and network security aspects.

This volume contains the papers presented at the 22nd International Conference on Cryptology and Network Security (CANS), which was held in Augusta, Georgia, USA from October 31st through November 2nd, 2023. The conference was run in cooperation with the International Association for Cryptologic Research (IACR).

The conference received 54 submissions, reviewed by the Program Committee of 43 cryptography and security experts, including the two Program Chairs. The committee's work was complemented by the contributions of 27 external reviewers. Out of these 54 submissions, 25 papers were accepted for presentation at the conference and publication in the proceedings. Papers were reviewed in the usual double-blind fashion. Program committee members were limited to two submissions, and their submissions were scrutinized more closely. The two program chairs were not allowed to submit papers.

The program also included two keynote addresses by Eric Toler, the Director of Georgia Cyber Center, and Vitaly Shmatikov, a Professor at Cornell Tech working on security of ML and censorship resistance.

CANS is relatively unique in that it aims to bring together researchers in both cryptography and security. While the PC's expertise evenly covered areas of both security and cryptography, we saw notably more crypto submissions, which is reflected in the final program. We would like to encourage more security submissions in future years.

Co-located with CANS, an International Workshop on Challenges in Cybersecurity Education was held on October 30th, 2023. The program included several invited presentations and a panel.

We express our sincere gratitude to all authors who submitted their work to the conference. We gratefully acknowledge the substantial effort of the track chairs and the Program Committee members invested in paper selection. Thanks are also due to the external reviewers for their valuable and insightful comments. We also thank the Steering Committee members for their valuable advice and guidance. Special thanks go to the Organizing Committee members for their work in ensuring a successful and pleasant meeting, including Caroline Eaker, Luca Mariot, Michelle McMolin, Michael Nowatkowski, Reza Rahaeimehr, Joanne Sexton, Edward Tremel, and Regina White.

We acknowledge with gratitude the highly professional editors and staff at Springer who have guided us in the production of these proceedings.

We also thank our sponsors: Augusta University, Georgia Cyber Center, and the National Science Foundation. Their generous support covered several student travel stipends and helped minimize registration fees, including reduced registration for all students.

Lastly, a big thanks to everyone who attended CANS 2023 and explored the slightly less beaten path, Augusta, Georgia – we hope you enjoyed the conference and your stay. The choice of this location is not entirely accidental: in addition to being one of the golf capitals of the world, Augusta was listed in recent years by *Fortune* magazine and *CSO Online* among 10 cities that could become the world's next Cybersecurity Capital due to the substantial momentum in cybersecurity in the area.

November 2023

Jing Deng
Vladimir Kolesnikov
Alexander A. Schwarzmann

Organization

General Chair

Alex Schwarzmann	Augusta University, USA

Program Committee Chairs

Jing Deng	UNC Greensboro, USA
Vlad Kolesnikov	Georgia Tech, USA

Steering Committee

Yvo G. Desmedt (Chair)	University of Texas, USA
Sara Foresti	Università degli Studi di Milano, Italy
Amir Herzberg	University of Connecticut, USA
Juan A. Garay	Texas A&M University, USA
Atsuko Miyaji	Osaka University, Japan
Panos Papadimitratos	KTH, Sweden
David Pointcheval	ENS, France
Huaxiong Wang	Nanyang Technological University, Singapore

Organizing Committee

Caroline Eaker	Augusta University, USA
Luca Mariot (Publicity Chair)	University of Twente, The Netherlands
Michelle McMolin	Augusta University, USA
Jeff Morris	Augusta University, USA
Michael Nowatkowski	Augusta University, USA
Meikang Qiu	Augusta University, USA
Reza Rahaeimehr (Web)	Augusta University, USA
Alex Schwarzmann (Chair)	Augusta University, USA
Joanne Sexton	Augusta University, USA
Edward Tremel	Augusta University, USA
Zi Wang	Augusta University, USA
Regina White	Augusta University, USA
Shungeng Zhang	Augusta University, USA

Program Committee

Cristina Alcaraz	University of Malaga, Spain
Subhadeep Banik	University of Lugano, Switzerland
Carlo Blundo	Università degli Studi di Salerno, Italy
Bo Chen	Michigan Technological University, USA
Arka Rai Choudhuri	Johns Hopkins University, USA
Sherman S. M. Chow	Chinese University of Hong Kong, China
Bei-Tseng Chu	UNC Charlotte, USA
Michele Ciampi	University of Edinburgh, UK
Bernardo David	IT University of Copenhagen, Denmark
Jing Deng	UNC Greensboro, USA
Shlomi Dolev	Ben-Gurion University of the Negev, Israel
Pooya Farshim	Durham University, UK
Satrajit Ghosh	IIT Kharagpur, India
Yong Guan	Iowa State University, USA
Zhou Haifeng	Zhejiang University, China
David Heath	UIUC, USA
Ashwin Jha	CISPA Helmholtz Center for Information Security, Germany
Elif Bilge Kavun	University of Passau, Germany
Vladimir Kolesnikov	Georgia Institute of Technology, USA
Ranjit Kumaresan	Visa Inc, USA
Shangqi Lai	Monash University, Australia
Riccardo Lazzeretti	Sapienza University of Rome, Italy
David Mohaisen	University of Central Florida, USA
Sergio Pastrana	Universidad Carlos III de Madrid, Spain
Sikhar Patranabis	IBM Research India, India
Constantinos Patsakis	University of Piraeus, Greece
Giuseppe Persiano	Università degli Studi di Salerno, Italy
Josef Pieprzyk	CSIRO/Data61, Australia
Lawrence Roy	Aarhus University, Denmark
Somitra Sanadhya	IIT Jodhpur, India
Dominique Schroeder	Friedrich-Alexander-Universität Erlangen-Nürnberg, Germany
Alberto Sonnino	Mysten Labs, UK
Angelo Spognardi	Sapienza Università di Roma, Italy
Christoph Striecks	AIT Austria, Austria
Ajith Suresh	Technology Innovation Institute, UAE
Willy Susilo	University of Wollongong, Australia
Ni Trieu	Arizona State University, USA

Giorgos Vasiliadis	Hellenic Mediterranean University and FORTH-ICS, Greece
Daniele Venturi	Sapienza University of Rome, Italy
Ivan Visconti	University of Salerno, Italy
Isabel Wagner	University of Basel, Switzerland
Edgar Weippl	University of Vienna, Austria
Yibin Yang	Georgia Institute of Technology, USA

Additional Reviewers

Avitabile, Gennaro
Botta, Vincenzo
Chauhan, Amit Kumar
Chen, Niusen
Choi, Gwangbae
Chu, Hien Thi Thu
Collins, Daniel
Dodd, Charles
Dutta, Priyanka
Fu, Huirong
Gerhart, Paul
Harasser, Patrick
Huguenin-Dumittan, Loïs
Kondi, Yashvanth
Neisarian, Shekoufeh
Pan, Ying-Yu
Ronge, Viktoria
Roy, Partha Sarathi
Sato, Shingo
Siniscalchi, Luisa
Slamanig, Daniel
Spyrakou, Marianna
Talayhan, Abdullah
Volkhov, Mikhail
Wu, Huangting
Xu, Depeng
Zecchini, Marco

Keynote Abstracts

Building Covert Communication Systems That Resist Traffic Analysis

Vitaly Shmatikov

Cornell Tech, USA
shmat@cs.cornell.edu

Covert, censorship-resistant communication in the presence of nation-state adversaries requires unobservable channels whose operation is difficult to detect via network-traffic analysis. One promising approach is traffic substitution: use an already-existing encrypted channel established by some application and replace that application's data with covert content.

In this talk, I will explain the challenges of traffic substitution and show how substitution channels can fail even against simple network adversaries. I will then discuss our experience designing and implementing Telepath, a new Minecraft-based covert communication system. Finally, I will present general principles for building covert channels that resist traffic analysis.

Cultivating a National Culture of Cybersecurity

Eric Toler

Georgia Cyber Center, USA
TTOLER@augusta.edu

Global cyber threats are outpacing the ability of Western democracies to mitigate or defeat those threats. The cyber capabilities of adversarial nation states have vastly improved in the last decade while cybercrime is set to become the third largest economy in the world by 2025. At the same time, the global cyber workforce gap continues to grow at an alarming pace. These trends, coupled with sluggish bureaucratic reaction speed, will nullify the U.S. and its ally's dominance in the information environment in the next few years – unless we do things differently. This presentation will highlight why the status quo has led to many national shortcomings in cybersecurity and discuss why it is an existential imperative to start cultivating a national culture of cybersecurity today.

Contents

MPC with Cards

Cryptanalysis

Blockchain

MPC and Secret Sharing

Schemes II

Schemes I

Forward Security Under Leakage Resilience, Revisited

Suvradip Chakraborty[1](✉), Harish Karthikeyan[2], Adam O'Neill[3], and C. Pandu Rangan[4]

[1] Visa Research, Palo Alto, CA, USA
suvchakr@visa.com
[2] J.P. Morgan AI Research, New York, USA
harish.karthikeyan@jpmchase.com
[3] Manning College of Information and Computer Sciences, University of Massachusetts Amherst, Amherst, USA
adamo@cs.umass.edu
[4] Kotak Mahindra, IISc Bangalore, Bengaluru, India

Abstract. As both notions employ the same key-evolution paradigm, Bellare *et al.* (CANS 2017) study combining forward security with leakage resilience. The idea is for forward security to serve as a hedge in case at some point the full key gets exposed from the leakage. In particular, Bellare *et al.* combine forward security with *continual* leakage resilience, dubbed FS+CL. Our first result improves on Bellare *et al.*'s FS+CL secure PKE scheme by building one from any continuous leakage-resilient binary-tree encryption (BTE) scheme; in contrast, Bellare *et al.* require extractable witness encryption. Our construction also preserves leakage rate of the underlying BTE scheme and hence, in combination with existing CL-secure BTE, yields the first FS+CL secure encryption scheme with optimal leakage rate from standard assumptions.

We next explore combining forward security with other notions of leakage resilience. Indeed, as argued by Dziembowski *et al.* (CRYPTO 2011), it is desirable to have a *deterministic* key-update procedure, which FS+CL does not allow for arguably pathological reasons. To address this, we combine forward security with *entropy-bounded* leakage (FS+EBL). We construct FS+EBL non-interactive key exchange (NIKE) with deterministic key update based on indistinguishability obfuscation ($i\mathcal{O}$), and DDH or LWE. To make the public keys constant size, we rely on the Superfluous Padding Assumption (SuPA) of Brzuska and Mittelbach (ePrint 2015) *without* auxiliary information, making it more plausible. SuPA notwithstanding, the scheme is also the first FS-secure NIKE from $i\mathcal{O}$ rather than multilinear maps. We advocate a future research agenda that uses FS+EBL as a hedge for FS+CL, whereby a scheme achieves the latter if key-update randomness is good and the former if not.

H. Karthikeyan—Work done while at New York University, New York, USA.
C. P. Rangan—Research partially supported by KIAC research grant.

J. Deng et al. (Eds.): CANS 2023, LNCS 14342, pp. 3–27, 2023.
https://doi.org/10.1007/978-981-99-7563-1_1

1 Introduction

1.1 Background and Motivation

Leakage Resilience. When a cryptographic algorithm is implemented and run, it must be done on some *physical* system. This introduces *side channel* attacks where the adversary obtains some leakage about secrets, via execution time, power consumption, and even sound waves [23,30,31]. The cryptographic community responded by extending the attack model so that the adversary gets some "bounded" leakage about the secrets [2,9,29,36]. Works further extended this new model to consider "continual" leakage (CL) attacks [10,14]. In that model, the life of a secret key is divided into time periods, and in time period $t+1$ one runs an update algorithm on the secret key of time period t to derive the new secret key for time period $t+1$. (The old secret key is erased.) In each time period, the adversary queries for a function with a bounded output length applied to the current secret key.

Forward Security. *Forward security* (FS) [5] employs the same key-evolution paradigm as CL to address the threat of exposure of the secret key *in whole.* This can happen due to too much leakage. If a break-in happens during time period i, it is required that security still holds relative to keys in time periods $1 \leq i' < i$. Initial work on forward security has been extended and optimized in numerous works, *e.g.* [1,7,8,21,22,27,32,35].

Combining Leakage Resilience and Forward Security. As advocated by Bellare *et al.* [6], one ought to use FS as a hedge in the context of leakage resilience. Specifically, one would like to "fall back" to forward security if the secret key at every time period up to some i' is partially leaked, but then in time period i' the leakage happens to be so much that this time period's entire key is revealed. This combination of forward security and continual leakage resilience was dubbed FS+CL by Bellare *et al.* [6]. For constructions, Bellare *et al.* start by examining tree-based constructs as in [5] and give such a construction of FS+CL signatures based on CL-signatures. They also provide a generic approach to construct FS+CL encryption and signature schemes by combining what they call a key-evolution scheme (KE) that is forward one-way under continual-leakage (FOWCL KE) with witness primitives, namely (extractable) witness encryption [20] and witness signatures [4,13] respectively.

1.2 Our Contributions in Brief

Our Goals. Extractable witness encryption is a suspect assumption [19] that we would like to eliminate. We would also like to improve the leakage rates of the Bellare *et al.*'s schemes. Finally, we would like to study complementary notions of leakage resilience in this context. In this paper, we focus on asymptotic efficiency and feasibility rather than practical efficiency. The design of more practical constructions is an interesting question for future work.

Improved FS+CL Encryption Scheme. We improve upon Bellare *et al.*'s FS+CL PKE scheme by carefully re-examining tree-based constructs. In particular, in their effort to construct FS+CL PKE, Bellare *et al.* explicitly dismissed the idea of using a CL-secure binary-tree encryption (BTE) [12], because the underlying hierarchical identity-based encryption scheme (HIBE) scheme must tolerate *joint* leakage on multiple keys, whereas CL-security only allows leakage on each such key *individually*. We show this intuition is *false* and construct an FS+CL-secure PKE scheme from any CL-secure BTE scheme. This, in turn, can be realized from any CL-secure HIBE. CL-secure HIBE is known from simple assumptions on composite-order bilinear groups [10].

We also show that our construction preserves the leakage rate of the base scheme. Hence, we obtain FS+CL encryption enjoying optimal leakage rate from standard assumptions.

Alternative Models: FS+(C)EBL. Dziembowski *et al.* [17] argue it is desirable to have a deterministic key-update procedure. Indeed, randomness generation in practice can be buggy, either subverted or by poor implementation. CL does not guarantee any security in such a case, as there is a trivial attack under it if key-update is deterministic: the adversary just leaks some future key bit-by-bit across time periods. Yet this attack is arguably contrived; if the key-update procedure is a complicated cryptographic operation, it's unlikely real-world leakage would compute it, let alone a non-noisy version of it. Accordingly, we seek meaningful security notion that can be achieved when key-update is deterministic.

At a high-level, we combine forward security with *entropic bounded leakage* (EBL) [36] instead of CL. To this end, we introduce a model called FS+EBL (pronounced *ee-bull*). The FS+EBL model is defined with respect to any key evolving scheme equipped with an update function. Our definition requires forward security in the presence of leakage such that the current key always meets an entropy bound. In particular, we require that the secret key in each time period prior to the period of exposure retain enough residual entropy conditioned on the leakage from each of the keys.

Such a restriction on key entropy seems overly severe, however, and motivates additional consideration of *computational entropy*. The point is that if considering information-theoretic entropy, leakage on the current key necessarily reduces the entropy of all other keys. But consider leaking (noisy) hamming weight or physical bits of the current key, or even some one-way function of the key. After an appropriate update function is applied, it is plausible that the computational entropy of the new key is restored. To profit in such a case, we introduce the FS+*C*EBL (pronounced *see-bull*—'C' for computational) that parallels FS+EBL but uses computational entropy.

FS+EBL and FS+CEBL NIKE. Broadening our set of primitives considered, we study non-interactive key exchange (NIKE) in the FS+(C)EBL model. We give an FS+EBL-secure NIKE in the common reference string (CRS) model from indistinguishability obfuscation ($i\mathcal{O}$), either DDH or LWE and a relaxed variant of the *Superfluous Padding Assumption* (SuPA) on $i\mathcal{O}$ introduced in [11].

We remark that, before this work, even *FS*-NIKE was not known from $i\mathcal{O}$. Similar to the prior FS-NIKE construction from multilinear maps [37], our construction of FS+EBL NIKE supports an a-priori bounded (but an arbitrary polynomial) number of time periods. However, our construction achieves much better parameters than the construction of [37]. In particular, the size of the public parameter in [37] is $O(T)$, the secret key size is $O(\log T)$, and the public key size is constant (here T denotes the maximum number of time periods supported by the scheme). In contrast, our FS+EBL NIKE achieves constant-size secret keys and public parameters, and the size of our public keys is $O(\log T)$. Ours also enjoys an optimal leakage rate. Hence, relaxed SuPA notwithstanding, our construction improves on [37].

NIKE in FS+CEBL Model. A nice feature of our FS+EBL NIKE construction is that the key update function can be instantiated by any entropic-leakage resilient one-way function [9]. In the FS+CEBL setting, we suggest using the PRG of Zhandry [39], because it is secure for any computationally unpredictable seed. The issue is that leakage from time period i could leak from secret key $i+1$ which is the output of the PRG. Existing results do not explore the case where the output of the PRG is also susceptible to leakage. We leave constructing FS+CEBL NIKE for future work.

Discussion. A drawback of FS+EBL and FS+CEBL is that they are *scheme-dependent*. This is because the entropy bound is required to hold with respect to the *specific* update function of the underlying key evolving primitive. Thus, the meaning of these security models in practice remains somewehat unclear. Therefore, we raise the open question of devising a notion combining forward security and leakage resilience that (1) admits schemes with deterministic key update, and (2) is *not* scheme dependent. We leave this for future work. Importantly, we conjecture that such a model would *not* deem our FS+EBL NIKE scheme insecure, but rather admit an improved security proof for it. We view our result as a step towards resolution of the above question. Another direction we suggest for future work is to design FS+CL schemes that simultaneously meet FS+(C)EBL or another notion as a hedge when key-update randomness is subverted or buggy.

2 Technical Overview

High-Level Idea of the FS+CL PKE. Recall that a binary-tree encryption (BTE) has a master public key (MPK) associated with the root node of a binary tree and all the nodes have an associated secret key. Moreover, the secret key of any node can be used to derive the secret keys for the children of that node. To encrypt a message for a particular node, one uses MPK and the identity of that node. The security notion requires the attacker to commit to a target node w^* in advance (i.e., before seeing MPK) and it gets the secret keys of all nodes except for those which lie on the path from the root to the "target" node (including both). Under CL, the adversary can also leak continuously from the secrets keys of all these nodes. The goal of the adversary is then to win the indistinguishability game with respect to the target node w^*.

To construct a FS+CL PKE scheme for $T \leq 2^\ell - 1$ time period, we use a continuous leakage-resilient BTE (CLR-BTE) scheme of depth ℓ and associate the time periods with all nodes of the tree according to a *pre-order* traversal.

Let w^i denote the node corresponding to time period i. The public key of the FS+CL PKE scheme consists of the root public key MPK and the secret key for time period i consists of sk_{w^i} (the secret key of w^i) and the secret keys of all right siblings of the nodes on the path from the root to w^i. At the end of time period i the secret key is updated as follows: If w^i is an internal node, then the secret keys of node w^{i+1} (the next node according to the pre-order traversal) and its sibling (i.e., the two children of w^i) are derived; otherwise the secret key for w^{i+1} is already stored as part of the secret key. In either case, sk_{w^i} is erased. The secret keys of the all the nodes corresponding to time period $i+1$ are then refreshed by running the key update algorithm of the underlying CLR-BTE scheme.

Proof Strategy. In our proof, the reduction (which is an adversary $\mathcal{A}_{\mathsf{clr\text{-}bte}}$ of the underlying CLR-BTE scheme) simply guesses the time period i^* in which the FS+CL adversary $\mathcal{A}_{\mathsf{kee}}$ will attack.[1] This corresponds to a challenge node w^{i^*} which $\mathcal{A}_{\mathsf{clr\text{-}bte}}$ forwards to its own challenger. If the guess is incorrect, the reduction aborts outputting a random bit. $\mathcal{A}_{\mathsf{clr\text{-}bte}}$ then receives the secret keys of all the nodes that are right siblings of the nodes that lie in the path $P_{w^{i^*}}$ from the root node to w^{i^*} (the target node) and also the secret keys of both the children of w^{i^*}. Using the knowledge of these keys $\mathcal{A}_{\mathsf{clr\text{-}bte}}$ can simulate the update queries of $\mathcal{A}_{\mathsf{kee}}$. Now, let us see how to simulate the leakage queries of $\mathcal{A}_{\mathsf{kee}}$. Note that, the secret key corresponding to some time period i in the FS+CL scheme is of the form $SK_i = (sk_{w^i}, \{sk_{rs(P_{w^i})}\})$, where sk_{w^i} and $\{sk_{rs(P_{w^i})}\}$ denote the (possibly refreshed versions of the) secret keys corresponding to the node w^i and the right siblings of all the nodes that lie on the path P_{w^i} respectively. Now, either of the following two cases arise: (i) either the node w^i lies in the path $P_{w^{i^*}}$ (the path from root to the target node w^{i^*}) or (ii) w^i does not lie in the path $P_{w^{i^*}}$. In the first case, $\mathcal{A}_{\mathsf{clr\text{-}bte}}$ already knows all the keys $\{sk_{rs(P_{w^i})}\}$ and hence it can translate the leakage function f (queried by $\mathcal{A}_{\mathsf{kee}}$) to a related leakage function f' *only* on the key sk_{w^i} (by hard-wiring the keys $\{sk_{rs(P_{w^i})}\}$ into f'). For the later case, $\mathcal{A}_{\mathsf{clr\text{-}bte}}$ knows the key sk_{w^i} and all the keys $\{sk_{rs(P_{w^i})}\}$, except exactly one key corresponding to a node w that lies in the path $P_{w^{i^*}}$. So, $\mathcal{A}_{\mathsf{clr\text{-}bte}}$ can again translate the joint leakage function f to leakage just on the secret key of node w.

To summarize, the key observation is that: in either case, the reduction knows the secret keys of all nodes except one, and hence it can simulate the joint leakage by leaking only on one node at a time. However, the adversary may also get multiple (continuous) leakages on the secret key of a node. For e.g., consider the secret key sk_1 (corresponding to the right child of the root node). The secret key sk_1 is included in each secret key sk_{0w} for any suffix w. However, note that, when the secret keys from one time period are updated to the next time period they are also refreshed by running the underlying key refresh algorithm of the CLR-BTE scheme. Hence the CLR property of the BTE scheme allows us to tolerate multiple leakages on the same node by making use of its leakage oracle.

[1] We stress that our scheme supports an *exponential* number of time periods; however, the adversary can only run for a polynomial number of them. Hence we incur a polynomial security loss in making this guess.

Constructing NIKE in the FS+EBL Model. The starting point of our NIKE construction is the bounded leakage-resilient NIKE construction of [34] (henceforth called the *LMQW protocol*) from indistinguishability obfuscation ($i\mathcal{O}$) and other standard assumptions (DDH/LWE) in the CRS model.

The main idea of the LMQW construction is as follows: Each user samples a random string s as its secret key and sets its public key as $x = G(s)$, where G is a function whose description is a part of the CRS and can be indistinguishably created in either *lossy* or in *injective* mode. In the real construction, the function G is set to be injective. To generate a shared key with an user j, user i inputs its own key pair (x_i, s_i) and the public key x_j of user j to an obfuscated program $\widehat{C}$ (which is also included as part of the CRS) which works as follows: The circuit C (which is obfuscated) simply checks if s_i is a valid pre-image of either x_i or x_j under G, i.e., it checks if either $x_i = G(s_i)$ or $x_j = G(s_i)$. If so, it returns $\mathsf{PRF}_K(x_i, x_j)$ (where the PRF key K is embedded inside the obfuscated program); else it outputs $\perp$.

Lifting the LMQW Protocol to the FS Setting. It is easy to see that the LMQW protocol is *not* forward-secure. This is because, each public key is an injective function of its corresponding secret key, and hence if a secret key s is updated to s', the public key no longer stays the same. We now describe how to modify the above construction to achieve security in the FS+EBL setting. Similarly to the LMQW protocol, the (initial) secret key of each user i in our construction is also a random string $s_i^{(1)}$. The CRS also contains the description of the obfuscated program $\widehat{C}$ and the function G (as described above). However, the public key of each party i is now an obfuscated circuit $\widehat{C_i}$ (corresponding to a circuit C_i, whose size is determined later) which has the initial/root secret key $s_i^{(1)}$ (corresponding to base time period 1) of party i embedded in it. It takes as input a key $s_j^{(t)}$ of user j (corresponding to some time period t) and works as follows: (a) First, it updates the secret key $s_i^{(1)}$ of user i (hard-coded in it) to $s_i^{(t)}$ by running the (deterministic) NIKE update function (to be defined shortly) $t-1$ times, (b) computes $x_i^{(t)} = G(s_i^{(t)})$ and $x_j^{(t)} = G(s_j^{(t)})$, and finally (c) internally invokes the obfuscated circuit $\widehat{C}$ (included as part of CRS) on input the tuple $(s_j^{(t)}, x_i^{(t)}, x_j^{(t)})$. To generate the shared key with an user i corresponding to time period t, user j runs $\widehat{C_i}$ with input its secret key $s_j^{(t)}$ corresponding to time period t to obtain the shared key $\mathsf{PRF}_K(x_i^{(t)}, x_j^{(t)})$. It is easy to see that user i also derives the same shared key for time period t by running the program $\widehat{C_j}$ (public key of user j) on input its own $s_i^{(t)}$ corresponding to time period t. The key update function for our FS+EBL NIKE can be any entropic-leakage resilient OWF [9]. This is so that it remains hard to compute the prior key even given entropic leakage on the pre-image of the OWF.

Security Proof. The security proof of our construction follows the proof technique of the LMQW protocol with some major differences as explained below. The main idea of the proof of the LMQW protocol follows the punctured programming paradigm [38], where they puncture the PRF key K at the point (x_i, x_j) and program a random output y. However, instead of hard-coding y directly they hard-core $y \oplus s_i$ and $y \oplus s_j$, i.e., the one-time pad encryption of y under s_i and s_j respectively. This allows the obfuscated program to decrypt y given either s_i or s_j as input. At this point, they switch the function G to be in *lossy* mode and argue that the shared key y retain high min-entropy, even given the obfuscated program with hard-coded ciphertexts, the public keys and leakages on the secret keys s_i and s_j. The entropic key k is then converted into a uniformly random string by using an appropriate extractor.

However, for our construction, we *cannot* argue the last step of the above proof, i.e., the shared key y (for time period t) retains enough entropy given all the public information (CRS and public keys) and entropic leakage on the keys. This is because the public keys $\hat{C}_i$ and $\hat{C}_j$ completely determine the keys $s_i^{(t)}$ and $s_j^{(t)}$ respectively, even after switching the function G to be in lossy mode. Indeed, the obfuscated programs $\hat{C}_i$ and $\hat{C}_j$ contains the base secret keys $s_i^{(1)}$ and $s_j^{(1)}$ hard-coded in them, and hence, given the public keys, the secret keys have no entropy left. To this end, we switch the public key $\hat{C}_i$ to an obfuscation of a program that, instead of embedding the base secret key $s_i^{(1)}$ embeds all possible public keys $(x_i^{(1)}, \cdots, x_i^{(T)})$ in it, where T is the total number of time period supported by our scheme and $x_i^{(j)} = G(s_i^{(j)})$ for $j \in [T]$. Note that this program is functionally equivalent but we need to pad C_i up to its size. Now, since, the function G is lossy the shared key y still retains enough entropy, even given the public key. A similar argument can be made for party j. By setting the parameters appropriately, we can prove FS+EBL security of our NIKE construction with optimal leakage rate.

Compressing the Size of the Public Key Using Relaxed SuPA. Note that, in the above proof step we needed to embed T values and hence the public key of each user (which consists of the above obfuscated and padded circuit) scales linearly with T. With linear public key size, FS is trivial. However, what makes our scheme different from the trivial one is that for us this issue is a *proof problem* formally captured via the *Superfluous Padding (SuP) Assumption* [11]. Intuitively the SuP assumption (SuPA) states that if two distributions are indistinguishable relative to an obfuscated circuit C which was padded before obfuscation, then the two distributions are also indistinguishable relative to the obfuscated circuit C without padding. Or in other words, if an obfuscation of a padded circuit hides something, then so does an obfuscation of the unpadded circuit.

Although non-standard, it is shown in [11] that SuPA holds for virtual black-box obfuscation (VBB) as evidence it holds for $i\mathcal{O}$. Unfortunately, as shown in [25], assuming $i\mathcal{O}$ and one-way functions SuPA does not hold for $i\mathcal{O}$ if the distinguisher is given *auxiliary information.* Crucially, we get around this by using a *relaxed* variant of SuPA that does not give the distinguisher auxiliary information. This relaxed SuPA is enough to prove the security of our NIKE construction. We stress the impossibility result of [25] does not apply to this relaxed SuPA, and in fact, we conjecture that, in the absence of any auxiliary information SuPA does hold for $i\mathcal{O}$. In this case, the size of the public keys in our NIKE scheme *is not linear in* T, but is only $O(\log T)$. This is because the obfuscated circuit just needs to know the maximum number of times it will need to update its keys.

3 Preliminaries

3.1 Notations

Let $x \in \mathcal{X}$ denote an element x in the support of $\mathcal{X}$. For a probability distribution $\mathcal{X}$, let $|\mathcal{X}|$ denote the size of the support of $\mathcal{X}$, i.e., $|\mathcal{X}| =| \{x \,|\, \mathsf{Pr}[\mathcal{X} = x] > 0\} |$. If x is a string , we denote $|x|$ as the length of x. Let $x \leftarrow \mathcal{X}$ be the process of sampling x from the distribution $\mathcal{X}$. For $n \in \mathbb{N}$, we write $[n] = \{1, 2, \cdots, n\}$. When A is an algorithm, we write $y \leftarrow A(x)$ to denote a run of A on input x and output y; if A is randomized, then y is a random variable and $A(x; r)$ denotes a run of A on input x and randomness r. An algorithm A is probabilistic polynomial-time (PPT) if A is randomized and for any input $x, r \in \{0,1\}^*$, the computation of $A(x; r)$ terminates in at most $poly(|x|)$ steps. For a set S, we let U_S denote the uniform distribution over S. For an integer $\alpha \in \mathbb{N}$, let U_α denote the uniform distribution over $\{0,1\}^\alpha$, the bit strings of length α. Throughout this paper, we denote the security parameter by κ, which is implicitly taken as input by all the algorithms. For two random variables X and Y drawn from a finite set $\mathcal{X}$, let $\delta(X, Y) = \frac{1}{2}|\sum_{x\in\mathcal{X}} \mathsf{Pr}(X = x) - \mathsf{Pr}(Y = x)|$ denote the statistical distance between them. Given a circuit D, define the computational distance δ^D between X and Y as $\delta^D(X, Y) = |\mathbb{E}[D(X)] - \mathbb{E}[D(Y)]|$.

3.2 Different Notions of Entropy

In this section, we recall some the definitions of information-theoretic and computational notions of entropy that are relevant to this work and also state the results related to them.

Unconditional (Information-Theoretic) Entropy

Definition 1 (Min-entropy). *The min-entropy of a random variable X, denoted as* $\mathrm{H}_\infty(\mathrm{X})$ *is defined as* $\mathrm{H}_\infty(\mathrm{X}) \stackrel{\text{def}}{=} -\log\big(\max_x \Pr[X = x]\big)$.

Definition 2 (Conditional Min-entropy [16]). *The average-conditional min-entropy of a random variable X conditioned on a (possibly) correlated variable Z, denoted as* $\widetilde{\mathrm{H}}_\infty(X|Z)$ *is defined as*

$$\widetilde{\mathrm{H}}_\infty(X|Z) = -\log\big(\mathbb{E}_{z\leftarrow Z}\,[\max_x \Pr[X = x|Z = z]\big) = -\log\big(\mathbb{E}_{z\leftarrow Z}\,[2^{-\mathrm{H}_\infty(X|Z=z)}]\big).$$

Lemma 1 (Chain Rule for min-entropy [16]). *For any random variable X, Y and Z, if Y takes on values in* $\{0,1\}^\ell$, *then*

$$\widetilde{\mathrm{H}}_\infty(X|Y, Z) \geq \widetilde{\mathrm{H}}_\infty(X|Z) - \ell \quad \text{and} \quad \widetilde{\mathrm{H}}_\infty(X|Y) \geq \widetilde{\mathrm{H}}_\infty(X) - \ell.$$

One may also define a more general notion of conditional min-entropy $\widetilde{H}_\infty(X|\mathcal{E})$, where the conditioning happens over an arbitrary experiment $\mathcal{E}$, and not just a "one-time" random variable Y [3].

Computational Entropy a.k.a Pseudo-entropy
Computational entropy or pseudo-entropy is quantified with two parameters- *quality* (i.e., how much distinguishable a random variable is from a source with true min-entropy to a size-bounded (poly-time) distinguisher)) and *quantity* (i.e., number of bits of entropy).

Definition 3 (Hill Entropy [24,26]**).** *A distribution* $\mathcal{X}$ *has* **HILL entropy** *at least* k*, denoted by* $\mathrm{H}^{\mathsf{HILL}}_{\epsilon,s}(\mathcal{X}) \geq k$*, if there exists a distribution* $\mathcal{Y}$*, where* $\mathrm{H}_\infty(\mathcal{Y}) \geq k$*, such that* $\forall \mathcal{D} \in \mathcal{D}^{\mathsf{rand},\{0,1\}}_s$, $\delta^{\mathcal{D}}(\mathcal{X},\mathcal{Y}) \leq \epsilon$*. By,* $\mathcal{D}^{\mathsf{rand},\{0,1\}}_s$ *we refer to the set of all probabilistic circuits without* $\{0,1\}$*.*

Let $(\mathcal{X},\mathcal{Y})$ *be a pair of random variables. Then, we say that* $\mathcal{X}$ *has* **conditional HILL entropy** *at least* k *conditioned on* $\mathcal{Y}$*, denoted* $\mathrm{H}^{\mathsf{HILL}}_{\epsilon,s}(\mathcal{X}|\mathcal{Y}) \geq k$*, if there exists a collection of distributions* $\mathcal{Z}_y$ *for each* $y \in \mathcal{Y}$*, yielding a joint distribution* $(\mathcal{Z},\mathcal{Y})$ *such that* $\widetilde{\mathrm{H}}_\infty(\mathcal{Z}|\mathcal{Y}) \geq k$*, and* $\forall \mathcal{D} \in \mathcal{D}^{\mathsf{rand},\{0,1\}}_s$*,* $\delta^{\mathcal{D}}\big((\mathcal{X},\mathcal{Y}),(\mathcal{Z},\mathcal{Y})\big) \leq \epsilon$*.*

3.3 Primitives Required for Our Constructions.

In this section, we briefly outline the primitives required for our constructions. A puncturable PRF (pPRF) allows one to evaluate the PRF on all but a subset of points (on which the master key is punctured). We require pseudorandomness to hold on the punctured points, even given the punctured key. We also require indistinguishability obfuscation ($i\mathcal{O}$), and lossy functions for our construction of the NIKE protocol in the $\mathsf{FS}+\mathsf{EBL}$ model. We refer the reader to the full version of our paper for the definitions of pPRF, $i\mathcal{O}$, and lossy functions. For our construction of $\mathsf{FS}+\mathsf{EBL}$-secure NIKE protocol, we also require an *entropic leakage-resilient* one-way function (ELR-OWF) to instantiate the update function. We also require the Superfluous padding assumption to hold for $i\mathcal{O}$. Below we present their formal definitions.

Entropic Leakage-Resilient OWF. In this section, we recall the definition of leakage-resilient one-way functions (LR-OWF) from [9]. Informally, a one-way function (OWF) $g : \{0,1\}^n \to \{0,1\}^m$ is leakage-resilient if it remains one-way, even in the presence of some leakage about pre-image. In entropy-bounded leakage model, instead of bounding the length of the output of leakage functions (as in bounded leakage model), we bound the entropy loss that happens due to seeing the output of the leakage functions. We follow the definition of [14] to consider the entropy loss over the uniform distribution as a measure of leakiness. We follow this definition since it has nice composability properties as stated below.

Definition 4 [14]**.** A (probabilistic) function $h : \{0,1\}^* \to \{0,1\}^*$ is ℓ-leaky, if for all $n \in \mathbb{N}$, we have $\widetilde{H}_\infty(U_n|h(U_n)) \geq n - \ell$, where U_n denote the uniform distribution over $\{0,1\}^n$.

As observed in [14], if a function is ℓ-leaky, i.e., it decreases the entropy of uniform distribution by at most ℓ bits, then it decreases the entropy of every distribution by at most ℓ bits. Moreover, this definition composes nicely in the sense that, if the adversary adaptively chooses different ℓ_i-leaky functions, it learns only $\sum_i \ell_i$ bits of information. We now define the security model for weak PRFs in this entropy-bounded leakage model.

Definition 5 (Entropic leakage-resilient one-wayness). *Let $\mathcal{A}$ be an adversary against $g : \{0,1\}^n \to \{0,1\}^m$. We define the advantage of the adversary $\mathcal{A}$ as* $\mathsf{Adv}_{\mathcal{A}}^{\mathsf{LR\text{-}OWF}}(\kappa) = \Pr[g(x) = y \,|\, x^* \xleftarrow{\$} \{0,1\}^n, y^* = g(x^*); x \leftarrow \mathcal{A}^{\mathcal{O}_{\mathsf{Leak}}(\cdot)}(y^*)]$.

Here $\mathcal{O}_{\mathsf{Leak}}$ is an oracle that on input $h : \{0,1\}^n \to \{0,1\}^*$ returns $f(x^*)$, subject to the restriction that h is λ-entropy leaky. We say that g is λ-entropic leakage-resilient one-way function (λ-ELR-OWF) if not any PPT adversary $\mathcal{A}$ its advantage defined as above is negligible in κ.

As shown in [15], a second-preimage resistant (SPR) function with $n(\kappa)$ bits input and $m(\kappa)$ bits output is also a $\lambda(\kappa)$-entropy leaky OWF for $\lambda(\kappa) = n(\kappa) - m(\kappa) - \omega(\log \kappa)$.

The Superfluous Padding Assumption. Following [11], we present the Superfluous Padding Assumption (SuPA). Intuitively SuPA states that if two distributions are indistinguishable relative to an obfuscated circuit C which was padded before obfuscation, then the two distributions are also indistinguishable relative to the obfuscated circuit C without padding. In other words, if an obfuscation of a padded circuit hides something, then so does an obfuscation of the unpadded circuit. Unfortunately, as shown in [25] assuming $i\mathcal{O}$ and one-way functions SuPA does not hold for $i\mathcal{O}$ if the distinguisher is given *arbitrary auxiliary* information. We present a relaxed version of the SuP assumption where the distinguisher is *not* given access to any auxiliary input and we observe that this relaxed variant of SuPA is enough to prove the security of our NIKE construction.

Following [11], we state the assumption in two steps: First, we define admissible sampler and then define the SuP assumption with respect to such an admissible sampler.

Definition 6 (Relaxed SuPA-admissible Samplers). *Let* Obf *be an obfuscation scheme and let* $\mathsf{PAD} : \mathbb{N} \times \{0,1\}^* \to \{0,1\}^*$ *be a deterministic padding algorithm that takes as input an integer s and and a description of a circuit C and outputs a functionally equivalent circuit of size $s + |C|$. We say that a pair of PPT samplers* $(\mathsf{Samp}_0, \mathsf{Samp}_1)$ *is* SuP*-admissible for obfuscator* Obf *, if there exists a polynomial s such that for any PPT distinguisher D its advantage in the* $\mathsf{SuP}[s]$ *game (see Fig. 1) is negligible:*

$$\mathsf{Adv}^{\mathsf{SuP}[s]}_{\mathsf{Obf},\mathsf{Samp}_0,\mathsf{Samp}_1,\mathcal{D}}(\kappa) = 2 \cdot \Pr\big[\mathsf{SuP}[s]^{\mathcal{D}}_{\mathsf{Obf},\mathsf{Samp}_0,\mathsf{Samp}_1}(\kappa)\big] - 1 \leq \mathsf{negl}(\kappa).$$

Definition 7 (The Relaxed SuPA assumption). *Let* Obf *be an obfuscation scheme and let* Samp_0 *and* Samp_1 *be two* SuP-admissible *samplers. Then, the relaxed* Superfluous Padding Assumption *states that no efficient distinguisher $\mathcal{D}$ has a non-negligible advantage in the* $\mathsf{SuP}[0]$ *game without padding:*

Game $\mathsf{SuP}[s]^{\mathcal{D}}_{\mathsf{Obf},\mathsf{Samp}_0,\mathsf{Samp}_1}$
$b \leftarrow \{0,1\}$
$C \leftarrow \mathsf{Samp}_b(1^\kappa)$
If $s(\kappa) > 0$, then return $\widehat{C} \leftarrow \mathsf{Obf}(\mathsf{PAD}(s(\kappa), C))$
Else, return $\widehat{C} \leftarrow \mathsf{Obf}(C))$
$b' \leftarrow \mathcal{D}(1^\kappa, s, \widehat{C}, \|C\|)$
Return $(b' = b)$

Fig. 1. The SuP game parameterized by a polynomial $s(\kappa)$. According to s, the circuit C is padded (if $s = 0$ the original circuit C is used) before it is obfuscated and given to distinguisher $\mathcal{D}$, who additionally gets s as well as the size of the original circuit C.

$$\mathsf{Adv}^{\mathsf{SuP}[0]}_{\mathsf{Obf},\mathsf{Samp}_0,\mathsf{Samp}_1,\mathcal{D}}(\kappa) = 2 \cdot \Pr\left[\mathsf{SuP}[0]^{\mathcal{D}}_{\mathsf{Obf},\mathsf{Samp}_0,\mathsf{Samp}_1}(\kappa)\right] - 1 \leq \mathsf{negl}(\kappa).$$

4 Our Results in the FS+CL Model

4.1 Encryption in the FS+CL Model

In this section, following [6] we recall the syntax and security definition of encryption schemes in the FS+CL Model.

Encryption in the FS+CL Model. A key-evolving encryption scheme KEE specifies the following PPT algorithms KEE.Kg, KEE.Upd, KEE.Enc, and KEE.Dec, where KEE.Dec is deterministic. The encryption scheme KEE is associated with the maximum number of time periods $T = T(\kappa)$. Here, $\mathsf{KEE.Kg}(1^\kappa)$ is used to generate the initial key pair (sk_1, pk). The key update algorithm $\mathsf{KEE.Upd}(1^\kappa, pk, i, sk_i)$ is used to evolve/update the key from time period i to $i+1$, outputting sk_{i+1} in the process. KEE.Enc is used to encrypt a message m in time period i using the public key pk. KEE.Dec is used to decrypt a ciphertext c, produced in time i, with the help of secret key sk_i. We require the standard correctness condition from KEE. The security game is presented in Fig. 2. In this game defining forward indistinguishability of key-evolving encryption scheme KEE under continual leakage (FINDCL), an attacker is given access to three oracles: Up (which it uses to update the key), Leak (which it uses to leak on the key with its choice of leakage function L, and a one-time access to Exp which gives the entire secret key sk_{t^*}. One additional constraint is that the attacker $\mathcal{A}$ is *δ-bounded*, i.e., $\mathcal{A}$ is allowed to leak at most $\delta(\kappa)$ bits from the secret keys *per time period.* The attacker provides challenge messages i, m_0, m_1 and a time period i. It receives an encryption of m_b for a randomly chosen bit b. $\mathcal{A}$ wins the game if it correctly guesses the bit b and if $i < t^*$. An encryption scheme is FINDCL-secure if the advantage of $\mathcal{A}$ in winning the above game is negligible.

4.2 Our Construction

In this section, we provide the details of our FS+CL encryption scheme. To this end, we first abstract out a notion of continuous leakage-resilient binary tree encryption (CLR-BTE) and use it to construct our FS+CL encryption scheme achieving optimal leakage rate, i.e., $1 - o(1)$.

Game $\text{FINDCL}^{\mathcal{A}}_{\mathsf{KEE}}(\kappa)$	$\underline{\mathsf{Up}()}$
$b \leftarrow\!\!\$ \{0,1\}$; $t \leftarrow 1$; $t^* \leftarrow T(\kappa)+1$	If $t < T(\kappa)$ then
$(pk, sk_1) \leftarrow\!\!\$ \mathsf{KEE.Kg}(1^\kappa)$	$\quad sk_{t+1} \leftarrow\!\!\$ \mathsf{KEE.Upd}(1^\kappa, pk, t, sk_t)$
$(i, m_0, m_1, state) \leftarrow\!\!\$ \mathcal{A}_1^{\mathsf{Up,Leak,Exp}}(1^\kappa, pk)$	$\quad t \leftarrow t+1$
If not $(1 \le i < t^*)$ then return false	Else return $\perp$
If $\lvert m_0 \rvert \neq \lvert m_1 \rvert$ then return false	$\underline{\mathsf{Leak}(L)}$
$(i, c) \leftarrow\!\!\$ \mathsf{KEE.Enc}(1^\kappa, pk, i, m_b)$	Return $L(sk)$
$b' \leftarrow\!\!\$ \mathcal{A}_2(1^\kappa, state, (i,c))$	
Return $(b' = b)$	$\underline{\mathsf{Exp}()}$
	$t^* \leftarrow t$; Return sk_t

Fig. 2. Game defining forward indistinguishability of key-evolving encryption scheme KEE under continual leakage.

Continuous Leakage-Resilient Binary Tree Encryption. We now introduce our notion of binary tree encryption in the continuous leakage model. Our security model of the CLR-BTE scheme generalizes the definition of binary tree encryption (BTE) (proposed by Canetti et al. [12]) in the setting of continuous leakage. A BTE can be seen as a restricted version of HIBE, where the identity tree is represented as a *binary* tree.[2] In particular, as in HIBE, a BTE is also associated with a "master" public key MPK corresponding to a tree, and each node in the tree has its respective secret keys. To encrypt a message for a node, one specifies the identity of the node and the public key MPK. The resulting ciphertext can be decrypted using the secret key of the target node.

Definition 8 *(Continuous leakage-resilient BTE).* A continuous leakage-resilient binary tree encryption scheme (CLR-BTE) consists of a tuple of the PPT algorithms $(\mathsf{Gen}, \mathsf{Der}, \mathsf{Upd}, \mathsf{Enc}, \mathsf{Dec})$ such that:

1. $\mathsf{Gen}(1^\kappa, 1^\ell)$: The key generation algorithm Gen takes as input the security parameter κ and a value ℓ for the depth of the tree. It returns a master public key MPK and an initial (root) secret key SK_ε.
2. $\mathsf{Der}(MPK, w, Sk_w)$: The key derivation algorithm Der takes as input MPK, the identity of a node $w \in \{0,1\}^{\le \ell}$, and its secret key SK_w. It returns secret keys SK_{w_0}, SK_{w_1} for the two children of w.
3. $\mathsf{Upd}(w, Sk_w)$: The key update algorithm Upd takes as input the secret key SK_w of a node w and outputs a re-randomized key SK'_w for the same node w, such that $|SK'_w| = |SK_w|$.
4. $\mathsf{Enc}(MPK, w, M)$: The encryption algorithm Enc takes as input MPK, the identity of a node $w \in \{0,1\}^{\le \ell}$ and a message M to return a ciphertext C.
5. $\mathsf{Dec}(MPK, w, Sk_w, C)$: The decryption algorithm Dec takes as input MPK, the identity of a node $w \in \{0,1\}^{\le \ell}$, its secret key SK_w, and a ciphertext C. It returns a message M or $\perp$ (to denote decryption failure).

[2] Recall that in HIBE the tree can have an arbitrary degree.

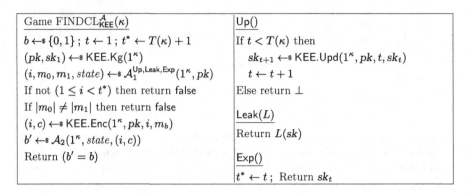

Correctness: For all (MPK, SK_ε) output by Gen, any node $w \in \{0,1\}^{\leq \ell}$, any secret key SK_w correctly generated for this node (which can be the output of (multiple invocations of) Upd also), and any message M, we have

$$\mathsf{Dec}(MPK, w, SK_w, \mathsf{Enc}(MPK, w, M)) = M.$$

Security Model for CLR-BTE. Our security model for CLR-BTE generalizes the notion of *selection-node chosen-plaintext attacks* (SN-CPA) put forward by Canetti et al. [12] to define the security of BTE. In our model, the adversary first specifies the identity of the target node[3] $w^* \in \{0,1\}^{\leq \ell}$. The adversary receives the public key MPK and the secret keys of all the nodes that do not trivially allow him/her to derive the secret key of w^*[4]. Besides, the adversary is also allowed to continuously leak from the secret keys of all the nodes that lie on the path from the root node and w^* (including both). The goal of the adversary is then to win the indistinguishability game with respect to the target node w^*.

Definition 9. A CLR-BTE scheme is secure against *continuous leakage selective-node, chosen-plaintext attacks* ($\lambda(\kappa)$-CLR-SN-CPA) if for all polynomially-bounded functions $\ell(\cdot)$, *and leakage bound* $\lambda(\kappa)$, the advantage of any PPT adversary $\mathcal{A}$ in the following game is negligible in the security parameter κ:

1. The adversary $\mathcal{A}(1^\kappa, \ell)$ outputs the name of a node $w^* \in \{0,1\}^{\leq \ell}$. We will denote the path from the root node to the target node w^* by P_{w^*}.
2. The challenger runs the algorithm $\mathsf{Gen}(1^\kappa, \ell)$ and outputs (MPK, SK_ε). In addition, it runs $\mathsf{Der}(\cdot,\cdot,\cdot)$ to generate the secret keys of all the nodes on the path P_{w^*}, and also the secret keys for the two children w_0^* and w_1^*. The adversary is given MPK and the secret keys $\{SK_w\}$ for all nodes w of the following form:
   - $w = w'\bar{b}$, where $w'b$ is a prefix of w^* and $b \in \{0,1\}$ (i.e., w is a sibling of some node in P_{w^*}).
   - $w = w_0^*$ or $w = w_1^*$ (i.e., w is a child of w^*; this is only when $|w^*| < \ell$).

   The challenger also creates a set $\mathcal{T}$ that holds tuples of all the (node) identities, secret keys and the number of leaked bits from each key so far.
3. The adversary $\mathcal{A}_{\mathsf{clr\text{-}bte}}$ may also ask leakage queries. The adversary runs for arbitrarily many leakage rounds. In each round:
   - The adversary provides the description of a probabilistic leakage function $h : \{0,1\}^* \to \{0,1\}^{\lambda(\kappa)}$, and an identity of a node w in the path P_{w^*}

[3] Note that, this model where the adversary specifies the target node w^* ahead of time is weaker than the model where the adversary may choose the target *adaptively* (analogous to the adaptive security of HIBE schemes). However, as we will show, this model already suffices to construct of a FS+CL encryption scheme.

[4] In particular, the adversary receives the secret keys of all the nodes that are siblings of all the nodes that are on the path from the root node to the target node w^*.

(that may also include both the root note and the target node w^*).[5] The challenger scans $\mathcal{T}$ to find the tuple with identity w. It should be of the form (w, SK_w, L_w). The challenger then checks if $L_w + |h(SK_w)| \leq \lambda(\kappa)$. If this is true, it responds with $h(SK_w)$ and updates $L_w = L_w + |h(SK_w)|$. If the check fails, it returns $\perp$ to the adversary.
- At the end of each round, the challenger computes $SK'_w \leftarrow \mathsf{Upd}(w, SK_w)$ and updates $SK_w = SK'_w$.

4. The adversary $\mathcal{A}$ then sends two messages M_0 and M_1 to the challenger such that $|M_0| = |M_1|$. The challenger samples a random bit $b \xleftarrow{\$} \{0, 1\}$, and computes $C^* \leftarrow \mathsf{Enc}(MPK, w^*, M_b)$. It then returns C^* to the adversary $\mathcal{A}$. The adversary is not allowed to ask any further leakage queries after receiving the challenge ciphertext C^*.[6]

At the end of this game, the adversary outputs a bit $b' \in \{0, 1\}$; it succeeds if $b' = b$. The advantage of the adversary is the absolute value of the difference between its success probability and 1/2.

Construction of CLR-BTE Scheme. Our construction of the CLR-BTE scheme can be instantiated in a straightforward manner from the continuous leakage-resilient HIBE (CLR-HIBE) construction of Lewko et al. [33], tuned to the setting of a binary tree. The resulting CLR-BTE is *adaptively secure*, since the CLR-HIBE of [33] enjoys security against adaptive adversaries employing the dual-system encryption technique. The security of the CLR-BTE scheme can be proven under static assumptions over composite-order bilinear groups. We refer the reader to [33] for the details of the CLR-HIBE construction and its proof. As shown in [33], for appropriate choice of parameters, their CLR-HIBE scheme achieves the optimal leakage rate of $1 - o(1)$.

FINDCL Encryption from CLR-BTE Scheme. We now show a generic construction of a FINDCL-secure encryption scheme starting from any CLR-BTE scheme. The main idea of our construction is very simple: use the Canetti-Halevi-Katz (CHK) transform [12] to the underlying CLR-BTE scheme to construct a FINDCL encryption scheme. In particular, we show the applicability of the CHK transform[7] even in the setting of continuous leakage. However, as we show later, the analysis of the CHK transform in the setting of leakage turns out to be quite tricky.

[5] This is equivalent to a definition where, in each round, the adversary asks for multiple leakage functions adaptively, such that the output length of all these functions sum up to $\lambda(\kappa)$.

[6] If the adversary is allowed to ask leakage queries after receiving the challenge ciphertext, it can encode the entire decryption algorithm of C^* as a function on a secret key, and thus win the game trivially.

[7] The original CHK transform [12] is used to construct a forward-secure PKE scheme starting from a BTE scheme.

Let (Gen, Der, Upd, Enc, Dec) be a CLR-BTE scheme. We construct our FINDCL PKE scheme (KEE.Kg, KEE.Upd, KEE.Enc, KEE.Dec) as shown below. The construction is identical to the CHK transform, with the underlying building blocks appropriately changed.

Some Additional Notation: To obtain a FINDCL-secure encryption scheme with $T = 2^\ell - 1$, time periods (labeled through 1 to T), we use a CLR-BTE of depth ℓ. We associate the time periods with all nodes of the tree according to a pre-order traversal. The node associated with time period i is denoted by w^i. In a pre-order traversal, $w^1 = \varepsilon$ (the root node), if w^i is an internal node then $w^{i+1} = w^i0$ (i.e., left child of w^i). If w^i is a leaf node and $i < T - 1$ then $w^{i+1} = w'1$, where w' is the longest string such that $w'0$ is a prefix of w^i.

1. $\mathsf{KEE.Kg}(1^\kappa, T)$: Run $\mathsf{Gen}(1^\kappa, \ell)$, where $T \leq 2^\ell - 1$, and obtain (MPK, SK_ε). Set $pk = (MPK, T)$, and $sk_1 = SK_\varepsilon$.
2. $\mathsf{KEE.Upd}(1^\kappa, pk, i, sk_i)$: The secret key sk_i is organized as a stack of node keys, with the secret key SK'_{w^i} on top, where SK'_{w^i} is obtained by running Upd of the CLR-BTE scheme (potentially multiple times) on the key SK_{w^i}. We first pop this key off the stack. If w^i is a leaf node, the next node key on top of the stack is $SK'_{w^{i+1}}$ (a refreshed version of the key $SK_{w^{i+1}}$). If w^i is an internal node, compute $(SK_{w^i0}, SK_{w^i1}) \leftarrow \mathsf{Der}(pk, w^i, SK_{w^i})$ Then for $b \in \{0,1\}$, compute $SK'_{w^ib} \leftarrow \mathsf{Upd}(w, SK_{w^ib})$. Further, for all other node keys SK_w remaining in the stack (corresponding to sk_{i+1}), run $SK'_w \leftarrow \mathsf{Upd}(w, SK_w)$. Then push SK'_{w^i1} and then SK'_{w^i0} onto the stack. In either case, the node key SK'_{w^i} is erased.
3. $\mathsf{KEE.Enc}(pk, i, m)$: Run $\mathsf{Enc}(pk, w^i, m)$. Note that w^i is publicly computable given i and T.
4. $\mathsf{KEE.Dec}(1^\kappa, pk_i, sk_i, c_i)$: Run $\mathsf{Dec}(pk, w, SK'_{w^i}, c_i)$. Note that, SK'_{w^i} is stored as part of sk_i.

Theorem 1. *Let* $\lambda : \mathbb{N} \rightarrow [0,1]$. *Let* $\Pi =$ (Gen, Der, Upd, Enc, Dec) *be a* $\lambda(\kappa)$-CLR-SN-CPA *continuous leakage-resilient binary-tree encryption* (CLR-BTE) *scheme. Let* $\ell : \mathbb{N} \rightarrow \mathbb{N}$ *be a polynomial such that* $T \leq 2^\ell - 1$. *Then* $\Pi' =$ (KEE.Kg, KEE.Upd, KEE.Enc, KEE.Dec) *is a* $\lambda(\kappa)$-FINDCL *secure encryption scheme supporting up to* T *time periods.*

Proof. Our proof follows the template of the CHK transformation for converting a BTE scheme to forward-secure encryption scheme, with the crucial difference in simulating the leakage queries.

Assume that we have an adversary $\mathcal{A}_{\mathsf{kee}}$ with advantage $\epsilon(\kappa)$ in an $\lambda(\kappa)$-FINDCL security game of $\Pi' =$ (KEE.Kg, KEE.Upd, KEE.Enc, KEE.Dec). We construct an adversary $\mathcal{A}_{\mathsf{clr\text{-}bte}}$ that obtains an advantage $\epsilon(\kappa)/T$ in the corresponding attack against the underlying the CLR-BTE scheme $\Pi =$ (Gen, Der, Upd, Enc, Dec). The leakage rate tolerated by Π is exactly the same as Π'. We now describe how $\mathcal{A}_{\mathsf{clr\text{-}bte}}$ simulates the environment for $\mathcal{A}_{\mathsf{kee}}$:

1. $\mathcal{A}_{\text{clr-bte}}$ chooses uniformly at random a time period $i^* \in [T]$. This define the node w^{i^*} (the identity of the node corresponding to i^*). $\mathcal{A}_{\text{clr-bte}}$ then forwards w^{i^*} to its challenger and obtains MPK and $\{SK_w\}$ for all the appropriate nodes w[8] from its challenger. $\mathcal{A}_{\text{clr-bte}}$ then sets $pk = (MPK, T)$, and forwards the public key pk to the adversary $\mathcal{A}_{\text{kee}}$.
2. When $\mathcal{A}_{\text{kee}}$ decides to break into the system, it provides the time period, say j. If $j \le i^*$, then $\mathcal{A}_{\text{clr-bte}}$ outputs a random bit and halts. Otherwise, $\mathcal{A}_{\text{clr-bte}}$ computes the appropriate secret key sk_j and gives it to $\mathcal{A}_{\text{kee}}$. Note that, $\mathcal{A}_{\text{clr-bte}}$ can efficiently compute the secret keys sk_j for any $j > i^*$ from the knowledge of $\{SK_w\}$ (the set of secret keys received in Step 1).
3. $\mathcal{A}_{\text{kee}}$ may ask leakage queries on the secret key corresponding to any time period, say i. The node associated with time period i is w^i. The secret key sk_i can be seen as a stack of node keys (derived using the underlying CLR-BTE scheme) with the key SK'_{w^i} on top of the stack. The other node keys in the stack are secret keys corresponding to the right siblings of all the nodes in the path P_{w^i} from the root node to w^i. Let us denote the secret key as $sk_i = (SK'_{w^i}, \{SK\}'_{rs(P_{w^i})})$, where $\{SK\}'_{rs(P_{w^i})}$ denote the (refreshed) secret keys of the right siblings of all nodes in path from the root to the node w^i (we denote this path by P_{w^i}). Now, either one of the two cases must be true: (1) $w^i \in P_{w^{i^*}}$ or (2) $w^i \notin P_{w^{i^*}}$, where $P_{w^{i^*}}$ is the path containing the nodes from the root node to the target node w^{i^*} (including both).
   For the first case, $\mathcal{A}_{\text{clr-bte}}$ already knows all the keys $\{SK\}_{rs(P_{w^i})})$ and it does the following:
   - Receive as input the leakage function f from $\mathcal{A}_{\text{kee}}$. Next, it calls Upd on all the node keys $\{SK\}_{rs(P_{w^i})}$ and receive the set of refreshed keys $\{SK\}'_{rs(P_{w^i})}$. It then modifies the description of the function as $h = f_{\{SK\}'_{rs(P_{w^i})}}(\cdot) = f(\cdot, \{SK\}'_{rs(P_{w^i})})$. In other words, $\mathcal{A}_{\text{clr-bte}}$ hardwires the secret keys $\{SK\}'_{rs(P_{w^i})}$ in the function f, and forwards h as the leakage function to its challenger.
   - On input the answer $h(SK'_{w^i}, \{SK\}'_{rs(P_{w^i})})$ from its challenger, $\mathcal{A}_{\text{clr-bte}}$ forwards this answer as the output of the leakage function f to $\mathcal{A}_{\text{kee}}$.

   For the second case (i.e., when $w^i \notin P_{w^{i^*}}$), there exists at most one node $w \in P_{w^{i^*}}$ whose secret key is included $\{SK\}'_{rs(P_{w^i})}$. Apart from the secret key of w, $\mathcal{A}_{\text{clr-bte}}$ knows the secret key of w^i, SK_{w^i}, and the keys $\{SK\}_{rs(P_{w^i})})$. Thus, similar to above it can transform the joint leakage function f to a leakage function h on SK'_w. It then returns the result to $\mathcal{A}_{\text{kee}}$.
   It is clear that in both cases, $\mathcal{A}_{\text{clr-bte}}$ perfectly simulates the answers to the leakage queries of the adversary $\mathcal{A}_{\text{kee}}$.
4. When $\mathcal{A}_{\text{kee}}$ asks an update query $\mathsf{KEE.Upd}(i)$, $\mathcal{A}_{\text{blr-bte}}$ can easily compute the key for the next time period using the knowledge of the keys $\{SK_w\}$ received from its challenger in the beginning.

[8] Recall that $\mathcal{A}_{\text{clr-bte}}$ receives the secret keys of all the nodes that are right siblings of the nodes that lie on the path P from the root node to w^{i^*}.

5. When $\mathcal{A}_{\mathsf{kee}}$ asks a challenge query with input (i, m_0, m_1), if $i \neq i^*$ then $\mathcal{A}_{\mathsf{clr\text{-}bte}}$ outputs a random bit and halts. Otherwise, it forwards the tuple (m_0, m_1) to its challenger and obtains the challenge ciphertext C^*. It then gives C^* to $\mathcal{A}_{\mathsf{kee}}$.
6. When $\mathcal{A}_{\mathsf{kee}}$ outputs b', $\mathcal{A}$ outputs b' and halts.

It is easy to see that, if $i = i^*$, the above simulation by $\mathcal{A}_{\mathsf{clr\text{-}bte}}$ is perfect. Since, $\mathcal{A}_{\mathsf{clr\text{-}bte}}$ guesses i^* with probability $1/T$, we have that $\mathcal{A}_{\mathsf{clr\text{-}bte}}$ correctly predicts the bit b with advantage $\epsilon(\kappa)/T$. □

5 Our Results in the FS+(C)EBL Model

In this section we present the FS+(C)EBL model and present a construction of NIKE in the FS+EBL model.

5.1 The FS+EBL Model

The Entropy Bounded Leakage (EBL) model was designed to capture security against adversary who leaked on the secret key. However, to make the attack non-trivial, it defines the legitimacy of the adversary. An adversary is legitimate if the secret key sk still contains enough min-entropy, parametrized by α, even after the leakage. This is a generalization of length-bounded leakage model where a leakage function can leak at most, say, δ bits. Implicitly, the EBL model is defined in the setting of a single time period (as there is only the one secret key). The notion of length bounded leakage model was extended to the setting of multiple time periods and this was called continual leakage model. In this setting, the secret key is updated (using a randomized update function) across time periods and an adversary can leak at most δ bits in every time period. In this section, we consider *deterministic* key update functions and take the idea of entropic bounded leakage model and extend it to the setting of multiple time periods. We consider the combined problem of FS+EBL, i.e., schemes that are forward secure and which are resilient to entropic bounded leakage. Specifically, we consider the Forward Secure + Entropic Bounded Leakage Model, abbreviated as FS+EBL. It is parametrized by T and α, where T is the maximum number of time periods and α is the minimum residual entropy required. As before, one can define the legitimacy of the attacker in this model.

Definition 10 (Definition of Legitimacy - FS+EBL Model). *Let Π be any key-evolving scheme with a* deterministic *key update algorithm. Let SK_i denote the random variable produced by the key update algorithm for time period i. Then, any PPT adversary $\mathcal{A}$ making leakage queries denoted by $\mathbb{L}_i(SK_i)$ for $i = 1, \ldots, T$, is legitimate in the (T, α)-FS+EBL model if:*

$$\forall j \in [t^*], \mathrm{H}_\infty(SK_j \,|\, \mathbb{L}_1, \cdots, \mathbb{L}_T, R_{L_1}, \cdots, R_{L_T}) \geq \alpha \quad (1)$$

where R_{L_i} denote the random coins of the adversary corresponding to the leakage function L_i, $t^* \leq T$ is the time period at which $\mathcal{A}$ is given sk_{t^*} in full.

5.2 NIKE in FS + EBL Model

Non-interactive key exchange (NIKE) protocols allow two (or more) parties to establish a shared key between them, without any interaction. It is assumed that the public keys of all the parties are pre-distributed and known to each other. In this work, we consider two-party NIKE protocols and extend them to the setting of *forward-security* under *entropy-bounded* leakage model (FS + EBL). We provide the definition of NIKE in this model (we will often call such a NIKE scheme as FS-EBLR-NIKE). To bypass the black-box impossibility result of constructing leakage-resilient NIKE protocol in the plain model [34], we consider the NIKE protocols in the *common reference string* (CRS) model, where we rely on leak-free randomness to generate the CRS. Our security model for FS-EBLR-NIKE scheme can be seen as a leakage-resilient adaptation of the model of forward-secure NIKE (FS-NIKE) of Pointcheval and Sanders (dubbed as $\mathcal{PS}$ model) [37]. Hence, we call our model of NIKE as the $\mathcal{EBL}$-$\mathcal{PS}$ model.

5.3 Syntax of FS-EBLR NIKE

A NIKE scheme NIKE in the FS + EBL model consists of the tuple of algorithms (NIKE.Setup, NIKE.Gen, NIKE.Upd, NIKE.Key). We associate to NIKE a public parameter space $\mathcal{PP}$, public key space $\mathcal{PK}$, secret key space $\mathcal{SK}$, shared key space $\mathcal{SHK}$, and an identity space $\mathcal{IDS}$. Identities are used to track which public keys are associated with which users; we are *not* in the identity-based setting.

- NIKE.Setup$(1^\kappa, (\alpha, T))$: This is a randomized algorithm that takes as input the security parameter κ (expressed in unary), parameters α and T of the (T, α)-FS + EBL model (where α is the leakage parameter and T denotes the maximum number of time period supported by the system[9]) and outputs public parameters $params \in \mathcal{PP}$.
- NIKE.Gen$(1^\kappa, ID)$: On input an identity $ID \in \mathcal{IDS}$, the key generation outputs a public-secret key pair (pk, sk_t) for the current time period t. We assume that the secret keys implicitly contain the time periods. The current time period t is initially set to 1.
- NIKE.Upd(sk_t): The (deterministic) update algorithm takes as input the secret key sk_t at time period t and outputs the updated secret key sk_{t+1} for the next time period $t + 1$, if $t < T$. We require that the updated key $sk_{t+1} \neq sk_t$. The key sk_t is then securely erased from memory. If $t = T$, then the secret key is erased and there is no new key.
- NIKE.Key$(ID_A, pk^A, ID_B, sk_t^B)$: On input an identity $ID_A \in \mathcal{IDS}$ associated with public key pk_A, and another identity $ID_B \in \mathcal{IDS}$ with secret key sk_t^B corresponding to the current time period t, output the shared key $shk_t^{AB} \in \mathcal{SHK}$ or a failure symbol $\perp$. If $ID_A = ID_B$, the algorithm outputs $\perp$. Since the secret key sk_t^B is associated with time period t, the shared key shk_t^{AB} between the two users ID_A and ID_B also corresponds to the same time period t.

[9] Our construction will achieve security for arbitrary polynomial T.

Game $\mathsf{EBL\text{-}PS}^{\mathcal{A}_{\mathsf{nike}}}_{\mathsf{NIKE}}(\kappa, \alpha, T)$

$params \leftarrow \mathsf{NIKE.Setup}(1^{\kappa}, \alpha, T)$; $S, C, Q \leftarrow \emptyset$ // S, C and Q maintains the list of *honest*, *corrupt* and *exposed* users respectively.

$(ID_A, ID_B, \tilde{t}) \leftarrow \mathcal{A}_1^{\mathsf{RegHon,RegCor,CorrReveal,Leak,Exp}}(params)$ // The descriptions of the oracles RegHon, RegCor, CorrReveal, Leak and Exp are provided below the description of this game.

$b \leftarrow_{\$} \{0, 1\}$
If $b = 0$ then Return $shk^{AB}_{\tilde{t}} \leftarrow \mathsf{NIKE.Key}(ID_A, pk_A, ID_B, sk^{B}_{\tilde{t}})$
Else Return $shk^{AB}_{\tilde{t}} \leftarrow_{\$} \mathcal{SHK}$
$b' \leftarrow_{\$} \mathcal{A}_2^{\mathsf{RegHon,RegCor,CorrReveal,Leak,Exp}}(shk^{AB}_{\tilde{t}})$

If $(ID_A, -, -, \mathsf{corrupt}) \in C$ or $(ID_B, -, -, , \mathsf{corrupt}) \in C$, then return $\perp$
If $(ID_A, t^*) \in Q$ and $t^* \leq \tilde{t}$, then return $\perp$
If $(ID_B, t^*) \in Q$ and $t^* \leq \tilde{t}$, then return $\perp$
Return $(b' = b)$

Fig. 3. Game defining security of NIKE scheme NIKE in the FS + EBL model.

Correctness: The correctness requirement states that the shared keys computed by any two users ID_A and ID_B in the *same* time period are *identical.* In other words, for any time period $t \geq 1$, and any pair (ID_A, ID_B) of users having key pairs (pk^A, sk^A_t) and (pk^B, sk^B_t) respectively, it holds that:

$$\mathsf{NIKE.Key}(ID_A, pk^B, ID_B, sk^A_t) = \mathsf{NIKE.Key}(ID_B, pk^A, ID_A, sk^B_t).$$

5.4 Security Model for FS-EBLR NIKE

Our security model for NIKE generalizes the model of forward-secure NIKE of [37] (often referred to as the $\mathcal{PS}$ model). We refer to our model as the $\mathcal{EBL}$-$\mathcal{PS}$ model. Security of a NIKE protocol NIKE in the $\mathcal{EBL}$-$\mathcal{PS}$ model is defined by a game EBL-PS between an adversary $\mathcal{A}_{\mathsf{nike}} = (\mathcal{A}_1, \mathcal{A}_2)$ and a challenger $\mathcal{C}$ (see Fig. 3). Before the beginning of the game, the challenger $\mathcal{C}$ also initializes three sets S, C and Q to be empty sets. The adversary $\mathcal{A}_{\mathsf{nike}}$ can query the following oracles:

1. $\mathsf{RegHon}(ID)$: This oracle is used by $\mathcal{A}_{\mathsf{nike}}$ to register a new honest user ID at the initial time period. The challenger runs the NIKE.Gen algorithm with the current time period as 1, and returns the public key pk to $\mathcal{A}_{\mathsf{nike}}$. It also adds the tuple $(ID, sk_1, pk, \mathsf{honest})$ to the set S. This implicitly defines all the future keys $sk_2, \cdots, sk_T$ (since the update function is deterministic). This query may be asked at most *twice* by $\mathcal{A}_{\mathsf{nike}}$. Users registered by this query are called "honest".
2. $\mathsf{RegCor}(ID, pk)$: This oracle allows the adversary to register a new corrupted user ID with public key pk. The challenger adds the tuple $(ID, --, pk, \mathsf{corrupt})$ to the set C. We call the users registered by this query as "corrupt".

3. $\mathsf{CorrReveal}(ID_A, ID_B, t)$: $\mathcal{A}_{\mathsf{nike}}$ supplies two indices where ID_A was registered as *corrupt* and ID_B was registered as *honest*. The challenger looks up the secret key sk_1^B (corresponding to ID_B) and computes the updated key sk_t^B corresponding to time period t. Then it runs $\mathsf{NIKE.Key}(ID_A, pk^A, ID_B, sk_t^B)$ to get the shared key shk_t^{AB} for time period t and returns shk_t^{AB} to $\mathcal{A}_{\mathsf{nike}}$.
4. $\mathsf{Leak}(L, ID, t)$: The adversary $\mathcal{A}_{\mathsf{nike}}$ submits a leakage function $L : \mathcal{PP} \times \mathcal{SK} \to \{0,1\}^*$ to leak on the secret key of user ID for time period t, provided that $\mathcal{A}_{\mathsf{nike}}$ belongs to the class of legitimate adversaries (see Definition 10).
5. $\mathsf{Exp}(ID, t^*)$: This query is used by $\mathcal{A}_{\mathsf{nike}}$ to get the secret key of an honestly registered user ID corresponding to time period t^*. The challenger looks for a tuple $(ID, sk_1, pk, \mathsf{honest})$. If there is a match, it computes sk_{t^*} corresponding to t^* and returns sk_{t^*} to $\mathcal{A}_{\mathsf{nike}}$. Else, it returns $\perp$. The challenger adds (ID, t^*) to the set Q.

The formal details of our EBL-PS game is given in Fig. 3.

Definition 11 (FS + EBL-secure NIKE). *A NIKE protocol* NIKE *is* (T, α)-forward-secure under computational-entropy-bounded leakage model *((T,α) - FS + EBL) with respect to any legitimate adversary $\mathcal{A}_{\mathsf{nike}}$ playing the above* EBL-PS *game (see Fig. 3), if the advantage defined below is negligible in κ.*

$$\mathsf{Adv}^{\mathsf{fs\text{-}ebl}}_{\mathcal{A}_{\mathsf{nike}}}(\kappa) = |\Pr[\mathsf{EBL\text{-}PS}^{\mathcal{A}_{\mathsf{nike}}}_{\mathsf{NIKE}}(\kappa, \alpha, T)) = 1] - 1/2|$$

.

In other words, the adversary $\mathcal{A}_{\mathsf{nike}}$ succeeds in the above experiment if it is able to distinguish a valid shared key between two users from a random session key. To avoid trivial win, some restrictions are enforced, namely: (i) both the targeted (or test) users needs to be *honestly registered* (ii) the adversary $\mathcal{A}_{\mathsf{nike}}$ is not allowed to obtain the secret keys corresponding to any of the test users prior to the challenge time period $\tilde{t}$, (iii) $\mathcal{A}_{\mathsf{nike}}$ is allowed to leak on the secret keys of both the target users ID_A and ID_B, as long as it satisfies the legitimacy condition (see Definition 10). We emphasize that the adversary can still obtain the secret keys of the target users ID_A and ID_B for time periods $t^* > \tilde{t}$, which models *forward security*.

Variants of NIKE. Similar to [34], we consider different variants of NIKE depending on whether the setup algorithm just outputs a uniformly random coins or sample from some structured distributions. In particular, we say a NIKE scheme is:

- a *plain* NIKE, if $\mathsf{NIKE.Setup}(1^\kappa)$ just outputs (some specified number of) uniform random coins. In particular, $\mathsf{NIKE.Setup}(1^\kappa; r) = r$.
- a NIKE in the *common reference string* model, if $\mathsf{NIKE.Setup}(1^\kappa)$ can be arbitrary (i.e., sample from an arbitrary distribution). In this case, we rely on *leak-free randomness* to run the setup algorithm.

Remark 1. We note that, in the original $\mathcal{PS}$ model of forward secure NIKE, there can be multiple honest users, and the adversary is allowed to obtain the secret keys of the honest users other than the target users (even prior to the challenge time period $\tilde{t}$). In this work, we consider a simplified version where there are only *two* honest users. The above simplified model can be shown to be polynomially equivalent to the full-fledged $\mathcal{PS}$ model by following the same reduction strategy as in [18] [Theorem 8, Appendix B], where they show that the CKS-light model (with two honest users) is polynomially equivalent to the CKS-heavy model (where they can be multiple honest users). We emphasize that, in our application of constructing FS + EBL-secure PKE scheme from FS-EBLR NIKE, we only require the above simplified model.

5.5 Construction of NIKE Scheme in the FS + EBL Model

In this section, we present our construction of forward-secure NIKE protocol resilient to entropy-bounded leakage in the common reference string model.

Let $i\mathcal{O}$ be an indistinguishability obfuscator for circuits, $\mathsf{pPRF} = (\mathsf{pPRF.keygen}, \mathsf{pPRF.puncture}, \mathsf{pPRF.eval})$ be a puncturable PRF with image space $\mathcal{Y} = \{0,1\}^y$, $\mathsf{LF} = (\mathsf{Inj}, \mathsf{Lossy}, f)$ be a (κ, k, m)[10]-lossy function, and $\mathsf{LF}' = (\mathsf{Inj}', \mathsf{Lossy}', f')$ be a (κ', k', m')-lossy function, where $\kappa' \geq m$.

- $\mathsf{NIKE.Setup}(1^\kappa, T)$: Choose a random key $K \leftarrow \mathsf{pPRF.keygen}(1^\kappa)$. Sample two injective evaluation keys $\mathsf{ek} \leftarrow \mathsf{Inj}(1^\kappa)$, $\mathsf{ek}' \leftarrow \mathsf{Inj}'(1^\kappa)$. Consider the circuit $C(r, X_i, X_j)$ that has the key K hard-coded (see Fig. 4) and compute $\widehat{C} = i\mathcal{O}(C)$. Set $params = (\widehat{C}, \mathsf{ek}, \mathsf{ek}')$.

Inputs: r, X_i, X_j.
Constant: $K, \mathsf{ek}, \mathsf{ek}'$
If $f_{\mathsf{ek}}(r) = X_i$ or $f_{\mathsf{ek}}(r) = X_j$, output $\mathsf{pPRF.eval}(K, (f'_{\mathsf{ek}'}(X_i), f'_{\mathsf{ek}'}(X_j)))$;
Else output $\perp$.

Fig. 4. The Circuit $C(r, X_i, X_j)$

- $\mathsf{NIKE.Gen}(1^\kappa, params, ID_i)$: To compute the key pair of an user ID_i, sample $sk_1^i \xleftarrow{\$} \{0,1\}^\kappa$. Consider the circuit $C_i(sk_t, t)$ that has the keys ek, ek', the base secret key sk_1^i, and the obfuscated circuit $\widehat{C}$ (which is part of $params$) hard-coded (See Fig. 5) and compute $\widehat{C_i} = i\mathcal{O}(C_i)$. Set the public key as $pk^i = \widehat{C_i}$.
- $\mathsf{NIKE.Upd}(1^\kappa, sk_t^i)$: On input of the user $ID_i's$ secret key sk_t^i at time period t, computes sk_{t+1}^i, the secret key for the next time period $t+1$. The instantiation of the update function is mentioned below.
- $\mathsf{NIKE.Key}(ID_i, pk^i = \widehat{C_i}, ID_j, sk_t^j)$: The user ID_j runs the obfuscated circuit $\widehat{C_i} = i\mathcal{O}(C_i)$ on inputs the secret key sk_t^j corresponding to time period t to obtain the shared key shk_t^{ij} at time period t.

---

[10] A (κ, k, m)-lossy function maps an input from $x \in \{0,1\}^\kappa$ to an output $y \in \{0,1\}^m$. In the lossy mode, the image size of the function is at most $2^{\kappa-k}$ with high probability.

Inputs: sk_t, t.
Constants: sk_1^i, ek, ek', $\hat{C}$, T.
1. Check if $t \leq T$. If not, output $\perp$.
2. Update $sk_t^i = \mathsf{NIKE.Upd}^{t-1}(sk_1^i)$.
3. Compute $X_t^i = f_{\mathsf{ek}}(sk_t^i)$ and $X_t^j = f_{\mathsf{ek}}(sk_t)$.

Output the shared key $shk_t^{ij} = \widehat{C}(sk_t, X_t^i, X_t^j)$.

Fig. 5. Circuit $C_i(sk_t, t)$

Note on Update Function: The update function NIKE.Upd is one which takes a secret key of the current period and produces a new secret key. As defined in the security model, the adversary can issue leakage queries provided the keys are α-entropic conditioned on the set of all leakage queries. It is not hard to see that the update function should necessarily satisfy the one-wayness property, essentially guaranteeing the non-invertibility of the earlier keys once the secret key is exposed. Interestingly, for the above construction, we can abstract away the update function to any *entropic leakage resilient one-way function*, i.e., $\mathsf{NIKE.Upd}(\cdot) = g(\cdot)$, where $g : \{0,1\}^\kappa \rightarrow \{0,1\}^\kappa$ be a α-entropic leakage-resilient one-way function (α-ELR-OWF). The definition of entropic leakage-resilient OWF is given in Sect. 3.3.

Correctness. It is not hard to see that both the parties ID_i and ID_j end up with the *same* shared key.

Shared key computation by party P_i: Party P_i computes the shared key as:

$$\begin{aligned} shk_t^{ij} &= \mathsf{NIKE.Key}(ID_j, pk^j = \widehat{C_j}, ID_i, sk_t^i) \\ &= \widehat{C_j}(sk_t^i, (X_t^i, X_t^j)) \\ &= \mathsf{pPRF.eval}\big(K, f'_{\mathsf{ek}'}(X_t^i), f'_{\mathsf{ek}'}(X_t^j)\big) \\ &= \mathsf{pPRF.eval}\big(K, f'_{\mathsf{ek}'}(f_{\mathsf{ek}}(sk_t^i)), f'_{\mathsf{ek}'}(f_{\mathsf{ek}}(\mathsf{NIKE.Upd}^{t-1}(sk_1^j)))\big) \\ &= \mathsf{pPRF.eval}\big(K, f'_{\mathsf{ek}'}(f_{\mathsf{ek}}(\mathsf{NIKE.Upd}^{t-1}(sk_1^i))), f'_{\mathsf{ek}'}(f_{\mathsf{ek}}(\mathsf{NIKE.Upd}^{t-1}(sk_1^j)))\big) \end{aligned}$$

Shared key computation by party P_j: Party P_j computes the shared key as:

$$\begin{aligned} shk_t^{ij'} &= \mathsf{NIKE.Key}(ID_i, pk^i = \widehat{C_i}, ID_j, sk_t^j) \\ &= \widehat{C_i}(sk_t^j, (X_t^i, X_t^j)) \\ &= \mathsf{pPRF.eval}\big(K, f'_{\mathsf{ek}'}(X_t^i), f'_{\mathsf{ek}'}(X_t^j)\big) \\ &= \mathsf{pPRF.eval}\big(K, f'_{\mathsf{ek}'}(f_{\mathsf{ek}}(\mathsf{NIKE.Upd}^{t-1}(sk_1^i))), f'_{\mathsf{ek}'}(f_{\mathsf{ek}}(sk_t^j))\big) \\ &= \mathsf{pPRF.eval}\big(K, f'_{\mathsf{ek}'}(f_{\mathsf{ek}}(\mathsf{NIKE.Upd}^{t-1}(sk_1^i))), f'_{\mathsf{ek}'}(f_{\mathsf{ek}}(\mathsf{NIKE.Upd}^{t-1}(sk_1^j)))\big) \end{aligned}$$

Hence, we can see that shared keys computed by both parties P_i and P_j corresponding to time period t are *same*, i.e., $shk_t^{ij} = shk_t^{ij'}$.

Instantiations. Our FS-EBLR NIKE construction from above can be instantiated based on the recent construction of $i\mathcal{O}$ from well-founded assumptions [28]. One can construct lossy functions from DDH or LWE [34]. Besides, we need to rely on the relaxed variant of the Superfluous Padding Assumption (SuPA). In particular we obtain FS+ECL NIKE from either DDH or LWE along with sub-exponential SXDH on asymmetric bilinear groups, sub-exponential LPN, Boolean PRGs in NC^0 and relaxed SuPA.

5.6 Security Proof

Theorem 2. *Let κ be the security parameter, and $T = T(\kappa)$ be an arbitrary but fixed polynomial. Assume that $i\mathcal{O}$ is an indistinguishability obfuscator for circuits, and the superfluous padding assumption holds for $i\mathcal{O}$. Let LF is an (κ, k, m)-lossy function, LF' is an (κ', k', m')-lossy function where $\kappa' \geq m$, pPRF is a family of puncturable PRFs with image size $\mathcal{Y} = \{0,1\}^y$. Then, Construction 5.5 is a (α, T)-forward-secure entropy-bounded leakage-resilient NIKE in the $\mathcal{EBL}$-$\mathcal{PS}$ model with $\alpha \geq y + rT + r' - 2\kappa$, where $r = (\kappa - k)$, $r' = (\kappa' - k')$, and T denote the total number of time periods supported by the scheme.*

The proof of the above theorem is presented in the full version of our paper. The high level idea of the proof strategy is presented in the introduction.

References

1. Abdalla, M., Reyzin, L.: A new forward-secure digital signature scheme. In: Okamoto, T. (ed.) ASIACRYPT 2000. LNCS, vol. 1976, pp. 116–129. Springer, Heidelberg (2000). https://doi.org/10.1007/3-540-44448-3_10
2. Akavia, A., Goldwasser, S., Vaikuntanathan, V.: Simultaneous hardcore bits and cryptography against memory attacks. In: Reingold, O. (ed.) TCC 2009. LNCS, vol. 5444, pp. 474–495. Springer, Heidelberg (2009). https://doi.org/10.1007/978-3-642-00457-5_28
3. Alwen, J., Dodis, Y., Wichs, D.: Leakage-resilient public-key cryptography in the bounded-retrieval model. In: Halevi, S. (ed.) CRYPTO 2009. LNCS, vol. 5677, pp. 36–54. Springer, Heidelberg (2009). https://doi.org/10.1007/978-3-642-03356-8_3
4. Bellare, M., Meiklejohn, S., Thomson, S.: Key-versatile signatures and applications: RKA, KDM and joint Enc/Sig. In: Nguyen, P.Q., Oswald, E. (eds.) EUROCRYPT 2014. LNCS, vol. 8441, pp. 496–513. Springer, Heidelberg (2014). https://doi.org/10.1007/978-3-642-55220-5_28
5. Bellare, M., Miner, S.K.: A forward-secure digital signature scheme. In: Wiener, M. (ed.) CRYPTO 1999. LNCS, vol. 1666, pp. 431–448. Springer, Heidelberg (1999). https://doi.org/10.1007/3-540-48405-1_28
6. Bellare, M., O'Neill, A., Stepanovs, I.: Forward-security under continual leakage. In: Capkun, S., Chow, S.S.M. (eds.) CANS 2017. LNCS, vol. 11261, pp. 3–26. Springer, Cham (2018). https://doi.org/10.1007/978-3-030-02641-7_1
7. Boyd, C., Gellert, K.: A modern view on forward security. Cryptology ePrint Archive, Report 2019/1362 (2019). http://eprint.iacr.org/2019/1362

8. Boyen, X., Shacham, H., Shen, E., Waters, B.: Forward-secure signatures with untrusted update. In: Juels, A., Wright, R.N., Vimercati, S. (eds.) ACM CCS 2006, pp. 191–200. ACM Press (2006)
9. Boyle, E., Segev, G., Wichs, D.: Fully leakage-resilient signatures. In: Paterson, K.G. (ed.) EUROCRYPT 2011. LNCS, vol. 6632, pp. 89–108. Springer, Heidelberg (2011). https://doi.org/10.1007/978-3-642-20465-4_7
10. Brakerski, Z., Kalai, Y.T., Katz, J., Vaikuntanathan, V.: Overcoming the hole in the bucket: public-key cryptography resilient to continual memory leakage. In: 51st FOCS, pp. 501–510. IEEE Computer Society Press (2010)
11. Brzuska, C., Mittelbach, A.: Universal computational extractors and the superfluous padding assumption for indistinguishability obfuscation. Cryptology ePrint Archive, Report 2015/581 (2015). http://eprint.iacr.org/2015/581
12. Canetti, R., Halevi, S., Katz, J.: A forward-secure public-key encryption scheme. In: Biham, E. (ed.) EUROCRYPT 2003. LNCS, vol. 2656, pp. 255–271. Springer, Heidelberg (2003). https://doi.org/10.1007/3-540-39200-9_16
13. Chase, M., Lysyanskaya, A.: On signatures of knowledge. In: Dwork, C. (ed.) CRYPTO 2006. LNCS, vol. 4117, pp. 78–96. Springer, Heidelberg (2006). https://doi.org/10.1007/11818175_5
14. Dodis, Y., Haralambiev, K., López-Alt, A., Wichs, D.: Cryptography against continuous memory attacks. In: 51st FOCS, pp. 511–520. IEEE Computer Society Press (2010)
15. Dodis, Y., Haralambiev, K., López-Alt, A., Wichs, D.: Efficient public-key cryptography in the presence of key leakage. In: Abe, M. (ed.) ASIACRYPT 2010. LNCS, vol. 6477, pp. 613–631. Springer, Heidelberg (2010). https://doi.org/10.1007/978-3-642-17373-8_35
16. Dodis, Y., Reyzin, L., Smith, A.: Fuzzy extractors: how to generate strong keys from biometrics and other noisy data. In: Cachin, C., Camenisch, J.L. (eds.) EUROCRYPT 2004. LNCS, vol. 3027, pp. 523–540. Springer, Heidelberg (2004). https://doi.org/10.1007/978-3-540-24676-3_31
17. Dziembowski, S., Kazana, T., Wichs, D.: Key-evolution schemes resilient to space-bounded leakage. In: Rogaway, P. (ed.) CRYPTO 2011. LNCS, vol. 6841, pp. 335–353. Springer, Heidelberg (2011). https://doi.org/10.1007/978-3-642-22792-9_19
18. Freire, E.S.V., Hofheinz, D., Kiltz, E., Paterson, K.G.: Non-interactive key exchange. In: Kurosawa, K., Hanaoka, G. (eds.) PKC 2013. LNCS, vol. 7778, pp. 254–271. Springer, Heidelberg (2013). https://doi.org/10.1007/978-3-642-36362-7_17
19. Garg, S., Gentry, C., Halevi, S., Wichs, D.: On the implausibility of differing-inputs obfuscation and extractable witness encryption with auxiliary input. Algorithmica **79**(4), 1353–1373 (2017)
20. Garg, S., Gentry, C., Sahai, A., Waters, B.: Witness encryption and its applications. In: Boneh, D., Roughgarden, T., Feigenbaum, J. (eds.) Symposium on Theory of Computing Conference, STOC 2013, Palo Alto, CA, USA, 1–4 June 2013, pp. 467–476. ACM (2013)
21. Green, M.D., Miers, I.: Forward secure asynchronous messaging from puncturable encryption. In: 2015 IEEE Symposium on Security and Privacy, pp. 305–320. IEEE Computer Society Press (2015)
22. Günther, F., Hale, B., Jager, T., Lauer, S.: 0-RTT key exchange with full forward secrecy. In: Coron, J.-S., Nielsen, J.B. (eds.) EUROCRYPT 2017. LNCS, vol. 10212, pp. 519–548. Springer, Cham (2017). https://doi.org/10.1007/978-3-319-56617-7_18

23. Halderman, J.A., et al.: Lest we remember: cold-boot attacks on encryption keys. Commun. ACM **52**(5), 91–98 (2009)
24. Håstad, J., Impagliazzo, R., Levin, L.A., Luby, M.: A pseudorandom generator from any one-way function. SIAM J. Comput. **28**(4), 1364–1396 (1999)
25. Holmgren, J.: On necessary padding with IO. Cryptology ePrint Archive (2015)
26. Hsiao, C.-Y., Lu, C.-J., Reyzin, L.: Conditional computational entropy, or toward separating pseudoentropy from compressibility. In: Naor, M. (ed.) EUROCRYPT 2007. LNCS, vol. 4515, pp. 169–186. Springer, Heidelberg (2007). https://doi.org/10.1007/978-3-540-72540-4_10
27. Itkis, G., Reyzin, L.: Forward-secure signatures with optimal signing and verifying. In: Kilian, J. (ed.) CRYPTO 2001. LNCS, vol. 2139, pp. 332–354. Springer, Heidelberg (2001). https://doi.org/10.1007/3-540-44647-8_20
28. Jain, A., Lin, H., Sahai, A.: Indistinguishability obfuscation from well-founded assumptions. In: Proceedings of the 53rd Annual ACM SIGACT Symposium on Theory of Computing, pp. 60–73 (2021)
29. Katz, J., Vaikuntanathan, V.: Signature schemes with bounded leakage resilience. In: Matsui, M. (ed.) ASIACRYPT 2009. LNCS, vol. 5912, pp. 703–720. Springer, Heidelberg (2009). https://doi.org/10.1007/978-3-642-10366-7_41
30. Kocher, P.C.: Timing attacks on implementations of Diffie-Hellman, RSA, DSS, and other systems. In: Koblitz, N. (ed.) CRYPTO 1996. LNCS, vol. 1109, pp. 104–113. Springer, Heidelberg (1996). https://doi.org/10.1007/3-540-68697-5_9
31. Kocher, P., Jaffe, J., Jun, B.: Differential power analysis. In: Wiener, M. (ed.) CRYPTO 1999. LNCS, vol. 1666, pp. 388–397. Springer, Heidelberg (1999). https://doi.org/10.1007/3-540-48405-1_25
32. Krawczyk, H.: Simple forward-secure signatures from any signature scheme. In: Jajodia, S., Samarati, P. (eds.) ACM CCS 2000, pp. 108–115. ACM Press (2000)
33. Lewko, A., Rouselakis, Y., Waters, B.: Achieving leakage resilience through dual system encryption. In: Ishai, Y. (ed.) TCC 2011. LNCS, vol. 6597, pp. 70–88. Springer, Heidelberg (2011). https://doi.org/10.1007/978-3-642-19571-6_6
34. Li, X., Ma, F., Quach, W., Wichs, D.: Leakage-resilient key exchange and two-seed extractors. In: Micciancio, D., Ristenpart, T. (eds.) CRYPTO 2020. LNCS, vol. 12170, pp. 401–429. Springer, Cham (2020). https://doi.org/10.1007/978-3-030-56784-2_14
35. Malkin, T., Micciancio, D., Miner, S.: Efficient generic forward-secure signatures with an unbounded number of time periods. In: Knudsen, L.R. (ed.) EUROCRYPT 2002. LNCS, vol. 2332, pp. 400–417. Springer, Heidelberg (2002). https://doi.org/10.1007/3-540-46035-7_27
36. Naor, M., Segev, G.: Public-Key cryptosystems resilient to key leakage. In: Halevi, S. (ed.) CRYPTO 2009. LNCS, vol. 5677, pp. 18–35. Springer, Heidelberg (2009). https://doi.org/10.1007/978-3-642-03356-8_2
37. Pointcheval, D., Sanders, O.: Forward secure non-interactive key exchange. In: Abdalla, M., De Prisco, R. (eds.) SCN 2014. LNCS, vol. 8642, pp. 21–39. Springer, Cham (2014). https://doi.org/10.1007/978-3-319-10879-7_2
38. Sahai, A., Waters, B.: How to use indistinguishability obfuscation: deniable encryption, and more. In: Shmoys, D.B. (ed.) 46th ACM STOC, pp. 475–484. ACM Press (2014)
39. Zhandry, M.: The Magic of ELFs. In: Robshaw, M., Katz, J. (eds.) CRYPTO 2016, Part I. LNCS, vol. 9814, pp. 479–508. Springer, Heidelberg (2016). https://doi.org/10.1007/978-3-662-53018-4_18

Anonymous Broadcast Authentication with Logarithmic-Order Ciphertexts from LWE

Yoshinori Aono[1,2](✉) and Junji Shikata[1,3]

[1] Institute of Advanced Sciences, Yokohama National University, 79-5 Tokiwadai, Hodogaya-ku, Yokohama 240-8501, Japan
aono-yoshinori-xf@ynu.ac.jp

[2] National Institute of Information and Communications Technology, 4-2-1, Nukui-Kitamachi, Koganei, Tokyo, Japan

[3] Graduate School of Environment and Information Sciences, Yokohama National University, 79-7 Tokiwadai, Hodogaya-ku, Yokohama 240-8501, Japan

Abstract. We propose an anonymous broadcast authentication (ABA) scheme to simultaneously control massive numbers of devices within practical resources. As a theoretical foundation, we find a barrier to construct an ABA working with a larger number of devices: there is a trilemma between (i) security, (ii) ciphertext length, and (iii) freedom in the target devices selection. For practical use, we propose ABAs with a ciphertext size of $O(\log N)$ where N is the number of target devices while we impose a certain restriction on (iii). We provide an ABA template and instantiate it into a specific scheme from the learning with errors (LWE) problem. Then, we give estimation of size and timing resources.

Keywords: Anonymous broadcast authentication · IoT Network · Learning with errors problem

1 Introduction

The ABA [25] is a one-way communication from a central server to multiple resource-limited devices. The server broadcasts a command to control a subset of devices. The following conditions (1) (2) are the minimum desired specifications for correctness. (1) A message from the server includes information on the IDs of the target devices and control commands. Each device that receives the message either executes the command if the device is included in the target devices or does nothing if otherwise. (2) The received message has integrity and authenticity.

Also, it should satisfy two additional security notions (3) (4). (3) Unforgeability: In a situation where secret information of some devices are leaked, an entity with the information cannot forge a legitimate command. (4) Anonymity: Each device can detect whether or not it is a target, but cannot determine whether another device is a target.

An application that we envision is sending emergency signals to reboot or shut down malware-infected devices. Thus, we assume that the space of commands is

J. Deng et al. (Eds.): CANS 2023, LNCS 14342, pp. 28–50, 2023.
https://doi.org/10.1007/978-981-99-7563-1_2

small (a few bits) to send reboot, shutdown, or other optional flags. We expect the number of devices to be about 10^6–10^9 to control all the devices within a wireless area (several square kilometers) simultaneously in the 5G IoT or the network beyond it. The entire process of command generation in a central server, communication, and authentication in target devices must also be completed within a few seconds for a fast response to an emergency.

For the application, the command should be encrypted to satisfy the above (3) and (4). However, several barriers are known regarding the ciphertext length. Assuming the atomic model [14,15], an ABA that has anonymity must have the ciphertext $\Omega(n)$, where n is the number of target or joined devices; it depends on the security requirement of anonymity. A similar bound is derived simply from Shannon's coding theorem because the condition (1) requires that the information amount contained in the ciphertext should exceed N under the assumption that the target device set is randomly selected from a family of any subset of N devices.

These observations deduce the following trilemma: In ABA, the three conditions (i) security (anonymity), (ii) ciphertext length, and (iii) freedom in the target devices selection are not simultaneously satisfied. For practical use, we propose an ABA with a ciphertext size of $O(\log N)$ while we impose a certain restriction on (iii). Concretely, our ABA protocol has the device IDs represented by a vector $(\mathsf{id}_1, \ldots, \mathsf{id}_K)$ where $\mathsf{id}_j \in [N_j] := \{1, 2, \ldots, N_j\}$ and ciphertext length $O(\sum N_j)$. It can control $\prod N_j$ devices, which is an exponential number to the ciphertext length.

We first construct an ABA template and provide instantiations from the LWE problem. With a parameter set controlling 10^9 devices with 128-bit security, the ciphertext length is about 1 MBytes and the expected processing timing of the verification in target devices is in a few seconds in ARM Cortex-M4 processors.

1.1 Related Work

Atomic model assumes that the server broadcasts a sequence of ciphertexts $\mathsf{ct}_1, \ldots, \mathsf{ct}_\ell$ that encrypts a control command. Each device j then tries to decrypt each ct_i using its key dk_j. The length ℓ of the sequence in this model is well-studied in the private key broadcast encryption (prBE) by Kiaias-Samari [14] and by Kobayashi et al. [15] including ABA. They showed that $\ell \geq N$ if an ABA controlling N devices has anonymity and it deduces the total bit-lengths of the ciphertexts is $\Omega(N \cdot \lambda)$ where λ is the security parameter. The bounds can be relaxed to $\ell \geq |S|$ and $\Omega(|S| \cdot \lambda)$ respectively if it considers the weak-anonymity instead of the anonymity where $\mathcal{S} \subset [N]$ is the set of target devices. In both cases, concrete constructions achieving the bounds are given by [15,25].

Broadcast encryption (BE) is considerably similar to ABA. At the formal definition level, the notion of ABA is equivalent to prBE in [21, Def. 3.1]. On the other hand, security notions are slightly changed whose reasons are mainly from the application. It is an authentication-oriented analog of anonymous BE (ANOBE).

The anonymity notion in the BE framework was first proposed by Barth et al. [2], which corresponds to the weak anonymity in the ABA framework. After, an efficient scheme from the DDH assumption over groups is given by Benoît et al. [18] with the notion of ANOBE, and its lattice interpretation is given in [12]. They keep the freedom in the choice of target devices and thus requires linear-sized ciphertexts, concretely, $O(N - r)$, where N and r are the numbers of joined and revoked devices. Fazio et al. [9] proposes a public key BE with outsider anonymity and CPA/CCA security with their notions. They achieved the log-order ciphertext size $O(r \log(N/r))$, but it is still linear in r.

For practical use on IoT devices, we have to consider the decryption timing. Efficient implementations of BE have been considered in many existing works. [5] reported a survey of several pairing-based BE systems and implementation results in the same environment on a standard laptop. In particular, sublinear ciphertext size BEs with some functionalities [4,11] can decrypt less than one second even for $N = 10^6$.

Following the existing works, we mention two issues when we import the techniques in BE to our ABA. First, constructing a practical scheme with short, i.e., $o(N)$ [bit] ciphertext with keeping reasonable anonymity has been one of the challenging problems in BE and its variants. It is not trivial to import an existing scheme and to prove an anonymity of ABA. On the other hand, a transformation technique to add the unforgeability is useful as explained in the next paragraph.

Interpreting the authentication result as the transmission of a one bit message, the framework of ABA can be considered as a prBE with additional functionalities. Our scheme in this paper can be considered as a new result of short ciphertext prBE, besides the context of ABA.

Transformation to add unforgeability can be done by a technique that converts a weak-security prBE to a CCA1 secure prBE. The simplest transformation should be adding a signature to the broadcasting ciphertext as in [17]. The proof of anonymity in our ABA is straightforward by considering similarity between the unforgeability of ABA and the CCA1 security of prBE.

Infeasibility of Naïve Atomic ABA Systems: Consider a size of an atomic type ABA constructed from a standard encryption and a signature scheme. For example, a standard (resp. structured) lattice-based encryption needs tens of kilobytes (resp. half a kilobyte) length ciphertexts; FrodoKEM [10] and FALCON [8] provide good examples of sizes after optimization. This implies that a system for controlling $N = 10^6$ devices requires a command ciphertext presented in gigabytes, which is too large to process on a low-resource device. Thus, an ABA with short ciphertexts is necessary to control millions of devices in the real world.

Anonymous multicast or anonymous message delivery invented in [3,6] is a similar terminology but is a different notion. It can broadcast a message to all the devices in a network whose connectivity is limited and represented by an undirected graph, and can hide who sends the message.

1.2 Our Contributions and Paper Organization

Trilemma in ABA Construction: Relations among considered limitations and the linear lower bound of the ciphertext length are organized as follows.

We use At and An to represent that an ABA is in the atomic model and has anonymity, respectively. LB represents that an ABA has ciphertext longer than N or $|\mathcal{S}|$ on average over the selection of target sets and messages. Then, the result of Kobayashi et al. [15] can be described as $[At \text{ AND } An] \Rightarrow LB$.

In addition, we denote F as the freedom in the choice of target devices, i.e., any $\mathcal{S} \subset [N]$ can be selected as a target device set, and assume it is randomly chosen from $2^{[N]}$. According to Shannon's coding theorem, the ciphertext must be longer than N bits on average because the broadcasting ciphertext entropy exceeds N bits. Thus, we have $F \Rightarrow LB$ and deduce the following relation

$$\neg LB \Rightarrow \neg F \text{ AND } [\neg At \text{ OR } \neg An].$$

It shows that the short ciphertext ($\neg LB$), anonymity (An) and the freedom in the choice of targets (F) are not satisfied simultaneously. In particular, an ABA with short ciphertexts must restrict conditions among F, At, and An.

Design Rationale: From the viewpoint of the aforementioned limitations, our construction satisfies $\neg F$, $\neg At$, and a nearly anonymity. We emphasize that it is on the borderline of the feasible area.

We explain why we restrict the strength of anonymity by introducing a new notion of anonymity which we named it single anonymity (Sect. 5.1), or shortly SA. It is a notion about information leakage on $\mathsf{id}' \overset{?}{\in} \mathcal{S}$, i.e., a binary information whether id' is contained in $\mathcal{S}$ or not, from other patterns $\{\mathsf{id} \overset{?}{\in} \mathcal{S}\}$. We proved that $\neg F \Rightarrow \neg SA$. Thus, combining with $F \Rightarrow LB$, we can conclude any short ciphertext ABA inherently lacks the single anonymity, and this is the reason that we do not investigate the complete anonymity.

Base atomic type ABA is constructed from a Vernam-styled multirecipient encryption (MRE) which is a fundamental gadget with information-theoretic security. Technically, the Vernam-styled gadget cannot be secure if the server sends ciphertexts with the same secret key many times. To address this problem, we transformed MRE to a computationally secure ABA with a template function f_{prm} using the technique of Kurosawa et al. [16]. Then, we instantiate it to a practical protocol by using an LWE-styled function. This template construction was within the atomic model that sends $M \geq N$ ciphertexts to N devices.

ABA with logarithmic-order ciphertext length is constructed by the concatenation of the base ABAs. However, it is easily seen that the concatenated ABA does not have anonymity. We propose a modification using the idea of Agrawal et al.'s inner-product encryption [1] to add anonymity in a limited sense. Finally, we add the unforgeability by adding a signature.

Each device is indexed by a vector $(i_1, \ldots, i_K)$ where $i_j \in [N_j] := \{1, 2, \ldots, N_j\}$ and each N_j is the size of each coordinate set as public parameters. The target set is defined by a sequence of sets $S_j \subset [N_j]$ and a device is a target if $i_j \in S_j$ for all j. A trade-off between the ciphertext length and the flexibility of target sets can be considered by changing N_j. For instance, $K = 1$ corresponds to an atomic ABA that can control N_1 devices. On the other hand, for $K \geq 2$

and setting all N_j equivalent, it derives an ABA controlling $N = N_1^K$ devices by $O(K \cdot N_1) = O(K \cdot N^{1/K})$ [bit] ciphertext. In particular, taking $N_j = 2$ for all j, it provides an ABA to control $N = 2^K$ devices by $O(K) = O(\log N)$ [bit] ciphertext.

We remark that the above setting of indexes and selecting method assume a realistic situation. For instance, the vector-style index can be recognized as an avatar of $ID = (company, model, serialnumber, \ldots)$. Assume *company* is one of $\{cA, cB, cC, \ldots\}$ and *model* is one of $\{mA, mB, mC, \ldots\}$. Then, suppose devices with model mA produced by cA found to be infected by malware, one can broadcast a shutdown command to the devices indicated by the wildcard $(mA, cA, *, *, \ldots)$.

Data sizes and expected timings to control 2^{20} to 2^{30} devices are given in Table 1. Besides the basic parameters, we give the sizes of a verification key and a control command and expected consuming cycles in verification in each target device assuming to include an ARM Cortex-M4 processor. In particular, assuming a processor working with 100MHz, it takes a few seconds in the setting of $K = 30$ and 128-bit security.

We remark that the verification process is dominated by the computation of SHA-3 in signature verification that requires 213 cycles/Byte [23]. It is possible to speed up the verification dramatically by employing a lightweight hash function. For instance, Chaskey [20] can work with 7 cycles/Byte in ARM Cortex-M4.

Table 1. Sizes of a verification key ($(4Kn)\lfloor \log_2 q \rfloor/8 + \mathsf{pksize}$) and command ciphertext ($(1 + 8Kn)\lfloor \log_2 q \rfloor/8 + \mathsf{sigsize}$) in Bytes in our lattice based ABA. K is the number of concatenated base ABAs, which makes it possible to control 2^K devices. n and q are the LWE dimension and modulus, respectively. L and Q are the variety of messages and the buffers to prevent overflow, respectively. $(\mathsf{pksize}, \mathsf{sigsize})$ is the size of public key and signature of a strongly and existentially unforgeable signature assumed to be (897, 666) and (1793, 1280) from 128 and 256 bit security FALCON signature [8] where the unit is in Bytes. The last two columns contain expected timings in the million clocks of signature verification and canceling computation to recover m in each target device with ARM Cortex-M4 processors. Other details will be given in Sect. 6.

Sec. Lev.	(K, L)	n	(q, Q)	Size($\mathsf{vk}_{\mathsf{id}}$) + pksize [Byte]	Size(cmd_S) +$\mathsf{sigsize}$ [Byte]	mil. cyc. (Σ.Vrfy)	mil. cyc. (Cancel)
128	(20,4)	926	(68588467, 428678)	250020 + 897	500052 + 666	107.1	0.1
	(20, 256)	1164	(4921551113, 480621)	384120 + 897	768245 + 666	164.2	0.4
	(30, 4)	961	(128364259, 534852)	389205 + 897	778414 + 666	166.4	0.2
	(30, 256)	1119	(9176392691, 597422)	611490 + 897	1222985 + 666	261.0	0.6
256	(20, 4)	1799	(95600731, 597505)	485730 + 1793	971464 + 1280	208.0	0.2
	(20, 256)	2238	(6824259821, 666432)	738540 + 1793	1477085 + 1280	315.7	0.8
	(30, 4)	1863	(178726489, 744694)	782460 + 1793	1564924 + 1280	334.3	0.3
	(30, 256)	2302	(12714961717, 827797)	1174020 + 1793	2348045 + 1280	501.2	1.2

Comparisons with existing works from the viewpoint on the performance and security are given as follows. Kobayashi et al. [15] provided the MAC-based constructions satisfying the anonymity (resp. weak-anonymity) whose command sizes are exactly $(N+2)\lambda$ (resp. $(|S|+2)\lambda$) that hits the non-asymptotic linear lower bound where λ is the security parameter. Watanabe et al. [26] proposed shorter command ABAs by relaxing the anonymity condition and employing improved Bloom filters whereas command size is still linear $O(N \cdot \log_2(1/\mu))$ to the number of devices. Here, μ is the false-positive rate, for which they assume 2^{-10} to 2^{-20}. For reference, to control $N = 10^6$ devices within the rate $\mu = 2^{-10}$, the size is about 1.8 MBytes. Our logarithmic-order constructions achieve much shorter commands than the previous construction by sacrificing anonymity.

Paper Organization: Section 2 introduces basic definitions, notations, LWE, and ABA. In Sect. 3, we provide a Vernam-styled multirecipient encryption (MRE) that broadcasts an encrypted message only for target devices with information-theoretic security. In Sect. 4, we convert the MRE to a template of computationally secure ABA. In Sect. 5, we propose an ABA of short command ciphertext by a concatenation of ABAs. Section 6 provides a lattice based protocol with concrete parameters, sizes of ciphertexts, and expected timings. Finally, in Sect. 7 we discuss future works.

2 Preliminaries

$\mathbb{Z}$ and $\mathbb{N}$ are the set of integers and natural numbers. For $N \in \mathbb{N}$, denote the set $[N] := \{1, \dots, N\}$. Define $\mathbb{Z}_q := \{0, 1, \dots, q-1\}$ and q is assumed to be an odd prime. $\mathbb{Z}_q^\times := \mathbb{Z}_q \setminus \{0\}$. For a finite set A, let the notation $a \xleftarrow{\$} A$ be the uniform sampling. Bold letters such as $\boldsymbol{c}$ represent a row vector and its transpose notation $\boldsymbol{c}^T$ represents a column vector. We use $\boldsymbol{u}_i$ to denote the i-th unit vector $(0, \dots, 1, \dots, 0)$ whereas the dimension is omitted if it is clear from the context. For vectors and matrices, the notation $||$ denotes the concatenation. For two sets $\mathcal{S}_0, \mathcal{S}_1$ of target devices, $\mathcal{S}_0 \triangle \mathcal{S}_1$ is the symmetric difference $(\mathcal{S}_0 \setminus \mathcal{S}_1) \cup (\mathcal{S}_1 \setminus \mathcal{S}_0)$.

The LWE problem [22] is a fundamental toolkit for constructing lattice based schemes. For a dimension parameter n, a modulo q, and an error distribution χ, the decision LWE is defined by the problem to distinguish the polynomial number of samples $\{(\boldsymbol{a}_i, \boldsymbol{a}_i \boldsymbol{s}^T + e_i)\}_{i=1,\dots,m}$ and $\{(\boldsymbol{a}_i, u_i)\}_{i=1,\dots,m}$ where $\boldsymbol{s}^T \in \mathbb{Z}_q^n$ is a random secret vector fixed at all the samples. $\boldsymbol{a}_i$, e_i, u_i are random vectors from $\mathbb{Z}_q^n$, random errors from χ, and random elements from $\mathbb{Z}_q$ respectively. χ is typically the discrete Gaussian distribution $D_{\mathbb{Z},\sigma}$ whose density function defined over $\mathbb{Z}$ is $\Pr[X = x] \propto \exp(-x^2/2\sigma^2)$. The goal of the search version of LWE is to recover $\boldsymbol{s}$ from legitimate samples $\{\boldsymbol{a}_i, \boldsymbol{a}_i \cdot \boldsymbol{s}^T + e_i\}_{i=1,\dots,m}$. The polynomial time equivalence between decision and search is known [22]. We set the lattice parameter using Albrecht et al.'s lattice estimator [7] as of May 2022.

2.1 Anonymous Broadcast Authentication (ABA)

We introduce the notion of ABA, and its correctness, unforgeability, and anonymity by Watanabe et al. [25]. They are essentially the same as in the original work whereas we explicitly mention t the number of colluded devices in the security notions.

Definition 1. *An ABA is formally defined by the tuple of four functions* $\Pi = (\mathsf{Setup}, \mathsf{Join}, \mathsf{Auth}, \mathsf{Vrfy})$.

- $\mathsf{Setup}(1^\lambda, N, \mathcal{D}) \rightarrow \mathsf{ak}$: *An algorithm that outputs the authorization key* ak. 1^λ *is a security parameter,* N *is the maximum number of joined devices, and* $\mathcal{D}$ *is a family of sets* $\mathcal{S} \subset [N]$ *allowed to use as a set of the target device.*
- $\mathsf{Join}(\mathsf{ak}, \mathsf{id}) \rightarrow \mathsf{vk}_{\mathsf{id}}$: *An algorithm that outputs a verification key* $\mathsf{vk}_{\mathsf{id}}$ *embedded to the device* id.
- $\mathsf{Auth}(\mathsf{ak}, \mathsf{m}, \mathcal{S}) \rightarrow \mathsf{cmd}_{\mathcal{S}}$: *It outputs a command ciphertext that encrypts the information of the message* m *and the set* $\mathcal{S}$ *of the target devices.*
- $\mathsf{Vrfy}(\mathsf{vk}_i, \mathsf{cmd}_{\mathcal{S}}) \rightarrow \mathsf{m}/\mathsf{reject}$: *It verifies the command ciphertext* $\mathsf{cmd}_{\mathcal{S}}$ *using the verification key* $\mathsf{vk}_{\mathsf{id}}$. *It returns the message or* reject *if it was accepted or rejected, respectively.*

The abovementioned algorithms, except for Vrfy are assumed to be probabilistic polynomials. The family $\mathcal{D}$ is typically set as $2^{[N]}$ in several early works whereas we restrict the freedom in the choice of a subset in $[N]$ to construct a short ciphertext ABA.

Definition 2. *We say an ABA* Π *has correctness if for any fixed* $(1^\lambda, N, \mathcal{D})$, ak *that are allowed to input,* $\mathcal{S} \in \mathcal{D}$, *and any* $\mathsf{m}, \mathsf{id} \in [N]$, *it holds that*

$$\Pr[\mathsf{Vrfy}(\mathsf{Join}(\mathsf{ak}, \mathsf{id}), \mathsf{Auth}(\mathsf{ak}, \mathsf{m}, \mathcal{S})) \rightarrow \mathsf{m}] = 1 - \mathsf{negl}(\lambda) \text{ if } \mathsf{id} \in \mathcal{S}, \text{ and}$$
$$\Pr[\mathsf{Vrfy}(\mathsf{Join}(\mathsf{ak}, \mathsf{id}), \mathsf{Auth}(\mathsf{ak}, \mathsf{m}, \mathcal{S})) \rightarrow \mathsf{reject}] = 1 - \mathsf{negl}(\lambda) \text{ if } \mathsf{id} \notin \mathcal{S}.$$

The probability is over the random coins in Join *and* Auth *(and possibly* Vrfy*).*

Below are the game-based formal definitions of unforgeability and anonymity within the situation where the receiver devices are colluded and can share their verification keys. We remark that a message security, i.e., whether an adversary can extract information on m, is not considered as in [25].

Definition 3 *(t-unforgeability [25]). Consider the game between a challenger* C *and an adversary* A.

0: C *and* A *share* $(1^\lambda, N, \mathcal{D})$ *and* C *runs* $\mathsf{Setup}(1^\lambda, N, \mathcal{D}) \rightarrow \mathsf{ak}$. *Let* $M_a = M_v = \phi$ *be the messages used in the authentication and verification queries. Also, let* $\mathcal{D} \subset [N]$ *and* $W \subset \mathcal{D}$ *be the set of considered devices during the game, and the set of colluded devices.* $\mathit{flag} \in \{0,1\}$ *is a variable that indicates whether the adversary gets the success forging.*

1: (Key generation) A *selects a set of considered devices* $\mathcal{D} \subset [N]$ *and send it to* C. C *runs* $\mathsf{Join}(\mathsf{ak}, \mathsf{id}) \rightarrow \mathsf{vk}_{\mathsf{id}}$ *for all* $\mathsf{id} \in \mathcal{D}$.

2: (Collusion query) A *selects* $\mathsf{id} \in D$ *and send it to* C. C *adds* id *to* W *and send back* $\mathsf{vk}_{\mathsf{id}}$ *to* A. A *can repeat this step until* $|W| < t$.

3: (Authentication query) A *sends* $(\mathsf{m}, \mathcal{S})$ *to* C *where the selection is limited within* $\mathcal{S} \subset D$ *and* $\mathsf{m} \notin M_v$. *Then,* C *runs* $\mathsf{Auth}(\mathsf{ak}, \mathsf{m}, \mathcal{S}) \rightarrow \mathsf{cmd}_{\mathcal{S}}$ *and returns it to* A.

4: (Verification query) A *generates a set* $(\mathsf{m}, \mathsf{id}, \mathsf{cmd}_{\mathcal{S}})$ *and send them to* C. C *runs* $\mathsf{Vrfy}(\mathsf{vk}_{\mathsf{id}}, \mathsf{cmd}_{\mathcal{S}})$ *and returns the output to* A. *If* $\mathsf{Vrfy}(\mathsf{vk}_{\mathsf{id}}, \mathsf{cmd}_{\mathcal{S}}) = \mathsf{m}$, $\mathsf{id} \notin W$ *and* $\mathsf{m} \notin M_a$, *set* $\mathit{flag} = 1$ *else set* $\mathit{flag} = 0$. *Add* m *to* M_v.

After repeating Steps 3 and 4, if there exists a verification trial such that $\mathit{flag} = 1$, *we define the output of the experiment* $\mathsf{Exp}^{\mathsf{CMA}}_{\Pi,\mathsf{A}}(\lambda, N, \ell)$ *is* 1, *and otherwise it is* 0. *The advantage of* A *on the protocol* Π *is*

$$\mathsf{Adv}^{\mathsf{CMA}}_{\Pi,\mathsf{A}}(\lambda, N, \ell) := \Pr[\mathsf{Exp}^{\mathsf{CMA}}_{\Pi,\mathsf{A}}(\lambda, N, \ell) \to 1].$$

We say the ABA protocol Π *has* t*-unforgeability if the advantage is a negligible function of* λ.

The above formal definition can be interpreted as follows. Suppose t devices are taken over and colluded. Under a situation where an attacker collects secret information in these devices, it cannot forge a legitimate command ciphertext that an uncolluded device accepts. We will construct our unforgeable ABA from a base ABA by adding a signature.

We deal with the following passive attack rather than the above active attack.

Definition 4 [25] *(t-anonymity). Consider the game between a challenger* C *and an adversary* A. *As the definition of unforgeability,* t *indicates the number of colluded devices.*

0: C *and* A *share* $(1^\lambda, N, \mathcal{D})$ *and* C *runs* $\mathsf{Setup}(1^\lambda, N, \mathcal{D}) \to \mathsf{ak}$. *Let* $M_a = \phi$ *be the set of the command used in the authentication. Also, let* $\mathcal{D} \subset [N]$ *and* $W \subset \mathcal{D}$ *be the set of considered devices during the game, and the set of colluded devices.*

1, 2: The same as the Steps 1, 2 in the unforgeability game (Definition 3).

3: (Authentication query) A *selects a pair* $(\mathsf{m}, \mathcal{S}), \mathcal{S} \subset \mathcal{D}, \mathsf{m} \notin M_a$ *and send it to* C. C *runs* $\mathsf{Auth}(\mathsf{ak}, \mathsf{m}, \mathcal{S}) \to \mathsf{cmd}_{\mathcal{S}}$ *and return the output and adds* m *to* M_a.

4: (Challenge query) A *selects a command* $\mathsf{m} \notin M_a$ *and two sets of devices* $\mathcal{S}_0, \mathcal{S}_1$ *and send them to* C. C *runs* $\mathsf{Auth}(\mathsf{ak}, \mathsf{m}, \mathcal{S}_b) \to \mathsf{cmd}_{\mathcal{S}_b}$ *where* $b \in \{0, 1\}$ *is a random bit. Return the ciphertext to* A. A *guesses* b' *for the random bit.*

We define the output of the game is 1 *if* $b = b'$, *i.e., the adversary succeeds in guessing, and the output is* 0 *if otherwise. The advantage is*

$$\mathsf{Adv}^{\mathsf{ANO}}_{\Pi,\mathsf{A}}(\lambda, N, \ell) := \left| 2 \Pr\left[\mathsf{Exp}^{\mathsf{ANO}}_{\Pi,\mathsf{A}}(\lambda, N, \ell)\right] - 1 \right|.$$

In Step 4, the considered sets $\mathcal{S}_0$ and $\mathcal{S}_1$ must satisfy

$$\mathcal{S}_d := (\mathcal{S}_0 \triangle \mathcal{S}_1) \cap W = \phi \tag{1}$$

to prevent a trivial distinguishing; if $\mathcal{S}_d \neq \phi$, A can check whether some $\mathsf{id} \in \mathcal{S}_d$ is in $\mathcal{S}_0$ or not via the decryption oracle.

We pointed out that the condition (1) does not hide the size of sets. The notion of weak anonymity is defined by adding the condition $|\mathcal{S}_0| = |\mathcal{S}_1|$ besides (1) in Step 4. Also, the outsider anonymity is defined by replacing (1) with $(\mathcal{S}_0 \cup \mathcal{S}_1) \cap W = \phi$ in Step 4. It is slightly weaker than the weak anonymity, though it has no restriction on the size of sets [25].

3 Vernam-Styled Multirecipient Encryption with Information-Theoretic Security

As a base gadget to construct our ABA, we introduce a simple multirecipient secret key encryption. It is a one-way protocol from a central server to N participant devices. The server packs a set of messages into one ciphertext and broadcasts it to the devices. Each device decrypts the ciphertext with its key. It has the information-theoretic security on messages; that is, each device i can recover the i-th message m_i whereas it can gain no information on the messages m_j $(j \neq i)$ to the other devices.

Definition 5. *A multirecipient encryption (MRE) is formally defined by a tuple of three functions* $\mathsf{MRE} = (\mathsf{KeyGen}, \mathsf{Enc}, \mathsf{Dec})$.

- $\mathsf{MRE.KeyGen}(N, \mathsf{pp}) \rightarrow (\mathsf{ek}, \mathsf{dk}_1, \ldots, \mathsf{dk}_N)$: *It outputs an encryption key* ek *and decryption keys* $\{\mathsf{dk}_i\}_{i \in [N]}$.
- $\mathsf{MRE.Enc}(\mathsf{ek}, \{m_i\}_{i \in S}) \rightarrow \mathsf{ct}$: *$S$ is the set of target devices to which messages are sent. m_i is a message sent to the i-th device and the server can take different m_i for each i. An encryption algorithm outputs* ct *to be broadcasted.*
- $\mathsf{MRE.Dec}(\mathsf{dk}_i, \mathsf{ct}) \rightarrow m_i'$: *A decryption algorithm that recovers a message in the i-th device from* ct *by using one's secret key* dk_i.

Construction: The public parameter $\mathsf{pp} = (M, q)$ is the pair of a vector dimension and a prime modulus. The decryption keys are randomly generated independent column vectors $\mathsf{dk}_i^T \in \mathbb{Z}_q^M$. The encryption key is the set $\mathsf{ek} = \{\mathsf{dk}_1^T, \ldots, \mathsf{dk}_N^T\}$. Each participant device i has pp and dk_i^T. For a set of target devices $\mathcal{S} \subset [N]$ and a set of messages $\{m_i\}_{i \in S}$ where $m_i \in \mathbb{Z}_q^\times$, the ciphertext ct is a randomly chosen vector in $\mathbb{Z}_q^M$ that satisfies $\mathsf{ct} \cdot \mathsf{dk}_i^T \equiv m_i \pmod q$ for all $i \in S$. The decryption at device i is the computation of inner-product $\mathsf{ct} \cdot \mathsf{dk}_i^T \pmod q$. Thus, the correctness is immediate.

Since each coordinate is of $\mathbb{Z}_q^M$, the sizes of the encryption key, decryption key, and ciphertext are $NM \log_2 q$, $M \log_2 q$, and $M \log_2 q$ in bits, respectively.

This construction can be regarded as a generalization of the concatenation of the Vernam cipher since under the situation where $N = M$ and all dk_i^T's are a multiple of i-th unit vector $\boldsymbol{u}_i^T$, the ciphertext $\mathsf{ct} = (c_1, \ldots, c_N)$ is the concatenation of c_i by which the i-th device can decrypt. We note the reason for setting dk_i^T independent vectors instead of $k_i \cdot \boldsymbol{u}_i^T$ where k_is are multiples. Consider a chosen plaintext attack that an attacker can obtain a pair (m_i, ct) for an index i. Then, the decryption key can be easily found by a simple division where $\mathsf{dk}_i^T = k_i \cdot \boldsymbol{u}_i^T$. However, in the case where dk_i's are independent, the information-theoretic security can be ensured using vectors until M pairs of (m_i, ct) are obtained by the attacker. Using the M pairs, one can recover all the dk_i^T's via the solution of simultaneous equations.

Information-Theoretic Security: Suppose the situation where the devices $1, 2, \ldots, t$ are colluded, and an attacker wants to recover the message m_{t+1} of the device $t+1$ from ct using the leaked keys $\mathsf{dk}_1^T, \ldots, \mathsf{dk}_t^T$. In this case, the attacker can know only the fact that dk_{t+1} is independent to $\mathsf{dk}_1^T, \ldots, \mathsf{dk}_t^T$.

Suppose that the attacker guesses a vector $\boldsymbol{v}^T$ and $m'_{t+1} = \mathsf{ct} \cdot \boldsymbol{v}^T$ as candidates of dk_{t+1}^T and m_{t+1}, respectively. Then, all the vectors $\boldsymbol{v}^T, 2\boldsymbol{v}^T, \ldots, (q-1)\boldsymbol{v}^T \bmod q$ can also be candidates for the secret keys with equal possibility. Thus, $\{m'_{t+1}, 2m'_{t+1}, \ldots, (q-1)m'_{t+1}\} = \mathbb{Z}_q^\times$, are also the set of candidates of the message with equal possibility. It means that the attacker gains no information about m_{t+1} from ct and colluded keys. A similar argument can prove the impossibility of forging ct that embeds a message to the device $t+1$.

Therefore, this MRE can be used as an ABA with information-theoretic security in one-time broadcasting whereas any security under chosen-plaintext attacks and key reusing situations does not hold. Specifically, suppose the situation where the attacker can obtain ct corresponding to any chosen $\{m_i\}_{i \in S}$ and any S with fixed decryption keys. The attacker can recover dk_i^Ts by solving linear equations from a sufficient number of pairs of messages and ciphertexts.

4 Template Construction of Base ABA

We transform the above information-theoretic MRE to ABA by adding a repeatable property. The main differences over the base MRE are: (1) it broadcasts the same message to a selected subset of participant devices, and (2) its security base is from a computational problem assumption. We give a template construction and discuss its security. Also, we will instantiate it to our lattice ABA.

4.1 A Template

We give a template of our base ABA using a function $f_{\mathsf{prm}}(\boldsymbol{c}^T)$ defined over an r-dimensional column vector with a parameter prm. We assume the function has the following "linear-like homomorphic" properties. For scalars a, b and vectors $\boldsymbol{x}, \boldsymbol{y}$, $f_{\mathsf{prm}}(a\boldsymbol{x}^T + b\boldsymbol{y}^T) = a \circ f_{\mathsf{prm}}(\boldsymbol{x}^T) \otimes b \circ f_{\mathsf{prm}}(\boldsymbol{y}^T)$ holds with operations $(\circ, \otimes)$ to compute a linear combination of vectors $f_{\mathsf{prm}}(\sum_{i=1}^{M} v_i \boldsymbol{y}_i^T)$ in verification. We also assume that an inverse $f_{\mathsf{prm}}(\boldsymbol{x}^T)^{-1}$ of $f_{\mathsf{prm}}(\boldsymbol{x}^T)$ that satisfies $f_{\mathsf{prm}}(\boldsymbol{x}^T) \otimes f_{\mathsf{prm}}(\boldsymbol{x}^T)^{-1} = I$ (an unit) is easily computable.

We will instantiate our LWE construction by setting $\mathsf{prm} = \boldsymbol{p} \in \mathbb{Z}_q^r$ and $f_{\boldsymbol{p}}(\boldsymbol{x}^T) = \boldsymbol{p}\boldsymbol{x}^T$. The homomorphic property holds with defining $a \circ \boldsymbol{x} = a\boldsymbol{x} \bmod q$ and $\boldsymbol{x} \otimes \boldsymbol{y} = \boldsymbol{x} + \boldsymbol{y} \bmod q$ for an integer a and vectors $\boldsymbol{x}, \boldsymbol{y}$. The above property holds for any vector $\boldsymbol{p}$ whereas we use a small $\boldsymbol{p}$ of which each coordinate is from a discrete Gaussian.

We remark that other functions can produce other schemes. For example, for a generator g of a finite group, taking $r = 1, \mathsf{prm} = g$ and $f_{\mathsf{prm}}(x) = g^x$ produces an ElGamal construction. The anonymity is from the DDH problem in the group. With the elliptic curve (Curve25519) group, it can construct an ABA controlling 2^{30} devices by a 10KBytes command while it is not quantum-resilient.

Definition 6 *(MRE-based ABA template). Assume the function $f_{\mathsf{prm}}(\cdot)$ has the above homomorphic property. A template of our ABA is defined as follows. Assume that $\mathsf{pp} = (M, q)$ in MRE is fixed from the security parameter λ.*

- $\mathsf{Setup}(1^\lambda, N, \mathcal{D}) \to \mathsf{ak}$: *Run* $\mathsf{MRE.Setup}(N, \mathsf{pp} = (M, q)) \to (\mathsf{ek}, \{\mathsf{dk}_i^T\}) =: \mathsf{ak}$
- $\mathsf{Join}(\mathsf{ak}, \mathsf{id}) \to \mathsf{vk_{id}}$: $\mathsf{vk_{id}} := \mathsf{dk}_{\mathsf{id}}^T$
- $\mathsf{Auth}(\mathsf{ak}, \mathsf{m}, \mathcal{S}) \to \mathsf{cmd}_{\mathcal{S}}$: *Randomly choose an r-dimensional column vector $\boldsymbol{x}^T$ from the domain of f_{prm}. Generate random small vectors $\boldsymbol{e}_1, \ldots, \boldsymbol{e}_N$ from some distribution. Randomly choose a matrix $CT \in \mathbb{Z}_q^{r \times M}$ that satisfies $CT \cdot \mathsf{dk}_i^T = \boldsymbol{x}^T + \boldsymbol{e}_i^T$ for $i \in \mathcal{S}$ and $CT \cdot \mathsf{dk}_i^T$ is far from $\boldsymbol{x}^T$ for $i \notin \mathcal{S}$. Parse CT into the column vectors $\mathsf{ct}_1^T, \ldots, \mathsf{ct}_M^T$, encode them by $F_i = f_{\mathsf{prm}}(\boldsymbol{ct}_i^T)$ and the command is $\mathsf{cmd}_{\mathcal{S}} = (\mathsf{m} \otimes f_{\mathsf{prm}}(\boldsymbol{x}), F_1, \ldots, F_M)$.*
- $\mathsf{Vrfy}(\mathsf{vk_{id}}, \mathsf{cmd}_{\mathcal{S}}) \to \mathsf{m}/\mathsf{reject}$: *For the device's key $\mathsf{dk}_i := (d_{i,1}, \ldots, d_{i,M})$, compute $f = d_{i,1} \circ F_1 \otimes \cdots \otimes d_{i,M} \circ F_M$, and $\mathsf{m}' = \mathsf{m} \otimes f_{\mathsf{prm}}(\boldsymbol{x}) \otimes f^{-1}$.*

For correctness, it is necessary to have some condition in f_{prm} and error vectors. For a legitimate command and decryption key

$$\begin{aligned} & d_{i,1} \circ F_1 \otimes \cdots \otimes d_{i,M} \circ F_M \\ &= f_{\mathsf{prm}}(d_{i,1}\boldsymbol{ct}_1^T + \cdots + d_{i,M}\boldsymbol{ct}_M^T) = f_{\mathsf{prm}}(CT \cdot \mathsf{dk}_i) = f_{\mathsf{prm}}(\boldsymbol{x}^T + \boldsymbol{e}_i^T) \end{aligned} \tag{2}$$

holds. Thus, by the homomorphic property, $(\mathsf{m} \otimes f_{\mathsf{prm}}(\boldsymbol{x}^T)) \otimes f_{\mathsf{prm}}(\boldsymbol{x}^T + \boldsymbol{e}_i^T)^{-1} = \mathsf{m} \otimes f(\boldsymbol{e}_i^T)^{-1}$. An optional decoding mechanism is required to recover m.

Note that an efficient sampling of matrix CT is possible via the precomputation. Let $\boldsymbol{c}_1, \ldots, \boldsymbol{c}_{M-N}$ be independent vectors and each $\boldsymbol{c}_j$ satisfies $\boldsymbol{c}_j \cdot \mathsf{dk}_i^T = 0$ for all $i \in [N]$. Define the matrix C by $C^T = (\boldsymbol{c}_1^T, \ldots, \boldsymbol{c}_{M-N}^T)$. For any matrix $R \in \mathbb{Z}_q^{(M-N) \times M}$, $RC \cdot \mathsf{dk}_i^T = \mathbf{0}^T$ holds. Then, fixing target vectors $\boldsymbol{y}_i^T = (y_{i,1}, \ldots, y_{i,r})^T$, which are set as $\boldsymbol{x}^T + \boldsymbol{e}_i^T$ or a vector far from $\boldsymbol{x}^T$, compute initial vectors $\boldsymbol{b}_j$ so that $\boldsymbol{b}_j \cdot \mathsf{dk}_i^T = y_{i,j}$ by solving simultaneous equations. Let $B = (\boldsymbol{b}_1^T, \ldots, \boldsymbol{b}_r^T)^T$ and then $CT = B + RC$ is the desired random matrix.

4.2 Anonymity

In the Step 4 of anonymity game (Definition 4), the adversary can select $\mathsf{m}, \mathcal{S}, \mathcal{S}'$. Due to the homomorphic property of f_{prm}, the adversary can remove m from the first coordinate, which is $\mathsf{m} \otimes f_{\mathsf{prm}}(\boldsymbol{x}^T)$ or $\mathsf{m} \otimes f_{\mathsf{prm}}((\boldsymbol{x}')^T)$, of a returned command ciphertext.

Thus, in the context of our template construction, breaking anonymity is the same as distinguishing the tuples

$$\begin{aligned} \mathsf{cmd}_{\mathcal{S}} &= (f_{\mathsf{prm}}(\boldsymbol{x}^T), f_{\mathsf{prm}}(\boldsymbol{ct}_1^T), \ldots, f_{\mathsf{prm}}(\boldsymbol{ct}_M^T)) \text{ and} \\ \mathsf{cmd}_{\mathcal{S}'} &= (f_{\mathsf{prm}}((\boldsymbol{x}')^T), f_{\mathsf{prm}}((\boldsymbol{ct}'_1)^T), \ldots, f_{\mathsf{prm}}((\boldsymbol{ct}'_M)^T)) \end{aligned}$$

under the situation where the adversary knows there exists an index $\mathsf{id} \in \mathcal{S} \setminus \mathcal{S}'$ such that $\mathsf{dk}_{\mathsf{id}}$ can recover $f_{\mathsf{prm}}(\boldsymbol{x}^T + \boldsymbol{e}_i^T)$ via the relation (2).

We transform the above problem into a distinguishing problem between legitimate sequences and random sequences.

Definition 7 *($(f_{\mathsf{prm}}, \chi, M)$-linear distinguishing problem). For a function $f_{\mathsf{prm}}(\cdot)$ used in the template construction, consider the computational problem to distinguish the sequence*

$$(f_{\mathsf{prm}}(\boldsymbol{x}^T), f_{\mathsf{prm}}(\boldsymbol{c}_1^T), \ldots, f_{\mathsf{prm}}(\boldsymbol{c}_M^T)) \text{ and } (f_{\mathsf{prm}}(\boldsymbol{r}^T), f_{\mathsf{prm}}(\boldsymbol{c}_1^T), \ldots, f_{\mathsf{prm}}(\boldsymbol{c}_M^T))$$

where $\boldsymbol{c}_1^T, \ldots, \boldsymbol{c}_M^T$ are randomly drawn from the domain of f_{prm}.

In the former case, $\boldsymbol{x}^T$ is computed $(\boldsymbol{c}_1^T || \boldsymbol{c}_2^T || \cdots || \boldsymbol{c}_M^T)\boldsymbol{d}^T + \boldsymbol{e}^T = \boldsymbol{c}_1^T d_1 + \cdots + \boldsymbol{c}_M^T d_M + \boldsymbol{e}^T$ by a fixed secret vector $\boldsymbol{d}^T = (d_1, \ldots, d_M)^T$ and a small random error $\boldsymbol{e}^T$ from χ^r. In the latter situation, $\boldsymbol{r}^T$ is random.

Theorem 1. *Using an adversary $\mathcal{A}$ that can win the anonymity game (Definition 4) with f_{prm}, noise distribution χ and dimension $2M$, it can solve the above distinguishing problem with parameters $(f_{\mathsf{prm}}, \chi, M)$ with high probability.*

Proof. Fix the parameters f_{prm}, χ and M, and suppose the existence of an adversary $\mathcal{A}$. After the game setup of the anonymity game with $2M$ dimensions, the challenger generates a $(2M) \times (2M)$ random invertible matrix U.

In the collusion query phase, suppose the adversary requires t verification keys; we can name them $\mathsf{dk}_1, \ldots, \mathsf{dk}_t$ without loss of generality. Upon the queries, generate random M-dimensional vectors $\boldsymbol{r}_1, \ldots, \boldsymbol{r}_t$ and set the fake verification keys to the adversary by $\mathsf{dk}_i^T = [(\boldsymbol{r}_i || \boldsymbol{u}_i)U]^T \in V^{2M}, i = 1, \ldots, t$.

Also, using the virtual secret vector $\boldsymbol{d}$ of the linear distinguishing problem, define tentative decryption keys $\mathsf{dk}_i^T = [(\boldsymbol{d} || \boldsymbol{u}_i)U]^T$ for $i = t+1, \ldots, M$, that are unknown by both the challenger and adversary. Upon requests from the adversary, the challenger sends the keys $\mathsf{dk}_1^T, \ldots, \mathsf{dk}_t^T$.

In the authentication query phase, the challenger generates the command ciphertext of a query $(\mathsf{m}, \mathcal{S})$ as follows. Call the problem oracle and get an instance $(f_{\mathsf{prm}}(\boldsymbol{y}^T), f_{\mathsf{prm}}(\boldsymbol{c}_1^T), \ldots, f_{\mathsf{prm}}(\boldsymbol{c}_M^T))$ where $\boldsymbol{y}^T$ is legitimate $\boldsymbol{x}^T$ or random $\boldsymbol{r}^T$. Denote $C = [\boldsymbol{c}_1^T || \cdots || \boldsymbol{c}_M^T]$. $F_i = f_{\mathsf{prm}}(\boldsymbol{c}_i^T)$ for $i = 1, \ldots, M$. Then, for $i = M+1, \ldots, M+t$, compute

$$f_{\mathsf{prm}}(C\boldsymbol{r}_i^T) = F_1 \circ r_{i,1} \otimes \cdots \otimes F_M \circ r_{i,M}$$

and

$$F_{M+i} := \begin{cases} f_{\mathsf{prm}}(C\boldsymbol{r}_i^T)^{-1} \otimes f_{\mathsf{prm}}(\boldsymbol{y}^T) \otimes f_{\mathsf{prm}}(\boldsymbol{\eta}_i^T) & (i \in S) \\ f_{\mathsf{prm}}(rand) & (i \notin S) \end{cases}$$

where $rand$ means a random sampling from the domain of f_{prm}. $\boldsymbol{\eta}_i$ is a random noise sampled from χ^r.

For $i = M+t+1, \ldots, 2M$, compute

$$F_{M+i} := \begin{cases} f_{\mathsf{prm}}(\boldsymbol{y}^T)^{-1} & (i \in S) \\ f_{\mathsf{prm}}(rand) & (i \notin S) \end{cases}$$

and let $(V_1, \ldots, V_{2M}) := (F_1, \ldots, F_{2M})U^{-1}$. Here, the vector-matrix operations are performed with the operations $(\circ, \otimes)$, i.e., $V_j = F_1 \circ u_{1,j} \otimes \cdots \otimes F_{2M} \circ u_{2M,j}$ where $u_{i,j}$ is the (i,j)-element of U^{-1}. The command to the adversary is $\mathsf{cmd}_{\mathcal{S}} = (\mathsf{m} \circ f_{\mathsf{prm}}(\boldsymbol{y}^T), V_1, \ldots, V_{2M})$.

It is easy to see that

$$\mathsf{Vrfy}(\mathsf{vk}_i, \mathsf{cmd}_{\mathcal{S}}) = \mathsf{m} \otimes f_{\mathsf{prm}}(\boldsymbol{y}^T) \otimes f_{\mathsf{prm}}^{-1}(\boldsymbol{y}^T) = \mathsf{m} \otimes \begin{cases} f_{\mathsf{prm}}(\boldsymbol{\eta}_i^T) & i = 1, \ldots, t \\ f_{\mathsf{prm}}(\boldsymbol{e}^T) & i = t+1, \ldots, M \end{cases}$$

for $i \in \mathcal{S}$ if problem instance is legitimate. On the other hand, if the problem instance is random, the relations on $i = t+1, \ldots, M$ do not hold.

In the challenge query phase, for $(\mathsf{m}, \mathcal{S}_0, \mathcal{S}_1)$, the challenger returns $\mathsf{cmd}_{\mathcal{S}_b}$ for $b = 0$ or 1 in the same manner and checks the adversary's response. Checking the adversary's advantage, the challenger distinguishes the problem instance. □

With the lattice setting $\mathsf{prm} = \boldsymbol{p} \in \mathbb{Z}_q^r$ and $f_{\boldsymbol{p}}(\boldsymbol{x}^T) = \boldsymbol{p}\boldsymbol{x}^T$, the problem is to distinguish $(\boldsymbol{p}\boldsymbol{x}^T, \boldsymbol{p}\boldsymbol{c}_1^T, \ldots, \boldsymbol{p}\boldsymbol{c}_M^T)$ and $(\boldsymbol{p}\boldsymbol{r}^T, \boldsymbol{p}\boldsymbol{c}_1^T, \ldots, \boldsymbol{p}\boldsymbol{c}_M^T)$ where $\boldsymbol{x}^T$ is computed by $\sum_{i=1}^M d_i \boldsymbol{c}_i^T + \boldsymbol{e}^T$ by a secret vector $\boldsymbol{d} = (d_1, \ldots, d_M)$ and an error vector $\boldsymbol{e}^T$, and $\boldsymbol{r}^T$ is a random vector. This is the decision LWE problem.

4.3 Unforgeability

A simple transformation technique has been known from a CPA-secure public-key BE to a CCA1-secure one [17]. Following these notions and techniques, we construct our version of the transformation method from our template ABA to an unforgeable ABA.

Definition 8 *(Transformation). For an ABA scheme ABA* = $(\mathsf{Setup}, \mathsf{Join}, \mathsf{Auth}, \mathsf{Vrfy})$ *and a strongly and existentially unforgeable signature* $\Sigma = (\mathsf{KeyGen}, \mathsf{Sign}, \mathsf{Vrfy})$, *the transformation of ABA, which we denote* ABA_Σ *is defined as follows.*

- $ABA_\Sigma.\mathsf{Setup}(1^\lambda, N, \mathcal{D}) \to (\mathsf{ak}, pk, sk)$: *Run* $ABA.\mathsf{Setup}(1^\lambda, N, \mathcal{D}) \to \mathsf{ak}$ *and* $\Sigma.\mathsf{KeyGen}(1^\lambda) \to (pk, sk)$.
- $ABA_\Sigma.\mathsf{Join}(\mathsf{ak}, \mathsf{id}) \to \mathsf{vk}_{\mathsf{id}}$: *Run* $ABA.\mathsf{Join}(\mathsf{ak}, \mathsf{id})$ *and let* $\mathsf{vk}_{\mathsf{id}} = (ABA.\mathsf{vk}_{\mathsf{id}}, pk)$.
- $ABA_\Sigma.\mathsf{Auth}(\mathsf{ak}, \mathsf{m}, \mathcal{S}) \to (\mathsf{cmd}_{\mathcal{S}}, \sigma)$: *Execute* $ABA.\mathsf{Auth}(\mathsf{ak}, \mathsf{m}, \mathcal{S}) \to \mathsf{cmd}_{\mathcal{S}}$. *Generate the signature for the base command* $\Sigma.\mathsf{Sign}(sk, \mathsf{cmd}_{\mathcal{S}}) \to \sigma$.
- $ABA_\Sigma.\mathsf{Vrfy}(\mathsf{vk}_i, (\mathsf{cmd}_{\mathcal{S}}, \sigma)) \to \mathsf{m}/\mathsf{reject}$: *Check the signature* $\Sigma.\mathsf{Vrfy}(pk, \sigma, \mathsf{cmd}_{\mathcal{S}})$. *If the check fails, return* reject. *Passing the verifications, execute* $ABA.\mathsf{Vrfy}(\mathsf{vk}_{\mathsf{id}}, \mathsf{cmd}_{\mathcal{S}})$ *and return the result.*

Security proof is straightforward. In the security game (Definition 3), an adversary can get verification keys and $\{(\mathsf{cmd}_{\mathcal{S}}, \sigma)\}$ upon one's queries. Suppose one can forge a command pair $(\mathsf{cmd}'_{\mathcal{S}'}, \sigma')$ with $(\mathsf{m}', \mathsf{id}')$ such that $\Sigma.\mathsf{Vrfy}(\mathsf{pk}, \sigma', \mathsf{cmd}'_{\mathcal{S}'})$ returns accept and $ABA.\mathsf{Vrfy}(\mathsf{vk}_{\mathsf{id}'}, \mathsf{cmd}'_{\mathcal{S}'})$ returns m'.

The forging is splitting into two situations. If $\mathsf{cmd}'_{\mathcal{S}'}$ is not equal to any commands returned from the challenger in the authentication query step, $(\mathsf{cmd}'_{\mathcal{S}'}, \sigma')$ is a valid pair to break the strong unforgeability of the signature game, which is assumed to be hard.

On the other hand, consider the situation where $\mathsf{cmd}'_{\mathcal{S}'}$ is equal to $\mathsf{cmd}_{\mathcal{S}_a}$, one of returned commands in the authentication queries. We show this situation is impossible. Recall that the corresponding message m' and m_a in the commands cannot be equal by the requirement $\mathsf{m} \notin M_v$ in Step 3. Thus, the first element of $\mathsf{cmd}'_{\mathcal{S}'} = \mathsf{cmd}_{\mathcal{S}_a}$ is $\mathsf{m}' \otimes f_{\mathsf{prm}}(\boldsymbol{x}'^T) = \mathsf{m}_a \otimes f_{\mathsf{prm}}(\boldsymbol{x}_a^T)$ which are different representations of different messages. Thus, the verification results by $\mathsf{vk}_{\mathsf{id}'}$ must satisfy $ABA.\mathsf{Vrfy}(\mathsf{vk}_{\mathsf{id}'}, \mathsf{cmd}'_{\mathcal{S}'}) = \mathsf{m}'$ and $ABA.\mathsf{Vrfy}(\mathsf{vk}_{\mathsf{id}'}, \mathsf{cmd}_{\mathcal{S}_a}) = \mathsf{m}_a$. This contradicts to the requirement $\mathsf{m}' \neq \mathsf{m}_a$ and $\mathsf{cmd}'_{\mathcal{S}'} = \mathsf{cmd}_{\mathcal{S}_a}$.

Therefore, forging a command ciphertext is hard due to the strong unforgeability of the signature.

5 Concatenation of ABAs

The sequential concatenation of small-size ABAs is a simple way to reduce the length of ciphertexts by restricting the choice of target devices. The plain construction which is immediately found to be insecure is described as follows.

Consider j base ABAs named $ABA_j = (\mathsf{Setup}_j, \mathsf{Join}_j, \mathsf{Auth}_j, \mathsf{Vrfy}_j)$ for $j \in [K]$. Let N_j be the maximum number of devices controlled by the j-th ABA. Execute $ABA_j.\mathsf{Setup}(1^\lambda, N, \mathcal{D})$ for all j and get all the authentication keys ak_j. These keys are used to generate components of verification keys $\mathsf{vk}_{j,i}$ for $i \in [N_j]$. For each device indexed by a vector $\mathsf{id} = (i_1, \ldots, i_K)$, its verification key is defined by $\mathsf{vk}_{\mathsf{id}} = (\mathsf{vk}_{1,i_1}, \ldots, \mathsf{vk}_{K,i_K})$. The set of target devices is indicated by $\mathcal{S} = \mathcal{S}_1 \times \cdots \times \mathcal{S}_K$ where $\mathcal{S}_j \subset [N_j]$. The command ciphertext $\mathsf{cmd}_{\mathcal{S}}$ is the concatenation of $\mathsf{cmd}_{\mathcal{S}_j} = \mathsf{Auth}(\mathsf{ak}_j, \mathsf{m}, \mathcal{S}_j)$ for $j \in [K]$. After the broadcast, each device executes $\mathsf{Vrfy}(\mathsf{vk}_{j,i_j}, \mathsf{cmd}_{\mathcal{S}_j})$ for all $j \in [K]$. If all the verifications have been accepted, output m, if otherwise, output reject.

Assuming the anonymity of the base ABA, we can see that the concatenated ABA also has anonymity on two sets of limited forms. For instance, consider two sets $\mathcal{S}_1 \times \cdots \times \mathcal{S}_K$ and $\mathcal{S}'_1 \times \cdots \times \mathcal{S}_K$ that are only the first coordinate are different. Then, messages that encode the sets are indistinguishable. However, one can break the anonymity in other situations as in the next section.

5.1 Anonymity in the Restricted Device Selection

Rearranging Attack: Consider the concatenation of $K = 2$ ABAs with $N_1 = N_2 = 2$. The composed ABA can control $N_1 N_2 = 4$ devices and we name them by $\mathsf{id} = (1,1), (1,2), (2,1)$ and $(2,2)$. Suppose that $(1,1)$ and $(2,2)$ are colluded and an attacker have $\mathsf{vk}_{1,1} = (\mathsf{vk}_{1,1}, \mathsf{vk}_{2,1})$ and $\mathsf{vk}_{2,2} = (\mathsf{vk}_{1,2}, \mathsf{vk}_{2,2})$. Then, it can generate other verification keys $\mathsf{vk}_{1,2} = (\mathsf{vk}_{1,1}, \mathsf{vk}_{2,2})$ and $\mathsf{vk}_{2,1} = (\mathsf{vk}_{1,2}, \mathsf{vk}_{2,1})$ via the recombination of components. Thus, it can recover any legitimate ciphertext and know which devices are in the target set. For instance, in the anonymity game, it can select $\mathcal{S}_0 = \{(1,2)\}$ and $\mathcal{S}_1 = \{(2,1)\}$ that satisfies the condition by the Eq. (1). Then $\mathsf{cmd}_{\mathcal{S}_b}$ can be easily verified to distinguish.

Non-cryptographic Attack: Another situation where one can break the anonymity from only the results of verification on the colluded devices. Denote the target indication by $(d_1, d_2) \in \{0, 1, *\}^2$ where $*$ is the wild-card; for example $(1, *)$ is the set $\{1\} \times \{1, 2\} = \{(1, 1), (1, 2)\}$. 9 patterns are possible as the rows in the table below.

(d_1, d_2)	(1, 1)	(1, 2)	(2, 1)	(2, 2)
(1, 1)	•			
(1, 2)		•		
(2, 1)			•	
(2, 2)				•

(d_1, d_2)	(1, 1)	(1, 2)	(2, 1)	(2, 2)
(1, *)	•	•		
(2, *)			•	•
(*, 1)	•		•	
(*, 2)		•		•
(*, *)	•	•	•	•

Consider the situation where $\mathsf{id} = (1, 2)$ and $(2, 1)$ are colluded and the attacker can know $\mathsf{vk}_{1,2}$ and $\mathsf{vk}_{2,1}$. Suppose the attacker decrypts a command ciphertext and knows that it targets both $\mathsf{id} = (1, 2)$ and $(2, 1)$. Then, from the table $d_1 d_2 = (*, *)$ is revealed and it can know $\mathsf{id} = (1, 1)$ and $(2, 2)$ are also target devices. We emphasize that such an attack is possible even if one cannot recover the other verification keys. It is independent of the cryptographic security of primitives.

The above examples illustrate how we consider anonymity in a situation where the freedom in the choice of targets is limited. In the notion of standard anonymity (Definition 4), the situation where no information leakage except for the colluded devices is considered via the indistinguishability property. We think the validity of this definition is based on the assumption that the target set is uniformly chosen from $2^{[N]}$ and information leakage is always caused by cryptographic vulnerability.

In our limited-freedom situation, information can be leaked regardless of the cryptographic vulnerability. To formulate this kind of anonymity, we introduce the notion of single anonymity.

Definition 9. *We say it has a single anonymity if for any $W \subsetneq [N]$ a pattern of $\{\mathsf{Vrfy}(\mathsf{vk}_{\mathsf{id}}, \mathsf{cmd}_{\mathcal{S}})\}_{\mathsf{id} \in W}$ does not reveal whether $\mathsf{id}' \overset{?}{\in} \mathcal{S}$ for some $\mathsf{id}' \notin W$.*

This condition is very tight so that it must be any subset of $[N]$ is selectable by the following proposition. We think one of our future works is to investigate the relationship between the restriction of target devices choice (that bounds ciphertext length) and the strength of anonymity.

Proposition 1. *If the freedom in the target devices selection is limited, it does not have the single anonymity.*

Proof. Let $\mathcal{D} \subset 2^{[N]}$ be a family of sets that can be specified as a target. We say $\mathcal{S} \subset [N]$ is selectable (resp. unselectable) if $\mathcal{S} \in \mathcal{D}$ (resp. $\mathcal{S} \notin \mathcal{D}$.)

We separate the situation. First, assume there are an unselectable $\mathcal{S}$ and selectable $\mathcal{S}'$ such that $\mathcal{S}' \supset \mathcal{S}$. Take the minimum such $\mathcal{S}'$, i.e., any proper subset of $\mathcal{S}'$ is unselectable. Then, suppose all the devices in $\mathcal{S} \cup ([N] \setminus \mathcal{S}')$ has been colluded and the server broadcasts a command $\mathsf{cmd}_{\mathcal{S}'}$ that targets all devices in $\mathcal{S}'$. The adversary can verify the commands in the infected devices and can know for $\mathsf{id} \in \mathcal{S}$ (resp. $\mathsf{id} \in [N] \setminus \mathcal{S}'$), they are in target (resp. non-target.) With the restriction of the choice of $\mathcal{S}$, the adversary also obtain that the devices in $\mathcal{S}' \setminus \mathcal{S}$ are in the target without using any cryptographic attacks.

Consider the other situation where for any selectable set $\mathcal{S}$, its subset is selectable. This condition derives that $[N]$ is divided into $\mathcal{T}_1 \cup \cdots \cup \mathcal{T}_k$ such that $\mathcal{T}_i \cap \mathcal{T}_j = \phi$ and any subsets of $\mathcal{T}_i$ are selectable. Thus, if one can know a device $\mathsf{id} \in \mathcal{T}_i$ is a target, it deduces all the devices in $\mathcal{T}_j, (j \neq i)$ are not selected. □

We remark that t-anonymity (Definition 4) and single anonymity do not imply each other. Also, even we construct a t-anonymity ABA for high t, information leakage from a pattern is possible. This is a motivation for our construction strategy in the next section; using a simple known technique and algebraic analysis.

5.2 Modification Against Recombination Attack

The anonymity and unforgeability of the concatenated ABA are broken by rearranging colluded keys. Also, a non-target device can recover the message. To prevent the attacks, we employ two methods. The first idea is to distribute m into K shares and recover it in a target device via the homomorphic property of f_{prm}. The other idea is from Agrawal et al.'s inner product encryption [1].

Definition 10 *(A modified concatenated template construction).*

- $\mathsf{Setup}(1^\lambda, K, \mathcal{D}) \to \mathsf{ak}$: *Fix a prime field* $\mathbb{Z}_q$ *and a dimension* M *of base MREs. Execute* $\mathsf{MRE}_j.\mathsf{KeyGen}(\mathsf{pp}) \to (\mathsf{ek}_j, \{\mathsf{dk}_{j,i}^T\}_{i \in [N_j]}\})$ *for* $j \in [K]$*, where* $\mathsf{ek}_j := \{\mathsf{dk}_{j,i}^T\}$*. Generate random matrices* $A_{j,i} \xleftarrow{\$} \mathbb{Z}_q^{r \times M}$ *for* $j \in [K], i \in [N_j]$*, a random invertible matrix* $W \in \mathbb{Z}_q^{2M \times 2M}$ *and a random vector* $\boldsymbol{u}^T \in \mathbb{Z}_q^r$*. The key is* $\mathsf{ak} = (\{\mathsf{dk}_{j,i}^T\}, \{\mathsf{ek}_j\}, \{A_{j,i}\}, W, \boldsymbol{u}^T)$.
- $\mathsf{Join}(\mathsf{ak}, \mathsf{id}) \to \mathsf{vk}_{\mathsf{id}}$: *For a device* $\mathsf{id} = (i_1, i_2, \ldots, i_K)$*, generate a random vector* $\mathsf{uk}_{\mathsf{id}}$ *such that* $\sum_{j=1}^K A_{j,i_j} \mathsf{uk}_{\mathsf{id}}^T = \boldsymbol{u}^T \pmod q$*. The verification key is* $\mathsf{vk}_{\mathsf{id}} = (W(\mathsf{dk}_{1,i_1}||\mathsf{uk}_{\mathsf{id}})^T, \ldots, W(\mathsf{dk}_{K,i_K}||\mathsf{uk}_{\mathsf{id}})^T)$.
- $\mathsf{Auth}(\mathsf{ak}, \mathsf{m}, \mathcal{S}) \to \mathsf{cmd}_{\mathcal{S}}$: *Suppose the target devices are indicated by* $\mathcal{S}_1 \times \cdots \times \mathcal{S}_K \subset \prod [N_j]$*. Pick random vectors* $\boldsymbol{t}_j^T \in \mathbb{Z}_q^r$ *and let* $\boldsymbol{x}^T := \boldsymbol{t}_1^T + \cdots + \boldsymbol{t}_K^T$*. Generate random matrices* $CT_{j,i}$ $(j \in [K], i \in [N_j])$ *such that*

$$CT_{j,i} \cdot \mathsf{dk}_{j,\ell} = \begin{cases} \boldsymbol{t}_j^T + \boldsymbol{e}_{j,i}^T \ (i = \ell \text{ and } i \in S_j) \\ rand \quad\ (i \notin S_j) \end{cases}$$

where rand represents a random element far from $\boldsymbol{t}_j^T$*. Define the matrix* $C_{j,i} := (CT_{j,i}||A_{j,i})W^{-1}$ *and split it into the* $2M$ *column vectors by* $C_{j,i} = (\boldsymbol{c}_{j,i,1}^T|| \cdots ||\boldsymbol{c}_{j,i,2M}^T)$*. Then, the command ciphertext* $\mathsf{cmd}_{\mathcal{S}}$ *is* $\mathsf{m} \otimes f_{\mathsf{prm}}(\boldsymbol{x}^T + \boldsymbol{u}^T)$ *and the sequence* $\{f_{\mathsf{prm}}(\boldsymbol{c}_{j,i,\ell}^T)\}$.

- $\mathsf{Vrfy}(\mathsf{vk}_{\mathsf{id}}, \mathsf{cmd}_{\mathcal{S}})$: *For* $\mathsf{id} = (i_1, \ldots, i_K)$*, denote* $\mathsf{vk}_{\mathsf{id}} = (\boldsymbol{v}_1, \ldots, \boldsymbol{v}_K)$ *and let the* ℓ*-th element of* $\boldsymbol{v}_j$ *be* $v_{j,\ell}$*. For the command* $(\mathsf{m} \otimes f_{\mathsf{prm}}(\boldsymbol{x}^T + \boldsymbol{u}^T), \{F_{j,i,\ell}\})$*, compute the sum* $T_j = \sum_{\ell=1}^{2M} v_{j,\ell} \otimes F_{j,i_j,\ell}$ *and* $\mathsf{m} \otimes f_{\mathsf{prm}}(\boldsymbol{x}^T + \boldsymbol{u}^T) \otimes (T_1 \otimes \cdots \otimes T_K)^{-1}$*.*

The correctness is as follows. For a target $\mathsf{id} = (i_1, \ldots, i_K)$, each T_j and the sum in the sense of $\otimes$ are

$$
\begin{aligned}
T_j &= \sum_{\ell=1}^{2M} v_{j,\ell} \otimes f_{\mathsf{prm}}(\boldsymbol{c}_{j,i_j,\ell}^T) = f_{\mathsf{prm}}\left(\sum_{\ell=1}^{2M} \boldsymbol{c}_{j,i_j,\ell}^T v_{j,\ell}\right) \\
&= f_{\mathsf{prm}}((CT_{j,i_j} || A_{j,i_j}) W^{-1} \cdot W(\mathsf{dk}_{j,i_j} || \mathsf{uk}_{\mathsf{id}})) = f_{\mathsf{prm}}(\boldsymbol{t}_j^T + \boldsymbol{e}_{j,i}^T + A_{j,i_j} \mathsf{uk}_{\mathsf{id}}), \\
\text{and } & T_1 \otimes \cdots \otimes T_K = f_{\mathsf{prm}}\left(\sum_{j=1}^K \boldsymbol{t}_j^T + \boldsymbol{u}^T + \sum_{j=1}^K \boldsymbol{e}_{j,i_j}\right).
\end{aligned}
$$

Therefore, it recovers $\mathsf{m} \otimes f_{\mathsf{prm}}\left(\sum_{j=1}^K \boldsymbol{e}_{j,i_j}^T\right)$.

For parameters K and N_i, rough estimations of key size and ciphertext length are given as follows. Each $\mathsf{vk}_{\mathsf{id}}$ for $\mathsf{id} = (i_1, i_2, \ldots, i_K)$ consists of K vectors in $\mathbb{Z}_q$ and each vector has dimension $2M$. Thus, each verification key is exactly $2MK$ elements in $\mathbb{Z}_q$ and represented by $O(MK \log q)$ [bits]. $\mathsf{cmd}_{\mathcal{S}}$ consists of the masked message $\mathsf{m} \otimes f_{\mathsf{prm}}(\boldsymbol{x}^T + \boldsymbol{u}^T)$ and $f_{\mathsf{prm}}(\boldsymbol{c}_{j,i,\ell}^T)$ for all $j \in [K], i \in [N_j]$ and $\ell \in [2M]$. Thus, a command consists exactly one masked message and $(N_1 + \cdots + N_K) \cdot 2M$ elements in the range space of f_{prm}.

In the next section, we give a lattice instantiation with extreme parameter sets $N_j = 2$ for all $j \in [K]$ and a function f_{prm} maps to an element of $\mathbb{Z}_q$. The size of a verification key and a command are represented by $2KM$ and $1+4KM$ elements in $\mathbb{Z}_q$, respectively.

5.3 Anonymity from the Dependency of Algebraic Systems

We discuss the necessary number of colluded keys and authentication queries to distinguish two commands $\mathsf{cmd}_{\mathcal{S}_0}$ and $\mathsf{cmd}_{\mathcal{S}_1}$ in the anonymity game. Assume that the attacker's strategy is to recover $\mathsf{vk}_{\mathsf{id}}$ for some $\mathsf{id} \in \mathcal{S}_0 \triangle \mathcal{S}_1$ and try to verify $\mathsf{cmd}_{\mathcal{S}_b}$. Let $\mathsf{id} = (1, 1, \ldots, 1)$ without loss of generality.

Split the matrix W into the upper and lower matrices with $M \times 2M$ dimensions: $W = \begin{bmatrix} W_1 \\ W_2 \end{bmatrix}$. Denote $\boldsymbol{w}_{j,i}^T = W_1 \mathsf{dk}_{j,i}^T$ and $\boldsymbol{u}_{\mathsf{id}}^T = W_2 \mathsf{uk}_{\mathsf{id}}^T$. Then, the verification key that one wants to recover is written as $\mathsf{vk}_{\mathsf{id}}^T = (\boldsymbol{w}_{1,1}^T + \boldsymbol{u}_{\mathsf{id}}^T, \ldots, \boldsymbol{w}_{K,1}^T + \boldsymbol{u}_{\mathsf{id}}^T)$. $\mathsf{uk}_{\mathsf{id}}^T$ also satisfies $\sum_{j=1}^K A_{j,1} \mathsf{uk}_{\mathsf{id}}^T = \boldsymbol{u}^T$ for unknown matrices $A_{j,1}$ and unknown vector $\boldsymbol{u}^T$. Then, consider simultaneous equations to recover $\mathsf{vk}_{\mathsf{id}}$.

The number of variables to fix is KM for $\boldsymbol{w}_{j,1}$ $(j = 1, \ldots, K)$, $K \cdot rM$ for $A_{j,i}$, $2M^2$ for W_2 and r for $\boldsymbol{u}$. Also, the number of unknown variables in $\mathsf{uk}_{\mathsf{id}}$ is r since the other $M - r$ variables can be random, i.e., have freedom, by construction. With a new colluded key $\mathsf{vk}_{\mathsf{id}'}^T$, MK equations can be obtained and it introduces new variables on $\boldsymbol{w}_{j,i}^T$ and $A_{j,i}$. An authentication query does not introduce new equations due to the random variables $\boldsymbol{t}_j$ in construction.

To minimize the number of unknown variables, when an attacker gets a new $\mathsf{vk}_{\mathsf{id}'}^T$, one can minimize the range of indexes. For $\mathsf{id} = (i_1, \ldots, i_N)$ that satisfies $i_j \in [2]$ for $j = 1, \ldots, s$ and $i_j = 1$ for $i = s+1, \ldots, K$, $t = 2^s - 1$ colluded keys are possible. Here, the number of variables is $2(K+s)M$ for $\boldsymbol{w}_{j,i_j}^T$, $2(K+s) \cdot rM$ for A_{j,i_j}, $2M^2$ for W_2, tr for $\mathsf{uk}_{\mathsf{id}}^T$, r for $\boldsymbol{u}^T$. The total number of variables from the public key and t colluded key is $V = 2M^2 + 2(K+s)rM + 2(K+s)M + tr + r$, and the attacker has to solve it by tKM simultaneous equations. To fix the unique solution and $\mathsf{vk}_{\mathsf{id}}^T$, it is necessary to satisfy

$$2M^2 + 2(K+s)rM + 2(K+s)M + tr + r < tKM$$
$$\Leftrightarrow t > \frac{2M^2 + 2(K+s)rM + 2(K+s)M + r}{KM - r}.$$

The last fraction is bounded by $M/K + 2r + 2$. Therefore, it has evidence of anonymity against $2 + 2r$ colluded devices. In the lattice instantiation, r is the number of samples in LWE which is greater than 900. We think the security against collusion of $2r = 1800$ devices is practically secure.

6 Concrete Scheme and Security Parameters

This section gives the concrete scheme, security parameters, and rough estimations of costs. Below we assume $N_j = 2$ for all j.

We discuss a relationship between the space of an ABA command and a cryptographic message. Each target device can recover m whereas a non-target device gets a random number which is possibly interpreted as a legitimate command. To prevent such accidents, we employ a gimmick in commands.

Recall that the LWE-based ABA is instantiated by setting $f_{\boldsymbol{p}}(\boldsymbol{x}) = \boldsymbol{x}\boldsymbol{p}^T \bmod q$ to Definition 8 and 10. M, K, r are parameters. Also, we use Q to the multiple of plaintext to avoid the effect of noises. Concretely, plaintext $\overline{\mathsf{m}}$ is an integer such that $0 \leq \overline{\mathsf{m}} < q/Q$ and embed it in the form of $\mathsf{m} = \overline{\mathsf{m}} \cdot Q$ in the command ciphertext. In verification, the device rounds the decoded message m' to $\overline{\mathsf{m}'} = \lfloor \mathsf{m}'/Q \rceil$. Also, we use an integer L to distinguish a legitimate and a nonlegitimate command. If the verification function returns $\overline{\mathsf{m}'} < L$, it is interpreted as a legitimate command and executes it. If otherwise, return the reject symbol. In our construction, we assume $q > 2KLQ$ to separate $\overline{\mathsf{m}}$.

Definition 11 *(LWE-based Construction).*

- $\mathsf{Setup}(1^\lambda, K, \mathcal{D}) \to \mathsf{ak}$: *Fix a prime field* $\mathbb{Z}_q$ *and a dimension* M *of base MREs. Execute* $\mathsf{MRE}_j.\mathsf{KeyGen}(\mathsf{pp}) \to (\mathsf{ek}_j, \{\mathsf{dk}_{j,i}^T\}_{i \in [2]})$ *for* $j \in [K]$*, where* $\mathsf{ek}_j := \{\mathsf{dk}_{j,i}^T\}$*. Generate random matrices* $A_{j,i} \xleftarrow{\$} \mathbb{Z}_q^{r \times M}$ *for* $j \in [K], i \in [2]$*, a random invertible matrix* $W \in \mathbb{Z}_q^{2M \times 2M}$ *and a vector* $\boldsymbol{u}^T \in \mathbb{Z}_q^r$*. Execute the key generation of signature* $\Sigma.\mathsf{KeyGen}(1^\lambda) \to (pk, sk)$*. The key is* $\mathsf{ak} = (\{\mathsf{dk}_{j,i}^T\}, \{\mathsf{ek}_j\}, \{A_{j,i}\}, W, \boldsymbol{u}^T, pk, sk)$*.*

- $\mathsf{Join}(\mathsf{ak}, \mathsf{id}) \to \mathsf{vk}_{\mathsf{id}}$: *For a device* $\mathsf{id} = (i_1, \ldots, i_K)$, *generate a random vector* $\mathsf{uk}_{\mathsf{id}}^T \in \mathbb{Z}_q^M$ *such that* $\sum_{j=1}^{K} A_{j,i_j} \mathsf{uk}_{\mathsf{id}}^T = \boldsymbol{u}^T \pmod q$. *The verification key is* $\mathsf{vk}_{\mathsf{id}}^T = \{(W(\mathsf{dk}_{1,i_1}^T || \mathsf{uk}_{\mathsf{id}}^T)^T, \ldots, W(\mathsf{dk}_{K,i_K}^T || \mathsf{uk}_{\mathsf{id}}^T)^T), pk\}$.
- $\mathsf{Auth}(\mathsf{ak}, \mathsf{m} \in \mathcal{M}, \mathcal{S}) \to \mathsf{cmd}_{\mathcal{S}}$: *Suppose the target devices are indicated by* $\mathcal{S}_1 \times \cdots \times \mathcal{S}_K \subset \prod[2]$. *Pick random vectors* $\boldsymbol{t}_j^T \in \mathbb{Z}_q^r$ *so that* $\boldsymbol{p}\boldsymbol{t}_j^T \in \{LQ, \ldots, 2LQ - 1\}$ *and let* $\boldsymbol{x}^T := \boldsymbol{t}_1^T + \cdots + \boldsymbol{t}_K^T$. *Here,* $\boldsymbol{p}\boldsymbol{x}^T$ *is greater than* KLQ *since there is no overflow in* $\mathbb{Z}_q$ *by the condition* $q > 2KLQ$. *Then, generate random matrices* $CT_{j,i} \in \mathbb{Z}_q^{r \times M}$ $(j \in [K], i \in [2])$ *such that*

$$CT_{j,i} \cdot \mathsf{dk}_{j,\ell}^T = \begin{cases} \boldsymbol{t}_j^T + \boldsymbol{e}_{j,i}^T & (i = \ell \text{ and } i \in S_j) \\ \boldsymbol{z}_{j,i}^T & (i \notin S_j) \end{cases} \tag{3}$$

  where $\boldsymbol{z}_{j,i}^T$ *is a random vector such that* $\boldsymbol{p}\boldsymbol{z}_{j,i}^T$ *is less than* LQ.
  For each i, j, *define the* $2M$ *column vectors* $\boldsymbol{c}_{j,i,1}^T$ *by* $C_{j,i} := (CT_{j,i} || A_{j,i}) W^{-1} = C_{j,i} = (\boldsymbol{c}_{j,i,1}^T || \cdots || \boldsymbol{c}_{j,i,2M}^T)$. *The command* $\mathsf{cmd}_{\mathcal{S}}$ *is the pair of vector* $\mathsf{vec} := (\mathsf{m} \cdot Q + \boldsymbol{p}(\boldsymbol{x}^T + \boldsymbol{u}^T), \{\boldsymbol{p}\boldsymbol{c}_{j,i,\ell}^T\})$ *and its signature* σ.
- $\mathsf{Vrfy}(\mathsf{vk}_{\mathsf{id}}, \mathsf{cmd}_{\mathcal{S}} = (\mathsf{vec}, \sigma))$: *Check the signature by* $\Sigma.\mathsf{Vrfy}(pk, \sigma, \mathsf{vec})$ *and if it is not valid, it stops with returning* reject. *If otherwise, execute the decryption process as follows. For* $\mathsf{id} = (i_1, \ldots, i_K)$, *denote the vector part of* $\mathsf{vk}_{\mathsf{id}}$ *be* $(\boldsymbol{v}_1, \ldots, \boldsymbol{v}_K)$ *and let the* ℓ*-th element of* $\boldsymbol{v}_j$ *be* $v_{j,\ell}$. *For a command* $(\mathsf{m} + \boldsymbol{p}(\boldsymbol{x}^T + \boldsymbol{u}^T), \{\boldsymbol{p} \cdot \boldsymbol{c}_{j,i,\ell}^T\} := \{F_{j,i,\ell}\})$, *compute*

$$T_j = \sum_{\ell=1}^{2M} v_{j,\ell} F_{j,i_j,\ell} \text{ and } \overline{\mathsf{m}'} = \mathsf{m} + \boldsymbol{p}(\boldsymbol{x}^T + \boldsymbol{u}^T) - (T_1 + \cdots + T_K). \tag{4}$$

  Decode the message by $\mathsf{m}' = \lfloor \overline{\mathsf{m}'} / Q \rceil$. *If it is greater than* L, *return* reject *and if otherwise, return* m'.

The correctness and securities are already discussed. We give detail on the separation of legitimate commands. In the computation of $\overline{\mathsf{m}'}$, we have

$$\boldsymbol{p}(\boldsymbol{x}^T + \boldsymbol{u}^T) - (T_1 + \cdots T_K) = \boldsymbol{p}\boldsymbol{x}^T - \sum_{j=1}^{K} \boldsymbol{p}(CT_{j,i_j} \cdot \mathsf{dk}_{j,i_j}^T). \tag{5}$$

after cancelling $\boldsymbol{u}^T$. Here, each factor is $\boldsymbol{p}(\boldsymbol{t}_j^T + \boldsymbol{e}_{j,i}^T)$ or $\boldsymbol{p}\boldsymbol{z}_{j,i}^T$ by (3). By the conditions $\boldsymbol{p}\boldsymbol{x}^T \geq KLQ$ and $\boldsymbol{p}\boldsymbol{z}_{j,i}^T < LQ$, if there is a factor from $\boldsymbol{p}\boldsymbol{z}_{j,i}^T$, the sum is greater than LQ and the resulting $\overline{\mathsf{m}'}$ is greater than L.

Example Parameter Sets: Assume $N_j = 2$ for all j and K is about 20 – 30. From Theorem 1 (with the lattice instantiation), the hardness of the decision LWE problem with parameters (n, m, q, σ) is the security base of the anonymity of lattice-based ABA with parameters $M = 2n$, modulus q, and the error parameter σ. We take such $(M = 2n, q, \sigma)$ for our ABA.

Besides the security, it needs to reduce the probability of decoding errors by changing q and Q. Following (5), the noise in the verification in a target device is

$\sum_{j=1}^{K} \boldsymbol{p} \cdot \boldsymbol{e}_{j,i_j}^T$. Approximating each coordinate of $\boldsymbol{e}_{j,i_j}^T$ by the continuous Gaussian $N(0, \sigma^2)$, the distribution of the error is $N(0, K||\boldsymbol{p}||^2\sigma^2)$. The approximation $\Pr[|N(0, s^2)| \geq \beta] = 1 - \mathrm{erf}\,(\beta/s) < \exp\left(-\beta^2/s^2\right)$ is accurate for low probability situations. Taking β so that the bound is very small, it derives a bound of the error in practice. For example, take the error bound by the inverse of $10^9 \cdot 2^{32} \cdot 2^{64} \approx e^{87.3}$, whose factors are the number of controlled devices, the number of seconds in 100 years, and safety margins, respectively. This derives $\beta > \sqrt{87.3}\,s$. Therefore, we can assume the absolute value of the noise (5) is smaller than $\sqrt{87.3} \cdot \sqrt{2K}||\boldsymbol{p}||\sigma$ in practice. Since $\boldsymbol{p}$ works as a secret vector of LWE in the security proof, it should be a discrete Gaussian [19] and its derivation is σ. As the same argument, we can assume $||\boldsymbol{p}|| < \sqrt{87.3}\sqrt{M}\sigma = 2\sqrt{2 \cdot 87.3 n}\sigma$ and thus we take Q so that $\sqrt{87.3} \cdot \sqrt{2K}\sigma \cdot 2\sqrt{2 \cdot 87.3 n}\sigma \approx 350\sqrt{Kn}\sigma^2 < Q$.

Communication Cost: As an example situation, we set $K = 20$ for controlling a million devices and set $\sigma = 3$. Let the space of legitimate message space be 4 (two bits). Then, q is a prime larger than $2KLQ > 2LK \cdot 350\sqrt{Kn}\sigma^2 \approx 2253956\sqrt{n}$. To achieve 128-bit security in ABA. We use Albrecht et al.'s lattice estimator [7] as of May 2022, and obtain the dimension 926.

For another set, we summarize the parameter in Table 1. As explained in the end of Sect. 5.2, one verification key and a command ciphertext consists of $2KM = 4Kn$ and $1 + 4KM = 1 + 8Kn$ elements of $\mathbb{Z}_q$ respectively, the sizes in Bytes are the smallest integers greater than $(4Kn)\lfloor \log_2 q \rfloor/8$ and $(1 + 8Kn)\lfloor \log_2 q \rfloor/8$.

Expected Timings in a Cortex-M4 Processor: The timing of signature verification is dominated by the computation of the SHA-3 hash function that requires 213 cycles/Byte [23] while FALCON-512 and 1024 for a short message takes less than 0.5M and 1M cycles in Cortex-M4, respectively [13].

The canceling-out computation (4) requires $2MK = 4nK$ additions and multiplications in $\mathbb{Z}_q$. For small q, this can be done by a sequence of the UMLAL instructions. For two 32bit unsigned numbers $r0, r1$ and one 64bit unsigned number $r2$, it computes $r0 \times r1 + r2$ and stores to a 64 bit register in 1 cycle [24]. Modular computations are not necessary after the addition. Theoretically, it is enough to compute the modulo in every $2^{64}/q^2$ term. Hence, about $4nK$ cycles are spent for the total computation. For a moderate q, divide the numbers in each 32bits, and we can use the schoolbook methods for multiplication and addition. Assume q is less than 64bit the total computing time would be 4 times the cost of small q and it would be about $16nK$ cycles. In Table 1, we assume the computation spends $4nK$ and $16nK$ cycles for $L = 4$ and 256, respectively.

7 Concluding Remarks

We proposed a template and its lattice instantiation of ABA that can control N devices with short length $O(\log N)$ ciphertext. Due to the trilemma on ABA construction, we imposed the restriction on the freedom in the target selection. It deduces the lack of single anonymity. However, we found that the single anonymity requires complete freedom in the target selection and thus, the ciphertext length has $\Omega(N)$. Throughout this study on ABA, we have clarified that the following problems are still open.

The initial motivation was to control millions to billions of IoT devices. Shannon's coding theorem (and also the lower bound discussions in [14,15]) bounds the ciphertext length from lower, which makes difficult to construct efficient protocols. To avoid the barrier, restrictions on the freedom in the target devices selection and anonymity are needed described as in Sect. 1.2. We think the set of restrictions that we choose is one possibility and we can investigate the relation among the ciphertext length and other properties for the practical use in the real world. For example, a lower bound of ABA that allows false-positive [26] should be expressed by an entropy function. Also, an information-theoretic-styled bound of outsider anonymity setting is not known.

In the lattice instanciation, the proposed LWE parameters have large margins to prevent accidents. However, the factor $\sqrt{87.3}$, which comes from $e^{87.3} \approx 10^9 \cdot 2^{32} \cdot 2^{64}$, may be unnecessarily large in some real situations. For instance, replacing it to $2^{32} \approx e^{22.2}$, the necessary size of Q if reduced by factor 4 and necessary dimension is reduced by about 10%. Setting appropriate margins for realistic situation would be jobs by collaborating the application and theoretical layers.

Acknowledgement. This research was in part conducted under a contract of "Research and development on IoT malware removal/make it non-functional technologies for effective use of the radio spectrum" among "Research and Development for Expansion of Radio Wave Resources (JPJ000254)", which was supported by the Ministry of Internal Affairs and Communications, Japan. This work was in part supported by JSPS KAKENHI Grant Number JP22H03590.

We thank the anonymous reviewers for their careful readings and insightful comments that improve the quality of the manuscript.

References

1. Agrawal, S., Freeman, D.M., Vaikuntanathan, V.: Functional Encryption for Inner Product Predicates from Learning with Errors. In: Lee, D.H., Wang, X. (eds.) ASIACRYPT 2011. LNCS, vol. 7073, pp. 21–40. Springer, Heidelberg (2011). https://doi.org/10.1007/978-3-642-25385-0_2
2. Barth, A., Boneh, D., Waters, B.: Privacy in encrypted content distribution using private broadcast encryption. In: Di Crescenzo, G., Rubin, A. (eds.) FC 2006. LNCS, vol. 4107, pp. 52–64. Springer, Heidelberg (2006). https://doi.org/10.1007/11889663_4
3. Beimel, A., Dolev, S.: Buses for anonymous message delivery. J. Cryptol. **16**(1), 25–39 (2003). https://doi.org/10.1007/s00145-002-0128-6
4. Boneh, D., Gentry, C., Waters, B.: Collusion resistant broadcast encryption with short ciphertexts and private keys. In: Shoup, V. (ed.) CRYPTO 2005. LNCS, vol. 3621, pp. 258–275. Springer, Heidelberg (2005). https://doi.org/10.1007/11535218_16

5. Chhatrapati, A., Hohenberger, S., Trombo, J., Vusirikala, S.: A performance evaluation of pairing-based broadcast encryption systems. In: Ateniese, G., Venturi, D. (eds.) ACNS 2022. LNCS, vol. 13269, pp. 24–44. Springer, Cham (2022). https://doi.org/10.1007/978-3-031-09234-3_2
6. Dolev, S., Ostrobsky, R.: XOR-trees for efficient anonymous multicast and reception. ACM Trans. Inf. Syst. Secur. **3**(2), 63–84 (2000). https://doi.org/10.1145/354876.354877
7. Estimate all the LWE, NTRU schemes!
8. Falcon: Fast-Fourier Lattice-based Compact Signatures over NTRU Specification v1.2 - 01/10/2020
9. Fazio, N., Perera, I.M.: Outsider-anonymous broadcast encryption with sublinear ciphertexts. In: Fischlin, M., Buchmann, J., Manulis, M. (eds.) PKC 2012. LNCS, vol. 7293, pp. 225–242. Springer, Heidelberg (2012). https://doi.org/10.1007/978-3-642-30057-8_14
10. FrodoKEM Learning With Errors Key Encapsulation Algorithm Specifications And Supporting Documentation (2021)
11. Garg, S., Kumarasubramanian, A., Sahai, A., Waters, B.: Building efficient fully collusion-resilient traitor tracing and revocation schemes. In: Proceedings of CCS 2010, New York, NY, USA, pp. 121–130 (2010)
12. Georgescu, A.: Anonymous lattice-based broadcast encryption. In: Mustofa, K., Neuhold, E.J., Tjoa, A.M., Weippl, E., You, I. (eds.) ICT-EurAsia 2013. LNCS, vol. 7804, pp. 353–362. Springer, Heidelberg (2013). https://doi.org/10.1007/978-3-642-36818-9_39
13. Kannwischer, M.J., Rijneveld, J., Schwabe, P., Stoffelen, K.: pqm4: testing and benchmarking NIST PQC on ARM Cortex-M4 (2019)
14. Kiayias, A., Samari, K.: Lower bounds for private broadcast encryption. In: Kirchner, M., Ghosal, D. (eds.) IH 2012. LNCS, vol. 7692, pp. 176–190. Springer, Heidelberg (2013). https://doi.org/10.1007/978-3-642-36373-3_12
15. Kobayashi, H., Watanabe, Y., Minematsu, K., Shikata, J.: Tight lower bounds and optimal constructions of anonymous broadcast encryption and authentication. Designs Codes Cryptogr. **91**, 2523–2562 (2023)
16. Kurosawa, K., Yoshida, T., Desmedt, Y., Burmester, M.: Some bounds and a construction for secure broadcast encryption. In: Ohta, K., Pei, D. (eds.) ASIACRYPT 1998. LNCS, vol. 1514, pp. 420–433. Springer, Heidelberg (1998). https://doi.org/10.1007/3-540-49649-1_33
17. Lee, J., Lee, S., Kim, J., Oh, H.: Combinatorial subset difference - IoT-friendly subset representation and broadcast encryption. Sensors **20**(11), 3140 (2020)
18. Libert, B., Paterson, K.G., Quaglia, E.A.: Anonymous broadcast encryption: adaptive security and efficient constructions in the standard model. In: Fischlin, M., Buchmann, J., Manulis, M. (eds.) PKC 2012. LNCS, vol. 7293, pp. 206–224. Springer, Heidelberg (2012). https://doi.org/10.1007/978-3-642-30057-8_13
19. Lindner, R., Peikert, C.: Better key sizes (and attacks) for LWE-based encryption. In: Kiayias, A. (ed.) CT-RSA 2011. LNCS, vol. 6558, pp. 319–339. Springer, Heidelberg (2011). https://doi.org/10.1007/978-3-642-19074-2_21
20. Mouha, N., Mennink, B., Van Herrewege, A., Watanabe, D., Preneel, B., Verbauwhede, I.: Chaskey: an efficient MAC algorithm for 32-bit microcontrollers. In: Joux, A., Youssef, A. (eds.) SAC 2014. LNCS, vol. 8781, pp. 306–323. Springer, Cham (2014). https://doi.org/10.1007/978-3-319-13051-4_19
21. Nuttapong, A.: Unified frameworks for practical broadcast encryption and public key encryption with high functionalities. Ph.D. thesis (2007)

22. Regev, O.: On lattices, learning with errors, random linear codes, and cryptography. In: Proceedings of STOC 2005, pp. 84–93 (2005)
23. Sobti, R., Ganesan, G.: Performance evaluation of SHA-3 final round candidate algorithms on ARM Cortex-M4 processor. Int. J. Inf. Secur. Priv. (IJISP) **12**(1), 63–73 (2018)
24. https://developer.arm.com/documentation/ddi0439/b/CHDDIGAC
25. Watanabe, Y., Yanai, N., Shikata, J.: Anonymous broadcast authentication for securely remote-controlling IoT devices. In: Barolli, L., Woungang, I., Enokido, T. (eds.) AINA 2021. LNNS, vol. 226, pp. 679–690. Springer, Cham (2021). https://doi.org/10.1007/978-3-030-75075-6_56
26. Watanabe, Y., Yanai, N., Shikata, J.: IoT-REX: a secure remote-control system for IoT devices from centralized multi-designated verifier signatures. In: Proceedings of ISPEC 2023. Springer, Cham (2023, to appear)

Traceable Policy-Based Signatures with Delegation

Ismail Afia(✉) and Riham AlTawy

University of Victoria, Victoria, BC, Canada
{iafia,raltawy}@uvic.ca

Abstract. In PKC 2014, a policy-based signature (PBS) scheme was proposed by Bellare and Fuchsbauer in which a signer can only sign messages conforming to some policy specified by an issuing authority and the produced signatures are verified under the issuer's public key. PBS construction supports the delegation of signing policy keys with possible restrictions to the original policy. Although the PBS scheme is meant to limit the signing privileges of the scheme's users, singers could easily abuse their signing rights without being held accountable since PBS does not have a tracing capability, and a signing policy key defines a policy that should be satisfied by the message only. In this work, we build on PBS and propose a traceable policy-based signature scheme (TPBS) where we employ a rerandomizable signature scheme, a digital signature scheme, and a zero-knowledge proof system as its building blocks. TPBS introduces the notion of identity keys that are used with the policy keys for signing. Thus it achieves traceability without compromising the delegatability feature of the PBS scheme. Additionally, TPBS ensures non-frameability under the assumption of a corrupted tracing authority. We define and formally prove the security notions of the generic TPBS scheme. Finally, we propose an instantiation of TPBS utilizing the Pointcheval-Sanders rerandomizable signature scheme, Abe *et al.*'s structure-preserving signature scheme, and Groth-Sahai NIZK system, and analyze its efficiency.

Keywords: policy-based signatures · attribute-based signatures · rerandomizable signatures · group signatures

1 Introduction

In policy-based signature (PBS) schemes, a signer can produce a valid signature of a message only if the message satisfies a specific hidden policy [5]. PBS schemes allow an issuer to delegate signing rights to specific signers under a particular policy (by sharing a signing policy key). Yet, the produced signature is verifiable under the issuer's public key. Besides unforgeability, the standard security notion for signature schemes, the privacy of the PBS scheme ensures that signatures do not reveal the policy under which they were created. Generally speaking, PBS schemes aim to extend the functionality of digital signature schemes by offering

J. Deng et al. (Eds.): CANS 2023, LNCS 14342, pp. 51–72, 2023.
https://doi.org/10.1007/978-981-99-7563-1_3

some form of delegation of signing rights under the issuer's policy signing key. Although there exist some primitives that offer signing rights delegation, such as group signatures (GS) [6] and attribute-based signatures (ABS) [4,15], PBS introduces some distinct features that other primitives do not fulfill. For instance, in GS schemes, a member signs any message on behalf of the whole group. However, PBS schemes give the issuer fine-grained control over who is allowed to sign which messages. On the other hand, in ABS schemes, the produced signature attests to a specific claim predicate (public policy) regarding certified attributes that the signer possesses. Additionally, ABS schemes do not impose any restrictions on the messages to be signed. PBS fulfills these gaps by hiding the policy under which the signature is created and requiring that the signed message conforms to the hidden policy.

Bellare and Fuchsbauer show that the PBS framework allows delegation, where a signer holding a key for some policy can delegate such a key to another signer with possible restrictions on the associated policy. Delegation enables the signing of messages that satisfy both the original and restricted policies which suites applications in hierarchical settings. For instance, if an issuer in a certain organization granted one of the managers the signing rights of contracts with clients X, Y, and Z, such a manager can delegate these signing rights to a team leader in his unit. Furthermore, the manager may restrict such rights and limit the team leader to signing contracts with client Z only.

The standard security requirements of PBS schemes are unforgeability and privacy [5]. Unforgeability ensures that an adversary cannot create a valid signature without having a policy key where the signed message conforms to such a policy. Privacy guarantees that a signature does not reveal the policy associated with the key. Privacy also implies unlinkability, where an adversary cannot decide whether two signatures were created using the same policy key. Although the PBS privacy definition ensures full signer anonymity, it permits key misuse without accountability. For instance, a signer of a given message may deny their responsibility for such a signature, especially in a delegatable setting where signers delegate their signing keys to others, signing accountability becomes of a vital value. Furthermore, policy key holders (delegated or not) may share their keys with anyone which authorizes them to sign messages under the issuer's name without any sort of liability over the signed message. Note, a straightforward way to overcome the latter problem could be by defining very restrictive policies and the issuer can keep track of all the generated policy keys, messages to be signed, and the identities of users who receive such keys. In case of a dispute, the issuer uses such information to determine who received the keys used in the signature generation of such a specific message. However, in this approach, the issuer can only identify the policy key receiver and not the signer. Also, the issuer is not able to prove such a claim, thus, unframeability is not ensured.

In an attempt to tackle the aforementioned problem, Xu *et al.* have proposed a traceable policy-based signature scheme [18]. In their proposal, the user's identity is attached to the policy. More precisely, the issuer generates signing keys for the user ensuring that the user's identity is part of the key, i.e. generating the signing keys for $id||p$, where id denotes the user identity and p, denotes the policy under which the signer is allowed to sign a specific message. To sign a message, the signer first encrypts their identity under the public key of an opener and provides a Non-Interactive Zero Knowledge (NIZK) proof of the issuer signature on $id||p$ such that p permits the message and id has been correctly encrypted to the given ciphertext. The generated signature contains the ciphertext in addition to the resulting NIZK proof. To trace a message to its original signer, the opener decrypts the ciphertext using its decryption key to reveal the signer's identity. Although Xu *et al.*'s proposal provides traceability, it does not protect against frameability because the issuer generates the signing keys of the scheme users. Moreover, attaching user identities to the policy seems counter-intuitive to the original goal of PBS schemes, where the signing rights are granted to users who have access to a policy key which allows them to sign messages that conform to the policy. Consequently, the issuer has to issue multiple signing keys to each scheme user to include their identities for the same policy. According to Xu *et al.* [18], a direct consequence of such an approach for traceability, is that the proposed scheme does not support policy key delegation because the policy is tied to a specific identity. More precisely, if a key holder delegates their key in the form $p' = id||p_1||p_2$ the signature generated with p' will always be traced back to the original key holder id.

Our Contributions. We propose a Traceable Policy-Based Signature (TPBS) scheme that supports delegation. TPBS extends the functionality of the original PBS scheme by adding a tracing mechanism to enforce accountability. We design TPBS where the generated signature of a given message does not reveal the policy nor the identity used in the signing process. The user's signing key in TPBS consists of an identity key and a policy key which are generated independently; thus, TPBS supports policy key delegation similar to the PBS scheme. In TPBS, each user generates a secret key which is used in an interactive protocol with the TA to generate the user's identity key. However, the user's secret key is never exchanged with the TA preventing a misbehaving tracing authority or any party intercepting the user's communication with the TA from framing such a user. We formally define the extractability, simulatability, non-framability, and traceability security notions for TPBS. Moreover, we propose a generic construction for TPBS employing a rerandomizable digital signature (RDS) scheme and a simulation-sound extractable non-interactive zero-knowledge (SE-NIZK) proof system. Then we prove that the generic construction achieves the defined security notions. Finally, we give a concrete instantiation for TPBS with Pointcheval-Sanders rerandomizable signature scheme and Groth-Sahai zero-knowledge proof system and analyze its efficiency.

2 Preliminaries and Building Blocks

Sampling x uniformly at random from $\mathbb{Z}_q$ is denoted by $x \xleftarrow{\$} \mathbb{Z}_p$. We denote by i an identity from the identity universe $\mathbb{I}$, $i \in \mathbb{I}$. Let $\lambda \in \mathbb{N}$ denotes our security parameter, then a function $\epsilon(\lambda) : \mathbb{N} \rightarrow [0, 1]$ denotes the negligible function if for any $c \in \mathbb{N}$, $c > 0$ there exists $\lambda_c \in \mathbb{N}$ s.t. $\epsilon(\lambda) < \lambda^{-c}$ for all $\lambda > \lambda_c$. We use $f(.)$ to denote a one-way function with a domain denoted by $\mathcal{F}$, and we use $\mathsf{PoK}(x : C = f(x))$ to denote an interactive perfect zero-knowledge proof of knowledge of x such that $C = f(x)$ [12]. Let a policy checker (PC) denote an NP-relation $\mathsf{PC} : \{0,1\}^* \times \{0,1\}^* \leftarrow \{0,1\}$, where the first input is a pair (p, m) representing a policy $p \in \{0,1\}^*$ and a message $m \in \{0,1\}^*$, while the second input is a witness $w_p \in \{0,1\}^*$. The signing of m is permitted under policy p if (p, m, w_p) is PC-valid such that $\mathsf{PC}((p, m), w_p) = 1$ [5].

2.1 Rerandomizable Digital Signature Scheme (RDS)

RDS schemes are digital signature algorithms that allow rerandomizing a signature such that the rerandomized version of the signature is still verifiable under the verification key of the signer [11,16,17,19]. An RDS scheme is a tuple of five polynomial-time algorithms, $\mathsf{RDS} = \{pp_{RDS} \leftarrow \mathsf{ppGenRDS}(1^\lambda)$, $(sk_{RDS}, pk_{RDS}) \leftarrow \mathsf{KeyGenRDS}(pp_{RDS}), \sigma_{RDS} \leftarrow \mathsf{SignRDS}(sk_{RDS}, m), \sigma'_{RDS} \leftarrow \mathsf{RandomizeRDS}(\sigma_{RDS}),\ \{\top, \bot\} \leftarrow \mathsf{VerifyRDS}(pk_{RDS}, m, \sigma_{RDS})\}$. Some RDS schemes include a $\sigma_{RDS} \leftarrow \mathsf{SignComRDS}(sk_{RDS}, C)$ procedure that enables the signing of a commitment C of a hidden message m such that the resulting σ_{RDS} is verifiable for m. Note that if σ_{RDS} is generated using SignComRDS, it could not be verified without the knowledge of m or some trapdoor information generated from m [10,16]. RDS schemes ensure existential unforgeability under chosen message attacks (EUF-CMA) and unlinkability where it is infeasible for adversaries to link a rereandomized version of a signature to its original one. RDS unlinkability also implies the indistinguishability of rereandomized signatures. The formal definition of such security notions and their associated experiments are given in [16,19] and in the full version of this paper [3].

2.2 Simulation-Sound Extractable NIZK (SE-NIZK)

A SE-NIZK system enables a prover with a witness w to prove non-interactively the truthfulness of a statement x to a verifier without conveying why [13]. For x in an $\mathbb{NP}$-language $\mathcal{L}$ such that $(x,\ w)$ in a relation $\mathbb{R}$ associated with $\mathcal{L}$, a SE-NIZK is a tuple of six polynomial-time algorithms, NIZK $= \{crs \leftarrow \mathsf{SetupNIZK}(1^\lambda),\ (crs, tr_{NIZK}) \leftarrow \mathsf{SimSetupNIZK}(1^\lambda),\ \pi_{NIZK} \leftarrow \mathsf{ProveNIZK}(crs, x, w),\ \pi_{NIZK} \leftarrow \mathsf{SimProveNIZK}(crs, x, tr_{NIZK}),\ \{\top, \bot\} \leftarrow \mathsf{VerifyNIZK}(crs, x, \pi_{NIZK}),\ w \leftarrow \mathsf{ExtrNIZK}(crs, x, \pi_{NIZK})\}$. SE-NIZK schemes ensure zero-knowledge which ensures a negligible success of an adversary that can distinguish between a proof for a statement x using a witness w from a simulated one. They also provide simulation-extractability which implies that it is hard for an adversary to output a verifiable proof for a statement x using a witness w such that $\mathbb{R}(x, w) = 0$. The formal definitions of such security notions are given in [5] and in the full version of this paper [3].

2.3 Digital Signature Schemes

A digital signature scheme is a tuple of four polynomial-time algorithms, $\mathsf{Sig} = \{pp_{Sig} \leftarrow \mathsf{ppGenSig}(1^\lambda),\ (pk_{Sig}, sk_{Sig}) \leftarrow \mathsf{KeyGenSig}(pp_{Sig}),\ \sigma_{Sig} \leftarrow$

$\mathsf{SignSig}(sk_{Sig}, m)$, $\{\top, \bot\} \leftarrow \mathsf{VerifySig}(pk_{Sig}, m, \sigma_{Sig})\}$. The standard security notion of a digital signature scheme is EUF-CMA [1] (see the full version of this paper [3]).

3 Traceable Policy-Based Signatures (TPBS)

We build on PBS and present a Traceable Policy-Based Signatures (TPBS) scheme. The main idea of our scheme is that in addition to the PBS issuer's policy key, we require the use of an identity key for signing a message that satisfies the policy defined by the issuer in the policy key. Hence, we introduce a Tracing Authority (TA) where every scheme user registers with to generate an identity key. The user then uses the identity key in addition to the policy key to sign a message that conforms to the policy set by the issuer. The produced signature allows the TA to trace it to the registration information acquired from the user during identity key generation. Note that contrary to the issuer's policy key, which could be shared among users allowed by the issuer to sign a specific message, the identity key is generated by individual users and is not shared with any other entity in the system. In what follows, we give the black box definitions of the proposed construction.

TPBS is a tuple of ten polynomial-time algorithms, TPBS = {ppGen, TASetup, IssuerSetup, UserKeyGen, IDKeyGen, PolicyKeyGen, Sign, Verify, Trace, Judge} which are defined as follows.

- ppGen. This algorithm outputs the public parameters of the scheme, which become an implicit input to all the other algorithms, $pp_{\mathsf{TPBS}} \leftarrow \mathsf{ppGen}(1^\lambda)$

- TASetup. This algorithm generates the TA's public secret key pair $(pk^{TA}_{\mathsf{TPBS}}, sk^{TA}_{\mathsf{TPBS}})$, initializes a private empty registry Reg, and defines the identity universe $\mathbb{I}$ such that $|\mathbb{I}| = |Reg|$, $(pk^{TA}_{\mathsf{TPBS}}, sk^{TA}_{\mathsf{TPBS}}, Reg) \leftarrow \mathsf{TASetup}(pp_{\mathsf{TPBS}})$

- IssuerSetup. This algorithm generates the issuer's public key secret key pair, $(pk^{Issuer}_{\mathsf{TPBS}}, sk^{Issuer}_{\mathsf{TPBS}}) \leftarrow \mathsf{IssuerSetup}(pp_{\mathsf{TPBS}})$

- UserKeyGen. For user identity $i \in \mathbb{I}$, this algorithm generates the user's secret public key pair (sk_i, pk_i). We assume that pk_i is authentically associated with i in a public registry $\mathcal{D}$ such that $\mathcal{D}[i] = pk_i$, a PKI system may be used for such a purpose. Moreover, this algorithm outputs the registration information ID_i generated from sk_i using a one-way function, $(pk_i, sk_i, ID_i) \leftarrow \mathsf{UserKeyGen}(pp_{\mathsf{TPBS}}, i)$

- IDKeyGen. This two-party interactive procedure runs between a scheme user and the TA to generate the user's identity key. The inputs of the user's routine are $(i, (sk_i))$, and the inputs to the TA's routine are $((sk^{TA}_{\mathsf{TPBS}}), i, ID_i)$, where i and ID_i are sent to the TA by the user. At the end of the interaction, the user obtains the TA's signature σ^i_{ID} over their hidden secret sk_i. Finally, the user sets $sk^i_{\mathsf{TPBS}} = (sk_i, \sigma^i_{ID})$ whereas the TA obtains some registration information $Reg[i] = ID_i$, $((Reg[i]), (sk^i_{\mathsf{TPBS}})) \leftarrow \mathsf{IDKeyGen}((sk^{TA}_{\mathsf{TPBS}}) \xleftrightarrow[\sigma^i_{ID}]{(i,ID_i)} (sk_i))$ where the first (resp. second) (.) in the input and output of IDKeyGen contains values that are only known to the TA (resp. user).

- PolicyKeyGen. The issuer runs this procedure to generate a secret key for a specific policy $p \in \{0,1\}^*$, $sk^p_{\mathsf{TPBS}} \leftarrow \mathsf{PolicyKeyGen}(sk^{Issuer}_{\mathsf{TPBS}}, p)$
- Sign. On input of a message m, a witness $w_p \in \{0,1\}^*$ that m conforms to a specific policy p, the secret signing key sk^p_{TPBS}, the user identity key sk^i_{TPBS}, this procedure generates a signature σ_m, $\sigma_m \leftarrow \mathsf{Sign}(pk^{TA}_{\mathsf{TPBS}}, pk^{Issuer}_{\mathsf{TPBS}}, sk^p_{\mathsf{TPBS}}, sk^i_{\mathsf{TPBS}}, m, p, w_p)$
- Verify. This algorithm verifies the signature σ_m over m using the issuer's and TA's public keys, $\{\top, \bot\} \leftarrow \mathsf{Verify}(pk^{TA}_{\mathsf{TPBS}}, pk^{Issuer}_{\mathsf{TPBS}}, m, \sigma_m)$
- Trace. This algorithm is run by the TA to trace a signature σ_m over m to its original signer and returns the signer identity along with proof confirming such a claim, $(i, \pi_{Trace}) \leftarrow \mathsf{Trace}(pk^{TA}_{\mathsf{TPBS}}, pk^{Issuer}_{\mathsf{TPBS}}, sk^{TA}_{\mathsf{TPBS}}, Reg, m, \sigma_m)$
- Judge. This algorithm verifies the output of the tracing algorithm, $\{\top, \bot\} \leftarrow \mathsf{Judge}(pk^{TA}_{\mathsf{TPBS}}, pk^{Issuer}_{\mathsf{TPBS}}, m, \sigma_m, i, \pi_{Trace})$

TPBS **Correctness** for the correctness of TPBS, we require that for all $\lambda \in \mathbb{N}$, all $pp_{\mathsf{TPBS}} \leftarrow \mathsf{ppGen}(1^\lambda)$, for all $(pk^{TA}_{\mathsf{TPBS}}, (sk^{TA}_{\mathsf{TPBS}}, Reg)) \leftarrow \mathsf{TASetup}(pp_{\mathsf{TPBS}})$, for all $(pk^{Issuer}_{\mathsf{TPBS}}, sk^{Issuer}_{\mathsf{TPBS}}) \leftarrow \mathsf{IssuerSetup}(pp_{\mathsf{TPBS}})$, for all $i \in \mathbb{I}$, for all $(pk_i, sk_i, ID_i) \leftarrow \mathsf{UserKeyGen}(pp_{\mathsf{TPBS}})$, for all $((Reg[i]),(sk^i_{\mathsf{TPBS}})) \leftarrow \mathsf{IDKeyGen}((sk^{TA}_{\mathsf{TPBS}}) \xleftrightarrow[\sigma^i_{ID}]{(i,ID_i)} (sk_i))$, for all $sk^p_{\mathsf{TPBS}} \leftarrow \mathsf{PolicyKeyGen}(sk^{Issuer}_{\mathsf{TPBS}}, p)$, and for all $(m, p, w_p) \in \{0,1\}^*$ s.t $\mathsf{PC}((p, m), w_p) = 1$, we have $\sigma_m \leftarrow \mathsf{Sign}(pk^{TA}_{\mathsf{TPBS}}, pk^{Issuer}_{\mathsf{TPBS}}, sk^p_{\mathsf{TPBS}}, sk^i_{\mathsf{TPBS}}, m, p, w_p)$ such that $\top \leftarrow \mathsf{Verify}(pk^{TA}_{\mathsf{TPBS}}, pk^{Issuer}_{\mathsf{TPBS}}, m, \sigma_m)$. Moreover, we have $(i, \pi_{Trace}) \leftarrow \mathsf{Trace}(pk^{TA}_{\mathsf{TPBS}}, pk^{Issuer}_{\mathsf{TPBS}}, Reg, m, \sigma_m)$ such that $\top \leftarrow \mathsf{Judge}(pk^{TA}_{\mathsf{TPBS}}, pk^{Issuer}_{\mathsf{TPBS}}, m, \sigma_m, i, \pi_{Trace})$.

To prevent a misbehaving TA or any party who has access to the policy key sk^p_{TPBS} from framing a user, we ensure that sk^i_{TPBS} contains sk_i which is generated by individual users and not shared with any entity in the scheme. Moreover, since our scheme segregates the identity keys from the policy keys, the delegatability of policy keys becomes a natural extension for our scheme and could be achieved seamlessly by applying the same technique of Bellare and Fuchsbauer [5]. Moreover, segregating the issuer and TA rules make our scheme a perfect fit for decentralized environments where multiple issuers may coexist.

3.1 TPBS Security Definitions

The security notions of PBS are privacy (policy-indistinguishability) and unforgeability [5]. Privacy of the policy ensures that a signature reveals nei-

$\mathcal{O}\mathsf{KeyGen}(i, p)$

---

if $i \in \mathcal{U}$ **return** $\perp$

$(pk_i, sk_i, ID_i) \leftarrow \mathsf{UserKeyGen}(pp_{\mathsf{TPBS}})$

$((Reg[i]), (sk^{i}_{\mathsf{TPBS}})) \leftarrow \mathsf{IDKeyGen}((sk^{TA}_{\mathsf{TPBS}}) \xleftrightarrow[\sigma^{i}_{ID}]{(i, ID_i)} (sk_i))$

$sk^{p}_{\mathsf{TPBS}} \leftarrow \mathsf{PolicyKeyGen}(sk^{Issuer}_{\mathsf{TPBS}}, p)$

$\mathcal{T} = \mathcal{T} \cup \{i, sk_i\}; \quad \mathcal{L} = \mathcal{L} \cup \{p\}$

return $(sk^{i}_{\mathsf{TPBS}}, sk^{p}_{\mathsf{TPBS}})$

$\mathcal{O}\mathsf{USign}(i_j, m, p, w_p)$

---

if $\mathsf{PC}((p, m), w_p) = 0 \vee i_j \notin \mathcal{U}$

  return $\perp$

$(sk^{i_j}_{\mathsf{TPBS}}) = (sk_{i_j}, \sigma^{i_j}_{ID}) \leftarrow \mathcal{Q}_i[i_j]$

$sk^{p}_{\mathsf{TPBS}} \leftarrow \mathsf{PolicyKeyGen}(sk^{Issuer}_{\mathsf{TPBS}}, p)$

$\sigma_m \leftarrow \mathsf{Sign}(pk^{TA}_{\mathsf{TPBS}}, pk^{Issuer}_{\mathsf{TPBS}}, sk^{p}_{\mathsf{TPBS}}, sk^{i_j}_{\mathsf{TPBS}}, m, p, w_p)$

$\mathcal{M} = \mathcal{M} \cup \sigma_m$

return $(\sigma_m, \sigma^{i_j}_{ID}, sk^{p}_{\mathsf{TPBS}})$

$\mathcal{O}\mathsf{IdLoRSign}(i_{j_0}, i_{j_1}, m, p, w_p)$

---

if $\mathsf{PC}((p, m), w_p) = 0 \vee i_{j_0}, i_{j_1} \notin \mathcal{U}$

  return $\perp$

$(sk^{i_0}_{\mathsf{TPBS}}) \leftarrow \mathcal{Q}_i[j_0][1]; \quad (sk^{i_1}_{\mathsf{TPBS}}) \leftarrow \mathcal{Q}_i[j_1][1]$

$sk^{p}_{\mathsf{TPBS}} \leftarrow \mathsf{PolicyKeyGen}(sk^{Issuer}_{\mathsf{TPBS}}, p)$

$\sigma_{m_b} \leftarrow \mathsf{Sign}(pk^{TA}_{\mathsf{TPBS}}, pk^{Issuer}_{\mathsf{TPBS}}, sk^{p}_{\mathsf{TPBS}}, sk^{i_b}_{\mathsf{TPBS}}, m, p, w_p)$

$\mathcal{M}' = \mathcal{M}' \cup (m, \sigma_{m_b})$

return σ_{m_b}

$\mathcal{O}\mathsf{Sign}(m, i, p, w_p)$

---

if $i \in \mathcal{T} \wedge p \in \mathcal{L}$

  return $\perp$

if $i \notin \mathcal{Q}_i \quad (pk_i, sk_i, ID_i) \leftarrow \mathsf{UserKeyGen}(pp_{\mathsf{TPBS}})$

  $((Reg[i]), (sk^{i}_{\mathsf{TPBS}})) \leftarrow \mathsf{IDKeyGen}((sk^{TA}_{\mathsf{TPBS}}) \xleftrightarrow[\sigma^{i}_{ID}]{(i, ID_i)} (sk_i))$

  $\mathcal{Q}_i[i] = sk^{i}_{\mathsf{TPBS}}$

  else $\quad sk^{i}_{\mathsf{TPBS}} = \mathcal{Q}_i[i]$

if $p \notin \mathcal{Q}_p \quad sk^{p}_{\mathsf{TPBS}} \leftarrow \mathsf{PolicyKeyGen}(sk^{Issuer}_{\mathsf{TPBS}}, p)$

  $\mathcal{Q}_p[p] = sk^{p}_{\mathsf{TPBS}}$

  else $\quad sk^{p}_{\mathsf{TPBS}} = \mathcal{Q}_p[p]$

$\sigma_m \leftarrow \mathsf{Sign}(pk^{TA}_{\mathsf{TPBS}}, pk^{Issuer}_{\mathsf{TPBS}}, sk^{p}_{\mathsf{TPBS}}, sk^{i}_{\mathsf{TPBS}}, m, p, w_p)$

$\mathcal{M} = \mathcal{M} \cup (m, \sigma_m)$

return σ_m

$\mathcal{O}\mathsf{PLoRSign}(i, m, p_0, w_{p_0}, p_1, w_{p_1})$

---

if $\mathsf{PC}((p_0, m), w_{p_0}) = 0 \vee \mathsf{PC}((p_1, m), w_{p_1}) = 0$

  return $\perp$

$(pk_i, sk_i, ID_i) \leftarrow \mathsf{UserKeyGen}(pp_{\mathsf{TPBS}})$

$((Reg[i]), (sk^{i}_{\mathsf{TPBS}})) \leftarrow \mathsf{IDKeyGen}((sk^{TA}_{\mathsf{TPBS}}) \xleftrightarrow[\sigma^{i}_{ID}]{(i, ID_i)} (sk_i))$

$sk^{p_0}_{\mathsf{TPBS}} \leftarrow \mathsf{PolicyKeyGen}(sk^{Issuer}_{\mathsf{TPBS}}, p_0)$

$sk^{p_1}_{\mathsf{TPBS}} \leftarrow \mathsf{PolicyKeyGen}(sk^{Issuer}_{\mathsf{TPBS}}, p_1)$

$\sigma_{m_b} \leftarrow \mathsf{Sign}(pk^{TA}_{\mathsf{TPBS}}, pk^{Issuer}_{\mathsf{TPBS}}, sk^{p_b}_{\mathsf{TPBS}}, sk^{i}_{\mathsf{TPBS}}, m, p_b, w_{p_b})$

$\mathcal{M} = \mathcal{M} \cup \{m, \sigma_m\}$

return σ_{m_b}

$\mathcal{O}\mathsf{Sim\text{-}or\text{-}Sign}(i_j, p, m, w_p)$

---

if $\mathsf{PC}((p, m), w_p) = 1$

  $(sk^{i_j}_{\mathsf{TPBS}}) \leftarrow \mathcal{Q}_i[i_j]$

  $sk^{p}_{\mathsf{TPBS}} \leftarrow \mathsf{PolicyKeyGen}(sk^{Issuer}_{\mathsf{TPBS}}, p)$

  $\sigma_{m_0} \leftarrow \mathsf{Sign}(pk^{TA}_{\mathsf{TPBS}_0}, pk^{Issuer}_{\mathsf{TPBS}_0}, sk^{p}_{\mathsf{TPBS}}, sk^{i_j}_{\mathsf{TPBS}}, m, w_p)$

  $\sigma_{m_1} \leftarrow \mathsf{SimSign}(tr_{NIZK}, pk^{TA}_{\mathsf{TPBS}_1}, pk^{Issuer}_{\mathsf{TPBS}_1}, m)$

  $\mathcal{M}' = \mathcal{M}' \cup \{m, \sigma_{m_b}\}$

  return σ_{m_b}

return $\perp$

$\mathcal{O}\mathsf{Trace}(m, \sigma_m)$

---

if $\sigma_m \in \mathcal{M}'$ **return** $\perp$

$(i, \pi_{Trace}) \leftarrow \mathsf{Trace}(pk^{TA}_{\mathsf{TPBS}}, pk^{Issuer}_{\mathsf{TPBS}}, sk^{TA}_{\mathsf{TPBS}}, Reg, m, \sigma_m)$

return (i, π_{Trace})

Fig. 1. TPBS Security Oracles

ther the policy associated with the policy key nor the witness that was used in creating such a signature. Unforgeability is defined as the infeasibility of creating a valid signature for a message m without holding a policy key for some policy p and a witness w_p such that $\mathsf{PC}((p, m), w_p) = 1$. In the same context, Bellare and Fuchsbauer have defined simulatability and extractability as stronger versions of the aforementioned security notions [5]. The main reason behind introducing such stronger notions is that the traditional notions of policy privacy and unforgeability are insufficient for all applications. For instance, a PBS scheme with a policy checker PC such that for every message m, there is only one policy

p where $\mathsf{PC}((p, m_i), w_i) = 1$ for $i \in \{0, \ldots, n\}$, such a scheme does not hide the policy, yet still satisfies indistinguishability.

Since TPBS signing requires the user's identity key and the produced signatures are traceable by the TA, we extend the definition of privacy to include user anonymity in addition to policy-privacy. Moreover, we define non-frameability and traceability to capture the newly introduced traceability feature. We also define simulatability and extractability as the stronger notions of privacy and unforgeability. Note that our definition of simulatability and extractability differs from those in PBS in that they include the newly introduced signer identity and tracing feature. In what follows, we give the formal definitions of the TPBS security notions. The oracles used in the security experiments are defined in Fig. 1 in which the lists, $\mathcal{U}$ contains all the honest users' identities in the system, $\mathcal{T}$ tracks all dishonest users in the system where the adversary has access to their identity secret key, and $\mathcal{L}$ tracks all the policies that the adversary has access to their policy keys. $\mathcal{Q}_i$ is a key-value pair matrix that contains the honestly generated identity keys defined by the user identity i. $\mathcal{Q}_p$ is a key-value pair matrix that contains the honestly generated policy keys defined by the policy p. $\mathcal{M}$ and $\mathcal{M}'$ are used to track signatures generated by the signing oracles.

Note that $\mathcal{O}\mathsf{KeyGen}$ is set up to generate the signer identity key from scratch and return it to the adversary along with the policy key. Such a setup allows the adversary to corrupt as many users as it wants without engaging with the oracle interactively.

3.2 Privacy

TPBS ensures privacy if it guarantees signer anonymity and policy-privacy, which are defined as follows.

Signer Anonymity. Anonymity is modeled by the indistinguishability experiment in Fig. 2, where the adversary has access to $\mathcal{O}\mathsf{KeyGen}(.)$, $\mathcal{O}\mathsf{USign}(.)$, $\mathcal{O}IdLoRSign$, and $\mathcal{O}\mathsf{Trace}(.)$ oracles. The challenge oracle $\mathcal{O}IdLoRSign$ is initialized with a random bit $b \in \{0,1\}$. The adversary inputs to $\mathcal{O}IdLoRSign$ are (i_0, i_1, m, p, w_p) where the adversary chooses i_0, i_1 from a predefined list of users $\mathcal{U}$ that it has no access to their signing keys. After verifying that $\mathsf{PC}((p, m), w_p) = 1$ and $i_0, i_1 \in \mathcal{U}$, the oracle generates σ_{m_b} for the message m using $(sk^p_{\mathsf{TPBS}}, sk^{i_b}_{\mathsf{TPBS}})$. Finally, the oracle returns σ_{m_b} to the adversary. The adversary wins if it can determine the bit b with more than the negligible probability. The adversary has access to $\mathcal{O}\mathsf{USign}(.)$ oracle, which on input $(i \in \mathcal{U}, m, p, w_p)$, it obtains a signature on message m under the identity key of $i \in \mathcal{U}$ and any policy of its choice. Furthermore, $\mathcal{O}\mathsf{USign}(.)$ returns the TA signature σ^i_{ID} of the user i to simulate the case where σ^i_{ID} is leaked without the knowledge of sk_i. Furthermore, we give the adversary access to $sk^{Issuer}_{\mathsf{TPBS}}$ to simulate the case of a corrupt issuer. Note, to prevent trivial attacks, the queries to $\mathcal{O}\mathsf{KeyGen}(.)$ are limited to users' identities not in $\mathcal{U}$ which models the set of honest users. Also, the adversary cannot query the $\mathcal{O}Trace$ with the output of $\mathcal{O}IdLoRSign$.

Anonymity is defined in a selfless setting where we do not provide the adversary with access to the identity keys of the two signers, $sk^{i_0}_{\mathsf{TPBS}}$ and $sk^{i_1}_{\mathsf{TPBS}}$, involved in the query to $\mathcal{O}IdLoRSign$ [9]. This models the case where an internal adversary should not be able to distinguish between two signatures generated under two identities different than its own, even if both signatures are generated using the same policy key. Such a restriction is essential to construct a significantly more efficient scheme [7].

Definition 1 *(*TPBS *Anonymity). The* TPBS *scheme is anonymous if for any PPT adversary $\mathcal{A}$, $|\Pr[\boldsymbol{Exp}^{Anonymity}_{\mathcal{A},\mathsf{TPBS}}(\lambda) = \top] - \frac{1}{2}| \leq \epsilon(\lambda)$, where $\boldsymbol{Exp}^{Anonymity}_{\mathcal{A},\mathsf{TPBS}}$ is defined in Fig. 2.*

$\mathbf{Exp}^{Anonymity}_{\mathcal{A},\mathsf{TPBS}}(\lambda)$

$b \xleftarrow{\$} \{0,1\}, \mathcal{U} = \{0,\ldots,n\}, \mathcal{M}' = \{\}, \mathcal{Q}_i = [\,], pp_{\mathsf{TPBS}} \leftarrow \mathsf{ppGen}(1^\lambda)$

$(pk^{TA}_{\mathsf{TPBS}}, sk^{TA}_{\mathsf{TPBS}}) \leftarrow \mathsf{TASetup}(pp_{\mathsf{TPBS}})$

$(pk^{Issuer}_{\mathsf{TPBS}}, sk^{Issuer}_{\mathsf{TPBS}}) \leftarrow \mathsf{IssuerSetup}(pp_{\mathsf{TPBS}})$

foreach $i_j \in \mathcal{U}$

  $(pk_{i_j}, sk_{i_j}, ID_{i_j}) \leftarrow \mathsf{UserKeyGen}(pp_{\mathsf{TPBS}})$

  $((Reg[i_j]), (sk^{i_j}_{\mathsf{TPBS}})) \leftarrow \mathsf{IDKeyGen}((sk^{TA}_{\mathsf{TPBS}}) \xleftrightarrow[\sigma^{i_j}_{ID}]{(i, ID_{i_j})} (sk_{i_j}))$

  $\mathcal{Q}_i[i_j] = sk^{i_j}_{\mathsf{TPBS}}$

$b' \leftarrow \mathcal{A}^{\mathcal{O}\mathsf{KeyGen}(.),\mathcal{O}\mathsf{USign}(.),\mathcal{O}\mathsf{Trace}(.),\mathcal{O}\mathsf{IdLoRSign}(.,b)}(\mathcal{U}, pp_{\mathsf{TPBS}}, pk^{TA}_{\mathsf{TPBS}}, pk^{Issuer}_{\mathsf{TPBS}}, sk^{Issuer}_{\mathsf{TPBS}})$

if $b = b'$

  return $\top$

return $\bot$

Fig. 2. TPBS Anonymity Experiment

Policy-Privacy. Policy-privacy is modeled by the indistinguishability experiment in Fig. 3, where the adversary has access to $\mathcal{O}\mathsf{KeyGen}(.)$ and $\mathcal{O}PLoRSign$ oracles. The challenge oracle $\mathcal{O}PLoRSign$ is initialized with a random bit $b \in \{0,1\}$. The adversary inputs to $\mathcal{O}PLoRSign$ oracle are $(i, m, p_0, w_{p_0}, p_1, w_{p_1})$. After verifying that $\mathsf{PC}((p_0, m), w_{p_0}) = 1$, and $\mathsf{PC}((p_1, m), w_{p_1}) = 1$, the oracle generates sk^{i}_{TPBS} and $sk^{p_b}_{\mathsf{TPBS}}$ for $b \in \{0,1\}$. It then signs m using $(sk^{p_b}_{\mathsf{TPBS}}, sk^{i}_{\mathsf{TPBS}})$ and returns σ_{m_b}. The adversary wins if it can determine the bit b with a probability better than the random guess. Note that we give the adversary access to sk^{TA}_{TPBS} and $sk^{Issuer}_{\mathsf{TPBS}}$ to simulate the case of a corrupt TA and\or issuer.

Definition 2 *(*TPBS *Policy-privacy). The* TPBS *scheme is policy-private if for any PPT adversary $\mathcal{A}$, $|\Pr[\boldsymbol{Exp}^{Policy-privacy}_{\mathcal{A},\mathsf{TPBS}}(\lambda) = \top] - \frac{1}{2}| \leq \epsilon(\lambda)$, where $\boldsymbol{Exp}^{Policy-privacy}_{\mathcal{A},\mathsf{TPBS}}$ is defined in Fig. 3.*

Consider a PBS scheme where for every message m there is only one policy p such that $\mathsf{PC}((p, m), w_p) = 1$; then the aforementioned policy-privacy definition

$\mathbf{Exp}^{Policy-privacy}_{\mathcal{A},\mathsf{TPBS}}(\lambda)$

$b \xleftarrow{\$} \{0,1\}, pp_{\mathsf{TPBS}} \leftarrow \mathsf{ppGen}(1^\lambda)$
$(pk^{TA}_{\mathsf{TPBS}}, sk^{TA}_{\mathsf{TPBS}}) \leftarrow \mathsf{TASetup}(pp_{\mathsf{TPBS}})$
$(pk^{Issuer}_{\mathsf{TPBS}}, sk^{Issuer}_{\mathsf{TPBS}}) \leftarrow \mathsf{IssuerSetup}(pp_{\mathsf{TPBS}})$
$b' \leftarrow \mathcal{A}^{\mathcal{O}\mathsf{KeyGen}(.),\mathcal{O}\mathsf{PLoRSign}(.,.,b)}(pp_{\mathsf{TPBS}}, pk^{TA}_{\mathsf{TPBS}}, pk^{Issuer}_{\mathsf{TPBS}}, sk^{TA}_{\mathsf{TPBS}}, sk^{Issuer}_{\mathsf{TPBS}})$
if $b = b'$
  return $\top$
return $\bot$

Fig. 3. TPBS Policy-privacy Experiment

can not hide the associated policy. It has been proven that simulatability is a stronger notion of policy-privacy that remedies the aforementioned limitation [5]. Since the same limitation is inherited in TPBS, thus, we also define simulatability, and we prove that our definition implies the privacy of TPBS, which is defined as both anonymity and policy-privacy.

Simulatability. This security notion requires the existence of a simulator that can create simulated signatures without having access to any of the users' signing keys or witnesses. Yet, such signatures are indistinguishable from real signatures. Thus, we assume that for every TPBS procedure, there exists a simulated procedure whose output is indistinguishable from the non-simulated one. We denote such a procedure with the Sim prefix. More precisely, we require the following algorithms, SimppGen, SimTASetup, SimIssuerSetup, SimUserKeyGenTPBS, SimIDKeyGen, SimPolicyKeyGen, SimSign, and SimTraceTPBS. Note that SimppGen, SimTASetup, and SimIssuerSetup also output the trapdoor information tr_{TPBS}, tr_{TA}, and tr_{Issuer}, respectively. Such trapdoor outputs are used as inputs to the other relevant simulated procedures instead of the secret inputs. We give the definitions of the simulated procedures in Fig. 9 after we present the generic construction

We formally define simulatability in a selfless setting by the experiment in Fig. 4, in which the adversary has access to $\mathcal{O}$KeyGen(.), $\mathcal{O}$USign(.), $\mathcal{O}$Trace(.), and $\mathcal{O}$Sim-or-Sign(.) oracles. $\mathcal{O}$Sim-or-Sign(.) is its challenge oracle which on the input of some i_j from a predefined list of honest users identities $\mathcal{U}$, a message m, a policy p, and a witness w_p that m conforms to p, the oracle outputs a signature σ_m. The adversary wins if it can determine whether σ_m is generated using i_j identity key and p policy key or it is a simulated signature. To prevent trivial attacks, the adversary cannot query the $\mathcal{O}$Trace(.) with the signatures generated by the challenging oracle.

Definition 3 (TPBS *Simulatability*). *The* TPBS *scheme is simulatable if for any PPT adversary* $\mathcal{A}$, $|\Pr[\boldsymbol{Exp}^{SIM}_{\mathcal{A},\mathsf{TPBS}}(\lambda) = \top] - \frac{1}{2}| \leq \epsilon(\lambda)$, *where the* $\boldsymbol{Exp}^{SIM}_{\mathcal{A},\mathsf{TPBS}}$ *is defined in Fig. 4.*

$\mathbf{Exp}^{SIM}_{\mathcal{A},\mathsf{TPBS}}(\lambda)$

$b \xleftarrow{\$} \{0,1\}, \mathcal{U} = \{0,\ldots,n\}, \mathcal{M}' = \{\}, \mathcal{Q}_i = [\,]$

$pp_{\mathsf{TPBS}_0} \leftarrow \mathsf{ppGen}(1^\lambda), (pp_{\mathsf{TPBS}_1}, tr_{\mathsf{TPBS}}) \leftarrow \mathsf{SimppGen}(1^\lambda)$

$(pk^{TA}_{\mathsf{TPBS}_0}, sk^{TA}_{\mathsf{TPBS}_0}) \leftarrow \mathsf{TASetup}(pp_{\mathsf{TPBS}_0})$

$(pk^{Issuer}_{\mathsf{TPBS}_0}, sk^{Issuer}_{\mathsf{TPBS}_0}) \leftarrow \mathsf{IssuerSetup}(pp_{\mathsf{TPBS}_0})$

$(pk^{TA}_{\mathsf{TPBS}_1}, sk^{TA}_{\mathsf{TPBS}_1}, tr_{TA}) \leftarrow \mathsf{SimTASetup}(pp_{\mathsf{TPBS}_1})$

$(pk^{Issuer}_{\mathsf{TPBS}_1}, sk^{Issuer}_{\mathsf{TPBS}_1}, tr_{Issuer}) \leftarrow \mathsf{SimIssuerSetup}(pp_{\mathsf{TPBS}_1})$

foreach $i_j \in \mathcal{U}$

$\quad (pk_{i_j}, sk_{i_j}, ID_{i_j}) \leftarrow \mathsf{UserKeyGen}(pp_{\mathsf{TPBS}})$

$\quad ((Reg[i_j]), (sk^{i_j}_{\mathsf{TPBS}})) \leftarrow \mathsf{IDKeyGen}((sk^{TA}_{\mathsf{TPBS}}) \underset{\sigma^{i_j}_{ID}}{\overset{(i, ID_{i_j})}{\longleftrightarrow}} (sk_{i_j}))$

$\quad \mathcal{Q}_i[i_j] = sk^{i_j}_{\mathsf{TPBS}}$

$b' \leftarrow \mathcal{A}^{\mathcal{O}\mathsf{KeyGen}(.), \mathcal{O}\mathsf{USign}(.), \mathcal{O}\mathsf{Trace}(.), \mathcal{O}\mathsf{Sim\text{-}or\text{-}Sign}(.)}(\mathcal{U}, pp_{\mathsf{TPBS}_b}, pk^{TA}_{\mathsf{TPBS}_b}, sk^{TA}_{\mathsf{TPBS}_b}, pk^{Issuer}_{\mathsf{TPBS}_b}, sk^{Issuer}_{\mathsf{TPBS}_b})$

if $b = b'$ **return** $\top$

return $\bot$

Fig. 4. TPBS Simulatability Experiment

3.3 Unforgeability

Intuitively unforgeability is the infeasibility of creating a valid signature on a message m without holding the policy key for policy p to which m conforms. To model users' corruption and collusion attacks where users could combine their policy keys to sign messages non of them is authorized to, Bellare and Fuchsbauer have defined the unforgeability of the PBS scheme by an experiment where the adversary is allowed to query a key generation oracle to generate user keys and gain access to some of them. However, in their definition, it becomes hard to efficiently determine if an adversary has won the unforgeability experiment by producing a valid signature such that $\mathsf{PC}((p,m), w_p) = 1$ using a queried policy key or not since policy-privacy requires hiding the policy and witness used in generating a specific signature. To overcome the aforementioned limitation, they defined extractability as a strengthened version of unforgeability and proved that extractability implies unforgeability [5]. Since TPBS privacy requires hiding the policy, witness, and signer's identity used in generating signatures over m, we define extractability and adapt it to imply the unforgeability for TPBS.

Extractability. We formally define TPBS extractability by the experiment in Fig. 5, where we assume the existence of an extractor algorithm Extr which upon inputting a valid message signature pair (m, σ_m) in addition to trapdoor information tr_{TPBS}, it outputs the tuple $(p, sk_i, sk^p_{\mathsf{TPBS}}, w_p)$. An adversary $\mathcal{A}$ who has access to $\mathcal{O}\mathsf{KeyGen}$ and $\mathcal{O}\mathsf{Sign}$ oracles (Fig. 1) wins $\mathbf{Exp}^{Ext}_{\mathcal{A},\mathsf{TPBS}}$ if it outputs a valid message signature pair (m^*, σ_{m^*}) such that either i) it does not hold some sk^{i*}_{TPBS} that is obtained from $\mathcal{O}\mathsf{KeyGen}$ oracle or for all p, it obtained sk^p_{TPBS} by querying $\mathcal{O}\mathsf{KeyGen}$ oracle, ii) it does not hold an sk^{p*}_{TPBS} corresponds to p^* such that $\mathsf{PC}((p^*, m^*), w^*_p) = 1$ or iii) $\mathsf{PC}((p^*, m^*), w^*_p) = 0$. Note that since tr_{TPBS} is required by Extr algorithm, the extractability experiment is initialized using

SimppGen(1^λ) algorithm rather than ppGen(1^λ), and all other algorithms are kept the same.

Definition 4 *(*TPBS *Extractability) a* TPBS *scheme is extractable if for any PPT adversary* $\mathcal{A}$, $\Pr[\boldsymbol{Exp}^{Ext}_{\mathcal{A},\mathsf{TPBS}}(\lambda) = \top] \leq \epsilon(\lambda)$, *where* $\boldsymbol{Exp}^{Ext}_{\mathcal{A},\mathsf{TPBS}}$ *is defined in Fig. 5.*

3.4 Non-frameability

This property ensures that even if the tracing authority, issuer, and all corrupt users in the scheme collude together, they cannot produce a valid signature that is traced back to an honest user. TPBS non-frameability is modeled by the experiment defined in Fig. 6, in which the adversary has access to both TA and issuer secret keys ($sk^{TA}_{\mathsf{TPBS}}, sk^{Issuer}_{\mathsf{TPBS}}$), in addition to $\mathcal{O}$KeyGen, $\mathcal{O}$USign, and $\mathcal{O}$Trace oracles. The adversary wins if it outputs a verifiable (m^*, σ_{m^*}) that has not been queried to $\mathcal{O}$USign and when (m^*, σ_{m^*}) is traced back to its signer, the tracing algorithm outputs an identity of one of the honest users in $\mathcal{U}$. Additionally, the output of $\mathcal{O}$Trace oracle should be verifiable using the Judge algorithm.

$\mathbf{Exp}^{Ext}_{\mathcal{A},\mathsf{TPBS}}(\lambda)$

$(pp_{\mathsf{TPBS}}, tr_{\mathsf{TPBS}}) \leftarrow \mathsf{SimppGen}(1^\lambda)$

$(pk^{TA}_{\mathsf{TPBS}}, sk^{TA}_{\mathsf{TPBS}}, Reg) \leftarrow \mathsf{TASetup}(pp_{\mathsf{TPBS}})$

$(pk^{Issuer}_{\mathsf{TPBS}}, sk^{Issuer}_{\mathsf{TPBS}}) \leftarrow \mathsf{IssuerSetup}(pp_{\mathsf{TPBS}})$

$\mathcal{Q}_i = \mathcal{Q}_p = [\,]$

$\mathcal{T} = \mathcal{L} = \mathcal{M} = \{\}$

$(m^*, \sigma_{m^*}) \leftarrow \mathcal{A}^{\mathcal{O}\mathsf{KeyGen}(.), \mathcal{O}\mathsf{Sign}(.)}(pp_{\mathsf{TPBS}}, pk^{TA}_{\mathsf{TPBS}}, pk^{Issuer}_{\mathsf{TPBS}})$

if $(m^*, \sigma_{m^*}) \in \mathcal{M} \vee \mathsf{Verify}(pk^{TA}_{\mathsf{TPBS}}, pk^{Issuer}_{\mathsf{TPBS}}, m^*, \sigma_{m^*}) = \bot$

  return $\bot$

$(p^*, sk^*_i, sk^p_{\mathsf{TPBS}}, w_{p^*}) \leftarrow \mathsf{Extr}(tr_{\mathsf{TPBS}}, m^*, \sigma_{m^*})$

if $sk^*_i \notin \mathcal{T} \vee p^* \notin \mathcal{L} \vee \mathsf{PC}((p^*, m^*), w^*_p) = 0$

  return $\top$

return $\bot$

Fig. 5. TPBS Extractability Experiment

Definition 5 *(*TPBS *Non-frameability) a* TPBS *scheme is non-frameable if for any PPT adversary* $\mathcal{A}$, $\Pr[\boldsymbol{Exp}^{Non-frameability}_{\mathcal{A},\mathsf{TPBS}}(\lambda) = \top] \leq \epsilon(\lambda)$, *where the non-frameability experiment is defined in Fig. 6.*

$\mathbf{Exp}_{\mathcal{A},\mathsf{TPBS}}^{Non-frameability}(\lambda)$

$\mathcal{U} = \{0,\ldots,n\}, \mathcal{M} = \{\}, \mathcal{Q}_i = [\,], pp_{\mathsf{TPBS}} \leftarrow \mathsf{ppGen}(1^\lambda)$

$(pk_{\mathsf{TPBS}}^{TA}, sk_{\mathsf{TPBS}}^{TA}) \leftarrow \mathsf{TASetup}(pp_{\mathsf{TPBS}}), (pk_{\mathsf{TPBS}}^{Issuer}, sk_{\mathsf{TPBS}}^{Issuer}) \leftarrow \mathsf{IssuerSetup}(pp_{\mathsf{TPBS}})$

foreach $i_j \in \mathcal{U}$

$(pk_{i_j}, sk_{i_j}, ID_{i_j}) \leftarrow \mathsf{UserKeyGen}(pp_{\mathsf{TPBS}})$

$((Reg[i_j]), (sk_{\mathsf{TPBS}}^{i_j})) \leftarrow \mathsf{IDKeyGen}((sk_{\mathsf{TPBS}}^{TA}) \xleftrightarrow[\sigma_{ID}^{i_j}]{(i,ID_{i_j})} (sk_{i_j}))$

$\mathcal{Q}_i[i_j] = sk_{\mathsf{TPBS}}^{i_j}$

$(m^*, \sigma_{m^*}) \leftarrow \mathcal{A}^{\mathcal{O}\mathsf{KeyGen}(.),\mathcal{O}\mathsf{USign}(.),\mathcal{O}\mathsf{Trace}(.)}(\mathcal{U}, pp_{\mathsf{TPBS}}, pk_{\mathsf{TPBS}}^{TA}, pk_{\mathsf{TPBS}}^{Issuer}, sk_{\mathsf{TPBS}}^{Issuer}, sk_{\mathsf{TPBS}}^{TA})$

if $(m^*, \sigma_{m^*}) \in \mathcal{M} \vee \mathsf{Verify}(pk_{\mathsf{TPBS}}^{TA}, pk_{\mathsf{TPBS}}^{Issuer}, m^*, \sigma_{m^*}) = \perp$

return $\perp$

$(i^*, \pi_{Trace}^*) \leftarrow \mathsf{Trace}(pk_{\mathsf{TPBS}}^{TA}, pk_{\mathsf{TPBS}}^{Issuer}, sk_{\mathsf{TPBS}}^{TA}, Reg, m, \sigma_m)$

if $i^* \notin \mathcal{U}$

return $\perp$

return $\mathsf{Judge}(pk_{\mathsf{TPBS}}^{TA}, pk_{\mathsf{TPBS}}^{Issuer}, m^*, \sigma_{m^*}, i^*, \pi_{Trace}^*)$

Fig. 6. TPBS Non-Frameability Experiment

3.5 Traceability

Traceability requires that even if all scheme users collude together, they cannot produce a signature that cannot be traced. We require the tracing authority to be honest, as knowing the secret key of the tracing authority would allow the adversary to sign a dummy sk_i under the tracing authority's secret key resulting in an untraceable signature. TPBS traceability is modeled by the experiment defined in Fig. 7, in which the adversary has access to $\mathcal{O}$KeyGen and $\mathcal{O}$Trace procedures. We omit the adversarial access to $\mathcal{O}$Sign oracle since the adversary could corrupt as many users as it wants and get access to their keys. Hence it could use the signing algorithm directly Sign(.) to produce signatures. The Adversary wins if it outputs a verifiable (m^*, σ_{m^*}), which when traced, the tracing algorithm Trace outputs $\perp$.

$\mathbf{Exp}_{\mathcal{A},\mathsf{TPBS}}^{Traceability}(\lambda)$

$(pp_{\mathsf{TPBS}}) \leftarrow \mathsf{ppGen}(1^\lambda), (pk_{\mathsf{TPBS}}^{TA}, sk_{\mathsf{TPBS}}^{TA}) \leftarrow \mathsf{TASetup}(pp_{\mathsf{TPBS}})$

$(pk_{\mathsf{TPBS}}^{Issuer}, sk_{\mathsf{TPBS}}^{Issuer}) \leftarrow \mathsf{IssuerSetup}(pp_{\mathsf{TPBS}})$

$(m^*, \sigma_{m^*}) \leftarrow \mathcal{A}^{\mathcal{O}\mathsf{KeyGen}(.),\mathcal{O}\mathsf{Trace}(.)}(pp_{\mathsf{TPBS}}, pk_{\mathsf{TPBS}}^{TA}, pk_{\mathsf{TPBS}}^{Issuer})$

if $\mathsf{Verify}(pk_{\mathsf{TPBS}}^{TA}, pk_{\mathsf{TPBS}}^{Issuer}, m^*, \sigma_{m^*})$

$(i^*, \pi_{Trace}^*) \leftarrow \mathsf{Trace}(pk_{\mathsf{TPBS}}^{TA}, pk_{\mathsf{TPBS}}^{Issuer}, Reg, m^*, \sigma_{m^*})$

if $i = \perp$

return $\top$

return $\perp$

Fig. 7. TPBS Traceability Experiment

Definition 6 *(*TPBS *Traceability) a* TPBS *scheme is traceable if for any PPT adversary* $\mathcal{A}$, $\Pr[\boldsymbol{Exp}_{\mathcal{A},\mathsf{TPBS}}^{Traceability}(\lambda) = \top] \leq \epsilon(\lambda)$*, where the traceability experiment is defined in Fig. 7.*

4 TPBS Generic Construction

The main building blocks of the new construction are a EUF-CMA RDS scheme capable of signing a commitment on a secret message, a SE-NIZK proof system, and a digital signature scheme. Figure 8 depicts the complete generic construction of TPBS.

User Setup. The general idea of the new scheme is that in addition to the policy key sk^p_{TPBS} that is generated by the issuer using PolicyKeyGen and shared with any user who is allowed to sign a message m conforming to p, each user has to run an interactive algorithm IDKeyGen with the TA to obtain an identity key sk^i_{TPBS}. Prior to engaging in IDKeyGen, the user runs the algorithm UserKeyGen where it selects some $sk_i \xleftarrow{\$} \mathcal{F}$ and generates the user's registration information ID_i. More precisely, ID_i contains $C_i = f(sk_i)$ and the user's digital signature τ_i over C_i. During the execution of IDKeyGen, the user obtains the TA's RDS signature σ^i_{ID} on the user-chosen secret value sk_i. However, to ensure non-framability, the TA uses the special form of RDS signing scheme SignComRDS to generate $\sigma^i_{ID} \leftarrow \mathsf{SignComRDS}(sk^{TA}_{RDS}, C)$ where the generated RDS signature is verifiable over sk_i without being shared with the TA. At the end of the interaction, the user stores σ^i_{ID} along with sk_i as the user's identity key sk^i_{TPBS} and the TA keeps track of users' registration information ID_i in a secret registry *Reg*.

Signing. To sign a message m, the user generates a rerandomized version of the TA signature σ'^i_{ID} along with a SE-NIZK proof π_m for the relation $\mathbb{R}'_{\mathbb{NP}}$ that is given by

$$((pk^{TA}_{\mathsf{TPBS}}, \sigma'^i_{ID}, pk^{Issuer}_{\mathsf{TPBS}}, m), (sk_i, p, sk^p_{\mathsf{TPBS}}, w_p)) \in \mathbb{R}'_{\mathbb{NP}} \Leftrightarrow$$

$$\mathsf{VerifyRDS}(pk^{TA}_{\mathsf{TPBS}}, sk_i, \sigma'^i_{ID}) = 1 \tag{1a}$$

$$\wedge\ \mathsf{VerifySig}(pk^{Issuer}_{\mathsf{TPBS}}, p, sk^p_{\mathsf{TPBS}}) = 1 \tag{1b}$$

$$\wedge\ \mathsf{PC}((p, m), w_p) = 1 \tag{1c}$$

whose statements $X = (pk^{TA}_{\mathsf{TPBS}}, \sigma'^i_{ID}, pk^{Issuer}_{\mathsf{TPBS}}, m)$ with witnesses $W = (sk_i, p, sk^p_{\mathsf{TPBS}}, w_p)$. Intuitively, π_m proves that a) σ'^i_{ID} is the TA signature over some signer-generated secret value sk_i, b) the user holds the issuer's signature over some policy p, and c) the message m conforms the policy p under some witness w_p, i.e. $\mathsf{PC}((p, m), w) = 1$.

Verifying and Tracing. Signature verification is done by verifying π_m over the statements X. To trace a signature to its signer, the TA associates σ'^i_{ID} in the signature to the original signer registration information in *Reg*. However, since the user's secret chosen value sk_i is never shared with the TA, the TA uses a tracing trapdoor C'_i for $f(sk_i)$ which is generated during the execution of the

UserKeyGen algorithm and shared with the TA as part of ID_i which is held secretly in Reg by the TA. To prove successful tracing, the TA produces a NIZK proof π for the relation $\mathbb{T}_{\mathbb{NP}}$ given by:

$$((pk^{TA}_{RDS}, {\sigma'}^{i}_{ID}, C_i), (C'_i)) \in \mathbb{T}_{\mathbb{NP}} \Leftrightarrow$$

$$\mathsf{VerifyRDS}(pk^{TA}_{RDS}, C'_i, {\sigma'}^{i}_{ID}) = 1 \quad \text{(2a)}$$

$$\wedge\, C_i \mapsto C'_i \quad \text{(2b)}$$

whose statements $X' = (pk^{TA}_{RDS}, {\sigma'}^{i}_{ID}, C_i)$ with witnesses $W' = C'_i$. Intuitively, π proves that a) ${\sigma'}^{i}_{ID}$ is verifiable under the TA public key using the trapdoor information C'_i, and b) C_i and C'_i are generated using the same secret value sk_i i.e., $C_i \mapsto C'_i$. One advantage of using a sign-rerandomize-proof paradigm

$\mathsf{ppGen}(1^\lambda)$

Choose a one-way function $f(.) : \mathcal{F} \rightarrow \mathcal{C}$
$crs \leftarrow \mathsf{SetupNIZK}(1^\lambda), pp_{RDS} \leftarrow \mathsf{ppGenRDS}(1^\lambda)$
$pp_{Sig} \leftarrow \mathsf{ppGenSig}(1^\lambda), pp_{Sig_\Sigma} \leftarrow \mathsf{ppGenSig}(1^\lambda)$
return $pp_{\mathsf{TPBS}} = \{f(.), crs, pp_{RDS}, pp_{Sig}, pp_{Sig_\Sigma}\}$

$\mathsf{TASetup}(pp_{\mathsf{TPBS}})$

$(pk^{TA}_{RDS}, sk^{TA}_{RDS}) \leftarrow \mathsf{KeyGenRDS}(pp_{RDS})$
$(pk^{TA}_{\mathsf{TPBS}}, sk^{TA}_{\mathsf{TPBS}}) = (pk^{TA}_{RDS}, sk^{TA}_{RDS}), Reg = [\,]$
return $(pk^{TA}_{\mathsf{TPBS}}, sk^{TA}_{\mathsf{TPBS}})$

$\mathsf{IssuerSetup}(pp_{Sig})$

$(pk^{Issuer}_{\mathsf{TPBS}}, sk^{Issuer}_{\mathsf{TPBS}}) \leftarrow \mathsf{KeyGenSig}(pp_{\mathsf{TPBS}})$
return $(pk^{Issuer}_{\mathsf{TPBS}}, sk^{Issuer}_{\mathsf{TPBS}})$

$\mathsf{UserKeyGen}(pp_{\mathsf{TPBS}}, i)$

$(pk^{i}_{Sig_\Sigma}, sk^{i}_{Sig_\Sigma}) \leftarrow \mathsf{KeyGenSig}(pp_{Sig_\Sigma})$
$\mathcal{D}[i] = pk_i = (pk^{i}_{Sig_\Sigma}), sk_i \xleftarrow{\$} \mathcal{F}, (C_i, C'_i) = f(sk_i)$
$\tau_i \leftarrow \mathsf{SignSig}(C_i, sk^{i}_{Sig_\Sigma}), ID_i = \{C_i, C'_i, \tau_i\}$
return (pk_i, sk_i, ID_i)

$\mathsf{IDKeyGen}((sk^{TA}_{\mathsf{TPBS}}) \underset{\sigma^{i}_{ID}}{\overset{(i, ID_i)}{\longleftrightarrow}} (sk_i))$

User		**TA**
(i, ID_i, sk_i)		$(sk^{TA}_{\mathsf{TPBS}})$
$\xrightarrow{i, ID_i}$		
		$\{C_i, C'_i, \tau_i\} \leftarrow ID_i, pk^{i}_{Sig_\Sigma} = \mathcal{D}[i]$
		if $Reg[i] = \emptyset$
		$\wedge\, \mathsf{VerifySig}(pk^{i}_{Sig_\Sigma}, C_i, \tau_i)$
		$\wedge\, C_i \mapsto C'_i$
$\xleftrightarrow{\mathsf{PoK}(sk_i : C_i = f(sk_i))}$		
$\xleftarrow{\sigma^{i}_{ID}}$		$\mathsf{SignComRDS}(sk^{TA}_{RDS}, C_i)$
$sk^{i}_{\mathsf{TPBS}} = (sk_i, \sigma^{i}_{ID})$		$Reg[i] = ID_i$

$\mathsf{PolicyKeyGen}(sk^{Issuer}_{\mathsf{TPBS}}, p)$

$sk^{p}_{\mathsf{TPBS}} \leftarrow \mathsf{SignSig}(sk^{Issuer}_{\mathsf{TPBS}}, p)$
return sk^{p}_{TPBS}

$\mathsf{Sign}(pk^{TA}_{\mathsf{TPBS}}, pk^{Issuer}_{\mathsf{TPBS}}, sk^{p}_{\mathsf{TPBS}}, sk^{i}_{\mathsf{TPBS}}, m, p, w_p)$

$(sk_i, \sigma^{i}_{ID}) = sk^{i}_{\mathsf{TPBS}}, {\sigma'}^{i}_{ID} \leftarrow \mathsf{RandomizeRDS}(\sigma^{i}_{ID})$
$\pi_m \leftarrow \mathsf{ProveNIZK}(crs, (pk^{TA}_{\mathsf{TPBS}}, {\sigma'}^{i}_{ID}, pk^{Issuer}_{\mathsf{TPBS}}, m),$
$(sk_i, p, sk^{p}_{\mathsf{TPBS}}, w_p))$
return $\sigma_m = ({\sigma'}^{i}_{ID}, \pi_m)$

$\mathsf{Verify}(pk^{TA}_{\mathsf{TPBS}}, pk^{Issuer}_{\mathsf{TPBS}}, m, \sigma_m)$

$({\sigma'}^{i}_{ID}, \pi_m) \leftarrow \sigma_m$
return $\mathsf{VerifyNIZK}(crs, (pk^{TA}_{\mathsf{TPBS}}, {\sigma'}^{i}_{ID}, pk^{Issuer}_{\mathsf{TPBS}}, m), \pi_m)$

$\mathsf{Trace}(pk^{TA}_{\mathsf{TPBS}}, pk^{Issuer}_{\mathsf{TPBS}}, Reg, m, \sigma_m)$

if $\mathsf{Verify}(pk^{TA}_{\mathsf{TPBS}}, pk^{Issuer}_{\mathsf{TPBS}}, m, \sigma_m)$
  $({\sigma'}^{i}_{ID}, \pi_m) = \sigma_m$
  foreach $C'_i \in Reg$
    if $\mathsf{VerifyRDS}(pk^{TA}_{RDS}, C'_i, {\sigma'}^{i}_{ID}) = 1 \wedge C_i \mapsto C'_i$
      $\pi \leftarrow \mathsf{ProveNIZK}(crs, (C_i, {\sigma'}^{i}_{ID}), C'_i)$
      return $(i, (\pi_{Trace})) = (i, (C_i, \tau_i, \pi))$
return $\perp$

$\mathsf{Judge}(pk^{TA}_{\mathsf{TPBS}}, pk^{Issuer}_{\mathsf{TPBS}}, sk^{TA}_{\mathsf{TPBS}}, m, \sigma_m, i, \pi_{Trace})$

if $\mathsf{Verify}(pk^{TA}_{\mathsf{TPBS}}, pk^{Issuer}_{\mathsf{TPBS}}, m, \sigma_m)$
  $pk^{i}_{Sig_\Sigma} = \mathcal{D}[i], (C_i, \tau_i, \pi) = \pi_{Trace}$
  if $(\mathsf{VerifySig}(pk^{i}_{Sig_\Sigma}, C_i, \tau_i)$
    $\wedge\, \mathsf{VerifyNIZK}(crs, (C_i, {\sigma'}^{i}_{ID}), \pi)) = 1$
    return $\top$
return $\perp$

Fig. 8. Generic Construction of TPBS

rather than a sign-encrypt-proof paradigm is that the former paradigm produces a significantly more efficient signature than the latter [7,16]. On the other hand, the tracing algorithm becomes a linear operation in the number of scheme users and requires a memory size linear in the number of scheme users as well, which is considered an affordable price since tracing is an infrequent operation and is run by a computationally powerful TA [7].

Note that in Fig. 8, we use two different instances of the digital signature scheme. The issuer uses one to sign a policy p in $\mathsf{PolicyKeyGen}$, and the scheme users use the other to sign the output of the one-way function to generate ID_i in $\mathsf{UserKeyGen}$. We label the latter with the subscript Σ. We also need different CRSs for each relation, $\mathbb{R}'_{\mathbb{NP}}$ (1) and $\mathbb{T}_{\mathbb{NP}}$ (2), However, we keep the description short, thus, we do not make it explicit. In Fig. 9, we show how $\mathsf{SimppGen}(.)$, $\mathsf{SimSign}(.)$, $\mathsf{Extr}(.)$ are constructed in accordance with the concrete construction in Fig. 8. Since tr_{TA}, and tr_{Issuer} is equal to sk^{TA}_{TPBS} and $sk^{Issuer}_{\mathsf{TPBS}}$, respectively, we omit the details of $\mathsf{SimTASetup}(.)$, $\mathsf{SimIssuerSetup}(.)$, $\mathsf{SimUserKeyGenTPBS}(.)$, $\mathsf{SimIDKeyGen}(.)$, $\mathsf{SimPolicyKeyGen}(.)$, and $\mathsf{SimTrace}(.)$ which are defined in the same way as $\mathsf{TASetup}(.)$, $\mathsf{IssuerSetup}(.)$, $\mathsf{IDKeyGen}(.)$, $\mathsf{PolicyKeyGen}(.)$, and $\mathsf{Trace}(.)$, respectively.

$\mathsf{SimppGen}(1^\lambda)$

$(crs, tr_{NIZK}) \leftarrow \mathsf{SimSetupNIZK}(1^\lambda), pp_{RDS} \leftarrow \mathsf{ppGenRDS}(1^\lambda)$

$pp_{Sig} \leftarrow \mathsf{ppGenSig}(1^\lambda), pp_{Sig_\Sigma} \leftarrow \mathsf{ppGenSig}(1^\lambda)$

return $pp_{\mathsf{TPBS}} \leftarrow (crs, pp_{RDS}, pp_{Sig}, pp_{Sig_\Sigma}),\ tr_{\mathsf{TPBS}} = tr_{NIZK}$

$\mathsf{SimSign}(tr_{NIZK}, (pk^{TA}_{\mathsf{TPBS}}, pk^{Issuer}_{\mathsf{TPBS}}, m))$

$sk'_i \xleftarrow{\$} \mathcal{F}, \sigma^i_{ID} \leftarrow \mathsf{SignRDS}(sk^{TA}_{\mathsf{TPBS}}, sk'_i)$

$\sigma'^i_{ID} \leftarrow \mathsf{RandomizeRDS}(\sigma^i_{ID})$

$\pi_m \leftarrow \mathsf{SimProveNIZK}(crs, tr_{NIZK}, (pk^{Issuer}_{\mathsf{TPBS}}, pk^{TA}_{\mathsf{TPBS}}, \sigma'^i_{ID}, m))$

return $\sigma_m = (\sigma'^i_{ID}, \pi_m)$

$\mathsf{Extr}(tr_{NIZK}, m, \sigma_m)$

$(\sigma'^i_{ID}, \pi_m) = \sigma_m$

$(p, sk_i, sk^p_{\mathsf{TPBS}}, w_p) \leftarrow \mathsf{Extr_{NIZK}}(crs, tr_{NIZK}, m, \pi_m)$

return $(p, sk_i, sk^p_{\mathsf{TPBS}}, w_p)$

Fig. 9. TPBS Simulated algorithms

5 TPBS Security

The definition of extractability of TPBS (see Definition 4) implies its unforgeability. The privacy of TPBS includes policy privacy and anonymity. Accordingly, we first prove that simulatability implies both anonymity and policy-privacy. Then we present a security proof for simulatability (implies privacy), extractability (implies unforgeability), non-frameability, and traceability. Note that due to the page limit, we only give proof sketch for Theorem 2. The corresponding formal proof is provided in the full version of the paper [3].

Theorem 1. *Simulatability implies both anonymity and policy-privacy*

Proof. Assuming an adversary $\mathcal{A}$ against TPBS anonymity in $\mathbf{Exp}^{Anonymity}_{\mathcal{A},\mathsf{TPBS}}$ in Fig. 2 (resp. policy-privacy in $\mathbf{Exp}^{Policy-privacy}_{\mathcal{A},\mathsf{TPBS}}$ in Fig. 3), we can construct an adversary $\mathcal{B}$ (resp. $\mathcal{B}'$) against the simulatability of TPBS. $\mathcal{B}$ receives

($\mathcal{U}$, pp_{TPBS_b}, $pk^{TA}_{\mathsf{TPBS}_b}$, $sk^{TA}_{\mathsf{TPBS}_b}$, $pk^{Issuer}_{\mathsf{TPBS}_b}$, $sk^{Issuer}_{\mathsf{TPBS}_b}$) from its challenger in the $\mathbf{Exp}^{SIM}_{\mathcal{A},\mathsf{TPBS}}$ in Fig. 4, chooses $d \xleftarrow{\$} \{0,1\}$, and runs $\mathcal{A}$ on ($\mathcal{U}$, pp_{TPBS_b}, $pk^{TA}_{\mathsf{TPBS}_b}$, $pk^{Issuer}_{\mathsf{TPBS}_b}$, $sk^{Issuer}_{\mathsf{TPBS}_b}$). Whenever $\mathcal{A}$ queries its challenging oracle $\mathcal{O}\mathsf{IdLoRSign}$ with $(i_{j_0}, i_{j_1}, m, p, w_p)$, if $\mathsf{PC}((p,m), w_p) = 0$ or $i_{j_0}, i_{j_1} \notin \mathcal{U}$, $\mathcal{B}$ returns $\perp$, otherwise it queries its challenger in the simulatability game with (i_{j_d}, m, p, w_p) and returns σ_{m_b} to $\mathcal{A}$. When $\mathcal{A}$ outputs b', $\mathcal{B}$ outputs 0 if $(b' = d)$, indicating that $\mathcal{A}$ returned the identity $\mathcal{B}$ queried $\mathcal{O}\mathsf{Sim\text{-}or\text{-}Sign}$ with; thus σ_{m_b} is not a simulated signature. $\mathcal{B}$ outputs 1 otherwise. $\mathcal{B}'$ could be constructed similarly as follows. It receives ($\mathcal{U}$, pp_{TPBS_b}, $pk^{TA}_{\mathsf{TPBS}_b}$, $sk^{TA}_{\mathsf{TPBS}_b}$, $pk^{Issuer}_{\mathsf{TPBS}_b}$, $sk^{Issuer}_{\mathsf{TPBS}_b}$) its challenger in the simulatability game in Fig. 4, chooses $d \xleftarrow{\$} \{0,1\}$, and runs $\mathcal{A}$ on (pp_{TPBS_b}, $pk^{TA}_{\mathsf{TPBS}_b}$, $sk^{TA}_{\mathsf{TPBS}_b}$, $pk^{Issuer}_{\mathsf{TPBS}_b}$, $sk^{Issuer}_{\mathsf{TPBS}_b}$). Whenever $\mathcal{A}$ queries its challenge oracle $\mathcal{O}\mathsf{PLoRSign}$ with $(i, m, p_0, w_{p_0}, p_1, w_{p_1})$, if $\mathsf{PC}((p_0,m), w_{p_0}) = 0$ or $\mathsf{PC}((p_1,m), w_{p_1}) = 0$ or $i \notin \mathcal{U}$, $\mathcal{B}'$ returns $\perp$, otherwise it queries its challenger in the simulatability game with (i, m, p_d, w_{p_d}) and returns σ_{m_b} to $\mathcal{A}$. When $\mathcal{A}$ outputs b', $\mathcal{B}'$ outputs 0 if $(b' = d)$ and 1 otherwise. In either case, if in $\mathbf{Exp}^{SIM}_{\mathcal{B},\mathsf{TPBS}}(\lambda)$ (resp. $\mathbf{Exp}^{SIM}_{\mathcal{B}',\mathsf{TPBS}}(\lambda)$) the challenger's bit is 0 indicating a signed signature, then $\mathcal{B}$ (resp. $\mathcal{B}'$) perfectly simulates $\mathbf{Exp}^{Anonymity}_{\mathcal{A},\mathsf{TPBS}}(\lambda)$ (resp. $\mathbf{Exp}^{Policy-privacy}_{\mathcal{A},\mathsf{TPBS}}(\lambda)$) for $\mathcal{A}$. However, if the bit is 1 indicating a simulated signature, then the bit d chosen by $\mathcal{B}$ (resp. $\mathcal{B}'$) has no relation to $\mathcal{A}$'s response. Hence, $\mathcal{B}$ outputs 1 with probability $\frac{1}{2}$. Therefore, the success probability of $\mathcal{B}$ (resp. $\mathcal{B}'$) is half that of $\mathcal{A}$ in the anonymity (resp. policy-privacy) experiment.

Theorem 2. *Given a zero-knowledge simulation-sound extractable NIZK system, an unlinkable RDS scheme, an unforgeable RDS scheme, an unforgeable digital signature scheme, a one-way function, and an interactive perfect zero-knowledge proof of knowledge, the traceable policy-based signature scheme in Fig. 8 is simulatable, extractable, non-frameable, and traceable.*

Proof (Sketch). Simulatability follows from the zero-knowledge property of the underlying SE-NIZK proof system, and the unlinkability of the used RDS scheme. Extractability directly follows from the unforgeability of both the used RDS scheme and digital signature scheme and the simulation-extractability of the underlying SE-NIZK proof system. Likewise, non-frameability follows from the unforgeability of the used digital signature scheme, and the zero-knowledge property of the underlying SE-NIZK proof system given a one-way function $f(.)$, and an interactive perfect zero-knowledge proof of knowledge PoK. Finally, traceability follows from the unforgeability of the used RDS scheme and the simulation-extractability of the underlying SE-NIZK proof system.

6 TPBS Instantiation and Performance

We instantiate TPBS with Pointcheval-Sanders (PS) RDS Scheme [16,17][1] because of its short signature size and low signing cost in addition to its ability

[1] PS scheme has two variants one is based interactive assumption to prove its security [16] and a slightly modified one [17] where its security is proved based on the SDH assumption both could be used to instantiate our scheme.

to sign a hiding commitment over a message using a special form of its signing algorithm. we consider the One-way function $f(.)$ over a type-3 bilinear group map defined by $(p, \mathbb{G}, \tilde{\mathbb{G}}, \mathbb{G}_T, e)$ where the SDH assumption holds to be simply the function $f(sk_i) = (g^{sk_i}, \tilde{g}^{sk_i})/$ for $(g, \tilde{g}) \in (\mathbb{G}, \tilde{\mathbb{G}})$ and $sk_i \in \mathbb{Z}_p^*$. We instantiate the issuer digital signature algorithm with the structure-preserving signature scheme in of Abe *et al.* [2]. We instantiate the SE-NIZK scheme with the Groth-Sahai proof system [14]. Any digital signature scheme can be utilized in TPBS, we keep it as a black box since it is not utilized in TPBS signature generation or verification. Finally, we instantiate the PoK with the four-move perfect zero-knowledge protocol of Cramer *et al.* [12]. We keep the original definition of Bellare and Fuchsbauer for a policy p that defines a set of Pairing Product Equations (PPEs) $(E_1, \ldots, E_n)$, such that the policy checker $\mathsf{PC}((p, m), w_p) = 1$ iff $E_j((p, m), w_p) = 1$ for all $j \in [n]$. The complete specifications of the algorithms used in instantiating TPBS are depicted in the full version of this paper [3]. In what follows, we give the concrete description of TPBS's instantiated procedures.

ppGen. for a security parameter λ, let $(p, \mathbb{G}, \tilde{\mathbb{G}}, \mathbb{G}_T, e, g, \tilde{g})$ defines a type-3 bilinear group map that is generated by $(g, \tilde{g})$ that is used by all the scheme algorithms, Run $pp_{Sig} \leftarrow \mathsf{ppGenAbe}(1^\lambda)$, $pp_{Sig_\Sigma} \leftarrow \mathsf{ppGenSig}(1^\lambda)$, $pp_{RDS} \leftarrow \mathsf{ppGenPS}(1^\lambda)$, and $crs \leftarrow \mathsf{SetupGS}$. Set $pp_{\mathsf{TPBS}} = \{crs, pp_{RDS}, pp_{Sig}, pp_{Sig_\Sigma}\}$, where pp_{TPBS} becomes an implicit input for all TPBS algorithms.

TASetup. $(pk^{TA}_{\mathsf{TPBS}}, sk^{TA}_{\mathsf{TPBS}}) \leftarrow \mathsf{KeyGenPS}(pp_{RDS})$ such that $pk^{TA}_{\mathsf{TPBS}} = (g_1, \tilde{A}, \tilde{B})$, $sk^{TA}_{\mathsf{TPBS}} = (a, b)$. Setup an empty $Reg = [\,]$.

IssuerSetup. $(pk^{Issuer}_{\mathsf{TPBS}}, sk^{Issuer}_{\mathsf{TPBS}}) \leftarrow \mathsf{KeyGenAbe}(pp_{Abe})$ such that $pk^{Issuer}_{\mathsf{TPBS}} = (U, V, H, Z)$, and $sk^{Issuer}_{\mathsf{TPBS}} = (u, v, h, z)$ for $U \in \mathbb{G}$, $(V, H, Z) \in \tilde{\mathbb{G}}$ and $(u, v, h, z) \in \mathbb{Z}_p^*$

UserKeyGen. Generates $(pk^i_{Sig_\Sigma}, sk^i_{Sig_\Sigma}) \leftarrow \mathsf{KeyGenSig}(pp_{Sig_\Sigma})$, sets $\mathcal{D}[i] = (pk^i_{Sig_\Sigma})$, picks $sk_i \xleftarrow{\$} \mathbb{Z}_p^*$, calculates $C_i = (C_i, C_i') = (g_1^{sk_i}, \tilde{B}^{sk_i})$, generates $\tau_i \leftarrow \mathsf{SignSig}(C_i, sk^i_{Sig_\Sigma})$, sets $ID_i = \{C_i, \tau_i\}$, finally return (pk_i, sk_i, ID_i).

IDKeyGen. The user sends (i, ID_i) to the TA, the TA parses ID_i as $\{(C_i, C_i'), \tau_i\}$ and obtains an authentic copy of $pk^i_{Sig_\Sigma}$, if $Reg[i] = \emptyset \wedge \mathsf{VerifySig}(pk^i_{Sig_\Sigma}, C_i, \tau_i) \wedge e(C_i, \tilde{B}) = e(g_1, C_i')$, the TA engages with the user to start the interactive zero-knowledge protocol $\mathsf{PoK}(sk_i : C_i = g_1^{sk_i})$, if TA verifies that the user knows sk_i such that the relation of PoK holds, the TA generates $\sigma^i_{ID} \leftarrow \mathsf{SignComPS}(sk^{TA}_{\mathsf{TPBS}}, C_i)$ as follows, the TA picks $r \xleftarrow{\$} \mathbb{Z}_p^*$ and generates $\sigma^i_{ID} = (\sigma^i_{ID_1}, \sigma^i_{ID_2}) \leftarrow (g_1^r, (g_1^a(C_i)^b)^r$, finally the TA sets $Reg[i] = ID_i$ and the user set his scheme identity key as $sk^i_{\mathsf{TPBS}} = (sk_i, \sigma^i_{ID})$.

PolicyKeyGen. For policy $p \in \{0,1\}^*$, which is presented by a set of PPE equations $(E_1, \ldots, E_n)$ for a number of secret group elements $(M, \tilde{N}) \in \mathbb{G}^{k_M} \times \tilde{\mathbb{G}}^{k_N}$, the issuer generates $sk^p_{\mathsf{TPBS}} \leftarrow \mathsf{SignAbe}(sk^{Issuer}_{\mathsf{TPBS}}, (M, \tilde{N}))$ such that $sk^p_{\mathsf{TPBS}} = (R, S, T)$.

Sign. To sign a message m, the signer first generates a rerandomized version of σ^i_{ID}, $\sigma'^i_{ID} \leftarrow \mathsf{RandomizePS}(\sigma^i_{ID})$, along with a SE-NIZK proof π_m for relation $\mathbb{R}'_{\mathbb{NP}}$ that is defined in 1 as follows:

$$((pk^{TA}_{\mathsf{TPBS}}, \sigma'^i_{ID}, pk^{Issuer}_{\mathsf{TPBS}}, m), (sk_i, p, sk^p_{\mathsf{TPBS}}, w_p)) \in \mathbb{R}'_{\mathbb{NP}} \Leftrightarrow$$

$$e(\sigma'_{ID1}, \tilde{A})e(\sigma'_{ID1}, \tilde{B}^{sk_i}) = e(\sigma'_{ID2}, \tilde{g}) \wedge e(g, \tilde{B}^{sk_i}) = e(g^{sk_i}, \tilde{B}) \quad (1a)$$

$$\wedge\, e(R, V)e(S, \tilde{g})e(M, H) = e(g, Z) \wedge e(R, T)e(U, N) = e(g, \tilde{g}) \quad (1b)$$

$$\wedge\, E_j(((M, \tilde{N}), m), (W_p, \tilde{W}_p)) = 1\ \forall j \in [n] \quad (1c)$$

Verify. To verify a message signature pair (m, σ_m), the verifier parses (σ'^i_{ID}, π_m) from σ_m and runs $\mathsf{VerifyNIZK}(crs, (pk^{TA}_{\mathsf{TPBS}}, \sigma'^i_{ID}, pk^{Issuer}_{\mathsf{TPBS}}, m), \pi_m)$. Finally, the verifier outputs $\top$ in case of verification success and $\perp$ otherwise.

Trace. To trace a message signature pair (m, σ_m) to its original signer, the TA verifies such pair. If the verification succeeds, it parses (σ'^i_{ID}, π_m) from σ_m and exhaustively searches Reg for a matching i as follows.
foreach $C'_i \in Reg$

if $e(\sigma'_{ID_2}, \tilde{g})e(\sigma'_{ID_1}, \tilde{A})^{-1} = e(\sigma'_{ID_1}, C'_i)$

$(i, ID_i) = Reg[i]$

$$\pi \leftarrow \mathsf{ProveNIZK}(crs, (C_i, \sigma'^i_{ID}), C'_i) \ni e(\sigma'_{ID_2}, \tilde{g})e(\sigma'_{ID_1}, \tilde{A})^{-1} = e(\sigma'_{ID_1}, C'_i) \wedge e(C_i, \tilde{B}) = e(g_1, C'_i)$$

$\pi_{Trace} \leftarrow (C_i, \tau_i, \pi)$

return (i, π_{Trace})

Judge. After verifying (m, σ_m), parses (C_i, τ_i, π) from π_{Trace} and outputs $\top$ if $\mathsf{VerifySig}(pk^i_{Sig_\Sigma}, C_i, \tau_i) \wedge \mathsf{VerifyNIZK}(crs, (C_i, \sigma'^i_{ID}), \pi))$ or $\perp$ otherwise.

Performance Analysis. Let TPBS be initialized with n users and the policy p be expressed in 1 PPE uniquely defined by $(M, \tilde{N}) \in \mathbb{G} \times \tilde{\mathbb{G}}$ group elements. To sign a message m that conforms to p, The proposed instantiation produces a total signature size of 14 elements in $\mathbb{G}$ + 16 elements in $\tilde{\mathbb{G}}$, where σ'^i_{ID} is a PS signature of size 2 elements in $\mathbb{G}$, and π_m is a Groth-Sahai proof of knowledge of size 12 elements in $\mathbb{G}$ + 16 elements $\tilde{\mathbb{G}}$. Signing costs two exponentiations in $\mathbb{G}$ to generate σ'^i_{ID} and approximately 40 exponentiations in $\mathbb{G}$ + 70 exponentiations in $\tilde{\mathbb{G}}$ to produce π_m. Verifying a given TPBS message signature pair costs approximately a total of 100 pairing operations to verify π_m[2]. For tracing a signature, the TA performs at most $n + 2$ pairing operations and produces a proof π of size 16 group elements in $\tilde{\mathbb{G}}$, which costs around 10 exponentiations in $\mathbb{G}$ and 20 exponentiations in $\tilde{\mathbb{G}}$. To verify the output of the tracing algorithm, the Judge performs around 40 pairing operations to verify π in addition to the verification cost of the TPBS signature and the verification cost of the signature τ_i of the user on the registration information.

[2] The verification cost of Groth-Sahai proofs could be enhanced using batch verification [8].

7 Comparisson with PBS and Xu *et al.*'s Schemes

TPBS builds on PBS and further provides traceability and non-frameability. Accordingly, in addition to the issuer in PBS, TPBS has a TA that can trace signatures back to their signers. Non-frameability of TPBS holds under the assumption of a misbehaving TA. TPBS black-box construction has four new algorithms when compared to PBS. Namely, UserKeyGen, and IDKeyGen, where the latter is run interactively between each scheme user and the TA to generate such user's identity key, Furthermore, we introduce the Trace, and Judge algorithms. Where Trace algorithm is used by the TA to trace a signature to its original signer and Judge algorithm is used to verify the output of the Trace algorithm. The security model of TPBS differs from that of PBS in that it includes formal definitions for traceability and non-frameability and, the definitions of simulatability and extractability capture the introduced notion of signer anonymity and identity features.

Xu *et al.* also builds on PBS by attaching the user's identity to the hidden policy and utilizing a sign-encrypt-proof paradigm to provide the traceability feature. On the other hand, TPBS utilizes sign-rerandomize-proof which produces more efficient signatures than the sign-encrypt-proof paradigm used in Xu *et al.*'s proposal. TPBS separates identity keys from policy keys, thus it supports the delegation of policy keys in the same way as PBS which is not applicable in Xu *et al.*'s proposal. The issuer Xu *et al.*'s scheme generates the signing keys of the user, thus, it does not ensure non-frameability. However, in TPBS the scheme users generate their identity keys using an interactive protocol with the TA, hence TPBS provides non-frameability. Xu *et al.*'s proposal does not give a formal definition for traceability.

Table 1 summarizes the comparison between TPBS, PBS, and Xu *et al.*'s proposal. We consider the utilized building blocks and the availability of the traceability feature. If traceability is ensured by a scheme, then we contrast

Table 1. Comparison between TPBS, PBS and Xu *et al.*'s proposal. N/A denotes an unavailable feature/entity.

	TPBS(this work)	PBS [5]	Xu *et al.* [18]
Building blocks	RDS SE-NIZK digital Sig.	SE-NIZK digital Sig.	encryption scheme SE-NIZK digital Sig.
Traceability	yes	no	yes
Identity	identity key	N/A	attached to the policy
Tracing Authority	standalone	N/A	issuer acts as the TA*
Delegatability	yes	yes	no
Security definitions	simulatability extractability traceability non-frameability	simulatability extractability	simulatability extractability

*Although the scheme defines two different entities issuer and opener, the issuer has to participate in the opening process since it generates policy keys that contain the users' identities.

the schemes in terms of how the signer identity is utilized. We also consider the structure of the TA, whether a scheme enables the delegation of signing keys, and finally what security definitions are considered in the scheme's security model.

8 Conclusion

We have proposed TPBS, a traceable policy-based signature scheme that supports delegatability. Our scheme fills the gap in the original policy-based schemes by linking a signature to the identity of its signer when needed, thus holding the signer of a specific message accountable for the produced signature. We have analyzed the security of TPBS and proved that it is an anonymous, policy-private, unforgeable, traceable, and non-frameable signature scheme. Moreover, we provided a concrete instantiation of TPBS using the Pointcheval-Sanders rerandomizable signature scheme, the structure-preserving signature scheme of Abe *et al.*, and the Groth-Sahai NIZK system and analyzed its efficiency. Following policy-based signature schemes which can be used in the construction of mesh signatures, ring signatures, etc., TPBS can be adapted for signature schemes that require traceability such as sanitizable and accountable redactable signatures.

References

1. Abe, M., Fuchsbauer, G., Groth, J., Haralambiev, K., Ohkubo, M.: Structure-preserving signatures and commitments to group elements. In: Rabin, T. (ed.) CRYPTO 2010. LNCS, vol. 6223, pp. 209–236. Springer, Heidelberg (2010). https://doi.org/10.1007/978-3-642-14623-7_12
2. Abe, M., Groth, J., Haralambiev, K., Ohkubo, M.: Optimal structure-preserving signatures in asymmetric bilinear groups. In: Rogaway, P. (ed.) CRYPTO 2011. LNCS, vol. 6841, pp. 649–666. Springer, Heidelberg (2011). https://doi.org/10.1007/978-3-642-22792-9_37
3. Afia, I., AlTawy, R.: Traceable policy-based signatures with delegation. Cryptology ePrint Archive, Paper 2023/193 (2023). https://eprint.iacr.org/2023/193
4. Afia, I., AlTawy, R.: Unlinkable policy-based sanitizable signatures. In: Rosulek, M. (ed.) CT-RSA 2023. LNCS, vol. 13871, pp. 191–221. Springer, Cham (2023). https://doi.org/10.1007/978-3-031-30872-7_8
5. Bellare, M., Fuchsbauer, G.: Policy-based signatures. In: Krawczyk, H. (ed.) PKC 2014. LNCS, vol. 8383, pp. 520–537. Springer, Heidelberg (2014). https://doi.org/10.1007/978-3-642-54631-0_30
6. Bellare, M., Micciancio, D., Warinschi, B.: Foundations of group signatures: formal definitions, simplified requirements, and a construction based on general assumptions. In: Biham, E. (ed.) EUROCRYPT 2003. LNCS, vol. 2656, pp. 614–629. Springer, Heidelberg (2003). https://doi.org/10.1007/3-540-39200-9_38
7. Bichsel, P., Camenisch, J., Neven, G., Smart, N.P., Warinschi, B.: Get shorty via group signatures without encryption. In: Garay, J.A., De Prisco, R. (eds.) SCN 2010. LNCS, vol. 6280, pp. 381–398. Springer, Heidelberg (2010). https://doi.org/10.1007/978-3-642-15317-4_24

8. Blazy, O., Fuchsbauer, G., Izabachène, M., Jambert, A., Sibert, H., Vergnaud, D.: Batch groth–sahai. In: Zhou, J., Yung, M. (eds.) ACNS 2010. LNCS, vol. 6123, pp. 218–235. Springer, Heidelberg (2010). https://doi.org/10.1007/978-3-642-13708-2_14
9. Boneh, D., Shacham, H.: Group signatures with verifier-local revocation. In: Proceedings of the 11th ACM Conference on Computer and Communications Security, pp. 168–177 (2004)
10. Camenisch, J., Lysyanskaya, A.: An efficient system for non-transferable anonymous credentials with optional anonymity revocation. In: Pfitzmann, B. (ed.) EUROCRYPT 2001. LNCS, vol. 2045, pp. 93–118. Springer, Heidelberg (2001). https://doi.org/10.1007/3-540-44987-6_7
11. Camenisch, J., Lysyanskaya, A.: Signature schemes and anonymous credentials from bilinear maps. In: Franklin, M. (ed.) CRYPTO 2004. LNCS, vol. 3152, pp. 56–72. Springer, Heidelberg (2004). https://doi.org/10.1007/978-3-540-28628-8_4
12. Cramer, R., Damgård, I., MacKenzie, P.: Efficient zero-knowledge proofs of knowledge without intractability assumptions. In: Imai, H., Zheng, Y. (eds.) PKC 2000. LNCS, vol. 1751, pp. 354–372. Springer, Heidelberg (2000). https://doi.org/10.1007/978-3-540-46588-1_24
13. Groth, J.: Simulation-sound NIZK proofs for a practical language and constant size group signatures. In: Lai, X., Chen, K. (eds.) ASIACRYPT 2006. LNCS, vol. 4284, pp. 444–459. Springer, Heidelberg (2006). https://doi.org/10.1007/11935230_29
14. Groth, J., Sahai, A.: Efficient noninteractive proof systems for bilinear groups. SIAM J. Comput. **41**(5), 1193–1232 (2012)
15. Maji, H., Prabhakaran, M., Rosulek, M.: Attribute-based signatures: achieving attribute-privacy and collusion-resistance. Cryptology ePrint Archive, Report 2008/328 (2008). https://ia.cr/2008/328
16. Pointcheval, D., Sanders, O.: Short randomizable signatures. In: Sako, K. (ed.) CT-RSA 2016. LNCS, vol. 9610, pp. 111–126. Springer, Cham (2016). https://doi.org/10.1007/978-3-319-29485-8_7
17. Pointcheval, D., Sanders, O.: Reassessing security of randomizable signatures. In: Smart, N.P. (ed.) CT-RSA 2018. LNCS, vol. 10808, pp. 319–338. Springer, Cham (2018). https://doi.org/10.1007/978-3-319-76953-0_17
18. Xu, Y., Safavi-Naini, R., Nguyen, K., Wang, H.: Traceable policy-based signatures and instantiation from lattices. Inf. Sci. **607**, 1286–1310 (2022). https://doi.org/10.1016/j.ins.2022.06.031, https://www.sciencedirect.com/science/article/pii/S0020025522006211
19. Zhou, S., Lin, D.: Unlinkable randomizable signature and its application in group signature, vol. 2007, p. 213 (2007). https://doi.org/10.1007/978-3-540-79499-8_26

Basic Primitives

How to Enumerate LWE Keys as Narrow as in KYBER/DILITHIUM

Timo Glaser(✉) and Alexander May

Ruhr-University Bochum, Bochum, Germany
{timo.glaser,alex.may}@rub.de

Abstract. In the Learning with Errors (LWE) problem we are given a matrix $A \in \mathbb{Z}_q^{N \times N}$ and a target vector $\boldsymbol{t} \in \mathbb{Z}_q^N$ such that there exists small-norm $\boldsymbol{s}, \boldsymbol{e} \in \mathbb{Z}_q^N$ satisfying $A \cdot \boldsymbol{s} = \boldsymbol{t} + \boldsymbol{e} \bmod q$. Modern cryptosystems often sample $\boldsymbol{s}, \boldsymbol{e}$ from narrow distributions that take integer values in a small range $[-\eta, \eta]$. KYBER and DILITHIUM both choose $\eta = 2$ and $\eta = 3$ using either a Centered Binomial distribution (KYBER), or a Uniform distribution (DILITHIUM).

In this work, we address the fundamental question how hard the enumeration of LWE secret keys for narrow distributions with $\eta \leq 3$ is. At Crypto 21, May proposed a representation-based algorithm for enumerating ternary keys, i.e. the case $\eta = 1$, with a fixed number of ± 1 entries. In this work, we extend May's algorithm in several ways.

First, we show how to deal with keys sampled from a probability distribution as in many modern systems like KYBER and DILITHIUM, rather than with keys having a fixed number of entries.

Second, we generalize to larger values $\eta = 2, 3$, thereby achieving asymptotic key guess complexities that are not far off from lattice estimates.

E.g. for KYBER's Centered Binomial distribution we achieve heuristic time/memory complexities of $\mathcal{O}(2^{0.36N})$ for $\eta = 2$, and $\mathcal{O}(2^{0.37N})$ for $\eta = 3$. For DILITHIUM's Uniform distribution we achieve heuristic complexity $\mathcal{O}(2^{0.38N})$ for $\eta = 2$.

Let $\mathcal{S}$ be the Shannon entropy of KYBER/DILITHIUM keys. Then our algorithms runs in time about $\mathcal{S}^{\frac{1}{6}}$, which greatly improves over the standard combinatorial Meet-in-the-Middle attack with complexity $\mathcal{S}^{\frac{1}{2}}$.

Our results also compare well to current lattice asymptotics of $2^{0.29\beta}$, where the lattice parameter β is roughly of size $\frac{4}{5}N$. Thus, our analysis supports that KYBER secret keys are indeed hard to enumerate. Yet, we find it remarkable that a purely combinatorial key search is almost competitive with highly evolved lattice sieving techniques.

Keywords: LWE Key Search · Representation Technique · Asymptotics

Funded by Deutsche Forschungsgemeinschaft (DFG) - Project number 465120249.

J. Deng et al. (Eds.): CANS 2023, LNCS 14342, pp. 75–100, 2023.
https://doi.org/10.1007/978-981-99-7563-1_4

1 Introduction

Since the introduction of the Learning with Errors (LWE) problem by Regev [20] into the cryptographic community, LWE has shown its amazing power to realize efficient cryptographic constructions, such as the Gödel Prize 22 award Fully Homomorphic Encryption schemes [6,7].

It does not come as a big surprise that LWE-type constructions play a central role in the current NIST initiative for identifying encryption/signature schemes resistant to quantum computers [5,8,9,15]. As solving LWE implies the solution to worst-case lattice problems, LWE is usually considered a lattice problem. However, this does not imply that lattice algorithms necessarily provide the best way for solving LWE. Moreover, many cryptosystems choose especially small secret keys for efficiency reasons, and to keep the probability of decryption errors low.

In this work we study the combinatorial complexity of recovering LWE keys chosen from a narrow range $\{-\eta, \ldots, \eta\}$. Our analysis also applies to common variants of LWE, such as Ring-LWE or Module-LWE, but we make no use of the additional structure that these LWE variants provide.

Previous Work on LWE Key Enumeration. There is still much to learn about directly enumerating LWE keys. A brute-force attack enumerates $\boldsymbol{s} \in \mathbb{Z}_q^N$, and checks whether $A\boldsymbol{s} - \boldsymbol{t}$ yields a small-norm error vector $\boldsymbol{e}$. If $\boldsymbol{s}$ has Shannon entropy $\mathcal{S}$, then the brute-force attack takes (expected) time $\mathcal{S}$, up to a polynomial runtime factor for checking key correctness. Throughout the paper, for ease of notation we ignore polynomial factors and round runtime exponents upwards.

In a Meet-in-the-Middle attack, attributed to Odlyzko [21], we split $\boldsymbol{s}$ in two $N/2$-dimensional vectors $\boldsymbol{s}_1, \boldsymbol{s}_2$ and check whether $A\boldsymbol{s}_1 \approx \boldsymbol{t} - A\boldsymbol{s}_2 \bmod q$. The approximate matching of $A\boldsymbol{s}_1$ and $\boldsymbol{t} - A\boldsymbol{s}_2$ is realized by a locality-sensitive hash function. Up to polynomial factors, Odlyzko's attack takes time $\mathcal{S}^{\frac{1}{2}}$.

Recently, May [17] showed that *ternary LWE keys* $\boldsymbol{s}, \boldsymbol{e} \in \{-1, 0, 1\}^N$ can be enumerated more efficiently in time roughly $\mathcal{S}^{\frac{1}{4}}$. His algorithm for NTRU-type schemes beats lattice reduction if $\boldsymbol{s}$ is overly sparse. May's technique is a natural recursive generalization of Odlyzko's Meet-in-the-Middle attack to search trees, using the so-called representation technique. This technique has been introduced in [16] and successfully applied in the cryptographic context of decoding algorithms [2,18].

Our Technical Contributions. We extend May's LWE key recovery algorithm in several ways.

- We first show that May's algorithm can be applied for LWE keys sampled from a probabilistic distribution. Since the purely combinatorial analysis in [17] requires to know for every element in $\{-\eta, \ldots, \eta\}$ the exact number of appearances in $\boldsymbol{s}$, we define for *any probability distribution* $\mathcal{P} = (p_{-\eta}, \ldots, p_{\eta})$ a so-called *core set* of vectors.

  We then show that length-N LWE keys randomly sampled coordinate-wise from $\mathcal{P}$ are in the core set with probability inverse polynomial in N. This core set density shows that our key enumeration already applies to a polynomial fraction of all keys.

- We then strengthen our result to almost all LWE keys $\boldsymbol{s}, \boldsymbol{e}$ by transforming almost any LWE instance in subexponential time $2^{\mathcal{O}(\sqrt{N})}$ to a permuted, weight-preserving LWE instance with keys $\boldsymbol{s}', \boldsymbol{e}'$ such that $\boldsymbol{s}'$ lies in the core set. Since our subsequent enumeration of $\boldsymbol{s}'$ takes time $2^{\mathcal{O}(N)}$, the transformation's subexponential overhead contributes only an $o(1)$-term to the runtime exponent.
- We generalize the combinatorics of [17] such that we can analyze secret vectors from $\{-2, \ldots, 2\}$ and even from $\{-3, \ldots, 3\}$. This introduces runtime optimization parameters whose amount grows quadratically with the digit sets and linearly in the search tree depth. The optimization complexity is the reason that we only analyze up to $\eta \leq 3$.
- Along this way we also generalize the ways in which the secret $\boldsymbol{s}$ can be represented. This is crucial in the representation technique, since more representations usually lead to better results. See as comparison the related subset sum literature that optimized runtimes by solely analyzing more powerful representations starting from $\{0, 1\}$ [16], over $\{-1, 0, 1\}$ [1], to $\{-1, 0, 1, 2\}$ [4]. In this work, we introduce four different representations, called REP-0 to REP-3, with increasing complexity. REP-3 representations are most powerful, and we eventually use REP-3 to show our best results for the KYBER/DILITHIUM distributions.
- We analyze different probability distributions $\mathcal{P} = (p_{-\eta}, \ldots, p_{\eta})$. For $\eta = 1$, we revisit weighted ternary key distributions and slightly improve over [17] by using larger search tree depths. For $\eta = 2, 3$ we study the *Centered Binomial* distribution $\mathcal{B}(\eta)$ used in KYBER, and the Uniform distribution used in DILITHIUM.

Our Results. Table 1 shows our runtimes for $\boldsymbol{s}, \boldsymbol{e} \in \mathcal{B}(\eta)^N$, KYBER's Centered Binomial distribution. KYBER uses $\eta = 3$ in combination with $N = 256 \cdot 2 = 512$, and $\eta = 2$ in combination with $N = 256 \cdot 3 = 768$ and $N = 256 \cdot 4 = 1024$.

As one would expect with increasing η—i.e., broader distributions—the key entropy $\mathcal{S}$ and our runtime $\mathcal{T}$ both increase. However, let us express our runtime as a polynomial function of the entropy $\mathcal{T} = \mathcal{S}^c$ for some constant $c = \log_{\mathcal{S}}(\mathcal{T})$. Then we see that the runtime exponent c actually decreases in Table 1 monotonously in η.

For $\eta = 2$ and $\eta = 3$ we have complexities around only $\mathcal{S}^{\frac{1}{6}}$, as opposed to the $\eta = 1$ ternary key case with complexity $\mathcal{S}^{0.225}$ (slightly improving over $\mathcal{S}^{0.232}$

Table 1. Runtime $\mathcal{T}$ and entropy $\mathcal{S}$ of our LWE key enumeration algorithm for $\boldsymbol{s}$ sampled from a *Centered Binomial* distribution $\mathcal{B}(\eta)^N$, $\eta = 1, 2, 3$.

η	$\mathcal{T}$	$\mathcal{S}$	$\log_{\mathcal{S}}(\mathcal{T})$
1	$2^{0.337N}$	$2^{1.500N}$	0.225
2	$2^{0.357N}$	$2^{2.031N}$	0.176
3	$2^{0.371N}$	$2^{2.334N}$	0.159

achieved in [17]). Thus, our generalizations for larger digit sets are *more effective for larger* η. This seems to be an artifact of the representation method. Our analysis shows that the entropy growth with larger digit sets is over-compensated by the growth of the number of representations, resulting in decreased runtime exponents $c = \log_{\mathcal{S}}(\mathcal{T})$.

These results demonstrate the power of our new combinatorial LWE key search algorithm. Recall that the best known combinatorial Meet-in-the-Middle algorithm by Odlyzko so far achieved square root complexity $\mathcal{S}^{\frac{1}{2}}$, independent of η. For the case $\eta = 1$ the exponent was lowered to $c = 0.232$ in [17]. Our work indicates that for Centered Binomials c as a function of η decreases strictly.

The effect of a strictly decreasing exponent $c(\eta)$ is also reflected in the absolute runtimes $\mathcal{T}$ in Table 1. More precisely, when choosing keys from $\mathcal{B}(3)^N$ rather than ternary keys $\mathcal{B}(1)^N$, then our key enumeration algorithm's runtime only mildly increases from $2^{0.337N}$ to $2^{0.371N}$. In other words, although we significantly increase the key entropy from $2^{1.5N}$ to $2^{2.334N}$ we do *not significantly increase the key security.*[1]

Other Distributions. Besides the Centered Binomial distribution we also study the enumeration of randomly sampled ternary LWE keys of different weight, thereby slightly improving the results of [17].

We also study the Uniform distribution $\mathcal{U}(\eta) = (p_{-\eta}, \ldots, p_\eta)$ with $p_i = \frac{1}{2\eta+1}$, widely used in cryptography, e.g. some NTRU variants [8] sample their keys from $\mathcal{U}(1)^N$. DILITHIUM chooses $\boldsymbol{s}, \boldsymbol{e} \in \mathcal{U}(2)^N$ for $N = 1024, 2048$.

Our results for the Uniform distribution are provided in Table 2. When comparing with Table 1, the lower entropy, more sharply zero-centered Binomial distribution yields slightly better runtimes than the Uniform distribution in Table 2, as one would expect. However, maybe somewhat surprisingly, our results for $\mathcal{U}(1)^N$ and $\mathcal{U}(2)^N$ are not far off, only $\mathcal{U}(3)^N$ is significantly worse.

Relative to the entropy $\mathcal{S}$ we achieve for $\eta = 2$ again runtime $\mathcal{S}^{\frac{1}{6}}$, but as opposed to the Centered Binomial distribution $c = \log_{\mathcal{T}} \mathcal{S}$ is for the Uniform distribution not strictly decreasing with growing η.

Notice that we achieve for DILITHIUM's $\mathcal{U}(2)^N$ a runtime $\mathcal{T}$ similar to KYBER's $\mathcal{B}(3)^N$. However, since DILITHIUM proposes much larger key lengths, our key enumeration is way more effective for KYBER parameter sets.

Table 2. Runtime $\mathcal{T}$ and entropy $\mathcal{S}$ of our enumeration algorithm for LWE keys sampled from a *Uniform* distribution $\mathcal{U}(\eta)^N$, $\eta = 1, 2, 3$.

η	$\mathcal{T}$	$\mathcal{S}$	$\log_{\mathcal{S}} \mathcal{T}$
1	$2^{0.345N}$	$2^{1.585N}$	0.218
2	$\mathbf{2^{0.378N}}$	$\mathbf{2^{2.322N}}$	**0.163**
3	$2^{0.493N}$	$2^{2.808N}$	0.176

[1] This conclusion is of course only valid relative to our algorithm. Relative to other algorithms like lattice reduction the key security might be behave differently.

Asymptotics. We would like to stress that our LWE key search algorithm is at this point mainly of theoretical interest. Our runtime analysis is asymptotic, and throughout our work we do not only generously supress polynomial runtime factors in soft-Oh notation $\tilde{\mathcal{O}}(\cdot)$, but we also supress two subexponential factors. First, as in [17] we have to guess $r = (N/\log N)$ coordinates of $\boldsymbol{e}$ in slightly subexponential time 2^r. Second, our transformation to the core set of $\boldsymbol{s}$ introduces another subexponential $2^{\mathcal{O}(\sqrt{N})}$ runtime factor.

Our analysis solely focuses on minimizing the runtime exponent. Our memory consumption is almost as large as the runtime exponent. Time-memory tradeoffs are possible, as in [17], but we do not consider them in this work.

Significant further work would be required to bring our results to practice. We would like to draw an analogy to decoding algorithms, which also first solely focused on asymptotic improvements [2,18]. It took a decade that these algorithms nowadays define the state-of-the-art in practical attacks against code-based cryptosystems [13].

LWE Representation Heuristic. Our LWE key enumeration uses the standard heuristic from representation based algorithms. Namely, we iteratively construct in our key search partial solutions as vectors sums, and treat these sums as independent in our analysis. This heuristic has been extensively verified experimentally in the context of subset sum and decoding algorithms [4,13]. On the theoretical side, it has been shown in [10] that the dependence between vectors sums merely affects the overall runtime exponent by an $o(1)$-term. Our own experimental results seem to validate this heuristic w.r.t. LWE.

In addition, we require that the LWE public key A is randomly chosen from $\mathbb{Z}_q^{N \times N}$, which is the case for standard LWE. In the case of Module-LWE (MLWE) we heuristically assume that A's structure does not affect our analysis.

When formulating theorems, we refer to these two heuristic assumptions as the *MLWE Representation Heuristic.*

Lattices. Our results are close to current lattice asymptotics of $2^{0.29\beta}$ from BKZ reduction, where the BKZ block length β is roughly of size $\frac{4}{5}N$. We find it quite remarkable that combinatorial key enumeration, at least in the case of quite narrow LWE keys as in KYBER and DILITHIUM, is not far off from highly evolved lattice reduction techniques. Even if key enumeration eventually cannot outperform lattice reduction, there exist other attack scenarios where direct key enumeration might be preferable over lattices, e.g. in the setting of partially known keys [4,12].

Organization of Paper. After fixing notations in Sect. 2, we give a short explanation of May's LWE-SEARCH's [17] in Sect. 3 and how to extend its analysis to probabilistically sampled keys in Sect. 4. In Sect. 5, we provide a first simple instantiation of LWE-SEARCH, called REP-0, for an introduction into the representation technique. We then strengthen our results by introducing more elaborated representations REP-1 to REP-3 in Sect. 6. Section 7 contains an overview of our results for the weighted ternary, the Centered Binomial, and the Uniform distribution. Section 8 covers the method of parameter searching as well as our experimental results.

We provide the source code for parameter optimization and our implementation of the attack via https://github.com/timogcgn/HTELWEK/.

2 Preliminaries

Unless explicitly stated otherwise, any log is base 2. For simplicity, we denote all vectors as column vectors and omit transposing them. The weight of i in some vector $\boldsymbol{v}$, i.e. the amount of times i appears in $\boldsymbol{v}$, is denoted $\mathrm{wt}_i(\boldsymbol{v})$.

Shannon Entropy. We denote with H the *n-ary entropy function* [19] where

$$H(p_1, \dots, p_n) = -\sum_{i=1}^{n} p_i \log(p_i) \qquad \text{for } \sum p_i = 1.$$

Using Stirling's Approximation, we find for constant p_i

$$\binom{N}{p_1 N, \cdots, p_n N} = \Theta(N^{-\frac{n-1}{2}} \cdot 2^{H(p_1,\cdots,p_n)N}) = \tilde{\Theta}(2^{H(p_1,\cdots,p_n)N}). \tag{1}$$

Distributions. Probability distributions are denoted $\mathcal{P} = (p_{-\eta}, \dots, p_\eta)$ where p_i denotes the probability to sample $i \in \{-\eta, \dots, \eta\}$. We only consider distributions symmetric around 0, i.e. where $p_i = p_{-i}$, so indices are generally unsigned.

Sampling from a probability distribution $\mathcal{P}$ will be denoted with $s \sim \mathcal{P}$. If $\boldsymbol{s} \in \mathbb{Z}_q^N$ has its N coefficients drawn i.i.d. from $\mathcal{P}$, we write $\boldsymbol{s} \sim \mathcal{P}^N$.

For some $\eta \in \mathbb{N}$, we denote the *Centered Binomial Distribution* with

$$p_i = \frac{\binom{2\eta}{\eta+i}}{2^{2\eta}}. \tag{2}$$

LWE Keys. We attack standard LWE keys, where both $\boldsymbol{s}$ and $\boldsymbol{e}$ are randomly drawn from some narrow probability distribution over $\mathbb{Z}_q$. More precisely, for some prime $q \in \mathbb{N}$ and some $N \in \mathbb{N}$, given a random $A \in \mathbb{Z}_q^{N\times N}$ and $\boldsymbol{t} \in \mathbb{Z}_q^N$ where $\boldsymbol{t} = A\boldsymbol{s} + \boldsymbol{e}$ for $\boldsymbol{s}, \boldsymbol{e} \in \mathbb{Z}_q^N$ drawn from $\mathcal{P}^N$, we want to find $(\boldsymbol{s}, \boldsymbol{e})$.

If we replace $\mathbb{Z}_q$ with $\mathbb{Z}_q[X]/P(X)$ and N with k, this becomes Module-LWE, abbreviated MLWE. Our results can be applied to MLWE with $N = \deg(P)k$.

3 How to Enumerate LWE Keys with May's Algorithm

Before we introduce May's algorithm for key enumeration [17], let us briefly recall some basic techniques.

3.1 Brute-Force and Meet-in-the-Middle LWE Key Enumeration

Let $q \in \mathbb{N}$ and let $(A, \boldsymbol{t}) \in \mathbb{Z}_q^{N \times N} \times \mathbb{Z}_q^N$ be an instance of LWE satisfying $A\boldsymbol{s} + \boldsymbol{e} = \boldsymbol{t} \bmod q$ for some $\boldsymbol{s}, \boldsymbol{e} \in \mathbb{Z}_q^N$ that have small coefficients (relative to q).

A *Brute-Force* LWE key enumeration searches over all potential secrets $\boldsymbol{s} \in \mathbb{Z}_q^N$, and checks whether the resulting error term $\boldsymbol{t} - A\boldsymbol{s}$ is sufficiently small. By construction, there is usually a unique $\boldsymbol{s}$ that satisfies this condition. If the potential $\boldsymbol{s}$ come from an exponential search space of size $\mathcal{S}$, then one has to iterate over $\Theta(\mathcal{S})$ potential $\boldsymbol{s}$, where each candidate can be tested in polynomial time. Thus, *Brute-Force* runs in time $\tilde{\mathcal{O}}(\mathcal{S})$. E.g. for random ternary $\boldsymbol{s} \in \{-1, 0, 1\}^N$ Brute-Force takes time $\tilde{\mathcal{O}}(3^N)$.

A classical *Meet-in-the-Middle* (MitM) LWE key enumeration equally splits $\boldsymbol{s} = (\boldsymbol{s}_1, \boldsymbol{s}_2) \in \mathbb{Z}_q^{N/2} \times \mathbb{Z}_q^{N/2}$ and $A = (A_1, A_2) \in \mathbb{Z}_q^{N \times N/2} \times \mathbb{Z}_q^{N \times N/2}$. One then enumerates pairs $(\boldsymbol{s}_1, \boldsymbol{s}_2)$ and checks whether $A_1\boldsymbol{s}_1$ approximately matches $\boldsymbol{t} - A_2\boldsymbol{s}_2$ modulo q, up to a small error term. The benefit is that $(\boldsymbol{s}_1, \boldsymbol{s}_2)$ have half the dimension of $\boldsymbol{s}$, and the terms $A_1\boldsymbol{s}_1, \boldsymbol{t} - A_2\boldsymbol{s}_2$ can be computed independently. The matching (up to the small error term) of $A_1\boldsymbol{s}_1, \boldsymbol{t} - A_2\boldsymbol{s}_2$ that finds the right pairs $(\boldsymbol{s}_1, \boldsymbol{s}_2)$ can usually be done in polynomial time, using a locality-sensitive hashing approach due to Odlyzko [21]. This implies that classical MitM runs for secret $\boldsymbol{s}$ from a search space of size $\mathcal{S}$ in time $\tilde{\mathcal{O}}(\sqrt{\mathcal{S}})$. For instance, for random ternary $\boldsymbol{s} \in \{-1, 0, 1\}^N$, classical MitM takes time $\tilde{\mathcal{O}}(3^{N/2})$.

3.2 High-Level Idea of the Algorithm

May's LWE key enumeration [17] can be seen as a Meet-in-the-Middle attack, where we *additively* split $\boldsymbol{s} = \boldsymbol{s}_1 + \boldsymbol{s}_2$ with $\boldsymbol{s}_1, \boldsymbol{s}_2 \in \mathbb{Z}_q^N$. As opposed to classical MitM the benefit of $\boldsymbol{s}$'s splitting does *not* come from dimension reduction, but from the following three properties.

Reduced Search Space. $\boldsymbol{s}_1, \boldsymbol{s}_2$ are usually easier to enumerate, i.e. they are defined over smaller search spaces. For instance, [17] uses for enumerating ternary keys $\boldsymbol{s}_1, \boldsymbol{s}_2$ of roughly half the Hamming weight of $\boldsymbol{s}$.

Recursion [17] recursively splits $\boldsymbol{s}_1, \boldsymbol{s}_2$ as sums of N-dimensional vectors that are (yet) defined over smaller search spaces. This recursion eventually results in a complete binary search tree of some optimal depth d. The optimization of the search spaces over all tree levels is a non-trivial optimization problem.

Ambiguous Representations. The secret $\boldsymbol{s}$ can be expressed in exponentially many ways as a sum $\boldsymbol{s}_1 + \boldsymbol{s}_2$. The algorithm uses these so-called *representations* of $\boldsymbol{s}$ to fix a special representation s.t. $A_1\boldsymbol{s}_1$, $\boldsymbol{t} - A_2\boldsymbol{s}_2$ take a fixed predefined value on certain coordinates.

In order to use representations, for some candidate $\boldsymbol{s}_1, \boldsymbol{s}_2$ we thus have to fix the values $A_1\boldsymbol{s}_1$, $\boldsymbol{t} - A_2\boldsymbol{s}_2$ on certain r coordinates. Let us fix zeros on these coordinates for simplicity. Recall however that the values $A_1\boldsymbol{s}_1$, $\boldsymbol{t} - A_2\boldsymbol{s}_2$ still

Algorithm 1: LWE-SEARCH [17]

Input : $A \in \mathbb{Z}_q^{N \times N}, \boldsymbol{t} \in \mathbb{Z}_q^N$
Output: Small norm $\boldsymbol{s} \in \mathbb{Z}_q^N$ s.t. $\boldsymbol{e} := A\boldsymbol{s} - \boldsymbol{t}$ has small norm
1 Guess r coordinates of $\boldsymbol{e}$, denoted $\boldsymbol{e}_r$.
2 **for** *all* $\boldsymbol{s}_1, \boldsymbol{s}_2$ *such that* $A\boldsymbol{s}_1 = \mathbf{0}^r = \boldsymbol{t} - A\boldsymbol{s}_2 + \boldsymbol{e}_r$ *on these* r *coordinates and* $A\boldsymbol{s}_1 \approx \boldsymbol{t} - A\boldsymbol{s}_2$ *on the remaining* $n - r$ *coordinates* **do**
3 | Output $\boldsymbol{s} = \boldsymbol{s}_1 + \boldsymbol{s}_2$
4 **end**

differ by the unknown error vector $\boldsymbol{e}$. Thus, May's algorithm first guesses r coordinates of $\boldsymbol{e}$. The algorithm's high-level structure is described in Algorithm 1.

Algorithm 1 was instantiated and analyzed in [17] only for ternary vectors $\boldsymbol{s} \in \{-1, 0, 1\}^N$ with a predefined number of ± 1-entries. However, the algorithm may as well be instantiated with any notion of smallness of $\boldsymbol{s}, \boldsymbol{e}$ (in comparison to q). Throughout the paper, we assume that $\boldsymbol{s}, \boldsymbol{e}$ are sampled from a constant size range $\{-\eta, \ldots, \eta\}$. I.e., the max-norm of $\boldsymbol{s}, \boldsymbol{e}$ does not grow as a function of q, as opposed to e.g. Regev's original cryptosystem [20].

The narrow max-norm distributions that we address in this work are typical for highly practical lattice-based schemes like KYBER and DILITHIUM. In the narrow max-norm distribution setting for $\boldsymbol{e}$ (we do not need constant max-norm $\boldsymbol{s}$ at this point) the following holds.

Subexponential Key Guessing. Let $\mathcal{R}$ be the number of representations of $\boldsymbol{s}$. In Algorithm 1 we choose r, the number of guessed error coordinates, such that on expectation at least one representation survives. The probability that a representation $(\boldsymbol{s}_1, \boldsymbol{s}_2)$ satisfies the condition $A\boldsymbol{s}_1 = \mathbf{0}^r$ in the last r coordinates in Algorithm 1 is q^{-r}. Thus, a representation survives if $\mathcal{R}q^{-r} \geq 1$. Since in the following $\mathcal{R} = 2^{\mathcal{O}(N)}$ and $q = \Theta(N)$, we obtain $r = \mathcal{O}(\frac{N}{\log N})$. Thus, for every constant max-norm $\boldsymbol{e}$, Algorithm 1 requires for the key guessing in step 1 subexponential time

$$(\mathcal{O}(1))^r = 2^{\mathcal{O}(N/\log N)}.$$

As a consequence, the (exponential) runtime of LWE-SEARCH includes an additional slightly subexponential factor. Asymptotically, this contributes a factor of $(1 + o(1))$ to the exponent, and can be ignored by rounding the runtime exponent upwards. However, in practice, this factor might affect concrete runtime estimates on a significant scale.

Efficient LSH. An approximate matching $A_1\boldsymbol{s}_1 \approx \boldsymbol{t} - A_2\boldsymbol{s}_2 \bmod q$ with Odlyzko's locality sensitive hash function (LSH) includes a constant runtime overhead $\mathcal{O}(1)$ over an exact matching of lists (via sorting), when we match up to a constant max-norm error vector $\boldsymbol{e}$, see [17]. Consequently, we can ignore LSH costs.

4 Enumerating Keys from a Probabilistic Distribution

Larger Range. LWE-SEARCH originally was instantiated and analyzed for ternary $\boldsymbol{s}, \boldsymbol{e} \in \{-1, 0, 1\}^N$, where $\boldsymbol{s}$ has a fixed number of $-1, 0, 1$ that sum to 0, i.e., we have to know the weights $\mathrm{wt}_{-1}(\boldsymbol{s}), \mathrm{wt}_0(\boldsymbol{s}), \mathrm{wt}_1(\boldsymbol{s})$. In subsequent sections, we extend it to vectors $\boldsymbol{s}, \boldsymbol{e} \in \{-\eta, \ldots, \eta\}^N$, where $\eta = 2, 3$. These calculations with wider ranges can be seen as a generalization of May's analysis for ternary keys.

Handling Probabilism. Motivated by our applications KYBER and DILITHIUM, we want to deal with keys $\boldsymbol{s}, \boldsymbol{e}$ that are sampled from a *probabilistic distribution* $\mathcal{P}$. This causes problems, since LWE-SEARCH requires explicit knowledge of the weights of $\boldsymbol{s}$. This case is not covered by [17], and per se it is not clear that LWE-SEARCH permits a proper analysis for probabilistic distributions.

In this section, we first show that for *any* probabilistic distribution $\mathcal{P} = (p_{-\eta}, \ldots, p_\eta)$ with constant η, a polynomial fraction of all secret keys $\boldsymbol{s} \in \mathcal{P}^N$ has weights $\mathrm{wt}_{-\eta}(\boldsymbol{s}) = p_{-\eta}N, \ldots, \mathrm{wt}_\eta(\boldsymbol{s}) = p_\eta N$. I.e., all weights achieve their expected values, ignoring rounding issues.

Thus, if we analyze LWE-SEARCH with weights fixed to their expectation, we already obtain an algorithm that succeeds for a *polynomial fraction of keys.*

Attacking (Almost) All Keys. In Sect. 5, we show that the runtime of LWE-SEARCH can be expressed as a function $\mathcal{T}(\mathrm{wt}_{-\eta}, \ldots, \mathrm{wt}_\eta)$ which grows exponentially in N. Instinctively, one might think that iterating LWE-SEARCH over all possible $\mathcal{O}(N^\eta)$ many weight distributions would solve the problem presented by randomly sampling keys. However, this would result in worst-case runtime

$$\mathcal{O}(N^\eta \cdot \max\{\mathcal{T}(\mathrm{wt}_{-\eta}, \ldots, \mathrm{wt}_\eta)) \mid \textstyle\sum \mathrm{wt}_i = N\},$$

where the latter term can be exponentially larger than the runtime of LWE-SEARCH for a vector with $\mathrm{wt}_i = p_i N$. Instead, we utilize a *permutation technique.* In a nutshell, we permute the entries of $\boldsymbol{s}, \boldsymbol{e} \in \mathcal{P}^N$, until $\boldsymbol{s}$ achieves its expected weights. It turns out than, on expectation, this happens within a subexponential number $2^{\mathcal{O}(\sqrt{N})}$ of iterations for all but a (tunably very small) fraction of keys and yields a runtime of

$$2^{\mathcal{O}(\sqrt{N})} \cdot \mathcal{O}(\mathcal{T}(p_{-\eta}N, \ldots, p_\eta N)),$$

i.e. subexponential many iterations of exponentially less runtime. In other words, we show that, for *any* probability distribution, one may analyze LWE-SEARCH w.l.o.g. with the weights of $\boldsymbol{s}$ fixed to their expectation. As a consequence, our results hold for a $(1 - o(1))$-fraction of all randomly sampled $\boldsymbol{s}, \boldsymbol{e} \sim \mathcal{P}^N$.

4.1 A Polynomial Fraction of All Keys Achieves Expectations

Let us define what we mean by the event that a vector $\boldsymbol{v}$ sampled from some probability distribution $\mathcal{P}$ achieves its expected number of entries. We call the set of these vectors a *core set.*

Definition 1 (core set). *Let $N, \eta \in \mathbb{N}$. Let $\mathcal{P} = (p_{-\eta}, \ldots, p_\eta)$ be a probability distribution. We define the* core set *of N-dimensional vectors over $\mathcal{P}$ as*

$$\mathcal{C}(\mathcal{P}) := \{\boldsymbol{v} \in \{-\eta, \ldots, \eta\}^N \mid \mathrm{wt}_i(\boldsymbol{v}) = p_i N \text{ for all } -\eta \leq i \leq \eta\},$$

where w.l.o.g. (asymptotically in N) we assume that $p_i N \in \mathbb{N}$ for all i.

Next, we show that for any discrete probability distribution $\mathcal{P} = (p_{-\eta}, \ldots, p_\eta)$ with constant η, a length-N vector $\boldsymbol{v}$ randomly sampled coordinate-wise according to $\mathcal{P}$ belongs to the core set $\mathcal{C}(\mathcal{P})$ with probability inverse polynomial in N.

Lemma 1. *Let $\mathcal{P} = (p_{-\eta}, \ldots, p_\eta)$ be some probability distribution, and let $N \in \mathbb{N}$ be such that $N_i := p_i N \in \mathbb{N}$ for all i. Then, $\boldsymbol{v} \sim \mathcal{P}^N$ is in the core set $\mathcal{C}(\mathcal{P})$ with probability at least $\Omega(\frac{1}{N^\eta})$.*

Proof. Let $\boldsymbol{v} \sim \mathcal{P}^N$. Then we have for all i that $\mathrm{wt}_i(\boldsymbol{v}) := N_i := p_i N$ with probability

$$\Pr[\boldsymbol{v} \in \mathcal{C}(\mathcal{P})] = \binom{N}{N_{-\eta}, \ldots, N_\eta} \cdot \prod_{-\eta \leq i \leq \eta} p_i^{N_i}.$$

We bound the multinomial coefficient using Eq. (1) as

$$\begin{aligned}\Pr[\boldsymbol{v} \in \mathcal{C}(\mathcal{P})] &= \Omega\left(\tfrac{1}{N^\eta} \cdot 2^{H(p_{-\eta}, \cdots, p_\eta)N}\right) \cdot 2^{\sum_{-\eta \leq i \leq \eta} N_i \log p_i} \\ &= \Omega\left(\tfrac{1}{N^\eta}\right) \cdot 2^{H(p_{-\eta}, \cdots, p_\eta)N} \cdot 2^{-H(p_{-\eta}, \cdots, p_\eta)N} = \Omega\left(\tfrac{1}{N^\eta}\right).\end{aligned}$$

□

By Lemma 1, any attack that works for LWE keys $\boldsymbol{s}$ from the core set $\mathcal{C}(\mathcal{P})$ with probability ε also works for any key $\boldsymbol{s} \sim \mathcal{P}^N$ with probability $\Omega(\frac{1}{N^\eta}) \cdot \varepsilon$, where the last probability is taken over the random choice of $\boldsymbol{s}$.

4.2 Attacking Almost All Keys via Permutations

In order to attack almost all keys we devise a simple permutation technique that exchanges coordinates in $\boldsymbol{s}$ and $\boldsymbol{e}$. Our goal is to show that for almost all keys a subexponential number of permutations yields a permuted $\boldsymbol{s}'$ from the core set.

Permutation Technique. Let $A\boldsymbol{s} + \boldsymbol{e} = \boldsymbol{t} \bmod q$ be an LWE instance with a square $A \in \mathbb{Z}_q^{N \times N}$. We can rewrite this equation in the form

$$(A \mid I_N) \cdot (\boldsymbol{s} \mid \boldsymbol{e}) = \boldsymbol{t} \bmod q.$$

Let $P \in \mathbb{Z}_q^{2N \times 2N}$ be a permutation matrix, and let $(A \mid I_n) \cdot P^{-1} = (B \mid C)$, where $B, C \in \mathbb{Z}_q^{N \times N}$. Then clearly

$$(B \mid C) \cdot P(\boldsymbol{s} \mid \boldsymbol{e}) = \boldsymbol{t} \bmod q.$$

Assume that C is invertible with inverse $C^{-1} \in \mathbb{Z}_q^{N \times N}$. Then

$$(C^{-1}B | I_N) \cdot P(\boldsymbol{s} \mid \boldsymbol{e}) = C^{-1}\boldsymbol{t} \bmod q.$$

Algorithm 2: PERMUTE-LWE

Input : LWE instance $(A, \boldsymbol{t})$ such that $A\boldsymbol{s} + \boldsymbol{e} = \boldsymbol{t} \bmod q$

Output: LWE instance $(A', \boldsymbol{t}')$ such that $A'\boldsymbol{s}' + \boldsymbol{e}' = \boldsymbol{t}' \bmod q$, where $(\boldsymbol{s}', \boldsymbol{e}')$ is a permutation of $(\boldsymbol{s}, \boldsymbol{e})$

repeat
  Choose a random permutation matrix $P \in \mathbb{Z}_q^{2N \times 2N}$. ;
  Compute $(B \mid C) = (A \mid I_N) \cdot P^{-1}$ with $B, C \in \mathbb{Z}_q^{N \times N}$.
until C *is invertible*;
$(A', \boldsymbol{t}') := (C^{-1}B, C^{-1}\boldsymbol{t})$;

Define $A' := C^{-1}B \in Z_q^{N \times N}$, $(\boldsymbol{s}', \boldsymbol{e}') := P(\boldsymbol{s} \mid \boldsymbol{e})$, and $\boldsymbol{t}' = C^{-1}\boldsymbol{t}$. Then we obtain a new LWE instance

$$A'\boldsymbol{s}' + \boldsymbol{e}' = \boldsymbol{t}',$$

where the coordinates of $(\boldsymbol{s}', \boldsymbol{e}')$ are a permutation of the coordinates of $(\boldsymbol{s}, \boldsymbol{e})$. Notice that a random matrix is invertible over $\mathbb{Z}_q$ with probability $\prod_{i=1}^{N}(1 - q^{-i}) \geq \frac{1}{4}$ [22].

This gives us the algorithm PERMUTE-LWE (Algorithm 2) with expected polynomial runtime $\mathcal{O}(N^3)$.

Any LWE key $\boldsymbol{v} = (\boldsymbol{s}, \boldsymbol{e}) \sim \mathcal{P}^{2N}$ has expected weight $\mathrm{wt}_i(\boldsymbol{v}) = 2Np_i$ for all i. Intuitively, if $\mathrm{wt}_i(\boldsymbol{v})$ is not significantly smaller than $2Np_i$ for any i, then PERMUTE-LWE should have a good chance to produce some $\boldsymbol{s}' \in \mathcal{C}(\mathcal{P})$. This motivates our following definition of well-balanced vectors.

Definition 2. *Let $\mathcal{P} = (p_{-\eta}, \ldots, p_\eta)$ be a probability distribution. We call an LWE key $(\boldsymbol{s}, \boldsymbol{e}) \sim \mathcal{P}^{2N}$* c-well-balanced *if for any $-\eta \leq i \leq \eta$ and some constant c, $(\boldsymbol{s}, \boldsymbol{e})$ contains at least $2Np_i - c\sqrt{Np_i}$ many i-entries.*

We want to show that any randomly sampled vector $(\boldsymbol{s}, \boldsymbol{e}) \sim \mathcal{P}^{2N}$ is c-well-balanced with constant probability.

Lemma 2. *Let $\mathcal{P} = (p_{-\eta}, \ldots, p_\eta)$ be a probability distribution. Then an LWE-key $(\boldsymbol{s}, \boldsymbol{e}) \sim \mathcal{P}^{2N}$ is* c-well-balanced *with probability at least $1 - (2\eta + 1)e^{-c^2/4}$.*

Proof. Let X_i be a random variable for the number of i-entries in $(\boldsymbol{s}, \boldsymbol{e}) \sim \mathcal{P}^{2N}$. Then $\mu := \mathbb{E}[X_i] = 2Np_i$. We apply the Chernoff bound

$$\Pr[X_i \leq (1 - \delta)\mu] \leq e^{-\frac{\mu\delta^2}{2}}$$

with the choice $\delta = \frac{c}{2\sqrt{Np_i}}$, which yields

$$\Pr[X_i \leq 2Np_i - c\sqrt{Np_i}] \leq e^{-\frac{c^2}{4}}.$$

An application of the union bound shows the statement. □

With Lemma 2, we know that, for large enough c, almost all keys are c-well-balanced. Now, we want to show that any LWE instance with c-well-balanced keys $(\boldsymbol{s}, \boldsymbol{e})$ can be turned via PERMUTE-LWE into an LWE-instance with a secret $\boldsymbol{s}'$ in the core set in subexponential time, for which we analyze our instantiations of LWE-SEARCH (Algorithm 1) in subsequent sections.

Lemma 3. *Let $\mathcal{P} = (p_{-\eta}, \dots, p_\eta)$ be a probability distribution, and $(A, \boldsymbol{t})$ be an LWE instance with* c-well-balanced *LWE-key $(\boldsymbol{s}, \boldsymbol{e}) \sim \mathcal{P}^{2N}$. Then on expectation* PERMUTE-LWE *outputs an LWE instance $(A, \boldsymbol{t}')$ with $\boldsymbol{s}' \in \mathcal{C}(\mathcal{P})$ after $2^{\mathcal{O}(\sqrt{N})}$ trials.*

Proof. Since $(\boldsymbol{s}, \boldsymbol{e})$ is c-well-balanced, we have $\mathrm{wt}_i(\boldsymbol{s}, \boldsymbol{e}) \geq 2Np_i - c\sqrt{Np_i}$ for any $i \in \{-\eta, \dots, \eta\}$. Thus, we obtain

$$\Pr[\boldsymbol{s} \in \mathcal{C}(\mathcal{P})] \geq \frac{\binom{2Np_{-\eta} - c\sqrt{Np_{-\eta}}}{Np_{-\eta}} \cdot \ldots \cdot \binom{2Np_\eta - c\sqrt{Np_\eta}}{Np_\eta}}{\binom{2N}{N}}.$$

Using Eq. (1) and neglecting polynomial terms we obtain for the exponent

$$\log \Pr[\boldsymbol{s} \in \mathcal{C}(\mathcal{P})] \geq -2N + \sum_{i=-\eta}^{\eta} H\left(\frac{1}{2 - \frac{c}{Np_i}}\right) \cdot \left(2 - \frac{c}{\sqrt{Np_i}}\right) Np_i.$$

For any $x \leq \frac{1}{2}$ we have $H(x, 1-x) \geq 2(1-x)$, leading to

$$\begin{aligned}\log \Pr[\boldsymbol{s} \in \mathcal{C}(\mathcal{P})] &\geq -2N + \sum_{i=-\eta}^{\eta} 2\left(1 - \frac{1}{2 - \frac{c}{Np_i}}\right) \cdot \left(2 - \frac{c}{\sqrt{Np_i}}\right) Np_i. \\ &= -2N + 2\sum_{i=-\eta}^{\eta} \left(1 - \frac{c}{\sqrt{Np_i}}\right) Np_i \\ &= -2c \sum_{i=-\eta}^{\eta} \sqrt{Np_i} = -\Theta(\sqrt{N}).\end{aligned}$$

Thus, we expect that after $(\Pr[\boldsymbol{s} \in \mathcal{C}(\mathcal{P})])^{-1} = 2^{\mathcal{O}(\sqrt{N})}$ iterations for PERMUTE-LWE to output an LWE-instance with a secret $\boldsymbol{s}$ in the core set $\mathcal{C}(\mathcal{P})$. □

5 Instantiating LWE-SEARCH with Simple (Rep-0) Representations

In this section, we show how to instantiate LWE-SEARCH (Algorithm 1) from Sect. 3 with both $\boldsymbol{s}, \boldsymbol{e}$ sampled from the Centered Binomial distribution $\mathcal{B}(3)^N$. In the previous Sect. 4 we showed that for any distribution $\mathcal{P}$ it suffices to instantiate LWE-SEARCH with secret $\boldsymbol{s}$ chosen from the core set $\mathcal{C}(\mathcal{P})$, that fixes all weights to their expectations, see Definition 1. Therefore, in the following we assume that $\boldsymbol{s} \in \mathcal{C}(\mathcal{P})^N$.

Our first LWE-SEARCH instantiation is mainly for didactic reasons. We assume that the reader is not familiar with the representation technique. Therefore, we define an especially simple representation, called REP-0, to illustrate the analysis. In subsequent sections, we further refine and parametrize our representations, called REP-1, REP-2 and REP-3. While these refinements complicate the analysis, they also lead to significantly stronger results.

Rep-0. Let us define simple representations, called REP-0, for $\boldsymbol{s} \in \{-3, \dots, 3\}^N$. Our representations are illustrated in Table 3. For instance, we represent a 3 in $\boldsymbol{s}$ as either $1+2$ or $2+1$, whereas a 2 is represented uniquely as $1+1$. For negative numbers we simply change sign, e.g. -1 is represented as either $0 + (-1)$ or $(-1) + 0$. If a coefficient i has two representations, then we represent half of its occurrences in $\boldsymbol{s}$ with either representation.

Counting Representations. Let $\mathcal{R}$ denote the number of representations of $\boldsymbol{s} \in \{-3, \dots, 3\}^N$. Let $\mathcal{R}_i$ denote the number of representations for entry i. Then $\mathcal{R} = \prod_{i=-3}^{3} \mathcal{R}_i$. Since we only consider distributions that are symmetric in 0, we obtain $\mathcal{R}_{-i} = \mathcal{R}_i$. For $i \in \{-2, 0, 2\}$ we have unique representations and therefore $\mathcal{R}_0 = \mathcal{R}_2 = \mathcal{R}_{-2} = 1$. For $i \in \{-3, -1, 1, 3\}$ we have two representations with equal splits instead, i.e.,

$$\mathcal{R}_1 = \mathcal{R}_{-1} = \binom{\mathrm{wt}_1(\boldsymbol{s})}{\frac{\mathrm{wt}_1(\boldsymbol{s})}{2}}, \quad \mathcal{R}_3 = \mathcal{R}_{-3} = \binom{\mathrm{wt}_3(\boldsymbol{s})}{\frac{\mathrm{wt}_3(\boldsymbol{s})}{2}}.$$

As a conclusion, using Eq. (1) the number $\mathcal{R}$ of REP-0 representations is

$$\mathcal{R} = \binom{\mathrm{wt}_1(\boldsymbol{s})}{\frac{\mathrm{wt}_1(\boldsymbol{s})}{2}}^2 \cdot \binom{\mathrm{wt}_3(\boldsymbol{s})}{\frac{\mathrm{wt}_3(\boldsymbol{s})}{2}}^2 = \tilde{\Theta}(2^{2\,\mathrm{wt}_1(\boldsymbol{s}) + 2\,\mathrm{wt}_3(\boldsymbol{s})}). \tag{3}$$

5.1 Rep-0 Instantiation of LWE-SEARCH

In a nutshell, LWE-SEARCH enumerates candidates for the LWE secret $\boldsymbol{s}$ in a list $L_1^{(0)}$. The candidates for $\boldsymbol{s}$ are represented as sums of $\boldsymbol{s}_1^{(1)}$ and $\boldsymbol{s}_2^{(1)}$, enumerated in lists $L_1^{(1)}$ and $L_2^{(1)}$, respectively, see Fig. 1 for an illustration. LWE-SEARCH constructs candidates recursively, i.e., on level j in the search tree of Fig. 1 we construct all candidates $\boldsymbol{s}_i^{(j)}$ in list $L_i^{(j)}$ as the sum of candidates $\boldsymbol{s}_{2i-1}^{(j+1)}$ and $\boldsymbol{s}_{2i}^{(j+1)}$ in lists $L_{2i-1}^{(j+1)}$ and $L_{2i}^{(j+1)}$. In the simplified illustration of Fig. 1 we stopped the recursion in depth $d = 3$, but in general we have to optimize d.

Weights. In the root list $L_1^{(0)}$ we eventually enumerate the candidates for $\boldsymbol{s}$. Recall that $\boldsymbol{s} \in \mathcal{B}(3)^N$ and $\mathcal{B}(3)$ has by Eq. (2) probability distribution

$$(p_{-3}, \dots, p_3) = \left(\tfrac{1}{64}, \tfrac{6}{64}, \tfrac{15}{64}, \tfrac{20}{64}, \tfrac{15}{64}, \tfrac{6}{64}, \tfrac{1}{64}\right).$$

Table 3. REP-0 representations of $i \in \{-3, \dots, 3\}$. Note the symmetry between i and $-i$, allowing us to omit negative values in later versions of this table.

i	Representations of i						
-3		$-2-1$	$-1-2$				
-2			$-1-1$				
-1			$-1+0$	$0-1$			
0				$0+0$			
1				$0+1$	$1+0$		
2					$1+1$		
3					$1+2$	$2+1$	

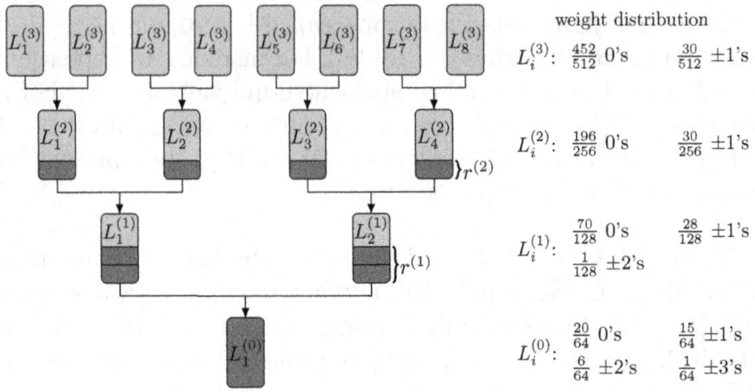

Fig. 1. LWE-Search tree in depth $d = 3$ with relative weights for $\mathcal{B}(3)$.

As shown in Sect. 4, in the root list $L_1^{(0)}$, it suffices to enumerate only vectors $\boldsymbol{s} \in \mathcal{C}(\mathcal{B}(3)^N)$ from the core set with weights $p_{-3}N, \ldots, p_3N$. For notational convenience let us define *relative (to N) weights* $\omega_i^{(j)} := \frac{\mathrm{wt}_i(\boldsymbol{s})}{N}$ for entry i on level j of our LWE-Search tree, see also Fig. 1. On the root level, we have relative weights $\omega_i^{(0)} = p_i$. Since we only consider symmetric distributions, for ease of exposition, we write $\omega_{-i}^{(j)} := \omega_i^{(j)}$ on all levels j.

From Table 3 we deduce the relative weights on level $j < d$ recursively as

$$\omega_0^{(j)} = \frac{2\omega_0^{(j-1)} + 2\omega_1^{(j-1)}}{2}, \quad \omega_1^{(j)} = \frac{\omega_1^{(j-1)} + 2\omega_2^{(j-1)} + \omega_3^{(j-1)}}{2}, \quad \omega_2^{(j)} = \frac{\omega_3^{(j-1)}}{2}, \quad \omega_3^{(j)} = 0.$$

On level d, LWE-Search uses a classical Meet-in-the-Middle strategy (without representations) that splits the weights evenly. Thus, we obtain

$$\omega_1^{(d)} = \frac{\omega_1^{(d-1)}}{2}, \quad \omega_2^{(d)} = \frac{\omega_2^{(d-1)}}{2}, \quad \omega_3^{(d)} = \frac{\omega_3^{(d-1)}}{2}, \quad \omega_0^{(d)} = 1 - 2(\omega_1^{(d)} + \omega_2^{(d)} + \omega_3^{(d)}).$$

The values of all relative weights for $\mathcal{B}(3)$ on all levels are summarized in Fig. 1.

As an example, in both level-1 lists $L_1^{(1)}$, $L_2^{(1)}$ all vectors $\boldsymbol{s}_i^{(1)}$ have $\mathrm{wt}_0(\boldsymbol{s}_i^{(1)}) = \frac{70}{128}N$ many 0-entries, $\mathrm{wt}_1(\boldsymbol{s}_i^{(1)}) = \frac{28}{128}N$ many ±1-entries each, $\mathrm{wt}_2(\boldsymbol{s}_i^{(1)}) = \frac{1}{128}N$ many ±2-entries each, and no ±3-entries.

Search Spaces. Now that we fixed the weight distributions on all levels of our LWE-Search tree we can define *search spaces*, i.e., the amount $\mathcal{S}^{(j)}$ of vectors on level j that satisfy our weight distributions. We obtain

$$\mathcal{S}^{(j)} = \binom{N}{\omega_0^{(j)}N,\ \omega_1^{(j)}N,\ \omega_1^{(j)}N,\ \ldots,\ \omega_3^{(j)}N,\ \omega_3^{(j)}N} = \tilde{\Theta}(2^{H(\omega_0^{(j)}, \omega_1^{(j)}, \omega_1^{(j)}, \ldots, \omega_3^{(j)}, \omega_3^{(j)})N}). \tag{4}$$

Representations and Lists. Recall that our secret $\boldsymbol{s}$ has many representations as the sum of two vectors. LWE-Search uses the representations to significantly reduce search spaces. More precisely, if on level j we have $\mathcal{R}^{(j)}$ representations, then we cut the search space by a random $\frac{1}{\mathcal{R}^{(j)}}$-factor such that on expectation only a single representation remains. This search space reduction is the representation technique's core idea.

From Eq. (3), we already know the amount of representations on level 1. Let $\mathcal{R}^{(j)}$ denote the amount of level-j representations, then $\mathcal{R}^{(1)} := \mathcal{R}$, and Eq. (3) easily generalizes to

$$\mathcal{R}^{(j+1)} = \tilde{\Theta}(2^{(2\omega_1^{(j)}+2\omega_3^{(j)})N}). \tag{5}$$

Recall that in the root list $L_1^{(0)}$ we store candidate secret keys $\boldsymbol{s}$, i.e.,

$$L_1^{(0)} = \{\boldsymbol{s} \in \mathcal{C}(\mathcal{B}(3)) \mid A \cdot \boldsymbol{s} - \boldsymbol{t} \in \{-3, \ldots, 3\}^N\}.$$

At level 1 of the search tree, we have $\mathcal{R}^{(1)}$ many representations of $\boldsymbol{s}$. Therefore, we have to cut the search space $\mathcal{S}^{(1)}$ by an $\frac{1}{\mathcal{R}^{(1)}}$-fraction. Let

$$r^{(1)} := \lfloor \log_q(\mathcal{R}^{(1)}) \rfloor = \mathcal{O}(\tfrac{N}{\log N}).$$

Let π_r denote the projection on the last r coordinates. In LWE-SEARCH we guess $\boldsymbol{e}_r := \pi_{r^{(1)}}(\boldsymbol{e})$ in subexponential time $\mathcal{O}(7^{r^{(1)}}) = 2^{\mathcal{O}(\frac{N}{\log N})}$.

Let $\boldsymbol{s}_1^{(1)}, \boldsymbol{s}_2^{(1)}$ be a representation of the secret key $\boldsymbol{s}$. Then $A\boldsymbol{s}_1^{(1)} + \boldsymbol{e} = \boldsymbol{t} - A\boldsymbol{s}_2^{(1)}$, which implies

$$\pi_{r^{(1)}}(A\boldsymbol{s}_1^{(1)}) + \boldsymbol{e}_r = \pi_{r^{(1)}}(\boldsymbol{t} - A\boldsymbol{s}_2^{(1)}). \tag{6}$$

By the randomness of A, the left and right hand side of Eq. (6) takes random values in $\mathbb{Z}_q^{r^{(1)}}$. Thus, for every target value $\boldsymbol{v} \in \mathbb{Z}_q^{r^{(1)}}$ any representation $\boldsymbol{s}_1, \boldsymbol{s}_2$ of $\boldsymbol{s}$ takes on both sides of Eq. (6) value $\boldsymbol{v}$ with probability $q^{-r^{(1)}}$. As a consequence, we expect that $\mathcal{R}^{(1)} \cdot q^{-r^{(1)}} \geq 1$ representations take value $\boldsymbol{v}$. For ease of exposition, we choose $\boldsymbol{v} = \boldsymbol{0}^{r^{(1)}}$ in the following, but in a real implementation one could randomize target values $\boldsymbol{v}$. Hence, we define level-1 lists

$$L_1^{(1)} := \{\boldsymbol{s}_1^{(1)} \mid \pi_{r^{(1)}}(A\boldsymbol{s}_1^{(1)}) = -\boldsymbol{e}_r\}, \quad L_2^{(1)} := \{\boldsymbol{s}_2^{(1)} \mid \pi_{r^{(1)}}(\boldsymbol{t} - A\boldsymbol{s}_2^{(1)}) = \boldsymbol{0}^{r^{(1)}}\}.$$

On level 2 to $d-1$, we algorithmically take the same approach as on level 1. As an example, let us derive the level-2 list descriptions. On level 2, we have $\mathcal{R}^{(2)}$ representations, and thus cut the search space $\mathcal{S}^{(2)}$ by an $\frac{1}{\mathcal{R}^{(2)}}$-fraction. To this end, define $r^{(2)} := \lfloor \log_q(\mathcal{R}^{(2)}) \rfloor$ (We generally assume that $r^{(j)} \geq r^{(j-1)}$, this can be achieved by using $\tilde{r}^{(j)} := \max_{j' \leq j}\{r^{(j')}\}$ instead). Let $\boldsymbol{s}_1^{(2)}, \boldsymbol{s}_2^{(2)}$ and $\boldsymbol{s}_3^{(2)}, \boldsymbol{s}_4^{(2)}$ be representations of $\boldsymbol{s}_1^{(1)}$ and $\boldsymbol{s}_2^{(1)}$, respectively. Then we obtain level-2 lists

$$L_1^{(2)} := \{\boldsymbol{s}_1^{(2)} \mid \pi_{r^{(2)}}(A\boldsymbol{s}_1^{(2)}) = \boldsymbol{0}^{r^{(2)}}\}, \qquad L_2^{(2)} := \{\boldsymbol{s}_2^{(2)} \mid \pi_{r^{(2)}}(A\boldsymbol{s}_2^{(2)} + \boldsymbol{e}_r) = \boldsymbol{0}^{r^{(2)}}\},$$
$$L_3^{(2)} := \{\boldsymbol{s}_3^{(2)} \mid \pi_{r^{(2)}}(\boldsymbol{t} - A\boldsymbol{s}_3^{(2)}) = \boldsymbol{0}^{r^{(2)}}\}, \quad L_4^{(2)} := \{\boldsymbol{s}_4^{(2)} \mid \pi_{r^{(2)}}(A\boldsymbol{s}_4^{(2)})) = \boldsymbol{0}^{r^{(2)}}\}.$$

Eventually, all level-d lists are constructed in a standard Meet-in-the-Middle manner by splitting each $\boldsymbol{s}_i^{(d-1)}$ in two $N/2$-dimensional vectors $\boldsymbol{s}_{2i-1}^{(d)}, \boldsymbol{s}_{2i}^{(d)}$.

Table 4. Rep-0 complexity exponents for $\mathcal{B}(3)^N$ using LWE-SEARCH with depths $d = 3, 4$. Bold exponents indicate the dominating term.

d	$\log \mathcal{T}^{(0)}$	$\log \mathcal{T}^{(1)}$	$\log \mathcal{T}^{(2)}$	$\log \mathcal{T}^{(3)}$	$\log \mathcal{T}^{(4)}$	$\log \mathcal{M}$
3	$1.090N$	$\mathbf{1.103N}$	$.583N$	$.510N$	-	$1.045N$
4	$1.090N$	$\mathbf{1.103N}$	$.605N$	$.405N$	$.320N$	$1.045N$

Runtime Analysis. The level-d lists are constructed by a classical square-root complexity Meet-in-the-Middle approach for a search space of size $\mathcal{S}^{(d-1)}$. On levels $1 \leq j < d$, we enumerate an $\frac{1}{\mathcal{R}^{(j)}}$-fraction of the search space size $\mathcal{S}^{(j)}$. Overall, we obtain lists of sizes

$$\mathcal{L}^{(d)} = \sqrt{\mathcal{S}^{(d-1)}}, \qquad \mathcal{L}^{(j)} = \frac{\mathcal{S}^{(j)}}{\mathcal{R}^{(j)}} \text{ for } 1 \leq j < d. \tag{7}$$

Since root list $L_1^{(0)}$ can be constructed on-the-fly and must not be stored, we obtain a total memory consumption of $\mathcal{M} = \max\{\mathcal{L}^{(j)}\}$.

Let $r^{(d)} = 0$. For constructing lists on level $1 \leq j < d$, we match two neighboring lists $L_{2i-1}^{(j+1)}, L_{2i}^{(j+1)}$ of size $\mathcal{L}^{(j+1)}$ on $r^{(j)} - r^{(j+1)}$ coordinates into a list $L_i^{(j)}$. Neglecting low order terms (e.g. for sorting), this can be done in time

$$\mathcal{T}^{(j)} = \max\{\mathcal{L}^{(j+1)}, \frac{(\mathcal{L}^{(j+1)})^2}{q^{r^{(j)} - r^{(j+1)}}}\}. \tag{8}$$

We then filter out all $\boldsymbol{s}_i^{(j)} \in L_i^{(j)}$ that do not have the correct weight distribution, resulting in list size $\mathcal{L}^{(j)}$.

The root list $L_1^{(0)}$ results from approximately matching both level-1 lists of size $\mathcal{L}^{(1)}$ via Odlyzko's hash function on the remaining $N - r^{(1)}$ coordinates that were previously unmatched. This can be done in time

$$\mathcal{T}^{(0)} = \max\{\mathcal{L}^{(1)}, \frac{(\mathcal{L}^{(1)})^2}{2^{N-r^{(1)}}}\}. \tag{9}$$

We obtain as total runtime complexity

$$\mathcal{T} = \max\{\mathcal{T}^{(0)}, \ldots, \mathcal{T}^{(d-1)}\}. \tag{10}$$

We analyzed LWE-SEARCH in depths $d = 3, 4$. All runtime exponents are given in Table 4. We observe that depth 3 is already sufficient, since depth 4 does not reduce the maximal exponent. The analysis for $d = 3$ is detailed in the proof of the following theorem.

Theorem 1. (REP-0). *Under the* MLWE Representation Heuristic *the following holds. Let* $(A, \boldsymbol{t}) \in \mathbb{Z}_q^{N \times N} \times \mathbb{Z}_q^N$ *be an (M)LWE instance with* $q = \Omega(N)$ *and secret keys* $\boldsymbol{s}, \boldsymbol{e} \sim \mathcal{B}(3)^N$*, where* $N = nk$ *for MLWE. Then* LWE-SEARCH *instantiated with* REP-0 *representations finds* $\boldsymbol{s}$ *(with constant probability) within time* $\mathcal{O}(2^{1.103N})$.

Proof. The correctness of LWE-SEARCH follows by the discussion above. It remains to show that LWE-SEARCH terminates in time $\mathcal{O}(2^{1.103N})$.

We use the runtime formulas from Eqs. (8) and (9). Using Eqs. (7), (4) and (5) for list size, search space size and representations, this results in

$$\mathcal{T}^{(0)} = \frac{(\mathcal{L}^{(1)})^2}{2^{N-r^{(1)}}} = 2^{(2(H(\frac{1}{128},\frac{28}{128},\frac{70}{128},\frac{28}{128},\frac{1}{128})-2\frac{15}{64}-2\frac{1}{64})-1+o(1))N} = \mathcal{O}(2^{1.090N}),$$
$$\mathcal{T}^{(1)} = \frac{(\mathcal{L}^{(2)})^2}{q^{r^{(1)}-r^{(2)}}} = \tilde{\Theta}(2^{(2H(\frac{30}{256},\frac{196}{256},\frac{30}{256})-2\frac{15}{64}-2\frac{1}{64}-2\frac{28}{128})N}) = \mathcal{O}(2^{1.103N}),$$
$$\mathcal{T}^{(2)} = \frac{(\mathcal{L}^{(3)})^2}{q^{r^{(2)}-r^{(3)}}} = \tilde{\Theta}(2^{(2H(\frac{30}{256},\frac{196}{256},\frac{30}{256})/2-2\frac{28}{128})N}) = \mathcal{O}(2^{0.583N}),$$
$$\mathcal{T}^{(3)} = \mathcal{L}^{(3)} = \tilde{\Theta}(2^{(H(\frac{30}{256},\frac{196}{256},\frac{30}{256})/2)N}) = \mathcal{O}(2^{0.51N}).$$

Thus, due to (10), LWE-SEARCH terminates in time $\max \mathcal{T}^{(j)} = \mathcal{O}(2^{1.103N})$. □

6 More Representations

In this section, we enhance our representations to significantly reduce the LWE-SEARCH runtime from Theorem 1. Our first refined representation REP-1 can be seen as an introduction to parametrization in the representation technique, where we add additional ±1's to represent 0-entries as $1 + (-1)$ and $(-1) + 1$.

We then parametrize to the full extent by adding in additional ±2's and ±3's in REP-2 and REP-3. The parameters used in Theorems 2 and 3 were found using the method described in Sect. 8.

6.1 REP-1 Representations

Our REP-1 representations are illustrated in Table 5. We introduce a parameter $\varepsilon^{(j)} \in [0,1], 1 \leq j < d$ for the additional number of ±1's on level j. I.e., if we have $\omega_0^{(j-1)}N$ many entries 0 on level $j-1$, we represent $\varepsilon^{(j)}N$ many as $1+(-1)$, and $\varepsilon^{(j)}N$ many as $(-1)+1$. The remaining $(\omega_0^{(j-1)} - 2\varepsilon^{(j)})N$ 0-entries are still represented as $0+0$. Accordingly, most formulas from Sect. 5 remain unchanged. We only increase the number of 0-representations

$$\mathcal{R}_0^{(j)} = \binom{\omega_0^{(j-1)}N}{\varepsilon^{(j)}N\ ,\ \varepsilon^{(j)}N\ ,\ \cdot}$$

at the cost of slightly increased search spaces $\mathcal{S}^{(j)}$, reflected by different weights

$$\omega_0^{(j)} = \frac{2\omega_0^{(j-1)}+2\omega_1^{(j-1)}-4\varepsilon^{(j)}}{2}, \qquad \omega_1^{(j)} = \frac{\omega_1^{(j-1)}+2\omega_2^{(j-1)}+\omega_3^{(j-1)}+2\varepsilon^{(j)}}{2}.$$

Theorem 2. (REP-1). *Under the* MLWE Representation Heuristic *the following holds. Let* $(A, t) \in \mathbb{Z}_q^{N\times N} \times \mathbb{Z}_q^N$ *be an (M)LWE instance with* $q = \Omega(N)$ *and secret keys* $s, e \sim \mathcal{B}(3)^N$, *where* $N = nk$ *for MLWE. Then* LWE-SEARCH *instantiated with* REP-1 *representations finds* s *(with constant probability) within time* $\mathcal{O}(2^{0.787N})$.

Table 5. Rep-1 representations of $i \in \{0,1,2,3\}$, magenta-colored representations are new.

i	Representations of i						
0			$-1+1$	$\mathbf{0+0}$	$1-1$		
1				$\mathbf{0+1}$	$\mathbf{1+0}$		
2					$\mathbf{1+1}$		
3					$\mathbf{1+2}$	$\mathbf{2+1}$	

Proof. Analogous to the proof of Theorem 1, parameters are presented in Table 6. The desired complexity $\mathcal{O}(2^{0.787N})$ is achieved with tree depth $d = 3$. □

Notice that the —in comparison to Rep-0— only slightly more advanced Rep-1 representations lowered the exponent $1.103N$ from Theorem 1 already significantly down to $0.787N$. In Sect. 6.2 we study way more advanced representations that lower to even $0.388N$ (Rep-2) and $0.371N$ (Rep-3). The small improvement from Rep-3 over Rep-2 however indicates that we are converging. We conjecture that even more complex representations would only provide marginal improvements over Rep-3.

6.2 Rep-2, Rep-3 Representations

Our Rep-2 and Rep-3 representations are illustrated in Table 7. While our Rep-1 representations only allowed for two more representations of 0, our Rep-2 and eventually Rep-3 representations heavily increase the number of representations (e.g. 7 representations for 0) for all elements (e.g. still 4 representations of 3).

Parametrization. Note that we define Rep-k such that for every $0 \leq \ell \leq k$ the parameters of Rep-ℓ are contained in Rep-k.

To express the amount of additionally added $\pm 1, \pm 2, \pm 3$, we define parameters $\varepsilon_{10}^{(j)}, \varepsilon_{20}^{(j)}, \varepsilon_{21}^{(j)}, \varepsilon_{22}^{(j)}, \varepsilon_{30}^{(j)}, \varepsilon_{31}^{(j)}, \varepsilon_{32}^{(j)}, \varepsilon_{33}^{(j)} \in [0,1]$, where $\varepsilon_{10}^{(j)} = \varepsilon^{(j)}$ from Rep-1 and $\varepsilon_{30}^{(j)}, \varepsilon_{31}^{(j)}, \varepsilon_{32}^{(j)}, \varepsilon_{33}^{(j)}$ are Rep-3 parameters only.

These parameters are to be understood as follows. Let $\boldsymbol{s}_i^{(j-1)}$ be a level-$(j-1)$ vector, represented by $\boldsymbol{s}_{2i-1}^{(j)}, \boldsymbol{s}_{2i}^{(j)}$. On level j, we replace $2\varepsilon_{ik}^{(j)}N$ of the Rep-0 representations of k with $\varepsilon_{ik}^{(j)}N$ representations $i + (k-i)$ and $\varepsilon_{ik}^{(j)}N$ representations $(k-i)+i$ in $\boldsymbol{s}_{2i-1}^{(j)}, \boldsymbol{s}_{2i}^{(j)}$.

Table 6. Rep-1 complexity exponents for $\mathcal{B}(3)^N$ using LWE-Search with depths $d = 2, 3, 4$ and optimized $\varepsilon^{(j)}$. Bold exponents indicate the dominating term.

d	j	$\varepsilon^{(j)}$	$\log \mathcal{T}^{(j)}$	$\log \mathcal{L}^{(j)}$
	0	-	$.810N$	0
2	1	.036	$\mathbf{.813}N$	$.810N$
	2	-	$\mathbf{.813}N$	$\mathbf{.813}N$

d	j	$\varepsilon^{(j)}$	$\log \mathcal{T}^{(j)}$	$\log \mathcal{L}^{(j)}$
	0	-	$.718N$	0
3	1	.073	$\mathbf{.787}N$	$\mathbf{.718}N$
	2	.028	$.655N$	$.436N$
	3	-	$.655N$	$.655N$

d	j	$\varepsilon^{(j)}$	$\log \mathcal{T}^{(j)}$	$\log \mathcal{L}^{(j)}$
	0	-	$.718N$	0
	1	.073	$\mathbf{.787}N$	$\mathbf{.718}N$
4	2	.028	$.503N$	$.436N$
	3		$.503N$	$.503N$
	4	-	$.433N$	$.433N$

Table 7. Representations of $i \in \{0, 1, 2, 3\}$ under REP-2 and REP-3; magenta-colored representations are added with REP-1; orange-colored representations are added with REP-2; blue-colored representations are added with REP-3.

i	Representations of i						
0	$-3+3$	$-2+2$	$-1+1$	$\mathbf{0+0}$	$1-1$	$2-2$	$3-3$
1		$-2+3$	$-1+2$	$\mathbf{0+1}$	$\mathbf{1+0}$	$2-1$	$3-2$
2			$-1+3$	$0+2$	$\mathbf{1+1}$	$2+0$	$3-1$
3				$0+3$	$\mathbf{1+2}$	$\mathbf{2+1}$	$3+0$

To unify notation, we always choose i such that $i \geq k - i$ (e.g. we write $\varepsilon_{22}^{(j)}$ instead of $\varepsilon_{02}^{(j)}$). In summary, $\varepsilon_{ik}^{(j)}$ is a parameter for REP-ℓ if and only if $\max\{0, \frac{k+1}{2}\} < i \leq \ell$.

For fixed $\varepsilon_{ik}^{(j)}$, we calculate the new formulas for $\mathcal{R}_i^{(j)}$ and for $\omega_i^{(j)}$ as

$$\mathcal{R}_0^{(j)} = \begin{pmatrix} \omega_0^{(j-1)}N \\ \varepsilon_{10}^{(j)}N\ ,\ \varepsilon_{10}^{(j)}N\ ,\ \varepsilon_{20}^{(j)}N\ ,\ \varepsilon_{20}^{(j)}N\ ,\ \varepsilon_{30}^{(j)}N\ ,\ \varepsilon_{30}^{(j)}N\ ,\ \cdot \end{pmatrix},$$

$$\mathcal{R}_1^{(j)} = \begin{pmatrix} \omega_1^{(j-1)}N \\ \varepsilon_{21}^{(j)}N\ ,\ \varepsilon_{21}^{(j)}N\ ,\ \varepsilon_{31}^{(j)}N\ ,\ \varepsilon_{31}^{(j)}N\ ,\ \frac{\omega_1^{(j-1)}-2\varepsilon_{21}^{(j)}-2\varepsilon_{31}^{(j)}}{2}N\ ,\ \frac{\omega_1^{(j-1)}-2\varepsilon_{21}^{(j)}-2\varepsilon_{31}^{(j)}}{2}N \end{pmatrix},$$

$$\mathcal{R}_2^{(j)} = \begin{pmatrix} \omega_2^{(j-1)}N \\ \varepsilon_{22}^{(j)}N\ ,\ \varepsilon_{22}^{(j)}N\ ,\ \varepsilon_{32}^{(j)}N\ ,\ \varepsilon_{32}^{(j)}N\ ,\ \cdot \end{pmatrix},$$

$$\mathcal{R}_3^{(j)} = \begin{pmatrix} \omega_3^{(j-1)}N \\ \varepsilon_{33}^{(j)}N\ ,\ \varepsilon_{33}^{(j)}N\ ,\ \frac{\omega_3^{(j-1)}-2\varepsilon_{33}^{(j)}}{2}N\ ,\ \frac{\omega_3^{(j-1)}-2\varepsilon_{33}^{(j)}}{2}N \end{pmatrix},$$

$$\omega_1^{(j)} = \frac{\omega_1^{(j-1)}+2\omega_2^{(j-1)}+\omega_3^{(j-1)}+2\varepsilon_{10}^{(j)}-4\varepsilon_{22}^{(j)}-2\varepsilon_{31}^{(j)}-2\varepsilon_{32}^{(j)}-2\varepsilon_{33}^{(j)}}{2},$$

$$\omega_2^{(j)} = \frac{\omega_3^{(j-1)}+2\varepsilon_{20}^{(j)}+2\varepsilon_{21}^{(j)}+2\varepsilon_{22}^{(j)}+2\varepsilon_{31}^{(j)}-2\varepsilon_{33}^{(j)}}{2},$$

$$\omega_3^{(j)} = \frac{2\varepsilon_{30}^{(j)}+2\varepsilon_{31}^{(j)}+2\varepsilon_{32}^{(j)}+2\varepsilon_{33}^{(j)}}{2},$$

$$\omega_0^{(j)} = \frac{2\omega_0^{(j-1)}+2\omega_1^{(j-1)}-4\varepsilon_{10}^{(j)}-4\varepsilon_{20}^{(j)}-4\varepsilon_{21}^{(j)}+4\varepsilon_{22}^{(j)}-4\varepsilon_{30}^{(j)}-4\varepsilon_{31}^{(j)}+4\varepsilon_{33}^{(j)}}{2}.$$

For a consistency check, verify that

$$\omega_0^{(j)} + 2\omega_1^{(j)} + 2\omega_2^{(j)} + 2\omega_3^{(j)} = \omega_0^{(j-1)} + 2\omega_1^{(j-1)} + 2\omega_2^{(j-1)} + 2\omega_3^{(j-1)}.$$

Inductively, by definition of level 0, we obtain

$$\omega_0^{(j)} + 2\omega_1^{(j)} + 2\omega_2^{(j)} + 2\omega_3^{(j)} = \omega_0^{(0)} + 2\omega_1^{(0)} + 2\omega_2^{(0)} + 2\omega_3^{(0)} = \sum_{-3}^{3} p_i = 1.$$

Optimization of parameters leads to our following main result.

Theorem 3 (main result). *Under the* MLWE Representation Heuristic *the following holds. Let* $(A, \mathbf{t}) \in \mathbb{Z}_q^{N\times N} \times \mathbb{Z}_q^N$ *be an (M)LWE instance with* $q = \Omega(N)$ *and secret keys* $\mathbf{s}, \mathbf{e} \sim \mathcal{B}(3)^N$*, where* $N = nk$ *for MLWE. Then* LWE-SEARCH *finds* $\mathbf{s}$ *(with constant probability) within time* $\mathcal{O}(2^{0.388N})$ (for REP-2)*, respectively* $\mathcal{O}(2^{0.371N})$ (for REP-3).

Proof. Analogous to the proof of Theorem 1. Optimization parameters for respective tree depths can be found in Table 8. □

7 Other Distributions – Ternary, $\mathcal{B}(2)$, and Uniform

We apply our in previous sections developed representation technique to other distributions of cryptographic interest. Throughout this section, we only focus on the best results that we achieve with REP-3 representations. Every parameter set was found by using the method described in Sect. 8.

First, we analyze ternary keys $\boldsymbol{s} \in \{-1, 0, 1\}^N$ of varying weight, as used e.g. in the cryptosystems NTRU [3,8], BLISS [11], and GLP [14]. We slightly improve over [17] for large weight keys.

Second, we study the Centered Binomial distribution $\mathcal{B}(\eta)$ for $\eta = 1, 2, 3$. Notice that $\mathcal{B}(3)^{nk}$ is used in KYBER with $nk = 512$, whereas $\mathcal{B}(2)^{nk}$ is used in KYBER with larger security parameters $nk = 768$ and $nk = 1024$.

Eventually, we study Uniform distributions in the range $[-\eta, \ldots, \eta]$ for $\eta = 1, 2, 3$. Naturally, uniformly distributed keys are widely used in cryptography, a prominent example being DILITHIUM with secret keys uniformly sampled from $\{-2, \ldots, 2\}^{nk}$, where $nk = 1024$ or $nk = 2048$.

7.1 Ternary Keys—Featuring NTRU, BLISS and GLP

We define a *weighted ternary* distribution as follows.

Definition 3. *Let* $0 \leq \omega \leq 1$. *We denote the* weighted ternary *distribution*

$$\mathcal{T}(\omega) := (p_{-1}, p_0, p_1) = \left(\tfrac{\omega}{2}, 1 - \omega, \tfrac{\omega}{2}\right).$$

Some NTRU versions [15] sample keys from the core set $\mathcal{C}(\mathcal{T}(\omega))$, see Definition 1, i.e., with fixed expected weights. Other NTRU versions [8] sample directly from $\mathcal{T}(\omega)^N$. Our new techniques also apply to the latter probabilistic versions.

Table 8. REP-2 and REP-3 complexity exponents for $\mathcal{B}(3)^N$ using LWE-SEARCH with optimized depths $d = 6$ (REP-2) and $d = 7$ (REP-3), and optimized $\varepsilon_{ik}^{(j)}$. Bold exponents indicate the dominating term.

Rep.	j	$\varepsilon_{10}^{(j)}$	$\varepsilon_{20}^{(j)}$	$\varepsilon_{21}^{(j)}$	$\varepsilon_{22}^{(j)}$	$\varepsilon_{30}^{(j)}$	$\varepsilon_{31}^{(j)}$	$\varepsilon_{32}^{(j)}$	$\varepsilon_{33}^{(j)}$	$\log \mathcal{T}^{(j)}$	$\log \mathcal{L}^{(j)}$
REP-2	0	-								$.316N$	0
	1	.075	.018	.032	.023					$.388N$	$.316N$
	2	.061	.004	.014	.019					$\mathbf{.388}N$	$.350N$
	3	.053	.001	.004	.007					$.388N$	$.366N$
	4	.028		.001	.002					$.388N$	$.382N$
	5	.007								$.388N$	$\mathbf{.388}N$
	6	-								$.382N$	$.382N$
REP-3	0	-								$.297N$	0
	1	.072	.011	.024	.020		.003	.003	.001	$.371N$	$.297N$
	2	.078	.004	.016	.015			.001	.001	$.371N$	$.316N$
	3	.070	.001	.007	.007					$\mathbf{.371}N$	$.329N$
	4	.046		.002	.002					$.371N$	$.348N$
	5	.023								$.371N$	$\mathbf{.360}N$
	6	.003								$.356N$	$.356N$
	7	-								$.316N$	$.316N$

Table 9. Ternary Key Results for different weights ω, and comparison with [17].

ω	0.3			0.375			0.441			0.5			0.62			0.667		
	d	$\log \mathcal{T}$	$\log \mathcal{M}$	d	$\log \mathcal{T}$	$\log \mathcal{M}$	d	$\log \mathcal{T}$	$\log \mathcal{M}$	d	$\log \mathcal{T}$	$\log \mathcal{M}$	d	$\log \mathcal{T}$	$\log \mathcal{M}$	d	$\log \mathcal{T}$	$\log \mathcal{M}$
[17]	4	$.295N$	$.294N$	4	$.318N$	$.316N$	4	$.334N$	$.333N$	4	$.348N$	$.346N$	4	$.371N$	$.371N$	4	$.379N$	$.379N$
Us	4	**.295N**	$.294N$	5	**.315N**	$.312N$	6	**.326N**	$.320N$	5	**.337N**	$.337N$	6	**.342N**	$.336N$	6	**.345N**	$.338N$

Our ternary key results are summarized in Table 9. More detailed optimization parameters are provided in Table 12, Appendix A. In particular, we see that for ternary keys REP-2 is sufficient, and REP-3 provides no further benefit.

Whereas [17] analyzed only depths $d \leq 4$, we obtain slightly better runtime exponents for increasing weights $\omega \geq 0.375$ in depths 5 and 6. In particular, we are interested in weights $\omega = \frac{1}{2}, \frac{2}{3}$, which denote $\mathcal{B}(1)$ and $\mathcal{U}(1)$, respectively.

7.2 $\mathcal{B}(2)$ and $\mathcal{B}(3)$—Featuring KYBER-512 and KYBER-768,1024

Our results for $\mathcal{B}(\eta)$, $\eta = 1, 2, 3$ are illustrated in Table 10. Our full optimization parameters can be found in Table 12, Appendix A.

We find it remarkable that despite a significant growth in entropy from $\mathcal{B}(1)$ with exponent $1.5N$ to $\mathcal{B}(3)$ with exponent $2.3N$, the actual key security against LWE-SEARCH with REP-3 increases only slightly with exponent $0.034N$. It appears that, in the case of Centered Binomial distributions, the number of representations grows much faster than the search space sizes. Consequently, whereas we obtain a $\sim \mathcal{S}^{\frac{1}{4}}$ algorithm for $\mathcal{B}(1)^N$, for $\mathcal{B}(3)^N$, we obtain an algorithm with approximate runtime $\mathcal{S}^{\frac{1}{6}}$, i.e., we achieve the 6th root of the search space.

7.3 Uniform Distribution—Featuring DILITHIUM-1024,2048

We define the *Uniform distribution* as follows.

Definition 4. *Let $\eta \in \mathbb{N}$. We denote by $\mathcal{U}(\eta)$ the* Uniform distribution *having for all $i = -\eta, \ldots, \eta$ constant probability $p_i = \frac{1}{2\eta+1}$.*

Notice that $\mathcal{U}(1) = \mathcal{T}(\frac{2}{3})$. Two DILITHIUM parameter sets use $\mathcal{U}(2)^{nk}$ for $nk = 1024$ and $nk = 2048$. Our $\mathcal{U}(\eta)$ results for $\eta = 1, 2, 3$ are provided in Table 10. Our optimization parameters can be found in Table 12, Appendix A.

The complexity exponent $0.378N$ for $\mathcal{U}(2)$ is of a similar size than $0.371N$ for $\mathcal{B}(3)$. But since KYBER uses significantly smaller key lengths $N = nk$ in comparison to DILITHIUM, our LWE-SEARCH algorithm can be considered much more effective for KYBER keys.

Table 10. Results for Centered Binomial distributions $\mathcal{B}(\eta)$ (left) and Uniform distribution $\mathcal{D}(\eta)$ (right) for $\eta = 1, 2, 3$.

	$\mathcal{B}(\eta)$					$\mathcal{U}(\eta)$				
η	d	$\log \mathcal{T}$	$\log \mathcal{M}$	$\log \mathcal{S}$	$\log_{\mathcal{S}} \mathcal{T}$	d	$\log \mathcal{T}$	$\log \mathcal{M}$	$\log \mathcal{S}$	$\log_{\mathcal{S}} \mathcal{T}$
1	5	**.337N**	$.337N$	$1.500N$	**.225**	6	**.345N**	$.338N$	$1.585N$	**.218**
2	7	**.357N**	$.357N$	$2.031N$	**.176**	8	**.378N**	$.372N$	$2.322N$	**.163**
3	7	**.371N**	$.360N$	$2.334N$	**.159**	6	**.493N**	$.481N$	$2.808N$	**.176**

8 Parameter Optimization and Implementation

In this section, we discuss our practical efforts, which include our parameter optimization method as well as our implementation of the algorithm. Either program can be accessed under https://github.com/timogcgn/HTELWEK/ and contains a readme with more in-depth description of its respective program.

8.1 Parameter Search

Let us first discuss our method of finding our (near)-optimal parameters.

Hill Climbing. Our goal was to find parameters which would minimize the runtime $\mathcal{T} = \max\{\mathcal{T}^{(j)}\}$, a function that is continuous but not differentiable in $\varepsilon_{ik}^{(j)}$. Therefore, applying a regular gradient descent search to find the optimal parameters is not possible. Instead, we opted to use a variant of the **Hill Climbing (HC)** method:

For some parameter set $\boldsymbol{\varepsilon} := (\varepsilon_{ik}^{(j)})$, consider the **set of** $\boldsymbol{\varepsilon}$**' neighbors**

$$\Gamma(\boldsymbol{\varepsilon}) := \{(\varepsilon_{ik}^{(j)'}) \mid \varepsilon_{ik}^{(j)'} = \varepsilon_{ik}^{(j)} \text{ or } |\varepsilon_{ik}^{(j)'} - \varepsilon_{ik}^{(j)}| = \gamma \text{ for all } ik, j\}$$

for some fixed γ, say 0.001. $\Gamma(\boldsymbol{\varepsilon})$ contains the parameter sets $\boldsymbol{\varepsilon}'$ where each singular parameter differs by either $\pm\gamma$ or not at all from their counterpart in $\boldsymbol{\varepsilon}$.

Let $\boldsymbol{\varepsilon}_0 := (0)^{8(d-1)}$. With HC, instead of trying to find the steepest descent by using the derivative of $\mathcal{T}$, we instead only look for the next best parameter set in $\Gamma(\boldsymbol{\varepsilon})$ greedily, i.e., given $\boldsymbol{\varepsilon}_i$, the next parameter set is

$$\boldsymbol{\varepsilon}_{i+1} = \arg\min_{\boldsymbol{\varepsilon}' \in \Gamma(\boldsymbol{\varepsilon}_i)} \mathcal{T}.$$

Since we only consider $\varepsilon_{ik}^{(j)}$ that are multiples of γ, this method guarantees to find a proximate local minimum after a finite amount of steps.

Partial Hill Climbing. It is easy to see that, ignoring invalid neighboring parameter sets (for example when $\varepsilon_{ik}^{(j)} < 0$), the size of $\Gamma(\boldsymbol{\varepsilon})$ is $3^{8(d-1)}$, as there are 8 parameters on a single level and every level from 1 to $d-1$ is parametrized. Even for moderate tree depths d, this is a search space that is impractical to traverse over multiple iterations, so we need a refined method that trades off runtime for result optimality, and then iterate this method multiple times.

The new idea is simple: Instead of optimizing all $8(d-1)$ parameters at once, fix, say, $(8-t)$ parameters per level and only optimize the remaining t parameters via Hill Climbing. Obviously, this implies a trade off between runtime and optimality of the resulting parameter set, where the parameters tuples considered per optimization step are now upper bounded by $3^{t(d-1)}$.

The parameters we present in Appendix A are the result of 100 iterations of this method per $t \in \{2, 3, 4\}$, i.e. 300 iterations overall (with t randomly drawn parameters per level per iteration). Additional iterations did not improve the runtime, so we assume that the parameters that we found are in close enough proximity to the optimal parameter set.

8.2 Implementation

In this section, we discuss the validity of the (M)LWE Representation Heuristic via an implementation of our algorithm. We would like to stress that our goal is not to show runtime superiority over the usual Meet-in-the-Middle algorithm (which follows from our runtime analysis), but to test our heuristic. Especially, we have to show that we obtain list sizes which do not differ too much from their expectation, which eventually guarantees that the final list contains solution with good probability.

We attack an LWE instance over $\mathcal{B}(2)$ and $N = 32, q = 3329$, a scaled-down version of KYBER. Aside from $\varepsilon_{10}^{(1)} = \frac{1}{16}$, every optimization parameter we found using our optimization tool from Sect. 8 is equal to 0. We use a search tree of depth $d = 3$. For a detailed description of each tree level, consider Table 11.

Table 11. Level description and resulting list sizes for parameters $d = 3, N = 32$, $q = 3329, \mathcal{P} = \mathcal{B}(2)$.

j	$\omega_0^{(j)}N$	$\omega_1^{(j)}N$	$\omega_2^{(j)}N$	$\mathcal{S}^{(j)}$	$\mathcal{R}^{(j)}$	$r^{(j)}$	$\mathbb{E}[\mathcal{L}^{(j)}]$	$\overline{\mathcal{L}^{(j)}}$
0	12	8	2	$\sim 8.4 \cdot 10^{16}$	1	–	1	0.65
1	16	8	0	$\sim 7.7 \cdot 10^{13}$	$\sim 1.5 \cdot 10^{8}$	2	698045.2	590153
2	24	4	0	$\sim 7.4 \cdot 10^{9}$	4900	1	221171.8	221187
3	28	2	0	215760	36	0	215760	215760

We removed the enumeration of $r^{(1)}$ coordinates of $\boldsymbol{e}$, and the permutation of $\boldsymbol{s}$ to an element from the core set $\mathcal{C}(\mathcal{B}(2))$ in our algorithm, since these procedures just affect the runtime, but not the success probability.

We let our algorithm run for 20 iterations. In 13 of those iterations, we successfully recovered the secret $\boldsymbol{s}$ from an element in $\mathcal{L}^{(0)}$. In the remaing 7 iterations $\mathcal{L}^{(0)}$ was empty.

Table 11 details the resulting average list sizes $\overline{\mathcal{L}^{(j)}}$ of these 20 iterations. Level 3 achieves its expectation, since we construct the list exhaustively, but level 2 also achieves its expectation. On level 1 we only get a $\frac{1}{7}$-fraction loss, and on level 0 we obtain a $\frac{1}{3}$-fraction loss. Therefore, we still have success probability $\frac{2}{3}$ showing that on expectation we have to run our algorithm only $\frac{3}{2}$ times, until we succeed to recover an LWE key. This implies the validity of our heuristic.

A Full Parameter Sets: Ternary, Binomial, and Uniform

Table 12. Parameter sets for Ternary distributions (left, REP-2) and Centered Binomial and Uniform distributions (right, REP-3).

$\mathcal{P}$	j	$\varepsilon_{10}^{(j)}$	$\varepsilon_{20}^{(j)}$	$\varepsilon_{21}^{(j)}$	$\varepsilon_{22}^{(j)}$	$\log \mathcal{T}^{(j)}$	$\log \mathcal{L}^{(j)}$
$\mathcal{T}(0.3)$	0	-				.239N	0
	1	.050		.001		.295N	.239N
	2	.026				**.295N**	.283N
	3	.006				.294N	**.294N**
	4	-				.288N	.288N
$\mathcal{T}(0.375)$	0	-				.251N	0
	1	.052	.001	.003		.313N	.251N
	2	.031		.001	.001	.315N	.299N
	3	.012				**.315N**	**.312N**
	4	.001				.275N	.275N
	5	-				.216N	.216N
$\mathcal{T}(0.441)$	0	-				.254N	0
	1	.056	.001	.005		.325N	.254N
	2	.042		.001	.001	**.326N**	.298N
	3	.019				.326N	**.320N**
	4	.002				.316N	.313N
	5					.220N	.220N
	6	-				.155N	.155N
$\mathcal{T}(0.5)$	0	-				.268N	0
	1	.049	.001	.009		.337N	.268N
	2	.040	.001	.002	.002	**.337N**	.311N
	3	.017		.001	.001	.337N	**.337N**
	4	.002				.333N	.333N
	5	-				.273N	.273N
$\mathcal{T}(0.62)$	0	-				.250N	0
	1	.063	.001	.011		.341N	.250N
	2	.061	.001	.003	.002	.342N	.290N
	3	.036		.001	.001	**.342N**	.324N
	4	.015				.342N	**.336N**
	5	.001				.313N	.313N
	6	-				.249N	.249N
$\mathcal{T}(0.667)$	0	-				.258N	0
	1	.056	.001	.013		**.345N**	.258N
	2	.060	.001	.004	.002	.345N	.294N
	3	.038		.001	.001	.345N	.325N
	4	.016				.345N	**.338N**
	5	.001				.321N	.321N
	6	-				.257N	.257N

$\mathcal{P}$	j	$\varepsilon_{10}^{(j)}$	$\varepsilon_{20}^{(j)}$	$\varepsilon_{21}^{(j)}$	$\varepsilon_{22}^{(j)}$	$\varepsilon_{30}^{(j)}$	$\varepsilon_{31}^{(j)}$	$\varepsilon_{32}^{(j)}$	$\varepsilon_{33}^{(j)}$	$\log \mathcal{T}^{(j)}$	$\log \mathcal{L}^{(j)}$
$\mathcal{B}(1)$	0	-								.268N	0
	1	.049	.001	.009						.337N	.268N
	2	.040	.001	.002	.002					**.337N**	.311N
	3	.017		.001	.001					.337N	**.337N**
	4	.002								.333N	.333N
	5	-								.273N	.273N
$\mathcal{B}(2)$	0	-								.264N	0
	1	.076	.007	.022	.014			.001		.357N	.264N
	2	.084	.003	.010	.009					.357N	.289N
	3	.061	.001	.004	.004					**.357N**	.315N
	4	.038		.001	.001					.357N	.340N
	5	.015								.357N	**.351N**
	6	.002								.316N	.316N
	7	-								.265N	.265N
$\mathcal{B}(3)$	0	-								.297N	0
	1	.072	.011	.024	.020		.003	.003	.001	.371N	.297N
	2	.078	.004	.016	.015			.001	.001	.371N	.316N
	3	.070	.001	.007	.007					**.371N**	.329N
	4	.046		.002	.002					.371N	.348N
	5	.023								.371N	**.360N**
	6	.003								.356N	.356N
	7	-								.316N	.316N
$\mathcal{U}(1)$	0	-								.258N	0
	1	.056	.001	.013						**.345N**	.258N
	2	.060	.001	.004	.002					.345N	.294N
	3	.038		.001	.001					.345N	.325N
	4	.016								.345N	**.338N**
	5	.001								.321N	.321N
	6	-								.257N	.257N
$\mathcal{U}(2)$	0	-								.308N	0
	1	.046	.014	.029	.040	.001	.005	.010		.377N	.308N
	2	.072	.007	.024	.020		.001	.002	.001	**.378N**	.322N
	3	.071	.003	.014	.012					.378N	.331N
	4	.051	.001	.005	.006					.378N	.351N
	5	.031		.001	.002					.375N	.370N
	6	.010								.378N	**.372N**
	7	.001								.307N	.307N
	8	-								.244N	.244N
$\mathcal{U}(3)$	0	-								.451N	0
	1	.030	.018	.025	.022	.006	.011	.013	.028	**.493N**	.451N
	2	.056	.007	.025	.027		.001	.001	.002	.492N	.475N
	3	.048	.001	.007	.012					.493N	**.481N**
	4	.023		.001	.001					.492N	.476N
	5	.004								.449N	.449N
	6	-								.423N	.423N

References

1. Becker, A., Coron, J.-S., Joux, A.: Improved generic algorithms for hard knapsacks. In: Paterson, K.G. (ed.) EUROCRYPT 2011. LNCS, vol. 6632, pp. 364–385. Springer, Heidelberg (2011). https://doi.org/10.1007/978-3-642-20465-4_21
2. Becker, A., Joux, A., May, A., Meurer, A.: Decoding random binary linear codes in $2^{n/20}$: how $1 + 1 = 0$ improves information set decoding. In: Pointcheval, D., Johansson, T. (eds.) EUROCRYPT 2012. LNCS, vol. 7237, pp. 520–536. Springer, Heidelberg (2012). https://doi.org/10.1007/978-3-642-29011-4_31
3. Bernstein, D.J., Chuengsatiansup, C., Lange, T., van Vredendaal, C.: NTRU prime: round 2 specification (2019)
4. Bonnetain, X., Bricout, R., Schrottenloher, A., Shen, Y.: Improved classical and quantum algorithms for subset-sum. In: Moriai, S., Wang, H. (eds.) ASIACRYPT 2020. LNCS, vol. 12492, pp. 633–666. Springer, Cham (2020). https://doi.org/10.1007/978-3-030-64834-3_22

5. Bos, J., et al.: Crystals-kyber: a CCA-secure module-lattice-based KEM. In: 2018 IEEE European Symposium on Security and Privacy (EuroS&P), pp. 353–367. IEEE (2018)
6. Brakerski, Z., Gentry, C., Vaikuntanathan, V.: (leveled) fully homomorphic encryption without bootstrapping. ACM Trans. Comput. Theory (TOCT) **6**(3), 1–36 (2014)
7. Brakerski, Z., Vaikuntanathan, V.: Efficient fully homomorphic encryption from (standard) LWE. SIAM J. Comput. **43**(2), 831–871 (2014)
8. Chen, C., et al.: NTRU algorithm specifications and supporting documentation. Brown University and Onboard security company, Wilmington, USA (2019)
9. D'Anvers, J.-P., Karmakar, A., Sinha Roy, S., Vercauteren, F.: Saber: module-LWR based key exchange, CPA-secure encryption and CCA-secure KEM. In: Joux, A., Nitaj, A., Rachidi, T. (eds.) AFRICACRYPT 2018. LNCS, vol. 10831, pp. 282–305. Springer, Cham (2018). https://doi.org/10.1007/978-3-319-89339-6_16
10. Devadas, S., Ren, L., Xiao, H.: On iterative collision search for LPN and subset sum. In: Kalai, Y., Reyzin, L. (eds.) TCC 2017. LNCS, vol. 10678, pp. 729–746. Springer, Cham (2017). https://doi.org/10.1007/978-3-319-70503-3_24
11. Ducas, L., Durmus, A., Lepoint, T., Lyubashevsky, V.: Lattice signatures and bimodal gaussians. In: Canetti, R., Garay, J.A. (eds.) CRYPTO 2013. LNCS, vol. 8042, pp. 40–56. Springer, Heidelberg (2013). https://doi.org/10.1007/978-3-642-40041-4_3
12. Esser, A., May, A., Verbel, J., Wen, W.: Partial key exposure attacks on bike, rainbow and NTRU. In: Dodis, Y., Shrimpton, T. (eds.) CRYPTO 2022. Lncs, vol. 13509, pp. 346–375. Springer, Cham (2022). https://doi.org/10.1007/978-3-031-15982-4_12
13. Esser, A., May, A., Zweydinger, F.: McEliece needs a break - solving McEliece-1284 and quasi-cyclic-2918 with modern ISD. In: Dunkelman, O., Dziembowski, S. (eds.) EUROCRYPT 2022. LNCS, vol. 13277, pp. 433–457. Springer, Cham (2022). https://doi.org/10.1007/978-3-031-07082-2_16
14. Güneysu, T., Lyubashevsky, V., Pöppelmann, T.: Practical lattice-based cryptography: a signature scheme for embedded systems. In: Prouff, E., Schaumont, P. (eds.) CHES 2012. LNCS, vol. 7428, pp. 530–547. Springer, Heidelberg (2012). https://doi.org/10.1007/978-3-642-33027-8_31
15. Hoffstein, J., Pipher, J., Silverman, J.H.: NTRU: a ring-based public key cryptosystem. In: Buhler, J.P. (ed.) ANTS 1998. LNCS, vol. 1423, pp. 267–288. Springer, Heidelberg (1998). https://doi.org/10.1007/BFb0054868
16. Howgrave-Graham, N., Joux, A.: New generic algorithms for hard knapsacks. In: Gilbert, H. (ed.) EUROCRYPT 2010. LNCS, vol. 6110, pp. 235–256. Springer, Heidelberg (2010). https://doi.org/10.1007/978-3-642-13190-5_12
17. May, A.: How to meet ternary LWE keys. In: Malkin, T., Peikert, C. (eds.) CRYPTO 2021, Part II. LNCS, vol. 12826, pp. 701–731. Springer, Cham (2021). https://doi.org/10.1007/978-3-030-84245-1_24
18. May, A., Meurer, A., Thomae, E.: Decoding random linear codes in $\tilde{\mathcal{O}}(2^{0.054n})$. In: Lee, D.H., Wang, X. (eds.) ASIACRYPT 2011. LNCS, vol. 7073, pp. 107–124. Springer, Heidelberg (2011). https://doi.org/10.1007/978-3-642-25385-0_6
19. Mitzenmacher, M., Upfal, E.: Probability and Computing: Randomization and Probabilistic Techniques in Algorithms and Data Analysis. Cambridge University Press, Cambridge (2017)

20. Regev, O.: On lattices, learning with errors, random linear codes, and cryptography. In: Proceedings of the Thirty-Seventh Annual ACM Symposium on Theory of Computing, STOC 2005, pp. 84–93. Association for Computing Machinery, New York (2005). https://doi.org/10.1145/1060590.1060603
21. Silverman, J.H., Odlyzko, A.: A meet-in-the-middle attack on an NTRU private key. Preprint (1997)
22. Waterhouse, W.C.: How often do determinants over finite fields vanish? Discret. Math. **65**(1), 103–104 (1987). https://doi.org/10.1016/0012-365X(87)90217-2

Towards Minimizing Non-linearity in Type-II Generalized Feistel Networks

Yuqing Zhao[1,2], Chun Guo[1,2,3(✉)], and Weijia Wang[1,2,4]

[1] School of Cyber Science and Technology, Shandong University, Qingdao, Shandong, China
yqzhao@mail.sdu.edu.cn, {chun.guo,wjwang}@sdu.edu.cn
[2] Key Laboratory of Cryptologic Technology and Information Security of Ministry of Education, Shandong University, Qingdao 266237, Shandong, China
[3] Shandong Research Institute of Industrial Technology, Jinan 250102, Shandong, China
[4] Quan Cheng Laboratory, Jinan 250103, Shandong, China

Abstract. Recent works have revisited blockcipher structures to achieve MPC- and ZKP-friendly designs. In particular, Albrecht et al. (EUROCRYPT 2015) first pioneered using a novel structure *SP networks with partial non-linear layers (*P-SPNs*)* and then (ESORICS 2019) repopularized using *multi-line generalized Feistel networks (GFNs)*. In this paper, we persist in exploring symmetric cryptographic constructions that are conducive to the applications such as MPC. In order to study the minimization of non-linearity in Type-II Generalized Feistel Networks, we generalize the (extended) GFN by replacing the bit-wise shuffle in a GFN with the stronger linear layer in P-SPN and introducing the key in each round. We call this scheme Generalized Extended Generalized Feistel Network (GEGFN). When the block-functions (or S-boxes) are public random permutations or (domain-preserving) functions, we prove CCA security for the 5-round GEGFN. Our results also hold when the block-functions are over the prime fields $\mathbb{F}_p$, yielding blockcipher constructions over $(\mathbb{F}_p)^*$.

Keywords: blockciphers · Generalized Feistel networks · substitution-permutation networks · provable security · prime fields

1 Introduction

The Feistel network has become one of the main flavors of blockciphers. A classical Feistel network, as shown in Fig. 1(a), proceeds with iterating a Feistel permutation $\Psi^F(A,B) := (B, A \oplus F(B))$, where F is a domain-preserving block-function. The generalized Feistel network (GFN) is a generalized form of the classical Feistel network. A popular version of GFN, called Type-II, show in Fig. 1(b), in which a single round uses a block-function F to map an input $(m_1, m_1, ..., m_w)$ to $(c_1, c_2, ..., c_w) = (m_2, m_3 \oplus F(m_4), m_4, m_5 \oplus$

J. Deng et al. (Eds.): CANS 2023, LNCS 14342, pp. 101–125, 2023.
https://doi.org/10.1007/978-981-99-7563-1_5

$F(m_6), ..., m_w, m_1 \oplus F(m_2))$. As we can see, this operation is equivalent to applying Feistel permutation for every two blocks and then performing a (left) cyclic shift of sub-blocks.

Type-II GFNs have many desirable features for implementation. In particular, they are *inverse-free*, i.e., they allow constructing invertible blockciphers from non-invertible block-functions with small domains. This reduces the implementation cost of deciphering and has attracted attention. A drawback, however, is the slow diffusion (when w is large), and security can only be ensured with many rounds [23,33,35]. To remedy this, a series of works [5,7,10,32] investigated replacing the block-wise cyclic shift with more sophisticated (though linear) permutations. These studies build secure GFN ciphers having fewer rounds than Type-II, while simultaneously ensuring simplicity of structure and without increasing the implementation cost as much as possible. Thus, a common feature of linear permutations is block-wise operations.

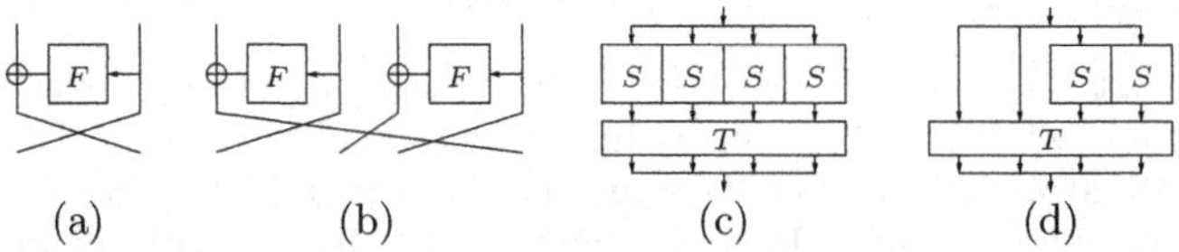

Fig. 1. Different blockcipher structures. (a) Feistel network; (b) multi-line generalized Feistel, with 4 chunks; (c) the classical SPN; (d) partial SPN.

Motivated by new applications such as secure Multi-Party Computation (MPC), Fully Homomorphic Encryption (FHE), and Zero-Knowledge proofs (ZKP), the need for symmetric encryption schemes that minimize non-linear operations in their natural algorithmic description is apparent. This can be primarily attributed to the comparatively lower cost of linear operations compared to non-linear operations.

In recent years, many works have been devoted to the research of construction strategies for symmetric cryptographic structures that are advantageous for applications such as secure MPC. Initiated by Zorro [14] and popularized by LowMC [2], a number of blockcipher designs followed an SPN variant depicted in Fig. 1(d). This structure was named *SP network with partial non-linear layers* [4] or *partial SPN* (P-SPN). Guo et al. [19] establish strong pseudorandom security for different instances of partial SPNs using MDS linear layers. The recent HADES design [16,18] combines the classical SPN (shown in Fig. 1(c)) with the P-SPN, where a middle layer that consists of P-SPN rounds is surrounded by outer layers of SPN rounds. Albrecht et al. [1] study approaches to generalized Feistel constructions with low-degree round functions and introduce a new variant of the generalized Feistel networks, which is called "Multi-Rotating Feistel network" that provides extremely fast diffusion.

Our Results. In this work, we continue the exploration of construction strategies for constructions for symmetric cryptography, which benefits applications such as MPC. Particular emphasis is placed on the investigation of the Type-II GFNs. By the nature of the problem, we are interested in two different metrics. One metric refers to what is commonly called multiplicative complexity (MC), and the other metric refers to the multiplicative depth (AND Depth). Our aim is to minimize both of these metrics as much as possible.

Due to the use of stronger diffusion layers, SPNs and P-SPNs enjoy much better diffusion than Type-II GFNs. This is also indicated by provable CCA security results: the best Type-II GFN variant [5] needs 10 rounds and $5w$ block-function applications, while the SPN, resp. P-SPN, requires only 3 rounds, resp. 5 rounds, and $3w$, resp. $5w/2$, block-function applications. It is thus natural to ask if the non-linear operations can reduce by leveraging the relatively cheaper linear operations, such as strong diffusion layers in SPNs and P-SPNs.

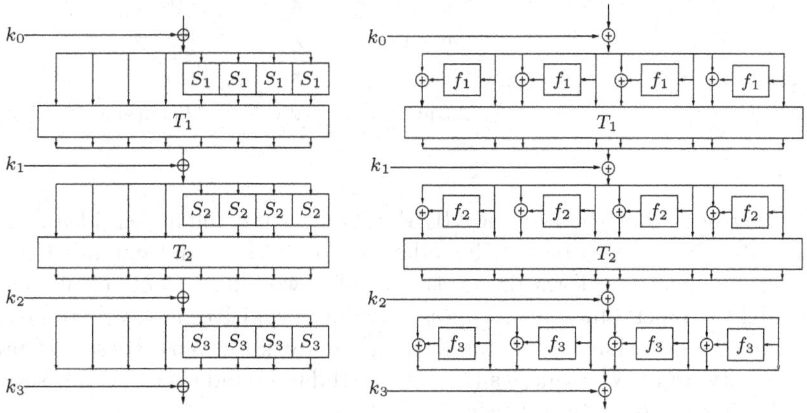

Fig. 2. Partial SPNs (with rate 1/2) and GEGFNs, with $w = 8$.

Regarding the above question, a natural idea is to "inject" the (strong) diffusion layers of SPNs/P-SPNs into Type-II GFNs, as shown in Fig. 2 (right). This model further generalizes the (extended) GFN by replacing the linear layer and permutation layer in [5] with strong diffusion layers in SPNs and P-SPNs, and introducing the key in each round. We call this scheme Generalized Extended Generalized Feistel Networks (GEGFNs).

From an alternative perspective, GEGFN is very similar to the so-called *rate-1/2 partial Substitution-Permutation Networks (*P-SPNs*)*, as shown in Fig. 2 (left). We can also get our construction by replacing the non-linear layer of P-SPN with the non-linear layer of Type-II GFN. GEGFN allows enjoying "the best of the two worlds"– the stronger diffusion provided by the P-SPN construction, along with the inverse-free of the Type-II GFN construction.

To provide a theoretical justification, we investigate the CCA security of GEGFNs. Noting that a number of recent MPC- and ZKP-friendly blockciphers operate on the prime field $\mathbb{F}_p$ [3,17], we consider general block-functions $f_i : \mathbb{F}_N \rightarrow \mathbb{F}_N$ with N equals 2^n or some prime p and addition $\bigoplus$ over $\mathbb{F}_N$ instead of the typical XOR action $\oplus$ (as indicated in Fig. 2 right).

Table 1. Comparison to existing wide SPRP structures. The *Rounds* column presents the number of rounds sufficient for birthday-bound security, where $\lambda(w) = \lceil \log_2 1.44w \rceil$. For Type-II GFN (i.e., GFNs with $w/2$ block-functions per round, see Fig. 1(b)), note that $2\lambda(w) = 2\lceil \log_2 1.44w \rceil \geq 6$ when $w \geq 4$. *Depth* stands for *AND Depth* and *Inv-free* means *Inverse-free.* Parameters in the *MC* and *AND Depth* columns are relative w.r.t. the S-box. The mode XLS [31] is excluded due to attacks [28,29]. Tweakable blockcipher-based modes [6,26,27] are also excluded due to incomparability.

Structure	Rounds	MC	Depth	Inv-free?	Reference
Optimal Type-II GFN	$2\lambda(w)$	$w\lambda(w)$	$2\lambda(w)$	✓	[10,32]
Extended GFN	10	$5w$	10	✓	[5]
Linear SPN	3	$3w$	3	✗	[11]
HADES	4	$3w$	4	✗	[13]
CMC	-	$2w$	$2w$	✗	[21]
EME & EME*	-	$2w+1$	3	✗	[20,22]
Rate 1/2 P-SPN	5	$2.5w$	5	✗	[19]
GEGFN	**5**	$\mathbf{2.5w}$	**5**	✓	Theorems 1 and 2

We first note that the 3-round GEGFN is insecure: the attack idea against 3-round P-SPN [19] can be (easily) adapted to GEGFN and extended to the more general field $\mathbb{F}_N$. Towards positive results, we follow Dodis et al. [11,12] and model the block-functions as public, random primitives available to all parties, while the diffusion layer T as linear permutations. With these, we prove CCA security up to $N^{1/2}$ queries (i.e., the birthday bound over $\mathbb{F}_N$) for 5-round GEGFNs, in two concrete settings:

(i) The block-functions are *random permutations* over $\mathbb{F}_N$;
(ii) The block-functions are *random functions* from $\mathbb{F}_N$ to $\mathbb{F}_N$.

In both cases, the linear layer T shall satisfy a certain property similar to [19] (generalized to the setting of $\mathbb{F}_N$), which is slightly stronger than an MDS transformation. To show the existence of such linear permutations, we exhibit examples in Appendix C.

Discussion. Being compatible with non-bijective block-functions is valuable for MPC-friendly ciphers. For example, as commented by Grassi et al. [15], if constructions incompatible with non-bijective block-functions (e.g., SPNs) are used then designers have to adopt functions of degree at least 3 over $\mathbb{F}_p$. They eventually resorted to a variant of Type-III GFNs. This work provides another choice.

On the other hand, while (GE) GFNs allow using non-bijective block-functions, our treatments include random permutation-based GEGFNs to justify using bijective block-functions. In fact, practical GFN blockciphers such as LBlock [34], Twine insist on using bijections, probably due to the difficulty in designing good non-bijective block-functions. Though, for certain bijections such as the power function $x \mapsto x^3$, $x \in \mathbb{F}_p$, designers are reluctant to use their inefficient inverse in deciphering. These motivated using inverse-free constructions, including blockcipher structures and protocols, and permutation-based GEGFNs may offer solutions.

As shown in Table 1, GEGFNs do enjoy fast diffusion, which is comparable with P-SPNs. In addition, in the CCA setting, its non-linearity cost is comparable with P-SPNs. This means it can be a promising candidate structure for blockciphers with low multiplicative complexities. In this respect, its inverse-freeness increases flexibility by allowing for more choices of S-boxes. On the other hand, the linear layer of GEGFNs is much more costly than the "ordinary" GFNs [7,10,32] (including the "extended" GFN [5]). Therefore, GEGFNs are better used in settings where non-linear operations are much more costly than linear ones (e.g., the MPC setting).

Lastly, as in similar works [5,9,12,19,24,32,35], provable security is limited by the domain of the block-functions and becomes meaningless when the block-functions are small S-boxes. E.g., the block-function in Twine is a 4-bit S-box, and our bounds indicate security up to 2^2 queries. Though, blockcipher structures are typically accomplished by such small-box provable security justification, and we refer to [5,24,32,35] as examples. Meanwhile, recent blockciphers such as the Rescue [3] also used large block-functions $f : \mathbb{F}_N \rightarrow \mathbb{F}_N$, $N \approx 2^{252}$, on which the provable result may shed more light.

Organization. Section 2 presents notations, definitions and tools. Then, we describe the attack against 3-round GEGFNs in Sect. 3. In Sect. 4 and Sect. 5, we prove SPRP security for 5-round GEGFNs with random permutations and functions, respectively. We finally conclude in Sect. 6.

2 Preliminaries

$(\mathbb{F}_N, +, \cdot) \equiv (\mathrm{GF}(N), +, \cdot)$, where N is either a power of 2 or a prime number and where $+$ and $\cdot$ are resp. the addition and the multiplication in GF(N). We view N as a cryptographic security parameter. For any positive integer w, we consider a string consisting of w field elements in $\mathbb{F}_N$, which is also viewed as a *column vector* in $\mathbb{F}_N^w$, where w is also called *width*. Indeed, strings and column vectors are just two sides of the same coin. Let x be a *column vector* in $\mathbb{F}_N^w$, then x^T is a row vector obtained by transposing x. Throughout the remaining, depending on the context, the same notation, e.g., x, may refer to both a string and a column vector, without additional highlight. In the same vein, the concatenation $x\|y$ is also "semantically equivalent" to the column vector $\binom{x}{y}$.

In this respect, for $x \in \mathbb{F}_N^w$, we denote the j-th entry of x (for $j \in \{1, ..., w\}$) by $x[j]$ and define $x[a..b] := (x[a], ..., x[b])$ for any integers $1 \leq a < b \leq w$. Let's assume that w is an even number. We define $x[\mathsf{even}] := (x[2], x[4], \ldots, x[w])$ and $x[\mathsf{odd}] := (x[1], x[3], \ldots, x[w-1])$. For $x, y \in \mathbb{F}_N^w$, we denote the difference of x and y by

$$(x[1] - y[1])\|(x[2] - y[2])\|...\|(x[w] - y[w]),$$

where $-$ represents $\oplus$ when N is a power of 2 and represents $\big((x[i] - y[i]) \bmod N\big)$ when N is a prime number.

The zero entry of $\mathbb{F}_N$ is denoted by $\mathsf{0}$ and we write $\mathsf{0}^w$ for the all-zero vector in $\mathbb{F}_N^w$. We write $\mathcal{P}(w)$ for the set of permutations of $\mathbb{F}_N^w$ and $\mathcal{F}(w)$ for the set of functions of $\mathbb{F}_N^w$.

Let T be a matrix. We denote by T_{OE} the submatrix composed of odd rows and even columns of matrix T, by T_{OO} the submatrix composed of odd rows and odd columns of matrix T, by T_{EE} the submatrix composed of even rows and even columns of matrix T, and by T_{EO} the submatrix composed of even rows and odd columns of matrix T.

Given a function $f : \mathbb{F}_N \to \mathbb{F}_N$, for any positive integer m and any vector $x \in \mathbb{F}_N^m$, we define $\overline{f}(x) := \big(f(x[1]), ..., f(x[m])\big)$. For integers $1 \le b \le a$, we write $(a)_b := a(a-1)...(a-b+1)$ and $(a)_0 := 1$ by convention.

MDS Matrix. For any (column) vector $x \in \mathbb{F}_N^w$, the *Hamming weight* of x is defined as the number of non-zero entries of x, i.e.,

$$\mathsf{wt}(x) := \big|\{i|x[i] \neq \mathsf{0}, i = 1, \ldots, w\}\big|.$$

Let T be a $w \times w$ matrix over $\mathbb{F}_N$. The *branch number* of T is the minimum number of non-zero components in the input vector x and output vector $u = T \cdot x$ as we search all non-zero $x \in \mathbb{F}_N^w$, i.e., the *branch number* of $w \times w$ matrix T is $\min_{x \in \mathbb{F}_N^w, x \neq 0}\{\mathsf{wt}(x) + \mathsf{wt}(T \cdot x)\}$. A matrix $T \in \mathbb{F}_N^{w \times w}$ reaching $w+1$, the upper bound on such branch numbers, is called *Maximum Distance Separable* (MDS). MDS matrices have been widely used in modern blockciphers, including the AES, since the ensured lower bounds on weights typically transform into bounds on the number of active S-boxes.

GEGFNs. When we replace the linear layer of Type-II GFN with the linear layer of P-SPN and introduce the key in each round, we get our construction $\mathcal{C}\lambda_{\mathbf{k}}^{\mathbf{f}}$ (shown in Fig. 2 (right)) that is defined by linear permutations $\{T_i \in \mathbb{F}_N^{w \times w}\}_{i=1}^{\lambda-1}$ and a distribution $\mathcal{K}$ over $K_0 \times \ldots \times K_\lambda$ and that take *oracle* access to λ public, random functions $\mathbf{f} = \{f_i : \mathbb{F}_N \to \mathbb{F}_N\}_{i=1}^{\lambda}$, where $\mathbf{k} = (k_0, \ldots, k_\lambda)$ and λ is the number of rounds. Given input $x \in \mathbb{F}_N^w$, the output of the GEGFN is computed as follows:

- Let $u_1 := k_0 + x$.
- for $i = 1, \ldots, \lambda - 1$ do:
  1. $v_i := \mathsf{PGF}^{f_i}(u_i)$, where
     $\mathsf{PGF}^{f_i}(u_i) = \big(u_i[1] + f_i(u_i[2])\big)\|u_i[2]\|\ldots\|\big(u_i[w-1] + f_i(u_i[w])\big)\|u_i[w]$.
  2. $u_{i+1} = k_i + T_i \cdot v_i$.
- $v_\lambda := \mathsf{PGF}^{f_\lambda}(u_\lambda)$.
- $u_{\lambda+1} = k_\lambda + v_\lambda$.
- Outputs $u_{\lambda+1}$.

SPRP Security of GEGFNs. Following [11], we consider GEGFN construction and analyze the security of the construction against unbounded-time attackers making a bounded number of queries to the construction and to $\mathbf{f}$. Formally, we consider the ability of an adversary D to distinguish two worlds: the "real world", in which it is given oracle access to $\mathbf{f}$ and $\mathcal{C}\lambda_{\mathbf{k}}^{\mathbf{f}}$ (for unknown keys $\mathbf{k}$ sampled according to $\mathcal{K}$), and an "ideal world" in which it has access to $\mathbf{f}$ and a random permutation $P : \mathbb{F}_N^w \to \mathbb{F}_N^w$. We allow D to make forward and inverse queries to $\mathcal{C}\lambda_{\mathbf{k}}^{\mathbf{f}}$ or P, and we always allow D to make forward queries to random functions $\mathbf{f} = \{f_1, ..., f_\lambda\}$. However, whether D makes inverse queries to $\mathbf{f}$ depends on whether $\mathbf{f}$ are random permutations. With these, for a distinguisher D, we define its *strong-PRP advantage* against the construction $\mathcal{C}\lambda_{\mathbf{k}}^{\mathbf{f}}$ as

$$\mathsf{Adv}^{\mathsf{sprp}}_{\mathcal{C}\lambda_{\mathbf{k}}^{\mathbf{f}}}(D) := \left| \Pr\left[\mathbf{k} \xleftarrow{\$} \mathcal{K} : D^{\mathcal{C}\lambda_{\mathbf{k}}^{\mathbf{f}}, \mathbf{f}} = 1\right] - \Pr\left[P \xleftarrow{\$} \mathcal{P}(w) : D^{P, \mathbf{f}} = 1\right] \right|,$$

where $\mathbf{f} = (f_1, \ldots, f_\lambda)$ are λ independent, uniform functions on $\mathbb{F}_N$. The *strong-PRP (SPRP) security* of $\mathcal{C}\lambda_{\mathbf{k}}^{\mathbf{f}}$ is

$$\mathsf{Adv}^{\mathsf{sprp}}_{\mathcal{C}\lambda_{\mathbf{k}}^{\mathbf{f}}}(q_C, q_f) := \max_D \left\{\mathsf{Adv}^{\mathsf{sprp}}_{\mathcal{C}\lambda_{\mathbf{k}}^{\mathbf{f}}}(D)\right\},$$

where the maximum is taken over all distinguishers that make most q_C queries to their left oracle and q_f queries to their right oracles.

A Useful Operator on the Linear Layer. We will frequently write $M \in \mathbb{F}_N^{w \times w}$ in the block form of 4 submatrices in $\mathbb{F}_N^{w/2 \times w/2}$. For this, we follow the convention using U, B, L, R for *upper*, *bottom*, *left*, and *right* resp., i.e.,

$$M = \begin{pmatrix} M_{\mathrm{UL}} & M_{\mathrm{UR}} \\ M_{\mathrm{BL}} & M_{\mathrm{BR}} \end{pmatrix}.$$

We use brackets, i.e., $(M^{-1})_{\mathrm{XX}}$, $\mathrm{XX} \in \{\mathrm{UL}, \mathrm{UR}, \mathrm{BL}, \mathrm{BR}\}$, to distinguish submatrices of M^{-1} (the inverse of M) from M_{XX}^{-1}, the inverse of M_{XX}.

As per our convention, we view $u, v \in \mathbb{F}_N^w$ as column vectors. During the proof, we will need to derive the "second halves" $u_2 := u[w/2+1..w]$ and $v_2 := v[w/2+1..w]$ from the "first halves" $u_1 := u[1..w/2], v_1 := v[1..w/2]$, and the equality $v = T \cdot u$. To this end, we follow [19] and define an operator on T:

$$\widehat{T} := \begin{pmatrix} -T_{\mathrm{UR}}^{-1} \cdot T_{\mathrm{UL}} & T_{\mathrm{UR}}^{-1} \\ T_{\mathrm{BL}} - T_{\mathrm{BR}} \cdot T_{\mathrm{UR}}^{-1} \cdot T_{\mathrm{UL}} & T_{\mathrm{BR}} \cdot T_{\mathrm{UR}}^{-1} \end{pmatrix}, \tag{1}$$

which satisfies

$$v = T \cdot u \Leftrightarrow \begin{pmatrix} u_2 \\ v_2 \end{pmatrix} = \widehat{T} \cdot \begin{pmatrix} u_1 \\ v_1 \end{pmatrix}.$$

3 A Chosen-Plaintext Attack on 3 Rounds

Guo et al. [19] showed a chosen-plaintext attack on 3-round P-SPN. We adapt that idea to our context.[1] Concretely, let $\mathcal{C}3_{\mathbf{k}}^{\mathbf{f}}$ be the 3-round GEGFN using any invertible linear transformations T_1, T_2. I.e.,

[1] We followed the attack idea in [19]. However, due to the difference between our construction and the P-SPN in the round function, the collision-inducing positions considered in our attack are distinct.

$$C3_{\mathbf{k}}^{\mathbf{f}}(x) := k_3 + \mathsf{PGF}^{f_3}(k_2 + T_2 \cdot (\mathsf{PGF}^{f_2}(k_1 + T_1 \cdot (\mathsf{PGF}^{f_1}(k_0 + x))))).$$

We show a chosen-plaintext attacker D, given access to an oracle $\mathcal{O} : \mathbb{F}_N^w \to \mathbb{F}_N^w$, that distinguishes whether $\mathcal{O}$ is an instance of $C3_{\mathbf{k}}^{\mathbf{f}}$ using uniform keys or a random permutation. The attacker D proceeds as follows:

1. Fix $\delta \in \mathbb{F}_N \backslash \{0\}$ in arbitrary, let $\Delta_3 = \delta \| 0^{w/2-1}$, and compute two differences $\Delta_1 := (T_1)_{\text{EO}}^{-1} \cdot \Delta_3$ and $\Delta_2 := (T_1)_{\text{OO}} \cdot \Delta_1$. Note that this means
$$\Big(T_1 \cdot (\Delta_1[1] \| 0 \| \Delta_1[2] \| 0 \| \ldots \| \Delta_1[w/2] \| 0)\Big)[\mathsf{odd}] = \Delta_2,$$
$$\Big(T_1 \cdot (\Delta_1[1] \| 0 \| \Delta_1[2] \| 0 \| \ldots \| \Delta_1[w/2] \| 0)\Big)[\mathsf{even}] = \Delta_3.$$
2. For all $\delta^* \in \mathbb{F}_N$ (we note that if f_2 is permutation, we have $\delta^* \in \mathbb{F}_N \backslash \{0\}$), compute
$$\begin{aligned}\Delta^* :&= T_2 \cdot (\Delta_2[1] \oplus \delta^* \| \Delta_3[1] \| \Delta_2[2] \| \Delta_3[2] \| \ldots \| \Delta_2[w/2] \| \Delta_3[w/2]) \\ &= T_2 \cdot (\Delta_2[1] \oplus \delta^* \| \delta \| \Delta_2[2] \| 0 \| \ldots \| \Delta_2[w/2] \| 0),\end{aligned}$$
and add $\Delta^*[\mathsf{even}]$ into a set Set.[2]
3. Choose inputs x, x' such that $(x - x')[\mathsf{odd}] = \Delta_1$ and $(x - x')[\mathsf{even}] = 0^{w/2}$, query $\mathcal{O}(x)$ and $\mathcal{O}(x')$ to obtain y and y' respectively, and compute the output difference $\Delta_4 := y - y'$.
4. If $\Delta_4[\mathsf{even}] \in \mathsf{Set}$ then output 1; otherwise, output 0.

It is not hard to see that if $\mathcal{O}$ is a w width random permutation then D outputs 1 with probability $O(N/N^{w/2})$. On the other hand, we claim that when $\mathcal{O}$ is an instance of the 3-round GEGFN then D always outputs 1.

For this, consider the propagation of the input difference Δ_1^*, where $\Delta_1^*[\mathsf{odd}] = \Delta_1$ and $\Delta_1^*[\mathsf{even}] = 0^{w/2}$. By step 1, the 2nd round input difference must be Δ_2^*, where $\Delta_2^*[\mathsf{odd}] = \Delta_2$ and $\Delta_2^*[\mathsf{even}] = \Delta_3$. Since $\Delta_3 = \delta \| 0^{w/2-1}$, the output difference of the 2nd function $\overline{f}(\Delta_3)$ action must be in the set $\{\delta^* \| 0^{w/2-1}\}_{\delta^* \in \mathbb{F}_N}$ of size at most N. This means the 3rd round input difference, denoted Δ_3^*, must be in a set of size N. Since the 3rd round PGF^{f_3} action does not affect $\Delta_3^*[\mathsf{even}]$, it can be seen $\Delta_4[\mathsf{even}]$, is also in a set of size N. Furthermore, this set *is* the set Set derived in step 2. This completes the analysis.

4 SPRP Security at 5 Rounds with Public Permutations

We will prove security for 5-round GEGFNs built upon 5 "S-boxes"/random permutations $\mathcal{S} = \{S_1, S_2, S_3, S_4, S_5\}$ and a *single linear layer* T. Formally,

$$\begin{aligned}C5_{\mathbf{k}}^{\mathcal{S}}(x) := k_5 + \mathsf{PGF}^{S_5}(k_4 + T \cdot (\mathsf{PGF}^{S_4}(k_3 + T \cdot (\mathsf{PGF}^{S_3}(k_2 + T \cdot (\mathsf{PGF}^{S_2}(\\ k_1 + T \cdot (\mathsf{PGF}^{S_1}(k_0 + x))))))))).\end{aligned} \quad (2)$$

[2] Here we consider the information-theoretic setting, with no limit on the time complexity. In practice, N is usually small, especially in the binary fields, and this enumeration remains feasible.

Using a single linear layer simplifies the construction. Recall from our convention that $T_{\mathrm{OE}}, \ldots, (T^{-1})_{\mathrm{EE}}$ constitute the eight submatrices of T and T^{-1}. In fact, $(T^{-1})_{\mathrm{OE}}, \ldots, (T^{-1})_{\mathrm{EE}}$ can be derived from $T_{\mathrm{OE}}, \ldots, T_{\mathrm{EE}}$, but the expressions are too complicated to use.

We next characterize the properties on T that are sufficient for security.

Definition 1 (Good Linear Layer for 5 Rounds with Permutations). *A matrix $T \in \mathbb{F}_N^{w \times w}$ is good if T is MDS, and the 6 induced matrices T_{EO}, $-T_{\mathrm{EO}}^{-1} \cdot T_{\mathrm{EE}} \cdot T_{\mathrm{EO}} - T_{\mathrm{OO}}$, $(T_{\mathrm{OE}} - T_{\mathrm{OO}} \cdot T_{\mathrm{EO}}^{-1} \cdot T_{\mathrm{EE}}) \cdot T_{\mathrm{EO}}$, $(T^{-1})_{\mathrm{EO}}$, $(T^{-1})_{\mathrm{OO}} - T_{\mathrm{OO}} \cdot T_{\mathrm{EO}}^{-1} \cdot (T^{-1})_{\mathrm{EO}}$, and $T_{\mathrm{EO}}^{-1} \cdot (T^{-1})_{\mathrm{EO}}$ are such that:*

1. *They contain no zero entries, and*
2. *Any column vector of the 6 induced matrices consists of $w/2$ distinct entries.*

We remark that, as T is MDS, all the four matrices $T_{\mathrm{OE}}, T_{\mathrm{OO}}, T_{\mathrm{EO}}$ and T_{EE} are all MDS (and invertible). A natural question is whether such a strong T exists at all. For this, we give several MDS matrices in Appendix C that follow our definition.

With such a good T, we have the following theorem on 5-round GEGFNs with public random permutations.

Theorem 1. *Assume $w \geq 2$, and $q_S + wq_C/2 \leq N/2$. Let $\mathcal{C}5_{\mathbf{k}}^{\mathcal{S}}$ be a 5-round, linear GEGFN structure defined in Eq. (2), with distribution $\mathcal{K}$ over keys $\mathbf{k} = (k_0, \ldots, k_5)$. If k_0 and k_5 are uniformly distributed and the matrix T fulfills Definition 1, then*

$$\mathsf{Adv}_{\mathcal{C}5_{\mathbf{k}}^{\mathcal{S}}}^{\mathsf{sprp}}(q_C, q_S) \leq \frac{12wq_Cq_S + 7w^2q_C^2}{2N} + \frac{2q_C^2}{N^{w/2}}. \quad (3)$$

All the remaining of this section devotes to proving Theorem 1. We employ Patarin's H-coefficient method [30], which we recall in Appendix A. Following the paradigm of H-coefficient, we first establish notations in the Sect. 4.1. We then complete the two steps of *defining and analyzing bad transcripts* and *bounding the ratio $\mu(\tau)/\nu(\tau)$ for good transcripts* in Sect. 4.2 and 4.3 resp.

4.1 Proof Setup

Fix a deterministic distinguisher D. Wlog assume D makes exactly q_C (non-redundant) forward/inverse queries to its left oracle that is either $\mathcal{C}5_{\mathbf{k}}^{\mathcal{S}}$ or P, and exactly q_S (non-redundant) forward/inverse queries to each of the oracle S_i on its right side. We call a query from D to its left oracle a *construction query* and a query from D to one of its right oracles an *S-box query*.

The interaction between D and its oracles is recorded in the form of 6 lists of pairs $Q_C \subseteq \mathbb{F}_N^w \times \mathbb{F}_N^w$ and $Q_{S_1}, \ldots, Q_{S_5} \subseteq \mathbb{F}_N \times \mathbb{F}_N$. Among them, $Q_C = ((x^{(1)}, y^{(1)}), \ldots, (x^{(q_C)}, y^{(q_C)}))$ lists the construction queries-responses of D *in chronological order*, where the i-th pair $(x^{(i)}, y^{(i)})$ indicates the i-th such query is either a forward query $x^{(i)}$ that was answered by $y^{(i)}$ or an inverse query $y^{(i)}$ that was answered by $x^{(i)}$. $Q_{S_1}, \ldots, Q_{S_5}$ are defined similarly with respect to queries to $S_1, \ldots, S_5$. Define $Q_S := (Q_{S_1}, \ldots, Q_{S_5})$. Note that D's interaction with its oracles can be unambiguously reconstructed from these sets since D is deterministic. For convenience, for $i \in \{1,2,3,4,5\}$ we define

$$\mathrm{Dom}_i := \{a : (a,b) \in Q_{S_i} \text{ for some } b \in \mathbb{F}_N\}, \quad \mathrm{Rng}_i := \{b : (a,b) \in Q_{S_i} \text{ for } a \in \mathbb{F}_N\}.$$

Following [8], we augment the transcript (Q_C, Q_S) with a key value $\mathbf{k} = (k_0, \ldots, k_5)$. In the real world, $\mathbf{k}$ is the actual key used by the construction. In the ideal world, $\mathbf{k}$ is a dummy key sampled independently from all other values according to the prescribed key distribution $\mathcal{K}$. Thus, a transcript τ has the final form $\tau = (Q_C, Q_S, \mathbf{k})$.

4.2 Bad Transcripts

Let $\mathcal{T}$ be the set of all possible transcripts that can be generated by D in the ideal world (note that this includes all transcripts that can be generated with non-zero probability in the real world). Let μ, ν be the distributions over transcripts in the real and ideal worlds, respectively (as in Appendix A).

We define a set $\mathcal{T}_2 \subseteq \mathcal{T}$ of *bad transcripts* as follows: a transcript $\tau = (Q_C, Q_S, \mathbf{k})$ is bad if and only if one of the following events occurs:

1. There exist a pair $(x,y) \in Q_C$ and an index $i \in \{2,4,\ldots,w\}$ such that $(x+k_0)[i] \in \mathrm{Dom}_1$ or $(y-k_5)[i] \in \mathrm{Dom}_5$.
2. There exist a pair $(x,y) \in Q_C$ and distinct $i, i' \in \{2,4\ldots,w\}$ such that $(x+k_0)[i] = (x+k_0)[i']$ or $(y-k_5)[i] = (y-k_5)[i']$.
3. There exist distinct $(x,y), (x',y') \in Q_C$ and distinct $i, i' \in \{2,4,\ldots,w\}$ such that $(x+k_0)[i] = (x'+k_0)[i']$ or $(y-k_5)[i] = (y'-k_5)[i']$.
4. There exist two indices $i, \ell \in \{1,\ldots,q_C\}$ such that $\ell > i$, and:
   - $(x^{(\ell)}, y^{(\ell)})$ was due to a forward query, and $y^{(\ell)}[\mathsf{even}] = y^{(i)}[\mathsf{even}]$; or,
   - $(x^{(\ell)}, y^{(\ell)})$ was due to a inverse query, and $x^{(\ell)}[\mathsf{even}] = x^{(i)}[\mathsf{even}]$.

Let $\mathcal{T}_1 := \mathcal{T} \backslash \mathcal{T}_2$ be the set of *good* transcripts.

To understand the conditions, consider a good transcript $\tau = (Q_C, Q_S, \mathbf{k})$ and let's see some properties (informally). First, since the 1st condition is not fulfilled, each construction query induces $w/2$ inputs to the 1st round S-box and $w/2$ inputs to the 5th round S-box, the outputs of which are *not* fixed by Q_S. Second, since neither the 2nd nor the 3rd condition is fulfilled, the inputs to the 1st round (5th round, resp.) S-boxes induced by the construction queries are distinct unless unavoidable. These ensure that the induced 2nd and 4th intermediate values are somewhat random and free from multiple forms of collisions. Finally, the last condition will be crucial for some structural properties of the queries that will be crucial in the subsequent analysis (see the full version, the proof of Lemma 2).

Let's then analyze the probabilities of the conditions in turn. Since, in the ideal world, the values k_0, k_5 are independent of Q_C, Q_S and (individually) uniform in $\mathbb{F}_N^w$, it is easy to see that the probabilities of the first three events do not exceed wq_Cq_S/N, $\binom{w/2}{2} \cdot \frac{2q_C}{N} \le w^2 q_C/4N$, and $\binom{w/2}{2} \cdot \binom{q_C}{2} \cdot \frac{2}{N} \le w^2 q_C(q_C-1)/8N \le w^2 q_C(q_C-1)/4N$, respectively.

For the 4-th condition, consider the ℓ-th construction query $(x^{(\ell)}, y^{(\ell)})$. When it is forward, in the ideal world, it means D issued $P(x^{(\ell)})$ to the w width random permutation P and received $y^{(\ell)}$, which is uniform in $N^w - \ell + 1$ possibilities. Thus, when $\ell \le q_C \le N^w/2$,

$$\Pr\Big[\exists i \le \ell - 1 : y^{(\ell)}[\mathsf{even}] = y^{(i)}[\mathsf{even}]\Big]$$
$$= \sum_{i \le \ell-1, z \in \mathbb{F}_N^{w/2}} \Pr\Big[y^{(\ell)} = \big(z \| y^{(i)}[\mathsf{even}]\big)\Big] \le \frac{(\ell-1)\cdot N^{w/2}}{N^w - \ell + 1} \le \frac{2(\ell-1)}{N^{w/2}}.$$

A similar result follows when $(x^{(\ell)}, y^{(\ell)})$ is inverse. A union bound thus yields

$$\Pr\big[\nu \in \mathcal{T}_2\big] \le \frac{wq_Cq_S}{N} + \frac{w^2 q_C^2}{4N} + \sum_{\ell=1}^{q_C} \frac{2(\ell-1)}{N^{w/2}} \le \frac{wq_Cq_S}{N} + \frac{w^2 q_C^2}{4N} + \frac{q_C^2}{N^{w/2}}. \quad (4)$$

4.3 Bounding the Ratio $\mu(\tau)/\nu(\tau)$

Let $\Omega_X = \big(\mathcal{P}(1)\big)^5 \times \mathcal{K}$ be the probability space underlying the real world, whose measure is the product of the uniform measure on $(\mathcal{P}(1))^5$ and the measure induced by the distribution $\mathcal{K}$ on keys. (Thus, each element of Ω_X is a tuple $(\mathcal{S}, \mathbf{k})$ with $\mathcal{S} = (S_1, \ldots, S_5)$, $S_1, \ldots, S_5 \in \mathcal{P}(1)$ and $\mathbf{k} = (k_0, \ldots, k_5) \in \mathcal{K}$.) Also, let $\Omega_Y = \mathcal{P}(w) \times \big(\mathcal{P}(1)\big)^5 \times \mathcal{K}$ be the probability space underlying the ideal world, whose measure is the product of the uniform measure on $\mathcal{P}(w)$ with the measure on Ω_X.

Let $\tau' = (Q_C^{\tau'}, Q_S^{\tau'}, \mathbf{k}^{\tau'})$ be a transcript. We introduce four types of *compatibility* as follows.

- First, an element $\omega = (\mathcal{S}^*, \mathbf{k}^*) \in \Omega_X$ is *compatible with* τ' if: (a) $\mathbf{k}^* = \mathbf{k}^{\tau'}$, and (b) $S_i^*(a) = b$ for all $(a, b) \in Q_{S_i}^{\tau'}$, and (c) $\mathcal{C}5_{\mathbf{k}^*}^{\mathcal{S}^*}(x) = y$ for all $(x, y) \in Q_C^{\tau'}$.
- Second, an element $\omega = (P^*, \mathcal{S}^*, \mathbf{k}^*) \in \Omega_Y$ is *compatible with* τ' if: (a) $\mathbf{k}^* = \mathbf{k}^{\tau'}$, and (b) $S_i^*(a) = b$ for all $(a, b) \in Q_{S_i}^{\tau'}$, and (c) $P^*(x) = y$ for all $(x, y) \in Q_C^{\tau'}$. We write
$$\omega \downarrow \tau'$$
to indicate that an element $\omega \in \Omega_X \cup \Omega_Y$ is compatible with τ'.
- Third, a tuple of S-boxes $\mathcal{S}^* \in (\mathcal{P}(1))^5$ is *compatible* with $\tau' = (Q_C^{\tau'}, Q_S^{\tau'}, \mathbf{k}^{\tau'})$, and write $\mathcal{S}^* \downarrow \tau'$, if $(\mathcal{S}^*, \mathbf{k}) \in \Omega_X$ is compatible with τ', where $\mathbf{k}$ is the key value of the fixed transcript τ.
- Last, we say that $(P^*, \mathcal{S}^*) \in \mathcal{P}(w) \times (\mathcal{P}(1))^5$ is *compatible* with $\tau' = (Q_C^{\tau'}, Q_S^{\tau'}, \mathbf{k}^{\tau'})$ and write $(P^*, \mathcal{S}^*) \downarrow \tau'$, if $(P^*, \mathcal{S}^*, \mathbf{k}^{\tau'}) \downarrow \tau'$.

For the rest of the proof, we fix a transcript $\tau = (Q_C, Q_S, \mathbf{k}) \in \mathcal{T}_1$. Since $\tau \in \mathcal{T}$, it is easy to see (cf. [8]) that

$$\mu(\tau) = \Pr[\omega \leftarrow \Omega_X : \omega \downarrow \tau], \qquad \nu(\tau) = \Pr[\omega \leftarrow \Omega_Y : \omega \downarrow \tau],$$

where the notation indicates that ω is sampled from the relevant probability space according to that space's probability measure. We bound $\mu(\tau)/\nu(\tau)$ by reasoning about the latter probabilities. In detail, with the third and fourth types of compatibility notions, the product structure of Ω_X, Ω_Y implies

$$\Pr[\omega \leftarrow \Omega_X : \omega \downarrow \tau] = \Pr[\mathbf{k}^* = \mathbf{k}] \cdot \Pr_{\mathcal{S}^*}[\mathcal{S}^* \downarrow \tau],$$
$$\Pr[\omega \leftarrow \Omega_Y : \omega \downarrow \tau] = \Pr[\mathbf{k}^* = \mathbf{k}] \cdot \Pr_{P^*,\mathcal{S}^*}[(P^*, \mathcal{S}^*) \downarrow \tau],$$

where $\mathcal{S}^*$ and $(P^*, \mathcal{S}^*)$ are sampled uniformly from $(\mathcal{P}(1))^5$ and $\mathcal{P}(w) \times (\mathcal{P}(1))^5$, respectively. Thus,

$$\frac{\mu(\tau)}{\nu(\tau)} = \frac{\Pr_{\mathcal{S}^*}[\mathcal{S}^* \downarrow \tau]}{\Pr_{P^*,\mathcal{S}^*}[(P^*, \mathcal{S}^*) \downarrow \tau]}.$$

By these, and by $|Q_C| = q_C, |Q_{S_1}| = \ldots = |Q_{S_5}| = q_S$, it is immediate that

$$\Pr_{P^*,\mathcal{S}^*}\big[(P^*, \mathcal{S}^*) \downarrow \tau\big] = \frac{1}{(N^w)_{q_C} \cdot \big((N)_{q_S}\big)^5}.$$

To compute $\Pr_{\mathcal{S}^*}[\mathcal{S}^* \downarrow \tau]$, we start by writing

$$\begin{aligned} \Pr_{\mathcal{S}^*}[\mathcal{S}^* \downarrow \tau] &= \Pr_{\mathcal{S}^*}[\mathcal{S}^* \downarrow (Q_C, Q_S, \mathbf{k})] \\ &= \Pr_{\mathcal{S}^*}[\mathcal{S}^* \downarrow (\emptyset, Q_S, \mathbf{k})] \cdot \Pr_{\mathcal{S}^*}[\mathcal{S}^* \downarrow (Q_C, Q_S, \mathbf{k}) \mid \mathcal{S}^* \downarrow (\emptyset, Q_S, \mathbf{k})] \\ &= \frac{1}{((N)_{q_S})^5} \cdot \Pr_{\mathcal{S}^*}[\mathcal{S}^* \downarrow (Q_C, Q_S, \mathbf{k}) \mid \mathcal{S}^* \downarrow (\emptyset, Q_S, \mathbf{k})]. \end{aligned}$$

To analyze $\Pr_{\mathcal{S}^*}[\mathcal{S}^* \downarrow (Q_C, Q_S, \mathbf{k}) \mid \mathcal{S}^* \downarrow (\emptyset, Q_S, \mathbf{k})]$, we proceed in two steps. First, based on Q_C and two outer S-boxes S_1^*, S_5^*, we derive the 2nd and 4th rounds intermediate values: these constitute a special transcript Q_{mid} on the middle 3 rounds. We characterize conditions on S_1^*, S_5^* that will ensure certain good properties in the derived Q_{mid}, which will ease the analysis. Therefore, in the second step, we analyze such "good" Q_{mid} to yield the final bounds. Each of the two steps will take a paragraph as follows.

The Outer 2 Rounds. Given a tuple of S-boxes $\mathcal{S}^*$, we let $\mathsf{Bad}(\mathcal{S}^*)$ be a predicate of $\mathcal{S}^*$ that holds if any of the following conditions is met:

- (B-1) There exist $(x, y) \in Q_C$ and $i \in \{2, 4, \ldots, w\}$ such that $\big(T \cdot (\mathsf{PGF}^{S_1^*}(x + k_0)) + k_1\big)[i] \in \mathrm{Dom}_2$ or $\big(T^{-1} \cdot (((\mathsf{PGF}^{S_5^*})^{-1}(y - k_5)) - k_4)\big)[i] \in \mathrm{Dom}_4$.
- (B-2) There exist $(x, y) \in Q_C$ and distinct indices $i, i' \in \{2, 4, \ldots, w\}$ such that $\big(T \cdot (\mathsf{PGF}^{S_1^*}(x + k_0)) + k_1\big)[i] = \big(T \cdot (\mathsf{PGF}^{S_1^*}(x + k_0)) + k_1\big)[i']$, or $\big(T^{-1} \cdot (((\mathsf{PGF}^{S_5^*})^{-1}(y - k_5)) - k_4)\big)[i] = \big(T^{-1} \cdot (((\mathsf{PGF}^{S_5^*})^{-1}(y - k_5)) - k_4)\big)[i']$.
- (B-3) There exist distinct pairs $(x, y), (x', y') \in Q_C$ and two indices $i, i' \in \{2, 4, \ldots, w\}$ such that:
  1. $x[\mathsf{even}] \neq x'[\mathsf{even}]$, yet $\big(T \cdot (\mathsf{PGF}^{S_1^*}(x + k_0)) + k_1\big)[i] = \big(T \cdot (\mathsf{PGF}^{S_1^*}(x' + k_0)) + k_1\big)[i']$; or

2. $x[\mathsf{even}] = x'[\mathsf{even}]$, $i \neq i'$, yet $\big(T \cdot (\mathsf{PGF}^{S_1^*}(x + k_0)) + k_1\big)[i] = \big(T \cdot (\mathsf{PGF}^{S_1^*}(x' + k_0)) + k_1\big)[i']$; or
3. $y[\mathsf{even}] \neq y'[\mathsf{even}]$, yet it holds $\big(T^{-1} \cdot (((\mathsf{PGF}^{S_5^*})^{-1}(y - k_5)) - k_4)\big)[i] = \big(T^{-1} \cdot (((\mathsf{PGF}^{S_5^*})^{-1}(y - k_5)) - k_4)\big)[i']$; or
4. $y[\mathsf{even}] = y'[\mathsf{even}]$, $i \neq i'$, yet $\big(T^{-1} \cdot (((\mathsf{PGF}^{S_5^*})^{-1}(y - k_5)) - k_4)\big)[i] = \big(T^{-1} \cdot (((\mathsf{PGF}^{S_5^*})^{-1}(y - k_5)) - k_4)\big)[i']$.

(B-1) captures the case that a 2nd round S-box input or a 4th round S-box input has been in Q_S, (B-2) captures collisions among the 2nd round S-box inputs & 4th round S-box inputs for a single construction query, while (B-3) captures various collisions between the 2nd round S-box inputs, resp. 4th round S-box inputs from two distinct queries. Note that essentially, $\mathsf{Bad}(\mathcal{S}^*)$ only concerns the randomness of the outer 2 S-boxes S_1^* and S_5^*. For simplicity, define $\mathsf{Good}(\mathcal{S}^*) := (\mathcal{S}^* \downarrow Q_S) \wedge \neg\mathsf{Bad}(\mathcal{S}^*)$. Then it holds

$$\begin{aligned}
&\Pr_{\mathcal{S}^*}\big[\mathcal{S}^* \downarrow (Q_C, Q_S, \mathbf{k}) \mid \mathcal{S}^* \downarrow (\emptyset, Q_S, \mathbf{k})\big] \\
\geq\ &\Pr_{\mathcal{S}^*}\big[\mathcal{S}^* \downarrow (Q_C, Q_S, \mathbf{k}) \wedge \mathsf{Good}(\mathcal{S}^*) \mid \mathcal{S}^* \downarrow (\emptyset, Q_S, \mathbf{k})\big] \\
=\ &\Pr_{\mathcal{S}^*}\big[\mathsf{Good}(\mathcal{S}^*) \mid \mathcal{S}^* \downarrow (\emptyset, Q_S, \mathbf{k})\big] \cdot \Pr_{\mathcal{S}^*}\big[\mathcal{S}^* \downarrow (Q_C, Q_S, \mathbf{k}) \mid \mathsf{Good}(\mathcal{S}^*)\big]. \quad (5)
\end{aligned}$$

Hence, all that remains is to lower bound the two terms in the product of (5). For the first term, we serve the result below and defer the proof to the full version.

Lemma 1. *When $q_S + w \leq N/2$, we have*

$$\Pr_{\mathcal{S}^*}\big[\mathsf{Bad}(\mathcal{S}^*) \mid \mathcal{S}^* \downarrow (\emptyset, Q_S, \mathbf{k})\big] \leq \frac{4wq_Cq_S + w^2q_C + w^2q_C^2}{2N}. \quad (6)$$

Analyzing the 3 Middle Rounds. Our next step is to lower bound the term $\Pr_{\mathcal{S}^*}\big[\mathcal{S}^* \downarrow (Q_C, Q_S, \mathbf{k}) \mid \mathsf{Good}(\mathcal{S}^*)\big]$ from Eq. (5). Given $\mathcal{S}^*$ for which $\mathsf{Good}(\mathcal{S}^*)$ holds, for every $(x^{(i)}, y^{(i)}) \in Q_C$, we define $u_1^{(i)} := x^{(i)} + k_0$, $v_1^{(i)} := \mathsf{PGF}^{S_1^*}(u_1^{(i)})$ (this means $v_1^{(i)}[\mathsf{even}] = u_1^{(i)}[\mathsf{even}]$), $u_2^{(i)} := T \cdot v_1^{(i)} + k_1$; $v_5^{(i)} := y^{(i)} - k_5$, $u_5^{(i)} := \big(\mathsf{PGF}^{S_5^*}\big)^{-1}(v_5^{(i)})$ (where $v_5^{(i)}[\mathsf{even}] = u_5^{(i)}[\mathsf{even}]$), $v_4^{(i)} := T^{-1} \cdot (u_5^{(i)} - k_4)$. With these, we obtain

$$Q_{mid} = \Big(\big(u_1^{(1)}, u_2^{(1)}, v_4^{(1)}, v_5^{(1)}\big), \ldots, \big(u_1^{(q_C)}, u_2^{(q_C)}, v_4^{(q_C)}, v_5^{(q_C)}\big)\Big),$$

in which the tuples follow exactly the same chronological order as in Q_C. Define

$$\mathcal{C}3^{\mathcal{S}^*}_{(k_2,k_3)}(u) = \mathsf{PGF}^{S_4^*}\big(T \cdot \big(\mathsf{PGF}^{S_3^*}\big(T \cdot \big(\mathsf{PGF}^{S_2^*}(u)\big) + k_2\big)\big) + k_3\big),$$

and write $\mathcal{S}^* \downarrow (Q_{mid}, Q_S, \mathbf{k})$ for the event that "$\mathcal{C}3^{\mathcal{S}^*}_{(k_2,k_3)}(u_2) = v_4$ for every (u_1, u_2, v_4, v_5) in the set Q_{mid}". Then it can be seen

$$\Pr_{\mathcal{S}^*}\big[\mathcal{S}^* \downarrow (Q_C, Q_S, \mathbf{k}) \mid \mathsf{Good}(\mathcal{S}^*)\big] = \Pr_{\mathcal{S}^*}\big[\mathcal{S}^* \downarrow (Q_{mid}, Q_S, \mathbf{k}) \mid \mathsf{Good}(\mathcal{S}^*)\big]. \quad (7)$$

To bound Eq. (7), we will divide Q_{mid} into multiple sets according to collisions on the "even halves" $u_1[\mathsf{even}]$ and $v_5[\mathsf{even}]$, and consider the probability that $\mathcal{S}^*$ is compatible with each set in turn. In detail, the sets are arranged according to the following rules:

- $Q_{m_1} := \{(u_1, u_2, v_4, v_5) \in Q_{mid} : u_1[\mathsf{even}] = u_1^{(1)}[\mathsf{even}]\}$;
- For $\ell = 2, 3, \ldots$, if $\cup_{i=1}^{\ell-1} Q_{m_i} = Q_{m_1} \cup Q_{m_2} \cup \ldots \cup Q_{m_{\ell-1}} \subset Q_{mid}$, then we define Q_{m_ℓ}. Let j be the minimum index such that $(u_1^{(j)}, u_2^{(j)}, v_4^{(j)}, v_5^{(j)})$ remains in $Q_{mid} \setminus \cup_{i=1}^{\ell-1} Q_{m_i}$. Then:
  - If $v_5^{(j)}$ has collisions, i.e., there exists $(u_1^*, u_2^*, v_4^*, v_5^*) \in \cup_{i=1}^{\ell-1} Q_{m_i}$ such that $v_5^*[\mathsf{even}] = v_5^{(j)}[\mathsf{even}]$, then we define $Q_{m_\ell} := \{(u_1, u_2, v_4, v_5) \in Q_{mid} \setminus \cup_{i=1}^{\ell-1} Q_{m_i} : v_5[\mathsf{even}] = v_5^{(j)}[\mathsf{even}]\}$. We call such sets **Type-II**.
  - Else, $Q_{m_\ell} := \{(u_1, u_2, v_4, v_5) \in Q_{mid} \setminus \cup_{i=1}^{\ell-1} Q_{m_i} : u_1[\mathsf{even}] = u_1^{(j)}[\mathsf{even}]\}$. We call such sets as well as Q_{m_1} **Type-I**.

Assume that Q_{mid} is divided into α disjoint sets by the above rules, with $|Q_{m_\ell}| = \beta_\ell$. Then $\sum_{\ell=1}^{\alpha} \beta_\ell = q_C$, and

$$\begin{aligned} &\Pr_{\mathcal{S}^*}\left[\mathcal{S}^* \downarrow (Q_{mid}, Q_{\mathcal{S}}, \mathbf{k}) \mid \mathsf{Good}(\mathcal{S}^*)\right] \\ &= \prod_{\ell=1}^{\alpha} \Pr_{\mathcal{S}^*}\left[\mathcal{S}^* \downarrow (Q_{m_\ell}, Q_{\mathcal{S}}, \mathbf{k}) \mid \mathcal{S}^* \downarrow (\cup_{i=1}^{\ell-1} Q_{m_i}, Q_{\mathcal{S}}, \mathbf{k}) \wedge \mathsf{Good}(\mathcal{S}^*)\right]. \end{aligned} \quad (8)$$

Now we could focus on analyzing the ℓ-th set Q_{m_ℓ}. Assume that

$$Q_{m_\ell} = \left((u_1^{(\ell,1)}, u_2^{(\ell,1)}, v_4^{(\ell,1)}, v_5^{(\ell,1)}), \ldots, (u_1^{(\ell,\beta_\ell)}, u_2^{(\ell,\beta_\ell)}, v_4^{(\ell,\beta_\ell)}, v_5^{(\ell,\beta_\ell)})\right).$$

The superscript (ℓ, i) indicates that it is the i-th tuple in this ℓ-th set Q_{m_ℓ}. For this index ℓ, we define six sets $\mathrm{ExtDom}_i^{(\ell)}$ and $\mathrm{ExtRng}_i^{(\ell)}$, $i = 2, 3, 4$, as follows:

$$\begin{aligned} &\mathrm{ExtDom}_2^{(\ell)} := \{u_2[j] : (u_1, u_2, v_4, v_5) \in \cup_{i=1}^{\ell-1} Q_{m_i}, j \in \{2, 4, \ldots, w\}\} \\ &\mathrm{ExtRng}_2^{(\ell)} := \{S_2^*(a) : a \in \mathrm{ExtDom}_2^{(\ell)}\} \\ &\mathrm{ExtDom}_3^{(\ell)} := \left\{(T \cdot (\mathsf{PGF}^{S_2^*}(u_2)) + k_2)[j] : (u_1, u_2, v_4, v_5) \in \cup_{i=1}^{\ell-1} Q_{m_i}, j \in \{2, 4, \ldots, w\}\right\} \\ &\mathrm{ExtRng}_3^{(\ell)} := \{S_3^*(a) : a \in \mathrm{ExtDom}_3^{(\ell)}\} \\ &\mathrm{ExtDom}_4^{(\ell)} := \left\{v_4[j] : (u_1, u_2, v_4, v_5) \in \cup_{i=1}^{\ell-1} Q_{m_i}, j \in \{2, 4, \ldots, w\}\right\} \\ &\mathrm{ExtRng}_4^{(\ell)} := \{S_4^*(a) : a \in \mathrm{ExtDom}_4^{(\ell)}\} \end{aligned}$$

Note that, conditioned on $\mathcal{S}^* \downarrow (\cup_{i=1}^{\ell-1} Q_{m_i}, Q_{\mathcal{S}}, \mathbf{k}) \wedge \mathsf{Good}(\mathcal{S}^*)$, the values in $\mathrm{ExtDom}_i^{(\ell)}$ and $\mathrm{ExtRng}_i^{(\ell)}$, $i = 2, 3, 4$, are compatible with the set $\cup_{i=1}^{\ell-1} Q_{m_i}$. For Q_{m_ℓ}, two useful properties regarding the arrangement of tuples and the derived intermediate values resp. could be exhibited.

Lemma 2. *Consider the ℓ-th set $Q_{m_\ell} = ((u_1^{(\ell,1)}, u_2^{(\ell,1)}, v_4^{(\ell,1)}, v_5^{(\ell,1)}), \ldots)$. If it is of* **Type-I**, *then the number of tuples $(u_1, u_2, v_4, v_5) \in \cup_{i=1}^{\ell-1} Q_{m_i}$ with $u_1[\mathsf{even}] = u_1^{(\ell,1)}[\mathsf{even}]$ is at most 1; if it is of* **Type-II**, *then the number of $(u_1, u_2, v_4, v_5) \in \cup_{i=1}^{\ell-1} Q_{m_i}$ with $v_5[\mathsf{even}] = v_5^{(\ell,1)}[\mathsf{even}]$ is also at most 1.*

The proof is deferred to the Appendix B.1.

Lemma 3. *Consider the* ℓ*-th set* Q_{m_ℓ} *and any two distinct elements* $(u_1^{(\ell,i_1)}, u_2^{(\ell,i_1)}, v_4^{(\ell,i_1)}, v_5^{(\ell,i_1)})$ *and* $(u_1^{(\ell,i_2)}, u_2^{(\ell,i_2)}, v_4^{(\ell,i_2)}, v_5^{(\ell,i_2)})$ *in* Q_{m_ℓ}. *Then, there exist two indices* $j_1, j_2 \in \{2, 4, \ldots, w\}$ *such that,*

- *when* Q_{m_ℓ} *is of* **Type-I**: $u_2^{(\ell,i_1)}[j_1] \notin Dom_2 \cup ExtDom_2^{(\ell)}$, $u_2^{(\ell,i_2)}[j_2] \notin Dom_2 \cup ExtDom_2^{(\ell)}$, *and* $(u_2^{(\ell,i_1)}[j_1], u_2^{(\ell,i_1)}[j_2]) \neq (u_2^{(\ell,i_2)}[j_1], u_2^{(\ell,i_2)}[j_2])$;
- *when* Q_{m_ℓ} *is of* **Type-II**: $v_4^{(\ell,i_1)}[j_1] \notin Dom_4 \cup ExtDom_4^{(\ell)}$, $v_4^{(\ell,i_2)}[j_2] \notin Dom_4 \cup ExtDom_4^{(\ell)}$, *and* $(v_4^{(\ell,i_1)}[j_1], v_4^{(\ell,i_1)}[j_2]) \neq (v_4^{(\ell,i_2)}[j_1], v_4^{(\ell,i_2)}[j_2])$.

The proof is deferred to the Appendix B.2. With the help of these two lemmas, we are able to bound the probability that the randomness is compatible with the ℓ-th set Q_{m_ℓ}.

Lemma 4. *For the* ℓ*-th set* Q_{m_ℓ}, *it holds*

$$\begin{aligned} &\Pr_{\mathcal{S}^*}\left[\mathcal{S}^* \downarrow (Q_{m_\ell}, Q_{\mathcal{S}}, \mathbf{k}) \mid \mathcal{S}^* \downarrow (\cup_{i=1}^{\ell-1} Q_{m_i}, Q_{\mathcal{S}}, \mathbf{k}) \wedge \mathsf{Good}(\mathcal{S}^*)\right] \\ \geq &\left(1 - \frac{12\beta_\ell w(q_S + wq_C/2) + 3\beta_\ell^2 w^2}{4N}\right) \cdot \frac{1}{N^{w\beta_\ell}}. \end{aligned} \tag{9}$$

The proof is deferred to the full version.

From Eq. (9), Eq. (8), and using $\sum_{\ell=1}^{\alpha} \beta_\ell = q_C$, we obtain

$$\begin{aligned} &\Pr_{\mathcal{S}^*}\left[\mathcal{S}^* \downarrow (Q_{mid}, Q_{\mathcal{S}}, \mathbf{k}) \mid \mathsf{Good}(\mathcal{S}^*)\right] \\ \geq &\prod_{\ell=1}^{\alpha}\left(\left(1 - \frac{12\beta_\ell w(q_S + wq_C/2) + 3\beta_\ell^2 w^2}{4N}\right) \cdot \frac{1}{N^{w\beta_\ell}}\right) \\ \geq &\left(1 - \sum_{\ell=1}^{\alpha} \frac{12\beta_\ell w(q_S + wq_C/2) + 3\beta_\ell^2 w^2}{4N}\right) \cdot \frac{1}{N^{w\sum_{\ell=1}^{\alpha}\beta_\ell}} \\ \geq &\left(1 - \frac{12wq_C(q_S + wq_C/2) + 3w^2 q_C^2}{4N}\right) \cdot \frac{1}{N^{wq_C}}. \end{aligned}$$

Gathering this and Eqs. (7) (6), and (5), we finally reach

$$\begin{aligned} \frac{\mu(\tau)}{\nu(\tau)} &\geq \left(1 - \frac{4wq_C q_S + w^2 q_C + w^2 q_C^2}{2N}\right)\left(1 - \frac{12wq_C(q_S + wq_C/2) + 3w^2 q_C^2}{4N}\right) \cdot \frac{(N^w)_{q_C}}{N^{wq_C}} \\ &\geq \left(1 - \frac{4wq_C q_S + w^2 q_C + w^2 q_C^2}{2N}\right)\left(1 - \frac{12wq_C(q_S + wq_C/2) + 3w^2 q_C^2}{4N}\right) \cdot \left(1 - \frac{q_C^2}{N^w}\right) \\ &\geq 1 - \frac{20wq_C q_S + 13w^2 q_C^2}{4N} - \frac{q_C^2}{N^w} \geq 1 - \frac{20wq_C q_S + 13w^2 q_C^2}{4N} - \frac{q_C^2}{N^{w/2}}. \end{aligned}$$

Further, using Eq. (4) yields the bound in Eq. (3) and completes the proof.

5 SPRP Security at 5 Rounds with Public Functions

In this section, we will prove security for 5-round GEGFNs built upon 5 random functions $\mathbf{F} = \{F_1, F_2, F_3, F_4, F_5\}$ and a *single linear layer* T. Firstly, we modify the Definition 1 to apply to the situation of using random functions.

Definition 2 (Good Linear Layer for 5 Rounds with Functions). *A matrix $T \in \mathbb{F}_N^{w \times w}$ is good if T is MDS, and the 2 induced matrices T_{EO} and $(T^{-1})_{\mathrm{EO}}$ are such that:*

1. *They contain no zero entries, and*
2. *Any column vector of the 2 induced matrices consists of $w/2$ distinct entries.*

With a good linear layer in Definition 2, we have the following theorem on 5-round GEGFNs with public random functions.

Theorem 2. *Assume $w \geq 2$. Let $C5_{\mathbf{k}}^{\boldsymbol{F}}$ be a 5-round, linear GEGFN structure defined in Eq. (10), with distribution $\mathcal{K}$ over keys $\mathbf{k} = (k_0, \ldots, k_5)$ and public functions $\boldsymbol{F} = (F_1, F_2, F_3, F_4, F_5)$.*

$$C5_{\mathbf{k}}^{\boldsymbol{F}}(x) := k_5 + \mathsf{PGF}^{F_5}\Big(k_4 + T \cdot \big(\mathsf{PGF}^{F_4}\big(k_3 + T \cdot \big(\mathsf{PGF}^{F_3}\big(k_2 + T \cdot \big(\mathsf{PGF}^{F_2}\big(k_1 + T \cdot \big(\mathsf{PGF}^{F_1}(k_0 + x)\big)\big)\big)\big)\big)\big)\big)\big)\Big). \tag{10}$$

If k_0 and k_5 are uniformly distributed and the matrix T fulfills Definition 2, then

$$\mathsf{Adv}^{\mathsf{sprp}}_{C5_{\mathbf{k}}^{F}}(q_C, q_F) \leq \frac{20wq_Cq_F + 9w^2q_C^2}{8N} + \frac{2q_C^2}{N^{w/2}}. \tag{11}$$

Since $C5_{\mathbf{k}}^{\mathbf{F}}$ is defined on random functions instead of random permutations, which slightly deviates from the permutation case, for the proof, we only need to make some moderate modifications to the previous proof for $C5_{\mathbf{k}}^{\mathcal{S}}$. We follow the proof idea of $C5_{\mathbf{k}}^{\mathcal{S}}$ and reduce proof as follows.

Proof Setup. Fix a deterministic distinguisher D. Similar to Sect. 4.1, we assume D makes exactly q_C (non-redundant) forward/inverse queries to its left oracle that is either $C5_{\mathbf{k}}^{\mathbf{F}}$ or P, and exactly q_F (non-redundant) forward queries to each of the oracle F_i on its right side. We call a query from D to its left oracle a *construction query* and a query from D to one of its right oracles a *function query*.

The interaction between D and its oracles is recorded in the form of 6 lists of pairs $Q_C \subseteq \mathbb{F}_N^w \times \mathbb{F}_N^w$ and $Q_{F_1}, \ldots, Q_{F_5} \subseteq \mathbb{F}_N \times \mathbb{F}_N$. The definition of Q_C remains unchange, $Q_{F_1}, \ldots, Q_{F_5}$ are defined similarly with respect to queries to $F_1, \ldots, F_5$. Define $Q_{\mathbf{F}} := (Q_{F_1}, \ldots, Q_{F_5})$. For convenience, for $i \in \{1, 2, 3, 4, 5\}$ we define

$$\mathrm{Dom}_i := \big\{a : (a, b) \in Q_{F_i} \text{ for some } b \in \mathbb{F}_N\big\}, \mathrm{Rng}_i := \big\{b : (a, b) \in Q_{F_i} \text{ for } a \in \mathbb{F}_N\big\}.$$

Similar to Sect. 4.1, we augment the transcript $(Q_C, Q_{\mathbf{F}})$ with a key value $\mathbf{k} = (k_0, \ldots, k_5)$. Thus, a transcript τ has the final form $\tau = (Q_C, Q_{\mathbf{F}}, \mathbf{k})$.

Completing the Proof. Note that since F_i is a random function, for a new input x, the function value $F_i(x)$ is uniform in $\mathbb{F}_N$, for $i = 1, 2, 3, 4, 5$, i.e., for any y, the probability of $F_i(x) = y$ is $1/N$. This is the main difference from the proof of $C5_{\mathbf{k}}^{\mathcal{S}}$.

In detail, we recall the definition of bad transcripts in Sect. 4.2 and we also have the same definition of bad transcripts in $C5_{\mathbf{k}}^{\mathbf{F}}$. Therefore,

Lemma 5. *The upper bounding of getting bad transcripts in the ideal world is*

$$\Pr\big[\nu \in \mathcal{T}_2\big] \le \frac{wq_Cq_S}{N} + \frac{w^2q_C^2}{4N} + \sum_{\ell=1}^{q_C} \frac{2(\ell-1)}{N^{w/2}} \le \frac{wq_Cq_F}{N} + \frac{w^2q_C^2}{4N} + \frac{q_C^2}{N^{w/2}}. \quad (12)$$

Then, following the idea as before, we bound the ratio $\mu(\tau)/\nu(\tau)$. Let $\Omega_X = \big(\mathcal{F}(1)\big)^5 \times \mathcal{K}$ be the probability space underlying the real world and $\Omega_Y = \mathcal{P}(w) \times \big(\mathcal{F}(1)\big)^5 \times \mathcal{K}$ be the probability space underlying the ideal world. We fix a transcript $\tau = (Q_C, Q_{\mathbf{F}}, \mathbf{k}) \in \mathcal{T}_1$. Since $\tau \in \mathcal{T}$, it is easy to see (cf. [8]) that

$$\mu(\tau) = \Pr[\omega \leftarrow \Omega_X : \omega \downarrow \tau] = \Pr[\mathbf{k}^* = \mathbf{k}] \cdot \Pr_{\mathbf{F}^*}[\mathbf{F}^* \downarrow \tau],$$
$$\nu(\tau) = \Pr[\omega \leftarrow \Omega_Y : \omega \downarrow \tau] = \Pr[\mathbf{k}^* = \mathbf{k}] \cdot \Pr_{P^*,\mathbf{F}^*}[(P^*, \mathbf{F}^*) \downarrow \tau],$$

where the notation indicates that ω is sampled from the relevant probability space according to that space's probability measure and $\mathbf{F}^*$ and $(P^*, \mathbf{F}^*)$ are sampled uniformly from $(\mathcal{F}(1))^5$ and $\mathcal{P}(w) \times (\mathcal{F}(1))^5$, respectively. Thus,

$$\frac{\mu(\tau)}{\nu(\tau)} = \frac{\Pr_{\mathbf{F}^*}[\mathbf{F}^* \downarrow \tau]}{\Pr_{P^*,\mathbf{F}^*}[(P^*, \mathbf{F}^*) \downarrow \tau]}.$$

By these, and by $|Q_C| = q_C, |Q_{F_1}| = \ldots = |Q_{F_5}| = q_F$, it is immediate that

$$\Pr_{P^*,\mathbf{F}^*}\big[(P^*, \mathbf{F}^*) \downarrow \tau\big] = \frac{1}{(N^w)_{q_C} \cdot \big(N^{q_F}\big)^5}.$$

To compute $\Pr_{\mathbf{F}^*}[\mathbf{F}^* \downarrow \tau]$ we start by writing

$$\begin{aligned}
\Pr_{\mathbf{F}^*}[\mathbf{F}^* \downarrow \tau] &= \Pr_{\mathbf{F}^*}[\mathbf{F}^* \downarrow (Q_C, Q_{\mathbf{F}}, \mathbf{k})] \\
&= \Pr_{\mathbf{F}^*}[\mathbf{F}^* \downarrow (\emptyset, Q_{\mathbf{F}}, \mathbf{k})] \cdot \Pr_{\mathbf{F}^*}[\mathbf{F}^* \downarrow (Q_C, Q_{\mathbf{F}}, \mathbf{k}) \mid \mathbf{F}^* \downarrow (\emptyset, Q_{\mathbf{F}}, \mathbf{k})] \\
&= \frac{1}{(N^{q_F})^5} \cdot \Pr_{\mathbf{F}^*}[\mathbf{F}^* \downarrow (Q_C, Q_{\mathbf{F}}, \mathbf{k}) \mid \mathbf{F}^* \downarrow (\emptyset, Q_{\mathbf{F}}, \mathbf{k})].
\end{aligned}$$

Now let's focus on $\Pr_{\mathbf{F}^*}[\mathbf{F}^* \downarrow (Q_C, Q_{\mathbf{F}}, \mathbf{k}) \mid \mathbf{F}^* \downarrow (\emptyset, Q_{\mathbf{F}}, \mathbf{k})]$. To analyze $\Pr_{\mathbf{F}^*}[\mathbf{F}^* \downarrow (Q_C, Q_{\mathbf{F}}, \mathbf{k}) \mid \mathbf{F}^* \downarrow (\emptyset, Q_{\mathbf{F}}, \mathbf{k})]$, we proceed in two steps. First, based on Q_C and two outer random functions F_1^*, F_5^*, we derive the 2nd and 4th rounds intermediate values: these constitute a special transcript Q_{mid} on the middle 3 rounds. We characterize conditions on F_1^*, F_5^* that will ensure certain good properties in the derived Q_{mid}, which will ease the analysis. Therefore, in the second step, we analyze such "good" Q_{mid} to yield the final bounds. Thus,

$$\begin{aligned}
&\Pr_{\mathbf{F}^*}\big[\mathbf{F}^* \downarrow (Q_C, Q_{\mathbf{F}}, \mathbf{k}) \mid \mathbf{F}^* \downarrow (\emptyset, Q_{\mathbf{F}}, \mathbf{k})\big] \\
\ge\ &\Pr_{\mathbf{F}^*}\big[\mathbf{F}^* \downarrow (Q_C, Q_{\mathbf{F}}, \mathbf{k}) \wedge \mathsf{Good}(\mathbf{F}^*) \mid \mathbf{F}^* \downarrow (\emptyset, Q_{\mathbf{F}}, \mathbf{k})\big] \\
=\ &\Pr_{\mathbf{F}^*}\big[\mathsf{Good}(\mathbf{F}^*) \mid \mathbf{F}^* \downarrow (\emptyset, Q_{\mathbf{F}}, \mathbf{k})\big] \cdot \Pr_{\mathbf{F}^*}\big[\mathbf{F}^* \downarrow (Q_C, Q_{\mathbf{F}}, \mathbf{k}) \mid \mathsf{Good}(\mathbf{F}^*)\big]. \quad (13)
\end{aligned}$$

In the first step, we define $\mathsf{Bad}(\mathbf{F}^*)$ the same as $\mathsf{Bad}(\mathcal{S}^*)$. So we have the following lemma,

Lemma 6.

$$\Pr_{F^*}\left[\mathsf{Bad}(F^*) \mid F^* \downarrow (\emptyset, Q_F, \mathbf{k})\right] \le \frac{4wq_Cq_F + w^2q_C + w^2q_C^2}{4N}. \tag{14}$$

The proof is deferred to the full version.

Then, in the second step, we analyze $\Pr_{\mathbf{F}^*}\left[\mathbf{F}^* \downarrow (Q_C, Q_{\mathbf{F}}, \mathbf{k}) \mid \mathsf{Good}(\mathbf{F}^*)\right]$. We define Q_{mid} as before and we have $\Pr_{\mathbf{F}^*}\left[\mathbf{F}^* \downarrow (Q_C, Q_{\mathbf{F}}, \mathbf{k}) \mid \mathsf{Good}(\mathbf{F}^*)\right] = \Pr_{\mathbf{F}^*}\left[\mathbf{F}^* \downarrow (Q_{mid}, Q_{\mathbf{F}}, \mathbf{k}) \mid \mathsf{Good}(\mathbf{F}^*)\right]$.

Lemma 7. *For the set Q_{mid}, it holds*

$$\Pr_{F^*}\left[F^* \downarrow (Q_{mid}, Q_F, \mathbf{k}) \mid \mathsf{Good}(F^*)\right] \ge \left(1 - \frac{4wq_C(q_F + wq_C/2) + w^2q_C^2}{8N}\right) \cdot \frac{1}{N^{wq_C}}. \tag{15}$$

The proof is deferred to the full version.

Gathering Eq. (13) and Eqs. (14) and (15), we finally reach

$$\begin{aligned}
\frac{\mu(\tau)}{\nu(\tau)} \ge & \left(1 - \frac{4wq_Cq_F + w^2q_C + w^2q_C^2}{4N}\right)\left(1 - \frac{4wq_C(q_F + wq_C/2) + w^2q_C^2}{8N}\right) \cdot \frac{(N^w)_{q_C}}{N^{wq_C}} \\
\ge & \left(1 - \frac{4wq_Cq_F + w^2q_C + w^2q_C^2}{4N}\right)\left(1 - \frac{4wq_C(q_F + wq_C/2) + w^2q_C^2}{8N}\right) \cdot \left(1 - \frac{q_C^2}{N^w}\right) \\
\ge & 1 - \frac{12wq_Cq_F + 7w^2q_C^2}{8N} - \frac{q_C^2}{N^w} \ge 1 - \frac{12wq_Cq_F + 7w^2q_C^2}{8N} - \frac{q_C^2}{N^{w/2}}.
\end{aligned}$$

Further, using Eq. (12) yield the bound in Eq. (11) and complete the proof.

6 Conclusion

In this paper, we explore the problem of minimizing non-linearity in Type-II Generalized Feistel Networks. Inspired by the fast diffusion of SPNs, we consider incorporating their (strong) diffusion layers into Type-II Generalized Feistel Networks and introduce the key in each round. Thus, we introduce a new variant of the generalized Feistel Networks, which we call GEGFN. To provide a theoretical justification, we study SPRP security of GEGFN using random permutation or function in binary fields $\mathbb{F}_{2^n}$ and prime fields $\mathbb{F}_p$, with p being prime. Our research proves birthday-bound security at 5 rounds.

Acknowledgments. Chun Guo was partly supported by the National Natural Science Foundation of China (Grant No. 62002202) and the Taishan Scholars Program (for Young Scientists) of Shandong. Weijia Wang was partly supported by the Program of Qilu Young Scholars (Grant No. 61580082063088) of Shandong University.

A The H-Coefficient Technique

We use Patarin's H-coefficient technique [30] to prove the SPRP security of GEGFNs. We provide a quick overview of its main ingredients here. Our presentation borrows heavily from that of [8]. Fix a distinguisher D that makes at most q queries to its oracles. As in the security definition presented above, D's aim is to distinguish between two worlds: a "real world" and an "ideal world". Assume wlog that D is deterministic. The execution of D defines a *transcript* that includes the sequence of queries and answers received from its oracles; D's output is a deterministic function of its transcript. Thus, if μ, ν denote the probability distributions on transcripts induced by the real and ideal worlds, respectively, then D's distinguishing advantage is upper bounded by the statistical distance

$$\mathsf{Dist}(\mu, \nu) := \frac{1}{2} \sum_{\tau} \left|\mu(\tau) - \nu(\tau)\right|, \tag{16}$$

where the sum is taken over all possible transcripts τ.

Let $\mathcal{T}$ denote the set of all transcripts such that $\nu(\tau) > 0$ for all $\tau \in \mathcal{T}$. We look for a partition of $\mathcal{T}$ into two sets $\mathcal{T}_1$ and $\mathcal{T}_2$ of "good" and "bad" transcripts, respectively, along with a constant $\epsilon_1 \in [0, 1)$ such that

$$\tau \in \mathcal{T}_1 \Longrightarrow \mu(\tau)/\nu(\tau) \geq 1 - \epsilon_1. \tag{17}$$

It is then possible to show (see [8] for details) that

$$\mathsf{Dist}(\mu, \nu) \leq \epsilon_1 + \Pr[\nu \in \mathcal{T}_2] \tag{18}$$

is an upper bound on the distinguisher's advantage.

B Deferred Proofs

B.1 Proof of Lemma 2

Wlog, consider the case of **Type-I** Q_{m_ℓ}, as the other case is just symmetric. Assume otherwise, and assume that $\mathsf{tuple}_1 = (u_1^{(j_1)}, u_2^{(j_1)}, v_4^{(j_1)}, v_5^{(j_1)})$ and $\mathsf{tuple}_2 = (u_1^{(j_2)}, u_2^{(j_2)}, v_4^{(j_2)}, v_5^{(j_2)})$ in $\cup_{i=1}^{\ell-1} Q_{m_i}$ are such two tuples with the smallest indices j_1, j_2. Wlog assume $j_2 > j_1$, i.e., tuple_2 was later. Then tuple_2 was necessarily a forward query, as otherwise $u_1^{(j_1)}[\mathsf{even}] = u_1^{(j_2)}[\mathsf{even}]$ would contradict the goodness of τ (the 4th condition). By this and further by the 4th condition, $v_5^{(j_2)}[\mathsf{even}]$ is "new", and tuple_2 cannot be in any **Type-II** set Q_{m_i}, $i \leq \ell - 1$. This means there exists a **Type-I** set Q_{m_i}, $i \leq \ell - 1$, such that $\mathsf{tuple}_2 \in Q_{m_i}$. By our rules, the tuples in the purported Q_{m_ℓ} should have been Q_{m_i}, and thus Q_{m_ℓ} should not exist, reaching a contradiction.

B.2 Proof of Lemma 3

Wlog consider a **Type-I** Q_{m_ℓ}. First, note that by $\neg$(B-1) (the 1st condition), $u_2^{(\ell,i_1)}[j] \notin \mathrm{Dom}_2$ and $u_2^{(\ell,i_2)}[j] \notin \mathrm{Dom}_2$ for any $j \in \{2, 4, \ldots, w\}$. We then distinguish two cases depending on $\cup_{i=1}^{\ell-1} Q_{m_i}$ (which contribute to $\mathrm{ExtDom}_2^{(\ell)}$):

Case 1: $\mathbf{u}_1^{(\ell,i_1)}[\mathsf{even}] \neq \mathbf{u}_1[\mathsf{even}]$ for all $(\mathbf{u}_1, \mathbf{u}_2, \mathbf{v}_4, \mathbf{v}_5) \in \cup_{i=1}^{\ell-1} \mathbf{Q}_{m_i}$. Then by $\neg$(B-3), $u_2^{(\ell,i_1)}[j], u_2^{(\ell,i_2)}[j] \notin \mathrm{ExtDom}_2^{(\ell)}$ *for all* $j \in \{2, 4, \ldots, w\}$. Among these $w/2$ indices, there exists j_1 such that $u_2^{(\ell,i_1)}[j_1] \neq u_2^{(\ell,i_2)}[j_1]$, as otherwise, it would contradict the "q_C non-redundant forward/inverse queries". Therefore, we complete the argument for this case.

Case 2: there exists $(\mathbf{u}_1^*, \mathbf{u}_2^*, \mathbf{v}_4^*, \mathbf{v}_5^*) \in \cup_{i=1}^{\ell-1} \mathbf{Q}_{m_i}$ with $\mathbf{u}_1^*[\mathsf{even}] = \mathbf{u}_1^{(\ell,i_1)}[\mathsf{even}]$.

Then by construction, we have $u_2^{(\ell,i_1)}[\mathsf{even}] = u_2^*[\mathsf{even}] + \Delta_{i_1}$ and $u_2^{(\ell,i_2)}[\mathsf{even}] = u_2^*[\mathsf{even}] + \Delta_{i_2}$, where $\Delta_{i_1} = T_{\mathrm{EO}} \cdot \left(u_1^{(\ell,i_1)}[\mathsf{odd}] - u_1^*[\mathsf{odd}]\right)$ and $\Delta_{i_2} = T_{\mathrm{EO}} \cdot \left(u_1^{(\ell,i_2)}[\mathsf{odd}] - u_1^*[\mathsf{odd}]\right)$. Let $\mathcal{J}_{i_1}$ be the subset of $\{2, 4, \ldots, w\}$ such that $\Delta_{i_1}[j] \neq 0$ iff. $j \in \mathcal{J}_{i_1}$, and $\mathcal{J}_{i_2} \subseteq \{2, 4, \ldots, w\}$ be such that $\Delta_{i_2}[j] \neq 0$ iff. $j \in \mathcal{J}_{i_2}$. We distinguish three subcases depending on $\mathcal{J}_{i_1}$ and $\mathcal{J}_{i_2}$:

- Subcase 2.1: $\mathcal{J}_{i_1} \backslash \mathcal{J}_{i_2} \neq \emptyset$. Then, let $j_1 \in \mathcal{J}_{i_1} \backslash \mathcal{J}_{i_2}$, and $j_2 \in \mathcal{J}_{i_2}$ in arbitrary. This means $j_1 \neq j_2$, $\Delta_{i_1}[j_1] \neq 0$ but $\Delta_{i_2}[j_1] = 0$, and then $u_2^{(\ell,i_1)}[j_1] \neq u_2^{(\ell,i_2)}[j_1]$. Moreover,
  - $u_2^{(\ell,i_1)}[j_1] \neq u_2^*[j_3]$ for any $j_3 \notin \{2, 4, \ldots, w\} \backslash \{j_1\}$, by $\neg$(B-3) (the 2nd condition); $u_2^{(\ell,i_1)}[j_1] \neq u_2^*[j_1]$ since $j_1 \in \mathcal{J}_{i_1}$. Thus $u_2^{(\ell,i_1)}[j_1] \notin \mathrm{ExtDom}_2^{(\ell)}$. Similarly for $u_2^{(\ell,i_2)}$.
  - $u_1^{(\ell,i_1)}[\mathsf{even}] \neq u_1^{**}[\mathsf{even}]$ for any $(u_1^{**}, u_2^{**}, v_4^{**}, v_5^{**}) \neq (u_1^*, u_2^*, v_4^*, v_5^*)$ in $\cup_{i=1}^{\ell-1} Q_{m_i}$ (by Lemma 2), and thus $u_2^{(\ell,i_1)}[j_1] \neq u_2^{**}[j']$ for any $j' \in \{2, 4, \ldots, w\}$ by $\neg$(B-3) (the 1st condition). Similarly for $u_2^{(\ell,i_2)}$.
- Subcase 2.2: $\mathcal{J}_{i_2} \backslash \mathcal{J}_{i_1} \neq \emptyset$. Then, let $j_2 \in \mathcal{J}_{i_2} \backslash \mathcal{J}_{i_1}$, and $j_1 \in \mathcal{J}_{i_1}$, and the argument is similar to subcase 2.1 by symmetry.
- Subcase 2.3: $\mathcal{J}_{i_1} = \mathcal{J}_{i_2}$. Then there exists $j \in \mathcal{J}_{i_1}$ such that $\Delta_{i_1}[j] \neq \Delta_{i_2}[j]$, as otherwise $\Delta_{i_1} = \Delta_{i_2}$, meaning a contradiction. Let $j_1 = j_2 = j$, then it's easy to see all the claims hold.

By the above, for **Type-I** sets, the claims hold in all cases. Thus the claim.

C MDS Candidates in $\mathbb{F}_N$

An important question is whether such a strong T in Definition 1 exists at all. Note that if a strong T in Definition 1 exists, then T in Definition 2 naturally exists. Therefore, we give candidates in $\mathbb{F}_N$, where N is either a power of 2 or a prime number.

C.1 MDS in Binary Field

Using the primitive polynomial $x^8 + x^4 + x^3 + x^2 + 1$, two candidates for $N = 2^8$ and $w = 8, 16$, respectively, are as follows. We employ Vandermonde matrices [25] to generate these MDS matrices.

$$\begin{pmatrix} 0x87 & 0xB3 & 0x1D & 0xC7 & 0x27 & 0x12 & 0x5A & 0x83 \\ 0x86 & 0x3C & 0xE6 & 0x3E & 0x0D & 0xBA & 0xE9 & 0x3D \\ 0x5D & 0xF4 & 0x4A & 0x1C & 0x0C & 0x3B & 0x79 & 0xB0 \\ 0x51 & 0xB1 & 0xA6 & 0xA5 & 0x34 & 0x6A & 0xA7 & 0x1B \\ 0x63 & 0x66 & 0xBC & 0x83 & 0x02 & 0xC9 & 0x63 & 0x93 \\ 0x61 & 0xB5 & 0xB6 & 0x97 & 0xEE & 0x67 & 0x09 & 0x74 \\ 0x62 & 0x9E & 0x42 & 0xC4 & 0x50 & 0x35 & 0xDA & 0xC4 \\ 0xA5 & 0x65 & 0xFB & 0x90 & 0xFC & 0x8E & 0xC9 & 0x11 \end{pmatrix},$$

$$\begin{pmatrix} 0x52 & 0xE7 & 0xAE & 0x82 & 0x5E & 0x47 & 0x66 & 0x1C & 0x7C & 0x35 & 0x68 & 0xBE & 0x96 & 0x13 & 0xD1 & 0x30 \\ 0xFB & 0xA2 & 0x7B & 0xAB & 0x2E & 0x8E & 0x5A & 0xF9 & 0x8C & 0x07 & 0xE2 & 0xC3 & 0x82 & 0xc8 & 0x89 & 0xE2 \\ 0xD4 & 0xFA & 0xEC & 0x33 & 0x7E & 0xE6 & 0x04 & 0xBC & 0x2D & 0x43 & 0x2B & 0x7E & 0xAB & 0xDF & 0x58 & 0xC7 \\ 0xC4 & 0xBF & 0xAF & 0x1A & 0x7A & 0xDF & 0xBD & 0xFE & 0x67 & 0x5F & 0xDB & 0x3E & 0x52 & 0xA7 & 0xDA & 0xE6 \\ 0xC1 & 0x18 & 0xDE & 0x5C & 0x1B & 0x26 & 0x3D & 0xC8 & 0x10 & 0x4D & 0xC4 & 0xD0 & 0x0D & 0x62 & 0x91 & 0x25 \\ 0x81 & 0xD8 & 0x77 & 0x92 & 0x12 & 0x6A & 0x92 & 0x3A & 0x8B & 0xCF & 0xAD & 0x43 & 0xC4 & 0xFD & 0x44 & 0xBA \\ 0xDF & 0x67 & 0x52 & 0xE2 & 0xCB & 0xCC & 0x8E & 0xEC & 0x1E & 0xEF & 0x71 & 0xDC & 0xD7 & 0xD1 & 0x95 & 0xA3 \\ 0xE4 & 0x3C & 0x88 & 0xE7 & 0xD2 & 0x41 & 0x01 & 0x20 & 0x3E & 0x56 & 0x11 & 0x9B & 0x09 & 0xFD & 0xD2 & 0xC0 \\ 0xF7 & 0x33 & 0x8F & 0x55 & 0x79 & 0x65 & 0x27 & 0x29 & 0x48 & 0x39 & 0x96 & 0xB9 & 0xF6 & 0xBF & 0xA5 & 0xBF \\ 0xAB & 0xEF & 0xA0 & 0x9C & 0xA7 & 0x6A & 0xF0 & 0x44 & 0x57 & 0x63 & 0xAF & 0x0F & 0x79 & 0x6A & 0xBA & 0x3D \\ 0x66 & 0x52 & 0x58 & 0xB5 & 0x17 & 0x1B & 0x58 & 0xBE & 0x9C & 0xBA & 0x77 & 0xD6 & 0x30 & 0xEA & 0xA1 & 0xCE \\ 0xC6 & 0x9D & 0x9C & 0xD2 & 0x89 & 0x02 & 0x5F & 0x25 & 0x90 & 0x25 & 0x34 & 0x21 & 0xD1 & 0xE9 & 0x2F & 0x52 \\ 0xE9 & 0x37 & 0xB1 & 0xF3 & 0x88 & 0x0F & 0x5F & 0xE7 & 0xCA & 0x0D & 0xF9 & 0x52 & 0x9F & 0x80 & 0xF5 & 0x24 \\ 0x13 & 0xB4 & 0xF3 & 0x71 & 0x0A & 0x7C & 0x13 & 0xCC & 0xC2 & 0x04 & 0x43 & 0xD3 & 0xC0 & 0xAC & 0x9B & 0x2C \\ 0xBE & 0x01 & 0x7B & 0x40 & 0x54 & 0x49 & 0x73 & 0xD9 & 0x2E & 0x47 & 0xA5 & 0x55 & 0x3B & 0x55 & 0xF7 & 0x32 \\ 0x5F & 0xA6 & 0x19 & 0x03 & 0x4D & 0x3F & 0x9E & 0xE8 & 0x9D & 0x54 & 0xC0 & 0xB6 & 0x62 & 0x5C & 0xE8 & 0x8F \end{pmatrix}.$$

Using the primitive polynomial $x^{11} + x^2 + 1$ a candidate for $N = 2^{11}$ and $w = 8$ is as follows:

$$\begin{pmatrix} 0x078 & 0x166 & 0x14D & 0x019 & 0x1C8 & 0x098 & 0x187 & 0x09C \\ 0x257 & 0x436 & 0x7F9 & 0x644 & 0x0F9 & 0x370 & 0x634 & 0x260 \\ 0x777 & 0x721 & 0x309 & 0x609 & 0x158 & 0x59B & 0x353 & 0x2C7 \\ 0x5FC & 0x6D8 & 0x63A & 0x21A & 0x78B & 0x483 & 0x252 & 0x65F \\ 0x74C & 0x4B3 & 0x068 & 0x1B5 & 0x103 & 0x273 & 0x263 & 0x330 \\ 0x568 & 0x45F & 0x401 & 0x5EE & 0x25B & 0x541 & 0x2D4 & 0x517 \\ 0x60C & 0x53B & 0x7EB & 0x30F & 0x0B8 & 0x52D & 0x35C & 0x11B \\ 0x67C & 0x77C & 0x388 & 0x749 & 0x216 & 0x742 & 0x52B & 0x5BF \end{pmatrix}.$$

We have also found plenty of candidates for other parameters, which are however omitted for the sake of space.

C.2 MDS in Prime Field

Rescue [3] is a symmetric cryptographic algorithm in the prime field. [3] offers to use $m \times 2m$ Vandermonde matrices using powers of an $\mathbb{F}_N$ primitive element. This matrix is then echelon reduced after which the $m \times m$ identity matrix is removed and the MDS matrix is obtained.

The field is $\mathbb{F}_N$ where $N = 2^{61} + 20 \cdot 2^{32} + 1$ and the state consists of $w = 12$ elements. We get an MDS matrix $T^{12\times12}$ that satisfies Definition 1. Because the matrix is large, we give four submatrices of $T^{12\times12}$ for convenience.

Remark 1. Our results also apply to some finite commutative rings if these rings exist MDS matrix. We assume that $\mathcal{R}$ is a finite commutative ring with identity and $\mathcal{U}(\mathcal{R})$ be the set of unit elements in $\mathcal{R}$. We note that a square matrix M over $\mathcal{R}$ is an MDS matrix if and only if the determinant of every submatrix of M is an element of $\mathcal{U}(\mathcal{R})$.

$$T_{\mathrm{EO}} = \begin{pmatrix} 2132424736362510249 & 272219690434835935 & 628384112905106413 & 1565489682189437819 & 1026477510185581666 & 2301513477475405913 \\ 760420574997441750 & 2035848417468001220 & 367912208253241944 & 547812474641127246 & 1612644506155170807 & 1039051613644087538 \\ 132726795077680251 & 276049002402132600 & 2062106681853038294 & 1798462318189496829 & 876966686293506264 & 287934944924422359 \\ 1264644276986552669 & 959231254313894919 & 1609867535685450063 & 600131831529382266 & 1620659942407802180 & 1917517751863507751 \\ 445000516669406821 & 999425300126380635 & 1424386583549059837 & 1840785481461661844 & 770207555826068291 & 1321685401225718358 \\ 639836024986482499 & 891641509416426249 & 85684006979349218 & 2009314248255768979 & 1461785329408795871 & 614526427234661302 \end{pmatrix},$$

$$T_{\mathrm{EE}} = \begin{pmatrix} 157114849226309962 & 2227517040482465911 & 187890826715913914 & 855185158248966901 & 1240231461853961953 & 52955405230 \\ 1609903324587312789 & 2102895942828698062 & 549219385545962688 & 1695153738293598915 & 2060362812156761441 & 1759676667219874712 \\ 923095709968000189 & 959338751046899491 & 244453736105668101 & 1406898979258649653 & 275447637214934490 & 2285734233230770845 \\ 1265639319216678149 & 697991249395296203 & 1704131864879019365 & 1685146518137773283 & 1060851437983461874 & 1755088683392460390 \\ 2093205648133558759 & 329637479548419001 & 301428008445525907 & 1513566306301422264 & 670626981701496916 & 2125103307689520606 \\ 875144587036228576 & 365539559403463513 & 595494090920351320 & 396294882845853692 & 733908538741415240 & 554203175223363034 \end{pmatrix},$$

$$T_{\mathrm{OE}} = \begin{pmatrix} 1785767748384713920 & 1176202705900433241 & 2002100411542386973 & 391614261697275974 & 360795585898440 & 265720 \\ 1911206489025036282 & 2288800061181620774 & 2022538467220806570 & 1528973107985342496 & 1329417068351153619 & 9741692640081640 \\ 1017975231587935907 & 458455469860708540 & 1509611069489431703 & 1431382453218999763 & 1603062934957270225 & 1154395161414073365 \\ 967955863044139674 & 606678741800936612 & 2152312119329458712 & 1922914078805331422 & 224816859858735634 & 1905450060424727813 \\ 1604595880107521285 & 1868014205588480988 & 2136423194693683476 & 1163035584930921200 & 1169104133940285381 & 398952898784904682 \\ 2174389749072740614 & 1890638126825797984 & 1260330357606851540 & 1134389307747653122 & 1180187000329492200 & 1245356238080565962 \end{pmatrix},$$

$$T_{\mathrm{OO}} = \begin{pmatrix} 648467820989193486 & 229302989012133557 & 1573754073982867168 & 1506606314453584238 & 2215038371668159819 & 2305843077461326703 \\ 1694082666618257031 & 1779960530227737406 & 2076188670648949015 & 68601033256903557 & 1078330817078159304 & 353061061557231418 \\ 2305116735606702210 & 1364902896243084334 & 693700034972091385 & 2150732365748590380 & 2047024234454902938 & 404543078237488362 \\ 1393210217904044083 & 475897447857635565 & 1964414678958219561 & 1764783251126283713 & 170610800668462953 & 286014450900263497 \\ 1004420887426787826 & 2132518609943871819 & 1328965370622617212 & 2032385826938959001 & 111192163100705374 & 1191292909712540868 \\ 1956705709965072738 & 260751610632947425 & 2287279591594228857 & 1266747282502070711 & 835240421619663589 & 648886269814194370 \end{pmatrix}.$$

References

1. Albrecht, M.R., et al.: Feistel structures for MPC, and more. In: Sako, K., Schneider, S., Ryan, P.Y.A. (eds.) ESORICS 2019. LNCS, vol. 11736, pp. 151–171. Springer, Cham (2019). https://doi.org/10.1007/978-3-030-29962-0_8
2. Albrecht, M.R., Rechberger, C., Schneider, T., Tiessen, T., Zohner, M.: Ciphers for MPC and FHE. In: Oswald, E., Fischlin, M. (eds.) EUROCRYPT 2015. LNCS, vol. 9056, pp. 430–454. Springer, Heidelberg (2015). https://doi.org/10.1007/978-3-662-46800-5_17
3. Aly, A., Ashur, T., Ben-Sasson, E., Dhooghe, S., Szepieniec, A.: Design of symmetric-key primitives for advanced cryptographic protocols. IACR Trans. Symm. Cryptol. **2020**(3), 1–45 (2020). https://doi.org/10.13154/tosc.v2020.i3.1-45
4. Bar-On, A., Dinur, I., Dunkelman, O., Lallemand, V., Keller, N., Tsaban, B.: Cryptanalysis of SP networks with partial non-linear layers. In: Oswald, E., Fischlin, M. (eds.) EUROCRYPT 2015. LNCS, vol. 9056, pp. 315–342. Springer, Heidelberg (2015). https://doi.org/10.1007/978-3-662-46800-5_13
5. Berger, T.P., Francq, J., Minier, M., Thomas, G.: Extended generalized Feistel networks using matrix representation to propose a new lightweight block cipher: Lilliput. IEEE Trans. Comput. **65**(7), 2074–2089 (2016). https://doi.org/10.1109/TC.2015.2468218
6. Bhaumik, R., List, E., Nandi, M.: ZCZ – achieving n-bit SPRP security with a minimal number of tweakable-block-cipher calls. In: Peyrin, T., Galbraith, S. (eds.) ASIACRYPT 2018. LNCS, vol. 11272, pp. 336–366. Springer, Cham (2018). https://doi.org/10.1007/978-3-030-03326-2_12
7. Cauchois, V., Gomez, C., Thomas, G.: General diffusion analysis: how to find optimal permutations for generalized type-II Feistel schemes. IACR Trans. Symm. Cryptol. **2019**(1), 264–301 (2019). https://doi.org/10.13154/tosc.v2019.i1.264-301
8. Chen, S., Steinberger, J.: Tight security bounds for key-alternating ciphers. In: Nguyen, P.Q., Oswald, E. (eds.) EUROCRYPT 2014. LNCS, vol. 8441, pp. 327–350. Springer, Heidelberg (2014). https://doi.org/10.1007/978-3-642-55220-5_19
9. Cogliati, B., et al.: Provable security of (tweakable) block ciphers based on substitution-permutation networks. In: Shacham, H., Boldyreva, A. (eds.) CRYPTO 2018. LNCS, vol. 10991, pp. 722–753. Springer, Cham (2018). https://doi.org/10.1007/978-3-319-96884-1_24
10. Derbez, P., Fouque, P., Lambin, B., Mollimard, V.: Efficient search for optimal diffusion layers of generalized Feistel networks. IACR Trans. Symmetric Cryptol. **2019**(2), 218–240 (2019). https://doi.org/10.13154/tosc.v2019.i2.218-240
11. Dodis, Y., Katz, J., Steinberger, J., Thiruvengadam, A., Zhang, Z.: Provable security of substitution-permutation networks. Cryptology ePrint Archive, Report 2017/016 (2017). https://eprint.iacr.org/2017/016
12. Dodis, Y., Stam, M., Steinberger, J., Liu, T.: Indifferentiability of confusion-diffusion networks. In: Fischlin, M., Coron, J.-S. (eds.) EUROCRYPT 2016. LNCS, vol. 9666, pp. 679–704. Springer, Heidelberg (2016). https://doi.org/10.1007/978-3-662-49896-5_24
13. Gao, Y., Guo, C.: Provable security Of HADES structure. In: Beresford, A.R., Patra, A., Bellini, E. (eds.) CANS 2022. LNCS, vol. 13641, pp. 258–276. Springer, Heidelberg (2022). https://doi.org/10.1007/978-3-031-20974-1_13
14. Gérard, B., Grosso, V., Naya-Plasencia, M., Standaert, F.-X.: Block ciphers that are easier to mask: how far can we go? In: Bertoni, G., Coron, J.-S. (eds.) CHES

2013. LNCS, vol. 8086, pp. 383–399. Springer, Heidelberg (2013). https://doi.org/10.1007/978-3-642-40349-1_22
15. Grassi, L., Hao, Y., Rechberger, C., Schofnegger, M., Walch, R., Wang, Q.: Horst meets fluid-SPN: griffin for zero-knowledge applications. Cryptology ePrint Archive, Paper 2022/403 (2022). https://eprint.iacr.org/2022/403. To appear at CRYPTO 2023
16. Grassi, L., Kales, D., Khovratovich, D., Roy, A., Rechberger, C., Schofnegger, M.: Starkad and Poseidon: new hash functions for zero knowledge proof systems. Cryptology ePrint Archive, Report 2019/458 (2019). https://eprint.iacr.org/2019/458
17. Grassi, L., Khovratovich, D., Rechberger, C., Roy, A., Schofnegger, M.: Poseidon: A new hash function for zero-knowledge proof systems. In: USENIX Security Symposium (2021)
18. Grassi, L., Lüftenegger, R., Rechberger, C., Rotaru, D., Schofnegger, M.: On a generalization of substitution-permutation networks: the HADES design strategy. In: Canteaut, A., Ishai, Y. (eds.) EUROCRYPT 2020. LNCS, vol. 12106, pp. 674–704. Springer, Cham (2020). https://doi.org/10.1007/978-3-030-45724-2_23
19. Guo, C., Standaert, F.X., Wang, W., Wang, X., Yu, Y.: Provable security of SP networks with partial non-linear layers. In: FSE 2021, pp. 353–388 (2021). https://doi.org/10.46586/tosc.v2021.i2.353-388
20. Halevi, S.: EME*: extending EME to handle arbitrary-length messages with associated data. In: Canteaut, A., Viswanathan, K. (eds.) INDOCRYPT 2004. LNCS, vol. 3348, pp. 315–327. Springer, Heidelberg (2004). https://doi.org/10.1007/978-3-540-30556-9_25
21. Halevi, S., Rogaway, P.: A tweakable enciphering mode. In: Boneh, D. (ed.) CRYPTO 2003. LNCS, vol. 2729, pp. 482–499. Springer, Heidelberg (2003). https://doi.org/10.1007/978-3-540-45146-4_28
22. Halevi, S., Rogaway, P.: A parallelizable enciphering mode. In: Okamoto, T. (ed.) CT-RSA 2004. LNCS, vol. 2964, pp. 292–304. Springer, Heidelberg (2004). https://doi.org/10.1007/978-3-540-24660-2_23
23. Hoang, V.T., Rogaway, P.: On generalized Feistel networks. In: Rabin, T. (ed.) CRYPTO 2010. LNCS, vol. 6223, pp. 613–630. Springer, Heidelberg (2010). https://doi.org/10.1007/978-3-642-14623-7_33
24. Iwata, T., Kurosawa, K.: On the pseudorandomness of the AES finalists - RC6 and serpent. In: Goos, G., Hartmanis, J., van Leeuwen, J., Schneier, B. (eds.) FSE 2000. LNCS, vol. 1978, pp. 231–243. Springer, Heidelberg (2001). https://doi.org/10.1007/3-540-44706-7_16
25. Lacan, J., Fimes, J.: Systematic MDS erasure codes based on Vandermonde matrices. IEEE Commun. Lett. **8**, 570–572 (2004)
26. Nakamichi, R., Iwata, T.: Iterative block ciphers from tweakable block ciphers with long tweaks. IACR Trans. Symm. Cryptol. **2019**(4), 54–80 (2019). https://doi.org/10.13154/tosc.v2019.i4.54-80
27. Nakaya, K., Iwata, T.: Generalized Feistel structures based on tweakable block ciphers. IACR Trans. Symmetric Cryptol. **2022**(4), 24–91 (2022). https://doi.org/10.46586/tosc.v2022.i4.24-91
28. Nandi, M.: XLS is not a strong pseudorandom permutation. In: Sarkar, P., Iwata, T. (eds.) ASIACRYPT 2014. LNCS, vol. 8873, pp. 478–490. Springer, Heidelberg (2014). https://doi.org/10.1007/978-3-662-45611-8_25
29. Nandi, M.: On the optimality of non-linear computations of length-preserving encryption schemes. In: Iwata, T., Cheon, J.H. (eds.) ASIACRYPT 2015. LNCS,

vol. 9453, pp. 113–133. Springer, Heidelberg (2015). https://doi.org/10.1007/978-3-662-48800-3_5
30. Patarin, J.: The "coefficients H" technique. In: Avanzi, R.M., Keliher, L., Sica, F. (eds.) SAC 2008. LNCS, vol. 5381, pp. 328–345. Springer, Heidelberg (2009). https://doi.org/10.1007/978-3-642-04159-4_21
31. Ristenpart, T., Rogaway, P.: How to enrich the message space of a cipher. In: Biryukov, A. (ed.) FSE 2007. LNCS, vol. 4593, pp. 101–118. Springer, Heidelberg (2007). https://doi.org/10.1007/978-3-540-74619-5_7
32. Suzaki, T., Minematsu, K.: Improving the generalized Feistel. In: Hong, S., Iwata, T. (eds.) FSE 2010. LNCS, vol. 6147, pp. 19–39. Springer, Heidelberg (2010). https://doi.org/10.1007/978-3-642-13858-4_2
33. Wu, S., Wang, M.: Automatic search of truncated impossible differentials for word-oriented block ciphers. In: Galbraith, S., Nandi, M. (eds.) INDOCRYPT 2012. LNCS, vol. 7668, pp. 283–302. Springer, Heidelberg (2012). https://doi.org/10.1007/978-3-642-34931-7_17
34. Wu, W., Zhang, L.: LBlock: a lightweight block cipher. In: Lopez, J., Tsudik, G. (eds.) ACNS 2011. LNCS, vol. 6715, pp. 327–344. Springer, Heidelberg (2011). https://doi.org/10.1007/978-3-642-21554-4_19
35. Zheng, Y., Matsumoto, T., Imai, H.: On the construction of block ciphers provably secure and not relying on any unproved hypotheses. In: Brassard, G. (ed.) CRYPTO 1989. LNCS, vol. 435, p. 10.1007/0-387-34805-0_42-480. Springer, New York (1990). https://doi.org/10.1007/0-387-34805-0_42

Hardness of Learning AES with Gradient-Based Methods

Kanat Alimanov[1] and Zhenisbek Assylbekov[2(✉)]

[1] Department of Computer Science, Nazarbayev University, Astana, Kazakhstan
[2] Department of Mathematical Sciences, Purdue University Fort Wayne, Fort Wayne, IN, USA
zassylbe@pfw.edu

Abstract. We show the approximate pairwise orthogonality of a class of functions formed by a single AES output bit under the assumption that all of its round keys except the initial one are independent. This result implies the hardness of learning AES encryption (and decryption) with gradient-based methods. The proof relies on the Boas-Bellman type of inequality in inner-product spaces.

Keywords: Advanced Encryption Standard · Block Ciphers · Gradient-based Learning

1 Introduction

The Advanced Encryption Standard (AES) is a widely used encryption algorithm in modern internet communication protocols such as TLS 1.3. However, its security is not based on any known hard mathematical problem. On the contrary, this algorithm is a heuristic proposed by Rijmen and Daemen [1] in the late 90 s. It is noteworthy that since then no one has managed to build a successful attack on the AES. State-of-the-art attacks are only marginally better than brute force: for example, a biclique attack of Tao and Wu [8] requires 2^{126} operations to recover a 128-bit AES key (compared to 2^{128} operations with a brute force attack).

A recent work by Liu et al. [5] shows that under the assumption of independence of keys at each round, the outputs of AES for distinct inputs are statistically close to pairwise independence, making it resistant to attacks based on differential and linear cryptanalysis. Our work shows that this result is also sufficient for establishing the resistance of AES to *gradient-based* machine learning attacks.

Related Work. The main source of inspiration for us is the work of Shalev-Shwartz et al. [6], which, among other things, shows the intractability of learning a class of orthogonal functions using gradient-based methods. We emphasize that their result is not directly applicable to the class of functions that we consider in this paper—a single bit of AES output—since these functions are not

Z. Assylbekov—Work done while at Nazarbayev University.

J. Deng et al. (Eds.): CANS 2023, LNCS 14342, pp. 126–133, 2023.
https://doi.org/10.1007/978-981-99-7563-1_6

necessarily orthogonal with respect to a uniform distribution over the domain. However, under certain assumptions, they are *approximately* pairwise orthogonal (Lemma 2). In addition, our adaptation of the proof method by Shalev-Shwartz et al. [6] using the Boas-Bellman type inequality [2] deserves special attention, as it allows us to extend the failure of gradient-based learning to a wider class of approximately orthogonal functions.

It should be noted that the relationship between orthogonal functions and hardness of learning is not new and has been established in the context of statistical query (SQ) learning model of Kearns [4]. It is noteworthy that gradient-based learning with an approximate gradient oracle can be implemented through the SQ algorithm [3], which means that our result on the approximate orthogonality of the considered class of functions (Lemma 2) immediately gives the hardness of learning this class with gradient-based methods. Nevertheless, we believe that the proof of this result directly (without resorting to the SQ proxy) deserves attention, since it allows us to establish that the low information content of the gradient is the very reason why gradient learning fails.

2 Preliminaries

Notation. Bold-faced lowercase letters ($\mathbf{x}$) denote vectors, bold-faced uppercase letters ($\mathbf{X}$) denote random vectors, regular lowercase letters (x) denote scalars, regular uppercase letters (X) denote random variables. $\|\cdot\|$ denotes the Euclidean norm: $\|\mathbf{x}\| := \sqrt{\mathbf{x}^\top \mathbf{x}}$. $\mathcal{U}(\mathcal{X})$ denotes uniform distribution over $\mathcal{X}$. When p is a prime or prime power, let $\mathbb{F}_p$ denote the finite field of size p, and $\oplus$ is an addition operation in such a field. We will use $\mathbb{F}_2$ and $\{0,1\}$ interchangeably. A sequence of elements $a_i, a_{i+1}, \dots, a_j$ is denoted by $a_{i:j}$. For two square-integrable functions f, g on a Boolean hypercube $\{0,1\}^n$, let $\langle f, g\rangle_{L_2} := \mathbb{E}_{\mathbf{X}\sim\{0,1\}^n}[f(\mathbf{X})\cdot g(\mathbf{X})]$ and $\|f\|_{L_2} := \sqrt{\langle f, f\rangle}$.

2.1 Advanced Encryption Standard

We give a brief overview of the AES algorithm. It can be considered as a special case of a substitution-permutation network (SPN), which in turn is a special case of a key alternating cipher (KAC), see Fig. 1. A KAC is parameterized by a block size n, number of rounds r, and a fixed permutation $\pi : \mathbb{F}_{2^n} \to \mathbb{F}_{2^n}$. A KAC is a family of functions indexed by $r+1$ sub-keys $\mathbf{k}_0, \mathbf{k}_1, \dots, \mathbf{k}_r$, and defined recursively as follows

$$
\begin{aligned}
F^{(0)}_{\mathbf{k}_0}(\mathbf{x}) &= \mathbf{x} \oplus \mathbf{k}_0, \\
F^{(i)}_{\mathbf{k}_{0:i}}(\mathbf{x}) &= \pi(F^{(i-1)}_{\mathbf{k}_{0:i-1}}(\mathbf{x})) \oplus \mathbf{k}_i.
\end{aligned}
\tag{1}
$$

The family of functions is $\mathcal{F} := \{F^{(r)}_{\mathbf{k}_{0:r}}(\mathbf{x}) : \mathbf{k}_i \in \mathbb{F}_2^n\}$. This can be naturally extended to have different permutations π_i in each round as depicted in Fig. 1. An SPN can be seen as a special case of a KAC, where $n = k \cdot b$, and the permutation π is obtained from an S-box $S : \mathbb{F}_{2^b} \to \mathbb{F}_{2^b}$ and a linear mixing

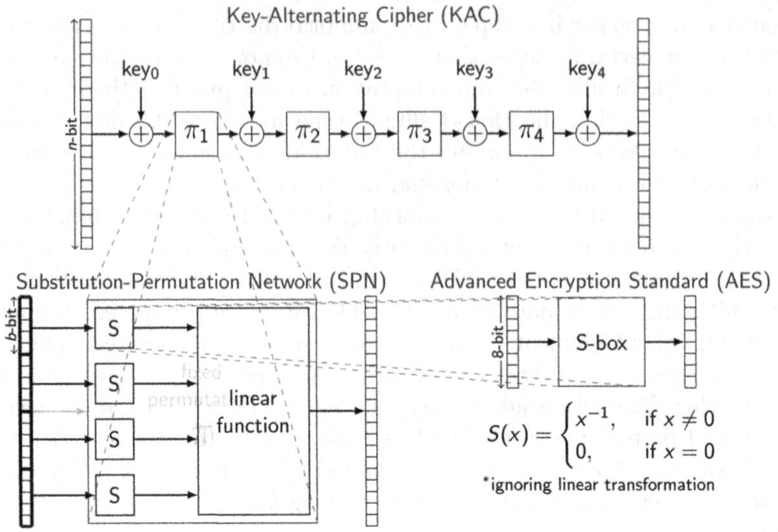

Fig. 1. KAC, SPN, and AES. Source: https://liutianren.com/static/slides/KAC.pdf. Reproduced with permission.

layer, described by a matrix $\mathbf{M} \in \mathbb{F}_{2^b}^{k\times k}$. In particular, π splits its input $\mathbf{x}$ into k b-bit blocks $x_1, \dots, x_k$ (treated as elements of $\mathbb{F}_{2^b}$), and computes first $y_\ell = S(x_\ell)$ for each $\ell \in \{1, \dots, k\}$, and then outputs $\mathbf{M} \cdot (y_1, \dots, y_k)$. Finally, AES is a special case of SPN with the block size $n = 128$, $k = 16$, and $b = 8$. The S-box is instantiated by $S(x) = A(x^{2^8-2})$, where $x \mapsto x^{2^8-2}$ is the patched inverse function over $\mathbb{F}_{2^8}$, A is an invertible affine function over $\mathbb{F}_2^8$.

2.2 Statistical Properties of AES

For the sake of brevity, $F_\mathbf{k}(\mathbf{x})$ denotes the output of AES with an initial key $\mathbf{k}$ on input $\mathbf{x}$. The rest of the round keys are assumed to be sampled uniformly at random from $\{0,1\}^n$, i.e. $\mathbf{K}_1, \dots, \mathbf{K}_r \overset{\text{iid}}{\sim} \mathcal{U}(\{0,1\}^n)$.[1] Under this assumption, Liu et al. [5] proved the following

Theorem 1 (Liu et al. [5]). *For a pair of distinct inputs* $\mathbf{x}, \mathbf{x}' \in \{0,1\}^n$, *and a uniformly sampled key* $\mathbf{K} \sim \mathcal{U}(\{0,1\}^n)$, *and given sufficiently large* r, *the distribution of the corresponding pair of outputs* $[F_\mathbf{K}(\mathbf{x}), F_\mathbf{K}(\mathbf{x}')]$ *can be made arbitrarily close in total variation distance to the uniform distribution of two random distinct* n*-bit strings* $[\mathbf{U}, \mathbf{U}']$. *That is, for any* $\epsilon > 0$, *there exists* $r \in \mathbb{N}$ *such that*

$$\frac{1}{2}\sum_{\mathbf{y},\mathbf{y}'}\left|\Pr_{\mathbf{K}}[F_\mathbf{K}(\mathbf{x}) = \mathbf{y}, F_{\mathbf{K}'}(\mathbf{x}) = \mathbf{y}'] - \Pr_{\mathbf{U},\mathbf{U}'}[\mathbf{U} = \mathbf{y}, \mathbf{U}' = \mathbf{y}']\right| \le \epsilon.$$

[1] This assumption is motivated by pseudo-randomness of the scheduler used in the real AES.

We can use the symmetry between the initial key and input at the 0th round of AES (1) to prove the following

Lemma 1. *For a pair of distinct keys* $\mathbf{k}, \mathbf{k}' \in \{0,1\}^n$, *and a uniformly sampled input* $\mathbf{X} \sim \mathcal{U}(\{0,1\}^n)$, *and any* $\epsilon > 0$, *the distribution of the corresponding pair* $[F_{\mathbf{k}}(\mathbf{X}), F_{\mathbf{k}'}(\mathbf{X})]$ *can be made* ϵ*-close to the distribution of two random distinct* n*-bit strings* $[\mathbf{U}, \mathbf{U}']$ *given sufficiently large* r, *i.e.*

$$\frac{1}{2}\sum_{\mathbf{y},\mathbf{y}'}\left|\Pr_{\mathbf{X}}[F_{\mathbf{k}}(\mathbf{X}) = \mathbf{y}, F_{\mathbf{k}'}(\mathbf{X}) = \mathbf{y}'] - \Pr_{\mathbf{U},\mathbf{U}'}[\mathbf{U} = \mathbf{y}, \mathbf{U}' = \mathbf{y}']\right| \leq \epsilon.$$

Proof. This follows from Theorem 1 and the chain of equalities:

$$\begin{aligned}
&\Pr_{\mathbf{K}}[F_{\mathbf{K}}(\mathbf{k}) = \mathbf{y}, F_{\mathbf{K}}(\mathbf{k}') = \mathbf{y}'] \\
&= \Pr_{\mathbf{K}}[F^{(r-1)}_{\mathbf{K}_{1:r}}(\pi(\mathbf{k} \oplus \mathbf{K})) = \mathbf{y}, F^{(r-1)}_{\mathbf{K}_{1:r}}(\pi(\mathbf{k}' \oplus \mathbf{K})) = \mathbf{y}'] \\
&= \Pr_{\mathbf{K}}[F_{\mathbf{k}}(\mathbf{K}) = \mathbf{y}, F_{\mathbf{k}'}(\mathbf{K}) = \mathbf{y}'] = \Pr_{\mathbf{X}}[F_{\mathbf{k}}(\mathbf{X}) = \mathbf{y}, F_{\mathbf{k}'}(\mathbf{X}) = \mathbf{y}'].
\end{aligned}$$

□

Let $h_{\mathbf{k}}(\mathbf{x})$ be defined as follows:

$$h_{\mathbf{k}}(\mathbf{x}) = \begin{cases} +1, & \text{if the first bit of } F_{\mathbf{k}}(\mathbf{x}) \text{ equals to 1,} \\ -1, & \text{otherwise} \end{cases} \tag{2}$$

The next lemma establishes the approximate pairwise orthogonality of the functions $\{h_{\mathbf{k}}(\mathbf{x}) \mid \mathbf{k} \in \{0,1\}^n\}$.

Lemma 2. *For any pair of distinct keys* $\mathbf{k}, \mathbf{k}' \in \{0,1\}^n$, *and any* $\epsilon > 0$ *there exists* $r \in \mathbb{N}$ *such that*

$$\left|\mathop{\mathbb{E}}_{\mathbf{X}}[h_{\mathbf{k}}(\mathbf{X})h_{\mathbf{k}'}(\mathbf{X})]\right| \leq 2\epsilon + \frac{1}{2^n - 1}.$$

Proof. Let $\mathbf{U}$, $\mathbf{U}'$ be sampled uniformly at random from $\{0,1\}^n$ without replacement. Then the first bits of $\mathbf{U}$ and $\mathbf{U}'$ (denoted as U_1 and U_1' respectively) differ with probability

$$\Pr[U_1 \neq U_1'] = \frac{2 \cdot 2^{n-1} \cdot 2^{n-1}}{2^n \cdot (2^n - 1)} = \frac{2^{n-1}}{2^n - 1}.$$

From this and Lemma 1, we have $\left|\Pr_{\mathbf{X}}[h_{\mathbf{k}}(\mathbf{X}) \neq h_{\mathbf{k}'}(\mathbf{X})] - \frac{2^{n-1}}{2^n-1}\right| \leq \epsilon$. Thus,

$$\begin{aligned}
&\left|\mathop{\mathbb{E}}_{\mathbf{X}}[h_{\mathbf{k}}(\mathbf{X})h_{\mathbf{k}'}(\mathbf{X})]\right| = \left|-1 \cdot \Pr_{\mathbf{X}}[h_{\mathbf{k}}(\mathbf{X}) \neq h_{\mathbf{k}'}(\mathbf{X})] + 1 \cdot \Pr_{\mathbf{X}}[h_{\mathbf{k}}(\mathbf{X}) = h_{\mathbf{k}'}(\mathbf{X})]\right| \\
&= \left|-1 \cdot \left(\Pr_{\mathbf{X}}[h_{\mathbf{k}}(\mathbf{X}) \neq h_{\mathbf{k}'}(\mathbf{X})] - \frac{2^{n-1}}{2^n - 1}\right) + (-1) \cdot \frac{2^{n-1}}{2^n - 1}\right. \\
&\left. +1 \cdot \left(\Pr_{\mathbf{X}}[h_{\mathbf{k}}(\mathbf{X}) = h_{\mathbf{k}}(\mathbf{X})] - \left(1 - \frac{2^{n-1}}{2^n - 1}\right)\right) + 1 \cdot \left(1 - \frac{2^{n-1}}{2^n - 1}\right)\right| \\
&\leq 2\epsilon + \left|1 - \frac{2^n}{2^n - 1}\right| = 2\epsilon + \frac{1}{2^n - 1}.
\end{aligned}$$

□

We will also need the following generalization of Bessel's inequality.

Lemma 3 (Boas-Bellman type inequality). *Let $h_1, \ldots, h_d, g$ be elements of an inner product space. Then*

$$\sum_{i=1}^{d} \langle h_i, g \rangle^2 \leq \|g\|^2 \left(\max_i \|h_i\|^2 + (d-1) \max_{i \neq j} |\langle h_i, h_j \rangle| \right).$$

Proof. Proof can be found in the work of Dragomir [2].

3 Main Result

Suppose we want to learn the first bit of AES output using a gradient-based method (e.g., deep learning). For this, consider the stochastic optimization problem associated with learning a target function $h_{\mathbf{k}}$ defined by (2),

$$L_{\mathbf{k}}(\mathbf{w}) := \mathbb{E}_{\mathbf{X}}[\ell(p_{\mathbf{w}}(\mathbf{X}), h_{\mathbf{k}}(\mathbf{X}))] \to \min_{\mathbf{w}}, \tag{3}$$

where ℓ is a loss function, $\mathbf{X}$ are the random inputs (from $\{0,1\}^n$), and $p_{\mathbf{w}}$ is some predictor parametrized by a parameter vector $\mathbf{w}$ (e.g. a neural network of a certain architecture). We will assume that $L_{\mathbf{k}}(\mathbf{w})$ is differentiable w.r.t. $\mathbf{w}$. We are interested in studying the *variance* of the gradient of $L_{\mathbf{K}}$ when $\mathbf{K}$ is drawn uniformly at random from $\{0,1\}^n$:

$$\mathrm{Var}[\nabla L_{\mathbf{K}}(\mathbf{w})] := \mathbb{E}_{\mathbf{K}} \|\nabla L_{\mathbf{K}}(\mathbf{w}) - \mathbb{E}_{\mathbf{K}'} \nabla L_{\mathbf{K}'}(\mathbf{w})\|^2 \tag{4}$$

The following theorem bounds this variance term.

Theorem 2. *Suppose that $p_{\mathbf{w}}(\mathbf{x})$ is differentiable w.r.t. $\mathbf{w}$, and for some scalar $G(\mathbf{w})$, satisfies $\mathbb{E}_{\mathbf{X}}\left[\|\frac{\partial}{\partial \mathbf{w}} p_{\mathbf{w}}(\mathbf{X})\|^2\right] \leq G(\mathbf{w})^2$. Let the loss function ℓ in (3) be either the square loss $\ell(\hat{y}, y) = \frac{1}{2}(\hat{y} - y)^2$ or a classification loss of the form $\ell(\hat{y}, y) = s(\hat{y} \cdot y)$ for some 1-Lipschitz function s. Then for any $\epsilon > 0$ there exists $r \in \mathbb{N}$ such that*

$$\mathrm{Var}[\nabla L_{\mathbf{K}}(\mathbf{w})] \leq \left(\frac{1}{2^{n-1}} + 2\epsilon \right) \cdot G(\mathbf{w})^2.$$

Proof. Define the vector-valued function

$$\mathbf{g}(\mathbf{x}) = \frac{\partial}{\partial \mathbf{w}} p_{\mathbf{w}}(\mathbf{x}),$$

and let $\mathbf{g}(\mathbf{x}) = (g_1(\mathbf{x}), g_2(\mathbf{x}), \ldots, g_d(\mathbf{x}))$ for real-valued functions $g_1, \ldots, g_d$. Then for the squared loss, we have $\mathbb{E}_{\mathbf{K}}[\nabla L_{\mathbf{K}}(\mathbf{w})] = \mathbb{E}_{\mathbf{X}}[p_{\mathbf{w}}(\mathbf{X})\mathbf{g}(\mathbf{X})]$, and

$$\begin{aligned}
\mathrm{Var}[\nabla L_{\mathbf{K}}(\mathbf{w})] &= \mathop{\mathbb{E}}_{\mathbf{K}} \left\| \nabla F_{\mathbf{K}}(\mathbf{w}) - \mathop{\mathbb{E}}_{\mathbf{X}}[p_{\mathbf{w}}(\mathbf{X})\mathbf{g}(\mathbf{X})] \right\|^2 \\
&= \mathop{\mathbb{E}}_{\mathbf{K}} \left\| \mathop{\mathbb{E}}_{\mathbf{X}}[(p_{\mathbf{w}}(\mathbf{X}) - h_{\mathbf{K}}(\mathbf{X}))\mathbf{g}(\mathbf{X})] - \mathop{\mathbb{E}}_{\mathbf{X}}[p_{\mathbf{w}}(\mathbf{X})\mathbf{g}(\mathbf{X})] \right\|^2 \\
&= \mathop{\mathbb{E}}_{\mathbf{K}} \left\| \mathop{\mathbb{E}}_{\mathbf{X}}[h_{\mathbf{K}}(\mathbf{X})\mathbf{g}(\mathbf{X})] \right\|^2 = \mathop{\mathbb{E}}_{\mathbf{K}} \sum_{j=1}^{d} \left(\mathop{\mathbb{E}}_{\mathbf{X}}[h_{\mathbf{K}}(\mathbf{X}) g_j(\mathbf{X})] \right)^2 = \mathop{\mathbb{E}}_{\mathbf{K}} \sum_{j=1}^{d} \langle h_{\mathbf{K}}, g_j \rangle_{L_2}^2 \\
&= \sum_{j=1}^{d} \left(\frac{1}{2^n} \sum_{\mathbf{k}\in\{0,1\}^n} \langle h_{\mathbf{k}}, g_j \rangle_{L_2}^2 \right) \overset{(*)}{\leq} \sum_{j=1}^{d} \frac{1}{2^n} \|g_j\|^2 \left(1 + (2^n - 1) \left(2\epsilon + \frac{1}{2^n - 1} \right) \right) \\
&= \frac{2 + 2\epsilon(2^n - 1)}{2^n} \sum_{j=1}^{d} \|g_j\|^2 \leq \left(\frac{1}{2^{n-1}} + 2\epsilon \right) \mathop{\mathbb{E}}_{\mathbf{X}} \|\mathbf{g}(\mathbf{X})\|^2 \leq \left(\frac{1}{2^{n-1}} + 2\epsilon \right) G(\mathbf{w})^2,
\end{aligned}$$

where $(*)$ follows from Lemmas 2 and 3. The case of the classification loss is handled analogously. □

Since ϵ can be made arbitrarily small, Theorem 2 says that the gradient of $L_{\mathbf{k}}(\mathbf{w})$ at any point $\mathbf{w}$ is extremely concentrated around a fixed point *independent* of the key $\mathbf{k}$. Using this one can show [7, Theorem 10] that a gradient-based method will fail in returning a reasonable predictor of the first bit of AES output unless the number of iterations is exponentially large in n (length of the key). This provides strong evidence that gradient-based methods cannot learn even a single bit of AES in poly(n) time. The result holds *regardless of which class of predictors we use* (e.g. arbitrarily complex neural networks)—the problem lies in using gradient-based method to train them.

Finally, we note that due to the one-to-one nature and symmetry of AES, we can replace $F_{\mathbf{k}}$ with its inverse $F_{\mathbf{k}}^{-1}$ in all our reasoning. This immediately implies the impossibility of learning even one bit of the inverse AES, and hence the entire AES decryption, in polynomial time using gradient-based methods.

4 Experiments

To validate the predictions of our theory, we generated a training sample as follows. We sampled $\mathbf{x}_1, \ldots, \mathbf{x}_m$ from $\{0,1\}^n$ uniformly at random. Next, we took a random key $\mathbf{k}$ and computed the ciphertexts $F_{\mathbf{k}}(\mathbf{x}_1), \ldots, F_{\mathbf{k}}(\mathbf{x}_m)$. We used the set $\{(F_{\mathbf{k}}(\mathbf{x}_1), x_1^1), \ldots, (F_{\mathbf{k}}(\mathbf{x}_m), x_m^1)\}$ for training, where x_i^1 denotes the first bit of i-th plaintext. The test sample was generated in the same way. The training and test sample sizes are 3.3M and 0.4M examples, respectively. We trained fully connected feedforward neural networks of depths 1–3[2] and evaluated their

[2] We used dropout 0.5 after each hidden layer, ReLU as the activation function, sigmoid as the output activation, and cross-entropy loss.

accuracies on the test set. The results of this experiment are shown in Table 1. Even though some architectures show some ability to fit the training set, this does not help them to generalize to new data, because in all cases the test accuracy is 0.5, which corresponds to randomly guessing the correct label by flipping a fair coin.

Table 1. The results of the experiments.

Depth	Architecture	Train Acc	Test Acc
1	128 → 2048 → 1	0.61	0.50
2	128 → 256 → 164 → 1	0.50	0.50
3	128 → 256 → 128 → 32 → 1	0.52	0.50

In order to visualize the hidden representations learned by the neural network with 1 hidden layer, we projected them from the hidden layer onto a 2D plane through the PCA. The results are shown in Fig. 2. As we can see, the neural network fails to separate the classes on both training and test samples. This supports implications from our Theorem 2.

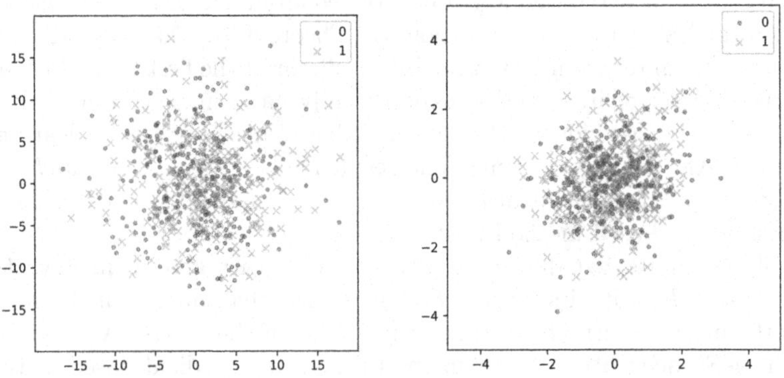

Fig. 2. PCA projections of representations from the 1-hidden-layer neural network for subsamples of size 600 from the training (left) and test sets.

5 Conclusion

Inspired by the recent result of Liu et al. [5] on statistical closeness of AES to pairwise independence under randomness of all round keys, we show closeness of AES to pairwise independence under randomness of the input and all round keys except the initial one. Based on this, we prove the resistance of AES against gradient-based machine learning attacks that aim to learn AES encryption (or decryption) from plaintext–ciphertext pairs (without recovering the key). Our proof is elementary and uses only college-level mathematics.

Acknowledgements. This work was supported by the Program of Targeted Funding "Economy of the Future" #0054/ПЦФ-НС-19.

References

1. Daemen, J., Rijmen, V.: The block cipher Rijndael. In: Quisquater, J.-J., Schneier, B. (eds.) CARDIS 1998. LNCS, vol. 1820, pp. 277–284. Springer, Heidelberg (2000). https://doi.org/10.1007/10721064_26
2. Dragomir, S.S.: On the boas-bellman inequality in inner product spaces. Bull. Aust. Math. Soc. **69**(2), 217–225 (2004)
3. Feldman, V., Guzmán, C., Vempala, S.S.: Statistical query algorithms for mean vector estimation and stochastic convex optimization. In: Klein, P.N. (ed.) Proceedings of the Twenty-Eighth Annual ACM-SIAM Symposium on Discrete Algorithms, SODA 2017, Barcelona, Spain, Hotel Porta Fira, 16–19 January 2017, pp. 1265–1277. SIAM (2017)
4. Kearns, M.J.: Efficient noise-tolerant learning from statistical queries. In: Kosaraju, S.R., Johnson, D.S., Aggarwal, A. (eds.) Proceedings of the Twenty-Fifth Annual ACM Symposium on Theory of Computing, 16–18 May 1993, San Diego, CA, USA, pp. 392–401. ACM (1993)
5. Liu, T., Tessaro, S., Vaikuntanathan, V.: The t-wise independence of substitution-permutation networks. In: Malkin, T., Peikert, C. (eds.) CRYPTO 2021, Part IV. LNCS, vol. 12828, pp. 454–483. Springer, Cham (2021). https://doi.org/10.1007/978-3-030-84259-8_16
6. Shalev-Shwartz, S., Shamir, O., Shammah, S.: Failures of gradient-based deep learning. In: Precup, D., Teh, Y.W. (eds.) Proceedings of the 34th International Conference on Machine Learning, ICML 2017, Sydney, NSW, Australia, 6–11 August 2017. Proceedings of Machine Learning Research, vol. 70, pp. 3067–3075. PMLR (2017)
7. Shamir, O.: Distribution-specific hardness of learning neural networks. J. Mach. Learn. Res. **19**, 32:1–32:29 (2018)
8. Tao, B., Wu, H.: Improving the biclique cryptanalysis of AES. In: Foo, E., Stebila, D. (eds.) ACISP 2015. LNCS, vol. 9144, pp. 39–56. Springer, Cham (2015). https://doi.org/10.1007/978-3-319-19962-7_3

Security

Privacy-Preserving Digital Vaccine Passport

Thai Duong[1], Jiahui Gao[2], Duong Hieu Phan[3], and Ni Trieu[2(✉)]

[1] Google LLC, Mountain View, USA
thai@calif.io
[2] Arizona State University, Tempe, USA
{jgao76,nitrieu}@asu.edu
[3] LTCI, Telecom Paris, Institut Polytechnique de Paris, Paris, France
hieu.phan@telecom-paris.fr

Abstract. The global lockdown imposed during the Covid-19 pandemic has resulted in significant social and economic challenges. In an effort to reopen economies and simultaneously control the spread of the disease, the implementation of contact tracing and digital vaccine passport technologies has been introduced. While contact tracing methods have been extensively studied and scrutinized for security concerns through numerous publications, vaccine passports have not received the same level of attention in terms of defining the problems they address, establishing security requirements, or developing efficient systems. Many of the existing methods employed currently suffer from privacy issues.

This work introduces PPass, an advanced digital vaccine passport system that prioritizes user privacy. We begin by outlining the essential security requirements for an ideal vaccine passport system. To address these requirements, we present two efficient constructions that enable PPass to function effectively across various environments while upholding user privacy. By estimating its performance, we demonstrate the practical feasibility of PPass. Our findings suggest that PPass can efficiently verify a passenger's vaccine passport in just 7 milliseconds, with a modest bandwidth requirement of 480 KB.

1 Introduction

As we navigate into the third year of the unprecedented global disruptions caused by the COVID-19 pandemic, there is a noticeable improvement in our circumstances. The accelerated development and widespread distribution of vaccines have played a vital role in expediting the pandemic's resolution and enhancing our preparedness for future outbreaks. However, it is crucial to recognize that privacy is equally significant in the context of vaccine passports as it is in contact tracing. Surprisingly, despite the multitude of proposals introduced by the scientific community last year for contact tracing, vaccine passports have not received the same level of attention when it comes to defining the problems they aim to address, establishing security requirements, or developing efficient systems. Consequently, many of the current methods employed in vaccine passport

J. Deng et al. (Eds.): CANS 2023, LNCS 14342, pp. 137–161, 2023.
https://doi.org/10.1007/978-981-99-7563-1_7

implementation suffer from privacy issues. In this study, we specifically focus on the privacy implications of a vaccine passport rollout (the term "vaccine passport" is used here to emphasize the privacy concern, but the discussion applies to all types of digital certificates).

It is important to acknowledge that the incentives for the general public to adopt a vaccine passport are considerably higher compared to those for using a contact tracing app. The use of a vaccine passport directly and immediately benefits the passport holder by allowing them to resume a normal life. On the other hand, the purpose of a contact tracing application primarily revolves around reducing the circulation of the virus in a more abstract manner. This disparity may explain why people tend to be more skeptical about the privacy and effectiveness of contact tracing while being more supportive of vaccine passports.

A survey conducted by Ipsos [17] further sheds light on public sentiment. The survey, which encompassed over 21,000 individuals across 28 countries between March 26 and April 9, 2021, revealed that 78% of respondents supported the requirement of COVID-19 vaccine passports for travelers. Interestingly, the same survey found that, on average across the 28 countries, only 50% of individuals felt comfortable with their government accessing their personal health information, with the number dropping to 40% in the case of private companies. Meanwhile, amidst the evolving landscape, several governments have made the decision to implement vaccine passports. Notably, we examine instances within countries known for their commitment to privacy:

- European leaders have reached an agreement to expedite the implementation of an EU-wide Digital Green Certificate as a matter of utmost importance.
- Some European countries, including Denmark, Sweden, and Iceland, have taken the initiative to launch their own vaccine passports. Denmark, for instance, has introduced the "Coronapas" vaccine passport domestically, with potential plans to utilize it for international travel purposes as well.
- Estonia has introduced the VaccineGuard, a distributed data exchange platform, to issue vaccination certificates in adherence to the EU's green certificate proposal. Additionally, in collaboration with the World Health Organization (WHO), Estonia has been involved in the creation of a "smart yellow card," which serves as a global vaccine certificate.
- In the United Kingdom, the primary National Health Service (NHS) has undergone updates to facilitate the presentation of COVID-19 vaccination or test results by the public when traveling or attending public events.

Essentially, the aforementioned solutions involve issuing a certificate to individuals after they have been vaccinated. This certificate is signed by the relevant authority and can be utilized for various purposes. In the case of the EU-wide Digital Green Certificate [1], it is specified that the certificate incorporates a QR code that is protected by a digital signature to prevent counterfeiting. During the verification process, the QR code is scanned and the signature is validated. To safeguard user privacy, the certificate contains only a limited set of information that cannot be retained by the visited countries, and all health data remains under the jurisdiction of the member state that issued the certificate.

However, it is important to note that this approach necessitates placing trust in the issuing authority. If the QR code is compromised or marked, it becomes possible to trace the movements of an individual. Moreover, even if the QR code is solely scanned by a machine, a security breach could result in the linkage of an individual's entire movement history. The reliance on trust in the authority and the potential linkability of data raise significant privacy concerns. Therefore, it is imperative to urgently address privacy concerns through a privacy-by-design approach rather than relying solely on trust. This entails proposing methods that offer the highest level of privacy protection.

1.1 Our Contribution

In this work, we present PPass, an innovative solution for safeguarding privacy in digital vaccine passports. Our system combines robust security measures with low resource requirements, ensuring an efficient and cost-effective approach. To enable PPass, we introduce two cryptographic constructions that function seamlessly both online and offline during the passport verification process. These constructions are specifically designed to optimize performance on resource-limited devices, such as mobile phones, while accommodating a substantial user base. Moreover, our proposed constructions fulfill all security and privacy objectives, which we will elaborate on in subsequent discussions. In summary, our contributions can be summarized as follows.

1. Problem Definition and Desirable Properties: We provide a formal definition of the digital vaccine passport problem and outline the essential security and performance requirements for an ideal scheme. To the best of our knowledge, this work represents the first formal study of this problem.
2. Efficient Constructions for PPass: Leveraging an untrusted cloud server, we propose two efficient constructions for PPass, namely a digital signature-based construction for offline verification and a PIR-based construction for online verification. For each construction, we conduct a thorough analysis of their security properties and assess their computational and communication costs.
3. Performance Evaluation: To demonstrate the feasibility of PPass, we estimate its performance in practical scenarios. Remarkably, the computational requirements for the involved entities-the health authority, the client/user (phone's holder), and the service (verifier)-are lightweight during the passport verification process. Specifically:
   - The authority needs a mere 0.054ms per client to generate/sign a valid vaccination certificate, with its runtime scaling linearly with the number of clients.
   - The client's computation cost is constant per redeemed token, requiring up to 13 milliseconds to redeem a vaccine passport certificate.
   - In the PIR-based construction, the service's computation cost grows logarithmically with the number of valid tokens held by the cloud server. However, in the signature-based construction, it remains constant per redeemed token, taking only 155 milliseconds.

Note that the cloud server bears the highest computation cost, but this can be mitigated by employing a more powerful machine or distributing the workload across multiple servers/cores. Importantly, PPass ensures no information leakage to the untrusted cloud server, enabling computation outsourcing without any privacy risks.

2 Problem Statement and Desirable Properties

In this section, we will elucidate the issue concerning digital vaccine passports that we aim to address. We will outline its security definition and expound upon the desirable properties of the system we propose.

Problem Definition. The problem at hand revolves around digital vaccine passports, which are mobile applications designed to verify an individual's vaccination status for a specific disease (e.g., COVID-19). The digital vaccine passport system comprises three primary participants: the client ($\mathcal{C}$), the health authority ($\mathcal{A}$), and the service or verifier ($\mathcal{S}$). When a client ($\mathcal{C}$) receives a vaccination, they obtain a vaccination certificate (σ) from a health authority ($\mathcal{A}$). The client ($\mathcal{C}$) can utilize this certificate (σ) to authenticate their vaccination status to a service without disclosing the actual certificate (σ) itself. The proof process involves leveraging information from the health authority ($\mathcal{A}$) that issued the certificate. In our proposed system, known as PPass, we employ an untrusted cloud server ($\mathcal{H}$) that performs the computational workload of the health authority ($\mathcal{A}$) to enhance system efficiency while ensuring the cloud server ($\mathcal{H}$) remains unaware of any sensitive information.

2.1 Security Definition

The vaccine passport system involves four types of participants: a client (or phone holder) $\mathcal{C}$, an authority $\mathcal{A}$, a cloud server $\mathcal{H}$, and a service (or verifier) $\mathcal{S}$. All participants have agreed upon a specific functionality, which is vaccine passport verification, and have consented to share the final result with a designated party. The computational process ensures that nothing is revealed except the final output.

For simplicity, we assume the presence of an authenticated secure channel (e.g., with TLS) between each pair of participants. In this work, we specifically focus on the semi-honest setting and the colluding model. In the ideal execution, the participants interact with a trusted party that evaluates the function while a simulator corrupts the same subset of participants. In the real-world execution, the protocol is performed in the presence of an adversary who can corrupt a subset of the participants. Privacy of the users is guaranteed as long as the adversary can only corrupt parties and does not compromise the authority server $\mathcal{A}$ and the service $\mathcal{S}$. Further details regarding the formal security definition and the security of our system can be found in Appendix D and Sect. 4, respectively.

2.2 Desirable Security

We outline the security and privacy requirements for the privacy-preserving digital vaccine passport system. One of the primary objectives is to ensure that the actions of honest clients, as well as other participants such as the authority server $\mathcal{A}$, cloud server $\mathcal{H}$, and service $\mathcal{S}$, are indistinguishable from each other. In other words, an ideal digital vaccine passport system would guarantee that executing the system in the real model is equivalent to executing it in an ideal model with a trusted party. This requirement aligns with the standard security definitions presented in [27]. Based on this definition, we consider the following security and privacy properties for the vaccine passport system:

- **Anonymous Identity:** The real identity of a client $\mathcal{C}$ should not be revealed to the untrusted cloud server $\mathcal{H}$. Furthermore, unless necessary, the service $\mathcal{S}$ should remain unaware of the client's identity. It is important to note that our PPass system does not maintain anonymity for clients if they willingly publish identifiable information. The authority $\mathcal{A}$ is only allowed to know the identity of a vaccinated client $\mathcal{C}$.
- **Token Unlinkability:** Valid tokens, generated from the same vaccination certificate σ, can be redeemed at multiple services $\mathcal{S}$. However, it should not be possible for any participant to link tokens belonging to the same client. Our PPass system does not guarantee token unlinkability if a group of services collude with the authority server $\mathcal{A}$.
- **Token Unforgeability:** All vaccination tokens must be unforgeable. A client should not be able to compute a valid token unless it corresponds to their valid vaccination certificate σ. Similarly, a client should not be able to compute a valid token generated from another client's vaccination certificate σ. Clients should be unable to redeem forged tokens, and any attempt to do so should be detected.
- **Token Unreusability:** Each valid token should be usable only once. Once a token is redeemed, it should be immediately deleted from the client's device. Clients and all participants, including services, should not be able to reuse redeemed tokens.

2.3 Desirable Performance

In addition to ensuring security and privacy, an ideal privacy-preserving digital vaccine passport system should possess certain performance requirements. We consider the following desirable performance properties:

- **Efficiency:** The digital vaccine passport system should be capable of processing a verification computation within a few seconds and should be scalable to accommodate a large number of users. Furthermore, participants, especially the authority $\mathcal{A}$ and the client $\mathcal{C}$, should perform lightweight tasks to ensure efficient operation.
- **Flexibility:** In certain scenarios where the client's ID is required to be collected by a service (e.g., at the airport), the vaccine passport system cannot maintain anonymous identity. Therefore, the system should be flexible enough

to provide a trade-off between performance and privacy in such cases. Similarly, the system can be optimized for efficiency in other scenarios where presenting an ID is not necessary.
- **Offline/Online Redeem:** In practice, a service may experience a slow network connection or be unable to connect to the internet during the verification process. The system should be designed to function correctly under different network conditions, supporting both offline and online redemption processes.

3 Cryptographic Preliminaries

This section introduces the notations and cryptographic primitives used in the later sections. For $n \in \mathbb{N}$, we write $[n]$ to denote the set of integers $\{1, \ldots, n\}$. We use '$||$' to denote string concatenation. In this work, the computational and statistical security parameters are denoted by κ, λ, respectively. Our PPass system is essentially based on the CDH or DDH assumption in a cyclic group [11].

3.1 Randomizable Signature Scheme

The use of digital signatures [25,33] in various applications has been crucial, serving as a fundamental building block. With the integration of advanced features like randomizability, digital signatures have become even more valuable. This added functionality allows for the derivation of a new valid signature $\sigma^\star$ on the same message, given an original valid signature σ. Importantly, randomizability ensures that these two signatures remain unlinkable, even for the signer themselves. The initial construction achieving this property was proposed by Camenisch and Lysyanskaya [7], which has since been further enhanced by Pointcheval and Sanders [31,32]. The use of randomizable signature schemes proves highly advantageous in our scenario as it enables the preservation of user privacy, even if the authority responsible for providing signed certificates is compromised.

Bilinear Group Setting. In the context of bilinear groups, a *bilinear group generator* $\mathcal{G}$ refers to an algorithm that takes a security parameter λ as input and produces a tuple $(\mathbb{G}_1, \mathbb{G}_2, \mathbb{G}_T, p, g_1, g_2, e)$. Here, $\mathbb{G}_1 = \langle g_1 \rangle$ and $\mathbb{G}_2 = \langle g_2 \rangle$ are cyclic groups of prime order p (a λ-bit prime integer), generated by g_1 and g_2 respectively. The function $e : \mathbb{G}_1 \times \mathbb{G}_2 \to \mathbb{G}_T$ is an *admissible pairing* satisfying the following properties:

- Bilinearity: For all $a, b \in \mathbb{Z}_p$, $e(g_1^a, g_2^b) = e(g_1, g_2)^{ab}$.
- Efficiency: e can be computed efficiently in polynomial time with respect to the security parameter λ.
- Non-degeneracy: $e(g_1, g_2) \neq 1$.

Additionally, the bilinear setting $(\mathbb{G}_1, \mathbb{G}_2, \mathbb{G}_T, p, g_1, g_2, e)$ is considered *asymmetric* when $\mathbb{G}_1 \neq \mathbb{G}_2$. There exist three types of pairings:

1. Type 1: $\mathbb{G}_1 = \mathbb{G}_2$.

2. Type 2: $e : \mathbb{G}_1 \times \mathbb{G}_2 \to \mathbb{G}_T$ is asymmetric, but an efficient homomorphism exists from $\mathbb{G}_2$ to $\mathbb{G}_1$, while no efficient homomorphism exists in the reverse direction.
3. Type 3: e is asymmetric, and no efficiently computable homomorphism exists between $\mathbb{G}_1$ and $\mathbb{G}_2$.

The Camenisch and Lysyanskaya signature scheme utilizes pairings of type 1, while the Pointcheval and Sanders signature scheme uses type 3 with a constant-size signature. The Pointcheval-Sanders scheme's unlinkability is based on the Decisional Diffie-Hellman (DDH) assumption in G_1, and its unforgeability relies on a complex assumption defined in [31]. In our PPass system, we rely on the Pointcheval-Sanders signature scheme because pairing type 3 offers the best performance among the three types.

3.2 Private Information Retrieval

Private Information Retrieval (PIR) allows a client to request information from one or multiple servers in such a way that the servers do not know which information the client queried. The basic concept of PIR is that the server(s) hold a database DB of N strings, and the client wishes to read data record $DB[i]$ without revealing the value of i. The construction of PIR [4] typically involves three procedures:

- PIR.Query$(pk, i) \to k$: a randomized algorithm that takes the index $i \in [N]$ and public key pk as input and outputs an evaluated key k.
- PIR.Answer$(pk, k, DB) \to c$: a deterministic algorithm that takes an evaluated key k, public key pk, and the DB as input and returns the response c.
- PIR.Extract$(sk, c) \to d$: a deterministic algorithm that takes the private key sk and the response c as input and returns the desired data d.

A PIR construction is correct if and only if $d = DB[i]$. We say that PIR is (symmetric) secure if an evaluated key k reveals nothing about the index i and the answer c reveals nothing about other database record $DB[j], j \in [N], j \neq i$.

Keyword-PIR. A variant of PIR called keyword-PIR was introduced by Chor, et al. [8]. In keyword-PIR, the client has an item x, the server has a database DB, and the client learns whether $x \in DB$. The most efficient keyword PIR [4] is implemented using bucketing with Cuckoo hashing [12]. In this paper, we are interested in Keyword PIR based on 1-server PIR [4,26,29], but our protocol can use multiple-server PIR [6,10,28] to speed up the system's performance.

Similar to traditional PIR, a keyword-PIR construction [4] comprises four procedures. However, in keyword-PIR, the PIR.Query(pk, x) procedure takes a keyword x as input, and PIR.Extract returns a bit d indicating whether x exists in the server's database DB. Utilizing hashing techniques [4,5], keyword-PIR exhibits similar computational and communication costs as traditional PIR. Angel et al.'s work [5, Figure 5] demonstrates that a PIR query on a database of size 2^{20} incurs approximately 7.62 milliseconds of client-side processing time and 80 milliseconds of server-side processing time (online time). Furthermore, the query requires 480KB of bandwidth for communication.

PIR-with-Default. Another variant of PIR, known as PIR-with-Default, was introduced by Lepoint et al. [20]. In PIR-with-Default, the server maintains a set of key-value pairs $P = (x_1, v_1), \ldots, (y_n, v_n)$, where y_i are distinct values and v_i are pseudo-random values. Additionally, there is a default (pseudo-random) value w. When the client submits an item x, it receives v_i if $x = v_i$, and w otherwise. The default value w needs to be refreshed for each query. This variant of PIR has found applications in private join and compute scenarios.

Similar to keyword-PIR, a PIR-with-Default construction also consists of the same procedures. However, in PIR-with-Default, the $\mathsf{PIR.Answer}(pk, k, P, w)$ procedure takes P and w as input, and $\mathsf{PIR.Extract}$ returns a value v. The PIR-with-Default protocol proposed by Lepoint et al. [20] is highly efficient, enabling 2^8 PIR with default lookups on a database of size 2^{20} with a communication cost of 7MB and an online computation time of 2.43 milliseconds.

3.3 Private Matching

A Private Matching (PM) is a two-party communication protocol where a sender possessing an input string m_0 interacts with a receiver who holds an input string m_1. The goal of this protocol is for the receiver to determine whether m_0 is equal to m_1, while ensuring that the sender learns nothing about m_1". The receiver obtains a single bit as output, indicating the equality result, but no additional information is revealed.

To the best of our knowledge, the concept of Private Equality Testing (PM) was first introduced in the works of Meadows [23] and FNW [14]. PM plays a crucial role in private set intersection (PSI) protocols [15]. Performing a batch of PM instances efficiently can be achieved using Oblivious Transfer (OT) extension techniques. For instance, a study by KKRT [19] demonstrates that the amortized cost of each PM instance, with an unbounded input domain $0, 1^*$, amounts to only a few symmetric-key operations and involves a communication of 488 bits. However, our protocol necessitates executing one PM instance at a time, rendering the construction of [19] unsuitable for our requirements. In our PPass system, we adopt a DH-based PM scheme, please refer Appendix E for the details.

4 Digital Vaccine Passport Constructions

We begin with describing the overview of our PPass system. We then present two cryptographic constructions: one for online verification and the other for offline verification.

4.1 System Overview

The purpose of a digital vaccine passport is to provide a means of verifying whether the individual holding the phone (referred to as the client) has been vaccinated for a specific disease. In this section, we present an overview of our proposed PPass system, which encompasses three primary procedures.

- `RegistrationRequest`$(\kappa, \text{inf}) \rightarrow \sigma$: The client $\mathcal{C}$ initiates this protocol by submitting a certificate request to the health authority $\mathcal{A}$. The $\mathcal{A}$ verifies whether the client has been vaccinated. If so, $\mathcal{A}$ generates a valid vaccination certificate σ and returns it to the client $\mathcal{C}$. Additionally, $\mathcal{A}$ sends certain anonymous information to the cloud server $\mathcal{H}$.
- `TokenGeneration`$(\sigma, n) \rightarrow \{tok_1, ..., tok_n\}$: The client $\mathcal{C}$ engages in this protocol with the cloud server $\mathcal{H}$ to generate a list of n vaccination tokens. The client $\mathcal{C}$ provides her vaccination certificate σ and specifies the number n, resulting in the generation of n tokens as output.
- `TokenRedeem`$(\text{tok}_t, \text{inf}) \rightarrow \{0, 1\}$: At time t, the client $\mathcal{C}$ redeems a token tok_t. The protocol takes as input the token tok_t and the client's information inf if required. Optionally, a service provider (verifier) $\mathcal{S}$ interacts with the cloud server $\mathcal{H}$ to verify the validity of tok_t and its association with the token holder. The output may be returned to the client $\mathcal{C}$. Once redeemed, the token tok_i becomes invalid (Fig. 1).

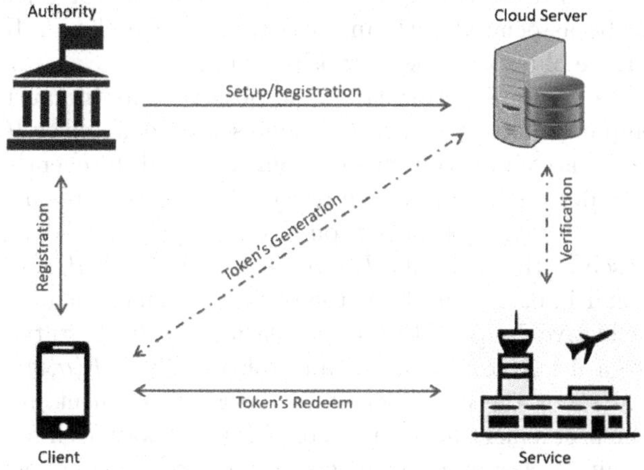

Fig. 1. The Overview of our PPass System. It consists of three main phases: Registration, Token's Generation, Token's Redeem. The solid and dashed lines show the required and optimal communication/connection between the participants, respectively.

4.2 PIR-Based Construction (Online Verification)

In this section, we present the vaccine passport construction where a service requires to be online for verifying whether a token is valid. The construction heavily relies on different PIR variants.

4.2.1 Technical Overview

At a starting point, we consider a blueprint solution in which a client $\mathcal{C}$ obtains a vaccination certificate σ from the authority $\mathcal{A}$, after being vaccinated. When visiting a location and needing to demonstrate vaccination status, the client $\mathcal{C}$

presents the certificate σ to a service, which securely communicates with the authority to validate σ in a privacy-preserving manner. A similar variation of this blueprint solution is currently implemented by the Smart Health Cards Framework, discussed in Sect. B.

Although the above solution provides a basic functionality for a digital vaccine passport, it falls short in terms of the desired security measures described in Sect. 2.2. For instance, it enables multiple compromised services to link tokens belonging to the same client. Moreover, the blueprint solution requires the authority to perform computationally intensive secure computations for token verification, contradicting the desired performance outlined in Sect. 2.3.

To meet the desirable security criteria of a vaccine passport system, we modify the blueprint construction to enable the client $\mathcal{C}$ to prove to the service $\mathcal{S}$ that she has been vaccinated, while keeping the vaccination certificate σ confidential. Specifically, we generate redeem tokens by computing a Pseudorandom Function (PRF), denoted as $tok \leftarrow F(\sigma, t)$, where t represents the token's redemption time. This process ensures that all generated tokens are unlinkable due to the underlying PRF, and each token can be redeemed individually. For certain locations, each token can be associated with an encryption of the client's ID to prevent unauthorized usage of a valid token by other clients.

Regarding the system's performance, we observe that the authority $\mathcal{A}$ can delegate its computations to an untrusted cloud server, denoted as $\mathcal{H}$. If the vaccination certificate σ is computed from a random key r and the client's information, revealing σ to $\mathcal{H}$ does not compromise privacy as long as r remains secret and known only to the authority $\mathcal{A}$. In our construction, $\sigma = F(r, I_2||...||I_n)$, where r is randomly chosen by the authority, I_1 represents the client's ID, and $I_i \in \{0,1\}^\star$ denotes additional information about the client's vaccine, such as the "type of vaccine" and "effective date." With the vaccination certificate σ, the cloud server $\mathcal{H}$ can generate a list T consisting of valid tokens $tok \leftarrow F(\sigma, t)$. Additionally, the authority $\mathcal{A}$ sends the cloud server $\mathcal{H}$ the group element $m = g^{H(I_1)}$ for anonymizing the user's identification where H is a one-way hash function. Based on the Diffie-Hellman assumption, m reveals no information about the client's actual ID.

To verify the token's validity, the service $\mathcal{S}$, possessing a token tok obtained from the client, aims to determine whether tok exists in the list of valid tokens held by the cloud server $\mathcal{H}$. This verification can be achieved using Keyword-PIR, as described in Sect. 3.2. Specifically, the service $\mathcal{S}$ sends a PIR request as $\mathsf{PIR.Query}(pk, tok) \rightarrow k$ and receives $\mathsf{PIR.Answer}(pk, k, T) \rightarrow c$ from the cloud server $\mathcal{H}$. By utilizing $\mathsf{PIR.Extract}(sk, c) \rightarrow 0, 1$, the service $\mathcal{S}$ can determine the validity of the token tok. Here, the public-private key pair pk, sk is generated by the service $\mathcal{S}$ using $\mathsf{PIR.Gen}(\kappa) \rightarrow (pk, sk)$.

Depending on whether the client's ID is required by the service, we consider two cases. In the first case, where the service $\mathcal{S}$ (e.g., an airline company) possesses the client's identity I_1 in clear, $\mathcal{S}$ can compute $m = g^{H(I_1)}$ and append it to the token as $tok||m$ before sending a PIR request. Similarly, the cloud server modifies T to include a set of $tok||m$ before returning a PIR answer to the service.

In the second case, where the service is not permitted to collect the client's ID, our construction relies on PIR-with-Default and Private Matching. Specifically, the cloud server $\mathcal{H}$ creates pairs (tok, m) and allows the service $\mathcal{S}$ to retrieve either m or a random default value using PIR-with-Default. Subsequently, the service $\mathcal{S}$ and the client $\mathcal{C}$, possessing m, engage in a private matching instance, leveraging the obtained PIR output, to determine whether the client redeemed a valid token generated from her vaccination certificate σ.

4.2.2 Construction

Figure 2 illustrates the construction of our PIR-based vaccine passport. The construction closely adheres to the technical overview described earlier. We organize the construction into three phases, aligning with the system overview detailed in Sect. 4.1. The first phase involves the computation and distribution of the vaccination certificate by the authority $\mathcal{A}$. In the second phase, each client $\mathcal{C}$ and the cloud server $\mathcal{H}$ independently generate valid tokens based on the obtained vaccination certificate. The final phase entails the redemption process of the tokens, wherein all participants except the authority $\mathcal{A}$ are involved (as the authority's role is limited to the first phase).

It is easy to see that correctness is obvious from the definitions of PIR variants, private matching, and Diffie-Hellman's assumption.

4.2.3 Security

We analyze the security of the proposed PIR-based construction according to our desirable security and privacy of a digital vaccine passport.

Anonymous Identity. To ensure anonymity, we demonstrate that the client's identity is not revealed to the cloud server. We assume that the corrupt cloud server $\mathcal{H}$ does not collude with the authority $\mathcal{A}$. The view of $\mathcal{H}$ includes the vaccination certificate σ, the exponentiation $m = g^{H(I_1)}$, and PIR transcripts. As $\mathcal{H}$ does not know the authority's secret value r, σ appears random to $\mathcal{H}$. Our construction relies on the difficulty of the discrete log problem. Therefore, given $m = g^{H(I_1)}$, $\mathcal{H}$ cannot recover the client's identity I_1.

We consider two cases: one where the service does not require collecting the client's identity I_1 but mandates presenting the ID (Step IV,3 in Fig. 2), and another where presenting the client's identity is not required. In the former case, the view of the corrupt service $\mathcal{S}$ consists of the redeemed token tok_t', PIR's and private matching transcripts. The token tok_t' is generated from the PRF key σ which is unknown to $\mathcal{S}$. Thus, tok_t' looks random to him. Because of PIR and private matching pseudorandomness property, the real identity of the client is protected. For the latter case, the analysis of anonymous identity security remains similar to the first one.

PARAMETERS:
- A client $\mathcal{C}$, an authority $\mathcal{A}$, a service $\mathcal{S}$, and a cloud server $\mathcal{H}$.
- A cyclic group $G = \langle g \rangle$ of prime order p
- A PRF function $F : (\{0,1\}^\kappa, \{0,1\}^*) \to \{0,1\}^\kappa$
- A hash function $H : \{0,1\}^* \to \{0,1\}^\kappa$
- A Keyword-PIR, PIR-with-Default, and Private Matching primitives.

INPUTS: When a client $\mathcal{C}$ is vaccinated, it is associated with an information vector $\boldsymbol{I} = \{I_1, \dots, I_n\} \in (\{0,1\}^*)^n$, where I_1 represent the client's ID, other $I_i \in \{0,1\}^*$ represents information about the vaccine taken by the client such as "type of vaccine", "effective date", etc.

PROTOCOL:

I. **Registration Phase**
- The client $\mathcal{C}$ sends $\boldsymbol{I} = \{I_1, \dots, I_n\}$ to the authority $\mathcal{A}$
- $\mathcal{A}$ chooses a random value r, computes $\sigma = F(r, I_2||...||I_n)$ and $m = g^{H(I_1)}$
- $\mathcal{A}$ distributes σ to both $\mathcal{C}$ and $\mathcal{H}$. Besides, $\mathcal{A}$ sends m to $\mathcal{H}$.

II. **Tokens Generation Phase**
- For each pair (σ, m) received from $\mathcal{A}$, the cloud server $\mathcal{H}$ computes a set T_m of valid tokens $F(\sigma, t)$, where t indicates the time of redeem (e.g. every 15 minutes).
- $\mathcal{C}$ generates a list of tokens $tok'_t = F(\sigma, t)$, where t is the redeem time.

III. **Token's Redeem Phase**: At the time t,
1. If presenting the client's identity I_1 is not required (light verification):
   - $\mathcal{C}$ sends tok'_t to $\mathcal{S}$
   - $\mathcal{S}$ and $\mathcal{H}$ involve a keyword-PIR instance:
     * $\mathcal{S}$ sends a PIR query $\mathsf{PIR.Query}(pk, tok'_t) \to k$ to $\mathcal{H}$
     * $\mathcal{H}$ replies $\mathsf{PIR.Answer}(pk, k, D) \to c$ to $\mathcal{S}$ where D is a set of tok, for all $tok \in T_m$
     * $\mathcal{S}$ outputs $\mathsf{PIR.Extract}(sk, c)$
2. If the client's identity I_1 is collected by the service $\mathcal{S}$
   - $\mathcal{C}$ sends (tok'_t, I_1) to $\mathcal{S}$ who computes $m' = g^{H(I_1)}$
   - $\mathcal{S}$ and $\mathcal{H}$ involve a keyword-PIR instance:
     * $\mathcal{S}$ sends a PIR query $\mathsf{PIR.Query}(pk, tok'_t||m') \to k$ to $\mathcal{H}$
     * $\mathcal{H}$ replies $\mathsf{PIR.Answer}(pk, k, D) \to c$ to $\mathcal{S}$ where D is a set of $tok||m$, for all $tok \in T_m$
     * $\mathcal{S}$ outputs $\mathsf{PIR.Extract}(sk, c)$
3. If presenting the client's identity I_1 is required, but the service does not allow to collect the client's identity I_1
   - $\mathcal{C}$ sends tok'_t to $\mathcal{S}$
   - $\mathcal{S}$ and $\mathcal{H}$ involve a PIR-with-Default instance:
     * $\mathcal{S}$ sends a PIR query $\mathsf{PIR.Query}(pk, tok'_t) \to k$ to $\mathcal{H}$
     * $\mathcal{H}$ replies $\mathsf{PIR.Answer}(pk, k, D, w) \to c$ to $\mathcal{S}$ where D is a set of pairs (tok, m), for all $tok \in T_m$, and w is a zero string.
     * $\mathcal{S}$ computes $\mathsf{PIR.Extract}(sk, c) \to v$
   - If v is a zero string, the $\mathcal{S}$ outputs 0 (i.e. tok'_t is invalid). Otherwise, the service $\mathcal{S}$ and the client $\mathcal{C}$ involve a private matching instance:
     * $\mathcal{C}$ acts as a sender with input $m' = g^{H(I_1)}$.
     * $\mathcal{S}$ acts as a receiver with input v and output whether $v = m'$.

Fig. 2. Our PIR-based Vaccine Passport Construction.

Token Unlinkability. Token unlinkability is crucial to prevent the disclosure of a user's travel history, safeguarding their privacy. In this section, we discuss how PPass ensures token unlinkability. We focus on the steps of the protocol and show the difficulty an attacker faces when attempting to link multiple individual tokens. We assume that clients use secure channels for communication with service providers and disregard attacks involving IP address matching.

- Phase 1. Registration Phase: During registration, the client and the cloud server communicate with the authority $\mathcal{A}$ to obtain a vaccination certificate σ and a value m. It is impractical for an attacker to recover the client's information $I_2, \ldots, I_n$ from the PRF value without the authority's secret value r, unless $\mathcal{A}$ is compromised. Additionally, due to the Diffie-Hellman assumption, the value m appears random to the attacker.
- Phase 2. This phase involves local computation by individual clients and the cloud server, without any communication or computation between the participants. Hence, no information is leaked. However, if an attacker compromises the cloud server, they can identify which tokens are generated from the same vaccination certificate σ, but they cannot determine where the tokens are redeemed (Phase 3).
- Phase 3. Token's Redeem Phase: During this phase, if an attacker controls a subset of service providers $\mathcal{S}$ who collect the client's IDs, PPass cannot provide unlinkability. However, if the attacker collects a list of redeemed tokens from different service providers $\mathcal{S}$, all the redeemed tokens appear random, even if they were generated from the same key σ. Furthermore, each token is designed for one-time use only. Therefore, no linkability can be established between tokens. If the attacker compromises the cloud server, they also gain no information due to the PIR ideal functionality. The cloud server does not know which tokens were redeemed at which places.

Token Unforgeability. According to our construction, if a token *tok* is not generated from a valid vaccination certificate, the service is able to detect this event via PIR. Recall that the cloud server $\mathcal{H}$ has a set of valid tokens, PIR functionality allows the service to check whether *tok* is in the $\mathcal{H}$'s database. Moreover, PIR-with-default allows $\mathcal{S}$ to retrieve anonymous information of the client's identity m. Private matching between $\mathcal{S}$ and $\mathcal{C}$ prevents an attacker to redeem tokens of another client.

Token Unreusability. Each token is associated with a specific redeem time, which prevents an attacker from reusing the token later. However, PPass cannot prevent an attacker from attempting to redeem the same token simultaneously at two different service providers, unless ID presentation is required. Therefore, we rely on end-user devices to delete the token after redemption. To eliminate the need for trust in end-user devices, secure deletion can be employed to obliviously remove redeemed tokens from the cloud server's database T. However, the cloud server can observe which token was deleted. To address this issue, multiple cloud servers can be used, with each holding secret shares of T. After executing an oblivious deletion event, all the shares must be re-randomized.

Finally, we state the security of our PIR-based construction using the following theorem. The proof of security straightforwardly follows from the security of its constituent building blocks and the security analysis presented above. Therefore, we omit the proof.

Theorem 1. *Given the Keyword-PIR, PIR-with-Defalt, Private Matching functionalities described in Sect. 3, the PIR-based construction of Fig. 2 securely implements the digitial vaccine passport described in Sect. 2 in semi-honest setting.*

4.2.4 Complexity

We begin with the analysis of the computational complexity. As desired, the authority only needs to perform one PRF (e.g. AES), and one exponentiation per client who was vaccinated.

The cloud server $\mathcal{H}$ requires to perform N AES calls to generate the set T_m. N can set to be 80 if assuming that a token is generated every 15 min for approximately 20 h a day. The $\mathcal{H}$ also involves PIR with the service in Phase 3. Denote the computational cost of PIR as $|\mathtt{PIR}|$ which is $O(Nn)$, where n is the number of vaccinated clients. The computational complexity of $\mathcal{H}$ is $N + |\mathtt{PIR}|$.

The client needs to compute N AES instances and one exponentiation in Phase 2. In the token redemption phase, she may need to perform private matching with the service, involving two additional exponentiations as described in Sect. 3.3. The computation on the service's side includes PIR, private matching (if the client presents their ID but doesn't allow the service to collect it), and one exponentiation (if the service can collect the ID).

In terms of communication complexity, the $\mathcal{A}$ sends a κ-bit σ to the client $\mathcal{C}$ and a 3κ-bit $\sigma||m$ to the cloud server. The client sends the service a κ-bit token along with 2κ-bits m, if required. Additionally, all participants except $\mathcal{A}$ send and receive transcripts/randomness from PIR or private matching executions.

4.3 Digital Signature-Based Construction (Offline Verification)

The vaccine passport construction described here eliminates the need for an online service provider, $\mathcal{S}$, to verify the authenticity of a token. It relies on randomized signatures and signatures on committed values.

4.3.1 Technical Overview

At the initial stage, the client $\mathcal{C}$ obtains a vaccination certificate σ from the authority after receiving the vaccination. In the PIR-based construction, the validation of a valid token requires an online interaction with the cloud server $\mathcal{H}$ to ensure client privacy. However, our construction eliminates the need for such online verification.

The central concept of our construction, based on digital signatures, involves randomizing the certificate σ into $\sigma^\star$ to ensure their unlinkability. The client can then utilize $\sigma^\star$ during the redemption process in a way that prevents the authority from linking it to the original certificate. The Pointcheval-Sander signature scheme perfectly aligns with our objective as it allows for randomization and offers a scalable solution with constant-sized signatures. Therefore, our signature-based construction relies on the Pointcheval-Sander signature scheme. The authority $\mathcal{A}$ generates a signature σ on the client's information $\boldsymbol{I}$, which includes details such as the client's identity, vaccine type, and effective date. To optimize system performance, the health authority $\mathcal{A}$ only issues a long-term certificate to the client and delegates the generation of short-lived temporary tokens to an untrusted cloud server $\mathcal{H}$.

The design of the system raises the question of how clients can request tokens from the cloud server $\mathcal{H}$. The simplest approach would be for the client to present the cloud server $\mathcal{H}$ with the randomized signature $\sigma^\star$ on the information $\boldsymbol{I}$. However, this would expose all personal information to the cloud server $\mathcal{H}$. Fortunately, the Pointcheval-Sander signature scheme enables us to transform the signature σ on the information $\boldsymbol{I}$ into a randomized signature $\sigma^\star$ on a committed value derived from $\boldsymbol{I}$. Consequently, the cloud server $\mathcal{H}$ can verify the validity of the client's certificate from the authority $\mathcal{A}$ without gaining access to any personal information. Subsequently, the $\mathcal{H}$ can issue tokens to the clients.

Each token includes a signature from the cloud server $\mathcal{H}$ on the committed value derived from $\boldsymbol{I}$, along with additional information t. This additional information t, appended by the cloud server $\mathcal{H}$, primarily comprises the redemption time for the token to prevent any potential reuse. To validate the token, the service $\mathcal{S}$ simply needs to check the validity of the signature, thereby enabling offline verification. For enhanced privacy, the client can also randomize the received token tok into $\mathsf{tok}^\star$ and store only $\mathsf{tok}^\star$ in memory. Consequently, even if the authority and the cloud server collude, they cannot link the utilized token $\mathsf{tok}^\star$ with personal information, ensuring strong privacy guarantees.

Additionally, we propose an optional "light verification" approach where services such as cinemas or restaurants can verify the validity of a token by checking if it is a valid signature from the cloud server $\mathcal{H}$. In this case, the client only needs to present their token tok to the service $\mathcal{S}$, along with aggregated information V related to their personal information, to demonstrate that the token tok is a valid signature issued by the cloud server $\mathcal{H}$. This allows the service $\mathcal{S}$ to quickly verify the token's validity without requiring any personal information from the client. While this approach benefits privacy, its drawback is that the token can be transferred between clients as personal information is not disclosed. For important checks, such as at airports or borders, where identity verification is necessary, the client must present their identity card and provide the information $\boldsymbol{I}$. This enables the service $\mathcal{S}$ to perform a thorough verification of the token against the personal information $\boldsymbol{I}$. In practice, a combination of light and full verification can be employed, wherein daily activities (e.g., restaurants, cinemas, public transport) mainly undergo light verification, with occasional random checks of full verification to mitigate the risk of token transfer between individuals.

4.3.2 Construction

The construction of our signature-based PPass system is outlined in Fig. 3, closely adhering to the technical overview provided earlier. Since our construction is based on the Pointcheval-Sander signature scheme [31], we will briefly explain the multi-message version of this signature below:

Setup: A type 3 bilinear map $e : G_1 \times G_2 \to G_T$ with $G_1 = \langle g_1 \rangle, G_2 = \langle g_2 \rangle$, and $G_T = \langle g_T \rangle$ are cyclic group of prime order p.
KeyGen: Choose a secret key $sk = (x, y_1, \ldots, y_n)$ and computes the public key $pk = (g_2, X, Y_1, \ldots, Y_n)$, where $X = g_2^x$ and $Y_i = g_2^{y_i}, i = 1, \ldots, n$.
Sign$(sk, \{m_1, \ldots, m_n\} \in (\mathbb{Z}_p^\star)^n)$: Choose a random $h \in G_1$, define $\sigma_1 = h$ and $\sigma_2 = h^{x + \Sigma_{j=1}^n y_j m_j}$, and output $\sigma = (\sigma_1, \sigma_2)$
Verify$(sk, \{m_1, \ldots, m_n\}, \sigma = (\sigma_1, \sigma_2))$: Check whether $\sigma_1 \neq 1_{G_1}$ and $e(\sigma_2, g_2) = e(\sigma_1, X \Pi_{j=1}^n Y_j^{m_j})$ are both satisfied, here 1_{G_1} denotes the identity in G_1. If yes, it accepts, otherwise, it rejects.

We use this signature for both authority server $\mathcal{S}$ and cloud server $\mathcal{H}$. In particular, the cloud server $\mathcal{H}$ utilizes the signature to sign the committed value of $m_1, \ldots, m_n$, ensuring that clients' personal information remains concealed from the cloud server $\mathcal{H}$. To accommodate space constraints, we defer the detailed security analysis of our PIR-based construction to Appendix C, where we elaborate on its security.

4.3.3 Complexity

The utilization of the Pointcheval-Sanders signature scheme is particularly advantageous for devices with limited storage capacity. This is because the signature size remains constant, allowing each token to contain only two elements in G_1. In terms of computational requirements, the following observations can be made:

- Client $\mathcal{C}$ performs 2 pairings and n exponentiations in G_1 to verify the validity of each credential or token. However, in practice, $\mathcal{C}$ may directly utilize credentials or tokens without the need for verification. $\mathcal{C}$ needs to randomize each credential or token for privacy, which requires only 2 exponentiations in G_1 per credential or token.
- The cloud server $\mathcal{H}$ performs $n + 2$ pairings to verify each credential because $\mathcal{C}$ only provides $\mathcal{H}$ with the committed values $com = (M_1, \ldots, M_n)$.
- Service $\mathcal{S}$ requires 2 pairings and n exponentiations in G_1 for verification (no exponentiation is necessary for light verification) of each token.
- The generation of credentials or tokens is efficient, requiring just one exponentiation in the group G_1.

5 Performance

In this section, we present an estimation of the performance of our PPass system to demonstrate its feasibility in practical scenarios. We assume that a redeem

PARAMETERS:

- A client $\mathcal{C}$, an authority $\mathcal{A}$, a service $\mathcal{S}$, and a cloud server $\mathcal{H}$.
- A bilinear map of type 3 $e : G_1 \times G_2 \rightarrow G_T$, where $G_1 = \langle g_1 \rangle, G_2 = \langle g_2 \rangle$, and $G_T = \langle g_T \rangle$ are cyclic groups of prime order p.
- A hash function $H : \{0,1\}^* \rightarrow \mathbb{Z}_p^*$
- $\mathcal{S}$ chooses a secret key $sk_{\mathcal{S}} = (x, y_1, \ldots, y_n)$ and computes the public key $pk_{\mathcal{S}} = (g_2, X, Y_1, \ldots, Y_n)$, where $X = g_2^x$ and $Y_i = g_2^{y_i}$, for $i \in [n]$.
- $\mathcal{H}$ chooses a secret key $sk_{\mathcal{H}} = (a, b_1, \ldots, b_n, , b_{n+1})$ and computes the public key $pk_{\mathcal{H}} = (g_2, A, B_1, \ldots, B_n, B_{n+1})$, where $A = g_2^a$ and $B_i = g_2^{b_i}$, for $i \in [n+1]$.

INPUTS:

- When a client $\mathcal{C}$ is vaccinated, it is associated with an information vector $\boldsymbol{I} = \{I_1, \ldots, I_n\} \in (\{0,1\}^*)^n$, where I_1 represent the client's ID, other $I_i \in \{0,1\}^*$ represents an information about the vaccine taken by the client such as "type of vaccine", "effective date" etc.

PROTOCOL:

I. **Registration Phase**
   - Client $\mathcal{C}$ sends $\boldsymbol{I} = \{I_1, \ldots, I_n\}$ to the authority $\mathcal{A}$ who computes $m_i = H(I_i)$ and gets the vector $\boldsymbol{m} = \{m_1, \ldots, m_n\} \in (\mathbb{Z}_p^*)^n$.
   - Authority $\mathcal{A}$ signs on $\boldsymbol{m}$ with the Pointcheval-Sanders signature and outputs $\sigma = (\sigma_1, \sigma_2)$, where:
     * $\sigma_1 = h$, for a random $h \in G_1$
     * $\sigma_2 = h^{x + \Sigma_{j=1}^n y_j m_j}$
   - Client receives the credential $\sigma = (\sigma_1, \sigma_2)$ and checks whether $\sigma_1 \neq 1_{G_1}$ and $e(\sigma_1, X\Pi_{j=1}^n Y_j^{m_j}) = e(\sigma_2, g_2)$. If it is positive (otherwise it aborts) then $\mathcal{C}$ randomizes it by randomly chooses $r \in \mathbb{Z}_p$ and outputs $\sigma^\star = (\sigma_1^\star = \sigma_1^r, \sigma_2^\star = \sigma_2^r)$.
   - The client computes a committed value of its data: $com = (M_1, \ldots, M_n)$, where $M_j = (\sigma_1^\star)^{m_j}$, for $j = 1, \ldots, n$.

II. **Tokens Generation Phase**
   - Client $\mathcal{C}$ sends to $\mathcal{H}$ the committed value com and $\sigma^\star$.
   - Upon receipt com and $\sigma^\star$, the server checks the validity whether $\sigma_1^\star \neq 1_{G_1}$ and $e(\sigma_1^\star, X)\Pi_{j=1}^n e(M_j, Y_j) = e(\sigma_2^\star, g_2)$.
   - If it is positive (otherwise it aborts), then $\mathcal{H}$ generates tokens for the client.
     * Define $t \in (\mathbb{Z}_p^*)$ to encode the redeem time for the token.
     * $\mathcal{H}$ randomly chooses $\lambda \in \mathbb{Z}_p^*$ and computes $f = (\sigma_1^\star)^\lambda$ (equivalently, f is randomly generated from G_1).
     * $\mathcal{H}$ sets $\mathsf{tok} = (\mathsf{tok}_1, \mathsf{tok}_2)$ where $\mathsf{tok}_1 = f$, $\mathsf{tok}_2 = f^a(\Pi_{j=1}^n M_j^{b_j})^\lambda f^{tb_{n+1}} = f^{a + \Sigma_{j=1}^n b_j m_j + b_{n+1} t}$. Each token is thus a Pointcheval-Sanders signature of $\mathcal{H}$ on $(m_1, \ldots, m_n, t)$
   - $\mathcal{H}$ sends back (tok, t) to the client $\mathcal{C}$.

III. **Token's Redeem Phase**:
   - Upon receipt a token $\mathsf{tok} = (\mathsf{tok}_1, \mathsf{tok}_2)$ and t, the client randomizes it as $\mathsf{tok}^\star = (\mathsf{tok}_1^\star = \mathsf{tok}_1^\gamma, \mathsf{tok}_2^\star = \mathsf{tok}_2^\gamma)$, for a random $\gamma \in \mathbb{Z}_p$.
   - Verification: the client shows $\mathsf{tok}^\star$ and its information $\boldsymbol{I} = \{I_1, \ldots, I_n\}$ and t to the service who checks the validity whether: $e(\mathsf{tok}_1^\star, A(\Pi_{j=1}^n B_j^{m_j})B_{n+1}^t) = e(\mathsf{tok}_2^\star, g_2)$, where $m_i = H(I_i)$ is computed by the service.
   - Light verification: The client pre-compute $V = A(\Pi_{j=1}^n B_j^{m_j})$ and then shows $\mathsf{tok}^\star$ and V, t to the service who simply checks the validity whether: $e(\mathsf{tok}_1^\star, VB_{n+1}^t) = e(\mathsf{tok}_2^\star, g_2)$.

Fig. 3. Our signature-based construction.

token is generated every 15 min, resulting in approximately 80 distinct tokens per day for each user (denoted as $N = 80$). We consider user information to consist of its identity I_1 and the concatenated vaccine information I_2, which gives us a value of $n = 2$.

For the PIR-based construction, we implement PRF and PRG instances using AES. Each AES operation costs 10 cycles, and on a 2.3 GHz machine, we can expect to compute an AES operation in approximately 0.005 microseconds. In our constructions, participants need to compute exponentiations. For example, the DH-based private matching consists of 3 exponentiation. [30, Table 2] reports the computation cost of DH-based PSI which computes 2^{21} exponentiations in 1148.1 s using the miracl library[1]. Using libsodium library[2] which is approximately 10× faster than miracl, we estimate that the time per exponentiation is 1148.1 s$/2^{21}/10 = 54$ microseconds. Our signature-based construction requires participants to compute pairings. We estimate that each pairing consists of about 30× exponentiations [9,16] which cost about 1620 microseconds.

As mentioned in Sect. 3.2, a Keyword-PIR query on a database of size 2^{20} requires 7.62 milliseconds on the client's side and 80 milliseconds on the server's side (online time). These queries necessitate a communication bandwidth of 480KB. The PIR-with-Default queries [20] with 2^8 queries on a database of size 2^{20} require a communication of at most 7MB and an online computation time of 2.43 milliseconds.

Table 1 (Appendix A) provides a summary of the estimated running time and communication/size for AES, exponentiation (Exp), two PIR variants (Keyword-PIR and PIR-with-Default) with different running times on the sender/client and receiver/server sides, private matching (PM), and pairing. It is important to note that Keyword-PIR includes a fixed cost for an offline phase on the cloud server's side, which is not included in Table 1.

Based on the information provided in Table 1, we have calculated the running time and communication costs for various implementation options in our PPass system. The estimated values are presented in Table 2 (Appendix A). Upon analysis, we observe that the PIR-based construction generally outperforms the signature-based construction in terms of speed. However, it does come with higher bandwidth costs and relies on an (online) connection between the cloud server $\mathcal{H}$ and the service $\mathcal{S}$. We observe that, a service such as an airport service counter can conduct an online verification to validate the authenticity of a token within just 7 milliseconds, leveraging its authorization to collect the passenger's ID. For offline verification, our protocol takes a maximum of 0.15 s. Based on these results, we conclude that the proposed PPass system is practical and feasible for real-world applications.

[1] Experiments were done on a machine with an Intel(R) Xeon(R) E5-2699 v3 2.30 GHz CPU and 256 GB RAM.

[2] https://doc.libsodium.org/.

Acknowledgment. The second and the fourth authors were partially supported by NSF awards #2101052, #2200161, #2115075, and ARPA-H SP4701-23-C-0074. The third author was partially supported by the BPI VisioConfiance Project.

A Performance

We show the running time of communication cost for building blocks in Table 1 and the performance of our PPass in Table 2.

Table 1. Estimated running time and communication cost (size) for building blocks and core operations used in our PPass constructions.

		AES	Exp.	Keyword-PIR	PIR-with-Default	PM	Pairing
Computation (microsecond)	**Sender**	0.005	54	80000	2430	108	1620
	Receiver			7620	2430	108	
Communication/Size (KB)		0.016	0.032	480	7000	0.096	0.064

Table 2. Estimated running time and communication cost for our PPass system across different implementation options. The client generates $N = 80$ tokens per day. The cloud server has 2^{20} tokens. The numbers with "star" indicate the cost for Step (III,3) where private matching and PIR-with-default are required in the PIR-based construction. The "star" also indicates the cost of light verification in the signature-based construction.

	PIR-based Construction		Signature-based Construction	
	Runtime (ms)	Comm. (KB)	Runtime (ms)	Comm. (KB)
Authority $\mathcal{A}$	0.054	0.064	0.054	0.064
Cloud Server $\mathcal{H}$	85.24	480	226492	67108
	5.24*	7000*		
Client $\mathcal{C}$	0.004	0.016	1.836	0.352
	12.99*	0.112*	1.944*	0.384
Service $\mathcal{S}$	7.62	480	142.56	7.68
	2.54*	7000.1*	13.82*	5.12*

B Related Work

In the realm of controlling the spread of COVID-19, privacy-preserving contact tracing [2,13,21,22] has garnered significant attention. However, there has been limited research on digital vaccine passports, and most existing solutions have privacy vulnerabilities. Notably, none of these solutions have been formally described with their construction and security guarantees.

There have been a few attempts to build digital vaccine passports such as in [3,24,34,35]. However, these works are in the blockchain setting and/or lack performance evaluations. In this section, we review the popular framework – Smart Health Cards Framework[3], which serves as a prominent system for digital

[3] https://smarthealth.cards.

vaccine passport cards. This open-source standard has been adopted by numerous companies and organizations, including Microsoft, IBM, and Mayo Clinic. The framework proposes a model involving three parties:

- Issuer (e.g., a lab, pharmacy, healthcare provider, public health department, or immunization information system) generates verifiable tokens (credentials).
- Client (e.g., a phone holder) stores the tokens and presents them when required.
- Verifier/Service (e.g., a restaurant, an airline) receives tokens from the client and verifies their authenticity through proper signatures.

In the Smart Health Cards system, the client is required to disclose personally identifiable information (PII) (e.g., full name and date of birth) and immunization status (e.g., vaccination location, date and time, vaccine type, lot number) to the issuer. Based on this information, the issuer generates multiple tokens, each containing a subset of the client's information along with a digital signature. By choosing which token to present to a verifier, the client can control the granularity of information disclosed to that specific verifier.

Although the Smart Health Cards framework aims to uphold end-user privacy, it fails to meet the desirable properties outlined in Sect. 2.2: token linkability and reusability. If a client presents tokens to two different verifiers, these verifiers can link the tokens together. Furthermore, if the verifiers collude with the issuer, they can potentially uncover the identity of the token holder.

C Security of Our Digital Signature-Based Construction

We proceed with the analysis of the security of our signature-based construction, considering the desired security and privacy properties of a digital vaccine passport system as described in Sect. 2.2.

Token Unlinkability and Unforgeability. These properties are directly inherited from the unlinkability and unforgeability of the Pointcheval-Sanders signature. Each token corresponds exactly to a signature generated by the cloud server $\mathcal{H}$.

Token Unreusability. To ensure token unreusability, the cloud server $\mathcal{H}$ appends additional information t to each token, indicating its redeem time. Therefore, the token's unreusability outside this redeem time is derived from the unforgeability of the Pointcheval-Sanders signature.

Anonymous Identity. In the digital signature-based construction, clients' anonymity is guaranteed against collusion between the authority $\mathcal{A}$ and the cloud server $\mathcal{H}$. We can outline the proof as follows:

- The authority $\mathcal{A}$ stores all the information $\boldsymbol{I} = \{I_1, \ldots, I_n\}$ of each client as well as the corresponding signature $\sigma = (\sigma_1, \sigma_2)$.
- The cloud server $\mathcal{H}$ stores all the clients' randomized signatures $\sigma^\star = (\sigma_1^\star, \sigma_2^\star)$

- The clients only use their randomized tokens given by the cloud server $\mathcal{H}$. After randomization, the clients do not need to store the original signature σ and the token tok.
- The tokens used by the client $\mathsf{tok}^\star$ are unlinkable to tok and thus unlikable to $\sigma^\star$ and σ.

The unlinkability directly stems from the unlinkability property of the Pointcheval-Sanders signature, which is guaranteed under the Decisional Diffie-Hellman (DDH) assumption. Consequently, client privacy is inherently preserved.

Clearly, when the client is required to present personal information to the $\mathcal{S}$, privacy cannot be guaranteed if the $\mathcal{S}$ is compromised. In this case, we offer the option of light verification, where the service $\mathcal{S}$ only receives $V = A(\Pi_{j=1}^{n} B_j^{m_j})$ and $\mathsf{tok}^\star, t$, without gaining access to any personal information. Even if the service $\mathcal{S}$ colludes with the cloud $\mathcal{H}$, they cannot obtain any personal information because $\mathsf{tok}^\star$ is unlinkable to $(M_1, \ldots, M_n)$ (due to the unlinkability property of Pointcheval-Sanders). However, if all three parties, $\mathcal{A}, \mathcal{H}, \mathcal{S}$, collude, the identity of the client matching the pre-calculated value V can be revealed. In this scenario, the authority $\mathcal{A}$ can perform an exhaustive search on the entire set of registered clients using their personal information $(m_1, \ldots, m_n)$ and check if V matches $A(\Pi_{j=1}^{n} B_j^{m_j})$. Finally, we state the security of our signature-based construction through the following theorem. The security proof of the construction straightforwardly follows from the security of its building blocks and the security discussion provided above. Therefore, we omit the proof.

Theorem 2. *Given the randomizable (Pointcheval-Sanders) signature scheme described in Sect. 3.1, the signature-based construction of Fig. 3 securely implements the digital vaccine passport described in Sect. 2 in semi-honest setting.*

D Formal Security Definition

There are two adversarial models and two models of collusion considered.

- **Adversarial Model:** The *semi-honest* adversary follows the protocol but tries to gain additional information from the execution transcript. The *malicious* adversary can employ any arbitrary polynomial-time strategy, deviating from the protocol to extract as much extra information as possible.
- **Collusion Security:** In the *non-colluding* model, independent adversaries observe the views of individual dishonest parties. The model is secure if the distribution of each view can be simulated independently. In the *colluding* model, a single monolithic adversary captures the possibility of collusion between dishonest parties. The model is secure if the joint distribution of these views can be simulated.

Following security definitions of [18,27], we formally present the security definition considered in this work.

Real-world Execution. The real-world execution of protocol Π takes place between a set of users $(\mathcal{C}_1, \ldots, \mathcal{C}_n)$, an authority server $\mathcal{A}$, a cloud server $\mathcal{H}$, a set of services $(\mathcal{S}_1, \ldots, \mathcal{S}_N)$, and a set of adversaries $(\mathsf{Adv}_1, \ldots, \mathsf{Adv}_m)$. Let H denote the honest participants, I denote the set of corrupted and non-colluding participants, and C denote the set of corrupted and colluding participants.

At the beginning of the execution, each participant receives its input x_i, an auxiliary input a_i, and random tape r_i. These values x_i, a_i can be empty. Each adversary $\mathsf{Adv}_{i \in [m-1]}$ receives an index $i \in I$ that indicates the party it corrupts. The adversary Adv_m receives C indicating the set of parties it corrupts.

For all $i \in H$, let out_i denote the output of honest party, let out'_i denote the view of corrupted party for $i \in I \cup C$ during the execution of Π. The ith partial output of a real-world execution of Π between participants in the presence of adversaries $\mathsf{Adv} = (\mathsf{Adv}_1, \ldots, \mathsf{Adv}_m)$ is defined as

$$\mathtt{real}^i_{\Pi,\mathsf{Adv},I,C,y_i,r_i}(x_i) \stackrel{\mathsf{def}}{=} \{\mathsf{out}_j \mid j \in H\} \cup \mathsf{out}'_i$$

Ideal-world Execution. All the parties interact with a trusted party that evaluates a function f in the ideal-world execution. Similar to the real-world execution, each participant receives its input x_i, an auxiliary input y_i, and random tape r_i at the beginning of the ideal execution. The values x_i, y_i can be empty. Each participant sends their input x'_i to the trusted party, where x'_i is equal to x_i if this user is semi-honest, and is an arbitrary value if he is malicious. If any honest participant sends an abort message $(\perp)$, the trusted party returns $\perp$. Otherwise, the trusted party then returns $f(x'_1, \ldots, x'_n)$ to some particular parties as agreed before.

For all $i \in H$, let out_i denote the output returned to the honest participant by the trusted party, and let out'_i denote some value output by corrupted participant $i \in I \cup C$. The ith partial output of a ideal-world execution of Π between participants in the presence of independent simulators $\mathsf{Sim} = (\mathsf{Sim}_1, \ldots, \mathsf{Sim}_m)$ is defined as

$$\mathtt{ideal}^i_{\Pi,\mathsf{Sim},I,C,z_i,r_i}(x_i) \stackrel{\mathsf{def}}{=} \{\mathsf{out}_j \mid j \in H\} \cup \mathsf{out}'_i$$

Definition 1. [18,27] *(Security) Suppose f is a deterministic-time n-party functionality, and Π is the protocol. Let x_i be the parties' respective private inputs to the protocol. Let $I \in [N]$ denote the set of corrupted and non-colluding parties and $C \in [N]$ denote the set of corrupted and colluding parties. We say that protocol $\Pi(I, C)$ securely computes deterministic functionality f with abort in the presence of adversaries $\mathsf{Adv} = (\mathsf{Adv}_1, \ldots, \mathsf{Adv}_m)$ if there exist probabilistic polynomial-time simulators $\mathsf{Sim}_{i \in m}$ for $m < n$ such that for all $\bar{x}, \bar{y}, \bar{r} \leftarrow \{0,1\}^*$, and for all $i \in [m]$,*

$$\{\mathtt{real}^i_{\Pi,\mathsf{Adv},I,C,\bar{y},\bar{r}}(\bar{x})\} \cong \{\mathtt{ideal}^i_{\Pi,\mathsf{Sim},I,C,\bar{y},\bar{r}}(\bar{x})\}$$

Where $\mathsf{Sim} = (\mathsf{Sim}_1, \ldots, \mathsf{Sim}_m)$ and $\mathsf{Sim} = \mathsf{Sim}_i(\mathsf{Adv}_i)$

E Diffie–Hellman-Based Private Matching

The DH-based PM operates as follows: The receiver computes $u \leftarrow H(m_1)^r$ using a random, secret exponent r and a one-way hash function H. The computed value u is then sent to the sender. The sender raises u to the power of the random secret k, obtaining u^k. This result is then sent back to the receiver. Upon receiving u^k, the receiver can compute $(u^k)^{1/r}$, which yields $H(m_1)^k$. Next, the sender sends $H(m_0)^k$ to the receiver. The receiver can check whether $H(m_0)^k$ is equal to $H(m_1)^k$ in order to determine the equality of m_0 and m_1. Importantly, in cases where $m_0 \neq m_1$, the receiver learns no information about m_1 from $H(m_1)^k$. This scheme relies on the Diffie-Hellman assumption [11] for its security guarantees. We introduce the Diffie-Hellman assumption in Definition 2. We describe the ideal functionality and the DH-based construction of PM in Fig. 4. The computation and communication cost of PM is 3 exponentiations and 3 group elements, respectively.

PARAMETERS: Two parties: sender and receiver
FUNCTIONALITY:
- Wait for input $m_0 \in \{0,1\}^*$ from the sender.
- Wait for input $m_1 \in \{0,1\}^*$ from the receiver.
- Give the receiver output 1 if $m_0 = m_1$ and 0 otherwise.

PROTOCOL:
- The receiver chooses a random exponent r, computes $u \leftarrow H(m_1)^r$ and sends it to the sender
- The sender chooses a random exponent k, computes $v \leftarrow u^k$ and sends it to the receiver
- The sender computes $w \leftarrow H(m_0)^k$ sends it to the receiver
- The receiver output 1 if $v^{1/r} = w$ and 0 otherwise.

Fig. 4. The Private Matching Functionality and DH-based Construction

Definition 2. [11] *Let $\mathbb{G}(\kappa)$ be a group family parameterized by security parameter κ. For every probabilistic adversary* Adv *that runs in polynomial time in κ, we define the advantage of* Adv *to be:*

$$|\Pr[\mathsf{Adv}(g, g^a, g^b, g^{ab}) = 1] - \Pr[\mathsf{Adv}(g, g^a, g^b, g^c) = 1]|$$

Where the probability is over a random choice $\mathbb{G}$ from $\mathbb{G}(\kappa)$, random generator g of $\mathbb{G}$, random $a, b, c \in [|G|]$ and the randomness of Adv. *We say that the Decisional Diffie-Hellman assumption holds for $\mathbb{G}$ if for every such* Adv*, there exists a negligible function ϵ such that the advantage of* Adv *is bounded by $\epsilon(\kappa)$.*

Definition 3. *Let $\mathbb{G}$ be a cyclic group of order N, and let g be its generator. The Computational Diffie-Hellman (CDH) problem is hard in $\mathbb{G}$ if no efficient algorithm given (g, g^a, g^b) can compute g^{ab}.*

References

1. European digital green certificates. https://ec.europa.eu
2. Apple and google privacy-preserving contact tracing (2020). https://www.apple.com/covid19/contacttracing
3. Abid, A., Cheikhrouhou, S., Kallel, S., Jmaiel, M.: Novidchain: blockchain-based privacy-preserving platform for COVID-19 test/vaccine certificates. Softw. Pract. Exp. **52**(4), 841–867 (2022)
4. Ali, A., et al.: Communication-computation trade-offs in PIR. Cryptology ePrint Archive, Report 2019/1483 (2019). https://eprint.iacr.org/2019/1483
5. Angel, S., Chen, H., Laine, K., Setty, S.: PIR with compressed queries and amortized query processing. In: 2018 IEEE Symposium on Security and Privacy, pp. 962–979. IEEE Computer Society Press, May 2018
6. Boyle, E., Gilboa, N., Ishai, Y.: Function secret sharing: improvements and extensions. In: Weippl, E.R., Katzenbeisser, S., Kruegel, C., Myers, A.C., Halevi, S. (eds.) ACM CCS 2016, pp. 1292–1303. ACM Press, October 2016
7. Camenisch, J., Lysyanskaya, A.: Signature schemes and anonymous credentials from bilinear maps. In: Franklin, M. (ed.) CRYPTO 2004. LNCS, vol. 3152, pp. 56–72. Springer, Heidelberg (2004). https://doi.org/10.1007/978-3-540-28628-8_4
8. Chor, B., Gilboa, N., Naor, M.: Private information retrieval by keywords. Cryptology ePrint Archive, Report 1998/003 (1998). https://eprint.iacr.org/1998/003
9. Clarisse, R., Duquesne, S., Sanders, O.: Curves with fast computations in the first pairing group. In: 19th CANS (2020)
10. Corrigan-Gibbs, H., Kogan, D.: Private information retrieval with sublinear online time. In: Canteaut, A., Ishai, Y. (eds.) EUROCRYPT 2020. LNCS, vol. 12105, pp. 44–75. Springer, Cham (2020). https://doi.org/10.1007/978-3-030-45721-1_3
11. Diffie, W., Hellman, M.: New directions in cryptography (2006)
12. Dong, C., Chen, L.: A fast single server private information retrieval protocol with low communication cost. In: Kutyłowski, M., Vaidya, J. (eds.) ESORICS 2014. LNCS, vol. 8712, pp. 380–399. Springer, Cham (2014). https://doi.org/10.1007/978-3-319-11203-9_22
13. Duong, T., Phan, D.H., Trieu, N.: Catalic: delegated PSI cardinality with applications to contact tracing. In: Moriai, S., Wang, H. (eds.) ASIACRYPT 2020. LNCS, vol. 12493, pp. 870–899. Springer, Cham (2020). https://doi.org/10.1007/978-3-030-64840-4_29
14. Fagin, R., Naor, M., Winkler, P.: Comparing information without leaking it. Commun. ACM **39**(5), 77–85 (1996)
15. Freedman, M.J., Nissim, K., Pinkas, B.: Efficient private matching and set intersection. In: Cachin, C., Camenisch, J.L. (eds.) EUROCRYPT 2004. LNCS, vol. 3027, pp. 1–19. Springer, Heidelberg (2004). https://doi.org/10.1007/978-3-540-24676-3_1
16. Guillevic, A.: Arithmetic of pairings on algebraic curves for cryptography. PhD thesis (2013)
17. IPSOS. Global public backs COVID-19 vaccine passports for international travel. https://www.ipsos.com/
18. Kamara, S., Mohassel, P., Riva, B.: Salus: a system for server-aided secure function evaluation. Cryptology ePrint Archive, Report 2012/542 (2012). https://eprint.iacr.org/2012/542
19. Kolesnikov, V., Kumaresan, R., Rosulek, M., Trieu, N.: Efficient batched oblivious PRF with applications to private set intersection. In: Weippl, E.R., Katzenbeisser,

S., Kruegel, C., Myers, A.C., Halevi, S. (eds.) ACM CCS 2016, pp. 818–829. ACM Press, October 2016

20. Lepoint, T., Patel, S., Raykova, M., Seth, K., Trieu, N.: Private join and compute from pir with default. Cryptology ePrint Archive, Report 2020/1011 (2020). https://eprint.iacr.org/2020/1011
21. Liu, X., Trieu, N., Kornaropoulos, E.M., Song, D.: Beetrace: a unified platform for secure contact tracing that breaks data silos. IEEE Data Eng. Bull. **43**(2), 108–120 (2020)
22. Madhusudan, P., Miao, P., Ren, L., Venkatakrishnan, V.: Contrail: privacy-preserving secure contact tracing (2020). https://github.com/ConTraILProtocols/documents/blob/master/ContrailWhitePaper.pdf
23. Meadows, C.A.: A more efficient cryptographic matchmaking protocol for use in the absence of a continuously available third party. In: IEEE Symposium on Security and Privacy, pp. 134–137 (1986)
24. Meng, W., Cao, Y., Cao, Y.: Blockchain-based privacy-preserving vaccine passport system. Secur. Commun. Netw. (2022)
25. Merkle, R.C.: A certified digital signature. In: Brassard, G. (ed.) CRYPTO 1989. LNCS, vol. 435, pp. 218–238. Springer, New York (1990). https://doi.org/10.1007/0-387-34805-0_21
26. Mughees, M.H., Chen, H., Ren, L.: OnionPIR: response efficient single-server PIR. In: Proceedings of the 2021 ACM SIGSAC Conference on Computer and Communications Security, CCS '21, pp. 2292–2306, New York, NY, USA. Association for Computing Machinery (2021)
27. Oded, G.: Foundations of Cryptography: Volume 2, Basic Applications, 1st ed. Cambridge University Press, USA (2009)
28. Patel, S., Persiano, G., Yeo, K.: Private stateful information retrieval. In: Lie, D., Mannan, M., Backes, M., Wang, X. (eds.) ACM CCS 2018, pp. 1002–1019. ACM Press, October 2018
29. Patel, S., Seo, J.Y., Yeo, K.: Don't be dense: efficient keyword PIR for sparse databases. In: 32nd USENIX Security Symposium (USENIX Security 23), pp. 3853–3870, Anaheim, CA, August 2023. USENIX Association (2023)
30. Pinkas, B., Rosulek, M., Trieu, N., Yanai, A.: SpOT-Light: lightweight private set intersection from sparse OT extension. In: Boldyreva, A., Micciancio, D. (eds.) CRYPTO 2019. LNCS, vol. 11694, pp. 401–431. Springer, Cham (2019). https://doi.org/10.1007/978-3-030-26954-8_13
31. Pointcheval, D., Sanders, O.: Short randomizable signatures. In: Sako, K. (ed.) CT-RSA 2016. LNCS, vol. 9610, pp. 111–126. Springer, Cham (2016). https://doi.org/10.1007/978-3-319-29485-8_7
32. Pointcheval, D., Sanders, O.: Reassessing security of randomizable signatures. In: Smart, N.P. (ed.) CT-RSA 2018. LNCS, vol. 10808, pp. 319–338. Springer, Cham (2018). https://doi.org/10.1007/978-3-319-76953-0_17
33. Schnorr, C.P.: Efficient identification and signatures for smart cards. In: Brassard, G. (ed.) CRYPTO 1989. LNCS, vol. 435, pp. 239–252. Springer, New York (1990). https://doi.org/10.1007/0-387-34805-0_22
34. Shakila, M., Rama, A.: Design and analysis of digital certificate verification and validation using blockchain-based technology. In: 2023 Eighth International Conference on Science Technology Engineering and Mathematics (ICONSTEM), pp. 1–9 (2023)
35. Shih, D.-H., Shih, P.-L., Wu, T.-W., Liang, S.-H., Shih, M.-H.: An international federal hyperledger fabric verification framework for digital COVID-19 vaccine passport. Healthcare **10**(10) (2022)

Exploiting Android Browser

Animesh Kar(✉) and Natalia Stakhanova

Department of Computer Science, University of Saskatchewan, Saskatoon, Canada
gqx108@usask.ca, natalia@cs.usask.ca

Abstract. Android permission is a system of safeguards designed to restrict access to potentially sensitive data and privileged components. While third-party applications are restricted from accessing privileged resources without appropriate permissions, mobile browsers are treated by Android OS differently. Android mobile browsers are the privileged applications that have access to sensitive data based on the permissions implicitly granted to them. In this paper, we present a novel attack approach that allows a permission-less app to access sensitive data and privileged resources using mobile browsers as a proxy. We demonstrate the effectiveness of our *proxy attack* on 8 mobile browsers across 12 Android devices ranging from Android 8.1 to Android 13. Our findings show that all current versions of Android mobile browsers are susceptible to this attack. The findings of this study highlight the need for improved security measures in Android browsers to protect against privilege escalation and privacy leakage.

Keywords: Android · Permissions · Overlay · Privilege Escalation

1 Introduction

Mobile phones have revolutionized the way we interact and exchange information. Android, one of the most prevalent mobile operating systems worldwide, has contributed significantly to this transformation, with over 2.5 billion active devices in 2021 [16]. The broad and convenient access to phone resources offered by Android has exposed shortcomings in the existing security measures. The Android permissions system is a crucial mechanism that aims to restrict an application's access to sensitive data and privileged components. However, several studies have highlighted its limitations [1,5,9,12,17,31,40].

The Android permission system has since evolved to a more regulated permission model enabling users to determine whether an app should access resources or not. Granting users the authority to accept or decline app permissions has not resolved the security concerns associated with Android permissions.

In this work, we investigate this transitive permission usage through mobile browsers. Although the Android permissions system has become more advanced, it appears to be still vulnerable to transitive permission usage, which enables attackers to perform actions that are prohibited for a third-party app.

We introduce the *proxy attack* which capitalizes on the absence of privileges for seemingly harmless operations (such as querying system information

J. Deng et al. (Eds.): CANS 2023, LNCS 14342, pp. 162–185, 2023.
https://doi.org/10.1007/978-981-99-7563-1_8

and launching an intent), thereby circumventing Android's permission framework. In our attack, we exploit a mobile browser as a proxy to request and gain unauthorized access to sensitive permission-protected data and resources on Android devices. Despite being limited in accessing sensitive data without explicit user consent, mobile browsers are granted certain permissions that regular user applications do not have. This is because browsers are viewed as less of a security threat since they present information to users in a controlled manner. In order to conceal the browser activity, we utilize overlay views, a form of UI deception technique that can manipulate users into performing specific actions. These techniques have been previously employed in attacks (e.g., phishing [13]) as users are unable to determine the source of a window they are interacting with on the screen. Although the abuse of overlays is not novel, the key aspect of the proxy attack involves obtaining unauthorized access to information that would typically be inaccessible to third-party apps but can be achieved through mobile browsers. Therefore, in the proxy attack, overlays primarily serve as a means to provide reassurance and conceal the use of browsers, which often goes unnoticed and does not raise suspicion among users.

In summary, we present the following contributions:

- We introduce a novel proxy attack that circumvents Android's permission model. We demonstrate that an unauthorized malicious app can leverage a mobile browser to gain privileged access to phone resources. By delegating the responsibility of acquiring permissions to the browser, which acts as a proxy and shields the attacker app, the malicious app is able to obtain the necessary permissions without raising suspicion. This attack methodology demonstrates the significant security risks posed to Android users and emphasizes the necessity of implementing effective security controls to counter such attacks.
- We show the effectiveness of our attack against eight popular mobile browsers on Android versions 8.1 to 13. Our findings reveal that most of the tested browsers disclose sensitive device-related information. We demonstrate that the proposed proxy attack is effective regardless of the updated security patches in older (Android 8.1–10) and newer devices (Android 11–12).
- We reexamine the vulnerabilities that enable our attack to succeed and suggest a set of countermeasures to establish a robust defense against such an attack.

The attacker app used in this study is publicly available[1]. The rest of our paper is organized as follows: Sect. 2 provides the required background information on Android. In Sect. 3, the overall attack scenario for this study is detailed. Our initial setup and overall evaluated findings are shown in Sect. 4. The consequences of our attack strategy and defenses against it are discussed in Sect. 5. Section 6 provides related studies, and the limitations of our work are discussed in Sect. 7 to conclude this work.

[1] https://github.com/thecyberlab/androidproxyattack.

2 Background

To govern access to sensitive data and privileged components, Android uses a system of safeguards called permissions. If an app requires access to any restricted device functionality, it must declare the corresponding permissions in its AndroidManifest.xml file. Historically, Android differentiated permissions with respect to the risk implied by requested permission. Currently, Android supports the following categories of permissions with respect to their protection level [19]: ① *normal permissions* that have the least risk associated with them. These permissions are granted to an app automatically during installation; ② *signature permissions* that are granted if an app is signed with the same signing key/certificate as the app defining them; ③ *dangerous permissions* that allow more substantial access to restricted data and interfaces; ③ *internal permissions* that are managed internally by the operating system.

Besides, these protections Android differentiates permissions based on the time they are granted [4]: ① *Install-time permissions* that are granted to the application when it is installed, these include normal permissions and signature permissions. ② *Runtime permissions* allow access to restricted data and functions, and hence, these are considered dangerous permissions. These permissions are requested at the runtime of the application. ③ *Special permissions* allowed for use only by the Android platform and original equipment manufacturers (OEM).

Components are the foundational elements of Android applications. An *Activity* is one of the main components managed by the Android system which is a single screen that a user can interact with in an Android application. Activities are the building blocks of an Android application responsible for presenting the user interface.

Inter-Process Communication (IPC) in Android refers to the method by which various parts of an application or various applications can communicate with one another. IPC can be used for a variety of things, including data exchange, calling methods from other processes, and messaging between processes.

An *Android intent* is a messaging object that is used to ask another app component or system tool for a certain action. The component name or fully qualified class name of the target component is specified in an *explicit intent*, which is used to start the component either within the same app or a separate app. An *implicit intent*, on the other hand, defines the kind of action to be taken and the data involved without specifying the precise component to begin with. Based on the action, category, and data specified in the intent in the AndroidManifest.xml file, the Android OS will look for the right component to handle the intent.

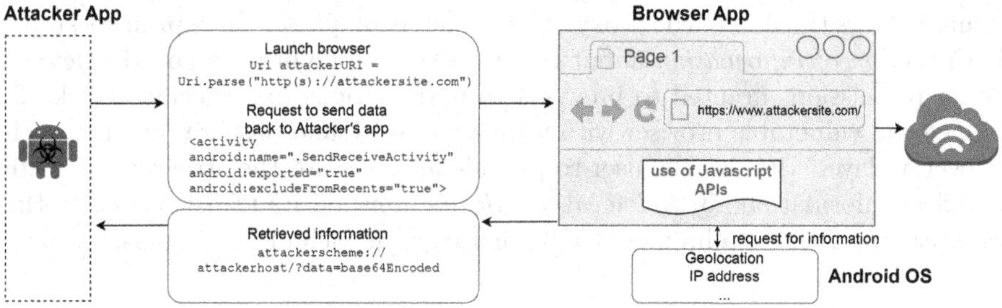

Fig. 1. The flow of the proxy attack

3 The Proxy Attack

3.1 Threat Model Overview

Android employs permissions as a primary system of safeguards to protect access to sensitive data or privileged resources. We adopt a typical threat model that assumes the attacker app has no permissions, i.e., no permissions are defined in the AndroidManifest.xml file, thus it appears benign with respect to the granted automatic permissions. In our attack, we assume that an attacker app may be any application installed on a device from a digital app distribution platform such as the Google Play Store. As such attacker app does not contain any malicious payload that may be recognized by anti-malware vendors. The target victim is the browser app that is pre-installed on a device or intentionally installed by a user.

3.2 Attack Overview

The goal of the *proxy attack* is to retrieve sensitive information or obtain protected access to phone resources without permission. The attacker app, installed on the user's device, exploits a specific browser by circumventing the `QUERY_ALL_PACKAGES` permission. The app delegates the responsibility of obtaining permissions to the browser, which then acts as a proxy hiding the attacker app. The app creates a deceptive customized toast overlay, a visual element that appears on top of other app interfaces. This overlay conceals the targeted browser and any malicious activities conducted by the attacker. By hiding the browser, the attacker gains access to protected information such as location coordinates or can initiate actions in system apps (e.g., sending an SMS message) on behalf of the attacker app. Once the sensitive data is collected, it is redirected back to the attacker app using implicit intent and deep linking, enabling the delivery of content directly to the attacker app without raising suspicion.

3.3 Attack Heuristics

The premise of the proxy attack is that an attacker app remains innocuous while interacting with a browser to obtain access to sensitive data on the device.

Figure 1 shows the flow of the proxy attack that encompasses three primary steps: ① *Collection of information* about the installed mobile browsers on the device, gather permissions granted to browsers to narrow focus to a specific attack; ② *Launch* the vulnerable browser with a target website and obscure the view with an overlay layer. Deceive the user to provide approval for the attacker's website to collect information; ③ *Retrieval of information* and its transfer back to the attacker app with deep linking. We further explain each of these steps.

3.4 Collection of Information

Since an attacker app does not request any permissions, the main goal of this phase is to choose a vulnerable proxy browser. Since different browsers may support different APIs and features or support them in different ways, the attacker app needs to gather information on the browsers that are installed on the user's device. Typically, scanning the 3rd party app information requires `QUERY_ALL_PACKAGES` permission. With this permission, an app can access other app's name, version code, granted/not granted permissions, component information (e.g., activities, services), etc. Given the sensitive nature of data, this permission allows to access, Google restricts the use of `QUERY_ALL_PACKAGES` permission to specific cases where interoperability with another app on the device is critical for the app to function [18]. For example, although `QUERY_ALL_PACKAGES` is an *install time* permission, an app developer wishing to place its app on the Google Play market has to obtain approval from Google first [27].

Listing 1.1. Bypassing a need for QUERY_ALL_PACKAGES permission

```
<queries>
    <intent>
        <action android:name="android.intent.action.MAIN"/>
        <category android:name="android.intent.category.LAUNCHER"/>
    </intent>
</queries>
```

To bypass this permission, we identified a loophole in using the *<queries>* element. The *<queries>* element specifies the content URI that the app is interested in, along with other additional parameters such as action and category. It allows the app to query the specified content URI and retrieve the data it needs.

Setting this *<queries>* element with the intent filter that uses the *action* element 'android.intent.action.MAIN' gives visibility into other apps installed on the device and their properties without requesting `QUERY_ALL_PACKAGES` permission. An example of this element usage is shown in Listing 1.1. The use of *<queries>* element is innocuous as almost all apps have this element in their AndroidManifest.xml file.

Listing 1.2. Search browsers in the device

```
Intent intent = new Intent();
intent.setAction(Intent.ACTION_VIEW);
intent.addCategory(Intent.CATEGORY_DEFAULT);
intent.addCategory(Intent.CATEGORY_BROWSABLE);
intent.setData(Uri.parse("http://www.google.com"));
List<ResolveInfo> list = null;
PackageManager pm = getPackageManager();
list = pm.queryIntentActivities(intent, PackageManager.MATCH_ALL);
for (ResolveInfo info: list) {
    String browserName = info.activityInfo.packageName;
}
```

The next step is to retrieve granted permission information on all browsers available on the device using a launchable intent that can be handled by the available browsers (Listing 1.2).

To view the permissions, we use the Android's *PackageManager* class which provides methods to retrieve information about the installed browser applications on a device, including the list of permissions granted to each application.

We retrieve the list of permissions for a specific application using the *getPackageInfo()* method of the PackageManager class. This method returns information about the specified browser package, including the list of permissions requested by the package (Listing 1.3).

Listing 1.3. Retrieve permissions granted to browsers

```
PackageManager pm = getPackageManager();
//replace with the package name of the browser app
String packageName = "com.android.chrome";

PackageInfo packageInfo = null;
try {
    packageInfo = pm.getPackageInfo(packageName, PackageManager.GET_PERMISSIONS);
} catch (PackageManager.NameNotFoundException e) {
    e.printStackTrace();
}
String[] permissions = packageInfo.requestedPermissions;

if (permissions != null && permissions.length > 0) {
    for (String permissioName : permissions) {
        int permissionStatus = pm.checkPermission(permissioName, packageName);
        if (permissionStatus == PackageManager.PERMISSION_GRANTED) {
            // permission is granted
            Log.i("permissions_granted", permissioName);
        } else {
            // permission is not granted
            Log.i("permissions_not_granted", permissioName);
        } } }
```

Once the vulnerable browser with the necessary permissions is identified, we are now ready to launch the proxy attack.

3.5 Launch

As the next step, we launch the targeted browser with an attacker-controlled website. We aim to deceive a user to grant the necessary permission to the attacker's website.

Browser Launch. Communication between apps in Android is realized through intent. At this stage, we know the specific browser's package name, so, rather than launching an implicit intent, we explicitly launch a chosen mobile browser app with a target URL.

When an intent with a target URL is sent by the attacker app, the system searches for browsers that can handle it based on their intent filters. *ResolveInfo.activityInfo.packageName* returns the package name and *ResolveInfo.activityInfo.name* returns the launcher activity of the browser used to handle the intent based on the current configuration of the device (see Table 1).

There are two ways how a target website can be opened on an Android device. Typically, when a user clicks on the link or an app launches an intent with a website request, the Android OS invokes the default mobile browser with

Table 1. Mobile browsers and their launchers retrieved using Listing 1.1

Browser Package	Browser Launcher
com.android.**chrome**	com.google.android.apps.chrome.IntentDispatcher
com.**duckduckgo**.mobile.android	com.duckduckgo.app.browser.BrowserActivity
com.**kiwibrowser**.browser	com.google.android.apps.chrome.IntentDispatcher
com.microsoft.emmx **(Edge)**	com.google.android.apps.chrome.IntentDispatcher
com.**opera**.mini.native	com.opera.mini.android.Browser
org.**mozilla**.firefox	org.mozilla.fenix.IntentReceiverActivity
com.**brave**.browser	com.google.android.apps.chrome.IntentDispatcher
com.sec.android.app.sbrowser **(Samsung)**	com.sec.android.app.sbrowser.SBrowserLauncherActivity

the target website. Alternatively, an app can embed a target website content as a part of its screen by asking the OS to load a website in a WebView. Since the attack aims to access sensitive data, it is critical to avoid requesting any privileges to not raise suspicions.

In the former approach, an Android app typically requires `android.permission.INTERNET` permission to access the internet service. However, the Android API provides several ways to request a target website and exfiltrate captured data without this permission. For example, requesting the URI of a website through Intent, allows the attacker's app to bypass this permission.

To incorporate web content within a mobile app's WebView, the originating app must possess the appropriate permissions for authorized access. However, if the app defers to a mobile browser to obtain such access, it essentially delegates the responsibility of obtaining permissions to the browser, which then acts as a proxy and shields the attacker app.

Due to the lack of restrictions in the Android OS, a URL activity can be initiated, enabling any website (even a malicious one controlled by an attacker) to be launched by a browser on behalf of the attacker's app.

In this proxy attack, we leverage the target website under the attacker's control. The website allows an attacker to embed Javascript (JS) code to collect location, microphone, camera, and device-related (e.g., operating system, device memory, and battery level) data. The *window.navigator* object in JS provides information about the user's device and environment(Table 2). For example, to collect location information, the *window.navigator* object can be used with the Geolocation API which allows websites to access the user's location. To collect microphone and camera information, the MediaDevices API can provide access to the user's microphone and camera. In both cases, appropriate permissions are expected to be granted.

At this point, an attacker is facing two challenges:

- *Permissions*: Some device information (e.g., device model, time zone) is available to any app without permissions, however, the more sensitive data is protected. The setup step ensures that the attacker app can see permissions already granted on the device's mobile browser apps, which significantly simplifies an attack and allows invoking the browser that was already granted permissions protecting the target data. For example, access to a phone's cam-

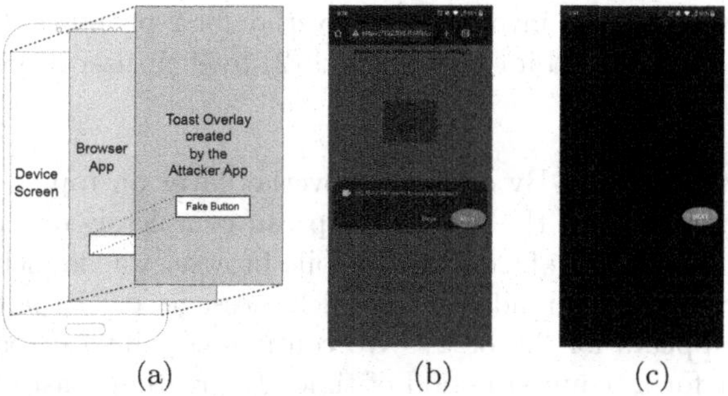

Fig. 2. Toast overlay on the attacker's website. (a) A conceptual view of overlay, (b) 50% overlay transparency and (c) 100% overlay shown on One Plus 7 Pro device.

era relies on run-time permission mandated by Android OS which means a user is prompted to grant this permission the first time the browser attempts to access it.

To provide an additional layer of protection, the browser mandates an extra confirmation when a website requests access to the camera. Subsequently, if the browser has permission, any website that attempts to access the camera triggers a prompt requiring the user to grant further consent. Consequently, if the attacker app can manipulate the user into granting this confirmation on their website, the attacker's site can gain access to the camera without any further prompts to the user.

It is possible, however, that none of the browsers have the necessary permissions yet. This requires attackers to obtain permissions first and subsequently prompt the user to approve access to the camera without raising the user's suspicions.

- *Browser visibility*: The browser with a target website appears in the foreground. Thus, its activity and the following user prompts are visible to a user.

We resolve both challenges with the use of overlays. Several studies have investigated Android UI deception techniques using overlays [6,14,42]. These techniques range from drawing toasts [34] to performing click-jack-style attacks [42]. The attacker app that we developed for this study uses a variation of these attacks to hide the browser's activity and silently obtain permissions.

Using Overlays. Figure 2(a) presents a conceptual view of using an overlay to deceive a user and access privileged data.

The attack combines an overlay layer with a *toast* window, i.e., a small text message pop-up window shown on screen for a limited amount of time. Toast messages can be drawn over the top view window even when an unrelated app controls the main screen without explicit permission.

In the proxy attack, we invoke a *toast* overlay for 2 purposes: (1) to hide the invoked mobile browser and its activity; and (2) to elicit user response to tap on the screen.

Hiding Browser Behavior. By adding an overlay layer on top of the host view (a mobile browser screen), the attacker app can completely obscure the target web page's content and the fact that a mobile browser was launched.

The toast window is intended for a quick message, e.g., a notification, and thus typically appears for 3.5 or 2 s. We continuously invoke toast to provide an overlay layer for a required period of time. To create a toast overlay, we use a *Handler* class and *Looper* object, which is responsible for creating a message queue (for our attack it is a customized toast) for our app thread.

The attacker app uses *Handler.postDelayed()* that starts both our custom toast overlaying (OuterHandler) and launches the targeted browser (InnerHandler) in a parallel thread so that our main user interface (UI) is non-blocking. This non-blocking mechanism allows long-running operations of toast to show on the screen of the device without blocking the main thread. This keeps our attacker app's overlay interface responsive and avoids ANR (Application Not Responding) errors.

The toast overlay is started right after the attacker app's main thread finishes scanning for the permission (e.g., camera) that is already granted on the targeted browser, the screen is taken over by the customized toast overlay, and then the targeted browser is launched. This sequence hides the underlying transitions and presents the workflow expected by a user.

Deceiving User. The toast overlay view also aims to deceive a user and elicit necessary taps on the screen. The toast overlay presents a legitimate-looking view, for example, mimicking an expected app view, without appearing suspicious (e.g., using *toast.setView(customiziedView)*). This view can include buttons to capture a user's taps. These taps are then transferred to a hidden browser requesting permissions or user approval. Note that the toast overlay does not get focus on the touch events and cannot be dismissed by a user, hence it is fully controlled by the attack app.

The use of toasts for user deception was noted by previous studies [15] using two signature protection level permissions `SYSTEM_ALERT_WINDOW` and the `BIND_ACCESSIBILITY_SERVICE`. To mitigate this vulnerability, Android introduced a timeout of a maximum of 3.5 s for a single toast and a single toast window per UserID (UID) at a time. This, however, does not address the underlying issue that an app does not require permission to show a toast window over any other app. Our use of toast overlay also bypasses any permissions that are required to draw over other apps as described in CVE-2017-0752.

If a targeted browser does not have the necessary permissions, upon request to access privileged resources, Android prompts the user twice to approve this access (once to grant this permission to a browser, and the second time to allow website access to this resource). The key weakness that our proxy attack exploits at this stage is the ability of any app to cover these permission prompts with the toast overlays.

Since the toast overlay presents a customized view, a user may be easily tricked into unknowingly approving permissions. As Fig. 2(a) shows a customized toast view can be easily mapped to the 'Allow' button on the underlying permission prompt. An example of a user prompt, when a website attempts to access sensitive data is shown in Fig. 2(b) and (c).

3.6 Retrieving Data

When an attacker's activities remain in the background hidden with an inescapable overlay view, there are many opportunities for exploiting device resources. We build an attacker app to obtain information and access services that require permissions. Once the permission-related data is gathered, it is redirected back to the attacker app through implicit intent using *deep linking*, which allows to programmatically delivery of content to an app. Deep links function as URIs links that guide users to a particular content of our attacker app. For example, the attacker app can specify what type of URIs links should be transferred back to this app.

Mobile browsers can invoke various activities, e.g., display link data, using a BROWSABLE intent. Thus, the attacker app specifies a BROWSABLE intent filter along with a URI *scheme* and a *host* in the app's AndroidManifest.xml file. An automatic click on any hyperlink on the website that fits the app's defined URI scheme and host triggers an intent to the attacker app that collects data sent by the browser (through .SendReceiveActivity).

For example, the hyperlink can be placed on the target website using an *anchor tag(<a>)*, i.e., *a.href = "attackerscheme://attackerhost/?data= base64EncodedData"*, where the specified URI 'scheme' is *attackerscheme*, the 'host' *attackerhost*, and 'base64Encoded' is transferred data.

There is no specific limit on the amount of data that an Android app can receive from a browser using a URI scheme, however, the device's available memory and processing power can impose limitations on how much data can be transferred, e.g., captured image and audio recordings can be resource consuming. For practical reasons, in our attack, we encode the collected data in base64 format.

Listing 1.4. Browsable intent-filter

```
<activity android:name=".SendReceiveActivity"
          android:exported="true"
          android:excludeFromRecents="true">
    <intent-filter>
        <action android:name="android.intent.action.VIEW" />
        <category android:name="android.intent.category.DEFAULT" />
        <category android:name="android.intent.category.BROWSABLE" />
        <data android:scheme="attackerscheme"
              android:host="attackerhost" />
    </intent-filter>
</activity>
```

The Listing 1.4, shows the BROWSABLE intent filter configuration provided in the attacker app's AndroidManifest.xml file. The collected data redirected by the browser is received by *SendReceiveActivity* in *onResume()* function. Finally, we extract the received intent with intent.getData() returning the data associated with the intent (Listing 1.5).

The *android:excludeFromRecents="true"* attribute used is to exclude the *SendReceiveActivity* from appearing in the list of recently used apps (the Overview screen). When this attribute is set to true for an activity in the AndroidManifest.xml file, the activity is removed from the list of recent tasks when the user navigates away from the app. This means that the user is not able to return to the activity using the Overview screen, and needs to restart the app. Though *android:excludeFromRecents="true"* is used to prevent sensitive data of activity from being exposed in the recent apps list, we use this attribute to hide *SendReceiveActivity* on the device.

Listing 1.5. Receiving data from a browser

```
@Override
protected void onResume() {
    super.onResume();
    handleIntetExtras(getIntent());
}
private void handleIntetExtras(Intent intent) {
    Uri uri = intent.getData();
    if(uri != null) {
        Log.i("Server_Response", "received some data");
        Log.i("Device_Data", uri.getQuery());
        //further logic to stop/continue toast overlay with
        //sharedPreference storage with a boolean flag
    }
}
```

Table 2. Information type and their navigator syntax

Device Information	JS Syntax
OS	- navigator.paltform - navigator.OS
Device Version	navigator.appVersion
GPU(Renderer)	canvas.getContext('#canvasID')
User Language	- navigator.languages - navigator.userLanguage - navigator.language
Network Information	navigator.connection
Battery*	navigator.getBattery()
Ram(memory)*	navigator.deviceMemory
Take Picture*	navigator.mediaDevices.getUserMedia()
Audio Record*	navigator.mediaDevices.getUserMedia()
Location*	navigator.geolocation.getCurrentPosition

* requires HTTPS protocol, the rest can be accessed through both HTTP and HTTPS.

Additional Attacks. Additional steps can allow us to mount more effective attacks accessing phone, SMS, and email services. These resources are typically accessed through the pre-installed system apps present on the device.

Listing 1.6. Launching system apps via browser

```
<!DOCTYPE html>
<html>
    <body>
      <a id="sendSms" style="display:none;">SMS</a>
      <a id="callPhone" style="display:none;">Call</a>
      <a id="sendEmail" style="display:none;">Email</a>
    </body>
    <script type="text/javascript">
      var aSms = document.getElementById('sendSms');
      aSms.href = "sms://+12345565444?body=I%27am%20Bob";
      //document.getElementById("sendSms").click();
      var aTel = document.getElementById('callPhone');
      aTel.href = "tel:12345565444";
      document.getElementById("callPhone").click();
      var aEmail = document.getElementById('sendEmail');
      aEmail.href = "mailto:person1@example.com?body=You%20are%20invited%20to%20The
          %20Party!";
     //document.getElementById("sendEmail").click();
   </script>
</html>
```

Table 3. Tested devices for proxy attack

Android version	Device model	The latest installed security patch
8.1	Huawei (P20 Pro)	June 1, 2018
9	Samsung (Galaxy A10 e)	December 1, 2020
10	LG (Phoenix 5)	July 1, 2020
10	Xiomi (Poco f1)	December 1, 2020
11	Umidigi (A9 Pro)	March 5, 2021
11	Ulefone (Armor 8 Pro)	July 5, 2022
11	Samsung (Galaxy A22)	March 1, 2022
12	Umidigi (BV4900 Pro)	May 5, 2022
12	One Plus 7 (Pro)	August 5, 2022
12	Ulefone (Note 14)	March 5, 2023
13	Samsusng (Galaxy A22 5g)	November 1, 2022
13	Google Pixel 7	February 5, 2022

Equivalently, these can be launched via browsers. When a hyperlink with a specific protocol is requested, for example, *tel:*, *sms:*, or *mailto:*, Android OS invokes an app that can handle the requested protocol. An attacker can pre-fill these schemes with corresponding information, thus, making a call, or sending an SMS or an email message.

To exploit these capabilities, predefined phone number, SMS, and email message with the receiver's contact information are placed on the target website called by the attacker app using the hyperlinks. We then follow the described deep link approach to automatically launch the corresponding system apps. Android allows the launching of the system apps via browsers without requiring any explicit permissions. A snippet is given in Listing 1.6. Android OS decides which apps can handle these implicit intents coming from the browser.

When an implicit intent is transmitted from a browser to the Android OS to carry out operations such as sending an SMS or making a phone call, a notification is not shown to the user. When a user clicks on an SMS link in a browser, for example, the implicit intent is delivered immediately to the SMS app without the user being notified. This strategy improves user experience and prevents interruptions by assuming that the user intentionally performs this operation.

4 Evaluation Study

4.1 Settings

Since some device information accessible by browsers requires an HTTPS connection to the server (Table 2), we installed an Apache/2.4.41 server with a self-signed certificate. Although all tested browsers gave an alert accessing the target HTTPS website, this did not prevent us from retrieving necessary information. To evaluate the proxy attack in the real world, we tested it on 12 mobile phones with Android versions 8.1 to 13 (Table 3).

For our evaluation, we have selected 6 most popular (based on the number of downloads) mobile browsers: Google Chrome, Samsung Internet browser, Opera Mini, Mozilla Firefox, Microsoft Edge, and Kiwi Browser. We also included 2 privacy-focused browsers: Brave Private Web Browser and DuckDuckGo Private browser.

Before proceeding with an attack, we verified permissions that were granted to mobile browsers by default on the Android devices using *Android Debug Bridge (adb)* [23]. The granted permissions were obtained using the *adb shell*

Table 4. Information generally accessible by mobile browsers

	Information Type	Chrome ←	Mozilla Firefox ←	Opera Mini	DDG	Edge ←	Brave ←	Samsung ←	Kiwi ←	Necessary Permissions
Category 1	TimeZone	✓	✓	✓	✓	✓	✓	✓	✓	N/A
	User Language	✓	✓	✓	✓	✓	✓	✓	✓	N/A
	Device Model, Android Version	✓	✓	✓	✓	✓	✓	✓	✓	N/A
	OS	✓	✓	✓	✓	✓	✓	✓	✓	N/A
	GPU	✓	✓	✓	✓	✓	✓	✓	✓	N/A
	Memory(RAM)	✓	X	✓	X	✓	✓	✓	✓	N/A
	Network Info - Internet Connection - Connection Type - EffectiveType - Downlink	✓	X	✓	✓	✓	X	✓	✓	ACCESS_NETWORK_STATE[a] ACCESS_WIFI_STATE[a] READ_PHONE_STATE[b]*
	Battery Status - Charging Status - Charge Level	✓	X	✓	X	✓	Wrong Value	✓	✓	BATTERY_STATS[c]*
Category 2	Camera	✓	✓	✓	✓	✓	✓	✓	✓	CAMERA[b]
	Microphone (Audio Recording)	✓	✓	✓	✓	✓	✓	✓	✓	RECORD_AUDIO[b]
	Location	✓	✓	✓	✓	✓	✓	✓	✓	ACCESS_FINE_LOCATION[b] ACCESS_COARSE_LOCATION[b]

DDG: DuckDuckGo browser
[a] Normal Permission
[b] Runtime Permission
[c] Signature Permission
* The 3rd party apps are required to obtain these permissions, while browsers granted them implicitly,

← Browsers that allow automatic hyperlink clicking from the attacker's site back to the attacker app through Android OS (deep link)

dumpsys package "browser.package.name". Although in practice browsers are likely to have at least some permissions granted, for our experiments, we made sure that browsers had no granted runtime permissions.

4.2 Accessible Information

Table 4 presents the devices' information availability on 8 mobile browsers tested on all analyzed Android devices. We observe fairly consistent results. Most browsers have direct access to this data. The exceptions are Mozilla Firefox, and two privacy-focused browsers: Brave and DuckDuckGo. Several device parameters can be retrieved by browsers and third-party apps without any permissions, e.g., timezone, user language, device model, Android version, OS, GPU, and memory-related information. We were able to retrieve network-related information from 6 out of 8 browsers without requiring to obtain any permissions.

We see that most of the browsers that provide network information (e.g., internet connection type, connection effective type, connection downlink) are granted `ACCESS_NETWORK_STATE` and `ACCESS_WIFI_STATE` permissions implicitly. Note that any third-party app requesting cellular information(e.g., 3g/4g) explicitly requires `READ_PHONE_STATE` permission which is a run-time permission and has dangerous level protection. Network information was unavailable from Mozilla Firefox and Brave (released under Mozilla) browsers as a part of defense from fingerprinting [38].

Memory (RAM) information was unavailable from Mozilla and DuckDuckGo browsers. According to Mozilla Developer Network(MDN), in order to reduce fingerprinting [10], the reported figure is inaccurate on web browsers and is not available on Android Firefox browser [10]. Similarly, due to anti-fingerprinting techniques, DuckDuckGo browser returns undefined for *navigator.deviceMemory* [29](hardware APIs).

Similarly, 6 browsers had access to battery-level information, while none of them had `BATTERY_STATS` permissions granted. Although this is signature-level permission, mobile browsers are exempt from it. Interestingly, Brave browser consistently provided incorrect battery level, i.e., 100% and the charging status is true even in cases when the device has a low charge level and was not being charged. The battery status API is deprecated in Mozilla due to tracking and fingerprinting. However, a third-party script found on multiple websites can quickly associate users' visits by exploiting battery information accessible to web scripts. These scripts can utilize battery level, discharging time, and charging time values, which remain constant across sites due to synchronized update intervals. Consequently, this approach enables the script to link concurrent visits effectively [35]. As a preventive measure, browsers like DuckDuckGO, Mozilla Firefox, and Brave have disabled the battery status API, thwarting this form of tracking.

All browsers provided geolocation information and also had access to the camera and microphone.

Table 5. The summary of the proxy attack on various Android devices

Device	Android Version	Browsers																			
		Chrome			Kiwi			Brave[a]			Edge			Samsung			Firefox[b]			Opera	DDG
		c1	c2	c3	c1	c2	c3	c1	c2	c3	c1	c2	c3	c1	c2	c3	c1	c2	c3		
Huawei	8.1 (API 27)	✓	✓	✓	✓	✓	✓	✓	✓	✓	✓	✓	✓	✓	✓	✓	✓	✓	✓	X	X
Samsung Galaxy	9 (API 28)	✓	✓	✓	✓	✓	✓	✓	✓	✓	✓	✓	✓	✓	✓	✓	✓	✓	✓	X	X
LG	10 (API 29)	✓	✓	✓	✓	✓	✓	✓	✓	✓	✓	✓	✓	✓	✓	✓	✓	✓	✓	X	X
Xiomi	10 (API 29)	✓	✓	✓	✓	✓	✓	✓	✓	✓	✓	✓	✓	✓	✓	✓	✓	✓	✓	X	X
Ulefone	11 (API 30)	✓	✓	✓	✓	✓	✓	✓	✓	✓	✓	✓	✓	✓	✓	✓	✓	✓	✓	X	X
Umidigi	11 (API 30)	✓	✓	✓	✓	✓	✓	✓	✓	✓	✓	✓	✓	✓	✓	✓	✓	✓	✓	X	X
Samsung Galaxy	11 (API 30)	✓	✓	✓	✓	✓	✓	✓	✓	✓	✓	✓	✓	✓	✓	✓	✓	✓	✓	X	X
One Plus	12 (API 31)	✓	✓	✓	✓	✓	✓	✓	✓	✓	✓	✓	✓	✓	✓	✓	✓	✓	✓	X	X
Ulefone	12 (API 31)	✓	X	✓[c]	✓	X	✓[c]	✓	X	✓[c]	✓	X	✓[c]	✓	X	✓[c]	✓	X	✓[c]	X	X
Umidigi	12 (API 31)	✓	X	X	✓	X	X	✓	X	X	✓	X	X	✓	X	X	✓	X	X	X	X
Samsung Galaxy	13 (API 33)	✓	X	X	✓	X	X	✓	X	X	✓	X	X	✓	X	X	✓	X	X	X	X
Google Pixel	13 (API 33)	✓	X	X	✓	X	X	✓	X	X	✓	X	X	✓	X	X	✓	X	X	X	X

DDG: DuckDuckGo browser
Category1(c1): TimeZone, User Language, Device Model, Android Version, OS, GPU, Ram, Network Info, Battery Status (no user interaction required)
Category2(c2): Permission-granted data - location, camera, microphone
Category3(c3): System app initiation: call, sms, email
[a] **Except** Network Info & Incorrect Battery status
[b] **Except** Ram, Battery Status, Network Info
[c] **Except** Email Sending

4.3 Evaluation Results

To evaluate the effectiveness of the proxy attack, we have installed all 8 browsers on each of the analyzed Android devices. Table 5 presents the results of our proxy attack. Browsers mostly displayed the same behavior on different devices. Although 6 of the 8 tested browsers, readily gave the attacker app all the data it needed, 2 of the browsers (such as DuckDuckGo and Opera Mini) did not allow the automatic click to occur using JS, making it impossible for the attacker app to automatically retrieve the information it had gathered from these browsers on the tested devices. We presume that these 2 browsers may, for security purposes, disable automatic navigation to native applications. This is most likely done to stop malicious websites from launching other apps on a user's device. The proxy attack failed on these 2 browsers. It should be noted that DuckDuckGo is a privacy-focused browser, hence stricter security measures are generally expected. However, Brave, another privacy-focused browser, did not exhibit this behavior, and in most cases provided information similar to the majority of browsers.

To see the smooth data flow from the browser to our attacker application, we set DuckDuckGo and Opera Mini as default browsers and changed the "href" value from `''attackerscheme://attackerhost/?data=base64Encoded''` to `''intent://attackerhost/#Intent;scheme=attackerscheme;package=attacker.package.name;S.data=''+base64Encoded+'';end;''` in JS to test data transmission specifically through intent. Even after this change, we were unable to retrieve data from Opera Mini and DuckDuckGo browsers however for the remaining browsers this strategy worked. This shows that, unlike other browsers that have used this strategy successfully, Opera Mini and DuckDuckGo do not provide seamless intent transfer to the 3rd party apps in the Android OS.

Accessing Category 1 Data. The first set of experiments was focused on accessing data that requires no user interaction. Some of this data requires no permissions (such as timezone, user language, Android model and version, etc.), while other needs runtime and signature permissions, e.g., accessing network information requires `READ_PHONE_STATE` run-time permission, while accessing battery status needs signature-level `BATTERY_STATS` permission.

Our attacker app did not obtain network information through Firefox and Brave browsers and memory and battery-level information through Firefox and DuckDuckGo browsers, as these browsers do not typically access this information even in non-attack context. In other browsers on all devices, our attack was successful, i.e., the attacker app was able to obtain data typically inaccessible by third-party apps without proper permissions.

We observed several noticeable variations in browser behavior when the attacker website was accessed through the attacker app beneath the overlay. No browsers alerted the user asking to confirm whether the attacker app should be launched through the automatic deeplink. Deeplinking did not succeed in the DuckDuckGo and Opera Mini browsers as they do not allow automatic deeplinking to happen.

Accessing Category 2 Data. With our proxy attack, we were able to retrieve permission-related data (location, camera, microphone) from browsers on devices with Android versions 8.1 to 11, and Android 12 (One Plus 7 Pro). We were unsuccessful on two Android 12 (Ulefone, Umidigi) and two Android 13 devices.

Retrieved Location Data. Apart from deceiving the user to give consent on the website's location prompt, we also examined the location coordinates of the Android devices using a public API and JavaScript code placed on the target website accessed by a browser. The user does not need to manually give consent to the location request. We use IP-based geolocation-db API [11] to get the latitude and longitude of the user's device. When the attacker app navigates to the target website, the browser automatically provides the IP address of the device. This API then retrieves the location by matching the IP address with geolocation in their database. We requested this information on each browser for 3 different locations. The retrieved information was imprecise by 2.06 km on average and varied against the data retrieved from browser apps. So, even if location data can be retrieved without the user's consent from the public API(s), the accuracy is not precise.

Initiating System Apps (Category 3). Our proxy attack was successful in triggering system apps to perform actions such as making a phone call, sending an SMS message, and sending an email across all browsers, except for Opera and DuckDuckGo, on devices running Android 8.1 to 11. However, the behavior observed on Android 12 exhibited some variability. Specifically, the attack was able to successfully make a phone call and send an SMS message on two devices, but it was unsuccessful on the Umidigi phone. Unfortunately, access to system apps failed on both Android 13 phones.

For all devices sending email message with the proxy attack was successful with a single tap (indicating the user's approval). An exception was the One Plus 7 (Pro) device that unexpectedly requested an additional confirmation after pressing the 'Send' button. Hence the overall attack required 2 clicks although permission was already granted to a browser. Knowing this behavior, however, does not prevent an attack, i.e., an attacker can craft an overlay view to obtain 2 clicks from the user within a few seconds. There was another interesting result we found analyzing an Android 12 Ulefone (Note 14) device. With a delay of 215–220 ms for notifying successive toasts with minimal flickering, we were able to successfully send an SMS message and dial phone numbers. However, the attack was inconsistent, 3 out of 10 attempts were successful.

We found that maintaining the duration of the toasts in the foreground for more than 3.5 s was challenging for Android versions 11 and up. However, setting the *targetSDK* version of the attacker app to 29 gave us more flexibility in maintaining the different duration of toast, i.e., more than 40 s on Android 11, approximately 16 s on Android 12, and 13 devices.

The observed behavior partially aligns with the official mitigation measures. In Android 11, Google implemented partial protection to prevent background custom toasts [26], and in Android 12, they introduced full *pass-through touch* protection to prevent touch events from reaching apps when they pass through a window from another app [24]. However, despite these measures, we consistently found that system apps could be accessed on Android 11 devices and inconsistently on Android 12 devices. Despite the introduction of Android 13, Android versions 10-12 continue to be widely used globally [41] underlying the devastating effects of the proxy attack.

Similarly, the use of overlays leading to privilege escalation has been reported before[2] and according to Android Security Bulletin, patched [20,21]. In our experiments, the tested devices had the latest patches installed (Table 3). These patches, however, did not prevent the use of overlays.

Although it was shown in [42] that *pass-through touch* and background toasts are still unresolved until Android 11, it's important to note that Android has effectively resolved the *pass-through touch* problem in Android 12 and 13. Android 12 automatically stops full occlusion attacks, and this protection is further enhanced in Android 13 and subsequent versions, where touch events from untrusted overlays originating from different UIDs are declined. The prevention of *fully covered* attacks is also feasible by adjusting the code. Specifically, developers need to ensure that *setFilterTouchesWhenObscured* is set to "true" in the

[2] CVE-2021-0954: https://www.cvedetails.com/cve/CVE-2021-0954/, CVE-2021-39692: https://www.cvedetails.com/cve/CVE-2021-39692/,.

code, or setting *android:filterTouchesWhenObscured* to true in the root layout, thereby prohibiting touch interactions while an overlay is active [28]. However, it's interesting to highlight that the *pass-through touch* problem remained under overlay even after the One Plus 7 Pro(Android 12) device was updated from Android 9 to Android 12. Moreover, The tested browsers that were compromised under toast overlay attack did not set the *setFilterTouchesWhenObscured/android:filterTouchesWhenObscured* to true in the launchers and layout files.

Through further examinations, we have discovered that when multiple applications share the same UID, they can experience pass-through touch due to being processed under a common process ID (PID). Additionally, we have identified that activities that utilize webviews are also vulnerable to toast overlay attacks within the confines of a single application.

Difficulty in Detecting Toast Overlay Behavior During App Review Process. Previous strategies to counter toast attacks have included actions like deprecating `TYPE_TOAST` since Android 8.0 and implementing a restriction on overlapping toasts [22]. Nonetheless, our research, as well as findings from [42], indicates that employing a brief delay in generating subsequent toasts can facilitate the execution of overlay attacks. Notably, Google's recent interventions to counter overlays predominantly occur after the application's release, focusing on stopping background toast bursts from Android 12. While app stores such as Google Play employ rigorous review processes to weed out potential threats before an app's release, the detection of sophisticated attacks like toast overlay attacks can sometimes pose challenges. However, while background toast blocking is a defense mechanism, Android provides a full-screen overlay in apps employing modules like *SurveyFragment.java* under *interaction* package for animation and tutorial purposes. So, the complexity of distinguishing between legitimate uses and malicious intent in apps under overlay can result in uncertainty during app review. Striking a balance between ensuring user safety and avoiding false positives remains a complex task for the app store. Moreover, Google employs advanced machine learning techniques to detect phishing activities within messaging apps, predominantly in the Pixel series. This system operates based on identifying suspicious requests and texts [25]. However, our toast overlay attack effectively circumvents these scanning mechanisms, as illustrated in Fig. 2.

We conducted an examination of our attacker app by subjecting it to scrutiny by two prominent antivirus programs, namely *AVG Antivirus & Security*[3] and *Malwarebytes Mobile Security*[4]. Despite huge downloads of these apps, neither application was able to identify the malicious intentions underlying the toast attack and the scan results indicated that the app was 'clean' and devoid of threats. To delve deeper into the detection process, we resorted to employing a specialized toast detection application named *Toast Source*[5]. However, it is

[3] https://play.google.com/store/apps/details?id=com.antivirus.
[4] https://play.google.com/store/apps/details?id=org.malwarebytes.antimalware.
[5] https://play.google.com/store/apps/details?id=pl.revanmj.toastsource.

worth noting that this app is designed to detect all types of toasts and does not possess the capability to differentiate between toast overlays and regular toasts. It is important to highlight that all these 3rd party apps required permission to AccessibilityService for their functioning.

Responsible Disclosure. We reached out to OnePlus[6] regarding the toast overlay vulnerability on the OnePlus 7 Pro(Android 12). They acknowledged it as a known problem on their end failing to give any kind of notification to users and asked us for device-specific details, including the IMEI. However, no concrete solution was provided following this initial communication.

5 Discussion and Lessons

Mitigation: Our evaluation of 8 mobile browsers across 12 mobile devices shows that the proposed proxy attack is effective in the real world in both older and newer devices regardless of the updated security patches. The attack relies on a few critical weaknesses that make this approach viable on the latest versions of mobile browsers and Android devices:

- *Query without permission*: Bypassing QUERY_ALL_PACKAGES permission in Android allows any third-party app to have visibility into other installed apps on the same device. As we showed, this can lead to several negative implications for user privacy and device security, including collecting information about other apps to craft targeted attacks or exploit known vulnerabilities. This information can be retrieved even for disabled apps. This weakness can be easily mitigated by modifying the app's default launcher activity settings to *android:exported="false"*, in this case, the activity is not launchable even after querying. Note, that the browsers' default activity launchers are set to *android:exported="true"*.
- *Overlays*: Overlaying presents a significant threat. Users are at risk of virtually any type of attack through these inescapable view-blocking layers that require no permissions to invoke. The fact that any app can draw a customized overlay with essentially any content on top of any other unrelated app allows a malicious attacker to convince the user to perform any action, e.g., provide credentials, or click on a phishing link. In spite of numerous studies showing the dangers of overlays [14,32], they still remain largely exploitable. Our proxy attack was successful in obtaining access to sensitive data and system apps on all Android devices versions 8.1–11 and partially successful on Android 12 and 13 phones.
  The touch protection introduced by Google for the new devices does not appear to be adopted uniformly by different OEMs, while the older devices that are prevalent worldwide have no protection. The impact of these weaknesses can be mitigated by introducing release patches for loop-based toast overlay attacks for both recent and older versions of Android.

[6] https://oneplus.custhelp.com/app/ask.

- *Lack of required permission for launching intent*: Android OS provides the mechanism for launching intents to browser apps without requiring any explicit permissions. To counter this Android OS should not allow third-party apps to launch browsers without explicit permissions defined in the AndroidManifest.xml. For example, the apps can be required to use *internet* permission to launch an intent using `Intent.ACTION_VIEW` along with some URI that starts with *http* or *https*.
- *Browser permissions*: The permissions only need to be granted once to a mobile browser regardless of whose behalf the browser is accessing the data. The user might choose to grant permission on the browser without any restrictions (Allow), once per session (Allowed once), for 24 h, or deny the browser-specific access. As our attack showed, only the 'Allowed once' option can be considered the safest. In this case, users are explicitly alerted when third-party apps attempt to access browsers.
- *Touch sensitivity of system apps*: Default phone and SMS applications need just a single click to function and trigger no additional confirmation before launching. While this allows for a seamless user experience, it presents many opportunities for malicious apps. Mitigation measures can include device button annotations with additional properties such as a long click duration, and confirmation prompts to prevent overlay-based clickjacking.

Limitations. In order to be successful, our proxy attack strategically positions buttons on the overlay using commonly observed coordinates from preliminary manual testing. For instance, for the dialer system app, the buttons are typically located in the lower middle section of the screen, while for the SMS system app, they are mostly placed in the lower right corner. However, there is some slight variation among different browsers. For example, Chrome, Edge, and Kiwi browsers display the alert in the middle of the screen, whereas Mozilla Firefox, Opera, and Samsung browsers show it at the bottom. It is possible that other browsers and system apps may exhibit further variations in button placement, potentially limiting the effectiveness of the attack. Nevertheless, we anticipate that a determined attacker can expand the testing pool and adjust the button coordinates based on specific browsers.

During our experimentation, we also observed another behavioral characteristic where multiple touches on the overlay were needed to perform a function in the target app. Among the devices we tested, only the OnePlus 7 phone required 2 clicks to send an email. It is reasonable to expect that other Original Equipment Manufacturers (OEMs) may have similar implementations that require multiple confirmations. While this does not prevent the attack, it does necessitate the attacker apps to anticipate and implement additional overlays.

6 Related Work

In the past decade, numerous studies examined attack paths and vulnerabilities unique to mobile browsers. Aldoseri et al. [2] showed security flaws in popular mobile browsers. Hassanshahi et al. [30] introduced web-to-app injection attacks that allow invoking installed apps on a mobile device when a user visits a malicious website in an Android browser.

Many studies investigated Android GUI deception techniques focused on exploiting the user's confusion and inability to verify which app is producing actions on the screen. These attack range from tapjacking [37], UI redressing [34], draw-and-destroy [42]. The mobile tapjacking attack is similar to traditional browser clickjacking which involves loading the victim webpage as a transparent frame on top of a harmless page, enticing the user to click on it. When the user clicks, the click event is transferred to the victim frame, allowing attackers to perform actions on behalf of the user.

Niemietz et al. [34] showed a UI redressing attack that allows to make a phone call without necessary permissions. The attack was relying on `SYSTEM_ALERT_WINDOW` permission explicitly requested in the AndroidManifest.xml. Fratantonio et al. [15] showed however that users can be deceived to grant `SYSTEM_ALERT_WINDOW` and the `BIND_ACCESSIBILITY_SERVICE` permissions enabling UI attacks. Rydstedt et al.'s [39] explored how different tapjacking attacks can be used against mobile browsers, e.g., for stealing WPA secret keys and geofencing the user. Felt et al. [13] demonstrated that in these cases users can be convinced to enter their sensitive information, such as their passwords. Bianchi et al. [6] explored different ways mobile users can be deceived and developed a defense mechanism to prevent GUI confusion attacks.

Starting Android API level 23, overlays have been significantly restricted, disabling most of these early attacks targeting GUI confusion. Focusing on more generic GUI properties, Alepis et al.'s [3] showed security standards of Android UI can be still bypassed. Wang et al. [42] introduced the draw-and-destroy overlay attack. Taking advantage of the Android animation mechanism, a malicious app can quickly draw and destroy a customized toast over a victim app stealing the user's input without triggering a system alert. In response to GUI confusion attacks, Possemato et al. [36] proposed the ClickShield defense mechanism based on an image analysis technique.

The impact of zero permission attacks have been noted before. For example, Block et al. [8] leveraged magnetic field communications in Android device location identification attack. Block et al. [7] showed that two apps can communicate with one another via an ultrasonic bridge using only two system-shared and permissionless resources, the speaker and the sensors. Narain et al. [33] demonstrated that an Android app with zero permissions can infer a user's location and route they have taken using accelerometer, gyroscope, and magnetometer information.

In this work, we also leverage overlays to hide browser behavior from the user, yet, our attack is fundamentally different as it exploits browsers to receive sensitive data and resources not accessible to third-party apps. As opposed to the existing approaches, our attack identifies permissions that have already been granted on the browser apps hence avoiding the need to request `QUERY_ALL_PACKAGES` permission at runtime.

7 Conclusion

In this work, we presented a proxy attack that bypasses Android's permission model to gain unauthorized access to sensitive data and resources of Android devices. Our attack uses toast overlay to silently exploit vulnerabilities in Android browsers and gain access to sensitive permissions not otherwise available to third-party apps. We demonstrate how an attack can be conducted quietly and covertly to extract sensitive information such as voice recordings, camera access, and location data with just one click using the browser as a proxy. We outline the weaknesses that enable the proxy attack and offer defense measures.

References

1. Aafer, Y., Tao, G., Huang, J., Zhang, X., Li, N.: Precise Android API protection mapping derivation and reasoning. In: Proceedings of the 2018 ACM SIGSAC CCS, pp. 1151–1164. ACM, New York (2018)
2. Aldoseri, A., Oswald, D.: Insecure://vulnerability analysis of URI scheme handling in Android mobile browsers. In: Proceedings of the Workshop on MADWeb (2022)
3. Alepis, E., Patsakis, C.: Trapped by the UI: the Android case. In: Dacier, M., Bailey, M., Polychronakis, M., Antonakakis, M. (eds.) RAID 2017. LNCS, vol. 10453, pp. 334–354. Springer, Cham (2017). https://doi.org/10.1007/978-3-319-66332-6_15
4. Android: Permissions on Android (2022). https://developer.android.com/guide/topics/permissions/overview#system-components
5. Backes, M., Bugiel, S., Derr, E., Mcdaniel, P., Octeau, D., Weisgerber, S.: On demystifying the Android application framework: re-visiting Android permission specification analysis. In: USENIX Security Symposium (2016)
6. Bianchi, A., Corbetta, J., Invernizzi, L., Fratantonio, Y., Kruegel, C., Vigna, G.: What the app is that? Deception and countermeasures in the Android user interface. In: 2015 IEEE Symposium on Security and Privacy, pp. 931–948 (2015)
7. Block, K., Narain, S., Noubir, G.: An autonomic and permissionless Android covert channel. In: Proceedings of the 10th ACM Conference on Security and Privacy in Wireless and Mobile Networks, pp. 184–194 (2017)
8. Block, K., Noubir, G.: My magnetometer is telling you where I've been? A mobile device permissionless location attack. In: Proceedings of the 11th ACM Conference on Security & Privacy in Wireless and Mobile Networks, pp. 260–270 (2018)
9. Calciati, P., Kuznetsov, K., Gorla, A., Zeller, A.: Automatically granted permissions in Android apps: an empirical study on their prevalence and on the potential threats for privacy. In: Proceedings of the 17th International Conference on MSR, pp. 114–124. ACM, New York (2020)
10. Contributors, M.: Navigator: devicememory property (2023). https://developer.mozilla.org/en-US/docs/Web/API/Navigator/deviceMemory
11. DB, G.: https://www.geolocation-db.com/documentation
12. Egners, A., Meyer, U., Marschollek, B.: Messing with Android's permission model. In: 2012 IEEE 11th International Conference on Trust, Security and Privacy in Computing and Communications, pp. 505–514. IEEE (2012)
13. Felt, A.P., Wagner, D.: Phishing on mobile devices. In: W2SP (2011)

14. Fernandes, E., et al.: Android UI deception revisited: attacks and defenses. In: Grossklags, J., Preneel, B. (eds.) FC 2016. LNCS, vol. 9603, pp. 41–59. Springer, Heidelberg (2017). https://doi.org/10.1007/978-3-662-54970-4_3
15. Fratantonio, Y., Qian, C., Chung, S.P., Lee, W.: Cloak and dagger: from two permissions to complete control of the UI feedback loop. In: 2017 IEEE Symposium on Security and Privacy (SP), pp. 1041–1057. IEEE (2017)
16. Garg, S., Baliyan, N.: Comparative analysis of Android and iOS from security viewpoint. Comput. Sci. Rev. **40**, 100372 (2021)
17. Gibler, C., Crussell, J., Erickson, J., Chen, H.: AndroidLeaks: automatically detecting potential privacy leaks in Android applications on a large scale. In: Katzenbeisser, S., Weippl, E., Camp, L.J., Volkamer, M., Reiter, M., Zhang, X. (eds.) Trust 2012. LNCS, vol. 7344, pp. 291–307. Springer, Heidelberg (2012). https://doi.org/10.1007/978-3-642-30921-2_17
18. GOOGLE: Permissions and APIs that Access Sensitive Information (2020). https://support.google.com/googleplay/android-developer/answer/9888170?hl=en&ref_topic=9877467
19. Google: Android developers reference (2022). https://developer.android.com/reference/android/R.attr#protectionLevel
20. Google: Android Security Bulletin-December 2021 (2022). https://source.android.com/docs/security/bulletin/2021-12-01#system
21. Google: Android Security Bulletin-March 2022 (2022). https://source.android.com/docs/security/bulletin/2022-03-01#framework
22. Google: Android Security Bulletin-September 2017 (2022). https://source.android.com/docs/security/bulletin/2017-09-01#2017-09-01-details
23. Google: Android Debug Bridge (ADB) (2023). https://developer.android.com/studio/command-line/adb
24. Google: Behavior changes: all apps (2023). https://developer.android.com/about/versions/12/behavior-changes-all#untrusted-touch-events
25. Google: Features and APIs Overview (2023). https://developer.android.com/about/versions/12/features#pixel-phishing-detection
26. Google: Tapjacking (2023). https://developer.android.com/topic/security/risks/tapjacking
27. GOOGLE: Use of the broad package (App) visibility (QUERY_ALL_PACKAGES) permission (2023). https://support.google.com/googleplay/android-developer/answer/10158779?hl=en
28. Google: View(Security) (2023). https://developer.android.com/reference/android/view/View#security
29. Hartzheim, A.: Technical analysis of duckduckgo privacy essentials (part 1) (2021). https://austinhartzheim.me/blog/2021/06/27/ddg-technical-analysis-part-1.html
30. Hassanshahi, B., Jia, Y., Yap, R.H.C., Saxena, P., Liang, Z.: Web-to-application injection attacks on Android: characterization and detection. In: Pernul, G., Ryan, P.Y.A., Weippl, E. (eds.) ESORICS 2015. LNCS, vol. 9327, pp. 577–598. Springer, Cham (2015). https://doi.org/10.1007/978-3-319-24177-7_29
31. Li, L., Bissyandé, T.F., Le Traon, Y., Klein, J.: Accessing inaccessible Android APIs: an empirical study. In: 2016 IEEE International Conference on Software Maintenance and Evolution (ICSME), pp. 411–422 (2016)
32. Luo, T., Jin, X., Ananthanarayanan, A., Du, W.: Touchjacking attacks on web in Android, iOS, and Windows phone. In: Garcia-Alfaro, J., Cuppens, F., Cuppens-Boulahia, N., Miri, A., Tawbi, N. (eds.) FPS 2012. LNCS, vol. 7743, pp. 227–243. Springer, Heidelberg (2013). https://doi.org/10.1007/978-3-642-37119-6_15

33. Narain, S., Vo-Huu, T.D., Block, K., Noubir, G.: Inferring user routes and locations using zero-permission mobile sensors. In: 2016 IEEE Symposium on Security and Privacy (SP), pp. 397–413. IEEE (2016)
34. Niemietz, M., Schwenk, J.: UI Redressing Attacks on Android Devices. Black Hat Abu Dhabi (2012)
35. Olejnik, Ł, Acar, G., Castelluccia, C., Diaz, C.: The leaking battery: a privacy analysis of the HTML5 battery status API. In: Garcia-Alfaro, J., Navarro-Arribas, G., Aldini, A., Martinelli, F., Suri, N. (eds.) DPM/QASA -2015. LNCS, vol. 9481, pp. 254–263. Springer, Cham (2016). https://doi.org/10.1007/978-3-319-29883-2_18
36. Possemato, A., Lanzi, A., Chung, S.P.H., Lee, W., Fratantonio, Y.: Clickshield: are you hiding something? Towards eradicating clickjacking on Android. In: Proceedings of the 2018 ACM SIGSAC Conference on Computer and Communications Security, pp. 1120–1136 (2018)
37. Qiu, Y.: Tapjacking: an untapped threat in Android. Trend Micro, [Ηλεκτρονικό] (2012). http://blog.trendmicro.com/trendlabs-security-intelligence/tapjacking-an-untapped-threat-inandroid/. [*Πρόσβαση* 7 12 2016]
38. Reardon, D.: Measuring the prevalence of browser fingerprinting within browser extensions (2018)
39. Rydstedt, G., Gourdin, B., Bursztein, E., Boneh, D.: Framing attacks on smart phones and dumb routers: tap-jacking and geo-localization attacks. In: Proceedings of the 4th USENIX Conference on Offensive Technologies, pp. 1–8 (2010)
40. Shao, Y., Chen, Q.A., Mao, Z.M., Ott, J., Qian, Z.: Kratos: discovering inconsistent security policy enforcement in the Android framework. In: NDSS (2016)
41. Statista: Mobile Android operating system market share by version worldwide from January 2018 to January 2023 (2023). https://www.statista.com/statistics/921152/mobile-android-version-share-worldwide/
42. Wang, S., et al.: Implication of animation on Android security. In: 2022 IEEE 42nd International Conference on Distributed Computing Systems (ICDCS), pp. 1122–1132 (2022)

Are Current CCPA Compliant Banners Conveying User's Desired Opt-Out Decisions? An Empirical Study of Cookie Consent Banners

Torsha Mazumdar, Daniel Timko, and Muhammad Lutfor Rahman(✉)

California State University San Marcos, San Marcos, USA
{mazum001,timko002,mlrahman}@csusm.edu

Abstract. The California Consumer Privacy Act (CCPA) secures the right to Opt-Out for consumers in California. However, websites may implement complex consent mechanisms that potentially do not capture the user's true choices. We investigated the user choices in Cookie Consent Banner of US residents, the plurality of whom were from California, through an online experiment of 257 participants and compared the results with how they perceived to these Cookie Consent Banner. Our results show a contradiction between how often participants self-report their Opt-Out rates and their actual Opt-Out rate when interacting with a complex, CCPA-compliant website. This discrepancy expands the context with which modern websites may implement the CCPA without providing users sufficient information or instruction on how to successfully Opt-Out. We further elaborate on how US residents respond to and perceive the GDPR-like Opt-In model. Our results indicate that even though very few consumers actually exercised their right to Opt-Out, the majority of US consumers desire more transparent privacy policies that the current implementation of CCPA on websites lacks.

Keywords: Cookie Consent Banner · CCPA · GDPR · Privacy Policy

1 Introduction

Over the past decade, there has been a significant increase in global awareness regarding data privacy. Personal information, as well as data on preferences, interests, and browsing behavior, is being captured, collected, sold to other companies, and analyzed in order to deliver personalized user experiences. While consumers are often curious or irritated by the sudden appearance of unsolicited advertisements on their screens or the constant influx of promotional emails in their inboxes, businesses also face the daunting challenge of ensuring data protection.

In response to escalating concerns about data privacy, the California Consumer Privacy Act (CCPA), which came into effect on January 1, 2020, grants

T. Mazumdar and D. Timko—Both authors contributed equally.

J. Deng et al. (Eds.): CANS 2023, LNCS 14342, pp. 186–207, 2023.
https://doi.org/10.1007/978-981-99-7563-1_9

consumers greater control over the personal information collected by businesses. The CCPA establishes regulations that offer guidance on the implementation of the law. Similar in many aspects to the European Union's General Data Protection Regulation (GDPR), the CCPA and GDPR share a common goal of safeguarding personal data by ensuring its fair, lawful, and transparent use.

However, despite these regulations, numerous businesses either fail to comply or intentionally create convoluted opt-out processes that are challenging for users to navigate [13]. Moreover, many users either remain unaware of their rights, exhibit reluctance to read privacy policies thoroughly, or simply do not prioritize data privacy to the same extent.

In this study, we conducted an online experiment involving 257 US residents to investigate how users react to consent notices. To enhance the experiment's realism, we employed a minor deception technique in the online task. Instead of explicitly focusing on the cookie banner consent popup, we instructed users to consider the browser's security indicators. By employing this minor deception, we aimed to minimize priming effects and obtain results that truly reflect users' authentic online behavior [16]. Additionally, to complement the online experiment, we administered a survey to gather users' perspectives on their data privacy rights and the data practices of corporations.

We further analyze the impact of various implementation choices commonly employed on websites subject to the CCPA on users' ability to make informed consent decisions [14]. It is important to note that the CCPA specifically applies to California residents and businesses operating within the state. Unlike the Opt-In model adopted by its European Union counterpart GDPR, the CCPA includes specific regulations regarding the right to Opt-Out. Through our online experiment, we closely observe and assess users' responses to the Opt-In and Opt-Out options, as well as capture their thoughts and opinions regarding these choices. In summary, we have the following contributions to our study.

1. We design a website that uses the pretense of a security indicator setup task to record the activity of participants with randomly assigned cookie consent mechanism. We conducted a user study to determine how different consent mechanisms affect user's Opt-Out rates.
2. We compare the rates of actual Opt-Out against the perception of how often the average user states they want to Opt-Out.
3. We analyze the user perspectives on the Opt-In model and their awareness of CCPA regulations among US residents.

2 Related Works

CCPA and Consent Mechanisms. The CCPA introduces a crucial right known as the *Right to Opt-Out of Sale or Share*, which is commonly implemented by offering users the option to withdraw their consent by clicking on a button or link within a website or application. It grants California residents the authority to file complaints with the Office of the Attorney General (OAG) in cases of suspected CCPA violations. However, it can be challenging for an average individual to ascertain whether a specific website is subject to or exempt from the CCPA [19].

O'Connor et al. [14] conducted a study that revealed the significant impact even minor differences in implementation decisions can have on user interactions with consent notices that appear on screens. The CCPA, which draws inspiration from the GDPR, mandates that Opt-Out links for sale must be *clear and conspicuous*. However, it has been observed that many websites adopt design and implementation choices that appear to *negatively* impact user privacy. Work by Utz et al. [18] explored how the developers use placement of notifications, notification choices, and persuasive design techniques like dark patterns and nudging to influence consent decisions. Dark patterns are malicious design choices that direct users into certain behavior or choices. These design implementations can be used to reduce Opt-Out rates by providing a link to the Opt-Out mechanism on a separate web page or requiring users to scroll to the bottom of the page to find the link, rather than offering a direct link.

Additionally, nudging techniques, low-contrast font colors, and smaller font sizes are used to divert users' attention. Some websites even place the Opt-Out mechanism solely within their privacy policy, disregarding the CCPA guideline that specifies the need for an Opt-Out link on the homepage of the website.

In their study, Chen et al. [6] conducted an analysis of 95 privacy policies from popular websites and discovered inconsistencies among them. They observed that not all disclosures provided the level of clarity mandated by the CCPA when describing data practices. Moreover, their findings indicated that different wording choices influenced how consumers interpreted the data practices of businesses and their own privacy rights. The presence of *Vagueness and ambiguity* in privacy policies significantly hampers consumers' ability to make informed choices [6].

It is worth noting that even for thoroughly tested designs, consumer education remains crucial for several reasons. Firstly, it helps *raise awareness among users, communicates the purpose of privacy icons, and dispels any misconceptions* [10]. Additionally, unifying privacy choices in a single, standardized location would likely enhance user accessibility to these controls [9]. The CCPA not only requires companies to provide privacy choices but also emphasizes the need to make these choices usable and user-friendly.

Opt-In systems require businesses to obtain an individual's *express, affirmative, and informed* consent before sharing or processing their data. In contrast, the Opt-Out rule places the responsibility on the individual to safeguard their own data [15]. Participants' responses can be influenced by the way questions are framed. Merely presenting the question as an Opt-Out instead of an Opt-In, or vice versa, often leads to different privacy preferences being recorded. Consent choices are frequently displayed with a pre-selected "Yes" or "Accept" response, exploiting individuals' inattention, cognitive biases, and tendency for laziness [3].

3 Methodology

Our study methodology was cleared by our university Institutional Review Board (IRB) and consisted of a presurvey questionnaire, online experiment and an exit survey. The average time required for this survey was 27 min. The time elapsed during the study was calculated from the start time of the presurvey questionnaire to the end time of the exit survey for each participant.

3.1 Participant Recruitment

Participants were recruited from the general US population. To be eligible, individuals had to be at least 18 years old and primarily English-speaking. While the main focus of this study is on the CCPA, which primarily affects the population of California, we also examined differences between residents in California and those in other states. We recruited participants for the "Study on Internet Users' Choice of Browser Security Indicators" through various channels, including flyers posted around the university campus, a call for participants on Craigslist, Reddit, and social media platforms such as Facebook, Instagram, and LinkedIn, as well as through the university email lists. As an incentive for participating in the study, two randomly selected participants out of the total 257 received a $50 Amazon gift card.

3.2 Presurvey Questionnaire

The presurvey questionnaire comprised a consent form and a Qualtrics questionnaire that collected participants' demographic information. The informed consent form, serving as the initial page of the Qualtrics questionnaire, provided a detailed overview of the study. Only participants who explicitly consented proceeded to the subsequent steps of the study. Each participant was assigned a unique 4-digit random number, generated within Qualtrics, which was referred to as the Participant ID throughout the paper.

The demographic questionnaire consisted of multiple-choice questions aimed at capturing participants' age, gender, education, income, occupation, weekly internet usage hours, state of residence in the US, as well as their preferred devices, browsers, and operating systems.

The inclusion of experiment variables, such as age, gender, education, income, occupation, and allowed us to assess the representativeness of our sample population and the generalizability of our results. Examining the participants' internet usage shed light on their familiarity with navigating various websites, thereby contributing to the existing literature on the relationship between online literacy, privacy awareness, and willingness to share data. Additionally, the inclusion of experiment variables like devices, browsers, and operating systems enabled us to analyze the impact of these choices on the implementation of the consent notice and subsequently the users' responses. Given that the CCPA exclusively applies to California residents, the participants' state of residence within the US served as an important variable in our study, allowing us to compare the tendencies of the US population residing outside of California.

3.3 Online Experiment

Participants who completed the presurvey questionnaire were subsequently directed to our experiment website. In order to maintain the integrity of the study, we employed a method of deception by using advertisements and instructions on the last page of the presurvey questionnaire. Although the study aimed to examine participants' responses to consent notices, participants were led to believe that the study focused on their preferences for browser security indicators. The use of deception in research has been the subject of ethical debates, but it can be implemented safely when carefully framed and reviewed [2,12,16]. Notably, several influential studies [17] have utilized deception to enhance the realism of experiments. The advantage of employing this deception is that it elicits more authentic responses from participants. If participants had been fully informed about the true purpose of our study, they might have approached the consent notices with increased attention and made choices that differ from their regular browsing tendencies. By incorporating an unrelated primary task in our experiment, we were able to observe how participants make consent decisions while simultaneously engaging in other prioritized tasks. This simulation reflects real-world scenarios, as users typically browse websites for personal, professional, or entertainment purposes rather than solely for accepting or rejecting cookies. The IRB granted approval for the use of deception in our study after determining that this aspect of the experiment would not cause any actual harm to participants. Furthermore, prior knowledge of the true purpose of the study was deemed likely to influence participants' behavior and potentially undermine the study's outcomes. At the conclusion of the exit survey, participants were provided with a debriefing that included information about the true purpose of the study, details about the CCPA, and suggestions for safeguarding their data.

Primary Task for the Participants. Participants were invited to participate in an online experiment framed as a study focusing on their preferred choices for browser security indicators. Browser security indicators serve the purpose of either alerting users to potentially suspicious URLs or assuring them of a secure connection. On the initial page of our website, participants were prompted to enter their Participant ID (generated in Qualtrics) and provided with context regarding the use of security indicators (see Fig. 1). They were then asked to indicate their preference for either the default browser security indicators or personalized ones (Fig. 1). Additionally, participants were asked to specify the type and color of the security indicators they would prefer to see in URLs (Fig. 1). The responses provided by participants were recorded and stored in our database. Although the users' choices were not directly related to our primary study on consent, they offer valuable insights into user preferences.

Consent Mechanisms. According to the CCPA, it is required that the Opt-Out links on websites should be *"clear and conspicuous"* on the homepage. As stated in the CCPA law document [4], *"You may request that businesses*

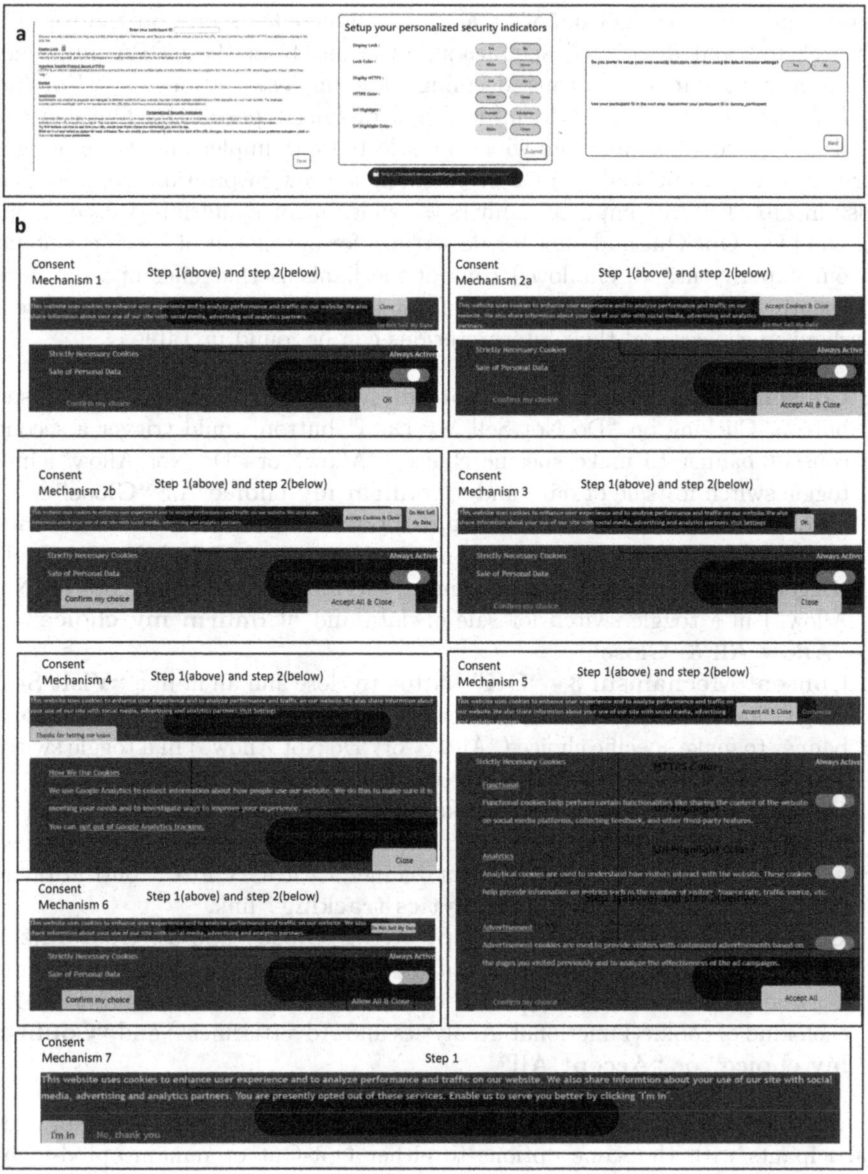

Fig. 1. a) Left: Welcome page screen. Middle: Security indicator selection task screen. Right: Exit page screen where participants are directed to the exit survey. b) 7 cookie consent mechanism banners and their steps used in the online experiment.

stop selling or sharing your personal information ("opt-out"), including via a user-enabled global privacy control.". However, many businesses have deliberately implemented mechanisms that impede users' ability to Opt-Out, resulting in lower Opt-Out rates. O'Connor et al. [14] conducted a study on the top 500 US websites and discovered significant deviations from the CCPA guidelines regarding Opt-Out mechanisms, deeming these implementations as *"(Un)clear and (In)conspicuous."* They identified eight distinct types of Opt-Out controls used in popular websites, from which we selected and implemented five designs for our study. Additionally, some of our designs drew inspiration from popular customizable CCPA compliant banners [7], which involve multiple decision steps for complete Opt-Out and offer toggle settings for opting out of specific content. In our experiment, we employed consent mechanisms that encompassed both the sharing and selling of personal information. The complete set of consent mechanism choices and their interpretations can be found in Table 1.

1. **Consent Mechanism 1 - "Do Not Sell My Data"** button and a **"Close"** button. Clicking on "Do Not Sell My Data" button would trigger a second consent banner to make specific choice ("Allow" or "Do Not Allow") in a toggle switch for sale of data and **"Confirm my choice"** or **"Close"**
2. **Consent Mechanism 2a - "Accept Cookies & Close"** and a **"Do not sell my data"** button. Clicking on "Do Not Sell My Data" button would trigger a second consent banner to make specific choice ("Allow" or "Do Not Allow") in a toggle switch for sale of data and **"Confirm my choice"** or **"Allow All & Close"**
3. **Consent Mechanism 3 - "OK"** button to close and an in-line **"Visit Settings"** link. Clicking on "Visit Settings" link would trigger a second consent banner to make specific choice ("Allow" or "Do Not Allow") in a toggle switch for sale of data and **"Confirm my choice"** or **"Close"**
4. **Consent Mechanism 4 - "Thanks for letting me know"** button and an in-line **"How We Use Cookies"** link. Clicking on "How We Use Cookies" link would trigger a second consent banner with a **"Close"** button or an in-line **"opt out of Google Analytics tracking"** link.
5. **Consent Mechanism 5 - "Accept All & Close"** and a **"Customize"** button. Clicking on "Customize" button would trigger a second consent banner to make specific choice ("Allow" or "Do Not Allow") in a toggle switch for each kind of cookie(Functional, Analytics and Advertisement) and **"Confirm my choice"** or **"Accept All"**

Although the aforementioned five consent mechanisms technically provide participants with the same options to either Opt-Out or remain opted-in by default for the sale or sharing of data, our study aims to investigate how the wording and implementation of each mechanism influence users' choices. Existing literature suggests that the format of questions plays a significant role [11], and our study seeks to verify this assertion. The remaining three Opt-Out controls described in O'Connor et al. [14] are not within the scope of this paper as they involve contacting third parties via email, filling out Opt-Out request forms, or adjusting account settings, which cannot be tested within a single experiment.

In their research, O'Connor et al. [14] also noted that nudging was commonly employed in direct links to subtly guide users away from successfully opting out. Digital Nudging [20] refers to a design approach where businesses highlight certain buttons to indirectly suggest, influence, or manipulate user behavior in a manner that benefits the businesses. In all of the above five consent mechanisms, we have incorporated nudging by highlighting options that do not allow users to Opt-Out. However, to examine all available conditions, we further expand Consent Mechanism 2 to include the following variation without nudging:

Consent Mechanism 2b - Neutral: Both the Opt-Out and accept options have the same design. Some websites employ an Anti-nudging design [14], wherein only the Opt-Out option is presented without any further steps. Clicking on this button directly opts the user out. We implemented this design as the initial decision in **Consent Mechanism 6**.

While the CCPA mandates the right to Opt-Out, we also included an Opt-In mechanism based on the GDPR model, allowing us to compare and contrast the two types of mechanisms. In **Consent Mechanism 7**, a banner was displayed with an "I'm in" and a "No, thank you!" button, enabling participants to explicitly provide single step consent to the sale of their data.

Participants were directed to our experiment website through a link provided at the end of the presurvey questionnaire. The website was designed to display a consent banner on the screen after 3 s of a participant visiting the web page hosting the primary task. Following a completely randomized experiment design [12], participants were randomly assigned one of the eight consent mechanisms developed for the study by selecting a random integer between 1 and 8. The assignment of consent mechanisms was counterbalanced [1] by selecting a different random consent mechanism from the last recorded one, ensuring that the same random number was not repeatedly selected. This approach allowed us to gather sufficient data for analyzing participant behavior across each consent mechanism. It is important to note that we did not actually place any cookies on participants' devices or require participants to consent to the sale of their personal data. Instead, we used HTML forms to replicate commercial consent banners and recorded participants' responses in our experiment database.

For the readers' reference, snapshots of our website screens, showcasing the unique design of each banner, are included in Fig. 1.

Response Collection and Interpretation. Prior to commencing our study, we conducted an analysis of the cookie consent banners displayed on 20 different websites. We observed that online businesses intentionally design complex consent mechanisms, which hinders users' ability to make informed choices. The presence of multiple buttons and switches often confuses or frustrates users, leading them to hastily dismiss the consent banner without fully understanding its implications in terms of data sale. In our experiment website, we have recreated this environment to capture participants' authentic behavior.

For instance, in consent mechanism 1, clicking on the "Do Not Sell My Data" button does not automatically indicate that participants have opted out. Instead, they are presented with a second banner where they need to explicitly slide the toggle switch until it turns grey, and then click on "Confirm my choice" to record

Table 1. Consent combinations and their interpretations. We present the Opt-Out path for each mechanism in bold.

Default	#CM	1st Decision	2nd Decision	2nd Decision Toggle	Interpretation
Opt-In	1	Close	NA	NA	Opt-In
	1	Do Not Sell My Data	Confirm my choice	Always Active(On)	Opt-In
	1	**Do Not Sell My Data**	**Confirm my choice**	**Do Not Allow**	**Opt-Out**
	1	Do Not Sell My Data	OK	Allow	Opt-In
	1	Do Not Sell My Data	OK	Do Not Allow	Opt-In
Opt-In	2a 2b	Accept Cookies & Close	NA	NA	Opt-In
	2a, 2b	Do Not Sell My Data	Allow All & Close	Allow	Opt-In
	2a, 2b	Do Not Sell My Data	Allow All & Close	Do Not Allow	Opt-In
	2a, 2b	Do Not Sell My Data	Confirm my choice	Allow	Opt-In
	2a, 2b	**Do Not Sell My Data**	**Confirm my choice**	**Do Not Allow**	**Opt-Out**
Opt-In	3	OK	NA	NA	Opt-In
	3	Visit Settings	Close	Allow	Opt-In
	3	Visit Settings	Close	Do Not Allow	Opt-In
	3	Visit Settings	Confirm my choice	Allow	Opt-In
	3	**Visit Settings**	**Confirm my choice**	**Do Not Allow**	**Opt-Out**
Opt-In	4	How We Use Cookies	Close	NA	Opt-In
	4	**How We Use Cookies**	**Opt-out of google analytics**	**NA**	**Opt-Out**
	4	Thanks for letting me know	NA	NA	Opt-In
Opt-In	5	Accept All & Close	NA	NA	Opt-In
	5	Customize	Accept All	Allow	Opt-In
	5	Customize	Accept All	Do Not Allow	Opt-In
	5	Customize	Confirm my choice	Allow	Opt-In
	5	**Customize**	**Confirm my choice**	**Do Not Allow**	**Opt-Out**
Opt-In	6	Do Not Sell My Data	Allow All & Close	Allow	Opt-In
	6	Do Not Sell My Data	Allow All & Close	Do Not Allow	Opt-In
	6	Do Not Sell My Data	Confirm my choice	Allow	Opt-In
	6	**Do Not Sell My Data**	**Confirm my choice**	**Do Not Allow**	**Opt-Out**
Opt-Out	7	I'm in	NA	NA	Opt-In
	7	**No, thank you!**	**NA**	**NA**	**Opt-Out**

their response as "Opted-Out." If participants either click on "Close" or click on "Confirm my choice" without disabling the toggle switch in the second banner, their response will still be recorded as "Opted-In," even though they initially selected "Do Not Sell My Data." This demonstrates that the combination of buttons and switches in the subsequent step either impairs participants' ability to make an informed decision or frustrates them, leading them to hastily dismiss or ignore the banner.

Participants who chose to ignore the consent banner in the first or second step for consent mechanisms 1 through 6 were categorized as "Opted-In." According to the CCPA, businesses are permitted to sell consumers' data unless consumers explicitly withdraw their consent. Conversely, participants who disregarded the consent banner for consent mechanism 7 were classified as "Opted-Out," as Opt-In models do not assume consent by default. Participant responses were recorded in our experiment database, indexed with the unique Participant ID assigned to them in the presurvey questionnaire.

3.4 Exit Survey

The exit questionnaire consisted of Likert scale, multiple-choice questions and few open ended questions. It was divided into three sections -

1. **Reflection on Completed Activity** In this section, we prompted participants to recall and reflect on the online experiment. Firstly, we inquired whether participants had noticed the presence of the consent banner and whether they believed their behavior was being tracked for the purpose of selling data to third parties. Secondly, we asked participants whether they were provided with the option to Opt-Out of the sale or share of their data. Thirdly, participants were asked to rate their comfort level regarding the website's tracking of their behavior and the potential sale of their information to third parties. Lastly, we inquired whether participants could recall their choices made within the cookie consent banner and to explain their choices.
2. **CCPA case examples** Participants were presented with two hypothetical scenarios, which were constructed based on real privacy complaints investigated by the Office of the Attorney General at the State of California Department of Justice [8]. The first scenario revolved around registering for an online dating platform and explored whether clicking a share button when creating an account constituted sufficient consent for the sale of personal information, especially in cases where no additional "Do Not Sell My Personal Information" links were provided on the platform's homepage. The second scenario involved an online pet adoption platform where submitting an Opt-Out request necessitated a third-party authorized agent to submit a notarized verification on behalf of the user. These scenarios were accompanied by Likert-scale questions [21] including: 1) "I think scenarios like this are likely to happen"; 2) "I would be concerned about my privacy in this scenario"; and 3) "Do you think the business acted appropriately and lawfully based on the situation described?" Additionally, participants were asked an open-ended question: 4) "Explain your reasoning above."
3. **Opt-In vs Opt-Out** Participants were initially queried regarding their familiarity with the distinction between Opt-In and Opt-Out consent mechanisms. Regardless of their prior response, they were subsequently provided with a debriefing explaining how each consent mechanism operates and its implications in terms of data sale. Participants were then asked to indicate their preferred consent mechanism. Following that, participants were given a debriefing on the economic implications [5] associated with Opt-In, and once again asked to specify their preferred consent mechanism. This economic implications debriefing can be found in the Opt-In vs Opt-Out section in the appendix.

4 Data Analysis and Results

In this section, we present participant demographics, compare the observations from our experiment with self-reported behavior in the exit survey, and discuss the results of our thematic analysis. Our findings provide insights into the level of concern or awareness among consumers regarding their privacy and privacy rights. Furthermore, we explore potential reasons why users are unable to successfully Opt-Out despite their intention to do so. To achieve this, we combine the findings from the online experiment, responses related to attitudes and concerns, reflections on the completed experiment, and explanations provided in a few open-ended questions. This comprehensive approach allows us to gain a deeper understanding of how users perceive the consent notices and why they make the choices they do. We reinforce our findings with participant quotes extracted from the responses to the open-ended questions.

After removing duplicate entries and rows with invalid data, a total of 360 participants responded to our invitation to participate in the study. 257 participants completed the primary task on our experiment website. After the primary task, we provided a link to an exit survey, which was completed by 232 participants. We utilized the data from the 257 participants who completed the primary task to examine the Opt-Out and Opt-In rates, as well as investigate the possible factors contributing to the low Opt-Out rates.

4.1 Participant Demographics

Our participant pool consisted of 163 (63.4%) males and 93 (36.2%) females. The age range varied from 18 to 75 years old, with the most common age group being 25 to 34 years, which accounted for 166 (64.6%) participants. The majority of participants, 106 (41.2%), held a bachelor's degree as their highest level of education. While the highest number of participants, 92 (35.8%), were from California, we also had participants from all other states in the US. The primary occupation for a significant portion of our participants was computer engineering, with 52 (20.2%) individuals, suggesting a higher level of overall online literacy. Among the participants, the highest number, 126 (49.0%), used a mobile device to complete the activity, while 167 (65.0%) preferred Google Chrome as their browser, and 128 (49.8%) used iOS/Mac as their operating system. In terms of self-reported internet usage, the most common range reported by participants was between 11 to 20 h per week, with 94 (36.6%) participants falling into this category.

4.2 Experiment Results

As a reminder, our experimental task primarily focused on participants indicating their preferred browser security indicators. Additionally, participants were randomly assigned one of the eight consent banners. They had the option to respond to the banners by clicking on the presented buttons or to ignore the banners altogether. Each participant's choices and the resulting interpretations were recorded and stored in our database.

Consent Mechanism Results. Table 2 provides a summary of the number of Opt-In and Opt-Out requests or preferences provided by participants on the experiment website. Our dataset is balanced due to the randomization and counterbalancing techniques discussed in the methodology, enabling us to compare the counts for each mechanism. It is important to note that our consent mechanism involved a two-step process.

Out of the total participants, we observed that 20.09% (45/224) interacted with the first step of our consent mechanism. However, only 0.45% (1/224) of users actually chose to Opt-Out in the second step for the consent mechanisms numbered 1 through 6. Consequently, 99.55% (223/224) of participants did not Opt-Out, resulting in their consent decision remaining as Opt-In by default. This aligns with real-world websites governed by the CCPA, where users' data is considered to be sold unless they explicitly Opt-Out.

For consent mechanism 7, which is an Opt-In mechanism, we received only 4 Opt-In requests out of the 34 participants assigned to this mechanism. This indicates that only 11.76% of users chose to Opt-In. Since this mechanism involved a one-step process, participants' first choice was sufficient to successfully Opt-In. In the next section, we will delve deeper into the analysis of our results.

Table 2. Opt-Out and Opt-In counts for each consent mechanism. Here, #Interact means the number of participant interact with cookie consent banner

Default Opt-In							
Mech.	#N	#Interact	1st Decision Opt-In	1st Decision Opt-Out	Default Opt-In	Opt-In	Opt-Out
1	34	6	6	0	28	34	0
2a	32	8	6	2	24	32	0
2b	34	8	6	2	26	34	0
3	26	8	8	0	18	26	0
4	30	6	6	0	24	30	0
5	28	6	5	1	22	28	0
6	40	3	0	3	37	39	1
Total Opt-In	224	45	37	8	179	223	1
Default Opt-Out							
7	33	6	4	2	27	4	29
Grand Total	257	51	41	10	206	227	30

Consent Mechanism Results Interpretation. In the related work, we have highlighted the significance of even minor differences in implementation choices and their impact on how users perceive and respond to consent notices. Furthermore, existing literature emphasizes the importance of the question format. Although the data collected was evenly distributed among the eight mechanisms, we observed variations in the number of Opt-Out requests for each mechanism, as shown in Table 2. In the following analysis, we will examine the influence of each consent mechanism on participants' consent decisions.

2-Step Opt-Out Mechanisms. Consent mechanisms 1 through 6 involved a 2-step Opt-Out process. In the first step, if participants accepted, closed, or ignored the banner, it indicated that they had not opted out. In the second step, participants were asked to make a specific choice regarding the sale of their data if they clicked on other available options such as "Do Not Sell My Data," "Visit Settings," "Customize," or "How We Use Cookies".

Table 2 reveals that a total of 31 participants clicked on the buttons labeled "Accept Cookies & Close," (#CM 2a,2b) "Close," (#CM 1) "OK," (#CM 3) or vAccept All & Close" (#CM 5) in the first step, indicating that they explicitly choose not to Opt-Out. This suggests that participants either made an informed decision, lacked sufficient understanding of online privacy, or were influenced by nudging factors that discouraged them from selecting the Opt-In buttons.

Furthermore, while 7 participants clicked on the more direct button "Do Not Sell My Data," one participant clicked on "Customize," and none on "How We Use Cookies" or "Visit Settings." This indicates that the direct buttons attracted more attention from users, while inline links were less commonly followed. In fact, this implementation choice, where businesses prioritize direct buttons over inline links, is one of the most common approaches employed by businesses (77.7% of the top 5000 US websites in 2021) to discourage users from opting out more frequently [14].

As a result, out of the participants who clicked on the "Not Accepted" options (grouped as "Not Accepted") in the first step, only 1 participant proceeded to Opt-Out in the final step. Consequently, 97.78% (44/45) of the participants who interacted with our Opt-In default consent banners remained in the Opt-In category. This suggests that although these participants did not immediately accept all cookies, they exhibited a higher level of curiosity or concern by exploring the other available options. However, their final decision did not align with their initial choice. Several factors could have influenced these decisions, including participants facing difficulty navigating the consent banners, altering their decision after reading the privacy policy, or losing interest in the privacy banner altogether.

Nudging, Neutral and Anti-Nudging. Among the Opt-Out mechanisms developed in our study, all except for consent mechanism 2b and consent mechanism 6 employed nudging techniques. Consent mechanism 2b, a variation of 2a, utilized a neutral format, while consent mechanism 6 employed an anti-nudging approach. We hypothesized that the use of nudging could potentially manipulate users into selecting the highlighted option. In the case of consent mechanism 6, we expected that the highlighting of the "Do Not Sell My Data" button would lead to a higher Opt-Out rate. Similarly, we anticipated a relatively higher Opt-Out rate for consent mechanism 2b since both Opt-In and Opt-Out options were presented in the same format without any push towards a specific choice. However, in our study, we did not receive any Opt-Out requests for consent mechanism 2b. To substantiate this observation, a larger dataset would be required. The counts for each mechanism can be found in Table 2, presented above.

Third-party Opt-Out Mechanism. Consent mechanism 4 featured two inline links in the second step of the Opt-Out process. Six participants clicked on "Thanks for letting me know," indicating that they did not choose to explore the available options for managing their privacy preferences further. Only one participant clicked on "How We Use Cookies" in the first step and also on "opt out of Google Analytics tracking" in the second step. In our experiment, selecting "opt out of Google Analytics tracking" was interpreted as the user's intention to Opt-Out of the sale of their data. However, in real websites, clicking on a similar link would redirect users to a new page with instructions to download and install an add-on for their browsers. It was not possible to determine in this study whether the participant who clicked on "opt out of Google Analytics tracking" would actually proceed with the installation of the add-on.

1-Step Opt-In Mechanism. In consent mechanism 7, we introduced a default Opt-In consent banner with a 1-step Opt-In mechanism. We observed that 27 participants ignored the banner, and 2 participants clicked on "No, thank you!" This indicates that only a few users actively chose to Opt-In, suggesting that they are not readily willing to share their data with businesses when they are not assumed to be Opt-In by default. However, under the current default model of CCPA, users' data remains accessible because the process of opting out can be confusing or cumbersome. On the other hand, 4 participants clicked on "I'm in." On real websites, clicking on similar buttons would provide businesses with explicit consent to sell or use their data. Although the number of participants who provided express consent in our experiment is small, it is noteworthy that these participants granted consent to an unknown website they visited for a research study on browser indicators. This could be attributed to participants' lack of online privacy literacy or the influence of nudging techniques.

We analyzed participants' explanations for their consent decisions (Section: Reflection on Completed Activity) and quote few of them that represent the most commonly reported reasons for:

1. Accepting Cookies - "If you do not select Accept, the site will not function properly", "Automatic click to the big button that says accept.", "Cause this one takes less time" and "I'm open to resource sharing".
2. Rejecting Cookies - "This is my personal data so I don't agree to sell it", "I pay more attention to information security", "I'm afraid they're selling it like crazy" and "I don't want to reveal my privacy to the outside world. I don't feel good about it".

Statistical Analysis. Significance tests were conducted for the below between-group studies. We used consent decision as the dependent variable and the miscellaneous factors as the independent variables and a 95% confidence interval for all our significance tests.

Residential Status in California. Since CCPA applies only to residents and businesses in California and only two other states in the US have similar privacy protection laws, we compare user behaviors from different states. 11.96% participants from California and 11.52% participants from all other states (49 states, Puerto Rico and District of Columbia) opted-out. A one-way ANOVA test suggests that there is no significant difference among how users from different states and territories in the US respond to consent notices ($F(39,217) = 0.792$, $p = .805$). However, as we discuss later in our survey results, 74.70% participants from California reported they are slightly to extremely concerned about their privacy and are not comfortable sharing their data with businesses.

Miscellaneous Platform Factors. We have learned that the design or implementation of the consent notices, or in other words how the consent banners are displayed on users' screens, impact users' choices or their ability to make these choices. The consent banners may have slight variations in look and feel depending upon the device, browser or operating system used. Using a one-way Anova test, we found that there was no observed statistically significant difference between groups of devices ($F(3,253) = 0.461$, $p = .710$), browsers ($F(5,251) = 0.962$, $p = .442$) and operating systems ($F(3,253) = 0.574$, $p = .632$).

Miscellaneous Demographic Factors. We analyze the impact of demographic factors into the consent decisions. We found that there was no statistically significant difference in the number of Opt-Outs or Opt-Ins when comparing males and females ($t=0.847$, $df=254$ $p = 0.389$), level of education ($F(7,249) = 0.597$, $p = .759$), hours spent on the internet ($F(4,252) = 1.439$, $p = .221$), occupation ($F(13,243) = 0.844$, $p = .613$), and age groups ($F(4,252) = 0.413$, $p = .799$).

4.3 Exit Survey Result

In the following section we present the results of the exit survey for Reflection on completed activity, CCPA case examples, and Opt-In vs Opt-Out.

Reflection on Completed Activity. In this section, we will analyze the participants' reflections on their completed activity. A majority of the participants, 71%, were able to recall that our experiment website provided them with the option to Opt-Out of the sale of their personal data. When asked about how often they notice websites offering the option to opt-out of data sale, 32.5% of participants stated that they rarely or never notice this option. Regarding their choice in the experiment, 57.2% of participants mentioned that they either accepted the cookies or closed the Opt-In consent banner. Additionally, 31.6% of participants indicated that they chose not to sell their data. The remaining participants were unsure about their choices or mentioned visiting the settings. In terms of comfort level, 14.7% of participants stated that they would be very comfortable if the experiment website tracked their behavior and sold their information to third parties, while 16.9% expressed being very uncomfortable with this idea.

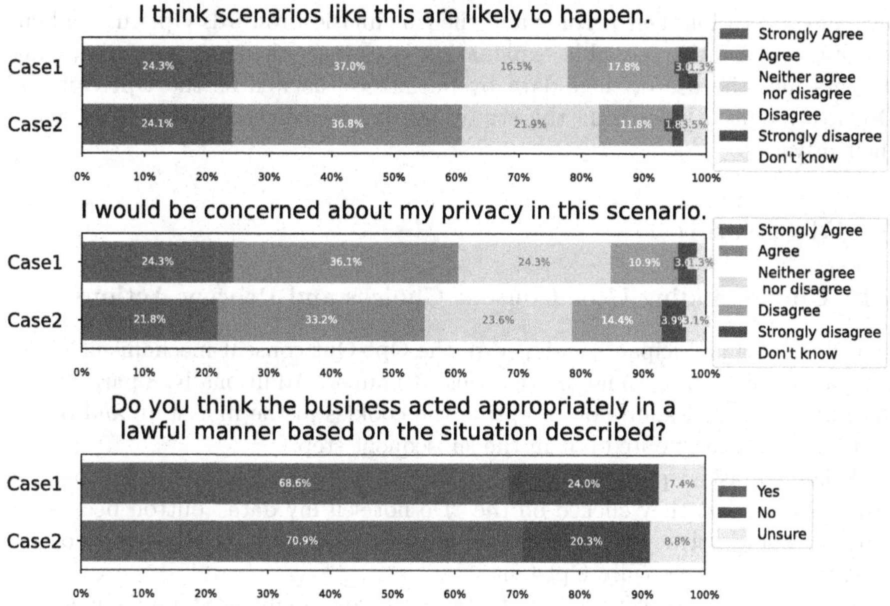

Fig. 2. Participants' responses to CCPA case examples.

CCPA Case Examples. The cases presented in this study depict two distinct scenarios involving how businesses handle and sell customer personal information, as well as a user's ability to Opt-Out of the sale or sharing of their data. While a majority of participants expressed concern in response to these scenarios, only 24% and 20.3% of participants correctly identified scenarios 1 and 2 as unlawful (see Fig 2). Many participants felt that since users were "warned in advance," the practices were deemed acceptable. This finding suggests that businesses can potentially exploit consumers' limited awareness to their advantage. It is important to note that these scenarios were based on real CCPA cases, in which the Office of the Attorney General notified the companies of alleged non-compliance and corrective actions were subsequently taken [8]. This observation highlights the lack of knowledge among users regarding their privacy rights.

Opt-In vs Opt-Out. A significant majority of participants, 85.7%, reported that they were aware of the distinction between Opt-In and Opt-Out models. After being presented with the differences between these models, 82.0% of participants indicated a preference for Opt-In. We found that 3.1% of participants changed their preference to Opt-Out after being informed about the potential economic implications associated with the Opt-In model. This suggests that 78.9% of participants still preferred Opt-In despite the awareness of these implications. Although there was a slight decrease in the number of individuals favoring Opt-In after being briefed about the economic implications, the overall preference for Opt-In remained higher. This could be attributed to users' high level of concern for their privacy and their inclination towards Opt-In in all circumstances. Another possible explanation is that participants gained valuable insights into the use of their data by businesses, as well as the Opt-Out and Opt-In systems, throughout the study, leading to heightened concerns about their privacy.

5 Discussion

5.1 Understanding User Consent Choices and Privacy Actions

Out of the 224 participants assigned to the Opt-Out consent mechanisms (1–6), 179 participants chose to ignore the consent banner. Additionally, 8 participants did not Opt-Out despite not accepting the cookies in the first step, and only 1 participant actually opted out in the subsequent step.

When we asked participants to explain their reasoning, the most common response was that they clicked on the "Do not sell my data" button because of concerns about privacy and their personal data. However, not all users who click on this button successfully Opt-Out.

Furthermore, we observed that the most commonly used implementation choices have a negative impact on Opt-Out rates, either due to the difficulty of navigating through multiple options or the influence of nudging techniques.

Although our study did not include consent mechanisms that require users to fill out forms or send requests via email, it is likely that even fewer users would go through the process due to the time-consuming nature of these methods. For example, one of our participants mentioned that they clicked on "Accept cookies & Close" because it was a quick option. Businesses have the ability to reduce Opt-Out rates through various design choices, as only a small percentage of users have the patience or willingness to complete the entire Opt-Out process.

Furthermore, we observed that very few users file complaints, and even fewer are able to identify if a website is acting unlawfully. Without significant pressure from users, companies and policymakers are likely to maintain the status quo and neglect necessary corrective changes.

5.2 Exploring User Interaction with Consent Banners

The Opt-Out mechanism, which assumes consent by default, typically has lower Opt-Out rates, and users remain opted-in. However, this does not necessarily mean that all users made an informed decision, fully understood the implications, or were aware of how the process works if they did not click on any button. When given an explicit option to Opt-In, users seldom choose to do so. This suggests that in an Opt-In regime, only a small number of users would actively opt-in for the use of their data, due to the default nature of the Opt-Out system.

Users generally prefer the Opt-In model because it provides them with power and control over their data. Interestingly, users rarely interacted with the consent banners at all. This aligns with the findings of O'Connor et al. [14], who observed a maximum interaction rate of 20.5% with their consent banners, compared with 19.84% in ours. In both Opt-In and Opt-Out scenarios, inaction was the most common outcome. By comparing the outcomes of Opt-In and Opt-Out banners, we can see that they lead to significantly different results based on the default condition. While further research is needed to explore the specific reasons for this inaction, it is clear that users' preferred mechanism differs from their chosen one due to the complexities of websites.

5.3 Limitations and Future Work

Given the small size of our sample population, the statistical power of our results is limited. To ensure the validity of these findings, it is necessary to replicate this study with a larger and more diverse sample that is representative of the general population. It is important to note that our survey results may not fully capture the tendencies of US residents outside of California, as CCPA primarily applies to California. Furthermore, the nature of our study being conducted within a university setting and utilizing a survey format may introduce biases, attracting younger and more educated participants who may be more inclined to consent to sharing their information compared to a real-world advertising context. Additionally, since our study was conducted exclusively in the US, the findings may not be applicable to other regions around the world. Furthermore, its important that we acknowledge the effect that utilizing pure HTML in our website design might have on the consent choices of participants. These choices contributed to an outdated appearance of our pages, and may have potentially influenced participant interaction rates with the banners or choices to consent. Future studies should aim to replicate these experiments with a non-Western, Educated, Industrialized, Rich, and Democratic (non-WEIRD) population to explore their perspectives and investigate potential differences between WEIRD and non-WEIRD populations regarding data privacy. Specifically, future research can tailor scenarios where participants have no pre-existing trust relationship with the website and where security indicators are not the primary focus. This would allow for a more comprehensive understanding of user behavior and decision-making in relation to consent banners.

5.4 Recommendations to Policy Makers

The feasibility of adopting the Opt-In model in the US market should be further explored. Under the current Opt-Out model, most users remain opted-in not because they want to, but due to either a lack of knowledge or the tedious and confusing Opt-Out process. The Opt-In model, as seen in GDPR, offers several benefits. Businesses can maintain a lean database of highly relevant leads who are genuinely interested, reducing data management overhead. Brands that are transparent and prioritize their customers' privacy gain consumer trust and can build stronger relationships. Adopting an Opt-In model can foster trust, open new opportunities, and provide internet users with a greater sense of safety and control over their data, without having to go through additional hurdles.

While the Opt-Out process under CCPA may seem promising, our study reveals that it is still far from effectively addressing consumer preferences. Standardizing the Opt-Out process is crucial. By establishing consistent formats, users will be relieved from the burden of navigating complex privacy forms and successfully opting out. Additionally, within this standardized setup, there should always be a single-step option available for users to easily opt out. Strict monitoring of businesses' compliance is necessary to ensure that users can make informed decisions based on their preferences, without the need to navigate through multiple buttons or web pages to submit an Opt-Out request. Awareness campaigns should also be launched to educate consumers about privacy laws, complaint filing procedures, and their privacy rights through mediums like radio and television. It is imperative that privacy laws, whether Opt-Out or Opt-In, are introduced in all states across the US to ensure consistency and protection for all consumers.

6 Conclusion

In this study, we conducted a deceptive experiment to evaluate user responses to CCPA compliant cookie consent banners. Our findings indicate that only 0.45% of participants chose to Opt-Out in the default opt-in model. Despite expressing a desire to Opt-Out, the current implementation of the Opt-Out mechanism hinders users from successfully doing so. Conversely, in the default Opt-Out mechanism, only 12.12% of participants opted-in. These results reveal a discrepancy between users' self-reported preferences to Opt-Out and the actual outcomes observed in our study. To address this issue, policymakers should establish clear guidelines for companies to follow in implementing the Opt-Out or Opt-In mechanisms, ensuring a standardized approach rather than allowing for variations in the steps involved.

Acknowledgement. ChatGPT was utilized to rectify grammatical errors and enhance the clarity and readability of the entire text. Primarily, we have used a common prompt: "Please correct grammatical errors, and improve the readability and clarity of this paragraph." We extend our gratitude to all study participants for their time. Furthermore, we are grateful to the anonymous reviewers for improving our paper for publication.

Appendix A

Reflection on Completed Activity

1. Answer the following (Yes, No, Unsure)
   (a) Did the website you visited for this activity track your behavior and sell this information to third parties?
   (b) Did the website you visited for this activity give you an option to opt out of the sale of your personal data?

2. If this website tracked your behavior and sold this information to third parties, how comfortable would you be with it? (Very Comfortable, Somewhat comfortable, Neutral, Somewhat uncomfortable, Very uncomfortable)
3. Which option for consent did you choose? (Do not sell my data, Opt-In, Close, Accept Cookies and Close, OK, Visit Settings, Unsure)

CCPA Case Examples

Imagine yourself in each of the following scenarios and indicate to what extent you agree or disagree with each statement.

1. You have registered on an online dating platform. A user clicking an "accept sharing" button when creating a new account is sufficient to establish blanket consent to sell personal information as per this business. There is no additional "Do Not Sell My Personal Information" link on its homepage.
   (a) I think scenarios like this are likely to happen. (Strongly Agree, Agree, Neither agree nor disagree, Disagree, Strongly Disagree, Don't know)
   (b) I would be concerned about my privacy in this scenario. (Strongly Agree, Agree, Neither agree nor disagree, Disagree, Strongly Disagree, Don't know)
   (c) Do you think the business acted appropriately in a lawful manner based on the situation described? (Yes, No, Unsure)
   (d) Explain your reasoning above. [Textbox]
2. A business that operates an online pet adoption platform requires your authorized agent to submit a notarized verification when invoking your privacy rights. The business directs you to a third-party trade association's tool in order to submit an opt-out request.
   (a) I think scenarios like this are likely to happen. (Strongly Agree, Agree, Neither agree nor disagree, Disagree, Strongly Disagree, Don't know)
   (b) I would be concerned about my privacy in this scenario. (Strongly Agree, Agree, Neither agree nor disagree, Disagree, Strongly Disagree, Don't know)
   (c) Do you think the business acted appropriately in a lawful manner based on the situation described? (Yes, No, Unsure)
   (d) Explain your reasoning above. [Textbox]

Opt-In vs Opt-Out

1. Do you understand the difference between Opt-in and Opt-out? (Yes, No, Unsure)
2. Which of the below options would you rather have businesses follow?

   – Option A : "Opt-In"

   (a) Default settings: Do not sell data
   (b) Explicitly ask user for consent before selling data
   (c) If user doesn't provide consent, do not sell data
   (d) User will not get customized recommendations
   (e) User will not get directed advertisements

- Option B : "Opt-Out"

(a) Default settings: Sell data
(b) Ask user if they want to revoke consent
(c) If user revokes consent, do not sell data
(d) By default, user will get the full experience of the service, customized recommendations and get directed advertisements

3. Research says "opt-in" impedes economic growth by raising the costs of providing services and consequently decreasing the range of products and services available to consumers. It would make it more difficult for new and often more innovative, firms and organizations to enter markets and compete. It would also make it more difficult for companies to authenticate customers and verify account balances. As a result, prices for many products would likely rise. Which option would you prefer with the information presented above? (Opt-In, Opt-Out)

References

1. The sage encyclopedia of communication research methods au - allen, mike, April 2017
2. Adar, E., Tan, D.S., Teevan, J.: Benevolent deception in human computer interaction. In: Proceedings of the SIGCHI Conference on Human Factors in Computing Systems, pp. 1863–1872 (2013)
3. Bellman, S., Johnson, E., Lohse, G.: To opt-in or opt-out? It depends on the question. Commun. ACM 25–27 (2001). https://doi.org/10.1145/359205.359241
4. Bonta, R.: California consumer privacy act (ccpa) (2023). https://oag.ca.gov/privacy/ccpa. Accessed 18 May 2023
5. Cate, F.H., Staten, M.E.: Protecting privacy in the new millennium: the fallacy of opt-in (2001)
6. Chen, R., Fang, F., Norton, T., McDonald, A., Sadeh, N.: Fighting the fog: evaluating the clarity of privacy disclosures in the age of CCPA, September 2021
7. Cookiefirst: Ccpa compliance - cookiefirst - cookie consent management (2023). https://cookiefirst.com/ccpa-compliance/. Accessed 20 May 2023
8. GENERAL, O.O.T.A.: CCPA Enforcement Case Examples (2021). https://oag.ca.gov/privacy/ccpa/enforcement. Accessed 7 June 2022
9. Habib, H., et al.: It's a scavenger hunt: usability of websites' opt-out and data deletion choices. In: Proceedings of the 2020 CHI Conference on Human Factors in Computing Systems, pp. 1–12 (2020)
10. Habib, H., et al.: Toggles, dollar signs, and triangles: how to (in) effectively convey privacy choices with icons and link texts. In: Proceedings of the 2021 CHI Conference on Human Factors in Computing Systems, pp. 1–25 (2021)
11. Johnson, E., Bellman, S., Lohse, G.: Defaults, framing and privacy: why opting in-opting out1. Mark. Lett. **13**, 5–15 (2002). https://doi.org/10.1023/A:1015044207315
12. Lazar, J., Feng, J.H., Hochheiser, H.: Research Methods in Human-Computer Interaction. Morgan Kaufmann, Cambridge (2017)
13. Liu, Z., Iqbal, U., Saxena, N.: Opted out, yet tracked: are regulations enough to protect your privacy? arXiv e-prints pp. arXiv-2202 (2022)

14. O'Connor, S., Nurwono, R., Siebel, A., Birrell, E.: (Un) clear and (in) conspicuous: the right to opt-out of sale under CCPA. In: Proceedings of the 20th Workshop on Workshop on Privacy in the Electronic Society, pp. 59–72 (2021)
15. Park, G.J.: The changing wind of data privacy law: a comparative study of the European union's general data protection regulation and the 2018 California consumer privacy act. UC Irvine Law Rev. 1455 (2020)
16. Salah El-Din, R.: To deceive or not to deceive! Ethical questions in phishing research (2012)
17. Schechter, S.E., Dhamija, R., Ozment, A., Fischer, I.: Emperor's new security indicators: an evaluation of website authentication and the effect of role playing on usability studies. In: In Proceedings of the 2007 IEEE Symposium on Security and Privacy (2007)
18. Utz, C., Degeling, M., Fahl, S., Schaub, F., Holz, T.: (Un)informed consent: studying GDPR consent notices in the field. In: Proceedings of the 2019 ACM SIGSAC Conference on Computer and Communications Security, pp. 973–990. CCS '19, Association for Computing Machinery, New York, NY, USA (2019). https://doi.org/10.1145/3319535.3354212
19. Van Nortwick, M., Wilson, C.: Setting the bar low: are websites complying with the minimum requirements of the CCPA? Proc. Priv. Enhanc. Technol. 608–628 (2022)
20. Weinmann, M., Schneider, C., Brocke, J.V.: Digital nudging. Bus. Inf. Syst. Eng. 433–436 (2016)
21. Zhang-Kennedy, L., Chiasson, S.: Whether it's moral is a whole other story: consumer perspectives on privacy regulations and corporate data practices. In: SOUPS@ USENIX Security Symposium, pp. 197–216 (2021)

MPC with Cards

Upper Bounds on the Number of Shuffles for Two-Helping-Card Multi-Input AND Protocols

Takuto Yoshida[1(✉)], Kodai Tanaka[2], Keisuke Nakabayashi[2], Eikoh Chida[1], and Takaaki Mizuki[2]

[1] National Institute of Technology, Ichinoseki College, Ichinoseki, Iwate, Japan
{a22706,chida+lncs}@g.ichinoseki.ac.jp
[2] Tohoku University, Sendai, Japan
mizuki+lncs@tohoku.ac.jp

Abstract. Card-based cryptography uses a physical deck of cards to achieve secure computations. To evaluate the performance of card-based protocols, the numbers of helping cards and shuffles required to execute are often used as evaluation metrics. In this paper, we focus on n-input AND protocols that use at most two helping cards, and investigate how many shuffles suffice to construct such a two-helping-card AND protocol. Since the Mizuki–Sone two-input AND protocol uses two helping cards and it can be repeatedly applied $n-1$ times to perform a secure n-input AND computation, an obvious upper bound on the number of required shuffles is $n-1$. In this paper, to obtain better bounds (than $n-1$), we consider making use of the "batching" technique, which was developed by Shinagawa and Nuida in 2020 to reduce the number of shuffles. Specifically, we first formulate the class of two-helping-card n-input AND protocols obtained by applying the batching technique to the Mizuki–Sone AND protocol, and then show n-input AND protocols requiring the minimum number of shuffles (among the class) for the case of $2 \le n \le 500$.

Keywords: Card-based cryptography · Secure computation · Real-life hands-on cryptography · AND protocols

1 Introduction

Secure computations [36] enable players holding individual private inputs to evaluate a predetermined function without revealing the input values more than necessary. The method of secure computation using a physical deck of cards is called *card-based cryptography* [7,19]. Typically, two types of cards are used,

The original version of this chapter was revised: The change was updated and the correct chapter title is "Upper Bounds on the Number of Shuffles for Two-Helping-Card Multi-Input AND Protocols". The correction to this chapter is available to https://doi.org/10.1007/978-981-99-7563-1_26

J. Deng et al. (Eds.): CANS 2023, LNCS 14342, pp. 211–231, 2023.
https://doi.org/10.1007/978-981-99-7563-1_10

where the reverse side is indistinguishable as [?] and the front side is either [♣] or [♡]. These cards are arranged in the following way to represent Boolean values:

[♣][♡] = 0, [♡][♣] = 1.

When two cards placed face down according to this encoding rule represent a bit $x \in \{0, 1\}$, these two cards are called a *commitment* to x and are represented as follows:

$\underbrace{\text{[?][?]}}_{x}$.

A two-input AND protocol takes as input two commitments to bits $x, y \in \{0, 1\}$ along with some helping cards like [♣][♡], and performs a secure computation of the AND value $x \wedge y$ via a series of actions such as shuffling, rearranging, and turning over cards. When the output is obtained as a commitment to $x \wedge y$, such a protocol is called a *committed-format* protocol:

$\underbrace{\text{[?][?]}}_{x}\underbrace{\text{[?][?]}}_{y}$[♣][♡] $\cdots \rightarrow \cdots \rightarrow$ $\underbrace{\text{[?][?]}}_{x \wedge y}$.

This paper deals with committed-format AND protocols, especially multi-input AND protocols, as seen later.

1.1 The Mizuki–Sone and Protocol

The most practical committed-format two-input AND protocol currently known would be the protocol proposed by Mizuki and Sone in 2009 [20]. Hereinafter, we refer to this as the *MS-AND protocol*, and the procedure is described below.

1. Place two input commitments to $x, y \in \{0, 1\}$ along with two helping cards, turning the middle two cards face down, as follows:

   $\underbrace{\text{[?][?]}}_{x}$[♣][♡]$\underbrace{\text{[?][?]}}_{y}$ $\rightarrow$ $\underbrace{\text{[?][?]}}_{x}\underbrace{\text{[?][?]}}_{0}\underbrace{\text{[?][?]}}_{y}$.

2. Rearrange the sequence as follows:

   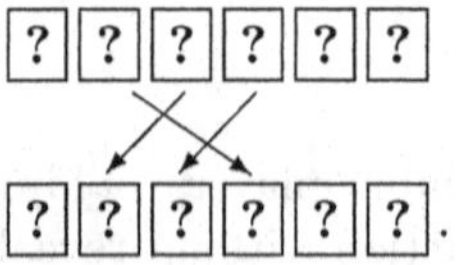

3. A *random bisection cut* (hereafter sometimes called an *RBC* for short), denoted by $[\cdots|\cdots]$, is applied to the sequence of six cards, meaning that we split the card sequence in half and randomly swap the left and right sides (until anyone loses track of the move):

   [[?][?][?] | [?][?][?]] $\rightarrow$ [?][?][?][?][?][?].

It is known that a random bisection cut can be securely implemented using familiar tools such as envelopes [35].

4. Rearrange the sequence as follows:

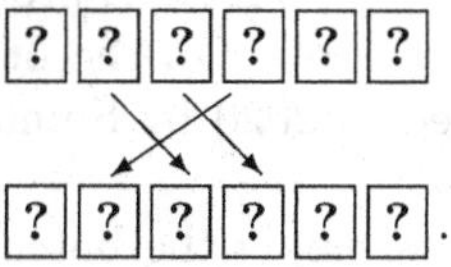

5. The two cards are turned over from the left. Depending on the order of the two revealed cards, we obtain a commitment to $x \wedge y$ as follows:

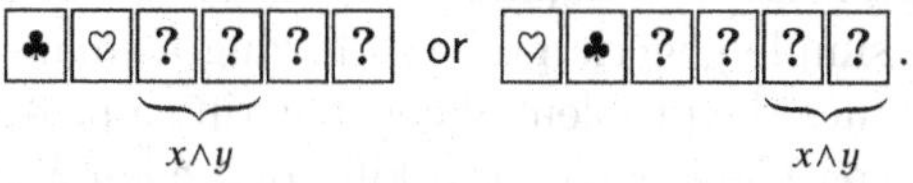

The above is the MS-AND protocol, which, given commitments to x and y, uses two helping cards and one random bisection cut to output a commitment to $x \wedge y$.

After the protocol terminates, the two cards that were turned over in Step 5 can be used as helping cards in another protocol run; we call such face-up cards *free cards*.

We will also call the two face-down cards that are not a commitment to $x \wedge y$ a *garbage commitment*[1]. A garbage commitment can be transformed into two free cards by applying a (normal) shuffle to the two cards (composing the garbage commitment) and turning them over.

1.2   Committed-Format Multi-input and Protocol

As mentioned above, the subject of this paper is to construct committed-format multi-input AND protocols. That is, given n input commitments

$$\underbrace{?\ ?}_{x_1}\ \underbrace{?\ ?}_{x_2}\ \cdots\ \underbrace{?\ ?}_{x_n},$$

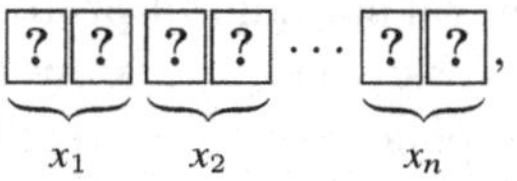

we want to produce a commitment to $x_1 \wedge x_2 \wedge \cdots \wedge x_n$.

Applying the MS-AND protocol described in Sect. 1.1 to commitments to x_1 and x_2 yields a commitment to $x_1 \wedge x_2$ together with two free cards. Thus, we can continue to apply the MS-AND protocol to commitments to $x_1 \wedge x_2$ and x_3. By repeating this a total of $n-1$ times, a committed-format n-input AND protocol can be constructed [15]:

$$\underbrace{?\ ?}_{x_1}\ \underbrace{?\ ?}_{x_2}\ \cdots\ \underbrace{?\ ?}_{x_n}\ \clubsuit\ \heartsuit\ \rightarrow \cdots \rightarrow\ \underbrace{?\ ?}_{x_1 \wedge x_2 \wedge \cdots \wedge x_n}.$$

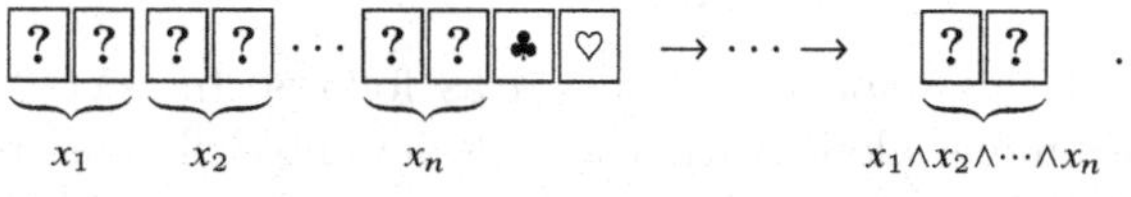

In this case, the number of required helping cards is two, and the number of required shuffles (namely, the number of random bisection cuts) is $n-1$.

---

[1] These two cards are actually a commitment to $\bar{x} \wedge y$.

1.3 Contribution of This Paper

As described in Sect. 1.2, an obvious upper bound on the number of required shuffles for a committed-format n-input AND protocol is $n-1$ under the condition that two helping cards are available. On the other hand, there is a technique called the "batching" proposed in 2020 by Shinagawa and Nuida [31] that can reduce the number of shuffles.

Therefore, in this paper, we apply the batching technique to the MS-AND protocol so that we can construct two-helping-card n-input AND protocols having a smaller number of shuffles. Such an application naturally formulates the class of committed-format two-helping-card n-input AND protocols. Within the class, we present a simple generic protocol having a smaller number of shuffles. Furthermore, we reduce the problem of constructing a protocol to the "MSbatching move-sequence" problem (which is a kind of a computational problem), and by analyzing the latter problem, we show the minimum number of shuffles among the class of protocols in the range of $2 \le n \le 500$. It turns out that the generic proposed protocol is optimal in terms of the number of shuffles for many cases of n. For every n, $2 \le n \le 500$, such that the proposed protocol is not optimal, we find optimal protocols, as well.

1.4 Related Works

The history of committed-format two-input AND protocols dates back to 1993 [2], and since then, a couple protocols have been invented [22,33], followed by the MS-AND protocol in 2009 [20] (which uses six cards and one random bisection cut as seen above). Subsequently, four- and five-card protocols have been developed using complex shuffles [8,9,25].

As for committed-format multi-input AND protocols, those using only one or two shuffles have recently been proposed [11] (although many helping cards are required). In addition, several specialized protocols have been known [6,15].

The research area of card-based cryptography has been growing rapidly in recent years [16,17]. Examples of active topics are: physical zero-knowledge proof protocols [4,10,23,24], private-model secure computations [1,12,21], symmetric function evaluation [26–28], information leakage due to operative or physical errors [18,29], graph automorphism shuffles [14,30], multi-valued protocols with a direction encoding [34], the half-open action [13], card-minimal protocols [3,8], and applications to private simultaneous messages protocols [32].

1.5 Organization of This Paper

The remainder of this paper is organized as follows. In Sect. 2, we introduce the batching technique along with the "pile-scramble shuffle" required for it. In Sect. 3, we show how the batching technique can be applied to multiple MS-AND protocols. In Sect. 4, we formulate the class of protocols obtained by applying the batching technique, and reduce the problem of finding protocols having fewer shuffles to the "MSbatching move-sequence" problem and propose a simple generic protocol in Sect. 5. In Sect. 6, the MSbatching move-sequence problem is analyzed by a dynamic programming algorithm, and we show optimal n-input AND protocols for $2 \leq n \leq 500$ in the sense that the number of shuffles is minimum among all the protocols in the class. Finally, the conclusion is given in Sect. 7.

2 Preliminaries

In this section, we first introduce the pile-scramble shuffle [5] and then explain the batching technique [31].

2.1 Pile-Scramble Shuffle

A *pile-scramble shuffle* [5] is a shuffling operation that divides a sequence of cards into multiple piles of the same size and then rearranges the order of those piles uniformly at random (while the order of cards inside each pile is kept unchanged).

As an example, applying a pile-scramble shuffle, denoted by $[\,\cdot\,|\,\cdot\,|\,\cdots|\,\cdot\,]$, to a sequence of nine cards consisting of three piles yields one of the following six sequences with a probability of exactly 1/6:

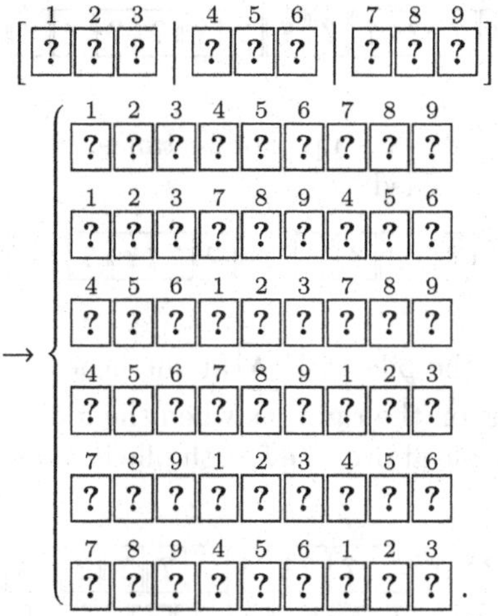

A pile-scramble shuffle can be easily implemented by placing each pile in an envelope and randomly stirring the envelopes.

A random bisection cut that appears in the MS-AND protocol can be said to be a pile-scramble shuffle for two piles (each consisting of three cards).

2.2 Batching Technique

The batching technique [31] combines multiple pile-scramble shuffles that can be executed in parallel into a single pile-scramble shuffle, thereby reducing the number of shuffles. Simply put, after adding "identifiers" with some helping cards to the piles of each pile-scramble shuffle, we perform a single pile-scramble shuffle together, and then open the identifier to return each pile to the position of its original pile-scramble shuffle.

As an example, suppose that we want to apply two random bisection cuts (RBCs) in parallel, which appear in the MS-AND protocol, and that we want to use the batching technique. In other words, we want to perform two RBCs

[? ? ? | ? ? ?], [? ? ? | ? ? ?]

simultaneously using a single shuffle by the batching technique.

1. To identify two RBCs, we use ♣ and ♡. That is, at the head of each pile, a helping card for identification is placed as follows:

   ♣ ? ? ? ♣ ? ? ? ♡ ? ? ? ♡ ? ? ?.

   In the sequel, we call such helping cards *identifier cards.*
2. Turn over the identifier cards and apply a pile-scramble shuffle to the four piles:

   [? ? ? ? | ? ? ? ? | ? ? ? ? | ? ? ? ?]
   → ? ? ? ? ? ? ? ? ? ? ? ? ? ? ? ?.

3. Turn the identifier cards face up. For instance, suppose that the following sequence of cards is obtained:

   ♣ ? ? ? ♡ ? ? ? ♡ ? ? ? ♣ ? ? ?.

4. Sort the piles so that the pile with ♣ at the head is on the left and the pile with ♡ at the head is on the right, as when the identifier cards were inserted in Step 1. In the example above, the fourth pile is moved in front of the second pile:

   ♣ ? ? ? ♡ ? ? ? ♡ ? ? ? ♣ ? ? ?
   → ♣ ? ? ? ♣ ? ? ? ♡ ? ? ? ♡ ? ? ?.

   Note that sorting the piles here is done publicly as seen just above (and hence, we need no additional shuffle).
5. Remove the face-up identifier cards; then, we have performed two RBCs by one pile-scramble shuffle.

In this example, two sets of ♣ ♡ were used to identify the two RBCs. If we want to identify four RBCs, two sets of

♣ ♣ ♣ ♡ ♡ ♣ ♡ ♡

suffice. That is, we can distinguish the piles by two binary digits according to the one-card-per-bit encoding: $\boxed{\clubsuit} = 0$, $\boxed{\heartsuit} = 1$. In general, when we want to apply the batching technique to k RBCs, we need $2k\lceil \log_2 k \rceil$ identifier cards (i.e., $k\lceil \log_2 k \rceil$ free cards for each of $\clubsuit$ and $\heartsuit$).

The batching technique can be applied not only to RBCs, but more generally to multiple pile-scramble shuffles. However, this paper only utilizes it for RBCs (of six cards each).

3 Application of Batching to MS-AND Protocol

As seen in Sect. 1.2, executing repeatedly the MS-AND protocol provides a two-helping-card n-input AND protocol using $n-1$ shuffles, namely $n-1$ RBCs. In this section, we utilize the batching technique to reduce the number of shuffles.

In Sect. 3.1, we mention the idea behind our approach. In Sect. 3.2, we present how to batch MS-AND protocols. In Sect. 3.3, we show an example of a protocol based on our approach.

3.1 Idea

As described in Sect. 2.2, the batching technique can be used to convert multiple RBCs into a single pile-scramble shuffle. This can be applied to the execution of multiple MS-AND protocols to reduce the number of shuffles. Remember that, in order to perform the batching technique, some free cards as identifier cards must be provided to identify each pile pair. Remember furthermore that in the problem setup, only two helping cards are available:

$$\underbrace{\boxed{?}\boxed{?}}_{x_1}\underbrace{\boxed{?}\boxed{?}}_{x_2}\cdots\underbrace{\boxed{?}\boxed{?}}_{x_n}\boxed{\clubsuit}\boxed{\heartsuit}.$$

Therefore, the batching technique cannot be applied immediately (because of shortage of free cards as identifier cards).

Let us recall the procedure of the MS-AND protocol described in Sect. 1.1; then, a garbage commitment arises in Step 5. That is, one execution of the MS-AND protocol yields one garbage commitment. Several garbage commitments can be turned into free cards by shuffling all the cards (of the garbage commitments) and revealing them. This leads to increasing the number of free cards to be used as identifier cards even if there are only two helping cards at the beginning.

More specifically, for the first m input commitments, if the MS-AND protocol is repeated $m-1$ times, we obtain $2m-2$ free cards:

$$\underbrace{\boxed{?}\boxed{?}}_{x_1}\cdots\underbrace{\boxed{?}\boxed{?}}_{x_m}\boxed{\clubsuit}\boxed{\heartsuit} \quad\rightarrow\quad \underbrace{\boxed{?}\boxed{?}}_{x_1\wedge x_2\wedge\cdots\wedge x_m}\ \boxed{\clubsuit}\boxed{\heartsuit}\ \underbrace{\boxed{\clubsuit}\boxed{\heartsuit}\cdots\boxed{\clubsuit}\boxed{\heartsuit}}_{2m-2 \text{ cards}}$$

Thus, some of the $2m$ free cards can be used as identifier cards for the batching technique. In this way, we first apply the MS-AND protocol for the first several input commitments to produce free cards enough for the batching technique to execute.

3.2 MSbatching: How to Batch MS-AND Protocols

This subsection describes in detail how the batching technique is applied to the execution of multiple MS-AND protocols.

Before we begin, let us define a couple of terms. As described in Sect. 3.1, free cards can be created by collecting garbage commitments, shuffling all the cards (constituting the garbage commitments), and then turning them over. This procedure is called the *garbage collection*. For convenience, we will refer to a pair of free cards (of different colors) $\boxed{\clubsuit}\boxed{\heartsuit}$ placed face up as a *free pair*.

First, as an example, assume that there are four commitments

$$\underbrace{\boxed{?}\boxed{?}}_{y_1}\underbrace{\boxed{?}\boxed{?}}_{y_2}\quad\underbrace{\boxed{?}\boxed{?}}_{y_3}\underbrace{\boxed{?}\boxed{?}}_{y_4}$$

and we want to produce commitments to $y_1 \wedge y_2$ and $y_3 \wedge y_4$ by executing the MS-AND protocol twice. Recalling the MS-AND protocol procedure, we need two helping cards, i.e., one free pair $\boxed{\clubsuit}\boxed{\heartsuit}$, per run; therefore, we require two free pairs:

$$\underbrace{\boxed{?}\boxed{?}}_{y_1}\boxed{\clubsuit}\boxed{\heartsuit}\underbrace{\boxed{?}\boxed{?}}_{y_2}\quad\underbrace{\boxed{?}\boxed{?}}_{y_3}\boxed{\clubsuit}\boxed{\heartsuit}\underbrace{\boxed{?}\boxed{?}}_{y_4}.$$

For each of these, an RBC is applied (after reordering). Using the batching technique, this can be achieved with a single shuffle. In this case, however, two more free pairs

$$\boxed{\clubsuit}\boxed{\heartsuit}\quad\boxed{\clubsuit}\boxed{\heartsuit}$$

are required (for identifier cards). After applying the batching technique and turning over the four identifier cards, we return to the two MS-AND protocols and terminate each protocol. Then, the following commitments are obtained:

$$\boxed{\clubsuit}\boxed{\heartsuit}\boxed{\clubsuit}\boxed{\heartsuit}\quad\boxed{\clubsuit}\boxed{\heartsuit}\underbrace{\boxed{?}\boxed{?}}_{y_1 \wedge y_2}\underbrace{\boxed{?}\boxed{?}}_{\text{garbage}}\quad\boxed{\clubsuit}\boxed{\heartsuit}\underbrace{\boxed{?}\boxed{?}}_{y_3 \wedge y_4}\underbrace{\boxed{?}\boxed{?}}_{\text{garbage}}.$$

In summary, given four commitments and four free pairs, one shuffle suffices to output two commitments (to the AND values), four free pairs, and two garbage commitments.

Next, more generally, consider running k MS-AND protocols in parallel (i.e., the number of input commitments is $2k$). As mentioned earlier, one MS-AND protocol requires one free pair, and hence, k free pairs are needed for this amount. In addition, when applying the batching technique, free cards are also needed for serving identifier cards; as mentioned in Sect. 2.2, we require $2k\lceil \log_2 k \rceil$ free cards, which are $k\lceil \log_2 k \rceil$ free pairs. Thus, a total of $k + k\lceil \log_2 k \rceil$ free pairs are required:

$$\underbrace{\boxed{?}\boxed{?}}_{y_1}\underbrace{\boxed{?}\boxed{?}}_{y_2}\cdots\underbrace{\boxed{?}\boxed{?}}_{y_{2k-1}}\underbrace{\boxed{?}\boxed{?}}_{y_{2k}}\quad\underbrace{\boxed{\clubsuit}\boxed{\heartsuit}}_{\text{free}}\times(k + k\lceil \log_2 k \rceil).$$

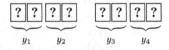

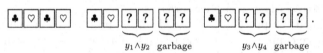

Applying the batching technique to this sequence of cards, the $2k$ commitments become k commitments (to the AND values) after one shuffle, resulting in k garbage commitments and no change in the number of free pairs:

$$\underbrace{\boxed{?}\boxed{?}}_{y_1\wedge y_2}\cdots\underbrace{\boxed{?}\boxed{?}}_{y_{2k-1}\wedge y_{2k}}\quad\underbrace{\boxed{\clubsuit}\boxed{\heartsuit}}_{\text{free}}\times(k+k\lceil\log_2 k\rceil)\quad\underbrace{\boxed{\clubsuit}\boxed{\heartsuit}}_{\text{garbage}}\times k.$$

This procedure will henceforth be referred to as *k-MSbatching.*

The number of free pairs required for k-MSbatching is given by $k+k\lceil\log_2 k\rceil$, where the specific numbers are shown in Table 1. Note that 1-MSbatching is the MS-AND protocol itself (i.e., one run of the protocol).

3.3 Example of Two-Helping-Card and Protocol by MSbatching

In this subsection, we illustrate a two-helping-card protocol by using MSbatching.

Table 1. The number of free pairs required for k-MSbatching

k	1	2	3	4	5	6	7	8	9
# of free pairs	1	4	9	12	20	24	28	32	45

Suppose that the number of inputs is 48, i.e., $n=48$. Then, 48 commitments and one free pair are the input sequence:

$$\underbrace{\boxed{?}\boxed{?}}_{x_1}\underbrace{\boxed{?}\boxed{?}}_{x_2}\underbrace{\boxed{?}\boxed{?}}_{x_3}\underbrace{\boxed{?}\boxed{?}}_{x_4}\cdots\underbrace{\boxed{?}\boxed{?}}_{x_{48}}\quad\underbrace{\boxed{\clubsuit}\boxed{\heartsuit}}_{\text{free}}.$$

Recall that the obvious upper bound on the number of shuffles is to repeat the MS-AND protocol 47 times, which is 47 shuffles. The following protocol requires a smaller number of shuffles to produce a commitment to the AND value of 48 inputs.

1. Perform 1-MSbatching 15 times for the commitments to $x_1,\ldots,x_{16}$ to obtain a commitment to $x_1\wedge\cdots\wedge x_{16}$ (by 15 shuffles):

$$\underbrace{\boxed{?}\boxed{?}}_{x_1\wedge\cdots\wedge x_{16}}\quad\underbrace{\boxed{?}\boxed{?}}_{x_{17}}\underbrace{\boxed{?}\boxed{?}}_{x_{18}}\cdots\underbrace{\boxed{?}\boxed{?}}_{x_{48}}\quad\underbrace{\boxed{\clubsuit}\boxed{\heartsuit}}_{\text{free}}\quad\underbrace{\boxed{?}\boxed{?}}_{\text{garbage}}\times 15.$$

2. The garbage collection is performed to generate 15 free pairs (by one shuffle):

$$\underbrace{\boxed{?}\boxed{?}}_{x_1\wedge\cdots\wedge x_{16}}\quad\underbrace{\boxed{?}\boxed{?}}_{x_{17}}\underbrace{\boxed{?}\boxed{?}}_{x_{18}}\cdots\underbrace{\boxed{?}\boxed{?}}_{x_{48}}\quad\underbrace{\boxed{\clubsuit}\boxed{\heartsuit}}_{\text{free}}\times 16.$$

3. Perform 4-MSbatching for $x_{17},\ldots,x_{24}$ and for $x_{25},\ldots,x_{32}$, followed by 4-MSbatching, 2-MSbatching, and 1-MSbatching, in this order, to obtain a commitment to $x_{17} \wedge \cdots \wedge x_{32}$ (by five shuffles):

$\underbrace{}_{x_1\wedge\cdots\wedge x_{16}} \underbrace{}_{x_{17}\wedge\cdots\wedge x_{32}} \underbrace{}_{x_{33}} \cdots \underbrace{}_{x_{48}} \underbrace{}_{\text{free}} \times 16 \quad \underbrace{}_{\text{garbage}} \times 15.$

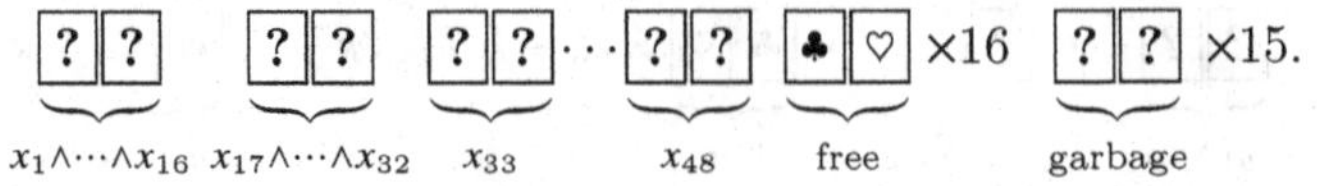

4. Perform 1-MSbatching for $x_1 \wedge \cdots \wedge x_{16}$ and $x_{17} \wedge \cdots \wedge x_{32}$ to obtain a commitment to $x_1 \wedge \cdots \wedge x_{32}$ (by one shuffle):

$\boxed{?}\boxed{?} \quad \boxed{?}\boxed{?} \cdots \boxed{?}\boxed{?} \quad \boxed{\clubsuit}\boxed{\heartsuit} \times 16 \quad \boxed{?}\boxed{?} \times 16.$

$\underbrace{}_{x_1\wedge\cdots\wedge x_{32}} \underbrace{}_{x_{33}} \cdots \underbrace{}_{x_{48}} \underbrace{}_{\text{free}} \quad \underbrace{}_{\text{garbage}}$

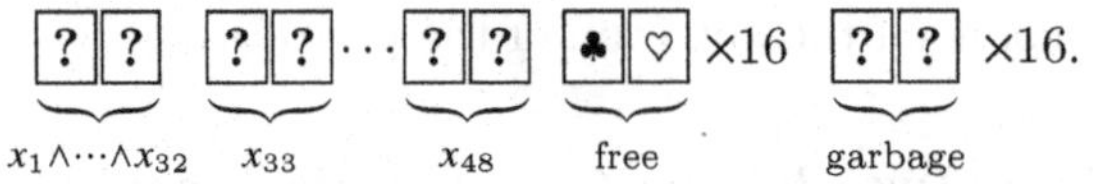

5. The garbage collection is performed (by one shuffle):

$\boxed{?}\boxed{?} \quad \boxed{?}\boxed{?} \quad \boxed{?}\boxed{?} \cdots \boxed{?}\boxed{?} \quad \boxed{\clubsuit}\boxed{\heartsuit} \times 32.$

$\underbrace{}_{x_1\wedge\cdots\wedge x_{16}} \underbrace{}_{x_{17}\wedge\cdots\wedge x_{32}} \underbrace{}_{x_{33}} \cdots \underbrace{}_{x_{48}} \underbrace{}_{\text{free}}$

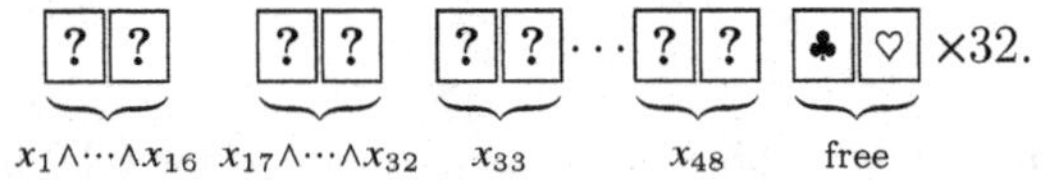

6. Execute 8-MSbatching, 4-MSbatching, 2-MSbatching, and 1-MSbatching for $x_{33},\ldots,x_{48}$ in this order to obtain a commitment to $x_{33} \wedge \cdots \wedge x_{48}$ (by four shuffles):

$\boxed{?}\boxed{?} \quad \boxed{?}\boxed{?} \quad \boxed{\clubsuit}\boxed{\heartsuit} \times 32 \quad \boxed{?}\boxed{?} \times 15.$

$\underbrace{}_{x_1\wedge\cdots\wedge x_{32}} \underbrace{}_{x_{33}\wedge\cdots\wedge x_{48}} \underbrace{}_{\text{free}} \quad \underbrace{}_{\text{garbage}}$

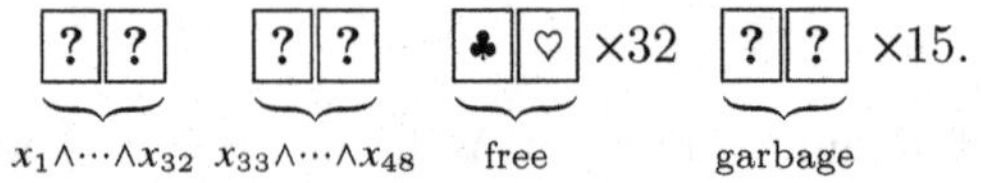

7. Perform 1-MSbatching for $x_1 \wedge \cdots \wedge x_{32}$ and $x_{33} \wedge \cdots \wedge x_{48}$ to obtain a commitment to $x_1 \wedge \cdots \wedge x_{48}$ (by one shuffle):

$\boxed{?}\boxed{?} \quad \boxed{\clubsuit}\boxed{\heartsuit} \times 32 \quad \boxed{?}\boxed{?} \times 16.$

$\underbrace{}_{x_1\wedge\cdots\wedge x_{48}} \underbrace{}_{\text{free}} \quad \underbrace{}_{\text{garbage}}$

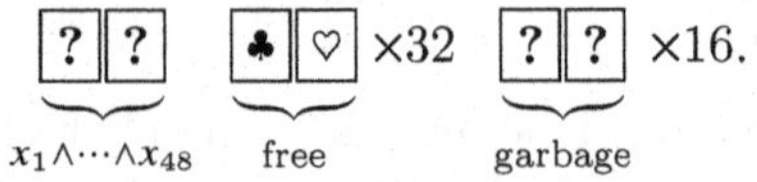

As shown above, the total number of shuffles is 28, which is a significant reduction from the obvious upper bound of 47 shuffles.

4   Class of MSbatching Protocols and Corresponding Problem

As seen in Sect. 3, given n input commitments and one free pair, we can produce a commitment to the AND value via a series of MSbatching (including 1-MSbatching) and the garbage collection with fewer shuffles than the obvious upper bound. In this section, we first formulate the class of two-helping-card AND protocols, called the "MSbatching protocols," naturally created by the combination of MSbatching and the garbage collection. We then introduce the "MSbatching move-sequence" problem; as seen soon, finding a protocol in the class corresponds to solving the problem.

4.1 MSbatching Protocols

This subsection clarifies the class of protocols obtained by MSbatching.

First, let $k \geq 1$ and consider the conditions under which k-MSbatching can be performed. As mentioned in Sect. 3.2, at least $k + k\lceil \log_2 k \rceil$ free pairs are required. Also, to be able to run the MS-AND protocol k times in parallel, there must be at least $2k$ input commitments.

Next, if we want to perform the garbage collection on g garbage commitments for $g \geq 1$, there must be at least g garbage commitments. Hereafter, the garbage collection for g garbage commitments is sometimes referred to as g-GC.

Bearing these in mind, we naturally obtain a class of one-free-pair n-input AND protocols, which we call the *MSbatching protocols*, as follows.

1. $a := n$, $b := 1$.
2. Now there are a commitments and b free pairs (and hence, there are $n-a-b+1$ garbage commitments). Perform one of the followings.
   (a) Apply k-MSbatching such that $a \geq 2k$ and $b \geq k + k\lceil \log_2 k \rceil$. In this case, the number of commitments decreases by k, the number of garbage commitments increases by k, and the number of free pairs remains the same. Thus, we set
   $$a := a - k,\ b := b.$$
   (b) Apply g-GC such that $1 \leq g \leq n - a - b + 1$. Since g free pairs arise, we set
   $$a := a,\ b := b + g.$$
3. If $a \geq 2$, then return to Step 2.

As described above, determining the strategy of selection in Step 2 stipulates one protocol. When $a \geq 2$, 1-MSbatching is always applicable, so it is never unselectable in Step 2. Note that the number of times Step 2 is executed is directly the number of shuffles the protocol uses.

4.2 MSbatching Move-Sequence Problem

Each protocol in the class of MSbatching protocols defined in Sect. 4.1 changes the current number of commitments a and the current number of free pairs b according to the selection in Step 2. Therefore, let us represent the current state at each iteration of Step 2 by a pair (a, b) and consider it as a point (a, b) on the ab-plane.

When $a = 1$, there is exactly one commitment and the protocol terminates; thus, we call any point $(1, b)$ a *terminal* point.

Assume a point (a, b) which is not terminal; from the point (a, b), we transition to another point by either of the following operations.

1. Transition to the point $(a-k, b)$ by k-MSbatching (provided that $a \geq 2k$ and $b \geq k + k\lceil \log_2 k \rceil$). Denote this by $B^k(a, b) = (a - k, b)$.
2. Transition to the point $(a, b+g)$ by g-GC (provided that $1 \leq g \leq n-a-b+1$). Denote this by $GC^g(a, b) = (a, b + g)$.

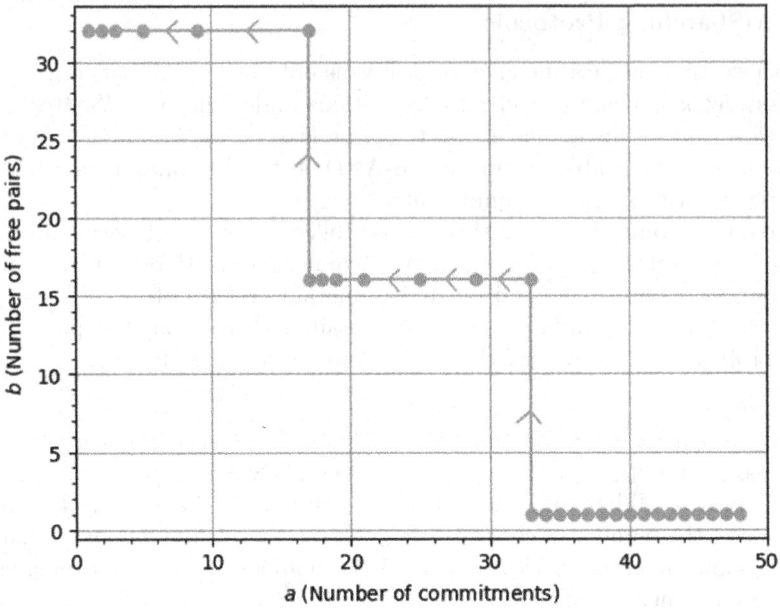

Fig. 1. The 48-input MSbatching protocol given in Sect. 3.3

In the ab-plane, starting from point $(n, 1)$, the current state (a, b) moves by Transition 1 or 2. Transition 1 moves horizontally (left) and Transition (2) moves vertically (up). The number of transitions required to reach a terminal point from the start $(n, 1)$ corresponds to the number of shuffles. That is, the length of the move-sequence connecting the start and terminal points corresponds to the number of shuffles used in the corresponding protocol. Figure 1 shows the move-sequence corresponding to the protocol illustrated in Sect. 3.3.

Figure 2 illustrates the area to which Transition 1 can be applied. From the lightest color to the darkest, they represent the regions to which k-MSbatching can be applied with $k = 2, 3, \ldots, 9$.

The *MSbatching move-sequence problem* is defined as easily imagined: given a start point $(n, 1)$, find a move-sequence to an terminal point on the ab-plane where only Transitions 1 and 2 are applicable. Such a move-sequence uniquely corresponds an MSbatching protocol, and the length of the move-sequence corresponds to the number of shuffles. Therefore, finding a shortest move-sequence is equivalent to constructing an optimal MSbatching protocol in terms of the number of shuffles.

5 Proposed Protocol

In this section, we propose a generic construction for an n-input MSbatching protocol by giving how to choose Transitions 1 and 2.

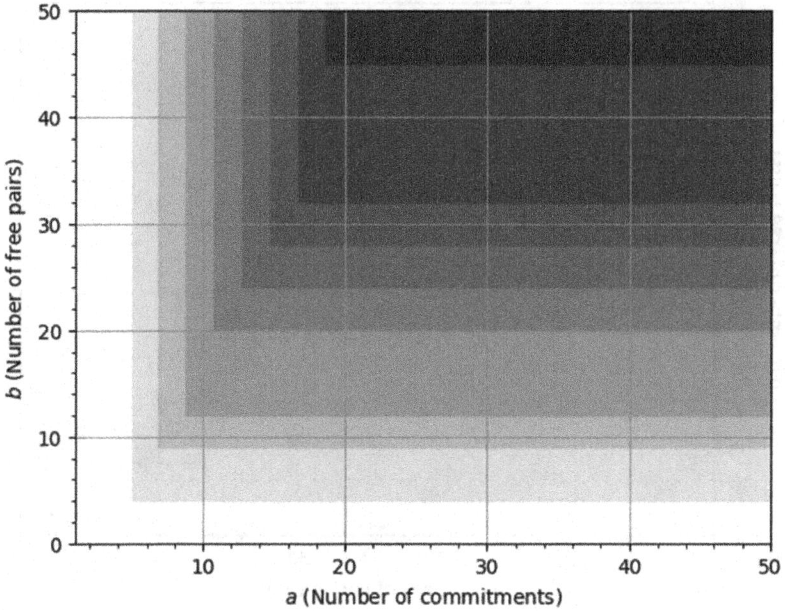

Fig. 2. The area to which k-MSbatching can be applied

5.1 Description of Proposed Protocol

First, we explain the idea of how to choose Transitions 1 and 2 in the proposed protocol. Basically, k-MSbatching to be applied is limited to those where k is a power of 2. If the garbage collection would allow for a larger MSbatching size compared to the currently applicable MSbatching, then perform the garbage collection.

To describe the above idea formally, the proposed protocol chooses a transition for a point (a, b) such that $a \geq 2$ as follows, where let k_b be the maximum value of k that satisfies $a \geq 2k$ and $b \geq k + k\lceil \log_2 k \rceil$, and let k_{b+g} be the maximum value of k that satisfies $a \geq 2k$ and $b + g \geq k + k\lceil \log_2 k \rceil$.

- If $k_{b+g} > k_b$ and $k_{b+g} = 2^i$ for some integer i, perform $(n - a - b + 1)$-GC and transition to $GC^{(n-a-b+1)}(a, b) = (a, n - a + 1)$.
- Otherwise, perform k_b-MSbatching and transition to $B^{k_b}(a, b) = (a - k_b, b)$.

5.2 Proposed Protocol for $n = 48$

Here, we illustrate the proposed protocol for the case of $n = 48$ as an example. That is, Fig. 3 shows the move-sequence of the proposed protocol in the case of 48 inputs.

For further explanation, 1-MSbatching is performed until enough garbage commitments have been accumulated for 2-MSbatching, i.e., for $a = 48, 47, 46$.

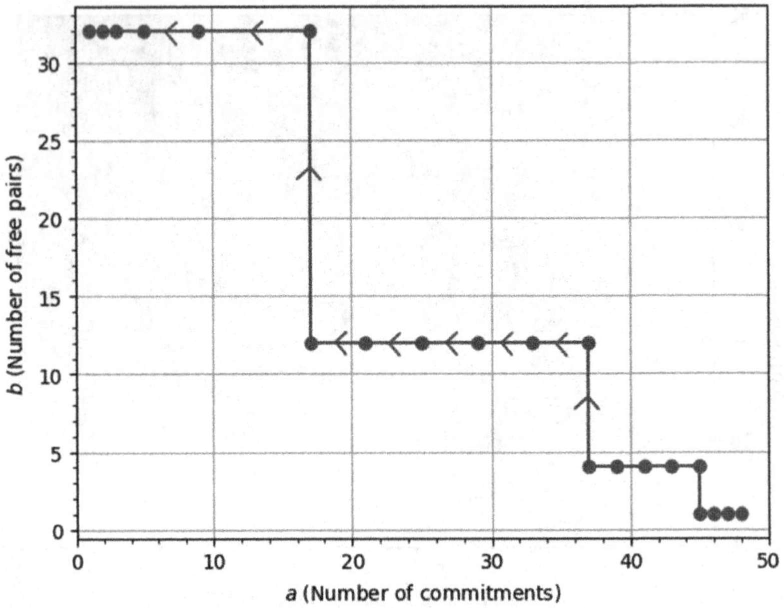

Fig. 3. Proposed protocol for $n = 48$

Next, after performing 3-GC when $a = 45$ is reached, 2-MSbatching is applied. Then, 2-MSbatching is performed until enough garbage commitments are accumulated for 4-MSbatching, i.e., until $a = 39$. When $a = 37$ is reached, 8-GC is performed and then 4-MSbatching is applied. In the same way, continue 4-MSbatching for a while and apply 8-MSbatching at $a = 17$. Then apply 4-MSbatching, 2-MSbatching, and 1-MSbatching for $a = 9, 5, 3, 2$.

Since the number of transitions above is 20, the number of shuffles in the proposed protocol is 20. Since the number of shuffles for the protocol introduced in Sect. 3.3 is 28, it is a successful improvement.

We show the number of shuffles in our protocol for $2 \leq n \leq 50$ in Fig. 4.

6 Search for Optimal Protocols

In this section, we verify whether the protocol proposed in Sect. 5 is optimal in the sense that it minimizes the number of shuffles among all the MSbatching protocols. Specifically, we find shortest move-sequences in the MSbatching move-sequence problem by a dynamic programming algorithm in the range up to $n = 500$.

First, in Sect. 6.1, two lemmas are given to narrow the space where we have to search. Next, in Sect. 6.2, we present the strategy for finding shortest move-sequences. After that, in Sect. 6.3, we compare the number of shuffles in the proposed protocol with the minimum number of shuffles.

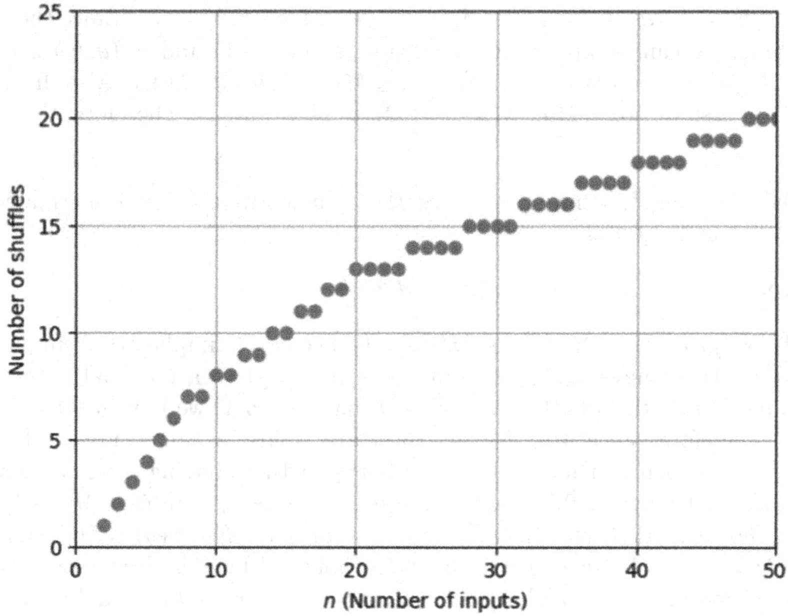

Fig. 4. Number of shuffles in our protocol for $2 \leq n \leq 50$

6.1 Lemmas to Narrow Search Space

When searching for shortest move-sequences in the MSbatching move-sequence problem presented in Sect. 4, the following two lemmas imply that there are transitions that do not need to be considered, narrowing the search space. Hereafter, n is fixed and $M(a, b)$ denotes the shortest move-sequence length from point (a, b) to a terminal point.

The following Lemma 1 indicates that whenever the garbage collection is performed, it should be done on all the remaining garbage commitments.

Lemma 1. *For any g and g' such that $1 \leq g < g' \leq n - a - b + 1$, $M(a, b + g) \geq M(a, b + g')$.*

Proof. We prove that $M(a, b+g) \geq M(a, b+g+1)$ because it implies the lemma. Let P be a shortest move-sequence from point $(a, b + g)$ to a terminal point, and use induction on the length of P. When P has length 1, $(a, b+g)$ is terminated by some k-MSbatching. Since the same k-MSbatching can be applied to $(a, b+g+1)$, $M(a, b + g) = M(a, b + g + 1) = 1$ and the claim holds. Assume inductively that when P has length 2 or more, the claim holds for those having a smaller length. When the first move of P transitions upward from the point $(a, b + g)$ to $GC^{g''}(a, b) = (a, b + g'')$, the point $(a, b + g + 1)$ can also transition to the same point $(a, b+g'')$ (or $b+g+1 = b+g''$), and hence, $M(a, b+g) = M(a, b+g'')+1$ and $M(a, b+g+1) \leq M(a, b+g'')+1$, from which we have $M(a, b+g) \geq M(a, b+g+1)$ as desired. When the first move of P is leftward, some k-MSbatching transitions to $B^k(a, b+g) = (a-k, b+g)$ and $M(a, b+g) = M(a-k, b+g)+1$. Since the same k-MSbatching can be applied to the point $(a, b+g+1)$ and $B^k(a, b+g+1) = (a-k, b+g+1)$, we have $M(a, b+g+1) \leq M(a-k, b+g+1)+1$. Also, from the induction assumption, $M(a-k, b+g) \geq M(a-k, b+g+1)$. Therefore, the claim holds. □

The following Lemma 2 indicates that when MSbatching is perfomed, it should be the largest size.

Lemma 2. *If $a < a'$, then $M(a, b) \leq M(a', b)$.*

Proof. We prove that $M(a, b) \leq M(a+1, b)$ because it implies the lemma. Let P be a shortest move-sequence from point $(a+1, b)$ to a terminal point, and use induction on the length of P. When P has length 1, we have $a+1 = 2$, i.e., $a = 1$. Therefore, since $M(a, b) = 0$, the claim holds. Assume inductively that when P has length 2 or more, the claim holds for those having a smaller length. When the first move of P is upward, there exists some g such that $M(a+1, b) = M(a+1, b+g)+1$. Also, from the induction assumption, $M(a, b+g) \leq M(a+1, b+g)$. Since $M(a, b) \leq M(a, b+g)+1$, the claim holds. When the first move of P is leftward, by some k-MSbatching, $M(a+1, b) = M(a-k+1, b)+1$ and $a+1 \geq 2k$. Therefore, $M(a, b) \leq M(a-(k-1), b)+1 = M(a-k+1, b)+1$ since $(k-1)$-MSbatching can be applied to the point (a, b). Therefore, the claim holds. □

6.2 Shortest Move-Sequence Search

Here, the shortest move-sequence length for each $n \leq 500$ is obtained by running a dynamic programming algorithm for the search space of the MSbatching move-sequence problem, which is narrowed by Lemmas 1 and 2 in Sect. 6.1. The pseudo code for the search is shown in Algorithm 1. The algorithm is explained below.

To search the entire move-sequence space from point $(n, 1)$ to a terminal point, we define a 2-dimensional array named SMS (Shortest Move Sequence) in Line 3 of Algorithm 1.

First, the search range is explained. Since it is assumed that the move-sequence is explored in reverse, a is processed in ascending order over the range of $1 \leq a \leq n$ and b is processed in descending order over the range of $1 \leq b \leq n-a+1$. When $b = n-a+1$, it means that there is no garbage commitment, which is the boundary. Figure 5 shows the search area (boundary) when $n = 48$, for example.

Next, the transition selection method is explained. Line 6 is the condition on the boundary $b = n-a+1$ shown in Fig. 5. Since no further GC can be performed on the boundary, add 1 to the value at the transition moved to the left by k_b-MSbatching, i.e., SMS$[a-k_b][b]$. The conditions from Line 8 are about the inside of the search area. Line 9 adds 1 to SMS$[a][n-a+1]$ since Transition 2 is better. Line 11 adds 1 to SMS$[a-k_b][b]$ because Transition 1 is better.

This algorithm was executed on a computer for up to $n = 500$.

Algorithm 1. Shortest move-sequence search

```
function MIN_ COST(n)
    n ← number of inputs
    SMS[n][n + 1]
    for 1 ≤ a ≤ n do
        for n − a + 1 ≥ b ≥ 1 do
            if b == n − a + 1 then
                SMS[a][b] = SMS[a − k_b][b] + 1
            else if b < n − a + 1 then
                if SMS[a][n − a + 1] ≤ SMS[a − k_b][b] then
                    SMS[a][b] = SMS[a][n − a + 1] + 1
                else
                    SMS[a][b] = SMS[a − k_b][b] + 1
                end if
            end if
        end for
    end for
end function
```

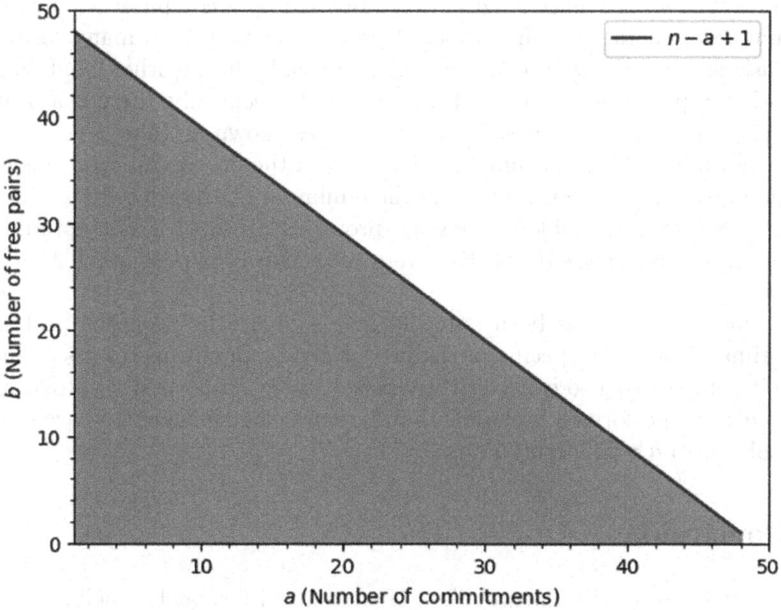

Fig. 5. Possible points to visit for $n = 48$

6.3 Comparison

Here, we compare the number of shuffles for the protocol proposed in Sect. 5 with the shortest move-sequence length calculated in Sect. 6.2.

Table 2. Numbers of inputs that do not minimize the number of shuffles in the proposed protocol

Number of inputs n	Proposed protocol's shuffles	Shortest length
48–49	20	19
56	21	20
104	27	26
112–115	28	27
128–129	29	28
240–247	36	35
256–271	37	36
288–295	38	37
320–323	39	38
352	40	39

As mentioned above, the search was performed within $n \leq 500$ of inputs, and the shortest move-sequence lengths were obtained by a computer. Compared to the number of shuffles for the proposed protocol in Sect. 5, in many cases they are consistent and the proposed protocol is optimal. On the other hand, in some cases, the proposed protocol is not optimal, and specifically, there is a protocol that is better than the proposed protocol at n as shown in Table 2.

As shown in Table 2, the number of shuffles of the proposed protocol is found to be minimum or only one more than the minimum. Although only the shortest lengths are shown in Table 2 when the proposed protocol is not optimal, the shortest move-sequences themselves were of course obtained for all the range $n \leq 500$.

No rule of thumb has been found for cases where the proposed protocol is not optimal. Nor is the specific procedure for giving an optimal protocol known. While it is interesting to consider these issues, since card-based cryptography is expected to be performed by human hands, it may be sufficient to have optimal protocols up to $n = 500$ figured out.

7 Conclusion

In this paper, we gave a natural class of committed-format two-helping-card n-input AND protocols based on the batching technique and the MS-AND protocol, and showed optimal protocols among them in terms of the minimum number of shuffles up to $n = 500$.

Note that the "optimality" here was discussed within the class of MSbatching protocols, and hence, it is still open to determine whether the upper bounds on the number of shuffles obtained in this paper are also lower bounds on the number of shuffles for *any* committed-format two-helping-card AND protocols (that are not necessarily based on the MS-AND protocol or the batching technique).

Acknowledgements. We thank the anonymous referees, whose comments have helped us to improve the presentation of the paper. This work was supported in part by JSPS KAKENHI Grant Numbers JP21K11881 and JP23H00479.

References

1. Abe, Y., et al.: Efficient card-based majority voting protocols. New Gener. Comput. 1–26 (2022). https://doi.org/10.1007/s00354-022-00161-7
2. Crépeau, C., Kilian, J.: Discreet solitary games. In: Stinson, D.R. (ed.) CRYPTO 1993. LNCS, vol. 773, pp. 319–330. Springer, Heidelberg (1994). https://doi.org/10.1007/3-540-48329-2_27
3. Haga, R., Hayashi, Y., Miyahara, D., Mizuki, T.: Card-minimal protocols for three-input functions with standard playing cards. In: Batina, L., Daemen, J. (eds.) Progress in Cryptology – AFRICACRYPT 2022. AFRICACRYPT 2022. LNCS, vol. 13503, pp. 448–468. Springer, Cham (2022). https://doi.org/10.1007/978-3-031-17433-9_19
4. Hand, S., Koch, A., Lafourcade, P., Miyahara, D., Robert, L.: Check alternating patterns: a physical zero-knowledge proof for Moon-or-Sun. In: Shikata, J., Kuzuno, H. (eds.) Advances in Information and Computer Security. IWSEC 2023. LNCS, vol. 14128, pp. 255–272. Springer, Cham (2023). https://doi.org/10.1007/978-3-031-41326-1_14
5. Ishikawa, R., Chida, E., Mizuki, T.: Efficient card-based protocols for generating a hidden random permutation without fixed points. In: Calude, C.S., Dinneen, M.J. (eds.) UCNC 2015. LNCS, vol. 9252, pp. 215–226. Springer, Cham (2015). https://doi.org/10.1007/978-3-319-21819-9_16
6. Isuzugawa, R., Toyoda, K., Sasaki, Yu., Miyahara, D., Mizuki, T.: A card-minimal three-input AND protocol using two shuffles. In: Chen, C.-Y., Hon, W.-K., Hung, L.-J., Lee, C.-W. (eds.) COCOON 2021. LNCS, vol. 13025, pp. 668–679. Springer, Cham (2021). https://doi.org/10.1007/978-3-030-89543-3_55
7. Koch, A.: The landscape of security from physical assumptions. In: IEEE Information Theory Workshop, pp. 1–6. IEEE, NY (2021). https://doi.org/10.1109/ITW48936.2021.9611501
8. Koch, A.: The landscape of optimal card-based protocols. Math. Cryptol. **1**(2), 115–131 (2022). https://journals.flvc.org/mathcryptology/article/view/130529
9. Koch, A., Walzer, S., Härtel, K.: Card-based cryptographic protocols using a minimal number of cards. In: Iwata, T., Cheon, J.H. (eds.) ASIACRYPT 2015. LNCS, vol. 9452, pp. 783–807. Springer, Heidelberg (2015). https://doi.org/10.1007/978-3-662-48797-6_32
10. Komano, Y., Mizuki, T.: Card-based zero-knowledge proof protocol for pancake sorting. In: Bella, G., Doinea, M., Janicke, H. (eds.) Innovative Security Solutions for Information Technology and Communications. SecITC 2022. LNCS, vol. 13809, pp. 222–239. Springer, Cham (2023). https://doi.org/10.1007/978-3-031-32636-3_13
11. Kuzuma, T., Toyoda, K., Miyahara, D., Mizuki, T.: Card-based single-shuffle protocols for secure multiple-input AND and XOR computations. In: ASIA Public-Key Cryptography, pp. 51–58. ACM, NY (2022). https://doi.org/10.1145/3494105.3526236

12. Manabe, Y., Ono, H.: Card-based cryptographic protocols with malicious players using private operations. New Gener. Comput. **40**, 67–93 (2022). https://doi.org/10.1007/s00354-021-00148-w
13. Miyahara, D., Mizuki, T.: Secure computations through checking suits of playing cards. In: Li, M., Sun, X. (eds.) Frontiers of Algorithmic Wisdom. IJTCS-FAW 2022. LNCS, vol. 13461, pp. 110–128. Springer, Cham (2022). https://doi.org/10.1007/978-3-031-20796-9_9
14. Miyamoto, K., Shinagawa, K.: Graph automorphism shuffles from pile-scramble shuffles. New Gener. Comput. 1–25 (2022). https://doi.org/10.1007/s00354-022-00164-4
15. Mizuki, T.: Card-based protocols for securely computing the conjunction of multiple variables. Theor. Comput. Sci. **622**(C), 34–44 (2016). https://doi.org/10.1016/j.tcs.2016.01.039
16. Mizuki, T.: Preface: special issue on card-based cryptography. New Gener. Comput. **39**(1), 1–2 (2021). https://doi.org/10.1007/s00354-021-00127-1
17. Mizuki, T.: Preface: special issue on card-based cryptography 2. New Gener. Comput. (1), 1–2 (2022). https://doi.org/10.1007/s00354-022-00170-6
18. Mizuki, T., Komano, Y.: Information leakage due to operative errors in card-based protocols. Inf. Comput. **285**, 104910 (2022). https://doi.org/10.1016/j.ic.2022.104910
19. Mizuki, T., Shizuya, H.: Computational model of card-based cryptographic protocols and its applications. IEICE Trans. Fundam. **E100.A**(1), 3–11 (2017). https://doi.org/10.1587/transfun.E100.A.3
20. Mizuki, T., Sone, H.: Six-card secure AND and four-card secure XOR. In: Deng, X., Hopcroft, J.E., Xue, J. (eds.) FAW 2009. LNCS, vol. 5598, pp. 358–369. Springer, Heidelberg (2009). https://doi.org/10.1007/978-3-642-02270-8_36
21. Nakai, T., Misawa, Y., Tokushige, Y., Iwamoto, M., Ohta, K.: Secure computation for threshold functions with physical cards: power of private permutations. New Gener. Comput. **40**, 95–113 (2022). https://doi.org/10.1007/s00354-022-00153-7
22. Niemi, V., Renvall, A.: Secure multiparty computations without computers. Theor. Comput. Sci. **191**(1–2), 173–183 (1998). https://doi.org/10.1016/S0304-3975(97)00107-2
23. Robert, L., Miyahara, D., Lafourcade, P., Mizuki, T.: Physical ZKP protocols for Nurimisaki and Kurodoko. Theor. Comput. Sci. **972**, 114071 (2023). https://doi.org/10.1016/j.tcs.2023.114071
24. Ruangwises, S.: Physical zero-knowledge proof for ball sort puzzle. In: Della Vedova, G., Dundua, B., Lempp, S., Manea, F. (eds.) Unity of Logic and Computation. CiE 2023. LNCS, vol. 13967, pp. 246–257. Springer, Cham (2023). https://doi.org/10.1007/978-3-031-36978-0_20
25. Ruangwises, S., Itoh, T.: AND protocols using only uniform shuffles. In: van Bevern, R., Kucherov, G. (eds.) CSR 2019. LNCS, vol. 11532, pp. 349–358. Springer, Cham (2019). https://doi.org/10.1007/978-3-030-19955-5_30
26. Ruangwises, S., Itoh, T.: Securely computing the n-variable equality function with 2n cards. Theor. Comput. Sci. **887**, 99–110 (2021). https://doi.org/10.1016/j.tcs.2021.07.007
27. Shikata, H., Miyahara, D., Mizuki, T.: Few-helping-card protocols for some wider class of symmetric Boolean functions with arbitrary ranges. In: 10th ACM Asia Public-Key Cryptography Workshop, pp. 33–41. APKC '23, ACM, New York (2023). https://doi.org/10.1145/3591866.3593073

28. Shikata, H., Toyoda, K., Miyahara, D., Mizuki, T.: Card-minimal protocols for symmetric Boolean functions of more than seven inputs. In: Seidl, H., Liu, Z., Pasareanu, C.S. (eds.) Theoretical Aspects of Computing – ICTAC 2022. ICTAC 2022. LNCS, vol. 13572, pp. 388–406. Springer, Cham (2022). https://doi.org/10.1007/978-3-031-17715-6_25
29. Shimano, M., Sakiyama, K., Miyahara, D.: Towards verifying physical assumption in card-based cryptography. In: Bella, G., Doinea, M., Janicke, H. (eds.) Innovative Security Solutions for Information Technology and Communications. SecITC 2022. LNCS, vol. 13809, pp. 289–305. Springer, Cham (2023). https://doi.org/10.1007/978-3-031-32636-3_17
30. Shinagawa, K., Miyamoto, K.: Automorphism shuffles for graphs and hypergraphs and its applications. IEICE Trans. Fundam. **E106.A**(3), 306–314 (2023). https://doi.org/10.1587/transfun.2022CIP0020
31. Shinagawa, K., Nuida, K.: A single shuffle is enough for secure card-based computation of any Boolean circuit. Discret. Appl. Math. **289**, 248–261 (2021). https://doi.org/10.1016/j.dam.2020.10.013
32. Shinagawa, K., Nuida, K.: Single-shuffle full-open card-based protocols imply private simultaneous messages protocols. Cryptology ePrint Archive, Paper 2022/1306 (2022). https://eprint.iacr.org/2022/1306, https://eprint.iacr.org/2022/1306
33. Stiglic, A.: Computations with a deck of cards. Theor. Comput. Sci. **259**(1–2), 671–678 (2001). https://doi.org/10.1016/S0304-3975(00)00409--6
34. Suga, Y.: A classification proof for commutative three-element semigroups with local AND structure and its application to card-based protocols. In: 2022 IEEE International Conference on Consumer Electronics - Taiwan, pp. 171–172. IEEE, NY (2022). https://doi.org/10.1109/ICCE-Taiwan55306.2022.9869063
35. Ueda, I., Miyahara, D., Nishimura, A., Hayashi, Y., Mizuki, T., Sone, H.: Secure implementations of a random bisection cut. Int. J. Inf. Secur. **19**(4), 445–452 (2019). https://doi.org/10.1007/s10207-019-00463-w
36. Yao, A.C.: Protocols for secure computations. In: Foundations of Computer Science, pp. 160–164. IEEE Computer Society, Washington, DC, USA (1982). https://doi.org/10.1109/SFCS.1982.88

Free-XOR in Card-Based Garbled Circuits

Yoshifumi Manabe[1(✉)] and Kazumasa Shinagawa[2,3]

[1] School of Informatics, Kogakuin University, Tokyo, Japan
manabe@cc.kogakuin.ac.jp

[2] Ibaraki University, 4-12-1 Nakanarusawa, Hitachi, Ibaraki 316-8511, Japan
kazumasa.shinagawa.np92@vc.ibaraki.ac.jp

[3] National Institute of Advanced Industrial Science and Technology (AIST), 2-3-26 Aomi, Koto, Tokyo 135-0064, Japan

Abstract. This paper shows a free-XOR technique in card-based garbled circuits. Card-based cryptographic protocols were proposed as a secure multiparty computation using physical cards instead of computers. They can be used when users cannot trust software on computers. Shinagawa and Nuida proposed card-based garbled circuits that compute any Boolean functions using a single shuffle. Their protocol uses $24g + 2n$ cards, where g is the number of gates and n is the number of inputs. Tozawa et al. reduced the number of cards to $8g + 2n$. This paper introduces the free-XOR technique for standard garbled circuits to card-based garbled circuits. It is unnecessary to prepare a garbled table for XOR gates. The number of cards is reduced to $8g_1 + 2g_2 + 2n$, where g_1 is the number of gates other than XOR and g_2 is the number of XOR gates whose output is used as a final output. The card-based garbled circuits proposed by Shinagawa and Nuida have one restriction the final outputs cannot be used for inputs to the other gates. This paper eliminates the restriction with two different techniques. The second technique uses the idea in free-XOR.

Keywords: Card-based cryptographic protocols · secure multiparty computation · garbled circuits · exclusive or · free-XOR

1 Introduction

Card-based cryptographic protocols [15,31,32] were proposed in which physical cards are used instead of computers to securely compute values. They can be used when computers cannot be used or users cannot trust the software on the computer. Also, the protocols are easy to understand, thus the protocols can be used to teach the basics of cryptography [4,27] to accelerate the social implementation of advanced cryptography [8]. den Boer [5] first showed a five-card

The first author was supported by JSPS KAKENHI Grant Number JP23H00479. The second author was supported during this work by JSPS KAKENHI Grant Numbers JP21K17702 and JP23H00479, and JST CREST Grant Number JPMJCR22M1.

J. Deng et al. (Eds.): CANS 2023, LNCS 14342, pp. 232–248, 2023.
https://doi.org/10.1007/978-981-99-7563-1_11

protocol to securely compute the logical AND of two inputs. Since then, many protocols have been proposed to realize primitives to compute any Boolean functions [14,17,22,33,38,44,45,52,53] and specific computations such as a specific class of Boolean functions [2,3,7,13,19–21,23,28,30,39,42,47,48,51,57], universal computation such as Turing machines [6,16], millionaires' problem [24,35,43], voting [1,29,36,37,40,56,60], random permutation [9,11,12,34], grouping [10], ranking [55], lottery [54], and so on.

Shinagawa and Nuida [53] proposed a protocol to compute any Boolean functions using the garbled circuit technique [61]. The number of shuffles used in the protocol is one. Their protocol uses $24g + 2n$ cards, where g is the number of gates and n is the number of inputs. Tozawa et al. [58] reduced the number of cards to $8g + 2n$.

To reduce the size of standard garbled tables, free-XOR technique [18] was shown, in which no garbled table is necessary for XOR gates. This paper introduces the technique to card-based garbled circuits. We show that garbled tables are also unnecessary for XOR gates in card-based garbled circuits. Thus no cards are necessary for internal XOR gates, where, the output of an XOR gate is not a final output. When the output of an XOR gate is a final output, two cards are necessary. The number of cards is thus reduced to $8g_1 + 2g_2 + 2n$, where g_1 is the number of gates other than XOR and g_2 is the number of XOR gates whose output is a final output. The number of shuffles is kept to one.

The card-based garbled circuits proposed by Shinagawa and Nuida [53] have one restriction the final outputs cannot be used for inputs to the other gates. Though each input value in the garbled tables is randomized to hide the value, the output data must not be randomized. That is the reason for the restriction. This paper considers eliminating the restriction with two different techniques. The first technique is preparing a copy of garbled table entries that is used for final outputs. The second technique is remembering the random value and undoing the randomization, whose idea is the same as the one in free-XOR. Though the former technique needs more cards, the total number of shuffles is kept to one. The latter technique needs one additional shuffle.

Section 2 shows basic notations and definitions of card-based cryptographic protocols. Section 3 shows Shinagawa-Nuida card-based garbled circuit whose size is reduced by [46]. Section 4 shows the new free-XOR technique for card-based garbled circuits. Section 5 discusses eliminating the output restriction in [53]. Section 6 concludes the paper.

2 Preliminaries

This section gives the notations and basic definitions of card-based cryptographic protocols. Most of the results are based on a two-color card model. In the two-color card model, there are two kinds of marks, $\boxed{\clubsuit}$ and $\boxed{\heartsuit}$. Cards of the same marks cannot be distinguished. In addition, the back of both types of cards is $\boxed{?}$. It is impossible to determine the mark on the back of a given card of $\boxed{?}$.

One-bit data is represented by two cards as follows: $\boxed{\clubsuit}\boxed{\heartsuit} = 0$ and $\boxed{\heartsuit}\boxed{\clubsuit} = 1$.

One pair of cards that represents one bit $x \in \{0, 1\}$, whose face is down, is called a commitment of x, and denoted as $commit(x)$. It is written as $\underbrace{\boxed{?}\boxed{?}}_{x}$.

Note that when these two cards are swapped, $commit(\bar{x})$ can be obtained. Thus, logical negation can be easily computed.

A set of cards placed in a row is called a sequence of cards. A sequence of cards S whose length is n is denoted as $S = s_1, s_2, \ldots, s_n$, where s_i is i-th card of the sequence. $S = \underbrace{\boxed{?}}_{s_1} \underbrace{\boxed{?}}_{s_2} \underbrace{\boxed{?}}_{s_3} \ldots, \underbrace{\boxed{?}}_{s_n}$.

All protocols are executed by two players, Alice and Bob. The players are semi-honest, that is, they obey the rule of the protocol, but they try to obtain secret values.

Next, we discuss the inputs and outputs of the protocols. Most protocols have committed inputs, that is, the inputs are given to the players in a committed manner. The players do not know the input values and they might try to obtain the input values during the protocol execution. The other type of protocol considers the case when each player inputs his/her input value that must be hidden from the other player. They are called non-committed input protocols. Note that committed-input protocols can be used when the players input their own values. Each player makes a commitment to his/her input in advance and they are used as inputs. Thus, committed-input protocols are desirable. On the other hand, non-committed input protocols can be simple and might reduce the number of cards used in the protocol.

Most protocols output the result in a committed manner. They are called committed-output protocols. On the other hand, several protocols terminate by opening some cards and obtaining the result from the sequence of the opened cards. Such protocols are called non-committed output protocols. Committed-output protocols are desirable since the committed output can be used as input for further secure computations.

Next, we show operations on the cards. Opening a card is turning a face-down card into a face-up, thus the players can see the mark on the card. Face-down a card is turning a face-up card to face-down. Rearrangement is a permutation of a sequence of cards, that is, the position of a given sequence of cards is changed.

A shuffle is executed on a sequence of cards S. Its parameter is $(\Pi, \mathcal{F})$, where Π is a set of permutations on S and $\mathcal{F}$ is a probability distribution on Π. For a given sequence S, each permutation $\pi \in \Pi$ is selected by the probability distribution $\mathcal{F}$ and π is applied to S. If π is applied on $S = s_1, s_2, \ldots, s_n$, the result is $s_{\pi^{-1}(1)}, s_{\pi^{-1}(2)}, \ldots, s_{\pi^{-1}(n)}$. Since π is selected from Π, the result is not deterministic. Non-deterministic execution is necessary for card-based protocols. If all operations are deterministic, the relation between the committed input value and the committed output value is known to the players. When the committed output cards are opened to see the final output, the private input data is known to the players using the relation between the input and the output. Thus non-deterministic execution is necessary to hide the private input values.

We show examples of shuffles used in the protocols shown below. A random shuffle is randomly changing the positions of the cards for the given sequence of cards. When $S = s_1, s_2, s_3$, the result of a random shuffle is $S_1 = s_1, s_2, s_3$, $S_2 = s_1, s_3, s_2$, $S_3 = s_2, s_1, s_3$, $S_4 = s_2, s_3, s_1$, $S_5 = s_3, s_1, s_2$, or $S_6 = s_3, s_2, s_1$. The probability of obtaining each result is $1/|S|!$.

A shuffle is uniform if $\mathcal{F}$ is a uniform distribution, that is, $\pi \in \Pi$ is selected uniformly at random. A shuffle is closed if multiple executions of a shuffle are also the same shuffle. Non-uniform shuffles are not desirable since they are difficult to execute by human hands. Using some additional cards or tools, protocols to execute any kinds of shuffles were shown [26,41,49,50,59].

Closed shuffles are desirable since each one of Alice and Bob can execute one instance of the shuffle to obtain one shuffle result. Even if Alice and Bob are not honest and each player knows the result of his/her shuffle, the final result of the two shuffles is unknown to the players. The random shuffle shown above is uniform and closed.

Next, we introduce piles of cards. A pile of cards is a sequence of cards whose order cannot be changed using some additional tools such as clips or envelopes. For example, consider a case when cards $s_{i,j} (i = 1, 2, \ldots, n,\ j = 1, 2, \ldots m)$ are given. The players make piles of cards such that $P_i = s_{i,1}, s_{i,2}, \ldots, s_{i,m} (i = 1, 2, \ldots, n)$ using clips or envelopes. The players treat each pile P_i just like a single card during shuffle operations. The order of cards in a pile cannot be changed because of the clip or envelope. Consider the case shuffle π is executed on the above piles $P_i (i = 1, 2, \ldots, n)$. The result is $P_{\pi^{-1}(1)}, P_{\pi^{-1}(2)}, \ldots, P_{\pi^{-1}(n)}$, where $P_{\pi^{-1}(i)} = s_{\pi^{-1}(i),1}, s_{\pi^{-1}(i),2}, \ldots, s_{\pi^{-1}(i),m}$. Random shuffles on piles are called pile-scramble shuffles.

Last, the efficiency of the protocol is evaluated by the number of cards used by the protocol. It corresponds to the space complexity of programs.

The number of shuffles is used to evaluate the time complexity of the protocols since the other operations are simple [25].

3 Card-Based Garbled Circuits

Garbled circuits [61] are a fundamental technique to securely compute any function by two semi-honest players. The original garbled circuits consider the case when Alice has input value x and Bob has input y. They want to compute $f(x, y)$ together without revealing each player's input value to the other player.

Shinagawa and Nuida [53] proposed a card-based cryptographic protocol to compute any Boolean functions using a single shuffle by using the garbled circuit technique. The problem definition differs from the above one. Alice and Bob have functions $f_i(x_1, x_2, \ldots, x_n) (i = 1, 2, \ldots, m)$ to compute from input $x_1, x_2, \ldots, x_n$. The inputs are given by cards in a committed manner. The outputs must be given in a committed manner. The number of cards used for each gate is 24.

Tozawa et al. [58] reduced the number of cards. Their protocol uses eight cards for each gate.

First, we show the outline of the computation with no security and the secure protocol shown in [58].

For each two-input logic gate, Alice and Bob prepare a table that represents the relation between the inputs and the output as in Fig. 1, which shows the case of $g_1 = x_1 \oplus x_2$. The first (or second) row has the values when $x_1 = 0$ (or 1), respectively. The first (or second) column has the values when $x_2 = 0$ (or 1), respectively.

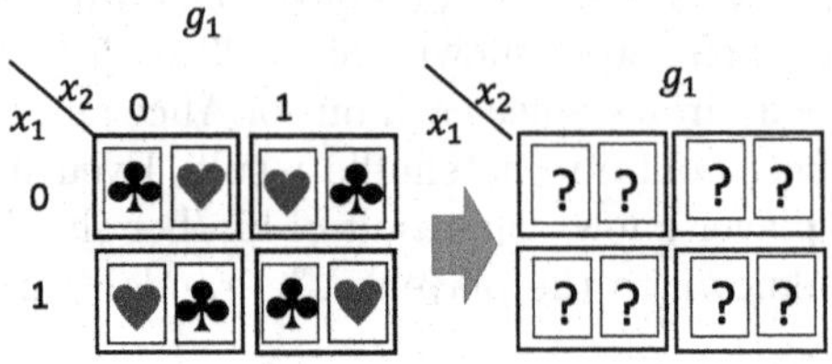

Fig. 1. Table to compute $g_1 = x_1 \oplus x_2$

All the cards are then set to face-down to hide the values of the table. Consider the simple case when x_1, x_2 are private inputs given to the players and $g_1 = x_1 \oplus x_2$ is a final output. The input value x_1 and x_2 are given by face-down cards. The players open the cards and search for the entry that corresponds to the input values. For example, if $x_1 = 1$ (♡♣) and $x_2 = 0$ (♣♡), the entry at the second row and the first column has the result. If the cards are opened, the value is ♡♣, which is the correct result of $x_1 \oplus x_2$. The result is obtained in a committed manner. Further computation of the other gates can be similarly executed. The final output can be obtained in a committed manner.

Since the players open the input values, the security of inputs is not realized. To solve the problem, Alice and Bob randomize the inputs of the tables and input values together. For each garbled table, make two piles P_1 and P_2. $P_1(P_2)$ consists of the first (second) row of the table and the left (right) card of input x_1, respectively. P_1 and P_2 consist of five cards. Alice and Bob execute a pile-scramble shuffle on P_1 and P_2 as in Fig. 2. With probability 1/2, P_1 and P_2 are swapped. With probability 1/2, they are unchanged. After the shuffle, the cards are set back to each position. The result can be represented by a random value $r_1 \in \{0, 1\}$ as follows: the cards that have the input x_1 is changed to $x_1 \oplus r_1$ and the first row of the garbled table has the values when the input is r_1.

Another pile-scramble shuffle is similarly executed for the input x_2 and the two columns of the table, as shown in Fig. 3. The result can be similarly represented by another random value $r_2 \in \{0, 1\}$. The cards that have the input x_2 is changed to $x_2 \oplus r_2$ and the first column of the garbled table has the values when the input is r_2.

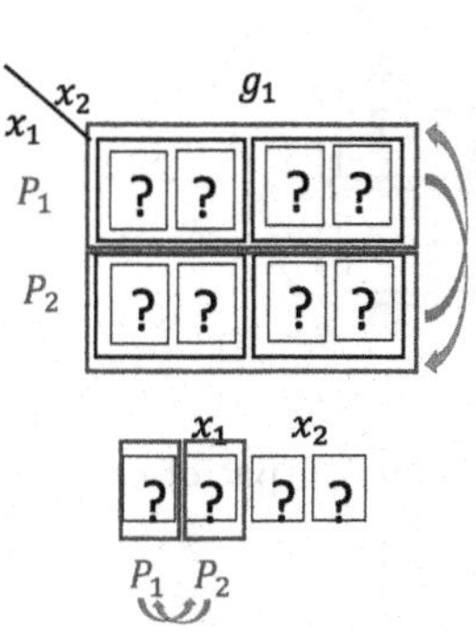

Fig. 2. Randomization for input x_1

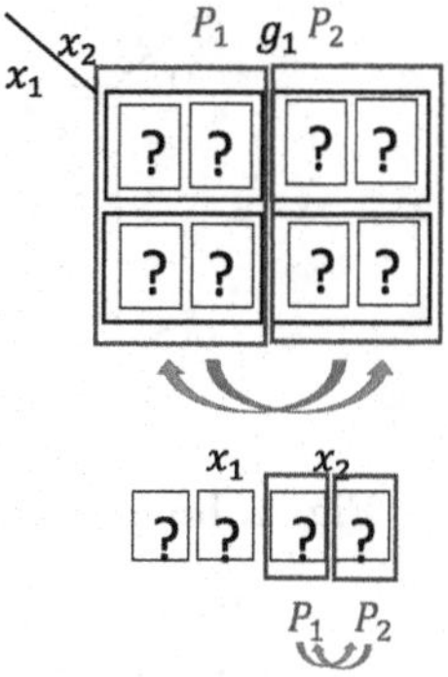

Fig. 3. Randomization for input x_2

When we execute the computation after the pile-scramble shuffles, the players can obtain the correct result of the computation of the gate. For example, consider the case when $x_1 = 1$, $x_2 = 0$, $r_1 = 1$, and $r_2 = 0$. The players see $0 = x_1 \oplus r_1$ and $0 = x_2 \oplus r_2$ when the input cards are opened. Thus the players select the element in the first row and the first column in the table. The result is correct since the entry was initially at the second row and the first column before the shuffles. The security of the input values is achieved because r_1 and r_2 are random values unknown to Alice and Bob.

Note that input x_1 might also be an input of another gate $g_2, g_3, \ldots, g_k$. In this case, when the players make piles P_1 and P_2, the entries of the table for $g_2, g_3, \ldots, g_k$ must also be added.

When the output of g_1 is the final output, the computation is finished and the players obtain the committed result. When the output of g_1 is an input of another gate, further computation is necessary. Let $g'_1, g'_2, \ldots, g'_i$ be the gates that input g_1's output. In this case, since the output cards of g_1 must be opened to select entries of g_j's garbled table, g_1's output value must also be randomized in advance to hide the output value. The randomization of the output must be executed together with the tables of $g'_1, g'_2, \ldots, g'_i$.

For example, Fig. 4 shows the case when the output of g_1 is used as the row input x_3 of gate g_2. Similar to the above case, the players make two piles P_1 and P_2. P_1 (P_2) consist of the left (right) card of each entry of table g_1 and the first (second) row of the table g_2, respectively. Execute a pile-scramble shuffle on P_1 and P_2 and the cards are set back to each position. Using a random value $r \in \{0, 1\}$, the output of g_1 is changed as $g_1 \oplus r$. When the players open the output card of g_1, the players obtain no information about the output since the value is randomized by r. In addition, the computation of g_2 is still correct since the entries of the tables are randomized using the same random value r.

Note that all shuffles of the inputs and table entries are executed in advance to compute.

In summary, the protocol is executed as follows.

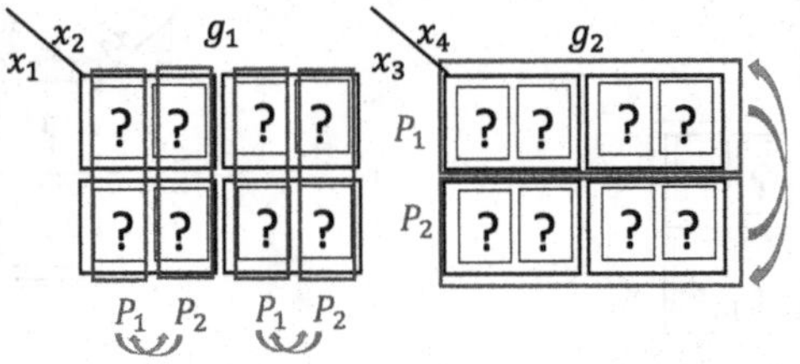

Fig. 4. Randomization when g_2's input x_3 is the output of g_1.

1. Prepare one table for each gate that is used to compute $f_i (i = 1, 2, \ldots, m)$.
2. When a value x (an input value or the output of a garbled table) is used for the row input of gate $g_1, g_2, \ldots, g_k$ and the column input of gate $g'_1, g'_2, \ldots, g'_{k'}$, make two piles P_1 (P_2) with the left (right) card(s) of x, the first (second) row of the garbled table of gate $g_1, g_2, \ldots, g_k$, and the first (second) column of the garbled table of gate $g'_1, g'_2, \ldots, g'_{k'}$, respectively. Execute a pile-scramble shuffle to P_1 and P_2. Set back the cards to the initial positions. Execute the above procedure for every value x that will be opened during computation.
3. For each gate, open (randomized) input cards and select the row and column entry that matches the opened value and obtain the committed output of the gate.
4. The final output cards are not opened and they are used as the result.

Though in this example the cards are set as a 2×2 table, they can also be set as one sequence of cards, for example, the output cards for input (0,0), (0,1) (1,0), and (1,1) can be placed in this order as in [58]. Since the players know each position, they can make two piles to be shuffled using the positions.

Note that any kind and any number of shuffles can be combined into one shuffle [53], thus the total number of shuffles is one. Since the final output must not be randomized, the output must not be used as an input of another gate.

4 Free-XOR in Card-Based Garbled Circuits

Free-XOR [18] is a technique for garbled circuits. It is unnecessary to prepare a garbled table for each XOR gate. This section shows that a garbled table is also unnecessary for XOR gates in the above card-based garbled circuits. Two cards are necessary when the output of an XOR gate is a final output. No cards are necessary when the output of an XOR gate is input to the other gates.

Before showing the protocol, we need to simplify the discussion. We need to eliminate the case when the output of an XOR gate is an input of another XOR gate. The output of an XOR gate $g_1 = x_1 \oplus x_2$ might be used as an input of another XOR gate such as $g_2 = g_1 \oplus x_3$. g_2 can be written as $g_2 = x_1 \oplus x_2 \oplus x_3$ to eliminate the case when the output of an XOR gate is an input of another XOR gate. A similar transformation can be executed when g_2 is also an input of another XOR gate. Thus, the cases to be considered are: the output of an

XOR gate is (1) a final output value or (2) an input of a non-XOR gate, where the number of inputs of the XOR gate is arbitrary (> 1) and the inputs of the XOR gate are not an output of another XOR gate, that is, they are initially-given inputs or outputs of a non-XOR gate. In the above example of g_1 and g_2, when g_2 is the final output and g_1 is an input of a non-XOR gate g_3, we need to compute (1) the output of $g_1 = x_1 \oplus x_2 \oplus x_3$ is a final output and (2) the output of $g_2 = x_1 \oplus x_2$ is an input of non-XOR gate g_3.

Note that the negation of an XOR might be needed. For example, consider the case when the players compute $g_4 = \overline{x_1 \oplus x_2}$. We note that we do not need to consider negation of the XOR gates[1]. As shown above, g_4 is a final output or an input of another non-XOR gate, for example, $g_5 = g_4 \wedge x_3$. In the former case, swap the pair of the cards that have the output $x_1 \oplus x_2$ and we can compute g_4. In the latter case, we can prepare a garbled table for g_5 in which the input of the first element is negated, just as $\bar{x} \wedge x_3$. Thus, we do not need to consider the negation of XOR gates.

Before showing the detail of the protocol, we show the basic idea. In the garbled circuits, every input value must be randomized in advance. Let us consider the case when we compute $g = x_1 \oplus x_2$. x_1 and x_2 are randomized as $x_1 \oplus r_1$ and $x_2 \oplus r_2$ where $r_1, r_2 \in \{0, 1\}$. We prepare one pair of cards G for g, which initially has 0(♣|♡). When x_1 is randomized using r_1, G is included in the randomization. When x_2 is randomized using r_2, G is included in the randomization. G has $r_1 \oplus r_2$ after the randomizations since $0 \oplus r_1 \oplus r_2 = r_1 \oplus r_2$. When the randomized input values, $x_1 \oplus r_1$ and $x_2 \oplus r_2$ are opened, swap G if $(x_1 \oplus r_1) \oplus (x_2 \oplus r_2) = 1$. Since G has $r_1 \oplus r_2$ after the randomizations, the value after the swap is $(r_1 \oplus r_2) \oplus ((x_1 \oplus r_1) \oplus (x_2 \oplus r_2)) = x_1 \oplus x_2$. Thus we can compute g without a garbled table. When the output of g is used as an input of non-XOR gate g', the input rows/columns of g''s garbled table can be used instead of the two cards of G.

First, consider the case when the output of XOR gate g is a final output value. Let $x_1, x_2, \ldots, x_k$ be inputs to compute $g = \bigoplus_{i=1}^{k} x_i$. $x_i (1 \leq i \leq k)$ are initially-given inputs or outputs of non-XOR garbled tables.

The protocol for XOR gate g is the following steps.

- For the computation of g, prepare one pair of cards, denoted as G. Initially, G is ♣|♡ and it is turned into a committed value.
- In Step 2 of the above protocol, when the left card and the right card for value x_i are included in a pile P_1 and P_2, the left card of G is also set into P_1 and the right card of G is also set into P_2 then a pile-scramble shuffle is executed. For each input $x_i (1 \leq i \leq k)$, the above procedure is executed. Figure 5 shows the randomization of $g = x_1 \oplus x_2$, where x_1 and x_2 are input values. Make P_1 (P_2) be the left (right) cards of G and x_1, respectively. Execute a Pile-scramble shuffle to P_1 and P_2. Then, make P'_1 (P'_2) be the left (right) cards of G and x_2, respectively. Execute a Pile-scramble shuffle to P'_1 and P'_2.

[1] By a similar argument, we can see that negation of gates is unnecessary for any gates.

Note that when x_i is an output of a garbled table, P_1 (P_2) consists of the left (right) cards of the garbled table.

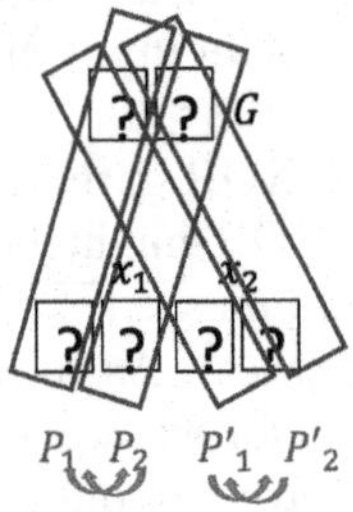

Fig. 5. Randomization of $g = x_1 \oplus x_2$'s input x_1 and x_2.

- When the players compute the gate $g = \bigoplus_{i=1}^{k} x_i$, the appropriate cards that have x_i are opened. Note that the value opened, x'_i, might not be x_i because of the randomization. Swap the two cards of G if the opened values x'_i satisfy $\bigoplus_{i=1}^{k} x'_i = 1$. The final committed pair G is used as the result of $g = \bigoplus_{i=1}^{k} x_i$.

Theorem 1. *The above protocol correctly computes* $g = \bigoplus_{i=1}^{k} x_i$.

Proof. Initially, G has value 0. By the pile-scramble shuffle of input x_i, the value is randomized as $x_i \oplus r_i$ for some $r_i \in \{0, 1\}$. At the same time, G is also randomized using r_i thus the value is changed from 0 to $0 \oplus (\bigoplus_{i=1}^{k} r_i) = \bigoplus_{i=1}^{k} r_i$. When the gate g is computed, cards of the inputs are opened. The opened values are $x_i \oplus r_i$. The two cards of G are swapped if $\bigoplus_{i=1}^{k} (x_i \oplus r_i) = 1$. Thus the value of G is changed from $\bigoplus_{i=1}^{k} r_i$ to $\bigoplus_{i=1}^{k} r_i \oplus (\bigoplus_{i=1}^{k} (x_i \oplus r_i)) = \bigoplus_{i=1}^{k} x_i$. Thus the result is correct. □

Next, consider the case when the output of $g = \bigoplus_{i=1}^{k} x_i$ is used as an input of another gate g'. The following protocol shows the case when g is the row input of g'. The case when g is the column input of g' can be similarly shown.

The protocol for XOR gate g is the following steps.

- For the computation of $g = \bigoplus_{i=1}^{k} x_i$, no cards are prepared. Instead, the cards for the input of g' are used. Suppose that g is the row input of g'.
- In Step 2 of the above protocol, when the left (right) card(s) of value x_i are included in a pile P_1 (P_2), respectively, the first (second) row of the table of g' is also set into P_1 (P_2), respectively. Then a pile-scramble shuffle is executed. For each input $x_i (1 \leq i \leq k)$, the above procedure is executed. Figure 6 shows the randomization of $g = x_1 \oplus x_2$, where x_1 and x_2 are input values and g is

the row input of g'. Make pile P_1 (P_2) by the left (right) card of x_1 and first (second) row of g', respectively. Execute pile-scramble shuffle to P_1 and P_2. Next. make pile P_1' (P_2') by the left (right) card of x_2 and first (second) row of g', respectively.
Note that when x_i is an output of a garbled table, P_1 (P_2) consists of the left (right) cards of the garbled table.

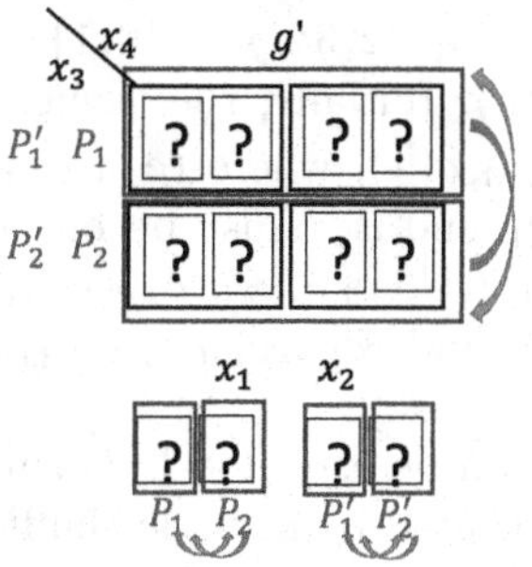

Fig. 6. Randomization of $g = x_1 \oplus x_2$'s input x_1 and x_2 when g is the row input of g'

- When the players compute the gate g', The appropriate cards that have x_i are opened. Note that the value opened, x_i', might not be x_i because of the randomization. The first row is used to compute g' if $\bigoplus_{i=1}^{k} x_i' = 0$. Otherwise, the second row is used. Note that the selection of the column of the garbled table g' is done using the value x_4 (in Fig. 6).

The output g might be inputs of multiple gates $g_1, g_2, \ldots, g_m$. In this case, all appropriate rows or columns of the tables for gate $g_1, g_2, \ldots, g_m$ are included to pile P_1 and P_2 to shuffle each input x_i.

Theorem 2. *The above protocol correctly computes the input value* $g = \bigoplus_{i=1}^{k} x_i$ *of gate* g'.

Proof. This proof assumes that g is the row input of gate g'. The case when g is the column input can be similarly proved. Initially, the first (or second) row of g''s garbled table has the values when the input is 0 (or 1), respectively.

By the pile-scramble shuffle of input x_i, the value is randomized as $x_i \oplus r_i$ for some $r_i \in \{0, 1\}$. At the same time, the rows of g' are also randomized using r_i thus the first row has the values when the input $0 \oplus (\bigoplus_{i=1}^{k} r_i) = \bigoplus_{i=1}^{k} r_i$ is 0. When the gate g' is computed, cards of g's inputs are opened. The opened values are $x_i \oplus r_i$. The players use the first row if $\bigoplus_{i=1}^{k}(x_i \oplus r_i) = 0$, otherwise, they use the second row to compute g'. $\bigoplus_{i=1}^{k}(x_i \oplus r_i) = 0$ implies that $\bigoplus_{i=1}^{k} x_i = \bigoplus_{i=1}^{k} r_i$. Thus, when the players select the first row, the first row has the values when the input $\bigoplus_{i=1}^{k} r_i$ is 0, that is, $\bigoplus_{i=1}^{k} x_i$ is 0. Therefore, the selection is correct. □

We need to show the detail of the shuffle operations. Even in our free-XOR protocol, each single shuffle is the same as the one in the original garbled circuit protocol: for each value x that will be opened during the computation, make two pile P_1 and P_2 and execute a pile-scramble shuffle (swap them or do nothing). It is possible to combine these shuffles into a single shuffle. Note that the combined single shuffle becomes complicated since a pair of cards is included in shuffles of multiple inputs. For example, consider the simple case when $x_3 = x_1 \oplus x_2$ needs to be computed, where x_1, x_2 are inputs and x_3 is the final output. Let $c_{i,j} (i \in \{1,2,3\}, j \in \{0,1\})$ be the cards for x_i, where $(c_{i,0}, c_{i,1})$ has the value of x_i. Initially, the sequence of these cards are written as $(c_{1,0}, c_{1,1}, c_{2,0}, c_{2,1}, c_{3,0}, c_{3,1})$, where $(c_{3,0}, c_{3,1})$ = (♣|♡). The result of the combined shuffle for x_1 and x_2 must be one of the following sequences: $(c_{1,0}, c_{1,1}, c_{2,0}, c_{2,1}, c_{3,0}, c_{3,1})$, $(c_{1,1}, c_{1,0}, c_{2,0}, c_{2,1}, c_{3,1}, c_{3,0})$, $(c_{1,0}, c_{1,1}, c_{2,1}, c_{2,0}, c_{3,1}, c_{3,0})$, and $(c_{1,1}, c_{1,0}, c_{2,1}, c_{2,0}, c_{3,0}, c_{3,1})$. The probability of each result is $1/4$.

However, these shuffles can be executed by a single shuffle since any combination of shuffles can be executed by a single shuffle [53]. The combined single shuffle is uniform and closed since each shuffle swaps two elements by the probability of $1/2$. The single shuffle can be executed with additional cards using the technique in [49]. Note that for the single shuffles for the garbled circuits in [53] and [58], no method to execute the shuffles only using human hands is known so far, thus additional cards are necessary to execute the shuffles.

The number of cards used by the protocol is $8g_1 + 2g_2 + 2n$, where g_1 is the number of non-XOR gates and g_2 is the number of XOR gates whose output is a final output.

5 Eliminating Restriction for Outputs

As shown above, the Shinagawa-Nuida protocol has a restriction that the output values cannot be used for inputs to the other circuits. This section discusses eliminating the restriction.

This section discusses the functions in the following form:

$$f_i(x_1, x_2, \ldots, x_n, f_1, f_2, \ldots, f_{i-1})(i = 1, 2, \ldots, m)$$

The definition considers the outputs $f_1, f_2, \ldots, f_{i-1}$ can be used as inputs of f_i. It is unnecessary to use the outputs of some functions as inputs of another function, but it might reduce the number of logic gates. For example, consider the case when we need to compute $f_1 = x_1 \vee x_2$ and $f_2 = (x_1 \vee x_2) \wedge x_3$. We can compute f_2 by $f_2 = f_1 \wedge x_3$.

Note that $f_j (j > i)$ cannot be used in f_i to avoid circular definition such as $f_2 = f_1 \wedge x_1$ and $f_1 = f_2 \wedge x_2$.

In the garbled circuits, each input of a gate must be randomized because the input cards are opened and the value is known to the players. On the other hand, the output value must not be randomized. Thus, Shinagawa and Nuida added the restriction that output cannot be used as an input of another gate. There are two ways to eliminate this restriction. The first technique is preparing cards for a non-randomized value and the second one is undoing randomization.

Before showing the technique, let us consider the case when the output of an XOR gate g is the final output. As shown in the previous section, no additional cards are necessary to input the output of g to a non-XOR gate or another XOR gate. Thus, we discuss the case when the output of a non-XOR gate is a final output.

The first technique is simple. If the output of a gate is a final output and input of another gate, prepare two pairs of each output value in the garbled table as in Fig. 7, where $g_{i,O}$ are cards for the output and $g_{i,I}$ are cards for the input of gate $g'_1, g'_2, \ldots, g'_k$. When $g'_1, g'_2, \ldots, g'_k$'s inputs are simultaneously randomized, $g_{i,I}$ are included in the randomization, but $g_{i,O}$ are not included. Note that $g_{i,O}$ are included in the shuffles of the rows or columns of the table of g_i. The values in $g_{i,O}$ are used as the final output, and the values in $g_{i,I}$ are used for the garbled table lookup. Since the value $g_{i,O}$ are not randomized, $g_{i,O}$ can be used as the output. Since the values in $g_{i,I}$ are randomized, $g_{i,I}$ can be opened for the garbled table lookup.

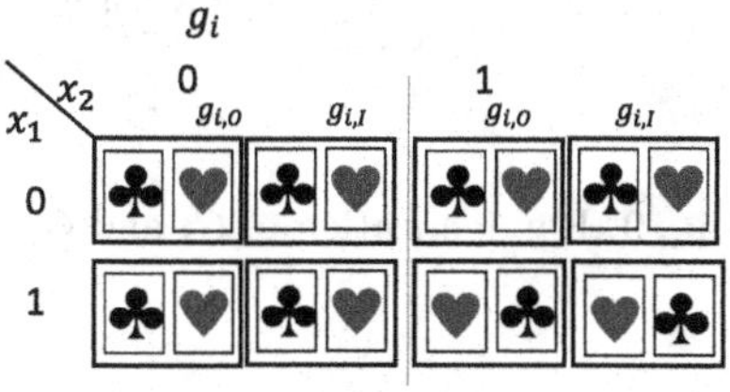

Fig. 7. Table for output gate g_i

The second technique is undoing randomization, whose basic idea is just the same as the one in free-XOR. If an output of a gate g_i is a final output and an input of another gate, prepare one pair of cards O_i whose initial value is ♣♡. The cards are set face-down. The change of the protocol is as follows.

- In Step 2 of the above protocol, when the left (right) card of the output of gate g_i are included in a pile P_1 (P_2), respectively, the left (right) card of O_i is also set into P_1 (P_2), respectively. Then a pile-scramble shuffle is executed. For example, O_i for gate g_i and their randomization is shown in Fig. 8.
- During the computation of gate g_i, one pair of cards, G_i, is selected as the output and opened because the value is used as an input of another gate. After the computation is finished, the cards for G_i are turned face-down.
- Make pile $P_{i,1}$ ($P_{i,2}$) that consists of the left (right) cards of O_i and G_i, respectively. Execute a pile-scramble shuffle on $P_{i,1}$ and $P_{i,2}$, as in Fig. 9, which shows the case when the output is the second row and the second column.

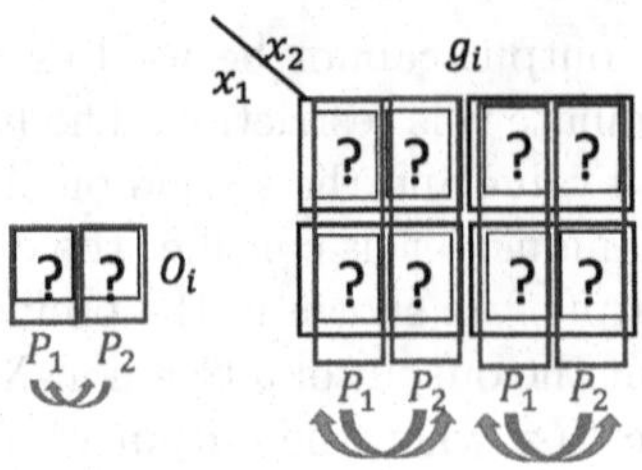

Fig. 8. O_i for output of gate g_i and randomization.

Open O_i and swap two cards of G_i if O_i has value 1, as shown in Fig. 10. G_i is used as a final output.

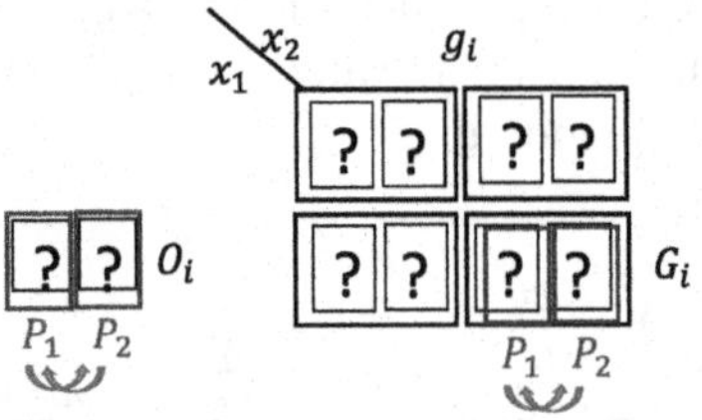

Fig. 9. Randomization of G_i and O_i.

Theorem 3. *The above protocol is secure and correctly outputs g_i.*

Proof. During the randomization of the output value of g_i, O_i is also randomized. The value that the output card G_i has is $g_i \oplus r_i$ for some unknown random value r_i. At the same time, the cards O_i have r_i since $0 \oplus r_i = r_i$. After G_i is turned face-down again, G_i and O_i are randomized using a random value $r'_i \in \{0, 1\}$. G_i has $g_i \oplus r_i \oplus r'_i$ and O_i has $r_i \oplus r'_i$. Then the players open O_i and swap the two cards of G_i if $O_i = 1$. The output is correct since G_i has $g_i \oplus r_i \oplus r'_i \oplus (r_i \oplus r'_i) = g_i$.

The protocol is secure since the players see $g_i \oplus r_i$ and $r_i \oplus r'_i$. The value g_i cannot be known from these values. □

Since the randomization of output G_i must be executed after the garbled table lookup, two shuffles are necessary for the total. Note that the shuffles for each O_i are combined into one shuffle.

The first technique needs eight cards for each output. The number of shuffles is one. The second technique needs two cards for each output, though the number of shuffles becomes two.

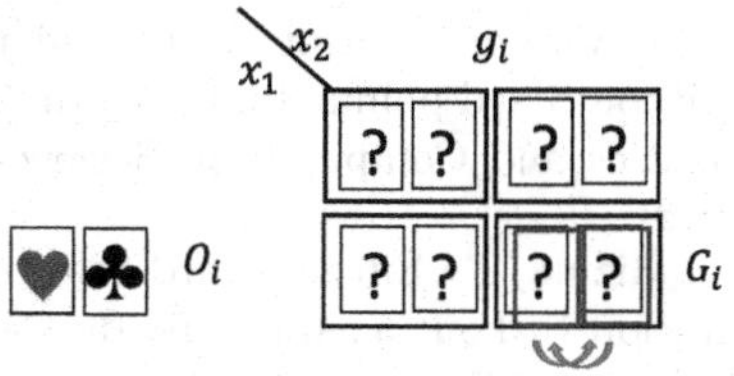

Fig. 10. Computation of the output using G_i and O_i.

6 Conclusion

This paper showed the free-XOR technique in card-based garbled circuits. The number of cards is reduced though the shuffle becomes complicated. This paper then showed techniques to eliminate the restriction that an output value cannot be used as an input of another gate. The remaining problem includes executing the combined single shuffle efficiently.

References

1. Abe, Y., et al.: Efficient card-based majority voting protocols. N. Gener. Comput. **40**(1), 173–198 (2022)
2. Abe, Y., Hayashi, Y.I., Mizuki, T., Sone, H.: Five-card and computations in committed format using only uniform cyclic shuffles. New Gener. Comput. **39**(1), 97–114 (2021)
3. Abe, Y., Mizuki, T., Sone, H.: Committed-format and protocol using only random cuts. Nat. Comput. **20**, 63–645 (2021)
4. Cheung, E., Hawthorne, C., Lee, P.: Cs 758 project: secure computation with playing cards (2013). http://cdchawthorne.com/writings/secure_playing_cards.pdf
5. den Boer, B.: More efficient match-making and satisfiability *the five card trick*. In: Quisquater, J.-J., Vandewalle, J. (eds.) EUROCRYPT 1989. LNCS, vol. 434, pp. 208–217. Springer, Heidelberg (1990). https://doi.org/10.1007/3-540-46885-4_23
6. Dvořák, P., Koucký, M.: Barrington plays cards: the complexity of card-based protocols. arXiv preprint arXiv:2010.08445 (2020)
7. Francis, D., Aljunid, S.R., Nishida, T., Hayashi, Y., Mizuki, T., Sone, H.: Necessary and sufficient numbers of cards for securely computing two-bit output functions. In: Phan, R.C.-W., Yung, M. (eds.) Mycrypt 2016. LNCS, vol. 10311, pp. 193–211. Springer, Cham (2017). https://doi.org/10.1007/978-3-319-61273-7_10
8. Hanaoka, G., et al.: Physical and visual cryptography to accelerate social implementation of advanced cryptographic technologies. IEICE Trans. Fundam. Electron. Commun. Comput. Sci. 214–228 (2023). (In Japanese)
9. Hashimoto, Y., Nuida, K., Shinagawa, K., Inamura, M., Hanaoka, G.: Toward finite-runtime card-based protocol for generating hidden random permutation without fixed points. IEICE Trans. Fundam. Electron. Commun. Comput. Sci. **101**-A(9), 1503–1511 (2018)
10. Hashimoto, Y., Shinagawa, K., Nuida, K., Inamura, M., Hanaoka, G.: Secure grouping protocol using a deck of cards. IEICE Trans. Fundam. Electron. Commun. Comput. Sci. **101**(9), 1512–1524 (2018)

11. Ibaraki, T., Manabe, Y.: A more efficient card-based protocol for generating a random permutation without fixed points. In: Proceedings of the 3rd International Conference on Mathematics and Computers in Sciences and in Industry (MCSI 2016), pp. 252–257 (2016)
12. Ishikawa, R., Chida, E., Mizuki, T.: Efficient card-based protocols for generating a hidden random permutation without fixed points. In: Calude, C.S., Dinneen, M.J. (eds.) UCNC 2015. LNCS, vol. 9252, pp. 215–226. Springer, Cham (2015). https://doi.org/10.1007/978-3-319-21819-9_16
13. Isuzugawa, R., Toyoda, K., Sasaki, Yu., Miyahara, D., Mizuki, T.: A card-minimal three-input and protocol using two shuffles. In: Chen, C.-Y., Hon, W.-K., Hung, L.-J., Lee, C.-W. (eds.) COCOON 2021. LNCS, vol. 13025, pp. 668–679. Springer, Cham (2021). https://doi.org/10.1007/978-3-030-89543-3_55
14. Kastner, J., et al.: The minimum number of cards in practical card-based protocols. In: Takagi, T., Peyrin, T. (eds.) ASIACRYPT 2017. LNCS, vol. 10626, pp. 126–155. Springer, Cham (2017). https://doi.org/10.1007/978-3-319-70700-6_5
15. Koch, A.: The landscape of optimal card-based protocols. Math. Cryptology **1**(2), 115–131 (2021)
16. Koch, A., Walzer, S.: Private function evaluation with cards. N. Gener. Comput. **40**(1), 115–147 (2022)
17. Koch, A., Walzer, S., Härtel, K.: Card-based cryptographic protocols using a minimal number of cards. In: Iwata, T., Cheon, J.H. (eds.) ASIACRYPT 2015. LNCS, vol. 9452, pp. 783–807. Springer, Heidelberg (2015). https://doi.org/10.1007/978-3-662-48797-6_32
18. Kolesnikov, V., Schneider, T.: Improved garbled circuit: free XOR gates and applications. In: Aceto, L., Damgård, I., Goldberg, L.A., Halldórsson, M.M., Ingólfsdóttir, A., Walukiewicz, I. (eds.) ICALP 2008. LNCS, vol. 5126, pp. 486–498. Springer, Heidelberg (2008). https://doi.org/10.1007/978-3-540-70583-3_40
19. Koyama, H., Toyoda, K., Miyahara, D., Mizuki, T.: New card-based copy protocols using only random cuts. In: Proceedings of the 8th ACM on ASIA Public-Key Cryptography Workshop, pp. 13–22. APKC 2021, Association for Computing Machinery, New York, NY, USA (2021)
20. Kuzuma, T., Isuzugawa, R., Toyoda, K., Miyahara, D., Mizuki, T.: Card-based single-shuffle protocols for secure multiple-input and and XOR computations. In: Proceedings of the 9th ACM on ASIA Public-Key Cryptography Workshop, pp. 51–58 (2022)
21. Manabe, Y., Ono, H.: Card-based cryptographic protocols for three-input functions using private operations. In: Flocchini, P., Moura, L. (eds.) IWOCA 2021. LNCS, vol. 12757, pp. 469–484. Springer, Cham (2021). https://doi.org/10.1007/978-3-030-79987-8_33
22. Manabe, Y., Ono, H.: Card-based cryptographic protocols with a standard deck of cards using private operations. In: Cerone, A., Ölveczky, P.C. (eds.) ICTAC 2021. LNCS, vol. 12819, pp. 256–274. Springer, Cham (2021). https://doi.org/10.1007/978-3-030-85315-0_15
23. Marcedone, A., Wen, Z., Shi, E.: Secure dating with four or fewer cards. In: IACR Cryptology ePrint Archive, Report 2015/1031 (2015)
24. Miyahara, D., Hayashi, Y.I., Mizuki, T., Sone, H.: Practical card-based implementations of Yao's millionaire protocol. Theoret. Comput. Sci. **803**, 207–221 (2020)
25. Miyahara, D., Ueda, I., Hayashi, Y.I., Mizuki, T., Sone, H.: Evaluating card-based protocols in terms of execution time. Int. J. Inf. Secur. **20**(5), 729–740 (2021)
26. Miyamoto, K., Shinagawa, K.: Graph automorphism shuffles from pile-scramble shuffles. N. Gener. Comput. **40**(1), 199–223 (2022)

27. Mizuki, T.: Applications of card-based cryptography to education. In: IEICE Technical Report ISEC2016-53, pp. 13–17 (2016). (In Japanese)
28. Mizuki, T.: Card-based protocols for securely computing the conjunction of multiple variables. Theoret. Comput. Sci. **622**, 34–44 (2016)
29. Mizuki, T., Asiedu, I.K., Sone, H.: Voting with a logarithmic number of cards. In: Mauri, G., Dennunzio, A., Manzoni, L., Porreca, A.E. (eds.) UCNC 2013. LNCS, vol. 7956, pp. 162–173. Springer, Heidelberg (2013). https://doi.org/10.1007/978-3-642-39074-6_16
30. Mizuki, T., Kumamoto, M., Sone, H.: The five-card trick can be done with four cards. In: Wang, X., Sako, K. (eds.) ASIACRYPT 2012. LNCS, vol. 7658, pp. 598–606. Springer, Heidelberg (2012). https://doi.org/10.1007/978-3-642-34961-4_36
31. Mizuki, T., Shizuya, H.: A formalization of card-based cryptographic protocols via abstract machine. Int. J. Inf. Secur. **13**(1), 15–23 (2014)
32. Mizuki, T., Shizuya, H.: Computational model of card-based cryptographic protocols and its applications. IEICE Trans. Fundam. Electron. Commun. Comput. Sci. **100**(1), 3–11 (2017)
33. Mizuki, T., Sone, H.: Six-card secure AND and four-card secure XOR. In: Deng, X., Hopcroft, J.E., Xue, J. (eds.) FAW 2009. LNCS, vol. 5598, pp. 358–369. Springer, Heidelberg (2009). https://doi.org/10.1007/978-3-642-02270-8_36
34. Murata, S., Miyahara, D., Mizuki, T., Sone, H.: Efficient generation of a card-based uniformly distributed random derangement. In: Uehara, R., Hong, S.-H., Nandy, S.C. (eds.) WALCOM 2021. LNCS, vol. 12635, pp. 78–89. Springer, Cham (2021). https://doi.org/10.1007/978-3-030-68211-8_7
35. Nakai, T., Misawa, Y., Tokushige, Y., Iwamoto, M., Ohta, K.: How to solve millionaires' problem with two kinds of cards. N. Gener. Comput. **39**(1), 73–96 (2021)
36. Nakai, T., Shirouchi, S., Iwamoto, M., Ohta, K.: Four cards are sufficient for a card-based three-input voting protocol utilizing private permutations. In: Shikata, J. (ed.) ICITS 2017. LNCS, vol. 10681, pp. 153–165. Springer, Cham (2017). https://doi.org/10.1007/978-3-319-72089-0_9
37. Nakai, T., Shirouchi, S., Tokushige, Y., Iwamoto, M., Ohta, K.: Secure computation for threshold functions with physical cards: power of private permutations. N. Gener. Comput. **40**(1), 95–113 (2022)
38. Nishida, T., Hayashi, Y., Mizuki, T., Sone, H.: Card-based protocols for any Boolean function. In: Jain, R., Jain, S., Stephan, F. (eds.) TAMC 2015. LNCS, vol. 9076, pp. 110–121. Springer, Cham (2015). https://doi.org/10.1007/978-3-319-17142-5_11
39. Nishida, T., Hayashi, Y., Mizuki, T., Sone, H.: Securely computing three-input functions with eight cards. IEICE Trans. Fundam. Electron. Commun. Comput. Sci. **98**(6), 1145–1152 (2015)
40. Nishida, T., Mizuki, T., Sone, H.: Securely computing the three-input majority function with eight cards. In: Dediu, A.-H., Martín-Vide, C., Truthe, B., Vega-Rodríguez, M.A. (eds.) TPNC 2013. LNCS, vol. 8273, pp. 193–204. Springer, Heidelberg (2013). https://doi.org/10.1007/978-3-642-45008-2_16
41. Nishimura, A., Hayashi, Y.I., Mizuki, T., Sone, H.: Pile-shifting scramble for card-based protocols. IEICE Trans. Fundam. Electron. Commun. Comput. Sci. **101**(9), 1494–1502 (2018)
42. Nishimura, A., Nishida, T., Hayashi, Y., Mizuki, T., Sone, H.: Card-based protocols using unequal division shuffles. Soft. Comput. **22**(2), 361–371 (2018)
43. Ono, H., Manabe, Y.: Efficient card-based cryptographic protocols for the millionaires' problem using private input operations. In: Proceedings of the 13th Asia Joint Conference on Information Security(AsiaJCIS 2018), pp. 23–28 (2018)

44. Ono, H., Manabe, Y.: Card-based cryptographic logical computations using private operations. N. Gener. Comput. **39**(1), 19–40 (2021)
45. Ono, H., Manabe, Y.: Minimum round card-based cryptographic protocols using private operations. Cryptography **5**(3), 17 (2021)
46. Ono, T., Nakai, T., Watanabe, Y., Iwamoto, M.: An efficient card-based protocol of any Boolean circuit using private operations. In: Proceedings of the Computer Security Symposium, pp. 72–77 (2022). (In Japanese)
47. Ruangwises, S., Itoh, T.: AND protocols using only uniform shuffles. In: van Bevern, R., Kucherov, G. (eds.) CSR 2019. LNCS, vol. 11532, pp. 349–358. Springer, Cham (2019). https://doi.org/10.1007/978-3-030-19955-5_30
48. Ruangwises, S., Itoh, T.: Securely computing the n-variable equality function with 2n cards. Theoret. Comput. Sci. **887**, 99–110 (2021)
49. Saito, T., Miyahara, D., Abe, Y., Mizuki, T., Shizuya, H.: How to implement a non-uniform or non-closed shuffle. In: Martín-Vide, C., Vega-Rodríguez, M.A., Yang, M.-S. (eds.) TPNC 2020. LNCS, vol. 12494, pp. 107–118. Springer, Cham (2020). https://doi.org/10.1007/978-3-030-63000-3_9
50. Shinagawa, K., Miyamoto, K.: Automorphism shuffles for graphs and hypergraphs and its applications. arXiv preprint arXiv:2205.04774 (2022)
51. Shinagawa, K., Mizuki, T.: The six-card trick: secure computation of three-input equality. In: Lee, K. (ed.) ICISC 2018. LNCS, vol. 11396, pp. 123–131. Springer, Cham (2019). https://doi.org/10.1007/978-3-030-12146-4_8
52. Shinagawa, K., Mizuki, T.: Secure computation of any Boolean function based on any deck of cards. In: Chen, Y., Deng, X., Lu, M. (eds.) FAW 2019. LNCS, vol. 11458, pp. 63–75. Springer, Cham (2019). https://doi.org/10.1007/978-3-030-18126-0_6
53. Shinagawa, K., Nuida, K.: A single shuffle is enough for secure card-based computation of any Boolean circuit. Discret. Appl. Math. **289**, 248–261 (2021)
54. Shinoda, Y., Miyahara, D., Shinagawa, K., Mizuki, T., Sone, H.: Card-based covert lottery. In: Maimut, D., Oprina, A.-G., Sauveron, D. (eds.) SecITC 2020. LNCS, vol. 12596, pp. 257–270. Springer, Cham (2021). https://doi.org/10.1007/978-3-030-69255-1_17
55. Takashima, K., et al.: Card-based protocols for secure ranking computations. Theoret. Comput. Sci. **845**, 122–135 (2020)
56. Toyoda, K., Miyahara, D., Mizuki, T.: Another use of the five-card trick: card-minimal secure three-input majority function evaluation. In: Adhikari, A., Küsters, R., Preneel, B. (eds.) INDOCRYPT 2021. LNCS, vol. 13143, pp. 536–555. Springer, Cham (2021). https://doi.org/10.1007/978-3-030-92518-5_24
57. Toyoda, K., Miyahara, D., Mizuki, T., Sone, H.: Six-card finite-runtime XOR protocol with only random cut. In: Proceedings of the 7th ACM Workshop on ASIA Public-Key Cryptography, pp. 2–8 (2020)
58. Tozawa, K., Morita, H., Mizuki, T.: Single-shuffle card-based protocol with eight cards per gate. In: Genova, D., Kari, J. (eds.) UCNC 2023. LNCS, vol. 14003, pp. 171–185. Springer, Cham (2023). https://doi.org/10.1007/978-3-031-34034-5_12
59. Ueda, I., Miyahara, D., Nishimura, A., Hayashi, Y.I., Mizuki, T., Sone, H.: Secure implementations of a random bisection cut. Int. J. Inf. Secur. **19**(4), 445–452 (2020)
60. Watanabe, Y., Kuroki, Y., Suzuki, S., Koga, Y., Iwamoto, M., Ohta, K.: Card-based majority voting protocols with three inputs using three cards. In: Proceedings of the 2018 International Symposium on Information Theory and Its Applications (ISITA), pp. 218–222. IEEE (2018)
61. Yao, A.C.C.: How to generate and exchange secrets. In: 27th Annual Symposium on Foundations of Computer Science (SFCS 1986), pp. 162–167. IEEE (1986)

Cryptanalysis

Hidden Stream Ciphers and TMTO Attacks on TLS 1.3, DTLS 1.3, QUIC, and Signal

John Preuß Mattsson(✉)

Ericsson Research, Stockholm, Sweden
john.mattsson@ericsson.com

Abstract. Transport Layer Security (TLS) 1.3 and the Signal protocol are very important and widely used security protocols. We show that the key update function in TLS 1.3 and the symmetric key ratchet in Signal can be modeled as non-additive synchronous stream ciphers. This means that the efficient Time Memory Tradeoff Attacks for stream ciphers can be applied. The implication is that TLS 1.3, QUIC, DTLS 1.3, and Signal offer a lower security level against TMTO attacks than expected from the key sizes. We provide detailed analyses of the key update mechanisms in TLS 1.3 and Signal, illustrate the importance of ephemeral key exchange, and show that the process that DTLS 1.3 and QUIC use to calculate AEAD limits is flawed. We provide many concrete recommendations for the analyzed protocols.

Keywords: TLS 1.3 · QUIC · DTLS 1.3 · Signal · Secret-key Cryptography · Key Derivation · Ratchet · Key Chain · Stream Cipher · Key Space · TMTO

1 Introduction

Transport Layer Security (TLS) is the single most important security protocol in the information and communications technology industry. The latest version, TLS 1.3 [26] is already widely deployed and is the default version on the Web and in many other industries. Several other very important protocols such as QUIC [16], EAP-TLS 1.3 [25], DTLS 1.3 [28], DTLS-SRTP [20], and DTLS/SCTP [32] are based on the TLS 1.3 handshake. The US National Institute of Standards and Technology (NIST) requires support for TLS 1.3 by January 1, 2024 [21]. Two nodes that support TLS 1.3 will never negotiate the obsolete TLS 1.2.

The Signal protocol [31] is very popular for end-to-end encryption of voice calls and instant messaging conversations. In addition to the Signal messaging service itself, the Signal protocol is used in WhatsApp, Meta Messenger, and Android Messages. The Signal messaging service is approved for use by the U.S. Senate and is recommended for the staff at the European Commission.

For efficient forward secure symmetric rekeying without Diffie-Hellman, TLS 1.3 and the Signal protocol use symmetric key ratchets in which a deterministic Key Derivation Function (KDF) $H()$ is frequently used to update and replace

J. Deng et al. (Eds.): CANS 2023, LNCS 14342, pp. 251–267, 2023.
https://doi.org/10.1007/978-981-99-7563-1_12

the current key $k = H(k)$. In Sect. 3 we show that the key update function in TLS 1.3 and the symmetric key ratchet in Signal can be modeled as non-additive synchronous stream ciphers. This means that the efficient Time Memory Tradeoff Attacks for stream ciphers can be applied [3,8]. The implication is that TLS 1.3, QUIC, DTLS 1.3, and Signal offer a lower security level against TMTO attacks than expected from the key sizes. In Sects. 4 and 5 we provide detailed analyses of the key update mechanisms in TLS 1.3 and Signal, illustrate the importance of ephemeral key exchange, and show that the process that DTLS 1.3 and QUIC use to calculate AEAD limits is flawed. We provide many concrete recommendations for the analyzed protocols. The upcoming revisions of the TLS 1.3 protocol [27] and DTLS/SCTP [33] have already been updated based on this work, see Sect. 5.2.

2 Preliminaries

2.1 Signal Protocol and the Symmetric-Key Ratchet

The Signal protocol [7,9,31] consists of the Extended Triple Diffie-Hellman (X3DH) key agreement protocol and the Double Ratchet algorithm. The Double Ratchet algorithm consists of a symmetric-key ratchet and a Diffie-Hellman ratchet. After the X3DH handshake is finished and at least one step of the Double Ratchet has been performed, a 256-bit initial chain key k_0 is derived (to simplify things we only discuss one of the directions). A chain of keys $k_0, k_1, k_2 \ldots$ derived from the initial chain key k_0 are used to protect all future messages sent in one direction until the Diffie-Hellman ratchet is used again. Message i is encrypted using a 256-bit message key K_i and an AEAD algorithm without nonce. Each message key K_i is only used once. The associated data contains identity information for both parties.

Before each message is sent, the message key and the next chain key are computed using the symmetric-key ratchet [31]. The message key K_i and the next chain key k_{i+1} are computed using a Key Derivation Function (KDF) as

$$\begin{aligned} K_i &= H'(k_i) = \mathrm{KDF}(k_i, label_1, n_2) \ , \\ k_{i+1} &= H(k_i) = \mathrm{KDF}(k_i, label_2, n) \ . \end{aligned} \tag{1}$$

Shortly after the symmetric-key ratchet, the old chain key k_i is deleted, which gives forward secrecy. Compromise of k_{i+1} does not allow an attacker to calculate k_i. The Signal Protocol does not mandate any specific KDF and labels but recommends HMAC-SHA256 or HMAC-SHA512 and suggests 0x01 and 0x02. The Signal Protocol does not mandate any specific AEAD algorithm but recommends AES-256-CBC with HMAC-SHA256 or HMAC-SHA512. Irrespectively of the used algorithms, the size n of the chain keys and the size n_2 of the message key are always 256 bits, i.e.,

$$n = n_2 = 256 \ . \tag{2}$$

Signal mandates that the symmetric-key ratchet is used for each message. When to use the Diffie-Hellman ratchet to derive a new initial chain key k_0 is left for the implementation. The Signal technical specification [31] does not give any recommendations or limits. Deriving a new initial chain key k_0 for each message or never deriving any new chain keys are both allowed according to the specification but the Double Ratchet algorithm is designed for quite frequent use of ephemeral Diffie-Hellman. Part of an example Double Ratchet key hierarchy is shown in Fig. 1.

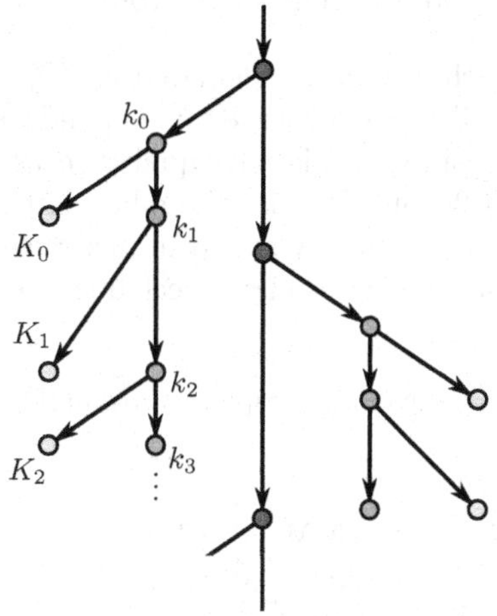

Fig. 1. Part of an example Double Ratchet key hierarchy.

2.2 TLS 1.3 and the Key Update Mechanism

TLS 1.3 [26] consists of a handshake protocol based on the theoretical SIGMA-I protocol [18] and a record protocol. After the TLS handshake is finished an initial traffic secret k_0 = application_traffic_secret_0 is derived (to simplify things we only discuss one of the directions). A chain of keys $k_0, k_1, k_2 \dots$ derived from the initial traffic secret k_0 are used by the record protocol to protect all future messages sent in one direction over the connection including application data, post-handshake messages, and alerts. The size of the traffic secrets depends on the output size n of the hash function in the selected cipher suite. The five initial TLS 1.3 cipher suites registered by the TLS 1.3 specification [26] are listed in Table 1. As there are two senders (client and server) each connection has two traffic secrets, one for each direction. For the rest of the connection, the keys in the two directions are independent of each other and in the rest of the paper we will only discuss one of the directions.

Once the handshake is complete, it is possible to update the traffic secret using the key update mechanism. The next traffic secret k_{i+1} is computed using a KDF based on HKDF-Expand [17] as

$$k_{i+1} = H(k_i) = \mathrm{KDF}(k_i, \text{"traffic upd"}, n) \ . \quad (3)$$

Shortly after key update, the old traffic secret k_i is deleted, which gives forward secrecy. Compromise of k_{i+1} does not allow an attacker to calculate k_i. The TLS 1.3 record protocol only uses ciphers with an Authenticated Encryption with Associated Data (AEAD) interface. The AEAD key K_i and initialization vector IV_i are derived from k_i as

$$\begin{aligned} K_i &= \text{KDF}(k_i, \text{"key"}, n_2) \ , \\ IV_i &= \text{KDF}(k_i, \text{"iv"}, 96) \ . \end{aligned} \tag{4}$$

The AEAD nonce for each record is calculated as IV_i XOR S where S is the record sequence number. The size of the key K_i depends on the AEAD key length n_2 in the selected cipher suite and is not equal to n as in the Signal Protocol. The size of the nonce is 96 bits for all the cipher suites listed in Table 1. The 64-bit sequence number S is initially set to 0, increased for each message, and then reset to 0 every time the key update mechanism is used.

Table 1. The five initial cipher suites in TLS 1.3 [26]

Cipher suite	n	n_2
TLS_AES_128_GCM_SHA256	256	128
TLS_AES_256_GCM_SHA384	384	256
TLS_CHACHA20_POLY1305_SHA256	256	256
TLS_AES_128_CCM_SHA256	256	128
TLS_AES_128_CCM_8_SHA256	256	128

A single AEAD key K_i is typically used to protect many record protocol messages. For each cipher suite, TLS 1.3 has a limit for the number of encryption queries q. Key update is recommended before the limit is reached (every $2^{24.5}$ records for AES-GCM), see Sect. 5.5 of [26]. Frequent use of the key update mechanism is therefore expected in connections where a large amount of data is transferred. TLS 1.3 does not restrict the number of key updates.

DTLS 1.3. Datagram Transport Layer Security (DTLS) 1.3 [28] is a datagram security protocol that uses the TLS 1.3 handshake and cipher suites. The only change to the key update mechanism is that DTLS 1.3 restricts the number of key updates to 2^{48}. DTLS 1.3 also increases the requirements on key usage limits to apply to both the sending and receiving side, i.e., key update is recommended based on both the number of encryption queries q and the number of failed decryption queries v.

QUIC. QUIC [16] is a general-purpose transport layer protocol with built in security used in e.g., HTTP/3. QUIC uses the TLS 1.3 handshake and cipher suites. Key update and key derivation are done in the same way as Eqs. (3) and (4) but with the labels "quic ku", "quic key", and "quic iv" and that both directions always do a key update at the same time instead of independently as in TLS 1.3 and DTLS 1.3. QUIC does not restrict the number of key updates. QUIC has similar key usage limits and requirements as DTLS 1.3.

3 Hidden Stream Ciphers and TMTO Attacks

3.1 Synchronous Stream Ciphers

As described in e.g., [19] the keystream z_i in a synchronous stream cipher depends only on the initial state σ_0 and the position i but is independent of the plaintexts p and the ciphertexts c. The output cycle of a synchronous stream cipher can be described by the equations

$$\begin{aligned} \sigma_{i+1} &= f(\sigma_i) \ , \\ z_i &= g(\sigma_i) \ , \\ c_i &= h(z_i, p_i) \ , \end{aligned} \tag{5}$$

where σ_0 is the initial state, f is the next-state (or update) function, g is the output function, and h is the function used to combine the keystream with the plaintext. In a binary additive stream cipher the function h is the exclusive or function (XOR). The schematic can be seen in Fig. 2.

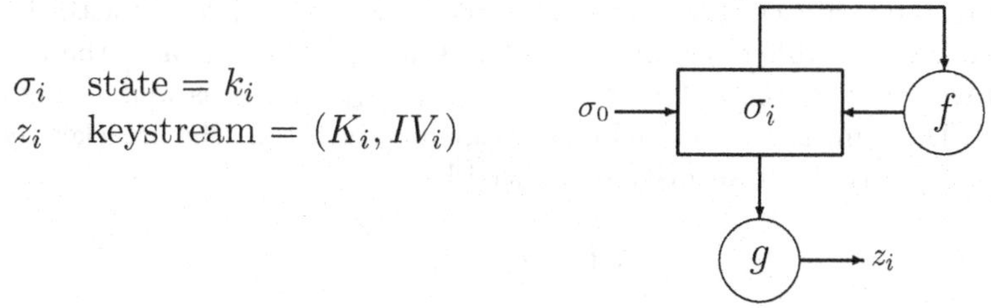

Fig. 2. Initiation and output cycle of a synchronous stream cipher.

It turns out that the symmetric-key ratchet in Signal [31] and the key update mechanism in TLS 1.3 [26] can be modeled as such (non-additive) synchronous stream ciphers. The initial internal state is k_0, the next-state function $k_{i+1} = H(k_i)$ modifies the inner state, the output function $z_i = (K_i, IV_i) = g(k_i)$ uses the inner state to produce "keystream" z_0, z_1, ..., and the ciphertexts are a function $c_i = h(z_i, p_i)$ of "keystream" and plaintext, where p_i is all the application data encrypted with the key K_i.

3.2 Time Memory Trade-Off Attacks

Stream ciphers with internal states are vulnerable to Time Memory Trade-Off (TMTO) attacks. There are various TMTO attacks on synchronous stream ciphers such as Babbage-Golić [3] and Biryukov-Shamir [8]. These attacks take advantage of the internal state and apply to the Signal symmetric-key ratchet and the TLS 1.3 key update as well. TMTO attacks allow an attacker to find an internal state k_i from a set of output strings $y_0, y_1, \ldots, y_{D-1}$. When the state k_i is found, the attacker can derive all the future states $k_{i+1}, k_{i+2}, \ldots$, key material (K_i, IV_i), $(K_{i+1}, IV_{i+1}), \ldots$, and plaintexts $p_i, p_{i+1}, \ldots$ by running the keystream generator forward from the known state k_i. Both TMTO attacks are summarized in [8].

Babbage-Golić. In Babbage-Golić [3], the attacker tries to find one of the many internal states instead of the key. The attacker generates M random states $k_0, k_1, \ldots, k_{M-1}$ from the total number of states N, calculates an output string y_j for each state k_j, and stores the pairs (k_j, y_j) ordered by y_j. In the real-time phase the attacker collects D output strings $y_0, y_1, \ldots, y_i, \ldots, y_{D-1}$. Requirements on the output strings are explained in Sect. 3.3. By the birthday paradox the attacker can find a collision $y_i = y_j$ and recover an inner state k_i in time $T = N/M$, memory M, data D, and preprocessing time $P = M$, where $1 \leq T \leq D$. Example points on this tradeoff relation is $P = T = M = D = N^{1/2}$, as well as and $T = D = N^{1/4}$ and $P = M = N^{3/4}$. This is very similar to a normal birthday attack where an attacker can recover a single key with the same complexities. The difference is that in the Babbage-Golić attack, the attacker, on average, recovers the last $D/2$ states $k_i, \ldots, k_{D-2}, k_{D-1}$ as well as any future states. If D is limited, a reasonable assessment (given that the attacker recovers $\approx D$ states) is that the security is reduced by

$$\min(d, n/2) \ , \tag{6}$$

where $d = \log_2 D$ and $n = \log_2 N$. If D is unlimited the security is reduced by $n/2$ bits when the attacker uses the tradeoff $P = T = M = D = N^{1/2}$.

Biryukov-Shamir. In Hellman's attack on block ciphers [12], the attacker generates tables covering the N possible keys, but only stores the leftmost and rightmost columns in the table. Biryukov-Shamir [8] combines the Hellman and Babbage-Golić attacks. The attacker generates tables covering N/D states instead of N keys in Hellman's attack [12]. In the real-time phase the attacker collects D output strings $y_0, y_1, \ldots, y_i, \ldots, y_{D-1}$ and can recover an inner state k_i in time $T = N^2/(M^2 D^2)$ and preprocessing time $P = N/D$, where $D^2 \leq T \leq N$. Example points on this tradeoff relation is $P = T = N^{2/3}$ and $M = D = N^{1/3}$, as well as $P = N^{3/4}$, $D = N^{1/4}$, and $M = T = N^{1/2}$. Compared to Hellman's attack on block ciphers [12], Biryukov-Shamir's attack on stream ciphers runs D^2 times faster and the attacker, on average, recovers the last $D/2$ states $k_i, \ldots, k_{D-2}, k_{D-1}$ as well as any future states. If D is unlimited the security is reduced by $n/2$ bits.

3.3 TMTO Attacks on Signal and TLS 1.3

The effective stream cipher specific time memory trade-offs (TMTO) will be possible as long as the state size is less than twice the security level. As the name implies, the trade-off attacks give the attacker many possibilities. In addition to the discussion above, an attacker might also launch attacks where the probability of recovering a key is notably less than 1.

Based on these attacks, modern stream ciphers such as SNOW-V [10] follow the design principle that the security level is at most $n/2$ and that the state size in bits n should therefore be at least twice the security level. In his attack paper, Babbage [3] states that this principle is desirable. Zenner [34] states that a state size at least twice the security level is a necessary requirement for security. This is a reasonable requirement, especially if the number of key updates is unlimited.

The requirements on the output strings $y_0, y_1, \ldots, y_{D-1}$ depend on the function $h()$ used to combine the keystream with the plaintext $c_i = h(z_i, p_i)$. If $h()$ like AES-GCM, AES-CCM, and ChaCha20-Poly1305 is a combination of an additive stream cipher and a MAC the attack can be done with partially known and different plaintexts where y_i is a substring of $c_i \oplus p_i$. If $h()$ is AES-CBC, the attack requires that all the plaintexts have the same known prefix and y_i is a prefix of the ciphertext c_i. See Sect. 3.4 for a discussion on the practicality of the equal plaintext prefix model. The standard requirement today is that protocols should provide confidentiality against adaptive chosen ciphertext attacks.

TLS 1.3 and Signal do not explicitly state the intended security level, but the key length of the AEAD key can typically be seen as the intended security level. If we use the key length of the AEAD keys K_i as the security level, we see that TLS 1.3 and Signal do not follow design principles for stream ciphers. The reason for this is likely that the non-obvious stream cipher structure was overseen. The state size in Signal is always equal to the security level and the state size in TLS 1.3 is in some cases equal or 1.5 times the security level. As a result, TLS 1.3 and Signal offer far less than the expected security against these types of TMTO attacks.

3.4 Equal Plaintext Prefix

Being able to make stronger assumptions than that plaintexts are in English, Italian, German, or some other language can significantly improve cryptanalysis. The cryptanalysis of Enigma ciphertext was e.g., improved by the assumption that certain German messages were likely to be the stereotypical phrase *"Keine besonderen Ereignisse"* or begin with the stereotypical prefix *"An die Gruppe"*.

In the computer age we can almost always make such stronger assumptions. The application data sent over TLS is almost always using some protocol, which most likely has (known) fixed information fields such as headers. One of many examples is HTTP/1.1 [11] where the header for each request and response might begin with a lot of partly known data elements such as

```
GET /somewhere/fun/ HTTP/1.1
Host: www.example.com
User-Agent: curl/7.16.3 libcurl/7.16.3 OpenSSL/0.9.71
Accept-Language: sv, tlh

HTTP/1.1 200 OK
Date: Thu, 12 August 2021 04:16:35 GMT
Server: Apache
Last-Modified: Mon, 5 August 2019 11:00:26 GMT
ETag: "34aa387-d-1568eb00"
Accept-Ranges: bytes
Content-Length: 51
Vary: Accept-Encoding
Content-Type: text/plain
```

Assuming partially known different plaintexts or that all the prefixes of the plaintexts are the same are very reasonable assumptions that are likely to apply in practice and can be used by an attacker. But note that protocols that do not provide confidentiality against adaptive chosen ciphertext attacks are typically to be considered broken.

4 Signal Protocol - Analysis and Recommendations

The Signal technical specification [31] does not aim for interoperability between different implementations and therefore has fewer details than the TLS 1.3 specification [26]. As the Signal protocol documentation does not give any recommendations or limits on how many times the symmetric-key ratchet can be used before the Diffie-Hellman ratchet is used we have to assume that in the worst case the symmetric-key ratchet can be used an unlimited number of times. We have not analyzed any implementations but even if attempts are made to transmit fresh ephemeral Diffie-Hellman keys as soon as possible, an attacker can hinder Diffie-Hellman to happen by blocking communication in one direction. In this case the Signal protocol gives a theoretical security level of 128 bits against TMTO attacks irrespectively of the used algorithms. This aligns with some of the recommended algorithms such as X25519 and SHA-256, but not other recommended algorithms such as X448, SHA-512, and AES-256, and not with the 256-bit key length of the message keys K_i.

A significant problem with the X3DH protocol [31] is that is does not mandate ephemeral Diffie-Hellman (as stated in the specification, the server might be all out of one-time Diffie-Hellman keys) and when ephemeral Diffie-Hellman is used the ephemeral Diffie-Hellman keys might be quite old. The X3DH specification [31] explains that this can be mitigated by quickly performing ephemeral Diffie-Hellman post-X3DH, but this is not mandated or even clearly recommended. The Double ratchet does not help as the initiating party can send messages before receiving an ephemeral public key from the responding party. Such messages provide neither forward secrecy with respect to long-term keys nor replay protection. Old ephemeral Diffie-Hellman keys are problematic as they are to be considered long term-keys and therefore cannot be used to provide *forward secrecy with respect to long-term keys*, which often is a desired property, promised for example by the TLS 1.3 handshake, see Appendix E.1 of [26].

As a first step we recommend that the Signal protocol documentation mandates a low limit on the number of times the symmetric-key ratchet can be used and gives clear security levels provided by the Signal protocol for different choices of algorithms. A limit on the number of times the symmetric-key ratchet can be used puts a limit on the data variable D, which following Eq. (6) improves the security level against TMTO attacks. With a low limit, the Signal protocol would provide a theoretical security level close to 256 bits when 256-bit algorithms are used, see Table 2.

We recommends that the Signal protocol documentation mandates quickly performing ephemeral Diffie-Hellman post-X3DH if the X3DH protocol did not include ephemeral Diffie-Hellman with recently generated keys. Before ephemeral Diffie-Hellman with fresh keys has been performed, the Initiator should restrict the type of messages that can be sent similar to zero round-trip time (0-RTT) data in TLS 1.3 [26], where HTTPS implementations typically only allow GET requests with no query parameters.

Mandating frequent use of ephemeral Diffie-Hellman also limits the impact of key compromise and forces an attacker to do dynamic exfiltration [5]. For IPsec, ANSSI [1] recommends enforcing periodic rekeying with ephemeral Diffie-Hellman every hour and every 100 GB of data, but we think that the Signal Protocol can and should have much stricter requirements than so. The impact of static key exfiltration with different rekeying mechanisms in TLS 1.3 is illustrated in Fig. 3. The symmetric-key ratchet in Signal has similar properties as the TLS 1.3 key_update and the Diffie-Hellman ratchet has similar properties as the TLS 1.3 rekeying with (EC)DHE.

We also recommend that the Signal protocol allows and recommends use of 512-bit chain keys together with the 256-bit message keys.

5 TLS 1.3 Family - Analysis and Recommendations

5.1 Time Memory Trade-Off Attacks

As TLS 1.3 [26] and QUIC [16] do not give any recommendations or limits on how many times key update can be used we have to assume that in the worst case the symmetric-key ratchet can be used an unlimited number of times (we have not analyzed any implementations). In this case TLS 1.3 and QUIC with TLS_CHACHA20_POLY1305_SHA256 gives a theoretical security level of 128

Table 2. Security level as a function of D

N	D	Security level
2^{256}	∞	128
2^{256}	2^{64}	192
2^{256}	2^{32}	224
2^{256}	2^{16}	240
2^{256}	2^{0}	256

bits against TMTO attacks and TLS_AES_256_GCM_SHA384 gives a maximum theoretical security level of 192 bits against TMTO attacks irrespectively of the used key exchange algorithm. This does not align with the 256-bit key length of the traffic secrets K_i. As stated in [24], the ChaCha20 cipher is designed to provide 256-bit security.

As DTLS 1.3 [28] restricts the number of key updates to 2^{48}, DTLS 1.3 with TLS_CHACHA20_POLY1305_SHA256 gives a theoretical security level of 208 bits, which does not align with the 256-bit key length of the traffic secrets K_i. Due to the restricted number of key updates, we assert that DTLS 1.3 with TLS_AES_256 _GCM_SHA384 gives 256 bits security if it is used with an equally secure key exchange algorithm.

As a first step we recommend that TLS 1.3 [26] and QUIC [16] mandate the same 2^{48} limit as DTLS 1.3 on the number of times a key update can be used and give clear security levels provided by different choices of algorithms. A limit on the number of key updates puts a limit on the data variable D, which following Eq. (6) improves the security level against TMTO attacks. With a 2^{48} limit, TLS 1.3 and QUIC would provide a theoretical security equal to the length of the traffic secrets K_i for all cipher suites except TLS_CHACHA20_POLY1305_SHA256. Note that the cipher CHACHA20_POLY1305_SHA256 does give 256-bit security in TLS 1.3 when key update is not used. CHACHA20_POLY1305_SHA256 also provides 256-bit security in TLS 1.2 when used with the rekeying mechanism renegotiation. We recommend that a new cipher suite TLS_CHACHA20_POLY1305_SHA512 is standardized for use with TLS 1.3.

TLS 1.3 should clearly state the intended security levels. We also recommend that TLS 1.3 mandates traffic secrets twice the AEAD key size for new cipher suites. As an alternative, the transcript hash could be used as context in the key update instead of the empty context used today.

5.2 Key Exfiltration Attacks and Frequent Ephemeral Diffie-Hellman

Instances of large-scale monitoring attacks involving key exfiltration have been documented [15]. Moreover, it's highly probable that numerous additional occurrences have transpired clandestinely, escaping public acknowledgment. The avenues through which malicious entities can acquire keys are diverse, encompassing methods such as physical attacks, hacking, social engineering attacks, espionage, or by simply demanding access to keying material with or without a court order. Exfiltration attacks pose a significant and pressing cybersecurity threat [2].

The impact of static key exfiltration [5] with different rekeying mechanisms in TLS 1.3 is illustrated in Fig. 3. As can be seen the key update mechanism gives significantly worse protection against key exfiltration attacks than ECDHE. An attacker can perform a single static key exfiltration and then passively eavesdrop on all information sent over the connection even if the key update mechanism is used. With frequent ephemeral key exchange such as ECDHE, an attacker is forced to do active man-in-the-middle attacks or to do dynamic key exfiltration, which significantly increases the risk of discovery for the attacker [5]. The cost and risk associated with discovery is intricately tied to deployment specifics and the nature of the employed attack. In instances of a compromised system, automating key exfiltration could normalize costs between static and dynamic approaches. However, an augmented risk still stems from increased amounts of traffic volumes and log entries. Contrarily, in attack scenarios like side-channel attacks on Internet of Things (IoT) devices mandating physical proximity, the distinction between static and dynamic key exfiltration is substantial - encompassing both cost implications and the risk of discovery.

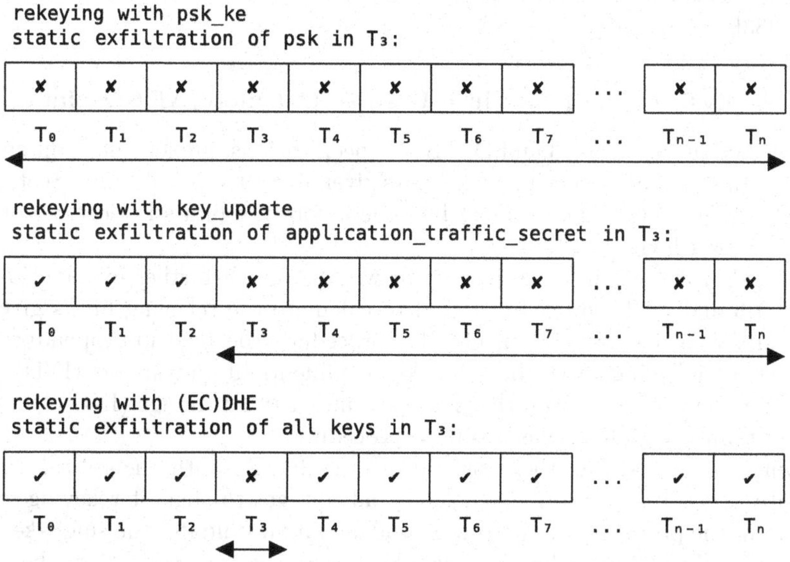

Fig. 3. TLS 1.3 - Impact of static key exfiltration in time period T_3 when psk_ke, key_update, and (EC)DHE are used.

Two essential zero trust principles are to assume that breach is inevitable or has likely already occurred [23], and to minimize impact when breach occur [22]. One type of breach is key compromise or key exfiltration. As the key update mechanism gives significantly worse protection against key exfiltration attacks than ECDHE, TLS 1.3, DTLS 1.3, and QUIC should mandate frequent use of ephemeral Diffie-Hellman. For IPsec, ANSSI [1] recommends enforcing periodic rekeying with ephemeral Diffie-Hellman every hour and every 100 GB of data, we recommend the TLS 1.3 handshake to recommend this for non-constrained implementations. Constrained implementations should also mandate periodic rekeying with ephemeral Diffie-Hellman but could have a maximum period of 1 day, 1 week, or 1 month depending on how constrained the device and the radio is.

From what we can gather from IETF mailing lists, the standardization of TLS 1.3 might have placed too much emphasis on forward secrecy, possibly overlooking the significance of the additional security properties offered by frequent ephemeral key exchanges. In addition to ephemeral key exchange during a connection, TLS 1.3 also removed the possibility to perform post-handshake server authentication. The implications are that TLS 1.3, DTLS 1.3, and QUIC are unsuitable for long-lived connections and that protocols like DTLS/SCTP have to be redesigned to be able to frequently set up new connections. The upcoming revisions of the TLS 1.3 protocol and DTLS/SCTP have already been updated with descriptions and recommendations for frequent use of ephemeral Diffie-Hellman based on this work. See Appendix F.1 of [27] and Sects. 3.4 and 9.1 of [33].

5.3 Analysis of the Procedure Used to Calculate AEAD Limits

As specified in the TLS 1.3 and DTLS 1.3 specifications, implementations should do a key update before reaching the limits given in Sect. 5.5 of [26] and Sect. 4.5.3 of [16]. In QUIC key update must be done before the limits in Sect. 6.6 of [16] have been reached.

In TLS 1.3 the limits are just given without much further explanation. In DTLS 1.3 and QUIC procedures used to calculate the rekeying limits given in Appendix B of [16,28]. The DTLS 1.3 procedure specified in Appendix B of [28] suggest rekeying when the single-key confidentiality advantage (IND-CPA) is greater than 2^{-60} or when the single-key integrity advantage (IND-CTXT) is greater than 2^{-57}. QUIC has a similar procedure.

Our analysis is that these procedures are flawed both theoretical and in practice. The procedures uses single-key advantages to suggest rekeying which transform the problem to a multi-key problem and invalidates the single-key calculation used to suggest the rekeying. Doing rekeying too early before the confidentiality or integrity of the algorithm decreases significantly faster than linear lowers the practical security and can create denial-of-service problems. The exact multi-key advantage depends on the algorithm but could be as much as m times its single-key advantage where m is the number of keys [6]. Multi-key advantages for the use of AES-GCM in TLS 1.3 is given by [6,13], which concludes that the nonce randomization do improve multi-key security for AES-GCM. We note that the nonce randomization do not improve security for ChaCha20-Poly1305 as $n = n_2$ and the 256-bit key K_i and the 96-bit IV are both derived from a 256-bit key k_i without any additional entropy. CHACHA20_POLY1305_SHA256 was suitable for TLS 1.2 but is not suitable for TLS 1.3. Requiring rekeying after a low number of forgery attempts might be a denial-of-service problem as an attacker can affect availability with a small number of forgeries.

In general, an algorithm with a confidentiality advantage that is linear in the number of encryption queries q, e.g., $CA = q/2^{97}$, and with an integrity advantage that is linear in the number of failed decryption queries v, e.g., $IA = v/2^{103}$, does not need rekeying because of the advantages. But as explained in Sect. 5.2, rekeying is beneficial to limit the impact of a key compromise.

The confidentiality rekeying limits for AES-GCM [26] and AES-CCM [28] and the integrity rekeying limit for AES-CCM [28] coincides pretty well with when the confidentiality and integrity advantages starts to grow significantly faster than linear. These rekeying limits do significantly improve security. We do not know if this was luck or if the magic numbers 2^{-60} and 2^{-57} were chosen to achieve this.

The integrity limits for AES-GCM and ChaCha20-Poly1305 do not improve security as the single-key integrity advantages are bounded by a function linear in v, the number of forgery attempts. The forgery probability is therefore independent of the rekeying. Rekeying likely lowers the multi-key security but is unlikely to happen in practice as the limits are 2^{36} forgery attempts.

For CCM_8 the procedure gives illogical results unsuitable for practical use. Looking at the bound for the CCM_8 integrity advantage it is easy to see that CCM_8 performs very close to an ideal MAC for quite large number of failed decryption queries v. CCM_8 in itself is not a security problem for use cases such as media encryption or the Internet of Things, but the recommendations in [28] and [16] for CCM_8 are significant security problems as they introduce a denial-of-service problem, lowers security against TMTO attacks, and likely lowers the multi-key security. The denial-of-service problem comes from the DTLS 1.3 procedure recommending rekeying after 128 forgery attempts instead of the correct value $v \approx 2^{36}$ when the CCM_8 integrity advantage starts to grow significantly faster than linear. Applying the procedure on an ideal MAC with tag length 64 bits, i.e., an algorithm with integrity advantage $v/2^{64}$, gives the same illogical result, that the ideal MAC should be rekeyed extremely often.

While the rekeying recommendations for CCM_8 are illogical, we do agree with the decision to make CCM_8 with its 64-bit tags not recommended for general usage. For constrained IoT, we do however not see any practical problems whatsoever. To have a 50% change of a single forgery, an attacker would need to send one billion packets per second for 300 years. This is completely unfeasible for constrained radio systems and the chance of this happening is negligible compared to the risk of data corruption due to hardware failure or cosmic rays.

We suggest that the procedures in Appendix B of [28] and [16] are deprecated in future versions. If any future procedure is needed it should be based on security per packet/byte/time instead of the practically irrelevant measures security per key/connection. Keeping some limit low per key or connection and then suggest rekeying or setting up a new connection will not increase practical security. If no good procedure can be found it is much better to just state limits as was done in [26], that is at least not wrong.

6 Conclusions, Recommendations, and Future Work

While we do not believe that the TMTO attacks pose a practical attack vector today, the attacks points to a fundamental design flaw in the key update mechanisms in TLS 1.3 and Signal, alternatively a lack of clearly stated security levels.

We find the design of the Signal protocol with a symmetric-key ratchet combined with a Diffie-Hellman ratchet very appealing as the protocol seems designed for frequent use of ephemeral Diffie-Hellman. It is possible that actual implementations already have hard limits on the number of times the symmetric-key ratchet can be used, meaning that they do provide close to 256-bit security and follows best practice when it comes to limit the impact of a key compromise.

We find several of the design choices in the TLS 1.3 handshake non-optimal resulting in that TLS 1.3 is problematic to use as a drop-in replacement of TLS 1.2. The standardization of TLS 1.3 might have placed too much emphasis on forward secrecy, possibly overlooking the significance of the additional security properties offered by frequent ephemeral key exchanges. Renegotiation was essential for frequent re-authentication and rekeying with ECDHE in DTLS/SCTP and the fourth flight in TLS 1.2 was essential for EAP-TLS. These problems can be overcome by using application data as a fourth flight [25] and by setting up new connections instead of using renegotiation [32].
Based on the analysis we recommend the Signal Protocol to:

- Introduce strict limits on the use of the symmetric-key ratchet.
- Mandate frequent use of the Diffie-Hellman ratchet based on time and data.
- Mandate ephemeral Diffie-Hellman with fresh keys before sending messages.
- Allow and recommend use of 512-bit chain keys.
- Clearly state the intended security level.

Based on the analysis we recommend TLS 1.3, DTLS 1.3, and QUIC to:

- Introduce strict limits on the use of the key update mechanism.
- Mandate frequent rekeying with EC(DHE) based on time and data.
- Standardize TLS_CHACHA20_POLY1305_SHA512.
- Mandate traffic secrets twice the AEAD key size for new cipher suites.
- Deprecate the procedure used for DTLS 1.3 and QUIC to calculate key limits.
- Clearly state the intended security levels.

Future work could evaluate the impact of this work on other protocols using symmetric ratchets such as MLS [4], EDHOC [29], and Key Update for OSCORE

[14,30] which have recently been standardized or are currently undergoing standardization. Future work should also evaluate implementations and deployments of the protocols. There is often significant differences between a specification, implementations of the specification, and actual deployments. One important aspect to investigate would be how often actual deployments perform symmetric key update and ephemeral Diffie-Hellman and if an active attacker can influence the frequency.

Acknowledgements. The authors would like to thank Patrik Ekdahl, Loïc Ferreira, Alexander Maximov, Ben Smeets, Erik Thormarker, and other reviewers for their helpful comments and suggestions.

References

1. Agence nationale de la sécurité des systèmes d'information: Recommendations for securing networks with IPsec (2015). https://www.ssi.gouv.fr/uploads/2015/09/NT_IPsec_EN.pdf
2. APNIC: how to: detect and prevent common data exfiltration attacks. https://blog.apnic.net/2022/03/31/how-to-detect-and-prevent-common-data-exfiltration-attacks/
3. Babbage, S.: Improved "exhaustive search" attacks on stream ciphers. In: 1995 European Convention on Security and Detection, pp. 161–166 (1995). https://doi.org/10.1049/cp:19950490
4. Barnes, R., Beurdouche, B., Robert, R., Millican, J., Omara, E., Cohn-Gordon, K.: The Messaging Layer Security (MLS) Protocol. RFC 9420 (2023). https://doi.org/10.17487/RFC9420
5. Barnes, R., et al.: Confidentiality in the face of pervasive surveillance: a threat model and problem statement. RFC 7624 (2015). https://doi.org/10.17487/RFC7624
6. Bellare, M., Tackmann, B.: The multi-user security of authenticated encryption: AES-GCM in TLS 1.3. In: Robshaw, M., Katz, J. (eds.) CRYPTO 2016. LNCS, vol. 9814, pp. 247–276. Springer, Heidelberg (2016). https://doi.org/10.1007/978-3-662-53018-4_10
7. Bienstock, A., Fairoze, J., Garg, S., Mukherjee, P., Raghuraman, S.: A more complete analysis of the signal double ratchet algorithm. Cryptology ePrint Archive, Report 2022/355 (2022). https://eprint.iacr.org/2022/355
8. Biryukov, A., Shamir, A.: Cryptanalytic time/memory/data tradeoffs for stream ciphers. In: Okamoto, T. (ed.) ASIACRYPT 2000. LNCS, vol. 1976, pp. 1–13. Springer, Heidelberg (2000). https://doi.org/10.1007/3-540-44448-3_1
9. Cohn-Gordon, K., Cremers, C., Dowling, B., Garratt, L., Stebila, D.: A formal security analysis of the signal messaging protocol. Cryptology ePrint Archive, Report 2016/1013 (2016). https://eprint.iacr.org/2016/1013
10. Ekdahl, P., Johansson, T., Maximov, A., Yang, J.: SNOW-Vi: an extreme performance variant of SNOW-V for lower grade CPUs. Cryptology ePrint Archive, Report 2021/236 (2021). https://eprint.iacr.org/2021/236
11. Fielding, R.T., Nottingham, M., Reschke, J.: HTTP Semantics. RFC 9110 (2022). https://doi.org/10.17487/RFC9110
12. Hellman, M.: A cryptanalytic time-memory trade-off. IEEE Trans. Inf. Theory **26**(4), 401–406 (1980). https://ee.stanford.edu/~hellman/publications/36.pdf

13. Hoang, V.T., Tessaro, S., Thiruvengadam, A.: The multi-user security of GCM, revisited: tight bounds for nonce randomization. In: Lie, D., Mannan, M., Backes, M., Wang, X. (eds.) ACM CCS 2018: 25th Conference on Computer and Communications Security, pp. 1429–1440. ACM Press, Toronto, ON, Canada, 15–19 October 2018. https://doi.org/10.1145/3243734.3243816
14. Höglund, R., Tiloca, M.: Key update for OSCORE (KUDOS). Internet-Draft draft-ietf-core-oscore-key-update-05, Internet Engineering Task Force (2023). https://datatracker.ietf.org/doc/draft-ietf-core-oscore-key-update/05/, work in Progress
15. Intercept, T.: How spies stole the keys to the encryption castle. https://theintercept.com/2015/02/19/great-sim-heist/
16. Iyengar, J., Thomson, M.: QUIC: a UDP-based multiplexed and secure transport. RFC 9000 (2021). https://doi.org/10.17487/RFC9000
17. Krawczyk, D.H., Eronen, P.: HMAC-based extract-and-expand key derivation function (HKDF). RFC 5869 (2010). https://doi.org/10.17487/RFC5869
18. Krawczyk, H.: SIGMA: the 'SIGn-and-MAc' approach to authenticated Diffie-Hellman and its use in the IKE protocols. In: Boneh, D. (ed.) CRYPTO 2003. LNCS, vol. 2729, pp. 400–425. Springer, Heidelberg (2003). https://doi.org/10.1007/978-3-540-45146-4_24
19. Mattsson, J.: Stream cipher design - an evaluation of the eSTREAM candidate Polar Bear. Master's thesis, Royal Institute of Technology (2006). https://citeseerx.ist.psu.edu/viewdoc/download?doi=10.1.1.108.40
20. McGrew, D., Rescorla, E.: Datagram transport layer security (DTLS) extension to establish keys for the secure real-time transport protocol (SRTP). RFC 5764 (2010). https://doi.org/10.17487/RFC5764
21. McKay, K., Cooper, D.: Guidelines for the selection, configuration, and use of transport layer security (TLS) implementations (2019). https://doi.org/10.6028/NIST.SP.800-52r2
22. National Institute of Standards and Technology: Implementing a zero trust architecture (2023). https://www.nccoe.nist.gov/sites/default/files/2023-07/zta-nist-sp-1800-35b-preliminary-draft-3.pdf
23. National Security Agency: Embracing a zero trust security model (2021). https://media.defense.gov/2021/Feb/25/2002588479/-1/-1/0/CSI_EMBRACING_ZT_SECURITY_MODEL_UOO115131-21.PDF
24. Nir, Y., Langley, A.: ChaCha20 and Poly1305 for IETF protocols. RFC 8439 (2018). https://doi.org/10.17487/RFC8439
25. Preuß Mattsson, J., Sethi, M.: EAP-TLS 1.3: using the extensible authentication protocol with TLS 1.3. RFC 9190 (2022). https://doi.org/10.17487/RFC9190
26. Rescorla, E.: The transport layer security (TLS) protocol version 1.3. RFC 8446 (2018). https://doi.org/10.17487/RFC8446
27. Rescorla, E.: The Transport layer security (TLS) protocol version 1.3. Internet-Draft draft-ietf-tls-rfc8446bis-09, Internet Engineering Task Force (2023). https://datatracker.ietf.org/doc/draft-ietf-tls-rfc8446bis/09/, work in Progress
28. Rescorla, E., Tschofenig, H., Modadugu, N.: The datagram transport layer security (DTLS) protocol version 1.3. RFC 9147 (2022). https://doi.org/10.17487/RFC9147
29. Selander, G., Preuß Mattsson, J., Palombini, F.: Ephemeral Diffie-Hellman over COSE (EDHOC). Internet-Draft draft-ietf-lake-edhoc-22, Internet Engineering Task Force (2023). https://datatracker.ietf.org/doc/draft-ietf-lake-edhoc/22/, work in Progress

30. Selander, G., Preuß Mattsson, J., Palombini, F., Seitz, L.: Object security for constrained RESTful environments (OSCORE). RFC 8613 (2019). https://doi.org/10.17487/RFC8613
31. Signal: signal technical documentation. https://signal.org/docs/
32. Tüxen, M., Rescorla, E., Seggelmann, R.: Datagram transport layer security (DTLS) for stream control transmission protocol (SCTP). RFC 6083 (2011). https://doi.org/10.17487/RFC6083
33. Westerlund, M., Preuß Mattsson, J., Porfiri, C.: Datagram transport layer security (DTLS) over stream control transmission protocol (SCTP). Internet-Draft draft-ietf-tsvwg-dtls-over-sctp-bis-06, Internet Engineering Task Force (2023). https://datatracker.ietf.org/doc/draft-ietf-tsvwg-dtls-over-sctp-bis/06/, work in Progress
34. Zenner, E.: On the role of the inner state size in stream ciphers. Cryptology ePrint Archive, Report 2004/003 (2004). https://eprint.iacr.org/2004/003

Differential Cryptanalysis with SAT, SMT, MILP, and CP: A Detailed Comparison for Bit-Oriented Primitives

Emanuele Bellini[2](✉), Alessandro De Piccoli[1], Mattia Formenti[2], David Gerault[2], Paul Huynh[2], Simone Pelizzola[1], Sergio Polese[1], and Andrea Visconti[1]

[1] Università degli Studi di Milano, Milan, Italy
{alessandro.depiccoli,simone.pelizzola,sergio.polese, andrea.visconti}@unimi.it

[2] Technology Innovation Institute, Abu Dhabi, UAE
{emanuele.bellini,mattia.formenti,david.gerault, paul.huynh}@tii.ae

Abstract. SAT, SMT, MILP, and CP, have become prominent in the differential cryptanalysis of cryptographic primitives. In this paper, we review the techniques for constructing differential characteristic search models in these four formalisms. Additionally, we perform a systematic comparison encompassing over 20 cryptographic primitives and 16 solvers, on both easy and hard instances of optimisation, enumeration and differential probability estimation problems.

Keywords: Differential cryptanalysis · SAT · SMT · MILP · CP

1 Introduction

The design and analysis of block ciphers is a time-consuming and error-prone task that involves tracing the propagation of bit-level or word-level patterns of all sorts, following intricate rules. Automatic tools have made such tasks significantly easier. In the case of differential cryptanalysis [9], one of the most widely used analysis technique, the studied patterns (differential characteristics) represent the propagation of a XOR difference between the inputs through the cipher, and are studied through the following methods: (1) *ad hoc* (include search algorithms implemented from scratch in general purpose programming languages, e.g. Matsui algorithm [34]); (2) *Boolean Satisfiability* and *Satisfiability Modulo Theory* (SAT/SMT); (3) *Mixed-Integer Linear Programming* (MILP); (4) *Constraint Programming* (CP). In this paper, we provide an extensive review and performance comparison for the last three techniques for the search of differential characteristics for various ciphers.

J. Deng et al. (Eds.): CANS 2023, LNCS 14342, pp. 268–292, 2023.
https://doi.org/10.1007/978-981-99-7563-1_13

Contributions. Our contributions are twofold:

- We provide an extensive review of modeling techniques in SAT, SMT, MILP and CP for the search of differential characteristics, in Sect. 3;
- We extensively compare these 4 methods on 3 different tasks: finding one optimal differential characteristic, enumerating all optimal differential characteristics, and estimating the probability of a differential. These tests are performed with 7 SAT solvers, 3 SMT solvers, 2 MILP solvers, 4 CP solvers, on over 20 primitives, resulting in the largest scale comparison of differential cryptanalysis models to date. The results are presented in Sect. 4.

The research community stands to benefit greatly from this extensive review and comparison of techniques, which provides a further steps towards a better understanding of how to solve the instances that are still out of reach.

2 Preliminaries

A symmetric cryptographic primitive is usually a sequence of linear and nonlinear *components* transforming a plaintext (possibly with a key) into a ciphertext, usually by applying a simple *round function* to update the state for a number of *rounds*, each round using a *round key* derived from a *key schedule* algorithm.

Differential cryptanalysis focuses on studying the probability of *differentials*, which map an XOR difference in the plaintexts to a differences in the ciphertexts. This probability is usually bounded by the probability of a *differential characteristics*, *i.e.*, a sequence of expected differences at each round (as described in Sect. A); the probability of the corresponding differential is related to the combined probabilities of all differential characteristics sharing the corresponding input and output differences, but varying in the internal rounds. Finding the optimal (highest probability) differential characteristic, or enumerating differential characteristics with given properties, is a highly combinatorial problem. In recent years, it has increasingly been tackled through declarative approaches (Sect. B), where the cryptographer describes the problem and leaves its resolution to a solver, usually SAT, SMT (Satisfiability Modulo Theories), MILP (Mixed Integer Linear Programming) and CP (Constraint Programming).

The search typically involves one set of variables per round to hold the difference state after each component of the primitive, as well as a set of variable for the probabilities. These variables usually contain the weights (base 2 logarithm of the reciprocal of the probabilities) for practical reasons. The problem of finding an optimal differential characteristic can then be expressed as assigning values for all state variables, such that known difference propagation rules are satisfied, and the sum of the probability weights is minimised, following the Markov cipher assumption of independent rounds.

The representation of these variables, and the expression of the propagation rules, vary between SAT, SMT, MILP and CP.

The propagation rules for linear components are simple, as differences propagate deterministically through them:

Proposition 1. *Let $f : \{0,1\}^m \to \{0,1\}^n$ be a linear function and let $\Delta\vec{x} \in \{0,1\}^m$ be an input difference; then $\Delta\vec{y} = f(\Delta\vec{x})$. (Proof: $f(\vec{x} + \Delta\vec{x}) = f(\vec{x}) + f(\Delta\vec{x})$)*

On the other hand, propagation through non-linear operations are stochastic, and represent the main difficulty of the problem, due to the resulting combinatorial explosion. In Sect. 3, we detail the models used for propagation of the linear and nonlinear components used by the analyzed ciphers.

Related Work. Differential cryptanalysis using declarative frameworks (SAT, SMT, MILP or CP) was introduced through MILP in [37], and has since then been an active research field (a review of techniques is given in Sect. 3). It is known [53] that the modeling choices for the search problem, independently of the chosen declarative framework, have a significant impact on the performance of the search. Additionally, within a given framework, it is difficult to predict what specific solver performs best: competitions such as the SAT competition [27] or the MiniZinc challenge for Constraint Programming solvers [36] pit existing solvers against each other on vast ranges of problems, but rarely cryptography-related ones. The choice of a model and a solver having such drastic impact on the ability to solve relevant differential cryptanalysis problems, research comparing the available options is important.

In [24,51], the authors use Constraint Programming tools to test the effectiveness of four solvers on PRESENT and AES, showing that for best differential characteristic search Chuffed is the best-performing solver on small instances, while Gurobi and Picat-SAT scale better. In [50], different SAT solvers are compared against a divide-and-conquer-based MILP model from [54] on a wide range of ciphers. In [18], the authors compare different models for the search of the best differential trails of SKINNY, including one for MILP, one for SAT, and one for CP. Following a two-stage search, their analysis showed that, in this case, this search is better performed with a MILP model in the first stage (enumerate the truncated trails with the smallest number of active S-box). CP performed best for the second stage, in which the truncated trails of the first stage are instantiated.

Despite extensive research in the area, many problems, such as the probabilities of differential characteristics for over 9 rounds of SPECK128 [50], are still out of reach. It is our hope that our large-scale comparison between solvers and modeling techniques will help chosing the right techniques to solving these.

3 Cipher Components Models

In this section, we review existing techniques to model different operations, in each of the studied declarative frameworks.

We use the following notation: x denotes inputs, y outputs and w weight; superscripts denote input numbers and subscripts bit positions. If no input number is given, the input is only one; if no bit position is given, the variable is intended to be a single bit. Finally, we will use the vector notation

$\vec{x} = (x_0, \ldots, x_{n-1})$ to denote the whole input, using 0 as the index of the Most Significant Bit (MSB). The models described in this section are *bit-based*, rather than *word-based*.

3.1 XOR Component

XOR is a linear function and Proposition 1 applies, so that we can directly apply the bitwise model $\Delta y = \bigoplus_{i=0}^{n-1} \Delta x^i$.

- **SAT:** for $n = 2$, the CNF is

$$(\neg\Delta x^0, \Delta x^1, \Delta y) \wedge (\Delta x^0, \neg\Delta x^1, \Delta y) \wedge (\Delta x^0, \Delta x^1, \neg\Delta y) \wedge (\neg\Delta x^0, \neg\Delta x^1, \neg\Delta y). \tag{1}$$

  When $n > 2$, one can operate in the following two ways: the first consists of the direct encoding without any additional variables; the second consists of performing a sequence of only two inputs XORs using intermediate variables that we will call d^i in the following way:

$$d^0 = \Delta x^0 \oplus \Delta x^1, \quad d^i = \Delta x^{i+1} \oplus d^{i-1} \text{ for } 1 \le i \le n-3, \quad \Delta y = \Delta x^{n-1} \oplus d^{n-3}. \tag{2}$$

  Note that the CNF in Eq. 1 represents every possible assignment verifying $\Delta y = \Delta x^0 \oplus \Delta x^1$. Therefore, a direct encoding of an XOR involving n variables will have 2^n clauses. In our analysis, when $n > 2$, we have preferred to use a sequential XOR, as depicted in Eq. 2, keeping the number of clauses linear in the number of variables, i.e. $4(n-1)$ clauses [50].
- **SMT:** a XOR theory is natively present for $n = 2$ or more.
- **MILP:** 2-input XOR is commonly modeled with four inequalities:

$$\{\Delta x^0 + \Delta x^1 \ge \Delta y\}, \ \{\Delta x^0 + \Delta y \ge \Delta x^1\}, \ \{\Delta x^1 + \Delta y \ge \Delta x^0\}, \{\Delta x^0 + \Delta x^1 + \Delta y \le 2\}. \tag{3}$$

  We also considered an alternative, with a dummy variable, which can easily be generalized to any arbitrary number of inputs:

$$\{\Delta x^0 + \cdots + \Delta x^{n-1} + \Delta y = 2d\} \tag{4}$$

  While this results in a smaller and constant number of inequalities, the *LP-relaxation* of the resulting problem—that is, the same optimization problem without integrality constraint on the variables—is weaker than the one obtained with Eq. 3. Indeed, any fractional solution of Eq. 3 is also a solution of Eq. 4. However, the converse is not true. For instance, for $n = 2$, $\Delta x^0 = \Delta x^1 = \frac{1}{5}, \Delta y = \frac{1}{2}$ is a solution for Eq. 4 when $d = \frac{9}{20}$ but does not satisfy Eq. 3. For this reason, we favored Eq. 3 over the more concise expression of Eq. 4. This was also backed by our experiments Midori64, whose linear layer contains several n-XORs: even though both expressions seemed to yield similar performance for 2 and 3 rounds, a difference started to be noticeable for 4 rounds as the search for the optimal trail with Gurobi took less than 2 min using Eq. 3, while it took more than 30 min with Eq. 4.

- **CP:** the XOR can be seen as the addition modulo 2, i.e. $\Delta y = \Delta x^0 + \Delta x^1 \pmod 2$. The same can be applied when dealing with more than 2 inputs:

$$\Delta y = \Delta x^0 + \Delta x^1 + \ldots + \Delta x^{n-1} \pmod 2.$$

3.2 Rotation and Shift Components

Rotation and shift are linear functions to which Proposition 1 directly applies.

- **SAT:** an equality can be translated in an if-and-only-if logic, so, the model that we have used is $(\Delta y_i \vee \neg f(\Delta x_i)) \wedge (\neg \Delta y_i \vee f(\Delta x_i))$.
- **MILP:** the equality is expressed as two inequalities: $\{\Delta y_i \geq f(\Delta x_i),\ \Delta y_i \leq f(\Delta x_i)\}$.
- **SMT, CP:** both formalisms natively include equality constraints.

3.3 Linear Layer Component

For the linear layer, Proposition 1 directly applies. Considering the linear function f represented as a vector-matrix product, the linear layer is simply a set of equalities of the form $\Delta y = \Delta x^0 \oplus \Delta x^1 \oplus \ldots \oplus \Delta x^{n-1}$.

If $n = 1$, then, we have no XOR and we can directly encode the equality. If $n \geq 2$, we refer to the XOR component for encoding the equality.

3.4 S-Box Component

An S-box is a nonlinear vectorial Boolean function that transforms an m-bit input into an n-bit output. Commonly, $m = n$ and usual values for n are up to 8. For instance, we take the 3-bit S-box defined as $S = (S_0, S_1, \ldots, S_7) = (3, 2, 7, 0, 4, 1, 6, 5)$, meaning that $S(i) = S_i$.

In order to study the differential of the S-box, it is usually affordable to consider its Difference Distribution Table (DDT). We start from a $m \times n$ table filled with zeros and for each input pair (i, j), we compute $\Delta\vec{x} = i \oplus j$ and $\Delta\vec{y} = S_i \oplus S_j$ and increase the $(\Delta\vec{x}, \Delta\vec{y})$ entry by one. Our SAT, SMT and MILP models also operate on other tables related to the DDT:

- $*$-DDT, using the same notation of [1], a truncated DDT, in which all the non-zero entries of the DDT are replaced by 1.
- w-DDT, which contains the weights[1] of the probability of the $(\Delta\vec{x}, \Delta\vec{y})$ entry.

Considering the previous 3-bit S-box S, we show its DDT in Table 1a and the associated w-DDT and $*$-DDT in Table 1b and Table 1c respectively.

[1] It should be noted that the entries of this table are not always integers, as a DDT might contain entries that are not powers of 2.

Table 1. DDT of the S-box $S = (3, 2, 7, 0, 4, 1, 6, 5)$ and its associated tables.

(a) DDT

$\Delta\vec{x}$ \ $\Delta\vec{y}$	0	1	2	3	4	5	6	7
0	8	0	0	0	0	0	0	0
1	0	2	0	2	0	2	0	2
2	0	0	4	0	4	0	0	0
3	0	2	0	2	0	2	0	2
4	0	2	0	2	0	2	0	2
5	0	0	4	0	0	0	4	0
6	0	2	0	2	0	2	0	2
7	0	0	0	0	4	0	4	0

(b) w-DDT

$\Delta\vec{x}$ \ $\Delta\vec{y}$	0	1	2	3	4	5	6	7
0	0	·	·	·	·	·	·	·
1	·	2	·	2	·	2	·	2
2	·	·	1	·	1	·	·	·
3	·	2	·	2	·	2	·	2
4	·	2	·	2	·	2	·	2
5	·	·	1	·	·	·	1	·
6	·	2	·	2	·	2	·	2
7	·	·	·	·	1	·	1	·

(c) $*$-DDT

$\Delta\vec{x}$ \ $\Delta\vec{y}$	0	1	2	3	4	5	6	7
0	1	0	0	0	0	0	0	0
1	0	1	0	1	0	1	0	1
2	0	0	1	0	1	0	0	0
3	0	1	0	1	0	1	0	1
4	0	1	0	1	0	1	0	1
5	0	0	1	0	0	0	1	0
6	0	1	0	1	0	1	0	1
7	0	0	0	0	1	0	1	0

- **SAT:** we will refer to the S-box presented above for concrete examples, thus, in the following, we will use the bit representation of values, i.e. $\Delta\vec{x} = (\Delta x_0, \Delta x_1, \Delta x_2)$, $\Delta\vec{y} = (\Delta y_0, \Delta y_1, \Delta y_2)$ and $\vec{w} = (w_0, w_1)$. The value for the *weight* has only two bits since from Table 1b, it is clear that the maximum weight $w_{\max}$ here is 2, so two bits will be enough to represent the weight. Generally speaking, we need $\lceil \log_2(w_{\max}) \rceil$ bits to encode the weight.
  Ankele and Kölbl presented a method to compute the CNF representing the w-DDT of an S-box [3]. Basically, they compute the $*$-DDT and, for every $(\Delta\vec{x}, \Delta\vec{y})$ having the relative entry equal to 0, they encode the constraint

$$\neg(\Delta\vec{x} \wedge \Delta\vec{y} \wedge w) \quad \Rightarrow \quad \neg\Delta\vec{x} \vee \neg\Delta\vec{y} \vee \neg w$$

  for every possible weight. For instance, for the pair (2, 3) in w-DDT, we use

$$\neg(\neg\Delta x_0 \wedge \Delta x_1 \wedge \neg\Delta x_2 \wedge \neg\Delta y_0 \wedge \Delta y_1 \wedge \Delta y_2 \wedge w_0 \wedge w_1)$$

  to avoid the triplet $(\Delta\vec{x}, \Delta\vec{y}, \vec{w}) = (2, 3, 2)$. The procedure must be repeated for every triplet that is not present in Table 1b. Summing up, we can say that they build the complementary set of the possible triplets shown in Table 1b. For a high number of cipher rounds, this method results in a number of constraints, i.e. clauses, which is not handy for SAT solvers.
  In order to reduce the number of constraints, we model the w-DDT as a sum of products. In this way, we directly encode only all allowed triplets. For instance, considering the triplet (2, 4, 1) in w-DDT, we use as a model

$$(\neg\Delta x_0 \wedge \Delta x_1 \wedge \neg\Delta x_2 \wedge \Delta y_0 \wedge \neg\Delta y_1 \wedge \neg\Delta y_2 \wedge \neg w_0 \wedge w_1) \\ \vee (\neg\Delta x_0 \wedge \Delta x_1 \wedge \neg\Delta x_2 \wedge \neg\Delta y_0 \wedge \Delta y_1 \wedge \Delta y_2 \wedge w_0 \wedge \neg w_1)$$

  Clearly, a SAT solver can not handle a sum of products. Therefore we have used the heuristic *Espresso* algorithm [11] in order to reduce it to a product-of-sum, i.e. a CNF. As already pointed out in [3], this technique is only applicable to DDTs containing entries that are powers of 2.
- **SMT:** we use the same model presented for SAT.

– **MILP:** The bitwise modeling of a differential propagation through an S-box of size greater than 6 bits remained a hard problem until the work of Abdelkhalek *et al.* was published [1]. Their approach relies on logical condition modeling, already introduced by Sun *et al.* [52], and uses the product-of-sums representation of the indicator function of the $*$-DDT, as in SAT and SMT. Taking the example again from Table 1a, let f be the 6-bit to 1-bit boolean function associated with the $*$-DDT shown in Table 1c. That is, $f(\Delta\vec{x}, \Delta\vec{y}) = 1$ only if the propagation is possible, where $\Delta\vec{x} = (\Delta x_0, \ldots, \Delta x_{n-1})$ and $\Delta\vec{y} = (\Delta y_0, \ldots, \Delta y_{n-1})$ denote the input and output difference, respectively. The product-of-sums representation of f is as follows:

$$f(\Delta\vec{x}, \Delta\vec{y}) = (\Delta x_0 \vee \Delta x_1 \vee \Delta x_2 \vee \Delta y_0 \vee \Delta y_1 \vee \overline{\Delta y_2}) \\ \wedge \cdots \wedge (\overline{\Delta x_0} \vee \overline{\Delta x_1} \vee \overline{\Delta x_2} \vee \overline{\Delta y_0} \vee \overline{\Delta y_1} \vee \overline{\Delta y_2}),$$

where $\overline{\Delta a}$ is the negation of Δa. Each term of the product represents one impossible transition in the $*$-DDT. For instance, the first term $(\Delta x_0 \vee \Delta x_1 \vee \Delta x_2 \vee \Delta y_0 \vee \Delta y_1 \vee \overline{\Delta y_2})$ corresponds to the impossible propagation $\mathtt{0} \times \mathtt{0} \rightarrow \mathtt{0} \times \mathtt{1}$. This means that the number of terms corresponds to the number of null entries in the $*$-DDT, which can be rather high for an 8-bit S-box. For this reason, finding a minimal, equivalent set of inequalities is a crucial step in the modeling of large S-boxes. Several algorithms have been described for the Boolean function minimization problem, such as the Quine-McCluskey algorithm [35,44,45] or the heuristic *Espresso* algorithm, already mentioned for SAT. Once a simplified product-of-sum is returned, each term can be rewritten as a linear inequality. For instance, $(\Delta x_0 \vee \Delta x_1 \vee \Delta x_2 \vee \Delta y_0 \vee \Delta y_1 \vee \overline{\Delta y_2}) = 1$ becomes:

$$\Delta x_0 + \Delta x_1 + \Delta x_2 + \Delta y_0 + \Delta y_1 + (1 - \Delta y_2) \geq 1.$$

After removing all impossible propagation for a given $*$-DDT table, the actual probabilities of the differential transitions of the S-box need to be taken into account. To do so, [1] proposed to separate the $*$-DDT into multiple w_k-DDT tables, such that w_k-DDT only contains entries with the same weight w_k, that is: $w_k\text{-DDT}[i,j] = 1$ if $w\text{-DDT}[i,j] = w_k$ and 0 otherwise.
The use of *indicator constraints* (such as the *big-M method*) ensures that only a single w_k-DDT is active:
  - for each S-box, we introduce a binary variable Q equal to 1 if the S-box is active, 0 otherwise;
  - similarly, for each w_k-DDT, a binary variable Q_{w_k} that equals 1 when the set of inequalities representing the w_k-DDT need to be effective.

Setting $\sum Q_{w_k} = Q$ ensures that whenever an S-box is active, only one w_k-DDT is effective; and the weight of the S-box can be modeled as $\sum w_k \cdot Q_{w_k}$.

– **CP:** *table constraints* allow for a straightforward representation of the S-box component. Indeed, they enforce a tuple of variables to take its value among a list of allowed tuples, explicitly defined as the rows of a table. In particular, each row will contain the following three elements concatenated:

an input difference, an output difference, and the weight of the probability for the input/output difference pair. In our bitwise representation, the input and output differences are the concatenations of m and n single-bit variables, respectively. An entry of the table is thus a $m + n + 1$ tuple.

Remark 1. We highlight that the S-box constraints represent a considerable amount of the constraints in SAT, SMT and MILP formalisms. In fact, the PRESENT S-box (4 bits) constraints are roughly one-half of the total constraints.

3.5 AND/OR Component

As the AND and OR are bitwise operations, one can easily build their DDTs. Indeed, they can be seen as 2-to-1 S-boxes repeated in parallel for as many times as the bit length of the inputs. This is equivalent to the approach explained in [2, Section 3].

- **SAT:** we reuse the techniques described in Subsect. 3.4 obtaining:

$$(\neg\Delta y \vee w) \wedge (\Delta x^0 \vee \Delta x^1 \vee \neg w) \wedge (\neg\Delta x^0 \vee w) \wedge (\neg\Delta x^1 \vee w).$$

- **SMT:** since satisfying a sum-of-products is easier than satisfying a product-of-sum, we encoded the AND component with the following model for a single bit:

$$(\neg\Delta x^0 \wedge \neg\Delta x^1 \wedge \neg\Delta y \wedge \neg w) \vee (\Delta x^0 \wedge w) \vee (\Delta x^1 \wedge w).$$

- **MILP, CP:** we reuse the techniques described in Subsect. 3.4 to model its DDT.

3.6 Modular Addition Component

Due to the intractable size of the DDT, even if using wordsize equal to 32 bits, the method adopted for the modular addition is the Lipmaa Moriai algorithm [31], based on two conditions:

1. $\mathsf{eq}(\Delta\vec{x}^0 \lll 1, \Delta\vec{x}^1 \lll 1, \Delta\vec{y} \lll 1) \wedge (\Delta\vec{x}^0 \oplus \Delta\vec{x}^1 \oplus \Delta\vec{y} \oplus (\Delta\vec{x}^1 \lll 1)) \neq 0$
2. $2^{-\mathsf{hw}(\neg\,\mathsf{eq}(\Delta\vec{x}^0, \Delta\vec{x}^1, \Delta\vec{y}) \wedge \mathsf{mask}(n-1))}$

with $\mathsf{eq}(x, y, z) := (\neg x \oplus y) \wedge (\neg x \oplus z)$, that is, $\mathsf{eq}(x, y, z) = 1 \Leftrightarrow x = y = z$, and for any n, $\mathsf{mask}(n) := 2^n - 1$.

- **SAT:** first of all, observe that $\mathsf{eq}(\Delta x_i^0, \Delta x_i^1, \Delta y_i)$ for $1 \leq i \leq n-1$ is used in both conditions, therefore, using w for the Hamming weight variable, we model

$$w_i = \neg\,\mathsf{eq}(\Delta x_i^0, \Delta x_i^1, \Delta y_i) \tag{5}$$

using the following CNF

$$(\Delta x_i^0 \vee \neg\Delta y_i \vee w_i) \wedge (\Delta x_i^1 \vee \neg\Delta x_i^0 \vee w_i) \wedge (\Delta y_i \vee \neg\Delta x_i^1 \vee w_i) \\ \wedge (\Delta x_i^0 \vee \Delta x_i^1 \vee \Delta y_i \vee \neg w_i) \wedge (\neg\Delta x_i^0 \vee \neg\Delta x_i^1 \vee \neg\Delta y_i \vee \neg w_i)$$

which is exhaustive for the second condition. By only considering the Least Significant Bit, the first condition can be encoded as

$$\Delta x_{n-1}^0 \oplus \Delta x_{n-1}^1 \oplus \Delta y_{n-1} = 0 \quad \Rightarrow \quad \Delta y_{n-1} = \Delta x_{n-1}^0 \oplus \Delta x_{n-1}^1 \tag{6}$$

for which we refer to the XOR component. Finally, taking the advantage of Eq. 5 and using a dummy variable, for $0 \leq i \leq n-2$, we need

$$(\neg w_i \wedge (d_i \oplus \Delta x_i^1) = 0) \wedge (d_i = \Delta x_{i+1}^0 \oplus \Delta x_{i+1}^1 \oplus \Delta y_{i+1}) \tag{7}$$

which turns into the following CNF

$$(\Delta x_i^1 \vee \neg d \vee w) \wedge (\neg\Delta x_i^1 \vee d \vee w) \\ \wedge(\Delta x_{i+1}^0 \vee \Delta x_{i+1}^1 \vee d \vee \neg\Delta y_{i+1}) \wedge (\Delta x_{i+1}^0 \vee \Delta x_{i+1}^1 \vee \neg d \vee \Delta y_{i+1}) \\ \wedge(\Delta x_{i+1}^0 \vee \neg\Delta x_{i+1}^1 \vee d \vee \Delta y_{i+1}) \wedge (\neg\Delta x_{i+1}^0 \vee \Delta x_{i+1}^1 \vee d \vee \Delta y_{i+1}) \\ \wedge(\Delta x_{i+1}^0 \vee \neg\Delta x_{i+1}^1 \vee \neg d \vee \neg\Delta y_{i+1}) \wedge (\neg\Delta x_{i+1}^0 \vee \Delta x_{i+1}^1 \vee \neg d \vee \neg\Delta y_{i+1}) \\ \wedge(\neg\Delta x_{i+1}^0 \vee \neg\Delta x_{i+1}^1 \vee d \vee \neg\Delta y_{i+1}) \wedge (\neg\Delta x_{i+1}^0 \vee \neg\Delta x_{i+1}^1 \vee \neg d \vee \Delta y_{i+1})$$

Note that this is a different approach from the one in [50]. Indeed, although our model has two more clauses in comparison, the number of variables per clause is reduced and can thus speed up the SAT solving process.

- **SMT:** since SMT has more expressive capability, we have encoded a bitwise model in a similar way to SAT. We simply report the implementation details:
  - we have used $\neg w_i = (\Delta x_i^0 = \Delta x_i^1 = \Delta y_i)$ instead of Eq. 5;
  - we have directly used $\Delta y_i \oplus \Delta x_i^0 \oplus \Delta x_i^1 = 0$ in Eq. 6;
  - we have used $w_i \vee \neg(\Delta x_{i+1}^0 \oplus \Delta x_{i+1}^1 \oplus \Delta y_{i+1} \oplus \Delta x_i^1)$ instead of Eq. 7.
- **MILP:** implementing the Lipmaa-Moriai as is in MILP would be rather inefficient, as expressing simple if-then-else statements requires extra variables and constraints. Instead, it is possible to directly derive a small set of linear constraints by listing all valid patterns for $(\Delta\vec{x}^0, \Delta\vec{x}^1, \Delta\vec{y}, \Delta\vec{x}^0 \ll 1, \Delta\vec{x}^1 \ll 1, \Delta\vec{y} \ll 1)$ that satisfy the conditions imposed by the Lipmaa-Moriai algorithm, as done by Fu *et al.* [21]. In their paper, the authors obtained 65 linear inequalities for each bit. This set of constraints was then reduced by using a greedy algorithm or the Espresso minimizer. As such, the differential behavior of addition modulo 2^n could be represented using $13(n-1)+5$ linear inequalities in total.
- **CP:** in the CP model, the constraints for modular addition involve the preliminary step of declaring three shifted arrays representing the carry (the shifts in the first condition) and an additional array `eq` with the results of the `eq` function. The constraint is then a straightforward implementation of the Lipmaa-Moriai algorithm. The `eq` function is easily defined thanks to the `all_equal()` global constraint. Then, the output difference constraints are derived from the first condition:

- if the eq constraint is satisfied, then the difference propagation is deterministic and its constraint is given by the second part of the condition, i.e. $\Delta\vec{x}^0 \oplus \Delta\vec{x}^1 \oplus \Delta\vec{y} \oplus (\Delta\vec{x}^1 \lll 1) = 0$. In other words, the output difference is the XOR of the inputs and carry differences;
- otherwise, no more constraints are needed, and the transition will have weight 1. The weight variable is constrained to be $n - sum(\texttt{eq})$.

4 Experimental Results

In this section, we present a comparison of formalisms and solvers for differential cryptanalysis problems. In particular, we examine the 3 following tasks:

1. **Task 1** the search for an optimal differential trail (easy and difficult instances);
2. **Task 2** the enumeration of all optimal trails;
3. **Task 3** the estimation of the probability of a differential.

For these three tasks we will present the results we obtained on different ciphers, based on the data available in literature and how accurately the corresponding graph would present the experimental comparison between the best solvers for each formalism.

It has been observed in previous works, such as [17], that the fastest solver on small instances does not always scale up to more difficult instances of the same problem; therefore, we study both cases for the search of an optimal trail.

In the first two cases, no constraints are imposed on the input and output; in the third case, the weight, or objective function, is fixed to the optimal value; in the last case, the input and output differences are fixed, and all trails with a probability greater than a fixed lower bound are enumerated.

Optimization is natively supported for CP and MILP, whereas increasing objective values are tested until the problem is satisfiable for SAT and SMT. The enumeration of solutions is performed natively in CP, by adding constraints forbidding each new solution after it is found for the other formalisms.
All tests were run on a server with the following configuration, on which no more than half the threads were used at any given time:

- `CPU`: 2 x Intel(R) Xeon(R) Gold 6258R;
- `Number of Cores/Threads`: 2×28 Cores/2×56 Threads
- `Base/Max CPU frequency achievable`: 2.7 GHz / 4.0 GHz
- `Cache`: 38.5 Mb
- `Memory`: 768GB @2933 MHz;
- `Operating System`: Ubuntu 18.04.5 LTS.

In this framework, many algorithms are taken into account, considering block ciphers, stream ciphers and hash functions. In particular, the following families of ciphers have been analyzed:

- Block ciphers: Simon and Speck, Threefish, LEA, DES, Midori, PRESENT, TEA, XTEA;
- Permutations: Gift, Gimli, Keccak, Ascon, ChaCha, Xoodoo,
- Hash functions: SHA1, SHA-224, SHA-256, SHA-384, SHA-512, Blake, Blake2, MD5.

For each cipher, we tested several rounds. We did not use results found in smaller rounds for the higher round case.

4.1 Choice of Solvers

In our testing activities, we not only compare formalisms but also try to identify which solver performs best for a given formalism and a given problem. Below is the list of solvers we used for each formalism.

- **SAT Solvers**: CaDiCal (1.5.3) [7]; CryptoMiniSat (5.11.4) [49]; Glucose Syrup (4.1) [4]; Kissat (3.0.0) [7]; MathSAT (5.6.9) [13]; Minisat (2.2.1) [20]; Yices2 (2.6.4) [19]. All solvers were run with their default parameters and options.
- **SMT Solvers**: MathSAT (5.6.9) [13]; Yices2 (2.6.4) [19]; Z3 (4.8.12) [38]. All solvers were run with their default parameters and options. Note that the SMT models developed in Sect. 3 need the `QF_UF` logic in SMT-LIB standard, therefore we excluded Boolector [40] and STP [22].
- **MILP Solvers**: GLPK [41], Gurobi [26]. SCIP [6] was considered, but since our MILP models were written using the solver interfaces provided by the `SageMath` MILP module, which do not include SCIP, it was not included.
- **CP Solvers**: Chuffed [12], Gecode [47], OR-tools [25], Choco [43]. Our model are written in the MiniZinc [39] language, which interfaces to these solvers.

4.2 Comparison for Task 1

The first problem of this comparison is that of the optimal objective value (and a satisfying trail).

We considered representatives of block ciphers, permutations and hash functions and fixed the number of rounds with two different ideas in mind: we wanted to compare the performances of the different formalisms and solvers on easier problems, obtained by considering instances of various ciphers on a low number of rounds (2 to 6). To make our results meaningful we set a minimum time threshold of 2 s: if any solver is able to finish the 6-round instance in less than that, we repeat the test for a higher number of rounds, until this threshold is crossed. These will be called *quick tests.* In addition, we ran a comparison on *slow tests*, composed of more difficult instances of Simon, Speck, and PRESENT.

For each test we measured the *solving time* (time to solve the model) and the *building time* (time to build the model). The sum of building and solving time will be referred to as the *combined time.*

Quick Tests. In this section, we present a comparison of solvers on easy cryptographic instances for all the primitives mentioned in Sect. 4. The solver with the lowest combined time for a given instance is awarded a *win*. The best solver for each cipher is the one with the highest number of wins. The winner of our *competition* (for every formalism) is the solver that performs best for the highest number of ciphers (more than 20, each from round 2 to 6).

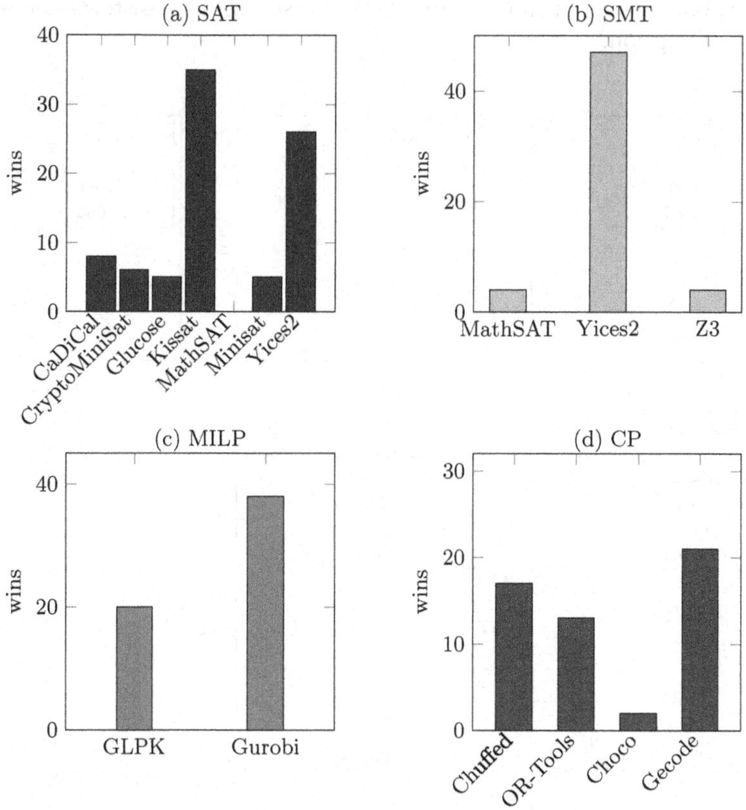

Fig. 1. Comparison of the number of victories of each solver, per formalism, on the set of easy instances.

The graphs in Fig. 1 report the results of these competitions:

- Among SAT solvers, Kissat and Yices2 emerge as the clear winners. It should also be noted that the timings reported from Glucose are computed taking multithreading into account, and thus do not faithfully represent the real time needed to obtain the results;
- In the SMT solvers category, Z3 and MathSAT are always inferior to Yices2, which is thus clearly the best SMT solver in our testing;

– In CP and MILP, the difference between different solvers is not as clear cut: while Gecode and Gurobi are the fastest solvers overall, Chuffed and GLPK often manage to be at least equal to them in their respective models.

In Fig. 2, we present the results of the quick tests for Simon32, Speck32, PRESENT, Gimli, and BLAKE[2], for the best solver of each formalism we found before. These tests were run with a timeout of 10 min, which was extended by another 10 min if no solver returned within the first time slot. We refer to Sect. C for the exhaustive list of timings. In all these cases, SAT consistently appears as the superior option.

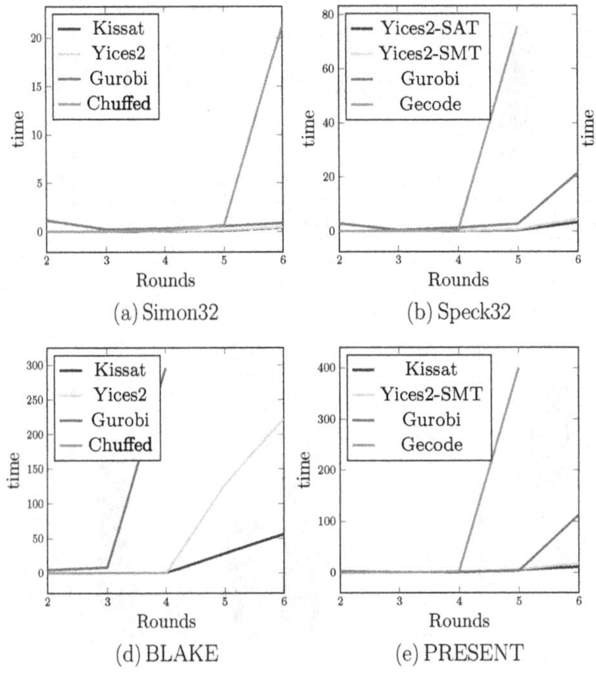

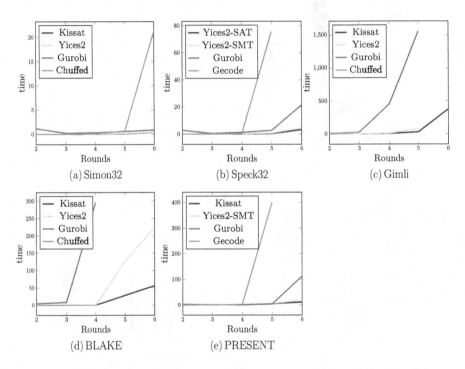

Fig. 2. Graph comparisons between the best solvers for each formalism on different ciphers testing the function `find_lowest_weight_trail`.

Figure 2a and Fig. 2b show very similar performances between SAT and SMT for Simon and Speck; the detailed times are given in Table 5 and 6 of Sect. C. On the other hand, SAT dominated on a primitive with a larger state, Gimli, as shown in Fig. 2c and Fig. 2d: SAT is the only formalism to complete the 6-round test within the 10 min time limit.

[2] As an example, we selected, respectively, three small state block ciphers, (one AndRX, one ARX, one S-Box based), one large state permutation (384 bits) and one large state ARX hash (512 bits).

Slow Tests. In this section, we run a comparison on longer instances, described in Table 2, with a timeout of 24 h.

Table 2. The instances of our long tests set; optimal weight for a fixed number of rounds is found and compared to known results for correctness.

Cipher	Rounds	Weight	Reference
PRESENT	18	78	[50]
Simon32	12	34	[33]
Simon64	19	64	[33]
Speck32	9	30	[5]
Speck64	13	55	[5]

The results are reported in Table 3; solving and building time are expressed in seconds, while the memory used is in megabytes. In the table, *inf* is reported when the solver does not provide a reliable way to measure its memory usage.

These tests were ran for all paradigms, but the solvers that returned within the 24 h timeout were mostly SAT, showing a clear advantage on this problem; MILP only finished within the timeout once (and came out on top) for SIMON32. We ran all tests with the best current known techniques for each for each formalism, except for MILP for which we use techniques from [1], even though we are aware of the improvements from [10,30] and plan to add them in the future. Chances are that the improvements from [10,30] will yield better performances for MILP solvers.

For 9 rounds of SPECK32, the known best trail was retrieved, but only SAT and SMT solvers finished within the time limit. For PRESENT and SPECK64, only SAT solvers finished within the time limit, with a clear advantage for Kissat.

These results contrast with the quick tests: Yices2, which was the best overall solver on the quick tests, is not able to find the Speck32 or Present64 trail, while CaDiCal, CryptoMiniSat and Glucose can.

We also see a notable increase in time when the state size is increased: while some SAT solvers can find the lowest known trail for Speck64 on 13 rounds, we can see that the time needed is much higher than the one needed for Speck32, and no solver among all formalisms is able to find the lowest weight trail for Speck128 within the timeout of 24 h.

4.3 Comparison for Task 2

It has been shown that a solver being fast at finding one solution is not always as fast for enumerating solutions with fixed variables, such as the objective value; for instance, in [23], a SAT solver is used to find solution patterns, which are then explored with a CP solver. In this experiment, we only tested the solvers that returned within the timeout in the `find_lowest_weight_trail` experiment.

Table 3. Results on the optimization problems on the difficult instances, for the solvers that finished within the timeout of 24 h.

(a) PRESENT 64/80, 18 rounds

Formalism	Building time	Solving time	Memory	Weight	Solver
SAT	**0.13**	**789.75**	**325.69**	**78**	**Kissat**
SAT	0.23	2761.93	311.17	78.0	CaDiCal
SAT	0.14	5757.36	163272.00	78.0	CryptoMiniSat
SAT	0.13	28624.79	inf	78.0	Glucose

(b) Simon 32/64, 12 rounds

Formalism	Building time	Solving time	Memory	Weight	Solver
MILP	**0.95**	**53.20**	**0**	**34.0**	**Gurobi**
SAT	0.03	86.43	208.72	34.0	CaDiCal
SAT	0.03	93.24	218.80	34.0	Kissat
SAT	0.03	132.63	inf	34.0	Glucose
SAT	0.03	432.77	14.39	34.0	Yices2
SAT	0.03	439.43	55.56	34.0	CryptoMiniSat
SMT	0.03	896.70	54.81	34.0	Z3
SAT	0.03	393369.00	56.82	34.0	MathSAT
SMT	0.03	469589.00	21277.00	34.0	Yices2
SMT	0.03	518824.00	100809.00	34.0	MathSAT

(c) Simon 64/128, 19 rounds

Formalism	Building time	Solving time	Memory	Weight	Solver
SAT	**0.11**	**533.09**	**257.62**	**64.0**	**Kissat**
SAT	0.13	64929.70	410.49	64.0	CaDiCal
SAT	0.07	346522.15	inf	64.0	Glucose

(d) Speck 32/64, 9 rounds

Formalism	Building time	Solving time	Memory	Weight	Solver
SAT	**0.04**	**99.01**	**220.45**	**30.0**	**Kissat**
SAT	0.03	764.28	209.79	30.0	CaDiCal
SAT	0.03	1963.10	inf	30.0	Glucose
SAT	0.03	3266.48	100.24	30.0	CryptoMiniSat
SMT	0.04	75977876.00	817426.00	30.0	MathSAT

(e) Speck 64/128, 13 rounds

Formalism	Building time	Solving time	Memory	Weight	Solver
SAT	**0.12**	**437.96**	**259.22**	**50.0**	**Kissat**
SAT	0.12	67051.43	300.97	50.0	CaDiCal

As we can see in Fig. 3a and Fig. 3b, SAT is still a suitable formalism for this problem, though with a different top performer (Yices over Kissat). Furthermore, this time CP's performances improve greatly and in Fig. 3c CP is actually the sole formalism to finish within the timeout.

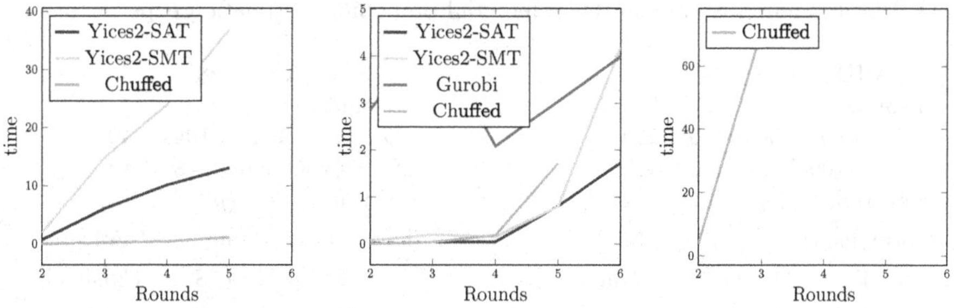

(a) Simon32 (b) Speck32 (c) Gimli

Fig. 3. Graph comparisons between the best solvers for each formalism on different ciphers testing `find_all_trails` function.

4.4 Comparison for Task 3

Our final test compares the time taken to estimate the probability of a differential: the input and output differences were fixed, along with a bound on the probability, and all satisfying trails were enumerated. We used the differentials reported in [3]; in particular, we tested the ones reported for 7 rounds of Speck64, and 14 rounds of Simon32. In addition, we ran this test on 4 rounds of Midori128 to evaluate the influence of a large S-box, which typically favors CP and its table constraints. The results, under a timeout of 6 h, are reported in Table 4.

For the case of SIMON, we were not able to enumerate all the weights reported in [28] within the timeout, so we only enumerated trails with weights between 38 and 49. As expected, due to the 8-bit S-box, CP was the fastest for Midori128, with all 4 solvers finishing under 12 s (Table 4a), followed by SAT solvers, from CryptoMiniSat, which runs in about 13 min to MiniSAT (1h24m). Lastly, SMT solvers exhibit even slower performance. With the exception of Yices2, where the performance difference between using SAT or SMT as a formalism is relatively small, all other solvers take over 2 h to complete, and MathSAT even times out. SPECK, an ARX block cipher, behaves differently: in Table 4b, the only formalism to finish the tests within the timeout is SAT, with the fastest being CaDiCal, which takes around 46 min. Due to the inherently boolean nature of ARX operations, an advantage for SAT was expected.

4.5 Speeding up CryptoMiniSat

In a final batch of experiments, we tested the differential probability estimation experiment using the `maxsol` option in CryptoMiniSat; this option lets CryptoMiniSat enumerate solutions up to a given maximum number. In this set of experiments, we set this number of solutions to 10^6, which is arbitrarily higher than the highest number of solutions we observed.

For the 3 ciphers under study, CryptoMiniSat becomes the fastest solver of all the tested ones with this strategy and finishes within 3 s for Midori, 40 min

Table 4. Timing results on the differential probability estimation experiments.

(a) MIDORI 64/128
4 rounds
$\Delta\vec{x} = \texttt{0x0002002000002000}$
$\Delta\vec{y} = \texttt{0x0000022222022022}$
896 trails, $-\log_2(p) = 23.7905$

Formalism	Time	Solver
CP	10.00	Chuffed
CP	10.28	Gecode
CP	10.49	OR Tools
CP	11.26	Choco
SAT	795.71	CryptoMiniSat
SAT	846.49	Yices2
SMT	874.31	Yices2
SAT	941.33	Kissat
SAT	960.07	CaDiCal
SAT	1168.56	Glucose
SAT	1206.09	MathSAT
SAT	5092.36	MiniSAT
SMT	8366.91	Z3

(b) SPECK 64/128
7 rounds
$\Delta\vec{x} = \texttt{0x4000409210420040}$
$\Delta\vec{y} = \texttt{0x8080a0808481a4a0}$
75 trails, $-\log_2(p) = 20.9538$

Formalism	Time	Solver
SAT	2789.58	CaDiCal
SAT	3400.27	Kissat
SAT	3416.21	Glucose
SAT	8785.10	CryptoMiniSat

for SPECK64, and 30 min for SIMON32. The significant increase in speed allows us to test larger weights, with a maximum of 58 in this experiment. As a result, we can enumerate a significantly greater number of trails than in our previous experiments, while still maintaining much faster solving times.

5 Conclusion

Differential cryptanalysis is one of the main techniques when testing the strength of symmetric ciphers, and fast evaluation helps designers set the parameters of new primitives; this paper reviews the existing modeling techniques for SAT, SMT, MILP and CP, and compares their performances through different solvers.

In the comparison, solvers from all categories were tested on finding an optimal differential trail, enumerating optimal trails, and estimating the probability of a differential, for block ciphers, permutations and hash functions.

Overall, SAT solvers were the winners of this comparison for ARX primitives and SPNs, such as PRESENT or Midori. In terms of solvers, Kissat dominated the SAT category, Yices2 the SMT pool, Gurobi in MILP and Chuffed won CP.

Even though SAT was the winner in most cases, CP obtained a victory when enumerating the trails of a differential for Midori, in line with previously observed results. On the other hand, when using the `maxsol` option, CryptoMiniSat took the win for enumeration problems.

This work is one further step towards a better understanding of what methods to use for solving differential cryptanalysis problems. A systematic study, with more primitives and more problems, would be extremely beneficial to the community. Indeed, in future works, we plan to extend similar comparisons for (1) other families of ciphers (such as SPNs or ciphers with large state) and (2) for other types of cryptanalysis, such as linear, differential-linear, and rotational-xor cryptanalysis.

A Differential Cryptanalysis

Differential cryptanalysis, first proposed by Biham and Shamir in 1990 [9], is a statistical cryptanalysis technique, very effective against many cryptographic primitives, such as block or stream ciphers or hash functions. Given two inputs to the primitive with difference Δx through a chosen operation (we use the XOR, the most common) the technique studies how this value propagates through the iterated operations to reach an output difference Δy.

The *differential probability* of a given input/output pair of differences for a vectorial Boolean function is the probability for that pair to yield over all the possible pairs of inputs with said input difference. For a function f and two differences Δx and Δy, we will denote this probability with $\mathsf{dp}^f(\Delta x \rightarrow \Delta y)$.

It is currently infeasible to compute the output difference for a block cipher for all the possible pairs of inputs, considering its large size, and building the table with all the frequencies for each pair of input/output difference (that is called *Difference Distribution Table*, in short DDT). To facilitate the analysis, we can use the fact that block ciphers are often *iterative functions*, i.e. they are the composition $f_{r-1} \circ \ldots \circ f_0$ of simpler keyed round functions f_i's.

We define a r-round *differential trail* (or *characteristic*) for an iterative function $f = f_{r-1} \circ \ldots \circ f_1 \circ f_0$, as a sequence of differences

$$\Delta_0 \xrightarrow{f_0} \Delta_1 \xrightarrow{f_1} \ldots \rightarrow \Delta_{r-1} \xrightarrow{f_{r-1}} \Delta_r$$

and a *differential* as a pair of input/output differences. In the case of the whole composite primitive, the differential

$$\Delta x \xrightarrow{f_0 \circ \ldots \circ f_{r-1}} \Delta y.$$

has probability equal to the sum of the probabilities of all the differential characteristics with $\Delta_0 = \Delta x$ and $\Delta_r = \Delta y$, where the probability of the characteristic is usually computed as the product of the probabilities of each intermediate differential of the chain. In particular, one can rely on the assumption of independence between each differential so that the resulting probability, when considering the composition of vectorial Boolean functions, is computed by the following:

Proposition 2. *Let f_1 and f_2 be two vectorial Boolean functions*

$$f_1 : \{0,1\}^l \to \{0,1\}^m, \quad f_2 : \{0,1\}^m \to \{0,1\}^n.$$

and let $\Delta\vec{x} \in \{0,1\}^l$, $\Delta\vec{y} \in \{0,1\}^m$ and $\Delta\vec{z} \in \{0,1\}^n$ be three differences such that

$$\mathsf{dp}^{f_1}(\Delta\vec{x} \to \Delta\vec{y}) = p_1 \qquad \mathsf{dp}^{f_2}(\Delta\vec{y} \to \Delta\vec{z}) = p_2.$$

Then, we have

$$\mathsf{dp}^{f_2 \circ f_1}(\Delta\vec{x} \to \Delta\vec{z}) = p_1 \cdot p_2.$$

To simplify the search for the most probable differential trail, it is common to search for the best differential characteristic instead, assuming its probability to be a good approximation of the target one, even if this is not always true [3].

In general, there is no efficient way to compute the precise probability of a differential characteristics. To do so, some fundamental assumptions on block ciphers are commonly used, such as the *Markov cipher* assumption, the *Hypothesis of stochastic equivalence* and the *Hypothesis of independent round keys* (see e.g. [32, Section 2.2.1]).

B Formalisms

In order to search for differential trails having the highest possible probability, we will make use of several constraints problems solvers adopting 4 different formalisms. The problem underlying the search of differential trails can be set from a general point of view.

Problem 1. Given a set of *variables* (unknown elements with a fixed domain) and a set of *constraints* (e.g. relations representing the propagation of the difference through the cipher), it is required to find an *assignment* of the variables to values in their domains, that is a mapping associating to each variable a value in its domain, that satisfies all the constraints.

We will call the resolution process *procedure*. In the following, we specialize the general terminology for each of the 4 formalisms we have used.

B.1 Satisfiability (SAT)

The terminology is as follows:

- *variables* are Boolean unknowns; a literal is either an unknown Boolean quantity v_i or its negation $\neg v_i$;
- *constraints* are clauses; a clause is a disjunction of literals, $\bigvee_{i=0}^{n-1} x_i$; the set of clauses is called Conjunctive Normal Form (CNF) and it is the conjunction of all the clauses, $\bigwedge_{j=0}^{m-1} \left(\bigvee_{i=0}^{n_j} x_{ij}\right)$;
- the main *procedures* are DPLL [15,16] or CDCL [48], improved in the actual implementations.

B.2 Satisfiability Modulo Theories (SMT)

The terminology is as follows:

- *variables* are unknown Booleans x_i coming from the quantifier free theory, i.e. the Boolean logic;
- *constraints* are formulae in the chosen theory involving Boolean symbols;
- the main *procedures* are Lazy or Eager [8]; due to the simplicity of implementation, Lazy is the most widely implemented.

B.3 Mixed-Integer Linear Programming (MILP)

The terminology is as follows:

- *variables* are unknown quantities x_i that can either be booleans, integers ($\mathbb{Z}$) or continuous ($\mathbb{R}$);
- *constraints* are linear inequalities of the form $a_0x_0+a_1x_1+\cdots+a_{n-1}x_{n-1} \leq b$ with $a_i, b \in \mathbb{Q}$; moreover we have an objective function of the form $z = c_0x_0 + c_1x_1 + \cdots + c_{n-1}x_{n-1}$ to be maximized or minimized, with $c_i \in \mathbb{Q}$;
- the main *procedures* are the Simplex algorithm [14], Branch-and-bound [29] and Branch-and-cut [42].

B.4 Constraint Programming (CP)

The terminology is as follows:

- *variables* are unknown quantities belonging to a specific domain, i.e. pairs (x_i, D_i). In our models we will either have Boolean variables ($D_i = \{0, 1\}$) or more generic integer variables ($D_i \subseteq \mathbb{N}$);
- *constraints* are relations which involve a subset of the variables. There are several types of constraints that can be used to model CP problems; in our models we used linear equations of integer variables (eventually modulo 2), logical combinations of linear equations of integer variables through the usual operators (AND, OR, NOT) and table constraints.
- the main *procedures* are Backtracking search, Local Search and Dynamic programming [46].

C Experimental Results Tables

In Table 5, we use the following notation: BT = Building Time, ST = Solving Time, NR = Number of Rounds, W = Weight, and similarly in Tables 6, 7, 8 and 9.

Table 5. Comparison results on Simon 32/64

Formalism	Solver	NR=2, W=2			NR=3, W=4			NR=4, W=6			NR=5, W=8			NR=6, W=12		
		BT	ST	Memory	BT	ST	Memory	BT	ST	Memory	BT	ST	Memory	BT	ST	Memory
SAT	Kissat	0.00	0.00	213.81	0.00	0.02	213.44	0.00	0.04	214.22	0.01	0.11	214.72	0.01	0.36	215.47
SAT	CaDiCal	0.00	0.00	203.40	0.00	0.02	203.61	0.00	0.07	204.23	0.01	0.16	205.01	0.02	0.45	206.13
SAT	CryptoMiniSat	0.00	0.00	5.59	0.00	0.03	5.80	0.01	0.06	5.82	0.01	0.15	6.12	0.01	0.51	6.84
SAT	MiniSAT	0.00	0.04	10.56	0.00	0.07	10.57	0.01	0.21	10.71	0.01	0.42	11.01	0.02	1.25	11.30
SAT	Yices2	0.00	0.00	3.50	0.00	0.01	3.63	0.00	0.04	3.76	0.01	0.08	3.76	0.01	0.23	4.02
SAT	MathSAT	0.00	0.01	8.60	0.01	0.03	8.60	0.00	0.06	9.11	0.01	0.14	9.37	0.01	0.41	10.14
SAT	Glucose	0.00	0.01	inf	0.01	0.04	inf	0.00	0.14	inf	0.01	0.25	inf	0.02	0.85	inf
SMT	Yices2	0.00	0.02	6.76	0.00	0.04	6.95	0.01	0.09	7.24	0.01	0.16	7.56	0.01	0.40	8.02
SMT	MathSAT	0.00	0.05	15.52	0.00	0.10	16.81	0.01	0.15	18.10	0.00	0.27	19.91	0.01	0.71	23.00
SMT	Z3	0.00	0.05	18.63	0.00	0.12	19.04	0.01	0.22	19.63	0.01	0.44	20.55	0.01	1.42	21.77
CP	Chuffed	0.00	0.00	0.12	0.00	0.01	0.19	0.00	0.09	0.28	0.00	0.63	0.28	0.00	20.46	0.42
CP	Gecode	0.00	0.00	inf	0.00	0.02	inf	0.00	0.16	inf	0.00	1.22	inf	0.00	30.34	inf
CP	Choco	0.00	0.03	inf	0.00	0.12	inf	0.00	0.49	inf	0.00	2.76	inf	0.00	63.79	inf
CP	OR Tools	0.00	0.02	inf	0.00	0.03	inf	0.00	0.20	inf	0.00	1.29	inf	0.00	33.13	inf
MILP	GLPK	0.06	0.11	0.00	0.07	1.03	0.00	2.85	0.19	0.00	2.96	0.41	0.00	-	-	-
MILP	Gurobi	2.78	0.01	0.00	2.92	0.09	0.00	0.08	7.60	0.00	0.15	38.71	0.00	3.07	0.66	0.00

Table 6. Comparison results on Speck 32/64

Formalism	Solver	NR=2, W=1			NR=3, W=3			NR=4, W=5			NR=5, W=9			NR=6, W=13		
		BT	ST	Memory	BT	ST	Memory	BT	ST	Memory	BT	ST	Memory	BT	ST	Memory
SAT	Kissat	0.00	0.00	213.46	0.00	0.02	214.79	0.01	0.07	215.38	0.01	0.47	216.47	0.02	2.46	218.04
SAT	CaDiCal	0.01	0.00	204.06	0.00	0.03	203.95	0.01	0.09	205.85	0.01	0.54	206.74	0.02	1.92	207.89
SAT	CryptoMiniSat	0.00	0.01	5.79	0.00	0.04	5.87	0.01	0.07	6.02	0.02	0.71	7.50	0.02	4.26	11.65
SAT	MiniSAT	0.00	0.03	10.56	0.01	0.10	10.73	0.01	0.27	10.84	0.01	1.94	10.30	0.02	15.88	11.54
SAT	Yices2	0.01	0.00	3.63	0.00	0.02	3.63	0.01	0.06	3.89	0.02	0.33	4.16	0.02	3.17	4.72
SAT	MathSAT	0.00	0.01	8.60	0.00	0.04	9.11	0.01	0.10	9.37	0.01	0.63	10.66	0.02	3.43	13.23
SAT	Glucose	0.00	0.01	inf	0.00	0.04	inf	0.01	0.19	inf	0.01	0.69	inf	0.02	3.42	inf
SMT	Yices2	0.00	0.01	6.79	0.01	0.04	7.07	0.01	0.10	7.55	0.01	0.66	8.27	0.02	4.38	10.22
SMT	MathSAT	0.00	0.03	16.04	0.01	0.14	19.39	0.01	0.41	25.58	0.01	1.53	35.89	0.02	9.25	65.57
SMT	Z3	0.00	0.04	18.67	0.01	0.12	19.30	0.01	0.36	20.27	0.01	2.17	22.66	0.02	12.88	26.92
CP	Chuffed	0.00	0.00	0.05	0.00	0.04	0.12	0.00	0.81	0.19	0.00	132.69	0.28	-	-	-
CP	Gecode	0.00	0.00	inf	0.00	0.01	inf	0.00	0.33	inf	0.00	74.62	inf	-	-	-
CP	Choco	0.00	0.04	inf	0.00	0.24	inf	0.00	17.41	inf	-	-	-	-	-	-
CP	OR Tools	0.00	0.02	inf	0.00	0.06	inf	0.00	0.47	inf	0.00	28.44	inf	-	-	
MILP	GLPK	0.04	14.92	-	-	-	-	-	-	-	-	-	-	-	-	-
MILP	Gurobi	2.70	0.05	0.00	2.93	0.29	0.00	3.02	1.33	0.00	2.84	3.27	0.00	3.09	21.44	0.00

Table 7. Comparison results on Blake 512

Formalism	Solver	NR=2, W=0			NR=3, W=0			NR=4, W=1			NR=5, W=6			NR=6, W=7		
		BT	ST	Memory	BT	ST	Memory	BT	ST	Memory	BT	ST	Memory	BT	ST	Memory
SAT	Kissat	0.04	0.02	173.08	0.05	0.03	181.31	0.06	0.21	191.15	0.08	18.40	225.68	0.11	55.87	237.44
SAT	CaDiCal	0.03	0.02	162.30	0.05	0.03	171.22	0.06	0.12	184.59	0.08	47.38	208.79	0.11	62.59	230.71
SAT	CryptoMiniSat	0.03	0.02	10.18	0.04	0.02	12.15	0.06	0.13	16.20	0.09	73.82	112.40	0.11	83.68	97.73
SAT	MiniSAT	0.04	0.21	14.57	0.05	0.31	16.07	0.06	1.01	21.82	0.09	280.28	103.45	0.11	367.98	235.89
SAT	Yices2	0.04	0.00	6.29	0.05	0.00	7.69	0.06	0.20	10.02	0.09	84.74	40.92	0.11	150.09	51.24
SAT	MathSAT	0.03	0.04	15.43	0.05	0.06	18.27	0.06	0.30	23.42	0.09	162.17	134.20	0.11	284.66	257.83
SAT	Glucose	0.04	0.04	119.50	0.05	0.04	124.34	0.06	0.18	inf	0.09	110.01	inf	0.11	166.23	inf
SMT	Yices2	0.02	0.05	12.22	0.03	0.07	15.21	0.05	0.21	23.92	0.09	127.53	71.81	0.11	222.02	94.72
SMT	MathSAT	0.02	0.28	37.68	0.03	0.81	56.50	0.05	1.01	92.64	0.10	174.88	268.01	0.12	331.54	307.70
SMT	Z3	0.02	0.21	37.20	0.03	0.34	68.50	0.05	2.12	76.78	0.09	448.57	163.91	0.13	666.45	254.68
CP	Chuffed	0.01	0.01	3.16	0.02	0.03	4.75	0.02	0.07	4.75	-	-	-	-	-	-
CP	Gecode	0.01	0.03	inf	0.01	0.05	inf	0.02	0.26	inf	-	-	-	-	-	-
CP	Choco	-	-	-	-	-	-	-	-	-	-	-	-	-	-	-
CP	OR Tools	-	-	-	-	-	-	-	-	-	-	-	-	-	-	-
MILP	GLPK	-	-	-	-	-	-	-	-	-	-	-	-	-	-	-
MILP	Gurobi	0.94	0.44	0.00	3.02	382.40	0.00	-	-	-	-	-	-	-	-	-

Table 8. Comparison results on Gimli 384

Formalism	Solver	NR=2, W=4			NR=3, W=6			NR=4, W=10			NR=5, W=16			NR=6, W=28		
		BT	ST	Memory	BT	ST	Memory	BT	ST	Memory	BT	ST	Memory	BT	ST	Memory
SAT	Kissat	0.04	0.14	225.93	0.05	0.88	233.74	0.09	5.47	245.46	0.08	27.92	262.10	0.12	355.12	302.89
SAT	CaDiCal	0.04	0.20	215.73	0.07	1.00	222.27	0.08	4.57	233.96	0.09	23.03	251.19	0.12	484.81	288.71
SAT	CryptoMiniSat	0.04	0.42	9.55	0.05	1.61	9.55	0.07	11.40	20.57	0.09	70.18	48.39	-	-	-
SAT	MiniSAT	0.03	1.14	13.90	0.05	3.53	16.64	0.07	24.27	21.23	0.09	217.81	45.50	-	-	-
SAT	Yices2	0.04	0.14	5.70	0.05	1.34	7.70	0.07	12.17	12.64	0.09	81.29	18.93	-	-	-
SAT	MathSAT	0.04	0.34	14.68	0.05	2.06	19.42	0.04	14.44	32.57	0.09	103.20	56.91	-	-	-
SAT	Glucose	0.04	0.21	inf	0.05	0.99	inf	0.07	7.21	inf	-	-	-	-	-	-
SMT	Yices2	0.03	0.34	12.98	0.05	1.62	18.63	0.07	9.16	27.50	0.11	75.54	42.49	-	-	-
SMT	MathSAT	0.04	0.87	52.13	0.05	2.89	80.23	0.07	14.35	125.35	0.11	99.44	208.36	-	-	-
SMT	Z3	0.04	1.47	39.06	0.05	5.10	72.12	0.07	33.32	136.04	0.11	569.40	149.982	-	-	-
CP	Chuffed	0.02	0.30	0.94	0.01	22.01	1.41	-	-	-	-	-	-	-	-	-
CP	Gecode	0.02	0.15	inf	0.03	22.39	inf	-	-	-	-	-	-	-	-	-
CP	Choco	0.02	46.04	inf	-	-	-	-	-	-	-	-	-	-	-	-
CP	OR Tools	0.02	0.72	inf	-	-	-	-	-	-	-	-	-	-	-	-
MILP	GLPK	0.57	75.56	0.00	-	-	-	-	-	-	-	-	-	-	-	-
MILP	Gurobi	4.50	1.45	0.00	5.92	22.49	0.00	7.62	452.57	0.00	-	-	-	-	-	-

Table 9. Comparison results on Present 64/80

Formalism	Solver	NR=2, W=4			NR=3, W=8			NR=4, W=12			NR=5, W=20			NR=6, W=24		
		BT	ST	Memory	BT	ST	Memory	BT	ST	Memory	BT	ST	Memory	BT	ST	Memory
SAT	Kissat	0.00	0.03	218.14	0.02	0.14	219.83	0.03	0.46	222.53	0.03	5.64	226.42	0.03	11.02	231.10
SAT	CaDiCal	0.02	0.04	207.43	0.02	0.19	209.20	0.02	1.08	212.66	0.03	5.78	216.67	0.04	11.25	220.55
SAT	CryptoMiniSat	0.02	0.04	6.08	0.02	0.04	6.08	0.03	0.81	7.99	0.03	9.37	13.23	0.03	31.09	21.76
SAT	MiniSAT	0.02	0.21	11.07	0.02	0.21	11.07	0.03	3.43	12.58	0.03	21.28	14.02	0.03	62.39	15.38
SAT	Yices2	0.01	0.01	3.89	0.02	0.13	4.29	0.03	0.49	4.73	0.03	5.74	6.04	0.03	18.47	7.27
SAT	MathSAT	0.02	0.05	9.37	0.02	0.89	33.57	0.03	0.80	11.95	0.03	7.08	16.59	0.04	18.93	18.91
SAT	Glucose	0.02	0.08	inf	0.02	0.42	inf	0.02	1.29	inf	0.03	8.12	inf	0.03	15.87	inf
SMT	Yices2	0.02	0.09	7.84	0.02	0.27	9.18	0.03	0.73	11.03	0.04	6.16	14.11	0.05	16.91	18.37
SMT	MathSAT	0.02	0.29	25.06	0.02	0.89	33.57	0.03	2.32	47.23	0.04	9.97	71.47	0.05	27.06	91.30
SMT	Z3	0.02	0.50	20.94	0.02	1.66	23.75	0.03	4.13	27.24	0.04	18.51	42.50	0.05	42.97	73.78
CP	Chuffed	0.01	0.00	0.19	0.01	0.11	0.28	0.01	3.13	0.42	-	-	-	-	-	-
CP	Gecode	0.01	0.00	inf	0.01	0.08	inf	0.01	2.43	inf	0.01	399.94	inf	-	-	-
CP	Choco	0.01	0.04	inf	0.01	0.31	inf	0.01	7.12	inf	-	-	-	-	-	-
CP	OR Tools	0.01	0.25	inf	0.01	0.47	inf	0.01	4.80	inf	-	-	-	-	-	-
MILP	GLPK	0.20	1.01	0.00	-	-	-	-	-	-	-	-	-	-	-	-
MILP	Gurobi	3.08	0.07	0.00	3.20	0.53	0.00	3.37	0.92	0.00	3.44	3.81	0.00	3.64	111.07	0.00

References

1. Abdelkhalek, A., Sasaki, Y., Todo, Y., Tolba, M., Youssef, A.M.: MILP modeling for (large) s-boxes to optimize probability of differential characteristics. IACR Trans. Symmetric Cryptol. **2017**(4), 99–129 (2017)
2. Abed, F., List, E., Lucks, S., Wenzel, J.: Differential cryptanalysis of round-reduced SIMON and SPECK. In: Cid, C., Rechberger, C. (eds.) FSE 2014. LNCS, vol. 8540, pp. 525–545. Springer, Heidelberg (2015). https://doi.org/10.1007/978-3-662-46706-0_27
3. Ankele, R., Kölbl, S.: Mind the gap - a closer look at the security of block ciphers against differential cryptanalysis. In: Cid, C., Jacobson Jr, M. (eds.) SAC 2018. LNCS, vol. 11349, pp. 163–190. Springer, Cham (2018). https://doi.org/10.1007/978-3-030-10970-7_8
4. Audemard, G., Simon, L.: Glucose and syrup: nine years in the sat competitions. In: Proceedings of SAT Competition, pp. 24–25 (2018)

5. Bellini, E., Gérault, D., Protopapa, M., Rossi, M.: Monte Carlo tree search for automatic differential characteristics search: application to SPECK. In: Isobe, T., Sarkar, S. (eds.) INDOCRYPT 2022. LNCS, vol. 13774, pp. 373–397. Springer, Cham (2022). https://doi.org/10.1007/978-3-031-22912-1_17
6. Bestuzheva, K., et al.: The SCIP Optimization Suite 8.0. ZIB-Report 21–41, Zuse Institute Berlin (2021)
7. Biere, A., Fazekas, K., Fleury, M., Heisinger, M.: CaDiCaL, Kissat, Paracooba, Plingeling and Treengeling entering the SAT Competition 2020. In: Balyo, T., Froleyks, N., Heule, M., Iser, M., Järvisalo, M., Suda, M. (eds.) Proceedings of the SAT Competition 2020 - Solver and Benchmark Descriptions. Department of Computer Science Report Series B, vol. B-2020-1, pp. 51–53. University of Helsinki (2020)
8. Biere, A., Heule, M., van Maaren, H., Walsh, T. (eds.): Handbook of Satisfiability, Frontiers in Artificial Intelligence and Applications, vol. 185. IOS Press (2009)
9. Biham, E., Shamir, A.: Differential cryptanalysis of des-like cryptosystems. J. Cryptol. **4**(1), 3–72 (1991)
10. Boura, C., Coggia, D.: Efficient MILP modelings for sboxes and linear layers of SPN ciphers. IACR Trans. Symmetric Cryptol. **2020**(3), 327–361 (2020)
11. Brayton, R.K., Hachtel, G.D., McMullen, C.T., Sangiovanni-Vincentelli, A.L.: Logic Minimization Algorithms for VLSI synthesis, The Kluwer International Series in Engineering and Computer Science, vol. 2. Springer, Heidelberg (1984)
12. Chu, G., Stuckey, P.J., Schutt, A., Ehlers, T., Gange, G., Francis, K.: Chuffed, a lazy clause generation solver. https://github.com/chuffed/chuffed. Accessed 19 Mar 2023
13. Cimatti, A., Griggio, A., Schaafsma, B.J., Sebastiani, R.: The MathSAT5 SMT solver. In: Piterman, N., Smolka, S.A. (eds.) TACAS 2013. LNCS, vol. 7795, pp. 93–107. Springer, Heidelberg (2013). https://doi.org/10.1007/978-3-642-36742-7_7
14. Dantzig, G.B.: Maximization of a linear function of variables subject to linear inequalities. Act. Anal. Prod. Allocat. **13**, 339–347 (1951)
15. Davis, M., Logemann, G., Loveland, D.W.: A machine program for theorem-proving. Commun. ACM **5**(7), 394–397 (1962)
16. Davis, M., Putnam, H.: A computing procedure for quantification theory. J. ACM **7**(3), 201–215 (1960)
17. Delaune, S., Derbez, P., Huynh, P., Minier, M., Mollimard, V., Prud'homme, C.: SKINNY with scalpel - comparing tools for differential analysis. IACR Cryptol. ePrint Arch. 1402 (2020)
18. Delaune, S., Derbez, P., Huynh, P., Minier, M., Mollimard, V., Prud'homme, C.: Efficient methods to search for best differential characteristics on SKINNY. In: Sako, K., Tippenhauer, N.O. (eds.) ACNS 2021. LNCS, vol. 12727, pp. 184–207. Springer, Cham (2021). https://doi.org/10.1007/978-3-030-78375-4_8
19. Dutertre, B.: Yices 2.2. In: Biere, A., Bloem, R. (eds.) Computer Aided Verification - 26th International Conference, CAV 2014, Held as Part of the Vienna Summer of Logic, VSL 2014, Vienna, Austria, 18–22 July 2014. Proceedings. LNCS, vol. 8559, pp. 737–744. Springer, Cham (2014)
20. Eén, N., Sörensson, N.: An extensible SAT-solver. In: Giunchiglia, E., Tacchella, A. (eds.) SAT 2003. LNCS, vol. 2919, pp. 502–518. Springer, Heidelberg (2004). https://doi.org/10.1007/978-3-540-24605-3_37
21. Fu, K., Wang, M., Guo, Y., Sun, S., Hu, L.: MILP-based automatic search algorithms for differential and linear trails for speck. In: Peyrin, T. (ed.) FSE 2016. LNCS, vol. 9783, pp. 268–288. Springer, Heidelberg (2016). https://doi.org/10.1007/978-3-662-52993-5_14

22. Ganesh, V., Dill, D.L.: A Decision procedure for bit-vectors and arrays. In: Damm, W., Hermanns, H. (eds.) CAV 2007. LNCS, vol. 4590, pp. 519–531. Springer, Heidelberg (2007). https://doi.org/10.1007/978-3-540-73368-3_52
23. Gérault, D., Lafourcade, P., Minier, M., Solnon, C.: Revisiting AES related-key differential attacks with constraint programming. Inf. Process. Lett. **139**, 24–29 (2018)
24. Gérault, D., Lafourcade, P., Minier, M., Solnon, C.: Computing AES related-key differential characteristics with constraint programming. Artif. Intell. **278**, 103183 (2020)
25. Google: Or-tools - google optimization tools. https://developers.google.com/optimization. Accessed 19 Mar 2023
26. Gurobi Optimization, LLC: Gurobi Optimizer Reference Manual (2023)
27. Heule, M., Iser, M., Jarvisalo, M., Suda, M., Balyo, T.: Sat competition 2022. https://satcompetition.github.io/2022/results.html. Accessed 2 Mar 2023
28. Kölbl, S., Leander, G., Tiessen, T.: Observations on the SIMON block cipher family. In: Gennaro, R., Robshaw, M. (eds.) CRYPTO 2015. LNCS, vol. 9215, pp. 161–185. Springer, Heidelberg (2015). https://doi.org/10.1007/978-3-662-47989-6_8
29. Land, A.H., Doig, A.G.: An automatic method for solving discrete programming problems. In: Jünger, M., et al. (eds.) 50 Years of Integer Programming 1958-2008, pp. 105–132. Springer, Heidelberg (2010). https://doi.org/10.1007/978-3-540-68279-0_5
30. Li, T., Sun, Y.: Superball: a new approach for MILP modelings of Boolean functions. IACR Trans. Symmetric Cryptol. **2022**(3), 341–367 (2022)
31. Lipmaa, H., Moriai, S.: Efficient algorithms for computing differential properties of addition. IACR Cryptol. ePrint Arch. 1 (2001)
32. Liu, Y.: Techniques for Block Cipher Cryptanalysis. Ph.D. thesis, KU Leuven, Faculty of Engineering Science (2018). https://www.esat.kuleuven.be/cosic/publications/thesis-306.pdf
33. Liu, Z., Li, Y., Wang, M.: Optimal differential trails in Simon-like ciphers. IACR Cryptol. ePrint Arch. 178 (2017)
34. Matsui, M., Yamagishi, A.: A new method for known plaintext attack of FEAL cipher. In: Rueppel, R.A. (ed.) EUROCRYPT 1992. LNCS, vol. 658, pp. 81–91. Springer, Heidelberg (1993). https://doi.org/10.1007/3-540-47555-9_7
35. McCluskey, E.J.: Minimization of Boolean functions. Bell Syst. Tech. J. **35**, 1417–1444 (1956)
36. MiniZinc: Minizinc challenge 2022 results. https://www.minizinc.org/challenge2022/results2022.html. Accessed 2 Mar 2023
37. Mouha, N., Wang, Q., Gu, D., Preneel, B.: Differential and linear cryptanalysis using mixed-integer linear programming. In: Wu, C.-K., Yung, M., Lin, D. (eds.) Inscrypt 2011. LNCS, vol. 7537, pp. 57–76. Springer, Heidelberg (2012). https://doi.org/10.1007/978-3-642-34704-7_5
38. de Moura, L., Bjørner, N.: Z3: an efficient SMT solver. In: Ramakrishnan, C.R., Rehof, J. (eds.) TACAS 2008. LNCS, vol. 4963, pp. 337–340. Springer, Heidelberg (2008). https://doi.org/10.1007/978-3-540-78800-3_24
39. Nethercote, N., Stuckey, P.J., Becket, R., Brand, S., Duck, G.J., Tack, G.: MiniZinc: towards a standard CP modelling language. In: Bessière, C. (ed.) CP 2007. LNCS, vol. 4741, pp. 529–543. Springer, Heidelberg (2007). https://doi.org/10.1007/978-3-540-74970-7_38
40. Niemetz, A., Preiner, M., Biere, A.: Boolector 2.0. J. Satisf. Boolean Model. Comput. **9**(1), 53–58 (2014)

41. Oki, E.: GLPK (gnu linear programming kit) (2012)
42. Padberg, M., Rinaldi, G.: A branch-and-cut algorithm for the resolution of large-scale symmetric traveling salesman problems. SIAM Rev. **33**(1), 60–100 (1991)
43. Prud'homme, C., Godet, A., Fages, J.G.: choco-solver. https://github.com/chocoteam/choco-solver. Accessed 19 Mar 2023
44. Quine, W.V.: The problem of simplifying truth functions. Amer. Math. Monthly **59**, 521–531 (1952)
45. Quine, W.V.: A way to simplify truth functions. Amer. Math. Monthly **62**, 627–631 (1955)
46. Rossi, F., van Beek, P., Walsh, T. (eds.): Handbook of Constraint Programming, Foundations of Artificial Intelligence, vol. 2. Elsevier (2006)
47. Schulte, C., Tack, G., Lagerkvyst, M.Z.: Gecode. https://www.gecode.org/index.html. Accessed 19 Mar 2023
48. Silva, J.P.M., Sakallah, K.A.: GRASP: a search algorithm for propositional satisfiability. IEEE Trans. Comput. **48**(5), 506–521 (1999)
49. Soos, M., Nohl, K., Castelluccia, C.: Extending SAT solvers to cryptographic problems. In: Kullmann, O. (ed.) SAT 2009. LNCS, vol. 5584, pp. 244–257. Springer, Heidelberg (2009). https://doi.org/10.1007/978-3-642-02777-2_24
50. Sun, L., Wang, W., Wang, M.: Accelerating the search of differential and linear characteristics with the SAT method. IACR Trans. Symmetric Cryptol. **2021**(1), 269–315 (2021)
51. Sun, S., et al.: Analysis of AES, SKINNY, and others with constraint programming. IACR Trans. Symmetric Cryptol. **2017**(1), 281–306 (2017)
52. Sun, S., Hu, L., Wang, P., Qiao, K., Ma, X., Song, L.: Automatic security evaluation and (related-key) differential characteristic search: application to SIMON, PRESENT, LBlock, DES(L) and other bit-oriented block ciphers. In: Sarkar, P., Iwata, T. (eds.) ASIACRYPT 2014. LNCS, vol. 8873, pp. 158–178. Springer, Heidelberg (2014). https://doi.org/10.1007/978-3-662-45611-8_9
53. Xu, S., Feng, X., Wang, Y.: On two factors affecting the efficiency of MILP models in automated cryptanalyses. IACR Cryptol. ePrint Arch. 196 (2023)
54. Zhou, C., Zhang, W., Ding, T., Xiang, Z.: Improving the MILP-based security evaluation algorithm against differential/linear cryptanalysis using a divide-and-conquer approach. IACR Trans. Symmetric Cryptol. **2019**(4), 438–469 (2019)

Key Filtering in Cube Attacks from the Implementation Aspect

Hao Fan[1], Yonglin Hao[2(✉)], Qingju Wang[3], Xinxin Gong[2], and Lin Jiao[2]

[1] School of Cyber Science and Technology, Shandong University, Qingdao, China
[2] State Key Laboratory of Cryptology, Beijing 100878, China
haoyonglin@yeah.net
[3] Telecom Paris, Institut Polytechnique de Paris, Paris, France

Abstract. In cube attacks, key filtering is a basic step of identifying the correct key candidates by referring to the truth tables of superpolies. When terms of superpolies get massive, the truth table lookup complexity of key filtering increases significantly. In this paper, we propose the concept of implementation dependency dividing all cube attacks into two categories: *implementation dependent* and *implementation independent*. The implementation dependent cube attacks can only be feasible when the assumption that *one encryption oracle query is more complicated than one table lookup* holds. On the contrary, implementation independent cube attacks remain feasible in the extreme case where encryption oracles are implemented in the full codebook manner making one encryption query equivalent to one table lookup. From this point of view, we scrutinize existing cube attack results of stream ciphers Trivium, Grain-128AEAD, Acorn and Kreyvium. As a result, many of them turn out to be implementation dependent. Combining with the degree evaluation and divide-and-conquer techniques used for superpoly recovery, we further propose new cube attack results on Kreyvium reduced to 898, 899 and 900 rounds. Such new results not only mount to the maximal number of rounds so far but also are implementation independent.

Keywords: Stream ciphers · Cube attacks · Division property · Superpoly · Key filtering

1 Introduction

Cube attack was proposed by Dinur and Shamir in [2] at EUROCRYPT 2009 and has become one of the most efficient cryptanalysis methods against primitives taking public initial values (IV) and secret key as inputs. For a cipher with public IV $\boldsymbol{v} = (v_0, v_1, \ldots, v_{m-1}) \in \mathbb{F}_2^m$ and secret key $\boldsymbol{x} = (x_0, x_1, \ldots, x_{n-1}) \in \mathbb{F}_2^n$, an output bit generated by the cipher can be regarded as a polynomial of $\boldsymbol{v}, \boldsymbol{x}$ denoted as $f(\boldsymbol{x}, \boldsymbol{v})$. In cube attacks, a set of IV indices, referred to as the *cube indices*, is selected as $I = \{i_0, i_1, \ldots, i_{|I|-1}\} \subset \{0, 1, \ldots, m-1\}$. Such a set I determines a specific structure called *cube*, denoted as C_I, containing $2^{|I|}$

J. Deng et al. (Eds.): CANS 2023, LNCS 14342, pp. 293–317, 2023.
https://doi.org/10.1007/978-981-99-7563-1_14

values: the cube variables in $\{v_{i_0}, v_{i_1}, \ldots, v_{i_{|I|-1}}\}$ take all possible combinations of values while the key and non-cube IV variables are static. It is proved that the summation of f over the cube C_I equals a particular polynomial $p(\boldsymbol{x}, \boldsymbol{v})$, commonly referred as the *superpoly* of cube I, denoted as $p_I(\boldsymbol{x}, \boldsymbol{v})$ or $p(\boldsymbol{x}, \boldsymbol{v})$ when I is clear from the context. The superpoly p_I also defines a set $J \subseteq \{0, \ldots, n-1\}$ such that the algebraic normal form ANF of p_I is only related to the key bit variable x_j for $j \in J$.

The general process of cube attacks can be naturally summarized into the 4 phases namely *superpoly recovery, key filtering, cube sum computation* and *exhaustive search*. The *superpoly recovery* recovery phase is carried out offline for determining I and the ANF (or truth table) of the corresponding superpoly p_I. Then, the cube summation over C_I, denoted as θ, is computed by querying the targeted encryption oracle for $2^{|I|}$ times. After that, the *key filtering* phase filter the correct key candidates satisfying $p(\boldsymbol{x}, \boldsymbol{v}) = \theta$ so as to recover 1 bit of secret key information. Finally, the *exhaustive search* recovers the remaining key bits through the exhaustive search with 2^{n-1} encryption oracle queries.

The superpoly recovery phase is crucial and used to dominate the overall complexity. Originally, the superpolies in cube attacks can only be recovered with repeated cube summation experiments restricting the superpoly ANFs to linear/quadratic form and limiting the cube dimensions within practical reach [2,13]. Theoretic deduction remains infeasible until the proposal of the division property based cube attack [18]: a combination of the division property [16,17,19,22] and cube attacks. Such a new cryptanalysis method enables us to conduct cube attacks with the mixed integer linear programming (MILP)–a mature technique that have been widely in the security evaluations of symmetric primitives against differential, linear and many other cryptanalysis methods [4,12,14]. The original division property based cube attacks suffer from extremely high offline complexities and a significant loss of accuracy [20,21]. After years' development, the state-of-art three-subset division property based cube attack [6] has been combined with the divide-and-conquer model solving technique [7,9,15] enabling us to recover the accurate ANFs of superpolies within a practical complexity, even when the superpolies are massive with $|J| \approx n$ and high algebraic degrees.

Motivations. Now that the superpoly recovery is no longer the complexity dominant, researchers turn to use smaller dimensional cubes with massive superpolies so as to conduct cube attacks covering more rounds. Following such a strategy, the current best cube attacks on TRIVIUM, Grain-128AEAD, KREYVIUM and ACORN, etc. [7,9] are all using massive superpolies related to almost all key bits, i.e., $|J| \approx n$, resulting in 2^n truth table lookups in the key filtering phase. Adding the 2^{n-1} queries in the exhaustive search phase, there is an obvious challenge that the overall complexity of cube attacks using massive superpolies may have exceeded the generic complexity bound of 2^n. According to the explanations in [7,9], the feasibility of such attacks is based on the assumption that 1 query to the encryption oracle is much more complicated than 1 table lookup: for example in [7], 1 query to the 848-round TRIVIUM encryption oracle is regarded as

$848 \times 9 = 7632$ XORs while a table lookup only contains 1 XOR. However, from the adversary's view, a query to the oracle does not take more effort than the execution of an XOR operation. Besides, such a bitwise and roundwise implementation is not the only way to realize cryptographic primitives: the selection of tags in TRIVIUM naturally supports a 64-time acceleration [1] for fast software speeds; the time for an unrolled hardware implementation of the full encryption is exactly 1 clock tick which is equal to that of a XOR. Therefore, the applicability of massive superpolies to cube attacks heavily relies on the implementations so the following 2 questions should be discussed in detail:

1. Whether the existing cube attacks are feasible for arbitrary implementations.
2. Whether there exist implementation-independent cube attacks that can reach more rounds.

Our Contributions. In this paper, we answer the above questions and scrutinize the existing cube attacks on several ciphers. Our contributions can be summarized as follows:

- We give the concept of implementation dependency and divide cube attacks into two categories, namely the *implementation dependent cube attacks* and the *implementation independent cube attacks.* Implementation dependent cube attacks can only be feasible when a query to the encryption oracle is more expensive than a table lookup while the implementation independent cube attacks remain feasible in the extreme case where the encryption oracle is implemented as the full codebook making one oracle query equivalent to one table lookup.
- Following the above new concepts for cube attacks, we revisit the latest three-subset division property based cube attacks on several symmetric primitives. According to our evaluations, many current best results using massive superpolies, such as all attacks on TRIVIUM in [9], are *implementation dependent.*
- We also propose new *implementation independent* results on 898-, 899-, 900-round KREYVIUM using the methods in [7,9]: superior to their massive-superpoly based, implementation dependent counterparts.

We list all our results in Table 1.

Organization of the Paper. Sect. 2 provides the necessary background information. Then, we describe our new three-subset division property based cube attacks on round-reduced KREYVIUM in Sect. 3. After that, we introduce the concept of implementation dependency and detail the evaluation of an existing cube attack on TRIVIUM in Sect. 4. Thorough implementation dependency evaluations of current best cube attack results for our targeted primitives are given in Sect. 5 and we conclude the paper in Sect. 6.

2 Preliminary

In this section, we first summarize the general procedure of cube attacks in Sect. 2.1. Then, we briefly review the technique details of division property based superpoly recovery (Sect. 2.2) and table-lookup based key filtering (Sect. 2.3).

Table 1. The complexity and implementation dependency of cube attacks. The complexities are evaluated with the number of instructions.

Cipher	#Rounds	Cube Attack	Exhaustive Search†	Implement. Dependency‡	Source
TRIVIUM	843	$2^{82.99}$	2^{81}	✓	[9]
	844	$2^{82.84}$	2^{81}	✓	[9]
	845	$2^{84.92}$	2^{81}	✓	[9]
	846	$2^{84.58}$	2^{81}	✓	[7]
	847	$2^{84.58}$	2^{81}	✓	[7]
	848	$2^{84.58}$	2^{81}	✓	[7]
Grain-128AEAD	191	$2^{131.55}$	2^{129}	✓	[9]
	192	$2^{133.17}$	2^{129}	✓	[7]
ACORN	776	$2^{128.58}$	2^{129}	×	[7]
KREYVIUM	894	2^{128}	2^{129}	×	[9]
	895	$2^{133.17}$	2^{129}	✓	[7]
	898	$\mathbf{2^{128.58}}$	$\mathbf{2^{129}}$	×	**Sect.** 3
	899	$\mathbf{2^{128.58}}$	$\mathbf{2^{129}}$	×	**Sect.** 3
	900	$\mathbf{2^{128.58}}$	$\mathbf{2^{129}}$	×	**Sect.** 3

† One query of the cipher considered is a table lookup and equals two instructions, then the brute force attack of the cipher needs $2^{\kappa+1}$ instructions where κ is the key size.
‡ ✓ denotes *implementation dependent* and × denotes *implementation independent.* The details of our analysis can be found in Sect. 5.

We first define some notations used in the remainder of this paper. We consider the stream ciphers with n-bit secret key $\boldsymbol{x} = (x_0, \ldots, x_{n-1})$ and m-bit public IV $\boldsymbol{v} = (v_0, \ldots, v_{m-1})$. For arbitrary positive integer $t > 1$, we denote the set of integers $\{0, \ldots, t-1\}$ as $[0, t)$ hereafter.

2.1 The Main Procedures of Cube Attacks

In cube attacks, the adversary is faced with an encryption oracle of the targeted stream cipher, denoted as E. The adversary can query E with a public IV vector $\boldsymbol{v}$ and acquire the key stream bits corresponding to $\boldsymbol{v}$ and an embedded secret key $\boldsymbol{x}_e$, denoted as $\boldsymbol{z}(\boldsymbol{v}, \boldsymbol{x}_e) = E(\boldsymbol{v})$. When queried with a key-IV pair $(\boldsymbol{x}, \boldsymbol{v})$, the oracle E outputs the corresponding key stream bits $\boldsymbol{z}(\boldsymbol{v}, \boldsymbol{x}) = E(\boldsymbol{v}, \boldsymbol{x})$. The target for the adversary is to retrieve the embedded key $\boldsymbol{x}_e$ within feasible complexity limits. The procedures of cube attacks for recovering $\boldsymbol{x}_e$ can be summarized as follows:

1. `Superpoly Recovery.` Recover the ANF of the superpoly $p_I(\boldsymbol{x}, \boldsymbol{IV})$ where IV is a known constant and p_I can be a simple and low-degree polynomial related to key bits $\boldsymbol{x}[J]$ where $J \subseteq [0, n-1]$. Such a superpoly can be recovered with division property based techniques that we will detail in.
2. `Cube Sum Computation.` For all $2^{|I|}$ $\boldsymbol{v} \in C_I(\boldsymbol{IV})$, query $E(\boldsymbol{v})$ and sum the output keystream bits for the exact value of superpoly $p_I(\boldsymbol{IV}, \boldsymbol{x}_e) = \theta$.

3. `Key Filtering`. For involved candidate bits: construct lookup tables for identifying the correct key candidate $\boldsymbol{x}_c$'s, s.t. $p_I(\boldsymbol{IV}, \boldsymbol{x}_c) = \theta$.
4. `Exhaustive Search`. find the only correct key $\boldsymbol{x}_e$ from the remaining keys.

2.2 Division Property Based Superpoly Recoveries

In the view of Boolean function for describing division property, the monomial prediction technique is developed to evaluate the degree of Boolean functions and is soon applied to recovery target polynomials, mainly for the polynomials after many rounds of iteration in stream or block ciphers. Hu et al. proposed the monomial prediction technique in [10], then developed it to the Nested Framework, which was used to recover the exact ANFs of massive superpolies [9].

(Bit-Based) Division Property. Before giving a brief introduction to division property, we need some notations for bit-vectors. For any bitvector $\boldsymbol{x} \in \mathbb{F}_2^m$, $x[i]$ denotes the ith bit of $\boldsymbol{x}$ where $i \in \{0, 1, \dots, m-1\}$. Given two bitvectors $\boldsymbol{x} \in \mathbb{F}_2^m$ and $\boldsymbol{u} \in \mathbb{F}_2^m$, $\pi_{\boldsymbol{u}}(\boldsymbol{x}) = \boldsymbol{x}^{\boldsymbol{u}} = \prod_{i=0}^{m-1} x[i]^{u[i]}$. Moreover, $\boldsymbol{x} \succeq \boldsymbol{u}$ denotes $x[i] \geq u[i]$ for all $i \in \{0, 1, \dots, m-1\}$; otherwise we denote $\boldsymbol{x} \not\succeq \boldsymbol{u}$.

The (conventional) division property, a.k.a two-subset division property, was proposed at Eurocrypt 2015 [17], and it is regarded as the generalization of the integral property.

Definition 1 (Two-subset division property). *Let $\mathbb{X}$ be a multiset whose elements take a value of $\mathbb{F}_2^m$, and $\mathbb{K} = \{\boldsymbol{k} \mid \boldsymbol{k} \in \mathbb{F}_2^m\}$ be a set of m-dimension bit vectors. When the multiset $\mathbb{X}$ has the division property $\mathcal{D}_{\mathbb{K}}^{1^m}$, it fulfills the following conditions:*

$$\bigoplus_{x \in \mathbb{X}} \boldsymbol{x}^{\boldsymbol{u}} = \begin{cases} \text{unknown} & \text{if there are } \boldsymbol{k} \in \mathbb{K} \text{ s.t. } \boldsymbol{u} \succeq \boldsymbol{k}, \\ 0 & \text{otherwise.} \end{cases}$$

To improve the accuracy of the division property propagation, the three-subset division property was proposed in [19], where the number of divided subsets is extended from two to three.

Definition 2 (Three-subset division property). *Let $\mathbb{X}$ be a multiset whose elements take a value of $\mathbb{F}_2^m$, and $\mathbb{K} = \{\boldsymbol{k} \mid \boldsymbol{k} \in \mathbb{F}_2^m\}$ and $\mathbb{L} = \{\boldsymbol{\ell} \mid \boldsymbol{\ell} \in \mathbb{F}_2^m\}$ be two sets of m-dimension bit vectors. Define $\boldsymbol{x}^{\boldsymbol{u}} := \prod_{i=0}^{m-1} x_i^{u_i}$, $\boldsymbol{u} \in \mathbb{F}_2^m$. When the multiset $\mathbb{X}$ has the three-subset division property $\mathcal{D}_{\mathbb{K},\mathbb{L}}^{1^m}$, it fulfills the following conditions:*

$$\bigoplus_{x \in \mathbb{X}} \boldsymbol{x}^{\boldsymbol{u}} = \begin{cases} \text{unknown} & \text{if there are } \boldsymbol{k} \in \mathbb{K} \text{ s.t. } \boldsymbol{u} \succeq \boldsymbol{k}, \\ 1 & \text{else if there is } \boldsymbol{\ell} \in \mathbb{L} \text{ s.t. } \boldsymbol{u} = \boldsymbol{\ell}, \\ 0 & \text{otherwise.} \end{cases}$$

Xiang et al. introduced MILP-based method to automatically search integral distinguishers (based on two-subset division property) for several block ciphers [22]. They modeled the propagation rules of basic operations such as COPY,

AND, and XOR by MILP. Later the MILP division property method was further applied to cube attacks on stream ciphers [18,20]. For the three-subset division property and the variant without unknown (removing the unknown set $\mathbb{K}$ from the Definition 2 for make cube attacks based on three-subset division property infeasible and/or practical), the detailed propagation rules and the MILP modelings can be found in [6,21].

Monomial Prediction. The monomial prediction technique [10] can be used to determine that the coefficient of an involved monomial is 0 or 1 in the ANF of a given Boolean function, which can be applied to the construction of SAT models for block ciphers taking the key schedule into consideration in order to find refined integral distinguishers [5], or to recover the ANF of the superpoly of the cube attacks. In this paper, we focus on the latter application.

Let $f : \mathbb{F}_2^n \to \mathbb{F}_2$ be a Boolean function whose *algebraic normal form* (ANF) is

$$f(\boldsymbol{x}) = f(x_0, x_1, \dots, x_{n-1}) = \bigoplus_{\boldsymbol{u} \in \mathbb{F}_2^n} a_{\boldsymbol{u}} \pi_{\boldsymbol{u}}(\boldsymbol{x})$$

where $a_{\boldsymbol{u}} \in \mathbb{F}_2$, $\pi_{\boldsymbol{u}}(\boldsymbol{x}) = \prod_{i=0}^{n-1} x_i^{u_i}$ is defined as before and is a monomial.

Let $\boldsymbol{f} : \mathbb{F}_2^n \to \mathbb{F}_2^m$ be a vectorial Boolean function with $\boldsymbol{y} = (y_0, y_1, \dots, y_{m-1}) = \boldsymbol{f}(\boldsymbol{x}) = (f_0(\boldsymbol{x}), f_1(\boldsymbol{x}), \dots, f_{m-1}(\boldsymbol{x}))$, where $f_i : \mathbb{F}_2^n \to \mathbb{F}_2$ is a Boolean function. For $\boldsymbol{u} \in \mathbb{F}_2^n$ and $\boldsymbol{v} \in \mathbb{F}_2^m$, we use $\boldsymbol{x}^{\boldsymbol{u}} \to \boldsymbol{y}^{\boldsymbol{v}}$ to denote that monomial $\boldsymbol{x}^{\boldsymbol{u}}$ appears in $\boldsymbol{y}^{\boldsymbol{v}}$.

We are interested in the following case: Let $\boldsymbol{f}$ be a composition of a sequence of r vectorial Boolean functions

$$\boldsymbol{y} = \boldsymbol{f}(\boldsymbol{x}) = \boldsymbol{f}^{(r-1)} \circ \boldsymbol{f}^{(r-2)} \circ \cdots \circ \boldsymbol{f}^{(0)}(\boldsymbol{x}).$$

For $0 \le i \le r-1$, suppose $\boldsymbol{x}^{(i)} \in \mathbb{F}_2^{n_i}$ and $\boldsymbol{x}^{(i+1)} \in \mathbb{F}_2^{n_i+1}$ are the input and output of the ith component function $\boldsymbol{f}^{(i)}$. We are interested in whether a monomial of $\boldsymbol{x}^{(0)}$, say $\pi_{\boldsymbol{u}^{(0)}}(\boldsymbol{x}^{(0)})$, appears in one monomial of $\boldsymbol{x}^{(r)}$, i.e., $\pi_{\boldsymbol{u}^{(0)}}(\boldsymbol{x}^{(0)}) \to \pi_{\boldsymbol{u}^{(r)}}(\boldsymbol{x}^{(r)})$. To make it happen, for one monomial in $\pi_{\boldsymbol{u}^{(i)}}(\boldsymbol{x}^{(i)})$, there must exist at least one monomial in $\pi_{\boldsymbol{u}^{(i+1)}}(\boldsymbol{x}^{(i+1)})$, i.e., for every $0 \le i \le r-1$, a transition $\pi_{\boldsymbol{u}^{(i)}}(\boldsymbol{x}^{(i)}) \to \pi_{\boldsymbol{u}^{(i+1)}}(\boldsymbol{x}^{(i+1)})$ must be guaranteed.

Definition 3 (Monomial Trail [10]). *Let $\boldsymbol{x}^{(i+1)} = \boldsymbol{f}^{(i)}(\boldsymbol{x}^{(i)})$ for $0 \le i \le r-1$. We call a sequence of monomials $(\pi_{\boldsymbol{u}^{(0)}}(\boldsymbol{x}^{(0)}), \pi_{\boldsymbol{u}^{(1)}}(\boldsymbol{x}^{(1)}), \dots, \pi_{\boldsymbol{u}^{(r)}}(\boldsymbol{x}^{(r)}))$ an r-round monomial trail connecting $\pi_{\boldsymbol{u}^{(0)}}(\boldsymbol{x}^{(0)})$ and $\pi_{\boldsymbol{u}^{(r)}}(\boldsymbol{x}^{(r)})$ under the composite function $\boldsymbol{f}(x) = \boldsymbol{f}^{(r-1)} \circ \boldsymbol{f}^{(r-2)} \circ \cdots \circ \boldsymbol{f}^{(0)}$ if there exist*

$$\pi_{\boldsymbol{u}^{(0)}}(\boldsymbol{x}^{(0)}) \to \cdots \pi_{\boldsymbol{u}^{(i)}}(\boldsymbol{x}^{(i)}) \to \cdots \to \pi_{\boldsymbol{u}^{(r)}}(\boldsymbol{x}^{(r)}).$$

If there exist at least one monomial trail connecting $\pi_{\boldsymbol{u}^{(0)}}(\boldsymbol{x}^{(0)})$ and $\pi_{\boldsymbol{u}^{(r)}}(\boldsymbol{x}^{(r)})$, we write $\pi_{\boldsymbol{u}^{(0)}}(\boldsymbol{x}^{(0)}) \rightsquigarrow \pi_{\boldsymbol{u}^{(r)}}(\boldsymbol{x}^{(r)})$. Otherwise, $\pi_{\boldsymbol{u}^{(0)}}(\boldsymbol{x}^{(0)}) \not\rightsquigarrow \pi_{\boldsymbol{u}^{(r)}}(\boldsymbol{x}^{(r)})$.

We describe the following theorem that is integrated from [6,8,10].

Theorem 1. *Let $\boldsymbol{f} = \boldsymbol{f}^{(r-1)} \circ \boldsymbol{f}^{(r-2)} \circ \cdots \circ \boldsymbol{f}^{(0)}$ defined as above. Denote all the trails from $\pi_{\boldsymbol{u}^{(0)}}(\boldsymbol{x}^{(0)})$ to $\pi_{\boldsymbol{u}^{(r)}}(\boldsymbol{x}^{(r)})$ by $\pi_{\boldsymbol{u}^{(0)}}(\boldsymbol{x}^{(0)}) \bowtie \pi_{\boldsymbol{u}^{(r)}}(\boldsymbol{x}^{(r)})$. Then $\pi_{\boldsymbol{u}^{(0)}}(\boldsymbol{x}^{(0)}) \rightsquigarrow \pi_{\boldsymbol{u}^{(r)}}(\boldsymbol{x}^{(r)})$ if and only if*

$$|\pi_{\boldsymbol{u}^{(0)}}(\boldsymbol{x}^{(0)}) \bowtie \pi_{\boldsymbol{u}^{(r)}}(\boldsymbol{x}^{(r)})| \equiv 1 \pmod 2.$$

Degree Evaluation for Superpoly. The technique of the superpoly degree evaluation for cube attacks was proposed in [20], to avoid constructing the whole truth table of the superpoly using cube summations which can eventually reduce the entire complexity of cube attacks.

Based on the MILP-aided two-subset division property, the upper bound for the algebraic degree, denoted as d, of the superpoly can be derived. With the knowledge of its degree d (and J as the set of the indices of key involved), the superpoly can be completely represented with its $\binom{|J|}{\leq d}$ coefficients rather than the whole truth table, where $\binom{|J|}{\leq d} := \sum_{i=0}^{d} \binom{|J|}{i}$. If $d < |J|$, which is true for lightweight ciphers because the algebraic degrees of their round functions are usually quite low, the coefficients of the monomials with degrees higher than d are constantly 0. Thus, the complexity of superpoly recovery can be reduced from $2^{|I|+|J|}$ to $2^{|I|} \times \binom{|J|}{\leq d}$. Therefore, the degrees d are often much smaller than $|J|$, especially when high-dimensional cubes are used.

Although such degree d's are only upper bounds for the degree of superpolies, the superpolies with a lower degree are more likely to be simpler than those with higher ones. This technique is used to help us heuristically filter out superpolies with a higher degree which potentially lead to massive superpolies. The effectiveness of using this technique is verified by simple superpolies we finally obtained for more rounds of KREYVIUM in Sect. 3.

Divide-and-Conquer Strategy for Recovering ANFs of Superpolies. As the number of rounds evaluated grows, the superpolies for certain cubes become increasingly complex. Many existing methods for superpoly recovery quickly hit their bottlenecks. Motivated by this, Hu et al. [9] proposed a framework with *nested monomial predictions* that scales well for massive superpoly recovery. The nested method actually is a hybrid of four popular methods in this area, namely Wang et al.'s pruning method [21], Ye and Tian's algebraic method [24], Tian's recursively-expressing method [23] and Hao et al.'s PoolSearchMode method [6]. Later, He et al. [7] improved the nested monomial prediction framework to further simplify the MILP model and speed up the model solving. Sun [15] also used a similar technique to handle the heavy search in the superpoly recovery. In this paper, we do not go deep into their respective details and uniformly called them the divide-and-conquer techniques, and we briefly describe the main idea of the strategy they follow.

In this kind of frameworks, the targeted output bit is first expressed as a polynomial of the bits of some intermediate state. For each term appearing in the polynomial, the monomial prediction technique is applied to determine its superpoly if the corresponding MILP model can be solved within a given time limit. Terms that cannot be resolved within the time limit are further expanded as polynomials of the bits of some deeper intermediate states with symbolic computation, whose terms are again processed with monomial predictions. The above procedure is iterated until all terms are resolved. Finally, all the sub-superpolies are collected and assembled into the superpoly of the targeted bit.

2.3 Table Lookup Based Key Filtering Techniques

In order to identify the $\boldsymbol{x}_c$'s satisfying $p_I(\boldsymbol{x}, \boldsymbol{IV}) = \theta$, one has to refer to the truth table of p_I, denoted as T_I. Such T_I is of size $2^{|J|}$. It also takes $2^{|J|}$ table lookups so as to identify the $\boldsymbol{x}[J]$ candidates. However, for the massive superpolies with $J = [0, n)$, tricks can be played to avoid storing and traversing the whole T_I. In [9], *the disjoint set* was used to decompose the whole superpoly into several sub-superpolies, thus the task of constructing a huge truth table for a massive superpoly can be divided into several smaller scale tasks of constructing smaller truth tables, which reduces the entirety of the complexity. We recall the idea of superpoly recovery using a disjoint set briefly in the following.

Disjoint Set Based Key Filtering. Given a polynomial $p(\boldsymbol{x})$ with n variables, if for $0 \le i \ne j < n$, x_i and x_j are never multiplied mutually in all monomials of $p(\boldsymbol{x})$, then we say x_i and x_j are disjoint. For a subset of variables $D \subseteq \{x_0, x_1, \cdots, x_{n-1}\}$, if every pair of variables like $(x_i, x_j) \in D$ are disjoint, we call D a disjoint set. Given the disjoint set $D = \{x_0, x_1, \ldots, x_{\ell-1}\}$, denote the set of the rest of the key variables not in D as $\overline{D} = \{x_0, x_1, \ldots, x_{n-1}\} \backslash D$, the superpoly can be re-written as a linear combination:

$$p(\boldsymbol{x}) = x_0 \cdot p_0(\overline{D}) + x_1 \cdot p_1(\overline{D}) + \cdots + x_{\ell-1} \cdot p_{\ell-1}(\overline{D}) + p_\ell(\overline{D}),$$

where $p(\overline{D})$ is a polynomial of the variables only in $\overline{D}$, which is usually simplier than $p(\boldsymbol{x})$. By this the huge truth table of $p(\boldsymbol{x})$ can be replaced by smaller sub-tables corresponding to $p_0(\overline{D}), p_1(\overline{D}), \ldots, p_{\ell-1}(\overline{D})$ and the residue $p_\ell(\overline{D})$. In the key filtering phase, the bits in disjoint set are guessed and refer to the corresponding sub-tables sequentially.

The key filtering procedures based on a single superpoly can easily be extended to multiple superpolies. In addition to the key filtering method based on the disjoint set, improvement was further proposed in [7] for key filtering: they choose to guess some key bits for simplifying the massive superpoly and construct truth tables on the fly for filtering keys.

Note that all truth tables are constructed using the Möbius transformation technique in [9]: for a Boolean function with n variables, the Möbius transformation algorithm can be used to construct its truth table with $n \cdot 2^{n-1}$ XOR operations.

3 New Attacks on Kreyvium

So far, cube attacks on stream ciphers are conducted the following two main strategies:

- The massive superpoly strategy uses low dimensional cubes but the superpolies are usually complicated;
- On the contrary, the conventional strategy turns to using high dimensional cubes so as to acquire low-degree superpolies related to very few key bits.

In the high-level view, our new cube attacks on 898-, 899- and 900-round KREYVIUM follow the conventional strategy. The reason we choose this strategy will be given in Sect. 4.1. In the low-level view, we propose our own specific procedures for constructing the cubes utilized in our cube attacks on KREYVIUM. We summarize them in the following:

- Since the key and IV of KREYVIUM share the same length of 128 bits, we decide to use the largest possible dimension of cubes as $|I| = m - 2 = 126$.
- The cube indices are selected so as to result in lower superpoly degrees which are evaluated naturally with the two-subset division property based degree evaluation technique [20].
- After finding cubes with low-degree superpolies, the superpolies recovery can be accomplished directly with the methods in [7,9].

In the following, we give the 898-, 899- and 900-round cube attacks on KREYVIUM, with the corresponding balanced superpolies. So far as we know, these are the best cube attacks on KREYVIUM.

3.1 New Results for 898-Round KREYVIUM

For 898-round KREYVIUM, there are plenty of 126-dimensional cubes with simple superpolies so we randomly pick several 126-dimensional cubes, run degree evaluation procedures and select the cubes with the lowest degrees. After examining several trials, we find two cubes, denoted as I_0 and I_1 respectively, with degree evaluations 2 and 3. The cube I_0 is defined as $I_0 = [0, 127]\backslash\{5, 56\}$, the superpoly $p_{I_0}(\boldsymbol{x}, \boldsymbol{0})$ of 898-round KREYVIUM is determined as the follows

$$p_{I_0}(\boldsymbol{x}, \boldsymbol{0}) = x_{11} + x_{13} + x_{28} + x_{37} + x_{38} + x_{39} + x_{53} + x_{53}x_{54} + x_{55} + x_{62}x_{63} + x_{70} + x_{72} + x_{87} + x_{97} + x_{98} + x_{112} + x_{54}x_{112} + x_{113} + x_{53}x_{113} + x_{112}x_{113} + x_{114} + x_{123}.$$

The definition of I_1 is $I_1 = [0, 127]\backslash\{38, 86\}$ and the superpoly $p_{I_1}(\boldsymbol{x}, \boldsymbol{0})$ is derived as Eq. (7) in Appendix A.2.

3.2 New Results for 899-Round KREYVIUM

Following the procedure for the 898-round case, we still hope to find a cube of dimension 126 whose superpoly has a considerably lower degree, for instance, 2 or 3. However, when we ran similar procedures directly for 899-round Kreyvium, we found that low-degree superpolies became quite rare given 126-dimensional cubes. Instead of constructing a 126-dimensional cube directly, we have to exploit new methods.

First, wes run degree evaluation procedure for all 127-dimensional cubes so as to find good indices for further exclusions. To be more specific, for all the 128 cubes $I_\lambda = [0, 127]\backslash\{\lambda\}$ with $\lambda = 0, \ldots, 127$, we acquire the degree upper bounds of their corresponding superpolies, denoted as $\deg(p_{I_\lambda})$, using the degree evaluation based on the conventional division property in [20]. We find that only 13 λ's satisfy $\deg(p_{I_\lambda}) \leq 3$ and we store such 13 λ's in the set Λ below:

$$\Lambda = \{\lambda \in [0, 127] : \deg(p_{I_\lambda}) \leq 3\} = \{28, 29, 41, 47, 48, 49, 52, 55, 60, 61, 70, 74, 75, 79\}.$$

Details of the 128 $\deg(p_{I_\lambda})$'s can be seen in Table 2 of Appendix A.1.

Next, we further construct the 126-dimensional cube $I = [0, 127]\backslash\{29, 47\}$ and the degree evaluation gives $\deg(p_I) = 3$. Therefore, we are able to recover p_I using the method of [9]. The ANF of $p_I(\boldsymbol{x}, \boldsymbol{0})$ is as follows:

$$p_I(\boldsymbol{x},\boldsymbol{0}) = x_2 + x_3 + x_8 + x_{10} + x_{11} + x_{10}x_{11} + x_{15} + x_{18} + x_{19} + x_{20} + x_6x_{20} + x_{21} + x_{24} + x_{28} + x_{29} + x_6x_{30} + x_{28}x_{34} + x_{20}x_{37} + x_{30}x_{37} + x_{34}x_{37} + x_{24}x_{38} + x_{39} + x_{20}x_{40} + x_{30}x_{40} + x_{41} + x_{28}x_{44} + x_{37}x_{44} + x_{45} + x_{51} + x_{52} + x_{39}x_{52} + x_{51}x_{52} + x_{34}x_{53} + x_{44}x_{53} + x_{34}x_{54} + x_{38}x_{54} + x_{44}x_{54} + x_{52}x_{54} + x_{34}x_{53}x_{54} + x_{44}x_{53}x_{54} + x_{34}x_{55} + x_{44}x_{55} + x_{20}x_{56} + x_{30}x_{56} + x_{62} + x_{54}x_{62} + x_{61}x_{62} + x_{63} + x_{34}x_{62}x_{63} + x_{44}x_{62}x_{63} + x_{34}x_{64} + x_{44}x_{64} + x_{63}x_{64} + x_{24}x_{63}x_{64} + x_{20}x_{65} + x_{24}x_{65} + x_{30}x_{65} + x_{20}x_{66} + x_{30}x_{66} + x_{66}x_{67} + x_{68} + x_{71} + x_{70}x_{71} + x_{72} + x_{74} + x_{77} + x_{78} + x_{77}x_{78} + x_{39}x_{77}x_{78} + x_{39}x_{79} + x_{80} + x_{79}x_{80} + x_{38}x_{79}x_{80} + x_{52}x_{79}x_{80} + x_{62}x_{79}x_{80} + x_{81} + x_{38}x_{81} + x_{52}x_{81} + x_{62}x_{81} + x_{83} + x_{38}x_{83} + x_{63}x_{64}x_{83} + x_{65}x_{83} + x_{86} + x_{87} + x_{34}x_{87} + x_{44}x_{87} + x_{88} + x_{87}x_{88} + x_{89} + x_6x_{89} + x_{37}x_{89} + x_{40}x_{89} + x_{56}x_{89} + x_{65}x_{89} + x_{66}x_{89} + x_{90}x_{91} + x_{92} + x_{95} + x_{20}x_{96} + x_{30}x_{96} + x_{89}x_{96} + x_{97} + x_{54}x_{97} + x_{79}x_{80}x_{97} + x_{81}x_{97} + x_{98} + x_{52}x_{98} + x_{77}x_{78}x_{98} + x_{79}x_{98} + x_{20}x_{99} + x_{30}x_{99} + x_{89}x_{99} + x_{28}x_{103} + x_{37}x_{103} + x_{53}x_{103} + x_{54}x_{103} + x_{53}x_{54}x_{103} + x_{55}x_{103} + x_{62}x_{63}x_{103} + x_{64}x_{103} + x_{87}x_{103} + x_{111} + x_{53}x_{111} + x_{112} + x_{34}x_{112} + x_{44}x_{112} + x_{52}x_{112} + x_{34}x_{54}x_{112} + x_{44}x_{54}x_{112} + x_{103}x_{112} + x_{54}x_{103}x_{112} + x_{111}x_{112} + x_{34}x_{113} + x_{44}x_{113} + x_{34}x_{53}x_{113} + x_{44}x_{53}x_{113} + x_{103}x_{113} + x_{53}x_{103}x_{113} + x_{34}x_{112}x_{113} + x_{44}x_{112}x_{113} + x_{103}x_{112}x_{113} + x_{34}x_{114} + x_{44}x_{114} + x_{103}x_{114} + x_{120} + x_{121} + x_{54}x_{121} + x_{79}x_{80}x_{121} + x_{81}x_{121} + x_{20}x_{124} + x_{30}x_{124} + x_{89}x_{124} + x_{20}x_{125} + x_{30}x_{125} + x_{89}x_{125}.$$

3.3 New Results for 900-Round Kreyvium

As for 900-round Kreyvium, the cube construction follows the same steps as 899-round in Sect. 3.2. The superpoly recovery is accomplished using the method in [7]. We take $I = [0, 127]\backslash\{38, 86\}$ as the cube for 900-round Kreyvium, and the superpoly $p_I(\boldsymbol{x}, \boldsymbol{0})$ is given in Appendix A.2.

4 Implementation Dependency

The stream cipher E in Sect. 2.1 can be implemented in many different ways. In codebook implementations, E is simply a lookup table storing all key-IV pairs $(\boldsymbol{x}, \boldsymbol{v})$'s along with the corresponding keystream $\boldsymbol{z}(\boldsymbol{x}, \boldsymbol{v})$ values. In round-wise implementations, E is simply executed by sequential assembly instructions describing the round functions of stream ciphers. In this case, E is implemented round by round so a query of E seems more complicated than a table lookup. However, for E's implemented in a codebook manner, a query of E is simply a table lookup. Therefore, for cube attacks, we propose the concept of implementation dependency revealing whether it can be feasible for both round-wise and codebook implementation oracles.

Implementation Dependent Cube Attacks. When the number of table lookups in the key filtering phase approaches the exhaustive search complexity, the cube attack may become infeasible for codebook-implemented oracles. We refer to the cube attacks that only work for round-wise implementations as implementation dependent cube attacks.

Implementation Independent Cube Attacks. On the contrary, those cube attacks work for both round-wise and codebook implementation attacks are therefore called the implementation independent cube attacks.

Consider a cube attack using ℓ cubes $I_0, \ldots, I_{\ell-1}$ with superpolies correlated to key bits $J_0, \ldots, J_{\ell-1}$. The cube attack in Sect. 2.1 requires $2^{|I_0|} + \ldots + 2^{|I_{\ell-1}|}$ oracle queries for `Cube Sum Computation` procedure, at least $2^{|J_0|} + \ldots + 2^{|J_{\ell-1}|}$ table lookups in `Key Filtering` and another $2^{n-\ell}$ oracle queries for the last `Exhaustive Search` procedure.

In fact, a table lookup takes two assembly instructions: one addition and one comparison. We further assume that the implementation of querying E takes α instructions. Besides, there may also involve basic operations such as XOR, for constructing the lookup tables used in the `Key Filtering` phase and the number of instructions for the table construction is denoted as β. Therefore, the complexity of the cube attack in Sect. 2.1 has now become:

$$C_{\text{new}} = \sum_{j=0}^{\ell-1} 2^{|I_j|} + 2^{n-\ell} + \frac{2}{\alpha} \sum_{j=0}^{\ell-1} 2^{|J_j|} + \frac{\beta}{\alpha} \tag{1}$$

The attack can only work when $C_{\text{new}} < 2^n$.

4.1 An Implementation Dependency Analysis Example

According to the concepts of implementation dependency, we find that the cube attack on 845-round TRIVIUM given in [9] is *implementation dependent*. We detail such an implementation dependency analysis here as an example and leave the same analysis of other cube attack results in Sect. 5.1.

TRIVIUM [1] is a hardware oriented stream cipher. It has been selected as part of the eSTREAM portfolio [3] and specified as an International Standard under ISO/IEC 29192-3 [11]. Then key and IV of TRIVIUM are both of 80 bits. Both key and IV are first loaded in a 288-bit internal state and run 1152-round initialization afterwards. The whole initialization process can be summarized as follows:

$$(s_0, s_1, \ldots, s_{92}) \leftarrow (K_0, K_1, \ldots, K_{79}, 0, \ldots, 0)$$
$$(s_{93}, s_{95}, \ldots, s_{177}) \leftarrow (IV_0, IV_1, \ldots, IV_{79}, 0, \ldots, 0)$$
$$(s_{177}, s_{179}, \ldots, s_{287}) \leftarrow (0, \ldots, 0, 1, 1, 1)$$

for $i = 0$ to 1151 **do**

$$t_1 \leftarrow s_{65} \oplus s_{90} \cdot s_{91} \oplus s_{92} \oplus s_{170} \tag{2}$$
$$t_2 \leftarrow s_{161} \oplus s_{174} \cdot s_{175} \oplus s_{176} \oplus s_{263} \tag{3}$$

$$t_3 \leftarrow s_{242} \oplus s_{285} \cdot s_{286} \oplus s_{287} \oplus s_{68} \tag{4}$$
$$(s_0, s_1, \ldots, s_{92}) \leftarrow (t_3, s_0, s_1, \ldots, s_{91})$$
$$(s_{93}, s_{95}, \ldots, s_{177} \leftarrow (t_1, s_{93}, s_{94}, \ldots, s_{175})$$
$$(s_{177}, s_{179}, \ldots, s_{287}) \leftarrow (t_2, s_{177}, s_{178} \ldots, s_{286})$$

end for

After the initialization phase, one key stream bit is generated by

$$z = s_{65} \oplus s_{92} \oplus s_{161} \oplus s_{176} \oplus s_{242} \oplus s_{287}. \tag{5}$$

When we say r-round TRIVIUM, we mean after r times of updates in the initialization phase, one key bit denoted by z_r is generated.

If implementing TRIVIUM bit-wisely, we can get quickly from Eqs. (2) to (5) that each round of TRIVIUM (one initialization and one keystream bit generation) requires 14 XORs, 3 ANDs and 288 rotates instructions, thus a total of 305 instructions. In fact, using parallel computing in a hardware environment could give 64 times speed up for the iterations, which leads to about just 4.8 instructions for each round. So considering a codebook-implemented oracle, one query of the TRIVIUM is just a table lookup.

In [9], Hu et al. found two cubes I_2 and I_3 (notations exactly follow [9]) which have the same disjoint set $D = \{k_1, k_{10}\}$, then they used 2 corresponding equations for the key recovery procedure of 845-round TRIVIUM, where $|I_2| = 55$ and $|I_3| = 54$. Obviously, we can filter keys by half for the remaining keys once we get another equation (if the equation is balanced). So three quarters of keys will be filtered by two equations. For the 845-round attack on TRIVIUM, the two equations are:

$$\begin{cases} p^{(2)} = k_1 \cdot p_0^{(2)} \oplus k_{10} \cdot p_1^{(2)} \oplus p_2^{(2)} \\ p^{(3)} = k_1 \cdot p_0^{(3)} \oplus k_{10} \cdot p_1^{(3)} \oplus p_2^{(3)} \end{cases} \tag{6}$$

There are 6 truth tables in the equations and recovering them needs using Möbius transformation technique. There are 3 tables for $p^{(2)}$ and 3 tables for $p^{(3)}$. Let T_1, T_2, T_0 are truth tables for $p_1^{(2)}$, $p_2^{(2)}$, $p_0^{(2)}$, the size of them are 2^{78}, 2^{77} and 2^{78}, and the probability of $p^{(2)}$ being balanced is 0.5. And there are four tables of 2^{78} size and 2 of 2^{77} size in the 6 tables. In the table constructing phase, the number of XORs is $4 \cdot 78 \cdot 2^{76} + 2 \cdot 77 \cdot 2^{75} \approx 1.51 \cdot 2^{84}$.

In the `Cube Sum Computation` phase, totally $2^{55} + 2^{54} = 1.5 \cdot 2^{55}$ queries and XORs are used to get $p^{(2)} = \theta_2$ and $p^{(3)} = \theta_3$, and this complexity could be ignored comparing with the `Key Filtering` and the `Exhaustive Search` phase. After we get the values of $p^{(2)}$ and $p^{(3)}$ by doing the `Cube Sum Computation` in the online phase, we can filter and search 2^{80} keys with the given equations. We simply consider the complexity of lookup for one equation (that is to say just use one single cube) first and then extend to that of two equations. There are totally four cases for the table lookup: $(k_1, k_{10}) = (0,0), (0,1), (1,0), (1,1)$. Consider three kinds of operations: lookup, XOR and judgement. Let k be a key which is filtered, and $k = *k_1 *** k_{10} ***$, where $*$ represents a bit not belonging to the disjoint set. That is to say, we should give three lookups each for T_0, T_1 and T_2. Firstly, consider the first equation in Eq. (6). For the four (k_1, k_{10}) situations in , we should compute the results and compare them with $p^{(2)}$, and if one key leads to $p^{(2)} = \theta_2 \oplus 1$, there is no need to do anything for the other equation with this key.

So the number of instructions of the first equation consists of three parts according to three kind of operations we considered:

1. Table lookups for T_0, T_1 and T_2. Totally $2^{78} + 2^{77} + 2^{78} = 1.25 \cdot 2^{79}$ lookups, and $1.25 \cdot 2^{80}$ instructions.
2. XORs in equation evaluation calculation. The four (k_1, k_{10}) cases need 0, 1, 1 and 2 XORs respectively. In total, there are $2^{78}+2^{78}+2\cdot2^{78} = 2^{80}$instructions.
3. Judgements. After calculating $k_1 \cdot p_0^{(2)} \oplus k_{10} \cdot p_1^{(2)} \oplus p_2^{(2)}$, give a judgement to check if it equals to $p^{(2)}$ so as to filter keys. There are totally 2^{80} judgements needed.

Now consider the situation for other equations. We need only to process the keys that are filtered by the first equation, about 2^{79} keys. This leads to a half number of XORs and half number of the judgements but full table lookups for the second equation. Totally it costs about $1.25 \cdot 2^{80}$ instructions for lookups, 2^{79} instructions for XORs and 2^{79} instructions for judgements.

After key filtering, we should exhaustively search the remaining $(1/4) \cdot 2^{80}$ keys, which needs $(1/4) \cdot 2^{80}$ oracle queries, scilicet, 2^{79} instructions.

Totally, the process of key filtering and searching uses $1.5 \cdot 2^{82}$ instructions and the full attack uses $1.89 \cdot 2^{84} = 2^{84.92}$ instructions. Instead, using brute force attack for the cipher needs 2^{80} oracle queries. One query of the Trivium is a table lookup and equals 2 instructions, then the full brute force attack of Trivium needs 2^{81} instructions. It means cube attack does not work for codebook implementation Trivium over 845-round. We also find some other cases to illustrate the universality of this phenomenon, and we put them in Sect. 5.1.

5 Further Analysis for Cube Attacks

Similar to the analysis in Sect. 4.1, we further scrutinize existing cube attack results of stream ciphers Trivium, Grain-128AEAD, Acorn and Kreyvium in Sect. 5.1 to see whether they are *implementation independent*. We also discuss if using multiple cubes (superpolies) can reduce the complexity of the key recovery in Sect. 5.2. For the convenience of the explanation, we give a brief introduction to Trivium in Sect. 4.1. However, due to page limits, we refer the specifications for Kreyvium, Grain-128AEAD and Acorn to the respective design papers.

5.1 Analysis for More Cases of Cube Attacks

We recall the corresponding relationship between operations and the number of instructions. All operations considered are: oracle query, table lookup, XOR, and judgment.

As has been explicit in Sect. 2.1, there are four procedures in cube attacks, namely `Superpoly Recovery`, `Cube Sum Computation`, `Key Filtering` and `Exhaustive Search`. Now that we consider the complexity between oracle and key filtering, which is important to justify what steps should be considered.

Oracle implementation is querying a stream cipher through a table lookup. One query for one key so that total 2^L queries for a cipher with an L-bit length key. One oracle query equals m-instructions so there are total $m \cdot 2^L$ instructions for the whole search. And in this section we let one oracle query equal to one table lookup, then we get $m = 2$. So in our analysis, we keep using: 1 oracle query $\approx$ 1 table lookup $\approx$ 2 instructions.

- The step `Superpoly Recovery` uses the nest framework [9] in the offline phase so its complexity is not involved.
- The step `Cube Sum Computation` needs to query the oracle $2^{|I|}$ times where $|I|$ is the number of indices of the cube. For someone who has much smaller cube sizes than L , the time cost for cube sum can be ignored. However, for those using heavy cubes , the time cost should be considered.
- The step `Key Filtering` uses superpoly and its value to eliminate wrong keys. One superpoly can filter half keys of the remaining keys (in most cases the balancedness of a superpoly is 0.5).
  Calculating instructions of the table lookups is easy, while the number of XORs is calculated as follows: Suppose the superpoly can be re-written using the common disjoint set containing ℓ keys $k_0, \ldots, k_{\ell-1}$, it means 2^ℓ keys share the same table and just change the values of $k_0, \ldots, k_{\ell-1}$. Obviously, there are $\ell \cdot 2^\ell/2$ XORs for 2^ℓ keys, so on average $\ell/2$ XORs for each key.
- Finally, we should execute `Exhaustive Search` procedure for the remaining keys. For one equation situation, there are still half of the total keys.

Note that for Trivium, we follow the same notations in [9]. The complexity of the steps of `Cube Sum Computation` in cube attacks for 843- and 848-round Trivium is negligible due to the small size of cubes.

The attack on 843-round Trivium **in** [9] uses three cubes I_0, I_2 and I_3 with sizes 56, 55, 54, and the corresponding superpolies p_0, p_2 and p_3 all have 5 sub truth tables(separated by their disjoint sets). The biggest truth table sizes of the three superpolies are 75, 74 and 75 respectively, so the number of instructions for table construction is $2 \cdot 75 \cdot 2^{73} + 74 \cdot 2^{72} = 1.46 \cdot 2^{80}$.

The `Key Filtering` uses three superpoly equations: the 1st equation involves $5 \cdot 2^{79}$ XORs, 2^{75} table lookups and 2^{80} judgements which is $3.5625 \cdot 2^{80}$ instructions in total; the 2nd involves $0.5 \cdot 5 \cdot 2^{79}$ XORs, $0.5 \cdot 2^{80}$ judgements and 2^{74} table lookups so there are $1.78125 \cdot 2^{80}$ instructions; the 3rd involves $0.25 \cdot 5 \cdot 2^{79}$ XORs, $0.25 \cdot 2^{80}$ judgements and 2^{75} table lookups, totally $0.9375 \cdot 2^{80}$ instructions.

The `Exhaustive Search` for the remaining $1/8 \cdot 2^{80}$ keys requires $1/8 \cdot 2^{80}$ encryption oracle queries which is equivalent to $1/4 \cdot 2^{80}$ instructions.

To sum up, the total amount of instructions for the whole attack is $(1.46 + 3.5625 + 1.78125 + 0.9375 + 0.25) \cdot 2^{80} = 2^{82.99}$ which is higher than that of the exhaustive search. So this is an *implementation dependent* result.

The attack on 844-round TRIVIUM **in** [9] uses 2 cubes I_2 and I_3 with size 55, 54, and the superpolies p_2 and p_3 have the same disjoint set with size 6. The truth table sizes of the two superpolies are both 74 respectively, so the number of instructions for table construction is $2 \cdot 74 \cdot 2^{72} = 0.58 \cdot 2^{80}$.

The `Key Filtering` uses two superpoly equations : the 1st equation involves $6 \cdot 2^{79}$ XORs, 2^{74} table lookups and 2^{80} judgements which is $4.03 \cdot 2^{80}$ instructions in total; the 2nd involves $0.5 \cdot 6 \cdot 2^{79}$ XORs, $0.5 \cdot 2^{80}$ judgements and 2^{74} table lookups, totally $2.03 \cdot 2^{80}$ instructions.

The `Exhaustive Search` for the remaining $1/4 \cdot 2^{80}$ keys requires $1/4 \cdot 2^{80}$ encryption oracle queries which is equivalent to $1/2 \cdot 2^{80}$ instructions.

To sum up, the total amount of instructions for the whole attack is $(0.58 + 4.03 + 2.03 + 0.5) \cdot 2^{80} = 2^{82.84}$ which is higher than that of exhaustive search. So this is an *implementation dependent* result.

The attacks on 846-, 847- and 848-round TRIVIUM **in** [7] use the same cube I with size 53, and the sizes of the corresponding superpolies are all 80 so the number of instructions for table construction is $80 \cdot 2^{78} = 20 \cdot 2^{80}$.

The `Key Filtering` uses one superpoly equation: the equation involves 2^{80} table lookups and 2^{80} judgements, totally $3.5625 \cdot 2^{80}$ instructions.

The `Exhaustive Search` for the remaining $1/2 \cdot 2^{80}$ keys requires $1/2 \cdot 2^{80}$ encryption oracle queries which is equivalent to 2^{80} instructions.

To sum up, the total amount of instructions for the whole attack is $(20+3+1) \cdot 2^{80} = 2^{84.58}$ which is higher than that of the exhaustive search. So these are *implementation dependent* results.

The attacks on 191-round Grain-128AEAD in [9] uses 2 cubes I_0 and I_1 with size 96 and 95, and the corresponding superpolies p_0 and p_1 have the same disjoint set with size 12. The biggest truth table sizes of the two superpolies are both 116 respectively, so the number of instructions for table construction can be ignored.

The `Key Filtering` uses two superpoly equations: the 1st equation involves $12 \cdot 2^{127}$ XORs, $2 \cdot 2^{116} + 2^{115}$ table lookups and 2^{128} judgements which is $7 \cdot 2^{128}$ instructions in total; the 2nd involves $0.58 \cdot 12 \cdot 2^{127}$ XORs, $0.58 \cdot 2^{128}$ judgements and $2 \cdot 2^{116} + 2^{115}$ table lookups, totally $0.58 \cdot 7 \cdot 2^{128} = 4.06 \cdot 2^{128}$ instructions.

The `Exhaustive Search` for the remaining $(1 - 0.42)^2 \cdot 2^{128}$ keys requires $(1 - 0.42)^2 \cdot 2^{128}$ encryption oracle queries which is equivalent to $0.67 \cdot 2^{128}$ instructions.

To sum up, the total amount of instructions for the whole attack is $7 \cdot 2^{128} + 4.06 \cdot 2^{128} + 0.67 \cdot 2^{128} = 2^{131.55}$ which is higher than that of the exhaustive search. So this is an *implementation dependent* result.

Remark 1. The balancedness for p_0 is 0.31 and 0.30 for p_1, so using the knowledge of classical models of probability, we can filter $0.3 \cdot 0.7 + 0.7 \cdot 0.3 = 0.42$ of the total keys using one equation with the mathematic expectation (more details referring to [9]). And it means the best balancedness is 0.5 in this attack.

The attacks on 192-round Grain-128AEAD [7] uses one cube I with size 94, and the size of the corresponding superpoly is 128 so the number of instructions for table construction is $128 \cdot 2^{126} = 32 \cdot 2^{128}$.

The `Key Filtering` uses one superpoly equation: the equation involves 2^{128} table lookups and 2^{128} judgements, totally $3 \cdot 2^{128}$ instructions.

The `Exhaustive Search` for the remaining $1/2 \cdot 2^{128}$ keys requires $1/2 \cdot 2^{128}$ encryption oracle queries which is equivalent to 2^{128} instructions.

To sum up, the total amount of instructions for the whole attack is $(32+3+1) \cdot 2^{128} = 2^{133.17}$ which is higher than that of the exhaustive search. So this is an *implementation dependent* result.

The attacks on 776-round ACORN in [7] uses 2 cubes I_1 and I_2 with both size 126, so the complexity of the two cubes sum computation is $2 \cdot 2^{126}$ encryption oracle queries which is equivalent to 2^{128} instructions, and the corresponding superpolies are p_0 and p_1. The biggest truth table sizes of the two superpolies are 120 and 119, so the number of instructions for table construction could be ignored and so as the `Key Filtering`.

The `Exhaustive Search` for the remaining $(1/4) \cdot 2^{128}$ keys requires $(1/4) \cdot 2^{128}$ encryption oracle queries which is equivalent to $(1/2) \cdot 2^{128}$ instructions.

To sum up, the total amount of instructions for the whole attack is $2^{128} + (1/2) \cdot 2^{128} = 2^{128.58}$ which is lower than that of the exhaustive search. So this is an *implementation independent* result.

The attacks on 894-round KREYVIUM in [9] uses 1 cube I with size 119, and the corresponding superpoly is p. The truth table size of the superpoly is 77, so the number of instructions for table construction could be ignored and so as the `Key Filtering`.

The `Exhaustive Search` for the remaining $1/2 \cdot 2^{128}$ keys requires $1/2 \cdot 2^{128}$ encryption oracle queries which is equivalent to 2^{128} instructions.

To sum up, the total amount of instructions for the whole attack is 2^{128} which is lower than that of the exhaustive search. So this is an *implementation independent* result.

The attacks on 895-round KREYVIUM in [7] uses one cube I with size 120, and the corresponding superpoly p has a single truth table. The truth table size of the superpoly is 128, so the number of instructions for table construction is $128 \cdot 2^{126} = 32 \cdot 2^{128}$.

The `Key Filtering` uses one superpoly equation: the equation involves 2^{128} table lookups and 2^{128} judgements, totally $3 \cdot 2^{128}$ instructions.

The `Exhaustive Search` for the remaining $1/2 \cdot 2^{128}$ keys requires $1/2 \cdot 2^{128}$ encryption oracle queries which is equivalent to 2^{128} instructions.

To sum up, the total amount of instructions for the whole attack is the equation involves 2^{128} table lookups and 2^{128} judgements, totally $3 \cdot 2^{128}$ instructions, which is higher than that of the exhaustive search. So this is an *implementation dependent* result.

The attack on 898-round KREYVIUM **in this paper** uses two cubes I_0 and I_1 with sizes both 126, so the complexity of the two cubes sum computation requires $2 \cdot 2^{126}$ encryption oracle queries which is equivalent to 2^{128} instructions, and the corresponding superpolies p_0 and p_1 both have one truth table. The truth table sizes of the superpolies are far smaller than 128, so the number of instructions for table construction can be ignored and so as the `Key Filtering`.

The `Exhaustive Search` for the remaining $1/4 \cdot 2^{128}$ keys requires $1/4 \cdot 2^{128}$ encryption oracle queries which is equivalent to $(1/2) \cdot 2^{128}$ instructions.

To sum up, the total amount of instructions for the whole attack is $2^{128} + (1/2) \cdot 2^{128} = 1.5 \cdot 2^{128} = 2^{128.58}$ which is lower than that of the exhaustive search. So this is an *implementation independent* result.

The attack on 899-round KREYVIUM **in this paper** uses one cube I with size 126, so the complexity of the cube sum computation requires 2^{126} encryption oracle queries which is equivalent to 2^{127} instructions, and the corresponding superpoly p have one truth table. The truth table size of the superpoly is far smaller than 128, so the number of instructions for table construction can be ignored and so as the `Key Filtering`.

The `Exhaustive Search` for the remaining $1/2 \cdot 2^{128}$ keys requires $1/2 \cdot 2^{128}$ encryption oracle queries which is equivalent to 2^{128} instructions.

To sum up, the total amount of instructions for the whole attack is $(1/2) \cdot 2^{128} + 2^{128} = 1.5 \cdot 2^{128} = 2^{128.58}$ which is lower than that of the exhaustive search. So this is an *implementation independent* result.

The attack on 900-round KREYVIUM **in this paper** uses one cube I with size 126, so the complexity of the cube sum computation requires 2^{126} encryption oracle queries which is equivalent to 2^{127} instructions, and the corresponding superpoly p have one truth table. The truth table size of the superpoly is far smaller than 128, so the number of instructions for table construction can be ignored and so as the `Key Filtering`.

The `Exhaustive Search` for the remaining $1/2 \cdot 2^{128}$ keys requires $1/2 \cdot 2^{128}$ encryption oracle queries which is equivalent to 2^{128} instructions.

To sum up, the total amount of instructions for the whole attack is $(1/2) \cdot 2^{128} + 2^{128} = 1.5 \cdot 2^{128} = 2^{128.58}$ which is lower than that of the exhaustive search. So this is an *implementation independent* result.

A summary of all the analyzed results is given in Table 1 in the Introduction.

5.2 Multiple Cubes Vs Single Cube

We find using multiple cubes may not result in more efficient key recoveries than its single-cube counterpart, and examples are 843, 844, 845-Round TRIVIUM, 898-round KREYVIUM and 776-round ACORN.

We find the interesting property firstly in studying key filtering. For a cipher with several cubes that can be exploited, such as N cubes, which correspond to N equations. Each equation could reduce half of the remaining keys. That means for an equation in the latter of the key filtering procedure, the cost of constructing its truth table and doing the cube summation might be unbearable. Though we handle corresponding fewer key bits for the equation in the back, we must pay for full time constructing its truth table and doing cube sum just like what we did for the first equation. And we give several examples.

The cube attack on 843-round TRIVIUM uses 3 cubes, which means the third equation could only filter 1/8 keys from the remaining 1/4 keys but should pay the whole expenses of truth table constructions.The cost is $75 \cdot 2^{73} = 1.17 \cdot 2^{79}$ XORs while the exhaustive search for (1/8) keys costs only $(1/8) \cdot 2^{80}$ oracle queries, equals to $0.5 \cdot 2^{79}$ instructions. And this does not consider the cost of table lookups, XORs and judgments for the third equation.

843, 844 and 845-round TRIVIUM are typical cases. And unexpectedly, even in the feasible cube attack on 898-round KREYVIUM, though the total complexity is less than exhaustive search, its second equation corresponds to a cube of size 126, which queries 2^{126} times KREYVIUM, and it just filters half of the rest keys, that is 2^{126} keys. And querying the KREYVIUM 2^{126} times is just the same as the exhaustive search. So using multiple cubes may not surpass using a single cube. A similar situation happens to the attack on 776-round ACORN, as the cube sum invokes oracle as that for an exhaustive search.

6 Conclusions

In this paper, we focused on the real performance of cube attacks for ciphers with massive superpolies or heavy cubes. We analyzed a dozen recent cube attack results on TRIVIUM, KREYVIUM, Grain-128AEAD and ACORN, and found cube attacks are ineffective against some of them in the situation of code-book implementation. We also gave some new results on 898-, 899- and 900-round KREYVIUM. In addition, we discussed the efficiency of cube attacks between multiple cubes and one single cube, and found sometimes the number of cubes used should be limited.

Acknowledgments. The authors thank all reviewers for their suggestions. This work is supported by the National Key Research and Development Program of China (Grant No. 2022YFA1004900), and by the National Natural Science Foundation of China (Grant No. 62002024, 62202062).

Appendix

A Details of Our Attacks on KREYVIUM

A.1 Degree Evaluations of 899-Round KREYVIUM

Table 2. The upper bound degree $\deg(p_{I_\lambda})$ of superpolies p_{I_λ} for 899-round KREYVIUM, with cube dimension 127.

λ	$\deg(p_{I_\lambda})$	λ	$\deg(p_{I_\lambda})$	λ	$\deg(p_{I_\lambda})$	λ	$\deg(p_{I_\lambda})$
0	5	32	6	64	4	96	4
1	6	33	5	65	5	97	5
2	6	34	4	66	6	98	4
3	4	35	5	67	4	99	5
4	4	36	4	68	4	100	4
5	5	37	5	69	4	101	5
6	5	38	5	**70**	**3**	102	5
7	4	39	4	71	4	103	6
8	7	40	4	72	4	104	6
9	6	**41**	**3**	73	4	105	5
10	4	42	4	**74**	**3**	106	5
11	5	43	4	**75**	**2**	107	6
12	4	44	4	76	4	108	4
13	5	45	5	77	5	109	4
14	4	46	4	78	5	110	4
15	5	**47**	**2**	**79**	**3**	111	4
16	5	**48**	**3**	80	4	112	4
17	5	**49**	**3**	81	4	113	6
18	5	50	4	82	6	114	6
19	5	51	4	83	7	115	6
20	5	**52**	3	84	5	116	6
21	6	53	4	85	4	117	5
22	5	54	4	86	4	118	5
23	4	**55**	**3**	87	4	119	5
24	6	56	4	88	5	120	4
25	6	57	4	89	4	121	5
26	6	58	4	90	5	122	5
27	4	59	4	91	5	123	6
28	**3**	**60**	2	92	5	124	5
29	**3**	**61**	**3**	93	4	125	4
30	5	62	4	94	6	126	4
31	4	63	5	95	6	127	4

A.2 The ANFs of Superpolies Corresponding to Attacks on 898-And 900-Round KREYVIUM

For $I_1 = [0,127]\backslash\{38,86\}$, the superpoly $p_{I_1}(\boldsymbol{x},\mathbf{0})$ for 898-round KREYVIUM is as Eq. (7)

$$
\begin{aligned}
p_{I_1}(\boldsymbol{x},\mathbf{0}) &= x_{12} + x_{20} + x_{21} + x_{20}x_{21} + x_{23} + x_{31} + x_{36} + x_{11}x_{36} + x_{12}x_{36} + x_{26}x_{36} \\
&+ x_{37} + x_{11}x_{37} + x_{12}x_{37} + x_{26}x_{37} + x_{38} + x_{11}x_{38} + x_{12}x_{38} + x_{26}x_{38} + x_{36}x_{38} \\
&+ x_{37}x_{38} + x_{41} + x_{45} + x_{45}x_{46} + x_{47} + x_{46}x_{47} + x_{48} + x_{47}x_{48} + x_{49} + x_{48}x_{49} + x_{50} \\
&+ x_{11}x_{55} + x_{12}x_{55} + x_{26}x_{55} + x_{38}x_{55} + x_{56} + x_{11}x_{56} + x_{12}x_{56} + x_{26}x_{56} + x_{38}x_{56} \\
&+ x_{57} + x_{58} + x_{59} + x_{64}x_{65} + x_{66} + x_{67} + x_{66}x_{67} + x_{68} + x_{36}x_{70} + x_{37}x_{70} + x_{38}x_{70} \\
&+ x_{55}x_{70} + x_{56}x_{70} + x_{71} + x_{36}x_{71} + x_{37}x_{71} + x_{38}x_{71} + x_{55}x_{71} + x_{56}x_{71} + x_{80}x_{81} \\
&+ x_{11}x_{80}x_{81} + x_{12}x_{80}x_{81} + x_{26}x_{80}x_{81} + x_{38}x_{80}x_{81} + x_{70}x_{80}x_{81} + x_{71}x_{80}x_{81} + x_{82} \\
&+ x_{11}x_{82} + x_{12}x_{82} + x_{26}x_{82} + x_{38}x_{82} + x_{70}x_{82} + x_{71}x_{82} + x_{81}x_{82} + x_{11}x_{81}x_{82} \\
&+ x_{12}x_{81}x_{82} + x_{26}x_{81}x_{82} + x_{38}x_{81}x_{82} + x_{70}x_{81}x_{82} + x_{71}x_{81}x_{82} + x_{83} + x_{11}x_{83} \\
&+ x_{12}x_{83} + x_{26}x_{83} + x_{38}x_{83} + x_{70}x_{83} + x_{71}x_{83} + x_{83}x_{84} + x_{85} + x_{84}x_{85} + x_{87} + x_{90} \\
&+ x_{89}x_{90} + x_{91} + x_{95} + x_{11}x_{95} + x_{12}x_{95} + x_{26}x_{95} + x_{38}x_{95} + x_{70}x_{95} + x_{71}x_{95} + x_{96} \\
&+ x_{11}x_{96} + x_{12}x_{96} + x_{26}x_{96} + x_{38}x_{96} + x_{70}x_{96} + x_{71}x_{96} + x_{97} + x_{11}x_{97} + x_{12}x_{97} \\
&+ x_{26}x_{97} + x_{36}x_{97} + x_{37}x_{97} + x_{55}x_{97} + x_{56}x_{97} + x_{70}x_{97} + x_{71}x_{97} + x_{80}x_{81}x_{97} \\
&+ x_{82}x_{97} + x_{81}x_{82}x_{97} + x_{83}x_{97} + x_{95}x_{97} + x_{96}x_{97} + x_{98} + x_{114} + x_{123} + x_{126}.
\end{aligned} \tag{7}
$$

For $I = [0,127]\backslash\{38,86\}$, the superpoly $p_I(\boldsymbol{x},\mathbf{0})$ for 900-round KREYVIUM is as Eq. (8).

$$
\begin{aligned}
p_I(\boldsymbol{x},\mathbf{0}) &= x_{125} + x_{122} + x_{121} + x_{116} + x_{113}x_{124} + x_{112} + x_{111} + x_{111}x_{112}x_{124} + \\
& x_{110}x_{124} + x_{110}x_{111}x_{124} + x_{106} + x_{105}x_{124} + x_{104} + x_{103} + x_{101} + x_{98}x_{125} + x_{98}x_{113} + \\
& x_{98}x_{111}x_{112} + x_{98}x_{110} + x_{98}x_{110}x_{111} + x_{98}x_{105} + x_{97}x_{124} + x_{97}x_{98} + x_{96} + x_{96}x_{120} + \\
& x_{96}x_{97} + x_{95} + x_{95}x_{123} + x_{94} + x_{92} + x_{92}x_{124} + x_{92}x_{98} + x_{91}x_{124} + x_{91}x_{98} + x_{90} + \\
& x_{90}x_{91} + x_{90}x_{91}x_{124} + x_{90}x_{91}x_{98} + x_{89}x_{121} + x_{89}x_{97} + x_{89}x_{96} + x_{89}x_{90} + x_{89}x_{90}x_{124} + \\
& x_{89}x_{90}x_{98} + x_{88} + x_{87} + x_{87}x_{88} + x_{87}x_{88}x_{121} + x_{87}x_{88}x_{97} + x_{87}x_{88}x_{96} + x_{87}x_{88}x_{95} + \\
& x_{86} + x_{86}x_{124} + x_{86}x_{98} + x_{85} + x_{85}x_{124} + x_{85}x_{98} + x_{84} + x_{83} + x_{82}x_{91} + x_{82}x_{89}x_{90} + \\
& x_{80}x_{81}x_{98} + x_{80}x_{81}x_{91} + x_{80}x_{81}x_{89}x_{90} + x_{80}x_{81}x_{83} + x_{80}x_{81}x_{82} + x_{79}x_{124} + x_{79}x_{98} + \\
& x_{79}x_{89} + x_{79}x_{88} + x_{79}x_{87}x_{88} + x_{79}x_{80} + x_{78}x_{89} + x_{77}x_{124} + x_{77}x_{98} + x_{77}x_{78} + \\
& x_{77}x_{78}x_{124} + x_{77}x_{78}x_{98} + x_{77}x_{78}x_{89} + x_{77}x_{78}x_{87}x_{88} + x_{76}x_{124} + x_{76}x_{98} + x_{76}x_{77} + \\
& x_{75}x_{76} + x_{75}x_{76}x_{78} + x_{75}x_{76}x_{77} + x_{73} + x_{72} + x_{72}x_{73} + x_{70} + x_{70}x_{89} + x_{70}x_{87}x_{88} + \\
& x_{70}x_{82} + x_{70}x_{80}x_{81} + x_{68}x_{125} + x_{68}x_{124} + x_{68}x_{121} + x_{68}x_{113}x_{124} + x_{68}x_{111}x_{112}x_{124} + \\
& x_{68}x_{110}x_{124} + x_{68}x_{110}x_{111}x_{124} + x_{68}x_{105}x_{124} + x_{68}x_{98}x_{125} + x_{68}x_{98}x_{113} + \\
& x_{68}x_{98}x_{111}x_{112} + x_{68}x_{98}x_{110} + x_{68}x_{98}x_{110}x_{111} + x_{68}x_{98}x_{105} + x_{68}x_{97} + x_{68}x_{92}x_{124} + \\
& x_{68}x_{92}x_{98} + x_{68}x_{91}x_{124} + x_{68}x_{91}x_{98} + x_{68}x_{90}x_{91}x_{124} + x_{68}x_{90}x_{91}x_{98} + \\
& x_{68}x_{89}x_{90}x_{124} + x_{68}x_{89}x_{90}x_{98} + x_{68}x_{86}x_{124} + x_{68}x_{86}x_{98} + x_{68}x_{85}x_{124} + x_{68}x_{85}x_{98} + \\
& x_{68}x_{80} + x_{68}x_{77}x_{124} + x_{68}x_{77}x_{98} + x_{68}x_{76}x_{124} + x_{68}x_{76}x_{98} + x_{67}x_{68} + x_{66} + x_{66}x_{98} +
\end{aligned}
$$

$$x_{66}x_{91} + x_{66}x_{89}x_{90} + x_{66}x_{88} + x_{66}x_{70} + x_{66}x_{68} + x_{66}x_{68}x_{98} + x_{65}x_{124} + x_{65}x_{113}+$$
$$x_{65}x_{111}x_{112} + x_{65}x_{110} + x_{65}x_{110}x_{111} + x_{65}x_{105} + x_{65}x_{98} + x_{65}x_{97} + x_{65}x_{92} + x_{65}x_{91}+$$
$$x_{65}x_{90}x_{91} + x_{65}x_{89}x_{90} + x_{65}x_{85} + x_{65}x_{79} + x_{65}x_{77} + x_{65}x_{77}x_{78} + x_{65}x_{76} + x_{65}x_{70}+$$
$$x_{65}x_{68}x_{124} + x_{65}x_{68}x_{113} + x_{65}x_{68}x_{111}x_{112} + x_{65}x_{68}x_{110} + x_{65}x_{68}x_{110}x_{111}+$$
$$x_{65}x_{68}x_{105} + x_{65}x_{68}x_{98} + x_{65}x_{68}x_{92} + x_{65}x_{68}x_{91} + x_{65}x_{68}x_{90}x_{91} + x_{65}x_{68}x_{89}x_{90}+$$
$$x_{65}x_{68}x_{86} + x_{65}x_{68}x_{85} + x_{65}x_{68}x_{77} + x_{65}x_{68}x_{76} + x_{64}x_{124} + x_{64}x_{98} + x_{64}x_{95}+$$
$$x_{64}x_{82} + x_{64}x_{80}x_{81} + x_{64}x_{68}x_{124} + x_{64}x_{68}x_{98} + x_{64}x_{66} + x_{64}x_{65}x_{91} + x_{64}x_{65}x_{89}x_{90}+$$
$$x_{64}x_{65}x_{88} + x_{64}x_{65}x_{70} + x_{64}x_{65}x_{68} + x_{63} + x_{63}x_{124} + x_{63}x_{98} + x_{63}x_{68}x_{124}+$$
$$x_{63}x_{68}x_{98} + x_{63}x_{65} + x_{63}x_{65}x_{68} + x_{63}x_{64}x_{86} + x_{63}x_{64}x_{70} + x_{63}x_{64}x_{66} + x_{63}x_{64}x_{65}+$$
$$x_{62} + x_{62}x_{124} + x_{62}x_{121} + x_{62}x_{98} + x_{62}x_{97} + x_{62}x_{96} + x_{62}x_{95} + x_{62}x_{89} + x_{62}x_{87}x_{88}+$$
$$x_{62}x_{79} + x_{62}x_{77}x_{78} + x_{62}x_{70} + x_{62}x_{68} + x_{62}x_{68}x_{124} + x_{62}x_{68}x_{98} + x_{62}x_{65}+$$
$$x_{62}x_{65}x_{68} + x_{62}x_{63} + x_{61}x_{96} + x_{61}x_{62}x_{124} + x_{61}x_{62}x_{98} + x_{61}x_{62}x_{68}x_{124}+$$
$$x_{61}x_{62}x_{68}x_{98} + x_{61}x_{62}x_{65} + x_{61}x_{62}x_{65}x_{68} + x_{60} + x_{60}x_{61}x_{124} + x_{60}x_{61}x_{98}+$$
$$x_{60}x_{61}x_{68}x_{124} + x_{60}x_{61}x_{68}x_{98} + x_{60}x_{61}x_{65} + x_{60}x_{61}x_{65}x_{68} + x_{58}x_{59} + x_{56}x_{98}+$$
$$x_{56}x_{82} + x_{56}x_{80}x_{81} + x_{56}x_{68} + x_{56}x_{68}x_{98} + x_{55} + x_{55}x_{113} + x_{55}x_{111}x_{112} + x_{55}x_{110}+$$
$$x_{55}x_{110}x_{111} + x_{55}x_{105} + x_{55}x_{98} + x_{55}x_{97} + x_{55}x_{92} + x_{55}x_{90}x_{91} + x_{55}x_{86} + x_{55}x_{85}+$$
$$x_{55}x_{83} + x_{55}x_{81}x_{82} + x_{55}x_{79} + x_{55}x_{77} + x_{55}x_{77}x_{78} + x_{55}x_{76} + x_{55}x_{70} + x_{55}x_{68}+$$
$$x_{55}x_{68}x_{113} + x_{55}x_{68}x_{111}x_{112} + x_{55}x_{68}x_{110} + x_{55}x_{68}x_{110}x_{111} + x_{55}x_{68}x_{105}+$$
$$x_{55}x_{68}x_{92} + x_{55}x_{68}x_{91} + x_{55}x_{68}x_{90}x_{91} + x_{55}x_{68}x_{89}x_{90} + x_{55}x_{68}x_{86} + x_{55}x_{68}x_{85}+$$
$$x_{55}x_{68}x_{77} + x_{55}x_{68}x_{76} + x_{55}x_{65} + x_{55}x_{65}x_{68} + x_{55}x_{64}x_{68} + x_{55}x_{63} + x_{55}x_{63}x_{68}+$$
$$x_{55}x_{62} + x_{55}x_{62}x_{68} + x_{55}x_{61}x_{62} + x_{55}x_{61}x_{62}x_{68} + x_{55}x_{60}x_{61} + x_{55}x_{60}x_{61}x_{68}+$$
$$x_{55}x_{56} + x_{54} + x_{54}x_{124} + x_{54}x_{98} + x_{54}x_{68}x_{124} + x_{54}x_{68}x_{98} + x_{54}x_{65} + x_{54}x_{65}x_{68}+$$
$$x_{54}x_{55} + x_{54}x_{55}x_{68} + x_{53} + x_{53}x_{111}x_{124} + x_{53}x_{98}x_{111} + x_{53}x_{68}x_{111}x_{124}+$$
$$x_{53}x_{68}x_{98}x_{111} + x_{53}x_{65}x_{111} + x_{53}x_{65}x_{68}x_{111} + x_{53}x_{55}x_{111} + x_{53}x_{55}x_{68}x_{111} + x_{52}+$$
$$x_{52}x_{124} + x_{52}x_{112}x_{124} + x_{52}x_{110}x_{124} + x_{52}x_{98} + x_{52}x_{98}x_{112} + x_{52}x_{98}x_{110} + x_{52}x_{68}+$$
$$x_{52}x_{68}x_{112}x_{124} + x_{52}x_{68}x_{110}x_{124} + x_{52}x_{68}x_{98}x_{112} + x_{52}x_{68}x_{98}x_{110} + x_{52}x_{65}+$$
$$x_{52}x_{65}x_{112} + x_{52}x_{65}x_{110} + x_{52}x_{65}x_{68}x_{112} + x_{52}x_{65}x_{68}x_{110} + x_{52}x_{55} + x_{52}x_{55}x_{112}+$$
$$x_{52}x_{55}x_{110} + x_{52}x_{55}x_{68}x_{112} + x_{52}x_{55}x_{68}x_{110} + x_{52}x_{53}x_{124} + x_{52}x_{53}x_{98}+$$
$$x_{52}x_{53}x_{68}x_{124} + x_{52}x_{53}x_{68}x_{98} + x_{52}x_{53}x_{65} + x_{52}x_{53}x_{65}x_{68} + x_{52}x_{53}x_{55}+$$
$$x_{52}x_{53}x_{55}x_{68} + x_{51}x_{124} + x_{51}x_{111}x_{124} + x_{51}x_{98} + x_{51}x_{98}x_{111} + x_{51}x_{96} + x_{51}x_{77}+$$
$$x_{51}x_{75}x_{76} + x_{51}x_{68}x_{124} + x_{51}x_{68}x_{111}x_{124} + x_{51}x_{68}x_{98} + x_{51}x_{68}x_{98}x_{111} + x_{51}x_{65}+$$
$$x_{51}x_{65}x_{111} + x_{51}x_{65}x_{68} + x_{51}x_{65}x_{68}x_{111} + x_{51}x_{55} + x_{51}x_{55}x_{111} + x_{51}x_{55}x_{68}+$$
$$x_{51}x_{55}x_{68}x_{111} + x_{51}x_{52}x_{124} + x_{51}x_{52}x_{98} + x_{51}x_{52}x_{68}x_{124} + x_{51}x_{52}x_{68}x_{98}+$$
$$x_{51}x_{52}x_{65} + x_{51}x_{52}x_{65}x_{68} + x_{51}x_{52}x_{55} + x_{51}x_{52}x_{55}x_{68} + x_{50} + x_{50}x_{78} + x_{50}x_{76}x_{77}+$$
$$x_{49} + x_{48} + x_{47}x_{48} + x_{46}x_{124} + x_{46}x_{98} + x_{46}x_{68}x_{124} + x_{46}x_{68}x_{98} + x_{46}x_{65}+$$
$$x_{46}x_{65}x_{68} + x_{46}x_{55} + x_{46}x_{55}x_{68} + x_{46}x_{47} + x_{45} + x_{44} + x_{42} + x_{40} + x_{39} + x_{39}x_{125}+$$
$$x_{39}x_{113} + x_{39}x_{111}x_{112} + x_{39}x_{110} + x_{39}x_{110}x_{111} + x_{39}x_{105} + x_{39}x_{97} + x_{39}x_{92}+$$
$$x_{39}x_{90}x_{91} + x_{39}x_{88} + x_{39}x_{86} + x_{39}x_{85} + x_{39}x_{80}x_{81} + x_{39}x_{79} + x_{39}x_{77} + x_{39}x_{77}x_{78}+$$
$$x_{39}x_{76} + x_{39}x_{70} + x_{39}x_{68}x_{125} + x_{39}x_{68}x_{113} + x_{39}x_{68}x_{111}x_{112} + x_{39}x_{68}x_{110}+$$

$$x_{39}x_{68}x_{110}x_{111} + x_{39}x_{68}x_{105} + x_{39}x_{68}x_{92} + x_{39}x_{68}x_{91} + x_{39}x_{68}x_{90}x_{91}+$$
$$x_{39}x_{68}x_{89}x_{90} + x_{39}x_{68}x_{86} + x_{39}x_{68}x_{85} + x_{39}x_{68}x_{77} + x_{39}x_{68}x_{76} + x_{39}x_{66}+$$
$$x_{39}x_{66}x_{68} + x_{39}x_{65}x_{68} + x_{39}x_{64}x_{68} + x_{39}x_{63} + x_{39}x_{63}x_{68} + x_{39}x_{63}x_{64} + x_{39}x_{62}+$$
$$x_{39}x_{62}x_{68} + x_{39}x_{61}x_{62} + x_{39}x_{61}x_{62}x_{68} + x_{39}x_{60}x_{61} + x_{39}x_{60}x_{61}x_{68} + x_{39}x_{56}+$$
$$x_{39}x_{56}x_{68} + x_{39}x_{55} + x_{39}x_{54} + x_{39}x_{54}x_{68} + x_{39}x_{53}x_{111} + x_{39}x_{53}x_{68}x_{111} + x_{39}x_{52}+$$
$$x_{39}x_{52}x_{112} + x_{39}x_{52}x_{110} + x_{39}x_{52}x_{68}x_{112} + x_{39}x_{52}x_{68}x_{110} + x_{39}x_{52}x_{53}+$$
$$x_{39}x_{52}x_{53}x_{68} + x_{39}x_{51} + x_{39}x_{51}x_{111} + x_{39}x_{51}x_{68} + x_{39}x_{51}x_{68}x_{111} + x_{39}x_{51}x_{52}+$$
$$x_{39}x_{51}x_{52}x_{68} + x_{39}x_{46} + x_{39}x_{46}x_{68} + x_{38}x_{124} + x_{38}x_{98} + x_{38}x_{96} + x_{38}x_{89}+$$
$$x_{38}x_{87}x_{88} + x_{38}x_{86} + x_{38}x_{70} + x_{38}x_{68} + x_{38}x_{66} + x_{38}x_{65} + x_{38}x_{64}x_{65} + x_{38}x_{62}+$$
$$x_{38}x_{55} + x_{37}x_{120} + x_{37}x_{97} + x_{37}x_{89} + x_{37}x_{87}x_{88} + x_{37}x_{62} + x_{37}x_{61} + x_{37}x_{51}+$$
$$x_{37}x_{38} + x_{36} + x_{36}x_{123} + x_{36}x_{87}x_{88} + x_{36}x_{64} + x_{36}x_{62} + x_{35}x_{124} + x_{35}x_{98}+$$
$$x_{35}x_{68}x_{124} + x_{35}x_{68}x_{98} + x_{35}x_{65} + x_{35}x_{65}x_{68} + x_{35}x_{55} + x_{35}x_{55}x_{68} + x_{35}x_{39}+$$
$$x_{35}x_{39}x_{68} + x_{34} + x_{33} + x_{32} + x_{31} + x_{30}x_{95} + x_{30}x_{78} + x_{30}x_{36} + x_{29}x_{79} + x_{29}x_{66}+$$
$$x_{29}x_{64}x_{65} + x_{29}x_{39} + x_{28} + x_{27} + x_{27}x_{124} + x_{27}x_{98} + x_{27}x_{68}x_{124} + x_{27}x_{68}x_{98}+$$
$$x_{27}x_{65}x_{68} + x_{27}x_{63}x_{64} + x_{27}x_{55} + x_{27}x_{55}x_{68} + x_{27}x_{39} + x_{27}x_{39}x_{68} + x_{27}x_{38} + x_{26}+$$
$$x_{26}x_{124} + x_{26}x_{98} + x_{26}x_{68}x_{124} + x_{26}x_{68}x_{98} + x_{26}x_{65} + x_{26}x_{65}x_{68} + x_{26}x_{55}+$$
$$x_{26}x_{55}x_{68} + x_{26}x_{39} + x_{26}x_{39}x_{68} + x_{25} + x_{23} + x_{23}x_{98} + x_{23}x_{39} + x_{22} + x_{21} + x_{21}x_{68}+$$
$$x_{20}x_{95} + x_{20}x_{88} + x_{20}x_{78} + x_{20}x_{36} + x_{20}x_{29} + x_{19}x_{89} + x_{19}x_{30} + x_{19}x_{20} + x_{18}x_{124}+$$
$$x_{18}x_{98} + x_{18}x_{68}x_{124} + x_{18}x_{68}x_{98} + x_{18}x_{65} + x_{18}x_{65}x_{68} + x_{18}x_{55} + x_{18}x_{55}x_{68}+$$
$$x_{18}x_{39} + x_{18}x_{39}x_{68} + x_{17}x_{124} + x_{17}x_{98} + x_{17}x_{68}x_{124} + x_{17}x_{68}x_{98} + x_{17}x_{65}+$$
$$x_{17}x_{65}x_{68} + x_{17}x_{55} + x_{17}x_{55}x_{68} + x_{17}x_{39} + x_{17}x_{39}x_{68} + x_{15} + x_{14} + x_{13} + x_{11}x_{89}+$$
$$x_{11}x_{87}x_{88} + x_{11}x_{82} + x_{11}x_{80}x_{81} + x_{11}x_{68} + x_{11}x_{66} + x_{11}x_{65} + x_{11}x_{64}x_{65}+$$
$$x_{11}x_{63}x_{64} + x_{11}x_{62} + x_{11}x_{55} + x_{11}x_{39} + x_{11}x_{38} + x_{10}x_{88} + x_{10}x_{29} + x_9x_{125} + x_9x_{124}+$$
$$x_9x_{121} + x_9x_{113}x_{124} + x_9x_{111}x_{112}x_{124} + x_9x_{110}x_{124} + x_9x_{110}x_{111}x_{124} + x_9x_{105}x_{124}+$$
$$x_9x_{98}x_{125} + x_9x_{98}x_{113} + x_9x_{98}x_{111}x_{112} + x_9x_{98}x_{110} + x_9x_{98}x_{110}x_{111} + x_9x_{98}x_{105}+$$
$$x_9x_{97} + x_9x_{92}x_{124} + x_9x_{92}x_{98} + x_9x_{91}x_{124} + x_9x_{91}x_{98} + x_9x_{90}x_{91}x_{124}+$$
$$x_9x_{90}x_{91}x_{98} + x_9x_{89} + x_9x_{89}x_{90}x_{124} + x_9x_{89}x_{90}x_{98} + x_9x_{86}x_{124} + x_9x_{86}x_{98}+$$
$$x_9x_{85}x_{124} + x_9x_{85}x_{98} + x_9x_{80} + x_9x_{77}x_{124} + x_9x_{77}x_{98} + x_9x_{76}x_{124} + x_9x_{76}x_{98}+$$
$$x_9x_{66} + x_9x_{66}x_{98} + x_9x_{65}x_{124} + x_9x_{65}x_{113} + x_9x_{65}x_{111}x_{112} + x_9x_{65}x_{110}+$$
$$x_9x_{65}x_{110}x_{111} + x_9x_{65}x_{105} + x_9x_{65}x_{98} + x_9x_{65}x_{92} + x_9x_{65}x_{91} + x_9x_{65}x_{90}x_{91}+$$
$$x_9x_{65}x_{89}x_{90} + x_9x_{65}x_{86} + x_9x_{65}x_{85} + x_9x_{65}x_{77} + x_9x_{65}x_{76} + x_9x_{64}x_{124} + x_9x_{64}x_{98}+$$
$$x_9x_{64}x_{65} + x_9x_{63}x_{124} + x_9x_{63}x_{98} + x_9x_{63}x_{65} + x_9x_{62} + x_9x_{62}x_{124} + x_9x_{62}x_{98}+$$
$$x_9x_{62}x_{65} + x_9x_{61}x_{62}x_{124} + x_9x_{61}x_{62}x_{98} + x_9x_{61}x_{62}x_{65} + x_9x_{60}x_{61}x_{124}+$$
$$x_9x_{60}x_{61}x_{98} + x_9x_{60}x_{61}x_{65} + x_9x_{56} + x_9x_{56}x_{98} + x_9x_{55} + x_9x_{55}x_{113}+$$
$$x_9x_{55}x_{111}x_{112} + x_9x_{55}x_{110} + x_9x_{55}x_{110}x_{111} + x_9x_{55}x_{105} + x_9x_{55}x_{92} + x_9x_{55}x_{91}+$$
$$x_9x_{55}x_{90}x_{91} + x_9x_{55}x_{89}x_{90} + x_9x_{55}x_{86} + x_9x_{55}x_{85} + x_9x_{55}x_{77} + x_9x_{55}x_{76}+$$
$$x_9x_{55}x_{65} + x_9x_{55}x_{64} + x_9x_{55}x_{63} + x_9x_{55}x_{62} + x_9x_{55}x_{61}x_{62} + x_9x_{55}x_{60}x_{61}+$$
$$x_9x_{54}x_{124} + x_9x_{54}x_{98} + x_9x_{54}x_{65} + x_9x_{54}x_{55} + x_9x_{53}x_{111}x_{124} + x_9x_{53}x_{98}x_{111}+$$
$$x_9x_{53}x_{65}x_{111} + x_9x_{53}x_{55}x_{111} + x_9x_{52} + x_9x_{52}x_{112}x_{124} + x_9x_{52}x_{110}x_{124}+$$

$$
\begin{aligned}
&x_9x_{52}x_{98}x_{112} + x_9x_{52}x_{98}x_{110} + x_9x_{52}x_{65}x_{112} + x_9x_{52}x_{65}x_{110} + x_9x_{52}x_{55}x_{112}+ \\
&x_9x_{52}x_{55}x_{110} + x_9x_{52}x_{53}x_{124} + x_9x_{52}x_{53}x_{98} + x_9x_{52}x_{53}x_{65} + x_9x_{52}x_{53}x_{55}+ \\
&x_9x_{51}x_{124} + x_9x_{51}x_{111}x_{124} + x_9x_{51}x_{98} + x_9x_{51}x_{98}x_{111} + x_9x_{51}x_{65} + x_9x_{51}x_{65}x_{111}+ \\
&x_9x_{51}x_{55} + x_9x_{51}x_{55}x_{111} + x_9x_{51}x_{52}x_{124} + x_9x_{51}x_{52}x_{98} + x_9x_{51}x_{52}x_{65}+ \\
&x_9x_{51}x_{52}x_{55} + x_9x_{46}x_{124} + x_9x_{46}x_{98} + x_9x_{46}x_{65} + x_9x_{46}x_{55} + x_9x_{39}x_{125}+ \\
&x_9x_{39}x_{113} + x_9x_{39}x_{111}x_{112} + x_9x_{39}x_{110} + x_9x_{39}x_{110}x_{111} + x_9x_{39}x_{105} + x_9x_{39}x_{92}+ \\
&x_9x_{39}x_{91} + x_9x_{39}x_{90}x_{91} + x_9x_{39}x_{89}x_{90} + x_9x_{39}x_{86} + x_9x_{39}x_{85} + x_9x_{39}x_{77}+ \\
&x_9x_{39}x_{76} + x_9x_{39}x_{66} + x_9x_{39}x_{65} + x_9x_{39}x_{64} + x_9x_{39}x_{63} + x_9x_{39}x_{62} + x_9x_{39}x_{61}x_{62}+ \\
&x_9x_{39}x_{60}x_{61} + x_9x_{39}x_{56} + x_9x_{39}x_{54} + x_9x_{39}x_{53}x_{111} + x_9x_{39}x_{52}x_{112} + x_9x_{39}x_{52}x_{110}+ \\
&x_9x_{39}x_{52}x_{53} + x_9x_{39}x_{51} + x_9x_{39}x_{51}x_{111} + x_9x_{39}x_{51}x_{52} + x_9x_{39}x_{46} + x_9x_{38}+ \\
&x_9x_{35}x_{124} + x_9x_{35}x_{98} + x_9x_{35}x_{65} + x_9x_{35}x_{55} + x_9x_{35}x_{39} + x_9x_{30} + x_9x_{27}x_{124}+ \\
&x_9x_{27}x_{98} + x_9x_{27}x_{65} + x_9x_{27}x_{55} + x_9x_{27}x_{39} + x_9x_{26}x_{124} + x_9x_{26}x_{98} + x_9x_{26}x_{65}+ \\
&x_9x_{26}x_{55} + x_9x_{26}x_{39} + x_9x_{21} + x_9x_{20} + x_9x_{18}x_{124} + x_9x_{18}x_{98} + x_9x_{18}x_{65}+ \\
&x_9x_{18}x_{55} + x_9x_{18}x_{39} + x_9x_{17}x_{124} + x_9x_{17}x_{98} + x_9x_{17}x_{65} + x_9x_{17}x_{55} + x_9x_{17}x_{39}+ \\
&x_9x_{11} + x_8x_{124} + x_8x_{98} + x_8x_{68}x_{124} + x_8x_{68}x_{98} + x_8x_{65} + x_8x_{65}x_{68} + x_8x_{55}+ \\
&x_8x_{55}x_{68} + x_8x_{39} + x_8x_{39}x_{68} + x_8x_9x_{124} + x_8x_9x_{98} + x_8x_9x_{65} + x_8x_9x_{55} + x_8x_9x_{39}+ \\
&x_7 + x_7x_{124} + x_7x_{98} + x_7x_{68}x_{124} + x_7x_{68}x_{98} + x_7x_{65} + x_7x_{65}x_{68} + x_7x_{55} + x_7x_{55}x_{68}+ \\
&x_7x_{39} + x_7x_{39}x_{68} + x_7x_9x_{124} + x_7x_9x_{98} + x_7x_9x_{65} + x_7x_9x_{55} + x_7x_9x_{39} + x_6+ \\
&x_5x_{95} + x_5x_{36}. \qquad (8)
\end{aligned}
$$

References

1. De Cannière, C., Preneel, B.: Trivium. In: Robshaw, M., Billet, O. (eds.) New Stream Cipher Designs. LNCS, vol. 4986, pp. 244–266. Springer, Heidelberg (2008). https://doi.org/10.1007/978-3-540-68351-3_18
2. Dinur, I., Shamir, A.: Cube attacks on tweakable black box polynomials. In: Joux, A. (ed.) EUROCRYPT 2009. LNCS, vol. 5479, pp. 278–299. Springer, Heidelberg (2009). https://doi.org/10.1007/978-3-642-01001-9_16
3. eSTREAM: the ECRYPT stream cipher project (2018). https://www.ecrypt.eu.org/stream/. Accessed 23 Mar 2021
4. Hadipour, H., Eichlseder, M.: Autoguess: a tool for finding guess-and-determine attacks and key bridges. In: Ateniese, G., Venturi, D. (eds.) ACNS 22. LNCS, vol. 13269, pp. 230–250. Springer, Heidelberg (2022). https://doi.org/10.1007/978-3-031-09234-3_12
5. Hadipour, H., Eichlseder, M.: Integral cryptanalysis of WARP based on monomial prediction. IACR Trans. Symmetric Cryptol. **2022**(2), 92–112 (2022). https://doi.org/10.46586/tosc.v2022.i2.92-112
6. Hao, Y., Leander, G., Meier, W., Todo, Y., Wang, Q.: Modeling for three-subset division property without unknown subset. In: Canteaut, A., Ishai, Y. (eds.) EUROCRYPT 2020. LNCS, vol. 12105, pp. 466–495. Springer, Cham (2020). https://doi.org/10.1007/978-3-030-45721-1_17

7. He, J., Hu, K., Preneel, B., Wang, M.: Stretching cube attacks: improved methods to recover massive superpolies. In: ASIACRYPT 2022, Part IV. LNCS, vol. 13794, pp. 537–566. Springer, Heidelberg (2022). https://doi.org/10.1007/978-3-031-22972-5_19
8. Hebborn, P., Lambin, B., Leander, G., Todo, Y.: Lower bounds on the degree of block ciphers. In: Moriai, S., Wang, H. (eds.) ASIACRYPT 2020, Part I. LNCS, vol. 12491, pp. 537–566. Springer, Heidelberg (2020). https://doi.org/10.1007/978-3-030-64837-4_18
9. Hu, K., Sun, S., Todo, Y., Wang, M., Wang, Q.: Massive superpoly recovery with nested monomial predictions. In: Tibouchi, M., Wang, H. (eds.) ASIACRYPT 2021, Part I. LNCS, vol. 13090, pp. 392–421. Springer, Heidelberg (2021). https://doi.org/10.1007/978-3-030-92062-3_14
10. Hu, K., Sun, S., Wang, M., Wang, Q.: An algebraic formulation of the division property: revisiting degree evaluations, cube attacks, and key-independent sums. In: Moriai, S., Wang, H. (eds.) ASIACRYPT 2020. LNCS, vol. 12491, pp. 446–476. Springer, Cham (2020). https://doi.org/10.1007/978-3-030-64837-4_15
11. ISO/IEC: 29192–3:2012: Information technology - Security techniques - Lightweight cryptography - part 3: Stream ciphers. https://www.iso.org/standard/56426.html
12. Mouha, N., Wang, Q., Gu, D., Preneel, B.: Differential and linear cryptanalysis using mixed-integer linear programming. In: Wu, C.-K., Yung, M., Lin, D. (eds.) Inscrypt 2011. LNCS, vol. 7537, pp. 57–76. Springer, Heidelberg (2012). https://doi.org/10.1007/978-3-642-34704-7_5
13. Mroczkowski, P., Szmidt, J.: The cube attack on stream cipher trivium and quadraticity tests. Fundam. Inform. **114**(3–4), 309–318 (2012). https://doi.org/10.3233/FI-2012-631
14. Sun, S., Hu, L., Wang, P., Qiao, K., Ma, X., Song, L.: Automatic security evaluation and (related-key) differential characteristic search: application to SIMON, PRESENT, LBlock, DES(L) and other bit-oriented block ciphers. In: Sarkar, P., Iwata, T. (eds.) ASIACRYPT 2014. LNCS, vol. 8873, pp. 158–178. Springer, Heidelberg (2014). https://doi.org/10.1007/978-3-662-45611-8_9
15. Sun, Y.: Cube attack against 843-round trivium. Cryptology ePrint Archive, Report 2021/547 (2021). https://eprint.iacr.org/2021/547
16. Todo, Y.: Integral cryptanalysis on full MISTY1. In: Gennaro, R., Robshaw, M. (eds.) CRYPTO 2015. LNCS, vol. 9215, pp. 413–432. Springer, Heidelberg (2015). https://doi.org/10.1007/978-3-662-47989-6_20
17. Todo, Y.: Structural evaluation by generalized integral property. In: Oswald, E., Fischlin, M. (eds.) EUROCRYPT 2015. LNCS, vol. 9056, pp. 287–314. Springer, Heidelberg (2015). https://doi.org/10.1007/978-3-662-46800-5_12
18. Todo, Y., Isobe, T., Hao, Y., Meier, W.: Cube attacks on non-blackbox polynomials based on division property. In: Katz, J., Shacham, H. (eds.) CRYPTO 2017. LNCS, vol. 10403, pp. 250–279. Springer, Cham (2017). https://doi.org/10.1007/978-3-319-63697-9_9
19. Todo, Y., Morii, M.: Bit-based division property and application to Simon family. In: Peyrin, T. (ed.) FSE 2016. LNCS, vol. 9783, pp. 357–377. Springer, Heidelberg (2016). https://doi.org/10.1007/978-3-662-52993-5_18
20. Wang, Q., Hao, Y., Todo, Y., Li, C., Isobe, T., Meier, W.: Improved division property based cube attacks exploiting algebraic properties of superpoly. In: Shacham, H., Boldyreva, A. (eds.) CRYPTO 2018. LNCS, vol. 10991, pp. 275–305. Springer, Cham (2018). https://doi.org/10.1007/978-3-319-96884-1_10

21. Wang, S., Hu, B., Guan, J., Zhang, K., Shi, T.: MILP-aided method of searching division property using three subsets and applications. In: Galbraith, S.D., Moriai, S. (eds.) ASIACRYPT 2019. LNCS, vol. 11923, pp. 398–427. Springer, Cham (2019). https://doi.org/10.1007/978-3-030-34618-8_14
22. Xiang, Z., Zhang, W., Bao, Z., Lin, D.: Applying MILP method to searching integral distinguishers based on division property for 6 lightweight block ciphers. In: Cheon, J.H., Takagi, T. (eds.) ASIACRYPT 2016. LNCS, vol. 10031, pp. 648–678. Springer, Heidelberg (2016). https://doi.org/10.1007/978-3-662-53887-6_24
23. Ye, C.D., Tian, T.: Revisit division property based cube attacks: key-recovery or distinguishing attacks? IACR Trans. Symm. Cryptol. **2019**(3), 81–102 (2019). https://doi.org/10.13154/tosc.v2019.i3.81-102
24. Ye, C.D., Tian, T.: Algebraic method to recover superpolies in cube attacks. IET Inf. Secur. **14**(4), 430–441 (2020)

New Techniques for Modeling SBoxes: An MILP Approach

Debranjan Pal(✉), Vishal Pankaj Chandratreya, and Dipanwita Roy Chowdhury

Crypto Research Lab, IIT Kharagpur, Kharagpur, India
debranjanpal@iitkgp.ac.in, vpaijc@kgpian.iitkgp.ac.in, drc@cse.iitkgp.ac.in

Abstract. Mixed Integer Linear Programming (MILP) is a well-known approach for the cryptanalysis of a symmetric cipher. A number of MILP-based security analyses have been reported for non-linear (SBoxes) and linear layers. Researchers proposed word- and bit-wise SBox modeling techniques using a set of inequalities which helps in searching differential trails for a cipher.

In this paper, we propose two new techniques to reduce the number of inequalities to represent the valid differential transitions for SBoxes. Our first technique chooses the best greedy solution with a random tiebreaker and achieves improved results for the 4-bit SBoxes of MIBS, LBlock, and Serpent over the existing results of Sun et al. [26]. Subset addition, our second approach, is an improvement over the algorithm proposed by Boura and Coggia. Subset addition technique is faster than Boura and Coggia [10] and also improves the count of inequalities. Our algorithm emulates the existing results for the 4-bit SBoxes of Minalpher, LBlock, Serpent, Prince, and Rectangle. The subset addition method also works for 5-bit and 6-bit SBoxes. We improve the boundary of minimum number inequalities from the existing results for 5-bit SBoxes of ASCON and SC2000. Application of subset addition technique for 6-bit SBoxes of APN, FIDES, and SC2000 enhances the existing results. By applying multithreading, we reduce the execution time needed to find the minimum inequality set over the existing techniques.

Keywords: Mixed Integer Linear Programming · Symmetric Key · Block Cipher · Active SBox · Differential Cryptanalysis · Convex Hull

1 Introduction

Differential cryptanalysis [7] and linear cryptanalysis [19] are the two most valuable methods in the cryptanalysis domain of symmetric-key cryptography. Differential cryptanalysis for block ciphers demonstrates the mapping of input differences in the plaintext to output differences in the ciphertext. The probabilistic linear relationships between the plaintext, ciphertext and key are expressed by linear cryptanalysis, on the other hand. For developing a distinguisher or identifying a key-recovery attack, we leverage the feature that an ideal cipher behaves differently from a random cipher for differential or linear cryptanalysis.

J. Deng et al. (Eds.): CANS 2023, LNCS 14342, pp. 318–340, 2023.
https://doi.org/10.1007/978-981-99-7563-1_15

For new ciphers, enforcing resistance against the linear and differential cryptanalysis is a common design criterion during the analysis of the cipher. The wide trail design [13] technique for block ciphers leads to prove the security against linear and differential cryptanalysis. Finding the minimum number of active SBoxes within the cipher is a useful way to assess the security of the scheme against differential attacks. Calculating the minimal amount of active SBoxes for block ciphers has received a lot of attention. But the time and effort by humans as well as by programs required to apply those techniques is huge. Here, MILP can be used to solve these issues. MILP is an optimization problem that restricts some of its variables to integral value. MILP offers a powerful and adaptable approach for handling large, significant and complicated problems. The attacker uses linear inequalities to define potential differential propagation patterns in a round function for differential search using MILP. The attacker then executes an MILP solver (in parallel), which yields the minimal number of active SBoxes for the specified propagation patterns. After generating a lower bound for the quantity of active SBoxes in differential and linear cryptanalysis, one may calculate an upper bound for the likelihood of the best characteristic by utilising the maximum differential probability (MDP) of the SBoxes. The probability of the best characteristic can be used to calculate the differential probability with accuracy by summing up all matching characteristics probabilities.

Typically, a cryptographic component's (like SBox) propagation characteristic can be expressed using Boolean functions. To model a Boolean function using the MILP method, a set of inequalities must be computed. Then some solutions to these inequalities also calculated which precisely corresponds to support the boolean function. In order to calculate a solution model of any boolean function, we must resolve two issues. To efficiently model a boolean function a set of inequalities to be created. Selecting a minimal set of possible inequalities which perfectly model the boolean function, if the first issue is resolved. To solve the these problems researchers proposes different techniques [10,18,20,21,24–26].

MILP models are frequently used in cryptanalysis, it is crucial to increase the effectiveness of MILP model solutions. Which kind of comprehensive model, though, would be the most effective is still a mystery. Different kinds of proposed models should be built and thoroughly investigated in order to fix this issue. Since different models are built from a varieties of possible inequalities, the first move towards achieving this goal is to generate a variety of inequalities.

To get optimized MILP model researchers observe reduction in number of inequalities by at least one unit is itself important. Because in a larger view, for a full round cipher, the total number of inequalities impacts a lot with respect to the computing resources and the timing requirements for the MILP solver.

1.1 Related Work

Mouha et al. [20] first described the problem of finding the smallest number of active SBoxes that can be modelled using MILP for assessing word-oriented ciphers. There are other ciphers that are not word-oriented, such as PRESENT, which applies a 4-bit SBox and then switches four bits from one SBox to four separate SBoxes using a bit-permutation.

Sun et al. [26] established a way to simulate all possible differential propagations bit by bit even for the SBox in order to apply MILP to such a structure. They used MILP-based techniques to assess a block cipher's security for related-key differential attacks. The methods are mainly applied for searching single-key or related-key differential [5] characteristics on PRESENT80, LBlock, SIMON48, DESL and PRESENT128. Sun et al. [26] report different methods to model differential characteristics of an SBox with linear inequalities. In the first technique, inequalities are produced based on some conditional differential characteristics of an SBox. Another method involves extracting the inequalities from the H-representation of the convex hull for all possible differential patterns of the SBox. To choose a certain number of inequalities from the convex hull, they devise a greedy algorithm for the second technique. They suggest an automated approach for assessing the security of bit-oriented block ciphers for differential attack. They propose many ways for getting tighter security limits using these inequalities along with the MILP methodology.

Sun et al. [25] look into the differential and linear behaviour of a variety of block ciphers using mixed-integer linear programming (MILP). They point out that a modest set of linear inequalities can precisely characterize the differential behaviour of every SBox. For a variety of ciphers, Sun et al. [25] build MILP models whose feasible zones are exactly the collections of all legitimate differential and linear properties. Any subset of $\{0,1\}^n \subset \mathbb{R}^n$ has an accurate linear-inequality description, according to them. They provide a technique that may be used to determine all differential and linear properties with certain specified features by converting the heuristic approach of Sun et al. [26] for finding differential and linear characteristics into an accurate one based on these MILP models.

Mouha's [20] technique is not suitable for SPN ciphers which contain diffusion layers with bitwise permutations, called S-bP structures. The problem occurs because of avoiding the diffusion effect calculated simultaneously by the non-linear substitution layers and bitwise permutation layers. Also the MILP constraints provided by Mouha are not sufficient for modeling the differential propagation of a linear diffusion layer derived from almost-MDS or non-MDS matrix. To automatically determine a lower constraint on the number of active SBoxes for block ciphers with S-bP structures, Sun et al. [24] expanded the method of Mouha et al. [20] and proposed a new strategy based on mixed-integer linear programming (MILP). They successfully applied the technique to PRESENT-80.

In order to automatically look for differential and linear characteristics for ARX ciphers, Kai Fu et al. [15] built a MILP model. By assuming independent inputs to the modular addition and independent rounds, they applied the differential and linear property of modular addition. They search for the differential properties and linear approximations of the Speck cipher using the new MILP model. Their identified differential characteristics for Speck64, Speck96, and Speck128 are prolonged for one, three, and five rounds, respectively, in comparison to the prior best differential characteristics for them, and the differential characteristic for Speck48 has a greater likelihood. Cui et al. [12] provide a novel automatic method to search impossible differential trails for ciphers containing SBoxes after taking into account the differential and linear features of non-linear components, like SBoxes themselves. They expand the tool's capabilities to include modulo addition and use it with ARX ciphers. For HIGHT, SHACAL-2, LEA, and LBlock, the tool enhances the best outcomes currently available. A new SBox modeling that can handle the likelihood of differential characteristics and reflect a condensed form of the Differential Distribution Table (DDT) of big SBoxes was presented by Ahmed Abdelkhalek et al. [2]. They increased the number of rounds needed to resist simple differential distinguishers by one round after evaluating the upper bound on SKINNY-128's differential features. For two AES-round based constructions, the upper bound on differential features are examined.

1.2 Our Contribution

In this paper we introduce two of MILP-based solutions for valid differential trail propagation through the non-linear layers, that is, SBoxes. The new approaches reduce the number of inequalities for modeling 4-bit SBoxes in comparison to the earlier algorithms [10,21,26,27]. Our techniques help cryptographic designers for providing a bound on finding minimum number of SBoxes and thus ensure resistance against differential cryptanalysis attacks.

- **Greedy random-tiebreaker algorithm** We propose a new algorithm by randomly choosing from the result of greedy algorithm. Our technique improves the boundary for minimum number of inequalities for 4-bit SBoxes of MIBS, LBlock and Serpent over the existing greedy algorithm [26].
- **Subset addition approach** A subset-addition-based algorithm is proposed by generating new inequalities from the results of H-representation of the convex hull. We add k-subset inequalities to generate new inequality, which removes more impossible propagation. Then replace some subset of old inequalities by the newer one, which results in an improvement over the existing algorithms for 4-bit SBoxes of Minalpher, LBlock, Serpent, Prince and Rectangle. The subset addition algorithm also works for 5- and 6-bit SBoxes. We also improve the boundary of inequalities for 5-bit SBoxes of ASCON, and SC2000. For 6-bit SBoxes of APN and SC2000, we reduce the number of inequalities from the existing results.
  We also improve the time for finding the minimum set of inequalities over Boura and Coggia's [10] approach by a significant percentage.

1.3 Organization of the Paper

The organization of the paper is as follows. Section 2 explains the background of our work. We describe the greedy random tiebreaker algorithm and its results in Sect. 3. In Sect. 4, we present the subset addition approach and the corresponding implementation process with the results. Section 5 concludes the paper.

2 Background

In this section we describe the earlier used methods and algorithms for modeling SBoxes using inequalities.

2.1 Representation of SBoxes Using Inequalities

An SBox S can be represented as $S : \mathbb{F}_2^n \rightarrow \mathbb{F}_2^n$. We can symbolize any operation on an SBox as $x \rightarrow y$ with $x, y \in \mathbb{F}_2^n$. Let $(x_0, \ldots, x_{n-1}, y_0, \ldots, y_{n-1}) \in \mathbb{R}^{2n}$ be a $2n$-dimensional vector, where $\mathbb{R}$ is the real number field, and for an SBox the input-output differential pattern is denoted using a point $(x_0, \ldots, x_{n-1}, y_0, \ldots, y_{n-1})$.

H-Representation of the Convex Hull. The convex hull of a set P of distance points in $\mathbb{R}^n$ is the smallest convex set that contains P. We compute the H-representation of the convex hull of all possible input-output differential patterns of the SBox by calculating the DDT. Applying SageMath [1] on the DDT, we compute the H-representation. From H-representation we get w linear inequalities, which can be written as

$$A \begin{bmatrix} x_0 \\ \vdots \\ x_{n-1} \\ y_0 \\ \vdots \\ y_{n-1} \end{bmatrix} \leq b$$

where A is a $w \times 2n$ matrix. Here, A and b contain only integer values. Every linear inequality also invalidates some points, which are associated with some impossible differential propagations. The H-representation also contains redundant inequalities associated with the MILP-based differential trail search; the reason is that the feasible points are constricted to $\{0,1\}^{2n}$, not $\mathbb{R}^{2n}$ As a result, a lot of extra linear inequalities force the MILP solver to work slower. To eliminate those redundant inequalities, researchers apply different techniques.

Conditional Differential Characteristics Modeling. The logical condition that $(x_0, \ldots, x_{m-1}) = (\delta_0, \ldots, \delta_{m-1}) \in \{0,1\}^m \subseteq \mathbb{Z}^m$ implies $y = \delta \in \{0,1\} \subseteq \mathbb{Z}$ can be modeled by using the following linear inequality,

$$\sum_{i=0}^{m-1} (-1)^{\delta_i} x_i + (-1)^{\delta+1} y - \delta + \sum_{i=0}^{m-1} \delta_i \geq 0 \tag{1}$$

Let (x_0, x_1, x_2, x_3) and (y_0, y_1, y_2, y_3) be MILP variables for the input and output differences of a 4-bit SBox. Let $(1010) \rightarrow (0111)$ be an impossible propagation in the DDT corresponding to the SBox. That is, the input difference (1010) is not propagating to (0111). By Eq. 1, the linear inequality which eliminates the impossible point (1001, 0111) is, $-x_0 + x_1 - x_2 + x_3 + y_0 - y_1 - y_2 - y_3 + 4 \geq 0$. Corresponding to an SBox, if in a DDT there occur n impossible paths, then at most n linear inequalities are needed to model the DDT correctly. But one can reduce the value of n by merging one or more available inequalities and therefore generating new inequalities. For example if we consider two impossible propagations $(1010) \rightarrow (0111)$ and $(1010) \rightarrow (0110)$, then the linear inequality: $-x_0 + x_1 - x_2 + x_3 + y_0 - y_1 - y_2 + y_3 \geq -3$ eliminates both the impossible points together.

Choosing the Best Inequalities from the Convex Hull

Applying an MILP model, generating a feasible solution is not guaranteed to be a legitimate differential path. We want to reduce the number of active SBoxes throughout a greater region and the optimal value achieved should be less than or equal to the actual minimum number of active SBoxes. Hence, we will look for any linear inequality that may be used to chop out a portion of the MILP model while maintaining the region of valid differential characteristics. Researchers proposed different algorithms (see Appendix A) for reducing number of inequalities for an SBox representation.

Greedy Algorithm Based Modeling [26]. The discrete points in the H-Representation (convex hull) generate a huge number of inequalities. A good approach is to filter the best valid inequalities which maximize the number of removed impossible differential patterns from the feasible region of the convex hull. Algorithm 5 explains the greedy approach proposed by Sun et al.

Modeling by Selecting Random Set of Inequalities [10]. A larger set of new inequalities (generated by randomly adding k inequalities) are worthless

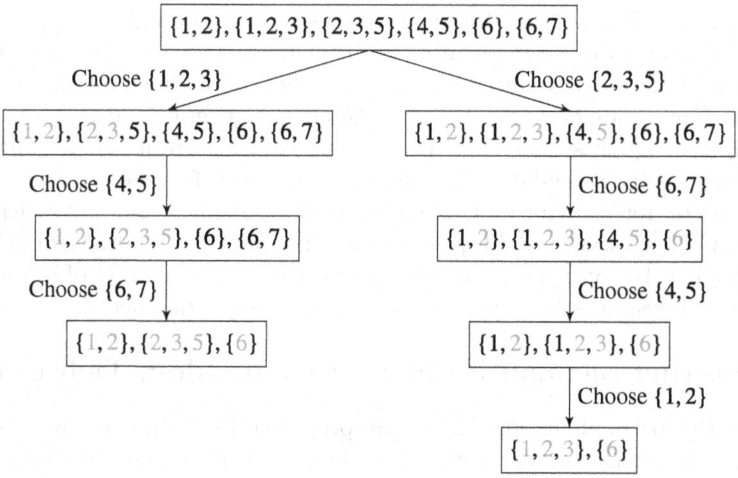

Fig. 1. Variation of the output of the greedy algorithm because of a random tiebreaker

as most probably they will satisfy the whole space $\{0,1\}^m$. If k-hyperplanes of the H-representation share a vertex on the cube $\{0,1\}^m$, then summing corresponding inequalities probably generates a new inequality Q_{new}. But the hyperplane corresponding Q_{new} should intersect with the cube by at least one point. In that case, Q_{new} possibly invalidates a different set of impossible points from H-representation than the older inequalities. Algorithm 6 briefs the whole procedure.

Algorithm 1. Randomly select inequalities from greedy set (Greedy Random-Tiebreaker)

Input:
H_{Rep}: Inequalities in the H-Representation of the convex hull of an SBox.
I_D: The set of all impossible differential paths of an SBox
Output:
I_{SR}: Set of n-best inequalities that generates more stricter feasible region after maximizing the removed impossible differential paths.

```
I_M ← φ, I_SR ← φ
while I_D ≠ φ do
    I_M ←The inequalities in H_Rep which maximizes the number of removed impossible differential paths from I_D.
    I_D ← I_D − {Removed impossible differential paths using I_M}
    if Degree(I_M) > 1 then                ▷ Returns the number of elements in a set
        Rand_I ← ChooseRandomInequality(I_M)   ▷ Chooses randomly an element from a set
    end if
    H_Rep ← H_Rep − Rand_I
    I_SR ← I_SR ∪ Rand_I
end while
return I_SR
```

MILP-Based Reduction Algorithm. Sasaki and Todo [21] propose a technique which generates a minimization problem, which they solve using a standard MILP solver to get the reduced set of inequalities. First they find all the impossible differential points from DDT of an SBox and generate impossible patterns applying those points. Next, for a given impossible pattern, check which subset of inequalities invalidates the pattern. Now, they form a constraint: every impossible pattern should be removed from the possible region by at least one inequality. They form an MILP problem which minimizes the total set of inequalities applying the constraints and solve it to get the minimized set of inequalities. Algorithm 4 describes the whole process in a step-wise manner.

3 Filtering Inequalities by Greedy Random-Tiebreaker

We use the original greedy algorithm proposed by S Sun et al. [26]. Our technique is similar to the original greedy algorithm, except that when multiple inequalities have the same rank, we choose one of them randomly. We

Algorithm 2. Generates a minimal subset of inequalities eliminating all impossible differential paths (Subset Addition)

Input:
H_{Rep}: Inequalities in the H-Representation of the convex hull of an SBox.
I_P: The set of all possible differential paths of an SBox
I_D: The set of all impossible differential paths of an SBox
Output:
I_{SR}: Set of n-best inequalities that generates more stricter feasible region after maximizing the removed impossible differential paths.

```
I_SR ← H_Rep
for p ∈ I_P do
    I_H ← all hyperplanes in H_Rep which the point p lies on
    for {h_1, h_2, ..., h_k} ∈ P_Set(I_H) do
        h ← h_1 + h_2 + ... + h_k
        if h is a good hyperplane (If satisfies condition of Type 1 or Type 2) then
            I_SR ← I_SR ∪ {h}
        end if
    end for
end for
return the smallest subset of I_SR removing all paths in I_D.
```

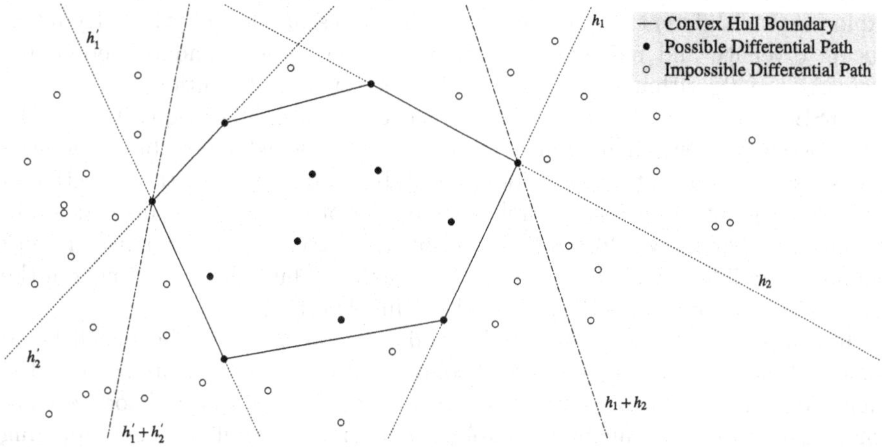

Fig. 2. Separating Type 1 and Type 2 inequalities in convex hull

claim that a random tiebreaker could result in a different number of inequalities across multiple runs, and prove it with an instance of the set cover problem (which is homomorphic to the problem of minimising the MILP model of an SBox). Consider the set $S = \{1,2,3,4,5,6,7\}$ and its subsets $\{\{1,2\},\{1,2,3\},\{2,3,5\},\{4,5\},\{6\},\{6,7\}\}$, which are to be used to find a cover of S. Two possible greedy approaches yield covers of sizes three, $\{\{1,2,3\},\{4,5\},\{6,7\}\}$ and four $\{\{2,3,5\},\{4,5\},\{6,7\},\{1,2\}\}$ (see Fig. 1).

After multiple runs of greedy random-tiebreaker, we choose the best (reduced) set of inequalities that invalidate all the impossible differential patterns. Thus, the greedy random-tiebreaker improves the performance of the greedy algorithm. Table 1 describes a comparative analysis of the number of reduced inequalities for different 4-bit SBoxes.

The overall technique is described in Algorithm 1. Let H_{Rep} be the set of inequalities that is generated from the SageMath method *inequality_generator*() as the H-representation of the convex hull of an SBox. Assume I_D be the set of all impossible differential points selected from difference distribution table (DDT) of an SBox. Let I_M stores the hyperplanes in H_{Rep} removing greatest number of paths from I_D. If I_M have more than one elements, then we are choosing an inequality randomly from I_M by applying *ChooseRandomInequality* method and collecting in I_{SR}. The best set of inequalities saved to I_{SR}. We execute the overall process multiple times to get the best set of inequalities.

3.1 Why Random Tiebreaking Improves the Performance of the Greedy Algorithm?

Random tiebreaking can improve the performance of a greedy algorithm by introducing an element of randomness, which helps to avoid certain pitfalls and issues that arise due to deterministic decision-making. This randomness helps to prevent the algorithm from getting stuck in predictable patterns, encourages exploration of different choices, and enables it to escape local optima. By introducing diversity and reducing sensitivity to input order, random tiebreaking increases the algorithm's chances of finding better overall solutions.

In SBox modeling, the greedy algorithm chooses an eligible inequality from the set of inequalities, which maximizes the number of removed impossible differential paths. Here, we notice that selecting the suitable inequality from the collection of possible inequalities affects the whole system's performance. Hence, instead of taking inequality greedily, one possible solution is to check the performance of every potential candidate and choose the best inequality. Thus, the randomness in the selection scheme improves the greedy algorithm's performance.

It's important to note that while random tiebreaking can be beneficial in some instances, it's not a guaranteed solution. It can help mitigate some of the limitations of deterministic greedy algorithms, but it might also introduce challenges related to reproducibility, stability, and unpredictability. When applying random tiebreaking, it's essential to analyze the specific problem, the characteristics of the input data, and the potential benefits and drawbacks to determine whether it's a suitable approach.

3.2 Implementations and Results

We implemented Algorithm 1 in SageMath (on a desktop computer with an Intel Core i5-6500 4C/4T CPU running Manjaro Linux Sikaris 22.0.0 Xfce Edition 64-bit) with a flag to randomise the list of inequalities.

Applications on 4-Bit SBoxes. We run our algorithm greedy random-tiebreaker on a large set 4-bit SBoxes used in ciphers. Now we describe the

Table 1. Minimum number of Inequalities for 4-bit SBoxes (Random Greedy-Tiebreaker)

Cipher	SageMath [1]	Sun et al. [26]	Random Greedy (Our Approach)
GIFT	237	–	22
KLEIN	311	22	22
Lilliput	324	–	26
MIBS	378	27	**24**
Midori S0	239	–	25
Midori S1	367	–	24
Minalpher	338	–	25
Piccolo	202	23	24
PRESENT	327	22	22
PRIDE	194	–	22
PRINCE	300	26	26
RECTANGLE	267	–	23
SKINNY	202	–	24
TWINE	324	23	25
LBlock S0	205	28	**25**
LBlock S1	205	27	**25**
LBlock S2	205	27	**25**
LBlock S3	205	27	**26**
LBlock S4	205	28	**25**
LBlock S5	205	27	**25**
LBlock S6	205	27	**26**
LBlock S7	205	27	**25**
LBlock S8	205	28	**26**
LBlock S9	205	27	**25**
Serpent S0	410	23	24
Serpent S1	409	24	25
Serpent S2	408	25	25
Serpent S3	396	31	**23**
Serpent S4	328	26	**24**
Serpent S5	336	25	**23**
Serpent S6	382	22	**21**
Serpent S7	470	30	**21**
Serpent S8	364	–	25
Serpent S9	357	–	24
Serpent S10	369	–	27
Serpent S11	399	–	21
Serpent S12	368	–	24
Serpent S13	368	–	24
Serpent S14	368	–	25
Serpent S15	368	–	23
Serpent S16	365	–	25
Serpent S17	393	–	31
Serpent S18	368	–	27
Serpent S19	398	–	23
Serpent S20	351	–	24
Serpent S21	447	–	25
Serpent S22	405	–	25
Serpent S23	328	–	24
Serpent S24	357	–	24
Serpent S25	366	–	22
Serpent S26	368	–	23
Serpent S27	523	–	24
Serpent S28	278	–	23
Serpent S29	394	–	24
Serpent S30	394	–	23
Serpent S31	357	–	27

comparison of our results with existing best known result against the minimum number of inequalities. The first block of Table 1 presents the results for 4-bit SBoxes for 14 different ciphers. We get mixed results, for instance in case of MIBS [17] we get 24 inequalities which is lesser in 3 numbers that of Sun et al. [26]; for Prince [9] the result is same but for other four ciphers it gives comparable results. The third block of Table 1 shows the result for all the SBoxes of Serpent [6]. Among the existing available results of eight SBoxes for four SBoxes ($S3, S4, S5, S7$) we are gaining, for S2 the results is same and for the remaining three ($S0, S1, S6$) we are loosing at most in two numbers. In Table 1 second block, for LBlock [28] the results are better over Sun et al [26] for all the SBoxes. For MIBS [17], the reduced 24 inequalities are provided in Appendix B.

4 Filtering Inequalities by Subset Addition

The main issue with the greedy algorithm is an optimal solution to minimisation problems is not guaranteed. Hence, we used Gurobi Optimizer [16], as described by Sasaki and Todo [21], to find the optimal solutions, and successfully replicated those results. Noting that solutions found in this manner are merely the optimal subsets of the H-representation, and not globally optimal, we attempt to follow the technique proposed by Boura and Coggia [10]. Their algorithm concentrates on producing a larger starting set of inequalities so that a smaller subset may more easily be found. They generates new inequalities by adding k-size subsets of inequalities. The new inequalities represents the hyperplanes which is the possible differential paths lie on. The newly generated inequalities are then discarded if they do not remove a new set of impossible differential paths. This is potentially slow, since it would necessitate comparing the lists of impossible differential paths removed by each of the constituent inequalities with that removed by the new inequality. Hence, we propose an alternative algorithm which differs from [10] in the way new inequalities are assessed. The concept is to add k inequalities representing the hyperplanes a possible differential path lies on (h_1 through h_k), thus generating a new inequality

$$h = \sum_{i=1}^{k} h_i$$

and keep it only if it is good. We propose that h is good if,

- **Type 1** New inequality h removes more impossible differential paths than the inequality in $h_1, h_2, h_3, \ldots, h_k$ which removes the fewest; or
- **Type 2** New inequality h invalidates at least as many impossible differential paths as the inequality in $h_1, h_2, h_3, \ldots, h_k$ which removes the most.

Algorithm 2 explains the overall process. Finally, we find an optimal subset using Gurobi Optimizer. Note that, unlike [10], no regard is given to which impossible differential paths are removed by h. We only check how many of them it removes. Examples of the two types of hyperplanes are shown in Fig. 2.

Algorithm 3. Subset Addition Algorithm

Input: The SBox and a positive integer k
Output: Minimized set of inequalities I_{SR}
1: $ddt \leftarrow DDT(SBox)$ ▷ Create and returns the difference distribution table
2: $impPoints \leftarrow GetImpossiblePaths\ (ddt)$ ▷ Returns the impossible transitions (points)
3: $validPoints \leftarrow GetValidPaths\ (ddt)$ ▷ Returns the valid transitions (points)
4: $I \leftarrow inequality\_generator\ (validPoints)$ ▷ Returns the inequalities
5: $Path \leftarrow \phi$ ▷ Each element of Path consists of two parts, an inequality and a point
6: **for** iq in I **do**
7:   $point\_iq \leftarrow \phi$
8:   **for** $point$ in $impPoints$ **do**
9:     **if** $Evaluate(iq,\ point) < 0$ **then**
10:       $point\_iq \leftarrow point\_iq \cup point$
11:     **end if**
12:   **end for**
13:   $Path \leftarrow Path \cup \{iq,\ point\_iq\}$
14: **end for**
15: **for** $point$ in $validPoints$ **do**
16:   **for** iq in $Path$ **do**
17:     **if** $Evaluate(iq,\ point) = 0$ **then**   ▷ Point lies in the line
18:       $I_p \leftarrow I_p \cup iq$
19:     **end if**
20:   **end for**
21: **end for**
22: $I_c \leftarrow GetAllkCombinations(I_p,\ k)$ ▷ Returns all k combinations from I_p
23: **for** each iq in I_c **do**
24:   $I_l \leftarrow GetAllSum(iq)$ ▷ Form a new inequality after summing of k inequalities. It is also a linear combination of the original inequalities
25:   $point\_iq \leftarrow \phi$
26:   **for** $point$ in $impPoints$ **do**
27:     **if** $Evaluate(I_l,\ point) < 0$ **then**
28:       $point\_iq \leftarrow point\_iq \cup point$
29:     **end if**
30:   **end for**
31:   $Path \leftarrow Path \cup \{I_l,\ point\_iq\}$
32: **end for**
33: **for** $point$ in $impPoints$ **do**
34:   **for** each $path$ in $Path$ **do**
35:     **if** $point$ is in $path$ **then**
36:       $coverMat[Path.inequality][Path.point] \leftarrow 1$
37:     **end if**
38:   **end for**
39: **end for**
40: Generate m binary variables such that $c_1, c_2, \ldots, c_m$ such that $c_i = 1$ means inequality i is included in the solution space else $c_i = 0$.
41: $constraintSet \leftarrow \phi$
42: **for each** $point \in impPoints$ **do**
43:   $constraintSet \leftarrow constraintSet \cup \{$Construct a constraint $c_k, \ldots, c_l >= 1$ such that p is removed by at least one inequality using matrix $coverMat\}$ ▷ Generate constraints
44: **end for**
45: Create an objective function $\sum_{i=1}^{m} c_i$ with constraints $constraintSet$ and solve to get best inequalities (I_{SR}) that generate a stricter feasible region after maximizing the removed impossible differential patterns.
46: **return** I_{SR}

These are only illustrative examples, since differential paths lie on the vertices of the unit hypercube. ($h_1 + h_2$ is of type 2 as it removes 12 impossible differential paths while h_1 removes removes 12, and h_2, 10; $h'_1 + h'_2$ is of type 1 as it removes 14 while h'_1 and h'_2 remove 16 and 10 respectively.

Now we describe our algorithm in details (see Algorithm 3). Assume *ddt* be the 2D matrix for difference distribution table corresponding to the given SBox. Define (u, v) as a point corresponding to the input difference (u) and output difference (v) in a *ddt*. Let $(\bar{u}, \bar{v})$ be a valid transition and $(\bar{\bar{u}}, \bar{\bar{v}})$ be any impossible transition for an SBox. Divide the *ddt* into two parts, $(\bar{u}, \bar{v}) \in$ *validPoints* and $(\bar{\bar{u}}, \bar{\bar{v}}) \in$ *impPoints*. Now apply *validPoints* to the sagemath method *inequality_generator()*, which returns the inequalities I, corresponding to the H-representation of *validPoints*. Assume a set *Path*, where each element consists of two parts, an inequality iq and a point (u, v).

Initially the set *Path* is empty. Traverse each inequality iq from set I. For each impossible point check if each inequality iq satisfies or not. Assume point_iq stores all the impossible points for an inequality iq. Finally, set *Path* have all the inequalities and for each inequality the corresponding impossible points. Next, for each point in *validPoints* perform a test if an inequality from set *Path* satisfies the point. Collect all such inequalities in set I_p. Now use method *GetAllkCombinations* to get all unique k-degree sets I_c. Next take elements from I_c one by one and compute the sum of all the k inequalities. This will create a new inequality, which is linear combination of the original inequalities. Let the resultant inequality (sum) be I_l. Again we perform the same satisfiablity checking for the new inequality I_l against all the impossible points from set *impPoints*. Assume I_l invalidates a subset point_iq form the set *impPoints*. We append I_l with point_iq to set *Path*. Now *Path* contains the original inequalities as well as the newly generated inequalities along with the corresponding impossible differential points. Create a two-dimensional array *coverMat* indicating which inequality removes which impossible differential paths.

$$coverMat_{i,j} = \begin{cases} 1 \text{ if } i^{th} \text{ inequality removes } j^{th} \text{ impossible point} \\ 0 \text{ otherwise} \end{cases}$$

Derive an MILP problem to find the minimum subset of those inequalities which removes all impossible differential paths. We generate m binary variables $c_1, c_2, \ldots, c_m$ such that $c_i = 1$ means inequality i is included in the solution space else $c_i = 0$. For each point p in *impPoints* generate a constraint $c_k, \ldots, c_l >= 1$, such that p is removed by at least one inequality using matrix *coverMat* and store the constraints in *constraintSet*. Here the objective function is $\sum_{i=1}^{m} c_i$ with constraints *constraintSet*. Now, solve the problem using an MILP tool to get the optimized set of inequalities I_{SR}, which generate a stricter feasible region after maximizing the removed impossible differential patterns.

4.1 Comparison with Boura and Coggia's [10] Approach

To create significant fresh linear inequalities based on the H-representation of the convex hull, Boura, and Coggia's observation reveals that when k hyperplanes within this representation intersect at a vertex, representing a potential transition, the addition of the corresponding k inequalities is likely to result in a new constraint. This outcome is driven by the associated hyperplane intersecting with the cube, particularly at this specific vertex. They expect the newly introduced inequality to eliminate a distinct and potentially broader range of infeasible transitions compared to the initial inequalities. The concept involves retaining an inequality if the collection of all points it eliminates is not encompassed within the set of points eliminated by another inequality. For instance, if an inequality I_1 removes precisely points $\{(u_1, v_1), (u_2, v_2), (u_3, v_3)\}$, while inequality I_2 only removes points $\{(u_1, v_1), (u_2, v_2)\}$, then I_2 lacks significance, and we solely retain I_1. On the other hand, the subset addition approach mainly concentrates on the count of the impossible transitions while comparing the original and newly generated inequalities rather than checking the entire list of impossible points of all the original inequalities. The newly introduced inequality either eliminates a greater number of infeasible differential paths than the initial inequality that removes the fewest paths or renders an equal or larger number of infeasible paths invalid as the original inequality that eliminates the most paths.

Boura and Coggia's process is potentially time-consuming, as it requires comparing the lists of excluded differential paths addressed by each of the initial inequalities and the list managed by the recently introduced inequality. However, instead of comparing the invalidated impossible paths, we compare the count of the removed paths. Hence, the running time is reduced in our approach. On the other way, there are significantly more hyperplanes on the potential differential path that leads to the origin [0, 0, 0, 0, 0, 0, 0, 0] than on any other path. However, it produces no fresh inequalities that ultimately make up the ideal subset. This path can be disregarded immediately, optimizing the overall time and performance.

4.2 Multithreading and Filtration

Each iteration of the loop (starting at line 4) of Algorithm 2 can run independently of any other. Consequently, the algorithm can be implemented in a multithreaded fashion, using a thread pool. Whenever any thread is free, it picks up the next available iteration of the loop and starts executing it. In doing so, we observed that one thread spends a noticeably longer time than the other threads, irrespective of the cipher under analysis. The reason is that the possible differential path corresponding to the origin: $[0, 0, 0, 0, 0, 0, 0, 0]$ appears to lie on significantly more hyperplanes than any other path; however, it does not generate any new inequalities which eventually form the optimal subset. As a result, the thread assigned to process it spends the longest amount of time doing nothing useful so that this path can be ignored from the outset.

4.3 Implementation and Results

We implemented Algorithm 3 in C++ (on a desktop computer with an Intel Core i5-6500 4C/4T CPU running Manjaro Linux Sikaris 22.0.0 Xfce Edition 64-bit),

Table 2. Minimum number of Inequalities for 4-bit SBoxes (Subset Addition)

Cipher	Sasaki and Todo [21]	Boura and Coggia [10]	Subset Addition ($k = 2$) (Our approach)	Subset Addition ($k = 3$) (Our approach)
GIFT	–	17	17	17
KLEIN	21	19	19	19
Lilliput	23	19	20	19
MIBS	23	20	20	20
Midori S0	21	16	17	16
Midori S1	22	20	20	20
Minalpher	22	19	19	**18**
Piccolo	21	16	16	16
PRESENT	21	17	17	17
PRIDE	–	16	17	17
PRINCE	22	19	19	**18**
RECTANGLE	21	17	17	**16**
SKINNY	21	16	16	16
TWINE	23	19	20	19
LBlock S0	24	17	17	**16**
LBlock S1	24	17	17	**16**
LBlock S2	24	17	17	**16**
LBlock S3	24	17	17	**16**
LBlock S4	24	17	17	**16**
LBlock S5	24	17	17	**16**
LBlock S6	24	17	17	**16**
LBlock S7	24	17	17	**16**
LBlock S8	24	17	17	**16**
LBlock S9	24	17	17	**16**
Serpent S0	21	17	18	17
Serpent S1	21	17	19	18
Serpent S2	21	18	18	**17**
Serpent S3	27	20	16	**14**
Serpent S4	23	19	19	19
Serpent S5	23	19	17	**17**
Serpent S6	21	17	16	**16**
Serpent S7	27	20	16	**16**
Serpent S8	–	–	18	18
Serpent S9	–	–	18	17
Serpent S10	–	–	17	16

(continued)

Table 2. (*continued*)

Cipher	Sasaki and Todo [21]	Boura and Coggia [10]	Subset Addition ($k = 2$) (Our approach)	Subset Addition ($k = 3$) (Our approach)
Serpent S11	–	–	15	15
Serpent S12	–	–	18	18
Serpent S13	–	–	18	18
Serpent S14	–	–	18	18
Serpent S15	–	–	18	18
Serpent S16	–	–	17	16
Serpent S17	–	–	19	19
Serpent S18	–	–	18	18
Serpent S19	–	–	18	17
Serpent S20	–	–	19	19
Serpent S21	–	–	18	17
Serpent S22	–	–	17	16
Serpent S23	–	–	19	19
Serpent S24	–	–	18	17
Serpent S25	–	–	17	16
Serpent S26	–	–	18	18
Serpent S27	–	–	17	16
Serpent S28	–	–	17	17
Serpent S29	–	–	17	17
Serpent S30	–	–	17	17
Serpent S31	–	–	18	17

and then extended the program to use Gurobi Optimizer to find the optimal subset of inequalities. We give the user the option to choose (by defining a macro while compiling) between good hyperplanes of types 1 and 2. Our experiments suggest that selecting type 1 is better than or as good as selecting type 2.

Application to 4-Bit SBoxes. Algorithm 3 is successfully applied to most of the 4-bit SBoxes. Among the 14 4-bit SBoxes provided in first block of Table 2, we are getting better results for Prince [9], Minalpher [22] and Rectangle [29] with setting $k = 3$. For 10 SBoxes the results are same as the existing one. Only for PRIDE [3] the minimum number of inequalities is one extra.

For all the ten LBlock [28] SBoxes the inequality count is decreased to 16 from 17 [10]. The results for LBlock are provided in block two in Table 2 for $k = 2$ and $k = 3$.

Block three of Table 2) explains the results of 32 Serpent [6] SBoxes. Comparing with the existing results of eight Serpent SBoxes ($S0$ to $S7$) we improve the results for five ($S2, S3, S5, S6, S7$) For two SBoxes ($S0, S4$) the results are same, though for $S2$ we are loosing. For the rest of the 24 SBoxes we provide new results. For Serpent S3 the inequalities are mentioned in Appendix B.

Application to 5- and 6-Bit SBoxes. We have applied Algorithm 3 for ASCON [14] and SC2000 [23], which use 5-bit SBoxes. In this case, by taking $k = 3$, the results are improved. For 6-bit SBoxes of APN [11] and SC2000 with $k = 2$, we can cross the existing boundary of Boura and Coggia [10]. For 5-bit SBox of FIDES [8] we are getting one extra inequality than the existing boundary. The results for 5 and 6-bit SBoxes are tabulated in Table 3 comparing with existing results.

Reducing Running Time over Boura and Coggia [10] Technique. As mentioned earlier, since each impossible differential path is processed independently, parallel processing can be employed to reduce the running time. A worker thread can independently process a possible differential path at a time.

Table 3. Minimum number of Inequalities for 5- and 6-bit SBoxes

SBox	SBox Size	SageMath [1]	Boura and Coggia [10]	Subset Addition $k = 2$ (Our approach)	Subset Addition $k = 3$ (Our approach)
ASCON	5	2415	32	**31**	**31**
FIDES		910	61	64	62
SC2000		908	64	65	**63**
APN	6	5481	167	**163**	–
FIDES		7403	180	184	
SC2000		11920	214	**189**	

For multithreading, we used the C++ POSIX Threads API (which is wrapped in the thread library). In Table 4 we have tabulated the running time of our algorithm (Algorithm 3) for some Sboxes. For LBlock S0 through S9 and Serpent S0 through S7, average running times are reported. In general, it appears that larger values of k lead to smaller subsets of inequalities. However, we were unable to confirm this. While $k = 3$ usually produced smaller subsets than $k = 2$ in our experiments, testing with $k = 4$ proved difficult. For Lilliput [4], MIBS [17] and Serpent S3, the outputs did not improve with $k = 4$, but the memory requirement shot up to around 10 GiB. We could not test any other ciphers because of this.

Boura and Coggia [10] reported that for $k = 2$, their algorithm implementation took a few minutes, while for $k = 3$, it took a few hours. They have yet to provide an exact running time estimation of different Sboxes for their approach. We have tried to regenerate their results, but it is taking longer running time than expected in our system. Still, we compare our algorithm for $k = 2$ and $k = 3$ with that of Boura and Coggia [10], and our results are provided in Table 4. Our implementation is faster by two orders of magnitude and gives comparable results. We achieve much better running times after making all the earlier mentioned optimizations in our program.

Table 4. Approximate running time of Subset Addition Algorithm

SBox	Required Time for Algorithm 3 (in sec)	
	No. of Inequality, k = 2	No. of Inequality, k = 3
Klein	0.16	2.5
LBlock S*	0.19	2.2
MIBS	1.9	4.5
Piccolo	0.15	2.0
PRESENT	0.28	3.9
PRINCE	0.17	4.8
Serpent S*	0.49	8.3
TWINE	0.16	3.4

5 Conclusion

In this paper, we propose two MILP-based techniques for finding the minimum set of inequalities for modeling differential propagations of an SBox. The algorithms we introduce for modeling the DDT of an SBox are more efficient than the other existing algorithms. Noting that a greedy algorithm is only complete with the notion of a tiebreaker, we implemented a new version of the greedy approach based on a random tiebreaker. The results of the greedy random tiebreaker outperform the original greedy one for some of the SBoxes. The subset addition algorithm can successfully model SBoxes up to 6-bit. The approach also provides better or almost identical results for most SBoxes. We also improved the execution time to find the minimized inequalities concerning the previous implementations.

A Existing Algorithm for Choosing Best Inequalities

Algorithm 4. MILP based reduction [21]

Inputs:
IDP: Impossible differential patterns corresponding to the impossible transitions from the DDT of an SBox.
P: Input set corresponding to the possible transitions in an SBox
Output:
I_{SR}: Set of inequalities that generates more stricter feasible region after maximizing the removed impossible differential patterns.

1: H $\leftarrow$ *ConvHull(P)*
2: $RI \leftarrow H$
3: Create a table PIT of size $|RI| \times |IDP|$ where $PIT_{i,j} = 1$ if inequality RI_i removes pattern IDP_j, else set $PIT_{i,j} = 0$
4: Set $m = |RI|$
5: Generate m binary variables such that $c_1, c_2, \ldots, c_m$ such that $c_i = 1$ means inequality i is included in the solution space else $c_i = 0$.
6: *constraintSet* $\leftarrow \phi$
7: **for each** *point* $\in IDP$ **do**
8: *constraintSet* $\leftarrow$ *constraintSet* $\cup$ {Construct a constraint $c_k, \ldots, c_l >= 1$ such that p is removed by at least one inequality applying table PIT} ▷ Generate constraints
9: **end for**
10: Create an objective function $\sum_{i=1}^{m} c_i$ with constraints *constraintSet* and solve to get best inequalities (I_{SR}) that generate a stricter feasible region after maximizing the removed impossible differential patterns.
11: **return** I_{SR}

Algorithm 5. Greedy Based Approach [26]

Input:
HI: Inequalities in the H-Representation of the convex hull of an SBox.
ID: The set of all impossible differential patterns of an SBox
Output:
RI: Set of inequalities that generates a stricter feasible region after maximizing the removed impossible differential patterns.

1: $l \leftarrow \phi, RI \leftarrow \phi$
2: **while** $ID \neq \phi$ **do**
3: $l \leftarrow$ The inequality in *HI* which maximizes the number of removed impossible differential patterns from *ID*.
4: $ID \leftarrow ID -$ {Removed impossible differential patterns using l}
5: $HI \leftarrow HI -$ {l}
6: $RI \leftarrow RI \cup$ {l}
7: **end while**
8: **return** *RI*

Algorithm 6. Modeling by selecting random set of inequalities [10]

Inputs:
P: Input set corresponding to the possible transitions in an SBox.
k: The number of inequalities to be added together.
Output:
RI: Set of inequalities that generates more stricter feasible region after maximizing the removed impossible differential patterns.

$H \leftarrow ConvHull(P)$
$RI \leftarrow H$
for all $p \in P$ **do**
  Choose k inequalities such that p belongs to the hyperplanes of $Q_1, Q_2, \ldots, Q_k$
  $Q_{new} = Q_1 + \ldots + Q_k$
  if Q_{new} removes new impossible transitions
  $RI \leftarrow RI \cup \{Q_{new}\}$
  end if
end for
return $\boldsymbol{RI}$

B Sample Reduced Inequalities

Applying random greedy tiebreaker Algorithm 1 for MIBS [17], the reduced 24 inequalities are as follows,

```
- 1x3 - 2x2 - 2x1 - 1x0 + 4y3 + 5y2 + 5y1 + 5y0 >= 0
+ 5x3 + 4x2 + 4x1 + 3x0 - 1y3 - 2y2 + 1y1 - 2y0 >= 0
- 2x3 + 2x2 + 4x1 + 1x0 + 3y3 + 1y2 - 3y1 - 3y0 >= -4
- 1x3 - 4x2 + 3x1 + 2x0 - 1y3 - 3y2 + 4y1 + 2y0 >= -5
- 2x3 + 1x2 - 3x1 - 1x0 - 1y3 - 3y2 - 2y1 - 2y0 >= -11
- 1x3 - 2x2 - 4x1 + 4x0 - 4y3 + 2y2 + 1y1 - 3y0 >= -10
+ 2x3 - 1x2 + 3x1 + 1x0 - 2y3 + 2y2 - 3y1 + 1y0 >= -3
+ 1x3 + 2x2 - 4x1 + 2x0 + 3y3 + 1y2 + 2y1 + 4y0 >= 0
+ 1x3 + 3x2 - 2x1 - 3x0 + 1y3 + 3y2 + 2y1 - 1y0 >= -3
+ 2x3 - 1x2 - 2x1 - 2x0 - 1y3 - 1y2 - 2y1 + 0y0 >= -7
+ 0x3 + 2x2 + 2x1 - 1x0 + 1y3 + 1y2 - 1y1 + 1y0 >= 0
- 3x3 - 3x2 + 1x1 - 2x0 + 1y3 - 2y2 + 1y1 + 2y0 >= -7
+ 2x3 - 1x2 + 2x1 - 1x0 + 1y3 + 1y2 + 2y1 - 1y0 >= -1
+ 1x3 - 2x2 - 2x1 + 2x0 + 1y3 + 1y2 - 1y1 - 2y0 >= -5
- 1x3 + 2x2 - 1x1 + 1x0 + 2y3 - 2y2 + 1y1 - 1y0 >= -3
- 1x3 + 1x2 + 0x1 - 1x0 - 1y3 - 1y2 + 0y1 + 1y0 >= -3
+ 1x3 - 2x2 - 1x1 - 1x0 + 1y3 - 2y2 - 2y1 + 1y0 >= -6
+ 2x3 - 1x2 + 0x1 - 2x0 - 2y3 + 2y2 - 1y1 + 1y0 >= -4
- 1x3 - 1x2 + 1x1 - 1x0 - 1y3 + 0y2 - 1y1 - 1y0 >= -5
- 1x3 + 1x2 - 1x1 + 2x0 + 1y3 + 2y2 - 1y1 + 2y0 >= -1
+ 2x3 + 1x2 + 2x1 + 3x0 - 2y3 - 1y2 - 1y1 + 2y0 >= -1
- 3x3 - 2x2 + 1x1 + 3x0 - 1y3 + 1y2 + 2y1 + 3y0 >= -3
+ 1x3 - 1x2 - 2x1 - 2x0 - 1y3 - 1y2 - 1y1 - 1y0 >= -7
- 1x3 + 1x2 + 0x1 - 1x0 - 1y3 + 1y2 + 1y1 - 1y0 >= -3
```

Applying subset addition Algorithm 3 for Serpent S3 the 14 inequalities are as follows,

```
- 5x3 + 4x2 + 4x1 - 5x0 + 2y3 + 10y2 + 3y1 + 10y0 >= 0
+ 6x3 - 1x2 - 2x1 + 2x0 + 1y3 +  7y2 - 3y1 +  7y0 >= 0
- 2x3 + 0x2 - 3x1 - 3x0 - 2y3 -  4y2 - 1y1 +  4y0 >= -11
+ 3x3 + 0x2 + 3x1 + 2x0 + 1y3 -  4y2 + 2y1 +  4y0 >= 0
- 3x3 - 3x2 + 0x1 - 2x0 - 1y3 +  4y2 - 2y1 -  4y0 >= -11
- 4x3 - 4x2 - 1x1 - 3x0 + 1y3 +  2y2 - 1y1 -  4y0 >= -13
+ 2x3 - 2x2 + 1x1 - 4x0 - 4y3 +  3y2 + 2y1 -  4y0 >= -10
+ 2x3 + 6x2 + 2x1 + 1x0 - 3y3 -  4y2 - 4y1 -  4y0 >= -10
- 2x3 + 8x2 + 4x1 - 1x0 + 5y3 -  7y2 + 6y1 -  7y0 >= -10
- 2x3 - 5x2 - 1x1 + 2x0 - 3y3 -  5y2 + 3y1 -  5y0 >= -17
+ 2x3 + 3x2 + 0x1 + 3x0 + 2y3 +  4y2 + 1y1 -  4y0 >= 0
+ 4x3 - 3x2 - 2x1 + 0x0 + 2y3 -  3y2 - 1y1 -  3y0 >= -9
- 2x3 - 1x2 + 2x1 + 4x0 + 4y3 -  4y2 - 2y1 +  3y0 >= -5
+ 0x3 - 1x2 - 1x1 + 5x0 - 2y3 +  5y2 + 2y1 +  5y0 >= 0
```

Applying subset addition Algorithm 3 for ASCON SBox the 31 inequalities are as follows,

```
- 9x5 +  8x4 +  6x3 + 11x2 - 6x1 + 4y5 - 5y4 - 3y3 - 1y2 +  3y1 >=  12
- 1x5 +  5x4 +  8x3 +  7x2 - 3x1 + 8y5 + 7y4 - 2y3 + 1y2 -  2y1 >=  0
+ 1x5 +  2x4 +  4x3 +  2x2 - 2x1 - 4y5 - 3y4 - 2y3 + 0y2 -  4y1 >=  11
+ 5x5 + 11x4 +  4x3 + 11x2 + 6x1 - 3y5 + 2y4 - 1y3 + 0y2 -  7y1 >=  0
+ 5x5 +  7x4 -  6x3 +  3x2 - 3x1 + 6y5 - 1y4 - 1y3 + 4y2 +  1y1 >=  4
- 1x5 +  7x4 +  7x3 +  9x2 - 3x1 + 9y5 - 3y4 - 2y3 - 1y2 +  9y1 >=  0
- 1x5 -  2x4 +  0x3 +  2x2 - 1x1 - 3y5 - 3y4 + 2y3 + 1y2 +  2y1 >=  7
- 1x5 +  7x4 +  9x3 +  8x2 - 3x1 - 3y5 + 9y4 - 2y3 - 1y2 + 10y1 >=  0
- 2x5 +  5x4 +  2x3 -  5x2 - 3x1 - 2y5 + 0y4 + 0y3 - 1y2 -  3y1 >=  11
+ 1x5 -  2x4 +  0x3 -  1x2 + 2x1 + 0y5 + 1y4 + 2y3 - 2y2 -  2y1 >=  5
+ 2x5 -  1x4 +  0x3 +  1x2 + 2x1 + 0y5 + 0y4 - 2y3 + 2y2 -  1y1 >=  2
+ 3x5 +  2x4 +  0x3 -  3x2 + 1x1 - 2y5 + 0y4 - 1y3 - 2y2 +  3y1 >=  5
+ 3x5 +  5x4 +  4x3 -  4x2 + 2x1 + 3y5 + 0y4 - 1y3 - 1y2 +  3y1 >=  0
- 2x5 +  0x4 -  1x3 -  2x2 - 2x1 + 1y5 + 1y4 + 3y3 + 3y2 +  0y1 >=  4
+ 2x5 -  3x4 +  3x3 -  3x2 - 2x1 + 0y5 + 0y4 + 1y3 + 3y2 +  1y1 >=  5
+ 2x5 +  2x4 -  2x3 -  2x2 - 1x1 + 0y5 + 0y4 + 0y3 + 2y2 +  1y1 >=  3
+ 1x5 -  4x4 -  4x3 +  3x2 + 2x1 + 2y5 + 2y4 - 1y3 - 1y2 +  2y1 >=  6
- 1x5 -  3x4 - 12x3 + 10x2 + 4x1 - 9y5 + 8y4 - 5y3 + 1y2 -  7y1 >=  25
- 3x5 -  1x4 -  6x3 +  6x2 - 1x1 - 5y5 - 5y4 - 3y3 + 2y2 +  7y1 >=  17
+ 0x5 +  3x4 -  2x3 +  3x2 + 2x1 - 1y5 - 1y4 + 2y3 + 0y2 -  1y1 >=  2
- 1x5 +  4x4 -  2x3 + 10x2 - 6x1 + 5y5 + 5y4 + 4y3 - 1y2 +  6y1 >=  0
- 2x5 +  2x4 -  2x3 -  2x2 + 1x1 + 2y5 + 0y4 + 0y3 + 0y2 -  1y1 >=  5
+ 6x5 -  5x4 -  6x3 -  2x2 + 3x1 - 1y5 - 6y4 + 0y3 - 3y2 +  1y1 >=  17
+ 2x5 -  2x4 -  2x3 -  3x2 - 2x1 + 0y5 + 3y4 + 1y3 + 1y2 +  1y1 >=  6
- 2x5 -  1x4 -  1x3 -  3x2 - 3x1 + 0y5 - 1y4 - 2y3 - 2y2 +  0y1 >=  12
+ 0x5 -  2x4 -  1x3 +  2x2 + 0x1 + 2y5 - 2y4 + 1y3 + 0y2 -  2y1 >=  5
+ 0x5 -  2x4 +  3x3 +  4x2 + 3x1 - 1y5 + 1y4 + 4y3 + 0y2 -  1y1 >=  0
- 2x5 -  2x4 +  2x3 -  1x2 + 1x1 + 0y5 - 2y4 + 1y3 + 2y2 -  2y1 >=  7
- 2x5 -  1x4 +  2x3 -  2x2 + 2x1 + 1y5 - 2y4 + 0y3 - 2y2 +  2y1 >=  7
- 3x5 -  3x4 -  1x3 -  1x2 - 2x1 + 0y5 + 2y4 - 4y3 - 4y2 -  3y1 >=  17
- 2x5 -  2x4 -  1x3 -  2x2 + 2x1 + 0y5 + 2y4 + 0y3 + 1y2 +  1y1 >=  5
```

References

1. The sage developers. sagemath, the sage mathematics software system (version 9.0) (2020). https://www.sagemath.org
2. Abdelkhalek, A., Sasaki, Y., Todo, Y., Tolba, M., Youssef, A.M.: MILP modeling for (large) s-boxes to optimize probability of differential characteristics. IACR Trans. Symmetric Cryptol. **2017**(4), 99–129 (2017). https://doi.org/10.13154/tosc.v2017.i4.99-129
3. Albrecht, M.R., Driessen, B., Kavun, E.B., Leander, G., Paar, C., Yalçın, T.: Block ciphers – focus on the linear layer (feat. PRIDE). In: Garay, J.A., Gennaro, R. (eds.) CRYPTO 2014, Part I. LNCS, vol. 8616, pp. 57–76. Springer, Heidelberg (2014). https://doi.org/10.1007/978-3-662-44371-2_4
4. Berger, T.P., Francq, J., Minier, M., Thomas, G.: Extended generalized feistel networks using matrix representation to propose a new lightweight block cipher: lilliput. IEEE Trans. Comput. **65**(7), 2074–2089 (2016). https://doi.org/10.1109/TC.2015.2468218
5. Biham, E.: New types of cryptanalytic attacks using related keys. In: Helleseth, T. (ed.) EUROCRYPT 1993. LNCS, vol. 765, pp. 398–409. Springer, Heidelberg (1994). https://doi.org/10.1007/3-540-48285-7_34
6. Biham, E., Anderson, R., Knudsen, L.: Serpent: a new block cipher proposal. In: Vaudenay, S. (ed.) FSE 1998. LNCS, vol. 1372, pp. 222–238. Springer, Heidelberg (1998). https://doi.org/10.1007/3-540-69710-1_15
7. Biham, E., Shamir, A.: Differential Cryptanalysis of the Data Encryption Standard. Springer, Heidelberg (1993). https://doi.org/10.1007/978-1-4613-9314-6
8. Bilgin, B., Bogdanov, A., Knežević, M., Mendel, F., Wang, Q.: Fides: lightweight authenticated cipher with side-channel resistance for constrained hardware. In: Bertoni, G., Coron, J.-S. (eds.) CHES 2013. LNCS, vol. 8086, pp. 142–158. Springer, Heidelberg (2013). https://doi.org/10.1007/978-3-642-40349-1_9
9. Borghoff, J., et al.: PRINCE - a low-latency block cipher for pervasive computing applications (full version). IACR Cryptol. ePrint Arch. 529 (2012)
10. Boura, C., Coggia, D.: Efficient MILP modelings for Sboxes and linear layers of SPN ciphers. IACR Trans. Symmetric Cryptol. **2020**(3), 327–361 (2020). https://doi.org/10.13154/tosc.v2020.i3.327-361
11. Browning, K., Dillon, J., McQuistan, M., Wolfe., A.: APN permutation in dimension six. In: Postproceedings of the 9th International Conference on Finite Fields and Their Applications (2010)
12. Cui, T., Jia, K., Fu, K., Chen, S., Wang, M.: New automatic search tool for impossible differentials and zero-correlation linear approximations. IACR Cryptol. ePrint Arch. 689 (2016), http://eprint.iacr.org/2016/689
13. Daemen, J., Rijmen, V.: The wide trail design strategy. In: Honary, B. (ed.) Cryptography and Coding 2001. LNCS, vol. 2260, pp. 222–238. Springer, Heidelberg (2001). https://doi.org/10.1007/3-540-45325-3_20
14. Dobraunig, C., Eichlseder, M., Mendel, F., Schläffer, M.: Ascon v1.2: lightweight authenticated encryption and hashing. J. Cryptol. **34**(3), 1–42 (2021). https://doi.org/10.1007/s00145-021-09398-9
15. Fu, K., Wang, M., Guo, Y., Sun, S., Hu, L.: MILP-based automatic search algorithms for differential and linear trails for speck. In: Peyrin, T. (ed.) FSE 2016. LNCS, vol. 9783, pp. 268–288. Springer, Heidelberg (2016). https://doi.org/10.1007/978-3-662-52993-5_14

16. Gurobi Optimization LLC.: Gurobi optimizer reference manual. 9.5.2 (2022). https://www.gurobi.com/, https://www.gurobi.com/
17. Izadi, M., Sadeghiyan, B., Sadeghian, S.S., Khanooki, H.A.: MIBS: a new lightweight block cipher. In: Garay, J.A., Miyaji, A., Otsuka, A. (eds.) CANS 2009. LNCS, vol. 5888, pp. 334–348. Springer, Heidelberg (2009). https://doi.org/10.1007/978-3-642-10433-6_22
18. Li, T., Sun, Y.: Superball: a new approach for MILP modelings of Boolean functions. IACR Trans. Symmetric Cryptol. **2022**(3), 341–367 (2022)
19. Matsui, M., Yamagishi, A.: A new method for known plaintext attack of FEAL cipher. In: Rueppel, R.A. (ed.) EUROCRYPT 1992. LNCS, vol. 658, pp. 81–91. Springer, Heidelberg (1993). https://doi.org/10.1007/3-540-47555-9_7
20. Mouha, N., Wang, Q., Gu, D., Preneel, B.: Differential and linear cryptanalysis using mixed-integer linear programming. In: Wu, C.-K., Yung, M., Lin, D. (eds.) Inscrypt 2011. LNCS, vol. 7537, pp. 57–76. Springer, Heidelberg (2012). https://doi.org/10.1007/978-3-642-34704-7_5
21. Sasaki, Yu., Todo, Y.: New algorithm for modeling S-box in MILP based differential and division trail search. In: Farshim, P., Simion, E. (eds.) SecITC 2017. LNCS, vol. 10543, pp. 150–165. Springer, Cham (2017). https://doi.org/10.1007/978-3-319-69284-5_11
22. Sasaki, Y., et al.: Minalpher. In: Directions in Authenticated Ciphers (DIAC 2014), pp. 23–24 (2014). https://info.isl.ntt.co.jp/crypt/minalpher/files/minalpher-diac2014.pdf
23. Shimoyama, T., et al.: The block cipher SC2000. In: Matsui, M. (ed.) FSE 2001. LNCS, vol. 2355, pp. 312–327. Springer, Heidelberg (2002). https://doi.org/10.1007/3-540-45473-X_26
24. Sun, S., Hu, L., Song, L., Xie, Y., Wang, P.: Automatic security evaluation of block ciphers with S-bP structures against related-key differential attacks. In: Lin, D., Xu, S., Yung, M. (eds.) Inscrypt 2013. LNCS, vol. 8567, pp. 39–51. Springer, Cham (2014). https://doi.org/10.1007/978-3-319-12087-4_3
25. Sun, S., et al.: Towards finding the best characteristics of some bit-oriented block ciphers and automatic enumeration of (related-key) differential and linear characteristics with predefined properties. Cryptology ePrint Archive, Paper 2014/747 (2014). https://eprint.iacr.org/2014/747
26. Sun, S., Hu, L., Wang, P., Qiao, K., Ma, X., Song, L.: Automatic security evaluation and (related-key) differential characteristic search: application to SIMON, PRESENT, LBlock, DES(L) and other bit-oriented block ciphers. In: Sarkar, P., Iwata, T. (eds.) ASIACRYPT 2014, Part I. LNCS, vol. 8873, pp. 158–178. Springer, Heidelberg (2014). https://doi.org/10.1007/978-3-662-45611-8_9
27. Udovenko, A.: MILP modeling of Boolean functions by minimum number of inequalities. IACR Cryptol. ePrint Arch. 1099 (2021). https://eprint.iacr.org/2021/1099
28. Wu, W., Zhang, L.: LBlock: a lightweight block cipher. In: Lopez, J., Tsudik, G. (eds.) ACNS 2011. LNCS, vol. 6715, pp. 327–344. Springer, Heidelberg (2011). https://doi.org/10.1007/978-3-642-21554-4_19
29. Zhang, W., Bao, Z., Lin, D., Rijmen, V., Yang, B., Verbauwhede, I.: RECTANGLE: a bit-slice ultra-lightweight block cipher suitable for multiple platforms. IACR Cryptol. ePrint Arch. 84 (2014)

Blockchain

LucidiTEE: Scalable Policy-Based Multiparty Computation with Fairness

Sivanarayana Gaddam[1], Ranjit Kumaresan[2], Srinivasan Raghuraman[2,3(✉)], and Rohit Sinha[4]

[1] Cohesity Inc., San Jose, USA
[2] Visa Research, Foster City, USA
srini131293@gmail.com
[3] MIT, Cambridge, USA
[4] Swirlds Labs, Dallas, USA

Abstract. Motivated by recent advances in exploring the power of hybridized TEE-blockchain systems, we present LucidiTEE, a unified framework for confidential, policy-compliant computing that guarantees fair output delivery. For context:

- Ekiden (EuroS&P'19) and FastKitten (Sec'19) use enclave-ledger interactions to enable privacy-preserving smart contracts. However, they store the contract's inputs on-chain, and therefore, are impractical for applications that process large volumes of data or serve large number of users. In contrast, LucidiTEE implements privacy-preserving computation while storing inputs, outputs, and state off-chain, using the ledger only to enforce policies on computation.
- Chaudhuri et al. (CCS'17) showed that enclave-ledger interactions enable fair secure multiparty computation. In a setting with n processors each of which possesses a TEE, they show how to realize fair secure computation tolerating up to t corrupt parties for any $t < n$. We improve upon their result by showing a novel protocol which requires only t out of the n processors to possess a TEE.
- Kaptchuk et al. (NDSS'19) showed that enclave-ledger interactions can enable applications such as one-time programs and rate limited logging. We generalize their ideas to enforcing arbitrary *history-based* policies within and across several multi-step computations, and formally specify a new functionality for policy-compliant multiparty computation.

Summarizing, LucidiTEE enables multiple parties to jointly compute on private data, while enforcing history-based policies even when input providers are offline, and fairness to all output recipients, in a malicious setting. LucidiTEE uses the ledger only to enforce policies; i.e., it does not store inputs, outputs, or state on the ledger, letting it scale to big data computation. We show novel applications including a personal finance app, collaborative machine learning, and policy-based surveys amongst an apriori-unknown set of participants.

Keywords: TEE · blockchain · policy compliance

Work done while all authors were at Visa Research.

J. Deng et al. (Eds.): CANS 2023, LNCS 14342, pp. 343–367, 2023.
https://doi.org/10.1007/978-981-99-7563-1_16

1 Introduction

Alice wishes to analyze her monthly spending behavior using a personal finance application, such as Mint [2]. Conscious of her privacy, she seeks to gauge, and even control, how her transaction records are stored, analyzed, and further shared with other parties — however, mainstream applications today only present a privacy policy written in legalese, without any technical means to enforce them. We discuss Alice's requirements from a new, transparent personal finance application that we build in this paper, called Acme.

Alice has the following requirements. Ideally, Alice prevents Acme from viewing her raw transaction data, allows computing only select analytics on her data (e.g. a monthly aggregate summary), and controls who can attain the output report[1]. Moreover, she does not wish to provision her own servers, and is expected to go offline at any time. For privacy, we must allow Acme to run only a single instance of the analysis, over an entire month's worth of transactions, as opposed to multiple, finer-grained analytics that can leak significantly more information about her spending behavior (this becomes a *one-time program* [34] policy). For correctness, we would like all of her transactions to be input to the computation.

As another example, Acme wishes to run a survey to collect feedback from users (such as Alice), without having to build a survey application but rather outsourcing it to a third-party service. Ideally, instead of trusting this service to collect genuine responses, Acme wishes to enforce the following policy: 1) only accept inputs from enrolled users of Acme; 2) all valid inputs are tallied in the output.

Alice's policy is expressed over the inputs and outputs of all computations in her history with Acme, while Acme's survey policy is expressed over multiple concurrent computations (over all users). We call them **history-based policies**, and it is an open research problem to efficiently enforce them in a multi-party setting, where the participants are not known in advance, may not be online, and may act maliciously.

In addition to enforcing policies, we wish to ensure **fair output delivery** to all participants, even when the computation is carried out by malicious parties (e.g. when Acme computes on Alice's data, or collaboration between businesses (see Sect. 7.1). It is an open problem how to provide fairness [22,36] — if any party gets the output, then so must all honest parties — in a multi-party computation (malicious setting), where participants have commodity devices without a trusted execution environment [22], such as end users.

In this work, we build on recent advances in exploring the power of a hybridized TEE-blockchain system (cf. [21,22,42] and references therein) to address the problem of *policy-compliance* on computations over user data. To that end, we provide a concrete **definition for policy-compliant computation**. Our definition takes the form of an ideal functionality $\mathcal{F}_{\text{PCC}}$ in the UC framework of [19]. $\mathcal{F}_{\text{PCC}}$ accepts user data and user-defined policies as inputs,

[1] While this is feasible with protocols for multiparty computation (MPC) [63,64], it requires Alice to remain online during the computation.

and guarantees (1) confidentiality of inputs on which computations are performed, and (2) fair output delivery to output recipients, and (3) execution of only policy-compliant computations.

$\mathcal{F}_{\text{PCC}}$ internally maintains a log of all function evaluations across all concurrent computations, and a computation-specific policy check uses this log to determine whether to allow any further function evaluation. Additionally, the interfaces provided by our $\mathcal{F}_{\text{PCC}}$ abstraction are well-suited to the practical setting of repeated (big data) computations on user data which may grow over time, thereby expressive enough to enforce policies on this important class of applications. In more detail, parties provide their input data to $\mathcal{F}_{\text{PCC}}$ once, and then bind it to an unbounded number of different computations, and also use it for an unbounded number of steps within a computation without having to resupply it. This interface is valuable for Acme, whose input database contains information of a large number of merchants and spans several GBs. $\mathcal{F}_{\text{PCC}}$ allows any (malicious) party to carry out the computation on behalf of the computation's input providers (e.g. a cloud compute provider), but the properties of policy compliance and fairness are ensured.

Next, we present LucidiTEE, a hybrid TEE-blockchain system that exploits enclave-ledger interactions to provide a **practical implementation of the abstractions provided by $\mathcal{F}_{\text{PCC}}$**. We assume a method that computes on encrypted data — for instance, MPC protocols or TEE-based systems such as VC3 [55], Opaque [66], StealthDB [38], Ryoan [40], Felsen et al. [28], etc. — and instead describe methods to enforce history-based policies and fair output delivery. While a variety of advanced cryptographic methods exist to enable confidentiality of computations [31,33,64], enclaves provide perhaps the most practical method for achieving this. Pure cryptographic methods also fall short of guaranteeing fair output delivery [23], or enforcing policies across computations involving different sets of parties. Also, secure computation does not apply to settings where participants are not known in advance or are offline or where confidentiality is required when different sets of users contribute input to different stages of a single computation [10,11].

Improvements upon Related Work

While enclaves address many of the problems above, they still suffer from other problems such as rollback protection in a multiparty computation. Prior work has employed blockchains for addressing state continuity, and also to support more robust designs involving a distributed network of TEE nodes [21,48]. Our work continues in the same vein. However, in addition to rollback protection, we rely on enclave-ledger interactions to (1) enforce policy compliance, and (2) guarantee fair output delivery. In the following, we first discuss how we extend ideas from Kaptchuk et al. [42] (see also [16]) to use enclave-ledger interactions to enforce policies in computations. After that, we discuss how we improve upon the work of Choudhuri et al. [22] to derive more practical protocols for fair output delivery and fair exchange. The latter may be of independent interest.

Kaptchuk et al. [42] showed that enclave-ledger interactions can enable applications such as one-time programs and "rate limited mandatory logging." To support applications such as one-time programs, [42]'s strategy is to record (the first) execution of the program on the blockchain. Then, the enclave running the program would first check the blockchain to see if the program was executed already (in which case it would abort), and if no record of program execution exists on the blockchain, then continue execution of the program. In the problem of rate limited mandatory logging, the goal is to log access to sensitive files before the necessary keys for an encrypted file can be accessed by the user. Here again, [42]'s strategy is to first check the blockchain to log the file access, and only then let the enclave release the key.

Extending [42], we provide general techniques to enforce arbitrary history-based policies within and across several multistage computations. At a high level, we implement such history-based policies by allowing the enclave executing a step of a computation to scan through the ledger to identify policies associated with the computation, and first check if the inputs to the computation step comply with the policies associated with the computation, and only then proceed with the execution of the computation step. In the following sections, we demonstrate several interesting practical applications which exploit the power of history-based policies. We note that such an extension is not straightforward from the "Enclave-Ledger Interaction" scheme suggested by [42]—among other things, concretely, their ExecuteEnclave function takes only a single ledger post, whereas our policies may involve multiple entries on the blockchain. Furthermore, unlike [42], LucidiTEE enforces policies across several computations. As an example, consider a survey application where one might wish to enforce a policy that only those users who have participated in a prior survey may participate in the current one.

Next, we discuss our contributions to the design of practical fair exchange and **fair computation** protocols. By fairness, we mean that either all output recipients obtain the output of a computation or none do. It is a well-known result [23] that fairness is impossible to achieve in a setting where a majority of the participants are corrupt. Faced with this result, several works have explored relaxed notions of fairness over the last few years [12,37,52]. However, very recently, Choudhuri et al. [22] showed that enclave-ledger interactions can enable fair secure computation. (Note that it is not known whether enclaves alone can enable the standard notion of fairness in secure computation [51].) In a setting with n processors each of which possesses a TEE, [22] show how to realize fair computation tolerating up to t corrupt parties for any $t < n$. We improve upon their result with a novel protocol which requires only t out of the n processors to possess a TEE. When $n = 2$ and $t = 1$, this provides practical fair computation in client-server settings, where clients may not possess TEEs. This contribution is of independent interest.

System Design

LucidiTEE provides a practical and scalable framework for privacy-preserving, policy-compliant computations. In our example applications, the inputs span large databases (see Sect. 7.1), and are provided by a large number of apriori-unknown users, such as in public surveys (see Sect. 7.1) and applications that provide a service based on aggregate data of its growing consumer base (see Sect. 7.1). Finally, the set of computations grow over time as parties enroll in new computations that consume results from prior computations.

LucidiTEE supports history-based policies with the use of a shared ledger or blockchain, which plays the role of the log in $\mathcal{F}_{\text{PCC}}$ — since rollback or tampering attacks on the log can violate policy compliance and fairness, we use a shared ledger (accessible by all parties) in lieu of a centralized database. LucidiTEE achieves scalability by minimizing use of the ledger. To support the above mentioned applications, we record only commitments (i.e., hash digests, which support membership queries) of the inputs, outputs, and the updated state on the ledger after each function evaluation. We note that the recent works of Ekiden [21] and FastKitten [24] also use enclave-ledger interactions to enable privacy-preserving smart contracts. However, Ekiden and FastKitten store the contract's inputs on-chain (during malicious behavior in the latter's case). In contrast, LucidiTEE stores inputs, outputs, and state off-chain (recall only commitments to these go on-chain), using the ledger only to enforce history-based policies.

We use remote attestation [18,51] to allow any party to act as a compute provider by providing a genuine TEE-equipped processor. For these reasons, we say that LucidiTEE embodies "bring-your-own-storage" and "bring-your-own-compute" paradigms, lending flexibility to the untrusted compute providers to manage storage and compute resources.

Contributions. In summary, our contributions are:

- formal specification of a functionality $\mathcal{F}_{\text{PCC}}$ for concurrent, multi-party computation, which guarantees history-based policies for offline parties and fairness for output recipients. For space reasons, we defer the $\mathcal{F}_{\text{PCC}}$ definition to the full version [27].
- LucidiTEE, a system that realizes this ideal functionality, using TEEs and a shared ledger
- protocol for fair n-party output delivery, requiring a shared ledger and t parties to allocate a TEE, for any corruption threshold $t < n$. We also prove security in the UC framework.
- evaluation of several applications, including a personal finance application (serving millions of users), federated machine learning over crowdsourced data, and a private survey. We also implement micro-benchmarks including one-time programs, digital lockboxes, and fair information exchange.

2 Overview of LucidiTEE

In this section, we introduce the components of our system, using the example of a personal finance application, called Acme. The design principles behind our system should be evident even when considering applications from different domains such as joint machine learning, surveys, etc.

2.1 Running Example: Personal Finance App

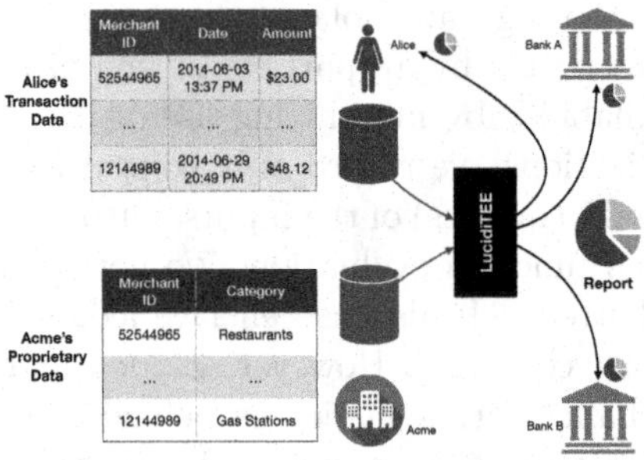

Fig. 1. Transparent Personal Finance Application

The open banking initiative [3] has fostered a variety of personal financial applications, such as Mint [2]. Figure 1 illustrates one such application by Acme, who provides a service for viewing aggregate spending behavior (i.e., the proportion of spending across categories for all transactions in a month), along with the feature to share this aggregate report with third parties. For instance, Alice may choose to share this report with lending institutions to avail lucrative mortgage offers.

To perform this joint computation, Acme maintains a proprietary database mapping merchant ids to category labels; Alice's data consists of a set of transaction records sorted by time, where each record contains several sensitive fields such as the merchant id, the amount spent, and the timestamp. The aggregation function (denoted hereon by f) is evaluated over inputs from Alice and Acme, and the output is shared with Alice and two lending institutions, BankA and BankB. Alice's data is either imported manually by her, or more conveniently, provided by Alice's bank, via an OAuth-based OFX API [3] that pushes transaction data one-by-one as they are generated by her. Today, an application like Acme often hosts the users' raw data, and is trusted by them to adhere to a legalese policy.

2.2 Requirements of Acme

Privacy Through Transparency

We find that transparency and control — i.e., enforcing which functions can be evaluated, and with whom the outputs are shared — are necessary for enforcing any measure of privacy. Without this basic enforcement, an attacker can proliferate arbitrary functions of user data. In our example, Alice wishes that the approved output recipients only learn the output of f (on one month of transaction data), and nothing else about her spending profile, such as her daily behavior or the location patterns. For this reason, f cannot be evaluated by sharing Alice's plaintext data with Acme, or vice versa as Acme also wishes to maintain secrecy of its proprietary database.

Strawman Approach

Both parties first encrypt their data before uploading it to a *compute provider* (e.g., Acme or cloud). Next, to allow the agreed-upon evaluation of function f on their data, both parties establish a secure channel with an **enclave program** (on Intel SGX, for example, using remote attestation), and share the decryption keys to that enclave — enclave is loaded with f and hosted on an untrusted compute provider's machine. Then, the enclave evaluates f, encrypts the output under the output recipients' public keys, and asks the compute provider to transmit the encrypted output.

As a first step towards transparency and control, this design ensures that only f is computed on inputs from Alice and Acme, and that no other party beyond Alice, BankA, and BankB can observe the output. Note that the input providers can go offline after providing their inputs, and the output recipients come online only to retrieve the outputs. There are several TEE-based systems that fit this general design, such as VC3 [55], Opaque [66], StealthDB [38], Ryoan [40], Felsen et al. [28], etc., which we can use to implement the function f. To restrict scope, f is assumed to be safe (e.g., without additional leaks via side channels), so we execute f as given.

History-Based Policies

While this strawman ensures that only f can be evaluated on Alice's data, we argue that this is insufficient for her privacy.

Recall that Alice's bank (we can treat Alice and her bank as one logical party) uploads encrypted transaction records to the compute provider (using the OFX API [3]), one-by-one as they are generated by Alice. The enclave's host software is controlled by an untrusted compute provider, who may perform attacks such as rewinding the persistent storage and launching multiple instances of the enclave program. Hence, an adversarial compute provider may repeat the computation with progressively smaller subsets of Alice's (encrypted) transaction data from that month (and collude to send the output to a corrupt party) — note that each of these computations is independently legal since it evaluates f on an input containing Alice's transactions that are timestamped to the same calendar month. By comparing any pair of output reports, the attacker infers more information about the transactions than what is leaked by the monthly aggregate report; for instance, one may learn that Alice tends to spend frivolously towards the end of the month[2]. In general, this form of a *rewind-and-fork* attack is detrimental for applications that maintain a privacy budget [41].

To counter such attacks, we enforce *history-based policies*, where the decision to execute the next step in a computation depends on that computation's history (and the history of any other computations over the input data) which contains some metadata about the inputs and outputs of a computation. In Acme's example, Alice uses the following history-based policy ϕ : all transactions must 1) be fresh, in that they have never been used by a prior evaluation of f, and 2) belong to the same month.

History-based policies find use in applications that maintain state, have privacy budgets, or make decisions based on prior inputs. We urge the reader to look at history-based policies in Sect. 7.1, such as private surveys amongst unknown participants with policies across computations (e.g. survey only open to users who participated in a previous survey, or only open to Acme users) — smart contracts on Ekiden [21] or FastKitten [24] cannot read the ledger entries (of other contracts), and therefore cannot implement such applications.

To our knowledge, this is the first work to study such policies in a multi-party setting (where participants may be offline or act maliciously), and enforcing them incurs the following challenges. For instance, multiple parties may compute concurrently, and attempt to append the computation's history on the shared ledger — there must be some conflict resolution to enable concurrency across computations, but also ensure policy compliance. Furthermore, we must develop efficient methods to check policies such as *k-time programs* and correct accounting of all inputs.

Fairness

A policy also enforces the set of output recipients: Alice, BankA, and BankB. Simply encrypting the output under their public keys ensures that other parties cannot observe the results of the computation (assuming confidentiality of enclave execution). However, a malicious compute provider can collude with a subset of output recipients, and deliver the encrypted outputs to only those parties — since all network communication is proxied via the compute provider, an enclave cannot ensure that an outbound message is sent, and therefore, must assume lossy links, making reliable message delivery impossible [30].

Without having to trust Acme, Alice wishes to have her monthly reports sent to a set of chosen banks, perhaps to get lucrative loan offers. For Acme to be transparent, we argue that it must also ensure fairness: if any party gets the output, then so must all honest parties. Moreover, a protocol for fair output delivery should ideally not require Alice to possess a device with a TEE — we

[2] While metadata, such as authenticated batched inputs, can remedy this attack, banks may be unwilling to create this data for each third-party app.

point out that the enclave-ledger protocol in [22] requires all parties to possess a TEE.

2.3 Acme on LucidiTEE

Specifying and Creating Computations

A computation's semantics is specified by a string, which anyone can post to the ledger for inspection by all parties. In Acme's case, we use the following specification:

```
computation { id: 42, /* unique id */
  inp: [("txs": pk_Alice), ("db": pk_Acme)],
  out: [("rprt": [pk_Alice, pk_BnkA, pk_BnkB])],
  policy: 0xcoff..eeee, /* ∀r∈txs: ¬consumed(r)*/
  func: 0x1337...c0de /* aggregate function */ }
```

Each computation on LucidiTEE has a unique `id`. The `in` field lists a set of named inputs, along with the public key of the input provider (who is expected to sign those inputs). Similarly, the `out` field lists a set of named outputs, where each output has one or more recipients. The evaluation function f and the policy function ϕ are implemented as enclave programs, for confidentiality and integrity, and we uniquely identify them using the hash of the enclave program binary.

A computation progresses via a potentially unbounded sequence of stateful evaluations of f, guarded by ϕ, and it is said to be *compliant* if all constituent steps use the function f and satisfy ϕ. Unlike f, ϕ takes the entire ledger as input. In our example, ϕ encodes the freshness property that no transaction within `txs` has been consumed by a prior evaluation of f; we can implement ϕ by performing membership test for each transaction (in `txs`) within the inputs consumed by prior evaluations of f in computation of `id` 42, or more efficiently, by maintaining state containing an accumulator (e.g. a Merkle tree) of all transactions previously consumed by f.

Enforcing Policies and Performing Computation

> **History-based Policy via Shared Ledger**
> We introduce an append-only ledger, which is shared at least between Alice and Acme, but more generally, a global set of users to enforce policies across multiple applications that process some data. The ledger fulfills a dual purpose. First, a protocol (see Sect. 5) forces the compute provider to record the enclave's evaluation of f on the ledger before extracting the output — for each function evaluation, we record a hash-based commitment of the encrypted inputs, outputs, and intermediate state. Second, enclave programs read the ledger to evaluate the policy ϕ.

The compute provider allocates a TEE machine, and downloads Alice's and Acme's encrypted inputs onto the machine's local storage — this expense may be amortized across several function evaluations. Next, Acme must convince an enclave that the requested function on Alice's inputs is compliant. To that end, Acme launches an enclave implementing the policy predicate ϕ, and provides it with a view of the ledger. Note that a malicious compute provider can provide a stale view of the ledger (by simply ignoring recent ledger entries), and our protocol defends against such attacks by requiring a proof that no relevant computation occurred since the ledger height at which ϕ is evaluated. On approval from ϕ, Acme launches an enclave to evaluate f, which gets the encrypted inputs' decryption keys from a key manager (also implemented as an enclave; see Sect. 5), and produces an output encrypted under the public keys of all output recipients. In Sect. 5, we discuss practical methods to enforce several classes of policies.

LucidiTEE is oblivious to how or where the encrypted data is stored, and the ledger size is independent of the size of the inputs. Therefore, we stress that LucidiTEE uses the ledger only to enforce policies, and embodies a "bring-your-own-storage" paradigm. Moreover, since LucidiTEE uses trusted enclaves and an append-only ledger to enforce the policy, any (malicious) compute provider can bring TEE nodes and evaluate ϕ and f. Hence, we emphasize that LucidiTEE also embodies a "bring-your-own-compute" paradigm.

Fair Reconstruction of Outputs

Since fairness is impossible to achieve in a setting where a majority of the participants are corrupt [23], several works have explored relaxed notions of fairness over the last few years [12,22,37,52] — specifically, Choudhuri et al. [22] showed that enclave-ledger interactions can enable fair secure computation. Our work continues in the same vein, and improves upon their result.

Inspired by [36,46], we reduce fair computation to fair reconstruction of an additive secret sharing scheme, as follows. The enclave's evaluation of f encrypts the output under a random key k. The enclave also emits shares of k for all output recipients: $\mathsf{Enc}(\mathsf{pk\_Alice}, \mathsf{k}_1)$, $\mathsf{Enc}(\mathsf{pk\_BankA}, \mathsf{k}_2)$, and $\mathsf{Enc}(\mathsf{pk\_BankB}, \mathsf{k}_3)$, such that $\mathsf{k} \doteq \mathsf{k}_1 \oplus \mathsf{k}_2 \oplus \mathsf{k}_3$, for random k_1, k_2, and k_3. All output recipients must engage in the reconstruction protocol with their shares. For best case security, we set the corruption threshold t in Acme's example to 2, thus withstanding byzantine behavior from any 2 of the 3 parties. Our protocol requires t parties to provide a TEE node (e.g., BankA and BankB).

Protocol for Fair Reconstruction
We develop a protocol that withstands an arbitrary corruption threshold $t < n$, and it requires any t recipients to allocate a TEE machine, and all n parties to access the shared ledger — in contrast, [22] needs all n parties to allocate a TEE machine and access the ledger, which is cumbersome for end users.

3 Building Blocks

3.1 Trusted Execution Environment (TEE)

An enclave program is an isolated region of memory, containing both code and data, protected by the TEE platform (where trust is only placed in the processor manufacturer). On TEE platforms such as Intel SGX and Sanctum, the CPU monitors all memory accesses to ensure that non-enclave software (including OS, Hypervisor, and BIOS or SMM firmware) cannot access the enclave's memory — SGX also thwarts hardware attacks on DRAM by encrypting and integrity-protecting the enclave's cache lines. In addition to isolated execution, we assume that the TEE platform provides a primitive for remote attestation. At any time, the enclave software may request a signed message (called a *quote*) binding an enclave-supplied value to that enclave's code identity (i.e., its hash-based measurement). We model the TEE hardware as an ideal functionality HW, adapted from [29]. HW maintains the memory of each enclave program in an internal variable $\mathtt{mem}$, and has the following interface:

- $\mathsf{HW.Load}(\mathsf{prog})$ loads the enclave code, denoted by prog, within the TEE-protected region. It returns a unique id eid for the loaded enclave program, and zero-initializes the enclave's private memory by setting $\mathtt{mem}[\mathsf{eid}] = \overrightarrow{0}$.
- $\mathsf{HW.Run}(\mathsf{eid}, \mathsf{in})$ executes enclave eid (from prior state $\mathtt{mem}[\mathsf{eid}]$) under input in, producing an output out while also updating $\mathtt{mem}[\mathsf{eid}]$. The command returns the pair $(\mathsf{out}, \mathsf{quote})$, where quote is a signature over $\mu(\mathsf{prog}) \parallel \mathsf{out}$, attesting that out originated from an enclave with hash measurement $\mu(\mathsf{prog})$ running on a genuine TEE. We also write the quote as $\mathsf{quote}_{\mathsf{HW}}(\mathsf{prog}, \mathsf{out})$. We assume no other information leaks to the adversary, such as from side channels.
- $\mathsf{HW.QuoteVerify}(\mathsf{quote})$ verifies the genuineness of quote and returns another signature σ (such that $\mathsf{Verify}_{\mathsf{HW}}(\sigma, \mathsf{quote}) = \mathsf{true}$) that is publicly verifiable. Any party can check $\mathsf{Verify}_{\mathsf{HW}}$ without invoking the HW functionality. For instance, SGX implements this command using Intel's attestation service, which verifies the CPU-produced quote (in a group signature scheme) and returns a publicly verifiable signature σ over $\mathsf{quote} \parallel b$, where $b \in \{0, 1\}$ denotes the validity of quote; then, any party can verify σ using Intel's public key without contacting Intel.

3.2 Shared, Append-Only Ledger

We borrow the bulletin board abstraction of a shared ledger, defined in [22], which lets parties get its contents and post arbitrary strings on it. Furthermore, on successfully publishing the string on the bulletin board, any party can request a (publicly verifiable) proof that the string was indeed published, and the bulletin board guarantees that the string will never be modified or deleted. Hence, the bulletin board is an abstraction of an append-only ledger. We model the shared ledger as an ideal functionality L, with internal state containing a list of entries, implementing the following interface:

- $\mathsf{L.getCurrentCounter}$ returns the height of the ledger
- $\mathsf{L.post}(e)$ appends e to the ledger and returns $(\sigma,\ \mathsf{t})$, where t is the new height and σ is the proof that e has been successfully posted to the ledger. Specifically, σ is an authentication tag (also called *proof-of-publication* in prior works [21]) over the pair $\mathsf{t}||\mathsf{e}$ such that $\mathsf{Verify_L}(\sigma, \mathsf{t}||\mathsf{e}) = \mathsf{true}$ — here, $\mathsf{Verify_L}$ is a public verification algorithm (e.g., verifying a set of signatures).
- $\mathsf{L.getContent(t)}$ returns the ledger entry $(\sigma,\ \mathsf{e})$ at height t.

The bulletin board abstraction can be instantiated using fork-less blockchains, such as permissioned blockchains [6], and potentially by blockchains based on proof-of-stake [32].

3.3 Cryptographic Primitives and Assumptions

We assume a hash function H (e.g. SHA-2) that is collision-resistant and pre-image resistant; we also assume a hash-based commitment scheme com with hiding and binding properties.

We use a *IND-CCA2* [39] public key encryption scheme PKE (e.g. RSA-OAEP) consisting of algorithms $\mathsf{PKE.Keygen}(1^\lambda)$, $\mathsf{PKE.Enc(pk,\ m)}$, $\mathsf{PKE.Dec(sk, ct)}$. Moreover, for symmetric key encryption, we use authenticated encryption AE (e.g. AES-GCM) that provides *IND-CCA2* and *INT-CTXT* [13], and it consists of polynomial-time algorithms $\mathsf{AE.Keygen}(1^\lambda)$, $\mathsf{AE.Enc(k, m)}$, $\mathsf{AE.Dec(k, ct)}$.

Finally, we use a *EUF-CMA* [35] digital signature scheme S (e.g. ECDSA) consisting of polynomial-time algorithms $\mathsf{S.Keygen}(1^\lambda)$, $\mathsf{S.Sig(sk, m)}$, $\mathsf{S.Verify}(\mathsf{vk}, \sigma, \mathsf{m})$.

4 Adversary Model

The attacker may corrupt any subset of the parties. We use a static corruption model wherein a party is said to be corrupt if it deviates from the protocol at any time. A corrupt party exhibits *byzantine* behavior, which includes aborts, and dropping or tampering any communication with other parties or the ledger. We discuss specific threats below.

TEE Threats. TEE machines can be operated by malicious hosts, who can abort the TEE's execution, and delay, tamper, or drop its inputs and outputs (including the communication with the ledger). The untrusted host can also launch multiple enclave instances containing the same program. We assume that the remote attestation scheme is existentially unforgeable under chosen message attacks [29]. Though side channels pose a realistic threat, we consider their defenses to be an orthogonal problem. This assumption is discharged in part by using safer TEEs such as RISC-V Sanctum, which implement defenses for several hardware side channels, and in part by compiling f and ϕ using software defenses (e.g., [54,57,58,60,65]).

Blockchain Threats. We draw attention to the subtlety of blockchain instantiations. While our fair delivery protocol tolerates an arbitrary corruption threshold of $t < n$, the ledger admits a weaker adversary (e.g. less than 1/3rd corruption in PBFT-based permissioned blockchains, or honest majority of collective compute power in permissionless blockchains). In permissioned settings, this means that the n parties cannot instantiate a shared ledger amongst themselves, and expect to achieve fairness; they need a larger set of participants on the ledger, and require more than 2/3rd of that set to be honest — this is reasonable on recently proposed consortium blockchains such as Libra [9].

With that said, [22] also has the same limitation. Fundamentally, forks on proof-of-work blockchains can violate policies, as computation records can be lost. Even the proof-of-publication scheme in Ekiden [21], which uses a trusted timeserver to enforce the rate of production of ledger entries, offers a probabilistic guarantee of rollback prevention, which worsens as the attacker's computational power increases. We restrict our scope to forkless ledgers (providing the bulletin-board abstraction L), such as HyperLedger [6] and Tendermint [5], and even blockchains based on proof-of-stake [32].

5 Policy-Compliant Computation

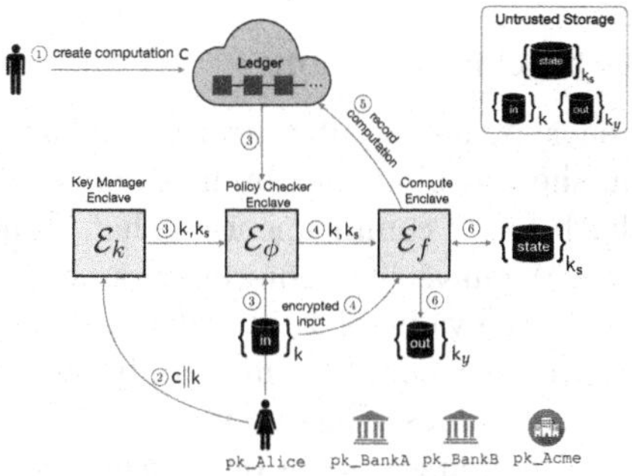

Fig. 2. Policy enforcement using TEEs and a shared ledger

In this section, we describe how computations are specified and setup, how inputs are bound to computations, how policies are evaluated prior to the computation, and how computations are recorded on the shared ledger.

Figure 2 illustrates the primary components of LucidiTEE. Each entry on the shared ledger records either the creation or revocation of a computation (along with its specification), or a function evaluation containing hash-based commitments of inputs, outputs, and state. We stress that the ledger does not store the inputs or state, and its entries only help us to enforce policies. Computation involves three types of enclave programs: 1) a *key manager enclave* $\mathcal{E}_k$ (responsible for handling keys that protect the computation's state and the offline users' input); 2) a *policy checker enclave* $\mathcal{E}_\phi$ (responsible for checking whether a requested evaluation f is compliant with the policy ϕ); 3) a *compute enclave* $\mathcal{E}_f$ (responsible for evaluating f). These enclaves are run on one or more physical TEE machines, managed by any untrusted party — hereon called the *compute provider* p_c — yet our protocols guarantee policy compliance and fairness to all parties (who may also act maliciously). Computation happens off-chain, and is decoupled from the ledger's consensus mechanism.

5.1 Specifying and Creating a Computation

A computation is specified using a structured string, denoted **c**, such as the one from Acme's application in Sect. 2.3. A party p can create a new multi-party computation by executing:

$$p \rightarrow \mathcal{E}_k : \mathbf{c} \parallel \sigma, \text{ where } (\sigma, \mathtt{t}) = \mathsf{L.post}(\mathtt{create} \parallel \mathbf{c})$$

Here, upon posting the specification **c** on the ledger, p contacts the compute provider p_c, who forwards the request to its local key manager enclave $\mathcal{E}_k$. $\mathcal{E}_k$ generates a key k_s to encrypt the computation's state across all function evaluations, using the TEE's entropy source (e.g. `rdrand` on SGX). Since **c** does not contain any secrets, any party can post it on the ledger, and it is up to the input providers to examine and choose to bind inputs to **c**. Any input provider listed in **c** can revoke a computation by executing $\mathsf{L.post}(\mathtt{revoke} \parallel \mathbf{c}.\mathtt{id})$.

5.2 Binding Inputs to Computations

LucidiTEE lets a user encrypt her input x and upload to an untrusted storage provider; from then on, she can bind that input to one or more computations **c** by referring only to a hash-based commitment on that input, without needing to store or upload the data. We have two requirements here: 1) the input provider must be able to commit to the value of x, in order to prevent any tampering by the storage or compute provider; and 2) x must only be used for evaluating $\mathbf{c}.f$, for each computation **c** that the user has bound x to.

The cryptographic protection must not only ensure confidentiality, integrity, and authenticity of the data, but also provide cryptographic binding to the commitment. To that end, the input provider chooses a random key k, and computes $\mathsf{AE.Enc}(\mathsf{k}, x)$. Then, the hash-based commitment h is computed over the ciphertext, using either plain hashing or accumulators. Accumulators, such as a Merkle trees, enable membership queries, which we find to be useful when enforcing policies such as one-time programs and vote counting.

The binding of key k, for input referred by h, to a computation **c** is established using an interaction between the input provider p, the compute provider p_c who is running the key manager enclave $\mathcal{E}_k$, and the ledger functionality L:

$$p : \mathsf{L.post}(\ \mathtt{bind} \parallel \mathbf{c}.\mathtt{id} \parallel h \parallel \mathsf{S.Sig}(\mathsf{sk}_p, \mathbf{c}.\mathtt{id} \parallel h)\ )$$
$$p_c \rightarrow p : \mathsf{quote}_{\mathsf{HW}}(\mathcal{E}_k, \mathsf{pk}), \text{where } \mathsf{pk} \leftarrow \mathsf{PKE.Keygen}$$
$$p \rightarrow p_c : \mathsf{PKE.Enc}(\mathsf{pk}, \mathbf{c}.\mathtt{id} \parallel \mathsf{k} \parallel \mathsf{S.Sig}(\mathsf{sk}_p, \mathbf{c}.\mathtt{id} \parallel \mathsf{k}))$$

First, p creates a ledger entry binding the commitment h to computation **c** using a signature. Next, p contacts p_c, whose instance of $\mathcal{E}_k$ generates a fresh public key pk along with a quote attesting to the genuineness of $\mathcal{E}_k$. Upon verifying the attestation, p signs and encrypts `c.id` and k. $\mathcal{E}_k$ will later reveal the key k only to that enclave which is evaluating $\mathbf{c}.f$.

By binding commitments to computations, we reuse inputs across function evaluations and computations, without having to repeatedly upload data or bind it on the ledger.

5.3 Enforcing Policy-Compliance

Any party p_c can act as a compute provider, and invoke $\mathbf{c}.f$ on chosen inputs (referenced by a vector of commitments H_{in}). Hence, we implement a protocol to ensure policy compliance even when input providers are offline and p_c acts maliciously.

Before evaluating f, p_c must first launch $\mathcal{E}_\phi$ to evaluate ϕ. Next, $\mathcal{E}_\phi$ must check whether the requested evaluation of f is compliant with ϕ, which requires checking three conditions:

1. active: **c** is created on the ledger, and not yet revoked
2. bound: data for each $h \in H_{\mathsf{in}}$ is bound to computation **c**
3. compliant: predicate $\phi(\text{ledger}, H_{\mathsf{in}})$ over ledger's contents

To perform these checks, p_c must provide $\mathcal{E}_\phi$ with a read-only view of L, by downloading the ledger's contents locally, in which case the enclave-ledger interaction is mediated by the host software controlled by p_c. Although using $\mathsf{Verify_L}$ allows $\mathcal{E}_\phi$ to detect arbitrary tampering of L's contents, an adversarial p_c may still present a stale view (i.e., a prefix) of L to $\mathcal{E}_\phi$. We mitigate this attack in Sect. 5.5. For now, we task ourselves with deciding compliance with respect to a certain (albeit potentially stale) view or height of L.

The policy ϕ is an arbitrary predicate. As an example, consider the policy ϕ from the Acme application: transactions in the input must *not* have been consumed by a prior evaluation of $\mathbf{c}.f$. Cryptographic accumulators, such as Merkle trees, play an important role in efficiently evaluating ϕ, as they support efficient membership queries. In Acme's case, we scan the ledger to construct an accumulator over the input handles from all prior evaluations of $\mathbf{c}.f$, and check absence of each input transaction within the accumulator.

Performance Optimizations. It is not practical to process the entire ledger for each evaluation of $\mathbf{c}.\phi$. Specifically, if the ledger L is naively stored as a sequence of entries, it would force us to perform a linear scan for evaluating the three aforementioned compliance checks.

Instead, our implementation stores L locally as an authenticated key-value database, whose index is the computation's id `c.id`. Each computation appends the ledger entry to the current value at `c.id`. Now, instead of scanning through the entire ledger, the first compliance check asserts the presence of key `c.id`, while the second check queries the list of records at key **c**.id. Finally, to evaluate ϕ, we maintain an accumulator as state, and update it on each entry of **c**.id — we let ϕ rely on an enclave that persists state, in the form of an authenticated key-value store [59], across several evaluations of ϕ. Note that this optimization does not impact security, as $\mathcal{E}_\phi$'s view of L is still controlled by p_c, and therefore potentially stale.

Consider other history-based policies used in apps from Sect. 7.1. In the survey app (Sect. 7.1), we check that the input includes *all* votes for which we find commitments on the ledger (produced by the user's binding of inputs); accumulators again suffice for this policy. Both the machine learning app (Sect. 7.1) and PSI apps (Sect. 7.1) compare commitments (i.e., equality check on hashes) for their policies.

5.4 Producing Encrypted Output

The compute provider launches the compute enclave $\mathcal{E}_f$, who then asks $\mathcal{E}_k$ for the keys to **c**'s state and all parties' input. $\mathcal{E}_k$ transmits these keys upon verifying that $\mathcal{E}_f$ has the expected hash-based measurement listed in **c**.

The computation can be performed using any enclave-based data processing system, such as Opaque [66], Ryoan [40], etc. A randomized f needs an entropy source. Recall that $\mathcal{E}_k$ generated a key k_s to protect the computation's state. Using a key derived from k_s, f can internally seed a pseudo-random generator (e.g. PRF with key $\mathsf{H}(\mathsf{t} \parallel \mathsf{k_s})$) to get a fresh pseudo-random bitstream at each step of the computation. (Note that t uniquely identifies the step.) This ensures that the random bits are private to $\mathcal{E}_f$, yet allows replaying computation from the ledger during crash recovery.

5.5 Recording Computation on Ledger

Recording the computation (specifically the commitments) on the ledger is a precursor to extracting the output, and is also necessary for enforcing our history-based policies.

Recall that $\mathcal{E}_\phi$ checked compliance of ϕ with respect to a certain height of the ledger. Since a malicious compute provider p_c can present a stale view of the ledger to $\mathcal{E}_\phi$, we show how we defend against this attack at the time of recording the computation on the ledger. The protocol works as follows. We first request the instance of $\mathcal{E}_\phi$ (from Sect. 5.3) for the ledger height t and input commitments H_{in} with which it evaluated **c**.ϕ; $\mathcal{E}_\phi$ sends these values as part of a quote.

$$\mathcal{E}_\phi \rightarrow \mathcal{E}_f : \mathsf{quote}_{\mathsf{HW}}(\mathcal{E}_\phi, \mathsf{t} \parallel H_{\mathsf{in}})$$

Next, to extract the encrypted output, the compute provider p_c must record the compliant evaluation of **c**.f on L by posting the following messages emitted by $\mathcal{E}_f$ and $\mathcal{E}_\phi$:

$$\mathsf{quote}_{\mathsf{HW}}(\mathcal{E}_\phi, \mathsf{t} \parallel H_{\mathsf{in}}) \parallel \mathsf{quote}_{\mathsf{HW}}(\mathcal{E}_f, \mathbf{c}.\mathtt{id} \parallel \mathsf{t} \parallel h_{s'} \parallel H_{\mathsf{out}})$$

The use of $\mathsf{quote_{HW}}$ ensures that the compute provider evaluated the functions $\mathbf{c}.f$ and $\mathbf{c}.\phi$ within a genuine TEE. It also ensures that the compute provider used inputs with commitments H_{in}, and produced outputs with commitments H_{out} and the next state with commitment $h_{s'}$.

However, by the time L receives the post command from p_c, it may have advanced by several entries from t to t′. This can be caused by a combination of reasons including: 1) ledger entries from concurrent evaluations of c and other computations on LucidiTEE; and, 2) malicious p_c providing a stale view of L to $\mathcal{E}_\phi$. This potentially invalidates $\mathcal{E}_\phi$'s check, but instead of rejecting the computation, which would unnecessarily limit concurrency even during honest behavior, we assert a *validity predicate* on the ledger's contents:

$$\forall \mathsf{t}, \mathsf{t}', \mathsf{t}^*.\ \mathsf{t}' = \mathsf{L.getCurrentCounter} \wedge \mathsf{t} < \mathsf{t}^* < \mathsf{t}' \Rightarrow$$
$$\neg((\sigma, \mathsf{e}) = \mathsf{L.getContent}(\mathsf{t}^*)\ \wedge\ \mathsf{Verify_L}(\sigma, \mathsf{t}^* \| \mathsf{e})\ \wedge$$
$$(\exists a \in \{\mathtt{compute}, \mathtt{bind}, \mathtt{revoke}\}.\ \mathsf{e} = a \parallel \mathbf{c}.\mathtt{id} \parallel \ldots))$$

Here, we check that the computation **c** is still active and that no new function evaluation or bind for **c** is performed in between t and the current height t′. The computation is rejected if the check fails, and no entry is recorded on L. This validity predicate may be checked by the ledger's participants before appending any entry, but that would be outside the scope of the bulletin-board abstraction; instead, we rely on our trusted enclaves, $\mathcal{E}_\phi$ and $\mathcal{E}_f$ (and $\mathcal{E}_r$) to assert the validity predicate, and abort any further computation or protocol execution atop an invalid ledger.

5.6 Fair Output Delivery

For lack of space, please see the full version [27].

6 Implementation

To help developers write enclave functions, we developed an enclave programming library libmoat, providing a narrow POSIX-style interface for common services such as file system, key-value databases, and channel establishment with other enclaves. libmoat is statically linked with application-specific enclave code, ϕ and f, which together form the enclaves, $\mathcal{E}_\phi$ and $\mathcal{E}_f$ respectively. libmoat transparently encrypts and authenticates all operations to the files and databases. LucidiTEE provides fixed implementations of $\mathcal{E}_r$ and $\mathcal{E}_k$, whose measurements are hard-coded within libmoat. Furthermore, libmoat implements the ledger interface L, which verifies signatures ($\mathsf{Verify_L}$) and TEE attestation of ledger entries. libmoat contains 3K LOC, in addition to Intel's SGX SDK [1].

We instantiate the ledger with a permissioned blockchain, and evaluate using both Hyperledger [6] and Tendermint [5]. The ledger participant's logic is implemented as a smart contract (in 200 lines of Go), which internally uses RocksDB [4].

7 Evaluation

7.1 Case Studies

We demonstrate applications which demonstrate novel history-based policies, and require fairness of output delivery. Though omitted for space reasons, we also build one-time programs [34], digital lockbox, and 2-party contract signing [14].

Personal Finance Application. We implement Acme's personal finance application, which Alice uses to generate a monthly report. The application uses a history-based policy that transaction records are fresh, i.e., they are not used in a prior evaluation of Acme's function (which would otherwise violate Alice's privacy). Acme's input is encoded as a key-value database indexed by the merchant id — with over 50 million merchants worldwide, this database can grow to a size of several GBs (we use a 1.6 GB synthetic database of 50 million merchants). We also built a client that uses the OFX API [3] to download the user's transactions from a bank, and encrypt and upload them to a public S3 bucket. This encrypted file is later decrypted within an enclave during compute.

Private Survey. Acme would like to conduct a privacy-preserving survey, such that Acme only learns the aggregate summary of the survey rather than individual responses. However, to maintain the integrity of the survey, we use a history-based policy consisting of two predicates. First, the survey is open only to users of their finance application to avoid fake reviews — specifically, the user (identified by her public key) that participates in the survey must have a ledger entry of type bind_input with Acme's finance application. Second, the survey's result must aggregate all submitted votes, until Acme closes the survey using another ledger entry.

Federated Machine Learning. A hospital sets up a service for any user to avail the prediction of a model (specifically the ECG class of a patient), in exchange for submitting their data for use in subsequent retraining of the model — we require a fair exchange of user's ECG data and the model's output, which our protocol achieves while only requiring the hospital to provision a TEE node. The service is split into two chained computations: training and inference. Retraining happens on successive batches of new users' data, so when a user submits their ECG data, they wish to use the output model from the latest evaluation of the retraining function — this acts as our history-based policy. For the experiment, we use the UCI Machine Learning Repository [25], and the side-channel resistant k-means clustering algorithm from [20].

One-Time Private Set Intersection. Two hospitals share prescription records about their common patients using private set intersection (PSI). Moreover, they require a guarantee of fair output delivery, and use a one-time program policy to prevent repeated (mis)use of their data. We implement oblivious set intersection by adapting Signal's private contact discovery service [47]. Our experiment uses a synthetic dataset with 1 million records for each hospital (totalling 15 GB).

7.2 Performance Measurement

We study the performance of our applications, and compare to a baseline version where the application runs without a ledger, and without our policy compliance and fairness protocols. The baseline versions of Acme, survey, ML, and PSI apps take on average 0.02, 0.41, 0.006, and 8.24 s, respectively, for each function evaluation of f (including the policy check ϕ), using the aforementioned inputs for each application.

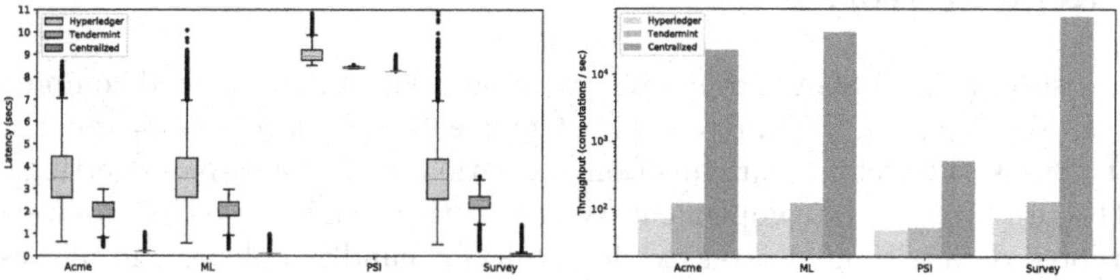

Fig. 3. Latency and Throughput Measurements

End-to-End Latency and Throughput. Figure 3 reports the latency and throughput (results aggregated over 100 runs) on both HyperLedger [6] and Tendermint [5] ledgers (running with 4 peers), with 500 enclave clients concurrently querying and posting ledger entries — we use a 4 core CPU to run the ledger, and a cluster with 56 CPU cores to run the enclaves. We measure end-to-end latency, from launching $\mathcal{E}_\phi$ to terminating $\mathcal{E}_r$. Recall that each evaluation on LucidiTEE performs at least one read query (often more in order to evaluate ϕ) and two writes (to record the `compute` and `deliver` entry) to the ledger. We found throughput to be bound by the performance of the ledger, which was highly dependent on parameters such as the batch size and batch timeout [6], with the exception of the PSI application which was compute bound (as each function evaluation took roughly 8.2 s). The latency also suffered by several seconds, as the ledger faced a high volume of concurrent read and write requests. We also evaluate on a "centralized" ledger, essentially a key-value store, thus demonstrating performance with an ideally-performant ledger on a single trusted node.

Application	Ledger	Input	Output	State
Acme Finance	2155 B	1.6 GB	1872 B	136 B
Federated ML	1835 B	132 KB	1088 B	-
Policy-based PSI	1835 B	30 MB	8 MB	-
Private Survey	100.1 MB	954.4 MB	2 KB	-

Fig. 4. On-chain and Off-chain Storage Requirements

Storage. Figure 4 shows the off-chain and on-chain ledger storage cost on each function evaluation; the ledger storage includes entries due to binding input, recording computation, and fair reconstruction protocol. Observe that the survey amongst 1 million participants incurred 1 million calls to bind_input, incurring a high on-chain storage cost. In other applications, inputs are orders of magnitude larger than the ledger storage. Since, Ekiden [21] and FastKitten [24] store inputs and state on-chain, LucidiTEE has orders of magnitude improvement.

8 Related Work

TEEs, such as Intel SGX, are finding use in systems for outsourced computing, such as M2R [26], VC3 [55], Ryoan [40], Opaque [66], EnclaveDB [53], etc. Felsen et al. [28] use TEEs for secure function evaluation in the multi-party setting. We find these systems to be complementary, in that they can be used to compute over encrypted data within enclaves, while LucidiTEE handles policies and fairness.

ROTE [48], Ariadne [61], Memoir [50], and Brandenburger et al. [17] address rollback attacks on TEEs. Similarly, Kaptchuk et al. [41] address rollback attacks by augmenting enclaves with ledgers. We extend their ideas to general history-based policies.

Ekiden [21], FastKitten [24], CCF [56], and Private Data Objects (PDO) [16] are closest to our work. FastKitten [24] provides fair distribution of coins in multi-round contracts such as poker and lotteries. Ekiden and PDO execute smart contracts within SGX enclaves, connected to a blockchain for persisting the contract's state. To our knowledge, none of these systems ([16,21,24,56]) provide complete fairness [22] or the expressivity of history-based policies. On the practical front, LucidiTEE improves efficiency by not placing inputs or state on the ledger, which is used only to enforce policies. In addition to the performance improvements, our history-based policies are expressed over the entire ledger, spanning multiple computations, whereas Ekiden, FastKitten, and CCF only support contract-specific state.

Hawk [44] and Zexe [15] enable parties to perform limited forms of private computation, while proving correctness by posting zero knowledge proofs on the ledger. In addition to Hawk, several works, namely [7,8,14,45], and [43], use Bitcoin [49] to ensure financial fairness in MPC applications.

MPC [63] [64] [62] protocols implement a secure computation functionality, but require parties to be online or trust one or more third parties. Choudhuri et al. [22] proposed a fair MPC protocol requiring each of the n parties to possess a TEE. We improve their result by requiring $t < n$ (for corruption threshold t) parties to possess a TEE. Moreover, [22] requires all parties to be online, and only considers one-shot MPC as opposed to stateful computation with policies.

9 Conclusion

We developed LucidiTEE, a TEE-blockchain system for policy-based, fair multiparty computation amongst possibly offline participants. Using novel use cases, we show that LucidiTEE scales to big data applications and large number of users.

Disclaimer

Case studies, comparisons, statistics, research and recommendations are provided "AS IS" and intended for informational purposes only and should not be relied upon for operational, marketing, legal, technical, tax, financial or other advice. Visa Inc. neither makes any warranty or representation as to the completeness or accuracy of the information within this document, nor assumes any liability or responsibility that may result from reliance on such information. The Information contained herein is not intended as investment or legal advice, and readers are encouraged to seek the advice of a competent professional where such advice is required.

These materials and best practice recommendations are provided for informational purposes only and should not be relied upon for marketing, legal, regulatory or other advice. Recommended marketing materials should be independently evaluated in light of your specific business needs and any applicable laws and regulations. Visa is not responsible for your use of the marketing materials, best practice recommendations, or other information, including errors of any kind, contained in this document.

References

1. Intel SGX for linux. https://github.com/intel/linux-sgx
2. Mint. https://www.mint.com
3. OFX: The payments API that lets you scale, simplify and save. https://developer.ofx.com/
4. Rocksdb. https://github.com/facebook/rocksdb
5. Tendermint core in go. https://github.com/tendermint/tendermint
6. Androulaki, E., et al.: Hyperledger fabric: a distributed operating system for permissioned blockchains. In: Proceedings of the Thirteenth EuroSys Conference, EuroSys 2018, pp. 30:1–30:15. ACM, New York, NY, US (2018)
7. Andrychowicz, M., Dziembowski, S., Malinowski, D., Mazurek, L.: Secure multiparty computations on bitcoin. In: Security and Privacy (SP), 2014 IEEE Symposium on, pp. 443–458. IEEE (2014)
8. Andrychowicz, M., Dziembowski, S., Malinowski, D., Mazurek, Ł.: Fair two-party computations via bitcoin deposits. Cryptology ePrint Archive, Report 2013/837 (2013). https://eprint.iacr.org/2013/837
9. Baudet, M., et al.: State machine replication in the libra blockchain (2019)

10. Beimel, A., Gabizon, A., Ishai, Y., Kushilevitz, E., Meldgaard, S., Paskin-Cherniavsky, A.: Non-interactive secure multiparty computation. In: Garay, J.A., Gennaro, R. (eds.) CRYPTO 2014. LNCS, vol. 8617, pp. 387–404. Springer, Heidelberg (2014). https://doi.org/10.1007/978-3-662-44381-1_22
11. Beimel, A., Ishai, Y., Kushilevitz, E.: Ad Hoc PSM protocols: secure computation without coordination. In: Coron, J.-S., Nielsen, J.B. (eds.) EUROCRYPT 2017. LNCS, vol. 10212, pp. 580–608. Springer, Cham (2017). https://doi.org/10.1007/978-3-319-56617-7_20
12. Beimel, A., Lindell, Y., Omri, E., Orlov, I.: $1/p$-secure multiparty computation without honest majority and the best of both worlds. In: Rogaway, P. (ed.) CRYPTO 2011. LNCS, vol. 6841, pp. 277–296. Springer, Heidelberg (2011). https://doi.org/10.1007/978-3-642-22792-9_16
13. Bellare, M., Namprempre, C.: Authenticated encryption: relations among notions and analysis of the generic composition paradigm. J. Cryptol. **21**(4), 469–491 (2008)
14. Bentov, I., Kumaresan, R.: How to use bitcoin to design fair protocols. In: Garay, J.A., Gennaro, R. (eds.) CRYPTO 2014. LNCS, vol. 8617, pp. 421–439. Springer, Heidelberg (2014). https://doi.org/10.1007/978-3-662-44381-1_24
15. Bowe, S., Chiesa, A., Green, M., Miers, I., Mishra, P., Wu, H.. Zexe: enabling decentralized private computation. Cryptology ePrint Archive, Report 2018/962 (2018). https://eprint.iacr.org/2018/962
16. Bowman, M., Miele, A., Steiner, M., Vavala, B.: Private data objects: an overview. arXiv preprint arXiv:1807.05686 (2018)
17. Brandenburger, M., Cachin, C., Lorenz, M., Kapitza, Rü.: Rollback and forking detection for trusted execution environments using lightweight collective memory. In: 2017 47th Annual IEEE/IFIP International Conference on Dependable Systems and Networks (DSN), pp. 157–168. IEEE (2017)
18. Brickell, E., Li, J.: Enhanced privacy id from bilinear pairing. Cryptology ePrint Archive, Report 2009/095 (2009)
19. Canetti, R.: Universally composable security: a new paradigm for cryptographic protocols. In: FOCS, pp. 136–145 (2001)
20. Chandra, S., Karande, V., Lin, Z., Khan, L., Kantarcioglu, M., Thuraisingham, B.: Securing data analytics on SGX with randomization. In: Foley, S.N., Gollmann, D., Snekkenes, E. (eds.) ESORICS 2017. LNCS, vol. 10492, pp. 352–369. Springer, Cham (2017). https://doi.org/10.1007/978-3-319-66402-6_21
21. Cheng, R., et al.: Ekiden: a platform for confidentiality-preserving, trustworthy, and performant smart contract execution. CoRR, abs/1804.05141 (2018)
22. Choudhuri, A.R., Green, M., Jain, A., Kaptchuk, G., Miers, I.: Fairness in an unfair world: Fair multiparty computation from public bulletin boards. In: Proceedings of the 2017 ACM SIGSAC Conference on Computer and Communications Security, CCS 2017, pp. 719–728. ACM, New York, NY, USA (2017)
23. Cleve, R.: Limits on the security of coin flips when half the processors are faulty. In: Proceedings of the Eighteenth Annual ACM Symposium on Theory of Computing, STOC 1986, pp. 364–369. ACM, New York, NY, USA (1986)
24. Das, P., et al.: FastKitten: practical smart contracts on bitcoin. In: 28th USENIX Security Symposium (USENIX Security 19), pp. 801–818. USENIX Association, Santa Clara, CA (2019)
25. Dheeru, D., Taniskidou, E.K.: UCI machine learning repository (2017)
26. Dinh, T.T.A., Saxena, P., Chang, E.C., Ooi, B.C., Zhang, C.: M2R: enabling stronger privacy in mapreduce computation. In: USENIX Security Symposium, pp. 447–462 (2015)

27. Gaddam, S., et al.: LucidiTEE: a tee-blockchain system for policy-compliant multiparty computation with fairness. Cryptology ePrint Archive, Report 2019/178 (2019)
28. Felsen, S., Kiss, Á., Schneider, T., Weinert, C.: Secure and private function evaluation with intel SGX (2019)
29. Fisch, B., Vinayagamurthy, D., Boneh, D., Gorbunov, S.: Iron: functional encryption using intel SGX. In: Proceedings of the 2017 ACM SIGSAC Conference on Computer and Communications Security, CCS 2017, pp. 765–782. ACM, New York, NY, USA (2017)
30. Fischer, M.J., Lynch, N.A., Paterson, M.S.: Impossibility of distributed consensus with one faulty process. J. ACM **32**(2), 374–382 (1985)
31. Gentry, C., et al.: Fully homomorphic encryption using ideal lattices. In: Stoc, vol. 9, pp. 169–178 (2009)
32. Gilad, Y., Hemo, R., Micali, S., Vlachos, G., Zeldovich, N.: Algorand: Scaling byzantine agreements for cryptocurrencies. In: Proceedings of the 26th Symposium on Operating Systems Principles, SOSP 2017, pp. 51–68. ACM, New York, NY, USA (2017)
33. Goldwasser, S., et al.: Multi-input functional encryption. In: Nguyen, P.Q., Oswald, E. (eds.) EUROCRYPT 2014. LNCS, vol. 8441, pp. 578–602. Springer, Heidelberg (2014). https://doi.org/10.1007/978-3-642-55220-5_32
34. Goldwasser, S., Kalai, Y.T., Rothblum, G.N.: One-time programs. In: Wagner, D. (ed.) CRYPTO 2008. LNCS, vol. 5157, pp. 39–56. Springer, Heidelberg (2008). https://doi.org/10.1007/978-3-540-85174-5_3
35. Goldwasser, S., Micali, S., Rivest, R.L.: A digital signature scheme secure against adaptive chosen-message attacks. SIAM J. Comput. **17**(2), 281–308 (1988)
36. Gordon, D., Ishai, Y., Moran, T., Ostrovsky, R., Sahai, A.: On complete primitives for fairness. In: Micciancio, D. (ed.) TCC 2010. LNCS, vol. 5978, pp. 91–108. Springer, Heidelberg (2010). https://doi.org/10.1007/978-3-642-11799-2_7
37. Gordon, S.D., Katz, J.: Partial fairness in secure two-party computation. In: Advances in Cryptology - EUROCRYPT 2010, 29th Annual International Conference on the Theory and Applications of Cryptographic Techniques, Monaco/French Riviera, May 30 - June 3, 2010. Proceedings, pp. 157–176 (2010)
38. Gribov, A., Vinayagamurthy, D., Gorbunov, S.: StealthDB: a scalable encrypted database with full SQL query support. Proc. Priv. Enhancing Technol. **2019**(3), 370–388 (2019)
39. Hofheinz, D., Hövelmanns, K., Kiltz, E.: A modular analysis of the fujisaki-okamoto transformation. Cryptology ePrint Archive, Report 2017/604 (2017). https://eprint.iacr.org/2017/604
40. Hunt, T., Zhu, Z., Xu, Y., Peter, S., Witchel, E.: Ryoan: a distributed sandbox for untrusted computation on secret data. In: Proceedings of the 12th USENIX Conference on Operating Systems Design and Implementation, OSDI 2016, pp. 533–549. USENIX Association, Berkeley, CA, USA (2016)
41. Kaptchuk, G., Miers, I., Green, M.: Giving state to the stateless: augmenting trustworthy computation with ledgers. In: 26th Annual Network and Distributed System Security Symposium, NDSS 2019, San Diego, California, USA, 24–27 February 2019 (2019)
42. Kaptchuk, G., Miers, I., Green, M.: Giving state to the stateless: augmenting trustworthy computation with ledgers (2019)
43. Kiayias, A., Zhou, H.-S., Zikas, V.: Fair and robust multi-party computation using a global transaction ledger. In: Fischlin, M., Coron, J.-S. (eds.) EUROCRYPT

2016. LNCS, vol. 9666, pp. 705–734. Springer, Heidelberg (2016). https://doi.org/10.1007/978-3-662-49896-5_25
44. Kosba, A., Miller, A., Shi, E., Wen, Z., Papamanthou, C.: Hawk: the blockchain model of cryptography and privacy-preserving smart contracts. In: 2016 IEEE Symposium on Security and Privacy (SP), pp. 839–858. IEEE (2016)
45. Kumaresan, R., Bentov, I.: How to use bitcoin to incentivize correct computations. In: Proceedings of the 2014 ACM SIGSAC Conference on Computer and Communications Security, pp. 30–41. ACM 2014
46. Kumaresan, R., Vaikuntanathan, V., Vasudevan, P.N.: Improvements to secure computation with penalties. In: Proceedings of the 2016 ACM SIGSAC Conference on Computer and Communications Security, Vienna, Austria, 24–28 October 2016, pp. 406–417 (2016)
47. Marlinspike, M.: Private contact discovery for signal (2017)
48. Matetic, S., et al.: ROTE: rollback protection for trusted execution. In: 26th USENIX Security Symposium (USENIX Security 2017), pp. 1289–1306. USENIX Association, Vancouver, BC (2017)
49. Nakamoto, S.: Bitcoin: a peer-to-peer electronic cash system (2008)
50. Parno, B., Lorch, J.R., Douceur, J.R., Mickens, J., McCune, J.M.: Memoir: practical state continuity for protected modules. In: Proceedings of the 2011 IEEE Symposium on Security and Privacy, SP 2011, pp. 379–394. IEEE Computer Society, Washington, DC, USA (2011)
51. Pass, R., Shi, E., Tramèr, F.: Formal abstractions for attested execution secure processors. In: Coron, J.-S., Nielsen, J.B. (eds.) EUROCRYPT 2017. LNCS, vol. 10210, pp. 260–289. Springer, Cham (2017). https://doi.org/10.1007/978-3-319-56620-7_10
52. Pinkas, B.: Fair secure two-party computation. In: Biham, E. (ed.) EUROCRYPT 2003. LNCS, vol. 2656, pp. 87–105. Springer, Heidelberg (2003). https://doi.org/10.1007/3-540-39200-9_6
53. Priebe, C., Vaswani, K., Costa, M.: EnclaveDB: a secure database using SGX. In: EnclaveDB: A Secure Database Using SGX. IEEE (2018)
54. Rane, A., Lin, C., Tiwari, M.: Raccoon: closing digital side-channels through obfuscated execution. In: 24th USENIX Security Symposium (USENIX Security 2015), pp. 431–446. USENIX Association, Washington, D.C. (2015)
55. Schuster, F., et al.: VC3: trustworthy data analytics in the cloud using SGX. In: Proceedings of the IEEE Symposium on Security and Privacy (2015)
56. Shamis, A., et al.: CCF: a framework for building confidential verifiable replicated services. Technical report MSR-TR-2019-16, Microsoft (2019)
57. Shih, M.-W., Lee, S., Kim, T., Peinado, M.: T-SGX: eradicating controlled-channel attacks against enclave programs (2017)
58. Shinde, S., Chua, Z.L., Narayanan, V., Saxena, P.: Preventing page faults from telling your secrets. In: Proceedings of the 11th ACM on Asia Conference on Computer and Communications Security, ASIA CCS 2016, pp. 317–328. ACM, New York, NY, USA (2016)
59. Sinha, R., Christodorescu, M.: VeritasDB: high throughput key-value store with integrity. Cryptology ePrint Archive, Report 2018/251 (2018). https://eprint.iacr.org/2018/251
60. Sinha, R., Rajamani, S., Seshia, S.A.: A compiler and verifier for page access oblivious computation. In: Proceedings of the 2017 11th Joint Meeting on Foundations of Software Engineering, ESEC/FSE 2017, pp. 649–660. ACM, New York, NY, USA (2017)

61. Strackx, R., Piessens, F.: Ariadne: a minimal approach to state continuity. In: 25th USENIX Security Symposium (USENIX Security 2016), pp. 875–892. USENIX Association, Austin, TX (2016)
62. Wang, X., Ranellucci, S., Katz, J.: Global-scale secure multiparty computation. In: Proceedings of the 2017 ACM SIGSAC Conference on Computer and Communications Security, CCS 2017, pp. 39–56. ACM, New York, NY, USA (2017)
63. Yao, A.C.: Protocols for secure computations. In: Proceedings of the 23rd Annual Symposium on Foundations of Computer Science, pp. 160–164. IEEE Computer Society, Washington, DC, USA (1982)
64. Yao, A.C.C.: How to generate and exchange secrets. In: Proceedings of the 27th Annual Symposium on Foundations of Computer Science, SFCS 1986, pp. 162–167. IEEE Computer Society, Washington, DC, USA (1986)
65. Zhang, D., Askarov, A., Myers, A.C.: Predictive mitigation of timing channels in interactive systems. In: Proceedings of the 18th ACM Conference on Computer and Communications Security, CCS 2011, pp. 563–574. ACM, New York, NY, USA (2011)
66. Zheng, W., Dave, A., Beekman, J.G., Popa, R.A., Gonzalez, J.E., Stoica, I.: Opaque: an oblivious and encrypted distributed analytics platform. In: Proceedings of the 14th USENIX Conference on Networked Systems Design and Implementation, NSDI 2017, pp. 283–298. USENIX Association, Berkeley, CA (2017)

Improving Privacy of Anonymous Proof-of-Stake Protocols

Shichen Wu[1,2], Zhiying Song[1,2], Puwen Wei[1,2,3](✉), Peng Tang[1,2], and Quan Yuan[4]

[1] Key Laboratory of Cryptologic Technology and Information Security, Ministry of Education, Shandong University, Qingdao, China
{shichenw,szyyz}@mail.sdu.edu.cn

[2] School of Cyber Science and Technology, Shandong University, Qingdao, China
{pwei,tangpeng}@sdu.edu.cn

[3] Quancheng Laboratory, Jinan, China

[4] The University of Tokyo, Tokyo, Japan
yuanquan@g.ecc.u-tokyo.ac.jp

Abstract. The proof of stake (PoS) mechanism, which allows stakeholders to issue a block with a probability proportional to their wealth instead of computational power, is believed to be an energy-efficient alternative to the proof of work (PoW). The privacy concern of PoS, however, is more subtle than that of PoW. Recent research has shown that current anonymous PoS (APoS) protocols do not suffice to protect the stakeholder's identity and stake, and the loss of privacy is theoretically inherent for any (deterministic) PoS protocol that provides liveness guarantees. In this paper, we consider the concrete stake privacy of PoS when considering the limitations of attacks in practice. To quantify the concrete stake privacy of PoS, we introduce the notion of (T, δ, ϵ)-privacy. Our analysis of (T, δ, ϵ)-privacy on Cardano shows to what extent the stake privacy can be broken in practice, which also implies possible parameters setting of rational (T, δ, ϵ)-privacy for PoS in the real world. The data analysis of Cardano demonstrates that the (T, δ, ϵ)-privacy of current APoS is not satisfactory, mainly due to the deterministic leader election predicate in current PoS constructions. Inspired by the differential privacy technique, we propose an efficient non-deterministic leader election predicate, which can be used as a plugin to APoS protocols to protect stakes against frequency analysis. Based on our leader election predicate, we construct anonymous PoS with noise (APoS-N), which can offer better (T, δ, ϵ)-privacy than state-of-the-art works. Furthermore, we propose a method of proving the basic security properties of PoS in the noise setting, which can minimize the impact of the noise on the security threshold. This method can also be applied to the setting of PoS with variable stakes, which is of independent interest.

Keywords: Blockchain · Proof of stake · Privacy · Verifiable random function

J. Deng et al. (Eds.): CANS 2023, LNCS 14342, pp. 368–391, 2023.
https://doi.org/10.1007/978-981-99-7563-1_17

1 Introduction

Proof of work (PoW) based blockchain protocols, such as bitcoin [1], provide a novel way to achieve consensus among users in a permissionless setting. However, one of the main concerns of PoW is its high energy consumption. To address this issue, Proof of Stake (PoS) protocols have emerged as a promising, energy-efficient alternative. In PoS protocols, users participate in a process to elect a leader who will propose the next block. The probability of a user winning the election is proportional to their wealth or relative stakes at any given time. The rationale behind PoS is that users with higher relative stakes have more economic incentives to keep the PoS system running, and their stakes would lose value if the system fails. In the past decade, a series of solid works focused on the candidates of PoS protocols [2–10]. In particular, [5–10] have presented PoS with rigorous security proofs and formal security models.

Due to the public nature of the permissionless setting, privacy has become a significant concern for blockchain users. For PoW based blockchains, privacy-preserving solutions such as ZCash [11] and Monero [12] have been developed to provide privacy protection for transactions, including the payer/payee identities and transaction amounts. However, achieving privacy in PoS based blockchains is more challenging. This is because in PoS, privacy not only needs to be ensured for transactions and identities but also for the leaders' stakes. In particular, a PoS user (or stakeholder) needs to provide public verifiable proof of his leadership, which is verified based on his public key and stakes. Even if this proof is realized in a zero-knowledge manner, as in the PoW setting, the number of times an anonymous leader wins the election implies an approximation of his stakes. To protect the stakeholders' identities and stakes, anonymous PoS protocols have been proposed [10,13,14].

Nevertheless, [15] has pointed out that current anonymous PoS protocols do not suffice to protect the stakeholder's identity and stake, and has shown the theoretical impossibility of a PoS blockchain protocol that guarantees both liveness and anonymity. Specifically, they introduce the tagging attack, which can leverage the network delay to distinguish the target stakeholder from others. Once the adversary can launch the tagging attack for the target stakeholder "enough" times, they can reveal the target stakeholder's stake since the frequency of winning the election is determined by participants' stakes in PoS. Theoretically, such leakage is inherent for deterministic PoS protocols when considering the network delay. In fact, the security loss through frequency attack (or frequency analysis) is inherent for any deterministic cryptographic schemes. To mitigate the tagging attack, [15] provides possible countermeasures, such as sanitization protocol and reliable broadcast mechanisms, which aim to ensure that all parties have the same view. These strategies, however, rely on additional assumptions on the network and have limitations on either privacy or practicality and scalability. As mentioned in [15], new technologies are needed to protect stakeholders' privacy against any potential network adversary.

It is worth noting that network attacks in the real world have limitations, as it takes time for an adversary to launch an attack, and the attack is not always successful. For instance, the success probability of eclipse attacks [16] is about 84%, and the attack may be stopped once the target user restarts the server. That means that the adversary of tagging attack may not be able to collect enough information to determine the target stakeholder's stake due to the limited duration of the attack. Therefore, it is natural to question the extent to which the frequency attacks (including tagging attack) can break the stake privacy of current anonymous PoS protocols and how to enhance the stake privacy of anonymous PoS against frequency attacks while preserving efficiency and scalability.

Our Contributions. In this work, we answer this question by proposing an effective method to enhance the privacy of stakes of anonymous PoS protocols. To that end, we first analyze the success probability of estimating the target stakeholder's stake using frequency attacks, such as repeated (reverse) tagging attacks or any attacks that exploit frequency analysis. We note that the estimation accuracy is heavily influenced by the number of attacks and the success probability of leader election in PoS system. The small number of attacks and success probability of leader election could lead to large estimation errors due to the inherent limitation of statistical methods. We then introduce the notion of (T, δ, ϵ)-privacy to quantify the concrete stake privacy of PoS. In particular, we analyze the (T, δ, ϵ)-privacy of Cardano, which is one of the largest PoS systems by market capitalization. Our results show that for the stake pools of Cardano with small relative stake, say $\leq 0.05\%$, the (T, δ, ϵ)-privacy it can achieve is $T = 432000$ slots, $\delta = 10\%$ and $\epsilon = 60.95\%$. That is, if the attack duration is restricted in one epoch (432000 slots), the probability that the adversary can approximate the target stake pool's stake with an error $\delta = 10\%$ is as high as 60.95%.

Furthermore, we find that the crux of the stake estimation by frequency analysis is the deterministic relation between the stakeholder's stake and his success probability of leader election. Inspired by the differential privacy technique [17,18], we propose an efficient non-deterministic leader election function that can randomize this relation by adding noise with a particular distribution such that the resulting stake estimation error can be increased significantly. Based on our noisy leader election function, we provide an anonymous PoS protocol with noise (APoS-N), which can enhance the stake privacy while preserving the stakeholders' long-term benefits. The main idea is to add "random" noise to the stakeholders' stakes, and the leader election function is evaluated using the noisy stake, where the expectation of the noise distribution is 0. Following Ganesh et al.'s framework [13] of constructing anonymous PoS, we can construct APoS-N by implementing the underlying leader election function with our noisy version. Due to the interference of the noise, it is difficult for the adversary to get the target stakeholder's accurate stake in APoS-N, resulting in better (T, δ, ϵ)-privacy being achieved. In addition, the privacy requirements defined by [13] are preserved in our APoS-N, as it follows the framework of [13].

The main challenge, however, is that the basic security properties of the underlying PoS blockchain, i.e., common prefix, chain growth and chain quality, may not hold due to the random noise. For instance, the noisy stakes of either all stakeholders or the adversary may be larger than the original one, which means the original threshold of adversarial relative stakes, say 1/2, could be broken in APoS-N. To address this problem, we improve the security analysis in [7,8], called characteristic string, to adapt to our noise setting. This improvement can minimize the impact of the noise on the security threshold. Our results show that the basic security properties of PoS can still be preserved in APoS-N if the noise is upper-bounded properly. It is worth noting that our proof can be applied to the setting of PoS with variable stakes, such as when the total active stakes of some slots are less than expected due to the absent stakeholders. This result is of independent interest.

Related Work. Our work is independent of another work by Wang et al. [19]. Their work extends the tagging attack model of [15] to the randomized PoS protocol and presents a practical stake inference attack with sublinear complexity. In our work, the analysis of frequency attack considers the concrete cost and accuracy of stake estimation, which are applicable to any attacks that rely on sampling frequency. Wang et al. [19] also propose a private PoS protocol using differential privacy techniques. However, we note that their protocol has security flaws. Specifically, we present an attack that allows the adversary to amplify his noisy stakes and gain more profits than required, breaking chain quality, which is one of the fundamental security requirements of the underlying PoS [8]. Even worse, this also implies the break of safety discussed in [8]. The presence of security flaws in Wang et al.'s approach is due to a limitation of the UC framework, which makes it difficult to capture all desired security requirements in the ideal functionality explicitly. In contrast, our protocol carefully controls the noisy stakes to preserve the fundamental security requirements of PoS, including common prefix, chain growth and chain quality. By explicitly considering these requirements, our protocol can provide stronger security guarantees than the approach used by Wang et al. [19].

2 Preliminaries

Notations. Let $\mathbb{N}$ denote the set of all natural numbers. Let $B(n, p)$ denote the binomial distribution with parameters n and p, where n denotes the total number of independent trials and p denotes the success probability of each trial. $Be(a, b)$ denotes the beta distribution with parameters a and b. $U(a, b)$ represents the uniform distribution on the interval $[a, b]$. We write $X \sim D$ to denote the random variable X following the distribution D.

Ouroboros Praos. We briefly recall *Ouroboros Praos* [8] and its anonymous version [13], which are typical PoS protocols with rigorous security proofs.

Ouroboros Praos works as follows: Suppose that n stakeholders $U_1, \ldots, U_n$ interact throughout the protocol. The stakeholders' initial stakes and related public keys, say $\{(stk_i, pk_i)\}_{i=1}^{n}$, are hardcoded into the genesis block. Let STK denote the total stakes of the PoS system. During the execution, the time is divided into discrete units called slots, and a set of n_e adjacent slots is called an epoch. Stakeholders participate in the leader election protocol in each slot to decide who is eligible to issue a block. In the process of leader election, each stakeholder locally evaluates a special verifiable random function (VRF) on the current slot and a nonce that is determined for an epoch. Let (y, π) denote the output of VRF, where y is pseudorandom and π is the proof. If y is less than a function of their stakes, then that stakeholder wins the election and can generate a new block. The probability of winning an election is proportional to the stakeholder's relative stake. More specifically, the leader election process can be captured by *Lottery Protocol*$^{\mathcal{E},LE}$ [13], where $\mathcal{E}$ is the set of the allowed entry parameters. The core of *Lottery Protocol*$^{\mathcal{E},LE}$ is a leader election predicate $LE(\cdot,\cdot)$. A stakeholder wins an election in a slot sl iff his $LE(stk, y) = 1$, where stk is the stakeholder's stake. The LE predicate has the following form:

$$LE(stk, y) = \begin{cases} 1, & \text{if } y < 2^{\ell_\alpha} \cdot (1 - (1-f)^{\frac{stk_i}{STK}}) \\ 0, & \text{otherwise.} \end{cases}$$

$\frac{stk_i}{STK}$ is the stakeholder's relative stake. ℓ_α denotes the output length of the VRF and f is called the active slots coefficient, which is the probability that a hypothetical party with 100% relative stake would be elected leader in a slot. A critical property of LE is that the probability of a stakeholder becoming a slot leader depends on his stake, whether this stakeholder acts as a single party or splits his stake among several virtual parties. Once a leader proposes a new block, all the stakeholders can check the validity of the block using the leader's public information, say stake, public key, π, etc., and update their local state by following the longest chain rule, which enables the honest users to converge to a unique view.

Anonymous PoS protocols (APoS) [10,13] focus on establishing a privacy-preserving election process that can protect the leader's identity and stakes. In order to hide the stakes, the stakeholders in APoS need to generate commitments to their stakes. Using these commitments and the list of all stakeholders' identities (ID), the stakeholder can execute *Lottery Protocol*$^{\mathcal{E},LE}$ in a zero-knowledge manner, which means all the users can check the validity of the leader election (or the block) without knowing the leader's identity and stake.

The related *Lottery Protocol*$^{\mathcal{E}}$ are described assuming hybrid access to ideal functionalities such as $\mathcal{F}_{Init}^{Com}$, $\mathcal{F}_{crs}$, $\mathcal{F}_{VRF}^{Com}$ and $\mathcal{F}_{ABC}^{\Delta}$. The functionality $\mathcal{F}_{Init}^{Com}$ initially contains a list of stakeholder's ID and their stakes. It computes the commitments to each stakeholder's stake and generates the corresponding public/secret key pairs. The functionality $\mathcal{F}_{crs}$ provides the common reference string for zero-knowledge proofs. To hide the identity of the sender, anonymous PoS protocols [10,13] need to rely on an ideal anonymous broadcast channel, which is captured by the functionality $\mathcal{F}_{ABC}^{\Delta}$. It takes as input a message m from a user and adds m to all users' buffers, where the adversary can influence the buffer of the user by introducing bounded delays. In particular, the adversary is allowed to send anonymous messages to specific users and impose an upper bound delay Δ on specific messages. Stakeholders use the functionality $\mathcal{F}_{VRF}^{Com}$ to generate the randomness for the leader election. For each stakeholder, $\mathcal{F}_{VRF}^{Com}$ generates a unique key as a private identity for accessing $\mathcal{F}_{VRF}^{Com}$ and a commitment to randomness y, which the stakeholder uses for the leader election. The commitment is used by users to check the validity of the claimed $\mathcal{F}_{VRF}^{Com}$ evaluation. More details of the above functionalities are shown in Appendix D.

Threat Model. The threat model in our paper is similar to that of [8], where the adversary $\mathcal{A}$'s capabilities are defined in the following three aspects:
Corruption: $\mathcal{A}$ is able to corrupt a set of stakeholders adaptively without delay and control these corrupted stakeholders to take any actions beyond the protocol, such as withholding blocks or publishing multiple blocks when they are leaders. In each slot, the fraction of the stake controlled by $\mathcal{A}$ cannot be greater than 50%, otherwise, the security of the PoS protocol can be broken directly.
Propagation: $\mathcal{A}$ can arbitrarily manipulate the propagation of honest messages within Δ slots. Specifically, for any honest message m sent in slot i, the adversary $\mathcal{A}$ can choose the time when each honest stakeholder receives m, but all honest must have received m at the end of slot $i + \Delta$. Notice that the messages sent by honest stakeholders could be new blocks, transactions, or other information.
Limitation: $\mathcal{A}$ has limited computing power so that it cannot violate the security properties of any underlying cryptographic component. For corruption and propagation, this means that the adversary cannot make the probability of corrupted stakeholders being elected leader exceed the adversary's stake proportion, nor can it tamper with honest messages, which requires $\mathcal{A}$ to break the security of the underlying VRF or digital signatures.

Security Requirements. The basic security properties of PoS follow that of [7]. A PoS protocol Π that implements a robust transaction ledger should satisfy the persistence and liveness. [20,21] demonstrate that persistence and liveness can be derived from the following three properties if the protocol Π uses the blockchain data structure to export the ledger.

- Common Prefix (CP) with parameters $k \in \mathbb{N}$. The chains C_1, C_2 possessed by two honest parties at the onset of the slots $sl_1 < sl_2$ are such that $C_1^{\neg k} \preceq C_2$, where $C_1^{\neg k}$ denotes the chain obtained by removing the last k blocks from C_1, and $\preceq$ denotes the prefix relation.
- Chain Quality (CQ) with parameters $\mu \in (0, 1]$ and $k \in \mathbb{N}$. Consider any portion of the length at least k of the chain possessed by an honest party at the onset of a slot, the ratio of blocks originating from the adversary is at most $1 - \mu$, where μ is the chain quality coefficient.
- Chain Growth (CG) with parameters $\tau \in (0, 1]$ and $s \in \mathbb{N}$. Consider the chains C_1 and C_2 possessed by two honest parties at the onset of two slots sl_1, sl_2

with sl_2 at least s slots ahead of sl_1. Then it holds that $len(C_2) - len(C_1) \geq \tau \cdot s$, where τ is the speed coefficient and $len(C_i)$ denotes the length of the chain C_i.

On the privacy of anonymous PoS, [13] introduces the private lottery functionality $\mathcal{F}_{Lottery}^{\mathcal{E},LE}$ to capture the privacy requirements of anonymous PoS in the universal composition (UC) setting. Loosely speaking, $\mathcal{F}_{Lottery}^{\mathcal{E},LE}$ can be considered as an ideal-world PoS protocol that can hide the leader's identity and stake. For more information of $\mathcal{F}_{Lottery}^{\mathcal{E},LE}$, we refer to [13]. We emphasize that the privacy defined by $\mathcal{F}_{Lottery}^{\mathcal{E},LE}$ does not rule out the possibility of privacy leakage by tagging attack described below.

3 Attack on Anonymous PoS and Its Limitations

In this section, we introduce frequency attack, which abstracts any attacks (including tagging attack) that estimate the target stakeholder's stake using frequency analysis. Then, we analyze the accuracy of the stake estimation and show its limitations in practice.

3.1 Frequency Attacks Against Stake Privacy

The frequency attack against stake privacy is an attack that may use various methods to determine the number of blocks proposed by the target stakeholder within a specific time period and then uses the frequency of proposed blocks to estimate the stakeholder's stake. The adversary can monitor either the physical or network layer to obtain the block frequency. A typical example of frequency attacks is the tagging attack [15], which can manipulate the targeted stakeholder's network delays to create a different view from others, enabling the adversary to distinguish blocks proposed by the targeted stakeholder and associate them with their stake. More precisely, the adversary creates a transaction tx_Δ for the purpose of tagging the targeted stakeholder P. By controlling the network delay, the adversary is capable of ensuring that stakeholder P receives tx_Δ at time t, while other stakeholders receive it after time $t + \Delta$. Notice that if a stakeholder succeeds in winning an election, then it adds all the transactions in his current view to the new block. For any block B that is produced between t and $t + \Delta$, the adversary is able to check whether tx_Δ is in B even if it can achieve privacy-preserving since the adversary is the owner of tx_Δ. As no one has tx_Δ before $t + \Delta$ except P, tx_Δ in B indicates that B is generated by P. By repetitively executing this attack, the adversary can determine the frequency of blocks proposed by P during a specific period. Then, the frequency can be exploited to uncover the relative stake of P, thereby compromising the stake privacy of the PoS system.

Theoretically, the relative stake of P can be approximated by statistical analysis, e.g., point estimation or interval estimation of the probability of success in a binomial distribution. Note that all the statistical methods have their limitations on the accuracy of the approximation due to the target probabilistic distributions and the number of samples. We show the accuracy of interval estimation, which is crucial to the stake privacy of anonymous PoS in practice. Interval estimation is an effective statistical method to estimate an interval of possible values of the unknown population parameters. For the stake estimation of PoS, which follows the binomial distribution with a small success probability, we adopt the Jeffreys interval rather than the standard interval in order to reduce the severity of the chaotic behavior of the confidence interval's coverage probability [22].

To illustrate the interval estimation for stakes, consider the following case. Suppose that the total number of slots during the attack is C and the target stakeholder's stake is fixed. Let $\mathsf{suc}[C, t]$ denote the event that t blocks proposed by P among C slots are observed by the adversary. Let p denote the relative stake of P. We use X to indicate whether P wins the election in a slot, where $X = 1$ if P wins the election. Otherwise, $X = 0$. We use $\Phi(\cdot)$ to denote the function which takes as inputs a stakeholder's relative stake and outputs the corresponding probability that he can win the election in a slot. The probability of P winning an election is $\Phi(p)$[1]. Since $\Phi(\cdot)$ is usually public and deterministic and p can be easily obtained given $\Phi(p)$, we focus on the estimation of $\Phi(p)$ to simplify our illustration. So X follows the Bernoulli distribution with $\Pr[X = 1] = \Phi(p)$ and t follows the binomial distribution with parameters C and $\Phi(p)$, i.e., $t \sim B(C, \Phi(p))$.

To estimate the unknown $\Phi(p)$, we apply the Jeffreys interval, which is the Bayesian confidence interval obtained using the non-informative Jeffreys prior of the binomial distribution $\Phi(p)$. The Jeffreys prior is a Beta distribution with parameters $(1/2, 1/2)$. The posterior distribution is derived from $\mathsf{suc}[C, t]$, which follows the Beta distribution $Be(t+1/2, C-t+1/2)$. The $100(1-\psi)\%$ equal-tailed Bayesian interval is $[Q(\psi/2; t+1/2, C-t+1/2), Q(1-\psi/2; t+1/2, C-t+1/2)]$, where Q is the quantile function of $Be(t + 1/2, C - t + 1/2)$.

3.2 Interval Estimation for Stakes in Practice

Following the above method, we estimate the stakes of Cardano [23] to show the accuracy of interval estimation in practice. We choose 100 stake pools with total relative stake $p \approx 26.732\%$ as the target stakeholder P with $\Phi(p) = \Pr[X = 1] \approx 1.362\%$. By analyzing the data of two different periods in epoch 325, which are $\mathsf{suc}[3000, 66]$ (1 h) and $\mathsf{suc}[345600, 4994]$ (96 h), we get the Jeffreys intervals for $\Phi(p)$, respectively. Figure 1 shows the estimation of $\Phi(p)$ using Jeffreys intervals, where the red line and the blue line represent the probability density functions of $\Phi(p)$ using $\mathsf{suc}[3000, 66]$ (1 h) and $\mathsf{suc}[345600, 4994]$ (96 h), respectively. When considering confidence level 95%, the Jeffreys intervals of the red line is [0.01721, 0.02773] with interval length 0.01052. For the blue line, the Jeffreys interval is [0.01406 0.01486] with interval length of 0.0008. So far, it follows the intuition that a large number of blocks that knew by the adversary can improve the

[1] In Ouroboros, the probability of P winning an election is defined by $\Phi(p) = 1 - (1 - f)^p$, which is close to $p \cdot f$.

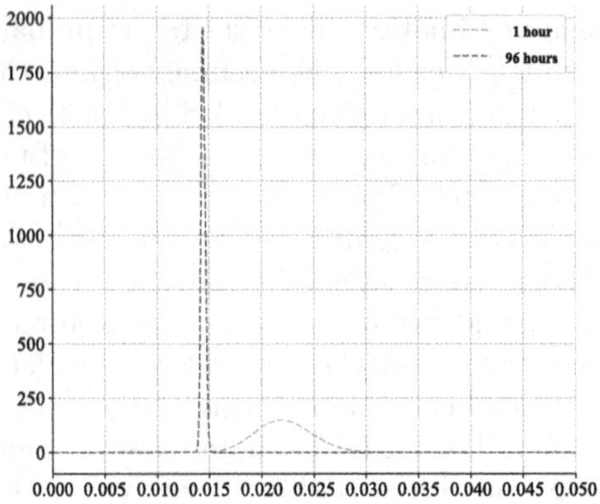

Fig. 1. Probability density function of $\Phi(p)$. (Color figure online)

estimation accuracy for p. However, we stress that the relative stake p of a stake pool in Cardano is only about 0.001%–0.35% and the corresponding $\phi(0.01\%)$–$\phi(0.35\%)$ is (0.000513%–0.0179%). That means even interval length 0.0008 is too large to distinguish stakeholders' $\Phi(p)$ in Cardano. So frequency attack and Jeffreys intervals is not accurate enough to distinguish most stakeholders' stake in Cardano when the attack duration is "short", say 96 h (345600 slots).

Furthermore, more trials do not necessarily imply a more accurate estimation. [22,24] reveal the degree of severity of the chaotic oscillation behavior of many intervals' coverage probability. Such chaotic oscillation behavior is more obvious for the binomial distribution with relatively small p. For instance, for a binomial distribution $B(C, p)$ with $p = 0.005$ [22], the coverage probability of the 95% confidence interval increases monotonically in C until $C = 591$ to 0.945, and drops to 0.792 when $C = 592$.

The above limitations of statistical analysis show the possibility of protecting the stakes of anonymous PoS in practice.

4 Privacy of PoS Against Frequency Attack

In this section, we introduce the notion of (T, δ, ϵ)-privacy to capture the concrete stake privacy of PoS and analyze the (T, δ, ϵ)-privacy of Cardano.

4.1 (T, δ, ϵ)-Privacy

In theory, if the adversary has an infinite amount of time to acquire the frequency of proposed blocks, they could precisely ascertain the stake of any stakeholder. However, in practice, the attack time for the adversary to gather information about the frequency of proposed blocks is usually limited. To conduct a more comprehensive evaluation of the costs and effects of frequency attacks in real-world scenarios, we need to consider the attack time. Let T denote the number of slots that an adversary can perform frequency attack. Hence, for a stakeholder with a relative stake p, the expected number of blocks generated by it during T slots is $T \cdot \Phi(p)$. We capture the concrete stake privacy of a PoS protocol Π by the following experiment, called $\mathsf{Exp}_{\Pi,\delta}^{\mathcal{A}}$.

- The challenger runs the protocol Π among n stakeholders.
- The adversary $\mathcal{A}$ chooses the target stakeholder (or stakeholders) S to launch the frequency attack, where the relative stake of S is p. Suppose that the frequency attack can last for T slots.
- Finally, $\mathcal{A}$ outputs X, which denotes the number of "tagged" and valid blocks generated by S.

We say the adversary $\mathcal{A}$ wins the experiment $\mathsf{Exp}_{\Pi,\delta}^{\mathcal{A}}$ if $(1-\delta) \cdot T \cdot \Phi(p) \leq X \leq (1+\delta) \cdot T \cdot \Phi(p)$, where $\delta \in (0,1)$. Let $\mathsf{Exp}_{\Pi,\delta}^{\mathcal{A}}(1^\lambda) = 1$ denote the event that $\mathcal{A}$ wins, where λ denotes the security parameter.

Definition 1. *(T, δ, ϵ)-privacy: A PoS protocol Π is (T, δ, ϵ)-privacy for a stakeholder with relative p if for any PPT adversary $\mathcal{A}$, $\Pr[\mathsf{Exp}_{\Pi,\delta}^{\mathcal{A}}(1^\lambda) = 1] \leq \epsilon$, where $0 < \epsilon < 1$ and δ is called the privacy error.*

Note that (T, δ, ϵ)-privacy captures to what extent the stake privacy of a PoS protocol can achieve no matter which statistical tool or strategies the adversary would use. Consider the case of Ouroboros Praos, we have $X \sim B(T, \Phi(p))$ and

$$\Pr[\mathsf{Exp}_{\Pi,\delta}^{\mathcal{A}}(1^\lambda) = 1] = \sum_{i=\lfloor(1-\delta)T\Phi(p)\rfloor}^{\lfloor(1+\delta)T\Phi(p)\rfloor} \Pr[X = i] \approx 60.95\%, \tag{1}$$

where the target stakeholder's relative stake $p = 0.3\%$ and $T = 432000$ (the number of slots in an epoch). In fact, due to the law of large numbers, typical PoS protocols usually cannot achieve (T, δ, ϵ)-privacy when T is large enough. Specifically, when $T \rightarrow \infty$ and Φ is deterministic, $\Pr[(1-\delta)T\Phi(p) \leq X \leq (1+\delta)T\Phi(p)] \rightarrow 1$. As shown in the previous section, when T and p are small, the accuracy of the estimation for target stakes is heavily influenced by the limitation of the underlying statistical analysis. So (T, δ, ϵ)-privacy depends on the duration of frequency attacks and the actual probability of the target stakeholder proposing a block.

4.2 (T, δ, ϵ)-Privacy in Practice

To measure the impact of frequency attacks on (T, δ, ϵ)-privacy in practice, we make a thorough analysis of the data of Cardano. Note that the underlying PoS protocol of Cardano is Ouroboros, which is also the core of anonymous PoS protocols [10,13]. While employing privacy-preserving techniques, the probability of stakeholder winning an election in [10,13] does not change. Hence, the block data of Cardano can reflect (T, δ, ϵ)-privacy of [10,13] in practice, although Cardano does not consider anonymity. We assume that the adversary can successfully find all the blocks generated by the target stakeholder during the attack. That is, X is the number of the blocks generated by the target stakeholder during the attack.

We investigate the transactions of Cardano for two months and focus on 600 pools, denoted by $\mathcal{S}_{total}$, which have more than 90% stakes of the entire system. To evaluate the error of frequency attack for stake estimation, we define the frequency attack error as $R = \left|1 - \frac{X}{T\Phi(p)}\right|$. Due to Definition 1, δ is the upper bound of R to break (T, δ, ϵ)-privacy.

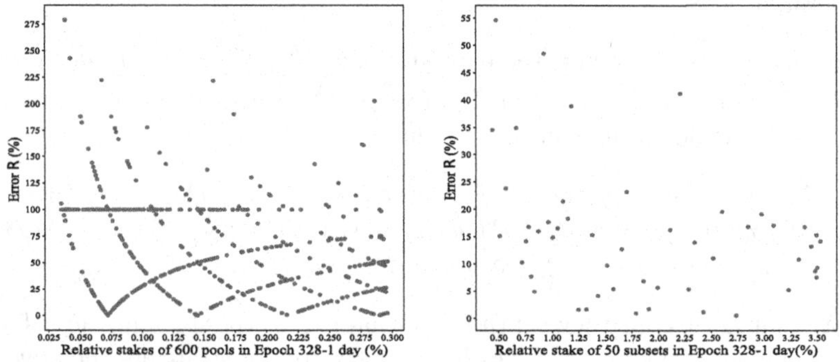

Fig. 2. Each blue dot represents a pool or a subset of pools where the x-coordinate denotes its relative stake and the y-coordinate denotes the corresponding frequency attack error during the first day of epoch 328. In the right figure, 600 pools are divided into 50 subsets, where each blue dot represents a subset of 12 pools. (Color figure online)

Figure 2 (left) shows the relation between each pool in $\mathcal{S}_{total}$ and its corresponding frequency attack error R in the first 24 h of epoch 328. In the horizontal axis, all the pools in $\mathcal{S}_{total}$ are sorted in ascending order of their relative stakes. For instance, there are stake pools with relative stake 0.3%, which have error 100.1%, 57.8% and 1.58%, respectively. By "merging" multiple pools in different ways, we can simulate multiple frequency attacks on different pools using the same transaction data. More precisely, 600 pools are randomly divided into subsets of equal size. In Fig. 2 (right), 600 pools are divided into 50 subsets, each of which has 12 pools. The horizontal coordinate and the vertical coordinate denote the total relative stake and the frequency attack error R of a subset, respectively. As illustrated in Fig. 2, the larger the relative stake, the less the frequency attack error is. In particular, all the subsets with relative stake about 3.5% in Fig. 2 (right) has error less than 20%, while most pools with relative stake about 0.05% in Fig. 2 (left) has error larger than 50%.

One may consider $\delta = 10\%$, since the difference of relative stake of most adjacent pools on the horizontal axis of Fig. 2 (left) is about 10%. So it is possible for pools with relative stake less than 0.3% to preserve (T, δ, ϵ)-privacy if $T =$ 432000 slots, $\delta = 10\%$ and $\epsilon = 60.95\%$.

Table 1. Proportion of pools (subsets of pools) such that $R > \delta$.

Epoch 328		Proportion s.t. $R > \delta$			
		$\delta = 0.1$	$\delta = 0.2$	$\delta = 0.3$	$\delta = 0.4$
24 h	600sets	86.5%	78.7%	66.2%	60.3%
	200sets	78.5%	63.5%	43.5%	32.0%
	100sets	72.0%	49.0%	32.0%	18.0%
	50sets	64.0%	18.0%	12.0%	6.0%
48 h	600sets	78.5%	60.3%	46.7%	32.8%
	200sets	66.0%	39.0%	18.5%	8.0%
	100sets	55.0%	23.0%	9.0%	1.0%
	50sets	36.0%	6.0%	4.0%	0%
72 h	600sets	74.8%	51.0%	31.8%	19.2%
	200sets	57.5%	26.5%	9.5%	3.0%
	100sets	35.0%	11.0%	3.0%	0%
	50sets	18.0%	2.0%	0%	0%
96 h	600sets	64.2%	38.2%	19.5%	9.8%
	200sets	48.5%	16.5%	4.5%	1.0%
	100sets	34.0%	7.0%	0%	0%
	50sets	12.0%	0%	0%	0%

Intuitively, the frequency attack error will be decreased when the adversary can extend the duration of frequency attack. Table 1 shows the effect of extending the duration of frequency attack for epoch 328. In Table 1, we show how the proportion of pools (or sets of pools) with $R > \delta$ changes over time in epoch 328. "200sets (resp. 100sets, 50sets)" means that we choose 3 (resp. 6, 12) pools as a set. Table 1 shows that the proportion of the subsets with $R > 0.1$ in the first 24 h of epoch 328 is greater than 50%, while the proportion of the subsets with $R > 0.4$ drops to about 0% by the first 96 h of epoch 328.

Similar phenomena occur in different epochs (shown in Table 2 in Appendix C), where the proportion such that $R > 0.1$ in the first 24 h of each epoch is greater than 83%. To sum up, comparing with larger relative stakes, say 2%–3%, smaller relative stakes, say 0.03%–0.3%, can dramatically reduce the accuracy of stake estimation in a short period of time, say 1 day. In addition, stakes in Cardano has "dense" distribution, where there are many pools with similar relative stakes. The above results implies the possibility for anonymous PoS protocols in practice to achieve (T, δ, ϵ)-privacy when considering $\delta = 0.1$–0.2.

As shown above, the corresponding ϵ of stakeholder with relative stake 0.3% can reach 60.95% in the first day of an epoch, which is too high for the privacy in practice. Next, we show how to reduce ϵ further.

5 Anonymous Proof-of-Stake with Noise

In this section, we construct the anonymous PoS with noise (APoS-N). In particular, we propose a non-deterministic leader election function, which can be used as a plug-in for PoS based blockchain to enhance stake privacy.

5.1 Adding Noise to Anonymous PoS

As shown in frequency attack, the adversary may determine the target stakeholder's stake by the frequency of "tagged" blocks, i.e., the frequency of $LE(stk, y) = 1$ for the target stakeholder. In order to hide the stakeholders' stake, we change the frequency of $LE(stk, y) = 1$ during a short period by adding noise to the stake stk. The main idea of our techniques is similar to differential privacy [17,18], which can preserve the data's privacy and statistical validity by adding noise with a particular distribution.

More specifically, we modify LE such that the probability of a stakeholder winning election depends on his "noisy" stake. The noise is generated by a noise function $\gamma(\cdot)$, which takes as input random value z and outputs a value following a particular distribution $\mathcal{D}$. The expectation of distribution $\mathcal{D}$ should be 0, e.g., the uniform distribution with expectation 0, so that the frequency of a stakeholder becoming a leader over the long term would not be changed. That means, the frequency of a stakeholder becoming a leader during a long period of time is still proportional to his stake, but during a short period of time, it is hard to estimate the probability of a stakeholder becoming a leader due to the noise. Our modified leader election predicate, called LE^*, is described as follows.

$$LE^*(stk; \eta) = \begin{cases} 1, \text{if } y < 2^{\ell_\alpha} \cdot (1 - (1 - f)^{\frac{stk \cdot (1+\gamma(z))}{STK}}) \\ 0, \text{otherwise} \end{cases}$$

where $\eta = y||z$ is generated by querying $\mathcal{F}_{VRF}^{Com}$.

Comparing with the definition of $\mathcal{F}_{VRF}^{Com}$ in [13], we make slight modifications that the randomness η returned by $\mathcal{F}_{VRF}^{Com}$ is divided into two parts, i.e., $\eta = y||z$, where y is the same as that of [13], and z is used for the noise function $\gamma(\cdot)$. Formal description of our $\mathcal{F}_{VRF}^{Com}$ is given below, where Com denotes the commitment scheme.

Functionality $\mathcal{F}_{VRF}^{Com}$

Key Generation

Upon input (KeyGen,sid) from a stakeholder uid, generate a unique key *vid* and set $U(vid) = uid$. Return (KeyGen, *sid*, *vid*) to *uid*.

VRF Evaluation

Upon receiving a request (Eval, *sid*, *vid*, *m*) from stakeholder *uid*, check whether $U(vid) \stackrel{?}{=} uid$. If not, ignore the request.

1. If $T(vid, m)$ is undefined, pick random η, r from $\{0,1\}^{\ell_{VRF}}$, where $\eta = y||z$.
2. Set $T(vid, m) = (\eta,\ Com(\eta; r),\ r)$.
3. Return (Evaluated, $sid, T(vid, m)$) to stakeholder *uid*.

VRF Verification

Upon receiving (Verify, sid, m, c) from some user, set $b = 1$ if there exists a *vid* such that $T(vid, m) = (\eta, c, r)$ for some η and r. Otherwise, set $b = 0$. Output (Verified, sid, m, c, b) to the user.

When instantiated with concrete VRF, the output of the corresponding VRF is longer than that of [13]. Note that $(1-(1-f)^{\frac{stk\cdot(1+\gamma(z))}{STK}}) \approx f \cdot (\frac{stk\cdot(1+\gamma(z))}{STK})$ still holds since $f \cdot (\frac{stk\cdot(1+\gamma(z))}{STK}) << 1$ if the slot and f is small enough.

Following the framework of [13], we present the modified *Lottery* $Protocol^{\mathcal{E},LE^*}$ below, where the main difference is that we use the noisy version of leader election predicate LE^*. Each stakeholder, say U, runs the modified *Lottery* $Protocol^{\mathcal{E},LE^*}$ to join the leader election. More details of related ideal functionalities $\mathcal{F}_{Init}^{Com}$, $\mathcal{F}_{crs}$, and $\mathcal{F}_{\Delta}^{ABC}$ are shown in Appendix D.

Lottery $Protocol^{\mathcal{E},LE^*}$

Suppose the underlying signature scheme consists of (SIG.keygen, SIG.sign, SIG.vrfy), which denote the key generation algorithm, the signing algorithm and the verification algorithm, respectively.

Initialzation

- Send (GetList, *sid*) to $\mathcal{F}_{Init}^{Com}$ to get the list $\mathcal{L}$ of stakeholders with committed stake and the corresponding signature verification key.
- Send (Setup, *sid*) to $\mathcal{F}_{crs}$ to get the common reference string crs for zero-knowledge proofs.
- If U is a stakeholder, send (Get-private-Data, *sid*) to $\mathcal{F}_{Init}^{Com}$ to get $\alpha_{uid}, r_{\alpha,uid}, sk_{uid}$, and send (KeyGen, *sid*) to $\mathcal{F}_{VRF}^{Com}$ to get *vid*. Initialize $V(\cdot) = \{\phi\}$.

Lottery and Publishing

- As a stakeholder upon receiving (Lottery, *sid*, *e*):

1. Ignore the request if e is not in $\mathcal{E}$, which is the set of allowed entry parameters.
2. If $V(e)$ is undefined, send (Eval, sid, vid, e) to $\mathcal{F}_{VRF}^{Com}$ and get (Evaluated, $sid, (\eta, c, r)$). Compute $b = LE^*(\alpha_{uid}, \eta)$, and set $V(e) = (b, \eta, c, r)$.
3. Return (Lottery, sid, e, b) where $V(e) = (b, \eta, c, r)$.

- As a stakeholder upon receiving (Send, sid, e, m)
  1. Ignore the request if $V(e) = (0, \cdots)$ or is undefined.
  2. If there exists $(1, \eta, c, r)$ such that $V(e) = (1, \eta, c, r)$,
     (a) Generate a signature σ on (e, m) under vk_{uid}.
     (b) Generate a zero-knowledge proof π_{zk} using crs for the following statement.

$$\begin{aligned}&\{(\alpha_{uid}, r_{\alpha,uid}, vk_{uid}, sk_{uid}, c_{\alpha,uid}, \sigma, \eta, r):\\&\mathsf{SIG.vrfy}_{vk_{uid}}((e,m),\sigma) = 1 \wedge LE^*(\alpha_{uid}, \eta) = 1\\&\wedge vk_{uid} = \mathsf{SIG.keygen}(sk_{uid}) \wedge c = Com(\eta; r)\\&\wedge c_{\alpha,uid} = Com(\alpha_{uid}; r_{\alpha,uid}) \wedge (c_{\alpha,uid}, vk_{uid}) \in \mathcal{L}\}\end{aligned}$$

  3. Send (Send, sid, (e, m, c, π_{zk})) to $\mathcal{F}_{ABC}^{\Delta}$.
- Upon receving (Fetch-New,sid)
  1. Send (Receive,sid) to $\mathcal{F}_{ABC}^{\Delta}$ and get $\vec{m}$.
  2. For each $(e, m, c, \pi_{zk}) \in \vec{m}$, do :
     (a) Check that $e \in \mathcal{E}$.
     (b) Send (Verify, sid, e, c) to $\mathcal{F}_{VRF}^{Com}$, and get the response (Verified, sid, e, c, b). Check that $b = 1$.
     (c) Check the validity of π_{zk}.
     (d) If all the above hold, add (e, m, c, π_{zk}) to $\vec{o}$
  3. Output (Feach-New, $sid, \vec{o}$).

To implement VRF Evaluation of $\mathcal{F}_{VRF}^{Com}$, [13] proposed the anonymous VRF (AVRF), which consists of (AVRF.gen, Update, AVRF.prov, AVRF.vrfy), in order to hide the identity of the stakeholder. Comparing with VRF, the special property of AVRF is that the stakeholder updates his public key without changing the corresponding private key, and two evaluations on different messages under the same secret key cannot be linked to a public key, while other properties of VRF can still be preserved. More details of the construction of AVRF are shown in Appendix B.

In our setting, AVRF with key k takes as input the public key pk and the slot sl and outputs the randomness η and the proof π_{AVRF}. For convenience, let $F_k(sl)$ denote randomness output by AVRF with k and slot sl. That is, $F_k(sl) = \eta$. To ensure the validity of an election, it remains to prove that the corresponding AVRF key is in the list $\mathcal{L}$ in a zero-knowledge manner. The overall ZK proof π_{zk} for APoS-N is similar to that of [13] except that we need to consider the ZK poofs for the consistency of the noise function $\gamma(z)$. More details of π_{zk} are shown in the full version of the paper.

Privacy defined by $\mathcal{F}^{\mathcal{E},LE}_{Lottery}$. The only difference between APoS proposed by [13] and our APoS-N is that we replace LE with our LE^*. Although the ZK proofs π_{zk} for APoS-N need to consider the noise z, π_{zk} is a special case of the description of π_{zk} in [13]. That means the construction of our APoS-N including the related ZK proof still follows the framework of [13] and the security proof for the privacy of APoS defined in [13] can be applied to APoS-N. By Theorem 1 and Corollary 1 in [13], we have the following theorem.

Theorem 1. *Lottery Protocol*$^{\mathcal{E},LE^*}$ *realizes the* $\mathcal{F}^{\mathcal{E},LE^*}_{Lottery}$ *functionality in the* ($\mathcal{F}^{ABC}_{\Delta}$, $\mathcal{F}^{Com}_{Init}$, $\mathcal{F}_{crs}$, $\mathcal{F}^{Com}_{VRF}$)*-hybrid world in the presence of a PPT adversary. APoS-N with Lottery Protocol*$^{\mathcal{E},LE^*}$ *results in a private PoS protocol.*

5.2 (T, δ, ϵ)-Privacy of APoS-N

Since the privacy defined by $\mathcal{F}^{\mathcal{E},LE}_{Lottery}$ does not rule out the possibility of the privacy leakage by frequency attack, we focus on the evaluation of (T, δ, ϵ)-privacy of APoS-N.

Notice that the frequency of changing $\gamma(z)$ will influence the effect of hiding stake. If $\gamma(z)$ is changed too frequently, e.g., $\gamma(z)$ takes as input fresh z in each slot, the interference effects of the noise will tend to be nullified in a short time. Because the expectation of the noise distribution is 0 and more noise samples make the sum of noise approximate to 0 much faster. Hence, we suggest that the same $\gamma(z)$ should be used for a period of time, say an epoch. In particular, we modify the first step of VRF Evaluation of $\mathcal{F}^{Com}_{VRF}$ as follows.

VRF Evaluation (Eval, sid, vid, m**)**

1. If $T(vid, m)$ is undefined, pick random η, r from $\{0,1\}^{\ell_{VRF}}$, where $\eta = y||z$ and $|y| = \ell_y$. If sid corresponds to the first slot of the corresponding epoch, the related randomness η is denoted as $y_1||z_1$. Otherwise, set $\eta = y||z_1$.

That is, the same randomness z will be used for the whole epoch and refreshed only at the beginning of each epoch. We stress that the above modification does not change the framework of APoS-N, where only minor modification on the concrete instantiations needs to be made. Let Π^* denote the resulting APoS-N. Hence, Theorem 1 still holds for Π^*.

To evaluate (T, δ, ϵ)-privacy of Π^* in practice, we consider the leader election process of a target stakeholder with stake p in an epoch, where the noise $\gamma(z)$ is fixed. Let $\Phi^*(p, \gamma(z))$ denote the probability of a stakeholder with noisy relative stake winning an election. So we have $\Pr[\mathsf{Exp}^{tag}_{\Pi^*,\delta}(1^\lambda) = 1] = \sum_{i=\lfloor(1-\delta)T\Phi(p)\rfloor}^{\lfloor(1+\delta)T\Phi(p)\rfloor}$

$\Pr[X = i]$, where $X \sim B(T, \Phi^*(p, \gamma(z)))$. Suppose $\gamma(z)$ follows the uniform distribution over $[-\gamma_{max}, \gamma_{max}]$. We need to consider the expectation of $\Pr[\mathsf{Exp}^{tag}_{\Pi^*,\delta}(1^\lambda) = 1]$, which is

$$\int_{-\gamma_{max}}^{\gamma_{max}} \Pr[\mathsf{Exp}^{tag}_{\Pi^*,\delta}(1^\lambda) = 1 | \gamma(z) = x] \Pr[\gamma(z) = x] dx.$$

Consider the concrete parameter $p = 0.3\%$, $\gamma_{max} = 0.3$, $T = 432000$ (an epoch) and $\delta = 0.1$. Recall that $\Pr[\mathsf{Exp}^{tag}_{\Pi,\delta}(1^\lambda) = 1] = 60.95\%$ for the APoS protocol Π (without noise) [10,13]. For APoS-N protocol Π^*, the expectation of $\Pr[\mathsf{Exp}^{tag}_{\Pi^*,\delta}(1^\lambda) = 1]$ is as low as 34.01%, which is decreased by 44.2% comparing with that of APoS. That means, the APoS-N protocol Π^* is expected to achieve $(432000, 0.1, 34.01\%)$-anonymity for a stakeholder with relative stake 0.3% in an epoch.

Long Term Benefits. Although larger noise bound γ_{max} can lead to better (T, δ, ϵ)-privacy, one may concern about the total number of proposed blocks of stakeholders during some periods deviates from their expectations too much due to the large noise. So the stakeholders' benefits in APoS-N may not match their stakes for some periods, which violates the intuition of proof of stake. It is obvious that the long-term block benefits of the stakeholder in APoS-N is similar to that of APoS, since the expectation of the noise distribution is 0. The problem is how long the stakeholder should wait to get what he deserves. Intuitively, the larger the noise the longer the stakeholder should wait. In Fig. 3, we simulate the block generation of a stakeholder with relative stake 0.3% over 60 days (12 epochs) in APoS and APoS-N, respectively, where $\gamma_{max} = 0.3$. The red curve and the green curve represent the deviation of the total number of blocks from the expectation, i.e., $\frac{X}{T \cdot \Phi(p)} - 1$, for APoS and APoS-N, respectively. As shown in Fig. 3, the difference of the deviations between APoS and APoSN is large during

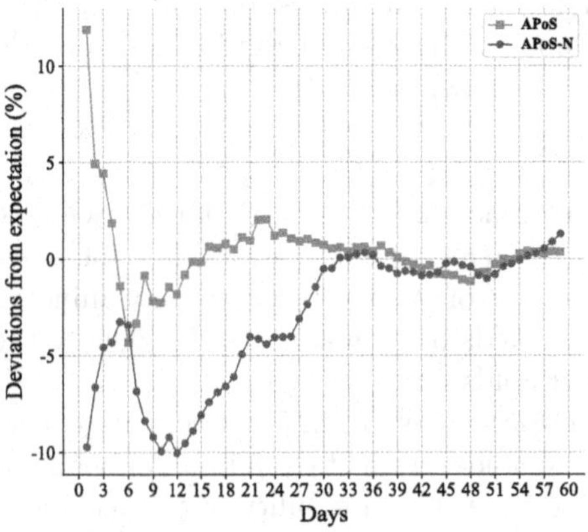

Fig. 3. Deviations from expectation in APoS and APoS-N during 12 epochs. (Color figure online)

the first 20 days, while it decreases to about 1% after the first 44 $\sim$ 47 days. That means, the time of the stakeholder with relative stake 0.3% to match his expectation is about 44–47 days.

Restriction on Individual's Maximum Relative Stake. To prevent the adversary from getting too much undeserved benefits in APoS-N for some period of time, e.g., winning an election with probability $\Phi(p \cdot (1+\gamma_{max}))$ for an epoch. We restrict the maximum relative stake of each stakeholder. That is, if a stakeholder's relative stake is larger than the maximum value, he should split his stake among multiple virtual parties, where each virtual party's stake p_i is less than the maximum value. Due to the randomness of the each virtual party's noise, it is hard for all the virtual parties to reach $\Phi(p_i \cdot (1+\gamma_{max}))$ simultaneously. In fact, such strategy is consistent with the saturation mechanism [25] in Cardano. The saturation mechanism is designed to prevent centralization by diminishing the stake pool's rewards if it reaches the saturation threshold, which is about 0.27%. Hence, no pool in Cardano has more than 0.4% relative stake.

We emphasize that the restriction on the maximum stake for each stakeholder is crucial for not only the stabilization of the benefits but also the security threshold of the adversarial stakes, which will be explained next.

Attack Against Wang et al.'s Protocol [19]**.** The work of [19] also proposes private PoS protocol using differential privacy technique, where the stake is distorted by adding noise. The noise in their stake distortion mechanisms follows the "same" Laplace distribution. As mentioned in [19], the noisy stake can be negative and a party with a negative stake is treated as having no stake. A direct attack on this mechanism involves an adversary dividing their stakes among multiple corrupted participants so that each participant has very small stakes. When applying their stake distortion mechanisms, some of the corrupted participants' noisy stakes are zero, while others may become larger. However, the expected total noisy stakes of the adversary are larger than his original stake due to the neglect of the negative stake. This gives the adversary a higher payoff, which violates the chain quality and even the safety of the resulting protocol and contradicts Theorem 17 in [19]. In our work, noise follows the uniform distribution and the amplitude of the noise is related to the stake. This allows for careful control of the noisy stake, preserving the fundamental security requirements of the underlying PoS protocol [8], such as chain quality.

5.3 Security Properties of Underlying PoS

Since the unpredictable noise changes the relation between stakes and the corresponding probability of proposing blocks in a short period of time, it is at the risk of breaking the basic security properties of underlying PoS, i.e., common prefix, chain growth, and chain quality. Recall that typical PoS protocols [7] are proven secure under the condition that the adversarial stakeholders' relative stakes should be less than a threshold, say 1/2. In some slots of our APoS-N, the adversarial stakeholders' noisy relative stakes may be larger than the threshold. Besides, the total noisy stakes may be also larger or less than the original total stakes STK. That means the security proof of previous works cannot be applied in our setting. Therefore, we will focus on examining the impact of noise on the security proof of PoS and prove the basic security properties of APoS-N.

Ensuring the safety and liveness of a PoS blockchain requires satisfying three essential properties: chain growth, chain quality, and common prefix. Chain growth is the requirement for the chain to grow at a certain rate, which can be proved by calculating the rate at which honest stakeholders extend the chain. Chain quality refers to the proportion of blocks on the chain proposed by honest stakeholders. If the chain growth rate surpasses the adversary block generation rate, there will eventually be blocks belonging to honest stakeholders, and the proportion of these blocks is the lower bound of chain quality. Common prefix captures the probability that chains in any two honest stakeholders' views are the same, except for the last few blocks. The proof for common prefix relies on the following events: the honest stakeholders proposing only one block within a certain period of time and the adversary's inability to propose a block with the same height within a certain period of time. The key to security analysis for APoS-N is how the noise affects the above three properties.

We first assume that the total number of stakeholders is large and make restrictions on the individual's maximum stake. The assumption is reasonable as there are thousands of stake pools in Cardano, none of which has more than 0.4% relative stake. Let α and β denote the relative honest and adversarial stakes in the system, respectively. Then we have the following two observations:

Observation 1: The total noisy honest relative stake in any slot is almost α. Note that the total honest relative stake is α and the noise of each stakeholder is uniformly distributed with an expected value of 0. According to the Chernoff-Hoeffding Bound in Appendix A, the total noisy honest stake will be very close to α with a high probability.

Observation 2: The probability that the adversarial relative stakes reach the maximum $\beta(1+\gamma_{\max})$ decreases exponentially with the number of adversarial stakeholders. The saturation mechanism prevents any single account from acquiring too much stakes. The adversary has to split its stake among numerous stakeholders. Otherwise, the probability of the adversary becoming a leader will decrease. By Chernoff-Hoeffding Bound, the probability of the adversary gaining a significant noise advantage is negligible.

The aforementioned observations imply that, if the noise can be carefully controlled, the presence of noise in our APoS-N is not expected to significantly change the overall block rate of honest or adversarial stakeholders, but it can increase the variance of the number of blocks proposed in a short period of time due to fluctuations in block proposal rates caused by the noise. However, with carefully controlled noise, it is still possible to prove the essential chain properties of the APoS-N protocol by carefully modeling and analyzing the impact of noise. On these properties, we have the following theorem, formal proof of which is shown in the full version of our paper due to space limitations.

Theorem 2. *APoS-N protocol satisfies chain growth, chain quality and common prefix.*

Acknowledgment. This work was supported by the National Key R&D Program of China (Grant No. 2022YFB2701700, 2018YFA0704702) and Shandong Provincial Natural Science Foundation (Grant No. ZR2020MF053). Quan Yuan is supported by JST CREST Grant Number JPMJCR2113, Japan.

Appendix

A Hoeffding Bound

Theorem 3 *(Hoeffding bound). Let $\{X_i\}_{i=1}^n$ be independent random variables ranging in $[a,b]$ where $a < b$, $X = \sum_{i=1}^n X_i$ and let $\mu = \mathbb{E}[x]$, then for any t:*

$$Pr[|X - \mu| > t] \leq 2e^{\frac{-t^2}{n(b-a)^2}}.$$

B AVRF

AVRF consists of (AVRF.gen, Update, AVRF.prov, AVRF.vrfy). Suppose that G is a group of prime order q such that $q = \Theta(2^{2m})$. Let $H(x)$ denote the hash function.

- $\mathsf{AVRF.gen}(1^{2m})$: Choose a generator $g \in G$, sample a random $k \in \mathbb{Z}_q$ and output(pk, k), where the public key $pk = (g, g^k)$.
- $\mathsf{Update}(pk)$: Let $v = g^k$. Randomly choose $r \in \mathbb{Z}_q$. Let $g' = g^r, v' = v^r$. Set $pk' = (g', v')$. Output pk'.
- $\mathsf{AVRF.prov}_k(pk', x)$: Let $pk' = (g, v)$. Compute $u = H(x)$, $\eta = u^k$ and π', which is the ZK proof of statement $\{(k) : \log_u(\eta) = \log_g(v)\}$. Set $\pi = (u, \pi')$. Output(pk', η, π).
- $\mathsf{AVRF.vrfy}_k(x, \eta, \pi)$: Output 1 if $u = H(x)$ and π verifies, and 0 otherwise.

C Frequency Attack over 12 Epochs

We investigate the transactions of Cardano for two months and focus on 600 pools. The proportion of the subsets with $R > \delta$ in different epochs is shown in Table 2.

Table 2. Proportion of 600 pools such that $R > \delta$ over 12 epochs.

Epoch		Proportion s.t. $R > \delta$				Epoch		Proportion s.t. $R > \delta$			
		$\delta = 0.1$	$\delta = 0.2$	$\delta = 0.3$	$\delta = 0.4$			$\delta = 0.1$	$\delta = 0.2$	$\delta = 0.3$	$\delta = 0.4$
325	24 h	86.8%	76.7%	66.0%	58.7%	331	24 h	83.2%	69.8%	57.1%	45.1%
	48 h	73.5%	53.3%	37.5%	22.3%		48 h	74.5%	52.8%	35.5%	23.5%
	72 h	69.0%	46.3%	31.0%	18.3%		72 h	70.3%	43.7%	26.2%	15.2%
	96 h	66.2%	39.8%	22.3%	12.8%		96 h	66.0%	34.0%	20.3%	10.7%
326	24 h	85.0%	68.0%	53.3%	44.5%	332	24 h	85.6%	69.0%	55.5%	45.8%
	48 h	82.5%	66.8%	51.2%	35.8%		48 h	75.7%	55.2%	39.8%	25.7%
	72 h	74.2%	50.0%	34.8%	22.0%		72 h	69.8%	44.7%	30.6%	17.7%
	96 h	62.7%	35.2%	16.8%	9.5%		96 h	66.5%	42.2%	23.8%	12.5%
327	24 h	92.5%	80.5%	72.5%	62.7%	333	24 h	88.8%	73.6%	63.7%	53.0%
	48 h	72.3%	50.5%	33.8%	21.3%		48 h	75.5%	55.5%	37.7%	22.8%
	72 h	71.5%	46.3%	29.2%	17.8%		72 h	66.8%	41.3%	24.1%	14.8%
	96 h	68.0%	41.7%	25.7%	13.3%		96 h	67.2%	38.2%	20.3%	9.2%
328	24 h	86.5%	78.7%	66.2%	60.3%	334	24 h	83.3%	68.5%	54.8%	43.8%
	48 h	78.5%	60.3%	46.7%	32.8%		48 h	74.3%	51.3%	33.2%	21.5%
	72 h	74.8%	51.0%	31.8%	19.2%		72 h	68.7%	42.0%	24.5%	12.8%
	96 h	64.2%	38.2%	19.5%	9.8%		96 h	65.2%	35.8%	18.8%	9.8%
329	24 h	84.3%	70.2%	57.0%	46.8%	335	24 h	82.7%	67.5%	55.3%	47.2%
	48 h	76.5%	56.0%	35.2%	22.8%		48 h	76.7%	58.3%	41.2%	28.5%
	72 h	67.3%	39.3%	22.8%	11.2%		72 h	69.2%	44.2%	25.2%	13.2%
	96 h	68.2%	38.3%	20.2%	10.0%		96 h	66.3%	36.2%	16.9%	9.3%
330	24 h	88.2%	73.3%	63.3%	52.5%	336	24 h	88.3%	79.5%	65.8%	58.3%
	48 h	74.5%	53.2%	34.5%	21.5%		48 h	74.6%	55.8%	35.3%	24.2%
	72 h	70.5%	43.3%	26.7%	15.3%		72 h	68.3%	43.3%	25.5%	14.5%
	96 h	63.5%	37.0%	19.7%	11.0%		96 h	66.8%	36.5%	20.2%	12.4%

D Functionalities

In this section, we recall functionalities $\mathcal{F}_{crs}$, $\mathcal{F}_{Init}^{Com}$ and $\mathcal{F}_{\Delta}^{ABC}$ defined in [13,15].

Functionality $\mathcal{F}_{crs}$

The functionality is parameterized by a distribution $\mathcal{D}$.

- Sample crs from the distribution $\mathcal{D}$.
- Upon receiving (Setup,sid) from a party, output(Setup,sid, crs).

Functionality $\mathcal{F}_{Init}^{Com}$

The functionality is parameterized by a signature scheme **Sig** =(SIG.keygen, SIG.sig, SIG.vrfy) and a commitment scheme **Com**.

Initialization

The Functionality $\mathcal{F}_{Init}^{Com}$ contains a list of each stakeholder unique id - uid, their election stake $\mathcal{S}_{uid}$. For each stakeholder uid, the functionality dose :

1. Execute **Com** with fresh randomness r_{uid} to get commitment **Com**($\mathcal{S}_{uid}$,r_{uid});
2. Randomly pick a secret key sk_{uid} and compute public key vk_{uid} = KeyGen(sk_{uid}).

Information

- Upon receiving an input message (GetPrivateData,sid) from a stakeholder uid, output (GetPrivateData, sid, $\mathcal{S}_{uid}$, r_{pid}, sk_{uid}).
- Upon receiving (GetList, sid) from a party, output $\mathcal{L} = (\mathcal{S}_{uid}, r_{uid})$.

Anonymous Broadcast Functionality: $\mathcal{F}_{\Delta}^{ABC}$

All parties can register or deregister at any time. The list $\mathcal{P}$ consists of registered parties $\{P_1, P_2, ..., P_n\}$. The functionality maintains a message buffer M.

Send Message

Upon receiving message (SEND, sid, m) from some party $P_i \in \mathcal{P}$, where $\mathcal{P} = \{P_1, P_2....P_n\}$ denotes the current party set, do:

1. Choose n new unique message-IDs: $mid_1, ..., mid_n$.
2. Initialize $2n$ new variables $D_{mid_1} = D_{mid_1}^{Max}, ..., D_{mid_n} = D_{mid_n}^{Max} = 1$, which are the delays and the maximum delays of the message for each party.
3. Set $M = M||(m, mid_i, D_{mid_i}, P_i)$ for each party $P_i \in \mathcal{P}$.
4. Send($SEND, m, sid, mid_1, ..., mid_n$) to the adversary.

Receive Message
Upon receiving message (FETCH,sid) from $P_i \in \mathcal{P}$:

1. For all tuples$(m, mid, D_{mid}, P_i) \in M$, set $D_{mid} = D_{mid} - 1$.
2. Let $M_0^{P_i}$ denote the subvector of M including all tuples of the (m, mid, D_{mid}, P_i) with $D_{mid} = 0$. Delete all $M_0^{P_i}$ from M and send $(sid, M_0^{P_i})$ to P_i

Adversarial Influence
Upon receiving message (DELAY,$sid, (T_{mid_1}, mid_1), \cdots, (T_{mid_\ell}, mid_\ell)$ from the adversary, do the following for each pair (T_{mid}, mid_i):

1. If $D_{mid_i}^{Max} + T_{mid_i} \leq \Delta$ and mid is a message-ID registered in the current M, set $D_{mid_i} = D_{mid_i} + T_{mid_i}$ and set $D_{mid_i}^{Max} = D_{mid_i}^{Max} + T_{mid_i}$; otherwise ignore this pair.

Adversarial multicast
Upon receiving (MSEND,$(m_1, P_1), \cdots, (m_\ell, P_\ell)$) from the adversary with $(P_1, \cdots, P_\ell \in \mathcal{P})$:

1. Choose ℓ new unique message-IDs: $mid_1, \cdots, mid_\ell$.
2. Initialize 2ℓ new variables $D_{mid_1} = D_{mid_1}^{Max}, \cdots D_{mid_\ell} = D_{mid_\ell}^{Max} = 1$.
3. Set $M = M||(m_1, mid_1, D_{mid_1}, P_1)|| \cdots ||(m_\ell, mid_\ell, D_{mid_\ell}, P_\ell)$.
4. Send (MSEND,$sid, m_1, mid_1, \cdots, m_\ell, mid_\ell$) to the adversary.

References

1. Nakamoto, S.: Cryptocurrencies without proof of work (2008)
2. King, S., Nadal, S.: Ppcoin: peer-to-peer crypto-currency with proof-of-stake (2012)
3. Bentov, I., Gabizon, A., Mizrahi, A.: Cryptocurrencies without proof of work. In: Clark, J., Meiklejohn, S., Ryan, P.Y.A., Wallach, D., Brenner, M., Rohloff, K. (eds.) FC 2016. LNCS, vol. 9604, pp. 142–157. Springer, Heidelberg (2016). https://doi.org/10.1007/978-3-662-53357-4_10
4. Bentov, I., Lee, C., Mizrahi, A., Rosenfeld, M.: Proof of activity: extending bitcoin's proof of work via proof of stake [extended abstract]y. SIGMETRICS Perform. Eval. Rev. **42**(3), 34–37 (2014)
5. Daian, P., Pass, R., Shi, E.: Snow white: robustly reconfigurable consensus and applications to provably secure proof of stake. Cryptology ePrint Archive, Paper 2016/919 (2016). https://eprint.iacr.org/2016/919
6. Chen, J., Micali, S.: Algorand: a secure and efficient distributed ledger. Theor. Comput. Sci. **777**, 155–183 (2019)
7. Kiayias, A., Russell, A., David, B., Oliynykov, R.: Ouroboros: a provably secure proof-of-stake blockchain protocol. In: Katz, J., Shacham, H. (eds.) CRYPTO 2017. LNCS, vol. 10401, pp. 357–388. Springer, Cham (2017). https://doi.org/10.1007/978-3-319-63688-7_12

8. David, B., Gaži, P., Kiayias, A., Russell, A.: Ouroboros praos: an adaptively-secure, semi-synchronous proof-of-stake blockchain. In: Nielsen, J.B., Rijmen, V. (eds.) EUROCRYPT 2018. LNCS, vol. 10821, pp. 66–98. Springer, Cham (2018). https://doi.org/10.1007/978-3-319-78375-8_3
9. Badertscher, C., Gazi, P., Kiayias, A., Russell, A., Zikas, V.: Ouroboros genesis: composable proof-of-stake blockchains with dynamic availability. In: CCS 2018, pp. 913–930. ACM (2018)
10. Kerber, T., Kiayias, A., Kohlweiss, M., Zikas, V.: Ouroboros crypsinous: privacy-preserving proof-of-stake. In: 2019 IEEE SP, pp. 157–174. IEEE (2019)
11. Ben-Sasson, E., et al.: Zerocash: decentralized anonymous payments from bitcoin. In: 2014 IEEE SP, pp. 459–474. IEEE Computer Society (2014)
12. Noether, S.: Ring signature confidential transactions for monero. Cryptology ePrint Archive, Paper 2015/1098 (2015). https://eprint.iacr.org/2015/1098
13. Ganesh, C., Orlandi, C., Tschudi, D.: Proof-of-stake protocols for privacy-aware blockchains. In: Ishai, Y., Rijmen, V. (eds.) EUROCRYPT 2019. LNCS, vol. 11476, pp. 690–719. Springer, Cham (2019). https://doi.org/10.1007/978-3-030-17653-2_23
14. Baldimtsi, F., Madathil, V., Scafuro, A., Zhou, L.: Anonymous lottery in the proof-of-stake setting. In: 33rd IEEE Computer Security Foundations Symposium, pp. 318–333. IEEE (2020)
15. Kohlweiss, M., Madathil, V., Nayak, K., Scafuro, A.: On the anonymity guarantees of anonymous proof-of-stake protocols. In: 42nd IEEE SP, pp. 1818–1833. IEEE (2021)
16. Heilman, E., Kendler, A., Zohar, A., Goldberg, S.: Eclipse attacks on bitcoin's peer-to-peer network. In: 24th USENIX Security Symposium, pp. 129–144. USENIX Association (2015)
17. Dwork, C.: Differential privacy. In: Bugliesi, M., Preneel, B., Sassone, V., Wegener, I. (eds.) ICALP 2006. LNCS, vol. 4052, pp. 1–12. Springer, Heidelberg (2006). https://doi.org/10.1007/11787006_1
18. Dwork, C., McSherry, F., Nissim, K., Smith, A.: Calibrating noise to sensitivity in private data analysis. In: Halevi, S., Rabin, T. (eds.) TCC 2006. LNCS, vol. 3876, pp. 265–284. Springer, Heidelberg (2006). https://doi.org/10.1007/11681878_14
19. Wang, C., Pujo, D., Nayak, K., Machanavajjhala, A.: Private proof-of-stake blockchains using differentially-private stake distortion. Cryptology ePrint Archive, Paper 2023/787 (2023). https://eprint.iacr.org/2023/787
20. Garay, J., Kiayias, A., Leonardos, N.: The bitcoin backbone protocol: analysis and applications. In: Oswald, E., Fischlin, M. (eds.) EUROCRYPT 2015. LNCS, vol. 9057, pp. 281–310. Springer, Heidelberg (2015). https://doi.org/10.1007/978-3-662-46803-6_10
21. Pass, R., Seeman, L., Shelat, A.: Analysis of the blockchain protocol in asynchronous networks. In: Coron, J.-S., Nielsen, J.B. (eds.) EUROCRYPT 2017. LNCS, vol. 10211, pp. 643–673. Springer, Cham (2017). https://doi.org/10.1007/978-3-319-56614-6_22
22. Brown, L.D., Cai, T.T., DasGupta, A.: Interval estimation for a binomial proportion. Stat. Sci. **16**(2), 101–133 (2001)
23. Cardano pooltool. https://pooltool.io/
24. Agresti, A.: On small-sample confidence intervals for parameters in discrete distributions. Biometrics **57**, 963–971 (2001)
25. Cardano official website. https://cardano.org/stake-pool-operation/

Compact Stateful Deterministic Wallet from Isogeny-Based Signature Featuring Uniquely Rerandomizable Public Keys

Surbhi Shaw(✉) and Ratna Dutta

Department of Mathematics, Indian Institute of Technology Kharagpur, Kharagpur 721302, India
surbhi_shaw@iitkgp.ac.in, ratna@maths.iitkgp.ac.in

Abstract. *Deterministic wallets* are promising cryptographic primitives that are employed in cryptocurrencies to safeguard user's fund. In CCS'19, a generic construction of deterministic wallets was proposed by Das et al. leveraging *signature schemes with rerandomizable keys*. This is an advanced form of signatures that enables separate but consistent rerandomization of secret and public keys. Das et al. instantiated their deterministic wallet construction from rerandomizable signatures based on BLS and ECDSA. However, these wallets are not quantum-resistant. In this work, we offer a strategy for post-quantum migration of secure deterministic wallets based on isogenies. Rerandomizable signatures being at the center of the wallet construction, we initially propose ways to design such signature schemes from isogenies. Employing the signature schemes CSI-FiSh and CSI-SharK, we present two quantum-resistant signature schemes with rerandomizable keys. We provide rigorous security proof showing our constructions are secure against *existential unforgeability under chosen-message attacks with honestly rerandomized keys*. Our rerandomized signature from CSI-SharK gives the most compact post-quantum secure rerandomized signature. Finally, we integrate our rerandomized signature scheme from CSI-FiSh to design the *first* isogeny-based deterministic wallet with compact key sizes. We present a detailed security analysis showing our wallet is secure against *wallet unlinkability* and *wallet unforgeability*.

Keywords: Deterministic wallet · Rerandomized signature · Blockchain protocols · Isogenies · Post-quantum cryptography

1 Introduction

Over the last decade, cryptocurrencies such as Bitcoin [20] and Ethereum [15] have facilitated the development of novel payment systems. To accomplish a fund transfer, from Alice to another user, Bob, Alice needs to authorize a new transaction that leads to the transfer of funds to Bob. A transaction is a tuple $\mathsf{tx}_{AB} = (\mathsf{pk}_A, \mathsf{pk}_B, v)$ which indicates the transfer of v coins from Alice with

J. Deng et al. (Eds.): CANS 2023, LNCS 14342, pp. 392–413, 2023.
https://doi.org/10.1007/978-981-99-7563-1_18

public key pk_A to Bob with public key pk_B. The transaction tx_{AB} is subsequently submitted to the network of miners for verification along with a signature on tx_{AB} under Alice's secret key sk_A. As only Alice, the possessor of the secret key sk_A, can compute a valid signature with respect to the public key sk_A, possession of sk_A implies complete control over the funds entrusted to pk_A. This renders Alice's secret key sk_A extremely vulnerable to attackers. Infact there are several instances of spectacular hacks where cryptocurrencies worth billions of dollars were stolen by means of unauthorized access to the secret key.

The natural question that follows is: Where to store these secret keys, then? Storing it in a digital wallet such as a smartphone is not a potential solution as it remains connected to the network and is open to hacking attempts. One viable solution is to store the keys in two different wallets – a *cold wallet* and a *hot wallet.* The secret key is held in a cold wallet, which is often kept offline and may be realized by specialized hardware [26]. On the other hand, the public key is stored in a hot wallet which is a software that works on some devices and is always connected to the network. However, this naive strategy has one significant problem. Since the transactions posted on the blockchain are public, all the transactions made to some particular public address can be linked to a hot wallet containing the public key which generates that particular public address. A widely used approach to make the transactions unlinkable is to generate as many fresh key pairs as the number of transactions. However, this requires a large wallet storage capacity and functions for a predetermined number of transactions.

Deterministic Wallets. In the cryptocurrency literature, a solution to address this problem is given by a primitive called *deterministic wallet* [11] which is standardized in the Bitcoin improvement proposal (BIP32) [27]. In the case of deterministic wallets, instead of computing fresh key pairs for each transaction, one computes a single master secret key and master public key and stores them in the cold wallet and hot wallet, respectively. Any deterministic wallet involves a deterministic public key derivation algorithm that generates a session public key in the hot wallet using the master public key. Likewise, the deterministic secret key derivation algorithm computes a session secret key in the cold wallet employing the master secret key. Consequently, one has to hold only one key in the hot/cold wallet to produce as many session keys as one wishes. The two main security attributes of a deterministic wallet are – *wallet unforgeability* and *wallet unlinkability.* Wallet unforgeability ensures that signatures used to validate new transactions cannot be forged as long as the cold wallet is not corrupted. Wallet unlinkability assures that no two transactions transferring money to the same wallet can be linked even if they are publicly posted on the blockchain. The notion of forward security in unlinkability assures that all transactions sent to the holder of session public keys generated before the hot wallet attack cannot be linked to the master public key. In order to achieve forward unlinkability, Das et al. [13] introduced the primitive *stateful deterministic wallet.* In this primitive, both the cold and hot wallet stores the initial state St_0 generated by the master key generation algorithm along with the master key pair (msk, mpk) and keeps updating the state deterministically for every new session key pair.

Related Works. The widespread application of wallets in cryptocurrencies has sparked a renewed interest in designing hot/cold wallets. In 2015, Gutoski and Stebila [19] identified shortcomings in BIP32 deterministic wallet scheme [27] used for Bitcoin and suggested a possible fix for it. However, they have not taken into account the standard model of unforgeability in which the adversary aims to forge a signature, but a much weaker model where the adversary intends to obtain the master secret key. Later, Fan et al. [16] analyze the security of deterministic wallets against secret session key leakage. Unfortunately, they did not provide a formal model or a security proof and their countermeasure is ad hoc. The notion of a stateful deterministic wallet was first formalized by defined by Das et al. [13]. They proposed a generic construction of a stateful deterministic wallet from *signature schemes with perfectly rerandomizable keys.*

A signature scheme with rerandomizable keys is an ideal cryptographic primitive that allows separate but consistent rerandomization of secret key sk and public key pk to sk' and pk', respectively. In addition to the four conventional algorithms Setup, KeyGen, Sign, Verify of a signature scheme, a rerandomizable signature scheme also includes the algorithm Randsk for rerandomization of the secret key sk and Randpk for rerandomization of the public key pk. More concretely, Randsk adds some randomness to the secret key sk to obtain randomized secret key sk' while Randpk computes the rerandomized public key pk' corresponding to sk' using the same randomness, without knowing the secret key sk. Signature with rerandomizable keys was built by Fleischhacker et al. [17] as the key component for developing efficient unlinkable sanitizable signatures [10], to facilitate a variety of applications, including outsourcing database and secure routing and multicast transmission. Such rerandomized signatures also play an important role in resolving the stealth address problem [18] in cryptocurrencies.

Das et al. [13] showed how BLS signatures [8] can be employed to develop signature scheme that exhibits rerandomizable keys and used it to construct a deterministic wallet. They also designed a provably secure ECDSA-based deterministic wallet. These wallets provide a simple and effective means to protect the fund of users. However, these wallets are not quantum-resistant as they derive their security from the hardness of the Discrete Logarithm Problem (DLP) which is easily solvable using Shor's algorithm [22]. Moreover, the ECDSA signature scheme used by the vast majority of prominent cryptocurrencies relies on DLP, leaving them open to quantum threats. In view of the devastating consequences that quantum computers have had on the security of cryptocurrencies [1], Alkadri et al. [2] developed the first signature scheme with rerandomizable public keys from lattices leveraging the Fiat-Shamir based signature schemes. They showed how the signature scheme qTESLA [3] could be used to instantiate the wallet construction of Das et al. [13]. However, their scheme has large key and signature sizes and is not suitable for applications in cryptocurrencies.

Contribution. The existing proposals for deterministic wallets are undesirable for practical applications. While some schemes lack formal security proof, others are susceptible to quantum attacks or necessitate impractically large parameters to achieve security. To design a quantum-immune deterministic wallet, a plausible way proposed by cryptocurrency projects Bitcoin Post-Quantum [4] and QRL [25] is to replace ECDSA with hash-based signature schemes. However, they are not suitable for building a wallet as these signature scheme does not exhibit key rerandomizability property. Thus, a natural question arises "*Is it possible to construct a post-quantum secure deterministic wallet with formal security proof in the strong model featuring small key sizes?*"

We respond positively to this question. Isogeny-based cryptosystems are one of the many promising systems that have the potential to be secure against quantum attacks. The main emphasis of this work is to develop an isogeny-based stateful deterministic wallet that is immune to quantum attacks. The challenge lies in the requirement of an efficient signature scheme with rerandomizable keys. The somewhat unsatisfactory state-of-art motivates our search for an isogeny-based instantiation of the signature scheme with rerandomizable keys.

We consider the two isogeny-based signature schemes: *Commutative Supersingular Isogeny based Fiat-Shamir signature* (CSI-FiSh) [7] and CSI-FiSh with Sharing-friendly Keys (CSI-SharK) [5]. The signature scheme CSI-FiSh introduced by Beullens et al. [7] gives the first practical signature scheme from isogenies with a small signature size. The signature scheme CSI-SharK is a new variant of CSI-FiSh developed by Atapoor et al. [5] adopts a different way of generating the public key used in CSI-FiSh.

Our contributions in this paper are listed below:

- *Firstly*, we initiate the study of a signature scheme with rerandomized keys in the isogeny realm. We propose two constructions of signature schemes with rerandomized keys, one based on CSI-FiSh and the other on CSI-SharK which we refer to as RCSI-FiSh and RCSI-SharK respectively. We also examine the security of each of these schemes and prove them to be secure against *existential unforgeability under chosen-message attack with honestly rerandomized keys* (UF-CMA-HRK). Each of our rerandomized signature schemes can be of independent interest in constructing sanitizable signatures and solving the stealth address problem in the post-quantum era.
- *Secondly*, we design the *first* construction of an isogeny-based stateful deterministic wallet with compact key sizes. We skillfully integrate our rerandomized signature scheme RCSI-FiSh to construct a deterministic wallet that will offer security in the post-quantum era. Our rerandomized signature RCSI-SharK is also a promising candidate to instantiate the wallet construction in [13]. We prove that our scheme achieves security against *wallet unlinkability* and *wallet unforgeability* under the Commutative Supersingular Decision Diffie-Hellman (CSSDDH) assumption.

We theoretically compare our isogeny-based schemes RCSI-FiSh and RCSI-SharK with existing works on the signature scheme with rerandomized keys in Table 1 in terms of signature size, key size and security. We compare our schemes with two Diffie-Hellman based constructions REC and RBLS proposed by Das et al. [13] as well as with the lattice-based rerandomizable signature given by Alkadri et al. [2]. When it comes to storage capacity and signature size, the rerandomizable signature schemes REC and RBLS are the most effective. However, none of these schemes is post-quantum secure. On the other hand, both of our schemes enjoy post-quantum security. Although the lattice-based signature scheme with rerandomized public keys of Alkadri et al. [2] is post-quantum secure under the Module Learning With Errors (MLWE) and Module Shortest Integer Solution with infinity norm (MSIS^{∞}) assumptions, it necessitated large key and signature size compared to our schemes. Moreover, the security of the lattice-based signature scheme with rerandomized public keys has been claimed in the weak security model where the distribution of secret key in rerandomized signature is not indistinguishable from the original distribution of secret key. On the positive side, both of our rerandomizable signature schemes RCSI-FiSh and RCSI-SharK are secure in the strong security model.

Table 1. Comparative analysis of key and signature size of signature scheme with rerandomized keys

Scheme	Quantum secure	Key Size		Signature	Security
		$\lvert\mathsf{sk}\rvert$	$\lvert\mathsf{pk}\rvert$	$\lvert\sigma\rvert$	
REC [13]	No	1 in $\mathbb{Z}_p$	1 in $\mathbb{G}$	2 in $\mathbb{Z}_p$	DLP
RBLS [13]	No	1 in $\mathbb{Z}_p$	1 in $\mathbb{G}$	1 in $\mathbb{G}$	CDH
Lattice-based RSig [2]	Yes	1 in $R_q^{k_1+k_2}$, 1 in $\{0,1\}^{\ell_G}$	1 in $R_q^{k_1}$	1 in $R_q^{k_1+k_2}$, 1 in $\mathbb{T}_\kappa^n$	MLWE, MSIS^{∞}
RCSI-FiSh	Yes	$S-1$ in $\mathbb{Z}_N$	$S-1$ in $\mathbb{F}_p$	$2T$ in $\mathbb{Z}_N$	CSSDDH
RCSI-SharK	Yes	1 in $\mathbb{Z}_N$	$S-1$ in $\mathbb{F}_p$	$2T$ in $\mathbb{Z}_N$	CSSDDH

$\lvert\mathsf{sk}\rvert$ = size of secret key, $\lvert\mathsf{pk}\rvert$ = size of public key, CDH = Computational Diffie-Hellman Problem, DLP = Discrete Logarithm Problem, CSSDDH = Commutative Supersingular Decision Diffie-Hellman Problem, MSIS^{∞} = Module Shortest Integer Solution with infinity norm, MLWE = Module Learning With Errors Problem. Here $\mathbb{G}$ = group of order p, $R = \mathbb{Z}[x]/(f(x))$ is a polynomial ring with $f(x)$ being a monic polynomial of degree n, $R_q = R/q$ for prime q, N = class number of $\mathsf{Cl}(\mathcal{O})$ and T, S are integers with $T < S$.

2 Preliminaries

Notation. Let $\lambda \in \mathbb{N}$ denotes the security parameter. By $\forall i \in [T]$, we mean for all $i \in \{1, 2, \ldots, T\}$. We write $\mathsf{sign}(x)$ to denote the sign of the integer x. We denote cardinality of a set S by $\#S$. A function $\epsilon(\cdot)$ is negligible if for every positive integer c, there exists an integer k such that for all $\lambda > k$, $|\epsilon(\lambda)| < 1/\lambda^c$.

2.1 Isogeny-Based Cryptography

Isogeny-based cryptography is a promising class of post-quantum cryptography that has attracted great interest over the last decade and has undergone a fast-paced development. It is appealing because of its rich mathematical structure and relatively small keys. *Isogenies* are non-constant homomorphisms between two elliptic curves [14,23]. The *degree* of an isogeny is its degree as a rational map. A non-zero isogeny is called *separable* if and only if the degree of the isogeny is equal to the cardinality of its kernel. An *endomorphism* of an elliptic curve E is referred to as an isogeny from the curve E to itself. The collection of all endomorphisms of E along with the zero map forms a ring called the *endomorphism ring* and is denoted by $\mathsf{End}(E)$. The endomorphism ring restricted to the field K is denoted by $\mathsf{End}_K(E)$. The *quadratic twist* of a curve $E : y^2 = f(x)$ defined over the field K is given by $E^{\mathsf{twist}} : dy^2 = f(x)$ where $d \in K$ has Legendre symbol value -1.

Theorem 2.11. [24] *For any finite subgroup H of an elliptic curve E_1, there exists up to isomorphism, a unique elliptic curve E_2 and a separable isogeny $\varphi : E_1 \longrightarrow E_2$ such that its kernel is H and $E_2 := E_1/H$.*

2.2 Class Group Action

In the Commutative Supersingular Diffie-Hellman (CSIDH) key exchange protocol introduced by Castryck et al. [12], the underlying field $K = \mathbb{F}_p$ is specified by a prime $p = 4\ell_1\ell_2 \ldots \ell_n - 1$, where the ℓ_i's are small primes. It makes use of supersingular elliptic curves for which $\mathsf{End}_{\mathbb{F}_p}(E)$ is isomorphic to an order $\mathcal{O}$ in the imaginary quadratic field and $\mathsf{End}_{\mathbb{F}_p}(E)$ is thus commutative. The ideal class group $\mathsf{Cl}(\mathcal{O})$ acts freely and transitively on the set $\mathsf{Ell}_p(\mathcal{O})$ of $\mathbb{F}_p$-isomorphic classes of supersingular curves E. The *action* $*$ of the ideal $[\mathfrak{a}] \in \mathsf{Cl}(\mathcal{O})$ on the curve $E \in \mathsf{Ell}_p(\mathcal{O})$ is the image curve $E/E[\mathfrak{a}]$ under the separable isogeny $\varphi_{\mathfrak{a}} : E \longrightarrow E/E[\mathfrak{a}]$ with kernel $E[\mathfrak{a}] = \bigcap_{\alpha \in \mathfrak{a}} \mathsf{ker}(\alpha)$ (See Theorem 2.11).

The isogeny-based signature CSI-FiSh introduced by Beullens et al. [7] was designed by precomputing the ideal class group structure of CSIDH-512 parameter set in the form of a relation lattice of generators with low norm. The knowledge of the class group structure and relation lattice enables unique representation and uniform sampling of the elements from $\mathsf{Cl}(\mathcal{O})$ which is isomorphic to $\mathbb{Z}_N$ where $N = \#\mathsf{Cl}(\mathcal{O})$. Thus, we can write any element $[\mathfrak{a}] \in \mathsf{Cl}(\mathcal{O})$ as $[\mathfrak{g}^a]$ for some $a \in \mathbb{Z}_N$ where $\mathsf{Cl}(\mathcal{O}) = \langle \mathfrak{g} \rangle$. Since the element $[\mathfrak{a}]$ is uniquely identified by the exponent $a \in \mathbb{Z}_N$, henceforth, we shall write $[a]E$ to denote $[\mathfrak{a}] * E$ and $[a + b]E$ to denote $[\mathfrak{a}] * [\mathfrak{b}] * E$.

Definition 2.21 (Multi-Target Group Action Inverse Problem (MT-GAIP)). [7] Given k elliptic curves $E_1, \ldots, E_k$, with $\mathsf{End}_{\mathbb{F}_p}(E_i) = \mathcal{O}$ for all $i = 1, \ldots, k$, the MT-GAIP is to find an element $a \in \mathbb{Z}_N$ such that $E_i = [a]E_j$ for some $i, j \in \{0, \ldots, k\}$ with $i \neq j$.

Definition 2.22 ((Super-)Exceptional set).[6] An exceptional set modulo N is a set $\mathfrak{R}_{S-1} = \{r_0 = 0, r_1 = 1, \ldots, r_{S-1}\} \subseteq \mathbb{Z}_N$ where the pairwise differences $r_i - r_j$ of all elements $r_i, r_j \in \mathfrak{R}_{S-1}$ with $r_i \neq r_j$ is invertible modulo N. A superexceptional set modulo N is an exceptional set $\mathfrak{R}_{S-1} = \{r_0 = 0, r_1 = 1, \ldots, r_{S-1}\}$ where the pairwise sums $r_i + r_j$ of all elements r_i, r_j (including $r_i = r_j$) is also invertible modulo N.

Definition 2.23 (($r_0, r_1, \ldots, r_{S-1}$)- **Vectorization Problem with Auxiliary Inputs** ($\mathfrak{R}_{S-1}$-VPwAI)). [6] Given $E \in \mathsf{Ell}_p(\mathcal{O})$ and the pairs $(r_i, [r_i a]E)_{i=1}^{S-1}$ where $\mathfrak{R}_{S-1} = \{r_0 = 0, r_1 = 1, \ldots, r_{S-1}\}$ is an exceptional set, the $\mathfrak{R}_{S-1}$-VPwAI problem is to find $a \in \mathbb{Z}_N$.

3 Signature Schemes

Definition 3.01 (Signature scheme). A *signature scheme* Sig = (Setup, KeyGen, Sign, Verify) is a tuple of probabilistic polynomial-time (PPT) algorithms associated with a message space $\mathcal{M}$ which are detailed below:

$\mathsf{Sig.Setup}(1^\lambda) \rightarrow \mathsf{pp}$: A trusted party on input the security parameter 1^λ outputs a public parameter pp.

$\mathsf{Sig.KeyGen}(\mathsf{pp}) \rightarrow (\mathsf{sk}, \mathsf{pk})$: On input a public parameter pp, each user runs this algorithm to generate its secret and public key pair (sk, pk).

$\mathsf{Sig.Sign}(\mathsf{pp}, \mathsf{sk}, m) \rightarrow \sigma$: By running this algorithm with a public parameter pp, secret key sk and a message $m \in \mathcal{M}$ as input, the signer computes a signature σ on the message m.

$\mathsf{Sig.Verify}(\mathsf{pp}, \mathsf{pk}, m, \sigma) \rightarrow 1/0$: The verifier on input a public parameter pp, public key pk, message $m \in \mathcal{M}$ and signature σ, returns 1 or 0 indicating the validity of the signature σ.

Correctness. For all $\mathsf{pp} \leftarrow \mathsf{Sig.Setup}(1^\lambda)$, all $(\mathsf{sk}, \mathsf{pk}) \leftarrow \mathsf{Sig.KeyGen}(\mathsf{pp})$ and $\sigma \leftarrow \mathsf{Sig.Sign}(\mathsf{pp}, \mathsf{sk}, m)$, we must have $\mathsf{Sig.Verify}(\mathsf{pp}, \mathsf{pk}, m, \sigma) = 1$.

Definition 3.02. A signature scheme Sig satisfies *existential unforgeability under chosen-message attacks* (UF-CMA) if the advantage $\mathsf{Adv}^{\mathsf{UF\text{-}CMA}}_{\mathsf{Sig}, \mathcal{A}}(\lambda)$ of any PPT adversary $\mathcal{A}$ defined as

$$\mathsf{Adv}^{\mathsf{UF\text{-}CMA}}_{\mathsf{Sig}, \mathcal{A}}(\lambda) = \Pr[\mathcal{A}\,\text{wins in}\ \mathsf{Exp}^{\mathsf{UF\text{-}CMA}}_{\mathsf{Sig}, \mathcal{A}}(\lambda)]$$

is negligible, where the unforgeability experiment $\mathsf{Exp}^{\mathsf{UF\text{-}CMA}}_{\mathsf{Sig}, \mathcal{A}}(\lambda)$ is depicted in Fig. 1.

Setup: The challenger $\mathcal{C}$ computes $\mathsf{pp} \leftarrow \mathsf{Sig.Setup}(1^\lambda)$ and secret-public key pair $(\mathsf{sk}, \mathsf{pk}) \leftarrow \mathsf{Sig.KeyGen}(\mathsf{pp})$. It forwards pp and pk to the adversary $\mathcal{A}$ while keeps sk secret to itself. It also sets the list SList to ϕ.

Query Phase: $\mathcal{A}$ issues polynomially many adaptive signature queries to the oracle $\mathcal{O}_{\mathsf{Sign}}(m)$.

- $\mathcal{O}_{\mathsf{Sign}}(m)$: Upon receiving a query on message m, the challenger $\mathcal{C}$ checks if $m \notin \mathcal{M}$. If the check succeeds, it returns $\perp$, or else it computes a signature $\sigma \leftarrow \mathsf{Sig.Sign}(\mathsf{pp}, \mathsf{sk}, m)$ on the message m under the secret key sk and sets $\mathsf{SList} \leftarrow \mathsf{SList} \cup \{m\}$. It returns the computed signature σ to $\mathcal{A}$.

Forgery: The adversary $\mathcal{A}$ eventually submits a forgery (m^*, σ^*). The adversary $\mathcal{A}$ wins the game if $1 \leftarrow \mathsf{Sig.Verify}(\mathsf{pp}, \mathsf{pk}, m^*, \sigma^*)$ and $m^* \notin \mathsf{SList}$.

Fig. 1. $\mathsf{Exp}^{\mathsf{UF\text{-}CMA}}_{\mathsf{Sig}, \mathcal{A}}(\lambda)$: Existential unforgeability under chosen-message attack

3.1 CSI-FiSh

In this section, we recall the CSI-FiSh signature scheme [7] that comprises of four PPT algorithms detailed below:

$\mathsf{CSI\text{-}FiSh.Setup}(1^\lambda) \rightarrow \mathsf{pp}_{\text{sgn}}$: A trusted party executes the following steps to generate the public parameter pp_{sgn}.

i. Choose a large prime $p = 4\ell_1\ell_2\ldots\ell_n - 1$ where ℓ_i's are small distinct odd primes with $n = 74$, $\ell_1 = 3$, $\ell_{73} = 373$ and $\ell_{74} = 587$.
ii. Fix a base curve $E_0 : y^2 = x^3 + x \in \mathsf{Ell}_p(\mathcal{O})$ over $\mathbb{F}_p$ and the generator $\mathfrak{g}$ of the class group $\mathcal{G} = \mathsf{Cl}(\mathcal{O})$ with class number N where $\mathcal{O} = \mathbb{Z}[\sqrt{-p}]$.
iii. Sample a hash function $\mathcal{H}_1 : \{0,1\}^* \rightarrow \{-S+1, \ldots, 0, \ldots, S-1\}^T$ where S, T are positive integers with $T < S$.
iv. Return $\mathsf{pp}_{\text{sgn}} = (p, \mathfrak{g}, N, E_0, \mathcal{H}_1, S, T)$.

$\mathsf{CSI\text{-}FiSh.KeyGen}(\mathsf{pp}_{\text{sgn}}) \rightarrow (\mathsf{sk}, \mathsf{pk})$: On input pp_{sgn}, a user computes its secret-public key pair $(\mathsf{sk}, \mathsf{pk})$ as follows:

i. Sample $a_i \in \mathbb{Z}_N$ and compute the curves $E_{A_i} = [a_i]E_0 \ \forall\, i \in [S-1]$.
ii. Set $\mathsf{sk} = \{a_i\}_{i=1}^{S-1}$ and $\mathsf{pk} = \{E_{A_i}\}_{i=1}^{S-1}$.

$\mathsf{CSI\text{-}FiSh.Sign}(\mathsf{pp}_{\text{sgn}}, \mathsf{sk}, m) \rightarrow \sigma$: Employing pp_{sgn}, and the secret key $\mathsf{sk} = \{a_i\}_{i=1}^{S-1}$, a signer computes a signature σ on $m \in \{0,1\}^*$ as follows:

i. Set $a_0 \leftarrow 0$ and samples $b_i \in \mathbb{Z}_N \ \forall\, i \in [T]$.
ii. Compute the curves $E_{B_i} = [b_i]E_0$, the challenge vector $(h_1, \ldots, h_T) = \mathcal{H}_1(E_{B_1}||\ldots||E_{B_T}||m)$ and the response vectors $z_i = (b_i \text{ - } \mathsf{sign}(h_i)a_{|h_i|}) \bmod N \ \forall\, i \in [T]$.
iii. Return $\sigma = (\mathsf{h}, \mathsf{z})$ where $\mathsf{h} = \{h_i\}_{i=1}^T$ and $\mathsf{z} = \{z_i\}_{i=1}^T$.

$\mathsf{CSI\text{-}FiSh.Verify}(\mathsf{pp}_{\text{sgn}}, \mathsf{pk}, m, \sigma) \rightarrow 1/0$: Employing the signer's public key $\mathsf{pk} = \{E_{A_i}\}_{i=1}^{S-1}$, the algorithm executes the following steps to verify the signature σ.

i. Parse $\sigma = (\mathsf{h}, \mathsf{z})$ where $\mathsf{h} = \{h_i\}_{i=1}^T$ and $\mathsf{z} = \{z_i\}_{i=1}^T$.
ii. Define $E_{A_{-i}} = E_{A_i}^{\mathsf{twist}} \ \forall i \in [S-1]$.
iii. Extract the curves $E_{A_{h_i}}$ from pk and compute the curves $E_{B_i} = [z_i]E_{A_{h_i}}$ $\forall\, i \in [T]$ and the challenge vector $(h'_1, \ldots, h'_T) = \mathcal{H}_1(E_{B_1}||\ldots||E_{B_T}||m)$.
iv. If $(h_1, \ldots, h_T) = (h'_1, \ldots, h'_T)$ return 1, else return 0.

Correctness. Correctness of $\mathsf{CSI\text{-}FiSh}$ follows from the fact that $E_{B_i} = [b_i]E_0$ is recovered by computing $[z_i]E_{A_{h_i}} \ \forall\ i \in [T]$ as follows: $[z_i]E_{A_{h_i}} = [b_i - \mathsf{sign}(h_i)\, a_{|\,h_i\,|}]E_{A_{h_i}} = [b_i - \mathsf{sign}(h_i)\, a_{|\,h_i\,|}][\mathsf{sign}(h_i)\, a_{|\,h_i\,|}]E_0 = [b_i]E_0$.

Theorem 3.11. [7] *The isogeny-based signature scheme* CSI-FiSh *is* UF-CMA *secure under the hardness of* MT-GAIP *problem defined in Definition 2.21, if the hash function* $\mathcal{H}_1$ *is modeled as a random oracle.*

Remark 3.12. Recent quantum attack on CSIDH by Bonnetain et al. [9] and Peikert et al. [21] reveals that CSIDH-512 does not attain the NIST security level 1. However, the CSIDH group operations require an expensive quantum circuit. Therefore, it appears that CSIDH is still quantum-secure when these external circuit overheads and its evaluation are taken into account.

3.2 CSI-SharK

The signature scheme CSI-SharK is a new variant of CSI-FiSh proposed by Atapoor et al. [5] that has more sharing-friendly keys.

CSI-SharK.Setup(1^λ) $\rightarrow$ pp_{sgn}: A trusted party on input 1^λ generate the public parameter pp_{sgn}.

i. Except for the involved hash function, it works same as the algorithm CSI-FiSh.Setup. Here, the algorithm selects a hash function $\mathcal{H}' : \{0,1\}^* \rightarrow \{0,\ldots,S-1\}^T$ where S, T are positive integers with $T < S$.
ii. Return $\mathsf{pp}_{\text{sgn}} = (p, \mathfrak{g}, N, E_0, \mathcal{H}', S, T)$.

CSI-SharK.KeyGen(pp_{sgn}) $\rightarrow$ (sk, pk): On input pp_{sgn}, this algorithm computes a secret key sk and the corresponding public key pk as follows:

i. Sample $a \in \mathbb{Z}_N$.
ii. Generate a (super)exceptional set $\mathfrak{R}_{S-1} = \{r_0 = 0, r_1 = 1, r_2, \ldots, r_{S-1}\}$.
iii. Compute the curve $E_{A_i} = [r_i a]E_0 \ \forall\, i \in [S-1]$.
iv. Set sk $= a$ and pk $= (\mathfrak{R}_{S-1}, \{E_{A_i}\}_{i=1}^{S-1})$.

CSI-SharK.Sign(pp_{sgn}, sk, m) $\rightarrow \sigma$: A signer employs public parameter pp_{sgn} and its secret key sk $= a$ to compute a signature σ on $m \in \{0,1\}^*$ as follows:

i. Sample $b_i \in \mathbb{Z}_N \ \forall\, i \in [T]$.
ii. Compute the curves $E_{B_i} = [b_i]E_0$, the challenge vector $(h_1, \ldots, h_T) = \mathcal{H}'(E_{B_1}||\ldots||E_{B_T}||m)$ and the response $z_i = (b_i - r_{h_i} \cdot a) \mod N \ \forall\, i \in [T]$.
iii. Return $\sigma = (\mathsf{h}, \mathsf{z})$ where $\mathsf{h} = \{h_i\}_{i=1}^T$ and $\mathsf{z} = \{z_i\}_{i=1}^T$.

CSI-SharK.Verify(pp_{sgn}, pk, m, σ) $\rightarrow$ 1/0: Employing the signer's public key pk $= (\mathfrak{R}_{S-1}, \{E_{A_i}\}_{i=1}^{S-1})$, this algorithm verifies the signature σ on m as follows:

i. Parse $\sigma = (\mathsf{h}, \mathsf{z})$ where $\mathsf{h} = \{h_i\}_{i=1}^T$ and $\mathsf{z} = \{z_i\}_{i=1}^T$.
ii. Compute $E_{B_i} = [z_i]E_{A_{h_i}} \ \forall\, i \in [T]$ and $(h'_1, \ldots, h'_T) = \mathcal{H}'(E_{B_1}||\ldots||E_{B_T}||m)$.
iii. If $(h_1, \ldots, h_T) = (h'_1, \ldots, h'_T)$ return 1, else return 0.

Correctness. Correctness of CSI-SharK follows from the fact that $E_{B_i} = [b_i]E_0$ is recovered by computing $[z_i]E_{A_{h_i}} \ \forall\, i \in [T]$ as follows: $[z_i]E_{A_{h_i}} = [\, b_i - r_{h_i} \cdot a\,]E_{A_{h_i}} = [b_i - r_{h_i} \cdot a][r_{h_i} \cdot a]E_0 = [b_i]E_0 = E_{B_i}$.

Theorem 3.21. [5] *Under the hardness of the* MT-GAIP *and* $\mathfrak{R}_{S-1}$-VPwAI *problem defined in Definition 2.21 and 2.23, respectively and assuming $\mathcal{H}'$ is modeled as a random oracle, the* CSI-SharK *signature scheme is* UF-CMA *secure.*

4 Signature Scheme with Perfectly Rerandomizable Keys

Definition 4.01 (Signature scheme with perfectly rerandomizable keys). A *signature scheme with perfectly rerandomizable keys* is a tuple RSig = (RSig.Setup, RSig.KeyGen, RSig.Sign, RSig.Verify, RSig. Randsk, RSig.Randpk) of PPT algorithms associated with a message space $\mathcal{M}$ and randomness space $\mathcal{R}$ that satisfy the following requirements:

Here the algorithms $\mathsf{RSig.Setup}$, $\mathsf{RSig.KeyGen}$, $\mathsf{RSig.Sign}$, $\mathsf{RSig.Verify}$ are like the algorithms in the signature scheme defined in Definition 3.01.

$\mathsf{RSig.Randsk}(\mathsf{pp}, \mathsf{sk}, \rho) \rightarrow \mathsf{sk}'$: The inputs to this probabilistic secret key rerandomization algorithm are a public parameter pp, a secret key sk and randomness $\rho \in \mathcal{R}$. It outputs a rerandomized secret key sk'.

$\mathsf{RSig.Randpk}(\mathsf{pp}, \mathsf{pk}, \rho) \rightarrow \mathsf{pk}'$: The inputs to this probabilistic public key rerandomization algorithm are a public parameter pp, a public key pk and randomness $\rho \in \mathcal{R}$. It outputs a rerandomized public key pk'.

Correctness. The scheme RSig is correct if the following conditions hold:

i. For all $\mathsf{pp} \leftarrow \mathsf{RSig.Setup}(1^\lambda)$, all $(\mathsf{sk}, \mathsf{pk}) \leftarrow \mathsf{RSig.KeyGen}(\mathsf{pp})$, all messages $m \in \mathcal{M}$ and all signatures $\sigma \leftarrow \mathsf{RSig.Sign}(\mathsf{pp}, \mathsf{sk}, m)$, it must hold that $\mathsf{RSig.Verify}(\mathsf{pp}, \mathsf{pk}, m, \sigma) = 1$.

ii. For all $\mathsf{pp} \leftarrow \mathsf{RSig.Setup}(1^\lambda)$, all $(\mathsf{sk}, \mathsf{pk}) \leftarrow \mathsf{RSig.KeyGen}(\mathsf{pp})$, all $m \in \mathcal{M}$, all randomness $\rho \in \mathcal{R}$ and signatures $\sigma \leftarrow \mathsf{RSig.Sign}(\mathsf{pp}, \mathsf{RSig.Randsk}(\mathsf{pp}, \mathsf{sk}, \rho), m)$, we must have $\mathsf{RSig.Verify}(\mathsf{pp}, \mathsf{RSig.Randpk}(\mathsf{pp}, \mathsf{pk}, \rho), m, \sigma) = 1$.

iii. For all $\mathsf{pp} \leftarrow \mathsf{RSig.Setup}(1^\lambda)$, all key pairs $(\mathsf{sk}, \mathsf{pk})$ and a uniformly chosen randomness $\rho \in \mathcal{R}$, the pairs $(\mathsf{sk}', \mathsf{pk}')$ and $(\mathsf{sk}'', \mathsf{pk}'')$ are identically distributed, where $\mathsf{pk}' \leftarrow \mathsf{RSig.Randpk}(\mathsf{pp}, \mathsf{pk}, \rho)$, $\mathsf{sk}' \leftarrow \mathsf{RSig.Randsk}(\mathsf{pp}, \mathsf{sk}, \rho)$ and $(\mathsf{sk}'', \mathsf{pk}'') \leftarrow \mathsf{RSig.KeyGen}(\mathsf{pp})$.

Definition 4.02. A signature scheme with perfectly rerandomizable (public) keys RSig satisfies *existential unforgeability under chosen-message attack with honestly rerandomized keys* (UF-CMA-HRK) if the advantage $\mathsf{Adv}^{\mathsf{UF\text{-}CMA\text{-}HRK}}_{\mathsf{RSig},\mathcal{A}}(\lambda)$ of any PPT adversary $\mathcal{A}$ defined as

$$\mathsf{Adv}^{\mathsf{UF\text{-}CMA\text{-}HRK}}_{\mathsf{RSig},\mathcal{A}}(\lambda) = \Pr[\mathcal{A} \text{ wins in } \mathsf{Exp}^{\mathsf{UF\text{-}CMA\text{-}HRK}}_{\mathsf{RSig},\mathcal{A}}(\lambda)]$$

is negligible, where the unforgeability experiment $\mathsf{Exp}^{\mathsf{UF\text{-}CMA\text{-}HRK}}_{\mathsf{RSig},\mathcal{A}}(\lambda)$ between a challenger $\mathcal{C}$ and adversary $\mathcal{A}$ is depicted in Fig. 2.

Setup: The challenger $\mathcal{C}$ computes $\mathsf{pp} \leftarrow \mathsf{RSig.Setup}(1^\lambda)$ and a secret-public key pair $(\mathsf{sk}, \mathsf{pk}) \leftarrow \mathsf{RSig.KeyGen}(\mathsf{pp})$. It forwards pp and pk to the adversary $\mathcal{A}$ while keeps sk secret to itself. It also sets the list of randomness RList to ϕ.

Query Phase: The adversary $\mathcal{A}$ issues polynomially many adaptive queries to the oracles $\mathcal{O}_{\mathsf{RSign}}(m, \rho)$ and $\mathcal{O}_{\mathsf{Rand}}(\cdot)$.

- $\mathcal{O}_{\mathsf{Rand}}(\cdot)$: In response to a query for randomness, the challenger $\mathcal{C}$ samples a randomness $\rho \leftarrow \mathcal{R}$, sets $\mathsf{RList} \leftarrow \mathsf{RList} \cup \{\rho\}$ and returns ρ to $\mathcal{A}$.
- $\mathcal{O}_{\mathsf{RSign}}(m, \rho)$: In response to a signature query on a message m and randomness ρ, $\mathcal{C}$ checks if $\rho \notin \mathsf{RList}$. If the check succeeds, it returns $\perp$; otherwise, it randomizes the secret key sk using ρ to generate a new secret key $\mathsf{sk}' \leftarrow \mathsf{RSig.Randsk}(\mathsf{pp}, \mathsf{sk}, \rho)$. It then computes a signature $\sigma \leftarrow \mathsf{RSig.Sign}(\mathsf{pp}, \mathsf{sk}', m)$ on the message m under the randomized secret key sk' and sets $\mathsf{MList} \leftarrow \mathsf{MList} \cup \{m\}$. It returns the computed signature σ to $\mathcal{A}$.

Forgery: The adversary $\mathcal{A}$ eventually submits a forgery (m^*, σ^*, ρ^*). $\mathcal{A}$ wins the game if $m^* \notin \mathsf{MList}$ and $1 \leftarrow \mathsf{RSig.Verify}(\mathsf{pp}, \mathsf{pk}', m^*, \sigma^*)$ where $\mathsf{pk}' \leftarrow \mathsf{RSig.Randpk}(\mathsf{pp}, \mathsf{pk}, \rho^*)$ and $\rho^* \in \mathsf{RList}$.

Fig. 2. $\mathsf{Exp}^{\mathsf{UF\text{-}CMA\text{-}HRK}}_{\mathsf{RSig},\mathcal{A}}(\lambda)$: Existential unforgeability under chosen-message attack with honestly rerandomized keys

Definition 4.03 (Signature with uniquely rerandomizable public keys). A rerandomizable signature scheme RSig with a randomness space $\mathcal{R}$ is said to have *uniquely rerandomizable public keys* if for all $(\rho, \rho') \in \mathcal{R}$, we have that $\mathsf{RSig.Randpk}(\mathsf{pp}, \mathsf{pk}, \rho) = \mathsf{RSig.Randpk}(\mathsf{pp}, \mathsf{pk}, \rho')$ implies $\rho = \rho'$.

4.1 Signature Scheme with Perfectly Rerandomizable Keys from CSI-FiSh

In this section, we explain our proposed signature scheme with perfectly rerandomizable keys from CSI-FiSh [7] and we call it *Rerandomized Commutative Supersingular Isogeny based Fiat-Shamir signatures* (RCSI-FiSh).
We set RCSI-FiSh.Setup = CSI-FiSh.Setup, RCSI-FiSh.KeyGen = CSI-FiSh.KeyGen, RCSI-FiSh.Sign = CSI-FiSh.Sign, RCSI-FiSh.Verify = CSI-FiSh.Verify.

$\mathsf{RCSI\text{-}FiSh.Randsk}(\mathsf{pp}_{\mathrm{sgn}}, \mathsf{sk}, \rho) \rightarrow \mathsf{sk}'$: This algorithm on input a public parameter $\mathsf{pp}_{\mathrm{sgn}}$, a secret key $\mathsf{sk} = \mathsf{a} = \{a_i\}_{i=1}^{S-1}$ and randomness $\rho = \mathsf{c} = \{c_i\}_{i=1}^{S-1} \xleftarrow{\$} \mathbb{Z}_N^{S-1}$ outputs a rerandomized secret key $\mathsf{sk}' = \mathsf{sk} + \rho = (\mathsf{a} + \mathsf{c}) \mod N = \{d_i\}_{i=1}^{S-1}$ where $d_i = a_i + c_i$.

$\mathsf{RCSI\text{-}FiSh.Randpk}(\mathsf{pp}_{\mathrm{sgn}}, \mathsf{pk}, \rho) \rightarrow \mathsf{pk}'$: This algorithm on input $\mathsf{pp}_{\mathrm{sgn}}$, a public key $\mathsf{pk} = \{E_{A_i}\}_{i=1}^{S-1}$ and randomness $\rho = \mathsf{c} = \{c_i\}_{i=1}^{S-1} \xleftarrow{\$} \mathbb{Z}_N^{S-1}$ outputs a rerandomized public key $\mathsf{pk}' = \{[c_i]E_{A_i}\}_{i=1}^{S-1} = \{E_{D_i}\}_{i=1}^{S-1}$ where $[c_i]E_{A_i} = [c_i][a_i]E_0 = [c_i + a_i]E_0 = [d_i]E_0 = E_{D_i}$.

Correctness. Our proposed scheme is correct as it satisfies all the requirements stated in Definition 4.01:

i. For all $\mathsf{pp}_{\mathrm{sgn}} = (p, \mathfrak{g}, N, E_0, \mathcal{H}_1, S, T) \leftarrow \mathsf{RCSI\text{-}FiSh.Setup}(1^\lambda)$, all $(\mathsf{sk} = \{a_i\}_{i=1}^{S-1}, \mathsf{pk} = \{E_{A_i}\}_{i=1}^{S-1}) \leftarrow \mathsf{RCSI\text{-}FiSh.KeyGen}(\mathsf{pp}_{\mathrm{sgn}})$, all $m \in \mathcal{M}$ and all $\sigma = (\mathsf{h}, \mathsf{z}) \leftarrow \mathsf{RCSI\text{-}FiSh.Sign}(\mathsf{pp}_{\mathrm{sgn}}, \mathsf{sk}, m)$ we have $\mathsf{RCSI\text{-}FiSh.Verify}(\mathsf{pp}_{\mathrm{sgn}}, \mathsf{pk}, m, \sigma) = 1$, which follows from the correctness of the CSI-FiSh signature.

ii. For all $\mathsf{pp}_{\mathrm{sgn}} = (p, \mathfrak{g}, N, E_0, \mathcal{H}_1, S, T) \leftarrow \mathsf{RCSI\text{-}FiSh.Setup}(1^\lambda)$, all $(\mathsf{sk} = \{a_i\}_{i=1}^{S-1}, \mathsf{pk} = \{E_{A_i}\}_{i=1}^{S-1}) \leftarrow \mathsf{RCSI\text{-}FiSh.KeyGen}(\mathsf{pp}_{\mathrm{sgn}})$, all messages $m \in \mathcal{M}$, all randomness $\rho = \mathsf{c} = \{c_i\}_{i=1}^{S-1} \in \mathbb{Z}_N^{S-1}$ and signatures $\sigma' = (\mathsf{h}', \mathsf{z}') \leftarrow \mathsf{RCSI\text{-}FiSh.Sign}(\mathsf{pp}_{\mathrm{sgn}}, \mathsf{sk}', m)$ it holds that $\mathsf{RCSI\text{-}FiSh.Verify}(\mathsf{pp}_{\mathrm{sgn}}, \mathsf{pk}', m, \sigma') = 1$ where $\mathsf{sk}' = (\mathsf{a} + \mathsf{c}) \bmod N$ and $\mathsf{pk}' = \{[c_i]E_{A_i}\}_{i=1}^{S-1}$. It follows from the fact that $E_{B_i'} = [b_i']E_0$ is recovered by computing $[z_i']E_{D_{h_i'}}$ $\forall\, i \in [T]$ as follows: $[z_i']E_{D_{h_i'}} = [b_i' - \mathsf{sign}(h_i')\, d_{|h_i'|}]E_{D_{h_i'}} = [b_i' - \mathsf{sign}(h_i')\, d_{|h_i'|}][\mathsf{sign}(h_i')\, d_{|h_i'|}]E_0 = [b_i']E_0$. Here, $\forall\, i \in [T]$, $E_{B_i'} = [b_i']E_0$ with $b_i' \in \mathbb{Z}_N$ are the commitment curves, $(h_1', \ldots, h_T') = \mathcal{H}'(E_{B_1'}||\ldots||E_{B_T'}||m)$ is the challenge vector and $z_i' = b_i' - \mathsf{sign}(h_i')d_{|h_i'|} \pmod N$ are the response vectors computed during the generation of $\sigma' = (\mathsf{h}', \mathsf{z}')$ on m under $\mathsf{sk}' = \{d_i\}_{i=1}^{S-1}$.

iii. Consider a randomized secret-public key pair $(\mathsf{sk}' = (\mathsf{a} + \mathsf{c}) \mod N, \mathsf{pk}' = \{[c_i]E_{A_i}\}_{i=1}^{S-1})$ which is a randomization of key pair $(\mathsf{sk} = \mathsf{a}, \mathsf{pk} = \{E_{A_i}\}_{i=1}^{S-1}) \leftarrow \mathsf{RCSI\text{-}FiSh.KeyGen}(\mathsf{pp}_{\mathrm{sgn}})$. We consider a freshly generated key pair $(\mathsf{sk}'', \mathsf{pk}'') \leftarrow \mathsf{RCSI\text{-}FiSh.KeyGen}(\mathsf{pp_{sgn}})$ where $\mathsf{sk}'' = \mathsf{u} = \{u_i\}_{i=1}^{S-1} \xleftarrow{\$} \mathbb{Z}_N^{S-1}$ and $\mathsf{pk}'' = \{E_{U_i}\}_{i=1}^{S-1}$ where $E_{U_i} = [u_i]E_0$. Note that sk' and sk'' are identically distributed as both of them are uniformly distributed in $\mathbb{Z}_N^{S-1}$. The public keys pk' and pk'' are identically distributed as the corresponding secret keys sk' and sk'' are identically distributed.

Lemma 4.11. *The proposed isogeny-based rerandomizable signature scheme* RCSI-FiSh *has uniquely rerandomizable public keys as per Definition 4.03.*

Proof. The proof of this lemma follows from the fact that the action of the ideal class group $\mathsf{Cl}(\mathcal{O})$ on $\mathsf{Ell}_p(\mathcal{O})$ is free and transitive. Hence, such a group action establishes a bijection between the group $\mathsf{Cl}(\mathcal{O})$ and the set $\mathsf{Ell}_p(\mathcal{O})$ given by the map $f_E : [a] \to [a]E$ for any $E \in \mathsf{Ell}_p(\mathcal{O})$. More precisely, consider two randomness $\rho = \mathsf{c} = \{c_i\}_{i=1}^{S-1}$, $\rho' = \mathsf{c}' = \{c_i'\}_{i=1}^{S-1} \xleftarrow{\$} \mathbb{Z}_N^{S-1}$ and $\mathsf{RCSI\text{-}FiSh.Randpk}(\mathsf{pp_{sgn}}, \mathsf{pk}, \rho) \to \mathsf{pk}_1' = \{[d_i]E_0\}_{i=1}^{S-1}$ and $\mathsf{RCSI\text{-}FiSh.Randpk}(\mathsf{pp_{sgn}}, \mathsf{pk}, \rho') \to \mathsf{pk}_2' = \{[d_i']E_0\}_{i=1}^{S-1}$ where $d_i = c_i + a_i$ and $d_i' = c_i' + a_i$. Let us consider $\mathsf{RCSI\text{-}FiSh.Randpk}(\mathsf{pp_{sgn}}, \mathsf{pk}, \rho) = \mathsf{RCSI\text{-}FiSh.Randpk}(\mathsf{pp_{sgn}}, \mathsf{pk}, \rho')$. This implies

$$
\begin{aligned}
& & [d_i]E_0 &= [d_i']E_0 \,\forall\, i \in [S-1] \\
&\Rightarrow & [-d_i' + d_i]E_0 &= [-d_i' + d_i']E_0 \,\forall\, i \in [S-1] \\
&\Rightarrow & [-d_i' + d_i]E_0 &= [0]E_0 \,\forall\, i \in [S-1] \\
&\Rightarrow & -d_i' + d_i &= 0 \,\forall\, i \in [S-1] \\
&\Rightarrow & d_i &= d_i' \,\forall\, i \in [S-1] \\
&\Rightarrow & c_i + a_i &= c_i' + a_i \,\forall\, i \in [S-1] \\
&\Rightarrow & \rho &= \rho'
\end{aligned}
$$

This completes the proof of this lemma. □

Theorem 4.12. *Our proposed signature scheme with perfectly rerandomizable keys* RCSI-FiSh *is* UF-CMA-HRK *secure as per Definition 4.02 as the signature scheme* CSI-FiSh *is* UF-CMA *secure as per Definition 3.02.*

Proof. On the contrary, we assume that there is an efficient adversary $\mathcal{A}$ that breaks the UF-CMA-HRK security of RCSI-FiSh. We will use the adversary $\mathcal{A}$ in the experiment $\mathsf{Exp}^{\mathsf{UF\text{-}CMA\text{-}HRK}}_{\mathsf{RCSI\text{-}FiSh}, \mathcal{A}}(\lambda)$ described in Fig. 2 as a procedure to design a forger $\mathcal{F}$ that breaks the UF-CMA security of CSI-FiSh. Playing the role of the challenger in the experiment $\mathsf{Exp}^{\mathsf{UF\text{-}CMA\text{-}HRK}}_{\mathsf{RCSI\text{-}FiSh}, \mathcal{A}}(\lambda)$, $\mathcal{F}$ interacts with $\mathcal{A}$.

In the experiment $\mathsf{Exp}^{\mathsf{UF\text{-}CMA}}_{\mathsf{CSI\text{-}FiSh}, \mathcal{A}}(\lambda)$ presented in Definition 3.02, the challenger computes $\mathsf{pp_{sgn}} = (p, \mathfrak{g}, N, E_0, \mathcal{H}_1, S, T) \leftarrow \mathsf{CSI\text{-}FiSh.Setup}(1^\lambda)$ where p is a 512-bit prime, $\mathfrak{g}$ is the generator and N is the class number of ideal class group $\mathsf{Cl}(\mathcal{O})$, E_0 is a base curve, $\mathcal{H}_1$ is a hash function and S and T are positive integers. It then computes a secret key $\mathsf{sk} = \{a_i\}_{i=1}^{S-1}$ and the corresponding public key $\mathsf{pk} = \{E_{A_i}\}_{i=1}^{S-1}$, where $E_{A_i} = [a_i]E_0$, by invoking the algorithm $\mathsf{CSI\text{-}FiSh.KeyGen}(\mathsf{pp_{sgn}})$ and forwards $\mathsf{pp_{sgn}}$, pk to $\mathcal{F}$. The forger $\mathcal{F}$ is also given access to the oracle $\mathcal{O}_{\mathsf{CSI\text{-}FiSh.Sign}}$.

Setup: In the setup phase, the forger $\mathcal{F}$ sends the public parameter $\mathsf{pp}_{\mathsf{sgn}}$ and public key pk received from its own challenger to the adversary $\mathcal{A}$. It also sets the list of randomness RList and list of message MList to ϕ.
Simulation of Query Phase: The adversary $\mathcal{A}$ issues polynomially many adaptive queries to the oracles $\mathcal{O}_{\mathsf{Rand}}(\cdot)$ and $\mathcal{O}_{\mathsf{RSign}}(m, \rho)$.

- *Simulating the oracle* $\mathcal{O}_{\mathsf{Rand}}(\cdot)$: Upon receiving a query to this oracle, the forger $\mathcal{F}$ samples a randomness $\rho = \mathsf{c} = \{c_i\}_{i=1}^{S-1} \xleftarrow{\$} \mathbb{Z}_N^{S-1}$, sets $\mathsf{RList} \leftarrow \mathsf{RList} \cup \{\rho\}$ and returns ρ to $\mathcal{A}$.
- *Simulating the oracle* $\mathcal{O}_{\mathsf{RSign}}(m, \rho)$: In response to a query on a message - randomness pair (m, ρ), the forger $\mathcal{F}$ checks if $\rho \notin \mathsf{RList}$. If the check succeeds it returns $\perp$; otherwise, it passes m to its signing oracle. Upon receiving a signature $\sigma = (\mathsf{h} = \{h_i\}_{i=1}^{T}, \mathsf{z} = \{z_i\}_{i=1}^{T})$ from its oracle, $\mathcal{F}$ computes $z_i' = z_i - \mathsf{sign}(h_i)c_{|h_i|} \pmod N$ and returns the signature $\sigma' = (\mathsf{h} = \{h_i\}_{i=1}^{T}, \mathsf{z}' = \{z_i'\}_{i=1}^{T})$ under randomized secret key $\mathsf{sk}' = \mathsf{sk} + \rho$ to $\mathcal{A}$. It then sets $\mathsf{MList} \leftarrow \mathsf{MList} \cup \{m\}$.

Extracting the forgery: $\mathcal{A}$ eventually submits a forgery (m^*, σ^*, ρ^*) where $\sigma^* = (\mathsf{h}^* = \{h_i^*\}_{i=1}^{T}, \mathsf{z}^* = \{z_i^*\}_{i=1}^{T})$ and $\rho^* = \mathsf{c}^* = \{c_i^*\}_{i=1}^{S-1}$. The forger $\mathcal{F}$ modifies the signature σ^* to frame a forgery under the key pk by adding $\mathsf{sign}(h_i^*)c^*_{|h_i^*|}$ to z_i^*. It thus computes $\bar{z}_i^* = (z_i^* + \mathsf{sign}(h_i^*)c^*_{|h_i^*|}) \mod N$ and outputs $(\mathsf{h}^* = \{h_i^*\}_{i=1}^{T}, \bar{\mathsf{z}}^* = \{\bar{z}_i^*\}_{i=1}^{T})$ as a forgery to its challenger.

For the analysis, we assume that the probability with which $\mathcal{A}$ wins in the experiment $\mathsf{Exp}_{\mathsf{RCSI\text{-}FiSh},\mathcal{A}}^{\mathsf{UF\text{-}CMA\text{-}HRK}}(\lambda)$ is non-negligible. We shall now demonstrate that the forger $\mathcal{F}$ provides a perfect simulation of the oracle $\mathcal{O}_{\mathsf{RSign}}$ on message-randomness pair (m, ρ) with $\rho = \mathsf{c} = \{c_i\}_{i=1}^{S-1}$. The signature on m under $\mathsf{pk} = \{E_{A_i}\}_{i=1}^{S-1}$ received by $\mathcal{F}$ from its own signing oracle consists of $\mathsf{h} = \{h_i\}_{i=1}^{T}$ and $\mathsf{z} = \{z_i\}_{i=1}^{T}$ where $(h_1, \ldots, h_T) = \mathcal{H}_1(E_{B_1}|| \ldots ||E_{B_T}||m)$ with $E_{B_i} = [b_i]E_0$ for $b_i \in \mathbb{Z}_N$ and $z_i = (b_i - \mathsf{sign}(h_i)a_{|h_i|}) \mod N$. The value h is independent of the secret key $\mathsf{sk} = \{a_i\}_{i=1}^{S-1}$, therefore only the z value needs to be adjusted and is computed as follows $z_i' = z_i - \mathsf{sign}(h_i)c_{|h_i|} \pmod N = b_i - \mathsf{sign}(h_i)a_{|h_i|} - \mathsf{sign}(h_i)c_{|h_i|} \pmod N = b_i - \mathsf{sign}(h_i)(a_{|h_i|} + c_{|h_i|}) \pmod N$. Thus, $\sigma' = (\mathsf{h} = \{h_i\}_{i=1}^{T}, \mathsf{z}' = \{z_i'\}_{i=1}^{T})$ is a signature on m under the rerandomized public key $\mathsf{pk}' = \{[c_i]E_{A_i}\}_{i=1}^{S-1}$ where $[c_i]E_{A_i} = [c_i][a_i]E_0 = [c_i + a_i]E_0$ with the same randomness as $\sigma = (\mathsf{h} = \{h_i\}_{i=1}^{T}, \mathsf{z} = \{z_i\}_{i=1}^{T})$. This indicates that the distribution of the signing queries is identical to that of the experiment $\mathsf{Exp}_{\mathsf{RCSI\text{-}FiSh},\mathcal{A}}^{\mathsf{UF\text{-}CMA\text{-}HRK}}(\lambda)$.

Similarly, the forgery of $\mathcal{F}$ is computed from the forgery of $\mathcal{A}$. Let the adversary $\mathcal{A}$ submit a valid message m^*, signature $\sigma^* = (\mathsf{h}^* = \{h_i^*\}_{i=1}^{T}, \mathsf{z}^* = \{z_i^*\}_{i=1}^{T})$ and randomness $\rho^* = \mathsf{c}^* = \{c_i^*\}_{i=1}^{S-1}$ where $(h_1^*, \ldots, h_T^*) = \mathcal{H}_1(E_{B_1^*}|| \ldots ||E_{B_T^*} ||m^*)$ with $E_{B_i^*} = [b_i^*]E_0$ for $b_i^* \in \mathbb{Z}_N$ and $z_i^* = (b_i^* - \mathsf{sign}(h_i^*)(a_{|h_i^*|} + c^*_{|h_i^*|}))$ mod N. The forger $\mathcal{F}$ computes $\bar{z}_i^* = z_i^* + \mathsf{sign}(h_i^*)c^*_{|h_i^*|} \pmod N = b_i^* - \mathsf{sign}(h_i^*)(a_{|h_i^*|} + c^*_{|h_i^*|}) + \mathsf{sign}(h_i^*)c^*_{|h_i^*|} \pmod N = b_i^* - \mathsf{sign}(h_i^*)a_{|h_i^*|} \pmod N$ and sets $\bar{\sigma}^* = (\mathsf{h}^* = \{h_i^*\}_{i=1}^{T}, \bar{\mathsf{z}}^* = \{\bar{z}_i^*\}_{i=1}^{T})$. Then $\bar{\sigma}^*$ is a valid signature on m^* under $\mathsf{pk} = \{E_{A_i}\}_{i=1}^{S-1}$. Moreover, $\mathcal{F}$ queries identical messages as $\mathcal{A}$ while responding signing queries for $\mathcal{A}$, and therefore whenever $\mathcal{A}$ wins in the experiment $\mathsf{Exp}_{\mathsf{RCSI\text{-}FiSh},\mathcal{A}}^{\mathsf{UF\text{-}CMA\text{-}HRK}}(\lambda)$, $\mathcal{F}$ wins in the experiment $\mathsf{Exp}_{\mathsf{CSI\text{-}FiSh},\mathcal{A}}^{\mathsf{UF\text{-}CMA}}(\lambda)$. $\square$

4.2 Signature Scheme with Perfectly Rerandomizable Keys from CSI-SharK

This section describes our signature scheme with perfectly rerandomizable keys from CSI-SharK and is referred as *rerandomized* CSI-SharK (RCSI-SharK).
We set RCSI-SharK.Setup = CSI-SharK.Setup, RCSI-SharK.KeyGen = CSI-SharK. KeyGen, RCSI-SharK.Sign = CSI-SharK.Sign, RCSI-SharK.Verify = CSI-SharK.Verify.

RCSI-SharK.Randsk($\mathsf{pp_{sgn}}$, sk, ρ) $\rightarrow$ sk$'$: On input a public parameter $\mathsf{pp_{sgn}}$, a secret key $\mathsf{sk} = a$ and randomness $\rho = c \xleftarrow{\$} \mathbb{Z}_N$, This algorithm outputs a rerandomized secret key $\mathsf{sk}' = \mathsf{sk} + \rho = (a + c) \mod N = d$.

RCSI-SharK.Randpk($\mathsf{pp_{sgn}}$, pk, ρ) $\rightarrow$ pk$'$: On input a public parameter $\mathsf{pp_{sgn}}$, a public key $\mathsf{pk} = (\mathfrak{R}_{S-1}, \{E_{A_i}\}_{i=1}^{S-1})$ and randomness $\rho = c \xleftarrow{\$} \mathbb{Z}_N$, this algorithm outputs a rerandomized public key $\mathsf{pk}' = \{\mathfrak{R}_{S-1}, [r_i c]E_{A_i}\}_{i=1}^{S-1}$ where $[r_i c]E_{A_i} = [r_i c][r_i a]E_0 = [r_i(c + a)]E_0 = [r_i d]E_0 = E_{D_i}$.

Correctness. The correctness of our scheme RCSI-SharK is similar to the correctness of our scheme RCSI-FiSh described in Sect. 4.1.

Theorem 4.21. *Our proposed signature scheme with perfectly rerandomizable keys* RCSI-SharK *is* UF-CMA-HRK *secure as per Definition 4.02 as the signature scheme* CSI-SharK *is* UF-CMA *secure as per Definition 3.02.*

Proof. Similar to the proof of Theorem 4.12. □

5 Stateful Deterministic Wallet

Definition 5.01. A stateful deterministic wallet is a tuple of algorithms SW = (SW.Setup, SW.MGen, SW.SKDer, SW.PKDer, SW.Sign, SW.Verify) which satisfy the following requirements:

SW.Setup(1^λ) $\rightarrow$ pp: A trusted party on input the security parameter 1^λ outputs a public parameter pp.

SW.MGen(pp) $\rightarrow$ (msk, mpk, St_0): This master key generation algorithm takes as input pp and outputs a master key pair (msk, mpk) and an initial state St_0.

SW.SKDer(pp, msk, id, St) $\rightarrow$ ($\mathsf{sk_{id}}$, St'): On input pp, msk, an identity id and a state St, this secret key derivation algorithm outputs a session secret key $\mathsf{sk_{id}}$ and a new state St'.

SW.PKDer(pp, mpk, id, St) $\rightarrow$ ($\mathsf{pk_{id}}$, St'): On input pp, mpk, an identity id and a state St, this public key derivation algorithm outputs a session public key $\mathsf{pk_{id}}$ and a new state St'.

SW.Sign(pp, $\mathsf{sk_{id}}$, $\mathsf{pk_{id}}$, m) $\rightarrow$ σ: This is a randomized algorithm that on input pp, a session secret key $\mathsf{sk_{id}}$, a session public key $\mathsf{pk_{id}}$ for some identity id and a message $m \in \mathcal{M}$ outputs a signature σ.

$\mathsf{SW.Verify}(\mathsf{pp}, \mathsf{pk}_{\mathsf{id}}, m, \sigma) \rightarrow 1/0$: This is a deterministic algorithm that on input pp, a session public key $\mathsf{pk}_{\mathsf{id}}$ for some identity id, a message $m \in \mathcal{M}$, and a signature σ verifies the validity of σ on the message m.

Correctness. For $n \in \mathbb{N}$, any $(\mathsf{msk}, \mathsf{mpk}, St_0) \leftarrow \mathsf{SW.MGen}(\mathsf{pp})$ and any identities $\{\mathsf{id}_1, \ldots, \mathsf{id}_n\} \in \{0,1\}^*$, we define the sequence $(\mathsf{sk}_{\mathsf{id}_i}, St_i)$ and $(\mathsf{pk}_{\mathsf{id}_i}, St_i)$ for $1 \leq i \leq n$ recursively as $(\mathsf{sk}_{\mathsf{id}_i}, St_i) \leftarrow \mathsf{SW.SKDer}(\mathsf{pp}, \mathsf{msk}, \mathsf{id}_i, St_{i-1})$, $(\mathsf{pk}_{\mathsf{id}_i}, St_i) \leftarrow \mathsf{SW.PKDer}(\mathsf{pp}, \mathsf{mpk}, \mathsf{id}_i, St_{i-1})$. A stateful deterministic wallet SW is said to be correct if $\forall\, m \in \mathcal{M}$ and i with $1 \leq i \leq n$, we have $\Pr[\mathsf{SW.Verify}(\mathsf{pp}, \mathsf{pk}_{\mathsf{id}_i}, m, \mathsf{SW.Sign}(\mathsf{pp}, \mathsf{sk}_{\mathsf{id}_i}, \mathsf{pk}_{\mathsf{id}_i}, m)) = 1] = 1$.
We now describe the two security requirements for a stateful deterministic wallet SW: *Wallet Unlinkability* and *Wallet Unforgeability*.

Definition 5.02. A stateful deterministic wallet SW satisfies against *wallet unforgeability* (WAL-UNF) if the advantage $\mathsf{Adv}^{\mathsf{WAL\text{-}UNF}}_{\mathsf{SW},\mathcal{A}}(\lambda)$ of any PPT adversary $\mathcal{A}$, defined as

$$\mathsf{Adv}^{\mathsf{WAL\text{-}UNF}}_{\mathsf{SW},\mathcal{A}}(\lambda) = \Pr[\mathcal{A} \text{ wins in } \mathsf{Exp}^{\mathsf{WAL\text{-}UNF}}_{\mathsf{SW},\mathcal{A}}(\lambda)]$$

is negligible, where unforgeability experiment $\mathsf{Exp}^{\mathsf{WAL\text{-}UNF}}_{\mathsf{SW},\mathcal{A}}(\lambda)$ between a challenger $\mathcal{C}$ and adversary $\mathcal{A}$ is depicted in Fig. 3.

Setup: The challenger $\mathcal{C}$ generates $\mathsf{pp} \leftarrow \mathsf{SW.Setup}(1^\lambda)$ and (msk, mpk) along with a state St by invoking the algorithm SW.MGen(pp). It forwards pp, mpk and St to the adversary $\mathcal{A}$ while keeps msk secret to itself. It also sets two lists KList and MsgList to ϕ.

Query Phase : $\mathcal{A}$ issues polynomially many adaptive queries to the oracles $\mathcal{O}_{\mathsf{PK}}(\mathsf{id})$ and $\mathcal{O}_{\mathsf{WalSign}}(m, \mathsf{id})$.

- $\mathcal{O}_{\mathsf{PK}}(\mathsf{id})$: In response to a query on identity id, the challenger $\mathcal{C}$ parallelly computes the session secret key $(\mathsf{sk}_{\mathsf{id}}, St') \leftarrow \mathsf{SW.SKDer}(\mathsf{pp}, \mathsf{msk}, \mathsf{id}, St)$ and corresponding session public key $(\mathsf{pk}_{\mathsf{id}}, St') \leftarrow \mathsf{SW.PKDer}(\mathsf{pp}, \mathsf{mpk}, \mathsf{id}, St)$ using the same current state St. It updates KList as $\mathsf{KList} = \mathsf{KList} \cup \{(\mathsf{id}, \mathsf{sk}_{\mathsf{id}}, \mathsf{pk}_{\mathsf{id}})\}$ and returns $\mathsf{pk}_{\mathsf{id}}$ to the adversary $\mathcal{A}$.
- $\mathcal{O}_{\mathsf{WalSign}}(m, \mathsf{id})$: In response to a query on some arbitrary message m and identity id, the challenger $\mathcal{C}$ extracts the session key pair $(\mathsf{sk}_{\mathsf{id}}, \mathsf{pk}_{\mathsf{id}})$ from KList, computes a signature $\sigma \leftarrow \mathsf{SW.Sign}(\mathsf{pp}, \mathsf{sk}_{\mathsf{id}}, \mathsf{pk}_{\mathsf{id}}, m)$ on m and returns the signature σ to $\mathcal{A}$. It also updates MsgList as $\mathsf{MsgList} = \mathsf{MsgList} \cup \{(\mathsf{id}, m)\}$. In case $(\mathsf{id}, \mathsf{sk}_{\mathsf{id}}, \mathsf{pk}_{\mathsf{id}}) \notin \mathsf{KList}$, it returns $\perp$.

Forgery: $\mathcal{A}$ eventually produces a forgery comprising of a message m^*, a signature σ^* and an identity id^*. $\mathcal{A}$ wins the game if (i) $(\mathsf{id}^*, m^*) \notin \mathsf{MsgList}$, (ii) $(\mathsf{id}^*, \mathsf{sk}_{\mathsf{id}^*}, \mathsf{pk}_{\mathsf{id}^*}) \in \mathsf{KList}$, (iii) σ^* is a valid signature on m^* under $\mathsf{pk}_{\mathsf{id}^*}$ where $(\mathsf{id}^*, \mathsf{sk}_{\mathsf{id}^*}, \mathsf{pk}_{\mathsf{id}^*}) \in \mathsf{KList}$.

Fig. 3. $\mathsf{Exp}^{\mathsf{WAL\text{-}UNF}}_{\mathsf{SW},\mathcal{A}}(\lambda)$: Wallet Unforgeability

Definition 5.03. A stateful deterministic wallet SW satisfies *wallet unlinkability* (WAL-UNL) if the advantage $\mathsf{Adv}^{\mathsf{WAL\text{-}UNL}}_{\mathsf{SW},\mathcal{A}}(\lambda)$ of any PPT adversary $\mathcal{A}$, defined as

$$\mathsf{Adv}^{\mathsf{WAL\text{-}UNL}}_{\mathsf{SW},\mathcal{A}}(\lambda) = |\Pr[\mathsf{Exp}^{\mathsf{WAL\text{-}UNL}}_{\mathsf{SW},\mathcal{A}}(\lambda) = 1] - \frac{1}{2}|$$

is negligible, where the unlinkability experiment $\mathsf{Exp}^{\mathsf{WAL\text{-}UNL}}_{\mathsf{SW},\mathcal{A}}(\lambda)$ is depicted in Fig. 4.

Setup: The challenger $\mathcal{C}$ generates $\mathsf{pp} \leftarrow \mathsf{SW.Setup}(1^\lambda)$ and $(\mathsf{msk}, \mathsf{mpk})$ along with a state St by running the algorithm $\mathsf{SW.MGen}(\mathsf{pp})$. It forwards pp and mpk to the adversary $\mathcal{A}$ while keeps msk and St secret to itself. It also sets KList to ϕ.

Query Phase 1: $\mathcal{A}$ issues polynomially many adaptive queries to the oracles $\mathcal{O}_{\mathsf{PK}}(\mathsf{id})$ and $\mathcal{O}_{\mathsf{WalSign}}(m, \mathsf{id})$.

- $\mathcal{O}_{\mathsf{PK}}(\mathsf{id})$: In response to a query on identity id, $\mathcal{C}$ parallelly computes the session secret key $(\mathsf{sk}_{\mathsf{id}}, St') \leftarrow \mathsf{SW.SKDer}(\mathsf{pp}, \mathsf{msk}, \mathsf{id}, St)$ and corresponding session public key $(\mathsf{pk}_{\mathsf{id}}, St') \leftarrow \mathsf{SW.PKDer}(\mathsf{pp}, \mathsf{mpk}, \mathsf{id}, St)$ using the same current state St. It updates KList as $\mathsf{KList} = \mathsf{KList} \cup \{(\mathsf{id}, \mathsf{sk}_{\mathsf{id}}, \mathsf{pk}_{\mathsf{id}})\}$ and returns $\mathsf{pk}_{\mathsf{id}}$ to $\mathcal{A}$.
- $\mathcal{O}_{\mathsf{WalSign}}(m, \mathsf{id})$: In response to a query on some arbitrary message $m \in \mathcal{M}$ and identity id, $\mathcal{C}$ extracts the session key pair $(\mathsf{sk}_{\mathsf{id}}, \mathsf{pk}_{\mathsf{id}})$ corresponding to id from KList, computes a signature $\sigma \leftarrow \mathsf{SW.Sign}(\mathsf{pp}, \mathsf{sk}_{\mathsf{id}}, \mathsf{pk}_{\mathsf{id}}, m)$ on m and returns the signature σ to $\mathcal{A}$. In case $(\mathsf{id}, \mathsf{sk}_{\mathsf{id}}, \mathsf{pk}_{\mathsf{id}}) \notin \mathsf{KList}$, it returns $\perp$.

Challenge: $\mathcal{A}$ submits an identity id^*. If none of the oracles $\mathcal{O}_{\mathsf{WalSign}}$ or $\mathcal{O}_{\mathsf{PK}}$ has been previously queried on id^*, $\mathcal{C}$ returns a session public key $\mathsf{pk}^b_{\mathsf{id}^*}$ that depends on a uniformly random bit b chosen by $\mathcal{C}$.

- If $b = 0$, the session key pair $(\mathsf{sk}^0_{\mathsf{id}^*}, \mathsf{pk}^0_{\mathsf{id}^*})$ is derived from the current state St and master secret-public key as follows:
  - $(\mathsf{sk}^0_{\mathsf{id}^*}, St^*) \leftarrow \mathsf{SW.SKDer}(\mathsf{pp}, \mathsf{msk}, \mathsf{id}^*, St)$
  - $(\mathsf{pk}^0_{\mathsf{id}^*}, St^*) \leftarrow \mathsf{SW.PKDer}(\mathsf{pp}, \mathsf{mpk}, \mathsf{id}^*, St)$
- If $b = 1$, the session key pair $(\mathsf{sk}^1_{\mathsf{id}^*}, \mathsf{pk}^1_{\mathsf{id}^*})$ is derived from a freshly-generated master key and state for the same identity id^* via the sequence of steps:
  - $(\widehat{\mathsf{msk}}, \widehat{\mathsf{mpk}}, \widehat{St}) \leftarrow \mathsf{SW.MGen}(\mathsf{pp})$
  - $(\mathsf{sk}^1_{\mathsf{id}^*}, St^*) \leftarrow \mathsf{SK.SKDer}(\mathsf{pp}, \widehat{\mathsf{msk}}, \mathsf{id}^*, \widehat{St})$
  - $(\mathsf{pk}^1_{\mathsf{id}^*}, St^*) \leftarrow \mathsf{SK.PKDer}(\mathsf{pp}, \widehat{\mathsf{mpk}}, \mathsf{id}^*, \widehat{St})$

The challenger then sets $\mathsf{KList} = \mathsf{KList} \cup \{\mathsf{id}^*, \mathsf{sk}^b_{\mathsf{id}^*}, \mathsf{pk}^b_{\mathsf{id}^*}\}$.

Query Phase 2: $\mathcal{A}$ gets access to oracles $\mathcal{O}_{\mathsf{PK}}(\mathsf{id})$, $\mathcal{O}_{\mathsf{WalSign}}(m, \mathsf{id})$ and $\mathcal{O}_{\mathsf{getSt}}(\cdot)$ where $\mathcal{O}_{\mathsf{getSt}}(\cdot)$ returns the current state of the wallet.

Guess : The adversary $\mathcal{A}$ eventually outputs a guess bit b' for bit b and wins the game if $b' = b$.

Fig. 4. $\mathsf{Exp}^{\mathsf{WAL\text{-}UNL}}_{\mathsf{SW}, \mathcal{A}}(\lambda)$: Wallet Unlinkability

6 Stateful Deterministic Wallet from Isogenies

This section describes our construction of a stateful deterministic wallet SW from isogenies using our rerandomized signature $\mathsf{RCSI\text{-}FiSh}$ given in Sect. 4.1.

$\mathsf{SW.Setup}(1^\lambda) \rightarrow \mathsf{pp}$: A trusted party on input 1^λ outputs pp.

i. Same as the algorithm $\mathsf{CSI\text{-}FiSh.Setup}$ which is described in Sect. 3.1. Additionally, it samples a hash function $\mathcal{H}_2 : \{0,1\}^* \rightarrow \mathbb{Z}_N^{S-1} \times \{0,1\}^\lambda$.
ii. Return $\mathsf{pp} = (\mathsf{pp}_{\mathrm{sgn}}, \mathcal{H}_2)$ where $\mathsf{pp}_{\mathrm{sgn}} = (p, \mathfrak{g}, N, E_0, \mathcal{H}_1, S, T)$.

$\mathsf{SW.MGen}(\mathsf{pp}) \rightarrow (\mathsf{msk}, \mathsf{mpk}, St_0)$: On input pp, this algorithm generates a master secret key msk, master public key mpk and an initial state St_0 as follows:

i. Sample an initial state $St_0 \xleftarrow{\$} \{0,1\}^\lambda$.
ii. Execute the $\mathsf{RCSI\text{-}FiSh.KeyGen}(\mathsf{pp}_{\mathrm{sgn}})$ algorithm to compute the master key pair as follows:
   - Sample $a_i \in \mathbb{Z}_N$ and compute the curve $E_{A_i} = [a_i]E_0 \ \forall i \in [S-1]$.
   - Set $\mathsf{msk} = \mathsf{a} = \{a_i\}_{i=1}^{S-1}$ and $\mathsf{mpk} = \{E_{A_i}\}_{i=1}^{S-1}$.
iii. Return $(\mathsf{msk}, \mathsf{mpk}, St_0)$.

$\mathsf{SW.SKDer}(\mathsf{pp}, \mathsf{msk}, \mathsf{id}, St)$: This algorithm takes as input pp, $\mathsf{msk} = \mathsf{a} = \{a_i\}_{i=1}^{S-1}$, an identity $\mathsf{id} \in \{0,1\}^*$, and a current state St. It outputs a session secret key $\mathsf{sk}_{\mathsf{id}}$ and an updated state St' as follows:

i. Compute $(\rho_{\mathsf{id}}, St') = \mathcal{H}_2(St, \mathsf{id})$ where $\rho_{\mathsf{id}} \in \mathbb{Z}_N^{S-1}$ and $St' \in \{0,1\}^\lambda$.
ii. Compute the session secret key by executing RCSI-FiSh.Randsk $(\mathsf{pp}_{\mathsf{sgn}}, \mathsf{msk}, \rho_{\mathsf{id}})$ as follows:
  - Let randomness $\rho_{\mathsf{id}} = \mathsf{c}_{\mathsf{id}} = \{c_{\mathsf{id},i}\}_{i=1}^{S-1} \xleftarrow{\$} \mathbb{Z}_N^{S-1}$.
  - Compute the rerandomized secret key $\mathsf{sk}_{\mathsf{id}} = \mathsf{msk} + \rho_{\mathsf{id}} = (\mathsf{a} + \mathsf{c}_{\mathsf{id}}) \bmod N = \{d_{\mathsf{id},i}\}_{i=1}^{S-1}$ where $d_{\mathsf{id},i} = a_i + c_{\mathsf{id},i}$.
iii. Return $\mathsf{sk}_{\mathsf{id}} = \{d_{\mathsf{id},i}\}_{i=1}^{S-1} = \mathsf{d}_{\mathsf{id}}$ and St'.

SW.PKDer(pp, mpk, id, St): This algorithm takes as input pp, $\mathsf{mpk} = \{E_{A_i}\}_{i=1}^{S-1}$, an identity $\mathsf{id} \in \{0,1\}^*$, and a current state St. It outputs a session public key $\mathsf{pk}_{\mathsf{id}}$ and an updated state St' as follows:

i. Compute $(\rho_{\mathsf{id}}, St') = \mathcal{H}_2(St, \mathsf{id})$.
ii. Compute the session public key by executing RCSI-FiSh.Randpk $(\mathsf{pp}_{\mathsf{sgn}}, \mathsf{mpk}, \rho_{\mathsf{id}})$ algorithm as follows:
  - Let randomness $\rho_{\mathsf{id}} = \mathsf{c}_{\mathsf{id}} = \{c_{\mathsf{id},i}\}_{i=1}^{S-1} \xleftarrow{\$} \mathbb{Z}_N^{S-1}$.
  - Compute a rerandomized public key $\mathsf{pk}_{\mathsf{id}} = \{[c_{\mathsf{id},i}]E_{A_i}\}_{i=1}^{S-1}$ where $[c_{\mathsf{id},i}]E_{A_i} = [c_{\mathsf{id},i}][a_i]E_0 = [c_{\mathsf{id},i} + a_i]E_0 = [d_{\mathsf{id},i}]E_0 = E_{D_{\mathsf{id},i}}$.
iii. Return $\mathsf{pk}_{\mathsf{id}} = E_{D_{\mathsf{id},i}}$ and the updated state St'.

SW.Sign(pp, $\mathsf{sk}_{\mathsf{id}}$, $\mathsf{pk}_{\mathsf{id}}$, m) $\to \sigma$: The algorithm generates a signature σ on a message $m \in \{0,1\}^*$ using a session secret key $\mathsf{sk}_{\mathsf{id}} = \{d_{\mathsf{id},i}\}_{i=1}^{S-1} = \mathsf{d}_{\mathsf{id}}$ and session public key $\mathsf{pk}_{\mathsf{id}} = E_{D_{\mathsf{id},i}}$ corresponding to an identity id as follows:

i. Set $\widehat{m} = (\mathsf{pk}_{\mathsf{id}}, m)$.
ii. Compute a signature σ on $\widehat{m}$ by executing the algorithm RCSI-FiSh.Sign $(\mathsf{pp}_{\mathsf{sgn}}, \mathsf{sk}_{\mathsf{id}}, \widehat{m})$ as follows:
  - Set $d_{\mathsf{id},0} \leftarrow 0$ and samples $b_i \in \mathbb{Z}_N \ \forall i \in [T]$.
  - Compute the curves $E_{B_i} = [b_i]E_0 \ \forall i \in [T]$, the challenge vector $(h_1, \dots, h_T) = \mathcal{H}_1(E_{B_1}||\cdots||E_{B_T}||\widehat{m}) \in \{-S+1, \dots, 0, \dots, S-1\}^T$ and the response $z_{\mathsf{id},i} = b_i$ - $\mathsf{sign}(h_i)d_{\mathsf{id},|h_i|} \pmod N \ \forall i \in [T]$.
  - Set the signature $\sigma = (\mathsf{h}, \mathsf{z}_{\mathsf{id}})$ where $\mathsf{h} = \{h_i\}_{i=1}^T$ and $\mathsf{z}_{\mathsf{id}} = \{z_{\mathsf{id},i}\}_{i=1}^T$.
iii. Return the signature σ.

SW.Verify(pp, $\mathsf{pk}_{\mathsf{id}}$, m, σ) $\to$ 1/0: Employing the session public key $\mathsf{pk}_{\mathsf{id}} = \{E_{D_{\mathsf{id},i}}\}_{i=1}^{S-1}$, the algorithm verifies the signature $\sigma = (\mathsf{h}, \mathsf{z}_{\mathsf{id}})$ on m as follows:

i. Set $\widehat{m} = (\mathsf{pk}_{\mathsf{id}}, m)$.
ii. Verify the signature σ on $\widehat{m}$ by running the algorithm RCSI-FiSh.Verify $(\mathsf{pp}_{\mathsf{sgn}}, \mathsf{pk}_{\mathsf{id}}, \widehat{m}, \sigma)$ as follows:
  - Parse $\sigma = (\mathsf{h} = \{h_i\}_{i=1}^T, \mathsf{z}_{\mathsf{id}} = \{z_{\mathsf{id},i}\}_{i=1}^T)$.
  - Define $E_{D_{\mathsf{id},-i}} = E_{D_{\mathsf{id},i}}^{\mathsf{twist}} \ \forall i \in [S-1]$.
  - Extract the curves $E_{D_{\mathsf{id},h_i}}$ from pk and computes $E_{B_i} = [z_i]E_{D_{\mathsf{id},h_i}} \ \forall i \in [T]$ and the challenge vector $(h_1', \dots, h_T') = \mathcal{H}_1(E_{B_1}||\cdots||E_{B_T}||\widehat{m})$.
  - If $(h_1, \dots, h_T) = (h_1', \dots, h_T')$ return 1, else return 0.

Correctness. The correctness of our stateful deterministic wallet SW follows from the correctness of RCSI-FiSh.

Theorem 6.01. *Let $\mathcal{A}$ be an algorithm that plays in the unforgeability experiment $\mathsf{Exp}^{\mathsf{WAL\text{-}UNF}}_{\mathsf{SW},\mathcal{A}}(\lambda)$ as described in Fig. 3. Then there exists a PPT adversary $\mathcal{B}$ that plays in the experiment $\mathsf{Exp}^{\mathsf{UF\text{-}CMA\text{-}HRK}}_{\mathsf{RCSI\text{-}FiSh},\mathcal{B}}(\lambda)$ shown in Fig. 2 running in roughly the same time as $\mathcal{A}$ such that $\mathsf{Adv}^{\mathsf{WAL\text{-}UNF}}_{\mathsf{SW},\mathcal{A}}(\lambda) \leq \mathsf{Adv}^{\mathsf{UF\text{-}CMA\text{-}HRK}}_{\mathsf{RCSI-FiSh},\mathcal{B}}(\lambda) + \frac{q^2_{\mathcal{H}_2}}{N}$ where RCSI-FiSh is the signature scheme with uniquely rerandomizable keys introduced in Sect. 4.1, $q_{\mathcal{H}_2}$ denotes the number of queries to $\mathcal{H}_2$ made by $\mathcal{A}$ and N is the class number of $\mathsf{Cl}(\mathcal{O})$.*

Proof. Let $\mathcal{A}$ be an adversary playing in the experiment $\mathsf{Exp}^{\mathsf{WAL\text{-}UNF}}_{\mathsf{SW},\mathcal{A}}(\lambda)$ as in Fig 3. By definition of the experiment $\mathsf{Exp}^{\mathsf{WAL\text{-}UNF}}_{\mathsf{SW},\mathcal{A}}(\lambda)$, $\mathcal{A}$ is provided the initial master public key mpk and the initial state St by the challenger. It is also provided access to the oracles $\mathcal{O}_{\mathsf{PK}}(\mathsf{id})$, $\mathcal{O}_{\mathsf{WalSign}}(m, \mathsf{id})$ and the random oracle $\mathcal{H}_2$. This theorem is proven via a hybrid argument that is based on two security games. The transition between the two games is detailed below:

Game G_0: This game is identical to the true unforgeability experiment $\mathsf{Exp}^{\mathsf{WAL\text{-}UNF}}_{\mathsf{SW},\mathcal{A}}(\lambda)$ as in Fig. 3. However, whenever $\mathcal{A}$ issues a query to the oracle $\mathcal{O}_{\mathsf{PK}}(\mathsf{id})$ for which $(\mathsf{id}, \mathsf{sk}_{\mathsf{id}}, \mathsf{pk}_{\mathsf{id}}), (\mathsf{id}', \mathsf{sk}_{\mathsf{id}'}, \mathsf{pk}_{\mathsf{id}'}) \in \mathsf{KList}$ with $\mathsf{sk}_{\mathsf{id}} = \mathsf{sk}_{\mathsf{id}'}$ and $\mathsf{pk}_{\mathsf{id}} = \mathsf{pk}_{\mathsf{id}'}$, the game G_0 internally sets $\mathsf{flag} \leftarrow \mathsf{true}$.

Game G_1: Except for one important modification, this game is almost identical to the preceding game. It aborts whenever flag is set to true.

For any adversary $\mathcal{A}$ and any $i \in \{0,1\}$, let $\wp_{\mathcal{A},i} : \mathbb{N} \rightarrow [0,1]$ denote the function such that $\forall\ \lambda \in \mathbb{N}$, $\wp_{\mathcal{A},i}(\lambda)$ is the probability that the adversary $\mathcal{A}$, on input 1^λ, outputs a forgery in game G_i. From the definition of game G_0, it follows that for all $\lambda \in \mathbb{N}$, $\wp_{\mathcal{A},0}(\lambda) = \Pr[\mathsf{Exp}^{\mathsf{WAL\text{-}UNF}}_{\mathsf{SW},\mathcal{A}}(\lambda) = 1]$. Hence, we have

$$\begin{aligned}\mathsf{Adv}^{\mathsf{WAL\text{-}UNF}}_{\mathsf{SW},\mathcal{A}}(\lambda) =& |\Pr[\mathsf{Exp}^{\mathsf{WAL\text{-}UNF}}_{\mathsf{SW},\mathcal{A}}(\lambda) = 1]| \\ \leq& |\wp_{\mathcal{A},0}(\lambda) - \wp_{\mathcal{A},1}(\lambda)| + |\wp_{\mathcal{A},1}(\lambda)| \\ \leq& \frac{q^2_{\mathcal{H}_2}}{N} + \mathsf{Adv}^{\mathsf{UF\text{-}CMA\text{-}HRK}}_{\mathsf{RCSI\text{-}FiSh},\mathcal{B}}\end{aligned}$$

by Lemma 6.02 and Lemma 6.03 proved below. □

Lemma 6.02. *We have $|\wp_{\mathcal{A},0}(\lambda) - \wp_{\mathcal{A},1}(\lambda)| \leq \frac{q^2_{\mathcal{H}_2}}{N}$ where $q_{\mathcal{H}_2}$ denotes the number of random oracle queries to $\mathcal{H}_2$ made by the adversary $\mathcal{A}$.*

Proof. A collision of session keys of the form $(\mathsf{sk}_{\mathsf{id}}, \mathsf{pk}_{\mathsf{id}}) = (\mathsf{sk}_{\mathsf{id}'}, \mathsf{pk}_{\mathsf{id}'})$ for different identities id and id′ would imply that $\mathsf{RCSI\text{-}FiSh.Randpk}(\mathsf{pp}_{\mathsf{sgn}}, \mathsf{mpk}, \rho_{\mathsf{id}}) = \mathsf{RCSI\text{-}FiSh.Randpk}(\mathsf{pp}_{\mathsf{sgn}}, \mathsf{mpk}, \rho_{\mathsf{id}'})$. Leveraging the property of uniquely rerandomizable public keys of RCSI-FiSh as proved in Lemma 4.11 in Sect. 4, we have $\rho_{\mathsf{id}} = \rho_{\mathsf{id}'}$ where $(\rho_{\mathsf{id}}, \cdot) = \mathcal{H}_2(\cdot, \mathsf{id})$ and $(\rho_{\mathsf{id}'}, \cdot) = \mathcal{H}_2(\cdot, \mathsf{id}')$. Since there are $q_{\mathcal{H}_2}$ queries issued to $\mathcal{H}_2$, we have $|\wp_{\mathcal{A},0}(\lambda) - \wp_{\mathcal{A},1}(\lambda)| \leq \frac{q^2_{\mathcal{H}_2}}{N}$. □

Lemma 6.03. *We have* $|\wp_{\mathcal{A},1}(\lambda)| \leq \mathsf{Adv}^{\mathsf{UF\text{-}CMA\text{-}HRK}}_{\mathsf{RCSI\text{-}FiSh},\mathcal{B}}(\lambda)$ *where* $\mathsf{Adv}^{\mathsf{UF\text{-}CMA\text{-}HRK}}_{\mathsf{RCSI\text{-}FiSh},\mathcal{B}}(\lambda)$ *is the advantage of adversary* $\mathcal{B}$ *in the experiment* $\mathsf{Exp}^{\mathsf{UF\text{-}CMA\text{-}HRK}}_{\mathsf{RCSI-FiSh},\mathcal{B}}$.

Proof. Let us assume that there exists a PPT adversary $\mathcal{A}$ that wins the game G_1. We will prove that $\mathcal{A}$ can be utilized as a procedure to design an adversary $\mathcal{B}$ which can break the UF-CMA-HRK security of the isogeny-based rerandomized signature scheme RCSI-FiSh introduced in Sect. 4. The adversary $\mathcal{B}$ takes on the role of a challenger in the game G_1 and simulates the random oracles queries, public key queries and signing queries.

On receiving a public parameter $\mathsf{pp}_{\mathsf{sgn}} = (p, \mathfrak{g}, N, E_0, \mathcal{H}_1, S, T)$ and public key $\mathsf{pk} = \{E_{A_i}\}_{i=1}^{S-1}$ from its own challenger, the adversary $\mathcal{B}$ simulates the game G_1 for $\mathcal{A}$ as follows:

Setup: The adversary $\mathcal{B}$ samples an initial state $St_0 \xleftarrow{\$} \{0,1\}^\lambda$ and a hash function $\mathcal{H}_2 : \{0,1\}^* \to \mathbb{Z}_N^{S-1} \times \{0,1\}^\lambda$. It uses its public parameter $\mathsf{pp}_{\mathsf{sgn}} = (p, \mathfrak{g}, N, E_0, \mathcal{H}_1, S, T)$ and public key $\mathsf{pk} = \{E_{A_i}\}_{i=1}^{S-1}$ to set the public parameter $\mathsf{pp} = (\mathsf{pp}_{\mathsf{sgn}}, \mathcal{H}_2)$ and master public key $\mathsf{mpk} = \mathsf{pk} = \{E_{A_i}\}_{i=1}^{S-1}$. It forwards pp, mpk and St to the adversary $\mathcal{A}$. In the entire course of the game, $\mathcal{B}$ updates the state whenever it responds to a query to the oracle $\mathcal{O}_{\mathsf{PK}}(\mathsf{id})$ from $\mathcal{A}$. It also set lists KList, HList, RList and MsgList to ϕ.
Simulation of Query Phase : $\mathcal{A}$ makes polynomially many adaptive queries to the oracles $\mathcal{O}_{\mathsf{PK}}(\mathsf{id})$ and $\mathcal{O}_{\mathsf{WalSign}}(m, \mathsf{id})$ and random oracle queries to $\mathcal{H}_2$.

- *Simulating the random oracle queries to* $\mathcal{H}_2$: In response to a query of the form $\mathcal{H}_2(s)$, $\mathcal{B}$ outputs $\mathcal{H}_2(s)$ if it was already set. Otherwise, $\mathcal{B}$ first queries its oracle $\mathcal{O}_{\mathsf{Rand}}(\cdot)$ to generate a randomness $\rho \leftarrow \mathbb{Z}_N^{S-1}$. Recall that the oracle $\mathcal{O}_{\mathsf{Rand}}$ internally refreshes the list of randomness $\mathsf{RList} = \mathsf{RList} \cup \{\rho\}$. $\mathcal{B}$ also samples $\varphi \xleftarrow{\$} \{0,1\}^\lambda$, returns $\mathcal{H}_2(s) = (\rho, \varphi)$ and updates $\mathsf{HList} = \mathsf{HList} \cup \{s, (\rho, \varphi)\}$.
- *Simulating the oracle* $\mathcal{O}_{\mathsf{PK}}(\mathsf{id})$: In response to a query on identity id, $\mathcal{B}$ simulates the hash value $(\rho_{\mathsf{id}}, St') = \mathcal{H}_2(St, \mathsf{id})$ as above where St is the current state, followed by computing the session public key $\mathsf{pk}_{\mathsf{id}} \leftarrow$ RCSI-FiSh.Randpk($\mathsf{pp}_{\mathsf{sgn}}$, mpk, ρ_{id}). If $\mathcal{B}$ detects a collision among secret-public key pair $(\rho_{\mathsf{id}}, \mathsf{pk}_{\mathsf{id}})$ and an existing record $(\mathsf{id}', (\rho_{\mathsf{id}'}, \mathsf{pk}_{\mathsf{id}'}))$ saved in KList, $\mathcal{B}$ terminates the simulation. Otherwise, it updates KList as KList = KList $\cup \{(\mathsf{id}, (\rho_{\mathsf{id}}, \mathsf{pk}_{\mathsf{id}}))\}$ and returns $\mathsf{pk}_{\mathsf{id}}$ to $\mathcal{A}$.
- *Simulating the oracle* $\mathcal{O}_{\mathsf{WalSign}}(m, \mathsf{id})$: In response to a query on an arbitrary message $m \in \{0,1\}^*$ and identity id, the adversary $\mathcal{B}$ extracts the tuple $(\mathsf{id}, (\rho_{\mathsf{id}}, \mathsf{pk}_{\mathsf{id}}))$ from KList. In case KList does not contain such a tuple corresponding to id, it returns $\perp$. Next, it sets $\widehat{m} = (\mathsf{pk}_{\mathsf{id}}, m)$ and submits $(\widehat{m}, \rho_{\mathsf{id}})$ to its own signing oracle $\mathcal{O}_{\mathsf{RSign}}(\widehat{m}, \rho_{\mathsf{id}})$. It also updates MsgList = MsgList $\cup \{(\mathsf{id}, m)\}$. Upon receiving a signature σ from $\mathcal{O}_{\mathsf{RSign}}(\widehat{m}, \rho_{\mathsf{id}})$ on $\widehat{m}$, it forwards it to $\mathcal{A}$. Note that the query $(\widehat{m}, \rho_{\mathsf{id}})$ on $\mathcal{O}_{\mathsf{RSign}}(\widehat{m}, \rho_{\mathsf{id}})$ does not return $\perp$ as the random oracle $\mathcal{H}_2()$ is programmed by issuing a query to the oracle $\mathcal{O}_{\mathsf{Rand}}(\cdot)$, which ensures that $\rho_{\mathsf{id}} \in$ RList. The simulated signatures are also correctly distributed as in

the real protocol which follows immediately from the correctness of RCSI-FiSh and we have $\mathsf{SW.Verify}(\mathsf{pp}, \mathsf{pk}_{\mathsf{id}}, m, \sigma) = \mathsf{RCSI\text{-}FiSh.Verify}(\mathsf{pp}_{\mathrm{sgn}}, \mathsf{RCSI\text{-}FiSh.Randpk}(\mathsf{pp}_{\mathrm{sgn}}, \mathsf{mpk}, \rho_{\mathsf{id}}), \widehat{m}, \sigma)$.

Extracting the forgery: $\mathcal{A}$ eventually submits a forgery comprising of a message m^*, a signature σ^* and an identity id^*. The adversary $\mathcal{B}$ aborts if it encounters any one of the following two cases:

- $\mathcal{O}_{\mathsf{WalSign}}$ has not been previously queried on m^*,
- $\mathcal{O}_{\mathsf{PK}}$ has not been previously queried on id^*.

If the check succeeds, the adversary $\mathcal{B}$ retrieves the key pair $(\rho_{\mathsf{id}^*}, \mathsf{pk}_{\mathsf{id}^*})$ from KList and submits $(\widehat{m}^* = (\mathsf{pk}_{\mathsf{id}^*}, m^*), \sigma^*, \rho_{\mathsf{id}^*})$ as a forgery to its own challenger. If $(m^*, \sigma^*, \mathsf{id}^*)$ is a valid forgery of $\mathcal{A}$, then $(\widehat{m}^* = (\mathsf{pk}_{\mathsf{id}^*}, m^*), \sigma^*, \rho_{\mathsf{id}^*})$ is indeed a valid forgery as:

- From the simulation, we have that $\mathsf{pk}_{\mathsf{id}^*} \leftarrow \mathsf{RCSI\text{-}FiSh.Randpk}(\mathsf{pp}_{\mathrm{sgn}}, \mathsf{mpk}, \rho_{\mathsf{id}^*})$ and $\rho_{\mathsf{id}^*} \in \mathsf{RList}$.
- Since $\mathsf{SW.Verify}(\mathsf{pp}, \mathsf{pk}_{\mathsf{id}^*}, m^*, \sigma^*) = 1$, we have $\mathsf{RCSI\text{-}FiSh.Verify}(\mathsf{pp}_{\mathrm{sgn}}, \mathsf{pk}_{\mathsf{id}^*}, \widehat{m}^*, \sigma^*) = 1$
- From the simulation, we observe that since $(\mathsf{id}^*, m^*) \notin \mathsf{MsgList}$ we have $\widehat{m}^* \notin \mathsf{MList}$.

Thus, the adversary $\mathcal{B}$ provides a perfect simulation of the game G_1 for $\mathcal{A}$. Therefore, we obtain $|\wp_{\mathcal{A},1}(\lambda)| \leq \mathsf{Adv}^{\mathsf{UF\text{-}CMA\text{-}HRK}}_{\mathsf{RCSI-FiSh}, \mathcal{B}}(\lambda)$. □

Theorem 6.04. *The isogeny-based stateful deterministic wallet* SW *is secure against wallet unlinkability as per Definition 5.03. In other words, for any PPT adversary $\mathcal{A}$ playing in the experiment $\mathsf{Exp}^{\mathsf{WAL\text{-}UNL}}_{\mathsf{SW}, \mathcal{A}}(\lambda)$ as described in Fig. 4, we have $\mathsf{Adv}^{\mathsf{WAL\text{-}UNL}}_{\mathsf{SW}, \mathcal{A}}(\lambda) \leq \frac{q_{\mathcal{H}_2}(q_P+2)}{2^\lambda}$, where $q_{\mathcal{H}_2}$ denotes the number of queries to $\mathcal{H}_2$ and q_P denotes the number of queries to $\mathcal{O}_{\mathsf{PK}}$ by $\mathcal{A}$.*

Proof. The adversary $\mathcal{A}$ playing in the experiment $\mathsf{Exp}^{\mathsf{WAL\text{-}UNL}}_{\mathsf{SW}, \mathcal{A}}(\lambda)$ has access to the oracles $\mathcal{O}_{\mathsf{PK}}(\mathsf{id})$, $\mathcal{O}_{\mathsf{WalSign}}(m, \mathsf{id})$ and $\mathcal{O}_{\mathsf{getSt}}(\cdot)$. As modelled in the experiment $\mathsf{Exp}^{\mathsf{WAL\text{-}UNL}}_{\mathsf{SW}, \mathcal{A}}(\lambda)$ in Fig. 4, the adversary $\mathcal{A}$ is supposed to produce its challenge identity id^* before making any query to the oracle $\mathcal{O}_{\mathsf{getSt}}(\cdot)$ and only on identity for which the oracle $\mathcal{O}_{\mathsf{PK}}(\cdot)$ has never been queried before. Otherwise, the adversary $\mathcal{A}$ would have no advantage in the experiment $\mathsf{Exp}^{\mathsf{WAL\text{-}UNL}}_{\mathsf{SW}, \mathcal{A}}(\lambda)$ and the theorem holds trivially. Recall that the session public key $\mathsf{pk}^0_{\mathsf{id}^*}$ or $\mathsf{pk}^1_{\mathsf{id}^*}$ submitted to the adversary $\mathcal{A}$ by the challenger $\mathcal{C}$ upon receiving the challenge identity id^* from $\mathcal{A}$ is obtained from the wallet state that is hidden from $\mathcal{A}$. Every time $\mathcal{A}$ sends a query to the oracle $\mathcal{O}_{\mathsf{PK}}(\mathsf{id})$, the state of the wallet gets updated. To win the unlinkability game, $\mathcal{A}$ can attempt to predict one of the wallet's state and issue a "problematic query" on such a state to the random oracle $\mathcal{H}_2$. This allows them to obtain one of $\mathsf{pk}^0_{\mathsf{id}^*}$ or $\mathsf{pk}^1_{\mathsf{id}^*}$ computed by the wallet and thereby distinguishing it from a randomly generated session public key. The challenger $\mathcal{C}$ maintains a list $\mathcal{T}$ of all the wallet states, ranging from the start state to the state that was determined by the last query issued to the oracle $\mathcal{O}_{\mathsf{PK}}(\cdot)$. Let us consider the set $\mathcal{T}$ of values taken by the variables St, $\widehat{St}$ before the adversary $\mathcal{A}$ outputs the challenger identity id^*.

We first analyze the case where the adversary $\mathcal{A}$ has not issued any problematic query to $\mathcal{H}_2$. If $\mathcal{A}$ does not send a problematic query to $\mathcal{H}_2$ on any $St' \in \mathcal{T}$, the distribution of the session public keys $\mathsf{pk}^0_{\mathsf{id}^*}$ and $\mathsf{pk}^1_{\mathsf{id}^*}$ are identical from the point of view of $\mathcal{A}$ as the states St, $\widehat{St}$ used to compute $\mathsf{pk}^0_{\mathsf{id}^*}$, $\mathsf{pk}^1_{\mathsf{id}^*}$, respectively, are uniformly distributed. We now employ the rerandomizability property of the underlying isogeny-based signature with rerandomizable keys RCSI-FiSh to guarantee that the distribution of both the session public key $\mathsf{pk}^0_{\mathsf{id}^*}$, $\mathsf{pk}^1_{\mathsf{id}^*}$ are identical to a freshly generated master public key $\widehat{\mathsf{mpk}}$ obtained by executing the algorithm RCSI-FiSh.KeyGen. Thus, there is no way $\mathcal{A}$ can get advantage in the unlinkability game in this case.

We now show that with negligible probability $\mathcal{A}$ issues the aforementioned problematic query to $\mathcal{H}_2$. Since throughout the experiment $\mathsf{Exp}^{\mathsf{WAL\text{-}UNL}}_{\mathsf{SW},\mathcal{A}}(\lambda)$, the adversary $\mathcal{A}$ issues maximum q_P queries to the oracle $\mathcal{O}_{\mathsf{PK}}(\mathsf{id})$, we have $|\mathcal{T}| \leq q_P + 2$. By the definition of experiment $\mathsf{Exp}^{\mathsf{WAL\text{-}UNL}}_{\mathsf{SW},\mathcal{A}}(\lambda)$, $\mathcal{A}$ always issue queries to the oracle $\mathcal{O}_{\mathsf{getSt}}(\cdot)$ after obtaining the challenge identity id^* from $\mathcal{A}$, Thus, from the adversary's point of view all values in $\mathcal{T}$ are distributed uniformly, until it gains the knowledge of any specific value $St' \in \mathcal{T}$. As a result, the probability that for any particular query to be of the form $\mathcal{H}_2(St', \mathsf{id})$, $St' \in \mathcal{T}$, is at most $\frac{q_P+2}{2^\lambda}$. Since the adversary $\mathcal{A}$ issue at most $q_{\mathcal{H}_2}$ many queries of the form $\mathcal{H}_2(St', \mathsf{id})$, the probability that for any of them, $St' \in \mathcal{T}$, is at most $\frac{q_{\mathcal{H}_2}(q_P+2)}{2^\lambda}$. □

References

1. Aggarwal, D., Brennen, G.K., Lee, T., Santha, M., Tomamichel, M.: Quantum attacks on Bitcoin, and how to protect against them. arXiv preprint arXiv:1710.10377 (2017)
2. Alkeilani Alkadri, N., et al.: Deterministic wallets in a quantum world. In: Proceedings of the 2020 ACM SIGSAC Conference on Computer and Communications Security, pp. 1017–1031 (2020)
3. Alkim, E., Barreto, P.S.L.M., Bindel, N., Krämer, J., Longa, P., Ricardini, J.E.: The lattice-based digital signature scheme qTESLA. In: Conti, M., Zhou, J., Casalicchio, E., Spognardi, A. (eds.) ACNS 2020. LNCS, vol. 12146, pp. 441–460. Springer, Cham (2020). https://doi.org/10.1007/978-3-030-57808-4_22
4. Anhao, N.: Bitcoin post-quantum (2018)
5. Atapoor, S., Baghery, K., Cozzo, D., Pedersen, R.: CSI-SharK: CSI-FiSh with sharing-friendly keys. Cryptology ePrint Archive (2022)
6. Baghery, K., Cozzo, D., Pedersen, R.: An isogeny-based ID protocol using structured public keys. In: Paterson, M.B. (ed.) IMACC 2021. LNCS, vol. 13129, pp. 179–197. Springer, Cham (2021). https://doi.org/10.1007/978-3-030-92641-0_9
7. Beullens, W., Kleinjung, T., Vercauteren, F.: CSI-FiSh: efficient isogeny based signatures through class group computations. In: Galbraith, S.D., Moriai, S. (eds.) ASIACRYPT 2019. LNCS, vol. 11921, pp. 227–247. Springer, Cham (2019). https://doi.org/10.1007/978-3-030-34578-5_9
8. Boneh, D., Lynn, B., Shacham, H.: Short signatures from the Weil pairing. J. Cryptol. **17**(4), 297–319 (2004)

9. Bonnetain, X., Schrottenloher, A.: Quantum security analysis of CSIDH. In: Canteaut, A., Ishai, Y. (eds.) EUROCRYPT 2020. LNCS, vol. 12106, pp. 493–522. Springer, Cham (2020). https://doi.org/10.1007/978-3-030-45724-2_17
10. Brzuska, C., Fischlin, M., Lehmann, A., Schröder, D.: Unlinkability of sanitizable signatures. In: Nguyen, P.Q., Pointcheval, D. (eds.) PKC 2010. LNCS, vol. 6056, pp. 444–461. Springer, Heidelberg (2010). https://doi.org/10.1007/978-3-642-13013-7_26
11. Buterin, V.: Deterministic wallets, their advantages and their understated flaws. Bitcoin Magazine (2013)
12. Castryck, W., Lange, T., Martindale, C., Panny, L., Renes, J.: CSIDH: an efficient post-quantum commutative group action. In: Peyrin, T., Galbraith, S. (eds.) ASIACRYPT 2018. LNCS, vol. 11274, pp. 395–427. Springer, Cham (2018). https://doi.org/10.1007/978-3-030-03332-3_15
13. Das, P., Faust, S., Loss, J.: A formal treatment of deterministic wallets. In: Proceedings of the 2019 ACM SIGSAC Conference on Computer and Communications Security, pp. 651–668 (2019)
14. De Feo, L.: Mathematics of isogeny based cryptography. arXiv preprint arXiv:1711.04062 (2017)
15. Ethereum, W.: Ethereum. org (2020)
16. Fan, C.I., Tseng, Y.F., Su, H.P., Hsu, R.H., Kikuchi, H.: Secure hierarchical bitcoin wallet scheme against privilege escalation attacks. In: 2018 IEEE Conference on Dependable and Secure Computing (DSC), pp. 1–8 (2018)
17. Fleischhacker, N., Krupp, J., Malavolta, G., Schneider, J., Schröder, D., Simkin, M.: Efficient unlinkable sanitizable signatures from signatures with re-randomizable keys. In: Cheng, C.-M., Chung, K.-M., Persiano, G., Yang, B.-Y. (eds.) PKC 2016. LNCS, vol. 9614, pp. 301–330. Springer, Heidelberg (2016). https://doi.org/10.1007/978-3-662-49384-7_12
18. Franco, P.: Understanding Bitcoin: Cryptography, Engineering and Economics. John Wiley & Sons, Hoboken (2014)
19. Gutoski, G., Stebila, D.: Hierarchical deterministic bitcoin wallets that tolerate key leakage. In: Böhme, R., Okamoto, T. (eds.) FC 2015. LNCS, vol. 8975, pp. 497–504. Springer, Heidelberg (2015). https://doi.org/10.1007/978-3-662-47854-7_31
20. Nakamoto, S.: Bitcoin: A peer-to-peer electronic cash system (2009). http://www.bitcoin.org/bitcoin.pdf
21. Peikert, C.: He gives C-sieves on the CSIDH. In: Canteaut, A., Ishai, Y. (eds.) EUROCRYPT 2020. LNCS, vol. 12106, pp. 463–492. Springer, Cham (2020). https://doi.org/10.1007/978-3-030-45724-2_16
22. Shor, P.W.: Polynomial-time algorithms for prime factorization and discrete logarithms on a quantum computer. SIAM Rev. **41**(2), 303–332 (1999)
23. Silverman, J.H.: The Arithmetic of Elliptic Curves. GTM, vol. 106. Springer, New York (2009). https://doi.org/10.1007/978-0-387-09494-6
24. Waterhouse, W.C.: Abelian varieties over finite fields. In: Annales scientifiques de l'École Normale Supérieure, vol. 2, pp. 521–560 (1969)
25. Waterland, P.: Quantum resistant ledger (QRL) (2016)
26. Wiki, B.: Hardware wallet (2020)
27. Wiki, B.: BIP32 proposal (2018)

CTA: Confidential Transactions Protocol with State Accumulator

Shumin Si[1,2], Puwen Wei[1,2,3](✉), Xiuhan Lin[1,2], and Li Liu[1,2]

[1] School of Cyber Science and Technology, Shandong University, Qingdao, China
{shuminsi,xhlin,sdu_liuli}@mail.sdu.edu.cn, pwei@sdu.edu.cn
[2] Key Laboratory of Cryptologic Technology and Information Security, Ministry of Education, Shandong University, Qingdao, China
[3] Quancheng Laboratory, Jinan, China

Abstract. Considering the increasingly large storage of post-quantum RingCT-like protocols, we construct a blockchain-based confidential transactions protocol with state accumulator (CTA), where each user only needs to store a concise state of the blockchain. More precisely, CTA can compress the historical data of all transactions into a short deterministic state, while preserving privacy and post-quantum security. The key component of our CTA is an efficient zero-knowledge lattice-based accumulator, which is based on Peikert et al.'s vector commitment scheme proposed in TCC 2021. We have modified their construction to ensure that the length of the underlying M-SIS parameters is kept short for the Merkle-tree structure. At a 128-bit security level, the membership proof size for our accumulator with 2^{20} members is only 225 KB under the Module-SIS and Extended-MLWE assumptions. Compared with previous lattice-based works where the time and storage complexity of each user is linear with the number of coins, our CTA is capable of achieving logarithmic storage space and computational time. Specifically, the concrete transaction size of spending a coin in CTA is around 236 KB, when the size of anonymity set is 2^{20}.

Keywords: confidential transactions · lattice-based accumulator · zero-knowledge proofs

1 Introduction

Blockchain-based confidential transactions (CT) protocols [23] allow users to create authenticated transactions without revealing sensitive information such as the users' identities and spending amounts. These protocols guarantee the authenticity and consistency of transactions by maintaining a globally distributed and synchronized ledger, i.e., the blockchain. Various research works [6,11,12,22,25] have proposed innovative solutions in this area. In particular, lattice-based ring signature confidential transactions (RingCT) protocols [11,22] can achieve post-quantum anonymity in an ad-hoc group without a trusted setup.

One inherent problem with RingCT is the increasing storage requirement for historical data, as the verification mechanism relies on the full records of

J. Deng et al. (Eds.): CANS 2023, LNCS 14342, pp. 414–439, 2023.
https://doi.org/10.1007/978-981-99-7563-1_19

transactions on the blockchain. Additionally, spent accounts cannot be removed from the history of the blockchain, as it is difficult to determine whether an account has been spent or simply used as part of the anonymity set in a RingCT transaction. This issue of increasing storage for historical records is a major concern for the scalability of blockchain systems. As of March 2023, there were over 460 gigabytes of historical data for Bitcoin. Another issue with relying on full transaction records is that the computational complexity of lattice-based ring signature [11,22] becomes prohibitive as the ring size approaches 2^{20} members, as pointed by [19]. Therefore, finding ways to prune the history blocks or generate compact expressions of all transactions is crucial for the practical deployment of confidential transactions protocols.

An intuitive solution to address the issue of increasing storage requirements for historical data in RingCT is to use an accumulator, which is a powerful tool for compressing transaction history [6]. By using accumulators, verification nodes of the blockchain can check transactions without retrieving the entire transaction history. This approach allows the nodes to maintain compressed states, which can significantly alleviate the storage shortage of the blockchain system. Accumulators constructed from lattice-based assumptions are preferred when considering post-quantum security. However, the proof size of lattice-based accumulators is much larger than their discrete logarithm (DL) based counterparts. In particular, the proof size of lattice-based Merkle-tree accumulators is in megabytes [16,27], which can lead to inefficient confidential transactions protocols.

1.1 Our Contributions

In this paper, we investigate the construction of a blockchain-based confidential transactions protocol with state accumulator (CTA), which compresses all transactions into a short state. Due to the compressed state, we need to consider a stronger security model than that of previous RingCT-like protocols. Specifically, we identify a new attack scenario called the "fake accounts" attack, where an adversary may break the balance of transactions by creating fake accounts, which can lead to the adversary obtaining benefits that they are not entitled to. In this type of attack, the adversary provides a membership proof of the accumulator for invalid members, exploiting the fact that the validity of accounts can only be checked by the compressed state.

For the concrete construction, we propose an efficient blockchain-based CTA that achieves 128-bit post-quantum security by using the Module Short Integer Solution (M-SIS) and Extended Module Learning With Errors (Extended-MLWE) assumptions. The key component of our construction is a lattice-based accumulator which allows short zero-knowledge proofs for large members. We use a shallow Merkle-tree of height l and branching factor $h \geq 2$, and instantiate the underlying hash function with lattice-based vector commitment (VC) schemes proposed by [26]. To further reduce the bandwidth, we modify the decomposition of the hash value for the internal nodes of the tree [26], so that the norm of each node is constant, enabling the underlying M-SIS parameters to remain short. Additionally, the statement for the membership proof of our accumulator can be expressed with concise multiplicative relations and linear relations over R_q, which allows for short zero-knowledge proofs. Through further optimization, the resulting membership proof size for our accumulator is only 225 KB with 2^{20} members. We compare the communication cost of our zero-knowledge lattice-based accumulator with other lattice-based constructions in Table 1, where N is the number of members of the accumulator.

Table 1. Comparison of zero-knowledge lattice-based accumulators.

	N	security level	assumption	proof size
[16]	2^{10}	100-bit	LWE & SIS	47.3 MB
[27]	2^{10}	128-bit	LWE & SIS	9.7 MB
This work	2^{20}	128-bit	Extended MLWE & MSIS	225 KB

The storage cost of the verification nodes (or miners) in our CTA protocol is 688 MB, significantly lower than the gigabyte-level storage required in previous works [11,22]. Additionally, the size of a spending transaction for one input and two output accounts with an anonymity set of size 2^{20} is approximately 236 KB. Our spending algorithm and verification algorithm follow the framework of Zerocash, which only relies on the authentication path from a leaf to the root, rather than all the public keys of members as in current lattice-based Ring-CT works [10,11,22]. This results in better asymptotic complexity in spending/verifying time and storage space, as shown in Table 2.

Table 2. Comparison of confidential transactions protocols. The "storage" column refers to the amount of data stored in order to validate new transactions among all users at all times. PQ indicates whether the scheme is plausibly secure against quantum attacks. N is the size of the anonymity set. The state of the blockchain in Quisquis [12] is compact UTXOs set, where UTXO is the unspent transaction outputs set in blockchain.

	storage	transaction size	spending time	verifying time	PQ
Quisquis [12]	UTXO	$\mathcal{O}(N)$	$\mathcal{O}(N)$	$\mathcal{O}(N)$	✗
Zerocash [6]	$\mathcal{O}(\log N)$	$\mathcal{O}(\log N)$	$\mathcal{O}(\log N)$	$\mathcal{O}(\log N)$	✗
MatRiCT [11]	$\mathcal{O}(N)$	$\mathcal{O}(\log N)$	$\mathcal{O}(N)$	$\mathcal{O}(N)$	✓
MatRiCT+ [10]	$\mathcal{O}(N)$	$\mathcal{O}(\log N)$	$\mathcal{O}(N)$	$\mathcal{O}(N)$	✓
SMILE [22]	$\mathcal{O}(N)$	$\mathcal{O}(\log N)$	$\mathcal{O}(N)$	$\mathcal{O}(N)$	✓
This work	$\mathcal{O}(\log N)$	$\mathcal{O}(\log N)$	$\mathcal{O}(\log N)$	$\mathcal{O}(\log N)$	✓

1.2 Technique Overview of ZK for Lattice-Based Accumulator

The main challenge of constructing CTA is to compress the ZK proofs for lattice-based accumulator, while making the underlying lattice-based assumptions preserve short parameters. Our accumulator adopts the structure of Merkle-tree with $N = h^l$ leaf nodes, where the height is l and the branching factor is h. We use VC [26] as the underlying hash function of our lattice-based accumulator, and its security is based on the M-SIS assumption. VC allows for concise commitment to an ordered sequence of messages, with the ability to later prove the messages at desired positions concisely. For instance, a VC which commits to a vector $(\boldsymbol{m}_0\|\cdots\|\boldsymbol{m}_{h-1})$ is of the form $\boldsymbol{c} = \sum_{i=0}^{h-1} \boldsymbol{U}_i \boldsymbol{m}_i$. For the openings of some $\boldsymbol{m}_i$, the verifier checks if the witness $\boldsymbol{w}_i$ is "short" and $\boldsymbol{c} = \boldsymbol{A}_i\boldsymbol{w}_i + \boldsymbol{U}_i\boldsymbol{m}_i$, where $\boldsymbol{U}_i$s and $\boldsymbol{A}_i$s are the public parameters of VC. Using VC has the advantage of effectively compressing the information of all the sibling nodes. However, the size of the underlying M-SIS parameters increases significantly with the number of committed messages. Specifically, the norm of related nodes increases linearly with the number of sibling nodes. As a result, VC is suitable for only moderately large h, due to the public parameters' quadratic dependence on h. For larger dimensions, we consider a tree transformation of VC. Based on techniques of [16], we construct the tree transformation with stateful updates. In particular, we transform VC with the "decomposition" function $\boldsymbol{G}^{-1}$ to keep the short norm, which is crucial for iteratively applying VC in a Merkle-tree.

The ZK proof of our accumulator demonstrates the membership of a leaf node in a zero-knowledge manner. In a nutshell, the root $\boldsymbol{v}_0$ and the target leaf nodes $\boldsymbol{v}_l$ along with the associated compressed siblings $\{\boldsymbol{w}_i\}_{i=1}^{l}$ satisfy a set of l verification equations. Specifically, the equations take the form of $\boldsymbol{G}\boldsymbol{v}_i = \sum_{k=0}^{h-1} b_{i+1,k}\boldsymbol{A}_k\boldsymbol{w}_{i+1} + \sum_{k=0}^{h-1} b_{i+1,k}\boldsymbol{U}_k\boldsymbol{v}_{i+1}$, where $i \in \{l-1, l-2, \cdots, 0\}$ and $\boldsymbol{b}_i = (b_{i,0}\ b_{i,1}\ \cdots\ b_{i,h-1})$ is the unary representation for the index j_i of the internal node on the path. The linear and multiplicative relations in the verification equation about $\{\boldsymbol{v}_i, \boldsymbol{w}_i, \boldsymbol{b}_i\}_{i=1}^{l}$ can be proven using the LANES framework for efficient arguments of knowledge [3,9,22]. However, a direct application of LANES leads to a proof size that is linear with the length of the witnesses $\{\boldsymbol{v}_i, \boldsymbol{w}_i, \boldsymbol{b}_i\}_{i=1}^{l}$ with a large factor, since the binary vector $\{\boldsymbol{b}_i\}_{i=1}^{l}$ in the multiplicative relation is not compatible with the method of NTT slots in [9,22], which can reduce the dimension of the committed messages.

To overcome this problem, we take advantage of an observation in [22] that vector $\boldsymbol{b}_i$ can be uniquely decomposed into vectors $\boldsymbol{o}_{i,1}, \cdots, \boldsymbol{o}_{i,e} \in \{0,1\}^{\log_e h}$ such that $\boldsymbol{b}_i = \boldsymbol{o}_{i,1} \otimes \cdots \otimes \boldsymbol{o}_{i,e}$ where $\|\boldsymbol{o}_{i,j}\|_1 = 1$, for all $i \in [l], j \in [e]$. So the prover only needs to commit to $\{\boldsymbol{o}_{i,1}, \cdots, \boldsymbol{o}_{i,e}\}_{i=1}^{l}$. As a result, the dimension of the masked opening of each $\boldsymbol{b}_i$ can be reduced to $e \cdot \log_e h$ instead of h.

Intuitively, applying the lattice-based bulletproofs [2] can further reduce the overall proof size. However, it leads to an increase in the total size of proofs. This is because the length of the extracted solution vector grows by a factor of $12d^3$, where d is the dimension of the polynomial ring for each level of Bulletproof folding. To optimize our scheme, we instead use the amortized protocol [3]. Although the asymptotic communication complexity of the amortized protocol is higher than that of Bulletproofs, the concrete cost of the amortized protocol for garbage commitments in our protocol can be significantly reduced. This reduction in cost further translates to a decrease in the total proof size. In addition, we find that sampling different masks for $(\boldsymbol{v}_1\|\cdots\|\boldsymbol{v}_l)$ and $(\boldsymbol{w}_1\|\cdots\|\boldsymbol{w}_l)$

also helps in reducing the proof size. Overall, these optimizations allow us to achieve efficient and secure membership verification of leaf nodes in our CTA, while maintaining a small proof size.

2 Preliminaries

Notations. The security parameter is denoted by λ. For an odd integer q, $Z_q = Z/qZ$ denotes the ring of integers modulo q, which is represented by the range $[-\frac{q-1}{2}, \frac{q-1}{2}]$. Cyclotomic rings are denoted by $R_q = Z_q/(X^d+1)$ of degree d where $d > 1$ is a power of 2. We use bold-face lower-case letters and bold-face capital letters to denote column vectors and matrices, respectively. $(\boldsymbol{a}\|\boldsymbol{b})$ and $[\boldsymbol{a}\|\boldsymbol{b}]$ denote the vertical concatenation and the horizon concatenation of vectors $\boldsymbol{a}$ and $\boldsymbol{b}$, respectively. Uniformly sampling from a set $\mathcal{S}$ is denoted by $\boldsymbol{a} \leftarrow \mathcal{S}$.

For positive integers a and b such that $a \le b$, $[a, b] = \{a, \cdots, b\}$. Specially, $[n] = \{0, \cdots, n-1\}$. For a matrix $\boldsymbol{V}$, we denote its maximum singular value as $s_1(\boldsymbol{V}) = \max_{\boldsymbol{u} \neq \boldsymbol{0}} \|\boldsymbol{V}\boldsymbol{u}\|/\|\boldsymbol{u}\|$. $\mathcal{S}^{d \cdot m}$ denotes a total of md coefficients from a set $\mathcal{S}$, which generates m polynomials in $R = Z[X]/(X^d+1)$ of degree d. We use $\mathcal{U}_\beta$ to denote the set of polynomials in R with infinity norm at most $\beta \in Z^+$.

Module-SIS and Module-LWE Problems. In this section, we provide a brief overview of the hard computational problems, which are Module-SIS (M-SIS) [15], Module-LWE (M-LWE) [15] and Extended M-LWE [21] problems.

Definition 1 (M-SIS$_{n,m,q,\beta_{SIS}}$). *Given a uniformly random matrix $\boldsymbol{A} \leftarrow R_q^{n \times m}$, the goal is to find $\boldsymbol{z} \in R_q^m$ such that $\boldsymbol{A}\boldsymbol{z} = \boldsymbol{0}$ over R_q and $0 < \|\boldsymbol{z}\| \le \beta_{SIS}$. An algorithm $\mathcal{A}$ has advantage ϵ in solving M-SIS$_{n,m,q,\beta_{SIS}}$ if*

$$\Pr\left[0 < \|\boldsymbol{z}\| \le \beta_{SIS} \wedge \boldsymbol{A}\boldsymbol{z} = \boldsymbol{0} | \boldsymbol{A} \leftarrow R_q^{n \times m}; \boldsymbol{z} \leftarrow \mathcal{A}(\boldsymbol{A})\right] \ge \epsilon.$$

Definition 2 (M-LWE$_{n,m,q,\beta}$). *Let $\boldsymbol{s} \leftarrow \mathcal{U}_\beta^n$ be a secret key. LWE$_{q,\boldsymbol{s}}$ is defined as the distribution obtained by outputting $(\boldsymbol{a}, \langle \boldsymbol{a}, \boldsymbol{s}\rangle + e)$ for $\boldsymbol{a} \leftarrow R_q^n$ and $e \leftarrow \mathcal{U}_\beta$. Then the goal is to distinguish between m samples from either LWE$_{q,\boldsymbol{s}}$ or $\mathcal{U}(R_q^n, R_q)$. An algorithm $\mathcal{A}$ has advantage ϵ in solving M-LWE$_{n,m,q,\beta}$ if*

$$\Big|\Pr\left[b = 1 | \boldsymbol{A} \leftarrow R_q^{m \times n}; \boldsymbol{s} \leftarrow \mathcal{U}_\beta^n; e \leftarrow \mathcal{U}_\beta^m; b \leftarrow \mathcal{A}(\boldsymbol{A}, \boldsymbol{A}\boldsymbol{s} + e)\right]$$
$$- \Pr\left[b = 1 | \boldsymbol{A} \leftarrow R_q^{m \times n}; \boldsymbol{t} \leftarrow R_q^m; b \leftarrow \mathcal{A}(\boldsymbol{A}, \boldsymbol{t})\right] \Big| \ge \epsilon.$$

Definition 3 (Extended M-LWE$_{n,m,\sigma}$). *The parameters $m, n > 0$ and the standard deviation σ are given. The goal is to distinguish the following two cases: $\boldsymbol{s}_0 = (\boldsymbol{B}, \boldsymbol{B}\boldsymbol{r}, c, \boldsymbol{z}, sign(\langle \boldsymbol{z}, c\boldsymbol{r}\rangle$*[1]*$))$ and $\boldsymbol{s}_1 = (\boldsymbol{B}, \boldsymbol{u}, c, \boldsymbol{z}, sign(\langle \boldsymbol{z}, c\boldsymbol{r}\rangle))$ where $\boldsymbol{B} \leftarrow R_q^{n \times (n+m)}$, a secret vector $\boldsymbol{r} \leftarrow \{-\beta, \beta\}^{n+m}$, $c \leftarrow \mathcal{C}$, $\boldsymbol{u} \leftarrow R_q^n$*

[1] Here, the inner product is over Z, i.e., $\langle \boldsymbol{z}, \boldsymbol{v}\rangle = \langle \boldsymbol{z}', \boldsymbol{v}'\rangle$ where vectors $\boldsymbol{z}'$ and $\boldsymbol{v}'$ are polynomial coefficients of $\boldsymbol{z}$ and $\boldsymbol{v}$, respectively.

and $\boldsymbol{z} \leftarrow D_\sigma^{(n+m)d}$, *where* $sign(a) = 1$ *if* $a \geq 0$ *and* 0 *otherwise. Then, adversary* $\mathcal{A}$ *has advantage* ϵ *in solving Extended M-LWE*$_{n,m,\sigma}$ *if*

$$\Big|Pr\Big[b = 1 | \boldsymbol{B} \leftarrow R_q^{n\times(n+m)}; \boldsymbol{r} \leftarrow \{-\beta, \beta\}^{n+m}; \boldsymbol{z} \leftarrow D_\sigma^{(n+m)d}; c \leftarrow \mathcal{C}; b \leftarrow \mathcal{A}(\boldsymbol{s}_0)\Big]$$
$$-Pr\Big[b = 1 | \boldsymbol{B} \leftarrow R_q^{n\times(n+m)}; \boldsymbol{u} \leftarrow R_q^n; \boldsymbol{z} \leftarrow D_\sigma^{(n+m)d}; c \leftarrow \mathcal{C}; b \leftarrow \mathcal{A}(\boldsymbol{s}_1)\Big]\Big| \geq \epsilon.$$

In [21], Extended M-LWE is assumed to be computationally hard, so that the new rejection Rej' shown in Appendix A.2 is simulatable, where the signal $sign(\langle \boldsymbol{z}, c\boldsymbol{r}\rangle))$ about the secret $\boldsymbol{r}$ is revealed.

Commitment Scheme. We briefly recall the ABDLOP commitment scheme in [18], which is computational hiding and computational binding based on the hardness of the M-LWE and M-SIS problem. As in [5], the commitment schemes Com consist of **CKeygen**,**Com** and **Open**. Suppose that n, m, β, q are positive integers. An instantiation of ABDLOP with $m > (n + v_2)$ is as follows.

- **CKeygen**(1^λ): Pick $\boldsymbol{A} \leftarrow R_q^{n\times v_1}$, $\boldsymbol{B}_1' \leftarrow R_q^{n\times(m-n)}$ and $\boldsymbol{B}_2' \leftarrow R_q^{v_2\times(m-n-v_2)}$. Set $\boldsymbol{B}_1 = [\boldsymbol{I}_n \| \boldsymbol{B}_1']$ and $\boldsymbol{B}_2 = [\boldsymbol{0}^{v_2\times n} \| \boldsymbol{I}_{v_2} \| \boldsymbol{B}_2']$. Output $ck = (\boldsymbol{B}_1, \boldsymbol{B}_2, \boldsymbol{A})$, where $\boldsymbol{I}_n$ denotes a n-dimensional square matrix in which all the principal diagonal elements are ones and all other elements are zeros.
- **Com**$_{ck}(\boldsymbol{m}_1, \boldsymbol{m}_2)$: Pick $\boldsymbol{r} \leftarrow \{-\beta, \cdots, \beta\}^{md}$. Output
$$\mathsf{COM}_{ck}(\boldsymbol{m}_1, \boldsymbol{m}_2; \boldsymbol{r}) = \begin{pmatrix} \boldsymbol{A} \\ \boldsymbol{0}^{v_2\times v_1} \end{pmatrix} \cdot \boldsymbol{m}_1 + \begin{pmatrix} \boldsymbol{B}_1 \\ \boldsymbol{B}_2 \end{pmatrix} \cdot \boldsymbol{r} + \begin{pmatrix} \boldsymbol{0}^n \\ \boldsymbol{m}_2 \end{pmatrix},$$
where $(\boldsymbol{m}_1, \boldsymbol{m}_2)$ are $(v_1 + v_2)$-dimensional vectors over R_q for $(v_1 + v_2) \geq 1$.
- **Open**$(C, (y, (\boldsymbol{m}_1', \boldsymbol{m}_2'), \boldsymbol{r}'))$: If C is a commitment such that $yC = \mathsf{COM}_{ck}$ $(\boldsymbol{m}_1', \boldsymbol{m}_2'; \boldsymbol{r}')$ and $\|(\boldsymbol{r}'\|\boldsymbol{m}_1')\| \leq \gamma_{com}$, return 1. Otherwise, return 0.

The algorithm **Open** is relaxed where $y \in R_q$ is called the relaxation factor.

Cryptographic Accumulators. An accumulator scheme Acc consists of the following algorithms [16].

- **Setup**(λ): On input security parameter λ, output public parameters pp.
- **Acc**$_{pp}(V)$: On input a set of N messages $V = (m_1, \cdots, m_N)$ and the public parameters pp, output the accumulator u.
- **Witness**$_{pp}(V, m, u)$: On input a set V, the accumulator u and a member m, output $\perp$ if $m \notin V$; otherwise output a witness w for the proof that m is accumulated in **Acc**$_{pp}(V)$.
- **Verify**$_{pp}(u, m, w)$: If w is a valid proof that u is accumulator to a sequence $(m_1, \cdots, m_N)$ such that $m = m_i$ for some $i \in \{1, \ldots, N\}$, output 1.

An accumulator scheme is correct if **Verify**$_{pp}$(**Acc**$_{pp}(V), m, w) = 1$ holds where $w =$ **Witness**$_{pp}(V, m,$ **Acc**$_{pp}(V))$, for all $pp \leftarrow$ **Setup**(λ) and all $m \in V$.

Definition 4. *An accumulator scheme is secure if for all PPT adversaries* $\mathcal{A}$:

$$\mathsf{Pr}\left[\begin{array}{c} pp \leftarrow \textbf{\textit{Setup}}(\lambda); (V, m', w') \leftarrow \mathcal{A}(pp): \\ m' \notin V \wedge \textbf{\textit{Verify}}_{pp}(\textbf{\textit{Acc}}_{pp}(V), m', w') = 1 \end{array}\right] \leq \mathsf{negl}(\lambda).$$

3 Lattice-Based ZK Proofs for Accumulators

In this section, we construct an M-SIS-based accumulator and provide an efficient zero-knowledge proof for its membership.

3.1 Construction of Lattice-Based Accumulator

The main structure of our lattice-based accumulator follows the idea of [26], which is a tree of height l and arity h. We modify the underlying "hash" for each node so that the resulting scheme allows more efficient proofs than that of [26]. Suppose that $V = \{\boldsymbol{d}_0 \in R_{\hat{p}}^{k\alpha}, \cdots, \boldsymbol{d}_{N-1} \in R_{\hat{p}}^{k\alpha}\}$ is the set to be accumulated, where $N = h^l$. Let $\boldsymbol{G} = \boldsymbol{I}_\alpha \otimes [1\|\hat{p}\| \cdots \|\hat{p}^{k-1}]$ denote the gadget matrix, where $\hat{p} = \lfloor \sqrt[k]{p} \rfloor$, with a set S. Our Acc is described as follows.

- **Setup**(λ): Choose $\boldsymbol{A}' \leftarrow R_p^{\alpha \times 2\alpha}$ and $\boldsymbol{T} \leftarrow \{-1,0,1\}^{2\alpha d \times (k+2)\alpha d}$. For $m^* \in S$, compute $\boldsymbol{A}_i = \boldsymbol{A}'\boldsymbol{T} + [\boldsymbol{0}\|(m^* - m_i)\boldsymbol{G}]$, where $m_i \neq m^* \in S$ for all $i \in [h]$. The definition of $S \subset R_p$ follows that of [19], which is set to be all polynomials in R_p of degree 0 such that, for any $m \neq m' \in S$, $m - m'$ is invertible in R_p. Randomly choose $\boldsymbol{U} = [\boldsymbol{U}_0\| \cdots \|\boldsymbol{U}_{h-1}] \in R_p^{\alpha \times kh\alpha}$, where each $\boldsymbol{U}_i \in R_p^{\alpha \times k\alpha}$. For all $i \in [h]$, set $\boldsymbol{R}_{i,i} = \boldsymbol{0}$ and use GPV [14,24] trapdoor $\boldsymbol{T}$ to sample $\boldsymbol{R}_{i,j} \in R_p^{(k+2)\alpha \times k\alpha}$, where each $j \in [h]/\{i\}$ such that $\boldsymbol{R}_{i,j}$ is short and $\boldsymbol{A}_i \boldsymbol{R}_{i,j} = \boldsymbol{U}_j$. Output the accumulator parameters $ap = (\boldsymbol{U}, \boldsymbol{R} = \{\boldsymbol{R}_{i,j}\}_{\ i,j \in [h]})$ and the verifier parameters $vp = (\boldsymbol{U}, \boldsymbol{B})$, where $\boldsymbol{B} = \boldsymbol{A}'\boldsymbol{T}$.
- **Acc**$_{ap}(V)$: Take $V = \{\boldsymbol{d}_0 \in R_{\hat{p}}^{k\alpha}, \cdots, \boldsymbol{d}_{N-1} \in R_{\hat{p}}^{k\alpha}\}$ as input. Let $\boldsymbol{u}_{j_1,\cdots,j_i}$ denote the node with path $(j_1, \cdots, j_i)$, where $i \in [1,l]$ and $j_i \in [h]$. Let $\boldsymbol{d}_j = \boldsymbol{u}_{j_1,\cdots,j_l}$ denote the leaf node with path $(j_1, \cdots, j_l) \in [h]^l$, where $j \in [N]$. All the internal nodes of the tree are generated in a bottoms-up manner. More precisely, for $i = l-1, l-2, \ldots, 0$,
  - compute $\boldsymbol{u}_{j_1,\cdots,j_i} = \boldsymbol{G}^{-1}(\sum_{b=0}^{h-1} \boldsymbol{U}_b \cdot \boldsymbol{u}_{j_1,\cdots,j_i,b})^2$, for all $(j_1, \cdots, j_i) \in [h]^i$.

  Note that the root $\boldsymbol{u}$ is defined as $\boldsymbol{G}^{-1}(\sum_{b=0}^{h-1} \boldsymbol{U}_b \cdot \boldsymbol{u}_b)$. Output $\boldsymbol{u}$.
- **Witness**$_{ap}(V, \boldsymbol{d}, \boldsymbol{u})$: If $\boldsymbol{d} \notin V$, return $\perp$. Otherwise, $\boldsymbol{d} = \boldsymbol{d}_j$ for some $j \in [N]$ with path $(j_1, \cdots, j_l)$. Output the witness w defined as:

$$w = ((j_1, \cdots, j_l), (\boldsymbol{w}_1, \cdots, \boldsymbol{w}_l)) \in \{0,1\}^l \times (R_p^{(k+2)\alpha})^l,$$

  where $\boldsymbol{w}_i = \sum_{b=0}^{h-1} \boldsymbol{R}_{j_i,b} \boldsymbol{u}_{j_1,\cdots,j_i,b}$ and $\|\boldsymbol{w}_i\| \leq \gamma$ for all $i \in [1,l]$.
- **Verify**$_{vp}(\boldsymbol{u}, \boldsymbol{d}, w)$: If $\|\boldsymbol{w}_i\| \leq \gamma$ for all $i \in [1,l]$, set $\boldsymbol{v}_l = \boldsymbol{d}$ and, for all $i \in \{l-1, \cdots, 1, 0\}$, compute $\boldsymbol{v}_{l-1}, \cdots, \boldsymbol{v}_1, \boldsymbol{v}_0 \in R_{\hat{p}}^{k\alpha}$ as follows,

$$\boldsymbol{v}_i = \boldsymbol{G}^{-1}(\boldsymbol{A}_{j_{i+1}} \boldsymbol{w}_{i+1} + \boldsymbol{U}_{j_{i+1}} \boldsymbol{v}_{i+1}). \quad (1)$$

  Then it returns 1 if $\boldsymbol{v}_0 = \boldsymbol{u}$. Otherwise, 0.

---

[2] We stress that $\boldsymbol{G}^{-1}$ is not a matrix, but rather a function which maps a mod-p input to a short integer vector such that $\boldsymbol{G}^{-1}[\boldsymbol{G}(\boldsymbol{u})] = \boldsymbol{u} \mod p$.

The main difference between our construction and that of [26] is the computation of $\boldsymbol{u}_{j_1,\cdots,j_i}$. In [26], $\boldsymbol{u}_{j_1,\cdots,j_i} = \sum_{i=0}^{h-1} \boldsymbol{G}^{-1}(\boldsymbol{U}_b) \cdot \boldsymbol{u}_{j_1,\cdots,j_i,b} \in R_{dk\alpha\hat{p}}^{k\alpha}$, the norm of which increases linearly with a factor $dk\alpha$. So the M-SIS parameters size of the underlying hash function in [26] need be increased to support the messages with larger norms. The M-SIS parameters size of our scheme is short, since the corresponding norm of our nodes is constant, i.e., $\|\boldsymbol{u}_{j_1,\cdots,j_i}\| \leq \hat{p}\sqrt{kd\alpha}$ for all $i \in [1, l]$. Note that our computation for $\boldsymbol{u}_{j_1,\cdots,j_i}$ can be transformed into $\boldsymbol{G} \cdot \boldsymbol{u}_{j_1,\cdots,j_i} = \sum_{i=0}^{h-1} \boldsymbol{U}_b \cdot \boldsymbol{u}_{j_1,\cdots,j_i,b}$, which has the same form as that of [26]. Hence, the security of our underlying hash function follows the security of vector commitments in [26].

Lemma 1 [26]. *The underlying hash function of the accumulator Acc is collision-resistant if M-SIS$_{\alpha,2(k+1)\alpha,p,\beta_s}$ is hard, where $\beta_s = 2\max\|(\boldsymbol{T}\boldsymbol{w}_i\|\boldsymbol{v}_i)\|$ for any $i \in [1, l]$.*

Due to Theorem 1 in [16], we have

Theorem 1 *Our accumulator scheme Acc is secure in sense of Definition 4, assuming the underlying hash functions are collision-resistant.*

Remark. The generation of trapdoor $\boldsymbol{T}$ requires a private-coin **Setup**. We can use a multi-party protocol [7] for securely generating the public parameters to alleviate the trust requirement.

3.2 Zero-Knowledge Proofs of Our Accumulator

In this section, we construct a zero-knowledge argument which allows a prover $\mathcal{P}$ to convince a verifier $\mathcal{V}$ for the following statement: $\mathcal{P}$ knows a secret element that is properly accumulated into the accumulator $\boldsymbol{u} = \boldsymbol{v}_0$. Specifically, the relation for the ZK system is defined as $\mathcal{R} = \Big\{((\boldsymbol{A}', \boldsymbol{B}, \boldsymbol{U}, \boldsymbol{v}_0 = \boldsymbol{u}); \boldsymbol{v}_l \in R_{\hat{p}}^{k\alpha}, w) : \boldsymbol{G}\boldsymbol{v}_i = \quad \boldsymbol{A}_{j_{i+1}}\boldsymbol{w}_{i+1} + \boldsymbol{U}_{j_{i+1}}\boldsymbol{v}_{i+1},\ \forall i \in [l]\Big\}$, where the witness $w = (j_1 \cdots, j_l, \boldsymbol{w}_1, \cdots, \boldsymbol{w}_l)$. Each element j_i of $(j_1 \cdots, j_l)$ can be represented as unary $\boldsymbol{b}_i$, such that $j_i = [0\|1\|\cdots\|h-1] \cdot \boldsymbol{b}_i$, where $\boldsymbol{b}_i = (b_{i,0}\|b_{i,1}\|\cdots\|b_{i,h-1}) \in \{0,1\}^h$ and $\|\boldsymbol{b}_i\|_1 = 1$. Based on the observation in [22], vector $\boldsymbol{b}_i$ can be uniquely decomposed into vectors $\boldsymbol{o}_1^i, \cdots, \boldsymbol{o}_e^i \in \{0,1\}^{\log_e h}$, which has exactly one 1 each, i.e., $\boldsymbol{b}_i = \boldsymbol{o}_1^i \otimes \cdots \otimes \boldsymbol{o}_e^i$. Then Eq. (1) for verifying the path in our accumulator is equivalent to the l verification equations, $\boldsymbol{G}\boldsymbol{v}_i = \sum_{k=0}^{h-1} b_{i+1,k}\boldsymbol{A}_k\boldsymbol{w}_{i+1} + \sum_{k=0}^{h-1} b_{i+1,k}\boldsymbol{U}_k\boldsymbol{v}_{i+1}$, where $i \in [l]$. For $\forall i \in [1, l]$, let $\boldsymbol{H}_i = (\sum_{k=0}^{h-1} b_{i,k}\boldsymbol{U}_k\| \sum_{k=0}^{h-1} b_{i,k}\boldsymbol{A}_k) \in R_p^{\alpha\times 2(k+1)\alpha}$,

$$\boldsymbol{a} = (\boldsymbol{v}_l\|\boldsymbol{w}_l\|\boldsymbol{v}_{l-1}\|\boldsymbol{w}_{l-1}\|\cdots\|\boldsymbol{v}_1\|\boldsymbol{w}_1) \in R_p^{2l(k+1)\alpha} \text{ and} \tag{2}$$

$$\boldsymbol{g} = (\boldsymbol{0}\|\cdots\|\boldsymbol{0}\|\boldsymbol{G}\cdot\boldsymbol{v}_0) \in R_p^{lk\alpha}. \tag{3}$$

Thus all the above l verification equations can be transformed into an equivalent quadratic relation $(\boldsymbol{H} - \hat{\boldsymbol{G}})\boldsymbol{a} = \boldsymbol{g}$ over R_p, where

$$H = \begin{pmatrix} H_l & & & \\ & H_{l-1} & & \\ & & \ddots & \\ & & & H_1 \end{pmatrix}, \hat{G} = \begin{pmatrix} 0\,0\,G\,0 & & & \\ & G\,0 & & \\ \vdots\ \vdots & & \ddots & \\ & & & G\,0 \\ 0\,0 & & \cdots & 0\,0 \end{pmatrix} \in R_q^{l\alpha \times 2(k+1)l\alpha}. \quad (4)$$

By [18], the above relation can be transformed into the final verification equation $q_1(\boldsymbol{H} - \hat{\boldsymbol{G}})\boldsymbol{a} = q_1\boldsymbol{g}$ over R_q further, where $q = q_1 p$.

Next, we construct the non-interactive zero-knowledge proofs, where the prover $\mathcal{P}$ proves the secrets $\boldsymbol{a} = (\boldsymbol{v}_l \| \boldsymbol{w}_l \| \cdots \| \boldsymbol{v}_1 \| \boldsymbol{w}_1)$ and each tensor product $\boldsymbol{b}_i$ of $\boldsymbol{o}_1^i, \cdots, \boldsymbol{o}_e^i \in \{0,1\}^{\log_e h}$ satisfying the final verification equation.

The Non-interactive ZK Protocol. Our non-interactive protocol Π_{acc} is described in Fig. 1. The first step is to commit the $\boldsymbol{a}$, $\{\boldsymbol{o}_1^i, \cdots, \boldsymbol{o}_e^i\}_{i=1}^l$ and some extra messages $\boldsymbol{g}_1'$, $\boldsymbol{g}_2$ and $\boldsymbol{t}_1$. The underlying commitment keys are $\{\boldsymbol{B}_i\}_{i=0}^4$, where $\{\boldsymbol{B}_i\}_{i=0}^4$ can be generated by $\mathcal{H}_0(\mathsf{seed})$. $\mathcal{H}_0$ is modeled as a random oracle and seed is a random string. We set $e = 2$ for an example, i.e., $\boldsymbol{b}_i = \boldsymbol{o}_1^i \otimes \boldsymbol{o}_2^i$ for all $i \in [1,l]$, where $\boldsymbol{b}_i \in \{0,1\}^h$, and $\boldsymbol{o}_1^i, \boldsymbol{o}_2^i \in \{0,1\}^{\log h}$. The second step is to compute the response. $\mathcal{P}$ computes the masked openings $\boldsymbol{f}$ and $\{\boldsymbol{f}_1^i, \boldsymbol{f}_2^i\}_{i=1}^l$ corresponding to the secret $\boldsymbol{a}$ and $\{\boldsymbol{o}_1^i, \boldsymbol{o}_2^i\}_{i=1}^l$, respectively. $\boldsymbol{z}$ is generated to mask $\boldsymbol{r}_a$ which is the randomness in the ABDLOP commitment. Then the rejection sampling algorithms Rej' and Rej shown in Appendix A.2, are applied to the corresponding masked openings.

In verification phase, the well-formness of C_0 is proved through the equation $D = \boldsymbol{B}_0(\boldsymbol{f} \| f_b) + \boldsymbol{B}_1\boldsymbol{z} - xC_0$. The masked form of $\boldsymbol{b}_i$ can be obtained by $\boldsymbol{f}_1^i \otimes \boldsymbol{f}_2^i = x^2\boldsymbol{b}_i + x\boldsymbol{p}_1^i + \boldsymbol{p}_0^i = (f_{i,0} \| \cdots \| f_{i,h-1})$ for all $i \in [1,l]$, where $\boldsymbol{p}_1^i = \boldsymbol{o}_1^i \otimes \boldsymbol{m}_2^i + \boldsymbol{m}_1^i \otimes \boldsymbol{o}_2^i$ and $\boldsymbol{p}_0^i = \boldsymbol{m}_1^i \otimes \boldsymbol{m}_2^i$. The secret $\boldsymbol{a}$ and $\{\boldsymbol{b}_i\}_{i=1}^l$ in final verification equation can be replaced by the masked openings $\boldsymbol{f}$ and $\{\boldsymbol{f}_1^i \otimes \boldsymbol{f}_2^i\}_{i=1}^l$.

We show how to generate the masked opening $\hat{\boldsymbol{H}}$ of matrix $\boldsymbol{H}$ through each $\hat{\boldsymbol{H}}_i$, where each $\hat{\boldsymbol{H}}_i = q_1\left[\sum_{k=0}^{h-1} f_{i,k}\boldsymbol{U}_k \| \sum_{k=0}^{h-1} f_{i,k}\boldsymbol{A}_k\right] = x^2 q_1 \boldsymbol{H}_i + x\boldsymbol{M}_i + \boldsymbol{N}_i$. For all $i \in [1,l]$, compute $\boldsymbol{M}_i = q_1\left[\sum_{k=0}^{h-1} \boldsymbol{p}_1^i[k]\boldsymbol{U}_k \| \sum_{k=0}^{h-1} \boldsymbol{p}_1^i[k]\boldsymbol{A}_k\right], \boldsymbol{N}_i = q_1\left[\sum_{k=0}^{h-1} \boldsymbol{p}_0^i[k]\boldsymbol{U}_k \| \sum_{k=0}^{h-1} \boldsymbol{p}_0^i[k]\boldsymbol{A}_k\right]$. Set

$$\boldsymbol{M} = \begin{pmatrix} \boldsymbol{M}_l & & \\ & \ddots & \\ & & \boldsymbol{M}_1 \end{pmatrix}, \boldsymbol{N} = \begin{pmatrix} \boldsymbol{N}_l & & \\ & \ddots & \\ & & \boldsymbol{N}_1 \end{pmatrix}, \text{and } \hat{\boldsymbol{H}} = \begin{pmatrix} \hat{\boldsymbol{H}}_l & & \\ & \ddots & \\ & & \hat{\boldsymbol{H}}_1 \end{pmatrix}. \quad (5)$$

Thus $\hat{\boldsymbol{H}}$ can be expressed as $\hat{\boldsymbol{H}} = x^2 q_1 \boldsymbol{H} + x\boldsymbol{M} + \boldsymbol{N}$. The equation $q_1(\boldsymbol{H} - \hat{\boldsymbol{G}})\boldsymbol{a} = q_1\boldsymbol{g}$ can be transformed to $(\hat{\boldsymbol{H}} - x^2 q_1 \hat{\boldsymbol{G}})\boldsymbol{f} = x^3 q_1(\boldsymbol{H} - \hat{\boldsymbol{G}})\boldsymbol{a} + x^2\boldsymbol{g}_2 + x\boldsymbol{g}_1 + \boldsymbol{g}_0 = x^3 q_1\boldsymbol{g} + x^2\boldsymbol{g}_2 + x\boldsymbol{g}_1 + \boldsymbol{g}_0$, where

$$\boldsymbol{g}_2 = q_1(\boldsymbol{H} - \hat{\boldsymbol{G}})\boldsymbol{m}_a + \boldsymbol{M}\boldsymbol{a}, \boldsymbol{g}_1 = \boldsymbol{M}\boldsymbol{m}_a + \boldsymbol{N}\boldsymbol{a} \text{ and } \boldsymbol{g}_0 = \boldsymbol{N}\boldsymbol{m}_a. \quad (6)$$

To ensure the confidentiality of the secret information $\boldsymbol{a}$, only the masked openings of $\boldsymbol{g}_2$ and $\boldsymbol{g}_1$ can be shown in verification. $\mathcal{V}$ computes the masked

Prove$(ap, \mathcal{H}, \mathcal{H}_0, \boldsymbol{u}, \mathsf{seed}, (\boldsymbol{o}_1^1, \boldsymbol{o}_2^1, \boldsymbol{v}_1, \boldsymbol{w}_1; \cdots; \boldsymbol{o}_1^l, \boldsymbol{o}_2^l, \boldsymbol{v}_l, \boldsymbol{w}_l))$

- Step 1: **Commit**
  1. Sample randomness: $\boldsymbol{r}_a \leftarrow \{-\beta, \cdots, \beta\}^{md}$; $\boldsymbol{m}_a \leftarrow D_{\phi_1 T_1}^{2l\alpha(k+1)d}$ for $T_1 = \eta\sqrt{l}(\hat{p}\sqrt{k\alpha d} + \gamma)$; $\boldsymbol{m} \leftarrow D_{\phi_2 T_2}^{2ld \log h}$ for $T_2 = \kappa\sqrt{2ld}$; $\boldsymbol{d} \leftarrow D_{\phi_3 T_3}^{md}$ for $T_3 = \eta\sqrt{md}$, where η and κ are shown in Appendix A.1.
  2. Compute $\boldsymbol{a}, \boldsymbol{H}, \hat{\boldsymbol{G}}, \boldsymbol{g}_2, \boldsymbol{g}_1', \boldsymbol{g}_0', \boldsymbol{t}_1, \boldsymbol{t}_0', \{\boldsymbol{t}_{i,1}, \boldsymbol{t}_{i,2}\}_{i=1}^l$ as described in (2) (4) (6) (7) (8) (9).
  3. Set $\boldsymbol{b} = \{\boldsymbol{o}_1^i \| \boldsymbol{o}_2^i\}_{i=l}^1$. Compute
  $$\begin{pmatrix} C_0 \\ C_1 \\ C_2 \\ C_3 \end{pmatrix} = \begin{pmatrix} \boldsymbol{B}_0 \\ \boldsymbol{0} \\ \boldsymbol{0} \\ \boldsymbol{0} \end{pmatrix} (\boldsymbol{a} \| \boldsymbol{b}) + \begin{pmatrix} \boldsymbol{B}_1 \\ \boldsymbol{B}_2 \\ \boldsymbol{B}_3 \\ \boldsymbol{B}_4 \end{pmatrix} \boldsymbol{r}_a + \begin{pmatrix} \boldsymbol{0}^n \\ \boldsymbol{g}_1' \\ \boldsymbol{g}_2 \\ \boldsymbol{t}_1 \end{pmatrix}; D = \boldsymbol{B}_0(\boldsymbol{m}_a \| \boldsymbol{m}) + \boldsymbol{B}_1 \boldsymbol{d} \in R_q^n,$$
  where $\boldsymbol{B}_0 \in R_q^{n \times 2l(k\alpha + \alpha + \log h)}$, $\boldsymbol{B}_1 \in R_q^{n \times m}$, $\boldsymbol{B}_2, \boldsymbol{B}_3 \in R_q^{lk\alpha \times m}$ and $\boldsymbol{B}_4 \in R_q^{2l \log h \times m}$.
  4. Compute the challenge $x = \mathcal{H}(C_0, C_1, C_2, C_3, D, \boldsymbol{g}_0', \boldsymbol{t}_0', \{\boldsymbol{t}_{i,1}, \boldsymbol{t}_{i,2}\}_{i=1}^l)$.
- Step 2: **Response**
  1. Let $\boldsymbol{m} = (\boldsymbol{m}_1^1 \| \boldsymbol{m}_2^1 \| \cdots \| \boldsymbol{m}_1^l \| \boldsymbol{m}_2^l)$. $\mathcal{P}$ computes $\boldsymbol{f} = x \cdot \boldsymbol{a} + \boldsymbol{m}_a, \boldsymbol{z} = x \cdot \boldsymbol{r}_a + \boldsymbol{d}$ and $\boldsymbol{f}_j^i = x \cdot \boldsymbol{o}_j^i + \boldsymbol{m}_j^i$, for all $i \in [1, l]$ and $j \in [1, 2]$.
  2. Denote $\boldsymbol{f}_b = \{\boldsymbol{f}_1^i \| \boldsymbol{f}_2^i\}_{i=l}^1$. Check the following equations, $\mathsf{Rej}'(\boldsymbol{z}, x \cdot \boldsymbol{r}_a, \phi_3, T_3) = 1$; $\mathsf{Rej}(\boldsymbol{f}_b, x \cdot \boldsymbol{b}, \phi_2, T_2) = 1$; $\mathsf{Rej}(\boldsymbol{f}, x \cdot \boldsymbol{a}, \phi_1, T_1) = 1$.
  3. If any of the above equations does not hold, then aborts. Otherwise, send $\pi_{zk} = (C_0, C_1, C_2, C_3, x, \boldsymbol{f}, \boldsymbol{f}_b, \boldsymbol{z})$ to $\mathcal{V}$.

Verify$(vp, \mathcal{H}, \mathcal{H}_0, \boldsymbol{u}, \mathsf{seed}, \pi_{zk})$

1. Parse $\pi_{zk} = (C_0, C_1, C_2, C_3, x, \boldsymbol{f}, \boldsymbol{f}_b, \boldsymbol{z})$ and compute $\boldsymbol{g}$, $\hat{\boldsymbol{H}}$, $\hat{\boldsymbol{G}}$ as in (3)(5)(4), and for all $i \in [1, l]$ and $j \in [1, 2]$,
$$\begin{aligned} D' =& \boldsymbol{B}_0(\boldsymbol{f} \| \boldsymbol{f}_b) + \boldsymbol{B}_1 \boldsymbol{z} - xC_0, \boldsymbol{g}_0'' = (\hat{\boldsymbol{H}} - x^2 q_1 \hat{\boldsymbol{G}})\boldsymbol{f} - x^3 q_1 \boldsymbol{g} - x(xC_2 - \boldsymbol{B}_3 \boldsymbol{z}) \\ & - (xC_1 - \boldsymbol{B}_2 \boldsymbol{z}), \\ \boldsymbol{t}_0'' =& \boldsymbol{f}_b \circ (\boldsymbol{x} - \boldsymbol{f}_b) - (xC_3 - \boldsymbol{B}_4 \boldsymbol{z}), \boldsymbol{t}_{i,j}' = \sum_{k=0}^{\log h - 1} \boldsymbol{f}_j^i[k] - x \end{aligned}$$
where $\boldsymbol{x} = (x \| x \| \cdots \| x) \in R_q^{2l \log h}$.
2. Output 1 iff all the following checks succeed:
   (a) $\|\boldsymbol{z}\| \le B_z = \phi_3 T_3 \sqrt{2md}$; $\|\boldsymbol{f}_b\| \le B_b = \phi_2 T_2 \sqrt{2ld \log h}$ and $\|\boldsymbol{f}\| \le B_f = 2\phi_1 T_1 \sqrt{(k+1)l\alpha d}$;
   (b) $x = \mathcal{H}(C_0, C_1, C_2, C_3, D', \boldsymbol{g}_0'', \boldsymbol{t}_0'', \{\boldsymbol{t}_{i,1}', \boldsymbol{t}_{i,2}'\}_{i=1}^l)$.

Fig. 1. Π_{acc}: Zero-knowledge proofs for lattice-based accumulator.

openings of $\boldsymbol{g}_2$ by $xC_2 - \boldsymbol{B}_3\boldsymbol{z}$, where C_2 is the commitment to $\boldsymbol{g}_2$ and $\boldsymbol{z}$ is the masked opening of the randomness used in the commitment. Note that $(\hat{\boldsymbol{H}} - x^2 q_1 \hat{\boldsymbol{G}})\boldsymbol{f} = x^3 q_1 \boldsymbol{g} + x(xC_2 - \boldsymbol{B}_3\boldsymbol{z}) + x\boldsymbol{g}_1 + x\boldsymbol{B}_3\boldsymbol{d} + \boldsymbol{g}_0$. We observe that the coefficient of x is transformed into $\boldsymbol{g}_1'$, as shown in (7). Similarly, the masked openings of $\boldsymbol{g}_1'$ can be obtained by $xC_1 - \boldsymbol{B}_2\boldsymbol{z}$. Eventually, all the secret information in the final verification equation are hidden, so the equation in **Verify** is $(\hat{\boldsymbol{H}} - x^2 q_1 \hat{\boldsymbol{G}})\boldsymbol{f} = x^3 q_1 \boldsymbol{g} + x(xC_2 - \boldsymbol{B}_3\boldsymbol{z}) + (xC_1 - \boldsymbol{B}_2\boldsymbol{z}) + \boldsymbol{g}_0'$, where

$$\boldsymbol{g}_1' = \boldsymbol{g}_1 + \boldsymbol{B}_3\boldsymbol{d} \text{ and } \boldsymbol{g}_0' = \boldsymbol{B}_2\boldsymbol{d} + \boldsymbol{g}_0. \tag{7}$$

Then we check that the element of $\boldsymbol{b}$ is binary, where $\boldsymbol{b} = \{\boldsymbol{o}_1^i \| \boldsymbol{o}_2^i\}_{i=l}^1$. Let $\circ$ denote component-wise product. We have $\boldsymbol{f}_b \circ (\boldsymbol{x} - \boldsymbol{f}_b) = x^2[\boldsymbol{b} \circ (\boldsymbol{1} - \boldsymbol{b})] + x[\boldsymbol{m} \circ (\boldsymbol{1} - 2\boldsymbol{b})] - \boldsymbol{m} \circ \boldsymbol{m} = x^2[\boldsymbol{b} \circ (\boldsymbol{1} - \boldsymbol{b})] + x\boldsymbol{t}_1 + \boldsymbol{t}_0$, where

$$\boldsymbol{x} = (x\|x\| \cdots \|x), \boldsymbol{t}_1 = \boldsymbol{m} \circ (\boldsymbol{1} - 2\boldsymbol{b}), \text{ and } \boldsymbol{t}_0 = -\boldsymbol{m} \circ \boldsymbol{m}. \tag{8}$$

Since C_3 is the commitment of $\boldsymbol{t}_1$, the statements that $\boldsymbol{b} \circ (\boldsymbol{1} - \boldsymbol{b}) = \boldsymbol{0}$ and $\|\boldsymbol{o}_j^i\|_1 = 1$ for all $i \in [1, l]$, $j \in [1, 2]$ can be transformed into $\boldsymbol{f}_b \circ (\boldsymbol{x} - \boldsymbol{f}_b) = xC_3 - \boldsymbol{B}_4\boldsymbol{z} + \boldsymbol{t}_0'$ and $\sum_{k=0}^{\log h - 1} \boldsymbol{f}_j^i[k] - x = \boldsymbol{t}_{i,j}$, respectively, where

$$\boldsymbol{t}_0' = -\boldsymbol{m} \circ \boldsymbol{m} + \boldsymbol{B}_4\boldsymbol{d}, \text{ and } \boldsymbol{t}_{i,j} = \sum_{k=0}^{\log h - 1} \boldsymbol{m}_j^i[k]. \tag{9}$$

Theorem 2. *The non-interactive protocol Π_{acc} for lattice-based accumulator is a zero-knowledge proof of knowledge for the relation $\mathcal{R}$ under the Extended-MLWE assumption and the M-SIS assumption.*

The proof is given in Appendix B.

Optimization of Protocol Π_{acc}

Amortized Protocol over All Relations. The verification is a product relation about the secret messages $\boldsymbol{a}$ and $\boldsymbol{b}$. The binary proof for $\boldsymbol{b}$ is also a product proof. Notice that the product proof will result in the garbage polynomials $\boldsymbol{g}_1'$, $\boldsymbol{g}_2 \in R_q^{lk\alpha}$ and $\boldsymbol{t}_1 \in R_q^{2l \log h}$. To reduce the size of the garbage polynomials, we can use amortized protocol [3,20] to linearly combine all the product relations into one product relation. Eventually, there will only be garbage polynomials of dimension 2, which act as the coefficients of x^2 and x in the verification equation.

Sampling Different Randomness to Mask. The randomness $\boldsymbol{m}_a$ is sampled from a gaussian distribution to mask both $\boldsymbol{v}_i$ and $\boldsymbol{w}_i$ for all $i \in [1, l]$ in Step 1 (1) of Π_{acc}. Note that the norm of $\boldsymbol{v}_i$ differs from that of $\boldsymbol{w}_i$ for all $i \in [1, l]$. The secret message $\boldsymbol{v}_i$ with a smaller norm does not necessarily need a larger randomness which can mask the $\boldsymbol{w}_i$ with a larger norm. Larger randomness will lead to higher communication costs. Hence, we sample different randomness to mask $\boldsymbol{v}_i$ and $\boldsymbol{w}_i$ to reduce the size of the corresponding masked opening. We replace $\boldsymbol{m}_a \leftarrow D_{\phi_1 T_1}^{2l\alpha(k+1)d}$ with $\boldsymbol{m}_v \leftarrow D_{\phi_1 T_1}^{l\alpha k d}$ and $\boldsymbol{m}_w \leftarrow D_{\phi_1' T_1'}^{l\alpha(k+2)d}$ in Step 1 (1) of Π_{acc}.**Prove**, where $T_1 \leq \eta\sqrt{l}\hat{p}\sqrt{k\alpha d}$ and $T_1' \leq \eta\sqrt{l}\gamma$. In Step 2 of Π_{acc}. **Prove**, $\boldsymbol{f} = x\boldsymbol{a} + \boldsymbol{m}_a$ is replaced with $\boldsymbol{f}_v = x(\boldsymbol{v}_l\|\cdots\|\boldsymbol{v}_1) + \boldsymbol{m}_v$ and $\boldsymbol{f}_w = x(\boldsymbol{w}_l\|\cdots\|\boldsymbol{w}_1) + \boldsymbol{m}_w$. Meanwhile, $\mathsf{Rej}(\boldsymbol{f}, x\cdot\boldsymbol{a}, \phi_1, T_1) = 1$ is replaced with $\mathsf{Rej}(\boldsymbol{f}_v, x\cdot(\boldsymbol{v}_l\|\cdots\|\boldsymbol{v}_1), \phi_1, T_1) = 1$ and $\mathsf{Rej}(\boldsymbol{f}_w, x\cdot(\boldsymbol{w}_l\|\cdots\|\boldsymbol{w}_1), \phi_1', T_1') = 1$. Thus, an honest prover does not abort with probability at least $1/(2\mu(\phi_1)\mu(\phi_1')\mu(\phi_2)\mu(\phi_3))$. The check $\|\boldsymbol{f}\| \leq B_f = 2\phi_1 T_1\sqrt{(k+1)l\alpha d}$ in Π_{acc}. **Verify** is replaced with $\|\boldsymbol{f}_v\| \leq B_v = \phi_1 T_1\sqrt{2kl\alpha d}$ and $\|\boldsymbol{f}_w\| \leq B_w = \phi_1' T_1' \sqrt{2(k+2)l\alpha d}$.

Instantiation. For the M-SIS and M-LWE assumption, we follow the methodology in [11,22] to offer 128-bit post-quantum security, where the root Hermite factor δ is around 1.0042. First, set $(q, p, d, N, \beta) = (\approx 2^{64}, \approx 2^{43}, 128, 2^{20}, 1)$ where $N = h^l$. To ensure the repetition rate of our protocol to be 32, i.e., $2\mu(\phi_1)\mu(\phi_1')\mu(\phi_2)\mu(\phi_3) = 32$, we set $\mu(\phi_1) = 3, \mu(\phi_1') = 4, \mu(\phi_2) = \sqrt{4/3}$ and $\mu(\phi_3) = \sqrt{4/3}$. Using the bimodal gaussian distribution [8,22] and the algorithm Rej' in Appendix A.2, we can compute the standard deviations $\sigma_1 \approx 0.675T_1$, $\sigma_1' \approx 0.6T_1', \sigma_2 \approx 1.32T_2$, and $\sigma_3 \approx 1.32T_3$ such that $\mu(\phi_1') = \mathsf{exp}(T_1'^2/2\sigma_1'^2)$ and $\mu(\phi_i) = \mathsf{exp}(T_i^2/2\sigma_i^2)$ for all $i \in [1,3]$.

Using upper-bounds for norms of random subgaussian matrices in [24], we can get $s_1(\boldsymbol{R}) \leq s_0(\sqrt{k\alpha d} + \sqrt{(k+2)\alpha d})$ with overwhelming probability, where s_0 is the parameter of the Gaussian distribution. Then, we have $\gamma \leq (h-1)s_1(\boldsymbol{R})\|\boldsymbol{v}_*\|$, where $\|\boldsymbol{v}_*\| \leq \hat{p}\sqrt{\alpha dk}$. We set $(\alpha, k) = (16, 4)$ so that $\text{M-SIS}_{\alpha, 2(k+1)\alpha, p, \beta_s}$ is hard, where $\beta_s = 2(k+2)\sqrt{d}\gamma + 2\hat{p}\sqrt{\alpha dk}$. For clarity, $e = 2$ in the description of Π_{acc} in Fig. 1. To reduce the proof size further, we set $e = 5$, i.e., $\boldsymbol{b}_i = \boldsymbol{o}_1^i \otimes \cdots \otimes \boldsymbol{o}_5^i$ for all $i \in [1, l]$. So the dimension of garbage polynomials is 5 and $T_2 = \kappa\sqrt{5ld}$. Then we set $(n, m) = (20, 26)$ such that the underlying problems, i.e., $\text{Extended-MLWE}_{n+5, m-n-5, \sigma_3}$ and $\text{M-SIS}_{n, 5l\log_5 h + m + 2(k+1)\alpha l, q, 4\eta(B_v+B_w+B_b+B_z)}$ are hard.[3]

Now we can evaluate the proof size of Π_{acc}. The size of the commitments $(C_0, \cdots, C_3)$ is $(n+5)d\log q$ bits. For $(\boldsymbol{f}_v, \boldsymbol{f}_w, \boldsymbol{f}_b, \boldsymbol{z})$, the coefficients of $\boldsymbol{f}_v, \boldsymbol{f}_w, \boldsymbol{f}_b, \boldsymbol{z}$ are upper-bounded by $6\sigma_1$, $6\sigma_1'$, $6\sigma_2$ and $6\sigma_3$ respectively, with high probability [21]. Notice that the dimension of $\boldsymbol{o}_j^i$ for all $j \in [1,5]$ and $i \in [1,l]$ is $\log_5 h$, where h is the dimension of each $\boldsymbol{b}_i$. So the size of $(\boldsymbol{f}_v, \boldsymbol{f}_w, \boldsymbol{f}_b, \boldsymbol{z})$ is $5l(\log_5 h)d\log(12\sigma_2) + md\log(12\sigma_3) + lk\alpha d\log(12\sigma_1) + l(k+2)\alpha d\log(12\sigma_1')$ bits. Hence, the total size of π_{zk} is $(n+5)d\log q + 5l(\log_5 h)d\ \log(12\sigma_2) + md\log(12\sigma_3) + lk\alpha d\log(12\sigma_1) + l(k+2)\alpha d\log(12\sigma_1')$ bits.

We note that the main part of the total proof size is $lk\alpha d\log(12\sigma_1) + l(k+2)\alpha d\log(12\sigma_1')$, which is linear with l, and the size of the public parameters, i.e., $\boldsymbol{U}$, is $\alpha^2 dkh\log p$ bits. Due to $l = \log_h N$, smaller l implies shorter proofs but a larger size of public parameters. We set $(h, l) = (2^{10}, 2)$.

To sum up, the proof size of the optimized Π_{acc} is around 225 KB, when the number of leaves of our accumulator tree is 2^{20}. The size of the public parameters, i.e., the length of $\boldsymbol{U}$, is 688 MB.

[3] More details are shown in the optimization of protocol Π_{acc} in Appendix 3.2.

4 Confidential Transactions with State Accumulator

In this section, we construct a blockchain-based confidential transactions protocol with state accumulator, called CTA, based on Π_{acc}.

4.1 Syntax

The syntax of our CTA is similar to that of RingCT-like protocols, say MatRiCT [11], where we make slight modifications to allow the state accumulator. In our CTA, the state st consists of the accumulator of all the valid accounts and a set of serial numbers sn, which are used to prevent double-spending. We assume that st is properly stored and maintained among all users or nodes of the blockchain system. The CTA protocol consists of the following tuple of polynomial time algorithms.

- **Setup**(1^λ): on input the security parameter λ, return public parameters pp, which is an implicit input to all the remaining functions.
- **CreateAddr**(pp): on input public parameters pp, output a address key pair $(\mathsf{pk}, \mathsf{sk})$.
- **SnGen**$(\mathsf{sk}_{\mathsf{old}})$: on input a secret key $\mathsf{sk}_{\mathsf{old}}$ of an input account, output a serial number sn. The serial number is unique to the input account.
- **Mint**$(\mathsf{amt}_{\mathsf{new}}, \mathsf{pk}_{\mathsf{new}})$: on input a output amount $\mathsf{amt}_{\mathsf{new}}$ and a output public key $\mathsf{pk}_{\mathsf{new}}$, output a coin cn and its coin key ck. A user runs **Mint** to generate a new coin.
- **UpdateSt**$(\mathsf{cn}, \mathsf{st})$: on input a coin cn, register a coin cn to the state st. Output a coin cn and the updated state st.
- **Spend**$(\mathsf{st}, \mathsf{Amt}_{\mathsf{new}}, \mathsf{Pk}_{\mathsf{new}}, \mathsf{Cn}_{\mathsf{old}}, \mathsf{Amt}_{\mathsf{old}}, \mathsf{Pk}_{\mathsf{old}}, \mathsf{Sk}_{\mathsf{old}}, \mathsf{Ck}_{\mathsf{old}})$: Run **Mint**$(\mathsf{Amt}_{\mathsf{new}}, \mathsf{Pk}_{\mathsf{new}})$ and **SnGen**$(\mathsf{Sk}_{\mathsf{old}})$ to generate new output coins $(\mathsf{Cn}_{\mathsf{new}}, \mathsf{Ck}_{\mathsf{new}})$ and serial numbers Sn, respectively. Generate a proof π of a transaction which is used to ensure the validity of a transaction. Output $(\mathsf{Tx}, \mathsf{Ck}_{\mathsf{new}}) = ((\mathsf{st}, \pi, \mathsf{Cn}_{\mathsf{new}}, \mathsf{Sn}), \mathsf{Ck}_{\mathsf{new}})$.
- **IfSpend**$(\mathsf{Sn}, \mathsf{st})$: on input a set Sn of serial numbers and st, if a serial number which belongs to Sn does not appear in st, output 1. Otherwise, output 0.
- **Verify**(Tx): on input a transaction Tx, if the proof π is not valid and **IfSpend**$(\mathsf{Sn}, \mathsf{st}) = 0$, output 0. Else, run $(\mathsf{Cn}_{\mathsf{new}}, \mathsf{st}) \leftarrow$ **UpdateSt**$(\mathsf{Cn}_{\mathsf{new}}, \mathsf{st})$, and output $\mathsf{Cn}_{\mathsf{new}}$ and updated st.

4.2 Security Model

The security requirements of CTA are captured by *Completeness*, *Ledger Indistinguishability* and *Balance*, the definitions of which almost follow that of MatRiCT [11]. The main modification is *Balance*, where we need to consider a new attack scenario, called fake account attack, due to the use of the state accumulator. The adversary $\mathcal{A}$'s abilities are modeled by the following oracles, where Orc denotes the set of all oracles defined below together with the random oracle. In addition, an adversary $\mathcal{A}$ cannot only induce honest parties to query Orc, but can also corrupt some honest parties.

- CreateAddr(i): on the i-th query, set $(\mathsf{pk}_i, \mathsf{sk}_i) \leftarrow$ **CreateAddr**(pp) and $\mathsf{sn}_i \leftarrow$ **SnGen**(sk_i). Return pk_i and sn_i. Insert $(\mathsf{pk}_i, \mathsf{sk}_i, \mathsf{sn}_i)$ to the list $\mathcal{T}$ defined by the structure of an account. The row tags in $\mathcal{T}$ are denoted by pk, sk, sn, cn, ck, amt and IsCrpt, where IsCrpt is set as the "is corrupted" tag. After inserting, IsCrpt tag is set to zero and the remaining information is left empty. We can retrieve a row in $\mathcal{T}$ by $\mathcal{T}[\mathsf{pk}]$ for some public key pk. Then, $\mathcal{T}[\mathsf{pk}].\mathsf{ck}$ corresponds to the coin key associate with the public key pk.
- Mint($\mathsf{amt}, \mathsf{pk}$): run $(\mathsf{cn}, \mathsf{ck}) \leftarrow$ **Mint**($\mathsf{amt}, \mathsf{pk}$) and return cn.
- ActGen($\mathsf{amt}, \mathsf{pk}, \mathsf{cn}, \mathsf{ck}, \mathsf{st}$): Add $(\mathsf{cn}, \mathsf{ck}, \mathsf{amt})$ to the list $\mathcal{T}[\mathsf{pk}]$ respectively. Run $(\mathsf{cn}, \mathsf{st}) \leftarrow$ **UpdateSt** $(\mathsf{cn}, \mathsf{st})$. Return pk, cn and updated st.
- Corrupt(act): For a $\mathsf{act} = (\mathsf{pk}, \mathsf{cn})$, if $\mathcal{T}[\mathsf{pk}]$ or $\mathcal{T}[\mathsf{cn}]$ cannot be found, output 0; else, set $\mathcal{T}[\mathsf{pk}]$.IsCrpt to 1, and output $\mathcal{T}[\mathsf{pk}].\mathsf{sk}$, $\mathcal{T}[\mathsf{pk}].\mathsf{ck}$ and $\mathcal{T}[\mathsf{pk}].\mathsf{amt}$.
- Spend($\mathsf{st}, \mathsf{Amt}_{\mathsf{new}}, \mathsf{Pk}_{\mathsf{new}}, \mathsf{Cn}_{\mathsf{old}}, \mathsf{Amt}_{\mathsf{old}}, \mathsf{Pk}_{\mathsf{old}}, \mathsf{Sk}_{\mathsf{old}}, \mathsf{Ck}_{\mathsf{old}}$): Retrieve from $\mathcal{T}$ all account secret keys corresponding to $\mathsf{Cn}_{\mathsf{old}}$. Run $(\mathsf{Tx}, \mathsf{Ck}_{\mathsf{new}}) \leftarrow$ **Spend**(st, $\mathsf{Amt}_{\mathsf{new}}, \mathsf{Pk}_{\mathsf{new}}, \mathsf{Cn}_{\mathsf{old}}$, $\mathsf{Amt}_{\mathsf{old}}, \mathsf{Sk}_{\mathsf{old}}, \mathsf{Ck}_{\mathsf{old}}$) and $B \leftarrow$ **Verify**(Tx). If the verification fails, i.e., $B = 0$, return $\perp$; otherwise, run $(\mathsf{Cn}_{\mathsf{new}}, \mathsf{st}) \leftarrow$ **UpdateSt** $(\mathsf{Cn}_{\mathsf{new}}, \mathsf{st})$, then output Tx and insert the output accounts information in the list $\mathcal{T}$, respectively.

Completeness requires that unspent coins generated with valid public keys and amounts honestly, can be spent. Ledger indistinguishability requires that the ledger reveals no secret information, e.g., the amount of minted coins, the real payers' and payees' addresses, to the adversaries (other than the payers and payees) beyond the publicly-revealed information, even if the adversary can adaptively query oracles according to his strategy. The above requirements are captured by an experiment, denoted as Exp-Anony, where the aim of the adversary $\mathcal{A}$ is to distinguish between two **Spend** output transactions Tx_0 and Tx_1.

Definition 5. *A CTA protocol is ledger indistinguishable if for all PPT adversaries $\mathcal{A}$ and $pp \leftarrow$ **Setup**(1^λ), Pr[$\mathcal{A}$ wins Exp-Anony] $\leq 1/2 + \mathsf{negl}(\lambda)$.*

More details of formal definitions of completeness and Exp-Anony refer to MatRiCT [11].

Balance. This property requires that no PPT adversary can spend a set χ of accounts under his control such that the sum of output amounts is more than the sum of the amounts in χ. To capture this property, we describe the experiment Exp-balance as follows. Given access to all the oracles Orc together with pp, the adversary $\mathcal{A}$ outputs a set of t transactions $((\mathsf{Tx}^1, {\mathsf{Amt}_{\mathsf{new}}}^1, {\mathsf{Ck}_{\mathsf{new}}}^1), \cdots, (\mathsf{Tx}^t, {\mathsf{Amt}_{\mathsf{new}}}^t, {\mathsf{Ck}_{\mathsf{new}}}^t))$, where $\mathsf{Tx}^i = (\mathsf{st}^i, \pi^i, {\mathsf{Cn}_{\mathsf{new}}}^i, \mathsf{Sn}^i)$ for all $i \in [1, t]$ and $({\mathsf{Amt}_{\mathsf{new}}}^i$, ${\mathsf{Ck}_{\mathsf{new}}}^i)$ are sets of output amounts and coin keys, respectively, for uncorrupted output public keys with $|{\mathsf{Amt}_{\mathsf{new}}}^i| = |{\mathsf{Ck}_{\mathsf{new}}}^i| \leq |{\mathsf{Pk}_{\mathsf{new}}}^i| = |{\mathsf{Cn}_{\mathsf{new}}}^i|$ for all $i \in [1, t]$. We say $\mathcal{A}$ wins Exp-balance if the following holds.

(1) $B^i \neq 0$ for all $i \in [1, t]$, where $B^i \leftarrow$ **Verify**(Tx^i).

(2) all input public keys and coins in $(\mathsf{Cn_{old}}^i, \mathsf{Pk_{old}}^i)$ for all $i \in [1, t]$, are generated by **CreateAddr** and **Mint**, respectively.
(3) $\cap_{i=1}^{t} \mathsf{Sn}_i = \emptyset$.
(4) for $S' = |\mathsf{Amt_{new}}^{j^*}|$ and $M = |\mathsf{Sn}^{j^*}|$, there exists a $j^* \in [1, t]$ such that $\sum_{i=0}^{S'-1} \mathsf{Amt_{new}}^{j^*}[i] > \sum_{i=0}^{M-1} \mathsf{amt_{old,i}}$, where for all $s_i \in \mathsf{Sn}^{j^*}$, if $s_i \in \mathcal{T}$ and $\mathcal{T}[s_i].\mathsf{IsCrpt} = 1$, $\mathsf{amt}_{\mathsf{in},i} = \mathcal{T}[s_i].\mathsf{amt}$, which corresponds to the attack scenario **Unbalanced amounts.** In this case, the attacker creates a valid transaction where the sum of input amounts being spent is not equal to the sum of output amounts to make a profit.
Otherwise, $\mathsf{amt}_{\mathsf{in},i} = 0$, which corresponds to the attack scenarios **Double spending**, **Forgery** and **Fake accounts.** The details of the above attack scenarios refer to MatRiCT [11].
(5) for any $i \in [1, t]$ and $0 \leq j < |\mathsf{Pk_{new}}^i|$, set $\mathsf{pk}_{i,j} = \mathsf{Pk_{new}}^i[j]$ and if $\mathcal{T}[\mathsf{pk}_{i,j}].\mathsf{IsCrpt} = 0$, then $\mathsf{Ck_{new}}^i[j] = \mathcal{T}[\mathsf{pk}_{i,j}].\mathsf{ck}$, $\mathsf{Amt_{new}}^i[j] = \mathcal{T}[\mathsf{pk}_{i,j}].\mathsf{amt}$ and $\mathsf{Cn_{new}}^i[j] = \mathbf{Mint}\ (\mathsf{Amt_{new}}^i[j], \mathsf{Ck_{new}}^i[j])$.

Definition 6. *A CTA protocol is balanced if for all PPT adversaries $\mathcal{A}$ and $pp \leftarrow$ **Setup**(1^λ), $\Pr[\mathcal{A}$ wins Exp-Balance$] \leq \mathsf{negl}(\lambda)$.*

We add a new attack scenario, called "Fake accounts", to the balance model. Note that all users of CTA only need to store the "compressed" state st, instead of the complete transaction records which contains the information of all valid accounts. It is possible that the adversary may try to create a transaction by some fake accounts which are not registered. MatRiCT [11] does not consider such an attack assuming that all input accounts are generated by ActGen oracle, i.e., all of them are registered in $\mathcal{T}$, while ours removes this assumption.

4.3 Construction of CTA

Without loss of generality, we show the construction of CTA for the case of one payer for clarity. In **Setup**, the commitment keys $ck = (\boldsymbol{H}_0, \boldsymbol{H}_1, \{\boldsymbol{G}_i\}_{i=0}^{2}, \{\boldsymbol{B}_i\}_{i=0}^{4})$ are generated by $\mathcal{H}_0(\mathsf{seed})$. **CreateAddr** generates a public-secret key pair. The secret key sk is a random vector over R_q with infinity norm β, and the public key pk is a commitment to zero. Set $\mathsf{pk} = \boldsymbol{H}_0 \cdot \mathbf{sk} \in R_q^{\hat{n}}$ where $\mathbf{sk} \leftarrow \{-\beta, \cdots, \beta\}^{\hat{m}d}$. **SnGen** generates a serial number sn for a given secret key to prevent double-spending, where $\mathsf{sn} = \boldsymbol{H}_1 \cdot \mathsf{sk} \in R_q$. **Mint** denotes that a payer mints the output coin cn, which is a commitment to the output amount $\mathsf{amt_{new}}$ and the output public key $\mathsf{pk_{new}}$. Set $\mathsf{cn} = (C_r \| C_a \| C_p) = (\boldsymbol{G}_0 \cdot \boldsymbol{k} \| \boldsymbol{G}_1 \cdot \boldsymbol{k} + \mathsf{amt_{new}} \| \boldsymbol{G}_2 \cdot \boldsymbol{k} + \mathsf{pk_{new}}) \in R_q^{2\hat{n}+1}$, where $\boldsymbol{k} \leftarrow \{-\beta, \cdots, \beta\}^{\hat{m}d}$.

The details of **Spend** which spends the old coin and mints new coins, and **Verify** which checks the validity of the transaction, are described in Fig. 2. When spending, the following NP statement for the underlying zero-knowledge proofs π is provided: Given the accumulator $\boldsymbol{u}$, serial number sn, and output coins $\{\mathsf{cn}_{\mathsf{new},i}\}_{i=0}^{S-1}$, I know $\mathsf{cn_{old}}$ and the corresponding account secret key $(\mathsf{sk_{old}}, \mathsf{ck_{old}}, \mathsf{amt_{old}})$ such that:

(s1) Every output coin $\mathsf{cn}_{\mathsf{new},i}$ is well-formed with a coin key $\boldsymbol{r}_{\mathsf{new},i}$, a positive amount $\mathsf{amt}_{\mathsf{new},i}$ and a public key $\mathsf{pk}_{\mathsf{new},i}$: it holds that $\mathsf{cn}_{\mathsf{new},i} = (C_{r,i}\|C_{a,i}\|C_{p,i}) = (\boldsymbol{G}_0 \cdot \boldsymbol{r}_{\mathsf{new},i}\|\boldsymbol{G}_1 \cdot \boldsymbol{r}_{\mathsf{new},i} + \mathsf{amt}_{\mathsf{new},i}\|\boldsymbol{G}_2 \cdot \boldsymbol{r}_{\mathsf{new},i} + \mathsf{pk}_{\mathsf{new},i})$.
(s2) The serial number is computed correctly and never appears in the blockchain before: it holds that $\mathsf{sn} = \boldsymbol{H}_1 \cdot \mathsf{sk}_{\mathsf{old}}$.
(s3) The spent coin belongs to some valid account: there exists a witness which can prove that $\mathsf{cn}_{\mathsf{old}}$ has been accumulated into $\boldsymbol{u}$, which is realized by our zero-knowledge accumulator.
(s4) $\mathsf{cn}_{\mathsf{old}}$ is well-formed with the coin key $\mathsf{ck}_{\mathsf{old}}$, the positive amount $\mathsf{amt}_{\mathsf{old}}$ and the public key $\mathsf{pk}_{\mathsf{old}}$: it holds that $\mathsf{cn}_{\mathsf{old}} = (\boldsymbol{G}_0 \cdot \mathsf{ck}_{\mathsf{old}}\|\boldsymbol{G}_1 \cdot \mathsf{ck}_{\mathsf{old}} + \sum_{i=0}^{S-1} \mathsf{amt}_{\mathsf{new},i}\|\boldsymbol{G}_2 \cdot \mathsf{ck}_{\mathsf{old}} + \boldsymbol{H}_0 \cdot \mathsf{sk}_{\mathsf{old}})$.

We omit the details for the range proof of the output amounts, which can be referred to the previous works [1,20].

Security Analysis. The completeness of CTA mainly follows from the completeness of the underlying ZKP.

Theorem 3. *CTA is ledger indistinguishable. More specifically, for any PPT adversary* $\mathcal{A}$*, the probability* $\varepsilon_{\mathcal{A}}^{\mathsf{Ano}}$ *that* $\mathcal{A}$ *wins* Exp-Anony *is at most* $\mathsf{Adv}_{\mathcal{A}}^{\mathsf{LWE}} + \mathsf{Adv}_{\mathcal{A}}^{\mathsf{LWE}_1} + S \cdot \mathsf{Adv}_{\mathcal{A}}^{\mathsf{LWE}_2} + \sum_{i=1}^{4} \varepsilon(\mu(\phi_i)) + 1/2$*, where* $\varepsilon(\mu(\phi_i)) \leq 2^{-100}/\mu(\phi_i)$ *and* $\mu(\phi_i)$ *for* $i = [1,4]$ *is defined in Appendix A.2, and* $\mathsf{Adv}_{\mathcal{A}}^{\mathsf{LWE}}$, $\mathsf{Adv}_{\mathcal{A}}^{\mathsf{LWE}_1}$ *and* $\mathsf{Adv}_{\mathcal{A}}^{\mathsf{LWE}_2}$ *denote the advantage of* $\mathcal{A}$ *over solving Extend M-LWE*$_{1,\hat{m}-1,\sigma_4}$*, Extend M-LWE*$_{n+5,m-n-5,\sigma_3}$ *and Extend M-LWE*$_{2\hat{n}+1,\hat{m}-2\hat{n}-1,\sigma_4}$*, respectively.*

Theorem 4. *CTA is balance, assuming the underlying zero-knowledge proof is sound.*

Lemma 2. *The underlying zero-knowledge proof of CTA is computational special sound under the M-SIS assumption.*

The proofs of Theorem 3, Theorem 4, and Lemma 2 are given in Appendix C, E and D, respecitively.

Transaction Size. We set the repetition rate of our CTA to be 64, i.e., $2\prod_{i=1}^{4} \mu(\phi_i) = 64$. Thus we get $\mu(\phi_4) = 2$. Similarly, using the algorithm Rej' in Appendix A.2, we can compute the standard deviations $\sigma_4 \approx 0.72T_4$ such that $\mu(\phi_i) = \mathsf{exp}(T_4^2/2\sigma_4^2)$. For 32-bit range, the size of range proof for the output amounts is approximately 5.9 KB when using the method in [3]. When $M = 1$ and $S = 2$, other than π_{zk}, the payer need to send $(\{\boldsymbol{z}_i\}_{i=0}^{S-1}, \boldsymbol{z}_{\mathsf{sk}}, \boldsymbol{z}_k)$, the size of which is $(S+2)\hat{m}d\log(12\sigma_4)$ bits. We set the parameters $(\hat{n}, \hat{m}) = (5, 12)$ such that the underlying problems, i.e., Extended-MLWE$_{\hat{m}-2\hat{n}-1,2\hat{n}+1,\sigma_4}$ and M-SIS$_{\hat{n},\hat{m},8\eta B}$, are hard.[4] Thus the proof size of our CTA is around 236 KB in the case of 1 input and 2 output accounts with anonymity set size 2^{20}.

[4] The details are shown in the proof of Lemma 2 in Appendix D.

Spend-I

Input: $S \in Z^+$; $\boldsymbol{u}$; $(\mathsf{pk}_{\mathsf{old}}, \mathsf{cn}_{\mathsf{old}})$; ck; $\mathcal{H}$; the secrets of input accounts $\mathsf{sk}_{\mathsf{old}}, \mathsf{amt}_{\mathsf{old}}, \mathsf{ck}_{\mathsf{old}}$; $\{\mathsf{pk}_{\mathsf{new},i}\}_{i=0}^{S-1}$; $\{\mathsf{amt}_{\mathsf{new},i}\}_{i=0}^{S-1}$.

1. Obtain the witness $w \leftarrow \mathsf{Acc}.\mathbf{Witness}(\mathsf{coinpool}, \mathsf{cn}_{\mathsf{old}}, \boldsymbol{u})$.
2. Sample randomness: $\boldsymbol{e}_0, \cdots, \boldsymbol{e}_{S-1}, \boldsymbol{m}_f, \boldsymbol{r}_k \leftarrow D_{\phi_4 T_4}^{\hat{m}d}$, where $T_4 = \eta\beta\sqrt{(S+2)\hat{m}d}$.
3. Run $\mathsf{sn} \leftarrow \mathbf{SnGen}(\mathsf{sk}_{\mathsf{old}})$, $(\mathsf{cn}_{\mathsf{new},i}, \boldsymbol{r}_{\mathsf{new},i}) \leftarrow \mathbf{Mint}(\mathsf{amt}_{\mathsf{new},i}, \mathsf{pk}_{\mathsf{new},i})$ where $\mathsf{cn}_{\mathsf{new},i} = (C_{r,i}\|C_{a,i}\|C_{p,i})$, for all $i \in [S]$ and $(\boldsymbol{a}, \boldsymbol{b}, \boldsymbol{r}_a, \boldsymbol{m}_a, \boldsymbol{m}, \boldsymbol{d}, C_0, C_1, C_2, C_3, D, \boldsymbol{g}_0', \boldsymbol{t}_0', \{\boldsymbol{t}_{i,1}, \boldsymbol{t}_{i,2}\}_{i=0}^{l-1}) \leftarrow$ Step 1 of $\Pi_{\mathsf{acc}}.\mathbf{Prove}$.
4. Compute $E_i = \boldsymbol{G}_0 \cdot \boldsymbol{e}_i$ for all $i \in [S]$, $F = \boldsymbol{H}_1 \cdot \boldsymbol{m}_f$ and $C_m = (\boldsymbol{G}_0\|\boldsymbol{G}_1\|\boldsymbol{G}_2) \cdot \boldsymbol{r}_k + (\boldsymbol{0}^n\| - \boldsymbol{G}_1 \sum_{i=0}^{S-1} \boldsymbol{e}_i\|\boldsymbol{H}_0 \cdot \boldsymbol{m}_f) - \boldsymbol{G} \cdot \boldsymbol{c}_l$, where $\boldsymbol{c}_l \in \boldsymbol{m}_a$.
5. Compute the challenge $x = \mathcal{H}(\{\mathsf{cn}_{\mathsf{new},i}, E_i\}_{i=0}^{S-1}, \mathsf{sn}, F, C_m, C_0, C_1, C_2, C_3, D, \boldsymbol{g}_0', \boldsymbol{t}_0', \{\boldsymbol{t}_{i,1}, \boldsymbol{t}_{i,2}\}_{i=1}^{l})$.

Spend-II

Input: $(\{\boldsymbol{e}_i, \boldsymbol{r}_{\mathsf{new},i}\}_{i=0}^{S-1}, \boldsymbol{m}_f, \boldsymbol{r}_k; \mathsf{sk}_{\mathsf{old}}, \mathsf{ck}_{\mathsf{old}}; \boldsymbol{a}, \boldsymbol{b}, \boldsymbol{r}_a, \boldsymbol{m}_a, \boldsymbol{m}, \boldsymbol{d}; x)$.

1. Compute $\boldsymbol{z}_i = x \cdot \boldsymbol{r}_{\mathsf{new},i} + \boldsymbol{e}_i$ for all $i \in [S]$, $\boldsymbol{z}_{\mathsf{sk}} = x \cdot \mathsf{sk}_{\mathsf{old}} + \boldsymbol{m}_f$ and $\boldsymbol{z}_k = x \cdot \mathsf{ck}_{\mathsf{old}} + \boldsymbol{r}_k$.
2. Check if $\mathsf{Rej}'((\boldsymbol{z}_0\| \cdots \|\boldsymbol{z}_{S-1}\|\boldsymbol{z}_{\mathsf{sk}}\|\boldsymbol{z}_k), (x\boldsymbol{r}_{\mathsf{new},0}\| \cdots \|x\boldsymbol{r}_{\mathsf{new},S-1}\|x \cdot \mathsf{sk}_{\mathsf{old}}\|x \cdot \mathsf{ck}_{\mathsf{old}}), \phi_4, T_4) = 1$ holds. If the equation does not hold, then aborts.
3. Run $(\boldsymbol{f}, \boldsymbol{z}, \boldsymbol{f}_b)/\perp \leftarrow$ Step 2 of $\Pi_{\mathsf{acc}}.\mathbf{Prove}$. If it outputs $\perp$, then aborts.

Spend outputs $((\pi = (C_0, C_1, C_2, C_3, x, \boldsymbol{f}, \boldsymbol{f}_b, \boldsymbol{z}, \boldsymbol{z}_{\mathsf{sk}}, \boldsymbol{z}_k, \{\boldsymbol{z}_i\}_{i=0}^{S-1}), \{\mathsf{cn}_{\mathsf{new},i}\}_{i=0}^{S-1}, \mathsf{sn}), \{\boldsymbol{r}_{\mathsf{new},i}\}_{i=0}^{S-1})$. Broadcast $(\{\mathsf{cn}_{\mathsf{new},i}\}_{i=0}^{S-1}, \mathsf{sn}, \pi)$ to the verification nodes.

Verify$(\boldsymbol{u}, ck, \mathcal{H}, \{\mathsf{cn}_{\mathsf{new},i}\}_{i=0}^{S-1}, \mathsf{sn}, \pi)$

1. Parse $\pi = (C_0, C_1, C_2, C_3, x, \boldsymbol{f}, \boldsymbol{f}_b, \boldsymbol{z}, \boldsymbol{z}_{\mathsf{sk}}, \boldsymbol{z}_k, \{\boldsymbol{z}_i\}_{i=0}^{S-1})$ and compute

$$E_i' = \boldsymbol{G}_0 \cdot \boldsymbol{z}_i - xC_{r,i} \text{ and } \boldsymbol{f}_i = xC_{a,i} - \boldsymbol{G}_1 \cdot \boldsymbol{z}_i, \text{ for all } i \in [S],$$
$$F' = \boldsymbol{H}_1 \cdot \boldsymbol{z}_{\mathsf{sk}} - x \cdot \mathsf{sn},$$
$$\boldsymbol{f}_c = (\boldsymbol{G}_0\|\boldsymbol{G}_1\|\boldsymbol{G}_2)\boldsymbol{z}_k + (\boldsymbol{0}^n\| \sum_{i=0}^{S-1} \boldsymbol{f}_i\|\boldsymbol{H}_0 \cdot \boldsymbol{z}_{sk}),$$
$$C_m' = \boldsymbol{f}_c - \boldsymbol{G}\boldsymbol{f}_l \text{ where } \boldsymbol{f}_l \subset \boldsymbol{f} \text{ and } \boldsymbol{f}_l = x\boldsymbol{v}_l + \boldsymbol{c}_l \text{ for } \boldsymbol{c}_l \subset \boldsymbol{m}_a.$$

2. Iff all the following checks succeed:
   (a) $\{\|\boldsymbol{z}_i\|\}_{i=0}^{S-1}$, $\|\boldsymbol{z}_{\mathsf{sk}}\|$ and $\|\boldsymbol{z}_k\| \leq B$ where $B = \phi_4 T_4\sqrt{2(S+2)\hat{m}d}$;
   (b) $1 \leftarrow \Pi_{\mathsf{acc}}.\mathbf{Verify}(vp, \mathcal{H}, \mathcal{H}_0, \boldsymbol{u}, \mathsf{seed}, C_0, C_1, C_2, C_3, x, \boldsymbol{f}, \boldsymbol{f}_b, \boldsymbol{z})$ except that (b) of Step 2.
   (c) $x = \mathcal{H}(\mathsf{cn}_{\mathsf{new},i}, E_i'\}_{i=0}^{S-1}, \mathsf{sn}, F', C_m', C_0, C_1, C_2, C_3, D', \boldsymbol{g}_0'', \boldsymbol{t}_0'', \{\boldsymbol{t}_{i,1}', \boldsymbol{t}_{i,2}'\}_{i=1}^{l})$.

Output $\{\mathsf{cn}_{\mathsf{new},i}\}_{i=0}^{S-1}$ and update the state.

Fig. 2. Spend and **Verify** of CTA.

5 Conclusions

The proposed lattice-based protocol CTA relies on the state accumulator, which follows from the blueprint of Zerocash. We consider a stronger security model than that of previous RingCT-like protocols, by identifying a new attack scenario, called "fake accounts" attack. If users have the complete records of transactions, which is the case in Ring-CT like protocols, it is not necessary to consider this attack. In our CTA, the validity of accounts is implied by the validity check of the compressed state. Our technical novelty lies in the concise zero-knowledge proofs for lattice-based accumulator, which enables optimized decomposition of hashes in the internal nodes and concise expression of the membership statement. Compared with state-of-the-art zero-knowledge lattice-based accumulators, the proposed protocol achieves better performance at 128-bit post-quantum security, i.e. the membership proof is only 225 KB with 2^{20} members. Compared with previous lattice-based protocols with linear storage space and computational time, CTA can achieve logarithmic storage space and computational time.

Acknowledgments. Puwen Wei was supported by National Key R&D Program of China (Grant No. 2022YFB2701700, 2018YFA0704702) and Shandong Provincial Natural Science Foundation (Grant No. ZR2020MF053). Shumin Si was supported by Shandong Key Research and Development Program (2020ZLYS09) and the Major Scientific and Technological Innovation Project of Shandong, China (2019JZZY010133). Xiuhan Lin was supported by the National Key Research and Development Program of China (2020YFA0309705,2018YFA0704701); and the Major Program of Guangdong Basic and Applied Research (2019B030302008).

A More on Preliminaries

A.1 Challenge Space

Let $q = q_1 q_2$ be a product of two odd primes where $q_1 < q_2$. Suppose each q_i splits into g prime ideals of degree d/g in R_q. That is, $X^d + 1$ can factor into g irreducible polynomials of degree d/g modulo q. Assuming Z_q contains a primitive $2g$-th root of unity $\zeta_i \in Z_q$ and $q_i \equiv 2g + 1 \pmod{4g}$, we have $X^d + 1 \equiv \prod_{j \in Z_g}(X^{d/g} - \zeta_i^{2j+1}) \bmod q_i$ where ζ_i^{2j+1} $(j \in Z_g)$ ranges over all the g primitive $2g$-th roots of unity. The ring R has a group of automorphisms $\mathsf{Aut}(R_q)$ which is isomorphic to $Z_{2d}^{\times}$. Let $\sigma_i \in \mathsf{Aut}(R_q)$ be defined by $\sigma_i(X) = X^i$, which is applied to the challenge set [18]. The challenge space $\mathcal{C}$ is defined as $\mathcal{C} = \{c \in S_\kappa^\sigma : \sqrt{\|\sigma_{-1}(c)c\|_1} \le \eta\}$, where $S_\kappa^\sigma = \{c \in R_q : \|c\|_\infty \le \kappa \wedge \sigma(c) = c\}$. We can compute $\|c\boldsymbol{r}\| \le \eta\|\boldsymbol{r}\|$ when $c \in \mathcal{C}$ and $\boldsymbol{r} \in R_q^n$. [18] shows that the difference of any two distinct elements of $\mathcal{C}$ is invertible over R_q if $\kappa < \frac{1}{2\sqrt{g}} q_1^{1/g}$. The concrete parameters proposed in [18] satisfy that for $d = 128, g = 4, \kappa = 2, \eta = 73, q_1 > 2^{20}$ and a automorphisms σ_{-1}, $|\mathcal{C}| = 2^{147}$ and the invertibility property of the challenge space holds.

A.2 Rejection Sampling

During the zero-knowledge proofs, the prover computes $\boldsymbol{z} = \boldsymbol{y} + c\boldsymbol{r}$ where $\boldsymbol{r}$ is the secret vector, $c \leftarrow \mathcal{C}$ is a challenge polynomial, and $\boldsymbol{y}$ is a masking vector. The distribution of the prover's output $\boldsymbol{z}$ should be independent of the secret randomness vector $\boldsymbol{r}$, so that any information on the prover's secret cannot be obtained from $\boldsymbol{z}$. To remove the dependency of $\boldsymbol{z}$ on $\boldsymbol{r}$, we use the rejection sampling technique by Lyubashevsky [17]. In order to reduce the standard deviation σ, recent work [21] modifies rejection sampling algorithm to force $\langle \boldsymbol{z}, \boldsymbol{v} \rangle$[5] ≥ 0 in Algorithm 2, which leaks one bit of information about the secret. We need to rely on the Extended-MLWE problem as analysed in [22] to show the advantage of distinguishability with the revealed one bit information.

Algorithm 1 $\mathsf{Rej}(\boldsymbol{z}, \boldsymbol{v}, \phi, T)$	Algorithm 2 $\mathsf{Rej}'(\boldsymbol{z}, \boldsymbol{v}, \phi, T)$
$\mu \leftarrow [0, 1)$;	$\mu \leftarrow [0, 1)$;
$\sigma = \phi T; \mu(\phi) = e^{12/\phi + 1/(2\phi^2)}$;	if $\langle \boldsymbol{z}, \boldsymbol{v} \rangle \leq 0$, **return** 0;
if $\mu > (\frac{1}{\mu(\phi)})\mathsf{exp}(\frac{-2\langle \boldsymbol{z}, \boldsymbol{v} \rangle + \|\boldsymbol{v}\|^2}{2\sigma^2})$,	$\sigma = \phi T; \mu(\phi) = e^{12/\phi + 1/(2\phi^2)}$;
return 0;	if $\mu > (\frac{1}{\mu(\phi)})\mathsf{exp}(\frac{-2\langle \boldsymbol{z}, \boldsymbol{v} \rangle + \|\boldsymbol{v}\|^2}{2\sigma^2})$,
else **return** 1.	**return** 0;
	else **return** 1.

B Proof for Theorem 2

Proof. **Completeness:** Completeness follows directly from the discussion in Sect. 3.2. Following [4] [Lemma 1.5(i)], with overwhelming probability, we have $\|\boldsymbol{f}\| \leq 2\phi_1 T_1 \sqrt{(k+1)l\alpha d}$, $\|\boldsymbol{f}_b\| \leq \phi_2 T_2 \sqrt{2ld \log h}$ and $\|\boldsymbol{z}\| \leq \phi_3 T_3 \sqrt{2md}$.

Zero-Knowledge: Firstly, randomly choose the challenges $x \in \mathcal{C}$. (Note that, in the random oracle model, the hash function $\mathcal{H}$ is modeled as a random oracle, which can be programmed by the simulator.) Compute $(C_0 \| C_1 \| \cdots \| C_3) = (\boldsymbol{B}_1 \| \boldsymbol{B}_2 \| \cdots \| \boldsymbol{B}_4) \cdot \boldsymbol{r}'$ by $\boldsymbol{r}' \leftarrow \{-\beta, \cdots, \beta\}^{md}$, i.e., the message committed in this commitment is $\boldsymbol{0}$. This commitment is computationally indistinguishable from the real case due to the computationally hiding property of the underlying commitment schemes, which are based on the Extended-MLWE$_{m-n-v,n,\sigma_3}$ assumption. Here v denotes the height of commitments $(C_1 \| C_2 \| C_3)$, i.e., it is the dimension of the committed messages of $(C_1 \| C_2 \| C_3)$. Then, generate $\boldsymbol{f} \leftarrow D_{\phi_1 T_1}^{2l\alpha(k+1)d}$, $\boldsymbol{z} \leftarrow D_{\phi_2 T_2}^{md}$ and also $\boldsymbol{f}_b \leftarrow D_{\phi_1 T_1}^{2ld \log h}$, which are computationally indistinguishable from that of the real execution due to the reject sampling technique. At last, compute D', $\boldsymbol{g}_0''$, $\boldsymbol{t}_0''$ and $\{\boldsymbol{t}_{i,1}', \boldsymbol{t}_{i,2}'\}_{i=0}^{l-1}$ as Step 1 of Π_{acc}.**Verify**. Therefore, D', $\boldsymbol{g}_0''$, $\boldsymbol{t}_0''$ and $\{\boldsymbol{t}_{i,1}', \boldsymbol{t}_{i,2}'\}_{i=0}^{l-1}$ are computationally indistinguishable from D, $\boldsymbol{g}_0'$, $\boldsymbol{t}_0'$ and $\{\boldsymbol{t}_{i,1}, \boldsymbol{t}_{i,2}\}_{i=0}^{l-1}$ of the real case. Thus we can obtain non-interactive Π_{acc} which is zero-knowledge through Fiat-Shamir transform [13].

[5] Here, the inner product is over Z, i.e.$\langle \boldsymbol{z}, \boldsymbol{v} \rangle = \langle \boldsymbol{z}', \boldsymbol{v}' \rangle$ where vectors $\boldsymbol{z}', \boldsymbol{v}'$ are polynomial coefficients of $\boldsymbol{z}$ and $\boldsymbol{v}$ respectively.

Soundness: The proof of soundess follows the idea of [2]. Define the matrix H, where the rows are indexed by all possible random tapes $\xi \in \{0,1\}^*$ and columns of H are indexed by all possible values for different challenge x. Let $H[\xi][x] = 1$ be the entry corresponding to randomness ξ and challenge $x \in \mathcal{C}$. Obviously, an extractor can check values of each entry in H in time at most T.

The extractor $\mathcal{E}$ is constructed as follows: Run $\mathcal{P}^*$ on random tape $\xi \leftarrow \{0,1\}^*$ and challenge x until it succeeds, which means $H[\xi][x] = 1$. Then, run $\mathcal{P}^*$ on ξ and new challenges x', x'' until $H[\xi][x'] = H[\xi][x''] = 1$. The expected time of $\mathcal{E}$ is at most $3T$ and $\mathcal{E}$ extracts three valid transcripts with probability at least $\epsilon - 2/|\mathcal{C}|$, where the success probability of the protocol is ϵ.

Considering the following two accepting protocol transcripts with $x \neq x'$, $t = \big((C_0\|C_1\|C_2\|C_3); x; \boldsymbol{f}; \boldsymbol{f}_b; \boldsymbol{z}\big), t' = \big((C_0\|C_1\|C_2\|C_3); x'; \boldsymbol{f}'; \boldsymbol{f}_b'; \boldsymbol{z}'\big)$. With the following verification equation

$$xC_0 + D' = \boldsymbol{B}_1 \boldsymbol{z} + \boldsymbol{B}_0(\boldsymbol{f}\|\boldsymbol{f}_b) \tag{10}$$

$$x'C_0 + D' = \boldsymbol{B}_1 \boldsymbol{z}' + \boldsymbol{B}_0(\boldsymbol{f}'\|\boldsymbol{f}_b'), \tag{11}$$

we have $(x - x') \cdot C_0 = \boldsymbol{B}_1 \cdot (\boldsymbol{z} - \boldsymbol{z}') + \boldsymbol{B}_0\big((\boldsymbol{f}\|\boldsymbol{f}_b) - (\boldsymbol{f}'\|\boldsymbol{f}_b')\big)$. So we extract the openings $(\boldsymbol{a}^*, \boldsymbol{b}^*, \boldsymbol{r}_a^*)$ of C_0, where $\boldsymbol{a}^* = \bar{x}^{-1}(\boldsymbol{f} - \boldsymbol{f}')$, $\boldsymbol{b}^* = \bar{x}^{-1}(\boldsymbol{f}_b - \boldsymbol{f}_b')$, $\boldsymbol{r}_a^* = \bar{x}^{-1}(\boldsymbol{z} - \boldsymbol{z}')$ and $\bar{x} := x - x'$.

Subtracting $x{\cdot}(11)$ from $x'{\cdot}(10)$, we get $(x - x') \cdot D' = \boldsymbol{B}_0 \cdot (x'\boldsymbol{z} - x\boldsymbol{z}') + \boldsymbol{B}_1(x'\boldsymbol{f} - x\boldsymbol{f}'\|x'\boldsymbol{f}_b - x\boldsymbol{f}_b')$. Thus, we can extract the openings $(\boldsymbol{m}_a^*, \boldsymbol{m}^*, \boldsymbol{d}^*)$ of D' such that $\boldsymbol{f} = x\boldsymbol{a}^* + \boldsymbol{m}_a^*$ and $\boldsymbol{f}_b = x\boldsymbol{b}^* + \boldsymbol{m}^*$ hold, where $\boldsymbol{m}_a^* = \bar{x}^{-1}(x\boldsymbol{f}' - x'\boldsymbol{f})$, $\boldsymbol{m}^* = \bar{x}^{-1}(x\boldsymbol{f}_b' - x'\boldsymbol{f}_b)$ and $\boldsymbol{d}^* = \bar{x}^{-1}(x\boldsymbol{z}' - x'\boldsymbol{z})$.

Consider an arbitrary accepting transcript with different challenge $x'' \neq x' \neq x$ and response $\boldsymbol{f}''$, $\boldsymbol{f}_b''$ and $\boldsymbol{z}''$. Define $\hat{x} = x - x''$, $\boldsymbol{a}^+ = \hat{x}^{-1}(\boldsymbol{f} - \boldsymbol{f}'')$, $\boldsymbol{b}^+ = \hat{x}^{-1}(\boldsymbol{f}_b - \boldsymbol{f}_b'')$ and $\boldsymbol{r}_a^+ = \hat{x}^{-1}(\boldsymbol{z} - \boldsymbol{z}'')$. We claim that $\boldsymbol{a}^+ = \boldsymbol{a}^*$, $\boldsymbol{b}^+ = \boldsymbol{b}^*$ and $\boldsymbol{r}_a^+ = \boldsymbol{r}_a^*$. Indeed, due to the opening equations of C_0, we have $\boldsymbol{B}_0\bar{x}\hat{x}(\boldsymbol{a}^* - \boldsymbol{a}^+\|\boldsymbol{b}^* - \boldsymbol{b}^+) + \boldsymbol{B}_1\bar{x}\hat{x}(\boldsymbol{r}_a^* - \boldsymbol{r}_a^+) = \boldsymbol{0}$.

Since $\|\bar{x}\hat{x}(\boldsymbol{a}^* - \boldsymbol{a}^+, \boldsymbol{b}^* - \boldsymbol{b}^+, \boldsymbol{r}_a^* - \boldsymbol{r}_a^+)\| \leq 8\eta(B_f + B_b + B_z)$ based on the challenge space in Appendix A.1, we have $\boldsymbol{a}^+ = \boldsymbol{a}^*$, $\boldsymbol{b}^+ = \boldsymbol{b}^*$ and $\boldsymbol{r}_a^+ = \boldsymbol{r}_a^*$ unless we find a M-SIS$_{8\eta(B_f+B_b+B_z)}$ solution for $[\boldsymbol{B}_0\|\boldsymbol{B}_1]$. Set $\boldsymbol{b}^* = \{\boldsymbol{o}_1^{*i}\|\boldsymbol{o}_2^{*i}\}_{i=l}^1$ and $\boldsymbol{o}_1^{*i} \otimes \boldsymbol{o}_2^{*i} = (b_{i,0}^*, \cdots, b_{i,h-1}^*)$ for all $i \in [1,l]$. The verification equation of Π_{acc}.**Verify** can be rewritten with $\boldsymbol{f} = x\boldsymbol{a}^* + \boldsymbol{m}_a^*$ and $\boldsymbol{f}_b = x\boldsymbol{b}^* + \boldsymbol{m}^*$ as follows, $(\hat{\boldsymbol{H}} - x^2 q_1 \hat{\boldsymbol{G}})\boldsymbol{f} = x^3 q_1(\boldsymbol{H} - \hat{\boldsymbol{G}})\boldsymbol{a}^* - x^2\mathsf{QuaT} - x\mathsf{PrimT} - \mathsf{ConsT}$, where the coefficient QuaT, PrimT and ConsT are independent from x. Recall Step 1 in Π_{acc}.**Verify**, the following equation holds $(\hat{\boldsymbol{H}} - x^2 q_1 \hat{\boldsymbol{G}})\boldsymbol{f} = x^3 q_1 \boldsymbol{g} + x(xC_2 - \boldsymbol{B}_3\boldsymbol{z}) + (xC_1 - \boldsymbol{B}_2\boldsymbol{z}) - \boldsymbol{g}_0''$.

The coefficient of x^3 in the above verification equation is $q_1\boldsymbol{g}$ which is independent from x, so we have $q_1(\boldsymbol{H} - \hat{\boldsymbol{G}})\boldsymbol{a}^* = q_1\boldsymbol{g}$. Similarly, we compute that $\boldsymbol{f}_b \circ (\boldsymbol{x} - \boldsymbol{f}_b) = (x\boldsymbol{b}^* + \boldsymbol{m}^*) \circ [x(\boldsymbol{1} - \boldsymbol{b}^*) - \boldsymbol{m}^*] = x^2\boldsymbol{b}^* \circ (\boldsymbol{1} - \boldsymbol{b}^*) + x\mathsf{P} + \mathsf{T}$. In verification, $\boldsymbol{f}_b \circ (\boldsymbol{x} - \boldsymbol{f}_b) = (xC_3 - \boldsymbol{B}_4\boldsymbol{z}) - t_0''$ holds, where the coefficient of x^2 is $\boldsymbol{0}$. Thus we get that $\boldsymbol{b}^* \circ (\boldsymbol{1} - \boldsymbol{b}^*) = \boldsymbol{0}$. For all $i \in [1,l]$ and $j \in [1,2]$, $\sum_{k=0}^{\log h} \boldsymbol{f}_j^i[k]$ can be computed as $x\sum_{k=0}^{\log h} \boldsymbol{o}_j^{*i}[k] + \mathsf{T}'$. Through the verification equation $\boldsymbol{t}_{i,j}' = \sum_{k=0}^{h_i} \boldsymbol{f}_j^i[k] - x$ in Step 1 in Π_{acc}.**Verify**, we obtain that the coefficient of x is equal to $\sum_{k=0}^{\log h} \boldsymbol{o}_j^{*i}[k]$, i.e., $\sum_{k=0}^{\log h} \boldsymbol{o}_j^{*i}[k] = 1$ holds.

C Proof of Theorem 3

Proof. Consider the following games. $\varepsilon_{\mathcal{A}}^{\mathsf{Game}_i}$ denotes the probability that $\mathcal{A}$ wins Game_i. Game_0: This is identical to the game Exp-Anony.

Game_1: same as Game_0 except that the challenger simulates the responses where the reject sampling is applied. In Algorithm **Spend**-II, it replaces $\boldsymbol{f}$ with random samples from $D_{\phi_1 T_1}^{2l\alpha(k+1)d}$, $\boldsymbol{f}_b$ with random samples from $D_{\phi_2 T_2}^{2ld\log h}$, $\boldsymbol{z}$ with random samples from $D_{\phi_3 T_3}^{md}$ and $\boldsymbol{z}_{i=0}^{S-1}, \boldsymbol{z}_{sk}, \boldsymbol{z}_k$ with random samples from $D_{\phi_4 T_4}^{\hat{m}d}$. This game is statistically indistinguishable from the previous game Game_0 due to rejection sampling. Thus $|\varepsilon_{\mathcal{A}}^{\mathsf{Game}_0} - \varepsilon_{\mathcal{A}}^{\mathsf{Game}_1}| \leq \sum_{i=1}^{4} \varepsilon(\phi_i)$.

Game_2: same as Game_1 except that the challenger replaces the serial number sn by uniformly random elements in R_q. This game is computationally indistinguishable from Game_1 by Extended M-LWE$_{1,\hat{m}-1,\sigma_4}$ assumption. We get that $|\varepsilon_{\mathcal{A}}^{\mathsf{Game}_2} - \varepsilon_{\mathcal{A}}^{\mathsf{Game}_1}| \leq \mathsf{Adv}_{\mathcal{A}}^{\mathsf{LWE}}$.

Game_3: same as Game_2 except that the challenger replaces the commitment $(C_0\|C_1\|\cdots\|C_3)$ by uniformly random elements in R_q^{n+5}. Considering the instantiation of Π_{acc}, the eventual dimension of the commitment is $n+5$. This game is computationally indistinguishable from Game_2 by Extended M-LWE$_{n+5,m-n-5,\sigma_3}$ assumption. Thus $|\varepsilon_{\mathcal{A}}^{\mathsf{Game}_3} - \varepsilon_{\mathcal{A}}^{\mathsf{Game}_2}| \leq \mathsf{Adv}_{\mathcal{A}}^{\mathsf{LWE}_1}$.

Game_4: same as Game_3 except that the challenger replaces each output coin $\mathsf{cn}_{\mathsf{new},i}$ by uniformly random elements in $R_q^{2\hat{n}+1}$, for all $i \in [S]$. This game is computationally indistinguishable from Game_3 by Extended M-LWE$_{2\hat{n}+1,\hat{m}-2\hat{n}-1,\sigma_4}$ assumption. Thus $|\varepsilon_{\mathcal{A}}^{\mathsf{Game}_3} - \varepsilon_{\mathcal{A}}^{\mathsf{Game}_2}| \leq S \cdot \mathsf{Adv}_{\mathcal{A}}^{\mathsf{LWE}_4}$. Thus, we can get $\varepsilon_{\mathcal{A}}^{\mathsf{Game}_0} - \varepsilon_{\mathcal{A}}^{\mathsf{Game}_4} \leq \mathsf{Adv}_{\mathcal{A}}^{\mathsf{LWE}} + \mathsf{Adv}_{\mathcal{A}}^{\mathsf{LWE}_1} + S \cdot \mathsf{Adv}_{\mathcal{A}}^{\mathsf{LWE}_2} + \sum_{i=1}^{4} \varepsilon(\mu(\phi_i))$.

Note that the output of Algorithm **Spend** in Game_4 is independent of $\mathsf{Act}_{\mathsf{new}}$, $\mathsf{Act}_{\mathsf{old}}$ and $\mathsf{Amt}_{\mathsf{old}}$, and thus independent of b. Hence $\mathcal{A}$ has probability $1/2$ of outputting $b = b'$ in Game_4. Finally, the probability $\varepsilon_{\mathcal{A}}^{\mathsf{Game}_0}$ that $\mathcal{A}$ wins Game_0 is $\varepsilon_{\mathcal{A}}^{\mathsf{Game}_0} \leq 1/2 + \mathsf{Adv}_{\mathcal{A}}^{\mathsf{LWE}} + \mathsf{Adv}_{\mathcal{A}}^{\mathsf{LWE}_1} + S \cdot \mathsf{Adv}_{\mathcal{A}}^{\mathsf{LWE}_2} + \sum_{i=1}^{4} \varepsilon(\mu(\phi_i))$.

D Proof for Lemma 2

Proof. With the same strategy as the soundness proof of Theorem 2, $\mathcal{E}$ can get the following two accepting protocol transcripts with two distinct challenges x_1, x_2, $t = (\mathsf{st}, x_1, \boldsymbol{z}_{\mathsf{sk}}, \{\boldsymbol{z}_i\}_{i=0}^{S-1}, \boldsymbol{z}_k; \mathsf{cn}_{\mathsf{new},0}, \cdots, \mathsf{cn}_{\mathsf{new},S-1}, \mathsf{sn})$, $t' = (\mathsf{st}, x_2, \boldsymbol{z}'_{\mathsf{sk}}, \{\boldsymbol{z}'_i\}_{i=0}^{S-1}, \boldsymbol{z}'_k; \mathsf{cn}_{\mathsf{new},0}, \cdots, \mathsf{cn}_{\mathsf{new},S-1}, \mathsf{sn})$.

For all $i \in [S]$ and $\mathsf{cn}_{\mathsf{new},i} = (C_{r,i}\|C_{a,i}\|C_{p,i})$, we get the following equations, $E'_i = \boldsymbol{G}_0 \cdot \boldsymbol{z}_i - x_1 C_{r,i}, E'_i = \boldsymbol{G}_0 \cdot \boldsymbol{z}'_i - x_2 C_{r,i}$. Subtracting one from the other, we get valid "unique" opening $\boldsymbol{r}_i^* = \bar{x}^{-1}(\boldsymbol{z}'_i - \boldsymbol{z}_i)$ of $C_{r,i}$ where $\bar{x}^{-1} = x_1 - x_2$, unless one can immediately compute a Module-SIS solution for $\boldsymbol{G}_0$ of length at most $8\eta B$. From the verification equation, the following holds $\boldsymbol{f}_i = x_1 C_{a,i} - \boldsymbol{G}_1 \cdot \boldsymbol{z}_i$, $\boldsymbol{f}'_i = x_2 C_{a,i} - \boldsymbol{G}_1 \cdot \boldsymbol{z}'_i$. Subtracting one from the other, we get $\boldsymbol{f}_i - \boldsymbol{f}'_i = \bar{x} C_{a,i} - \boldsymbol{G}_1(\boldsymbol{z}'_i - \boldsymbol{z}_i) \Rightarrow \bar{x}^{-1}(\boldsymbol{f}_i - \boldsymbol{f}'_i) = C_{a,i} - \boldsymbol{G}_1 \boldsymbol{r}_i^*$.

Let $\boldsymbol{a}_i^* = \bar{x}^{-1}(\boldsymbol{f}_i - \boldsymbol{f}'_i)$. There can only be a "unique" opening $(\boldsymbol{a}_i^*, \boldsymbol{r}_i^*)$ for $C_{a,i}$ such that $C_{a,i} = \boldsymbol{G}_1 \boldsymbol{r}_i^* + \boldsymbol{a}_i^*$. As the same way, there can only be a "unique" opening $(\boldsymbol{p}_i^*, \boldsymbol{r}_i^*)$ for $C_{p,i}$ such that $C_{p,i} = \boldsymbol{G}_2\boldsymbol{r}_i^* + \boldsymbol{p}_i^*$, where $\boldsymbol{p}_i^* = C_{p,i} - \bar{x}^{-1}\boldsymbol{G}_2 \cdot (\boldsymbol{z}_i' - \boldsymbol{z}_i)$. Thus we get the "unique" opening $(\boldsymbol{a}_i^*, \boldsymbol{p}_i^*; \boldsymbol{r}_i^*)$ of the output coin $\mathsf{cn}_{\mathsf{out},i}$ such that $\mathsf{cn}_{\mathsf{out},i} = (\boldsymbol{G}_0 \cdot \boldsymbol{r}^* \| \boldsymbol{G}_1 \cdot \boldsymbol{r}^* + \boldsymbol{a}^* \| \boldsymbol{G}_2 \cdot \boldsymbol{r}^* + \boldsymbol{p}^*)$.

We can also get the following verification equations $C_m' = (\boldsymbol{G}_0 \cdot \boldsymbol{z}_k \| \boldsymbol{G}_1 \cdot \boldsymbol{z}_k + \sum_{i=0}^{S-1} \boldsymbol{f}_i \| \boldsymbol{G}_2 \cdot \boldsymbol{z}_k + \boldsymbol{H}_0 \cdot \boldsymbol{z}_{\mathsf{sk}}) - \boldsymbol{G}\boldsymbol{f}_l, C_m' = (\boldsymbol{G}_0 \cdot \boldsymbol{z}_k' \| \boldsymbol{G}_1 \cdot \boldsymbol{z}_k' + \sum_{i=0}^{S-1} \boldsymbol{f}_i' \| \boldsymbol{G}_2 \cdot \boldsymbol{z}_k' + \boldsymbol{H}_0 \cdot \boldsymbol{z}_{\mathsf{sk}}') - \boldsymbol{G}\boldsymbol{f}_l'$. Due to the soundness proof of Π_{acc}, $\boldsymbol{f}_l$ and $\boldsymbol{f}_l'$ can be denoted by $\boldsymbol{f}_l = x_1\boldsymbol{v}_l^* + \boldsymbol{c}_l^*$, and $\boldsymbol{f}_l' = x_2\boldsymbol{v}_l^* + \boldsymbol{c}_l^*$. Subtracting one from the other, let $\boldsymbol{k}^* = \bar{x}^{-1}(\boldsymbol{z}_k' - \boldsymbol{z}_k)$ and $\boldsymbol{s}^* = \bar{x}^{-1}(\boldsymbol{z}_{\mathsf{sk}}' - \boldsymbol{z}_{\mathsf{sk}})$, thus we can get that $(\boldsymbol{G}_0 \cdot \boldsymbol{k}^* \| \boldsymbol{G}_1 \cdot \boldsymbol{k}^* + \sum_{i=0}^{S-1} \boldsymbol{a}_i^* \| \boldsymbol{G}_2 \cdot \boldsymbol{k}^* + \boldsymbol{H}_0 \cdot \boldsymbol{s}^*) = \boldsymbol{G} \cdot \boldsymbol{v}_l^*$.

That is, the "unique" leaf node $\boldsymbol{v}_l^*$ in Π_{acc} are equal to the well-formed input coin with the opening $\boldsymbol{k}^*$, $\boldsymbol{s}^*$ and $\sum_{i=0}^{S-1} \boldsymbol{a}_i^*$. The opening $\boldsymbol{k}^*$ is "unique" unless one can immediately compute a Module-SIS solution for $\boldsymbol{G}_0$ of length at most $8\eta B$. Then we can infer the "uniqueness" of the opening $\boldsymbol{s}^*$ can be guaranteed unless one can compute a Module-SIS solution for $\boldsymbol{H}_0$ of length at most $8\eta B$.

Subtracting the verification equation from the other, $F' = \boldsymbol{H}_1 \cdot \boldsymbol{z}_{\mathsf{sk}} - x \cdot \mathsf{sn}, F' = \boldsymbol{H}_1 \cdot \boldsymbol{z}_{\mathsf{sk}}' - x \cdot \mathsf{sn}$. We get that $\mathsf{sn} = \boldsymbol{H}_1 \cdot \bar{x}^{-1}(\boldsymbol{z}_{\mathsf{sk}}' - \boldsymbol{z}_{\mathsf{sk}})$. Thus the opening of serial number sn is also $\boldsymbol{s}^*$.

E Proof of Theorem 4

Proof. – **Unbalanced amounts**: Let $\mathsf{E}_{\mathsf{unb}}$ denote the event that $\mathcal{A}$ wins the game $\mathsf{Exp\text{-}balance}$. Note that $\mathsf{E}_{\mathsf{unb}}$ occurs when $\mathcal{A}$ outputs t transactions $\{\mathsf{Tx}^j, \mathsf{Amt_{new}}^j, \mathsf{Ck_{new}}^j\}_{j=0}^{t-1}$ which satisfy:

- there exists $j^* \in [t]$, such that $\sum_{i=0}^{S-1} \mathsf{Amt_{new}}^{j^*}[i] > \mathsf{amt}_{\mathsf{old}}^{j^*}$ where $S = |\mathsf{Amt_{new}}^{j^*}|$ and $\mathcal{T}[\mathsf{sn}].\mathsf{IsCrpt} = 1$.
- **Verify**$(\mathsf{Tx}^j) \neq 0$ for all $j \in [t]$.
- all input public keys and coins in $(\mathsf{cn_{old}}^j, \mathsf{pk_{old}}^j)$ for all $j \in [t]$ are generated by **CreateAddr** and **Mint**, respectively, and all accounts in $(\mathsf{cn_{old}}^j, \mathsf{pk_{old}}^j)$ are generated by ActGen.

If $\mathsf{E}_{\mathsf{unb}}$ happens with non-negligible probability, we can construct an efficient algorithm $\mathcal{E}$ to break the MSIS problem. $\mathcal{E}$ simulates $\mathsf{Exp\text{-}balance}$ for $\mathcal{A}$ as follows.

(1) $\mathcal{E}$ runs $pp \leftarrow$ **Setup**(1^λ), randomly picks index $j^* \in [t]$ to guess that $\mathsf{E}_{\mathsf{unb}}$ occurs in the j^*-th transaction.

(2) When $\mathcal{A}$ makes queries for Orc, $\mathcal{E}$ responds by maintaining a list $\mathcal{T}$ which is initially empty.

∗ CreateAddr(i): on the i-th query, $\mathcal{E}$ runs $(\mathsf{pk}_i, \mathsf{sk}_i) \leftarrow$ **CreateAddr**(pp), $\mathsf{sn}_i \leftarrow$ **SnGen**(sk_i) and returns $(\mathsf{pk}_i, \mathsf{sn}_i)$ to $\mathcal{A}$. Insert $(\mathsf{pk}_i, \mathsf{sk}_i, \mathsf{sn}_i)$ to the list $\mathcal{T}$ where IsCrpt tag is set to zero and the remaining information is left empty.

∗ Mint$(\mathsf{amt}, \mathsf{pk})$: $\mathcal{E}$ runs $(\mathsf{cn}, \mathsf{ck}) \leftarrow$ **Mint**$(\mathsf{amt}, \mathsf{pk})$ and returns cn.

ActGen$(\mathsf{amt}, \mathsf{pk}, \mathsf{cn}, \mathsf{ck}, \mathsf{st})$: For pk, add $(\mathsf{cn}, \mathsf{ck}, \mathsf{amt})$ to the list $\mathcal{T}[\mathsf{pk}]$ respectively and run $(\mathsf{cn}, \mathsf{st}) \leftarrow$ **UpdateSt**$(\mathsf{cn}, \mathsf{st})$. Return $(\mathsf{pk}, \mathsf{cn})$ and updated st.

$*$ Corrupt(act): For a act $= (\mathsf{pk}, \mathsf{cn})$, if $\mathcal{T}[\mathsf{pk}]$ or $\mathcal{T}[\mathsf{cn}]$ cannot be found, indicating failure, return 0; else, update $\mathcal{T}[\mathsf{pk}]$.IsCrpt to 1, and output $\mathcal{T}[\mathsf{pk}].\mathsf{sk}$, $\mathcal{T}[\mathsf{pk}].\mathsf{ck}$ and $\mathcal{T}[\mathsf{pk}].\mathsf{amt}$.

$*$ Spend$(\mathsf{st}, \mathsf{Amt}_{\mathsf{new}}, \mathsf{Pk}_{\mathsf{new}}, \mathsf{Cn}_{\mathsf{old}}, \mathsf{Amt}_{\mathsf{old}}, \mathsf{Pk}_{\mathsf{old}}, \mathsf{Sk}_{\mathsf{old}}, \mathsf{Ck}_{\mathsf{old}})$: Retrieve from $\mathcal{T}$ all account secret keys associated to $\mathsf{Cn}_{\mathsf{old}}$. Run $(\mathsf{Tx}, \mathsf{Ck}_{\mathsf{new}}) \leftarrow$ **Spend** $(\mathsf{st}, \mathsf{Amt}_{\mathsf{new}}, \mathsf{Pk}_{\mathsf{new}}, \mathsf{Cn}_{\mathsf{old}}, \mathsf{Amt}_{\mathsf{old}}, \mathsf{Sk}_{\mathsf{old}}, \mathsf{Ck}_{\mathsf{old}})$ and $B \leftarrow$ **Verify** (Tx). If the verification fails, i.e., $B = 0$, return $\perp$; otherwise, run $(\mathsf{Cn}_{\mathsf{new}}, \mathsf{st}) \leftarrow$ **UpdateSt** $(\mathsf{Cn}_{\mathsf{new}}, \mathsf{st})$, then output Tx and insert the output accounts information in the list $\mathcal{T}$, respectively.

By the rewinding technique, $\mathcal{E}$ runs $\mathcal{A}$ until $\mathsf{E}_{\mathsf{unb}}$ occurs twice with the distinct challenges, the same instances and witnesses, and the index j^* is the same. Hence, $\mathcal{E}$ gets two accepting transcripts of CTA protocol with distinct challenges. Based on the soundness proof of the underlying ZKP in CTA, $\mathcal{E}$ can recover an opening $(\boldsymbol{a}_i, \boldsymbol{r}_i, \boldsymbol{p}_i)$ for the $\mathsf{Cn}_{\mathsf{new}}{}^{j^*}[i]$ such that $\mathsf{Cn}_{\mathsf{new}}{}^{j^*}[i] = (\boldsymbol{G}_0\|\boldsymbol{G}_1\|\boldsymbol{G}_2) \cdot \boldsymbol{r}_i + (\boldsymbol{0}^{\hat{n}}\|\boldsymbol{a}_i\|\boldsymbol{p}_i)$ for all $i \in [S]$ and $\sum_{i=0}^{S-1} \boldsymbol{a}_i = \mathsf{amt}_{\mathsf{old}}^{j^*}$. Due to $\sum_{i=0}^{S-1} \mathsf{Amt}_{\mathsf{new}}{}^{j^*}[i] \geq \mathsf{amt}_{\mathsf{old}}^{j^*}$, there exists at least one of the corrupted output coins such that $\mathsf{Amt}_{\mathsf{new}}{}^{j^*}[i] \neq \boldsymbol{a}_i$. That implies that there exists $\boldsymbol{r}' \neq \boldsymbol{r}_i$ and $\boldsymbol{p}'$ such that $\mathsf{Cn}_{\mathsf{new}}{}^{j^*}[i] = (\boldsymbol{G}_0\|\boldsymbol{G}_1\|\boldsymbol{G}_2) \cdot \boldsymbol{r}' + (\boldsymbol{0}^{\hat{n}}\|\mathsf{Amt}_{\mathsf{new}}{}^{j^*}[i]\|\boldsymbol{p}')$. This gives a solution $(\boldsymbol{r}' - \boldsymbol{r}_i)$ for M-SIS problem under the matrix $\boldsymbol{G}_0$, which yields a contradiction with the M-SIS$_{\hat{n},\hat{m},q,8\eta B}$ assumption.

- **Double spending**: Let $\mathsf{E}_{\mathsf{2sp}}$ denote the event that $\mathcal{A}$ wins the game Exp-balance. $\mathsf{E}_{\mathsf{2sp}}$ means that when $\mathcal{A}$ outputs t transactions $\{\mathsf{Tx}^j\}_{j=0}^{t-1}$, there exists $j^* \in [t]$, such that $\mathsf{sn}^{j^*} \notin \mathcal{T}$, where
  - **Verify**$(\mathsf{Tx}^j) \neq 0$ for all $j \in [t]$.
  - all input public keys and coins in $(\mathsf{cn}_{\mathsf{old}}{}^j, \mathsf{pk}_{\mathsf{old}}{}^j)$ for all $j \in [t]$ are generated by **CreateAddr** and **Mint**, respectively, and all accounts in $(\mathsf{cn}_{\mathsf{old}}{}^j, \mathsf{pk}_{\mathsf{old}}{}^j)$ are generated by ActGen.

  If $\mathsf{E}_{\mathsf{2sp}}$ happens with non-negligible probability, we can construct an efficient algorithm $\mathcal{E}$ to break the M-SIS assumption. The way that $\mathcal{E}$ simulates Exp-balance for $\mathcal{A}$ is just like that of $\mathsf{E}_{\mathsf{unb}}$. By the rewinding technique, $\mathcal{E}$ runs $\mathcal{A}$ with distinct challenges, the same instances x and witnesses w, and the same index j^*.

  For the j^*-th transaction output by $\mathcal{A}$, $\mathcal{E}$ recovers an opening $\boldsymbol{s}$ of sn^{j^*} such that $\mathsf{sn}^{j^*} = \boldsymbol{H}_1 \cdot \boldsymbol{s}$, $\mathsf{pk}_{\mathsf{old}} = \boldsymbol{H}_0 \cdot \boldsymbol{s}$ and $\mathcal{T}[\mathsf{pk}_{\mathsf{old}}].\mathsf{sn} \neq \mathsf{sn}^{j^*}$. So, there exists some $\boldsymbol{s}' \neq \boldsymbol{s}$ such that $\mathcal{T}[\mathsf{pk}_{\mathsf{old}}].\mathsf{sn} = \boldsymbol{H}_1 \cdot \boldsymbol{s}'$ and $\mathsf{pk}_{\mathsf{old}} = \boldsymbol{H}_0 \cdot \boldsymbol{s}'$. This gives a solution $(\boldsymbol{s}' - \boldsymbol{s})$ for M-SIS problem under the matrix $\boldsymbol{H}_0$, which yield a contradiction with the M-SIS$_{\hat{n},\hat{m},q,8\eta B}$ assumption.
- **Forgery**: Let $\mathsf{E}_{\mathsf{forge}}$ denote the event that $\mathcal{A}$ wins the game Exp-balance. $\mathsf{E}_{\mathsf{forge}}$ occurs when $\mathcal{A}$ outputs t transactions $\{\mathsf{Tx}^j\}_{j=0}^{t-1}$, there exists $j^* \in [t]$, such that $\mathsf{sn}^{j^*} \in \mathcal{T}$ and $\mathcal{T}[\mathsf{sn}^{j^*}].\mathsf{IsCrpt} = 0$, where
  - $0 \neq$ **Verify**(Tx^j) for all $j \in [t]$.
  - all input public keys and coins in $(\mathsf{cn}_{\mathsf{old}}{}^j, \mathsf{pk}_{\mathsf{old}}{}^j)$ for all $j \in [t]$, are generated by **CreateAddr** and **Mint**, respectively, and all accounts in $(\mathsf{cn}_{\mathsf{old}}{}^j, \mathsf{pk}_{\mathsf{old}}{}^j)$ are generated by ActGen.

Let Q be the number of CreateAddr queries that $\mathcal{A}$ makes. $\mathcal{E}$ picks $a \in [Q]$, then return $\mathsf{pk}_a = \boldsymbol{H}_0 \boldsymbol{s} + (1\|0\|\cdots\|0)$ for the a-th query from $\mathcal{A}$ to CreateAddr oracle, where $\boldsymbol{s} \in \{-\beta, \cdots, \beta\}^{\hat{m}d}$. Note that the attacker's view in this modified game is computationally indistinguishable from its view in the original attack by the hiding property of commitment pk_a, i.e., the M-LWE$_{\hat{n},\hat{m}-\hat{n},q,\beta}$ assumption. $\mathcal{E}$ simulates the $\mathsf{Exp\text{-}balance}$ until $\mathsf{E}_{\mathsf{forge}}$ occurs twice by the rewinding technique with the distinct challenges, the same instances x and witnesses w, and the indices j^* and a are the same.
By the soundness of the underlying ZKP, $\mathcal{E}$ recovers an opening sk such that $\mathsf{pk}_a = \boldsymbol{H}_0 \cdot \mathsf{sk}$. This also gives a solution $\big((\mathsf{sk} - \boldsymbol{s})\| - (1\|0\|\cdots\|0)\big)$ for M-SIS problem under the matrix $[\boldsymbol{H}_0\|\boldsymbol{I}_{\hat{n}}]$, which yield a contradiction with the M-SIS$_{\hat{n},\hat{m}+\hat{n},q,8\eta B}$ assumption.

- **Fake accounts**: Let $\mathsf{E}_{\mathsf{fake}}$ be the event that $\mathcal{A}$ wins the game $\mathsf{Exp\text{-}balance}$. $\mathsf{E}_{\mathsf{fake}}$ occurs when $\mathcal{A}$ outputs t transactions $\{\mathsf{Tx}^j\}_{j=0}^{t-1}$, there exists $j^* \in [t]$, such that $\mathsf{sn}^{j^*} \notin \mathcal{T}$ where
  - $0 \neq \mathbf{Verify}(\mathsf{Tx}^j)$ for all $j \in [t]$.
  - all input public keys and coins in $({\mathsf{cn}_{\mathsf{old}}}^j, {\mathsf{pk}_{\mathsf{old}}}^j)$ for all $j \in [t]$, are generated by **CreateAddr** and **Mint**, respectively.
  - ${\mathsf{cn}_{\mathsf{in}}}^{j^*}$ is not the output by the ActGen oracle.

  $\mathcal{E}$ simulates the $\mathsf{Exp\text{-}balanced}$ until $\mathsf{E}_{\mathsf{fake}}$ occurs twice by the rewinding technique with distinct challenges, the same instances x and witnesses w, and the same index j^*. Retrieving all the $\mathcal{T}[\mathsf{cn}]$ to form the set V. Therefore, for the j^*-th transaction output by $\mathcal{A}$, $\mathcal{E}$ recovers an opening cn^{j^*} such that $\mathsf{cn}^{j^*} \notin V$ and $\mathsf{Acc}.\mathbf{Acc}(V) = \boldsymbol{u}_0 \in \mathsf{st}$. This yields a contradiction with the security of the accumulator schemes Acc by returning $(\mathsf{cn}^{j^*}, \boldsymbol{u}_0, V)$.

References

1. Attema, T., Cramer, R.: Compressed Σ-protocol theory and practical application to plug & play secure algorithmics. In: Micciancio, D., Ristenpart, T. (eds.) CRYPTO 2020. LNCS, vol. 12172, pp. 513–543. Springer, Cham (2020). https://doi.org/10.1007/978-3-030-56877-1_18
2. Attema, T., Cramer, R., Kohl, L.: A compressed Σ-protocol theory for lattices. In: Malkin, T., Peikert, C. (eds.) CRYPTO 2021. LNCS, vol. 12826, pp. 549–579. Springer, Cham (2021). https://doi.org/10.1007/978-3-030-84245-1_19
3. Attema, T., Lyubashevsky, V., Seiler, G.: Practical product proofs for lattice commitments. In: Micciancio, D., Ristenpart, T. (eds.) CRYPTO 2020. LNCS, vol. 12171, pp. 470–499. Springer, Cham (2020). https://doi.org/10.1007/978-3-030-56880-1_17
4. Banaszczyk, W.: New bounds in some transference theorems in the geometry of numbers. Math. Ann. **296**(1), 625–635 (1993)
5. Baum, C., Damgård, I., Lyubashevsky, V., Oechsner, S., Peikert, C.: More efficient commitments from structured lattice assumptions. In: Catalano, D., De Prisco, R. (eds.) SCN 2018. LNCS, vol. 11035, pp. 368–385. Springer, Cham (2018). https://doi.org/10.1007/978-3-319-98113-0_20
6. Ben-Sasson, E., et al.: Zerocash: decentralized anonymous payments from bitcoin. In: SP 2014, pp. 459–474. IEEE (2014)

7. Cheon, J.H., Kim, D., Lee, K.: MHz2k: MPC from HE over $\mathbb{Z}_{2^k}$ with new packing, simpler reshare, and better ZKP. In: Malkin, T., Peikert, C. (eds.) CRYPTO 2021. LNCS, vol. 12826, pp. 426–456. Springer, Cham (2021). https://doi.org/10.1007/978-3-030-84245-1_15
8. Ducas, L., Durmus, A., Lepoint, T., Lyubashevsky, V.: Lattice signatures and bimodal Gaussians. In: Canetti, R., Garay, J.A. (eds.) CRYPTO 2013. LNCS, vol. 8042, pp. 40–56. Springer, Heidelberg (2013). https://doi.org/10.1007/978-3-642-40041-4_3
9. Esgin, M.F., Nguyen, N.K., Seiler, G.: Practical exact proofs from lattices: new techniques to exploit fully-splitting rings. In: Moriai, S., Wang, H. (eds.) ASIACRYPT 2020. LNCS, vol. 12492, pp. 259–288. Springer, Cham (2020). https://doi.org/10.1007/978-3-030-64834-3_9
10. Esgin, M.F., Steinfeld, R., Zhao, R.K.: Matrict$^+$: more efficient post-quantum private blockchain payments. In: SP 2022, pp. 1281–1298. IEEE (2022)
11. Esgin, M.F., Zhao, R.K., Steinfeld, R., Liu, J.K., Liu, D.: MatRiCT: efficient, scalable and post-quantum blockchain confidential transactions protocol. In: CCS 2019, pp. 567–584. ACM (2019)
12. Fauzi, P., Meiklejohn, S., Mercer, R., Orlandi, C.: Quisquis: a new design for anonymous cryptocurrencies. In: Galbraith, S.D., Moriai, S. (eds.) ASIACRYPT 2019. LNCS, vol. 11921, pp. 649–678. Springer, Cham (2019). https://doi.org/10.1007/978-3-030-34578-5_23
13. Fiat, A., Shamir, A.: How to prove yourself: practical solutions to identification and signature problems. In: Odlyzko, A.M. (ed.) CRYPTO 1986. LNCS, vol. 263, pp. 186–194. Springer, Heidelberg (1987). https://doi.org/10.1007/3-540-47721-7_12
14. Gentry, C., Peikert, C., Vaikuntanathan, V.: Trapdoors for hard lattices and new cryptographic constructions. In: STOC 2008, pp. 197–206. Association for Computing Machinery, New York (2008)
15. Langlois, A., Stehlé, D.: Worst-case to average-case reductions for module lattices. Des. Codes Cryptogr. **75**(3), 565–599 (2015). https://doi.org/10.1007/s10623-014-9938-4
16. Libert, B., Ling, S., Nguyen, K., Wang, H.: Zero-knowledge arguments for lattice-based accumulators: logarithmic-size ring signatures and group signatures without trapdoors. In: Fischlin, M., Coron, J.-S. (eds.) EUROCRYPT 2016. LNCS, vol. 9666, pp. 1–31. Springer, Heidelberg (2016). https://doi.org/10.1007/978-3-662-49896-5_1
17. Lyubashevsky, V.: Lattice signatures without trapdoors. In: Pointcheval, D., Johansson, T. (eds.) EUROCRYPT 2012. LNCS, vol. 7237, pp. 738–755. Springer, Heidelberg (2012). https://doi.org/10.1007/978-3-642-29011-4_43
18. Lyubashevsky, V., Nguyen, N.K., Plançon, M.: Lattice-based zero-knowledge proofs and applications: shorter, simpler, and more general. In: Dodis, Y., Shrimpton, T. (eds.) CRYPTO 2022. LNCS, vol. 13508, pp. 71–101. Springer, Cham (2022). https://doi.org/10.1007/978-3-031-15979-4_3
19. Lyubashevsky, V., Nguyen, N.K., Plancon, M., Seiler, G.: Shorter lattice-based group signatures via "almost free" encryption and other optimizations. In: Tibouchi, M., Wang, H. (eds.) ASIACRYPT 2021. LNCS, vol. 13093, pp. 218–248. Springer, Cham (2021). https://doi.org/10.1007/978-3-030-92068-5_8
20. Lyubashevsky, V., Nguyen, N.K., Seiler, G.: Practical lattice-based zero-knowledge proofs for integer relations. In: CCS 2020, pp. 1051–1070. ACM (2020)
21. Lyubashevsky, V., Nguyen, N.K., Seiler, G.: Shorter lattice-based zero-knowledge proofs via one-time commitments. In: Garay, J.A. (ed.) PKC 2021. LNCS, vol.

12710, pp. 215–241. Springer, Cham (2021). https://doi.org/10.1007/978-3-030-75245-3_9
22. Lyubashevsky, V., Nguyen, N.K., Seiler, G.: SMILE: set membership from ideal lattices with applications to ring signatures and confidential transactions. In: Malkin, T., Peikert, C. (eds.) CRYPTO 2021. LNCS, vol. 12826, pp. 611–640. Springer, Cham (2021). https://doi.org/10.1007/978-3-030-84245-1_21
23. Maxwell, G.: Confidential transactions (2015). https://people.xiph.org/$~greg/confidential_values$.txt
24. Micciancio, D., Peikert, C.: Trapdoors for lattices: simpler, tighter, faster, smaller. In: Pointcheval, D., Johansson, T. (eds.) EUROCRYPT 2012. LNCS, vol. 7237, pp. 700–718. Springer, Heidelberg (2012). https://doi.org/10.1007/978-3-642-29011-4_41
25. Noether, S.: Ring signature confidential transactions for monero. IACR Cryptology ePrint Archive 2015:1098 (2015)
26. Peikert, C., Pepin, Z., Sharp, C.: Vector and functional commitments from lattices. In: Nissim, K., Waters, B. (eds.) TCC 2021. LNCS, vol. 13044, pp. 480–511. Springer, Cham (2021). https://doi.org/10.1007/978-3-030-90456-2_16
27. Yang, R., Au, M.H., Zhang, Z., Xu, Q., Yu, Z., Whyte, W.: Efficient lattice-based zero-knowledge arguments with standard soundness: construction and applications. In: Boldyreva, A., Micciancio, D. (eds.) CRYPTO 2019. LNCS, vol. 11692, pp. 147–175. Springer, Cham (2019). https://doi.org/10.1007/978-3-030-26948-7_6

MPC and Secret Sharing

A Plug-n-Play Framework for Scaling Private Set Intersection to Billion-Sized Sets

Saikrishna Badrinarayanan[1], Ranjit Kumaresan[2], Mihai Christodorescu[3], Vinjith Nagaraja[2], Karan Patel[2], Srinivasan Raghuraman[2,4(✉)], Peter Rindal[2], Wei Sun[5], and Minghua Xu[2]

[1] LinkedIn, Sunnyvale, USA
[2] Visa Research, Foster City, USA
srini131293@gmail.com
[3] Google, Mountain View, USA
[4] MIT, Cambridge, USA
[5] The University of Texas at Austin, Austin, USA

Abstract. Motivated by the recent advances in practical secure computation, we design and implement a framework for scaling solutions for the problem of private set intersection (PSI) into the realm of big data. A protocol for PSI enables two parties each holding a set of elements to jointly compute the intersection of these sets without revealing the elements that are not in the intersection. Following a long line of research, recent protocols for PSI only have ≈5× computation and communication overhead over an insecure set intersection. However, this performance is typically demonstrated for set sizes in the order of ten million. In this work, we aim to scale these protocols to efficiently handle set sizes of one billion elements or more.

We achieve this via a careful application of a *binning* approach that enables parallelizing any arbitrary PSI protocol. Building on this idea, we designed and implemented a framework which takes a pair of PSI executables (i.e., for each of the two parties) that typically works for million-sized sets, and then scales it to billion-sized sets (and beyond). For example, our framework can perform a join of billion-sized sets in 83 min compared to 2000 min of Pinkas et al. (ACM TPS 2018), an improvement of 25×. Furthermore, we present an *end-to-end* Spark application where two enterprises, each possessing private databases, can perform a restricted class of database join operations (specifically, join operations with only an *on* clause which is a conjunction of equality checks involving attributes from both parties, followed by a *where* clause which can be split into conjunctive clauses where each conjunction is a function of a single table) without revealing any data that is not part of the output.

Keywords: Spark · Private Set Intersection · Plug-n-Play Framework

This work was done while all authors were at Visa Research.

J. Deng et al. (Eds.): CANS 2023, LNCS 14342, pp. 443–467, 2023.
https://doi.org/10.1007/978-981-99-7563-1_20

1 Introduction

Private set intersection (PSI) enables two parties, each holding a private set of elements to compute the intersection of the two sets while revealing nothing more than the intersection itself. PSI is an extremely well-motivated problem and has found applications in a variety of settings. For instance, PSI has been used to measure the effectiveness of online advertising [33], private contact discovery [11,19,53], privacy-preserving location sharing [42], privacy-preserving ride sharing [26], remote diagnostics [9] and botnet detection [41]. In the last few years, PSI has become truly practical with extremely fast implementations [13,17,19–21,23,28,29,34–36,43,45–49,51,55,56]. In terms of performance, the most computationally efficient PSI protocol [35] can privately compute the intersection of two million size sets in about 4 s. On the other hand, and for settings where only low bandwidth communication is available, one can employ the communication-optimal PSI protocol [4] whose communication is only marginally more than an insecure set intersection protocol. Several recent works, most notably [10,45,46] have studied the balance between computation and communication, and even optimize for *monetary cost* of running PSI protocols in the cloud.

While significant progress has been made in advancing the efficiency of PSI protocols, almost all documented research in this area has so far focused on settings with set sizes of at most $2^{24} \approx 16$ million.[1] One notable exception is the work of [58] who demonstrate the feasibility of PSI over billion sized sets albeit in the non-standard *server-aided* model where a mutually trusted third party server aids in the computation. Another notable exception is the recent work of [50,51] whose implementation on 2 servers each with <16 GB memory takes 34.2 h to compute the intersection of two billion-element sets. Clearly, this leaves a lot of room for improvement. This is the gap we aspire to fill in this paper.

(Issues in) Scaling Existing PSI Protocols. Broadly speaking, memory consumption is a big problem when implementing cryptographic schemes that operate on large amounts of data. In fact, many if not all implemented PSI protocols (e.g., those based on garbled circuits, or bloom filters, or cuckoo hashing) quickly exceed the main memory, thereby requiring more engineering effort. Even computing the plaintext intersection for billions of elements becomes a nontrivial problem. That said, many of the PSI protocols somewhat benefit from thread-level parallelism (e.g., for preprocessing OTs, generating garbled circuits) and hardware support (e.g., AES-NI). Some of the steps that do not parallelize well are those dealing with data structures (such as cuckoo hashing or bloom filters), however these may be preprocessed since only one party's input is required.

Concretely, we discuss the implementation of the OT-based PSI protocol of [51] running on billion-sized sets containing 128-bit elements. The work of [51]

[1] This does not necessarily apply to the setting of unbalanced PSI where the set sizes can be orders of magnitude apart [3,7,11,27,48]. For instance, [14] do unbalanced PSI with 2^{28} elements on one side and say 1024 elements on the other side.

makes use of solid state drives in their PSI execution on billion-sized sets. As documented in [51], the total execution time is 34.2 h.[2] In comparison, the (insecure) naive hashing protocol for set intersection required 74 mins, of which 19 min (26%) are for hashing and transferring data and 55 min (74%) are for computing the plaintext intersection.

1.1 Our Contributions

We study the possibility of parallelizing PSI protocols by distributing a party's workload into *multiple worker nodes* running within its premises. Towards this, we propose a simple technique that can parallelize any PSI protocol in a blackbox way. Finally, we build a framework to test out the feasibility of our technique in scaling PSI via Spark in a practical use case involving private database join operations. Comparing to the work of [51], our protocols for the same setting of billion-sized sets containing 128-bit elements, we require a total execution time of 83 min in total, a 25× improvement compared to [51]. We explain these in more detail below.

Techniques to Parallelize PSI. We describe a few approaches at a high level and analyze their security and generality.

Self-reduction. A natural approach is to reduce an instance of PSI on large sets to multiple instances of PSI on smaller sets. Some care needs to be taken to ensure that privacy is still preserved. Specifically, note that PSI protocols are not guaranteed to hide the size of the input sets. For instance, if the sets are partitioned based on lexicographic ordering of the elements, then this would likely result in partitions being of unequal size, and thus either party could learn how the elements of the other party's set are distributed. We avoid such issues by proposing a natural random self-reduction which we refer to as our *binning technique* (see Sect. 3 for a formal description). Loosely speaking, our binning technique proceeds by asking each party to (1) locally randomize its input set (by applying a random oracle), (2) locally partition the randomized set, say lexicographically, into smaller sets, (3) locally pad each of these smaller sets with dummy elements so that they are all of the same size, (4) feed each small set into an independent PSI instance with the other party, and (5) finally use each PSI instance's output to recover the intersection in the original input set.

Important Note. Partitioning elements into bins is a standard technique that appears several times and in several forms in the PSI literature. For instance, in [48] such a binning strategy is used to enable a reduction from PSI to *private set membership* by partitioning n elements into m bins for $m \approx n$. Among other similar works, the protocols of [35,49] enjoy high efficiency by employing cuckoo hashing which partitions n elements into $m \approx 1.2n$ bins. A similar partitioning

[2] For a further breakdown of this number, [51] note that 30.0 h (88%) are for simple hashing (cuckoo hashing runs in parallel and requires 16.3 h), 3 h (9%) are for computing the OTs, and 1.2 h (4%) are for computing the plaintext intersection.

approach is also used in the case of unbalanced sets of sizes n_0 and n_1 with $n_0 \gg n_1$ and even there (cf. [51]) the set of size n_0 is partitioned into $\approx 2.4n_1$ bins.

Where our approach differs from prior work is that we perform a *self-reduction* (i.e., PSI to itself) with a choice of parameters that differs from prior works mentioned above. In particular, for large n, we will be partitioning a set of size n into m bins for $n \gg m$ (e.g., $n = 10^9$ and $m = 64$).[3] While our PSI self-reduction is very simple and straightforward, to the best of our knowledge, we are not aware of any prior work documenting or implementing the self-reduction for the parameters that we employ in this paper. In particular, while the binning technique that we described above appears (nearly) verbatim in Section 3.1.1 of [51], the corresponding analysis in Section 3.1.2 of [51] focuses on $m = n$ resulting in n instances of PSI each of size $\frac{\ln n}{\ln \ln n}(1 + o(1))$ (see Table 3 in [51] for exact numbers).[4] On the other hand, we provide a hybrid approach where we employ the binning technique (referred to as *simple hashing* in Section 3.1.1 of [51]) to set up input sets (for independent PSI instances) which are large enough to enable application of a fast PSI protocol [35] (for independent PSI instances) that employs cuckoo hashing. To see how this affects performance, note that in Section 6.2.4 of [51], which details the performance of their best PSI protocol on billion element sets, the authors note that the cuckoo hashing step requires 16.3 h. In contrast, applying our binning technique with our choice of parameters, i.e., $m = 64$ for $n = 10^9$, even **serially** would likely result in significant improvements since the best known PSI protocols on instances of size $n/m \approx 2^{24}$ use cuckoo hashing and still complete in under 2 min [35].

Big Data Frameworks. Another approach to parallelize a PSI protocol Π is to implement it in a big data framework like Spark which will distribute the work among many nodes. The downside is the lack of generality, in that each protocol must be rewritten in Scala to scale it. For instance, there exist efficient PSI protocols based on a variety of techniques and assumptions. Choice of what protocol to implement may also depend on the setting (e.g., client-server), set sizes (balanced or unbalanced), network bandwidth, or whether the PSI output needs to be kept secret-shared in order to pipeline it into other MPC protocols. Also, recent PSI protocols rely on data structures such as cuckoo hashing whose efficient scaling may be nontrivial [61] and may depend on the underlying big data framework.

In this paper, we show how our binning technique allows us to leverage a big data framework like Spark in a protocol agnostic way. The high level idea is to express (PSI) protocols in terms of its *round functions* aka *next message functions*.[5] These round functions are to be executed by a designated party at

[3] Using $m \approx n$ in our self-reduction would incur an unacceptable overhead due to padding. Please see Sect. 3.1 on how to choose the optimum value of m.

[4] In that Section, they also analyze the choice of m for PSI with unbalanced sets.

[5] This is a standard technique to capture protocols in cryptography, for example while designing zero-knowledge compilers that transform a semi-honest secure protocol into a maliciously secure protocol.

a particular round to determine the next message that needs to be sent by that party. More concretely, a round function takes as input the current state of the protocol, and the inputs and randomness of the designated party, and outputs the next message that the designated party sends to the other party.[6] Expressing PSI protocols in this way, allows a protocol agnostic[7] way of orchestrating on each Spark cluster. Please see Section 5 for specific implementation of KKRT protocol [35]. Furthermore, such an orchestration does not require reconfiguring the clusters or modifying the internals of Spark (c.f. unlike [65]).

Private Database Joins. Building on our techniques to parallelize PSI protocols, we describe how to implement an *end-to-end private database join application*. We consider a setting where two enterprises wish to perform a *data exchange*. That is, each of these two parties have databases storing sensitive information, and they wish to enrich their data based on information from the database tables of the other party. More concretely, the operation they wish to perform can be expressed succinctly as a join operation (inner, outer, left, or right) which specifies the attributes that need to be matched, and additional attributes that need to be fetched on the matched rows. A necessary privacy requirement in this setting is that either enterprise wishes to not reveal any information other than what is revealed by the output of the join operation.

Since enterprises often have (access to) dedicated clusters supporting their big data frameworks, an import design goal is to leverage these frameworks to (1) increase the efficiency of the join operation, and also to (2) integrate with existing data pipelines for pre- or post-processing. In this work, we focus specifically on Spark. We picked Spark because it is open-source and widely adopted big data analytics engine for large-scale data processing. Additionally, it comes with higher-level libraries and extensions which makes it an ideal choice for various use cases beyond PSI. We assume that the two enterprises each employ a Spark cluster consisting of multiple nodes co-ordinated by an *orchestrator* (that may be on either side). Note that each Spark cluster has complete access to that party's input dataset only. Communication between the clusters that is required for private database join will be facilitated via dedicated edge servers. More details about our system architecture can be found in Sect. 4.2. Functionally, an analyst may connect to the orchestrator and use, for instance, a JupyterLab interface to issue private database join instructions to initiate and run our protocol on the specified datasets.

Plug-n-Play Framework. By itself, Spark does not provide any privacy guarantees for computations that cross data boundaries. In Sect. 4, we describe a natural transformation of the private database join problem into a PSI problem. (The transformation itself can be carried out locally, and additionally admits

[6] Most PSI protocols have very few rounds (exceptions include circuit PSI protocols that rely on the GMW compiler).

[7] We support any PSI protocol irrespective of the underlying cryptographic assumptions or algorithmic techniques.

parallelization via Spark.) Then, to solve the resultant PSI problem, we implement a generic framework that can apply our binning technique on top of any existing PSI implementation. Our framework is generic in that one could plug in any C/C++ PSI implementation (say from [54]) to our framework. Using the Java Native Interface (JNI) [60] technology, our framework integrates the native implementation with the rest of our Spark pipeline. We refer to Sect. 4.3 for additional details.

1.2 Related Work

Private Set Intersection. Several protocols have been proposed to realize PSI such as the efficient but insecure naive hashing solution, public key cryptography based protocols [4,11,17,22,23,31,39,55], those based on oblivious transfer [10, 20,35,45,46,49] and other circuit-based solutions [7,30,47,48]. Another popular model for PSI is to introduce a semi-trusted third party that aids in efficiently computing the intersection [1,2,58]. We refer to [50] for a more detailed overview on the various approaches taken to solve PSI. In addition, other variants of PSI have also been extensively studied such as multi-party PSI [29,36], PSI cardinality [12,33], PSI sum [32,33], threshold PSI [6,24] to name a few. Apart from PSI, there is also a line of work on performing other set operations such as union privately [8,16,34,37].

Privacy-Preserving Frameworks. A set of privacy-preserving frameworks makes use of hardware enclaves. Opaque [65] is an oblivious distributed data analytics platform which utilized Intel SGX hardware enclaves to provide strong security guarantees. OCQ [15] further decreases communication and computation costs of Opaque via an oblivious planner. Unlike these methods, Spark-PSI does not depend on hardware. Other recent works include CryptDB [52] and Seabed [44] which provide protocols for the secure execution of analytical queries over encrypted big data. Senate [57] describes a framework for enabling privacy preserving database queries in a multiparty setting. For more related work, we refer the reader to the full version of this work [5].

2 Preliminaries

2.1 Private Set Intersection

In the problem of private set intersection (PSI), two parties (sometimes referred to as "sender" and "receiver") each hold a set of items and wish to learn nothing more than the intersection of these sets. In this paper, we present generic techniques to *securely* parallelize any PSI protocol, with security against semi-honest (aka honest-but-curious) adversaries. For our experiments, we apply our parallelization technique on the KKRT PSI protocol [35]. The KKRT protocol is an OT-based PSI (like [43,49,51]) and relies heavily on modern OT extension protocols [25,59,62]. We chose KKRT because it is currently the fastest PSI protocol against semihonest adversaries.

2.2 Apache Spark

Apache Spark is an open-source, fast, and distributed computing framework used for large-scale data workloads. It utilizes in-memory caching and optimizes query execution for any size of data. It is faster and more flexible than other systems such as Google's MapReduce [18], as it runs in memory, which makes processing much faster than disk [64], and allows for complex processing schemes, instead of MapReduce's linear model. On top of Spark, there are libraries for running distributed computations ranging from SQL queries, to machine-learning algorithms, to graph analytics, and to data streaming.

A Spark application consists of a *driver program* that translates user-provided data processing pipelines into individual tasks and distributes these tasks to *worker nodes*. The basic abstractions available in Spark are built on a distributed data structure called *resilient distributed dataset* (RDD) [63] and these abstraction offer distributed data processing operators such as map, filter, reduce, broadcast, etc. Higher-level abstractions expose popular APIs such as SQL, streaming, and graph processing.

Implementing state-of-art PSI protocols on top of Spark holds the promise of using the demonstrated capabilities of Spark and similar data platforms to achieve significant performance gains. Unfortunately Spark lacks any multi-tenant concepts, running all applications and scheduling all tasks in one security domain. This is incompatible with the basic settings of PSI protocols which involve two or more untrusted parties, which require multiple security domains with strong isolation between them. We address this problem by assigning each party to one Spark cluster, thus achieving isolation by physically separating each party's computation, and then introducing an *orchestrator* component that coordinates multiple independent Spark clusters in different data centers to jointly perform the PSI tasks. Section 4 describes our multi-cluster architecture and motivates our design.

A second security challenge in Apache Spark is the default data-partitioning scheme, which can reveal information about a party's dataset. For example, if data partitioning relies on the first byte in each record to distribute data records to nodes, an adversary can learn how many records start with `0x00`, how many with `0x01`, and so on. This leaks information about the data distribution in a dataset and undermines the security guarantees offered by a PSI protocol. We address this problem by introducing a *secure binning approach* (described in Sect. 3) that makes such leaks statistically inconsequential while still allowing each Spark cluster to partition data and distribute tasks as is locally optimal.

Finally, adding an orchestrator outside of the Spark clusters and treating individual Spark clusters' schedulers as black boxes, which are convenient for operational purposes, can lead to sub-optimal execution plans. In particular, the local optimization of schedules at each cluster may contradict with desired performance from collaborative computing across multiple clusters with different data sizes and hardware configurations. We take advantage of Spark's lazy evaluation capability, which can be used to delay the execution of a task until a certain action is triggered. Section 4.3 presents how we effectively use lazy evaluation to loosely and efficiently coordinate across clusters.

2.3 Threat Model

We consider a semi-honest adversary and detail its capabilities with respect to the PSI protocol we wish to deploy on Spark, to the Spark framework, and to our overall Spark-PSI system.

Threat Model of the PSI Protocol. In standard cryptography terminology, we assume that the PSI protocol is secure against *semi-honest* (aka honest-but-curious) adversaries. That is, we expect the participants to faithfully follow the instructions of the protocol but allow the parties to learn as much as they can from the protocol messages. We believe that this assumption fits many use cases, where parties are likely already under certain agreements to participate honestly. We further assume that all cryptographic primitives are secure. Finally, we note that the PSI protocol does reveal the sizes of the sets to both parties, as well as the final outputs in the clear (see [4] for size-hiding PSI, and [40,48] for protecting the outputs).

Threat Model of the Spark Framework. We assume that every Spark cluster's built-in security features are enabled and that the Spark implementation is free of vulnerabilities. These features include data-at-rest encryption, access management, quota management, queue management, etc. We further assume that these features guarantee a locally secure computing environment at each local cluster, such that an attacker cannot gain access to a Spark cluster unless authorized.

Threat Model of Spark-PSI. We assume that only authorized users can issue commands to the orchestrator and we further assume that the orchestrator is operated by one of the two parties. We note that it could be operated by some (semi-honest) third party without impacting security.

The adversary can observe the network communication between different parties during execution of the protocol. It may also control some of the parties to observe data present in the storage and memory of their clusters, as well as the order of memory accesses.

Our semi-honest adversary model implies that we expect participants to supply correct inputs to the PSI protocol. While in practice input validity is important, it is outside the scope of this work as we believe it can be tackled as a future, separate layer on top of Spark-PSI.

3 Parallelizing PSI via Binning

We describe an efficient technique to scale any PSI protocol Π. For simplicity, we assume that both parties have equal sized sets, say of size n. Each set contains elements of length κ bits (typically and wlog $\kappa = 128$). Then, for a given parameter m, we show how to solve PSI on instances of size n, via m invocations of Π on set sizes $\approx n/m$ with minimal overhead. Our parallelization technique will be statistically secure. To aid in the analysis, we use σ to denote the statistical security parameter (typically, set to 80).

Our idea is to first let each party to locally partition their set into $m > 1$ subsets. That is, the parties first locally sample a random hash function $h : \{0,1\}^* \to \{1, \ldots, m\}$. Each party P transforms its set $S = \{s_1, \ldots, s_n\}$ into subsets $T_1, \ldots, T_m$ such that for all $s \in S$ it holds that $s \in T_{h(s)}$. Modeling h as a random function ensures that the elements $\{h(s) \mid s \in S\}$ are all distributed uniformly. This directly implies that $\mathbb{E}[\text{size of } T_i] = n/m$.

However, observe that the number of elements in any given bin T_i does in fact leak information about the distribution of the input set. For example, say there are no items in T_i, then this implies that the set S does not contain any element s that s.t. $h(s) = i$. To maintain the security guarantees of PSI, it is critical that this information is not leaked.

Now given that the parties have locally partitioned their sets into $T_1, \ldots, T_m$, next they pad each T_j with uniformly random dummy elements to ensure that the size of each padded set equals $(1 + \delta_0)n/m$ for some parameter δ_0. Since $S \subset \{0,1\}^\kappa$, there are 2^κ possible elements and the probability of a dummy item being in the intersection is negligible. Alternatively, if κ is large enough, we can ensure that no dummy item is in the intersection by asking each party to pad its j-th bin with dummy items s' sampled from non-overlapping subsets of $\{0,1\}^\kappa$ such that $h(s') = j' \neq j$. Then, the two parties engage in m *parallel* instances of Π, where in the i-th instance π_i, parties input their respective i-th padded tokenized set. Once all m instances of Π deliver output, parties then by simply combining these m individual outputs to obtain the final output.

In summary, our binning technique proceeds by asking each party to (1) locally tokenize the sets, (2) locally map the set elements into m bins, (3) locally pad each bin with dummy elements to ensure that each bin contains exactly $(1 + \delta_0)n/m$ elements, (4) execute m instances of a PSI protocol with the other party, (5) finally combine the outputs of the individual PSI protocols to get the final output.

3.1 Analysis

We compute the value of the parameter δ_0 that ensures that the binning step does not fail except with negligible probability. This turns out to be $\delta_0 \stackrel{\text{def}}{=} \sqrt{3m/n \cdot (\sigma \ln 2 + \ln m)}$ (detailed analysis in the full version [5]). More concretely, suppose set size $n = 10^9$ and statistical parameter $\sigma = 80$, then choosing parameter $m = 64$, we see that the max bin size of any of the 64 bins is at most $n' \approx 15.68 \times 10^6$ (with $\delta_0 = 0.0034$) with probability $(1 - 2^{-80})$. Note that existing PSI protocols [10,35,46] can already efficiently handle set sizes of n'. Therefore, in principle, we can use 64 instances of PSI protocol of say [35] to implement a PSI protocol that operates on 1 billion sized sets.

We prove the security of this scheme in the so-called *simulation paradigm* in the full version of this work [5].

3.2 Applying Our Binning Technique

We emphasize that our technique works for any PSI protocol (no matter what assumption it is based on) for all settings including cases where the sets are unbalanced. Furthermore, the PSI instances operating on different bins could in principle use different PSI protocols or implementations (which can be useful if the underlying infrastructure is heterogeneous).

By design our technique is highly conducive for an efficient Spark implementation (or in any other big data framework). Also, large input sets may already be distributed across several nodes in a Spark cluster. We provide a quick overview of how our protocol would operate in such a setting. At the beginning of the protocol the hash function h is sampled and distributed to the nodes in both clusters. Within each cluster, each node uses h as a mapping function to define the new partitions $T_1, \ldots, T_m$ which are each assigned to some worker node in the same cluster. The main phase of the protocol proceeds as described by running m parallel instances[8] of the PSI protocol across the two clusters which outputs the intersection sets $I_1, \ldots, I_m$ such that the final output is defined as $I' = \cup_i I_i$. In the next sections, we describe our system Spark-PSI that applies our binning technique in a real-world application.

4 Scalable Private Database Joins

In this section, we describe how to perform SQL styled join queries with the use of our parallel PSI protocol implemented via Spark. In Sect. 4.1, we describe the problem of private database joins across different data domains, and outline a solution which leverages our binning technique for parallelizing PSI. Then, in Sect. 4.2, we describe the architecture of our system Spark-PSI that solves the database join problem. Finally, in Sect. 4.3, we describe the various techniques we employ to efficiently implement our binning technique in Spark.

4.1 Database Joins Across Data Domains

In the problem of private database joins, we have two distinct parties A, B, who wish to perform a join operation on their private data. To model the problem, we denote Domain A as the data domain of party A, and likewise Domain B for party B. We assume that one of the parties hosts an *orchestrator* which is essentially a server that exposes metadata such as schemas of the data sets that are available for the join operation. (For more details, see Sect. 4.2). This way parties discover the available types of queries and can submit them via the

[8] If we have k worker nodes on each side, then we can run k instances of Π in parallel, and repeat this m/k times to complete the PSI portion of the execution.

orchestrator API. When a query is submitted, the orchestrator will validate the correctness of the query and forward to request to the other party for approval. While many types of query languages could be supported, we have chosen to implement a subset of SQL.

More precisely we support any query which can be divided into the following. A *select* clause which specifies one more columns among the two tables. A *join on* clause which compares one or more columns for equality between the two sets. A *where* clause which can be split into conjunctive clauses where each conjunction is a function of a single table. For example, we support the following query:

```
SELECT DomainB.table0.col4, DomainA.table0.col3
FROM DomainA.table0
JOIN DomainB.table0
ON DomainA.table0.col1 = DomainB.table0.col2
AND DomainA.table0.col2 = DomainB.table0.col6
WHERE DomainA.table0.col3 > 23.
```

In this example a column from both parties is being selected where they are being joined on the equality of the join keys

```
DomainA.table0.col1 = DomainB.table0.col2
DomainA.table0.col2 = DomainB.table0.col6
```

along with the added constraint

```
DomainA.table0.col3 > 23.
```

Our framework transforms this query by first filtering the local data sets based on the `WHERE` clause. We require that each of the where clauses be a function of a single table. For example, we do not support a where clause such as

```
WHERE DomainA.table0.col0 > DomainB.table0.col7
```

because this predicate compares across the two data sets.[9]

Once the local *where* clauses have filtered the input tables, the parties *tokenize* the join key columns. The join key columns refer to the columns which appear in the `JOIN ON` clause. In the example above these are `DomainA.table0.col1`, `DomainA.table0.col2` from the first party (Domain A) and `DomainB.table0.col2`, `DomainB.table0.col6` from the second party (Domain B). For each row of the respective data sets, the parties generate a

[9] Restricting clauses this way enables us to reduce the above problem to the PSI problem. We note that the restriction above can be lifted if we use more sophisticated PSI protocols that can keep the PSI output in secret shared form without revealing it. We leave this for future work.

set of tokens by hashing together their join keys. For example, Domain A can generate their set A as

$$A = \{H(\texttt{DomainA.table0.col1}[i], \texttt{DomainA.table0.col2}[i]) \mid i \in \{1, \ldots, n\}\}$$

Let B denote the analogous set of tokens for Domain B. We note that rows with the same join keys will have the same token and that the A, B sets will contain only a single copy of that token. Later we will need to map elements of A, B back to the rows which they correspond to. For this task we will logically add an additional column to each input table which we label as `token` and stores that row's token value. That is, for the example above we have

$$\texttt{DomainA.table0.token} = H(\texttt{DomainA.table0.col1}[i], \texttt{DomainA.table0.col2}[i])$$

Now the parties can execute a PSI protocols on their respective A, B sets as inputs. The protocol outputs the intersection $I = A \cap B$ to both parties. As described in the previous section, this phase is parallelized with the use of our binning technique.

In the final phase the parties use the intersection I to construct the output table. Here we will assume that only Domain A should obtain the output table but note that this general procedure can provide output to both. Both parties take subsets of their tables such that only rows which have a token value in I remain. This can efficiently be implemented using the `token` column that was appended to the input tables. From this subset, Domain B sends their columns which appear in the select clause along with the token value. Let this table be denoted as `table`*. Domain A then joins their table with `table`* to construct the final output table.

In summary, the private database join operation can be performed via the following three phases. The first phase, referred to as tokenization, translates a possibly complex join query into a set intersection problem. In the second phase our parallel PSI protocol runs and outputs the intersection to both parties. The final phase is referred to as reverse-lookup which instructs the parties to use the intersection to construct the final join output which may contain significantly more information than the intersection alone, e.g. additional attributes being selected. In the next section, we will see the design of an architecture that enables us to efficiently execute these several phases in a setting where parties have Spark clusters.

4.2 System Architecture

Figure 1 describes the overall architecture of our system where we connect two distinct parties (or data domains) each having a Spark cluster. To solve the private database join problem, we need to co-ordinate the two Spark clusters to implement the various phases described in the previous section.

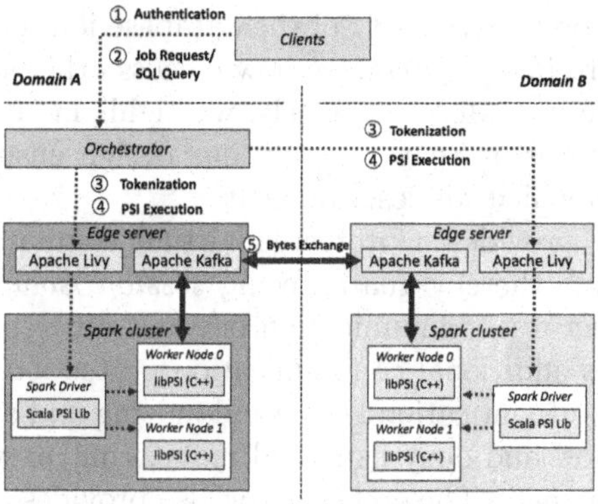

Fig. 1. Spark-PSI Framework.① Clients need authentication first so that they can talk to the orchestrator ② Clients have two modes to start a job: a JSON style request or a SQL style query. ③ The orchestrator parses the query for tokenization of related columns. ④ Execute Spark PSI pipelines ⑤ Intermediate bytes are exchanged through Kafka brokers deployed on edge servers.

This co-ordination is carried out by an *orchestrator* that exposes an interface (such as UI application/portal/Jupyter Lab) to specify the database join operation and to receive the results. Our orchestrator interfaces with each party's Spark cluster via Apache Livy [38].

In more detail, the orchestrator is responsible for storing various metadata such as the schemas of the data sets. We assume that these schemas are made available to the orchestrator by the parties in an initialization phase. Following this, either party can authenticate itself to the orchestrator and submit a SQL styled query. The orchestrator is then responsible for parsing the query and compiling Spark jobs for two clusters for different phases of the private database join operation, including the PSI protocols. The orchestrator then initiates the protocol by sending both clusters the relevant parameters for different phases of the protocol, e.g. data sets identifiers, join columns, network configuration, etc. Once the database join protocol completes, the orchestrator will record audit logs and potentially facilitate access to the output of the join.

The Apache Livy [38] interface helps internally to manage Spark session and submission of Spark code for PSI computation. Communication between the two clusters for various phases of the join protocol (e.g., for the PSI subprotocols) is facilitated via dedicated edge servers which work as Kafka brokers to establish a secure data transmission channel. While we have chosen Apache Kafka for implementing the communication pipeline, our architecture allows the parties to plug their own communication channel of choice to read/write data back and forth. Additionally, our architecture doesn't change any internals of Spark that makes easier to adopt and deploy at scale.

Security Implications. We discuss some security considerations and highlight some security implications that are a consequence of our architecture described above. While the theoretical security of the database join protocol is guaranteed by employing a secure PSI protocol, we now discuss other security features provided by our architecture. More concretely, we highlight that in addition to the built-in security features of Spark cluster, our design ensures *cluster isolation* and *session isolation* which we describe next.

The orchestrator provides a protected virtual computing environment for each database join job thereby guaranteeing *session isolation.* While standard TLS is used to protect the communication between different Spark clusters, the orchestrator provides additional communication protection such as session specific encryption and authentication keys, randomizing and anonymizing the endpoints, managing allow and deny lists, and monitoring/preventing DOS/DDOS attack to the environments. The orchestrator also provides an additional layer of user authentication and authorization. All of the computing resources, including tasks, cached data, communication channels, and metadata are protected within this session. No foreign user or job may peek or alter the internal state of the session. Each parties' Spark session is isolated from each other and only reports execution state back to orchestrator.

On the other hand, *cluster isolation* aims at protecting computing resources from each parties from misuse or abuse in the database join jobs. To accomplish this, the orchestrator is the only node in the environment that controls and is visible to the end-to-end processing flows. It is also the only party that has the metadata for Spark clusters involved in the session. Recall that a separate secure communication channel is employed via Livy and Kafka that limits the parties from accessing each other's Spark cluster. This keeps the orchestrator out of the data flow pipeline thereby preventing the party operating the orchestrator from gaining advantages over other parties involved. It also ensures that each Spark cluster is self-autonomous and requires little or no changes to participate in a database join protocol with other parties. The orchestrator also takes care of job failures or uneven computing speed to ensure out-of-the-box reusability of Spark clusters that typically already exist in enterprise organizations.

Finally, we remark that the low level APIs calling cryptographic libraries and exchanging data between C++ instances and Spark dataframes, lie in each party's data cluster and thus do not introduce any information leakage. The high level APIs package the secure Spark execution pipeline as a service, and are responsible for mapping independent jobs to each executor and collecting the results from them. See Sect. 4.3 for more details.

Taken together, our architecture essentially provides the theoretical security that is guaranteed by the underlying PSI subprotocol. More concretely, when one party is compromised by the adversary, the other party's data remains completely private except whatever is revealed by the output of the computation.

4.3 Spark-PSI Implementation

We provide details on how we leverage Spark to implement the binning technique. Our underlying PSI protocol is the KKRT protocol implemented in C++.

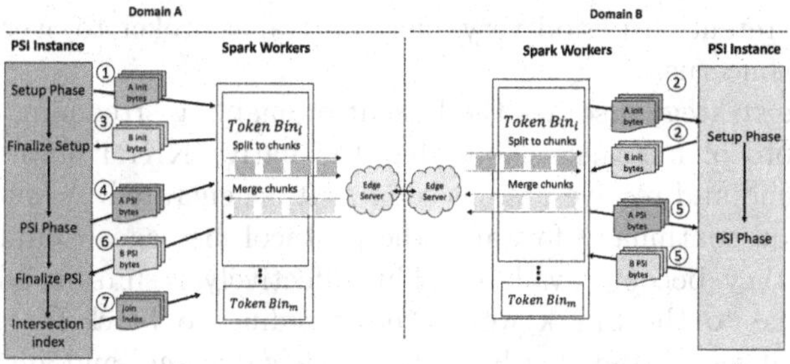

Fig. 2. KKRT Implementation Workflow. ① [DomainA.setup1] Domain A in its setup phase generates encrypted data and transmits them to Domain B. ② [DomainB.setup1] Domain B performs its setup phase with data received from Domain A and in turn generates encrypted data and transmits them to Domain A. ③ [DomainA.setup2] Domain A finalizes setup phase. ④ [DomainA.psi1] and ⑤ [DomainB.psi1] Domains A and B execute the online PSI phase, which proceeds over multiple rounds. ⑥ [DomainA.psi2] Domain A enters the Finalize PSI phase and computes the intersection with Domain B as row indices. ⑦ Domain A retrieves matching records by doing a reverse lookup into its dataset using the computed indices.

KKRT Workflow. Figure 2 shows the detailed data flows in our SPARK-PSI framework instantiated with the KKRT protocol. All of the phases shown in Fig. 2 are invoked by the orchestrator sequentially. The orchestrator starts the native KKRT execution by submitting metadata information about the datasets to both parties. Based on the request, both parties start executing their Spark code which creates new dataframes by loading the required data set using the supported JDBC driver. This dataframe is then hashed into the tokens of fixed length by both parties. This *token dataframe* is then mapped to m number of bins (in Spark terminology partitions) using the custom partitioner by both parties, which is basically distributing tokens evenly on both side. Then the final intersection is obtained by taking the union of each bin intersection. Note that tokenization and binning are generic functionalities in our framework and can be used by any other PSI algorithm. This way Spark achieves parallel execution of multiple bins on both sides.

The native KKRT protocol is executed via a generic JNI interface that connects to the Spark code. Specifically, the JNI interface is in terms of round functions, and therefore is agnostic about internal protocol implementation. Note that there is a one-time setup phase for KKRT (this setup is required only once for a pair of parties). This is described in Steps ①, ②, ③ in Fig. 2. Later, the online PSI phase that actually computes the intersection between the bins is shown in Steps ④, ⑤, ⑥, and ⑦. The parties use edge servers to mirror data whenever there is a write operation on any of the Kafka brokers. Note that the main PSI phase consists of sending the encrypted data sets and can be a performance bottleneck as Kafka is optimized for small size messages. To overcome this issue, we are chunking encrypted data sets into smaller partitions on both sides so that we can utilize Kafka's capability efficiently. We also keep the intermediate data retention period very short on Kafka broker to overcome storage and security concerns.

The above strategy also has the benefit of enabling streaming of the underlying PSI protocol messages. Note that the native KKRT implementation is designed to send and receive data as soon as it is generated. As such, our Spark implementation continually forwards the protocol messages to and from Kafka the moment they become available. This effectively results in additional parallelization due to the Spark worker not needing to block for slow network I/O. Note that we also explicitly cache *token dataframe* and *instance address dataframe* which are used in multiple phases to avoid any re-computation. This way we take advantage of Spark's lazy evaluation that optimizes execution plan based on DAG and RDD persistence.

Reusable Components for Parallelizing Other PSI Protocols. Our code is packaged as a Spark-Scala library which includes an end-to-end example implementation of native KKRT protocol. This library itself has many useful reusable components such as JDBC connectors to work with multiple data sources, methods for tokenization and binning approach, general C++ interface to link other native PSI algorithms and a generic JNI interface between Scala and C++ interface. All these functions are implemented in base class of the library, which may be reused for other native PSI implementations. Additionally, our library decouples networking methods from actual PSI computation which adds flexibility to the framework to support other networking channels if required.

Any PSI implementation can be plugged into SPARK-PSI by exposing a C/C++ API that can be invoked by the framework. The API is structured around the concept of setup rounds and online rounds and does not make assumptions about the cryptographic protocol executed in these rounds. The following functions are part of the API:

- `get-setup-round-count() -> count` – retrieves the total number of setup rounds required by this PSI implementation;
- `setup( id, in-data ) -> out-data` – invokes round `id` on the appropriate party with data received from the other party in the previous round of the setup and returns the data to be sent;
- `get-online-round-count() -> count` – retrieves the total number of online rounds required by this PSI implementation;
- `psi-round( id, in-data ) -> out-data` – invokes the online round `id` on the appropriate party with data received from the other party in the previous round of the PSI protocol and returns the data to be sent.

The data passed to an invocation of `psi-round` is the data from a single bin, and SPARK-PSI orchestrates the parallel invocations of this API over all of the bins. For example, KKRT has three setup rounds (which we label for clarity in the rest of the paper as DomainA.setup1, DomainB.setup1, and DomainA.setup2) and three online rounds (labeled DomainA.psi1, DomainB.psi1, and DomainA.psi2). When running KKRT with 256 bins (as done in one of the experiments detailed in Sect. 5), the setup rounds DomainA.setup1, DomainB.setup1, and

DomainA.setup2 each invoke `setup` once with the appropriate round id, and the online rounds DomainA.psi1, DomainB.psi1, and DomainA.psi2 each invoke `psi-round` with the appropriate round id 256 times.

5 Experimental Evaluation

In this section, we describe the performance of our SPARK-PSI implementation, and provide detailed benchmarks for various steps. Then, we provide our end-to-end performance numbers and study the impact of number of bins on the running time. The highlight of this section is our running time of 82.88 min for sets of size 1 billion. We obtain this when we use $m = 2048$ bins.[10]

5.1 System Setup

Our experiments are evaluated on a setup similar to the one described in Fig. 1. Each party runs an independent standalone six-node Spark (v2.4.5) cluster with 1 server for driver and 5 servers for workers. Additionally we have an independent Kafka (v2.12-2.5.0) VM on each side for inter-cluster communication. The orchestrator server, which triggers the PSI computation, is on Domain A. All servers have 8 vCPUs (2.6 GHz), 64 GB RAM and run Ubuntu 18.04.4 LTS.

5.2 Microbenchmarking

We first benchmark the performance of the various steps in the binning pipeline and the KKRT implementation workflow (cf. Fig. 2). For these experiments, we assume that each party uses a dataset of size 100M as input.

Table 1 describes the total time required for the individual phases of our protocol when the number of bins equals 2048. For example, DomainA.tokenize (resp. DomainB.tokenize) denotes the time taken for tokenizing A's input (resp. B's input) and mapping these tokens into different bins and padding each bin to be of the same size. Note that the tokenization step is done in parallel. DomainA.psi1 denotes the time taken for executing Step ④ for all the bins. In this step, Domain A generates and transfers approximately $60n$ bytes for dataset size n (i.e., 100M) to Domain B. Likewise, DomainB.psi1 denotes the time taken for executing Step ⑤ for all the bins. In this step, Domain B generates and transfers approximately $22n$ bytes back to Domain A. Finally, DomainA.psi2 denotes the time taken for executing Steps ⑥ and ⑦, where the intersection is determined for all the bins. Note that we have excluded benchmarking Steps ①, ②, ③ in Fig. 2 as these correspond to the setup functions which have a constant cost, and more importantly these functions need to be executed only once between a pair of parties (and can be reused for subsequent PSI executions).

[10] This corresponds to $\delta_0 = 0.019$ for a bin size of ≈500K (cf. Sect. 3.1).

Table 1. Microbenchmark of Spark-PSI when using KKRT PSI and 2048 bins.

Spark-PSI step	Time (s) by dataset size		
	$10M$	$50M$	$100M$
DomainA.tokenize	47.21	91.20	124.68
DomainB.tokenize	45.90	92.89	121.64
DomainA.psi1	8.40	20.64	31.55
DomainB.psi1	40.83	121.73	247.30
DomainA.psi2	14.92	47.49	88.05

Table 2. Network latency for a dataset of size 100M.

KKRT PSI round	Time (s) by number of bins	
	256	2048
DomainA.psi1.write	36.44	**13.36**
DomainB.psi1.read	178.76	**98.77**
DomainB.psi1.write	15.24	**8.12**
DomainA.psi2.read	25.61	**21.35**

Communication vs. Number of Bins. Table 2 describes the impact of bin size on the time taken for reading and writing data via Kafka (i.e., inter-cluster communication). (Note that the numbers in Table 1 include the time taken for reading and writing data.)

Here, DomainA.psi1 produces intermediate data of size 9.1GB which is sent to Doman B, while DomainB.psi1 produces 3.03GB intermediate data that is sent to A. As evident from the benchmarks in Table 2, more bins improve networking performance as the message chunks become smaller. In more detail, when we go with 256 bins, individual messages of size 35.55MB are sent over Kafka for DomainA.psi1. With 2048 bins, the corresponding individual message size is only 4.44MB.

5.3 End-to-End Performance

Table 3. Total execution time for different joins over datasets of size 100M. Fastest times in each column are highlighted.

Number of bins	Time (m)		
	Insecure single-cluster Spark join	Insecure cross-cluster Spark join	Spark-PSI
256	**3.76**	7.60	11.41
4096	5.62	**4.90**	**8.71**
8192	10.83	10.26	9.79

Shuffle Overhead of Our Protocol. In Table 3, we compare the performance of our protocol with the performance of insecure joins on datasets of size 100M. To evaluate and compare with the performance of insecure joins, we consider two variants. In the first variant, which we call *single-cluster Spark join*, we employ a single cluster with six nodes (one server for driver and five servers for workers) to perform the join on two datasets each of size 100M. Here, we assume that both datasets reside on the same cluster. The join computation then proceeds by partitioning the data into multiple bins and then computing the intersection directly using a *single* Spark join call. In the second variant, which we call *cross-cluster Spark join*, we employ two clusters each with six nodes, and each containing only one 100M tokenized dataset. Now, to perform the join, each cluster partitions its dataset into multiple bins. Then one of the clusters sends the partitioned dataset to the other cluster, which then aggregates the received data into one dataset, and then computed the final join using a *single* Spark join call.

In the case of insecure join on a single cluster, we observe that increasing the number of bins leads to an increase in the number of data shuffling operations (shuffle read/write), which ends up slowing down the execution. When we split the insecure join across two clusters, we incur the overhead of network communication across clusters and the additional shuffling on the destination cluster, but gain a parallelism because we have twice the compute resources.

When we switch to Spark-PSI, we maintain the overhead of cross-cluster communication and incur additional overhead of the PSI computation, but we avoid the extra data shuffling (as we employ broadcast join). We believe the effect of the broadcast join appears most significant when we have smaller per-bin data (as is the case with 8,192 bins) making Spark-PSI faster than the insecure cross-cluster join in some cases. Our secure system introduces an overhead of up to 77% in the worst case on top of the insecure cross-cluster join.

Table 4. Total execution time for PSI with various dataset sizes and bin sizes. Fastest times in each column are highlighted.

Number of bins	Time (m) by dataset size			
	$1M$	$10M$	$100M$	$1B$
1	1.07	12.04	–	–
16	**0.75**	2	–	–
64	0.78	1.66	15.27	154.10
256	0.99	**1.47**	11.41	116.89
1024	1.03	1.63	8.57	86.54
2048	1.11	1.86	**8.12**	**82.88**
4096	1.4	1.94	8.71	90.46
8192	2.45	3.07	9.79	94.74

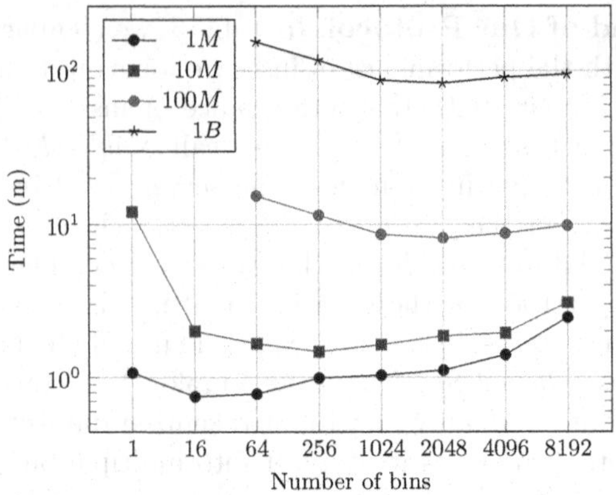

Fig. 3. Different input sizes achieve optimal execution time for different number of bins.

Choosing the Optimal Bin Size. In Table 4 we report the running time of the PSI as a function of the number of bins and dataset size, and plot the same in Fig. 3. The highlight of this table is our running time of 82.88 min for dataset size 1B, roughly a 25× speedup over the prior work of Pinkas et al. [51]. As evident from the table, we obtain this running time when we set the number of bins $m = 2048$. Also as evident from the table and from the corresponding plot in Fig. 3, the performance of our protocol on datasets of a given size first begins to improve as we increase the number of bins, and then hits an inflection point after which the performance degrades. The initial improvement is a result of parallelization. Higher number of bins results in smaller bin size on Spark and this is ideal especially for larger datasets, but the strategy of increasing the number of bins doesn't continue to work as the task scheduling overhead in Spark (and the padding overhead of the binning technique itself) slows down the execution. Also, we believe that better performance is possible if we use more executor cores (i.e., a larger cluster) as this is likely to allow better parallelization.

Disclaimer

Case studies, comparisons, statistics, research and recommendations are provided "AS IS" and intended for informational purposes only and should not be relied upon for operational, marketing, legal, technical, tax, financial or other advice. Visa Inc. neither makes any warranty or representation as to the completeness or accuracy of the information within this document, nor assumes any liability or responsibility that may result from reliance on such information. The Information contained herein is not intended as investment or legal advice, and readers are encouraged to seek the advice of a competent professional where such advice is required.

These materials and best practice recommendations are provided for informational purposes only and should not be relied upon for marketing, legal, regulatory or other advice. Recommended marketing materials should be independently evaluated in light of your specific business needs and any applicable laws and regulations. Visa is not responsible for your use of the marketing materials, best practice recommendations, or other information, including errors of any kind, contained in this document.

References

1. Abadi, A., Terzis, S., Dong, C.: O-PSI: delegated private set intersection on outsourced datasets. In: Federrath, H., Gollmann, D. (eds.) SEC 2015. IAICT, vol. 455, pp. 3–17. Springer, Cham (2015). https://doi.org/10.1007/978-3-319-18467-8_1
2. Abadi, A., Terzis, S., Dong, C.: VD-PSI: verifiable delegated private set intersection on outsourced private datasets. In: Grossklags, J., Preneel, B. (eds.) FC 2016. LNCS, vol. 9603, pp. 149–168. Springer, Heidelberg (2017). https://doi.org/10.1007/978-3-662-54970-4_9
3. Kiss, A., Liu, J., Schneider, T., Asokan, N., Pinkas, B.: Private set intersection for unequal set sizes with mobile applications. In: Proceedings on Privacy Enhancing Technologies, no. 4, pp. 177–197 (2017)
4. Ateniese, G., De Cristofaro, E., Tsudik, G.: (If) size matters: size-hiding private set intersection. In: Catalano, D., Fazio, N., Gennaro, R., Nicolosi, A. (eds.) PKC 2011. LNCS, vol. 6571, pp. 156–173. Springer, Heidelberg (2011). https://doi.org/10.1007/978-3-642-19379-8_10
5. Badrinarayanan, S., et al.: A plug-n-play framework for scaling private set intersection to billion-sized sets. Cryptology ePrint Archive, Paper 2022/294 (2022)
6. Badrinarayanan, S., Miao, P., Rindal, P.: Multi-party threshold private set intersection with sublinear communication. IACR Cryptology ePrint Archive 2020, 600 (2020). https://eprint.iacr.org/2020/600
7. Pinkas, B., Schneider, T., Tkachenko, O., Yanai, A.: Efficient circuit-based PSI with linear communication. In: Ishai, Y., Rijmen, V. (eds.) EUROCRYPT 2019. LNCS, vol. 11478, pp. 122–153. Springer, Cham (2019). https://doi.org/10.1007/978-3-030-17659-4_5
8. Blanton, M., Aguiar, E.: Private and oblivious set and multiset operations. Int. J. Inf. Sec. **15**(5), 493–518 (2016). https://doi.org/10.1007/s10207-015-0301-1
9. Brickell, J., Porter, D.E., Shmatikov, V., Witchel, E.: Privacy-preserving remote diagnostics. In: CCS (2007)
10. Chase, M., Miao, P.: Private set intersection in the internet setting from lightweight oblivious PRF. In: Micciancio, D., Ristenpart, T. (eds.) CRYPTO 2020. LNCS, vol. 12172, pp. 34–63. Springer, Cham (2020). https://doi.org/10.1007/978-3-030-56877-1_2
11. Chen, H., Laine, K., Rindal, P.: Fast private set intersection from homomorphic encryption. In: Thuraisingham, B.M., Evans, D., Malkin, T., Xu, D. (eds.) Proceedings of the 2017 ACM SIGSAC Conference on Computer and Communications Security, CCS 2017, Dallas, TX, USA, 30 October–03 November 2017, pp. 1243–1255. ACM (2017). https://doi.org/10.1145/3133956.3134061

12. De Cristofaro, E., Gasti, P., Tsudik, G.: Fast and private computation of cardinality of set intersection and union. In: Pieprzyk, J., Sadeghi, A.-R., Manulis, M. (eds.) CANS 2012. LNCS, vol. 7712, pp. 218–231. Springer, Heidelberg (2012). https://doi.org/10.1007/978-3-642-35404-5_17
13. De Cristofaro, E., Kim, J., Tsudik, G.: Linear-complexity private set intersection protocols secure in malicious model. In: Abe, M. (ed.) ASIACRYPT 2010. LNCS, vol. 6477, pp. 213–231. Springer, Heidelberg (2010). https://doi.org/10.1007/978-3-642-17373-8_13
14. Kales, D., Rechberger, C., Schneider, T., Senker, M., Weinert, C.: Mobile private contact discovery at scale. In: USENIX Annual Technical Conference, pp. 1447–1464 (2019)
15. Dave, A., Leung, C., Popa, R.A., Gonzalez, J.E., Stoica, I.: Oblivious coopetitive analytics using hardware enclaves. In: Proceedings of the Fifteenth European Conference on Computer Systems, pp. 1–17 (2020)
16. Davidson, A., Cid, C.: An efficient toolkit for computing private set operations. In: Pieprzyk, J., Suriadi, S. (eds.) ACISP 2017. LNCS, vol. 10343, pp. 261–278. Springer, Cham (2017). https://doi.org/10.1007/978-3-319-59870-3_15
17. De Cristofaro, E., Tsudik, G.: Practical private set intersection protocols with linear complexity. In: Sion, R. (ed.) FC 2010. LNCS, vol. 6052, pp. 143–159. Springer, Heidelberg (2010). https://doi.org/10.1007/978-3-642-14577-3_13
18. Dean, J., Ghemawat, S.: MapReduce: simplified data processing on large clusters. In: Sixth Symposium on Operating System Design and Implementation, OSDI 2004, San Francisco, CA, pp. 137–150 (2004)
19. Demmler, D., Rindal, P., Rosulek, M., Trieu, N.: PIR-PSI: scaling private contact discovery. Proc. Priv. Enhancing Technol. **2018**(4), 159–178 (2018). https://doi.org/10.1515/popets-2018-0037
20. Dong, C., Chen, L., Wen, Z.: When private set intersection meets big data: an efficient and scalable protocol. In: Proceedings of the 2013 ACM SIGSAC Conference on Computer & Communications Security, pp. 789–800 (2013)
21. Falk, B.H., Noble, D., Ostrovsky, R.: Private set intersection with linear communication from general assumptions. In: Cavallaro, L., Kinder, J., Domingo-Ferrer, J. (eds.) Proceedings of the 18th ACM Workshop on Privacy in the Electronic Society, WPES@CCS 2019, London, UK, 11 November 2019, pp. 14–25. ACM (2019). https://doi.org/10.1145/3338498.3358645
22. Freedman, M.J., Hazay, C., Nissim, K., Pinkas, B.: Efficient set intersection with simulation-based security. J. Cryptol. **29**(1), 115–155 (2016). https://doi.org/10.1007/s00145-014-9190-0
23. Freedman, M.J., Nissim, K., Pinkas, B.: Efficient private matching and set intersection. In: Cachin, C., Camenisch, J.L. (eds.) EUROCRYPT 2004. LNCS, vol. 3027, pp. 1–19. Springer, Heidelberg (2004). https://doi.org/10.1007/978-3-540-24676-3_1
24. Ghosh, S., Simkin, M.: The communication complexity of threshold private set intersection. In: Boldyreva, A., Micciancio, D. (eds.) CRYPTO 2019. LNCS, vol. 11693, pp. 3–29. Springer, Cham (2019). https://doi.org/10.1007/978-3-030-26951-7_1
25. Asharov, G., Lindell, Y., Schneider, T., Zohner, M.: More efficient oblivious transfer and extensions for faster secure computation. In: CCS, pp. 535–548 (2013)
26. Hallgren, P.A., Orlandi, C., Sabelfeld, A.: PrivatePool: privacy-preserving ridesharing. In: CSF (2017)
27. Chen, H., Huang, Z., Laine, K., Rindal, P.: Labeled PSI from fully homomorphic encryption with malicious security. In: CCS, pp. 1223–1237 (2018)

28. Hazay, C., Nissim, K.: Efficient set operations in the presence of malicious adversaries. In: Nguyen, P.Q., Pointcheval, D. (eds.) PKC 2010. LNCS, vol. 6056, pp. 312–331. Springer, Heidelberg (2010). https://doi.org/10.1007/978-3-642-13013-7_19
29. Hazay, C., Venkitasubramaniam, M.: Scalable multi-party private set-intersection. In: Fehr, S. (ed.) PKC 2017. LNCS, vol. 10174, pp. 175–203. Springer, Heidelberg (2017). https://doi.org/10.1007/978-3-662-54365-8_8
30. Huang, Y., Evans, D., Katz, J., Malka, L.: Faster secure two-party computation using garbled circuits. In: 20th USENIX Security Symposium, San Francisco, CA, USA, 8–12 August 2011, Proceedings. USENIX Association (2011). http://static.usenix.org/events/sec11/tech/full_papers/Huang.pdf
31. Huberman, B.A., Franklin, M.K., Hogg, T.: Enhancing privacy and trust in electronic communities. In: Feldman, S.I., Wellman, M.P. (eds.) Proceedings of the First ACM Conference on Electronic Commerce (EC-99), Denver, CO, USA, 3–5 November 1999, pp. 78–86. ACM (1999). https://doi.org/10.1145/336992.337012
32. Ion, M., et al.: On deploying secure computing commercially: private intersection-sum protocols and their business applications. IACR Cryptology ePrint Archive 2019, 723 (2019). https://eprint.iacr.org/2019/723
33. Ion, M., et al.: Private intersection-sum protocol with applications to attributing aggregate ad conversions (2017). ia.cr/2017/735
34. Kissner, L., Song, D.: Privacy-preserving set operations. In: Shoup, V. (ed.) CRYPTO 2005. LNCS, vol. 3621, pp. 241–257. Springer, Heidelberg (2005). https://doi.org/10.1007/11535218_15
35. Kolesnikov, V., Kumaresan, R., Rosulek, M., Trieu, N.: Efficient batched oblivious PRF with applications to private set intersection. In: Proceedings of the 2016 ACM SIGSAC Conference on Computer and Communications Security, pp. 818–829 (2016)
36. Kolesnikov, V., Matania, N., Pinkas, B., Rosulek, M., Trieu, N.: Practical multi-party private set intersection from symmetric-key techniques. In: CCS (2017)
37. Kolesnikov, V., Rosulek, M., Trieu, N., Wang, X.: Scalable private set union from symmetric-key techniques. In: Galbraith, S.D., Moriai, S. (eds.) ASIACRYPT 2019. LNCS, vol. 11922, pp. 636–666. Springer, Cham (2019). https://doi.org/10.1007/978-3-030-34621-8_23
38. Livy, A.: Apache Livy (2017). https://livy.apache.org/
39. Meadows, C.A.: A more efficient cryptographic matchmaking protocol for use in the absence of a continuously available third party. In: Proceedings of the 1986 IEEE Symposium on Security and Privacy, Oakland, California, USA, 7–9 April 1986, pp. 134–137. IEEE Computer Society (1986). https://doi.org/10.1109/SP.1986.10022
40. Ciampi, M., Orlandi, C.: Combining private set-intersection with secure two-party computation. In: Catalano, D., De Prisco, R. (eds.) SCN 2018. LNCS, vol. 11035, pp. 464–482. Springer, Cham (2018). https://doi.org/10.1007/978-3-319-98113-0_25
41. Nagaraja, S., Mittal, P., Hong, C.Y., Caesar, M., Borisov, N.: BotGrep: finding P2P bots with structured graph analysis. In: USENIX Security Symposium (2010)
42. Narayanan, A., Thiagarajan, N., Lakhani, M., Hamburg, M., Boneh, D.: Location privacy via private proximity testing. In: Proceedings of the Network and Distributed System Security Symposium, NDSS 2011, San Diego, California, USA, 6th February–9th February 2011. The Internet Society (2011). https://www.ndss-symposium.org/ndss2011/privacy-private-proximity-testing-paper

43. Orrù, M., Orsini, E., Scholl, P.: Actively secure 1-out-of-N OT extension with application to private set intersection. In: Handschuh, H. (ed.) CT-RSA 2017. LNCS, vol. 10159, pp. 381–396. Springer, Cham (2017). https://doi.org/10.1007/978-3-319-52153-4_22
44. Papadimitriou, A., et al.: Big data analytics over encrypted datasets with seabed. In: 12th USENIX Symposium on Operating Systems Design and Implementation (OSDI 2016), pp. 587–602 (2016)
45. Pinkas, B., Rosulek, M., Trieu, N., Yanai, A.: SpOT-light: lightweight private set intersection from sparse OT extension. In: Boldyreva, A., Micciancio, D. (eds.) CRYPTO 2019. LNCS, vol. 11694, pp. 401–431. Springer, Cham (2019). https://doi.org/10.1007/978-3-030-26954-8_13
46. Pinkas, B., Rosulek, M., Trieu, N., Yanai, A.: PSI from PaXoS: fast, malicious private set intersection. In: Canteaut, A., Ishai, Y. (eds.) EUROCRYPT 2020. LNCS, vol. 12106, pp. 739–767. Springer, Cham (2020). https://doi.org/10.1007/978-3-030-45724-2_25
47. Pinkas, B., Schneider, T., Segev, G., Zohner, M.: Phasing: private set intersection using permutation-based hashing. In: USENIX (2015)
48. Pinkas, B., Schneider, T., Weinert, C., Wieder, U.: Efficient circuit-based PSI via cuckoo hashing. In: Nielsen, J.B., Rijmen, V. (eds.) EUROCRYPT 2018. LNCS, vol. 10822, pp. 125–157. Springer, Cham (2018). https://doi.org/10.1007/978-3-319-78372-7_5
49. Pinkas, B., Schneider, T., Zohner, M.: Faster private set intersection based on OT extension. In: USENIX (2014)
50. Pinkas, B., Schneider, T., Zohner, M.: Scalable private set intersection based on OT extension. IACR Cryptology ePrint Archive 2016, 930 (2016). http://eprint.iacr.org/2016/930
51. Pinkas, B., Schneider, T., Zohner, M.: Scalable private set intersection based on OT extension. ACM Trans. Priv. Secur. **21**(2), 7:1–7:35 (2018). https://doi.org/10.1145/3154794
52. Popa, R.A., Redfield, C.M., Zeldovich, N., Balakrishnan, H.: CryptDB: protecting confidentiality with encrypted query processing. In: Proceedings of the Twenty-Third ACM Symposium on Operating Systems Principles, pp. 85–100 (2011)
53. Resende, A.C.D., Aranha, D.F.: Unbalanced approximate private set intersection. IACR Cryptology ePrint Archive 2017, 677 (2017). http://eprint.iacr.org/2017/677
54. Rindal, P.: libPSI: an efficient, portable, and easy to use Private Set Intersection Library. https://github.com/osu-crypto/libPSI
55. Rindal, P., Rosulek, M.: Improved private set intersection against malicious adversaries. In: Coron, J.-S., Nielsen, J.B. (eds.) EUROCRYPT 2017. LNCS, vol. 10210, pp. 235–259. Springer, Cham (2017). https://doi.org/10.1007/978-3-319-56620-7_9
56. Rindal, P., Rosulek, M.: Malicious-secure private set intersection via dual execution. In: CCS (2017)
57. Poddar, R., Kalra, S., Yanai, A., Deng, R., Popa, R.A., Hellerstein, J.M.: Senate: a maliciously-secure MPC platform for collaborative analytics. IACR Cryptology ePrint Archive 2020, 1350 (2020)
58. Kamara, S., Mohassel, P., Raykova, M., Sadeghian, S.: Scaling private set intersection to billion-element sets. In: Financial Cryptography and Data Security, pp. 195–215 (2014)

59. Kolesnikov, V., Kumaresan, R.: Improved OT extension for transferring short secrets. In: Canetti, R., Garay, J.A. (eds.) CRYPTO 2013. LNCS, vol. 8043, pp. 54–70. Springer, Heidelberg (2013). https://doi.org/10.1007/978-3-642-40084-1_4
60. Wikipedia: Java native interface - Wikipedia (2020). https://en.wikipedia.org/wiki/Java_Native_Interface
61. Sun, Y., Hua, Y., Jiang, S., Li, Q., Cao, S., Zuo, P.: SmartCuckoo: a fast and cost-efficient hashing index scheme for cloud storage systems. In: USENIX Annual Technical Conference, pp. 553–565 (2017)
62. Ishai, Y., Kilian, J., Nissim, K., Petrank, E.: Extending oblivious transfers efficiently. In: Boneh, D. (ed.) CRYPTO 2003. LNCS, vol. 2729, pp. 145–161. Springer, Heidelberg (2003). https://doi.org/10.1007/978-3-540-45146-4_9
63. Zaharia, M., et al.: Resilient distributed datasets: a fault-tolerant abstraction for in-memory cluster computing. In: Presented as Part of the 9th USENIX Symposium on Networked Systems Design and Implementation (NSDI 2012), pp. 15–28 (2012)
64. Zaharia, M., Chowdhury, M., Franklin, M.J., Shenker, S., Stoica, I.: Spark: cluster computing with working sets. In: Proceedings of the 2nd USENIX Conference on Hot Topics in Cloud Computing, HotCloud 2010, USA, p. 10. USENIX Association (2010)
65. Zheng, W., Dave, A., Beekman, J.G., Popa, R.A., Gonzalez, J.E., Stoica, I.: Opaque: an oblivious and encrypted distributed analytics platform. In: 14th USENIX Symposium on Networked Systems Design and Implementation (NSDI 2017), pp. 283–298 (2017)

Lower Bounds on the Share Size of Leakage Resilient Cheating Detectable Secret Sharing

Sabyasachi Dutta[1](✉), Shaoquan Jiang[2], and Reihaneh Safavi-Naini[1]

[1] Department of Computer Science, University of Calgary, Calgary, Canada
{sabyasachi.dutta,rei}@ucalgary.ca

[2] School of Computer Science, University of Windsor, Windsor, Canada
jiangshq@uwindsor.ca

Abstract. Cheating detectable secret sharing schemes (CDSS) detects changes in the secret that is caused by an adversary who modifies shares of an unauthorized subset of participants. We consider leakage resilient cheating detectable secret sharing schemes (LRCDSS) where protection is against an adversary who, in addition to the shares of an unauthorized set, has access to the leakages from all other shares. We give lower bounds on the share size of these schemes when the scheme provides ϵ-indistinguishability security, and the adversary's modification of shares can be detected with probability at least $1-\delta$. We discuss our bounds in relation to other known results, relate CDSS with non-malleable secret sharing, and suggest directions for future work.

Keywords: secret sharing · leakage resilience · cheating detection · information theoretic security

1 Introduction

Secret sharing (SS) was independently proposed by Blakely [9] and Shamir [40], and forms a fundamental building block of important cryptographic systems including threshold cryptography [17,39] and multiparty computation [7,23], and their applications to securing distributed and decentralized systems [22,38].

A secret sharing scheme consists of two algorithms: a share generation algorithm Share that generates shares of a secret for n users $U = \{1, 2, \ldots, n\}$, and a Rec algorithm that takes the shares of a *qualified subset* of parties and reconstruct the original secret. The most widely used and studied secret sharing scheme is (k, n)-*threshold secret sharing* [9,40] where any subset of at least k parties is a qualified subset and can reconstruct the secret.

A secret sharing scheme in its basic form provides perfect *correctness* that guarantees the secret can always be correctly recovered by the shares of a qualified subset of participants, and *perfect (information theoretic) privacy* that guarantees no information will be leaked to the adversary who has access to the shares of a (maximal) unauthorized subset of participants. Perfect correctness

J. Deng et al. (Eds.): CANS 2023, LNCS 14342, pp. 468–493, 2023.
https://doi.org/10.1007/978-981-99-7563-1_21

and perfect privacy have been relaxed to β-correctness and ϵ-privacy, respectively, allowing reconstruction and privacy properties to fail with probabilities β and ϵ, respectively.

Security against Active Adversaries. We consider a setting where shares are generated and distributed by a trusted dealer, and an active adversary controls an unauthorized subset of parties. The adversary's goal is to change the reconstructed secret by modifying the shares of the parties that they control. In this paper we consider the problem of cheater detection which requires reconstruction algorithm to detect any tampering with the reconstructed secret.

Cheater detection was first introduced by Tompa and Woll [42], and later studied in [4,13,37,42]. Cheater detection is a basic security requirement against active attackers, and is important in practice as it prevents a wrong secret being used in the system. Schemes that provide cheater detection, *a.k.a cheater detectable secret sharing (CDSS)* have been proposed in [4,37,42]. Lower bounds on the share size of CDSS are derived in [13,37], where optimal constructions that satisfy the bounds with equality are presented.

Non-malleable Secret Sharing. Recently a weaker security notion against active adversaries, called *non-malleability*, has been proposed that uses a randomized coding scheme called *Non-malleable Codes (NMC)* [2,3,14,19,21,31,32] to ensure tampering with the coded secret does not lead to the decoding of a "related" secret. This security notion was later used to define Non-malleable Secret Sharing (NMSS) that has been widely studied [1,5,10,20,24,25,28,29,41].

In NMSS the adversary has access to a *class of tampering functions* $\mathcal{T}$ that can modify possibly all shares. Non-malleability protection requires that the reconstruction algorithm, when applied to the tampered shares, output a message (secret) that is either the same as the original secret or is "unrelated" to the secret (*see* Definition 11, and Definition 6).

A widely studied class of tampering functions is *the class of component-wise independent tampering* ($\mathcal{T}_{ind}$) where a tampering function g is defined by a vector of component tampering functions $\mathsf{g} = (\mathsf{g}_1, \cdots, \mathsf{g}_n)$. Here $\mathsf{g}_i, i = 1 \cdots n$ is the tampering function that is applied to the share S_i, and is chosen independent of the share values (i.e. before shares are generated). Stronger classes of tampering functions $\mathcal{T}_{\text{joint}}$ allow *joint tampering* with subsets of shares [10,11,24,25].

Security against both independent and joint tampering attacks were first considered for *single* round tampering, and later extended to multiple round tampering in information theoretic setting [1,5], and in computational setting [10,20].

Leakage-Resilient Secret Sharing (LRSS). Leakage-resilient cryptography [12,18,35] models adversaries that have access to the implementation of cryptographic systems and can obtain partial leakages of the secret state. We refer to the survey in [27] and references therein for more details on leakage-resilient cryptography.

Leakage resilience in secret sharing was first implicitly considered in [16] for a (2, 2) secret sharing. The surprising result of [26] showed that leaking a single physical bit from all shares in a Shamir SS over a binary (extension) field can break the privacy property of the secret sharing where privacy is defined in terms of distinguishability of two secrets. Formal definition of leakage resilience for (k, n) threshold secret sharing schemes was first considered in [24] in the context of non-malleable secret sharing, and in [8,33,34] in the context of linear secret sharing schemes that are used in leakage resilient secure multiparty computation. Leakage adversaries that can use leakage functions in the *class of leakage functions* $\mathcal{L}$, has been defined for static and adaptive adversaries in [1,41] and [29], respectively.

Local Leakage Model. In the *local* leakage model of secret sharing [1,24,41] the attacker defines a vector of leakage functions $\mathsf{f} = (\mathsf{f}_1, \mathsf{f}_2, \ldots, \mathsf{f}_n)$ independent of the secret and share values (before the secret is chosen, and the Share function is called). Each function f_j, $j \in [n]$ has an ℓ bit output that gives ℓ-bit leakage $\mathsf{f}_j(share_j)$ to the adversary. *We refer to this class of leakage functions as* `Local`.

The model in [1,41] allows a subset of component functions $\{\mathsf{f}_j\}_{j \in F}$ that correspond to an unauthorized set of parties, F, be identity functions and leak the whole shares. The remaining f_j's have ℓ-bit outputs. *We refer to this class of leakage functions as* `Local`$^+$. In this paper, we focus on `Local`$^+$ model; see Definition 3 for more details.

Leakage resilience of an SS against a class of leakage function $\mathcal{L}$ is formalized using the notion of indistinguishability that requires for any two secrets, the adversary's *views of the system* remain statistically close, where the view consists of public values of the system and the leakages of shares according to a function in $\mathcal{L}$.

Lower Bounds on the Share Size of CDSS. There are a number of lower bounds on the share sizes of cheater detectable secret sharing schemes. The best (tightest) lower bounds are due to Ogata *et al.* [37] who considered two models for tampering attacks - the OKS model where a secret is uniformly chosen from the secret set, and CDV model where the secret can have any distribution. The bounds are obtained by lower bounding the success probability of the adversary in a particular attack, and results in the following bounds,

$$|\mathcal{S}_i| \geq \frac{|\mathcal{S}| - 1}{\delta} + 1, \text{ in the OKS model and,}$$

$$|\mathcal{S}_i| \geq \frac{|\mathcal{S}| - 1}{\delta^2} + 1, \text{ in the CDV model.}$$

In these bounds, $\mathcal{S}_i$ and $\mathcal{S}$ are the share space and the secret space, respectively, and $1-\delta$ is the detection probability of cheating (or tampering) where probability in the CDV model is over the random coins of the Share function only, while in OKS model it is over the randomness of the Share function and uniform secret from secret space. Both bounds are tight and can be achieved with equality. Both bounds assume perfect correctness, and perfect privacy for the secret.

1.1 Contributions

We consider a (k, n)-threshold leakage resilient CDSS with security in the Local$^+$ model. The class of leakage functions in this model, denoted by $\mathcal{L}$, consists of vector functions $\mathbf{f}$ where each vector consists of component functions that each leak either ℓ bits from the share, or leak the whole share, and the number of the latter type is at most $k-1$, where k is the reconstruction threshold. A (k, n, ϵ, δ)-LRCDSS with security against an against an adversary who has access to leakages of a function $\mathbf{f} \in \mathcal{L}$, guarantees (i) ϵ indistinguishability security for the secret, and (ii) detection with probability at least $1-\delta$, of an incorrectly reconstructed secret, resulting from tampering of the shares that are controlled by the adversary.

Our main results are stated as follows.

Theorem 1 [Informal].
In a (k, n, ϵ, δ)-LRCDSS, to ensure detection probability of tampering is at most δ, the share size must be at least, $|\mathcal{S}_u| \geq 2^\ell \cdot \frac{|\mathcal{S}|(1-\epsilon)-1}{\delta}$. Otherwise there is an adversary that uses ℓ bits of leakage of a single share to modify that share, and remains undetected with probability at least δ.

Theorem 2 [Informal]. For a (k, n, ϵ, δ)-LRCDSS the share size must be at least $|\mathcal{S}_u| \geq 2^\ell \cdot \frac{1-\frac{1}{|\mathcal{S}|}}{(\delta+\epsilon)^2}$.

Otherwise there is an adversary that uses the shares of a maximal unauthorized set A, and ℓ bit leakage output of a specially constructed function f applied to the share S_i where $A \cup \{S_i\}$ is a minimal qualified set, and has success probability at least δ.

The theorems as stated above, are for threshold access structure and give bounds on the share size of LRCDSS when $\mathcal{L}$ is the family of all functions in the Local^+ model. Our attacks to obtain the bounds only use a weak leakage function in $\mathcal{L}$. This is further detailed as follows.

(i) For Theorem 1*:* The adversary obtains ℓ bit leakage that is the output of the application of a leakage function f to a share S_i which belongs to a minimal qualified set. Adversary can only tamper with S_i, and in particular replaces it with S_i'. The function f is known to the adversary, and satisfies a property *P1* (See Sect. 4), that can be satisfied by many functions.

(ii) For Theorem 2*:* The adversary learns shares of a maximal unauthorized set A, and receives ℓ bit leakage output of a function f applied on a share S_i, where $A \cup \{S_i\}$ is a (minimal) qualified set. The function f must satisfy the same property as (i) above. The adversary uses their information to tamper with a share $S_j \in A$.

Note that in (i) the adversary only needs to have the leaked information of a single share that belongs to a minimal qualified set, and be able to tamper with the same share. In (ii) the adversary uses the information of the shares of a maximal unauthorized set A together with ℓ bit leakage from the a share S_i where $A \cup \{S_i\}$ is a (minimal) authorized set used by the reconstruction algorithm, and tampers with one of the shares in A. The adversary in both cases is permissible for all access structures and all leakage classes that include a leakage function with a component function f_i with ℓ bit leakage, which is a very basic leakage function.

Technical Overview. In Theorem 1 the adversary uses only the ℓ bit leakage of a single share to devise a strategy to flip that share. The attack does not use all the information of an unauthorized set, and is available to the adversary in practice in a wide range of scenarios. For example in the case of a file that is broken into shares and each shares is stored on a different server, an adversary who obtains partial information about only one share (possibly through a side-channel) and is able to modify the share, can undetectably modify that reconstructed file.

Our main observation towards proving Theorem 1 is that the ϵ-privacy in Local^+ leakage model guarantees that $k-1$ full shares (say, $S_2, \ldots, S_k$) with leakage $v_1 = \mathsf{f}_1(S_1)$ of share S_1, give almost no information about the secret S. This means that all elements of the secret space $\mathcal{S}$ are possible secrets. In other words, a randomly chosen pre-image $S_1' \in \mathsf{f}_1^{-1}(v_1)$ w.r.t. f_1, together with the $k-1$ shares, will reconstruct a random secret. Thus the cheating attacker can revise S_1 to a randomly chosen pre-image of v_1. This is a valid/admissible cheating strategy for the attacker. With this cheating strategy, the adversary can succeed with probability of roughly $(|\mathcal{S}|-1)/|\mathsf{f}_1^{-1}(v_1)|$.

Bounding the success probability of the adversary in terms of the amount of leakage ℓ, and the privacy parameter ϵ however needs a number of steps that are given in the proof of the Theorem 1.

Theorem 2 lower bounds the success probability of an (inefficient) adversary that uses the information of shares of a maximal unauthorized set A and the leakage of an additional share that completes A to a qualified set, and replaces one of the a shares in A with a fraudulent one. For this, we first observe that the number of possible S_1' in the share space of S_1, that together with the $k-2$ other shares in A and a specific share S_K reconstruct a valid secret, is at most $\delta|\mathcal{S}_1|$ (otherwise, taking a random s_1' will allow to obtain the cheating probability better than δ, where the attacker controls the first $k-1$ shares and the honest user has the share S_K). We note that the expected size of the preimage set of $\mathsf{f}_1(S_1)$ for a randomly selected ℓ-bit leakage function f_1 is $2^{-\ell}|\mathcal{S}_1|$, and so for a fixed leakage value $\mathsf{f}_1(S_1)$, the number of possible preimages S_1', is $\delta 2^{-\ell}|\mathcal{S}_1|$.

The adversary can then use a guessing attack from the smaller space and replaces S_1 with a randomly chosen value from the set of $\delta 2^{-\ell}|\mathcal{S}_1|$ possible S_1'. The success probability of this attack is lower bounded by $1/(\delta 2^{-\ell}|\mathcal{S}_1|)$. Since this is upper bounded by δ, we obtain a relation between $1/(\delta 2^{-\ell}|\mathcal{S}_1|)$ and δ and hence a lower bound for δ. The computation details and establishing the relation with ϵ (privacy parameter) and δ (maximum cheating probability) is given in the proof of Theorem 2.

The bound shows the share size grows inversely to the quadratic value of the sum of the leakage resilience and cheating detection parameters.

Discussion and Comparison. For $\ell = 0$ (no leakage from the uncorrupted shares) and $\epsilon = 0$ (the secret is perfectly hidden), the bound in **Theorem** 1 is the same as the lower bound for the OKS model in [37] (*see* Page 3). **Theorem** 2 however for $\ell = 0$ and $\epsilon = 0$ gives a bound $\frac{1-1/|\mathcal{S}|}{\delta^2}$ in the OKS model. This bound is also applicable to the share size in the CDV model because of the relation between the models (CDV can be seen as the worst case while OKS is average case), but it is weaker than the CDV bound $\frac{|S|-1}{\delta^2}+1$ in [37].

We note that CDV bound applies to systems with for perfect privacy while our derived bound applies to ϵ-privacy. The bound in Theorem 2 shows that the share size of an (k,n,ϵ,δ)-LRCDSS where the leakage function $\mathbf{f} \in \mathcal{L}$, is lower bounded by $\frac{2^{\ell-1}}{(\epsilon+\delta)^2}$ for $|S| \geq 2$ and for large enough secret space it is approximately $\frac{2^{\ell}}{(\epsilon+\delta)^2}$.

Relation to Non-malleable Secret Sharing (NMSS). In [19] it was noted that error detection implies non-malleability if for any tampering function, the probability that the tampered codeword is invalid is the same for all messages.

In Sect. 6 we show that cheating detection property can be formulated as non-malleability against a special class of tampering functions. Proposition 1 shows that if a (k,n)-threshold secret sharing with perfect correctness and perfect privacy is a (k,n,σ)-$NMSS_{cd}$, it is also a (k,n,σ)-CDSS, in CDV model. This result can be extended to the case that the adversary also has access to leakages of $\mathbf{f} \in \mathcal{L}$.

Combining this result with Theorems 1 and 2, we obtain lower bounds on the share size of non-malleable secret sharing when the tampering class consists of the set of joint tampering of the shares of an unauthorized set, and the tampering function is selected after obtaining leakages from all the shares according to a leakage function $\mathbf{f} \in \mathcal{L}$ (see Sect. 6).

In Sect. 6 we compare this bound with the only other known bound on the share size of LRNMSS due to Brian et al. [10]. We show that the two bounds although both applicable to LRNMSS but are not directly comparable because (i) they are for two different classes of tampering functions that do not have inclusion relationship (i.e. one class is not contained in the other), and (ii) although both are lower bounds on the share size, they are stated in terms of different sets of parameters of secret sharing schemes. More details is in Sect. 6.

1.2 Related Works

Lower bounds on the share size of CDSS are given in [13,37]. Theorem 1 and Theorem 2 are inspired by the approach in [37] that provide tight lower bounds for OKS and CDV models.

Bounds on the share size of LRSS are given in [36] for Local and Local$^+$ leakage models, and are implied using compiler constructions for LRSS [41]. Srinivasan and Vasudevan [41] also considered *strong local leakage* where the leakage of the *uncorrupted shares* (not in the unauthorized set of shares seen by the adversary) is allowed to depend on the shares of the unauthorized set. This allows the adversary to choose the vector of leakage functions after learning the shares of an unauthorized set. Kumar, Meka and Sahai [29] proposed a general *adaptive leakage* model for ℓ-bit leakage that is described as a multi-round communication protocol, and gave a secure construction for the model.

Share tampering with the goal of providing non-malleability is considered in [1,5,25,29,41]. Share efficiency in these works is measured in terms of rate of the scheme which is defined as the ratio of the secret length to the maximum size of a share. Our bounds give concrete bounds on the share size of NM secret sharing and leakage resilient secret sharing.

Leakage resilience of non-malleable SS was studied by Kumar, Meka and Sahai [29] and Lin *et al.* [30]. Kumar *et al.* [29] defined and constructed LR NMSS that allows an adversary to have adaptive leakage from shares to choose the tampering functions. Lin *et al.* considered affine leakage functions and gave constructions for LR-NMSS for that class. Brian *et al.* [10] while considering the question of constructing continuously non-malleable secret sharing also proved an important result. They showed that every one-time statistically non-malleable secret sharing against joint tampering is also a leakage-resilient non-malleable (with some loss in the security parameter) where the adversary first leaks jointly from the shares and then tampers with them.

Organization. Section 2 gives background models and definitions. Section 3, 4 and 5 give some preliminary results needed for proving the lower bounds and lower bounds on share size of LRCDSS in two cases: with and without considering the share information of an unauthorized set, respectively. Section 6 relates CDSS and non-malleable secret sharing and discusses the implication of the bounds. Section 7 is the conclusion.

2 Model and Definitions

We use capital letters such as X to denote random variables and lower case letters such as x to show the realizations of X. For a vector $\boldsymbol{v}$ and index set T, we use $\boldsymbol{v}_T$ to denote the sub vector of $\boldsymbol{v}$ with components v_i for every $i \in T$.

Statistical Distance. Let X and Y denote two random variables that are defined over a set S. The statistical distance between the two variables is defined as $\Delta(X, Y) = \sum_{s \in S} |\Pr[X = s] - \Pr[Y = s]|$. Sometimes it is also denoted by $\Delta(P_X, P_Y)$, or even $\Delta(P, Q)$ if only distributions P, Q are specified.

We say X and Y are ϵ-close if $\Delta(X, Y) \leq \epsilon$ and is denoted by $X \approx_\epsilon Y$. It is well-known that if $X \approx_{\epsilon_1} Y$ and $Y \approx_{\epsilon_2} Z$ then $X \approx_{\epsilon_1+\epsilon_2} Z$.

2.1 Secret Sharing

In a secret sharing system a secret is distributed among a user set U such that authorized subsets of users can reconstruct the secret, and the secret is statistically hidden from an unauthorised set. Let Γ be a subset of the power set, 2^U, that specifies the subsets of users that form an authorized set; *i.e.* the set of their shares can recover the secret. A subset $F \subset U$ which is not in Γ, *i.e.* $F \notin \Gamma$, is called an unauthorized set and the set of shares $(S_u)_{u \in F}$ will be independent of secret S. We only consider *monotone* access structures: if $A_1 \in \Gamma$ and $A_1 \subseteq A_2$, then $A_2 \in \Gamma$. Moreover, the collection of unauthorized sets is denoted by $\mathcal{F}$. Note that, in our model $\Gamma \cap \mathcal{F} = \emptyset$ and $\Gamma \cup \mathcal{F} = 2^U$. A formal definition of secret sharing [6] is as follows.

Definition 1 **($(\Gamma, U, \beta, \epsilon)$ Secret Sharing Scheme).** *Let U be a set of n users labeled by $[n] = \{1, 2, \ldots, n\}$. Let $(\Gamma, \mathcal{F})$ denote an access structure on these n users with $\mathcal{F} = 2^U \backslash \Gamma$. A secret sharing scheme Π for an access structure $(\Gamma, \mathcal{F})$ consists of a pair of algorithms (Share, Rec). Share is a randomized algorithm that gets as input a secret S (from a domain of secrets $\mathcal{S}$ with at least two elements), Γ and the number of parties n, and generates n shares $(S_1, \ldots, S_n) \longleftarrow \mathsf{Share}(S)$. Rec is a deterministic algorithm that gets as input the shares of a subset B of parties and outputs a string. The requirements for defining a secret sharing scheme are as follows:*

- β-Correctness: *If $\{S_u\}_u \leftarrow \mathsf{Share}(S)$ for some secret $S \in \mathcal{S}$, then for any $B \in \Gamma$, we always have $Pr[\mathsf{Rec}(\{S_u\}_{u \in B}) = S] \geq 1 - \beta$.*
- ϵ-privacy: *Let $\{S_u\}_u = \mathsf{Share}(S)$. For $F \in \mathcal{F}$, let $S_F = \{S_u\}_{u \in F}$. Then, for any $s', s'' \in \mathcal{S}$, the statistical distance between the conditional random variables $S_F|S$ satisfies $\Delta(P_{S_F|S}(\cdot|s'), P_{S_F|S}(\cdot|s'')) \leq \epsilon$*

In this paper, we consider $\beta = 0$, that is perfect correctness, and statistical privacy, that is $\epsilon \neq 0$. In a (k, n)-threshold secret sharing any subset of at least k shares reconstructs the secret, and any set of $k - 1$ or less shares does not reveal any information about the secret. Furthermore, Γ consists of the set of all subsets of U of size at least k. In the above definition of secret sharing scheme the adversary is passive and follows the protocol.

2.2 Cheater Detection

Cheater detection in threshold secret sharing, was first proposed in [42], and considers security against an active adversary that does not follow the protocol. A *cheating adversary* is defined for a maximal unauthorised set C. and works as follows. For a secret $s \in \mathcal{S}$ that is shared by an honest dealer using the algorithm $\mathsf{Share}(s)$, the adversary takes the shares of C and replaces them with an arbitrary set of share values. The adversary succeeds if the reconstruction algorithm applied to a minimal authorized set T, where $C \subset T$, outputs a secret $s' \neq s$, without being detected. That is, $\mathsf{Rec}(\{S_u\}_{u \in T \backslash C}, \{S'_u\}_{u \in C}) \notin \{S, \perp\}$.

There are two commonly used types of cheating detection, OKS where the secret is chosen from a uniform distribution on secret space, and CDV where the property holds for any secret that is known to the adversary. We consider OKS model and a cheating detectable scheme is defined as follows (adapted from [37]).

Definition 2 **(Cheating Detectable Secret Sharing [37]).** *Let SS = (Share, Rec) be a (k, n)-threshold secret sharing scheme. The scheme SS is said to be (k, n, δ)-cheating detectable secret sharing (or (k, n, δ)-CDSS for short) in the OKS model if besides correctness and perfect privacy of a general secret sharing, it additionally satisfies the following.*

- *cheating detection: for s uniformly random over $\mathcal{S}$, for every $F \subset \{1, \ldots, n\}$ of size $|F| = k-1$ and for any $i \notin F$, the reconstruction $\mathsf{Rec}(\widetilde{\mathsf{sh}}_F, \mathsf{sh}_i) \in \{s, \perp\}$ holds, except with probability δ, where the modified shares $\widetilde{\mathsf{sh}}_F$ only depend on the shares in F i.e. sh_F.*

Note 1. In the cheating detection property of the above definition, the secret is uniformly random and unknown to adversary. If the secret s is known to adversary, then the corresponding model is as (k, n, δ)-CDSS in the CDV model.

2.3 Leakage Resilient Secret Sharing

We consider the local leakage model proposed by Srinivasan *et al.* [41] (and concurrently by Aggarwal *et al.* [1]) which has been used in numerous follow-up works [10,30,33,36].

Definition 3 (Local leakage family [41]). *Let $\mathcal{S}_1 \times \cdots \times \mathcal{S}_n$ be the domain of shares for some secret sharing scheme realizing a (k, n)-threshold access structure. The family $\mathcal{H}_{k,\ell}$ parameterized by threshold k and the number of leaked bits ℓ per share, consists of leakage functions $\mathbf{f}_H = (f_1, \ldots, f_n)$ where $H \subset [n]$ such that*

- $|H| = k - 1$
- *f_i is identity function for all $i \in H$ and $f_j : \mathcal{S}_j \longrightarrow \{0,1\}^\ell$ for all $j \notin H$. More precisely, the function $\mathbf{f}_H$ when given input $(\mathsf{sh}_1, \ldots, \mathsf{sh}_n)$, outputs*
  - *sh_i for all $i \in H$ and*
  - *ℓ-bit leakages $f_j(\mathsf{sh}_j)$ for all $j \in \{1, \ldots, n\} \backslash H$.*

We now introduce the leakage-resilient secret sharing (adapted from [24,41]).

Definition 4 (Local$^+$ Leakage-Resilient Secret Sharing Scheme). *A (k, n)-threshold secret sharing scheme for secret space $\mathcal{S}$ and share and reconstruction algorithms $(\mathsf{Share}, \mathsf{Rec})$ is ϵ-leakage resilient against a (local) leakage family $\mathcal{H}_{k,\ell}$ if it satisfies correctness and privacy as defined below.*

- *(Perfect Correctness) for every $s \in \mathcal{S}$ and every $Q \subset \{1, \ldots, n\}$ of size $|Q| = k$, it holds that for $\{\mathsf{sh}_i\}_{i \in [n]} \leftarrow \mathsf{Share}(s)$ that $Pr[\mathsf{Rec}(\{\mathsf{sh}_i\}_{i \in Q}) = s] = 1$.*

- *(ϵ-Privacy against Leakage) For all function $\mathbf{f}_H \in \mathcal{H}_{k,\ell}$ and for any two secrets $m_0, m_1 \in \mathcal{S}$, we have $\Delta\left(\mathbf{f}_H(\mathsf{Share}(m_0)), \mathbf{f}_H(\mathsf{Share}(m_1))\right) \leq \epsilon$.*

2.4 Leakage Resilient Cheating Detectable Secret Sharing

In this section, we define leakage resilient cheating detectable secret sharing (LRCDSS). Essentially, it is leakage resilient secret sharing against leakage family $\mathcal{H}_{k,\ell}$ (i.e., in the Local^+ model) with cheating detection capability. Since this is the main definition in this paper, we present it in details.

Definition 5 (Leakage Resilient Cheating Detectable Secret Sharing). *A (k, n)-threshold secret sharing scheme $SS = (\mathsf{Share}, \mathsf{Rec})$ is said to be $(k, n, \ell, \epsilon, \delta)$-leakage resilient and cheating detectable (or $(k, n, \ell, \epsilon, \delta)$-LRCDSS) in the OKS model if the following three conditions are satisfied.*

- *Correctness: for every $s \in \mathcal{S}$ and every minimal authorized set $Q \subset \{1, \dots, n\}$ of size $|Q| = k$, it holds that for $\mathsf{sh} \leftarrow \mathsf{Share}(s)$ that* $\Pr[\mathsf{Rec}(\mathsf{sh}_Q) = s] = 1$.
- *ϵ-Privacy against Local^+ Leakage: For all function $\mathbf{f}_H \in \mathcal{H}_{k,\ell}$ for some $H \subset [n]$ with $|H| = k - 1$ and for any two secrets $m_0, m_1 \in \mathcal{S}$ the statistical distance: $\Delta(\mathbf{f}_H(\mathsf{Share}(m_0)), \mathbf{f}_H(\mathsf{Share}(m_1))) \leq \epsilon$.*
- *OKS cheating detection: Let $s \in \mathcal{S}$ be uniformly random over $\mathcal{S}$ and $\mathsf{sh} = \mathsf{Share}(s)$. The adversary is given access to $\mathbf{f}_H(\mathsf{sh})$, and modifies sh_H to $\widetilde{\mathsf{sh}}_H$. The scheme is cheating detectable if for any $i \notin H$, the reconstruction $\mathsf{Rec}(\widetilde{\mathsf{sh}}_H, \mathsf{sh}_i) \in \{s, \perp\}$ except with probability δ.*

Note 2. We can also define (k, n, ϵ, δ)-**LRCDSS in the CDV model**, with the only difference in the definition of cheating detection.

- CDV cheating detection: Same as OKS cheating detection except that the secret $s \in \mathcal{S}$ is chosen using any distribution.

Note 3. Definition 5 generalizes the Definition 2 in two ways. Firstly, it generalizes perfect privacy to ϵ-privacy; secondly, both privacy and cheating detection hold against an adversary who chooses a leakage family $\mathcal{H}_{k,\ell}$ (instead leakage of $k - 1$ shares) and after seeing the output of the leakage function, chooses their tampering function.

3 Preliminaries

In this section we introduce two basic lemmas which will be used in proving our lower bounds. The following lemma by Csiszár [15] gives the relation between probability distance and mutual information.

Lemma 1 *(Lemma 1 of [15]). Let X, Y be random variables over $\mathbb{X}, \mathbb{Y}$ respectively. Let $D = \Delta(P_{XY}; P_X P_Y)$. Then*

$$\frac{1}{2 \ln 2} D^2 \leq I(X;Y) \leq D \log \frac{|\mathbb{X}|}{D}, \tag{1}$$

where the second inequality holds under condition $|\mathbb{X}| \geq 4$.

From this result, we prove a lemma that will be used in analyzing the privacy or leakage resilience. The proof is deferred to Appendix B.

Lemma 2. *Let S, Y be two variables over $\mathcal{S}$ and $\mathcal{Y}$ respectively with $|\mathcal{S}| \geq 4$. If for any $s', s'' \in \mathcal{S}$,*

$$\Delta(P_{Y|S}(\cdot|s'), P_{Y|S}(\cdot|s'')) \leq \epsilon, \tag{2}$$

then $\Delta(P_{SY}, P_S P_Y) \leq \epsilon$ and $I(S;Y) \leq \epsilon \log \frac{|\mathcal{S}|}{\epsilon}$.

In a ϵ-secret sharing scheme, let S denote the secret and Y denote the vector of shares corresponding to an unauthorized set. From the above lemma, we know that $I(S;Y) < \epsilon \log \frac{|\mathcal{S}|}{\epsilon}$ and $\Delta(P_{SY}; P_S P_Y) < \epsilon$. This provides the ϵ-privacy with an information theoretical interpretation: unauthorized shares have little information about the secret and they are almost statistically independent.

4 A Lower Bound Using Leakage and Tampering of a Single Share

In this section we derive a lower bound on the share size for (k, n, ϵ, δ)-LRCDSS in the OKS model. Our strategy is to prove a lower bound on the cheating probability which involves the share size and can hence be used to get a lower bound on share size. Our lower bound on cheating probability of a leakage resilient secret sharing scheme is obtained by considering a rather weak attacker who does not use the leakage from all shares and instead uses the leakage from a *single* share. We show that this minimal amount of information suffices for an adversary to launch an attack that has a non-trivial cheating probability and hence obtain a lower bound on δ.

In the following we show a share tampering strategy for an adversary that has the leakage only from a single share of a minimal qualified set, where the leakage function of this share satisfies a certain property. The adversary has the ability to arbitrarily modify this share.

Let $\{S_1, \cdots, S_k\}$ be the share set of a minimal qualified set, and let $\mathsf{f}_1(S_1)$ be an ℓ-bit leakage function on S_1, where f_1 is known by the attacker, and satisfies

Property P1: Preimage set $\mathsf{f}_1^{-1}(\mathsf{f}_1(S_1))$ has a size of about $2^{-\ell}|\mathcal{S}_1|$ for all $S_1 \in \mathcal{S}_1$.

This property can be be easily satisfied using functions that partition the domain $\mathcal{S}_1$ into 2^ℓ parts of (almost) equal size, and map all elements of one part to a single ℓ-bit value. We can fix f_1 as any function satisfying this property (so the attacker does not need to adaptively choose this).

Technical Observation. By ϵ-privacy of LRCDSS , $(\mathsf{f}_1(S_1), S_2, \cdots, S_k)$ does not significantly reduce the uncertainty of S (*see* Lemma 2 for interpreting). That is to say, S is almost independent of this vector *i.e.* given this leakage vector, almost every element of $\mathcal{S}$ remains a candidate for the secret S and with almost the same probability. To get hold of the idea, we can assume every element in $\mathcal{S}$ is a candidate. Since $(S_1, \cdots, S_k)$ determines S, it follows that for each possible candidate secret S', there must exist an S_1' such that $\mathsf{Rec}(S_1', S_2, \cdots, S_k) = S'$ with $f_1(S_1') = f_1(S_1)$ (otherwise, S' is not possible to be a candidate, given $f_1(S_1), S_2, \cdots, S_k$).

Since, for every S', there exists S_1' such that $\mathsf{Rec}(S_1', S_2, \cdots, S_k) = S'$, there are at least $|\mathcal{S}| - 1$ choices of S_1' such that $\mathsf{Rec}(S_1', S_2, \cdots, S_k))$ is different from the original S.

Attack Strategy. For a function f_1 that is known to the attacker and satisfies property *P1*. Assume $(S_1, \cdots, S_k)$ will be used in the reconstruction algorithm, where only S_1 is known to attacker. The attacker then computes $\mathsf{f}_1(S_1)$ and replaces S_1 by S_1' which is chosen randomly from the preimage set $\mathsf{f}_1^{-1}(\mathsf{f}_1(S_1))$. Attacker succeeds if $\mathsf{Rec}(S_1', S_2, \cdots, S_k)$ differs from the original secret S.

The above technical observation reveals that the cheating probability δ is at least $\frac{|\mathcal{S}|-1}{|\mathsf{f}_1^{-1}(\mathsf{f}_1(S_1))|}$ which can be approximated by $\frac{|\mathcal{S}|-1}{2^{-\ell}|\mathcal{S}_1|}$, as the size of $\mathsf{f}_1^{-1}(\mathsf{f}_1(S_1))$ is roughly $2^{-\ell}|\mathcal{S}_1|$.

In the following we state our results for threshold LRCDSS scheme. We emphasize that our result can be generalized to a general access structure LRCDSS setting, by using shares of a minimal authorised set instead of k shares.

Theorem 1. *Let $SS = (\mathsf{Share}, \mathsf{Rec})$ be (k, n, ϵ, δ)-LRCDSS in the OKS model. Then, $\delta \geq \frac{|\mathcal{S}|(1-\epsilon)-1}{\lceil |\mathcal{S}_u| 2^{-\ell} \rceil - 1}$, where $\mathcal{S}_u$ is the space of the uth share. Therefore, the share size $|\mathcal{S}_u| \geq 2^{\ell} \cdot \frac{|\mathcal{S}|(1-\epsilon)-1}{\delta}$.*

Proof. Deferred to Appendix B

Remark 1. When there is no leakage (i.e., $\ell = 0$) and the privacy is perfect (i.e., $\epsilon = 0$), the lower bound in the above theorem is degenerated to $\delta \geq \frac{|\mathcal{S}|-1}{|\mathcal{S}_u|-1}$. This is exactly the bound on δ in [37] for (k, n, δ)-CDSS in the OKS model.

5 A Lower Bound Using Shares of an Unauthorized Set and Leakage of a Single Share

In the previous section, we obtained a lower bound on the cheating probability from a weaker adversary who only uses one share and chooses the modified share from the preimage of this share's leakage value. The attacker did not consider the leakages from the uncorrupted shares when tampering his own share. This is a very special case of the cheating adversary in Definition 5. In this section, we derive a lower bound on δ using the leakage from uncorrupted shares. As before, let us consider the minimal number of qualified shares $S_1, \cdots, S_k$ of secret S. We start with two important observations and then outline the intuition behind our proof strategy.

Observation 1. The number of s_1' in $\mathcal{S}_1$ such that $\mathsf{Rec}(s_1', S_2, \cdots, S_k) \neq \perp$ is at most about $\delta|\mathcal{S}_1|$, where δ denotes the maximum cheating probability. Otherwise, an attacker, who corrupts S_1, can break the cheating threshold δ by simply sampling $s_1' \leftarrow \mathcal{S}_1$ as his modified share. Then, $S' \stackrel{\text{def}}{:=} \mathsf{Rec}(s_1', S_2, \cdots, S_k)$ is not $\perp$ with probability significantly larger than δ. On the other hand, it is unlikely that $S' = S$ (as S' is random and can be any value in $\mathcal{S}$). Thus, attacker's success probability is larger than δ, which is a contradiction to the definition of δ.

Observation 2. We consider a *random* leakage function f_1 of S_1 in the following manner – randomly partition $\mathcal{S}_1$ into 2^{ℓ} subsets and define the f_1 value of every element in set i to be i. Since each s_1' is assigned to set i with probability $2^{-\ell}$, set i (i.e., $\mathsf{f}_1^{-1}(i)$) on average has a size $2^{-\ell}|\mathcal{S}_1|$. If we only look at the elements of s_1' in set i so that $\mathsf{Rec}(s_1', S_2, \cdots, S_k) \neq \perp$, then this restricted set has a size at most about $2^{-\ell}\delta|\mathcal{S}_1|$ (by Observation 1).

Idea to Lower Bound δ. Lower bounding on δ is actually just to present an attack achieving the desired success probability. Assume $\{S_1, \cdots, S_k\}$ is the shares of a minimal qualified set. Attacker corrupts $S_2, \cdots, S_k$ and obtains the leakage $\mathsf{f}_1(S_1)$ of an uncorrupted share S_1. Then, he computes $\mathsf{f}_1^{-1}(\mathsf{f}_1(S_1)) \stackrel{def}{=} \{v_1, \cdots, v_N\}$ from the leakage $\mathsf{f}_1(S_1)$ (Note: N is a random variable, depending on corrupted shares and f_1). Then, the attacker randomly samples v_u from $\{v_1, \cdots, v_N\}$ (hoping that $v_u = S_1$) and then try to find x_u in $\mathcal{S}_2$ so that $\mathsf{Rec}(v_u, x_u, S_3, \cdots, S_k) \neq \perp$. If there are more than one such x_u's, choose one randomly. Attacker then outputs x_u as his modified share for S_2. He will succeed if $\mathsf{Rec}(v_u, x_u, S_3, \cdots, S_k) \neq \mathsf{Rec}(v_u, S_2, S_3, \cdots, S_k)$ and $v_u = S_1$. In the proof, we show that if $v_u = S_1$, then the attacker will succeed with high probability. Notice that $v_u = S_1$ occurs with probability $1/N \approx \frac{1}{2^{-\ell}\delta|\mathcal{S}_1|}$ (by Observation 2). Since the cheating probability is upper bounded by δ, it follows that δ has a lower bound about $1/N \approx \frac{1}{2^{-\ell}\delta|\mathcal{S}_1|}$ and so δ has a lower bound about $\sqrt{\frac{1}{2^{-\ell}|\mathcal{S}_1|}}$.

In the following theorem, we make the above intuitive analysis rigorous.

Theorem 2. *Let SS = (Share, Rec) be (k, n, ϵ, δ)-LRCDSS in the OKS model. Then, $\delta \geq \sqrt{\frac{1-1/|\mathcal{S}|}{2^{-\ell}|\mathcal{S}_u|}} - \epsilon$ and hence the share size $|\mathcal{S}_u| \geq 2^{\ell} \cdot \frac{1-\frac{1}{|\mathcal{S}|}}{(\delta+\epsilon)^2}$. For $|\mathcal{S}| \geq 2$, we note that the lower bound on the share size is at least $2^{\ell-1} \cdot \frac{1}{(\delta+\epsilon)^2}$.*

Proof. Deferred to Appendix B.

Remark 2. When there is no leakage (i.e., $\ell = 0$) and the privacy is perfect (*i.e.*, $\epsilon = 0$), the lower bound in Theorem 2 implies that $|\mathcal{S}_u| \geq \frac{1-\frac{1}{|\mathcal{S}|}}{\delta^2} \geq \frac{1}{2\delta^2}$. That is, the share size increases as a quadratic in the parameter $1/\delta$. This result has resemblance with the bound $|\mathcal{S}_u| \geq \frac{|\mathcal{S}|-1}{\delta^2} + 1$ for the cheating detectable (but no leakage from uncorrupted shares) secret sharing in [37] in the CDV model (where S can be known to attacker). Note our bound is for a weaker adversary (i.e., OKS model where S is uniformly random and unknown to attacker).

6 Cheater Detectability and Non-Malleability in Secret Sharing

Non-malleable secret sharing schemes (NMSS) were introduced by Goyal and Kumar [24] to protect the secret against tampering by requiring that the attacker cannot tamper with the shares of the secret such that a related but different secret can be reconstructed. The reconstructed secret (if any) must be "unrelated" to the original one. They defined non-malleability using a simulation-based approach that requires the statistical distance between two random variables where one is the output of a real world tampering experiment, and the second one is the output of an ideal world simulator that samples from a fixed distribution, be a small value σ. The quantity σ is referred to as the "simulation error".

We first recall the definition of non-malleable secret sharing by Goyal and Kumar [24,25], that follows the approach of Dziembowski *et al.* [19] in defining non-malleable codes. (Definition of NM codes is recalled in the Appendix.)

Definition 6 (Non-malleable threshold Secret Sharing [24]). *Let (Share, Rec) be a secret sharing scheme realizing a (k, n)-threshold access structure for secret space $\mathcal{S}$. Let $\mathcal{T}$ be some family of tampering functions. For each $g \in \mathcal{T}$, secret $s \in \mathcal{S}$ and authorized set T containing k indices, define the tampering experiment*

$$Tamper_s^{g,T} = \left\{ \begin{array}{l} share \longleftarrow Share(s) \\ \widetilde{share} \longleftarrow g(share) \\ \widetilde{s} \longleftarrow Rec(\widetilde{share_T}) \\ output\ : \widetilde{s} \end{array} \right\}$$ *with associated random variable*

$Tamper_s^{g,T}$, which is a random variable over the randomness of the sharing function Share. The secret sharing scheme (Share, Rec) is σ-non-malleable with respect to the function class $\mathcal{T}$, if for every $g \in \mathcal{T}$ and every authorized set T of k shares, there exists a distribution $D^{g,T}$ over $\mathcal{S} \cup \{\mathsf{same}^*, \perp\}$ such that for every secret $s \in \mathcal{S}$, the following holds :

$$Tamper_s^{g,T} \approx_\sigma \left\{ \begin{array}{l} \widetilde{s} \longleftarrow D^{g,T} \\ output\text{: } s \text{ if } \widetilde{s} = \mathsf{same}^* \text{ and } \widetilde{s} \text{ otherwise.} \end{array} \right\}$$

In the above, "$\approx_\sigma$" means that the statistical distance between the two distributions is at most σ. The distribution $D^{g,T}$ should be efficiently samplable given oracle access to $g(\cdot)$.

Defining Cheating Detection Using Simulation-Based Approach. Cheating detectability and non-malleability both consider active unbounded adversaries. To relate the two security notions, we first provide a simulation based approach to capture cheating detection. Cheating detectability is defined for a class of functions where the adversary has access to the shares of a maximal unauthorized set, and jointly tampers with the shares, keeping the rest of the shares unaltered. The cheating detection property can be formulated as non-malleability of the secret sharing for the following tampering function family.

Definition 7 (Joint Tampering function family). *We consider (k, n)-threshold access secret sharing. For any maximal unauthorized set $H \subset [n]$ (i.e. $|H| = k - 1$), define a* joint tampering function g_H *as a function that takes a vector of n shares and outputs a vector of n shares, $g_H : \mathcal{S}_1 \times \cdots \times \mathcal{S}_n \longrightarrow \mathcal{S}_1 \times \cdots \times \mathcal{S}_n$, which is determined by H and a joint tampering function $g_{[H]}$ defined on shares of the index set H, $g_{[H]} : \times_{j \in H} \mathcal{S}_j \longrightarrow \times_{j \in H} \mathcal{S}_j$ that takes $k-1$ shares corresponding to the indices in H, and outputs a vector of $k-1$ shares for the same indices. Given input $(sh_1, \cdots, sh_n)$, the output of function g_H is given by,*

- $sh'_i = sh_i$ *for all* $i \in [n] \backslash H$, *and*
- $sh'_i = g_{[H]}((sh_j)_{j \in H})[i]$, *for* $i \in H$

where $g_{[H]}((sh_j)_{j \in H})[i]$ is the component of $g_{[H]}$ output for index $i \in H$.

That is, for any maximal unauthorized set H, a joint tampering function acts on all the shares, keeping the shares in $[n] \backslash H$ unaltered and jointly modifies the shares with indexes in H using an arbitrary function $g_{[H]}$.

For a maximal unauthorized set H, define $\mathcal{T}_H^{cdss}$ to be the set of all joint tampering functions as defined in Definition 7, and let $\mathcal{T}^{cdss}$ denote the union of $\mathcal{T}_H^{cdss}$ for all H. That is, $\mathcal{T}^{cdss} = \cup_H \mathcal{T}_H^{cdss}$. Thus a function in $\mathcal{T}^{cdss}$ is indexed by a maximal unauthorized set H.

Cheating detectability for secret sharing is captured by requiring the reconstructed secret to be either the original secret, or $\perp$. In terms of non-malleable secret sharing at Definition 6, this is modeled by requiring the distribution $D^{g_H,T}$ be on the set $\{\mathsf{same}^*, \perp\}$. where T is any minimal authorized set that contains H (*i.e.* $H \subset T$).

Definition 8. *Let* (Share, Rec) *be a* (k, n)*-threshold secret sharing scheme for secret space* $\mathcal{S}$. (Share, Rec) *is called* (k, n, σ)*-NMSS*$_{cd}$ *against tampering family* $\mathcal{T}^{cdss}$, *if*

- *for any* H *with* $|H| = k - 1$, *for any* k*-sized set* T *containing* H, *and any tampering function* $g_H \in \mathcal{T}^{cdss}$, *there is a distribution* $D^{g_H,T}$ *on* $\{\mathsf{same}^*, \perp\}$ *such that*

$$Tamper_s^{g_H,T} \approx_\sigma \left\{ \begin{array}{l} \widetilde{s} \longleftarrow D^{g_H,T} \\ output\text{: } s \text{ if } \widetilde{s} = \mathsf{same}^* \text{ and } \perp \text{ otherwise.} \end{array} \right\}$$

Here, the tampering experiment $Tamper_s^{g_H,T}$ *is defined as*

$$Tamper_s^{g_H,T} = \left\{ \begin{array}{l} \mathsf{share} \longleftarrow \mathsf{Share}(s) \\ \widetilde{\mathsf{share}} \longleftarrow g_H(\mathsf{share}) \\ \widetilde{s} \longleftarrow \mathsf{Rec}(\widetilde{\mathsf{shares}}_T) \\ output\ :\ \widetilde{s} \end{array} \right\}$$

Also, $D^{g_H,T}$ *is efficiently samplable given oracle access to* $g_H(\cdot)$.

We note that (k, n, σ)-NMSS$_{cd}$ property is defined for the same adversary of Sect. 2.2 but uses a different way of quantifying security. The proposition below relates insecurity measure and simulation error of Definition 2 and Definition 8 respectively.

Proposition 1. *Let* SS = (Share, Rec) *be a* (k, n)*-threshold secret sharing on a secret space* $\mathcal{S}$ *with perfect correctness and perfect privacy. Then, if* SS *is* (k, n, σ)*-NMSS*$_{cd}$*, according to Definition 8, then it is* (k, n, σ)*-CDSS, according to Definition 2 in the CDV model.*

Proof. Deferred to Appendix B.

Leakage and Tampering. In Definition 3, we have defined the leakage function family $\mathcal{H}_{k,\ell}$ for a (k, n)-threshold secret sharing: for a maximal unauthorized set H, $\mathbf{f}_H \in \mathcal{H}_{k,\ell}$ has the form $\mathbf{f}_H = (\mathsf{f}_1, \ldots, \mathsf{f}_n)$, a vector of functions such that f_i is the leakage function acting on share S_i. More precisely, for any $i \in H$, $\mathsf{f}_i(S_i) = S_i$ and for $j \notin H$, $\mathsf{f}_j(S_j)$ is a ℓ bit string which is the leakage of the share S_j.

Let $\mathsf{Leak}_{\mathbf{f}_H}$ denote the leakage vector that is the output of the function $\mathbf{f}_H$, that is $\mathsf{Leak}_{\mathbf{f}_H} = ((\mathsf{f}_1(S_1), \mathsf{f}_2(S_2), \ldots, \mathsf{f}_n(S_n)))$.

The set of such leakage vectors is denoted by $\mathcal{L}_{k,\ell} = \cup_{\mathbf{f}_H \in \mathcal{H}_{k,\ell}} \mathsf{Leak}_{\mathbf{f}_H}$

Definition 9 (Joint tampering with leakage). *Consider a (k,n)-threshold secret sharing with secret space $\mathcal{S}$ and share spaces $\mathcal{S}_1,\ldots,\mathcal{S}_n$.*

For a maximal unauthorized set $H \subset [n]$ (i.e. $|H| = k-1$), let $\mathcal{L}_{k,\ell}$ be defined as above.

For any $\mathbf{f}_H \in \mathcal{H}_{k,\ell}$ (see Definition 3), define a joint tampering function $g_H^{\mathbf{f}_H}$ that takes a vector of shares generated by an honest dealer and a leakage vector that is the output of $\mathbf{f}_H \in \mathcal{H}_{k,\ell}$ on the share vector, and outputs a vector of shares,

$$g_H^{\mathbf{f}_H} : \mathcal{S}_1 \times \cdots \times \mathcal{S}_n \times \mathcal{L}_{k,\ell} \longrightarrow \mathcal{S}_1 \times \cdots \times \mathcal{S}_n$$

which is determined by a function

$$g_{[H]}^{\mathbf{f}_H} : \times_{j\in H}\mathcal{S}_j \times \mathcal{L}_{k,\ell} \longrightarrow \times_{j\in H}\mathcal{S}_j$$

that is defined on the shares with indices in H and leakage $\mathcal{L}_{k,\ell}$, with the output being a vector of shares with indices in H. Precisely, given shares $(sh_1,\cdots,sh_n)$ and leakage $\tau = f_H(sh_1,\ldots,sh_n)$,

$$g_H^{f_H}(sh_1,\ldots,sh_n,\tau) = (sh'_1,\ldots,sh'_n),$$

where

- $sh'_i = sh_i$ *for all* $i \in [n]\backslash H$, *and*
- $sh'_i = g_{[H]}((sh_j)_{j\in H},\tau)[i]$, *for* $i \in H$

where $g_{[H]}((sh_j)_{j\in H},\tau)[i]$ is the component of $g_{[H]}$ output for $i \in H$.

For a maximal unauthorized set H and a leakage function $\mathbf{f}_H \in \mathcal{H}_{k,\ell}$, let $\mathcal{T}_{H,\mathbf{f}_H}^{leak,cdss}$ denote the set of all joint leakage and tampering functions (*see* Definition 9), and let $\mathcal{T}^{leak,cdss}$ denote the union of all such sets for all H and $\mathbf{f}_H$.

The tampering experiment for a LRNMSS is informally defined as follows. For an secret s, tampering function $g_H^{\mathbf{f}_H}$ and minimal authorized set T where $H \subset T$, (i) use $\mathsf{Share}(s)$ to generate a vector of shares $(\mathsf{sh}_1,\ldots,\mathsf{sh}_n)$ for s, (ii) apply $g_H^{\mathbf{f}_H}$ on the share vector to obtain the vector $(\mathsf{sh}'_1,\ldots,\mathsf{sh}'_n)$, and (iii) apply Rec using the shares of T.

A secret sharing is leakage resilient cheating detectable SS, if the output of Rec is either the original secret s or a special symbol $\perp$.

Definition 10. *Let $(\mathsf{Share},\mathsf{Rec})$ be a (k,n,ℓ,ϵ)-LR threshold secret sharing scheme for secret space $\mathcal{S}$ with respect to Definition 4. $(\mathsf{Share},\mathsf{Rec})$ is called $(k,n,\ell,\epsilon,\sigma)$-$NMSS_{LRCD}$ against tampering family $\mathcal{T}^{leak,cdss}$ if for any maximal unauthorized set H, for any function $g_H^{\mathbf{f}_H} \in \mathcal{T}^{leak,cdss}$ and any minimal authorized set T with $|T| = k$ containing H, there exists a distribution $D^{g_H^{\mathbf{f}_H},T}$ over $\{\mathsf{same}^*,\perp\}$ such that for any secret $s \in \mathcal{S}$,*

$$Tamper_s^{g_H^{f_H},T} \approx_\sigma \left\{ \begin{array}{l} \widetilde{s} \longleftarrow D^{g_H^{f},T} \\ output\text{: } s \text{ if } \widetilde{s} = \mathsf{same}^* \text{ and } \perp \text{ otherwise.} \end{array} \right\}$$

In the above, the random variable $Tamper_s^{g_H^{f_H},T}$ *is defined by the tampering experiment that is described below, over the randomness of the sharing function* Share,

$$Tamper_s^{g_H^{f_H},T} = \left\{ \begin{array}{l} (sh_1, \ldots, sh_n) \longleftarrow Share(s) \\ (sh'_1, \ldots, sh'_n) \leftarrow g_H^{f_H}(sh_1, \ldots, sh_n, \tau) : \tau = f_H(sh_1, \ldots, sh_n) \\ \widetilde{s} \longleftarrow Rec(\{sh'\}_T) \\ output\ : \widetilde{s} \end{array} \right\}$$

We require $D^{g_H^{f_H},T}$ *should be efficiently samplable given oracle access to* $g_H^{f_H}(\cdot)$.

In Definition 10 the secret has arbitrary distribution. Using argument similar to Proposition 1 we can show that a $(k, n, \ell, \epsilon, \delta)$-NMSS$_{LRCD}$ is a LRCDSS in the CDV model with cheating probability at most δ. This results in the following corollary.

Corollary 1. *If* $SS = (Share, Rec)$ *is* $(k, n, \ell, \epsilon, \delta)$*-NMSS*$_{LRCD}$ *according to Definition 10, then SS is also a* $(k, n, \ell, \epsilon, \delta)$*-LRCDSS according to Definition 5 in the CDV model.*

The corollary shows that a $(k, n, \ell, \epsilon, \delta)$-NMSS$_{LRCD}$, is a $(k, n, \ell, \epsilon, \delta)$-LRCDSS, and so the share size of any such NMSS$_{LRCD}$ must also satisfy the lower bound in Theorem 2. To our knowledge, this is the lower bound on share size of LRNMSS where tampering functions is a joint tampering. Brian *et al.* [10] obtained a lower bound on the share size of non-malleable secret sharing with respect to independent tampering (Corollary 4 of [10]). The lower bound (in bits) is $\frac{(\log \frac{1}{\delta} - 1)(1 - k/n)}{\widehat{k}}$ which relates the share size to the total number of shares n, the number of shares $\widehat{k}$ (that is the minimal number of shares required to uniquely recover all shares,) and the non-malleability simulation error δ. Our bound relates the share size to the secret size, leakage parameter ℓ, privacy parameter ϵ and non-malleability simulation error δ. The two bounds are not directly comparable: Brian et al.'s bound is obtained assuming Local model of leakage and for independent tampering functions whereas our bound is for Local$^+$ model of leakage and some restricted model of joint tampering.

7 Conclusion

We derived bounds on the share size of leakage resilient secret sharing with security against tampering adversary. We used the security notion of detectability of tampering which is a natural notion and widely used in coding theory, in particular error detecting codes. We discussed the relationship of this notion to non-malleability of secret sharing schemes under a particular class of tampering, and showed our results also applied to leakage resilient NMSS.

Acknowledgements. This work is in part supported by Natural Sciences and Engineering Research Council of Canada Discovery Grant program, and MITACS Accelerate Fellowship, Canada wide Ref. No. IT25625, FR66861.

A Non-malleable Codes

Definition of non-malleable code introduced by Dziembowski *et al.* [19] is given below. We refer to the original paper [19] for more background on non-malleable codes.

Definition 11 (Non-malleable Code [19]). *Let (Enc, Dec) be a coding scheme where Enc is a randomized function and Dec is deterministic and $\mathcal{F}$ be some family of tampering functions. For each $f \in \mathcal{F}$ and message $s \in \mathcal{S}$, define the tampering experiment*

$$Tamper_s^f = \left\{ \begin{array}{c} c \leftarrow Enc(s); \qquad \widetilde{c} \leftarrow f(c), \widetilde{s} \leftarrow Dec(\widetilde{c}) \\ output : \widetilde{s} \end{array} \right\}$$

which is a random variable over the randomness of the encoding function Enc. The coding scheme (Enc, Dec) is said to be non-malleable with respect to $\mathcal{F}$ if for every $f \in \mathcal{F}$ there exists a distribution D_f over $\mathcal{S} \cup \{\mathsf{same}^*, \perp\}$ such that for every message $s \in \mathcal{S}$ the following holds:

$$Tamper_s^f \approx_\delta \left\{ \begin{array}{c} \widetilde{s} \leftarrow D_f \\ output\text{: } s \text{ if } \widetilde{s} = \mathsf{same}^* \text{ and } \widetilde{s} \text{ otherwise.} \end{array} \right\}$$

and D_f is efficiently samplable given oracle access to $f(\cdot)$. In the above indistinguishability "$\approx$" can refer to statistical or computational indistinguishability. In case of statistical indistinguishability,the scheme is said to have exact-security δ, if the statistical distance above is at most δ.

B Proofs

Proof of Lemma 2. We assume that $P_S(s) \neq 0$ (otherwise, it can be removed from $\mathcal{S}$). Notice that

$$\begin{aligned} \Delta(P_{SY}, P_Y P_S) &= \sum_{y,s} |P_{SY}(s,y) - P_Y(y)P_S(s)| \\ &= \sum_s P_S(s) \sum_y |P_{Y|S}(y|s) - P_Y(y)| \\ &\leq \sum_s P_S(s) \sum_y \sum_{s'} P_S(s')|P_{Y|S}(y|s) - P_{Y|S}(y|s')| \\ &= \sum_s P_S(s) \sum_{s'} P_S(s') \sum_y |P_{Y|S}(y|s) - P_{Y|S}(y|s')| \\ &\leq \sum_s P_S(s) \sum_{s'} P_S(s')\epsilon = \epsilon. \end{aligned}$$

Also, by Lemma 1, we now have that $I(S;Y) \leq \epsilon \log \frac{|S|}{\epsilon}$. □

Proof of Theorem 1

For simplicity, let $u = 1$ and we consider $|\mathcal{S}_1|$. We only need to lower bound δ. Without loss of generality, let us assume an attacker corrupts the share of user 1. It needs to specify a leakage function with ℓ-bit output from the share and requests a secret sharing from dealer. The dealer then samples $S \leftarrow \mathcal{S}$, computes $\{S_i\}_i \longleftarrow \mathsf{Share}(S)$, and provides the leakage information on the first share to the attacker. In the following, A denotes a minimal qualified set participating in the reconstruction protocol containing k users such that user $1 \in A$.

Let $\mathcal{S}_1$ be the space of S_1 and let $\mathsf{f}_1 : \mathcal{S}_1 \to \{0,1\}^\ell$ be an arbitrary but fixed mapping with $|\mathsf{f}_1^{-1}(z)| = \lceil |\mathcal{S}_1| 2^{-\ell} \rceil$ or $\lfloor |\mathcal{S}_1| 2^{-\ell} \rfloor$ for any $z \in \{0,1\}^\ell$, where $\mathsf{f}_1^{-1}(z)$ is the set of preimage s_1 with $\mathsf{f}_1(s_1) = z$. Let $Y = \{S_u\}_{u \in A - \{1\}}$ and $X = S_1$. Then, attacker samples $X' \leftarrow \mathsf{f}_1^{-1}(\mathsf{f}_1(X)) - \{X\}$. That is, X' is a random preimage of $\mathsf{f}_1(X)$ other than X. Attacker then outputs X' as user $1's$ modified share (i.e., the substitute of the original share X). Define the recovered secret from (Y, X') as $S' = \mathsf{Rec}(Y, X')$. The success probability of this attack is $\Pr(S' \notin \{S, \perp\})$. We now focus on bounding the probability. Before we proceed, we present an important observation.

Claim 1. $P_{XYS}(x, y, s) > 0$ if and only if there is some randomness R so that $\mathsf{Share}(s; R)$ has the share x for user 1 and shares y for $A - \{1\}$ (which implies $\mathsf{Rec}(x, y) = s$ by perfect correctness).

Assuming **Claim 1**, we first claim that the attack success probability is[1]

$$\Pr(S' \notin \{S, \perp\}) = \sum_{\substack{(x',x,y,s):\mathsf{Rec}(x',y)\notin\{s,\perp\} \\ x' \in \mathsf{f}_1^{-1}(\mathsf{f}_1(x))}} \frac{P_{XYS}(x, y, s)}{|\mathsf{f}_1^{-1}(\mathsf{f}_1(x))| - 1}. \tag{3}$$

To see this, notice that $P_{XYS}(x, y, s) > 0$ if and only if $\mathsf{Rec}(x, y) = s$ by **Claim 1**. Further, $X' = x'$ is uniformly random over $\mathsf{f}_1^{-1}(\mathsf{f}_1(x)) - \{x\}$. Hence, each event $\mathsf{Rec}(x', y) \notin \{s, \perp\}$ implies a successful attack.

For ease of our analysis, we introduce the notation $Z = \mathsf{f}_1(X)$ into P_{XYS} of Eq. (3). Notice $P_{XYZS}(x, y, z, s) = 0$ (in case $\mathsf{f}_1(x) \neq z$) and $P_{XYZS}(x, y, z, s) = P_{XYS}(x, y, s)$ (in case $\mathsf{f}_1(x) = z$). Therefore, we have

$$\Pr(S' \notin \{S, \perp\}) = \sum_{\substack{(x',x,y,z,s):\mathsf{Rec}(x',y)\notin\{s,\perp\} \\ x' \in \mathsf{f}_1^{-1}(z)}} \frac{P_{XYZS}(x, y, z, s)}{|\mathsf{f}_1^{-1}(z)| - 1}. \tag{4}$$

[1] if $f^{-1}(f(x)) = \{x\}$ only, then x' w.r.t. this x does not exist and so the equation is still well-defined.

Let $L_{x'}$ be the set of (y, s) such that $\mathsf{Rec}(x', y) \neq s, \perp$. Hence, Eq. (4) can be written as

$$\Pr(S' \notin \{S, \perp\}) = \sum_{\substack{(x',x,y,z,s):(y,s)\in L_{x'}\\ x'\in \mathsf{f}_1^{-1}(z)}} \frac{1}{|\mathsf{f}_1^{-1}(z)|-1} P_{XYZS}(x,y,z,s),$$

$$= \sum_{(x,y,z,s)} \frac{1}{|\mathsf{f}_1^{-1}(z)|-1} \sum_{\substack{x':(y,s)\in L_{x'}\\ x'\in \mathsf{f}_1^{-1}(z)}} P_{XYZS}(x,y,z,s). \quad (5)$$

Given y, z, let $s_1, \cdots, s_N$ be the all possible secrets such that $P_{YZSX}(y, z, s_j, x_j) > 0$ for some $x_j \in \mathsf{f}_1^{-1}(z)$. By **Claim 1**, $\mathsf{Rec}(y, x_j) = s_j$ for each j. Thus, $(y, s_i) \in L_{x_j}$ for $i \neq j$ (as $\mathsf{Rec}(x_j, y) = s_j \neq s_i$).

Define $\mathbb{N}_{y,z} = \{s_1, \cdots, s_N\}$ and so $\mathbb{N}_{y,z}\backslash\{s_j\} \subseteq L_{x_j}$. Let us denote the random variable $N_{y,z} = |\mathbb{N}_{y,z}|$.

Continue Eq. (5), counting over j for $x' = x_j$ in Eq. (5) we get

$$\Pr(S' \notin \{S, \perp\}) \geq \sum_{(x,y,z,i)} \frac{1}{|\mathsf{f}_1^{-1}(z)|-1} \sum_{\substack{x_j:(y,s_i)\in L_{x_j}\\ x_j\in \mathsf{f}_1^{-1}(z)}} P_{XYZS}(x,y,z,s_i)$$

$$\geq \sum_{x,y,z,i} \frac{P_{XYZS}(x,y,z,s_i)}{|\mathsf{f}_1^{-1}(z)|-1}(N_{y,z}-1) \quad (6)$$

$$= \sum_{x,y,z,s} \frac{P_{XYZS}(x,y,z,s)}{|\mathsf{f}_1^{-1}(z)|-1}(N_{y,z}-1) \quad (7)$$

$$= \sum_{y,z} \frac{1}{|\mathsf{f}_1^{-1}(z)|-1}(N_{y,z}-1)P_{YZ}(y,z), \quad (8)$$

where Eq. (7) is by the definition of $s_1, \cdots, s_N$ (that implies $P_{XYZS}(x, y, z, s) = 0$ for $s \notin \mathbb{N}_{y,z}$) and Eq. (8) is obtained by summing over s, x on P_{XYZS} to get the marginal distribution P_{YZ}.

According to the definition of f_1, the restriction that either $|\mathsf{f}_1^{-1}(z)| = \lceil |\mathcal{S}_1| \cdot 2^{-\ell} \rceil$ or $\lfloor |\mathcal{S}_1| \cdot 2^{-\ell} \rfloor$ gives,

$$\Pr(S' \notin \{S, \perp\}) \geq \sum_{y,z} \frac{1}{\lceil |\mathcal{S}_1| \cdot 2^{-\ell} \rceil - 1}(N_{y,z}-1)P_{YZ}(y,z). \quad (9)$$

Dividing both sides of the Equation of **Claim 2** (*see* below) by $\lceil |\mathcal{S}_1| 2^{-\ell} \rceil - 1$ and add to Eq. (9), we know that $\Pr(S' \notin \{S, \perp\})$ is lower bounded by

$$\frac{|\mathcal{S}|-1}{\lceil |\mathcal{S}_1| 2^{-\ell} \rceil - 1} \sum_{y,z} P_{YZ}(y,z) - \frac{|\mathcal{S}|}{\lceil |\mathcal{S}_1| 2^{-\ell} \rceil - 1}\epsilon \quad (10)$$

$$= \frac{|\mathcal{S}|-1}{\lceil |\mathcal{S}_1| 2^{-\ell} \rceil - 1} - \frac{|\mathcal{S}|}{\lceil |\mathcal{S}_1| 2^{-\ell} \rceil - 1}\epsilon. \quad (11)$$

Reformatting Eq. (11), we conclude our theorem. □

Claim 2. $\sum_{y,z}(|\mathcal{S}| - N_{y,z})P_{YZ}(y,z) \leq \epsilon|\mathcal{S}|$.

Proof. From the ϵ-privacy of LRCDSS (with secret S, unauthorized shares Y and leakage Z) and Lemma 2 (where YZ here is variable Y in that lemma),

$$\sum_{s,yz} |P_{SYZ}(s,y,z) - P_S(s)P_{YZ}(y,z)| \leq \epsilon. \tag{12}$$

Recall that $\mathbb{N}_{y,z}$ is the set of s with $P_{XYZS}(x,y,z,s) > 0$ for some $x \in \mathsf{f}_1^{-1}(z)$. Note that $P_{XYZS}(x,y,z,s) > 0$ implies $z = \mathsf{f}_1(x)$ (and hence $x \in \mathsf{f}_1^{-1}(z)$). Thus, $\mathbb{N}_{y,z}$ is actually the set of s with $P_{XYZS}(x,y,z,s) > 0$ for some $x \in \mathcal{S}_1$. This also implies that $P_{YZS}(y,z,s) = 0$ for each $s \in \mathcal{S}\backslash\mathbb{N}_{y,z}$. Denote $\mathcal{S}\backslash\mathbb{N}_{y,z}$ by $\bar{\mathbb{N}}_{y,z}$. Therefore, looking the partial sum in Eq. (12) with $s \in \bar{\mathbb{N}}_{y,z}$, we have

$$\sum_{(y,z,s):\ s\in\bar{\mathbb{N}}_{y,z}} |0 - P_{YZ}(y,z)P_S(s)| \leq \epsilon. \tag{13}$$

Since $P_S(s) = 1/|\mathcal{S}|$ and $|\bar{\mathbb{N}}_{y,z}| = |\mathcal{S}| - |N_{y,z}|$, we have $\epsilon|\mathcal{S}| \geq \sum_{(y,z,s):s\in\bar{\mathbb{N}}_{y,z}} P_{YZ}(y,z) = \sum_{y,z}(|\mathcal{S}| - N_{y,z})P_{YZ}(y,z)$. This completes the proof of Claim 2. □

Proof of Theorem 2. For simplicity, let $u = 1$ and we consider $|\mathcal{S}_1|$. It suffices to derive a lower bound $\delta \geq \sqrt{\frac{1-1/|\mathcal{S}|}{2^{-\ell}|\mathcal{S}_1|}} - \epsilon$ for δ. Assume there are k users with shares $S_1, \cdots, S_k$. Attacker does as follows: it corrupts $S_2, \cdots, S_k$ and obtains leakage $Z = \mathsf{f}_1(V)$.

Let $X = S_2, V = S_1$ and $\mathsf{f}_1(\cdot) : \mathcal{S}_1 \to \{0,1\}^\ell$ is a purely random function chosen by attacker (i.e., for each $w \in \mathcal{S}_1$, $\mathsf{f}_1(w)$ is purely random in $\{0,1\}^\ell$). Let $Y = (S_3, \cdots, S_k)$. So attacker has $k-1$ shares X, Y and leakages $Z = f_1(S_1)$. He will try to modify X to X' using Y, Z while preserving Y unchanged.

Let $\{v_1, \cdots, v_N\} = \mathsf{f}_1^{-1}(Z)$, where N is a random variable (depending on Z and randomness of f_1). Attacker than samples $v_u \leftarrow \{v_1, \cdots, v_N\}$ (hope that $v_u = S_1$). Then, he tries to find $x_u \in \mathcal{S}_2$ such that $\mathsf{Rec}(Y, x_u, v_u) \notin \{\perp, \mathsf{Rec}(Y, X, v_u)\}$; defines $x_u =\perp$ if such x_u does not exist. Finally, the attacker outputs $X' = x_u$ as the modified share of X and keeps Y unchanged. This completes the description of the attack. By our description, he succeeds if $v_u = V$ and $x_u \neq\perp$.

We now analyze the success probability of the attacker. This equals $P(v_u = V) - P(v_u = V \wedge x_u =\perp) \geq \mathbf{E}(1/N) - P(\mathbf{Bad})$, where **Bad** is the event that there does not exist x', x such that $\mathsf{Rec}(Y, x', V)$ and $\mathsf{Rec}(Y, x, V)$ are distinct and not $\perp$.

By Cauchy-Schwarz inequality, $\mathbf{E}(1/N)\mathbf{E}(N) = [\sum_i P_N(i)/i] \times [\sum_i P_N(i)i] \geq (\sum_i \sqrt{P_N(i)/i} \times \sqrt{P_N(i)i})^2 = 1$. So $\mathbf{E}(1/N) \geq 1/\mathbf{E}(N)$.

We note that in **Claim 4** shown below, $\lambda_{XY}|\mathcal{S}_1|$ is the number of v so that $\mathsf{Rec}(X, Y, v) \neq\perp$. Further, since $\mathsf{f}_1(\cdot)$ is a purely random function (independent of randomness in secret sharing), each of such v belongs to $\mathsf{f}_1^{-1}(Z)$ with probability exactly $2^{-\ell}$. Hence, $\mathbf{E}(N) = 2^{-\ell} \cdot \mathbf{E}(\lambda_{XY}|\mathcal{S}_1|) \leq 2^{-\ell}|\mathcal{S}_1|(\delta + \epsilon/2)/(1 - 1/|\mathcal{S}|)$.

From $\mathbf{E}(1/N) \geq 1/\mathbf{E}(N)$ and **Claim 3** (*see* below), the success probability is lower bounded by $\frac{1-1/|\mathcal{S}|}{2^{-\ell}|\mathcal{S}_1|(\delta+\epsilon)} - \frac{\epsilon}{2(1-1/|\mathcal{S}|)}$. Since the attacker success probability is upper bounded by δ, we have $\delta \geq \frac{1-1/|\mathcal{S}|}{2^{-\ell}|\mathcal{S}_1|(\delta+\epsilon)} - \frac{\epsilon}{2(1-1/|\mathcal{S}|)}$. Since $|\mathcal{S}| \geq 2$, reformatting the inequality we conclude the result. ■

Claim 3. $P(\mathbf{Bad}) \leq \frac{\epsilon}{2(1-1/|\mathcal{S}|)}$.

Proof. Denote Ω be the set of (v, y) so that there does not exist x, x' such that $\mathsf{Rec}(x, y, v), \mathsf{Rec}(x', y, v)$ are distinct and not $\perp$. So $P(\mathbf{Bad}) = P_{VY}(\Omega)$. Note that if **Bad** event happens to $Y = y, V = v$ with $P_{VY}(v, y) > 0$, then (y, v) can compute the secret S, because there is only one s that can be recovered from (v, y) (together with some x); otherwise, **Bad** will not occur to v, y. Therefore,

$$\Delta(P_{VYS}, P_{VY}P_S) = \sum_{v,y,s} P_{VY}(v, y) \cdot |P_{S|VY}(s|v, y) - P_S(s)| \tag{14}$$

$$\geq 2 \sum_{(y,v)\in\Omega} P_{VY}(v, y) \cdot (1 - 1/|\mathcal{S}|) \tag{15}$$

$$= 2P(\mathbf{Bad}) \cdot (1 - 1/|\mathcal{S}|), \tag{16}$$

where the inequality uses the standard fact $\Delta(P_X, P_Y) \geq 2(P_X(A) - P_Y(A))$ for any subset A of the domain of X, Y and also uses the fact: if $(v, y) \in \Omega$, then either $P_{VY}(v, y) = 0$ or (v, y) determines $S = s$ for some s which means $P_{S|VY}(s|v, y) = 1$. As $\Delta(P_{VYS}, P_{VY}P_S) \leq \epsilon$, it follows that $P(\mathbf{Bad}) \leq \frac{\epsilon}{2(1-1/|\mathcal{S}|)}$. This completes the proof of **Claim 3**. □

Claim 4. Let $\lambda_{x,y}$ be the fraction of v in $\mathcal{S}_1$ satisfying $\mathsf{Rec}(x, y, v) \neq \perp$. Then, $\mathbf{E}(\lambda_{XY}) \leq \frac{\delta+\epsilon/2}{1-1/|\mathcal{S}|}$, where the expectation is with respect to P_{XY}.

Proof. To prove the claim, we construct a simple attacker against cheating resistance. Assume the challenger generates $(S_1, \cdots, S_k)$. Recall that $X = S_2, Y = (S_3, \cdots, S_k), V = S_1)$. Let $\mathbb{V} = \mathcal{S}_1$. Attacker corrupts Y and V and takes $V' \leftarrow \mathbb{V}$. He outputs (Y, V') during the reconstruction stage. The attack is successful if and only if $\mathsf{Rec}(X, Y, V') \notin \{\mathsf{Rec}(X, Y, V), \perp\}$. Let $\mathbb{V}(x, y, v)$ be the set of v' so that $\mathsf{Rec}(x, y, v') = \mathsf{Rec}(x, y, v)$. Then, the attack success probability is (i..e, the reconstructed secret is neither $\perp$ nor S)

$$\sum_{x,y,v} P_{XYV}(x, y, v)(\lambda_{xy} - |\mathbb{V}(x, y, v)|/|\mathbb{V}|) \tag{17}$$

$$= \mathbf{E}(\lambda_{XY}) - \sum_{x,y,v} P_{XYV}(x, y, v)|\mathbb{V}(x, y, v)|/|\mathbb{V}|. \tag{18}$$

Notice that for fixed s, $\mathbb{V}(x,y,v)$ is invariant over v satisfying $\mathsf{Rec}(x,y,v)=s$. So we can denote $\mathbb{V}(x,y,v)$ by $\mathbb{V}_s(x,y)$. Thus,

$$\begin{aligned}
Eq.(18) =& \mathbf{E}(\lambda_{XY}) - \sum_{x,y,s} P_{X,Y}(x,y)P_{V|XY}(\mathbb{V}_s(x,y)|x,y)\cdot|\mathbb{V}_s(x,y)|/|\mathbb{V}| \\
=& \mathbf{E}(\lambda_{XY}) - \sum_{x,y,s} P_{X,Y}(x,y)P_{S|XY}(s|x,y)\cdot|\mathbb{V}_s(x,y)|/|\mathbb{V}| \\
& (\mathbb{V}_s(x,y) \text{ and } s \text{ are in one-one correspondence, given } x,y) \\
\overset{*}{\geq}& \mathbf{E}(\lambda_{XY}) - \sum_{x,y,s} P_{X,Y}(x,y)P_S(s)\cdot|\mathbb{V}_s(x,y)|/|\mathbb{V}| - D(P_{XYS},P_{XY}P_S)\cdot 1 \\
\geq& \mathbf{E}(\lambda_{XY}) - \sum_{x,y,s} P_{X,Y}(x,y)P_S(s)\cdot|\mathbb{V}_s(x,y)|/|\mathbb{V}| - \epsilon \\
=& \mathbf{E}(\lambda_{XY}) - \sum_{x,y} P_{X,Y}(x,y)\lambda_{x,y}\cdot 1/|\mathcal{S}| - \epsilon \\
& (\text{observe that } \sum_s |\mathbb{V}_s(x,y)|/|\mathbb{V}| = \lambda_{x,y}) \\
=& \mathbf{E}(\lambda_{XY})(1-1/|\mathcal{S}|) - \epsilon
\end{aligned}$$

where (*) uses facts that $|\mathbb{V}_s(x,y)|/|\mathbb{V}| \leq 1$ and that $\mathbf{E}_{P_Z}(F(Z)) \geq \mathbf{E}_{Q_Z}(F(Z)) - D(P_Z,Q_Z)\cdot\max_z F(z)$ for distributions P_Z and Q_Z of variable Z and non-negative function $F(z)$. Further, since the attack success probability (hence Eq. (18)) is upper bounded by δ, $\mathbf{E}(\lambda_{XY}) \leq \frac{\delta+\epsilon}{1-1/|\mathcal{S}|}$. This proves **Claim 4.** □

Proof of Proposition 1. Since SS has perfect correctness and perfect privacy, to prove SS is (k,n,δ)-CDSS, it remains to show the cheating probability is upper bounded by δ. Let S_H be the unauthorized set of shares chosen by the adversary $\mathcal{A}$ and $\mathbf{g}_H$ be a joint tampering function (that modifies shares in $H \subset T$, where $|T|=k$) used in Definition 2 in the CDV model (for some $s \in \mathcal{S}$). In the CDV model, let the output of $Tamper_s^{\mathbf{g}_H,T}$ be S' and the output of simulation corresponding to $D^{\mathbf{g}_H,T}$ be S''. Then, $\Pr(S' \notin \{s,\perp\}|S=s)$ will be the cheating probability in Definition 2 as the tampering process in $Tamper_s^{\mathbf{g}_H,T}$ is identical to that in Definition 2. Since SS is (k,n,σ)-NMSS$_{cd}$, then by definition of $D^{\mathbf{g}_H,T}$, $\Pr(S'' \notin \{s,\perp\}|S=s)=0$. Therefore,
$\sigma \geq \Delta(P_{S'|S=s}, P_{S''|S=s}) = \sum_v |P_{S'|S}(v|s) - P_{S''|S}(v|s)|$
$= \Pr(S' \notin \{s,\perp\}|S=s) + |P_{S'|S}(\perp|s) - P_{S''|S}(\perp|s)| + |P_{S'|S}(s|s) - P_{S''|S}(s|s)|$
$\geq \Pr(S' \notin \{s,\perp\}|S=s)$.
As the inequality holds for any s, it follows that $\max_s P(S' \notin \{s,\perp\}|S=s) \leq \sigma$. That is, SS is CDSS with a cheating probability at most σ. We also note that the above result is valid for OKS model also. It suffices to show that if SS is CDSS in the CDV model with cheating probability at most δ, then it is CDSS in the OKS model with cheating probability at most δ. This is immediate as CDSS has a cheating probability $\Pr(S' \notin \{S,\perp\}) = \sum_s P_S(s)P(S' \notin \{s,\perp\}|S=s) \leq \max_s P(S' \notin \{s,\perp\}|S=s)$, which is the CDSS cheating probability in the CDV model. This completes our proof. □

References

1. Aggarwal, D., et al.: Stronger leakage-resilient and non-malleable secret sharing schemes for general access structures. In: Boldyreva, A., Micciancio, D. (eds.) CRYPTO 2019. LNCS, vol. 11693, pp. 510–539. Springer, Cham (2019). https://doi.org/10.1007/978-3-030-26951-7_18
2. Aggarwal, D., Dodis, Y., Lovett, S.: Non-malleable codes from additive combinatorics. In STOC 2014, pp. 774–783 (2014)
3. Aggarwal, D., Dziembowski, S., Kazana, T., Obremski, M.: Leakage-resilient non-malleable codes. In: Dodis, Y., Nielsen, J.B. (eds.) TCC 2015. LNCS, vol. 9014, pp. 398–426. Springer, Heidelberg (2015). https://doi.org/10.1007/978-3-662-46494-6_17
4. Araki, T.: Efficient (k,n) threshold secret sharing schemes secure against cheating from n–1 cheaters. In: Pieprzyk, J., Ghodosi, H., Dawson, E. (eds.) ACISP 2007. LNCS, vol. 4586, pp. 133–142. Springer, Heidelberg (2007). https://doi.org/10.1007/978-3-540-73458-1_11
5. Badrinarayanan, S., Srinivasan, A.: Revisiting non-malleable secret sharing. In: Ishai, Y., Rijmen, V. (eds.) EUROCRYPT 2019. LNCS, vol. 11476, pp. 593–622. Springer, Cham (2019). https://doi.org/10.1007/978-3-030-17653-2_20
6. Beimel, A.: Secret-sharing schemes: a survey. In: Chee, Y.M., et al. (eds.) IWCC 2011. LNCS, vol. 6639, pp. 11–46. Springer, Heidelberg (2011). https://doi.org/10.1007/978-3-642-20901-7_2
7. Ben-Or, M., Goldwasser, S., Wigderson, A.: Completeness theorems for non-cryptographic fault-tolerant distributed computation. In STOC 1988, pp. 1–10, ACM New York (1988)
8. Benhamouda, F., Degwekar, A., Ishai, Y., Rabin, T.: On the local leakage resilience of linear secret sharing schemes. J. Cryptol. **34**(2), 1–65 (2021). https://doi.org/10.1007/s00145-021-09375-2
9. Blakley, G.R.: Safeguarding cryptographic keys. In: AFIPS, vol. 1979, pp. 313–317 (1997)
10. Brian, G., Faonio, A., Obremski, M., Simkin, M., Venturi, D.: Non-malleable secret sharing against bounded joint-tampering attacks in the plain model. In: Micciancio, D., Ristenpart, T. (eds.) CRYPTO 2020. LNCS, vol. 12172, pp. 127–155. Springer, Cham (2020). https://doi.org/10.1007/978-3-030-56877-1_5
11. Brian, G., Faonio, A., Venturi, D.: Continuously non-malleable secret sharing: joint tampering, plain model and capacity. In: Nissim, K., Waters, B. (eds.) TCC 2021. LNCS, vol. 13043, pp. 333–364. Springer, Cham (2021). https://doi.org/10.1007/978-3-030-90453-1_12
12. Canetti, R., Dodis, Y., Halevi, S., Kushilevitz, E., Sahai, A.: Exposure-resilient functions and all-or-nothing transforms. In: Preneel, B. (ed.) EUROCRYPT 2000. LNCS, vol. 1807, pp. 453–469. Springer, Heidelberg (2000). https://doi.org/10.1007/3-540-45539-6_33
13. Carpentieri, M., De Santis, A., Vaccaro, U.: Size of shares and probability of cheating in threshold schemes. In: Helleseth, T. (ed.) EUROCRYPT 1993. LNCS, vol. 765, pp. 118–125. Springer, Heidelberg (1994). https://doi.org/10.1007/3-540-48285-7_10
14. Chattopadhyay, E., Goyal, V., Li. X.: Non-malleable extractors and codes, with their many tampered extensions. In: Proceedings of the Forty-Eighth Annual ACM Symposium on Theory of Computing, pp. 285–298 (2016)

15. Csiszár, I.: Almost independence of random variables and capacity of a secrecy channel. Probl. Inf. Transm. **32**(1), 40–47 (1996)
16. Davì, F., Dziembowski, S., Venturi, D.: Leakage-resilient storage. In: Garay, J.A., De Prisco, R. (eds.) SCN 2010. LNCS, vol. 6280, pp. 121–137. Springer, Heidelberg (2010). https://doi.org/10.1007/978-3-642-15317-4_9
17. Desmedt, Y.: Threshold cryptosystems. In: Seberry, J., Zheng, Y. (eds.) AUSCRYPT 1992. LNCS, vol. 718, pp. 1–14. Springer, Heidelberg (1993). https://doi.org/10.1007/3-540-57220-1_47
18. Dodis, Y., Sahai, A., Smith, A.: On perfect and adaptive security in exposure-resilient cryptography. In: Pfitzmann, B. (ed.) EUROCRYPT 2001. LNCS, vol. 2045, pp. 301–324. Springer, Heidelberg (2001). https://doi.org/10.1007/3-540-44987-6_19
19. Dziembowski, S., Pietrzak, K., Wichs, D.: Non-malleable codes. J. ACM (JACM) **65**(4), 1–32 (2018)
20. Faonio, A., Venturi, D.: Non-malleable secret sharing in the computational setting: adaptive tampering, noisy-leakage resilience, and improved rate. In: Boldyreva, A., Micciancio, D. (eds.) CRYPTO 2019. LNCS, vol. 11693, pp. 448–479. Springer, Cham (2019). https://doi.org/10.1007/978-3-030-26951-7_16
21. Faust, S., Mukherjee, P., Nielsen, J.B., Venturi, D.: Continuous non-malleable codes. In: Lindell, Y. (ed.) TCC 2014. LNCS, vol. 8349, pp. 465–488. Springer, Heidelberg (2014). https://doi.org/10.1007/978-3-642-54242-8_20
22. Gennaro, R., Goldfeder, S., Narayanan, A.: Threshold-optimal DSA/ECDSA signatures and an application to bitcoin wallet security. In: Manulis, M., Sadeghi, A.-R., Schneider, S. (eds.) ACNS 2016. LNCS, vol. 9696, pp. 156–174. Springer, Cham (2016). https://doi.org/10.1007/978-3-319-39555-5_9
23. Goldreich, O., Micali, S., Wigderson, A.: How to play any mental game. In: Proceedings of, STOC 1987, pp. 218–229, ACM. New York (1987)
24. Goyal, V., Kumar, A.: Non-malleable secret sharing. In Proceedings of STOC 2018, pp. 685–698, ACM. New York (2018)
25. Goyal, V., Kumar, A.: Non-malleable secret sharing for general access structures. In: Shacham, H., Boldyreva, A. (eds.) CRYPTO 2018. LNCS, vol. 10991, pp. 501–530. Springer, Cham (2018). https://doi.org/10.1007/978-3-319-96884-1_17
26. Guruswami, V., Wootters, M.: Repairing reed-solomon codes. IEEE Trans. on Information Theory **63**(9), 5684–5698 (2017)
27. Kalai, Y.T., Reyzin, L.: A survey of leakage-resilient cryptography. In Providing Sound Foundations for Cryptography: On the Work of Shafi Goldwasser and Silvio Micali, pp. 727–794 (2019)
28. Kanukurthi, B., Obbattu, S.L.B., Sekar, S., Tomy, J.: Locally reconstructable non-malleable secret sharing. In: ITC 2021. Schloss Dagstuhl-Leibniz-Zentrum für Informatik (2021)
29. Kumar, A., Meka, R., Sahai, A.: Leakage-resilient secret sharing against colluding parties. In: FOCS, vol. 2019, pp. 636–660 (2019)
30. Lin, F., Cheraghchi, M., Guruswami, V., Safavi-Naini, R., Wang, H.: Leakage-resilient secret sharing in non-compartmentalized models. In: ITC 2020. Schloss Dagstuhl-Leibniz-Zentrum für Informatik (2020)
31. Lin, F., Safavi-Naini, R., Cheraghchi, M., Wang, H.: Non-malleable codes against active physical layer adversary. In: ISIT 2019, pp. 2753–2757, IEEE (2019)
32. Liu, F.-H., Lysyanskaya, A.: Tamper and leakage resilience in the split-state model. In: Safavi-Naini, R., Canetti, R. (eds.) CRYPTO 2012. LNCS, vol. 7417, pp. 517–532. Springer, Heidelberg (2012). https://doi.org/10.1007/978-3-642-32009-5_30

33. Maji, H.K., Nguyen, H.H., Paskin-Cherniavsky, A., Suad, T., Wang, M.: Leakage-resilience of the Shamir secret-sharing scheme against physical-bit leakages. In: Canteaut, A., Standaert, F.-X. (eds.) EUROCRYPT 2021. LNCS, vol. 12697, pp. 344–374. Springer, Cham (2021). https://doi.org/10.1007/978-3-030-77886-6_12
34. Maji, H.K., Paskin-Cherniavsky, A., Suad, T., Wang, M.: Constructing locally leakage-resilient linear secret-sharing schemes. In: Malkin, T., Peikert, C. (eds.) CRYPTO 2021. LNCS, vol. 12827, pp. 779–808. Springer, Cham (2021). https://doi.org/10.1007/978-3-030-84252-9_26
35. Micali, S., Reyzin, L.: Physically observable cryptography. In: Naor, M. (ed.) TCC 2004. LNCS, vol. 2951, pp. 278–296. Springer, Heidelberg (2004). https://doi.org/10.1007/978-3-540-24638-1_16
36. Nielsen, J.B., Simkin, M.: Lower bounds for leakage-resilient secret sharing. In: Canteaut, A., Ishai, Y. (eds.) EUROCRYPT 2020. LNCS, vol. 12105, pp. 556–577. Springer, Cham (2020). https://doi.org/10.1007/978-3-030-45721-1_20
37. Ogata, W., Kurosawa, K., Stinson, D.R.: Optimum secret sharing scheme secure against cheating. SIAM J. Dis. Math. **20**(1), 79–95 (2006)
38. Raman, R.K., Varshney, L.R.: Distributed storage meets secret sharing on the blockchain. In: 2018 Information Theory and Applications Workshop (ITA), pp. 1–6. IEEE (2018)
39. De Santis, A., Desmedt, Y., Frankel, Y., Yung, M.: How to share a function securely. In STOC 1994 (1994)
40. Shamir, A.: How to share a secret. Commun. ACM **22**(11), 612–613 (1979)
41. Srinivasan, A., Vasudevan, P.N.: Leakage resilient secret sharing and applications. In: Boldyreva, A., Micciancio, D. (eds.) CRYPTO 2019. LNCS, vol. 11693, pp. 480–509. Springer, Cham (2019). https://doi.org/10.1007/978-3-030-26951-7_17
42. Tompa, M., Woll, H.: How to share a secret with cheaters. J. Cryptology **1**(2), 133–138 (1988)

Schemes II

Lattice-Based Key-Value Commitment Scheme with Key-Binding and Key-Hiding Properties

Hideaki Miyaji[1(✉)] and Atsuko Miyaji[2]

[1] Department of Information Science and Engineering, Ritsumeikan University, Kusatsu, Japan
h-miyaji@fc.ritsumei.ac.jp
[2] Graduate School of Engineering, Osaka University, Suita, Japan
miyaji@comm.eng.osaka-u.ac.jp

Abstract. Blockchain plays an important role in distributed file systems, such as cryptocurrency. One of the important building blocks of blockchain is the key-value commitment scheme, which constructs a commitment value from two inputs: a key and a value. In an ordinal commitment scheme, a single user creates a commitment value from an input value, whereas, in a key-value commitment scheme, multiple users create a commitment value from their own key and value. Both commitment schemes need to satisfy both binding and hiding properties. The concept of a key-value commitment scheme was first proposed by Agrawal et al. in 2020 using the strong RSA assumption. They also proved its key-binding property of their key-value commitment scheme. However, the key-hiding property was not yet proved. The key-hiding property was then proposed by Campaneli et al. in 2022. In this paper, we propose two lattice-based key-value commitment schemes, $\mathsf{Insert\text{-}KVC}_{m/2,n,q,\beta}$, and $\mathsf{KVC}_{m,n,q,\beta}$. Furthermore, we prove the key-binding and key-hiding of both lattice-based $\mathsf{Insert\text{-}KVC}_{m/2,n,q,\beta}$ and $\mathsf{KVC}_{m,n,q,\beta}$ for the first time. We prove the key-binding of both $\mathsf{Insert\text{-}KVC}_{m/2,n,q,\beta}$ and $\mathsf{KVC}_{m,n,q,\beta}$ based on the short integer solutions ($\mathsf{SIS}^{\infty}_{n,m,q,\beta}$) problem. Furthermore, we prove key-hiding of both $\mathsf{Insert\text{-}KVC}_{m/2,n,q,\beta}$ and $\mathsf{KVC}_{m,n,q,\beta}$ based on the Decisional-$\mathsf{SIS}^{\infty}_{n,m,q,\beta}$ form problem, which we first introduced in this paper. We also discuss the difficulty of the Decisional-$\mathsf{SIS}^{\infty}_{n,m,q,\beta}$ form problem.

Keywords: lattice-based key-value commitment scheme · key-binding · key-hiding · blockchain

1 Introduction

With the rapid development of cryptocurrency in recent years, blockchain has become a widely researched field. Blockchain is mainly used in cryptocurrency, especially in Ethereum [2] and Bitcoin [1], which have a significant amount of users. Consequently, many studies have been conducted to make blockchain more

J. Deng et al. (Eds.): CANS 2023, LNCS 14342, pp. 497–515, 2023.
https://doi.org/10.1007/978-981-99-7563-1_22

convenient. The commitment scheme is used to make the blockchain more convenient. For example, a commitment scheme is used to share the data between two blockchains (cross-chain communication) [17], and a key-value commitment scheme is proposed to compress and verify the data in a blockchain.

1.1 Commitment Scheme and Key-Value Commitment Scheme

The commitment scheme was proposed by Blum in 1982 [6], and the key-value commitment scheme was formally proposed in 2020 by Agrawal et al. [3]. A commitment scheme plays a crucial role in cryptography and involves two parties: a sender and a receiver. It comprises two main phases: the commitment phase, where the sender transforms a message into a commitment string and sends it to the receiver, and the decommitment phase, where the sender reveals the original message and its key by providing a decommitment string. This enables the receiver to verify the integrity of the commitment and confirm whether it corresponds to the revealed message. The security of a commitment scheme is established based on two properties: hiding and binding [8,11]. The hiding property ensures that the receiver gains no partial information about the message from the commitment string prior to the decommitment phase. Conversely, the binding property guarantees that the sender cannot produce more than two valid decommitment strings for a given commitment string, thereby preventing the sender from changing or modifying the original message without detection.

The key-value commitment scheme inherits the same characteristics as the commitment scheme. Key-hiding and key-binding must be satisfied to prevent malicious user acts. Furthermore, the key-value commitment scheme has one commitment value per n users. In other words, it creates one commitment value from "key" and "value" inputs. In general commitment schemes [6,10,12,15], there is one commitment value per user; however, in the key-value commitment scheme, one commitment value is created for the users who construct the commitment value. Each user creates his/her own commitment value C. Other users can insert their own commitment value C' into C to realize a single commitment value for all users. Because one commitment value is constructed only from many users, it is possible to reduce the space. Consequently, the key-value commitment scheme is more highly applicable to blockchain than general commitment schemes.

Apart from the key-value commitment scheme, additional protocols applicable to blockchain include the vector commitment scheme and the accumulator. Catalano et al. constructed the vector commitment scheme in 2013 [7], and the accumulator was constructed by Benaloh et al. in 1993 [5]. Both comprise a single output value (the vector commitment value and accumulator value), regardless of the number of users. However, the vector commitment scheme requires all user input values to be collected to form a single commitment value. In other words, the vector commitment requires a trusted setup that collects all input values. The commitment value in the vector commitment scheme is constructed by $Enc(m_1, \ldots, m_n)$ from some encryption function Enc and input values $(m_1, \ldots, m_n)$. In an accumulator, although it is possible to create one's accumulator value (output value), users who create the same accumulator value can see each other's input values. Consequently, most of the existing vector commitment schemes and accumulators require a trusted setup, which is often undesirable [16].

1.2 Construction Without a Trusted Setup Based on Lattice Assumption with Key-Binding and Key-Hiding Properties

Because the key-value commitment scheme can be constructed without a trusted setup, it can be applied to other protocols, such as blockchain. Agrawal constructed a key-value commitment scheme based on RSA with satisfying key-binding [3]. However, this scheme is designed to send the user's input key-value (k, v) in the commitment phase to construct a vector commitment or accumulator from their key-value commitment scheme. In other words, this method requires a trusted setup considering users can view each other's (k, v), and hence, does not overcome the problems of vector commitment and accumulator.

Additionally, Agrawal's key-value commitment scheme only proposes a key-binding and does not show that it satisfies key-hiding; by demonstrating key-hiding in the key-value commitment scheme, it can be concluded that the verifier cannot act as malicious in the commitment phase. In a blockchain, the user who verifies the value is not necessarily honest. As a result, the verifier in the blockchain must demonstrate their inability to engage in malicious activities. Consequently, to apply the key-value commitment scheme to the blockchain, key-hiding must be shown.

Furthermore, the emergence of quantum computing poses a threat to blockchain protocols and other cryptography, considering they rely on cryptographic algorithms that are not post-quantum. Allende et al. constructed the method of blockchain based on post-quantum cryptography [4]. Consequently, it is extremely important to propose a scheme using post-quantum cryptography. The key-value commitment scheme constructed by Agrawal et al. is based on RSA and is not constructed using a post-quantum cryptography. Consequently, it is essential to construct a key-value commitment scheme using post-quantum cryptography to apply blockchain based on post-quantum cryptography.

1.3 Contribution

In this paper, we propose two lattice-based Key-Value Commitment schemes, $\mathsf{Insert\text{-}KVC}_{m/2,n,q,\beta}$ and $\mathsf{KVC}_{m,n,q,\beta}$. $\mathsf{Insert\text{-}KVC}_{m/2,n,q,\beta}$ and $\mathsf{KVC}_{m,n,q,\beta}$ satisfy the following:

- In the commitment phase, the user can create their commitment value C without a trusted setup.
- Both $\mathsf{Insert\text{-}KVC}_{m/2,n,q,\beta}$ and $\mathsf{KVC}_{m,n,q,\beta}$ satisfy both key-hiding and key-binding.
- Both key-binding properties are proven under $\mathsf{SIS}^{\infty}_{n,m,q,\beta}$ problem. Conversely, both key-hiding properties are proven under the newly proposed Decisional-$\mathsf{SIS}^{\infty}_{n,m,q,\beta}$ form problem.

$\mathsf{Insert\text{-}KVC}_{m/2,n,q,\beta}$ comprises four functions: Keygen, Insert, ProofUpdate, and Ver. By adding one more function of Update, $\mathsf{KVC}_{m,n,q,\beta}$ comprising five functions: Keygen, Insert, Update, ProofUpdate, and Ver. By excluding the Update function, $\mathsf{Insert\text{-}KVC}_{m/2,n,q,\beta}$ can be constructed more simply than $\mathsf{KVC}_{m,n,q,\beta}$; therefore, the computational complexity (multiplication and addition cost) of $\mathsf{Insert\text{-}KVC}_{m/2,n,q,\beta}$ reduces to half of $\mathsf{KVC}_{m,n,q,\beta}$. $\mathsf{KVC}_{m,n,q,\beta}$ provides Update while sacrificing the computational complexity.

To demonstrate the key-hiding of the proposed $\mathsf{Insert\text{-}KVC}_{m/2,n,q,\beta}$ and $\mathsf{KVC}_{m,n,q,\beta}$, we newly define the Decisional-$\mathsf{SIS}^{\infty}_{n,m,q,\beta}$ form problem. We also discuss the difficulty of the Decisional-$\mathsf{SIS}^{\infty}_{n,m,q,\beta}$ problem. To guarantee the difficulty of the Decisional-$\mathsf{SIS}^{\infty}_{n,m,q,\beta}$ form problem, we newly proposed the One-Way-$\mathsf{SIS}^{\infty}_{n,m,q,\beta}$ problem, which is a one-way version of the $\mathsf{SIS}^{\infty}_{n,m,q,\beta}$ problem. Then, we prove that the Decisional-$\mathsf{SIS}^{\infty}_{n,m,q,\beta}$ form problem is secure when the One-Way-$\mathsf{SIS}^{\infty}_{n,m,q,\beta}$ problem is secure, and guarantees the difficulty of the Decisional-$\mathsf{SIS}^{\infty}_{n,m,q,\beta}$ form problem.

We prove both $\mathsf{Insert\text{-}KVC}_{m/2,n,q,\beta}$ and $\mathsf{KVC}_{m,n,q,\beta}$ of key-binding based on $\mathsf{SIS}^{\infty}_{n,m,q,\beta}$ problem, and $\mathsf{Insert\text{-}KVC}_{m/2,n,q,\beta}$ and $\mathsf{KVC}_{m,n,q,\beta}$ of key-hiding based on Decisional-$\mathsf{SIS}^{\infty}_{n,m,q,\beta}$ form problem.

1.4 Paper Organization

The remainder of this paper is organized as follows. Section 2 summarizes the notations and security assumptions used in this paper. Our contribution is presented from Sect. 3. Section 3 presents the novel definition of our proposal and discusses the difficulty associated with this new definition. Section 4 describes our $\mathsf{Insert\text{-}KVC}_{m/2,n,q,\beta}$ and its key-binding and key-hiding. Section 5 describes our $\mathsf{KVC}_{m,n,q,\beta}$ and its key-binding and its key-hiding. Section 6 compares our two proposed key-value commitment schemes, $\mathsf{Insert\text{-}KVC}_{m/2,n,q,\beta}$ and $\mathsf{KVC}_{m,n,q,\beta}$. We conclude our paper in Sect. 7.

2 Preliminary

In this section, we present the notation used in this paper and describes the definitions.

- λ: security parameter
- N: a positive number
- q: a prime number
- $\mathbb{Z}_q$:a set $\{0, \dots, q-1\}$
- $[a||b]$: concatenation of a and b
- $\varepsilon(n)$: negligible function in n
- $poly(n)$: polynomial function in n
- pp: public parameter

- $||f||_\infty(=\max_i|f_i|)$: ℓ_∞-norm of $f = \Sigma_i f_i X^i$
- $||f||_2 = \left(\Sigma_i|f_i|^2\right)^{1/2}$: ℓ_2-norm of $f = \Sigma_i f_i X^i$
- C: proposed key-value commitment value
- $H : \mathbb{Z}^\ell \to \mathbb{Z}^m_{\beta/2}$: Hash function
- $\mathcal{M}$: message map
- $\mathcal{C}$: commitment map
- verifier: a person who verifies the commitment value

Definition 1 (Shortest Independent Vectors Problem ($SIVP_\gamma$) [9]). *Given a full-rank basis B of an n-dimensional lattice B, the problem of finding a set of n linearly independent vectors $S \subset L(B)$ such that $||S||_2 <= \gamma(n) \cdot \lambda_n(L(B))$, where $\lambda_n(L(B))$ is the n-th vector with the ℓ_2-norm of the lattice $L(B)$ consisting of B.*

Definition 2 (Short Integer Solutions ($\mathsf{SIS}^\infty_{n,m,q,\beta}$) problem [9]). *Given a uniform random matrix $A \in \mathbb{Z}_q^{n\times m}$, the problem is to find a nonzero vector $x \in \mathbb{Z}^m$ such that $A \cdot x = 0 \pmod q$ and $||x||_\infty \leq \beta$.*

If $m, \beta = poly(n)$ and $q > \beta \cdot \widetilde{O}(\sqrt{n})$, then $\mathsf{SIS}^\infty_{n,m,q,\beta}$ is at least as hard as SIVP_γ such that $\gamma = \beta \cdot \widetilde{O}(\sqrt{mn})$ [9]. Next, we define a key-value commitment scheme [3].

Definition 3 (Key-value commitment scheme [3]). *A key-value commitment allows one to commit to a key-value map and later open the commitment with respect to any specific key. It is possible to update the map $\mathcal{M}$ by either adding new key-value pairs or updating the value corresponding to an existing key. A key-value map $\mathcal{M} \subseteq \mathcal{K}\times\mathcal{V}$ is a collection of key-value pairs $(k, v) \in \mathcal{K}\times\mathcal{V}$. Let $\mathcal{K}_\mathcal{M} \subseteq \mathcal{K}$ denote the set of keys for which values have been stored in the map $\mathcal{M}$. We define a key-value map $\mathsf{KVC}_{m,n,q,\beta}$ as a non-interactive primitive that can be formally described via the following algorithms:*

- $\mathsf{Keygen}(1^\lambda) \to (\mathsf{pp}, \mathsf{C})$*: On input the security parameter λ, the key generation algorithm outputs certain public parameters* pp *(which implicitly define the key space $\mathcal{K}$ and value space $\mathcal{V}$) and the initial commitment $\mathbb{C}$ to the empty key-value map. All other algorithms have access to the public parameters.*
- $\mathsf{Insert}(\mathsf{C}, (\mathsf{k}, \mathsf{v})) \to (\mathsf{C}, \Lambda_\mathsf{k}, \mathsf{upd})$*: On inputting a commitment string C and a key-value pair $(k, v) \in \mathcal{K} \times \mathcal{V}$, the insertion algorithm outputs a new commitment string C, a proof Λ_k (that v is the value corresponding to k), and update information* upd.
- $\mathsf{Update}(\mathsf{C}, (\mathsf{k}, \delta)) \to (\mathsf{C}, \mathsf{upd})$*: On inputting a commitment string C, a key $k \in \mathcal{K}$ and an update value δ, the update algorithm outputs an updated string C and update information* upd. *Note that this algorithm does not need the value corresponding to the key k.*

- $\mathsf{ProofUpdate}(\mathsf{k}, \Lambda_\mathsf{k}, \mathsf{upd}) \to \Lambda_\mathsf{k}$: *On inputting a key $k \in \mathcal{K}$, a proof Λ_k for some value corresponding to the key k and update information* upd, *the proof update algorithm outputs an updated proof Λ_k.*
- $\mathsf{Ver}(\mathsf{C}, (\mathsf{k}, \mathsf{v}), \Lambda_\mathsf{k}) \to 1/0$: *On inputting a commitment string C, a key-value pair $(k, v) \in \mathcal{K} \times \mathcal{V}$ and a proof Λ_k, the verification algorithm either outputs* 1 *(denoting accept) or* 0 *(denoting reject).*

In $\mathsf{KVC}_{m,n,q,\beta}$, we require correctness. For all honestly generated public parameters $\mathsf{Keygen}(1^\lambda) \to \mathsf{pp}$, if C is a commitment to a key-value map $\mathcal{M}$, obtained by running a sequence of calls to Insert and Update, then Λ_k is a proof corresponding to key k for any $k \in \mathcal{K}_\mathcal{M}$, generated during the call to Insert and updated by appropriate calls to ProofUpdate, then $\mathsf{Ver}(\mathsf{C}, (\mathsf{k}, \mathsf{v}), \Lambda_\mathsf{k})$ outputs 1 with probability 1 if $(k, v) \in \mathcal{M}$. Next, we define key-binding, which is the security requirement of our $\mathsf{KVC}_{m,n,q,\beta}$. We define a game to prove key-binding in Definition 4, and define the key-binding in Definition 5, a security feature of the proposed $\mathsf{KVC}_{m,n,q,\beta}$.

Definition 4 (Key-binding game [3]). *For a key-value commitment $\mathsf{KVC}_{m,n,q,\beta}$ and an adversary $\mathcal{A}$, we define a random variable $\mathcal{G}^{\mathsf{bind}}_{\mathsf{KVC}_{m,n,q,\beta},\lambda,\mathcal{A}}$ through a game between a challenger* CH *and $\mathcal{A}$ as follows.*

- $\mathcal{G}^{\mathsf{bind}}_{\mathsf{KVC}_{m,n,q,\beta},\lambda,\mathcal{A}}$:

1. CH *samples* $\mathsf{Keygen} \to (\mathsf{pp}, \mathsf{C})$ *and sends them to $\mathcal{A}$.* CH *also maintains its own state that comprises a key-value map $\mathcal{M} \subseteq \mathcal{K} \times \mathcal{V}$ initialized to the empty map and the initial commitment value C.*
2. *$\mathcal{A}$ issues queries of one of the following forms:*
   - $(\mathsf{Insert}, (\mathsf{k}, \mathsf{v}))$: CH *checks if $\mathcal{M}$ contains a tuple of the form $(k, \cdot)$. If yes,* CH *responds with $\perp$. Else,* CH *updates $\mathcal{M}$ to $\mathcal{M} \cup \{(k, v)\}$ and executes* $\mathsf{Insert}(\mathsf{C}, (\mathsf{k}, \mathsf{v}))$ *to obtain a new commitment C.*
   - $(\mathsf{Update}, (\mathsf{k}, \delta))$: CH *checks if $\mathcal{M}$ contains a tuple of the form (k, v). If yes,* CH *responds with $\perp$. Else,* CH *updates $\mathcal{M}$ to $\mathcal{M} \cup \{(k, v + \delta)\} \backslash \{(k, v)\}$ and executes* $\mathsf{Update}(\mathsf{C}, (\mathsf{k}, \delta))$ *to obtain a new commitment C.*
3. *$\mathcal{A}$ sends a final output to* CH *of the following forms:*
   - *A key k such that $\mathcal{M}$ contains a tuple of the form $(k, \cdot)$, a pair of values (v, v') where $v \neq v'$, and a pair of proofs (Λ_k, Λ'_k).*
4. CH *performs the following checks corresponding to $\mathcal{A}$'s output:*
   - *If* $\mathsf{Ver}(\mathsf{C}, (\mathsf{k}, \mathsf{v}), \Lambda_\mathsf{k}) = \mathsf{Ver}(\mathsf{C}, (\mathsf{k}, \mathsf{v}'), \Lambda'_\mathsf{k}) = 1$, *then* CH *outputs $\perp$. Else,* CH *outputs* 1.

Definition 5 (Key-binding property [3]). *A key-value commitment $\mathsf{KVC}_{m,n,q,\beta}$ is key-binding if for every PPT adversary $\mathcal{A}$, the following probability is negligible in λ:*

$$\mathsf{Adv}^{\mathsf{bind}}_{\mathsf{KVC}_{m,n,q,\beta},\mathcal{A}}(\lambda) = \Pr\left[\mathcal{G}^{\mathsf{bind}}_{\mathsf{KVC}_{m,n,q,\beta},\lambda,\mathcal{A}} \to 0\right] < \varepsilon(\lambda)$$

3 New Security Assumption and Its Difficulty Proof

In this section, we define our new terminologies and discuss their difficulty.

3.1 New Definitions as Defined in This Paper

Because this paper proves the key-hiding property of the proposed key-value commitment schemes, we define the key-hiding property. To prove key-hiding, we also define the decision version of $\mathsf{SIS}^{\infty}_{n,m,q,\beta}$ problem.

Definition 6 (Key-hiding game). *For a key-value commitment $\mathsf{KVC}_{m,n,q,\beta}$ and an adversary $\mathcal{A}$, we define a random variable $\mathcal{G}^{\mathsf{hid}}_{\mathsf{KVC}_{m,n,q,\beta},\lambda,\mathcal{A}}$ by conducting a game between a challenger* CH *and* $\mathcal{A}$ *as follows:*

- $\mathcal{G}^{\mathsf{hid}}_{\mathsf{KVC}_{m,n,q,\beta},\lambda,\mathcal{A}}$:

1. CH *samples* Keygen $\rightarrow$ (pp, C) *and sends them to* $\mathcal{A}$. CH *also maintains its own state that comprises a key-value map* $\mathcal{M} \subseteq \mathcal{K} \times \mathcal{V}$ *and its commitment map* $\mathcal{C}$. *They first output the initial commitment value* $C \in \mathcal{C}$.
2. CH *sends* (pp, C) *to* $\mathcal{A}$.
3. $\mathcal{A}$ *collects* $y_1 \in U$ *and* $y_2 \in \mathcal{C}$.
4. $\mathcal{A}$ *chooses either* y_1 *or* y_2 *and set as* y_b.
5. $\mathcal{A}$ *computes* $C' = C + y_b$.
6. $\mathcal{A}$ *sends* C' *to* CH.
7. CH *performs the following checks corresponding to* $\mathcal{A}$*'s output:*
   - *If* $y_b = y_1$*: If they can distinguish* C' *as a uniform random, they output* $\perp$*. Else,* CH *outputs* 1.
   - *If* $y_b = y_2$*: If they can distinguish* C' *as in the commitment value, then they output outputs* $\perp$*. Else,* CH *outputs* 1.

From the key-hiding game, a new definition of key-hiding property is provided.

Definition 7 (Key-hiding property). *A key-value commitment* $\mathsf{KVC}_{m,n,q,\beta}$ *is key-hiding if for every PPT adversary* $\mathcal{A}$*, the following probability is negligible in* λ*:*

$$\mathsf{Adv}^{\mathsf{hid}}_{\mathsf{KVC}_{m,n,q,\beta},\mathcal{A}}(\lambda) = \Pr\left[\mathcal{G}^{\mathsf{hid}}_{\mathsf{KVC}_{m,n,q,\beta},\lambda,\mathcal{A}} \rightarrow 0\right] < \varepsilon(\lambda)$$

Next, we newly define Decisional-$\mathsf{SIS}^{\infty}_{n,m,q,\beta}$ form problem to prove key-hiding property.

Definition 8 (Decisional-$\mathsf{SIS}^{\infty}_{n,m,q,\beta}$ form problem). *Let* $\mathcal{A}$ *denote the probabilistic polynomial time adversary. Given a uniform random matrix* $\mathsf{A} \in \mathbb{Z}_q^{n\times m}$*, the Decisional-*$\mathsf{SIS}^{\infty}_{n,m,q,\beta}$ *form problem asserts such that for every* $x \in \mathbb{Z}_\beta^m$*, it satisfies*

$$\left| \Pr_{\mathsf{A},\mathsf{C}=\mathsf{A}\cdot\mathsf{x}\wedge||\mathsf{x}||_\infty\leq\beta}[\mathcal{A}(\mathsf{A},\mathsf{C})=1] - \Pr_{\mathsf{A},\mathsf{C}\in\mathsf{U}}[\mathcal{A}(\mathsf{A},\mathsf{C})=1] \right| < \varepsilon(\mathsf{n}).$$

We then discuss the difficulty of the Decisional-$\mathsf{SIS}^{\infty}_{n,m,q,\beta}$ form problem. To guarantee the difficulty of Decisional-$\mathsf{SIS}^{\infty}_{n,m,q,\beta}$ form problem, we newly introduce the One-Way-$\mathsf{SIS}^{\infty}_{n,m,q,\beta}$ problem.

Definition 9 (One-Way-$\mathsf{SIS}^{\infty}_{n,m,q,\beta}$ problem). *Let $\mathcal{A}$ be a PPT adversary. Given a uniform random matrix $\mathsf{A} \in \mathbb{Z}_{\mathsf{q}}$, and $y \in \mathbb{Z}^n$, the One-Way-$\mathsf{SIS}^{\infty}_{n,m,q,\beta}$ problem asserts that for every $x \in \mathbb{Z}^m$, $\mathsf{A} \cdot \mathsf{x} = \mathsf{y} \pmod{\mathsf{q}}$ and $||x||_\infty \leq \beta$, it satisfies*

$$\Pr[\mathcal{A}(\mathsf{A}, \mathsf{y}) = \mathsf{x} \ s.t. \ \mathsf{A} \cdot \mathsf{x} = \mathsf{y} \pmod{\mathsf{q}} \wedge ||\mathsf{x}||_\infty \leq \beta] < \varepsilon(\lambda)$$

The $\mathsf{SIS}^{\infty}_{n,m,q,\beta}$ problem is similar to collision resistance, and the One-Way-$\mathsf{SIS}^{\infty}_{n,m,q,\beta}$ problem is similar to preimage resistance [13]. As demonstrated in [13], when collision resistance is satisfied, preimage resistance is also satisfied. If the $\mathsf{SIS}^{\infty}_{n,m,q,\beta}$ problem is secure, the One-Way-$\mathsf{SIS}^{\infty}_{n,m,q,\beta}$ problem is also secure from the relation between collision resistance and preimage resistance. Therefore, we can guarantee the difficulty of the One-Way-$\mathsf{SIS}^{\infty}_{n,m,q,\beta}$ problem under the $\mathsf{SIS}^{\infty}_{n,m,q,\beta}$ problem.

Next, we discuss the difficulty of the Decisional-$\mathsf{SIS}^{\infty}_{n,m,q,\beta}$ form problem. We follow the method of Miyaji et al. proposed in 2021 [14]. Miyaji et al. proposed the reduction from (M, δ)-bSVP assumption to Decisional-(M, δ)-bSVP assumption in 2021 [14]. Note that (M, δ)-bSVP assumption is a binary SVP problem and Decisional-(M, δ)-bSVP assumption is a decision version of (M, δ)-bSVP assumption. To guarantee the difficulty of the Decisional-$\mathsf{SIS}^{\infty}_{n,m,q,\beta}$ form problem, we prove that the Decisional-$\mathsf{SIS}^{\infty}_{n,m,q,\beta}$ form problem is secure when the One-Way-$\mathsf{SIS}^{\infty}_{n,m,q,\beta}$ problem is secure. In other words, to guarantee the difficulty of Decisional-$\mathsf{SIS}^{\infty}_{n,m,q,\beta}$ form problem, we prove Decisional-$\mathsf{SIS}^{\infty}_{n,m,q,\beta}$ form problem is as secure as the One-Way-$\mathsf{SIS}^{\infty}_{n,m,q,\beta}$ problem, as demonstrated in Theorem 1.

Theorem 1. *Let $y : \mathbb{Z}^m_\beta \rightarrow \mathbb{Z}^n_{\mathsf{q}}$ be a function and q be the integer, we define $\mathsf{SIS}^{\infty}_{n,m,q,\beta}$ distribution by choosing $x \in \mathbb{Z}^m_\beta$ and outputting $y = \mathsf{A} \cdot \mathsf{x}$. Suppose there exists a PPT adversary $\mathcal{A}$ that can distinguish the input y sampled from the distribution of $\mathsf{SIS}^{\infty}_{n,m,q,\beta}$ distribution or sampled from a uniform distribution U with polynomial time. Then, we prove that another PPT adversary $\mathcal{B}$ can break the One-Way-$\mathsf{SIS}^{\infty}_{n,m,q,\beta}$ problem with maximum βm approaches within the polynomial time.*

Proof: We assume there exists an adversary $\mathcal{A}$ that can break Decisional-$\mathsf{SIS}^{\infty}_{n,m,q,\beta}$ form problem. First, $\mathcal{B}$ gains (A, y) from One-Way-$\mathsf{SIS}^{\infty}_{n,m,q,\beta}$ problem oracle where $\mathsf{A} \in \mathbb{Z}^{\mathsf{n} \times \mathsf{m}}_{\mathsf{q}}$ and $y \in \mathbb{Z}^n$. Let x denote as $x = [x_1, \ldots, x_n]$, and let A denote as Eq. (1) where $c_{ij} \in \mathbb{Z}_q$.

$$\mathsf{A} = \begin{pmatrix} c_{11} & \cdots & c_{1j} & \cdots & c_{1n} \\ \vdots & \ddots & & & \vdots \\ c_{i1} & & c_{ij} & & c_{in} \\ \vdots & & & \ddots & \vdots \\ c_{m1} & \cdots & c_{mj} & \cdots & c_{mn} \end{pmatrix}. \tag{1}$$

Then $y = \mathsf{Ax} \in \mathbb{Z}^{\mathsf{n}}$ can be written as

$$y = \begin{pmatrix} c_{11} \cdot x_1 + c_{12} \cdot x_2 + & \cdots & + c_{1n} \cdot x_n \\ & \vdots & \\ c_{m1} \cdot x_1 + c_{m2} \cdot x_2 + & \cdots & + c_{mn} \cdot x_n \end{pmatrix}.$$

We randomly select $k \in \mathbb{Z}_\beta$ and $l_{i1} \in \mathbb{Z}_q$ $(i = 1, \ldots, n)$, and compute a pair

$$A' = \left(\mathsf{A} - \begin{pmatrix} l_{11} & 0 \cdots 0 \\ \vdots & \vdots \ddots \vdots \\ l_{m1} & 0 \cdots 0 \end{pmatrix}, \mathsf{y} - \begin{pmatrix} l_{11} \cdot k \\ \vdots \\ l_{m1} \cdot k \end{pmatrix} \right), \tag{2}$$

where $\mathsf{A}' = \mathsf{A} - \begin{pmatrix} l_{11} & 0 \cdots 0 \\ \vdots & \vdots \ddots \vdots \\ l_{m1} & 0 \cdots 0 \end{pmatrix}$ and $y' = y - \begin{pmatrix} l_{11} \cdot k \\ \vdots \\ l_{m1} \cdot k \end{pmatrix}$. The value obtained in Eq. (2) as $A' = (\mathsf{A}', \mathsf{y}')$. Now, $\mathcal{B}$ sends $A' = (\mathsf{A}', \mathsf{y}')$ to $\mathcal{A}$. If $k = x_1$, then y' can be written as Eq. (3)

$$y' = \begin{pmatrix} (c_{11} - l_{11}) \cdot x_1 + & \cdots & + c_{1n} \cdot x_n \\ & \vdots & \\ (c_{m1} - l_{m1}) \cdot x_1 + & \cdots & + c_{mn} \cdot x_n \end{pmatrix}. \tag{3}$$

Because Eq. (3) can be expressed in the form $y' = \mathsf{A}'\mathsf{x}$, $\mathcal{A}$ can confirm that Eq. (3) is contained in the $\mathsf{SIS}^{\infty}_{n,m,q,\beta}$ distribution. Then, $\mathcal{A}$ can distinguish that A' is in the $\mathsf{SIS}^{\infty}_{n,m,q,\beta}$ distribution. In contrast, if $k \neq x_1$, then y' cannot expressed as the $\mathsf{SIS}^{\infty}_{n,m,q,\beta}$ distribution. Then, $\mathcal{A}$ can distinguish that A' is in the uniform distribution. $\mathcal{A}$ sends this result to $\mathcal{B}$ to gain the following result.

- If A' distinguish as $\mathsf{SIS}^{\infty}_{n,m,q,\beta}$ distribution: $x_1 = k$
- Else: $x_1 \neq k$.

By proceeding with a similar approach for the remaining $[x_2, \ldots, x_m]$, $\mathcal{B}$ can obtain the value of x where $y = \mathsf{A} \cdot \mathsf{x}$. Now, we analyze the number of iterations $\mathcal{B}$ to be performed until obtaining x. $\mathcal{B}$ can gain the value of x_1 within a maximum of β attempts. Consequently, to obtain all the values of x, a total of βm iterations are required, which is a polynomial number. ∎

From the contraposition of Theorem 1, we can show Decisional-$\mathsf{SIS}^{\infty}_{n,m,q,\beta}$ form problem is as secure as One-Way-$\mathsf{SIS}^{\infty}_{n,m,q,\beta}$ problem.

4 Proposed Insert-KVC Based on SIS

In this section, we propose our SIS-based Insert-$\mathsf{KVC}_{m/2,n,q,\beta}$. In Insert-$\mathsf{KVC}_{m/2,n,q,\beta}$, the user can only insert key-value pairs (k_i, v_i) into the commitment C, and cannot update the value corresponding to the user's key (No Update function). Conversely, by not including the Update function, the construction becomes simpler.

In this section, we first propose the concrete design of $\mathsf{Insert\text{-}KVC}_{m/2,n,q,\beta}$ in Sect. 4.1. Subsequently, we explain the feature of $\mathsf{Insert\text{-}KVC}_{m/2,n,q,\beta}$. We prove its key-binding of $\mathsf{Insert\text{-}KVC}_{m/2,n,q,\beta}$ in Sect. 4.2 and key-hiding of $\mathsf{Insert\text{-}KVC}_{m/2,n,q,\beta}$ in Sect. 4.3.

Construction 1 (Construction method of $\mathsf{Insert\text{-}KVC}_{m/2,n,q,\beta}$). *In* $\mathsf{Insert\text{-}KVC}_{m/2,n,q,\beta}$*, the proposal comprises four functions:* Keygen, Insert, ProofUpdate *and* Ver. *We now explain the construction method of the proposed* $\mathsf{Insert\text{-}KVC}_{m/2,n,q,\beta}$*. First, the public parameters* pp *and the initial commitment value* C *are created using* Keygen. *Each user inserts their own key-value using the* Insert *function and* (pp, C). *Note that each user cannot change their value after they execute* Insert. *The user's key-value is encrypted using the* Insert *function and stored in the commitment value* C. *Following the insertion of their commitment value into* C*, users create a proof* Λ *to verify their commitment value using* ProofUpdate. *Considering the commitment value* C *is updated every time by inserting a new commitment value from each user, each user needs to update their* Λ *using* ProofUpdate *every time* C *is updated. Finally, when each user wants to open their key-value, they send their key-value and* Λ *to the verifier, who performs verification on the key-value and* Λ *to ensure their validity.*

4.1 Concrete Explanation of Proposed $\mathsf{Insert\text{-}KVC}_{m/2,n,q,\beta}$

Here, we describe the concrete function of our proposed $\mathsf{Insert\text{-}KVC}_{m/2,n,q,\beta}$. We first show the concrete function of $\mathsf{Insert\text{-}KVC}_{m/2,n,q,\beta}$ then analyze the completeness and efficiency of $\mathsf{Insert\text{-}KVC}_{m/2,n,q,\beta}$.

- $\mathsf{Insert\text{-}KVC}_{m/2,n,q,\beta}$

- $\mathsf{Keygen}(1^\lambda) \to (\mathsf{pp}, \mathsf{C_M})$: Sample the description q, m, n, β, which satisfies $m, \beta = poly(n)$ and $q > \beta \cdot \tilde{O}(\sqrt{n})$. Sample the uniform random matrix $\mathsf{A} \in \mathbb{Z}_q^{n \times m}$ for public parameter pp. Set $\mathcal{V} = \mathbb{Z}^m$ and $\mathcal{K} = \mathbb{Z}^m$. Let E as the identity matrix, choose $u \in \mathcal{V}$. Output $(\mathsf{pp}, \mathsf{C}) = ((\mathsf{q}, \mathsf{m}, \mathsf{n}, \beta, \mathsf{u}), (\mathsf{E} \cdot \mathsf{u}, \mathsf{A} \cdot \mathsf{u}))$.
- $\mathsf{Insert}(\mathsf{C}, (\mathsf{k_i}, \mathsf{v_i})) \to (\mathsf{C}, \Lambda_{\mathsf{k_i}}, \mathsf{upd})$: Parse C as $(\mathsf{C_1}, \mathsf{C_2})$, and parse Λ_{k_i} as $(\Lambda_{k_{i,1}}, \Lambda_{k_{i,2}})$. Let $k_i \in \mathbb{Z}^\ell$, $v_i \in \mathbb{Z}_{\beta/2}^{m/2}$, and let $z_i = H(k_i)$, which satisfies $z_i \in \mathbb{Z}_{\beta/2}^{m/2}$, where H is a hash function $H : \mathbb{Z}^\ell \to \mathbb{Z}_{\beta/2}^{m/2}$. User computes $x_i = (z_i \| v_i)\mathrm{v}$, and the commitment value and its proof Λ_{k_i}

are inserted as

$$\begin{aligned} \Lambda'_{k_i} &= (\mathsf{C}_1, \mathsf{C}_2) \\ \mathsf{C}' &= (\mathsf{C}_1 + \mathsf{A} \cdot \mathsf{x}_\mathsf{i}, \mathsf{C}_2 + \mathsf{A} \cdot \mathsf{x}_\mathsf{i}) \\ \mathsf{upd} &= (z_i, v_i) \\ \Lambda_{k_{i,1}} &\leftarrow \Lambda'_{k_{i,1}} \\ \Lambda_{k_{i,2}} &\leftarrow \Lambda'_{k_{i,2}} \\ \mathsf{C}_1 &\leftarrow \mathsf{C}'_1 \\ \mathsf{C}_2 &\leftarrow \mathsf{C}'_2 \end{aligned}$$

Output $(\mathsf{C}, \Lambda_{\mathsf{k_i}}, \mathsf{upd})$.

- $\mathsf{ProofUpdate}(\mathsf{k_i}, \Lambda_{\mathsf{k_i}}, \mathsf{upd}) \rightarrow \Lambda'_{\mathsf{k_i}}$: Parse upd as $(\mathsf{upd}_1, \mathsf{upd}_2)$. Let $z = H(\mathsf{upd}_1)$, and computes $x = (z||\mathsf{upd}_2)$. Set

$$\begin{aligned} \Lambda_{k_{i,1}} &= \Lambda_{k_i} + A \cdot x \\ \Lambda_{k_{i,2}} &= \Lambda_{k_i} + A \cdot x \\ \Lambda_{k_{i,1}} &\leftarrow \Lambda'_{k_{i,1}} \\ \Lambda_{k_{i,2}} &\leftarrow \Lambda'_{k_{i,2}} \end{aligned}$$

Output Λ_{k_i}.

- $\mathsf{Ver}(\mathsf{C}, (\mathsf{k_i}, \mathsf{v_i}), \Lambda_{\mathsf{k_i}}) \rightarrow 1/\perp$: Parse C as $(\mathsf{C}_1, \mathsf{C}_2)$ and Λ_{k_i} as $(\Lambda_{k_{i,1}}, \Lambda_{k_{i,2}})$. Let $z = H(k_i)$, which computes $x_i = (z||v_i)$. The user who wants to open the commitment value sends (k_i, v_i) to the verifier, who checks the following.
  * $v_i \in \mathcal{V}$ and $k_i \in \mathcal{K}$,
  * $\Lambda_{k_{i,1}} + A \cdot x_i = \mathsf{C}_1$,
  * $\Lambda_{k_{i,2}} + A \cdot x_i = \mathsf{C}_2$,
  * $\Lambda_{k_{i,2}} - \Lambda_{k_{i,1}} = u \cdot (\mathsf{A} - \mathsf{E})$

  If the above equation satisfies, the verifier outputs 1. Else, they output $\perp$.

The correctness of $\mathsf{Insert\text{-}KVC}_{m/2,n,q,\beta}$ can be determined immediately by following the construction method in Construction 1. In the commitment phase, the user sends its commitment value C and upd. In the decommitment phase, user sends their own decommitment value $((k_i, v_i), \Lambda_{k_i})$. Note that in the commitment phase, the user's key k_i is sent in the form of hashed z_i in upd. Consequently, each user's key k_i is not disclosed until the decommitment phase. In our $\mathsf{Insert\text{-}KVC}_{m/2,n,q,\beta}$, the Update function cannot be executed. Consequently, the construction of $\mathsf{Insert\text{-}KVC}_{m/2,n,q,\beta}$ can be simpler compared to that of $\mathsf{KVC}_{m,n,q,\beta}$.

Analyze $\mathsf{Insert\text{-}KVC}_{m/2,n,q,\beta}$: From Construction 1, multiplication and addition cost in each function satisfy the following.

- Insert: one hash computation, multiplication cost: $2mn$, addition cost: $4n$,
- ProofUpdate: one hash computation, multiplication cost: $2mn$, addition cost: $4n$,
- Ver: one hash computation, multiplication cost: $2mn$, addition or subtraction cost: $3n$.

We assume that there is only one user, and each function is executed once. Furthermore, the size of the key-value commitment is constant.

4.2 Key-Binding of Proposed $\mathsf{Insert\text{-}KVC}_{m/2,n,q,\beta}$

In this subsection, we prove the key-biding property of $\mathsf{KVC}_{m,n,q,\beta}$.

Theorem 2. *Suppose there exists a PPT adversary $\mathcal{A}$ that can break the key-binding of $\mathsf{Insert\text{-}KVC}_{m/2,n,q,\beta}$. Subsequently, we prove that another PPT adversary $\mathcal{B}$ can break the $\mathsf{SIS}^{\infty}_{n,m,q,\beta}$ problem.*

Proof: We assume that there exists an adversary $\mathcal{A}$ that can break the key-binding property of $\mathsf{KVC}_{m,n,q,\beta}$. In other words, $\mathcal{A}$ performs the adversary in Definition 4. For some k, create a value $x, x'(x \neq x')$ and a proof value $\Lambda_k, \Lambda'_k(\Lambda_k = \Lambda'_k)$ for the verifier to output $\mathsf{Ver}(\mathsf{C}, (\mathsf{k}, \mathsf{v}), \Lambda_\mathsf{k}) = \mathsf{Ver}(\mathsf{C}, (\mathsf{k}, \mathsf{v}'), \Lambda'_\mathsf{k}) = 1$.

Another adversary $\mathcal{B}$ gains $\mathsf{pp} = \mathsf{A} \in \mathbb{Z}_\mathsf{q}^{\mathsf{n} \times \mathsf{m}}$ from $\mathsf{SIS}^{\infty}_{n,m,q,\beta}$ oracle. Subsequently, $\mathcal{B}$ sends pp to challenger CH of the key-binding game in Definition 4. Challenger CH sends $(\mathsf{pp}, \mathsf{C})$ to $\mathcal{A}$. $\mathcal{A}$ chooses $k_i \in \mathcal{K}$ and computes $z_i = H(k_i)$ which satisfies $z_i \in \mathbb{Z}^m_{\beta/2}$. $\mathcal{A}$ also chooses $v_i \in \mathbb{Z}^m_{\beta/2}$ and computes $x_i = (z_i || v_i)$. Furthermore, it issues k_i queries to CH whether $\mathcal{M}$ contains a tuple of $(k_i, \cdot)$. If yes, CH responds with $\perp$; else, CH updates $\mathcal{M}$ to $\mathcal{M} \cup \{(k_i, v_i)\}$ and executes $\mathsf{Insert}(\mathsf{C}, (\mathsf{k_i}, \mathsf{v_i})) \rightarrow \mathsf{C}'$ to obtain a new commitment C'. Subsequently, $\mathcal{A}$ gains new C'. $\mathcal{A}$ can break the key-binding property to construct a pair of values $((k_i, v_i), (k_i, v'_i))$ and a pair of proofs $(\Lambda_{k_i}, \Lambda'_{k_i})$, where $v_i \neq v'_i \wedge \Lambda_{k_i} = \Lambda'_{k_i}$, which CH outputs $\mathsf{Ver}(\mathsf{C}', (\mathsf{k_i}, \mathsf{v_i}), \Lambda_{\mathsf{k_i}}) = \mathsf{Ver}(\mathsf{C}', (\mathsf{k_i}, \mathsf{v'_i}), \Lambda'_{\mathsf{k_i}}) = 1$. Then, $\mathcal{A}$ computes $z_i = H(k_i)$, $x_i = (z_i || v_i)$, and $x'_i = (z_i || v'_i)$. Parse Λ_{k_i} as $(\Lambda_{k_{i,1}}, \Lambda_{k_{i,2}})$, $\mathcal{A}$ sends a tuple of the form $((x_i, \Lambda_{k_i}), ((x'_i, \Lambda'_{k_i}))$ to CH and $\mathcal{B}$. From the assumption that the key-binding property can be broken, $\mathcal{B}$ can derive the following equation with considering the $\Lambda_{k_{i,1}} = \Lambda'_{k_{i,1}}$.

$$\Lambda_{k_{i,1}} + \mathsf{A} \cdot \mathsf{x_i} = \Lambda'_{k_{i,1}} + \mathsf{A} \cdot \mathsf{x'_i}$$
$$\mathsf{A} \cdot (\mathsf{x_i} - \mathsf{x'_i}) = 0$$

From the condition $x_i \neq x'_i$, it can be observed that $x_i - x'_i \neq 0$. Additionally, considering the condition $\forall x_i \in \mathbb{Z}^m_{\beta/2}$, it satisfies $||x_i - x'_i|| \leq \beta$. In other words, the pair (x_i, x'_i) serves as a solution to the $\mathsf{SIS}^{\infty}_{n,m,q,\beta}$ oracle. Consequently, $\mathcal{B}$ sends (x_i, x'_i) to $\mathsf{SIS}^{\infty}_{n,m,q,\beta}$ oracle and break $\mathsf{SIS}^{\infty}_{n,m,q,\beta}$ problems. ∎

By using the contraposition of Theorem 2, the key-binding property of $\mathsf{KVC}_{m,n,q,\beta}$ satisfies based on the difficulty of $\mathsf{SIS}^{\infty}_{n,m,q,\beta}$ problem.

4.3 Key-Hiding of Insert-KVC$_{m/2,n,q,\beta}$

In this subsection, we prove the key-hiding of Insert-KVC$_{m/2,n,q,\beta}$.

Theorem 3. *Suppose there exists a PPT adversary $\mathcal{A}$ that can break the key-hiding of* Insert-KVC$_{m/2,n,q,\beta}$. *Subsequently, we prove that another PPT adversary $\mathcal{B}$ can break the Decisional-*$\mathsf{SIS}^{\infty}_{n,m,q,\beta}$ *form problem.*

Proof: We assume that there exists an adversary $\mathcal{A}$ that can break the key-hiding property of Insert-KVC$_{m/2,n,q,\beta}$. In other words, $\mathcal{A}$ performs the adversary in Definition 6. First, Decisional-$\mathsf{SIS}^{\infty}_{n,m,q,\beta}$ oracle gain $y_1 \in U$ and $y_2 = \mathsf{A} \cdot \mathsf{x_i}$. Subsequently, it chooses one of them and selects it as y_b. Decisional-$\mathsf{SIS}^{\infty}_{n,m,q,\beta}$ oracle sends (y_b, pp) to $\mathcal{B}$.

$\mathcal{B}$ gains pp and sends it to challenger CH of the key-hiding game in Definition 6. $\mathcal{B}$ sends y_b to $\mathcal{A}$. $\mathcal{A}$ gains $(\mathsf{pp}, \mathsf{C})$ from a challenger CH. Because C is commitment value, C can be expressed in the form $\mathsf{A} \cdot (\mathsf{x_1} + \cdots \mathsf{x_n})$ where $x_i = (z_i || v_i)$ where $z_i \in \mathbb{Z}^{m/2}_{\beta/2}$ and $v_i \in \mathbb{Z}^{m/2}_{\beta/2}$. Subsequently, it computes $\mathsf{C}' = \mathsf{C} + \mathsf{y_b}$. $\mathcal{A}$ assumes to break the key-hiding of Insert-KVC$_{m/2,n,q,\beta}$ so it can distinguish C' constructed from key-value commitment, if C is constructed from key-value commitment. C can be divided into two cases.

- If $y_b = y_2 = \mathsf{A} \cdot \mathsf{x_i}$:

$$\mathsf{C}' = \mathsf{A} \cdot (\mathsf{x_1} + \cdots + \mathsf{x_i} + \mathsf{x_n})$$

  Considering C' can be expressed as $\mathsf{A} \cdot \mathsf{x}$, which is in the form of a key-value commitment scheme, $\mathcal{A}$ can consequently distinguish C' as a key-value commitment map.
- Else: it cannot express C' as a form of key-value commitment scheme. Consequently, $\mathcal{A}$ can distinguish C' as a uniform distribution.

$\mathcal{A}$ sends either result to $\mathcal{B}$, and based on the received result, $\mathcal{B}$ can identify the value of y_b as follows.

- If C' is distinguished as key-value commitment map: y_b is constructed from $y_b = y_2 = \mathsf{A} \cdot \mathsf{x_i}$.
- If C' is distinguish as a uniform distribution: y_b is constructed from uniform distribution.

Finally, $\mathcal{B}$ sends the solution to Decisional-$\mathsf{SIS}^{\infty}_{n,m,q,\beta}$ oracle and break Decisional-$\mathsf{SIS}^{\infty}_{n,m,q,\beta}$ form problem. ∎

By using the contraposition of Theorem 3, the key-hiding property of KVC$_{m,n,q,\beta}$ satisfies based on the difficulty of Decisional-$\mathsf{SIS}^{\infty}_{n,m,q,\beta}$ form problem.

5 Proposed Key-Value Commitment Based on SIS

In this section, we propose our SIS-based KVC$_{m,n,q,\beta}$. In KVC$_{m,n,q,\beta}$, the Update function allows each user to update the committed value v_i. Consequently, KVC$_{m,n,q,\beta}$ is more applicable to applications such as blockchain.

First, we propose the concrete design of $\mathsf{KVC}_{m,n,q,\beta}$ in Sect. 5.1. Then, we explain the feature of $\mathsf{KVC}_{m,n,q,\beta}$ by proving its key-binding of $\mathsf{KVC}_{m,n,q,\beta}$ in Sect. 5.2 and key-hiding of $\mathsf{KVC}_{m,n,q,\beta}$ in Sect. 5.3.

Construction 2 (Construction method of $\mathsf{KVC}_{m,n,q,\beta}$). *In $\mathsf{KVC}_{m,n,q,\beta}$, the proposal comprises of five functions:* Keygen, Insert, Update, ProofUpdate, *and* Ver. *We now explain the construction method of the proposed $\mathsf{KVC}_{m,n,q,\beta}$. First, the public parameters* pp *and the initial commitment value* C *are created using* Keygen. *Each user inserts their own key-value using the* Insert *function and* (pp, C). *At this point, the user's key-value is encrypted using the* Insert *function and stored in the commitment value* C. *Following the insertion of their commitment value into* C, *users create a proof Λ to verify their commitment value using* ProofUpdate. *Because the commitment value* C *is updated every time by inserting a new commitment value from each user, each user needs to update their Λ using* ProofUpdate *whenever* C *is updated. Finally, when each user wants to open their key-value, they send their key-value and Λ to the verifier, who performs verification on the key-value and Λ to ensure their validity.*

5.1 Concrete Explanation of Proposed $\mathsf{KVC}_{m,n,q,\beta}$

This subsection describes the concrete function of our proposed $\mathsf{KVC}_{m,n,q,\beta}$. We first show the concrete function of $\mathsf{KVC}_{m,n,q,\beta}$, then analyze the completeness and efficiency of $\mathsf{KVC}_{m,n,q,\beta}$.

- $\mathsf{KVC}_{m,n,q,\beta}$

- $\mathsf{Keygen}(1^\lambda) \to (\mathsf{pp}, \mathsf{C})$: Sample the description q, m, n, β, which satisfies $m, \beta = poly(n)$ and $q > \beta \cdot \tilde{O}(\sqrt{n})$. Sample the uniform random matrix $\mathsf{A} \in \mathbb{Z}_\mathsf{q}^{\mathsf{n}\times\mathsf{m}}$ for public parameter pp. Set $\mathcal{V} = \mathbb{Z}^m_{\beta/2}$ and $\mathcal{K} = \mathbb{Z}^\ell$. Let E as the identity matrix, and choose $u \in \mathcal{V}$. Output $(\mathsf{pp}, \mathsf{C}) = ((\mathsf{q}, \mathsf{m}, \mathsf{n}, \beta, \mathsf{u}), (\mathsf{E} \cdot \mathsf{u}, \mathsf{A} \cdot \mathsf{u}))$.
- $\mathsf{Insert}(\mathsf{C}, (\mathsf{k_i}, \mathsf{v_i})) \to (\mathsf{C}, \Lambda_{\mathsf{k_i}}, \mathsf{upd})$: Parse C as $(\mathsf{C}_1, \mathsf{C}_2)$, and parse Λ_{k_i} as $(\Lambda_{k_{i,1}}, \Lambda_{k_{i,2}})$. Let $k_i \in \mathbb{Z}^m$, $v_i \in \mathbb{Z}^m_{\beta/2}$, and compute $z_i = H(k_i)$ which satisfies $z_i \in \mathbb{Z}^m_{\beta/2}$, where H is a hash function $H : \mathbb{Z}^\ell \to \mathbb{Z}^m_{\beta/2}$. The commitment value and its proof Λ_{k_i} are inserted as

$$
\begin{aligned}
\Lambda'_{k_i} &= (\mathsf{C}_1, \mathsf{C}_2) \\
\mathsf{C}' &= (\mathsf{C}_1 + \mathsf{A} \cdot (\mathsf{z_i} + \mathsf{v_i}), \mathsf{C}_2 + \mathsf{A} \cdot (\mathsf{z_i} + \mathsf{v_i})) \\
\mathsf{upd} &= (z_i, v_i) \\
\Lambda_{k_{i,1}} &\leftarrow \Lambda'_{k_{i,1}} \\
\Lambda_{k_{i,2}} &\leftarrow \Lambda'_{k_{i,2}} \\
\mathsf{C}_1 &\leftarrow \mathsf{C}'_1 \\
\mathsf{C}_2 &\leftarrow \mathsf{C}'_2
\end{aligned}
$$

Output $(\mathsf{C}, \Lambda_{\mathsf{k_i}}, \mathsf{upd})$.

- $\mathsf{Update}(\mathsf{C}, (\mathsf{k_i}, \delta)) \rightarrow (\mathsf{C}, \mathsf{upd}))$: Parse C as $(\mathsf{C_1}, \mathsf{C_2})$, and parse upd as $(\mathsf{upd}_1, \mathsf{upd}_2)$. The updated value of the commitment, when v_i updates to $v_i' = v_i + \delta$, is

$$\mathsf{C}_1' = \mathsf{C}_1 + \mathsf{A} \cdot \delta$$
$$\mathsf{C}_2' = \mathsf{C}_2 + \mathsf{A} \cdot \delta$$
$$\mathsf{C}_1 \leftarrow \mathsf{C}_1'$$
$$\mathsf{C}_2 \leftarrow \mathsf{C}_2'$$
$$\mathsf{upd} = (z_i, \delta)$$

Output $(\mathsf{C}, \mathsf{upd})$.

- $\mathsf{ProofUpdate}(\mathsf{k_i}, \Lambda_{\mathsf{k_i}}, \mathsf{upd}) \rightarrow \Lambda_{\mathsf{k_i}}$: Parse upd as $(\mathsf{upd}_1, \mathsf{upd}_2)$, and Λ_{k_i} as $(\Lambda_{k_{i,1}}, \Lambda_{k_{i,2}})$. Let $z = H(\mathsf{upd}_1)$.
  * If $z < \mathsf{upd}_1$: Set

$$\Lambda_{k_i}' = (\Lambda_{k_{i,1}} + \mathsf{A} \cdot (\mathsf{upd}_1 + \mathsf{upd}_2), \Lambda_{k_{i,2}} + \mathsf{A} \cdot (\mathsf{upd}_1 + \mathsf{upd}_2))$$
$$\Lambda_{k_i} \leftarrow \Lambda_{k_i}'$$

  Output Λ_{k_i}.
  * If $z > \mathsf{upd}_1$: Set

$$\Lambda_{k_i}' = (\Lambda_{k_{i,1}} + \mathsf{A} \cdot \mathsf{upd}_2, \Lambda_{k_{i,2}} + \mathsf{A} \cdot \mathsf{upd}_2)$$
$$\Lambda_{k_i} \leftarrow \Lambda_{k_i}'$$

  Output Λ_{k_i}.
  * Elif $z = \mathsf{upd}_1$: Output Λ_{k_i}.
- $\mathsf{Ver}(\mathsf{C}, (\mathsf{k_i}, \mathsf{v_i}), \Lambda_{\mathsf{k_i}}) \rightarrow 1/\perp$: Parse C as $(\mathsf{C_1}, \mathsf{C_2})$, and parse Λ_{k_i} as $(\Lambda_{k_{i,1}}, \Lambda_{k_{i,2}})$, and let z as $z = H(k_i)$. The user who wants to open the commitment value sends (k_i, v_i) to the verifier, which checks the following.
  * $v_i \in \mathcal{V}$ and $k_i \in \mathcal{K}$,
  * $\Lambda_{k_{i,1}} + \mathsf{A} \cdot (\mathsf{z} + \mathsf{v_i}) = \mathsf{C}_1$,
  * $\Lambda_{k_{i,2}} + \mathsf{A} \cdot (\mathsf{z} + \mathsf{v_i}) = \mathsf{C}_2$,
  * $\Lambda_{k_{i,2}} - \Lambda_{k_{i,1}} = u \cdot (\mathsf{A} - \mathsf{E})$

  If the aforementioned equation satisfies, the verifier outputs 1. Else, they output $\perp$.

The correctness of $\mathsf{KVC}_{m,n,q,\beta}$ can be determined immediately by following the construction method in Construction 2. In the commitment phase, the user sends its commitment value C and upd. In the decommitment phase, user sends their own value $((k_i, v_i), \Lambda_{k_i})$. In upd, Note that in the commitment phase, the user's key k_i is sent in the form of hashed z_i. Consequently, each user's key k_i is not disclosed until the decommitment phase.

Analyze $\mathsf{KVC}_{m,n,q,\beta}$: From Construction 2, multiplication and addition cost in each function satisfy the following.

- Insert: one hash computation, multiplication cost: $4mn$, addition cost: $6n$,
- Update : zero hash computation, multiplication cost: $2mn$, addition cost: $2n$,
- ProofUpdate: one hash computation, at most multiplication cost: $6mn$, addition cost: $6n$,
- Ver: one hash computation, multiplication cost: $4mn$, addition or subtraction cost: $7n$.

We assume that there is only one user, and each of the five functions is executed once. Furthermore, the size of the key-value commitment is constant.

5.2 Key-Binding of Proposed $\mathsf{KVC}_{m,n,q,\beta}$

In this subsection, we prove the key-biding property of $\mathsf{KVC}_{m,n,q,\beta}$.

Theorem 4. *Suppose there exists a PPT adversary $\mathcal{A}$ that can break the key-binding of $\mathsf{KVC}_{m,n,q,\beta}$. We then prove that another PPT adversary $\mathcal{B}$ can break the $\mathsf{SIS}^{\infty}_{n,m,q,\beta}$ problem.*

Proof: We assume that there exists an adversary $\mathcal{A}$ that can break the key-binding property of $\mathsf{KVC}_{m,n,q,\beta}$. In other words, $\mathcal{A}$ performs the adversary in Definition 4. For some k, create a value $v, v'(v \neq v')$ and a proof value $\Lambda_k, \Lambda'_k(\Lambda_k = \Lambda'_k)$ such that the verifier can output $\mathsf{Ver}(\mathsf{C}, (\mathsf{k}, \mathsf{v}), \Lambda_\mathsf{k}) = \mathsf{Ver}(\mathsf{C}, (\mathsf{k}, \mathsf{v}'), \Lambda'_\mathsf{k}) = 1$.

Another adversary $\mathcal{B}$ first gains $\mathsf{pp} = \mathsf{A} \in \mathbb{Z}_\mathsf{q}^{\mathsf{n} \times \mathsf{m}}$ from $\mathsf{SIS}^{\infty}_{n,m,q,\beta}$ oracle. Subsequently, $\mathcal{B}$ sends pp to challenger CH of key-binding game in Definition 4. Challenger CH sends $(\mathsf{pp}, \mathsf{C})$ to $\mathcal{A}$. $\mathcal{A}$ chooses $k_i \in \mathcal{K}$ and computes $z_i = H(k_i)$ which satisfies $z_i \in \mathbb{Z}^m_{\beta/2}$. $\mathcal{A}$ chooses $v_i \in \mathbb{Z}^m_{\beta/2}$. It issues k_i queries to CH whether $\mathcal{M}$ contains a tuple of $(k_i, \cdot)$. If yes, CH responds with $\perp$. Else, CH updates $\mathcal{M}$ to $\mathcal{M} \cup \{(k_i, v_i)\}$ and executes $\mathsf{Insert}(\mathsf{C}, (\mathsf{k_i}, \mathsf{v_i})) \to \mathsf{C}'$ to obtain a new commitment C'. Then, $\mathcal{A}$ gains new C'. $\mathcal{A}$ can break the key-binding property so it can construct a pair of values $((k_i, v_i), (k_i, v'_i))$ and a pair of proofs $(\Lambda_{k_i}, \Lambda'_{k_i})$ where $v_i \neq v'_i \wedge \Lambda_{k_i} = \Lambda'_{k_i}$ which CH outputs $\mathsf{Ver}(\mathsf{C}', (\mathsf{k_i}, \mathsf{v_i}), \Lambda_{\mathsf{k_i}}) = \mathsf{Ver}(\mathsf{C}', (\mathsf{k_i}, \mathsf{v}'_\mathsf{i}), \Lambda'_{\mathsf{k_i}}) = 1$. Parse Λ_{k_i} as $(\Lambda_{k_{i,1}}, \Lambda_{k_{i,2}})$, $\mathcal{A}$ sends a tuple of the form $((k_i, v_i, \Lambda_{k_i}), ((k_i, v'_i, \Lambda'_{k_i}))$ to CH and $\mathcal{B}$. From the assumption that the key-binding property can be broken, $\mathcal{B}$ can derive the following equation with considering the $\Lambda_{k_{i,1}} = \Lambda'_{k_{i,1}}$ and computing $z_i = H(k_i)$.

$$\Lambda_{k_{i,1}} + \mathsf{A} \cdot (\mathsf{z_i} + \mathsf{v_i}) = \Lambda'_{k_{i,1}} + \mathsf{A} \cdot (\mathsf{z_i} + \mathsf{v}'_\mathsf{i})$$
$$\mathsf{A} \cdot (\mathsf{z_i} + \mathsf{v_i}) = \mathsf{A} \cdot (\mathsf{z_i} + \mathsf{v}'_\mathsf{i})$$
$$\mathsf{A} \cdot (\mathsf{v_i} - \mathsf{v}'_\mathsf{i}) = 0$$

From the condition $v_i \neq v_i'$, it can be observed that $v_i - v_i' \neq 0$. Additionally, considering the condition $\forall v_i \in \mathbb{Z}^m_{\beta/2}$, it satisfies $||v_i - v_i'|| \leq \beta$. In other words, the pair (v_i, v_i') serves as a solution to the $\mathsf{SIS}^{\infty}_{n,m,q,\beta}$ oracle. Consequently, $\mathcal{B}$ sends (v_i, v_i') to $\mathsf{SIS}^{\infty}_{n,m,q,\beta}$ oracle and break $\mathsf{SIS}^{\infty}_{n,m,q,\beta}$ problems. ∎
By using the contraposition of Theorem 4, the key-binding property of $\mathsf{KVC}_{m,n,q,\beta}$ is satisfied based on the difficulty of $\mathsf{SIS}^{\infty}_{n,m,q,\beta}$ problem.

5.3 Key-Hiding of $\mathsf{KVC}_{m,n,q,\beta}$

In this subsection, we prove its key-hiding of $\mathsf{KVC}_{m,n,q,\beta}$.

Theorem 5. *Suppose there exists a PPT adversary $\mathcal{A}$ that can break the key-hiding of $\mathsf{KVC}_{m,n,q,\beta}$. We then prove that another PPT adversary $\mathcal{B}$ can break the Decisional-$\mathsf{SIS}^{\infty}_{n,m,q,\beta}$ form problem.*

Proof: We assume that there exists an adversary $\mathcal{A}$ that can break the key-hiding property of $\mathsf{KVC}_{m,n,q,\beta}$. In other words, $\mathcal{A}$ performs the adversary in Definition 6. First, Decisional-$\mathsf{SIS}^{\infty}_{n,m,q,\beta}$ oracle gain $y_1 \in U$ and $y_2 = \mathsf{A} \cdot \mathsf{x_i}$. Then, it chooses one of them as y_b. Decisional-$\mathsf{SIS}^{\infty}_{n,2m,q,\beta}$ oracle sends (y_b, pp) to $\mathcal{B}$.

$\mathcal{B}$ gains pp and sends it to challenger CH of key-hiding game in Definition 6. $\mathcal{B}$ sends y_b to $\mathcal{A}$. $\mathcal{A}$ gains $(\mathsf{pp}, \mathsf{C})$ from a challenger CH. Since C is commitment value, C can be expressed in the form $\mathsf{A} \cdot (\mathsf{x_1} + \cdots \mathsf{x_n})$ where $x_i = z_i + v_i$. Then, it computes $\mathsf{C}' = \mathsf{C} + \mathsf{y_b}$. $\mathcal{A}$ assume to break the key-hiding of $\mathsf{KVC}_{m,n,q,\beta}$, thus, it can distinguish C' is constructed from key-value commitment if C is constructed from key-value commitment. C can be divided into two cases.

- If $y_b = y_2 = \mathsf{A} \cdot \mathsf{x_i}$:

$$\mathsf{C}' = \mathsf{A} \cdot (\mathsf{x_1} + \cdots \mathsf{x_n} + \mathsf{x_i})$$

  Because C' can be expressed as $\mathsf{A} \cdot \mathsf{x}$, which is in the form of a key-value commitment scheme, $\mathcal{A}$ can consequently distinguish C' as a key-value commitment map.
- Else: it cannot express C' as the form of key-value commitment scheme. Consequently, $\mathcal{A}$ can distinguish C' as a uniform distribution.

$\mathcal{A}$ sends either result to $\mathcal{B}$ and based on the received result, $\mathcal{B}$ can identify the value of y_b as follows,

- If C' is distinguish as a key-value commitment map: y_b is constructed from $y_b = y_2 = \mathsf{A} \cdot \mathsf{x_i}$.
- If C' is distinguish as a uniform distribution: y_b is constructed from uniform distribution.

Finally, $\mathcal{B}$ sends the solution to Decisional-$\mathsf{SIS}^{\infty}_{n,m,q,\beta}$ oracle and break Decisional-$\mathsf{SIS}^{\infty}_{n,m,q,\beta}$ form problem. ∎
By using the contraposition of Theorem 5, the key-hiding property of $\mathsf{KVC}_{m,n,q,\beta}$ satisfies based on difficulty of Decisional-$\mathsf{SIS}^{\infty}_{n,m,q,\beta}$ form problem.

6 Comparison

In this section, we compare our two key-value commitment schemes in Table 1. In $\mathsf{Insert\text{-}KVC}_{m/2,n,q,\beta}$, Update function is not included, making the construction of $\mathsf{Insert\text{-}KVC}_{m/2,n,q,\beta}$ much simpler than $\mathsf{KVC}_{m,n,q,\beta}$. In the $\mathsf{Insert\text{-}KVC}_{m/2,n,q,\beta}$ construction, the total multiplication and addition cost can be reduced by 1/2 compared to the $\mathsf{KVC}_{m,n,q,\beta}$ construction from Table 1. Consequently, if you use a key-value commitment scheme that does not need to update values, $\mathsf{Insert\text{-}KVC}_{m/2,n,q,\beta}$ is more suitable.

Conversely, $\mathsf{KVC}_{m,n,q,\beta}$ includes a Update function that can update the value after creating the commitment value. Therefore, if you use a key-value commitment scheme to apply to certain applications such as blockchain, $\mathsf{KVC}_{m,n,q,\beta}$ is more suitable.

Table 1. Comparison of $\mathsf{Insert\text{-}KVC}_{m/2,n,q,\beta}$ and $\mathsf{KVC}_{m,n,q,\beta}$

Scheme	key-binding	key-hiding	total multiplication cost	total addition cost
$\mathsf{Insert\text{-}KVC}_{m/2,n,q,\beta}$	$\mathsf{SIS}^{\infty}_{n,m,q,\beta}$ problem	Decisional-$\mathsf{SIS}^{\infty}_{n,m,q,\beta}$ form problem	$6mn$	$11n$
$\mathsf{KVC}_{m,n,q,\beta}$	$\mathsf{SIS}^{\infty}_{n,m,q,\beta}$ problem	Decisional-$\mathsf{SIS}^{\infty}_{n,m,q,\beta}$ form problem	$16mn$	$21n$

7 Conclusion

In this paper, we propose two key-value commitment schemes, $\mathsf{Insert\text{-}KVC}_{m/2,n,q,\beta}$ and $\mathsf{KVC}_{m,n,q,\beta}$ by achieving the following.

- Prove the Decisional-$\mathsf{SIS}^{\infty}_{n,m,q,\beta}$ form problem is secure based on the hardness of One-Way-$\mathsf{SIS}^{\infty}_{n,m,q,\beta}$ problem.
- Propose the construction of $\mathsf{Insert\text{-}KVC}_{m/2,n,q,\beta}$ based on lattice assumption.
- Prove the key-binding of $\mathsf{Insert\text{-}KVC}_{m/2,n,q,\beta}$ based on the $\mathsf{SIS}^{\infty}_{n,m,q,\beta}$ problem, and prove the key-hiding of $\mathsf{Insert\text{-}KVC}_{m/2,n,q,\beta}$ based on the Decisional-$\mathsf{SIS}^{\infty}_{n,m,q,\beta}$ form problem.
- Analyze the multiplication and addition cost of $\mathsf{Insert\text{-}KVC}_{m/2,n,q,\beta}$.
- Propose the construction of $\mathsf{KVC}_{m,n,q,\beta}$ based on lattice assumption.
- Prove the key-binding of $\mathsf{KVC}_{m,n,q,\beta}$ based on the $\mathsf{SIS}^{\infty}_{n,m,q,\beta}$ problem, and prove the key-hiding of $\mathsf{KVC}_{m,n,q,\beta}$ based on the Decisional-$\mathsf{SIS}^{\infty}_{n,m,q,\beta}$ form problem.
- Analyze the multiplication and addition cost of $\mathsf{KVC}_{m,n,q,\beta}$.

Acknowledgment. This work is partially supported by JSPS KAKENHI Grant Number JP21H03443 and SECOM Science and Technology Foundation.

References

1. Bitcoin. https://bitcoin.org/
2. Ethereum. https://www.ethereum.org/
3. Agrawal, S., Raghuraman, S.: KVaC: key-value commitments for blockchains and beyond. In: Moriai, S., Wang, H. (eds.) ASIACRYPT 2020. LNCS, vol. 12493, pp. 839–869. Springer, Cham (2020). https://doi.org/10.1007/978-3-030-64840-4_28
4. Allende, M., et al.: Quantum-resistance in blockchain networks. CoRR, abs/2106.06640 (2021)
5. Benaloh, J., de Mare, M.: One-way accumulators: a decentralized alternative to digital signatures. In: Helleseth, T. (ed.) EUROCRYPT 1993. LNCS, vol. 765, pp. 274–285. Springer, Heidelberg (1994). https://doi.org/10.1007/3-540-48285-7_24
6. Blum, M.: Coin flipping by telephone - a protocol for solving impossible problems. In: COMPCON 1982, Digest of Papers, Twenty-Fourth IEEE Computer Society International Conference, San Francisco, California, USA, 22–25 February 1982, pp. 133–137. IEEE Computer Society (1982)
7. Catalano, D., Fiore, D.: Vector commitments and their applications. In: Kurosawa, K., Hanaoka, G. (eds.) PKC 2013. LNCS, vol. 7778, pp. 55–72. Springer, Heidelberg (2013). https://doi.org/10.1007/978-3-642-36362-7_5
8. Damgård, I.: Commitment schemes and zero-knowledge protocols. In: Damgård, I.B. (ed.) EEF School 1998. LNCS, vol. 1561, pp. 63–86. Springer, Heidelberg (1999). https://doi.org/10.1007/3-540-48969-X_3
9. Gentry, C., Peikert, C., Vaikuntanathan, V.: Trapdoors for hard lattices and new cryptographic constructions. In: Dwork, C. (ed.) Proceedings of the 40th Annual ACM Symposium on Theory of Computing, Victoria, British Columbia, Canada, 17–20 May 2008, pp. 197–206. ACM (2008)
10. Goldwasser, S., Micali, S., Rivest, R.L.: A digital signature scheme secure against adaptive chosen-message attacks. SIAM J. Comput. **17**(2), 281–308 (1988)
11. Haitner, I., Nguyen, M., Ong, S.J., Reingold, O., Vadhan, S.P.: Statistically hiding commitments and statistical zero-knowledge arguments from any one-way function. SIAM J. Comput. **39**(3), 1153–1218 (2009)
12. Halevi, S., Micali, S.: Practical and provably-secure commitment schemes from collision-free hashing. In: Koblitz, N. (ed.) CRYPTO 1996. LNCS, vol. 1109, pp. 201–215. Springer, Heidelberg (1996). https://doi.org/10.1007/3-540-68697-5_16
13. Katz, J., Lindell, Y.: Introduction to Modern Cryptography, 2nd edn. CRC Press, Boca Raton (2014)
14. Miyaji, H., Wang, Y., Kawachi, A., Miyaji, A.: A commitment scheme with output locality-3 fit for IoT device. Secur. Commun. Netw. 2949513, 1–10 (2021)
15. Pedersen, T.P.: Non-interactive and information-theoretic secure verifiable secret sharing. In: Feigenbaum, J. (ed.) CRYPTO 1991. LNCS, vol. 576, pp. 129–140. Springer, Heidelberg (1992). https://doi.org/10.1007/3-540-46766-1_9
16. Yuen, T.H., Esgin, M.F., Liu, J.K., Au, M.H., Ding, Z.: *DualRing*: generic construction of ring signatures with efficient instantiations. In: Malkin, T., Peikert, C. (eds.) CRYPTO 2021. LNCS, vol. 12825, pp. 251–281. Springer, Cham (2021). https://doi.org/10.1007/978-3-030-84242-0_10
17. Zamyatin, A., Al-Bassam, M., Zindros, D., Kokoris-Kogias, E., Moreno-Sanchez, P., Kiayias, A., Knottenbelt, W.J.: SoK: communication across distributed ledgers. In: Borisov, N., Diaz, C. (eds.) FC 2021. LNCS, vol. 12675, pp. 3–36. Springer, Heidelberg (2021). https://doi.org/10.1007/978-3-662-64331-0_1

A Practical Forward-Secure DualRing

Nan Li[1], Yingjiu Li[2], Atsuko Miyaji[3], Yangguang Tian[4(✉)], and Tsz Hon Yuen[5]

[1] School of Computing and Information Technology, University of Wollongong, Wollongong, Australia
[2] Computer and Information Science, University of Oregon, Eugene, USA
[3] Graduate School of Engineering, Osaka University, Suita, Japan
[4] Department of Computer Science, University of Surrey, Guildford, UK
yangguang.tian@surrey.ac.uk
[5] Department of Computer Science, University of Hong Kong, Pok Fu Lam, Hong Kong

Abstract. Ring signature allows a signer to generate a signature on behalf of a set of public keys, while a verifier can verify the signature without identifying who the actual signer is. In Crypto 2021, Yuen et al. proposed a new type of ring signature scheme called DualRing. However, it lacks forward security. The security of DualRing cannot be guaranteed if the signer's secret key is compromised. To address this problem, we introduce forward-secure DualRing, in which a signer can periodically update their secret key using a "split-and-combine" method. A practical instantiation of our scheme enjoys a logarithmic complexity in signature size and key size. Implementation and evaluation further validate the practicality of our proposed scheme.

Keywords: DualRing · Forward Security · Practical Scheme

1 Introduction

Ring signatures [31] allow a signer to sign messages on behalf of a set of public keys, and a verifier cannot identify who the real signer is. Since ring signatures provide anonymity, they are widely used in the privacy-preserving scenarios such as whistleblowing, e-voting, and privacy-preserving cryptocurrencies. The classic ring signature scheme [31] requires a signer first to compute n-1 pseudo-signatures for a set of n public keys PK. Then, the signer generates a real signature on a challenge value c using his signing key. The n signatures together with the challenge value c form a ring signature under PK.

The state-of-the-art ring signature scheme is called DualRing [33] proposed in Crypto 2021. The construction of DualRing takes a different approach, which achieves a significant saving in terms of signature size. Specifically, a signer first chooses n-1 pseudo-challenge values. Next, the signer derives a real challenge value c from the n-1 pseudo-challenge values and a set of n public keys PK. The last step is the signer generating a signature on the challenge value c using his signing key. The resulting DualRing consists of a single signature and n challenge

J. Deng et al. (Eds.): CANS 2023, LNCS 14342, pp. 516–537, 2023.
https://doi.org/10.1007/978-981-99-7563-1_23

values compared to the classical ring signature that consists of a single challenge value and n signatures. The n challenge values in DualRing can be further compressed to a $O(\log n)$-size argument of knowledge in the discrete logarithm (DL) setting. However, DualRing lacks forward security. Forward secrecy [14] means that the unforgeability of the message-signature pair generated in the past is still guaranteed after the current secret key is leaked (e.g., due to side-channel attacks).

1.1 Motivations

Forward-secure ring signature is important for privacy-preserving applications. In the case of whistleblowing, an employee Alice intends to leak a secret as a whistleblower on behalf of all public keys in her company while she is still in the company, and she does not want to be identified before leaving the company. If Alice uses a ring signature to reveal the secret, the unforgeability of the ring signature assumes that no adversary can obtain any secret key from the members of the ring. However, due to the nature of dynamic ring formation in ring signatures, it is difficult for such assumption to hold over time. In our example, Alice may not know each and every user in the company, and she may not have any control to ensure that all users in her company would keep their secret keys secure over a certain period of time. Therefore, it is beneficial to design a cryptographic solution, such that the unforgeability of a ring signature is guaranteed if and only if the secret keys of the members of the ring are not compromised *at the time of signing.*

Forward-secure ring signatures (FS-RS) can be used in the case of remote (or internet) voting. The internet voting systems like Helios [5], Remotegrity [35], and VOTOR [22] allow anyone to set up an election, invite voters to cast a secret ballot, compute a tally, and provide a verifiable tally for the election. Our forward-secure ring signature scheme is suitable for internet voting for two reasons: 1) On the usability side, the voters register their credentials once to a voting authority. The registered credentials can be re-used in different elections without being identified. 2) On the security side, the voters submit their votes in an election and (privately) updates their credentials for future elections. The forward security of our ring signature scheme ensures that no user's updated credentials can be misused by adversary for tracing or revealing the vote submissions of the user, even if the user is under coercion to reveal their updated credentials.

1.2 Overview of Our Construction

In this work, we introduce forward-secure DualRing and extend it to forward-secure linkable DualRing. The proposed construction is built from DualRing [33] and a key update technique [11,20]. First, we review a Type-T signature (three-move type such as Schnorr signature [32]), which is used in building our scheme. We focus on the DL-based Type-T signature in this work. The signing process of the Type-T signature includes three functions: 1) a commit function, which outputs a commitment $R = g^{\widehat{r}}$, where $\widehat{r}$ denotes randomness; 2) a hash function, which outputs a challenge $\widehat{c} = \mathtt{H}(R||\mathtt{pk}||m)$, where $\mathtt{pk} = g^{\mathtt{sk}}$ denotes a public key, sk denotes a secret key, and m denotes the signing message. 3) a response function, which outputs a response $z = \widehat{r} - \widehat{c} \cdot \mathtt{sk}$. The resulting signature is $\sigma = (\widehat{c}, z)$. For verification, one can check $\widehat{c} \stackrel{?}{=} \mathtt{H}(R' || \mathtt{pk} || m)$, where $R' = g^z \cdot \mathtt{pk}^{\widehat{c}}$.

Second, we show a key update technique, which was used in building the forward-secure schemes [11,20]. We assume that a secret key at epoch (i.e., a fixed time period) t includes the following elements,

$$\mathtt{sk}_t = (c, d, e_{t+1}, \cdots, e_T) = (g^r, \underline{h^{\mathtt{sk}} \cdot F(t)^r}, h_{t+1}^r, \cdots, h_T^r)$$

where T denotes the upper bound of time periods, r denotes randomness (due to security reasons), $F(t)$ represents a public function for time t, and $h_{t+1}^r, \cdots, h_T^r$ is used for key updates. The key update process at epoch t' is shown as follows.

$$\mathtt{sk}_{t'} = (c', d', e_{t+2}, \cdots, e_T) = (g^{r+r'}, \underline{h^{\mathtt{sk}} \cdot F(t')^{r+r'}}, h_{t+2}^{r+r'}, \cdots, h_T^{r+r'})$$

where t' denotes a new time period (note that t is a prefix of t'), r' denotes a new randomness. For each key update, it requires a new randomness r' to ensure forward security.

The challenge of designing forward-secure Type-T signature (and forward-secure DualRing) is to replace the static secret key sk by a time-dependent secret key $\mathtt{sk}_t$ for signing, while the public key pk is fixed. However, the secret key $\mathtt{sk}_t$ is not suitable to be used directly in generating the response z in forward-secure DualRing because $\mathtt{sk}_t$ consists of group elements that cannot work with the response function on finite field $\mathbb{F}_q$ (q is prime number). We propose a novel technique to apply $\mathtt{sk}_t$ in generating forward-secure DualRing signatures. The key idea is that we use group elements (c, d) as the signing keys, and we use the randomness $\widehat{r}$ involved in the commit function to *link* the signing keys (c, d). We call it "split-and-combine" method. Specifically, we first *split* the randomness $\widehat{r}$ used in the commit function into two shares $(\widehat{r_1}, \widehat{r_2})$, where $\widehat{r} = \widehat{r_1} + \widehat{r_2}$. Then, we use signing keys (c, d) to "sign" two randomness shares $(\widehat{r_1}, \widehat{r_2})$ respectively, and output two response values. The resulting signature includes a challenge $\widehat{c}$ (i.e., the hash function's output) and two response values. The verification of the signature is performed by computing a commitment R' from the two response values, and checking $\widehat{c} \stackrel{?}{=} \mathtt{H}(R' || \mathtt{pk} || m)$. Note that the two randomness shares can be *combined* in the generation of R'. To conclude, this split-and-combine method allows a signer to use the split randomness shares to link group elements (c, d). The linked group elements are used in generating the response values for forward-secure DualRing signatures. In the process of signature verification, the split randomness shares can be combined as a verifier computes a commitment R' from the response values.

1.3 Related Work

Ring Signatures. Ring signatures [31] allow a signer to sign messages over a chosen set of public keys (including his/her own) without revealing who the real signer is. Since ring signatures provide anonymity (i.e., signer-ambiguity), they can be used in constructing various privacy-preserving protocols, including whistleblowing, electric voting, and privacy-preserving cryptocurrencies (e.g., Monero and Zcash).

Abe et al. [4] introduced a generic framework that allows a signer to choose different types of public keys to form a ring (i.e., public-key set). Specifically, a signer can choose both RSA-keys and Discrete logarithm (DL)-keys to generate ring signatures. The ring signature scheme is efficient if it is used only with a single type of public keys.

Dodis et al. [19] introduced an accumulator-based ring signature scheme. The resulting signature size is constant, which is independent of the size of the ring. Specifically, the proposed scheme allows the signer to "compress" n public keys into a single value, and rely on a *witness* showing that the signer's public key is in the public-key set. However, their scheme requires a trusted setup for generating system parameters.

Groth and Kohlweiss [21] proposed efficient ring signatures based on one-out-of-many proofs. The one-out-of-many approach requires a zero-knowledge proof to prove the knowledge of the secret key with respect to one of the public keys in the ring. The proof size of this scheme is $\mathcal{O}(\log n)$, and it is setup-free. The follow-up works are various. For example, Bootle et al. [13] presented an accountable ring signature scheme, which extends Groth and Kohlweiss's scheme to support accountability. Libert et al. [24] introduced a tightly secure ring signature scheme. Their scheme is derived from Groth and Kohlweiss's ring signature scheme and DDH-based Elgamal encryptions. Recently, Lai et al. [23] introduced Omniring (i.e., Ring Confidential Transactions or RingCT) for RingCT, and Yuen et al. [34] proposed a new ring signature scheme for RingCT3.0. Both signature schemes require no trusted setup, and the proof size is $\mathcal{O}(\log n)$.

Forward Security. Forward security states that the compromise of entities at the present time will not affect the security of cryptographic primitives in the past. It is regarded as a basic security guarantee for many cryptographic primitives, including encryptions, signatures and key exchanges. Here, we focus on forward-secure signatures. If an attacker compromises a signer (e.g., via side-channel attacks), she cannot forge a signature from the signer at an earlier time. Specifically, when the attacker compromises a signer's signing key for the current time period, the signing keys from earlier time periods cannot be recovered. In this case, a one-way key update process is needed.

Bellare and Miner [8] formalized the security for forward-secure signatures. They also proposed a scheme with a squaring-based key update. So, its forward security is based on the hardness of factoring ($N = pq$, where p, q are two primes). Later, forward-secure ring signature (FS-RS) schemes have been proposed in the literature [15,26,27]. However, they have certain limitations. For example, the squaring-based key update in [26] is not suitable for the standard RSA/DL-based forward-secure schemes. The scheme in [27] involves composite-order group operations, thus it is less practical. The forward-secure linkable ring signature proposed in [15] is constructed from hypothetical multilinear maps. However, it remains unclear how to instantiate such multilinear maps. We also notice that the forward-secure ring signature scheme proposed in [26] is setup-free, and those in [15,27] require a trusted setup. Our proposed scheme can operate without any trusted setup by leveraging an indifferentiable hash-to-curve algorithm [16], as suggested in [20].

2 Preliminaries

In this section, we present the complexity assumptions and the building blocks for constructing our proposed protocol.

2.1 Complexity Assumptions

Bilinear Maps. We define a group generation as $(q, \mathbb{G}, \mathbb{H}, \mathbb{G}_T, \hat{e}) \leftarrow \mathsf{GroupGen}(1^\lambda)$, where q is a prime number, g, h are two group generators, $\mathbb{G}$, $\mathbb{H}$ and $\mathbb{G}_T$ are cyclic groups of order q. The asymmetric bilinear map $\hat{e} : \mathbb{G} \times \mathbb{H} \rightarrow \mathbb{G}_T$ has the following properties: 1) Bilinearity: for $g, h \in \mathbb{G}$ and $a, b \in \mathbb{Z}_q$, we have $\hat{e}(g^a, h^b) = \hat{e}(g, h)^{ab}$. 2) Non-degeneracy: $\exists g \in \mathbb{G}$ such that $\hat{e}(g, h)$ has order q in $\mathbb{G}_T$.
We introduce a variant of wBDHI assumption, which is used in the unforgeability analysis.

Definition 1. *Given group generators $g \in \mathbb{G}, h \in \mathbb{H}$, and $a, b \in \mathbb{Z}_q$, we define the advantage of the adversary $\mathcal{A}$ in solving the wBDHI problem as*

$$\mathtt{Adv}_{\mathcal{A}}^{wBDHI}(\lambda) = \Pr[\mathcal{A}(g, h, g^a, g^b, h^a, h^b, \underline{h^{b^2}, \cdots, h^{b^\ell}}) = \hat{e}(g, h)^{a \cdot b^{\ell+1}} \in \mathbb{G}_T]$$

The wBDHI assumption is secure if $\mathtt{Adv}_{\mathcal{A}}^{wBDHI}(\lambda)$ is negligible in λ.

The wBDHI assumption holds for Type-3 pairings (i.e., $\mathbb{G} \neq \mathbb{H}$), which is shown in [20]. The difference between this variant and the existing wBHDI assumption [20] is small. If we give $g^{b^2}, \cdots, g^{b^\ell}$ (as well as the above underline part in group $\mathbb{H}$) to $\mathcal{A}$, it is equal to the wBDHI assumption described in [20]. We omit the security analysis of this variant since the reduction is straightforward. The decisional version of the wBDHI problem requires $\mathcal{A}$ to distinguish $\hat{e}(g, h)^{a \cdot b^{\ell+1}}$ from a random value in $\mathbb{G}_T$. For simplicity, we use wBDHI to represent the variant used in this work.

2.2 DualRing

The DL-based DualRing signature scheme consists of the following algorithms [33].

- $\mathsf{Setup}(1^\lambda)$: It takes a security parameter λ as input, outputs public parameters PP, which are the implicit input for all the following algorithms. It also defines a hash function $\mathtt{H} : \{0, 1\}^* \rightarrow \mathbb{Z}_q$.
- $\mathsf{KeyGen}(\mathsf{PP})$: It takes the public parameters PP as input, output a key pair $(\mathtt{sk}_i, \mathtt{pk}_i)$, where $\mathtt{pk}_i = g^{\mathtt{sk}_i}$.

- $\mathsf{Sign}(\mathsf{PP}, \mathbf{sk}_i, m, \mathsf{PK})$: It takes a signer's secret key $\mathbf{sk}_i$, a message m, and a set of public keys $\mathsf{PK} = (\mathbf{pk}_1, \cdots, \mathbf{pk}_n)$, outputs a signature $\sigma = (z, c_1, \cdots, c_n)$. Specifically, the signer $\mathbf{pk}_i$ performs the following operations.
  1. Choose $r \in \mathbb{Z}_q$, $\{c_j\}_{j=1}^{n-1} \in \mathbb{Z}_q$, and compute a commitment $R = g^r \cdot \prod_{j=1}^{n-1} \mathbf{pk}_j^{c_j}$, where $j \neq i$.
  2. Compute a challenge $c_i = \mathtt{H}(R||\mathsf{PK}||m) - \sum_{j=1}^{n-1} c_j$.
  3. Compute a response $z = r - \mathbf{sk}_i \cdot c_i$.
- $\mathsf{Verify}(\mathsf{PP}, \mathsf{PK}, m, \sigma)$: It outputs 1 if $\mathtt{H}(R'||\mathsf{PK}||m) = \sum_{i=1}^{n} c_i$, where $R' = g^z \cdot \prod_{i=1}^{n} \mathbf{pk}_i^{c_i}$.

We present the high-level idea of DL-based DualRing as follows. First, a signer adds the decoy public keys $\{\mathbf{pk}_j\}_{j=1}^{n-1}$ and the corresponding challenge values $\{c_j\}_{j=1}^{n-1}$ to the commitment R. Second, after computing a hash value $\mathtt{H}(R||\mathsf{PK}||m)$, the signer can compute a challenge c_i from $\mathtt{H}(R||\mathsf{PK}||m)$ and the challenge values $\{c_j\}_{j=1}^{n-1}$. Third, the signer computes a response z according to Type-T signature scheme. To verify, the commitment R is reconstructed from all public keys and all challenge values. The sum of the challenge values is equal to the hash value $\mathtt{H}(R||\mathsf{PK}||m)$. For security, DualRing needs to achieve unforgeability and anonymity. Specifically, unforgeability means that the adversary cannot produce a valid signature without accessing the secret key, even if s/he can adaptively corrupt other honest participants and obtain their secret keys. Anonymity requires that the adversary cannot pinpoint the actual signer given a valid signature and a group of public keys, even if s/he is given all randomness to generate the secret keys. The formal definition is given in [33].

DualRing relies on the sum of argument of knowledge to achieve logarithmic complexity in signature size. The sum argument relation is given below:

$$\{(\mathbf{g} \in \mathbb{G}^n, P \in \mathbb{G}, c \in \mathbb{Z}_q; \mathbf{a} \in \mathbb{Z}_q^n) : P = \mathbf{g}^{\mathbf{a}} \bigwedge c = \sum \mathbf{a}\}$$

In this sum argument, a prover convinces a verifier that s/he has the knowledge of a vector of scalars $\mathbf{a}$, such that $P = \mathbf{g}^{\mathbf{a}}$ and $c = \sum \mathbf{a}$. For some $a_i \in \mathbb{Z}_q$, given $g_i, P \in \mathbb{G}$ and $c \in \mathbb{Z}_q$: $P = \prod_{i=1}^{n} g_i^{a_i} \bigwedge c = \sum_{i=1}^{n} a_i$. Second, since Type-T signature contains $\mathbf{pk}_i^{c_i}$, we can rewrite the sum argument for the relation:

$$R \cdot (g^z)^{-1} = \prod_{i=1}^{n} \mathbf{pk}_i^{c_i} \bigwedge \mathtt{H}(R||\mathsf{PK}||m) = \sum_{i=1}^{n} c_i.$$

Eventually, a logarithmic size DL-based DualRing can be constructed from Type-T signature and the non-interactive sum argument (NISA). The resulting signature is (c, z, R, π), where $\pi \leftarrow NISA.Proof(\{\mathsf{param}, \mathsf{PK}, u, P, c\}, \mathbf{a})$, $\mathsf{param} = (\mathsf{PP}, u)$, $u \in \mathbb{G}$, $c = \sum_{i=1}^{n} c_i$, $P = R \cdot (g^z)^{-1}$, $\mathbf{a} = (c_1, \cdots, c_n)$. In particular, π has $\log(n)$ complexity. The detailed algorithms are referred to [33] (Sect. 6).

2.3 Forward Security

In this sub-section, we show non-interactive forward security. Non-interactive means that the key holder updates their keys locally, without interacting with any third parties. First, we show the forward security technique based on the hierarchical identity-based encryption scheme (HIBE) in [11]. Second, we show the forward security technique with logarithmic complexity $\mathcal{O}(\log(T)^2)$ using the binary tree-based approach in [17,20], where T denotes the upper-bound of time periods (or epochs). We mainly focus on *how to generate and update keys* because they determine the forward security. We assume a secret key $\mathtt{sk}_t$ is of the following form:

$$\mathtt{sk}_t = (g^r, \underline{h^{\mathtt{sk}} \cdot (h_0 \prod h_i^{t_i})^r}, h_{i+1}^r, \cdots, h_T^r)$$

where r is randomness, $t = t_1||t_2||\cdots||t_i$ denotes the current time, $(g, h_0, h_1, \cdots, h_T)$ denotes the public parameters, and $(h_0 \prod h_i^{t_i})^r = (h_0 \cdot h_1^{t_1} \cdot h_2^{t_2} \cdots h_i^{t_i})^r$. Note that these public parameters can be generated using an indifferentiable hash-to-curve algorithm [16], thus avoiding any trusted setup. To derive a new key $\mathtt{sk}_{t'}$ at the next time $t' = t||t_{i+1}$ from $\mathtt{sk}_t$, the secret key holder performs the following operation on the underlined element above

$$h^{\mathtt{sk}} \cdot (h_0 \prod h_{i+1}^{t_{i+1}})^{r+r'} = \underline{h^{\mathtt{sk}} \cdot (h_0 \prod h_i^{t_i})^r} \cdot h_{i+1}^{r \cdot t_{i+1}} \cdot (h_0 \prod h_{i+1}^{t_{i+1}})^{r'}$$

where r' is a new randomness, and the underline part is the second element of secret key $\mathtt{sk}_t$. For the first and other elements of the new secret key $\mathtt{sk}_{t'}$, the key holder can easily update them by multiplying $g^{r'}, h_{i+2}^{r'}, \cdots, h_T^{r'}$, respectively. So, the new secret key is $\mathtt{sk}_{t'} = (g^{r+r'}, h^{\mathtt{sk}} \cdot (h_0 \prod h_{i+1}^{t_{i+1}})^{r+r'}, h_{i+2}^{r+r'}, \cdots, h_T^{r+r'})$.

The above approach shows that each key update requires new randomness to unlink the original and the new secret keys, and the complexity is linear to the number of epochs: $\mathcal{O}(T)$. Now, we use a tree-based approach [17,20] to compress the secret keys down to $\mathcal{O}(\log(T)^2)$. First, we assume the secret key $\mathtt{sk}_t$ for the current time t is of the following form:

$$\mathtt{sk}_t = \tilde{\mathtt{sk}}_t, \tilde{\mathtt{sk}}_{t+1}, \cdots, \tilde{\mathtt{sk}}_T.$$

where each sub-key $\tilde{\mathtt{sk}}_t$ is generated using independent randomness. Second, we explain the tree-based approach in Fig. 1.

Specifically, a tree of depth $\ell - 1$ consists of $2^\ell - 1$ nodes, which corresponds to time periods in $[1, 2^\ell - 1]$. We use $\{1,2\}$-string to represent time period, where 1 denotes taking the left branch and 2 denotes taking the right branch. For instance, for $\ell = 4$, the string $(\epsilon, 1, 11, \cdots, 222)$ corresponds to time period $(1, 2, 3, \cdots, 15)$, where ϵ denotes the root node or the first time period. Suppose the current time is $t = 121$ (a leaf node in color blue in Fig. 1), the tree traversal method states that the key holder will use the sub-key $\tilde{\mathtt{sk}}_{121}$ to represent time 121, and locally store the secret keys of the "right siblings" (or siblings on the right) of the nodes on the path from the root to 121 for subsequent

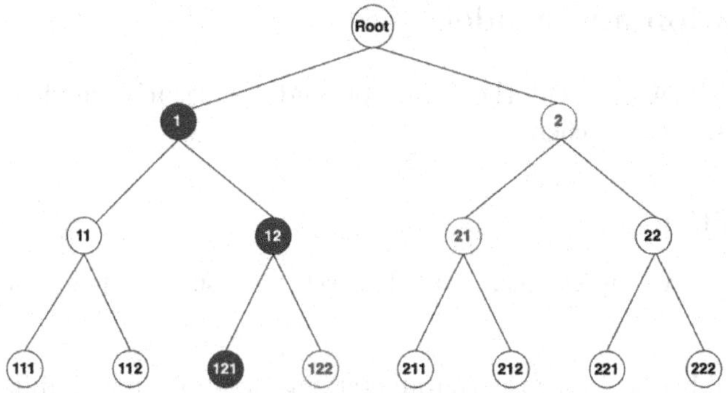

Fig. 1. Tree Traversal Method.

key updates. As a result, the key holder stores a set of sub-keys at epoch 121: $\mathtt{sk}_t = (\tilde{\mathtt{sk}}_{121}, \tilde{\mathtt{sk}}_{122}, \tilde{\mathtt{sk}}_{21}, \tilde{\mathtt{sk}}_2)$. In particular, the sub-keys are organized as a stack of node keys, with the sub-key $\tilde{\mathtt{sk}}_{121}$ on top. The sub-keys at epoch 121 are described below

$$\begin{aligned}
\tilde{\mathtt{sk}}_{121} &= (g^{r_{121}}, h^{\mathtt{sk}} \cdot (h_0 \cdot h_1^1 \cdot h_2^2 \cdot h_3^1)^{r_{121}}, \bot) \\
\tilde{\mathtt{sk}}_{122} &= (g^{r_{122}}, h^{\mathtt{sk}} \cdot (h_0 \cdot h_1^1 \cdot h_2^2 \cdot h_3^2)^{r_{122}}, \bot) \\
\tilde{\mathtt{sk}}_{21} &= (g^{r_{21}}, h^{\mathtt{sk}} \cdot (h_0 \cdot h_1^2 \cdot h_2^1 \cdot h_3^0)^{r_{21}}, h_3^{r_{21}}) \\
\tilde{\mathtt{sk}}_{2} &= (g^{r_{2}}, h^{\mathtt{sk}} \cdot (h_0 \cdot h_1^2 \cdot h_2^0 \cdot h_3^0)^{r_{2}}, h_2^{r_2}, h_3^{r_2})
\end{aligned}$$

where $r_{121}, r_{122}, r_{21}, r_2$ are independent randomness, and (g, h_0, h_1, h_2, h_3) are public parameters.

Third, we show the key update from $\mathtt{sk}_t$ to $\mathtt{sk}_{t+1}$. The sub-keys $\tilde{\mathtt{sk}}_{121}, \tilde{\mathtt{sk}}_{122}$ cannot be updated further once they are used because their third elements are empty values $\bot$. But, we can derive a new sub-key $\tilde{\mathtt{sk}}_{211}$ from the sub-key $\tilde{\mathtt{sk}}_{21}$ (which is stored locally) using the following equation.

$$\begin{aligned}
\tilde{\mathtt{sk}}_{211} &= (g^{r_{21}} \cdot g^{r_{211}}, \underline{h^{\mathtt{sk}} \cdot (h_0 \cdot h_1^2 \cdot h_2^1 \cdot h_3^0)^{r_{21}}} \cdot h_3^{r_{21} \cdot 1} \cdot (h_0 \cdot h_1^2 \cdot h_2^1 \cdot h_3^1)^{r_{211}}, \bot) \\
&= (g^{r_{21}+r_{211}}, h^{\mathtt{sk}} \cdot (h_0 \cdot h_1^2 \cdot h_2^1 \cdot h_3^1)^{r_{21}+r_{211}}, \bot)
\end{aligned}$$

where r_{211} is a new randomness used in this key update. We can derive all the following sub-keys shown in the tree using the same method described above. Specifically, $\mathtt{sk}_{212}$ is derived from $\mathtt{sk}_{21}$, and $\mathtt{sk}_{22}, \mathtt{sk}_{221}, \mathtt{sk}_{222}$ are derived from $\mathtt{sk}_2$.

Next, we show the complexity of key updates, which includes storage cost and computational cost. The storage cost is $\mathcal{O}(\log(T)^2)$, meaning that each key $\mathtt{sk}_t$ contains $\mathcal{O}(\log(T))$ sub-keys and each sub-key $\tilde{\mathtt{sk}}_t$ consists of $\mathcal{O}(\log(T))$ group elements. Since all tree nodes are used to represent time periods, the amortized key update requires $\mathcal{O}(1)$ exponentiations.

3 Definition and Models

In this section, we present the definition and the security models of forward-secure ring signature scheme.

3.1 Definition

A forward-secure ring signature (FS-RS) scheme consists of the following algorithms.

- $\mathsf{Setup}(1^\lambda)$: It takes a security parameter λ as input, outputs public parameters PP that include the maximum number of epoch T.
- $\mathsf{KeyGen}(\mathsf{PP})$: It takes public parameters PP as input, outputs an initial key pair $(\mathtt{pk}_i, \mathtt{sk}_{(i,0)})$ for any user. We use $\mathtt{pk}_i$ to represent this user.
- $\mathsf{KeyUp}(\mathsf{PP}, \mathtt{sk}_{(i,t)}, t')$: It takes a user $\mathtt{pk}_i$'s key $\mathtt{sk}_{(i,t)}$ and an epoch t' as input, outputs an updated key $\mathtt{sk}_{(i,t')}$, where $t \leq t'$.
- $\mathsf{Sign}(\mathsf{PP}, \mathtt{sk}_{(i,t)}, m, \mathsf{PK}, t)$: It takes a user $\mathtt{pk}_i$'s key $\mathtt{sk}_{(i,t)}$, a message m, a set of public keys $\mathsf{PK} = (\mathtt{pk}_1, \cdots, \mathtt{pk}_n)$, and an epoch t as input, outputs a signature σ.
- $\mathsf{Verify}(\mathsf{PP}, \mathsf{PK}, m, \sigma, t)$: It takes a message-signature pair (m, σ), a public key set PK, and an epoch t as input, outputs 1 to indicate that the signature is valid and 0 otherwise.

Correctness. The FS-RS is *correct* if for all security parameters λ, all public parameters $\mathsf{PP} \leftarrow \mathsf{Setup}(1^\lambda)$, for all keys $(\mathtt{pk}_i, \mathtt{sk}_{(i,0)}) \leftarrow \mathsf{KeyGen}(\mathsf{PP})$, for all $t \leq t'$, $\mathtt{sk}_{(i,t')} \leftarrow \mathsf{KeyUp}(\mathsf{PP}, \mathtt{sk}_{(i,t)}, t')$, for all m and $\mathsf{PK} = (\mathtt{pk}_1, \cdots, \mathtt{pk}_n)$, $\sigma \leftarrow \mathsf{Sign}(\mathsf{PP}, \mathtt{sk}_{(i,t)}, m, \mathsf{PK}, t)$, we have $1 = \mathsf{Verify}(\mathsf{PP}, \mathsf{PK}, m, \sigma, t)$.

3.2 Security Models

Forward-Secure Unforgeability. Informally, an attacker cannot forge a message-signature pair, even if the attacker can adaptively corrupt some honest participants and obtain their epoch-based secret keys. The formal security game between a probabilistic polynomial-time (PPT) adversary $\mathcal{A}$ and a simulator $\mathcal{S}$ is defined as follows.

- $\mathcal{S}$ sets up the game by creating n users with the corresponding key pairs $\{(\mathtt{pk}_i, \mathtt{sk}_{(i,0)})\} \leftarrow \mathsf{KeyGen}(\mathsf{PP})$, where $\mathsf{PP} \leftarrow \mathsf{Setup}(1^\lambda)$, and $\{\mathtt{sk}_{(i,0)}\}$ denotes user i's initial secret key. For each user $\mathtt{pk}_i$, $\mathcal{S}$ can update the epoch-based secret keys to $\{\mathtt{sk}_{(i,t)}\}_{t=1}^{T}$. Eventually, $\mathcal{S}$ returns all public keys to $\mathcal{A}$, and $\mathcal{S}$ maintains a set $\mathcal{Q}$ to record the corrupted users.
- During the game, $\mathcal{A}$ can make the following queries to $\mathcal{S}$.
  - $\mathsf{Key\ Update}$. If $\mathcal{A}$ issues a key update query with respect to a user $\mathtt{pk}_i$ at epoch t, then $\mathcal{S}$ updates the key $\mathtt{sk}_{(i,t)}$ to $\mathtt{sk}_{(i,t+1)}$ and increases t, where $t \leq T$.

- Signing. If $\mathcal{A}$ issues a signing query on a message m and a public key set $\mathsf{PK} = \{\mathbf{pk}_i, \cdots\}$ at epoch t, then $\mathcal{S}$ computes a signature σ using the secret key $\mathtt{sk}_{(i,t)}$ and returns it to $\mathcal{A}$.
- Break In. If $\mathcal{A}$ issues a break-in query at epoch $\bar{t}$ with respect to a user $\mathbf{pk}_i$, then $\mathcal{S}$ returns the corresponding secret key $\mathtt{sk}_{(i,\bar{t})}$ to $\mathcal{A}$. This query can be issued once for each user, and after this query, $\mathcal{A}$ can make no further key update or signing queries to that user. In addition, we allow $\mathcal{A}$ to issue different break-in queries with respect to different users.
- Corrupt. If $\mathcal{A}$ issues a corrupt query on a user $\mathbf{pk}_i$, then $\mathcal{S}$ returns the user's initial secret key $\mathtt{sk}_{(i,0)}$ to $\mathcal{A}$, and updates the set $\mathcal{Q}$ by including the corrupted public key $\mathbf{pk}_i$.

– At some point, $\mathcal{A}$ outputs a forgery $(\mathsf{PK}^*, t^*, m^*, \sigma^*)$. $\mathcal{A}$ wins the game if the following conditions hold.
  1. The message-signature pair (m^*, σ^*) is a valid under PK^* at t^*.
  2. For any user $\mathbf{pk}^* \in \mathsf{PK}^*$, but $\mathbf{pk}^* \notin \mathcal{Q}$.
  3. The forgery $(\mathsf{PK}^*, t^*, m^*, \cdot)$ was not previously queried to the signing oracle.
  4. If the break in oracle has been queried at epoch $\bar{t}$ with respect to any user in PK^*, the break in epoch must satisfy $\bar{t} > t^*$.

  We define the advantage of $\mathcal{A}$ in the above game as

$$\mathtt{Adv}_{\mathcal{A}}(\lambda) = |\Pr[\mathcal{A}\ wins]|.$$

Definition 2. *A forward-secure ring-signature scheme is unforgeable if for any PPT $\mathcal{A}$, $\mathtt{Adv}_{\mathcal{A}}(\lambda)$ is a negligible function in λ.*

Anonymity Against Full Key Exposure. Informally, an attacker cannot identify a specific signer given a valid signature and a set of public keys, even if the attacker can access all randomnesses that were used in generating each user's secret key. Note that we consider an anonymity model in [10] that the attacker can access all randomnesses that were used in generating each user's secret key (i.e., full key exposure). The formal anonymity game between a PPT adversary $\mathcal{A}$ and a simulator $\mathcal{S}$ is defined as follows.

– $\mathcal{S}$ sets up the game using the same method described in the above unforgeability game except the following differences. First, $\mathcal{S}$ generates a user's key pair as $(\mathbf{pk}_i, \mathsf{sk}_i) \leftarrow \mathsf{KeyGen}(\mathsf{PP}; w_i)$, where w_i denotes the randomness used in generating user's secret key. Second, $\mathcal{S}$ returns all users' public keys to $\mathcal{A}$, and tosses a random coin b which is used later in the game.
– $\mathcal{A}$ can make signing queries to $\mathcal{S}$ during the training phase. In the end, $\mathcal{A}$ outputs two indices $i_0, i_1 \notin \mathcal{Q}$, where $\mathcal{Q}$ denotes the set of queries to the corrupt oracle.
– During the challenge phase, $\mathcal{A}$ can issue a signing query on a message m^* under a public key set $\mathsf{PK}^* = \{\mathbf{pk}_{i_0}, \mathbf{pk}_{i_1}, \cdots\}$ at epoch t^*, then $\mathcal{S}$ returns a signature $\sigma \leftarrow \mathsf{Sign}(\mathsf{PP}, \mathtt{sk}_{(i_b,t^*)}, m^*, \mathsf{PK}^*, t^*)$ and all witness $\{w_i\}$ to $\mathcal{A}$. Finally, $\mathcal{A}$ outputs b' as its guess for b. If $b' = b$, then $\mathcal{S}$ outputs 1; Otherwise, $\mathcal{S}$ outputs 0. We define the advantage of $\mathcal{A}$ in the above game as

$$\mathtt{Adv}_{\mathcal{A}}(\lambda) = |\Pr[\mathcal{S} \rightarrow 1] - 1/2|.$$

Definition 3. *A forward-secure ring-signature scheme is anonymous if for any PPT $\mathcal{A}$, $\mathtt{Adv}_{\mathcal{A}}(\lambda)$ is a negligible function in λ.*

Remark. We consider two types of randomnesses for (forward-secure) Type-T ring signatures. One is the randomnesses $\{w_i\}$ that are used in generating/updating users' secret keys, and another is the randomnesses $Rand_s$ that are used in generating ring signatures. Our anonymity is held even if attackers can access all $\{w_i\}$ (note that $\mathcal{S}$ can record all $\{w_i\}$ for key update queries) and corrupt all users in a ring during the challenge phase. However, if attackers get access to the randomness $Rand_s$ associated with a ring signature, this ring signature's anonymity is lost. Our anonymity model disallows attackers to access any $Rand_s$ in the entire game.

4 Our Construction

We denote an epoch-based function as $F(t) = h_0 \prod h_i^{t_i}$, where $t = t_1||t_2||\cdots||t_i = \{1,2\}^i$. Let $\mathtt{H} : \{0,1\}^* \rightarrow \mathbb{Z}_q$ be a collision-resistant hash function. Below, we show a construction with linear complexity. We can easily convert it to a practical scheme with logarithmic complexity using the sum argument and the tree-based approach described in Sect. 2.2 and Sect. 2.3, respectively. The logarithmic complexity here means that the signature size and the signing key size are logarithmic in both the number of public keys involved in a ring and the maximum number of epochs.

- $\mathsf{Setup}(1^\lambda)$: Let $\hat{\mathsf{e}} : \mathbb{G} \times \mathbb{H} \rightarrow \mathbb{G}_T$ be a bilinear pairing. The common system parameters include $\mathsf{PP} = (g, h, T, \{h_i\}^\ell)$, where $g \in \mathbb{G}$, $h, \{h_i\}^\ell \in \mathbb{H}$, and $T = 2^\ell - 1$ denotes the upper bound of epochs. The first epoch is $\epsilon = 0$, and the last epoch is $t_1||\cdots||t_{\ell-1}$.
- $\mathsf{KeyGen}(\mathsf{PP})$: A user chooses a secret key $\mathbf{sk}_i$ and computes $h^{\mathbf{sk}_i}$. It computes an initial key as $\mathbf{sk}_{(i,\epsilon)} = (g^{r_0}, h^{\mathbf{sk}_i} \cdot h_0^{r_0}, h_1^{r_0}, \cdots h_\ell^{r_0})$, where $r_0 \in \mathbb{Z}_q$. It also sets its public key as $\mathbf{pk}_i = g^{\mathbf{sk}_i}$. We denote the second element of $\mathbf{sk}_{(i,\epsilon)}$ as $\mathbf{sk}_{(i,\epsilon,2)}$.
- $\mathsf{KeyUp}(\mathsf{PP}, \mathbf{sk}_{(i,t)}, t')$: Given a key $\mathbf{sk}_{(i,t)} = (g^r, h^{\mathbf{sk}_i} \cdot F(t)^r, h_{i+1}^r, \cdots, h_\ell^r)$, where $t = t_1||\cdots||t_i$, the user creates a new key $\mathbf{sk}_{(i,t')} = (g^r \cdot g^z, \mathbf{sk}_{(i,t,2)} \cdot h_{i+1}^{r \cdot t_{i+1}} \cdot (h_0 \cdot \prod h_{i+1}^{t'})^z, h_{i+2}^r \cdot h_{i+2}^z, \cdots, h_\ell^r \cdot h_\ell^z)$, where $z \in \mathbb{Z}_q$, and epoch $t' = t_1||\cdots||t_i||t_{i+1}$.
- $\mathsf{Sign}(\mathsf{PP}, \mathbf{sk}_{(i,t)}, m, \mathsf{PK}, t)$: Given a signing key $\mathbf{sk}_{(i,t)}$, a message m, and a set of public keys $\mathsf{PK} = (\mathbf{pk}_1, \cdots, \mathbf{pk}_n)$, a signer performs the following operations.
  1. Choose challenge values $\{c_j\}_{j=1}^{n-1} \in \mathbb{Z}_q$, and compute a commitment value $R = \hat{\mathsf{e}}(\prod_{j=1}^{n-1} \mathbf{pk}_j^{c_j}, h)/\hat{\mathsf{e}}(g, F(t))^{\widehat{r}}$, where $\widehat{r} = \widehat{r_1} + \widehat{r_2}$, and $\widehat{r_1}, \widehat{r_2} \in \mathbb{Z}_q$.
  2. Compute a challenge value $c_i = \mathtt{H}(R||m||\mathsf{PK}) - \sum_{j=1}^{n-1} c_j$.
  3. Output a ring signature $\sigma = (\sigma_1, \sigma_2, c_1, \cdots, c_n)$, where $\sigma_1 = [h^{\mathbf{sk}_i} \cdot F(t)^r]^{c_i} \cdot F(t)^{\widehat{r_1}}$ and $\sigma_2 = g^{\widehat{r_2}}/g^{r \cdot c_i}$.

– Verify(PP, PK, m, σ, t): Anyone can verify $\mathtt{H}(R'||m||\mathsf{PK}) \stackrel{?}{=} \sum_{i=1}^{n} c_i$, where R' is computed as follows.

$$\begin{aligned}
A &= \hat{\mathtt{e}}(g, \sigma_1) = \hat{\mathtt{e}}(g, h^{\mathtt{sk}_i})^{c_i} \cdot \hat{\mathtt{e}}(g, F(t)^r)^{c_i} \cdot \hat{\mathtt{e}}(g, F(t))^{\widehat{r_1}} \\
B &= \hat{\mathtt{e}}(\sigma_2, F(t)) = \hat{\mathtt{e}}(g^{\widehat{r_2}}, F(t))/\hat{\mathtt{e}}(g^{rc_i}, F(t)) \\
AB &= \hat{\mathtt{e}}(g, h^{\mathtt{sk}_i})^{c_i} \cdot \hat{\mathtt{e}}(g^{\widehat{r}}, F(t)), \triangleright \widehat{r} = \widehat{r_1} + \widehat{r_2} \\
R' &= C/AB = \hat{\mathtt{e}}(\prod_{j=1}^{n-1} \mathsf{pk}_j^{c_j}, h)/\hat{\mathtt{e}}(g, F(t))^{\widehat{r}}, \textit{where } C = \hat{\mathtt{e}}(\prod_{i=1}^{n} \mathsf{pk}_i^{c_i}, h)
\end{aligned}$$

Correctness. We associate a user pk_i's signing key at epoch $t = t_1||\cdots||t_i$ of the form

$$\mathtt{sk}_{(i,t)} = (c, d, e_{i+1}, \cdots, e_\ell) = (g^r, h^{\mathtt{sk}_i} \cdot (h_0 \cdot \prod h_i^{t_i})^r, h_{i+1}^r, \cdots, h_\ell^r) \quad (1)$$

where r is an independent uniformly distributed exponent. We say that a signing key $\mathtt{sk}_{(i,t)}$ is *well-formed* if it satisfies the equation (1). Now, we show the honestly generated and updated secret keys are well-formed. For simplicity, we assume a key update from epoch $t = t_1||\cdots||t_i$ to $t' = t_1||\cdots||t_i||t_{i+1}$, where t' contains t as a prefix (e.g., $t = 12$ and $t' = 121$ or $t' = 122$). Note that the epoch cannot contain bit 0 due to technical reasons such as $h_i^0 = 1$.

First, the initial key $\mathtt{sk}_{(i,\epsilon)}$ for $\epsilon = 1$ is trivially well-formed. Then, we show that the key $\mathtt{sk}_{(i,t')}$ is also well-formed after a key update from t to t'. Specifically, we show two cases of key update. The first case is of the form

$$\mathtt{sk}_{(i,t')} = (c, d \cdot e_{i+1}^{t_{i+1}}, e_{i+2}, \cdots, e_\ell) = (g^r, h^{\mathtt{sk}_i} \cdot (h_0 \cdot \prod h_{i+1}^{t_{i+1}})^r, h_{i+2}^r, \cdots, h_\ell^r)$$

which satisfies Eq. (1) with an independent randomness r. The second case is of the form

$$\begin{aligned}
\mathtt{sk}_{(i,t')} &= (c \cdot g^z, d \cdot e_{i+1}^{t_{i+1}} \cdot (h_0 \cdot \prod h_{i+1}^{t'})^z, e_{i+2} \cdot h_{i+2}^z, \cdots, e_\ell \cdot h_\ell^z) \\
&= (g^{r+z}, h^{\mathtt{sk}_i} \cdot (h_0 \cdot \prod h_i^{t_i})^r \cdot h_{i+1}^{r \cdot t_{i+1}} \cdot (h_0 \cdot \prod h_{i+1}^{t'})^z, h_{i+2}^{r+z}, \cdots, h_\ell^{r+z}) \\
&= (g^{r+z}, h^{\mathtt{sk}_i} \cdot (h_0 \cdot \prod h_{i+1}^{t'})^{r+z}, h_{i+2}^{r+z}, \cdots, h_\ell^{r+z}).
\end{aligned}$$

The above form also satisfies equation (1) with randomness $r + z$, which is an independent exponent due to the uniform choice of z. The last step to obtain $\mathtt{sk}_{(i,t')}$ is crucial to forward security, the signer deletes $\mathtt{sk}_{(i,t)}$ and the re-randomization exponent z used in the second case of key update. The verification of signatures for epoch $t' = t_1||\cdots||t_{i+1}$ is straightforward. The signer generates a signature using $F(t')$, while the verifier computes $F(t')$ and uses it in computing B of the Verify algorithm.

Forward Deniability and Claimability. Consider an internet voting system that includes a voter (or sender) and a voting authority (or receiver), and assume they authenticate each other successfully. It is required that (i) the authority know that the voter has the right to vote and (ii) the voter know that his/her vote is counted after voting. Forward deniability is important here because it prevents either party from walking away with a non-deniable proof of the actual vote (i.e., authenticated message) [18]. Specifically, the authority should not prove to a third party how the voter voted, and the voter should not prove that s/he authenticated a message *at a later stage* to prevent coercion and vote-selling.

Forward deniability is not equal to the original notion of deniability. The deniability prevents a receiver from proving to a third party that s/he received an authenticated message from a sender, while forward deniability prevents the sender from generating any non-deniable proofs. Forward deniability is comparable to the notion of forward security. In forward security, if a party's key is compromised, the security of past sessions remains secure. Forward deniability states that if a party is compromised at some time t, s/he cannot revoke the deniability from sessions happened before time t.

To ensure forward security of ring signatures, a signer should erase any internal randomness used in updating his/her signing keys, apart from his/her signing keys. Similarly, forward-deniable ring signatures require the signer to erase any internal randomness used in generating signatures. One may argue that such randomness erasure (from local memory) is a strong assumption to make. If the signer keeps the randomness, s/he may claim authorship of generated signatures (i.e., claimability [30]). So, the erasure of internal randomness used in generating ring signatures is critical for achieving forward deniability and claimability. This work focuses on forward-secure unforgeability and anonymity against full key exposure. Forward deniability may be considered as a desired feature if one applies our proposed scheme to deniable authentication protocols and deniable authenticated key exchanges (or Signal protocols [1,3]).

4.1 Security Analysis

Theorem 1. *The FS-DR signature scheme Σ is unforgeable if the wBDHI assumption holds in the underlying asymmetric groups.*

Theorem 2. *The FS-DR signature scheme Σ is anonymous in the random oracle model.*

Please refer to Appendix for the detailed proofs.

5 Extension

Extending our construction, we now introduce a forward-secure linkable Dual-Ring. The linkability means that anyone can link multiple signatures generated by a same signer. Based on the technique used in [28], we adapt the proposed FS-DR as follows

- The setup is almost same as FS-DR, except that the algorithm additionally generates a one-time signature scheme $\Sigma_{ots} = (\mathsf{OKGen}, \mathsf{OSig}, \mathsf{OVer})$.
- The key generation proceeds as follows. A user generates a key pair $(\mathsf{osk}, \mathsf{opk}) \leftarrow \mathsf{OKGen}(1^\lambda)$, computes a linkability tag $R_i = \mathtt{H}(\mathsf{opk})$. The user's secret key is of the form $\mathbf{sk}_{(i,t)} = (g^r, h^{\mathsf{sk}_i + R_i} \cdot h_0^r, h_1^r, \cdots h_\ell^r)$, where $r \in \mathbb{Z}_q$. The user's public key is $\mathbf{pk}_i = g^{\mathsf{sk}_i + R_i}$. The key update remains the same as FS-DR.
- For signing, a signer with a signing key $\mathbf{sk}_{(i,t)}$, a message m, and a set of public keys $\mathsf{PK} = (\mathbf{pk}_1, \cdots, \mathbf{pk}_n)$, performs the following operations.
  1. Generate a new set of public keys using its linkability tag R_i, such that $\mathbf{pk}'_i = \mathbf{pk}_i / g^{R_i} = g^{\mathsf{sk}_i}$, and $\mathbf{pk}'_j = \mathbf{pk}_j / g^{R_i} = g^{\mathsf{sk}_j - R_i}$.
  2. Choose challenge values $\{c_j\}_{j=1}^{n-1} \in \mathbb{Z}_q$, and compute a commitment value $R = \hat{\mathsf{e}}(\prod_{j=1}^{n-1} \mathbf{pk}_j'^{c_j}, h) / \hat{\mathsf{e}}(g, F(t))^{\widehat{r}}$, where $\widehat{r} = \widehat{r_1} + \widehat{r_2}$, and $\widehat{r_1}, \widehat{r_2} \in \mathbb{Z}_q$.
  3. Compute a challenge value $c_i = \mathtt{H}(R||m||\mathsf{PK}') - \sum_{j=1}^{n-1} c_j$, where $\mathsf{PK}' = (\mathbf{pk}'_1, \cdots, \mathbf{pk}'_n)$.
  4. Generate a ring signature $\sigma = (\sigma_1, \sigma_2, c_1, \cdots, c_n)$, where $\sigma_1 = [h^{\mathsf{sk}_i} \cdot F(t)^r]^{c_i} \cdot F(t)^{\widehat{r_1}}$ and $\sigma_2 = g^{\widehat{r_2}} / g^{r \cdot c_i}$. Note that $h^{\mathsf{sk}_i} \cdot F(t)^r = \frac{h^{\mathsf{sk}_i + R_i} \cdot F(t)^r}{h^{R_i}}$.
  5. Generate a one-time signature $s \leftarrow \mathsf{OSig}(\mathsf{osk}; m, \sigma, \mathsf{PK})$.
  6. Output $(\mathsf{PK}, m, \sigma, \mathsf{opk}, s)$.
- For verification, anyone first computes $\mathsf{PK}' = (\mathbf{pk}'_1, \cdots, \mathbf{pk}'_n)$ from the public-key set $\mathsf{PK} = (\mathbf{pk}_1, \cdots, \mathbf{pk}_n)$ and g^{R_i}, where $R_i = \mathtt{H}(\mathsf{opk})$. Next, the user runs the Verify algorithm described in FS-DR under public key set PK'. Last, the user verifies the signature $1 \leftarrow \mathsf{OVer}(\mathsf{opk}; m, \sigma, \mathsf{PK})$.
- The link process takes two message-signature pairs $(\mathsf{PK}_1, m_1, \sigma_1, \mathsf{opk}_1, s_1)$, $(\mathsf{PK}_2, m_2, \sigma_2, \mathsf{opk}_2, s_2)$ as input, output either *linked* or *unlinked.* Specifically, the algorithm first verify (m_1, σ_1) under PK_1 and (m_2, σ_2) under PK_2, respectively. Then, the algorithm outputs *linked* if $\mathsf{opk}_1 = \mathsf{opk}_2$. Otherwise, it outputs *unlinked.*

Correctness and Security. The correctness of linkable FS-DR is held if: 1) the FS-DR and the one-time signature Σ_{ots} are correct. 2) two legally signed signatures are linked if they share a same signer. The security of linkable FS-DR should include the following aspects.

- *Forward-secure Unforgeability.* The forward-secure unforgeability for linkable FS-DR remains the same as in Sect. 3.2.
- *Forward-secure Anonymity.* Informally, an attacker cannot identify a specific signer given a valid signature and a set of public keys at epoch t^*, even if the attacker can corrupt all users' secret keys after t^*. The formal definition is adopted from Boyen and Haines [15]. We claim that, the linkable FS-DR is forward-secure anonymous in the random oracle model if the decisional wBDHI is held in the asymmetric pairing group. The security proof is similar to Theorem 5 described in [15], except that the hard problem is replaced by the decisional wBDHI problem.

- *Linkability and Non-slanderability.* Linkability means that the link process always outputs "linked" for two signatures generated by a same signer. The non-slanderability states that a signer cannot frame other honest signers for generating a signature linked with another signature not signed by the signer. The formal definitions are adopted from Liu et al. [25]. We claim that, the linkable FS-DR is linkable and non-slanderable in the random oracle model if the FS-DR scheme and the one-time signature scheme Σ_{ots} are unforgeable. This assumption is valid because if a linkable ring signature scheme is linkable and non-slanderable, it is also unforgeable [7]. The security proofs are similar to Theorem 4 and 5 described in [28].

6 Implementation and Evaluation

In this section, we focus on the implementation and evaluation. Specifically, we compare the proposed scheme with two closely related research work [15,27] in terms of execution time and storage cost. First, we remove the linkability described in [15] for a fair comparison. We stress that the extension to a linkable FS-DualRing is not our major contribution. Second, we remove the implementation of the forward-secure key update described in [15]. They use multilinear maps [12] to update key pairs for different time periods or epochs. But, multilinear maps are not available in practice due to various attacks [15]. Therefore, they suggest using (symmetric) bilinear maps to give a forward-secure scheme that supports a key update for two epochs.

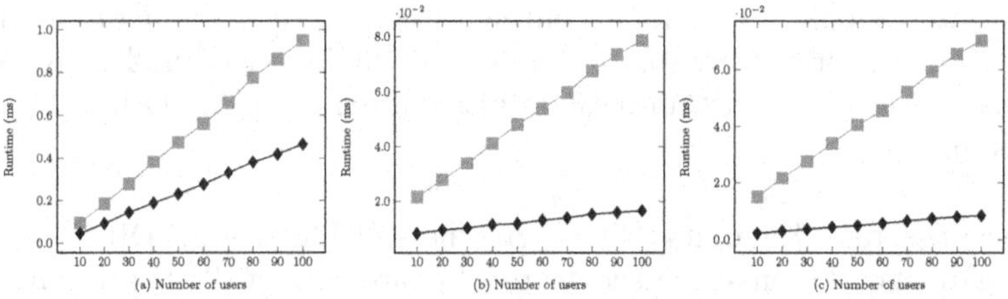

Fig. 2. Execution time of KeyGen, Sign, Verify algorithms. Red (with solid square) is for our scheme, Blue (with solid dot) is for [15]. (Color figure online)

We implement our proposed scheme using Charm framework [6] and evaluate its performance on a PC with Intel Core i9. We use MNT224 curve [29] for pairing, which is the commonly-used asymmetric pairing in PBC library, and it has around 100-bit security level. Our source code is available at Github [2].

First, we provide a performance comparison between our scheme and [15]. The execution time of KeyGen, Sign, and Verify algorithms are shown in Fig. 2. The execution time of our scheme is relatively slow compared to [15]. This is because their pairing relies on the symmetric SS512 curve, which is short (thus fast). But, the security level of SS512 is incomparable to MNT224 (note that our scheme is insecure in the symmetric pairing setting). We stress that our scheme's execution time is acceptable. The signing and verifying processes take approximately 0.07ms to handle a group of 100 public keys.

Second, we compare the storage costs of our scheme with those proposed in [27] and [15] in Table 1. We evaluate the sizes of signing keys, public keys, and signatures. One can see that the public/signing key sizes between [27] and our proposed scheme are close because both rely on the same forward-secure technique described in Sect. 2.3. However, our scheme's signature size is much smaller compared to [27]. Specifically, our scheme's signature is $(c, \sigma_1, \sigma_2, R, \pi)$, and its size is $\mathbb{Z}_q + \mathbb{G} + \mathbb{H} + \mathbb{G}_T + \log(n)(\mathbb{Z}_q + \mathbb{G})$ (we use $*$ to represent those single elements in Table 1), where the size of π is $\log(n)(\mathbb{Z}_q + \mathbb{G})$. The signature size in [27] is linear to the number of public keys because their construction is based on the classic ring signature scheme [31]. The signature size in [15] is also larger than our proposed scheme because their ring signature is linear to the number of public keys. Besides, the public key in [15] is not a single group element as in [27] and in our proposed scheme. Our proposed scheme is the most practical forward-secure (linkable) ring signature in a sense that the signature and the signing key sizes are logarithmic in the number of public keys and the maximum number of time periods.

Table 1. Storage comparison with two existing works. n denotes the number of public keys involved in a signature. T denotes the upper bound for time periods. Subgroup means subgroup decision problem. (k_1, b)-GMDP means generalized multilinear decoding problem, where k_1 is a combinatorial constant, and b (we assume $b = 1$ here) is an initial public key level. (k_1, b)-(GMDDH) means that generalized sub-exponent multilinear decisional Diffie-Hellman problem.

	$\|pk\|$	$\|sk\|$	$\|\sigma\|$	Assumption
[27]:	$\mathbb{G}$	$(2 + (\log(T)^2)\mathbb{G}$	$(2n + 3)\mathbb{G}$	CDH/Subgroup
[15]:	$k_1\mathbb{G}$	$k_1\mathbb{Z}_q + 2k_1\mathbb{G}$	$\mathbb{Z}_q + \mathbb{G}_T + n\mathbb{Z}_q$	(k_1, b)-GMDP/GMDDH
Ours:	$\mathbb{G}$	$\mathbb{G} + \log(T)^2(1 + \mathbb{H})$	$* + \log(n)(\mathbb{Z}_q + \mathbb{G})$	wBDHI

7 Conclusion

In this work, we proposed a forward-secure DualRing scheme and extended it to a forward-secure linkable DualRing scheme. We relied on a non-interactive key update mechanism described in the hierarchical identity-based encryption (HIBE) [17,20] to ensure forward security. We proposed a novel "split-and-combine" method in building our practical schemes. This method is suitable for the Type-T based (or random oracle based) signature schemes such as DualRing [33].

Acknowledgements. This work is supported by the EU's research and innovation program: 952697 (ASSURED) and 101095634 (ENTRUST). These projects are funded by the UK government Horizon Europe guarantee and administered by UKRI. Yangguang Tian is partially supported by the National Natural Science Foundation of China under Grant No. 61872264. Yingjiu Li is supported in part by the Ripple University Blockchain Research Initiative.

A Proof of Theorem 1

Proof. We define a sequence of games $\mathbb{G}_i$, $i = 0, \cdots, 2$ and let $\mathtt{Adv}_i^{\Sigma}$ denote the advantage of the adversary in game $\mathbb{G}_i$. Assume that $\mathcal{A}$ issues at most q signing queries in each game.

- $\mathbb{G}_0$: This is original unforgeability game.
- $\mathbb{G}_1$: This game is identical to game $\mathbb{G}_0$ except the following difference: $\mathcal{S}$ randomly chooses a challenge epoch t^* and a challenge user $\mathtt{pk}_i$ regards a forgery from $\mathcal{A}$. $\mathcal{S}$ will output a random bit if $\mathcal{A}$'s forgery does not occur at epoch t^* and user $\mathtt{pk}_i$. In this game, $\mathcal{S}$ honestly generates all initial signing keys during setup. In particular, $\mathcal{S}$ sets the break in epoch as $\bar{t} = t^* + 1$. If $\mathcal{A}$ issues a break-in query at epoch $\bar{t}'$ with respect to user $\mathtt{pk}_i$, such that $\bar{t}' \geq \bar{t}$, then $\mathcal{S}$ returns $\mathtt{sk}_{(i,\bar{t}')}$ to $\mathcal{A}$. Since at most T epochs and n users exist in the system, we have
$$\mathtt{Adv}_0^{\Sigma} = T \cdot n \cdot \mathtt{Adv}_1^{\Sigma}$$
- $\mathbb{G}_2$: This game is identical to game $\mathbb{G}_1$ except that $\mathcal{S}$ outputs a random bit if a **Forge** event happens where $\mathcal{A}$'s forgery is valid at epoch t^* under a public key set PK^* (that includes $\mathtt{pk}_i$) while the corresponding signing key $\mathtt{sk}_{(i,t^*)}$ is not corrupted. Then we have
$$\left|\mathtt{Adv}_1^{\Sigma} - \mathtt{Adv}_2^{\Sigma}\right| \leq \Pr[\mathbf{Forge}].$$

Let $\mathcal{S}$ be a challenger, who is given $(g, h, g^a, g^b, h^a, h^b, \cdots, h^{b^\ell}, \hat{\mathsf{e}})$, aiming to compute $\hat{\mathsf{e}}(g, h)^{ab^{\ell+1}}$. $\mathcal{S}$ sets up the game for $\mathcal{A}$ by creating n users and T epochs. We assume that each epoch $t = t_1||t_2||\cdots||t_\ell$ is a $\{1, 2\}$-string of length ℓ. $\mathcal{S}$ pads zeros if an epoch's length is less than ℓ. $\mathcal{S}$ randomly selects a challenge user and sets its public key as $\mathtt{pk}_i = g^b$. $\mathcal{S}$ honestly generates key pairs for n-1 users. To complete the setup, $\mathcal{S}$ computes the system parameters as $h = h^{b^\ell} \cdot \bar{H}^{\gamma}$, $h_1 = \bar{H}^{\gamma_1}/h^{b^\ell}, \cdots, h_\ell = \bar{H}^{\gamma_\ell}/h^b$, and $h_0 = \bar{H}^{\delta} \cdot h^{b^\ell \cdot t_1^*} \cdots \cdot h^{b \cdot t_\ell^*}$, where $t^* = t_1^*||t_2^*||\cdots||t_\ell^*$, and $\gamma, \gamma_1, \cdots \gamma_\ell, \delta, \bar{z} \in \mathbb{Z}_q$, $\bar{H} = h^{\bar{z}} \in \mathbb{H}$. Note that the value $h^{b^{\ell+1}} \cdot \bar{H}^{b \cdot \gamma}$ associated with user $\mathtt{pk}_i$'s signing key is unknown to $\mathcal{S}$. During the game, $\mathcal{S}$ can honestly answer $\mathcal{A}$'s corrupt queries with respect to all users except the challenge user $\mathtt{pk}_i$. If $\mathcal{A}$ queries corrupt oracle on $\mathtt{pk}_i$, $\mathcal{S}$ aborts. Next, we show $\mathcal{S}$ can simulate a signing key at epoch $t = t_1||\cdots||t_k||\cdots||t_\ell$, where $k \in [1, \ell]$. Note that $t_k \neq t_k^*$ means that t is not prefix of t^*, and k is the smallest index at epoch t.

Specifically, $\mathcal{S}$ first chooses $z \in \mathbb{Z}_q$, and sets $r = \frac{b^k}{t_k - t_k^*} + z$. Then, $\mathcal{S}$ computes a signing key with the following form

$$(g^r, h^b \cdot \underline{(h_0 \cdot h_1^{t_1} \cdots h_k^{t_k})^r}, h_{k+1}^r, \cdots, h_\ell^r) \quad (2)$$

This is a well-formed key for epoch $t = t_1 || \cdots || t_k$. We show that $\mathcal{S}$ can compute the underline term in (2).

$$\begin{aligned}(h_0 \cdot h_1^{t_1} \cdots h_k^{t_k})^r &= [\bar{H}^\delta \cdot h^{b^\ell \cdot t_1^*} \cdots \cdot h^{b \cdot t_\ell^*} \cdot (\bar{H}^{\gamma_1}/h^{b^\ell})^{t_1} \cdots (\bar{H}^{\gamma_k}/h^{b^{\ell-k+1}})^{t_k}]^r \\ &= [\bar{H}^{\delta + \Sigma_{i=1}^k t_i \cdot \gamma_i} \cdot \prod_{i=1}^{k-1} h_{\ell-i+1}^{t_i^* - t_i} \cdot h_{\ell-k+1}^{t_k^* - t_k} \cdot \prod_{i=k+1}^{\ell} h_{\ell-i+1}^{t_i^*}]^r \\ &= Z \cdot h_{\ell-k+1}^{r(t_k^* - t_k)}\end{aligned}$$

where Z is shown as follows

$$Z = [\bar{H}^{\delta + \Sigma_{i=1}^k t_i \cdot \gamma_i} \cdot \underline{\prod_{i=1}^{k-1} h_{\ell-i+1}^{t_i^* - t_i}} \cdot \prod_{i=k+1}^{\ell} h_{\ell-i+1}^{t_i^*}]^r$$

$\mathcal{S}$ can compute all the terms in Z and the underline term in Z is equal to 1 because $t_i = t_i^*$ for all $i < k$. The remaining term in $(h_0 \cdot h_1^{t_1} \cdots h_k^{t_k})^r$ is $h_{\ell-k+1}^{r(t_k^* - t_k)}$. Since we set $r = \frac{b^k}{t_k - t_k^*} + z$, we rewrite it as follows

$$h_{\ell-k+1}^{r \cdot (t_k^* - t_k)} = h_{\ell-k+1}^{z(t_k^* - t_k)} \cdot h_{\ell-k+1}^{(t_k^* - t_k)\frac{b^k}{t_k - t_k^*}} = \frac{h_{\ell-k+1}^{z(t_k^* - t_k)}}{h^{b^{\ell+1}}}$$

Hence, the second element in (2) is equal to

$$h^b \cdot \underline{(h_0 \cdot h_1^{t_1} \cdots h_k^{t_k})^r} = h^{b^{\ell+1}} \cdot \bar{H}^{b \cdot \gamma} \cdot Z \cdot \frac{h_{\ell-k+1}^{z(t_k^* - t_k)}}{h^{b^{\ell+1}}} = \bar{H}^{b \cdot \gamma} \cdot Z \cdot h_{\ell-k+1}^{z(t_k^* - t_k)}$$

To this end, $\mathcal{S}$ can simulate the second element in (2) because the unknown value $h^{b^{\ell+1}}$ is cancelled out. Besides, the first element g^r in (2), and other elements $(h_{k+1}^r, \cdots, h_\ell^r)$ can be easily computed by $\mathcal{S}$ since they do not involve $h^{b^{\ell+1}}$. This completes the simulation of signing key at epoch $t \neq t^*$. $\mathcal{S}$ can simulate signing queries on different messages using the simulated signing keys at epoch $t \neq t^*$.

Another case is that $\mathcal{S}$ can simulate message-signature pairs at epoch t^*. If $\mathcal{A}$ issues a signing query on a message m for a public key set $\mathsf{PK} = \{\mathtt{pk}_1 \cdots, \mathtt{pk}_n\}$ (note that if $\mathtt{pk}_i \notin \mathsf{PK}$, $\mathcal{S}$ aborts) at epoch t^*, $\mathcal{S}$ performs the following operations to simulate a valid signature.

- Choose $c_i, \{c_j\}_{j=1}^{n-1}, \widehat{r_1}, \widehat{r_2} \in \mathbb{Z}_q$ and $h^* \in \mathbb{H}$, compute $\sigma_1 = h^* \cdot F(t^*)^{\widehat{r_1}}, \sigma_2 = g^{\widehat{r_2}}$, where $F(t^*) = h_0 \cdot h_1^{t_1^*} \cdots h_\ell^{t_\ell^*}$.
- Set $c_i = \mathtt{H}(R || m || \mathsf{PK}) - \sum_{j=1}^{n-1} c_j$, where $R = \frac{\hat{\mathsf{e}}(\mathtt{pk}_i^{c_i} \cdot \prod_{j=1}^{n-1} \mathtt{pk}_j^{c_j}, h)}{\hat{\mathsf{e}}(g, h^* \cdot F(t^*)^{\widehat{r}})}$ and $\widehat{r} = \widehat{r_1} + \widehat{r_2}$.

- Return (m, σ) to $\mathcal{A}$, where $\sigma = (c_1, \cdots, c_n, \sigma_1, \sigma_2)$.

The simulator $\mathcal{S}$ can simulate the case $(\mathsf{PK}^*, t^*, m, \sigma)$ using the same method described above. Specifically, $\mathcal{S}$ sets $c_i = \mathtt{H}(R||m||\mathsf{PK}^*) - \sum_{j=1}^{n-1} c_j$ (i.e., replaces PK with PK^*).

For key update, $\mathcal{S}$ keeps track of the current epoch t without returning anything to $\mathcal{A}$. For break in query, $\mathcal{S}$ needs to simulate a signing key $\mathbf{sk}_{(i,\bar{t})}$ with respect to user $\mathbf{pk}_i$, such that $t^* < \bar{t}$. $\mathcal{S}$ can simulate $\mathbf{sk}_{(i,\bar{t})}$ using the same method described in the case of $t \neq t^*$, and return it to $\mathcal{A}$.

At some point, if $\mathcal{A}$ outputs a forgery on a message m^* for a public key set PK^* and t^* in the form of $(m^*, c_1^*, \cdots, c_n^*, \sigma_1^*, \sigma_2^*)$, such that

$$\sigma_1^* = [h^{b^{\ell+1}} \cdot \bar{H}^{b \cdot \gamma} \cdot \bar{H}^{r^*(\delta + \sum_{i=1}^{|t^*|} \gamma_i \cdot t_i^*)}]^{c_i^*} \cdot (\bar{H}^{\delta + \sum_{i=1}^{|t^*|} \gamma_i \cdot t_i^*})^{\widehat{r_1^*}}$$
$$\sigma_2^* = g^{\widehat{r_2^*}} / g^{r^* \cdot c_i^*}$$

where $c_i^* = \mathtt{H}(R^*||m^*||\mathsf{PK}^*) - \sum_{j=1}^{n-1} c_j^*, R^* = \hat{\mathsf{e}}(\prod_{j=1}^{n-1} \mathbf{pk}_j^{c_j^*}, h) \cdot \hat{\mathsf{e}}(g, (\bar{H}^{\delta + \sum_{i=1}^{|t^*|} \gamma_i \cdot t_i^*})^{\widehat{r^*}})$, and $\widehat{r^*} = \widehat{r_1^*} + \widehat{r_2^*}$ (note that $r^*, \widehat{r_1^*}, \widehat{r_2^*}$ are chosen by $\mathcal{A}$), then $\mathcal{S}$ checks the following conditions.

- The public key set PK^* includes the challenge user $\mathbf{pk}_i$.
- The message-signature pair $(m^*, c_1^*, \cdots, c_n^*, \sigma_1^*, \sigma_2^*)$ was not previously generated by $\mathcal{S}$.
- The signature (σ_1^*, σ_2^*) is valid on message m^* and public key set PK^* according to the Verify process.

If all the above conditions hold, $\mathcal{S}$ regards it as a valid forgery. The next step is that $\mathcal{S}$ rewinds the game according to the forking lemma [9], and obtains another valid forgery (σ_1', σ_2') with a different $c_i^{*'} = \mathtt{H}(R^*||m^*||\mathsf{PK}^*) - \sum_{j=1}^{n-1} c_j^*$ (note that the different value $c^{*'}$ happens with probability $1/n$). Eventually, $\mathcal{S}$ computes the following equations

$$E = (\sigma_1/\sigma_1')^{1/(c_i^* - c_i^{*'})} = h^{b^{\ell+1}} \cdot \bar{H}^{b \cdot \gamma} \cdot \bar{H}^{r^*(\delta + \sum_{i=1}^{|t^*|} \gamma_i \cdot t_i^*)}$$
$$F = (\sigma_2'/\sigma_2)^{1/(c_i^{*'} - c_i^*)} = g^{r^*}$$
$$D = \frac{\hat{\mathsf{e}}(g^a, E)}{\hat{\mathsf{e}}(g^a, \bar{H}^{b \cdot \gamma}) \hat{\mathsf{e}}(F, h^{a \cdot (\delta + \sum_{i=1}^{|t^*|} \gamma_i \cdot t_i^*)})}$$
$$= [\frac{\hat{\mathsf{e}}(g^a, h^{b^{\ell+1}}) \hat{\mathsf{e}}(g^a, \bar{H}^{b \cdot \gamma}) \hat{\mathsf{e}}(g^a, \bar{H}^{r^*(\delta + \sum_{i=1}^{|t^*|} \gamma_i \cdot t_i^*)})}{\hat{\mathsf{e}}(g^a, h^{b \cdot \bar{r} \cdot \gamma}) \hat{\mathsf{e}}(g^{r^*}, h^{a \cdot (\delta + \sum_{i=1}^{|t^*|} \gamma_i \cdot t_i^*)})}]$$
$$= \hat{\mathsf{e}}(g, h)^{ab^{\ell+1}}$$

It is easy to see that D is the solution to the wBDHI problem. Therefore, we have

$$|\Pr[\mathbf{Forge}]| \leq \mathtt{Adv}_{\mathcal{A}}^{\mathrm{wBDHI}}(\lambda).$$

By combining the above results together, we have

$$\mathtt{Adv}_{\mathcal{A}}^{\Sigma}(\lambda) \leq T \cdot n \cdot \mathtt{Adv}_{\mathcal{A}}^{\mathrm{wBDHI}}(\lambda).$$

B Proof of Theorem 2

Proof. The simulation is performed between an adversary $\mathcal{A}$ and a simulator $\mathcal{S}$. The goal of simulator $\mathcal{S}$ is to break anonymity. In this simulation, $\mathcal{S}$ simulates $\mathtt{H}$ as a random oracle.

$\mathcal{S}$ setups the game for $\mathcal{A}$ by creating n users with the corresponding key pairs $\{(\mathtt{pk}_i, \mathtt{sk}_i) \leftarrow \mathsf{KeyGen}(\mathsf{PP}; w_i)\}$, where $\mathsf{PP} \leftarrow \mathsf{Setup}(1^\lambda)$. $\mathcal{S}$ gives $\{\mathtt{pk}_i\}^n$ to $\mathcal{A}$. $\mathcal{S}$ also chooses a random bit b.

During the training phase, if $\mathcal{A}$ issues a signing query on a message m, a set of public keys PK with the signer index j at epoch t, then $\mathcal{S}$ generates $\sigma \leftarrow \mathsf{Sign}(\mathsf{PP}, \mathtt{sk}_{(j,t)}, m, \mathsf{PK}, t)$ and returns it to $\mathcal{A}$.

During the challenge phase, if $\mathcal{A}$ issues a signing query on a message m^*, a set of public keys PK^*, two indices (i_0, i_1) and an epoch t^*, then $\mathcal{S}$ simulates the signature $\sigma^* = (\sigma_1^*, \sigma_2^*, c_1^*, \cdots, c_n^*)$ using the same method described in the above game $\mathbb{G}_2$ (i.e., the case of $t = t^*$). Eventually, $\mathcal{S}$ returns σ^* and $\{w_i\}^n$ to $\mathcal{A}$. Recall that in the simulation of signature σ^*, $\mathcal{S}$ picks $c_1^*, \cdots, c_n$ at random in $\mathbb{Z}_q$, and sets $c_i = \mathtt{H}(R^*||m^*||\mathsf{PK}^*) - \sum_{j=1}^{n-1} c_j$ in the random oracle. The distribution of message-signature pair (m^*, σ^*) is correct. Note that the commutative operation $\sum_{i=1}^{n} c_i$ is also uniformly distributed in $\mathbb{Z}_q$, and $\mathcal{S}$ aborts if the hash value $\mathtt{H}(R^*||m^*||\mathsf{PK}^*)$ is already set by the random oracle $\mathtt{H}$.

Finally, $\mathcal{S}$ outputs whatever $\mathcal{A}$ outputs. Since b is not used in the simulation of message-signature pair in the challenge phase (i.e., $\mathcal{S}$ simulates a valid signature without using the signing key $\mathtt{sk}_{(i_b,t^*)}$), $\mathcal{A}$ wins only with probability 1/2.

References

1. Double Ratchet Algorithm. https://www.signal.org/docs/specifications/doubleratchet
2. Our Source Code. https://github.com/SMC-SMU/Forward-secure-DualRing
3. X3DH Key Agreement Protocol. https://signal.org/docs/specifications/x3dh
4. Abe, M., Ohkubo, M., Suzuki, K.: 1-out-of-n signatures from a variety of keys. In: Zheng, Y. (ed.) ASIACRYPT 2002. LNCS, vol. 2501, pp. 415–432. Springer, Heidelberg (2002). https://doi.org/10.1007/3-540-36178-2_26
5. Adida, B.: Helios: web-based open-audit voting. In: USENIX Security Symposium, 17, pp. 335–348 (2008)
6. Akinyele, J.A., et al.: Charm: a framework for rapidly prototyping cryptosystems. J. Cryptogr. Eng. **3**(2), 111–128 (2013)
7. Au, M.H., Susilo, W., Yiu, S.-M.: Event-oriented k-times revocable-iff-linked group signatures. In: Batten, L.M., Safavi-Naini, R. (eds.) ACISP 2006. LNCS, vol. 4058, pp. 223–234. Springer, Heidelberg (2006). https://doi.org/10.1007/11780656_19
8. Bellare, M., Miner, S.K.: A forward-secure digital signature scheme. In: Wiener, M. (ed.) CRYPTO 1999. LNCS, vol. 1666, pp. 431–448. Springer, Heidelberg (1999). https://doi.org/10.1007/3-540-48405-1_28
9. Bellare, M., Neven, G.: Multi-signatures in the plain public-key model and a general forking lemma. In: CCS, pp. 390–399 (2006)

10. Bender, A., Katz, J., Morselli, R.: Ring signatures: stronger definitions, and constructions without random oracles. In: Halevi, S., Rabin, T. (eds.) TCC 2006. LNCS, vol. 3876, pp. 60–79. Springer, Heidelberg (2006). https://doi.org/10.1007/11681878_4
11. Boneh, D., Boyen, X., Goh, E.-J.: Hierarchical identity based encryption with constant size ciphertext. In: Cramer, R. (ed.) EUROCRYPT 2005. LNCS, vol. 3494, pp. 440–456. Springer, Heidelberg (2005). https://doi.org/10.1007/11426639_26
12. Boneh, D., Silverberg, A.: Applications of multilinear forms to cryptography. Contemp. Math. **324**(1), 71–90 (2003)
13. Bootle, J., Cerulli, A., Chaidos, P., Ghadafi, E., Groth, J., Petit, C.: Short accountable ring signatures based on DDH. In: Pernul, G., Ryan, P.Y.A., Weippl, E. (eds.) ESORICS 2015. LNCS, vol. 9326, pp. 243–265. Springer, Cham (2015). https://doi.org/10.1007/978-3-319-24174-6_13
14. Boyd, C., Gellert, K.: A modern view on forward security. Comput. J. **64**(4), 639–652 (2021)
15. Boyen, X., Haines, T.: Forward-secure linkable ring signatures. In: Susilo, W., Yang, G. (eds.) ACISP 2018. LNCS, vol. 10946, pp. 245–264. Springer, Cham (2018). https://doi.org/10.1007/978-3-319-93638-3_15
16. Brier, E., Coron, J.-S., Icart, T., Madore, D., Randriam, H., Tibouchi, M.: Efficient indifferentiable hashing into ordinary elliptic curves. In: Rabin, T. (ed.) CRYPTO 2010. LNCS, vol. 6223, pp. 237–254. Springer, Heidelberg (2010). https://doi.org/10.1007/978-3-642-14623-7_13
17. Canetti, R., Halevi, S., Katz, J.: A forward-secure public-key encryption scheme. In: Biham, E. (ed.) EUROCRYPT 2003. LNCS, vol. 2656, pp. 255–271. Springer, Heidelberg (2003). https://doi.org/10.1007/3-540-39200-9_16
18. Di Raimondo, M., Gennaro, R.: New approaches for deniable authentication. In: CCS, pp. 112–121 (2005)
19. Dodis, Y., Kiayias, A., Nicolosi, A., Shoup, V.: Anonymous identification in *Ad Hoc* groups. In: Cachin, C., Camenisch, J.L. (eds.) EUROCRYPT 2004. LNCS, vol. 3027, pp. 609–626. Springer, Heidelberg (2004). https://doi.org/10.1007/978-3-540-24676-3_36
20. Drijvers, M., Gorbunov, S., Neven, G., Wee, H.: Pixel: multi-signatures for consensus. In: USENIX, pp. 2093–2110 (2020)
21. Groth, J., Kohlweiss, M.: One-out-of-many proofs: or how to leak a secret and spend a coin. In: Oswald, E., Fischlin, M. (eds.) EUROCRYPT 2015. LNCS, vol. 9057, pp. 253–280. Springer, Heidelberg (2015). https://doi.org/10.1007/978-3-662-46803-6_9
22. Haines, T., Boyen, X.: Votor: conceptually simple remote voting against tiny tyrants. In: Proceedings of the Australasian Computer Science Week Multiconference, pp. 1–13 (2016)
23. Lai, R.W., Ronge, V., Ruffing, T., Schröder, D., Thyagarajan, S.A.K., Wang, J.: Omniring: scaling private payments without trusted setup. In: ACM CCS, pp. 31–48 (2019)
24. Libert, B., Peters, T., Qian, C.: Logarithmic-size ring signatures with tight security from the DDH assumption. In: Lopez, J., Zhou, J., Soriano, M. (eds.) ESORICS 2018. LNCS, vol. 11099, pp. 288–308. Springer, Cham (2018). https://doi.org/10.1007/978-3-319-98989-1_15
25. Liu, J.K., Au, M.H., Susilo, W., Zhou, J.: Linkable ring signature with unconditional anonymity. IEEE Trans. Knowl. Data Eng. **26**(1), 157–165 (2013)
26. Liu, J.K., Wong, D.S.: Solutions to key exposure problem in ring signature. Int. J. Netw. Secur. **6**(2), 170–180 (2008)

27. Liu, J.K., Yuen, T.H., Zhou, J.: Forward secure ring signature without random oracles. In: Qing, S., Susilo, W., Wang, G., Liu, D. (eds.) ICICS 2011. LNCS, vol. 7043, pp. 1–14. Springer, Heidelberg (2011). https://doi.org/10.1007/978-3-642-25243-3_1
28. Lu, X., Au, M.H., Zhang, Z.: Raptor: a practical lattice-based (linkable) ring signature. In: Deng, R.H., Gauthier-Umaña, V., Ochoa, M., Yung, M. (eds.) ACNS 2019. LNCS, vol. 11464, pp. 110–130. Springer, Cham (2019). https://doi.org/10.1007/978-3-030-21568-2_6
29. Miyaji, A., Nakabayashi, M., Takano, S.: Characterization of elliptic curve traces under FR-reduction. In: Won, D. (ed.) ICISC 2000. LNCS, vol. 2015, pp. 90–108. Springer, Heidelberg (2001). https://doi.org/10.1007/3-540-45247-8_8
30. Park, S., Sealfon, A.: It wasn't me! In: Boldyreva, A., Micciancio, D. (eds.) CRYPTO 2019. LNCS, vol. 11694, pp. 159–190. Springer, Cham (2019). https://doi.org/10.1007/978-3-030-26954-8_6
31. Rivest, R.L., Shamir, A., Tauman, Y.: How to leak a secret. In: Boyd, C. (ed.) ASIACRYPT 2001. LNCS, vol. 2248, pp. 552–565. Springer, Heidelberg (2001). https://doi.org/10.1007/3-540-45682-1_32
32. Schnorr, C.P.: Efficient signature generation by smart cards. J. Cryptol. **4**(3), 161–174 (1991). https://doi.org/10.1007/BF00196725
33. Yuen, T.H., Esgin, M.F., Liu, J.K., Au, M.H., Ding, Z.: *DualRing*: generic construction of ring signatures with efficient instantiations. In: Malkin, T., Peikert, C. (eds.) CRYPTO 2021. LNCS, vol. 12825, pp. 251–281. Springer, Cham (2021). https://doi.org/10.1007/978-3-030-84242-0_10
34. Yuen, T.H., et al.: RingCT 3.0 for blockchain confidential transaction: shorter size and stronger security. In: Bonneau, J., Heninger, N. (eds.) FC 2020. LNCS, vol. 12059, pp. 464–483. Springer, Cham (2020). https://doi.org/10.1007/978-3-030-51280-4_25
35. Zagórski, F., Carback, R.T., Chaum, D., Clark, J., Essex, A., Vora, P.L.: Remotegrity: design and use of an end-to-end verifiable remote voting system. In: Jacobson, M., Locasto, M., Mohassel, P., Safavi-Naini, R. (eds.) ACNS 2013. LNCS, vol. 7954, pp. 441–457. Springer, Heidelberg (2013). https://doi.org/10.1007/978-3-642-38980-1_28

Dually Computable Cryptographic Accumulators and Their Application to Attribute Based Encryption

Anaïs Barthoulot[1,2(✉)], Olivier Blazy[3], and Sébastien Canard[4]

[1] Orange Innovation, Caen, France
anais.barthoulot@gmail.com
[2] Université de Limoges, XLim, Limoges, France
[3] École Polytechnique, Palaiseau, France
olivier.blazy@polytechnique.edu
[4] Télécom Paris, Palaiseau, France
sebastien.canard@telecom-paris.fr

Abstract. In 1993, Benaloh and De Mare introduced cryptographic accumulator, a primitive that allows the representation of a set of values by a short object (the accumulator) and offers the possibility to prove that some input values are in the accumulator. For this purpose, so-called *asymmetric* accumulators require the creation of an additional cryptographic object, called a *witness*. Through the years, several instantiations of accumulators were proposed either based on number theoretic assumptions, hash functions, bilinear pairings or more recently lattices. In this work, we present the first instantiation of an asymmetric cryptographic accumulator that allows private computation of the accumulator but public witness creation. This is obtained thanks to our unique combination of the pairing based accumulator of Nguyen with *dual pairing vector spaces*. We moreover introduce the new concept of *dually computable* cryptographic accumulators, in which we offer two ways to compute the representation of a set: either privately (using a dedicated secret key) or publicly (using only the scheme's public key), while there is a unique witness creation for both cases. All our constructions of accumulators have constant size accumulated value and witness, and satisfy the accumulator security property of *collision resistance*, meaning that it is not possible to forge a witness for an element that is not in the accumulated set. As a second contribution, we show how our new concept of dually computable cryptographic accumulator can be used to build a Ciphertext Policy Attribute Based Encryption (CP-ABE). Our resulting scheme permits policies expressed as disjunctions of conjunctions (without "NO" gates), and is adaptively secure in the standard model. This is the first CP-ABE scheme having both constant-size user secret keys and ciphertexts (i.e. independent of the number of attributes in the scheme, or the policy size). For the first time, we provide a way to use cryptographic accumulators for both key management and encryption process.

Keywords: Cryptographic accumulators · Attribute based encryption · Pairing · Dual pairing vector spaces

J. Deng et al. (Eds.): CANS 2023, LNCS 14342, pp. 538–562, 2023.
https://doi.org/10.1007/978-981-99-7563-1_24

1 Introduction

Cryptographic Accumulator. Cryptographic accumulators were introduced in 1993 by Benaloh and De Mare [7] as a compact way to represent a set of elements, while permitting to prove the membership for each element in the set. Since their introduction, lots of new functionalities and properties were introduced and we refer interested readers to the work of Derler *et al.* [15] for more details on cryptographic accumulators. In this work, we focus on asymmetric accumulators, which are composed of four algorithms: Gen, the generation algorithm that outputs a public key and a master secret key; Eval, the evaluation algorithm that from a set of elements outputs the compact representation of this set (which is called the "accumulator"); $\mathsf{WitCreate}$, the witness creation algorithm that creates a witness that an element is the set; Verify, the verification algorithm that outputs 1 if the given witness proves that the element is indeed in the accumulated set. If the algorithm Eval (resp. $\mathsf{WitCreate}$) takes as input the master secret key we say that the evaluation (resp. witness generation) is done privately, otherwise it is done publicly. The main purpose of cryptographic accumulators is to produce accumulators and witnesses that have constant size. Regarding security, there are several properties but in this work we will consider the notion of *collision resistance* meaning that given the accumulator public key it is hard for an adversary to find a set $\mathcal{X}$ and a value $y \notin \mathcal{X}$ and build a witness wit_y such that $\mathsf{Verify}(\mathsf{pk}_{\mathsf{acc}}, \mathsf{acc}_{\mathcal{X}}, \mathsf{wit}_y) = 1$, where $\mathsf{acc}_{\mathcal{X}} = \mathsf{Eval}((\mathsf{sk}_{\mathsf{acc}}), \mathsf{pk}_{\mathsf{acc}}, \mathcal{X})$.

Improving Accumulator's State of the Art. Regarding the literature, one surprising thing is that there is no accumulator with private evaluation and public witness generation: either both evaluation and witness creation are either public [29] or private [20], or witness generation is private while evaluation is public [30]. As soon as the accumulator has been secretly computed and publish, it could be relevant for some use cases to consider the case where anyone can prove that one element is in the chosen set. In the sequel, we show how this property can be used to construct encryption schemes from a cryptographic accumulator. Therefore, we propose the first instantiation of such accumulator, based on asymmetric pairings in prime order group and using dual pairing vector spaces. We also introduce the notion of *dually computable* accumulator, which permits both a private (Eval) and a public ($\mathsf{PublicEval}$) accumulator generation, such that both accumulators are distinguishable. From a unique witness generation algorithm, we add two associated verifications (Verify and $\mathsf{PublicVerify}$ respectively) to verify set membership. Using our previous accumulator instantiation, we derive the first dually computable accumulator scheme. We then show how such new concept can be used to provide an efficient Attribute Based Encryption (ABE) scheme.

Attribute Based Encryption. ABE, introduced by Sahai and Waters in 2005 [35], is an encryption scheme in which secret keys and ciphertexts are associated to some subset of attributes, and decryption is possible if there exists a relation between the secret key's attributes and the ciphertext's attributes. In more details, in a *Ciphertext Policy ABE* (CP-ABE) the ciphertext is associated to an access policy while the secret key is associated to a set of attributes. Decryption becomes possible if the set of attributes satisfies the policy. There exist several ways to define an access policy in the literature: through threshold structure [35], tree-based structure [22], boolean formulas [28], linear secret sharing schemes [40], circuits [10], ... Regarding security, ABE schemes must satisfy *indistinguishability*, meaning that an adversary who is given an encryption of one of two messages he previously chose, cannot tell which message was encrypted. The main aim of research in ABE is to build efficient schemes in terms of both time and space complexities, while supporting complex access policies. Unfortunately, most existing schemes propose ciphertexts with a size linear in the number of attributes in the scheme [22,25,26], while some other constructions succeed in proposing constant size ciphertext, but at the cost of quadratic-size user private key [4].

ABE from Dually Computable Accumulators. In this paper, we propose a way to obtain an ABE scheme for which both the ciphertext and the user secret key are constant, while obtaining very good time complexities. For that, our idea is to use cryptographic accumulators. Curiously, while the purpose of the latter is to make constant the size of cryptographic objects, few attempts have been done to use them for encryption schemes. Indeed, [2,19] propose broadcast encryption schemes that use (RSA based) cryptographic accumulator, and more recently, Wang and Chow [38] present an identity based broadcast encryption scheme that uses a degenarated notion of accumulators. However, [2,19] are using accumulators only to manage users' secret key while [38] is using their notion of accumulator for encryption only, whereas in our scheme, accumulators are used for both secret keys and ciphertexts. Plus, (identity based) broadcast encryption is one particular case of ABE, which makes our scheme more general.

To reach such objective of compactness, our idea is to employ our notion of dually computable accumulators in the following manner: the secret key, computed by the authority, corresponds to a privately computed accumulator of the users' attributes set, while the encryption corresponds to a one-time-pad with a mask derived from a publicly computed accumulator of the access policy. Decryption is then possible if the decryptor can demonstrate that the intersection of their accumulator and the one associated with the ciphertext is not empty, utilizing membership witnesses for both the privately computed and the publicly computed accumulators. However, while it is relatively straightforward to use accumulators to represent sets of attributes, understanding how they can serve as a concise representation of access policies is more complex. In this study, we introduce a way to represent monotone boolean formulas that is compatible with the use of accumulators, and then show how to employ dually computable accumulators to obtain a compact, efficient and secure ABE.

Our Contributions. As a summary, our work gives the three following contributions:

- a new accumulator scheme, based on [31]'s work. It is the first accumulator in the literature that has private evaluation while having public witness creation. This scheme is based on asymmetric pairings in prime order groups and dual pairing vector spaces (DPVS) of dimension 2, and satisfies *collision resistance* under the q-Strong Bilinear Diffie-Hellman assumption. This is the first construction of cryptographic accumulators that uses DPVS. See Sect. 3;
- a new functionality of *dually computable* cryptographic accumulators, together with an instantiation of a such accumulator, based on our first accumulator instantiation. Details are given in Sect. 4;
- a new bounded CP-ABE scheme, with both constant size for ciphertexts and user secret keys where access policies are monotone NC^1 circuits. Our scheme moreover gives very good time complexities, and is proven adaptively secure in the standard model, under the standard SXDH assumption. See Sect. 5.

2 Preliminaries

This section introduces the notations, the building blocks and the security assumptions used throughout this paper. Let "PPT" denote "probabilistic polynomial-time". For every finite set S, $x \leftarrow S$ denotes a uniformly random element x from the set S. Vectors are written with **bold face** lower case letters and matrices with **bold face** upper case letters.

2.1 Cryptographic Accumulators

In the following we present a simplified definition of accumulator, presenting only properties used in this work, for simplicity of reading. Refer to [15] for a complete definition of cryptographic accumulators.

Definition 1. ***Static accumulator*** *[7,15,17]. A static cryptographic accumulator scheme is a tuple of efficient algorithms defined as follows:*

- $\mathsf{Gen}(1^\kappa, \mathfrak{b})$: *this algorithm takes as input a security parameter κ and a bound $\mathfrak{b} \in \mathbb{N} \cup \{\infty\}$ such that if $\mathfrak{b} \neq \infty$ then the number of elements that can be accumulated is bounded by $\mathfrak{b}$. It returns a key pair $(\mathsf{sk_{acc}}, \mathsf{pk_{acc}})$, where $\mathsf{sk_{acc}} = \varnothing$ if no trapdoor exists and $\mathsf{pk_{acc}}$ contains the parameter $\mathfrak{b}$.*
- $\mathsf{Eval}((\mathsf{sk_{acc}},)\mathsf{pk_{acc}}, \mathcal{X})$: *this algorithm takes as input the accumulator (secret key $\mathsf{sk_{acc}}$ and) public key $\mathsf{pk_{acc}}$ and a set $\mathcal{X}$ to be accumulated. It returns an accumulator $\mathsf{acc}_\mathcal{X}$ together with some auxiliary information* aux.
- $\mathsf{WitCreate}((\mathsf{sk_{acc}},)\mathsf{pk_{acc}}, \mathcal{X}, \mathsf{acc}_\mathcal{X}, \mathsf{aux}, x)$: *this algorithm takes as input the accumulator (secret key $\mathsf{sk_{acc}}$ and) public key $\mathsf{pk_{acc}}$, an accumulator $\mathsf{acc}_\mathcal{X}$, the associated set $\mathcal{X}$, auxiliary information* aux, *and an element x. It outputs a membership witness $\mathsf{wit}_x^\mathcal{X}$ if $x \in \mathcal{X}$, otherwise it outputs a reject symbol $\perp$.*
- $\mathsf{Verify}(\mathsf{pk_{acc}}, \mathsf{acc}_\mathcal{X}, \mathsf{wit}_x^\mathcal{X}, x)$: *this algorithm takes as input the accumulator public key $\mathsf{pk_{acc}}$, an accumulator $\mathsf{acc}_\mathcal{X}$, a witness $\mathsf{wit}_x^\mathcal{X}$ and an element x. If $\mathsf{wit}_x^\mathcal{X}$ is correct it returns* 1, *otherwise it returns* 0.

Definition 2. *If in the above definition x can be replaced by a set S, we say that the accumulator supports* subset queries. *If any element in $\mathcal{X}$ can be present more than once, and witnesses can be made to prove that the element is present a given number of times in $\mathcal{X}$, we say that the accumulator supports* multisets *setting.*

Note 1. Sometimes $\mathsf{wit}_x^\mathcal{X}$ is simply written wit_x.

Definition 3. ***Correctness of accumulators.*** *A static accumulator is said to be* correct *if for all security parameters κ, all integer $\mathfrak{b} \in \mathbb{N} \cup \{\infty\}$, all set of values $\mathcal{X}$, and all element x such that $x \in \mathcal{X}$:*

$$\Pr\left[\begin{array}{c}\mathsf{sk_{acc}}, \mathsf{pk_{acc}} \leftarrow \mathsf{Gen}(1^\kappa, \mathfrak{b}), \mathsf{acc}_\mathcal{X}, \mathsf{aux} \leftarrow \mathsf{Eval}((\mathsf{sk_{acc}},)\mathsf{pk_{acc}}, \mathcal{X}),\\ \mathsf{wit}_x^\mathcal{X} \leftarrow \mathsf{WitCreate}((\mathsf{sk_{acc}},)\mathsf{pk_{acc}}, \mathcal{X}, \mathsf{acc}_\mathcal{X}, \mathsf{aux}, x) :\\ \mathsf{Verify}(\mathsf{pk_{acc}}, \mathsf{acc}_\mathcal{X}, \mathsf{wit}_x, x) = 1\end{array}\right] = 1$$

Regarding security, we will only consider the following definition in this work.

Definition 4. ***Collision resistance.*** *A static accumulator scheme is* collision resistant, *if for all PPT adversaries $\mathcal{A}$ there is a negligible function $\epsilon(.)$ such that:*

$$\Pr\left[\begin{array}{c}\mathsf{sk_{acc}},\mathsf{pk_{acc}} \leftarrow \mathsf{Gen}(1^\kappa,\mathfrak{b}), \mathcal{O} \leftarrow \{\mathcal{O}^E, \mathcal{O}^W\}, (\mathcal{X}, \mathsf{wit}_x, x) \leftarrow \mathcal{A}^{\mathcal{O}}(\mathsf{pk_{acc}}): \\ \mathsf{Verify}(\mathsf{pk_{acc}}, \mathsf{acc}_{\mathcal{X}}, \mathsf{wit}_x, x) = 1 \wedge x \notin \mathcal{X}\end{array}\right] \leq \epsilon(\kappa),$$

where $\mathsf{acc}_{\mathcal{X}} \leftarrow \mathsf{Eval}((\mathsf{sk_{acc}},)\mathsf{pk_{acc}}, \mathcal{X})$ *and $\mathcal{A}$ has oracle access to $\mathcal{O}$, where $\mathcal{O}^E$ and $\mathcal{O}^W$ that represent the oracles for the algorithms* Eval *and* WitCreate. *An adversary is allowed to query it an arbitrary number of times.*

2.2 Other Preliminaries

Definition 5. ***Asymmetric bilinear pairing groups*** *[13].* Asymmetric bilinear groups *$\Gamma = (p, \mathbb{G}_1, \mathbb{G}_2, \mathbb{G}_T, g_1, g_2, e)$ are tuple of prime p, cyclic (multiplicative) groups $\mathbb{G}_1, \mathbb{G}_2$, $\mathbb{G}_T$ (where $\mathbb{G}_1 \neq \mathbb{G}_2$) of order p, $g_1 \neq 1 \in \mathbb{G}_1$, $g_2 \neq 1 \in \mathbb{G}_2$, and a polynomial-time computable non-degenerate bilinear pairing $e : \mathbb{G}_1 \times \mathbb{G}_2 \rightarrow \mathbb{G}_T$, i.e. $e(g_1^s, g_2^t) = e(g_1, g_2)^{st}$ and $e(g_1, g_2) \neq 1$.*

Note 2. For any group element $g \in \mathbb{G}$, and any vector $\boldsymbol{v}$ of size $l \in \mathbb{N}$, we denote by $g^{\boldsymbol{v}}$ the vector $(g^{v_1}, \cdots, g^{v_l})$. Let $\boldsymbol{u}, \boldsymbol{v}$ be two vectors of length l. Then by $g^{\boldsymbol{u}\cdot\boldsymbol{v}}$, we denote the element g^α, where $\alpha = \boldsymbol{u} \cdot \boldsymbol{v} = u_1 \cdot v_1 + u_2 \cdot v_2 + \cdots + u_l \cdot v_l$. Then we define $e(g_1^{\boldsymbol{v}}, g_2^{\boldsymbol{u}}) := \prod_{i=1}^{l} e(g_1^{v_i}, g_2^{u_i}) = e(g_1, g_2)^{\boldsymbol{v}\cdot\boldsymbol{u}}$.

Definition 6. ***Dual pairing vector spaces (DPVS).*** *[13] For a prime p and a fixed (constant) dimension n, we choose two random bases $\mathbb{B} = (\boldsymbol{b}_1, \cdots, \boldsymbol{b}_n)$ and $\mathbb{B}^* = (\boldsymbol{b}_1^*, \cdots, \boldsymbol{b}_n^*)$ of $\mathbb{Z}_p^n$, subject to the constraint that they are* **dual orthonormal**, *meaning that $\boldsymbol{b}_i \cdot \boldsymbol{b}_j^* = 0 \pmod p$ whenever $i \neq j$, and $\boldsymbol{b}_i \cdot \boldsymbol{b}_i^* = \psi \pmod p$ for all i, where ψ is a uniformly random element of $\mathbb{Z}_p$. Here the elements of $\mathbb{B}, \mathbb{B}^*$ are vectors and $\cdot$ corresponds to the scalar product. We denote such algorithm as* $\mathsf{Dual}(\mathbb{Z}_p^n)$. *For generators $g_1 \in \mathbb{G}_1$ and $g_2 \in \mathbb{G}_2$, we note that $e(g_1^{\boldsymbol{b}_i}, g_2^{\boldsymbol{b}_j^*}) = 1$ whenever $i \neq j$.*

Note 3. In our constructions we will use the notation $(\mathbb{D}, \mathbb{D}^*)$ to also denote dual orthonormal bases, as in our ABE security proof, we will handle more than one pair of dual orthonormal bases at a time, and we think that a different notation will avoid confusion. The notation $(\mathbb{F}, \mathbb{F}^*)$ will also be used in the proof for dual orthonormal bases.

Definition 7. ***Characteristic Polynomial.*** *[18,20]. A set $\mathcal{X} = \{x_1, \cdots, x_n\}$ with elements $x_i \in \mathbb{Z}_p$ can be represented by a polynomial. The polynomial $\mathsf{Ch}_{\mathcal{X}}[z] = \prod_{i=1}^{n}(x_i + Z)$ from $\mathbb{Z}_p[Z]$, where Z is a formal variable, is called the* characteristic polynomial *of $\mathcal{X}$. In what follows, we will denote this polynomial simply by $\mathsf{Ch}_{\mathcal{X}}$ and its evaluation at a point y as $\mathsf{Ch}_{\mathcal{X}}(y)$.*

Definition 8. ***Elementary symmetric polynomial.*** *The* elementary symmetric polynomial *on $n \in \mathbb{N}$ variables $\{X_i\}$ of degree $k \leq n$ is the polynomial $\sigma_k(X_1, \cdots, X_n) = \sum_{1 \leq i_1 \nleq \cdots \nleq i_k \leq n} X_{i_1} \cdots X_{i_k}$. Notice that $\sigma_1(X_1, \cdots, X_N) = \sum_{i=1}^{n} X_i$ and $\sigma_n = \prod_{i=1}^{n} X_i$.*

Note 4. Let $\mathcal{X} = \{X_1, \cdots, X_n\}$. Notice that $\mathsf{Ch}_{\mathcal{X}}[Z]$, which is equals to $\prod_{i=1}^{n} (X_i + Z)$ by definition, is also equals to $Z^n + \sigma_1(X_1, \cdots, X_n)Z^{n-1} + \sigma_2(X_1, \cdots, X_n)Z^{n-2} + \cdots + \sigma_n(X_1, \cdots, X_n)$.

Definition 9. ***Decisional Diffie-Hellman assumption in*** $\mathbb{G}_1$ (DDH_1). *[13] Given an asymmetric bilinear pairing group* $\Gamma = (p, \mathbb{G}_1, \mathbb{G}_2, \mathbb{G}_T, g_1, g_2, e)$*, we define the following distribution:* $a, b, c \leftarrow \mathbb{Z}_p$, $D = (\Gamma, g_1, g_2, g_1^a, g_2^b)$. *We assume that for any PPT algorithm* $\mathcal{A}$, $\mathsf{Adv}_{\mathcal{A}}^{\mathsf{DDH}_1}(\lambda) = \left|\Pr\left[\mathcal{A}(D, g_1^{ab})\right] - \Pr\left[\mathcal{A}(D, g_1^{ab+c})\right]\right|$ *is negligible in the security parameter* λ.

The dual of above assumption is Decisional Diffie-Hellman assumption in $\mathbb{G}_2$ (denoted as DDH_2), which is identical to DDH_1 with the roles of $\mathbb{G}_1$ and $\mathbb{G}_2$ reversed.

Definition 10. ***Symmetric External Diffie-Hellman*** (SXDH). *[13] The* SXDH *assumption holds if* DDH *problems are intractable in both* $\mathbb{G}_1$ *and* $\mathbb{G}_2$.

Definition 11. ***q-strong Bilinear Diffie-Hellman*** (q-SBDH). *[9] Let* $\Gamma = (p, \mathbb{G}_1, \mathbb{G}_2, \mathbb{G}_T, g_1, g_2, e)$ *be a bilinear group. In* Γ*, the* q-SBDH *problem is stated as follows: given as input a* $(2q+2)$*-tuple of elements* $(g_1, g_1^{\alpha}, g_1^{(\alpha^2)}, \cdots, g_1^{(\alpha^q)}, g_2, g_2^{\alpha}, g_2^{(\alpha^2)}, \cdots, g_2^{(\alpha^q)}) \in \mathbb{G}_1^{q+1} \times \mathbb{G}_2^{q+1}$*, output a pair* $(\gamma, e(g_1, g_2)^{1/(\alpha+\gamma)}) \in \mathbb{Z}_p \times \mathbb{G}_T$ *for a freely chosen value* $\gamma \in \mathbb{Z}_p \backslash \{-\alpha\}$. *The* q-SBDH *assumption states that for any PPT adversary* $\mathcal{A}$*, there exists negligible function* $\epsilon(.)$ *such that*

$$\Pr\left[\mathcal{A}(\Gamma, g_1^{\alpha}, g_1^{(\alpha^2)}, \cdots, g_1^{(\alpha^q)}, g_2^{\alpha}, g_2^{(\alpha^2)}, \cdots, g_2^{(\alpha^q)}) = (\gamma, e(g_1, g_2)^{1/(\alpha+\gamma)})\right] \leq \epsilon$$

where the probability is over the random choice of generator $g_1 \in \mathbb{G}_1$ *and* $g_2 \in \mathbb{G}_2$*, the random choice of* $\alpha \in \mathbb{Z}_p^*$*, and the random bits consumed by* $\mathcal{A}$.

Note 5. The above definition is a slightly modified version of the original assumption of [9]. Following the work of [36], our version can be reduced to the original one.

Definition 12. ***Decisional subspace assumption in*** $\mathbb{G}_1$ **(DS1).** *[13] Given an asymmetric bilinear group generator* $\mathcal{G}(.)$*, define the following distribution*

$$\begin{aligned}
&\Gamma = (p, \mathbb{G}_1, \mathbb{G}_2, \mathbb{G}_T, g_1, g_2, e) \leftarrow \mathcal{G}(1^{\kappa}), (\mathbb{B}, \mathbb{B}^*) \leftarrow \mathsf{Dual}(\mathbb{Z}_p^n), \tau_1, \tau_2, \mu_1, \mu_2 \leftarrow \mathbb{Z}_p,\\
&\boldsymbol{u}_1 = g_2^{\mu_1.\boldsymbol{b}_1^* + \mu_2.\boldsymbol{b}_{k+1}^*}, \cdots, \boldsymbol{u}_k = g_2^{\mu_1.\boldsymbol{b}_k^* + \mu_2 \boldsymbol{b}_{2k}^*}, \boldsymbol{v}_1 = g_1^{\tau_1.\boldsymbol{b}_1}, \cdots, \boldsymbol{v}_k = g_1^{\tau_1.\boldsymbol{b}_k},\\
&\boldsymbol{w}_1 = g_1^{\tau_1.\boldsymbol{b}_1 + \tau_2 \boldsymbol{b}_{k+1}}, \cdots, \boldsymbol{w}_k = g_1^{\tau_1.\boldsymbol{b}_k + \mu_2 \boldsymbol{b}_{2k}},\\
&\Delta = (\Gamma, g_2^{\boldsymbol{b}_1^*}, \cdots, g_2^{\boldsymbol{b}_k^*}, g_2^{\boldsymbol{b}_{2k+1}^*}, \cdots, g_2^{\boldsymbol{b}_n^*}, g_1^{\boldsymbol{b}_1}, \cdots, g_1^{\boldsymbol{b}_n}, \boldsymbol{u}_1, \cdots, \boldsymbol{u}_k, \mu_2),
\end{aligned}$$

where k, n *are fixed positive integers that satisfy* $2k \leq n$. *We assume that for any PPT algorithm* $\mathcal{A}$*, the following is negligible in* 1^{κ}.

$$\mathsf{Adv}_{\mathcal{A}}^{DS1}(\kappa) = |\Pr[\mathcal{A}(\Delta, \boldsymbol{v}_1, \cdots, \boldsymbol{v}_k) = 1] - \Pr[\mathcal{A}(\Delta, \boldsymbol{w}_1, \cdots, \boldsymbol{w}_k) = 1]|$$

Lemma 1. *If the decisional Diffie Hellman assumption* (DDH) *in* $\mathbb{G}_1$ *holds, then the decisional subspace assumption in* $\mathbb{G}_1$ *(DS1) also holds.*

For the proof, refer to [13]. The **decisional subspace assumption** in $\mathbb{G}_2$ is defined as identical to DS1 with the roles of $\mathbb{G}_1$ and $\mathbb{G}_2$ reversed. DS2 holds if DDH in $\mathbb{G}_2$ holds. The proof is done as for $\mathbb{G}_1$. Thus, DS1 and DS2 hold if SXDH hold.

3 A New Accumulator Scheme

We here present a new cryptographic accumulator scheme based on a unique combination of Nguyen's accumulator [31] and dual pairing vector spaces. We also briefly compare our scheme to the literature, concluding that this is the first cryptographic accumulator permitting a private evaluation and a public witness generation.

Intuition. In a bilinear environment, Nguyen's accumulator for a set $\mathcal{X}$ is the element $\mathsf{acc}_{\mathcal{X}} = g_1^{\prod_{x \in \mathcal{X}}(x+s)}$ where s is the secret key. A witness for an element $\underline{x} \in \mathcal{X}$ is then the object $\mathsf{wit}_{\underline{x}} = g_2^{\prod_{x \in \mathcal{X} \setminus \{\underline{x}\}}(x+s)}$. Verification is done by checking that $e(\mathsf{acc}_{\mathcal{X}}, g_2) = e(g_1^{\underline{x}} \cdot g_1^s, \mathsf{wit}_{\underline{x}})$. If only g_1, g_2 and g_1^s are published, evaluation *and* witness generation are *private*. If the public key contains $g_1, g_1^s, \cdots, g_1^{s^q}, g_2, g_2^s, \cdots, g_2^{s^q}$, then both evaluation *and* witness generation are *public*, using characteristic polynomials (see Definition 7).

One basic idea to obtain a secret evaluation and a public witness generation is to keep secret the elements in $\mathbb{G}_1$ for the evaluation and to publicly use the elements in $\mathbb{G}_2$ for the witness creation. But this does not work as we need to have g_1^s for verification. Our idea is hence to go in a Dual Pairing Vector Space (DPVS) setting, as introduced above, in dimension $n = 2$. By playing with the bases $\boldsymbol{d}_1, \boldsymbol{d}_1^*, \boldsymbol{d}_2$ and $\boldsymbol{d}_2^*$, we can keep secret some elements and publish some others as follows:

- $g_1^{\boldsymbol{d}_1}, g_1^{\boldsymbol{d}_1 s}, \cdots g_1^{\boldsymbol{d}_1 s^q}$ are not publicly given since used for private evaluation;
- $g_2^{\boldsymbol{d}_2^*}, g_2^{\boldsymbol{d}_2^* s}, \cdots g_2^{\boldsymbol{d}_2^* s^q}$ are publicly used for witness creation; and
- $g_2^{\boldsymbol{d}_1^*}, g_1^{\boldsymbol{d}_2}, g_1^{\boldsymbol{d}_2 s}$ are publicly used for verification.

Thanks to that and the transformation from $\prod_{x \in \mathcal{X}}(x+s)$ to $\sum_{i=0}^{q} a_i s^i$, using the characteristic polynomial given in Definition 7, the above public elements are easily computable from the knowledge of the successive powers of s in groups $\mathbb{G}_1$ or $\mathbb{G}_2$, as it is done in Nguyen's. We obtain our scheme below. To be exhaustive, the resulting comparison between our scheme and Nguyen's is given in Table 1.

Table 1. Comparison between Nguyen's accumulator and ours.

Operation	Nguyen [31]	Ours
Evaluation	$\mathsf{acc}_{\mathcal{X}} = g_1^{\prod_{x \in \mathcal{X}}(x+s)}$	$\mathsf{acc}_{\mathcal{X}} = g_1^{\boldsymbol{d}_1 \prod_{x \in \mathcal{X}}(x+s)}$
Witness	$\mathsf{wit}_{\underline{x}} = g_2^{\prod_{x \in \mathcal{X} \setminus \{\underline{x}\}}(x+s)}$	$\mathsf{wit}_{\underline{x}} = g_2^{\boldsymbol{d}_2^* \prod_{x \in \mathcal{X} \setminus \{\underline{x}\}}(x+s)}$
Verification	$e(\mathsf{acc}_{\mathcal{X}}, g_2) = e(g_1^{\underline{x}} \cdot g_1^s, \mathsf{wit}_{\underline{x}})$	$e(\mathsf{acc}_{\mathcal{X}}, g_2^{\boldsymbol{d}_1^*}) = e(g_1^{\boldsymbol{d}_2 \underline{x}} \cdot g_1^{\boldsymbol{d}_2 s}, \mathsf{wit}_{\underline{x}})$

Regarding efficiency, notice that our scheme is slightly less efficient than Nguyen's scheme [31]. Indeed in the latter accumulators and witnesses are respectively composed of one element of $\mathbb{G}_1$ and $\mathbb{G}_2$ while in our scheme they are respectively composed of *two* elements of $\mathbb{G}_1$ and $\mathbb{G}_2$. Regarding the number of pairing in verification, Nguyen's requires one pairing while our scheme requires *two* pairing.

Construction. Following the above intuition, our full scheme is presented in Fig. 1. In a nutshell, our construction is a static, bounded, and supports multisets and subsets queries.

- $\mathsf{Gen}(1^\kappa, q)$: run a bilinear group generation algorithm to get $\Gamma = (p, \mathbb{G}_1, \mathbb{G}_2, \mathbb{G}_T, e, g_1, g_2)$. Then choose a random $s \leftarrow \mathbb{Z}_p^*$, and run $\mathsf{Dual}(\mathbb{Z}_p^2)$ to get $\mathbb{D} = (\boldsymbol{d}_1, \boldsymbol{d}_2), \mathbb{D}^* = (\boldsymbol{d}_1^*, \boldsymbol{d}_2^*)$. Let $\psi \in \mathbb{Z}_p$ be the random such that $\boldsymbol{d}_1 \cdot \boldsymbol{d}_1^* = \boldsymbol{d}_2 \cdot \boldsymbol{d}_2^* = \psi$. Set $\mathsf{sk}_{\mathsf{acc}} = (s, \mathbb{D}, \mathbb{D}^*)$, $\mathsf{pk}_{\mathsf{acc}} = \left(\Gamma, g_1^{\boldsymbol{d}_2}, g_1^{\boldsymbol{d}_2 s}, \cdots, g_1^{\boldsymbol{d}_2 s^q}, g_2^{\boldsymbol{d}_1^*}, g_2^{\boldsymbol{d}_2^*}, g_2^{\boldsymbol{d}_2^* s}, \cdots, g_2^{\boldsymbol{d}_2^* s^q}\right)$, and return $\mathsf{sk}_{\mathsf{acc}}, \mathsf{pk}_{\mathsf{acc}}$.
- $\mathsf{Eval}(\mathsf{sk}_{\mathsf{acc}}, \mathsf{pk}_{\mathsf{acc}}, \mathcal{X})$: compute the coefficients $\{a_i\}_{i=0,\cdots,q}$ of the polynomial $\mathsf{Ch}_{\mathcal{X}}[Z] = \prod_{x \in \mathcal{X}}(Z + x)$. Then compute $\mathsf{acc}_{\mathcal{X}} = g_1^{\boldsymbol{d}_1 \sum_{i=0}^q a_i s^i}$, and return $\mathsf{acc}_{\mathcal{X}}$.
- $\mathsf{WitCreate}(\mathsf{pk}_{\mathsf{acc}}, \mathcal{X}, \mathsf{acc}_{\mathcal{X}}, \mathcal{I})$: let $\{b_i\}_{i=0,\cdots,q}$ be the coefficients of the polynomial $\mathsf{Ch}_{\mathcal{X}\setminus\mathcal{I}}[Z] = \prod_{x \in \mathcal{X}\setminus\mathcal{I}}(x + Z)$. Compute $\mathsf{wit}_{\mathcal{I}} = g_2^{\boldsymbol{d}_2^* \sum_{i=0}^q b_i s^i}$, and return $\mathsf{wit}_{\mathcal{I}}$.
- $\mathsf{Verify}(\mathsf{pk}_{\mathsf{acc}}, \mathsf{acc}_{\mathcal{X}}, \mathsf{wit}_{\mathcal{I}}, \mathcal{I})$: let $\{c_i\}_{i=0,\cdots,q}$ be the coefficients of the polynomial $\mathsf{Ch}_{\mathcal{I}}[Z] = \prod_{x \in \mathcal{I}}(x + Z)$ and return 1 if $e(\mathsf{acc}_{\mathcal{X}}, g_2^{\boldsymbol{d}_1^*}) = e(g_1^{\boldsymbol{d}_2 \sum_{i=0}^q c_i s^i}, \mathsf{wit}_{\mathcal{I}})$, 0 otherwise.

Fig. 1. Our first accumulator scheme, with private evaluation and public witness generation.

Security. In short, the correctness comes from both (i) the one of Nguyen scheme (indeed, the same pairing equation is used), and (ii) the properties of DPVS ($\boldsymbol{b}_i \cdot \boldsymbol{b}_j^* = 0 \pmod p$) whenever $i \neq j$, and $\boldsymbol{b}_i \cdot \boldsymbol{b}_i^* = \psi \pmod p$ for all i). More formally, we prove the following theorem.

Theorem 1. *Our accumulator scheme is correct.*

Proof. Let $\mathcal{X}, \mathcal{I}$ be two sets such that $\mathcal{I} \subset \mathcal{X}$. Let $\{a_i, b_i, c_i\}_{i=0}^q$ be respectively the coefficients of polynomials $\mathsf{Ch}_{\mathcal{X}}[Z] = \prod_{x \in \mathcal{X}}(x + Z)$, $\mathsf{Ch}_{\mathcal{X}\setminus\mathcal{I}}[Z] = \prod_{x \in \mathcal{X}\setminus\mathcal{I}}(x + Z)$ and $\mathsf{Ch}_{\mathcal{I}}[Z] = \prod_{x \in \mathcal{I}}[Z](x + Z)$. Let $\mathsf{acc}_{\mathcal{X}} \leftarrow \mathsf{Eval}(\mathsf{sk}_{\mathsf{acc}}, \mathcal{X})$ and $\mathsf{mwit}_{\mathcal{I}} \leftarrow \mathsf{WitCreate}(\mathsf{pk}_{\mathsf{acc}}, \mathsf{acc}_{\mathcal{X}}, \mathcal{X}, \mathcal{I})$. We have that

$$e(g_1^{d_2 \sum_{i=0}^q c_i s^i}, \mathsf{mwit}_{\mathcal{I}}) = e(g_1^{d_2 \sum_{i=0}^q c_i s^i}, g_2^{d_2^* \sum_{i=0}^q b_i s^i}) = e(g_1, g_2)^{\psi \sum_{i=0}^q c_i s^i \cdot \sum_{i=0}^q b_i s^i}.$$

As $\mathcal{I} \subset \mathcal{X}$, then $\sum_{i=0}^q c_i s^i \cdot \sum_{i=0}^q b_i s^i = \sum_{i=0}^q a_i s^i$. Thus,

$$e(g_1^{d_2 \sum_{i=1}^q c_i s^i}, \mathsf{mwit}_{\mathcal{I}}) = e(g_1, g_2)^{\psi \sum_{i=0}^q a_i s^i} = e(\mathsf{acc}_{\mathcal{X}}, g_2^{\boldsymbol{d}_1^*}).$$

□

Theorem 2. *Our scheme satisfies collision resistance under q-SBDH assumption.*

Proof. We prove the contrapositive. Let $\mathcal{C}$ be the q-SBDH challenger, $\mathcal{B}$ an adversary against collision resistance of the accumulator, that wins with non-negligible advantage. We build, in Fig. 2, $\mathcal{A}$ an adversary against the q-SBDH assumption, using $\mathcal{B}$.

- On input $1^\kappa, q \in \mathbb{N}$, $\mathcal{C}$ runs bilinear group generation to get $\Gamma = (p, \mathbb{G}_1, \mathbb{G}_2, \mathbb{G}_T, e, g_1, g_2)$ and chooses $\alpha \leftarrow \mathbb{Z}_p^*$. It sends $\Gamma, g_1^\alpha, \cdots, g_1^{\alpha^q}, g_2^\alpha, \cdots, g_2^{\alpha^q}$ to $\mathcal{A}$.
- $\mathcal{A}$ runs $\mathsf{Dual}(\mathbb{Z}_p^2)$ to get $\mathbb{D} = (\boldsymbol{d}_1, \boldsymbol{d}_2)$ and $\mathbb{D}^* = (\boldsymbol{d}_1^*, \boldsymbol{d}_2^*)$ such that $\boldsymbol{d}_1 \cdot \boldsymbol{d}_1^* = \boldsymbol{d}_2 \cdot \boldsymbol{d}_2^* = \psi$, where $\psi \in \mathbb{Z}_p$. Then it sets $\mathsf{pk}_{\mathsf{acc}} = \left(\Gamma, g_1^{\boldsymbol{d}_2}, g_1^{\boldsymbol{d}_2\alpha}, \cdots, g_1^{\boldsymbol{d}_2\alpha^q}, g_2^{\boldsymbol{d}_1^*}, g_2^{\boldsymbol{d}_2^*}, g_2^{\boldsymbol{d}_2^*\alpha}, \cdots, g_2^{\boldsymbol{d}_2^*\alpha^q}\right)$ and sends it to $\mathcal{B}$.
- $\mathcal{B}$ makes an accumulator query: it chooses set $\mathcal{X}$ and sends it to $\mathcal{A}$. The latter uses its knowledge of $\boldsymbol{d}_1$ to return to $\mathcal{B}$ $\mathsf{acc}_\mathcal{X} = g_1^{\boldsymbol{d}_1 \mathsf{Ch}_\mathcal{X}(\alpha)}$. This step can be repeat an unbounded number of times.
- At some point, $\mathcal{B}$ answers with $\underline{\mathcal{X}}, \underline{x}, \mathsf{wit}_{\underline{x}}$ where $\underline{x} \notin \underline{\mathcal{X}}$ and $\mathsf{wit}_{\underline{x}}$ is a membership witness of $\underline{x}$ for set $\underline{\mathcal{X}}$.
- $\mathcal{A}$ returns to $\mathcal{C}$ $(\underline{x}, e(g_1, (\mathsf{wit}_{\underline{x}}^{\boldsymbol{d}_2})^{1/\psi r} \cdot (g_2^{-Q(\alpha)})^{1/r}))$ as its answer to break the assumption.

Fig. 2. Construction of q-SBDH adversary from collision resistance adversary.

Let us see that the solution output by $\mathcal{A}$ is correct. As $\underline{x} \notin \underline{\mathcal{X}}$, there exist polynomial $Q[Z]$ and integer r such that $\mathsf{Ch}_{\underline{\mathcal{X}}}[Z] = Q[Z](\underline{x} + Z) + r$. As $\mathsf{wit}_{\underline{x}}$ is a membership witness, we have that $e(g_1^{\boldsymbol{d}_2(\underline{x}+\alpha)}, \mathsf{wit}_{\underline{x}}) = e(\mathsf{acc}_{\underline{\mathcal{X}}}, g_2^{\boldsymbol{d}_1^*})$.

Therefore, we have that $e(g_1^{\boldsymbol{d}_2(\underline{x}+\alpha)}, \mathsf{wit}_{\underline{x}}) = e(g_1, g_2)^{\psi(\alpha+\underline{x})Q(\alpha)+\psi r}$ and

$$
\begin{aligned}
&(e(g_1, (\mathsf{wit}_{\underline{x}}^{\boldsymbol{d}_2})^{1/\psi r} \cdot (g_2^{-Q(\alpha)})^{1/r}))^{(\alpha+\underline{x})} \\
&= e(g_1, g_2)^{\frac{(\alpha+\underline{x})Q(\alpha)}{r}+1} \cdot (g_1, g_2)^{\frac{-(\alpha+\underline{x})Q(\alpha)}{r}} \\
&= e(g_1, g_2)
\end{aligned}
$$

Notice that $\mathcal{A}$ knows $\boldsymbol{d}_2, \psi$ and r and can compute $g_2^{-Q(\alpha)}$ from the challenge tuple. Thus, $\underline{x}, e(g_1, (\mathsf{wit}_{\underline{x}}^{\boldsymbol{d}_2})^{1/\psi r} \cdot (g_2^{-Q(\alpha)})^{1/r})$ is a solution to the q-SBDH problem.

As $\mathcal{A}$ breaks the assumption when $\mathcal{B}$ breaks the collision resistance of the accumulator, we have that $\mathcal{A}$'s advantage is equal to $\mathcal{B}$'s advantage, meaning that $\mathcal{A}$ breaks the q-SBDH assumption with non-negligible advantage. □

Comparison. Our accumulator is the first to propose a private evaluation while having a public witness generation. Indeed, we compare in Table 2 for the four families of accumulators instantiations how evaluation and witness creation are done. The only exception could be a construction given by Zhang *et al.* in [41]. More precisely, the studied primitive is called an *Expressive Set Accumulator* and is presented with private evaluation and some kind of public witness creation: their scheme does not have a WitCreate algorithm but a Query that takes as input some sets along with a set operation query, and returns the result of the query along with a proof of correctness. However, as stated in their work, in their construction the evaluation can actually be done only with the public key.

Having both private evaluation and public witness creation helps us build an encryption scheme where the accumulator is used as a secret key computed by an author-

Table 2. Comparison of evaluation and witness creation according to the type of accumulator instantiation.

Type	Evaluation	Witness Generation
Hash based	Public	Public
	Public	Public
Lattices	Public	Private
Number Theoretic	Public	Public[a]
Pairing based	Public	Public
	Private	Private
Ours	Private	Public

[a] Secret key can be given for witness generation in order to improve efficiency. Creation is still possible without it.

ity, from which user can derive some information (the witness) for decryption. Moreover, accumulators can satisfy a lot of additional properties: universal, dynamic, asynchronous, ... and verify a lot of security properties: undeniability, indistinguishability, ...(see e.g., [15]). The above construction focuses on static accumulators that satisfy collision resistance, and in this work, we do not consider those additional features and security properties. We leave as an open problem the modifications to satisfy other properties of accumulators. The only exception is when accumulators are used in the context of authenticated set operations [20,29,34]. See the full version of this work [6] for more details on sets operations. Regarding pairing-based accumulators, we refer the interested reader to several works such as [1,5,11,14,15,20] among others.

In the next section, we present our main new functionality, namely dually computable accumulator, and show how to transform the above construction into a new one that satisfies it.

4 Dually Computable Cryptographic Accumulators

In this section, we introduce a new kind of cryptographic accumulator that we call *dually computable* accumulator. In such case, there are two separate evaluation algorithms that give two different outputs: the first one (Eval) uses the accumulator secret key while the second one ($\mathsf{PublicEval}$) uses solely the public key. Using the unique unmodified witness generation algorithm, we also define two different verification algorithms, one for each type of accumulator. Following the work done in the previous section, we focus on accumulator schemes that have private evaluation and public witness generation. We start by formally defining dually computable accumulators, then we present an instantiation.

4.1 Definitions

Definition 13. ***Dually computable accumulator.*** *Starting from a static accumulator* $\mathsf{Acc} = (\mathsf{Gen}, \mathsf{Eval}, \mathsf{WitCreate}, \mathsf{Verify})$, *we say that* Acc *is* dually computable *if it also provides two algorithms* $\mathsf{PublicEval}$, $\mathsf{PublicVerify}$ *such that:*

- $\mathsf{PublicEval}(\mathsf{pk}_{\mathsf{acc}}, \mathcal{X})$: *it takes as input the accumulator public key* $\mathsf{pk}_{\mathsf{acc}}$ *and a set* $\mathcal{X}$. *It outputs an accumulator* $\mathsf{accp}_{\mathcal{X}}$ *of* $\mathcal{X}$ *and auxiliary information* auxp.
- $\mathsf{PublicVerify}(\mathsf{pk}_{\mathsf{acc}}, \mathsf{accp}_{\mathcal{X}}, \mathsf{witp}_x, x)$: *it takes as input the accumulator public key* $\mathsf{pk}_{\mathsf{acc}}$, *a publicly computed accumulator* $\mathsf{accp}_{\mathcal{X}}$ *of* $\mathcal{X}$, *an element* x, *a witness* witp_x *for* x, *computed from* $\mathsf{WitCreate}(\mathsf{pk}_{\mathsf{acc}}, \mathcal{X}, \mathsf{accp}_{\mathcal{X}}, \mathsf{auxp}, x)$. *It outputs* 1 *if* witp_x *is a membership witness and* $x \in \mathcal{X}$, 0 *otherwise.*

A dually computable accumulator must satisfy four properties: *correctness*, *collision resistance*, *distinguishability* and *correctness of duality*.

Definition 14. ***Correctness of dually computable accumulator.*** *A dually computable accumulator is said to be* correct *if for all security parameters* κ, *all integer* $\mathfrak{b} \in \mathbb{N} \cup \{\infty\}$, *all set of values* $\mathcal{X}$ *and all element* x *such that* $x \in \mathcal{X}$

$$\Pr\left[\begin{array}{c} \mathsf{sk}_{\mathsf{acc}}, \mathsf{pk}_{\mathsf{acc}} \leftarrow \mathsf{Gen}(1^{\kappa}, \mathfrak{b}),\\ \mathsf{acc}_{\mathcal{X}}, \mathsf{aux} \leftarrow \mathsf{Eval}(\mathsf{sk}_{\mathsf{acc}}, \mathsf{pk}_{\mathsf{acc}}, \mathcal{X}),\\ \mathsf{accp}_{\mathcal{X}}, \mathsf{auxp} \leftarrow \mathsf{PublicEval}(\mathsf{pk}_{\mathsf{acc}}, \mathcal{X}),\\ \mathsf{wit}_x \leftarrow \mathsf{WitCreate}(\mathsf{pk}_{\mathsf{acc}}, \mathcal{X}, \mathsf{acc}_{\mathcal{X}}, \mathsf{aux}, x)\\ \mathsf{witp}_x \leftarrow \mathsf{WitCreate}(\mathsf{pk}_{\mathsf{acc}}, \mathcal{X}, \mathsf{accp}_{\mathcal{X}}, \mathsf{auxp}, x) :\\ \mathsf{Verify}(\mathsf{pk}_{\mathsf{acc}}, \mathsf{acc}_{\mathcal{X}}, \mathsf{wit}_x, x) = 1\\ \wedge \mathsf{PublicVerify}(\mathsf{pk}_{\mathsf{acc}}, \mathsf{accp}_{\mathcal{X}}, \mathsf{witp}_x, x) = 1 \end{array}\right] = 1$$

Definition 15. ***Collision resistance.*** *A dually computable accumulator is* collision resistant, *if for all PPT adversaries* $\mathcal{A}$ *there is a negligible function* $\epsilon(.)$ *such that:*

$$\Pr\left[\begin{array}{c} (\mathsf{sk}_{\mathsf{acc}}, \mathsf{pk}_{\mathsf{acc}}) \leftarrow \mathsf{Gen}(1^{\kappa}, \mathfrak{b}), (\mathsf{wit}_x, x) \leftarrow \mathcal{A}^{\mathcal{O}^E}(\mathsf{pk}_{\mathsf{acc}}) :\\ (\mathsf{Verify}(\mathsf{pk}_{\mathsf{acc}}, \mathsf{acc}_{\mathcal{X}}, \mathsf{wit}_x, x) = 1 \wedge x \notin \mathcal{X})\\ \vee (\mathsf{PublicVerify}(\mathsf{pk}_{\mathsf{acc}}, \mathsf{accp}_{\mathcal{X}}, \mathsf{wit}_x, x) = 1 \wedge x \notin \mathcal{X}) \end{array}\right] \leq \epsilon(\kappa),$$

where $\mathsf{acc}_{\mathcal{X}} \leftarrow \mathsf{Eval}(\mathsf{sk}_{\mathsf{acc}}, \mathsf{pk}_{\mathsf{acc}}, \mathcal{X})$, $\mathsf{accp}_{\mathcal{X}} \leftarrow \mathsf{PublicEval}(\mathsf{pk}_{\mathsf{acc}}, \mathcal{X})$ *and* $\mathcal{A}$ *has oracle access to* $\mathcal{O}^E$ *that represents the oracle for the algorithm* Eval. *An adversary is allowed to query it an arbitrary number of times and can run* $\mathsf{PublicEval}$, $\mathsf{WitCreate}$ *as the two algorithms only use the accumulator public key, that is known by the adversary.*

Definition 16. ***Distinguishability.*** *A dually computable accumulator satisfies* distinguishability, *if for any security parameter* κ *and integer* $\mathfrak{b} \in \mathbb{N} \cup \{\infty\}$, *any keys* $(\mathsf{sk}_{\mathsf{acc}}, \mathsf{pk}_{\mathsf{acc}})$ *generated by* $\mathsf{Gen}(1^{\kappa}, \mathfrak{b})$, *and any set* $\mathcal{X}$, $\mathsf{acc}_{\mathcal{X}} \leftarrow \mathsf{Eval}(\mathsf{sk}_{\mathsf{acc}}, \mathsf{pk}_{\mathsf{acc}}, \mathcal{X})$ *and* $\mathsf{accp}_{\mathcal{X}} \leftarrow \mathsf{PublicEval}(\mathsf{pk}_{\mathsf{acc}}, \mathcal{X})$ *are distinguishable.*

The last property states that a witness computed for a privately (resp. publicly) computed accumulator as input of the $\mathsf{WitCreate}$ algorithm must pass the $\mathsf{PublicVerify}$ (resp. Verify) algorithm, with publicly (resp. privately) computed accumulator for the same set as the privately (resp. publicly) computed accumulator.

Definition 17. ***Correctness of duality.*** *A dually computable accumulator is said to satisfy* correctness of duality *if for all security parameters* κ, *all integer* $\mathfrak{b} \in \mathbb{N} \cup \{\infty\}$, *all set of values* $\mathcal{X}$ *and all value* x *such that* $x \in \mathcal{X}$

$$\Pr\left[\begin{array}{c} \mathsf{sk_{acc}}, \mathsf{pk_{acc}} \leftarrow \mathsf{Gen}(1^\kappa, \mathfrak{b}), \\ \mathsf{acc}_{\mathcal{X}}, \mathsf{aux} \leftarrow \mathsf{Eval}(\mathsf{sk_{acc}}, \mathsf{pk_{acc}}, \mathcal{X}), \\ \mathsf{accp}_{\mathcal{X}}, \mathsf{auxp} \leftarrow \mathsf{PublicEval}(\mathsf{pk_{acc}}, \mathcal{X}), \\ \mathsf{wit}_x \leftarrow \mathsf{WitCreate}(\mathsf{pk_{acc}}, \mathcal{X}, \mathsf{acc}_{\mathcal{X}}, \mathsf{aux}, x) \\ \mathsf{witp}_x \leftarrow \mathsf{WitCreate}(\mathsf{pk_{acc}}, \mathcal{X}, \mathsf{accp}_{\mathcal{X}}, \mathsf{auxp}, x): \\ (\mathsf{PublicVerify}(\mathsf{pk_{acc}}, \mathsf{accp}_{\mathcal{X}}, \mathsf{wit}_x, x) = 1) \\ \wedge(\mathsf{Verify}(\mathsf{pk_{acc}}, \mathsf{acc}_{\mathcal{X}}, \mathsf{witp}_x, x) = 1) \end{array}\right] = 1$$

4.2 Our First Dually Computable Cryptographic Accumulator

We now present our instantiation of a dually computable cryptographic accumulator. We also present some variants in the next section (for our construction of an ABE), and in our the extended version of this work [6]. We consider that the version we propose in this section is the simplest and more efficient one, but the others, as we will see, can be used for different other contexts.

Intuition. Using our previous accumulator instantiation (see Sect. 3), we can obtain a dually computable accumulator scheme by adding $g_2^{d_1^*}, g_2^{d_1^* s}, \cdots, g_2^{d_1^* s^q}$ to the public key. Then, the public evaluation corresponds to the generation of $\mathsf{accp}_{\mathcal{X}} = g_2^{d_1^* \prod_{x \in \mathcal{X}}(x+s)}$. With the description of Eval as in the previous scheme, we directly obtain what we need. Moreover, the two accumulators are easily distinguishable as the secretly computed one is two elements in $\mathbb{G}_1$ while the publicly generated one is two elements in $\mathbb{G}_2$.

From those two accumulators, and the witness as generated in our first accumulator scheme (i.e., $\mathsf{wit}_{\underline{x}} = g_2^{d_2^* \prod_{x \in \mathcal{X} \setminus \{\underline{x}\}}(x+s)}$), we are able to provide two very close verification equations. In fact, we remark that we obtain a sort of symmetry between the two accumulators, as $e(\mathsf{acc}_{\mathcal{X}}, g_2^{d_1^*}) = e(g_1^{d_1}, \mathsf{accp}_{\mathcal{X}})$, which two are equals to $e(g_1^{d_2 \underline{x}} \cdot g_1^{d_2 s}, \mathsf{wit}_{\underline{x}})$, which is computable from the knowledge of the witness[1].

Construction. In Fig. 3, we present the full description of our first dually computable scheme, from the above intuition, and using again the characteristic polynomial result (see Definition 7).

Security. We can now focus on the security of our construction, by providing the following full theorem.

Theorem 3. *Our scheme is correct, collision resistant under* q-SBDH *assumption, and satisfies both* distinguishability *and correctness of duality.*

Proof. Correctness and collision resistance (for privately and publicly computed accumulators) can be done as for our cryptographic accumulator in Sect. 3. Indeed, the algorithms Eval, $\mathsf{WitCreate}$ and Verify are not changed compare to what we provided in Fig. 1. For the publicly computed part, the proof still holds. The only modification

[1] We could have also chosen to define $\mathsf{PublicEval}$ such that it returns $g_2^{d_2^* a_i s^i}$, and $\mathsf{PublicVerify}$ such that the left part of the equation is $e(g_1^{d_2}, \mathsf{accp})$.

- $\mathsf{Gen}(1^\kappa, q)$: run a bilinear group generation algorithm to get $\Gamma = (p, \mathbb{G}_1, \mathbb{G}_2, \mathbb{G}_T, e, g_1, g_2)$. Then choose a random $s \leftarrow \mathbb{Z}_p^*$, and run $\mathsf{Dual}(\mathbb{Z}_p^2)$ to get $\mathbb{D} = (\boldsymbol{d}_1, \boldsymbol{d}_2), \mathbb{D}^* = (\boldsymbol{d}_1^*, \boldsymbol{d}_2^*)$. Let $\psi \in \mathbb{Z}_p$ be the random such that $\boldsymbol{d}_1 \cdot \boldsymbol{d}_1^* = \boldsymbol{d}_2 \cdot \boldsymbol{d}_2^* = \psi$. Set $\mathsf{sk}_{\mathsf{acc}} = (s, \mathbb{D}, \mathbb{D}^*)$,

$$\mathsf{pk}_{\mathsf{acc}} = \left(\begin{array}{c} \Gamma, g_1^{\boldsymbol{d}_1}, g_1^{\boldsymbol{d}_2}, g_1^{\boldsymbol{d}_2 s}, \cdots, g_1^{\boldsymbol{d}_2 s^q}, g_2^{\boldsymbol{d}_1^*}, \\ g_2^{\boldsymbol{d}_1^* s}, \cdots, g_2^{\boldsymbol{d}_1^* s^q}, g_2^{\boldsymbol{d}_2^*}, g_2^{\boldsymbol{d}_2^* s}, \cdots, g_2^{\boldsymbol{d}_2^* s^q} \end{array} \right).$$

Return $\mathsf{sk}_{\mathsf{acc}}, \mathsf{pk}_{\mathsf{acc}}$.
- $\mathsf{Eval}(\mathsf{sk}_{\mathsf{acc}}, \mathsf{pk}_{\mathsf{acc}}, \mathcal{X})$: compute the coefficients $\{a_i\}_{i=0,\cdots,q}$ of the polynomial $\mathsf{Ch}_{\mathcal{X}}[Z] = \prod_{x \in \mathcal{X}}(Z + x)$. Then compute $\mathsf{acc}_{\mathcal{X}} = g_1^{\boldsymbol{d}_1 \sum_{i=0}^{q} a_i s^i}$, and return $\mathsf{acc}_{\mathcal{X}}$.
- $\mathsf{PublicEval}(\mathsf{pk}_{\mathsf{acc}}, \mathcal{X})$: compute the coefficients $\{a_i\}_{i=0,\cdots,q}$ of the polynomial $\mathsf{Ch}_{\mathcal{X}}[Z] = \prod_{x \in \mathcal{X}}(Z + x)$. Then compute $\mathsf{accp}_{\mathcal{X}} = g_2^{\boldsymbol{d}_1^* \sum_{i=0}^{q} a_i s^i}$, and return $\mathsf{accp}_{\mathcal{X}}$.
- $\mathsf{WitCreate}(\mathsf{pk}_{\mathsf{acc}}, \mathcal{X}, \mathsf{acc}_{\mathcal{X}}/\mathsf{accp}_{\mathcal{X}}, \mathcal{I})$: let $\{b_i\}_{i=0,\cdots,q}$ be the coefficients of the polynomial $\mathsf{Ch}_{\mathcal{X}\backslash\mathcal{I}}[Z] = \prod_{x \in \mathcal{X}\backslash\mathcal{I}}(x + Z)$. Compute $\mathsf{wit}_{\mathcal{I}} = \mathsf{witp}_{\mathcal{I}} = g_2^{\boldsymbol{d}_2^* \sum_{i=0}^{q} b_i s^i}$, and return $\mathsf{wit}_{\mathcal{I}}$.
- $\mathsf{Verify}(\mathsf{pk}_{\mathsf{acc}}, \mathsf{acc}_{\mathcal{X}}, \mathsf{wit}_{\mathcal{I}}, \mathcal{I})$: let $\{c_i\}_{i=0,\cdots,q}$ be the coefficients of the polynomial $\mathsf{Ch}_{\mathcal{I}}[Z] = \prod_{x \in \mathcal{I}}(x + Z)$ and return 1 if $e(\mathsf{acc}_{\mathcal{X}}, g_2^{\boldsymbol{d}_1^*}) = e(g_1^{\boldsymbol{d}_2 \sum_{i=0}^{q} c_i s^i}, \mathsf{wit}_{\mathcal{I}})$, 0 otherwise.
- $\mathsf{PublicVerify}(\mathsf{pk}_{\mathsf{acc}}, \mathsf{accp}_{\mathcal{X}}, \mathsf{wit}_{\mathcal{I}}, \mathcal{I})$: let $\{c_i\}_{i=0,\cdots,q}$ be the coefficients of the polynomial $\mathsf{Ch}_{\mathcal{I}}[Z] = \prod_{x \in \mathcal{I}}(x + Z)$ and return 1 if $e(g_1^{\boldsymbol{d}_1}, \mathsf{accp}_{\mathcal{X}}) = e(g_1^{\boldsymbol{d}_2 \sum_{i=0}^{q} c_i s^i}, \mathsf{wit}_{\mathcal{I}})$, 0 otherwise.

Fig. 3. Our first dually computable accumulator scheme.

is that $e(\mathsf{acc}_{\underline{\mathcal{X}}}, g_2^{\boldsymbol{d}_1^*})$ and $e(\mathsf{acc}_{\mathcal{X}}, g_2^{\boldsymbol{d}_1^*})$ are replaced by $e(g_1^{\boldsymbol{d}_1}, \mathsf{acc}_{\underline{\mathcal{X}}})$ and $e(g_1^{\boldsymbol{d}_1}, \mathsf{acc}_{\mathcal{X}})$ respectively.

Additionally, our accumulator satisfies *distinguishability* as a privately computed accumulator is composed of an element in $\mathbb{G}_1$ while a publicly computed accumulator is an element in $\mathbb{G}_2$. In fact, in a bilinear environment, we know that there are efficient algorithms for computing group operations, evaluating the bilinear map, deciding membership of the groups, deciding equality of group elements and sampling generators of the groups (see e.g., [23]). Correctness of duality is satisfied as we have one unique witness and, as explained above, we have a symmetry between the two accumulators:

$$\underbrace{e(\mathsf{acc}_{\mathcal{X}}, g_2^{\boldsymbol{d}_1^*})}_{\text{from Eval}} = \underbrace{e(g_1^{\boldsymbol{d}_2 \sum_{i=0}^{q} c_i s^i}, \mathsf{wit}_{\mathcal{I}})}_{\text{from WitCreate}} = \underbrace{e(g_1^{\boldsymbol{d}_1}, \mathsf{accp}_{\mathcal{X}})}_{\text{from PublicEval}}.$$

Thus, the proof for $\mathsf{acc}_{\mathcal{X}}$ is exactly the same than in Theorem 1. For $\mathsf{accp}_{\mathcal{X}}$ the proof can proceed as in Theorem 1 by replacing $\mathsf{acc}_{\mathcal{X}}$ and Verify by $\mathsf{accp}_{\mathcal{X}}$ and PublicVerify.

5 Application of Dually Computable Accumulator: Attribute Based Encryption

In this section, our purpose is to show how we can transform our new notion of dually computable cryptographic accumulator to design Attribute Based Encryption (ABE). More precisely, first showing that due to security reasons, it cannot directly be used to obtain an ABE, and then show how to transform it into a dually computable accumulator that can be used to obtain the first Ciphertext Policy ABE (CP-ABE) for monotone NC^1 circuits with both constant size for ciphertexts and secret keys. We start by formally presenting the notion of ABE, then we explain briefly the intuitions of our construction. Finally we present our scheme and compare it to existing ones.

5.1 Security Definitions for ABE

We start by formally introducing attribute based encryption scheme and the related security notions. In this work we will focus on *bounded* attribute based encryption schemes, meaning that during the setup phase a bound in the number of attributes allowed in the scheme is given and keys and ciphertexts can be created for an arbitrarily number of attributes at the condition that this number is lower than the bound.

Definition 18. ***Bounded (ciphertext policy) attribute based encryption.*** *[21,35] A ciphertext policy attribute based encryption scheme consists of four algorithms:*

- $\mathsf{Setup}(1^\kappa, q) \to (\mathsf{pk}, \mathsf{msk})$*: the setup algorithm takes as input a security parameter* κ *and an integer* q *which represent the bound of the number of attributes, and outputs a master public key* pk *and a master secret key* msk.
- $\mathsf{KeyGen}(\mathsf{pk}, \mathsf{msk}, \Upsilon) \to \mathsf{sk}_\Upsilon$*: the key generation algorithm takes as input the master public key* pk*, the master secret key* msk*, and a key attribute* Υ *and outputs a private key* sk_Υ.
- $\mathsf{Encrypt}(\mathsf{pk}, \Pi, \mathsf{m} \in \mathcal{M}) \to \mathsf{ct}$*: the encryption algorithm takes as input a master public key* pk*, an access policy* Π*, and a message* m *and outputs a ciphertext* ct_Π.
- $\mathsf{Decrypt}(\mathsf{pk}, \mathsf{sk}_\Upsilon, \Upsilon, \mathsf{ct}_\Pi, \Pi) \to \mathsf{m}$ *or* $\perp$*: the decryption algorithm takes as input the master public key* pk*, a private key* sk_Υ *along with the associated set of attributes* Υ*, a ciphertext* ct_Π *and its associated access policy* Π*. It outputs the message* m *if* Υ *satisfies* Π *or reject symbol* $\perp$ *otherwise.*

Definition 19. ***Correctness of ABE.*** *A CP-ABE scheme is correct if for all security parameter* $\kappa \in \mathbb{N}$*, all integer* q *that represents the bound in the number of attributes, all attributes set* Υ *and all access policy* Π *such that* Υ *satisfies* Π *and for all messages* m*,*

$$\Pr\left[\begin{array}{c}(\mathsf{pk}, \mathsf{msk}) \leftarrow \mathsf{Setup}(1^\kappa, q)\\ \mathsf{sk}_\Upsilon \leftarrow \mathsf{KeyGen}(\mathsf{pk}, \mathsf{msk}, \Upsilon)\\ \mathsf{ct}_\Pi \leftarrow \mathsf{Encrypt}(\mathsf{pk}, \Pi, \mathsf{m})\\ \mathsf{Decrypt}(\mathsf{pk}, \mathsf{sk}_\Upsilon, \Upsilon, \mathsf{ct}_\Pi, \Pi) = \mathsf{m}\end{array}\right] = 1$$

where the probability is taken over the coins of Setup*,* KeyGen*, and* $\mathsf{Encrypt}$.

Definition 20. ***Adaptive indistinguishability security.*** *(Ada-IND) A (CP-)ABE scheme is said to satisfy* adaptive indistinguishability *security if for all PPT adversary $\mathcal{A}$, there exists a negligible function $\epsilon(.)$ such that $\mathsf{Adv}_{\mathcal{A}}^{Ada-IND}(1^\kappa) \leq \epsilon(\kappa)$ where $\mathsf{Adv}_{\mathcal{A}}^{Ada-IND}(1^\kappa)$ is the advantage of $\mathcal{A}$ to win the security game presented in Fig. 4, and is defined as $\mathsf{Adv}_{\mathcal{A}}^{Ada-IND}(1^\kappa) = \left|\Pr\left[b' = b\right] - \frac{1}{2}\right|$. Let $\mathcal{C}$ be the challenger.*

1. **Setup phase**: on input $1^\kappa, q$, $\mathcal{C}$ samples $(\mathsf{pk}, \mathsf{msk}) \leftarrow \mathsf{Setup}(1^\kappa, q)$ and gives pk to $\mathcal{A}$.
2. **Query phase**: during the game, $\mathcal{A}$ makes the following queries, in an arbitrary order. $\mathcal{A}$ can make unbounded many key queries, but can make only single challenge query.
   (a) **Key Queries**: $\mathcal{A}$ chooses an attributes set Υ and sends it to $\mathcal{C}$ who replies with $\mathsf{sk}_\Upsilon \leftarrow \mathsf{KeyGen}(\mathsf{pk}, \mathsf{msk}, \Upsilon)$.
   (b) **Challenge Query**: at some point, $\mathcal{A}$ submits a pair of equal length messages $\mathsf{m}_0, \mathsf{m}_1$ and the challenge access policy Π^* to $\mathcal{C}$. The latter samples a random bit $b \leftarrow \{0, 1\}$ and replies to $\mathcal{A}$ with $\mathsf{ct}_{\Pi^*} \leftarrow \mathsf{Encrypt}(\mathsf{pk}, \Pi^*, \mathsf{m}_b)$.

   We require that Υ does not satisfy Π^* in order to avoid trivial attacks, for any queried Υ.
3. **Output phase**: $\mathcal{A}$ outputs a guess bit b' s the output of the experiment.

Fig. 4. Adaptive indistinguishability security game.

5.2 ABE from Dualy Computable Accumulator: Intuition

Basic Idea. As said previously, having both private evaluation and public witness creation permits us to transform a cryptographic accumulator into an encryption scheme. More precisely, in our CP-ABE, the user secret key is a privately computed accumulator $\mathsf{acc}_\mathcal{X} = g_1^{d_1 \prod_{x \in \mathcal{X}}(x+s)}$, where $\mathcal{X}$ is a representation of the user's attributes. In parallel, the ciphertext is a one-time-pad between the message m and a mask $\boldsymbol{H}$ that is computed using a publicly computable accumulator $\mathsf{accp}_\mathcal{Y}$, where $\mathcal{Y}$ is a representation of the access policy. However, with the dually computable accumulator of the previous section as given in Fig. 3, this construction is not efficient and secure. Due to lack of space, we here give only a summary of all the changes we have to make on the accumulator scheme, and we detail them in our extended work [6]. Before going into those details, we first explain how we can define $\mathcal{X}$ and $\mathcal{Y}$. In the sequel let $Q = 2^q - 1$, where $q \in \mathbb{N}$ is the bound on the number of attributes in the ABE.

Representation of Boolean Formulas and Attributes with Cryptographic Accumulators. In our ABE, access policies are expressed as disjunctions of conjunctions (DNF), without "NO" gates. Hence, a policy could be noted $\Pi = \pi_1 \vee \pi_2 \vee \cdots \vee \pi_l$, where $l \in \mathbb{N}$, and π_i is a conjunction of attributes. Let $\mathcal{Y}_i$ be the set of attributes present in clause π_i, for $i = 1, \cdots, l$. Our idea is to define $\mathcal{Y}$ as the set $\{\mathcal{H}(\mathcal{Y}_i)\}_{i=1}^l$, where $\mathcal{H}$ is a hash function that takes as input a set of elements and returns an element in $\mathbb{Z}_p$, for a prime p. During the encryption process, we create the accumulator $\mathsf{accp}_\mathcal{Y}$ using $\mathsf{PublicEval}$ (see below).

For a set Υ of attributes for a given user, we create $\mathcal{X}$ as the set of hash values (using $\mathcal{H}$) of all non-empty subsets of Υ[2]. During the key generation process, the authority hence creates the accumulator $\mathsf{acc}_{\mathcal{X}}$ using Eval.

Encryption and Decryption. For a given user, if her set of attributes Υ satisfies the policy Π, it means that there exists a non-empty subset of Υ that corresponds to a clause π_i in Π. As $\mathcal{H}$ is deterministic, it follows that one element, called ξ in the sequel, is present in both accumulators: $\mathsf{acc}_{\mathcal{X}}$ (the one corresponding to the non-empty subsets of Υ) and $\mathsf{accp}_{\mathcal{Y}}$ (the one that corresponds to Π). Based on that, we propose that during the encryption process, the mask $\boldsymbol{H}$ is computed using the public verification equation $\mathsf{PublicVerify}$, as $e(g_1^{d_1}, \mathsf{accp}_{\mathcal{Y}})^{\alpha}$, where α is some randomness.

During decryption, a user having a valid set of attributes precisely knows both the clause π_i and the element in Υ that match together. The next step is then for the user to generate a witness for such element, and thanks to the verification algorithms, retrieve $\boldsymbol{H}$ and then the message. But as both accumulators are not related to the same sets, we cannot directly use the properties of a dually computable accumulator. The user hence needs to compute two witnesses (one for each accumulator), and we need to find a way to combine them appropriately for the decryption to work.

Managing the Randomness α and a Constant-Size Ciphertext. The first problem we need to solve is that the element for which the witnesses need to be computed is only known during decryption time, and that we should manage the randomness α. A trivial solution could consist in given as many $g_2^{\alpha d_2^* s^k}$ as necessary to permit the user computing all the possible witnesses. But this option obviously results in (at least) a linear ciphertext. To reach a constant-size ciphertext, we need a way to "anticipate" witnesses during encryption. Here, our trick is to use a specificity of accumulators based on Nguyen's construction, that is the fact that accumulators and witnesses are constructed with the coefficients of polynomials of the form $\mathsf{Ch}[Z] = \prod_{i=1}^{q}(x_i + Z)$. Yet, we know that elementary symmetric polynomials for q variables appear in $\mathsf{Ch}[Z]$ (see Definition 8 and Note 4) and that the coefficient of lowest degree is equal to $\sigma_q = \prod_{i=1}^{q} x_i$. We decide to accumulate in the secret key accumulator a public value, denoted x_0, which is not related to any user attribute, hence having no impact on the decryption capability. From the above observation, we know that x_0 will always be a factor of $\mathsf{Ch}[Z]$'s lowest degree coefficient, no matter the element for which the witness is generated and the user attributes. We proceed similarly for the access policy, introducing the public value y_0 that will be attached to the witness corresponding to the public accumulator. To give the user the possibility to introduce α in the decryption process we then give in the ciphertext the value $\alpha(x_0 + y_0)$.

But this trick necessitates us to modify the way we have computed the witness in our construction in Sect. 4 so that we can manage the values x_0 and y_0 independently of the other. For that, for a subset $\mathcal{I}$ in $\mathcal{X}$, the witness is now divided into two parts: $\mathsf{wit}_{\mathcal{I}} = (W_1, W_2)$ where $W_1 = g_1^{d_1 b_0}$ and $W_2 = g_2^{d_2^* \sum_{i=1}^{q} b_i s^i}$. Again, we proceed similarly for the publicly computable accumulator with witness $\mathsf{witp}_{\mathcal{I}} = (W_1', W_2')$.

[2] It follows that if $|\Upsilon| = k$, then $|\mathcal{X}| = 2^k - 1$.

Auxiliary Information in the Ciphertext. From the previous issue, we now know that the ciphertext should include a first auxiliary information to permit decryption: $\mathsf{aux}_1 = g_1^{\boldsymbol{d}_1\alpha(x_0+y_0)}$. At this step, we also need to give $\mathsf{aux}_2 = g_2^{-\alpha\boldsymbol{d}_1^*}$ with the ciphertext, so that the Verify algorithm, on input such value and the secretly computed accumulator now includes the randomness α.

But from aux_1 and $\left\{g_2^{\boldsymbol{d}_1^* s^i}\right\}_{i=0}^{Q}$, anyone can compute $e(g_1^{\boldsymbol{d}_1(x_0+y_0)}, \mathsf{acc}_{\mathcal{Y}}) = \boldsymbol{H}^{x_0+y_0}$. As x_0, y_0 are publicly known, this permits to recover $\boldsymbol{H}$ and hence the message. To avoid that, our idea is to split α into two randoms α_1, α_2, and modify the auxiliary information accordingly, as $\mathsf{aux}_1 = g_1^{\boldsymbol{d}_1\alpha_2(x_0+y_0)}$ and $\mathsf{aux}_2 = g_2^{-\alpha_1\alpha_2\boldsymbol{d}_1^*}$. For the same reason as above, we cannot directly include α_1 and need to find another trick.

We use the same "anticipation" trick that we used for the witnesses. More precisely, we add an additional public value z_0 in both accumulators. The consequence is that, at the time of decryption, the users obtains that the element ξ and the value z_0 are both in the two accumulators. Hence, in the verification process, we necessarily have the term $s^2 + s(z_0 + \xi) + z_0\xi$ which can be divided in two parts: $s^2 + sz_0$ and $s + z_0$. It follows that during encryption, we additionally give the terms $ele_1 = g_2^{\alpha_1\boldsymbol{d}_1(z_0+s)}$ and $ele_2 = g_2^{\alpha_1\boldsymbol{d}_1(z_0 s+s^2)}$ that are associated to aux_1 using a pairing during the decryption process. This indirectly brings α_1 to aux_1 without revealing it. We now have fully treated the case of W_1 and W_1' but we also need to add the randomness (α_1, α_2) to W_2 and W_2'. To solve that we simply need to add two new auxiliary information: $ele_3 = g_1^{\alpha_1\alpha_2\boldsymbol{d}_2(z_0 s+s^2)}$ and $ele_4 = g_1^{\alpha_1\alpha_2\boldsymbol{d}_2(z_0+s)}$.

Managing the Dual System Encryption Framework. To prove the security of our ABE, we need to use the dual system encryption framework [39]. In a nutshell, during the security proof, such technique introduces the notion of semi-functional (SF) keys and ciphertexts, which should be indistinguishable from normal keys and ciphertexts. Such new elements behave exactly the same as their normal counterparts, except that no semi-functional key can decrypt an SF ciphertext. During the security proof, the simulator changes all the keys issued to the adversary into SF ones, and make the challenge answer to the adversary an SF ciphertext. This way, the adversary cannot extract any information from the challenge ciphertext: it has no advantage.

To manage semi-functional ciphertexts and secret keys in our own proof, we need to increase by one the dimension of the DPVS. More precisely, we rely on the decisional subspace assumptions in $\mathbb{G}_1$ (DS1) and in $\mathbb{G}_2$ (DS2) [13], which necessitate to guess between $g_1^{\tau_1\boldsymbol{d}_i}$ (resp. $g_2^{\tau_1\boldsymbol{d}_i^*}$) and $g_1^{\tau_1\boldsymbol{d}_i+\tau_2\boldsymbol{d}_{i+k}}$ (resp. $g_2^{\tau_1\boldsymbol{d}_i^*+\tau_2\boldsymbol{d}_{i+k}^*}$) for $i = 1, \cdots, k$, where $k \in \mathbb{N}$ is one parameter of the assumption, and $\tau_1, \tau_2 \in \mathbb{Z}_p$ are random elements chosen by the challenger. To avoid disturbance with the base used in the accumulator, we will not use $\boldsymbol{d}_1$ to bring SF space. Instead we consider $\boldsymbol{d}_2$ in the secret key and $\boldsymbol{d}_2^*$ in aux_2. More precisely, we generate two randoms $r, z \in \mathbb{Z}_p$ and generate $r \cdot \boldsymbol{d}_2$ and $z \cdot \boldsymbol{d}_2^*$ to have the same semi-functional part in the ciphertext than the one we have in the secret key. The randoms r and z are used to match the assumptions in which $\boldsymbol{d}_2$ (resp. $\boldsymbol{d}_2^*$) are randomized (by τ_1). But this results in an additional term $e(g_1, g_2)^{\psi r z \alpha_1\alpha_2}$ during decryption. To avoid this, we need to introduce a new dimension in the DPVS, and then $(\boldsymbol{d_3}, \boldsymbol{d_3}^*)$. It follows that the secret accumulator becomes $\mathsf{acc}_{\mathcal{X}} = g_1^{\boldsymbol{d_1} \sum_{i=0}^{Q} a_i s^i + r(\boldsymbol{d_2} - \gamma \boldsymbol{d_3})}$ and $\mathsf{aux}_2 = g_2^{-\boldsymbol{d_1}^* \alpha + z(\gamma \boldsymbol{d}_2^* + \boldsymbol{d}_3^*)}$.

Managing the Third Bases. There is one last change we need to do in our accumulator. Indeed, in the last part of the CP-ABE security proof, we need to randomize the dual orthonormal bases $(\mathbb{D}, \mathbb{D}^*)$ to new bases $(\mathbb{F}, \mathbb{F}^*)$, so that with the latter, the adversary has no more possibility to win the game. This modification implies that we need to express $\boldsymbol{d}_1$ as $\boldsymbol{f}_1 + \eta \boldsymbol{f}_5$, which means that any element having $\boldsymbol{d}_1$ in the exponent will have a SF part when expressed in bases $(\mathbb{F}, \mathbb{F}^*)$. It results that the elements aux_1 and $g_1^{\boldsymbol{d}_1}$ used in $\boldsymbol{H}$ have now a SF part, while we defined a SF ciphertext such that only aux_2 contains the SF components. Our idea here is then to replace $\boldsymbol{d}_1$ by $\boldsymbol{d}_3$ in the witness creation: hence, the witness element W_1 goes from $g_1^{\boldsymbol{d}_1 b_0}$ to $g_1^{\boldsymbol{d}_3 b_0}$. To keep the orthonormality of the DPVS, we also replace $\boldsymbol{d}_1^*$ by $\boldsymbol{d}_3^*$ in the public evaluation of the accumulator and the publicly computed accumulator goes from $g_2^{\boldsymbol{d}_1^* \sum_{i=0}^{Q} m_i s^i}$ to $g_2^{\boldsymbol{d}_3^* \sum_{i=0}^{Q} m_i s^i}$. We then change aux_1 to $g_1^{\boldsymbol{d}_3 (x_0 + y_0)}$, $ele_1 = g_2^{\alpha_1 \boldsymbol{d}_3^* (z_0 s + s^2)}$, and $ele_2 = g_2^{\alpha_1 \boldsymbol{d}_3^* (z_0 + s)}$. This gives us the final dually computable accumulator that we use to design our CP-ABE, fully given in our extended work [6]. Thus we will use DS1 and DS2 with parameter $k = 2$ and $n = 2k = 6$, and so DPVS of dimension 6.

5.3 Our CP-ABE Scheme

The resulting CP-ABE is fully given in Fig. 5. As said above, it permits to manage access policies expressed as disjunctions of conjunctions without "NO" gates. For sake of clarity, we highlight the underlying dually computable accumulator scheme with colors as follows: the privately computed accumulator is in green, the publicly computed accumulator is in blue, the anticipation of the first element of the witnesses is in orange, the second parts of the witnesses are in purple and the anticipation of the intersection of both sets is in red.

Theorem 4. *Our CP-ABE scheme is correct.*

Proof.

$$
\begin{aligned}
& e(\mathsf{aux}_1^{\delta\delta'}, ele_1 \cdot ele_2^{\xi}) \\
= \; & e((g_1^{\alpha_2 \boldsymbol{d}_3 (x_0 + y_0)})^{\delta\delta'}, g_2^{\alpha_1 \boldsymbol{d}_3^* (z_0 s + s^2)} \cdot (g_2^{\alpha_1 \boldsymbol{d}_3^* (z_0 + s)})^{\xi}) \\
= \; & e(g_1^{\alpha_2 \boldsymbol{d}_3 \delta\delta' (x_0 + y_0)}, g_2^{\alpha \boldsymbol{d}_3^* (s^2 + s(z_0 + \xi) + z_0 \xi)}) \\
= \; & e(g_1, g_2)^{\psi \alpha_1 \alpha_2 (s^2 + s(z_0 + \xi) + z_0 \xi) c_0 \delta'} \cdot e(g_1, g_2)^{\psi \alpha_1 \alpha_2 (s^2 + s(z_0 + \xi) + z_0 \xi) t_0 \delta}
\end{aligned}
$$

$$
\begin{aligned}
& e(ele_3 \cdot ele_4^{\xi}, W_2^{\delta'} \cdot W_2'^{\delta}) \\
= \; & e(g_1^{\alpha_1 \alpha_2 \boldsymbol{d}_2 (z_0 s + s^2)} \cdot (g_1^{\alpha_1 \alpha_2 \boldsymbol{d}_2 (z_0 + s)})^{\xi}, (g_2^{\boldsymbol{d}_2^* \sum_{i=1}^{Q} c_i s^i})^{\delta'} \cdot (g_2^{\boldsymbol{d}_2^* \sum_{i=1}^{Q} t_i s^i})^{\delta}) \\
= \; & e(g_1^{\alpha_1 \alpha_2 \boldsymbol{d}_2 (s^2 + s(z_0 + \xi) + z_0 \xi)}, g_2^{\boldsymbol{d}_2^* \delta' \sum_{i=1}^{Q} c_i s^i + \boldsymbol{d}_2^* \delta \sum_{i=1}^{Q} t_i s^i}) \\
= \; & e(g_1, g_2)^{\psi \alpha_1 \alpha_2 (s^2 + s(z_0 + \xi) + z_0 \xi) \delta' \sum_{i=1}^{Q} c_i s^i} \\
& \cdot e(g_1, g_2)^{\psi \alpha_1 \alpha_2 (s^2 + s(z_0 + \xi) + z_0 \xi) \delta \sum_{i=1}^{Q} t_i s^i}
\end{aligned}
$$

- Setup$(1^\lambda, q)$: generate bilinear group $\Gamma = (\mathbb{G}_1, \mathbb{G}_2, \mathbb{G}_T, p, e, g_1, g_2)$, dual pairing vector spaces $(\mathbb{D}, \mathbb{D}^*) \leftarrow \mathsf{Dual}(\mathbb{Z}_p^6)$ such that $\mathbb{D} = (\boldsymbol{d}_1, \cdots, \boldsymbol{d}_6)$, $\mathbb{D}^* = (\boldsymbol{d}_1^*, \cdots, \boldsymbol{d}_6^*)$ and $\boldsymbol{d}_i \cdot \boldsymbol{d}_i^* = \psi$, for $i = 1, \cdots, 6$ and $\psi \in \mathbb{Z}_p$. Also choose $\gamma, s, x_0, y_0, z_0 \leftarrow \mathbb{Z}_p$ and a hash function $\mathcal{H}$ that takes as input an attributes set and outputs an element of $\mathbb{Z}_p \setminus \{\gamma, s, x_0, y_0, z_0\}$. Set $Q = 2^q - 1$, $\mathsf{msk} = \left(\gamma, s, g_2^{\boldsymbol{d}_2^*}, \left\{g_1^{\boldsymbol{d}_1 s^i}\right\}_{i=0}^{Q}, \left\{g_1^{\boldsymbol{d}_3 s^i}\right\}_{i=1}^{Q}\right)$ and

$$\mathsf{pk} = \begin{pmatrix} \Gamma, g_1^{\boldsymbol{d}_3}, g_1^{\boldsymbol{d}_2}, g_1^{\boldsymbol{d}_2 s}, \cdots, g_1^{\boldsymbol{d}_2 s^Q}, g_2^{\boldsymbol{d}_1^*}, g_2^{\boldsymbol{d}_1^* s}, \cdots, g_2^{\boldsymbol{d}_1^* s^Q}, g_2^{\boldsymbol{d}_2^* \gamma}, \\ g_2^{\boldsymbol{d}_2^* s}, \cdots, g_2^{\boldsymbol{d}_2^* s^Q}, g_2^{\boldsymbol{d}_3^*}, g_2^{\boldsymbol{d}_3^* s}, \cdots, g_2^{\boldsymbol{d}_3^* s^Q}, \mathcal{H}, x_0, y_0, z_0 \end{pmatrix}.$$

Return msk, pk.
- KeyGen(pk, msk, Υ): let $k \in \mathbb{N}$ be the number of attributes in Υ. Compute $p_1, \cdots, p_{2^k-1}$ all the non-empty subsets of Υ and set $\mathcal{X} = \{\mathcal{H}(p_i)\}_{i=1}^{2^k-1} \cup \{x_0, z_0\}$. Compute $\{a_i\}_{i=0,\cdots,Q}$ the coefficients of the polynomial $\mathsf{Ch}_{\mathcal{X}}[Z] = (x_0 + Z) \cdot (z_0 + Z) \cdot \prod_{i=1}^{2^k-1}(\mathcal{H}(p_i) + Z)$. Pick $r \leftarrow \mathbb{Z}_p$ and set

$$\mathsf{sk}_{\Upsilon} = \mathsf{acc}_{\mathcal{X}} = g_1^{\boldsymbol{d}_1 \sum_{i=0}^{Q} a_i s^i + r(\boldsymbol{d}_2 - \gamma \boldsymbol{d}_3)}.$$

- Encrypt(pk, Π, m): let $\Pi = \pi_1 \vee \pi_2 \vee \cdots \vee \pi_l$ be the access policy, where $l \in \mathbb{N}$ is the number of clauses in the policy, and π_i for $i = 1, \cdots, l$ is a conjunction of attributes. Define $\mathcal{Y}_i$ for $i = 1, \cdots, l$ as the set of attributes associated to clause π_i and $\mathcal{Y} = \cup_{i=1}^{l} \mathcal{H}(\mathcal{Y}_i) \cup \{y_0, z_0\}$. Let $\{m_i\}_{i=0}^{Q}$ be the coefficients of polynomial $\mathsf{Ch}_{\mathcal{Y}}[Z]$.
  - *Mask computation:* choose $z, \alpha_1, \alpha_2 \leftarrow \mathbb{Z}_p$ and define $\mathsf{acc}_{\mathcal{P}_\mathcal{Y}} = g_2^{\boldsymbol{d}_3^* \sum_{i=0}^{Q} m_i s^i}$ and $\boldsymbol{H} = e(g_1^{\boldsymbol{d}_3}, \mathsf{acc}_{\mathcal{P}_\mathcal{Y}})^{\alpha_1 \alpha_2}$.
  - *Auxiliary information computation:* $\mathsf{aux}_1 = g_1^{\alpha_2 \boldsymbol{d}_3 (x_0 + y_0)}$ and $\mathsf{aux}_2 = g_2^{-\boldsymbol{d}_1^* \alpha_1 \alpha_2 + z(\gamma \boldsymbol{d}_2^* + \boldsymbol{d}_3^*)}$.
  - *Anticipation of the element computation:* $ele_1 = g_2^{\alpha_1 \boldsymbol{d}_3^*(z_0 s + s^2)}$, $ele_2 = g_2^{\alpha_1 \boldsymbol{d}_3^*(z_0 + s)}$, $ele_3 = g_1^{\alpha_1 \alpha_2 \boldsymbol{d}_2 (z_0 s + s^2)}$, and $ele_4 = g_1^{\alpha_1 \alpha_2 \boldsymbol{d}_2 (z_0 + s)}$.

  Set $\mathsf{ct}_\Pi = (ele_1, ele_2, ele_3, ele_4, \mathsf{aux}_1, \mathsf{aux}_2, \mathsf{m} \cdot \boldsymbol{H})$ and return ct_Π.
- Decrypt(pk, $\mathsf{sk}_\Upsilon, \Upsilon, \mathsf{ct}_\Pi, \Pi$): find p_{j^*} (for $j^* \in \{1, \cdots, 2^k - 1\}$) the non-empty subset of Υ that satisfies Π (if no such subset exists, then return reject symbol $\perp$). It means that there exist $j \in [1, \cdots, l]$ such that $\mathcal{Y}_j = p_{j^*}$ and $\mathcal{H}(\mathcal{Y}_j) = \mathcal{H}(p_{j^*}) = \xi$. Let $\{c_i\}_{i=0}^{Q}$ be the coefficients of the polynomial $\mathsf{Ch}_{\mathcal{X}}[Z]/((z_0 + Z)(\xi + Z))$. Let $\{t_i\}_{i=0}^{Q}$ be the coefficients of the polynomial $\mathsf{Ch}_{\mathcal{Y}}[Z]/((z_0 + Z)(\xi + Z))$. Find $\delta, \delta' \in \mathbb{Z}_p$ such that $c_0 = x_0 \delta$ and $t_0 = y_0 \delta'$. Set $W_2 = g_2^{\boldsymbol{d}_2^* \sum_{i=1}^{Q} c_i s^i}$, $W_2' = g_2^{\boldsymbol{d}_2^* \sum_{i=1}^{Q} t_i s^i}$ and compute

$$\frac{\mathsf{m} \cdot \boldsymbol{H}}{\left(e(\mathsf{aux}_1^{\delta\delta'}, ele_1 \cdot ele_2^{\xi}) \cdot e(ele_3 \cdot ele_4^{\xi}, W_2^{\delta'} \cdot W_2'^{\delta}) \cdot e(\mathsf{acc}_{\mathcal{X}}, \mathsf{aux}_2)^{\delta'}\right)^{\delta^{-1}}}$$

to get m or $\perp$.

Fig. 5. Our CP-ABE scheme.

Therefore

$$
\begin{aligned}
& e(\mathsf{aux}_1^{\delta\delta'}, ele_1 \cdot ele_2^{\xi}) \cdot e(ele_3 \cdot ele_4^{\xi}, W_2^{\delta'} \cdot W_2'^{\delta}) \\
= \quad & e(g_1, g_2)^{\psi\alpha_1\alpha_2(s^2+s(z_0+\xi)+z_0\xi)\delta' \sum_{i=0}^{Q} c_i s^i} \\
& \cdot e(g_1, g_2)^{\psi\alpha_1\alpha_2(s^2+s(z_0+\xi)+z_0\xi)\delta \sum_{i=0}^{Q} t_i s^i}
\end{aligned}
$$

If ξ belongs to $\mathcal{X}$ and ξ belongs to $\mathcal{Y}$, then

$$
\begin{aligned}
& e(\mathsf{aux}_1^{\delta\delta'}, ele_1 \cdot ele_2^{\xi}) \cdot e(ele_3 \cdot ele_4^{\xi}, W_2^{\delta'} \cdot W_2'^{\delta}) \\
& = e(g_1, g_2)^{\psi\alpha_1\alpha_2\delta' \sum_{i=0}^{Q} a_i s^i} \cdot e(g_1, g_2)^{\psi\alpha_1\alpha_2\delta \sum_{i=0}^{Q} m_i s^i}
\end{aligned}
$$

The last pairing is equal to

$$
\begin{aligned}
& e(\mathsf{acc}_{\mathcal{X}}, \mathsf{aux}_2)^{\delta'} \\
= \quad & e(g_1^{d_1 \sum_{i=0}^{Q} a_i s^i + r(d_2 - \gamma d_3)}, g_2^{-d_1^* \alpha_1\alpha_2 + z(\gamma d_2^* + d_3^*)})^{\delta'} \\
& = e(g_1, g_2)^{-\alpha_1\alpha_2\psi \sum_{i=0}^{Q} a_i s^i \delta'} \cdot e(g_1, g_2)^{rz\gamma\psi} \cdot e(g_1, g_2)^{-rz\gamma\psi} \\
= \quad & e(g_1, g_2)^{-\alpha_1\alpha_2\psi \sum_{i=0}^{Q} a_i s^i \delta'}
\end{aligned}
$$

so multiplying it with $e(\mathsf{aux}_1^{\delta\delta'}, ele_1 \cdot ele_2^{\xi}) \cdot e(ele_3 \cdot ele_4^{\xi}, W_2^{\delta'} \cdot W_2'^{\delta})$ gives $e(g_1, g_2)^{\psi\alpha_1\alpha_2\delta \sum_{i=0}^{Q} m_i s^i}$. As we know δ we can recover the mask of the message and then the message. Therefore, the scheme is correct.

Theorem 5. *Our ABE satisfies adaptive indistinguishability under* SXDH *assumption.*

To prove the security of our scheme, we prove that the encryption of challenge message is indistinguishable from the encryption of a random message. To do so, we use a sequence of games (our proof is inspired of Chen *et al.* [13]'s IBE security proof) and Water's dual system encryption framework [39]. Let $N_q \in \mathbb{N}$ be the number of secret keys that the adversary is allowed to query.[3]

- Game_{Real} is the original security game, as presented in Fig. 4.
- Game_0 is the same as Game_{Real} except that the challenge ciphertext is a *semi-functional* ciphertext.
- Game_i for $i = 1, \cdots, N_q$ is the same as Game_0 except that the first i keys are semi-functional.
- Game_{Final} is the same as Game_{N_q} except that the challenge ciphertext is an encryption of a random message.

Now we define semi-functional (SF) keys and ciphertexts. Let $t_5, t_6, z_5, z_6 \leftarrow \mathbb{Z}_p$.

- a semi-functional key for Υ, $\mathsf{sk}_{\Upsilon}^{(SF)}$, is computed from normal key sk_{Υ} as $\mathsf{sk}_{\Upsilon}^{(SF)} = \mathsf{sk}_{\Upsilon} \cdot g_1^{t_5 d_5^+ t_6 d_6} = g_1^{d_1 \sum_{i=0}^{Q} a_i s^i + r(d_2 - \gamma d_3) + t_5 d_5 + t_6 d_6}$

[3] As the number of attributes in the scheme is bounded, so is the number of keys that an adversary can query.

- a semi-functional ciphertext for Π, $\mathsf{ct}_{\Pi}^{(SF)}$, is computed as a normal ciphertext ct_{Π} except that $\mathsf{aux}_2^{(SF)} = \mathsf{aux}_2 \cdot g_2^{z_5 \boldsymbol{d}_5^* + z_6 \boldsymbol{d}_6^*}$.

Notice that normal keys can decrypt SF ciphertexts, and normal ciphertexts can be decrypted by SF keys. However, decryption of a SF ciphertext by a SF key leads to an additional term: $1/e(g_1, g_2)^{(t_5 z_5 \psi + t_6 z_6 \psi)\delta^{-1}}$. Due to lack of place, we only present the intuition of our proof here. Refer to our full paper [6] for more details. Briefly, the proof is done as follows.

First we prove that if there exists an adversary that can distinguish Game_{Real} from Game_0 we can build an adversary that breaks the DS2 assumption with parameters $k = 3$ and $n = 6$. To do so the main idea is to use the assumption's challenge to build the challenge ciphertext. Depending on the value of the challenge we will either obtain a normal form ciphertext or a semi-functional form one.

Then we prove that if there exists an adversary that can distinguish Game_{j-1} from Game_j for $j = 1, \cdots, N_q$ we can build an adversary that breaks the DS1 assumption with $k = 3$ and $n = 6$. The idea is to use the assumption's challenge to build the j-th key. Thus, depending on the value of the challenge we will either obtain a normal form key or a semi-functional form one. To build the challenge ciphertext, we use the assumption's parameters to obtain a semi-functional ciphertext.

Finally, we prove that Game_{N_q} is computationally indistinguishable from Game_{Final}, with a change of dual orthonormal bases. Doing so, we randomized the coefficient of $\boldsymbol{d}_1$ in the aux_2 term of the ciphertext, thereby severing its link with the blinding factor. That gives us the encryption of a random message.

5.4 Comparison

It is known that monotone boolean formulas can be put under DNF form, where the latter represents the minterm of the formula, *i.e.* a minimal set of variables which, if assigned the value 1, forces the formula to take the value 1 regardless of the values assigned to the remaining variables [16]. For more details on the transformation of monotone boolean formulas into DNF and its probable efficiency loss we refer the interested reader to [8,37]. It is also known that the circuit complexity class monotone NC^1 is captured by monotone boolean formulas of log-depth and fan-in two [24]. Therefore, our CP-ABE can directly deal with monotone NC^1 circuits. We present in Table 3 a comparison of (bounded) CP-ABE scheme for monotone NC^1 circuits, based on pairings[4]. All schemes in this table overpass the one-use restriction on attributes, which imposes that each attribute is only present once in the access policy. All schemes are single authority, and secure in the standard model.

As we can see our scheme is the first one to obtain constant size for both ciphertexts and secret keys. However, this is done at the cost of the public key size, which become exponential. This drawback comes from the fact that for accumulating user's attributes set we are running the hash function $\mathcal{H}$ on each non-empty subset of this set. Doing so we obtain an easy way to check if an attributes set verifies an access policy: if it does,

[4] Some works are expressing their monotone boolean formula through Linear Secret Sharing Scheme (LSSS) matrix, see [27] for more details on this transformation.

Table 3. Comparison of CP-ABE schemes for monotone NC^1 circuits, based on pairings. Here q is the bound on the number of attributes in the scheme, and l is the number of rows in the access matrix when the policy is expressed with LSSS matrix.

Schemes	$\vert pk\vert$	$\vert ct\vert$	$\vert sk\vert$	Adaptive Security	Assumption	Group Order	Pairing
[40]	$O(q)$	$O(l)$	$O(q)$	×	Non Static	Prime	Symmetric
[25]	$O(q)$	$O(l)$	$O(q)$	✓	Static	Composite	Symmetric
[28]	$O(q)$	$O(l)$	$O(q)$	✓	Non Static	Prime	Symmetric
[24]	$O(q)$	$O(q)$	$O(l)$	✓	Static	Prime	Asymmetric
Our	$O(2^q)$	$O(1)$	$O(1)$	✓	Static	Prime	Asymmetric

one of non-empty subsets of the set is equal to one clause of the access policy. We argue that the size of the public key is less important than the size of the other parameters, as it can easily be stored on-line. Additionally, while the sets (and access policies) representation might be scary at first glance, this is not an issue in practice as (i) it is not necessary to keep all elements in memory and (ii) for each decryption, only the useful part will have to be computed again. Finding another way to accumulate attributes sets and access policies in order to have efficient membership verification may lead to a more efficient CP-ABE, with shorter public key size. Also notice that our scheme is dealing with DNF access policies which have small expressiveness. We leave as an open problem to reduce the size of the public key in our scheme and also to modify it so that it can deal with fine-grained access policies. We also leave as an open problem the case of unbounded ABE schemes [3, 12], and the case of non-monotonic access formulas [32, 33]. In our extended work [6], we also show how the above construction can be transformed into a Key Policy ABE (KP-ABE), in which the secret key is attached to the access policy and the ciphertext is given by a set of attributes.

6 Conclusion

In this work, we improved the state of the art of cryptographic accumulator schemes by proposing a new scheme that has private evaluation while having public generation. This scheme is the first (as far as we know) accumulator that uses dual pairing vector spaces. We also introduced the new notion of *dually computable* cryptographic accumulators, allowing two ways to evaluate an accumulator: either privately or publicly. We instantiate a dually computable accumulator for our first scheme. Furthermore, we built a new CP-ABE scheme, that deals with monotone NC^1 circuits. This is the first scheme in the literature that has both constant size ciphertexts and users secret keys. We achieve such compactness by using cryptographic accumulators for both key management and encryption. Unfortunately, as our construction strongly relies on the fact that Nguyen's accumulator uses polynomial representation of sets, we cannot generalized our idea. Hence, we leave as an open problem the way to generically transform a cryptographic accumulator into an (attribute-based) encryption scheme.

Acknowledgments. We would like to thank anonymous reviewers for their helpful discussions and valuable comments. Part of this work has received funding from the French National Research Agency (ANR), PRESTO project number ANR-19-CE39-0011-01.

References

1. Acar, T., Chow, S.S.M., Nguyen, L.: Accumulators and U-prove revocation. In: Sadeghi, A.-R. (ed.) FC 2013. LNCS, vol. 7859, pp. 189–196. Springer, Heidelberg (2013). https://doi.org/10.1007/978-3-642-39884-1_15
2. Asano, T.: A revocation scheme with minimal storage at receivers. In: Zheng, Y. (ed.) ASIACRYPT 2002. LNCS, vol. 2501, pp. 433–450. Springer, Heidelberg (2002). https://doi.org/10.1007/3-540-36178-2_27
3. Attrapadung, N.: Dual system encryption framework in prime-order groups via computational pair encodings. In: Cheon, J.H., Takagi, T. (eds.) ASIACRYPT 2016 Part II. LNCS, vol. 10032, pp. 591–623. Springer, Heidelberg (2016). https://doi.org/10.1007/978-3-662-53890-6_20
4. Attrapadung, N., Libert, B., de Panafieu, E.: Expressive key-policy attribute-based encryption with constant-size ciphertexts. In: Catalano, D., Fazio, N., Gennaro, R., Nicolosi, A. (eds.) PKC 2011. LNCS, vol. 6571, pp. 90–108. Springer, Heidelberg (2011). https://doi.org/10.1007/978-3-642-19379-8_6
5. Au, M.H., Wu, Q., Susilo, W., Mu, Y.: Compact E-cash from bounded accumulator. In: Abe, M. (ed.) CT-RSA 2007. LNCS, vol. 4377, pp. 178–195. Springer, Heidelberg (2006). https://doi.org/10.1007/11967668_12
6. Barthoulot, A., Blazy, O., Canard, S.: Dually computable cryptographic accumulators and their application to attribute based encryption. Cryptology ePrint Archive, Paper 2023/1277 (2023). https://eprint.iacr.org/2023/1277
7. Benaloh, J., de Mare, M.: One-way accumulators: a decentralized alternative to digital signatures. In: Helleseth, T. (ed.) EUROCRYPT 1993. LNCS, vol. 765, pp. 274–285. Springer, Heidelberg (1994). https://doi.org/10.1007/3-540-48285-7_24
8. Blais, E., Håstad, J., Servedio, R.A., Tan, L.-Y.: On DNF approximators for monotone Boolean functions. In: Esparza, J., Fraigniaud, P., Husfeldt, T., Koutsoupias, E. (eds.) ICALP 2014. LNCS, vol. 8572, pp. 235–246. Springer, Heidelberg (2014). https://doi.org/10.1007/978-3-662-43948-7_20
9. Boneh, D., Boyen, X.: Short signatures without random oracles and the SDH assumption in bilinear groups. J. Cryptol. **21**(2), 149–177 (2008). https://doi.org/10.1007/s00145-007-9005-7
10. Boneh, D., et al.: Fully key-homomorphic encryption, arithmetic circuit ABE and compact garbled circuits. In: Nguyen, P.Q., Oswald, E. (eds.) EUROCRYPT 2014. LNCS, vol. 8441, pp. 533–556. Springer, Heidelberg (2014). https://doi.org/10.1007/978-3-642-55220-5_30
11. Camenisch, J., Kohlweiss, M., Soriente, C.: An accumulator based on bilinear maps and efficient revocation for anonymous credentials. In: Jarecki, S., Tsudik, G. (eds.) PKC 2009. LNCS, vol. 5443, pp. 481–500. Springer, Heidelberg (2009). https://doi.org/10.1007/978-3-642-00468-1_27
12. Chen, J., Gong, J., Kowalczyk, L., Wee, H.: Unbounded ABE via bilinear entropy expansion, revisited. In: Nielsen, J.B., Rijmen, V. (eds.) EUROCRYPT 2018. LNCS, vol. 10820, pp. 503–534. Springer, Cham (2018). https://doi.org/10.1007/978-3-319-78381-9_19
13. Chen, J., Lim, H.W., Ling, S., Wang, H., Wee, H.: Shorter IBE and signatures via asymmetric pairings. In: Abdalla, M., Lange, T. (eds.) Pairing 2012. LNCS, vol. 7708, pp. 122–140. Springer, Heidelberg (2013). https://doi.org/10.1007/978-3-642-36334-4_8

14. Damgard, I., Triandopoulos, N.: Supporting non-membership proofs with bilinear-map accumulators. Cryptology ePrint Archive, Report 2008/538 (2008). https://eprint.iacr.org/2008/538
15. Derler, D., Hanser, C., Slamanig, D.: Revisiting cryptographic accumulators, additional properties and relations to other primitives. In: Nyberg, K. (ed.) CT-RSA 2015. LNCS, vol. 9048, pp. 127–144. Springer, Cham (2015). https://doi.org/10.1007/978-3-319-16715-2_7
16. Elbassioni, K., Makino, K., Rauf, I.: On the readability of monotone Boolean formulae. J. Comb. Optim. **22**, 293–304 (2011)
17. Fazio, N., Nicolosi, A.: Cryptographic accumulators: definitions, constructions and applications (2002)
18. Freedman, M.J., Nissim, K., Pinkas, B.: Efficient private matching and set intersection. In: Cachin, C., Camenisch, J.L. (eds.) EUROCRYPT 2004. LNCS, vol. 3027, pp. 1–19. Springer, Heidelberg (2004). https://doi.org/10.1007/978-3-540-24676-3_1
19. Gentry, C., Ramzan, Z.: RSA accumulator based broadcast encryption. In: Zhang, K., Zheng, Y. (eds.) ISC 2004. LNCS, vol. 3225, pp. 73–86. Springer, Heidelberg (Sep (2004). https://doi.org/10.1007/978-3-540-30144-8_7
20. Ghosh, E., Ohrimenko, O., Papadopoulos, D., Tamassia, R., Triandopoulos, N.: Zero-knowledge accumulators and set algebra. In: Cheon, J.H., Takagi, T. (eds.) ASIACRYPT 2016. LNCS, vol. 10032, pp. 67–100. Springer, Heidelberg (2016). https://doi.org/10.1007/978-3-662-53890-6_3
21. Goyal, V., Jain, A., Pandey, O., Sahai, A.: Bounded ciphertext policy attribute based encryption. In: Aceto, L., Damgård, I., Goldberg, L.A., Halldórsson, M.M., Ingólfsdóttir, A., Walukiewicz, I. (eds.) ICALP 2008. LNCS, vol. 5126, pp. 579–591. Springer, Heidelberg (2008). https://doi.org/10.1007/978-3-540-70583-3_47
22. Goyal, V., Pandey, O., Sahai, A., Waters, B.: Attribute-based encryption for fine-grained access control of encrypted data. In: Juels, A., Wright, R.N., De Capitani di Vimercati, S. (eds.) ACM CCS 2006, pp. 89–98. ACM Press (2006). https://doi.org/10.1145/1180405.1180418. available as Cryptology ePrint Archive Report 2006/309
23. Groth, J.: On the size of pairing-based non-interactive arguments. In: Fischlin, M., Coron, J.-S. (eds.) EUROCRYPT 2016. LNCS, vol. 9666, pp. 305–326. Springer, Heidelberg (2016). https://doi.org/10.1007/978-3-662-49896-5_11
24. Kowalczyk, L., Wee, H.: Compact adaptively secure ABE for NC^1 from *k*-Lin. In: Ishai, Y., Rijmen, V. (eds.) EUROCRYPT 2019. LNCS, vol. 11476, pp. 3–33. Springer, Cham (2019). https://doi.org/10.1007/978-3-030-17653-2_1
25. Lewko, A., Okamoto, T., Sahai, A., Takashima, K., Waters, B.: Fully secure functional encryption: attribute-based encryption and (hierarchical) inner product encryption. In: Gilbert, H. (ed.) EUROCRYPT 2010. LNCS, vol. 6110, pp. 62–91. Springer, Heidelberg (2010). https://doi.org/10.1007/978-3-642-13190-5_4
26. Lewko, A.B., Sahai, A., Waters, B.: Revocation systems with very small private keys. In: 2010 IEEE Symposium on Security and Privacy, pp. 273–285. IEEE Computer Society Press (2010). https://doi.org/10.1109/SP.2010.23
27. Lewko, A., Waters, B.: Decentralizing attribute-based encryption. In: Paterson, K.G. (ed.) EUROCRYPT 2011. LNCS, vol. 6632, pp. 568–588. Springer, Heidelberg (2011). https://doi.org/10.1007/978-3-642-20465-4_31
28. Lewko, A., Waters, B.: New proof methods for attribute-based encryption: achieving full security through selective techniques. In: Safavi-Naini, R., Canetti, R. (eds.) CRYPTO 2012. LNCS, vol. 7417, pp. 180–198. Springer, Heidelberg (2012). https://doi.org/10.1007/978-3-642-32009-5_12
29. Libert, B., Ramanna, S.C., Yung, M.: Functional commitment schemes: from polynomial commitments to pairing-based accumulators from simple assumptions. In: Chatzigiannakis,

I., Mitzenmacher, M., Rabani, Y., Sangiorgi, D. (eds.) ICALP 2016. LIPIcs, vol. 55, pp. 30:1–30:14. Schloss Dagstuhl (Jul 2016). https://doi.org/10.4230/LIPIcs.ICALP.2016.30
30. Mahabir, J., Reihaneh, S.N.: Compact accumulator using lattices. In: International Conference on Security, Privacy, and Applied Cryptography Engineering (2015)
31. Nguyen, L.: Accumulators from bilinear pairings and applications. In: Menezes, A. (ed.) CT-RSA 2005. LNCS, vol. 3376, pp. 275–292. Springer, Heidelberg (2005). https://doi.org/10.1007/978-3-540-30574-3_19
32. Okamoto, T., Takashima, K.: Fully secure functional encryption with general relations from the decisional linear assumption. In: Rabin, T. (ed.) CRYPTO 2010. LNCS, vol. 6223, pp. 191–208. Springer, Heidelberg (2010). https://doi.org/10.1007/978-3-642-14623-7_11
33. Okamoto, T., Takashima, K.: Fully secure unbounded inner-product and attribute-based encryption. In: Wang, X., Sako, K. (eds.) ASIACRYPT 2012. LNCS, vol. 7658, pp. 349–366. Springer, Heidelberg (2012). https://doi.org/10.1007/978-3-642-34961-4_22
34. Papamanthou, C., Tamassia, R., Triandopoulos, N.: Optimal verification of operations on dynamic sets. In: Rogaway, P. (ed.) CRYPTO 2011. LNCS, vol. 6841, pp. 91–110. Springer, Heidelberg (2011). https://doi.org/10.1007/978-3-642-22792-9_6
35. Sahai, A., Waters, B.: Fuzzy identity-based encryption. In: Cramer, R. (ed.) EUROCRYPT 2005. LNCS, vol. 3494, pp. 457–473. Springer, Heidelberg (2005). https://doi.org/10.1007/11426639_27
36. Tanaka, N., Saito, T.: On the q-Strong Diffie-Hellman problem. IACR Cryptol. ePrint Arch. **2010**, 215 (2010)
37. Venema, M., Alpár, G., Hoepman, J.H.: Systematizing core properties of pairing-based attribute-based encryption to uncover remaining challenges in enforcing access control in practice. Des. Codes Crypt. **91**(1), 165–220 (2023). https://doi.org/10.1007/s10623-022-01093-5
38. Wang, X., Chow, S.S.M.: Cross-domain access control encryption: arbitrary-policy, constant-size, efficient. In: 2021 IEEE Symposium on Security and Privacy, pp. 748–761. IEEE Computer Society Press (2021). https://doi.org/10.1109/SP40001.2021.00023
39. Waters, B.: Dual system encryption: realizing fully secure IBE and HIBE under simple assumptions. In: Halevi, S. (ed.) CRYPTO 2009. LNCS, vol. 5677, pp. 619–636. Springer, Heidelberg (2009). https://doi.org/10.1007/978-3-642-03356-8_36
40. Waters, B.: Ciphertext-policy attribute-based encryption: an expressive, efficient, and provably secure realization. In: Catalano, D., Fazio, N., Gennaro, R., Nicolosi, A. (eds.) PKC 2011. LNCS, vol. 6571, pp. 53–70. Springer, Heidelberg (2011). https://doi.org/10.1007/978-3-642-19379-8_4
41. Zhang, Y., Katz, J., Papamanthou, C.: An expressive (zero-knowledge) set accumulator, pp. 158–173 (2017). https://doi.org/10.1109/EuroSP.2017.35

A Minor Note on Obtaining Simpler iO Constructions via Depleted Obfuscators

Răzvan Roşie(✉)

Lombard International, Luxembourg, Luxembourg
razvan.rosie@lombardinternational.com

Abstract. This paper puts forth a simple construction for indistinguishability obfuscation (iO) for general circuits. The scheme is obtained from four main ingredients: (1) selectively indistinguishably-secure functional encryption for general circuits having its encryption procedure in the complexity class NC^1; (2) universal circuits; (3) puncturable pseudorandom functions having evaluation in NC^1; (4) indistinguishably-secure affine-determinant programs, a notion that particularizes iO for specific circuit classes and acts as "depleted" obfuscators. The scheme can be used to build iO for all polynomial-sized circuits in a simplified way.

Keywords: affine determinant programs · branching programs · FE · iO

1 Introduction

Indistinguishability obfuscation (iO) [3] is a central goal in the cryptographic community. Its prime purpose is to make functionally equivalent circuits indistinguishable. Its plethora of applications includes functional encryption, searchable encryption or non-interactive key-exchange protocols [10]. iO can be realized from multilinear maps [13], multi-input functional encryption [16] or compact functional encryption [25]. Nowadays schemes achieving security under well-established assumptions exist [22].

Functional Encryption and iO. Functional encryption (FE) provides targeted access over encrypted data. Using the public parameters (abbreviated mpk), any input inp taken from a specified domain can be encrypted as ciphertext CT. Using FE's secret key (abbreviated msk), a functional key – sk_f – can be issued for any function f represented as a polynomial-sized circuit $\mathscr{C}$. One recovers $\mathscr{C}(\mathsf{inp})$ whenever CT is decrypted under sk_f. The major security notion to be accomplished is indistinguishability: as long as $\mathscr{C}(\mathsf{m}_0) = \mathscr{C}(\mathsf{m}_1)$ for two different messages m_0 and m_1, it is hard for any computationally bounded adversary to distinguish if CT encrypts m_0 or m_1, given access to sk_f and mpk (and CT).

Indistinguishability obfuscation appears, at first sight, unrelated to functional encryption. Its interface has the following specification: consider two functionally equivalent circuits – $\mathscr{C}_0$ and $\mathscr{C}_1$ – both implementing the same function f. An

J. Deng et al. (Eds.): CANS 2023, LNCS 14342, pp. 563–587, 2023.
https://doi.org/10.1007/978-981-99-7563-1_25

indistinguishability obfuscator iO takes as input one of them – say $\mathscr{C}_b$ – for a bit b sampled uniformly at random. It releases $\overline{\mathscr{C}}$, such that it is hard for any computationally bounded adversary to distinguish if $\overline{\mathscr{C}}$ was obtained from $\mathscr{C}_0$ or $\mathscr{C}_1$ (the indistinguishability property). We will use the term *depleted* obfuscator to refer to an iO obfuscator for very restricted subclasses of P.

1.1 Our Result

Placing Our Work in the Context of iO Schemes. This work follows, from a high level, the recipe put forth in [25]: an obfuscator is used to compute a functional ciphertext, and a functional key is issued to decrypt iO's outputs. There are, though, *major* differences: [25] builds a *compact* functional encryption (cFE) scheme using *generically* an exponentially-efficient obfuscator (XiO); the cFE is then used through a sequence of convoluted transforms to build iO. XiO is an obfuscator that is slightly smaller than a lookup table (the trivial obfuscator). Perhaps, at the time, the line of thought therein was focused on *provably* obtaining iO through means involving the realization of a less demanding XiO.

Herein, the energy is put on building an indistinguishable obfuscator for a very restricted (depleted) class of circuits. We depart from the usage of an XiO and go for a direct construction assuming the existence of (1) FE with encryption in NC^1 [17], universal circuits (Uc)[1], puncturable pseudorandom functions (pPRF) with evaluation in NC^1 and affine determinant programs (ADP).

The main idea is to generate a functional key for the Uc. Then, using a different type of obfuscator[2] – the ADP – we can produce functional ciphertexts for messages having their form: "$\mathscr{C}||\mathsf{inp}$" for some binary representation of circuit $\mathscr{C}$ and input inp. By the correctness of FE we get that:

$$\mathsf{FE.Dec}(\mathsf{FE.KGen}(\mathsf{msk}, \mathsf{Uc}), \mathsf{FE.Enc}(\mathsf{mpk}, \mathscr{C}||\mathsf{inp})) = \mathscr{C}(\mathsf{inp}) \; . \tag{1}$$

The ADP (our depleted obfuscator) is used having the master public key of an FE scheme and a (puncturable) PRF key hardcoded. It will produce functional ciphertexts, to be decrypted under the functional key evaluating Uc. A preview of the inner working of our obfuscator is in Eq. (2).

$$\begin{aligned} \mathsf{iO.Setup}(\mathscr{C}) &:= \Big(\mathsf{ADP.Setup}(\mathsf{mpk}, \mathscr{C}, \mathsf{k}),\ \mathsf{FE.KGen}(\mathsf{msk}, \mathsf{Uc})\Big) \\ \mathsf{iO.Eval}(\mathsf{inp}) &:= \mathsf{FE.Dec}(\mathsf{sk}_{\mathsf{Uc}}, \mathsf{ADP.Eval}(\mathsf{FE.Enc}(\mathsf{mpk}, \mathscr{C}||\mathsf{inp}; \mathsf{pPRF}(\mathsf{k}, \mathsf{inp})))) \end{aligned} \tag{2}$$

Before exploring the main question – how to build such an ADP able to provide "fresh" FE ciphertexts while hiding $\mathscr{C}$ – we provide the intuition behind the indistinguishability proof for our iO obfuscator.

The proof for the obfuscator described in Eq. (2) goes by hybridizing over all inputs (similar to [25]): considering two functionally equivalent $\mathscr{C}_0$ and $\mathscr{C}_1$, we

[1] To recap, a universal circuit Uc is itself a circuit that takes as input a description of another circuit $\mathscr{C}$ computing some (abstract) function f as well as the input inp to $\mathscr{C}$ and returns the value of $\mathscr{C}(\mathsf{inp})$; Thus $\mathsf{Uc}(\mathscr{C}, \mathsf{inp}) = \mathscr{C}(\mathsf{inp})$.

[2] We show how to build and prove its indistinguishability herein.

will use the indistinguishability of ADP to switch to a setting where pPRF's key is replaced by one punctured in the hybrid game's input. Then, we use pPRF's security to replace the randomness used to produce the FE ciphertext in the current challenge point by true random coins. Next, we use the indistinguishability of the functional encryption for the current input, to replace the ciphertext encoding $\mathcal{C}_0||\mathsf{inp}^*$ with $\mathcal{C}_1||\mathsf{inp}^*$. Finally we switch back. Clearly, the number of hybrids is exponential in input length.

1.2 How to Use ADPs to Obfuscate Specific Classes of Circuits

Affine determinant programs [6] were defined to target more efficient and direct obfuscators. The original construction was heuristic and is already broken for the general case using simple, specially-crafted counterexamples [30]. Our work describes how to instantiate a different flavour of ADPs using *augmented* branching programs, thus incurring topological transforms on the underlying graph structure. More importantly, Sect. 5 discusses constraints needed to prove security for *peculiar* classes of circuits.

Consider a binary input of length n. An ADP is a set of $n+1$ square matrices having entries in $\mathbb{F}_2$. The first one $\mathbf{T}_0$ is referred to as the "base" matrix. Altogether they allow to encode and evaluate one function f representable as an NC^1 circuit. The evaluation procedure computes the determinant obtained by summing up the base matrix to subsets of matrices that are input dependent:

$$f(\mathsf{m}) = \det\left(\mathbf{T}_0 + \sum_{i=1}^{n} \mathsf{inp}_i \cdot \mathbf{T}_i\right) , \tag{3}$$

where inp_i is the ith bit of inp. The operation is done over $\mathbb{F}_2$.

A High-Level View on ADPs. To build the matrices that form an ADP, one should consider a function in NC^1, as its branching program [7,28] will have polynomial size [4]. The branching program consists of a start node, two terminal nodes denoted 0 and 1 and a set – variable in size – of regular nodes. The start node has two potential outgoing edges and no incoming edge. The terminal nodes have no or multiple incoming edges and no outgoing edges. The regular nodes receive at least an incoming edge and have two outgoing edges (potentially pointing to the same node). The crux point is that each node (except terminals) is associated (or labelled) to some input bit value inp_i. If $\mathsf{inp}_i = 0$ one of the two outgoing edges is selected, when $\mathsf{inp}_i = 1$ the other one gets used. The selection (or settling) of one of the two possible arcs corresponding to each input bit induces an adjacency matrix where on each line, only one out of two possible entries are set to one. If we fix an input – say $\vec{0}$ – we get the core of the base matrix of the ADP from the adjacency matrix of the branching program. Let this core matrix be denoted $\mathbf{G}_0$.

Next, we can obtain "difference" matrices: to evaluate input $1||0\ldots||0$, we subtract from the adjacency matrix that we obtained for $1||0\ldots||0$ the "base" matrix $\mathbf{G}_0$. Let this "difference" matrix be $\mathbf{G}_1 \leftarrow \mathbf{G}_{1||0\ldots||0} - \mathbf{G}_{0||0\ldots||0}$ (in general $\mathbf{G}_i$, i is the index of the bit set to 1). This constitutes the core of a *simplified* ADP.

After an intermediate simple post-processing step, a randomization phase is applied: left and right invertible matrices sampled over $\mathbb{F}_2^{m\times m}$ – denoted by $\mathbf{L}$ and $\mathbf{R}$ – are multiplied to each of the $n+1$ matrices.

1.3 The Usage of ADPs in Our Scheme

As mentioned before, the idea is to employ ADPs to generate FE ciphertexts. To this end, FE's encryption procedure itself must be in NC^1. The random coins used by FE.Enc are generated through a pPRF – which itself must be in NC^1. The circuit is described in Fig. 2. Note that we use a limiting variable ρ, originally set to the maximum input (and used in the security proof), while the circuit returns an FE ciphertext for the inp that will change during the proof.

Given that each ADP outputs a single bit, we employ the usage of ℓ such circuits, where ℓ is the length of an FE ciphertext. This functional ciphertext, will, in turn, support decryption for functions of t bits length.

One of the major predicaments we face in our indistinguishability proof for ADPs is a different structure of circuits evaluating a pPRF under its *normal* and *punctured* keys[3]. Generally for pPRFs these evaluations circuits differ (see for instance the case of the GGM-based pPRF [27]). To cope with this issue we use a trick that artificially expands the pPRF's input domain with one bit. The key is punctured in an input starting with 0, while always evaluating in an input starting with 1. Thus, we are guaranteed to be able to evaluate the pPRF on the entire original domain. In the proof, we will switch to the usage of a key puncture in point "$1||\mathsf{inp}^*$" for some challenge inp^*, while preserving the same topology of branching program, a crux point in the indistinguishability proof for the ADP acting as "depleted obfuscator".

By reusing the previous argument, the strategy we put forth is to retain the same topology for the underlying BP. The only change occurs for a designated set of "sensitive" variables – the nimv – which can be regarded as hardcoded inputs. To this end our security proof will switch values for k, the limit ρ and $\mathscr{C}$'s representation, while preserving the branching program's structure.

Security Considerations for ADPs: Topology, Behaviour and "nimvs". In order to prove the security of our iO-obfuscator, we use a nested level of hybrids. We iterate over the entire input space, and for each challenge input we switch from the encoding of the first circuit $\mathscr{C}_0$ to the representation of $\mathscr{C}_1$. For each challenge inp^*, we first rely on the indistinguishability of the ADP obfuscator to switch the key to one punctured in the current input. Then, we rely on pPRF's security to switch the randomness terms used to compute the challenge ciphertext c corresponding to inp^*. Once we are in a setting where fresh random coins are used, we rely on FE's security to switch to a setting

[3] A puncturable PRF is a pseudorandom function with a normal evaluation mode using a key k and an input m, producing (pseudo-) random values y; a special evaluation mode uses a punctured key k^*, punctured in some point m^* and can compute all PRF values except for $\mathsf{PRF}(\mathsf{k}, \mathsf{m}^*)$.

where $\mathscr{C}_1$ is encoded. Finally, we have reverse hybrids that will undo the changes related to pPRF keys and decrease limit ρ.

It should be noted that values such as $\mathsf{k}, \mathscr{C}_0, \mathscr{C}_1$ or ρ are highly sensitive. Revealing them incurs a trivial distinguisher. One of the goals of IND-ADP indistinguishability is, indirectly, to protect such variables, denoted here as *non-input mutable variables*, or nimv. More detailed, one can think at the circuit in Fig. 2 as taking 2-inputs: i and nimvs. We will denote by $|\mathsf{nimv}|$ the cumulative length of the binary description of all nimvs.

This work offers a view on ADP as being built from a "proto"-ADP having $|\mathsf{nimv}|+n+1$ matrices. In the setup phase, the nimv values are settled, and the actual base matrix is obtained by summing up the "proto"-ADP base matrix with the $|\mathsf{nimv}|$-matrices obtained by assigning values to nimv variables. In this way, we are guaranteed that the *topology* of the "proto"-branching program will remain the same even if the nimv variables are going to change (which is the case during the security proof). We sometimes write that ADPs have "embedded" nimv values.

Theorem 1 (Informal). *Assume the existence of an* IND-ADP*-secure* ADP *for the class $\mathfrak{C}_{d,|\mathsf{nimv}|+(n+1)}$. Moreover, assuming the existence of universal circuits, puncturable pseudorandom functions with evaluation in* NC^1 *and* FE *with encryption in* NC^1 *there is an indistinguishably-secure* iO *scheme for functions in class $\mathfrak{C}_{d',|\mathsf{nimv}|+(n+1)}$. The advantage of any adversary $\mathcal{A} := (\mathcal{A}_1, \mathcal{A}_2, \mathcal{A}_3)$ running in polynomial time against the security of the scheme is bounded as follows:* $\mathbf{Adv}^{\mathsf{IND}}_{\mathcal{A},\mathsf{iO}}(\lambda) \le 2^n \cdot \Big((2\ell+1)\cdot \mathbf{Adv}^{\mathsf{IND\text{-}ADP}}_{\mathcal{A}_1,\mathsf{ADP}}(\lambda) + \mathbf{Adv}^{\mathsf{s\text{-}IND\text{-}FE\text{-}CPA}}_{\mathcal{A}_2,\mathsf{FE}}(\lambda) + 2\cdot \mathbf{Adv}^{\mathsf{puncture}}_{\mathcal{A}_3,\mathsf{pPRF}}(\lambda)\Big)$ *where ℓ represents the output length of the* FE *ciphertext, λ is the security parameter and* pPRF *stands for a puncturable* PRF.

How to Read this Paper. Section 2 introduces the standard notations and definitions. Section 2.2 reviews the construction of randomized encodings from branching programs. In Sect. 3 we introduce our scheme and prove the iO based on ADPs' indistinguishability, while in Sect. 4 we provide the security proof. In Appendices A and B we analyse the efficiency of a puncturable PRF's punctured evaluation procedure, as well as of an FE encryption procedure and conclude their punctured evaluation procedure are in NC^1.

2 Background

Notation. An algorithm is equivalent to a Turing machine and receives the security parameter denoted by $\lambda \in \mathbb{N}^*$ in unary representation (denoted by 1^λ). Unless mentioned, an algorithm herein is randomized, and in many cases we use PPT algorithms: their runtime is "probabilistic polynomial-time" in the security parameter. Given an algorithm $\mathcal{A}$ running $\mathcal{A}$ on input(s) $(1^\lambda, x_1, \dots)$ with uniform random coins r and assigning the output(s) to $(y_1, \dots)$ is defined as $(y_1, \dots) \leftarrow_\$ \mathcal{A}(1^\lambda, x_1, \dots; r)$. If $\mathcal{A}$ has access to an oracle $\mathcal{O}$, we write $\mathcal{A}^{\mathcal{O}}$. For $k \in$

$\mathbb{N}^*$, we define $[k] := \{1, \ldots, k\}$; $|S|$ is the cardinality of a finite set S; the action of sampling an uniformly at random element x from X by $x \leftarrow_\$ X$. Bold lowercase variables – $\mathbf{w}$ – represent column vectors and bold upercase matrices – $\mathbf{A}$. A subscript $\mathbf{A}_{i,j}$ indicates an entry in the matrix. A real-valued function $\textsc{Negl}(\lambda)$ is negligible if $\textsc{Negl}(\lambda) \in \mathcal{O}(\lambda^{-\omega(1)})$. $||$ stands for concatenation. Circuits are used to represent (abstract) functions. Unless mentioned, n stands for the input length of the circuit, s for its size and d for its depth.

2.1 Basic Definitions

Definition 1 (Learning with Errors [26]). *Given $q = q(\lambda) \geq 2$ in $\mathbb{N}^*$ and an error distribution $\chi = \chi(\lambda)$ defined on $\mathbb{Z}_q$, the learning-with-errors problem asks to distinguish the following distributions:* $\{(\mathbf{A}, \mathbf{A}^\top \cdot \mathbf{s} + \mathbf{e})\}$ *and* $\{(\mathbf{A}, \mathbf{u})\}$, *where* $\mathbf{A} \leftarrow_\$ \mathbb{Z}_q^{n \times m}, \mathbf{s} \leftarrow_\$ \mathbb{Z}_q^n, \mathbf{e} \leftarrow_\chi \mathbb{Z}_q^m, \mathbf{u} \leftarrow_\$ \mathbb{Z}_q^m$.

Definition 2 (Puncturable PRFs [27]). *A puncturable pseudorandom function* pPRF *is a set of* PPT *procedures* $(\mathsf{pPRF.Setup}, \mathsf{pPRF.Eval}, \mathsf{pPRF.Puncture})$:

$K_{\mathsf{pPRF}} \leftarrow_\$ \mathsf{pPRF.Setup}(1^\lambda)$: *samples K_{pPRF} uniformly at random over keyspace.*
$K^*_{\mathsf{pPRF}} \leftarrow \mathsf{pPRF.Puncture}(K_{\mathsf{pPRF}}, \mathsf{m}^*)$: *given a point m^* from the input space, and K_{pPRF}, returns the punctured key K^*_{pPRF}.*
$Y \leftarrow \mathsf{pPRF.Eval}(K_{\mathsf{pPRF}}, \mathsf{m})$: *returns the output of the pseudorandom function.*

Correctness: *given any $\mathsf{m}^* \in \mathcal{M}$, any $K_{\mathsf{pPRF}} \in \mathcal{K}$ and any $\mathsf{m} \neq \mathsf{m}^* \in \mathcal{M}$:* $\mathsf{pPRF.Eval}(K_{\mathsf{pPRF}}, \mathsf{m}) = \mathsf{pPRF.Eval}(K^*_{\mathsf{pPRF}}, \mathsf{m})$, *where* $K^*_{\mathsf{pPRF}} \leftarrow \mathsf{pPRF.Puncture}(K_{\mathsf{pPRF}}, \mathsf{m}^*)$. *Moreover,* pPRF*'s output distribution is indistinguishable (computationally) from the uniform one. Even when punctured key K^*_{pPRF} is revealed, no* PPT *adversary can distinguish between* $\mathsf{pPRF.Eval}(K_{\mathsf{pPRF}}, \mathsf{m}^*)$ *and* $R \leftarrow_\$ \mathcal{R}$.

Definition 3 (Functional Encryption - Public Key Setting [9]). *A public-key functional encryption scheme* FE *defined for a set of functions* $\{\mathcal{F}_\lambda\}_{\lambda \in N} = \{f : \mathcal{M}_\lambda \to Y_\lambda\}$ *is a tuple of* PPT *algorithms* $(\mathsf{Setup}, \mathsf{KGen}, \mathsf{Enc}, \mathsf{Dec})$:

- $(\mathsf{msk}, \mathsf{mpk}) \leftarrow_\$ \mathsf{FE.Setup}(1^\lambda)$: *for the unary representation of the security parameter λ, a pair of master secret/public keys is released.*
- $\mathsf{sk}_f \leftarrow_\$ \mathsf{FE.KGen}(\mathsf{msk}, f)$: *for the master secret key and a function f taken as input, the key-derivation method releases a corresponding sk_f.*
- $\mathsf{CT} \leftarrow_\$ \mathsf{FE.Enc}(\mathsf{mpk}, \mathsf{m})$: *the encryption method releases a plaintext m corresponding to mpk.*
- $\mathsf{FE.Dec}(\mathsf{CT}, \mathsf{sk}_f)$: *for a ciphertext CT and a functional key sk_f, either a valid message $f(\mathsf{m})$ is released or a an error symbol $\perp$, if decryption fails.*

We say that FE *satisfies correctness if for all* $f : \mathcal{M}_\lambda \to Y_\lambda$:

$$\Pr\left[y = f(M) \,\middle|\, \begin{array}{l} (\mathsf{msk}, \mathsf{mpk}) \leftarrow_\$ \mathsf{FE.Setup}(1^\lambda) \wedge \mathsf{sk}_f \leftarrow_\$ \mathsf{FE.KGen}(\mathsf{msk}, f) \wedge \\ \mathsf{CT} \leftarrow_\$ \mathsf{FE.Enc}(\mathsf{mpk}, \mathsf{m}) \wedge y \leftarrow \mathsf{FE.Dec}(\mathsf{CT}, \mathsf{sk}_f) \end{array}\right] = 1 - \textsc{Negl}(\lambda) .$$

We call a scheme selectively indistinguishably secure if for any PPT *adversary* $\mathcal{A}$, $\mathbf{Adv}^{\mathsf{s\text{-}IND\text{-}FE\text{-}CPA}}_{\mathcal{A},\mathsf{FE}}(\lambda) := |\Pr[\mathsf{s\text{-}IND\text{-}FE\text{-}CPA}^{\mathcal{A}}_{\mathsf{FE}}(\lambda) = 1] - \frac{1}{2}|$ *is negligible; the game* s-IND-FE-CPA *is presented in Fig. 1 (left).*

Definition 4 (Indistinguishability Obfuscation [25]**).** *A* PPT *algorithm* iO *is an indistinguishability obfuscator for a class* $\{\mathscr{C}_\lambda\}_{\lambda\in\mathbb{N}^*}$ *if the followings hold:*

- ***Correctness:*** $\Pr\left[\forall x \in \mathcal{D}, \mathscr{C}(x) = \overline{\mathbf{C}}(x) | \overline{\mathbf{C}} \leftarrow_{\$} \mathsf{iO}(\mathscr{C})\right] = 1$.
- ***Indistinguishability:*** *for* $\mathcal{D}$ *the input domain of the circuits* C*, the following quantity is negligible:*

$$\left|\Pr\left[b = b' \,\middle|\, \begin{array}{l}\forall C_1, C_2 \in \{C\}_\lambda \wedge \forall x \in \mathcal{D} : C_1(x) = C_2(x) \wedge \\ b \leftarrow_{\$} \{0,1\} \ \wedge\ \overline{\mathbf{C}} \leftarrow_{\$} \mathsf{iO}(\mathscr{C}_b) \wedge b' \leftarrow_{\$} \mathcal{A}(1^\lambda, \overline{\mathbf{C}}, \mathscr{C}_0, \mathscr{C}_1)\end{array}\right] - \frac{1}{2}\right|$$

$b \leftarrow_{\$} \{0,1\}$ $\mathsf{L} \leftarrow \emptyset$ $(\mathsf{m}_0, \mathsf{m}_1, \mathsf{state}) \leftarrow_{\$} \mathcal{A}(1^\lambda)$ $(\mathsf{mpk}, \mathsf{msk}) \leftarrow_{\$} \mathsf{FE.Setup}(1^\lambda)$ $\mathsf{CT}^* \leftarrow_{\$} \mathsf{FE.Enc}(\mathsf{mpk}, \mathsf{m}_b)$ $b' \leftarrow_{\$} \mathcal{A}^{\mathsf{KGenO}_{\mathsf{msk}}(\cdot)}(1^\lambda, \mathsf{mpk}; \mathsf{state})$ if $\exists f \in \mathsf{L}$ s.t. $f(\mathsf{m}_0) \neq f(\mathsf{m}_1)$: return 0 return $b = b'$ Proc. $\mathsf{KGenO}_{\mathsf{msk}}(f)$: $\mathsf{L} \leftarrow \mathsf{L} \cup \{f\}$ $\mathsf{sk}_f \leftarrow_{\$} \mathsf{FE.KGen}(\mathsf{msk}, f)$ return sk_f	$\mathsf{PRF}^{\mathcal{A}}_{\mathsf{PRF}}(\lambda)$: $b \leftarrow_{\$} \{0,1\}$; $\mathsf{L} \leftarrow \emptyset$ $K \leftarrow_{\$} \mathsf{Setup}(1^\lambda)$ $b' \leftarrow_{\$} \mathcal{A}^{\mathsf{Prf}(\cdot)}(1^\lambda)$ **return** $(b' \stackrel{?}{=} b)$ Proc. $\mathsf{Prf}(\mathsf{m})$: **if** $\mathsf{m} \in \mathsf{L}$ **then return** $\mathsf{L}[\mathsf{m}]$ $Y \leftarrow \mathsf{PRF}(K, \mathsf{m})$ **if** $b = 0$ **then** $Y \leftarrow_{\$} \{0,1\}^{\lvert Y \rvert}$ $\mathsf{L} \leftarrow \mathsf{L} \cup \{(\mathsf{m}, Y)\}$ **return** Y

Fig. 1. Security for pseudorandom functions (right), as well as FE security (left).

2.2 Direct ADPs from Randomized Encodings

Definition 5 (Affine Determinant Programs [6]**).** *Given the input length* n *and dimension* m*, an affine determinant program over* $\mathbb{F}_p$ *has two algorithms:*

$\mathsf{Prog} \leftarrow_{\$} \mathsf{ADP.Setup}(1^\lambda, \mathscr{C})$: *the* Setup *is a randomized algorithm s.t. given a circuit description* $\mathscr{C}$ *of a function* f *with* $\mathscr{C} : \{0,1\}^n \rightarrow \{0,1\}$*, outputs a set of* $n+1$ *matrices as the* ADP *program:* $\mathsf{Prog} := (\mathbf{T}_0,\ \mathbf{T}_1,\ \ldots,\ \mathbf{T}_n) \in \mathbb{F}_p^{m\times m}$.

$b \leftarrow \mathsf{ADP.Eval}(\mathsf{Prog}, \mathsf{inp})$: *is a deterministic procedure, that given the program* Prog *and some input* m*, returns a binary value* b*, defined as:*

$$b := \det\left(\mathbf{T}_0 + \sum_{i=1}^{n} \mathsf{inp}_i \cdot \mathbf{T}_i\right) .$$

Correctness: $\forall \mathsf{m} \in \{0,1\}^n$, $\Pr[\mathscr{C}(\mathsf{m}) = \mathsf{Prog}(\mathsf{m}) | \mathsf{Prog} \leftarrow_\$ \mathsf{ADP.Setup}(\lambda, \mathscr{C})] = 1$

Security: *We say that an* ADP *is* IND-ADP *secure with respect to a class of circuits* $\mathcal{C}_\lambda$, *if* $\forall(\mathscr{C}_1, \mathscr{C}_2) \in \mathcal{C}_\lambda \times \mathcal{C}_\lambda$ *such that* $\forall \mathsf{m} \in \{0,1\}^\lambda \mathscr{C}_1(\mathsf{m}) = \mathscr{C}_2(\mathsf{m})$, *the following quantity is negligible:*

$$\left| \Pr\left[b \leftarrow_\$ \mathcal{A}(1^\lambda, \mathsf{Prog}) \,\middle|\, b \leftarrow_\$ \{0,1\} \wedge \mathsf{Prog} \leftarrow_\$ \mathsf{ADP.Setup}(1^\lambda, \mathscr{C}_b) \right] - \frac{1}{2} \right|$$

Randomized Encodings through Branching Programs. This part covers the implementation of randomized encodings [21] from branching programs, and recaps the description from [5].

A BP puts forth a method to (sequentially) compute an abstract function (represented as a circuit). Constructing branching programs for circuits is straightforward and largely described in literature [24]. In this work we use only single-bit output functions, but we can view non-boolean functions as concatenations of boolean ones. The branching program itself is (close to) a digraph such that each node has two potential outgoing arcs (except for terminal nodes). Each bit within input is linked to a corresponding node and based on input's value, one out of two corresponding arcs is followed until a terminal node – 0 or 1 – is visited. The value of the terminal node is the function's output for the provided input (that determined a path in digraph). Barrington provides a proof in [4] that the depth of the circuit representation of f is linked to the size of the corresponding branching program.

Set $\mathbf{G}_\mathsf{m}$ to be the adjacency matrix for the branching program corresponding to some $f : \{0,1\}^{|\mathsf{m}|} \to \{0,1\}$. Set the entries in the main diagonal to 1. Note that every row has at most one extra 1 apart from the 1 occurring on the main diagonal. Let $\overline{\mathbf{G}}_\mathsf{m}$ stand for the matrix post-processed by eliminating the first column and the last row within $\mathbf{G}_\mathsf{m}$. In [20] it is shown that $f(\mathsf{m}) = \mathbf{det}(\overline{\mathbf{G}}_\mathsf{m})$. Furthermore, matrices $\mathbf{R}_l$ and $\mathbf{R}_r$ having a special form exist, and the following relation holds:

$$\mathbf{R}_l \cdot \overline{\mathbf{G}}_\mathsf{m} \cdot \mathbf{R}_r = \left(\begin{array}{c|c} \vec{0} & f(\mathsf{m}) \\ \hline -\mathbf{I} & \vec{0} \end{array} \right) = \begin{pmatrix} 0 & 0 & \ldots & 0 & f(\mathsf{m}) \\ -1 & 0 & \ldots & 0 & 0 \\ 0 & -1 & \ldots & 0 & 0 \\ \vdots & \vdots & & \vdots & \vdots \\ 0 & 0 & \ldots & -1 & 0 \end{pmatrix} = \overline{\mathbf{G}}_{f(\mathsf{m})} \in \mathbb{F}_p^{m \times m}$$

This representation of $f(\mathsf{m})$, as a product of two matrices $\mathbf{R}_l$ and $\mathbf{R}_r$, is advantageous when considering randomized encodings' simulation security. Notable, the value $f(\mathsf{m})$ is given to the simulator while it can simulate a product of (1) either full-ranked matrices or (2) of rank $m-1$ matrices. Thus, such a representation is a direct, natural randomized encoding. During the decoding phase of the randomized encoding, the determinant of $\mathbf{R}_l \cdot \overline{\mathbf{G}}_\mathsf{m} \cdot \mathbf{R}_r$ is obtained, allowing to get $f(\mathsf{m})$. Correctness follows given that both $\mathbf{R}_l, \mathbf{R}_r$ are non-singular.

We consider $\mathbf{R}_r, \mathbf{R}_l \in \mathbb{F}_p^{m\times m}$ having the subsequent pattern:

$$\mathbf{R}_l = \begin{pmatrix} 1\,\$\,\$\ldots\$\,\$ \\ 0\,1\,\$\ldots\$\,\$ \\ \vdots\;\vdots\;\vdots\quad\;\vdots\;\vdots \\ 0\,0\,0\ldots1\,\$ \\ 0\,0\,0\ldots0\,1 \end{pmatrix}, \; \mathbf{R}_r = \begin{pmatrix} 1\,0\,0\ldots0\,\$ \\ 0\,1\,0\ldots0\,\$ \\ \vdots\;\vdots\;\vdots\quad\;\vdots\;\vdots \\ 0\,0\,0\ldots1\,\$ \\ 0\,0\,0\ldots0\,1 \end{pmatrix}.$$

To generalize the previous observation, one can use different distributions for $\mathbf{R}_l, \mathbf{R}_r$. Put differently, consider $\mathbf{L} \in \mathbb{F}_p^{m\times m}$ and $\mathbf{R} \in \mathbb{F}_p^{m\times m}$ being sampled uniformly at random over the space of non-singular matrices. We can write them as: $\mathbf{R} \leftarrow \mathbf{R}_r \cdot \mathbf{R}'$ and $\mathbf{L} \leftarrow \mathbf{L}' \cdot \mathbf{R}_l$. Note that:

$$\mathbf{L}\cdot\overline{\mathbf{G}}_{\mathsf{m}}\cdot\mathbf{R} = (\mathbf{L}'\cdot\mathbf{R}_l)\cdot\overline{\mathbf{G}}_{\mathsf{m}}\cdot(\mathbf{R}_r\cdot\mathbf{R}) = \mathbf{L}'\cdot(\mathbf{R}_l\cdot\overline{\mathbf{G}}_{\mathsf{m}}\cdot\mathbf{R}_r)\cdot\mathbf{R} = \mathbf{L}'\cdot\overline{\mathbf{G}}_{f(\mathsf{m})}\cdot\mathbf{R}'$$

Since the matrices $\mathbf{L}'$ and $\mathbf{R}'$ have full-rank, $\det\left(\mathbf{L}\cdot\overline{\mathbf{G}}_{\mathsf{m}}\cdot\mathbf{R}\right) = \det\left(\overline{\mathbf{G}}_{\mathsf{m}}\right) = f(\mathsf{m})$. Also, observe that all entries in the resulting $m \times m$ matrix $\mathbf{T}_{\mathsf{m}} \leftarrow \mathbf{L}\cdot\overline{\mathbf{G}}_{\mathsf{m}}\cdot\mathbf{R}$, can be written as a sum of degree-three monomials. [20] shows that when decomposing every entry within $\mathbf{T}_{i,j}$ in monomials, no monomial depends on more than one input bit of m. Moreover, each monomial has one component stemming from $\mathbf{L}$ and $\mathbf{R}$.

Augmenting NC^1 BPs for Keyed Functions. The next part (Sect. 3) describes how ADPs can be used to instantiate iO. We will not use ADPs directly as described before. We will first apply transformations at the branching program level resulting in an "augmented" branching program, taken from [5] and described herein. The nuts and bolts of "augmented ADP" may be used only in the indistinguishability proof for ADPs, while Sect. 3 needs only the interface of ADPs – so they can regarded as black-box objects enjoying indistinguishability (Definition 5).

Nimvs and Augmenting BPs. [5] puts forth a method to *augment* a branching program with a set of intermediate nodes. This step is done without changing the underlying function's behaviour. The reason for doing so is to isolate the "sensitive" variables – called *non-input mutable variables* or nimv. For the problem of building iO, nimv should be imagined as pPRFs keys, m, ρ or c, or any other variables on which ADPs may differ while preserving their functionality. Hiding such variables is instrumental in constructing iO.

Consider the branching program BP that implements a bivariate function $f(\mathsf{nimv}, \mathsf{inp})$ that is represented as a circuit by $\mathscr{C}(\mathsf{nimv}||\mathsf{inp})$; BP's directed acyclic graph representation has two complementary sets of nodes: the first contains the vertices depending on nimv, the second contains vertices linked to input (the message inp). Any other non-terminal vertex – if any – that is not linked to input is added to the first set. Moreover, the nimvs are hardcoded (i.e. fixed) to some values. This hardcoding step implies that all nodes depending on nimv in BP are assigned a binary value.

The augmented branching program is simply a BP that has an additional ensemble of nodes injected into its original graph.

Auxiliary Nodes. The transform proposed in [5] concerns auxiliary nodes. Given v a vertex settled by bit in some nimv variable's binary representation, and let u stand for another vertex s.t. an arc $v \to u$ exists in the graph representation of the BP. The digraph's structure is changed (augmented) by injecting an auxiliary node α between v and u, such that v is no longer directly connected to u. The path between the two variables becomes $v \to \alpha \to u$.

Definition 6 (Augmented branching programs for circuits in NC^1 with auxiliary nodes [5]), *Let* BP *be the branching program corresponding to some circuit* $\mathscr{C}_{\mathsf{nimv}} \in \mathsf{NC}^1$ *that embeds* nimv. *Let* $\mathcal{V}$ *denote the set of vertices settled by* nimv. *For each vertex* $v \in \mathcal{V}$ *let* u *be a vertex such that there exists an arc from* v *to* u. *A branching program augmented with auxiliary nodes* ABP *is defined by extending the* BP *graph and introducing an intermediate vertex* α *on the path between any node* v *depending on* nimv *and any child vertex* u.

It can be noted that using auxiliary nodes to augment a branching program upholds its correctness. Over $\mathbb{F}_2$ computing the determinant (in order to evaluate the ADP) is in fact a sum of $m!$ permutations. Given that a path originating in the start vertex and ending in the terminal node 1 exists, it must be the case that this path as well as the 1s placed on the second diagonal will force one of the $m!$ sums appearing in the explicit determinant formulation to be 1.

Related to the size of the augmented branching program, [5] notes an upper bound of $3 \cdot |\mathsf{BP}|$. This happens because every nimv-dependent node injects two other nodes, the number of nodes being at most triple.

The primary advantage offered by auxiliary nodes is a way to decouple the nimv dependent rows (or columns) appearing within the randomizing matrices $\mathbf{R}$ (or $\mathbf{L}$), from the other nodes. To see this, when the post-processed augmented matrix $\overline{\mathbf{G}}$ (obtained from ABP) gets multiplied with $\mathbf{R}$, the rows of $\mathbf{R}$ triggered by nimv-depending variables are isolated from the rows within $\mathbf{R}$ that depend on input inp. Somehow similarly, the columns of $\mathbf{L}$ can be partitioned in three disjoint sets: columns that are triggered by nimv, the inp or the auxiliary variables (there is an *asymmetry* to the splitting of rows in the randomizing matrix $\mathbf{R}$ – we only split its lines in two disjoint sets).

3 Our Indistinguishability Obfuscator

Definition 7. *Let* $C_{d,g} : \{0,1\}^n \to \{0,1\}^t$ *stand for a class of circuits having depth* d, *size* g, *input length* n *and output length* t. *Let* $\mathsf{Uc}^{d,g}_{d',g'}$ *stand for a universal circuit supporting the evaluation of circuits of depth* $\leq d$ *and gates* $\leq g$ *and itself having depth* d' *and* g' *gates. Let* FE *denote a functional encryption scheme for a class of circuits* $C_{d',g'} : \{0,1\}^{n+\mathsf{poly}(d',g')} \to \{0,1\}^t$ *having depth* d' *and gates* g'. *Let* ℓ *stand for the size of a ciphertext of* FE. *Assume the encryption procedure of* FE *can be described by an* NC^1 *circuit. Let* pPRF *stand for a puncturable pseudorandom function keyed by* k *and having its length of output matching the length of* FE*'s encryption randomness term. Let* ADP *denote an affine* *determinant program supporting circuits matching the depth and width of* FE*'s encryption procedure. The following construction represents an* iO*-obfuscator for circuits in class $C_{d,g}$.*

iO.Setup($1^\lambda, \mathscr{C}$): *Let* m *stand for the representation of $\mathscr{C}$ as a binary string. Consider the decomposition of an* FE *ciphertext into ℓ components. For every $j \in [\ell]$, consider the circuit described in Fig. 2.*

1. *Sample* (msk, mpk)$\leftarrow_\$$ FE.Setup($1^{g'}, 1^{d'}$). *Set* $\rho \leftarrow 2^n - 1$.
2. *Compute* $c \leftarrow_\$$ FE.Enc(mpk, m$||2^n - 1$).
3. *Sample a* pPRF *key* $\mathsf{k}_{\mathsf{pPRF}}$ *and puncture it in a random point* $0||\$$.
4. *For each j in $[\ell]$, run* ADP.Setup$\left(1^\lambda, \mathscr{C}^j_{\mathsf{mpk},\mathsf{k}_{\mathsf{pPRF}},\mathsf{m},\perp,\rho,c}\right)$ *and obtain* ADP^j.
5. *Run* FE.KGen(msk, Uc) *and obtain* $\mathsf{sk}_{\mathsf{Uc}}$.
6. *Return* $\left(\mathsf{sk}_{\mathsf{Uc}}, \{\mathsf{ADP}^j\}_{j\in[\ell]}\right)$.

iO.Eval(inp):

1. *For each j in $[\ell]$, evaluate* ADP^j.Eval(inp) *and obtain* CT^j.
2. *Run* FE.Dec($\mathsf{sk}_{\mathsf{Uc}}, \mathsf{CT}^1||\ldots||\mathsf{CT}^\ell$).

Proposition 1 (Correctness). *The obfuscator in Definition 7 is correct.*

Proof (Proposition 1).

$$\begin{aligned}\mathsf{iO.Eval(inp)} &= \mathsf{FE.Dec}(\mathsf{sk}_{\mathsf{Uc}}, \mathsf{ADP}^1.\mathsf{Eval(inp)}||\ldots||\mathsf{ADP}^\ell.\mathsf{Eval(inp)} = ||_{i=1}^\ell \mathsf{ADP}^i.\mathsf{Eval(inp)})\\ &= \mathsf{FE.Dec}(\mathsf{sk}_{\mathsf{Uc}}, ||_{i=1}^\ell \mathsf{ADP}^i.\mathsf{Eval}(\mathsf{FE.Enc}(\mathsf{mpk}, \mathscr{C}||\mathsf{inp}; \mathsf{pPRF}(\mathsf{k}, \mathsf{inp}))))\\ &= \mathsf{FE.Dec}(\mathsf{sk}_{\mathsf{Uc}}, \mathsf{FE.Enc}(\mathsf{mpk}, \mathscr{C}||\mathsf{inp}; \mathsf{pPRF}(\mathsf{k}, \mathsf{inp}))) = \mathsf{Uc}(\mathscr{C}||\mathsf{inp}) = \mathscr{C}(\mathsf{inp}) = f(\mathsf{inp})\ .\end{aligned}$$

$\mathscr{C}^j_{\mathsf{mpk},\mathsf{k},\mathsf{m},\perp,\rho,c}(b||i)$:

if $b = 0$: return 0
if $i < \rho$: return $\mathsf{FE}_j.\mathsf{Enc}(\mathsf{mpk}, \mathsf{m}||i; \mathsf{pPRF}(\mathsf{k}, 1||i))$
if $i = \rho$: return c
if $i > \rho$: return $\mathsf{FE}_j.\mathsf{Enc}(\mathsf{mpk}, \perp||i; \mathsf{pPRF}(\mathsf{k}, 1||i))$

Fig. 2. The circuit outputs (bits of) a functional encryption (FE) ciphertext. ρ is a limit set to $2^n - 1$. The main input range is $\{0,1\}^n$, artificially extended by 1.

4 Security of Our iO Scheme

The proof is akin to the one published in [25]. Its structure can be summarized as follows: we hybridize over every single input inp taken over $\{0,1\}^n$ (which incurs an exponential security loss in n). For each input, we will: i) use the indistinguishability of ADP to switch the pPRF key to one[4] punctured in $1||\mathsf{inp}$;

[4] This happens once for all of the $[\ell]$ circuits.

ii) then, based on pPRF indistinguishability, we switch the pPRF's value in the punctured point to true randomness[5]; iii) then based on FE's indistinguishability we switch to an FE ciphertext corresponding to $\mathsf{m}_1||\mathsf{inp}$, where m_1 is the binary representation of $\mathscr{C}_1$; iv) we then revert the changes, and switch the random coins back to the ones generated by the pPRF under a key punctured in inp; v) finally, we use the ADP's indistinguishability to switch back the punctured key and also decrease the limit ρ.

Theorem 2 (iO-Security). *The obfuscator presented in Definition 7 reaches indistinguishability, as per Definition 4.*

Proof (Theorem 2). The proof follows through a standard hybrid argument. We present the hybrid games and then provide the reductions that justify the transitions between these distributions.

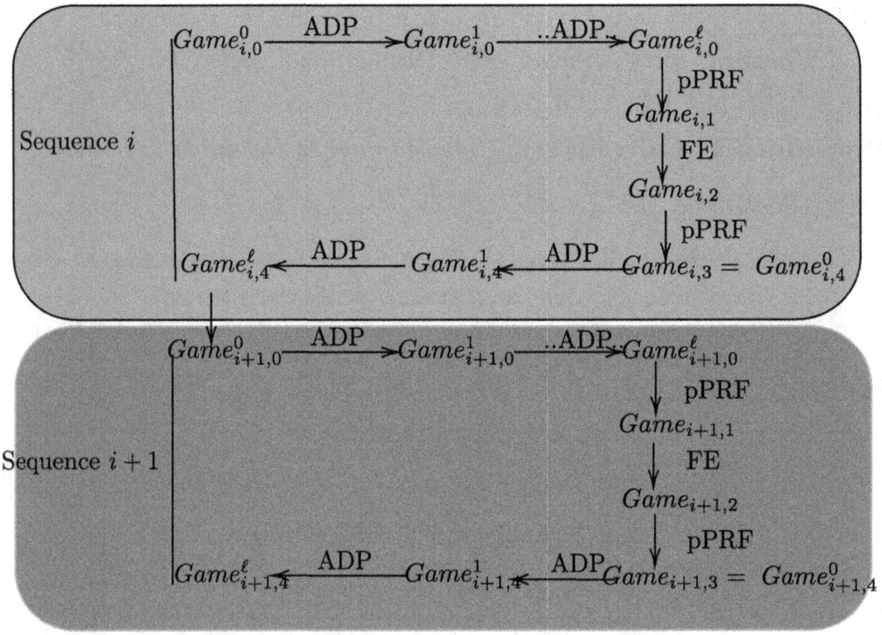

Game_0: the real game corresponding to $\mathscr{C}_0$ encoded as m_0. Identical to $\mathsf{Game}_{1,0}$.

$\mathsf{Game}^0_{i,0}$: identical to $\mathsf{Game}_{i,0}$. In forthcoming games, i indexes elements of set $[2^n - 1]$.

$\mathsf{Game}^j_{i,0}$: for all $j \in [\ell]$ using ADP's indistingishability, replace the pPRF key k (punctured in $0||\$$) with a key punctured in $1||(2^n - i)$.

$\mathsf{Game}_{i,1}$: based on pPRF's security in the punctured point, replace the actual pPRF's value used to compute FE's ciphertext c in the challenge point with an actual truly randomly sampled value r.

[5] Note that the output corresponding to the challenge inp is an FE ciphertext encrypting $\mathscr{C}_0||\mathsf{inp}$.

$\mathsf{Game}_{i,2}$: based on FE's indistinguishability, replace the FE ciphertext c corresponding to the challenge point with a ciphertext encrypting $\mathsf{m}_1 := \mathscr{C}_1$.

$\mathsf{Game}_{i,3}$: is the inverse of $\mathsf{Game}_{i,1}$.

$\mathsf{Game}^j_{i,4}$: is the inverse of $\mathsf{Game}^j_{i,0}$ (the punctured key is replaced by k, and the limit ρ is decreased to $2^n - (i+1)$.

$\mathsf{Game}^\ell_{2^n-1,4}$: is the last game in the sequence, where the ciphertext corresponds to $\mathsf{m}_1 := \mathscr{C}_1$ and the limit ρ is 0.

$\mathsf{Game}_{\mathsf{final}}$: based on ADP's indistinguishability, we switch the places between m_0 and m_1 and replace ρ's value of 0 with $2^n - 1$.

We prove the transitions between each pair of consecutive hybrids.

$\mathsf{Game}^{j-1}_{i,0} \rightarrow \mathsf{Game}^j_{i,0}$: for any $j \in [\ell]$, in $\mathsf{Game}^{j-1}_{i,0}$ the circuit will compute the jth-bit of the FE ciphertexts using k, a punctured key punctured in $0||\$$; while in $\mathsf{Game}^j_{i,0}$, a punctured key punctured in $1||(2^n - i)$ is going to be used. The two circuits are equivalent due to the functional preservation under punctured keys of a puncturable PRF as well as due to the fact that in the challenge point, the ciphertext is computed using the normal key. Formally, the reduction algorithm $\mathcal{B}$ crafts the two functionally-equivalent circuits, sends them to the ADP challenger, and receives an ADP-obfuscated version of one of them. The received version stands for the jth ADP that is sent to the adversary $\mathcal{A}_1$. The adversary $\mathcal{A}_1$ impersonates an iO distinguisher, and returns its guess b (that is next returned by $\mathcal{B}$ to the security experiment). Clearly, the simulation is perfect and the winning advantage against the hybrid transition is identical to the advantage against ADP's indistinguishability.

$\mathsf{Game}^\ell_{i,0} \rightarrow \mathsf{Game}_{i,1}$: in this setting, the punctured key used by the ℓ circuits is punctured in the input point $1||(2^n - i)$. The hardcoded ciphertext corresponding to $\rho = 2^n - i$ cannot be computed without the challenge value received from the pPRF game. Our reduction $\mathcal{B}$ takes from the pPRF game: i) a key punctured in $1||(2^n - i)$ and ii) a value corresponding to point $1||(2^n - i)$ which is either sampled uniformly at random or generated using the normal pPRF key. The reduction $\mathcal{B}$ uses challenge value to build the FE ciphertext in ρ and the punctured key in $1||(2^n - i)$ to further build all ADPs, which is perfectly possible. The set of ADPs as well as the FE functional key are then sent to the adversary $\mathcal{A}$ that outputs a guess b, which is $\mathcal{B}$'s guess. As for the previous case, the reduction is tight. Note that in adversary's view, both iO obfuscators are functionally equivalent, as decrypting FE ciphertexts generated under different random coins will provide the same result.

$\mathsf{Game}_{i,1} \rightarrow \mathsf{Game}_{i,2}$: we use the indistinguishability of the functional encryption to switch the encoded message, which should correspond to $\mathscr{C}_1$ for the challenge input. The reduction $\mathcal{B}$ will receive the mpk, $\mathsf{sk}_{\mathsf{Uc}}$, will construct the challenge ciphertext corresponding to $\rho = 2^n - i$. It will sample on its own the pPRF keys and build the ADPs. The resulting obfuscator represents the input to the adversary. Clearly, if the adversary distinguishes with non-negligible probability, the same will do $\mathcal{B}$.

$\underline{\mathsf{Game}^{\ell}_{i,2} \rightarrow \mathsf{Game}_{i,3}}$: is virtually the inverse of the transition between $\mathsf{Game}^{\ell}_{i,0}$ and $\mathsf{Game}_{i,1}$.

$\underline{\mathsf{Game}_{i,3} \rightarrow \mathsf{Game}^{0}_{i,4}}$: these games are identical.

$\underline{\mathsf{Game}^{j-1}_{i,4} \rightarrow \mathsf{Game}^{j}_{i,4}}$: is almost the inverse of the transition between $\mathsf{Game}^{j-1}_{i,0}$ and $\mathsf{Game}^{j}_{i,0}$, up to the difference that the limit ρ is decreased by 1 and a ciphertext corresponding to m_0 is computed for this position $\rho - 1$. Clearly the two settings are identical, as for inputs $(\rho - 1, \rho)$ the first ADP outputs the ciphertexts corresponding to $(\mathsf{m}_0, \mathsf{m}_1)$, while the ADPs in the other setting outputs ciphertexts corresponding exactly to the same pair $(\mathsf{m}_0, \mathsf{m}_1)$.

In the last but one game, the circuit will have $\rho = 0$. We do an extra game hop and will output only ciphertexts corresponding to m_1 (and thus $\mathscr{C}_1$). We add the extra hybrid that switches ρ back to $2^n - 1$ and inverses m_0 and m_1. Clearly this follows from ADP indistinguishability.

We apply the union bound and conclude that the advantage of any PPT adversary $\mathcal{A} = (\mathcal{A}_1, \mathcal{A}_2, \mathcal{A}_3)$ is upper bounded by: $\mathbf{Adv}^{\mathsf{IND}}_{\mathcal{A},\mathsf{iO}}(\lambda) \leq 2^n \cdot \Big((2\ell + 1) \cdot \mathbf{Adv}^{\mathsf{IND\text{-}ADP}}_{\mathcal{A}_1,\mathsf{ADP}}(\lambda) + \mathbf{Adv}^{\mathsf{s\text{-}IND\text{-}FE\text{-}CPA}}_{\mathcal{A}_2,\mathsf{FE}}(\lambda) + 2 \cdot \mathbf{Adv}^{\mathsf{puncture}}_{\mathcal{A}_3,\mathsf{pPRF}}(\lambda)\Big) + \mathbf{Adv}^{\mathsf{IND\text{-}ADP}}_{\mathcal{A}_1,\mathsf{ADP}}(\lambda)$. This completes the proof. □

Instantiation from Learning With Errors. Somehow expected, the primitives used herein are realizable from the sub-exponentially secure Learning with Errors assumption. Universal circuits able to evaluate circuits of the same depth exists unconditionally. Puncturable PRFs can be realized from LWE, by referring to a work of Brakerski and Vaikuntanathan that builds single-key constrained PRFs [11,12] (thus puncturable PRFs) where the evaluation is in NC^1. Sub-exponentially secure LWE suffices to instantiate succinct single-key functional encryption [1,17].

5 ADPs as Depleted Obfuscators

In our view, indistinguishability obfuscation is related to hiding structure for circuits. The goals are similar for ADPs: preserve the structure/topology while "shielding" the nimvs. Given the *lack* of average-case assumptions related to ADPs, our work considers a different approach – perfect security[6]:

$$\mathsf{ADP.Setup}(1^\lambda, \mathscr{C}_{\mathsf{nimv}_0}; R_0) = \mathsf{ADP.Setup}(1^\lambda, \mathscr{C}_{\mathsf{nimv}_1}; R_1) \tag{4}$$

The equation above states that for any random coins R_0 used during the ADP.Setup w.r.t. circuit $\mathscr{C}_0$, there is a term R_1 that can be used by ADP.Setup to produce the same program output, but with respect to $\mathscr{C}_1$. [5] puts forth a

[6] Note that this approach will **not** provide a perfectly secure obfuscator (which is impossible), the scheme relying on the security of FE and puncturable PRFs.

series of requirements on the function considered[7] which, if fulfilled, would have been sufficient to prove the security of IND-ADP. These conditions are to be introduced below, all but the 6th being unchanged. Formally, we have to assume the existence of IND-ADP-secure programs for circuit classes fulfilling the conditions below[8]. Caveat: the circuit description has input length incremented by 1.

Assumption 1 (Informal). *Let* $f : \{0,1\}^{|\mathsf{nimv}|+n} \rightarrow \{0,1\}$ *denote a binary function and let* $\mathfrak{C}_{d,|\mathsf{nimv}|+(n+1)}$ *stand for a class of circuits of depth d with input length* $|\mathsf{nimv}| + (n+1)$*, satisfying conditions (1)* $\rightarrow$ *(6) below:*

> ***Condition 1.*** *Every* $\mathscr{C} \in \mathfrak{C}_{d,|\mathsf{nimv}|+(n+1)}$ *implements the two-input function* $f : \{0,1\}^{|\mathsf{nimv}|+n} \rightarrow \{0,1\}$.
>
> ***Condition 2.*** *A condition for* $\mathfrak{C}_{d,|\mathsf{nimv}|+(n+1)}$ *to admit a* IND-ADP*-secure implementation is* $d \in O(\log_2(|\mathsf{nimv}| + (n+1)))$.
>
> ***Condition 3.*** *For every* $\mathscr{C} \in \mathfrak{C}_{d,|\mathsf{nimv}|+(n+1)}$ *implementing some* $f : \{0,1\}^{|\mathsf{nimv}|+n} \rightarrow \{0,1\}$*, there exists a* PPT *algorithm* $\mathcal{R}$ *such that:*
>
> $$\Pr\left[\mathscr{C}(|\mathsf{nimv}|, \mathsf{inp}) = 1 \middle| (|\mathsf{nimv}|, \mathsf{inp}) \leftarrow \mathcal{R}(1^\lambda, \mathscr{C})\right] > \frac{1}{\mathsf{poly}(|\mathsf{nimv}| + (n+1))} .$$
>
> ***Condition 4.*** *For every* $\mathscr{C} \in \mathfrak{C}_{d,|\mathsf{nimv}|+(n+1)}$ *modelling some f, there exists a* PPT *algorithm* $\mathcal{R}$ *such that* $\forall\ \mathsf{inp} \in \{0,1\}^{(n+1)}$, $\Pr[\mathsf{nimv} \neq \mathsf{nimv}' \wedge \mathscr{C}(\mathsf{nimv}, \mathsf{inp}) = \mathscr{C}(\mathsf{nimv}', \mathsf{inp}) | (\mathsf{nimv}, \mathsf{nimv}') \leftarrow \mathcal{R}(1^\lambda, f)] > \frac{1}{\mathsf{poly}(|\mathsf{nimv}|+(n+1))}$.
>
> ***Condition 5.*** *For every* $\mathscr{C} \in \mathfrak{C}_{d,|\mathsf{nimv}|+(n+1)}$ *modelling some* $f : \{0,1\}^{|\mathsf{nimv}|+n} \rightarrow \{0,1\}$*, there exists and is "easy to find"* nimv *such that:*
>
> $$\mathscr{C}(\mathsf{nimv}, b||\mathsf{inp}') := \begin{cases} 1\ , & \text{if } b = 0. \\ f(\mathsf{nimv}, \mathsf{inp}')\ , & \text{if } b = 1 \text{ and } \forall \mathsf{inp}' \in \{0,1\}^n \end{cases} .$$
>
> ***Condition 6.*** *Considering the underlying branching program representation of some* $\mathscr{C} \in \mathfrak{C}_{d,|\mathsf{nimv}|+(n+1)})$*, on any local path, any index of a vertex depending on input is greater than any index of a vertex depending on* nimv*.*

We assume there is an IND-ADP*-secure* ADP *for the class* $\mathfrak{C}_{d,|\mathsf{nimv}|+(n+1)}$.

We note that the first four requirements above are fulfilled by any circuit representation that: (1) represents a bivariate function, (2) is in NC^1, (3) represents a non-constant function and (4) is functionally equivalent to a circuit built under different nimvs. The fifth condition is needed in order to ensure the existence of well-defined inverse matrices for ADPs, while the most challenging part is achieving (6). In the forthcoming part we put forward a new transform that produces augmented BPs respecting constraints (5) and (6) having its purpose to allow an indistinguishability proof to go through. We present below a transformation that allows to tackle condition (6) above.

---

[7] E.g., it should be non-zero, a finding independently meeting an earlier result of [18].

[8] This part is included from a different work and has not yet been peer reviewed.

Flare Vertices. A second transform, similar to auxiliary nodes, introduced herein is to inject *flare* vertices. The purpose is to handle node ordering constraints on each of BP's paths. We consider the following problem: (1) take BP's structure augmented with auxiliary vertices; (2) choose any vertex that depends on nimvs; (3) choose any path that visits the nimv-dependent vertex from step (2); (4) enforce that on the path chosen in (3), no vertices that depend on inp-dependent vertices appear "before" vertices that depend on nimvs. Equivalently, on any local path, all low-indexed vertices must be linked to nimvs (similarly for auxiliary nodes) and all high-indexed nodes must be linked to inp dependent nodes. This is done by injecting artificial vertices that redirect to the terminal node 1, whenever the condition stated above fails. To restore the "normal evaluation mode", we add complementary arcs when summing up the matrix $\overline{\mathbf{G}}_1$ (that corresponds to the first input bit) to the base matrix $\overline{\mathbf{G}}_0$. This observation is made precise in what follows.

Take any path within the BP, and consider 3 non-empty lists of vertices $\mathtt{L}_1$, $\mathtt{L}_2$, $\mathtt{L}_3$. $\mathtt{L}_1$ includes only vertices linked to nimvs or auxiliary vertices, $\mathtt{L}_2$ includes only vertices linked to inputs, and $\mathtt{L}_3$ includes only vertices linked to nimvs or auxiliary vertices like $\mathtt{L}_1$. Assume that there is an arc between any two pair of neighbour vertices occurring in $\mathtt{L}_1$ (resp. $\mathtt{L}_2$ and $\mathtt{L}_3$); furthermore assume that arc between the last vertex in $\mathtt{L}_1$ and the first vertex in $\mathtt{L}_2$ exists; assume that an arc between the last vertex in $\mathtt{L}_2$ and the first vertex in $\mathtt{L}_3$ (thus a "path") exists. We introduce a natural ordering relation of vertices within BP: $v_i \prec v_j$ holds iff $i < j$. This ordering relationship is extended to paths and such that $\mathtt{L}_1 \prec \mathtt{L}_2$ iff $\max\{\mathsf{index}(v) : v \in \mathtt{L}_1\} < \min\{\mathsf{index}(v) : v \in \mathtt{L}_2\}$. According to the ordering defined above, every vertex in $\mathtt{L}_1$ has a lower index than any vertex in $\mathtt{L}_2$, and this transitive relation is kept amongst $\mathtt{L}_2$ and $\mathtt{L}_3$. We decouple vertices in $\mathtt{L}_2$ from the vertices in $\mathtt{L}_3$. We introduce flares, after each "ending" vertex from $\mathtt{L}_2$. An "ending" vertex $v \in \mathtt{L}_2$ is a vertex that has an arc to some node $v' \in \mathtt{L}_3$. Flare nodes $\mathit{fl}^1, \mathit{fl}^0$ depending on input bit in position 1 are introduced s.t. the following arcs exist: $v \to \mathit{fl}^0 \to 1$ and $v \to \mathit{fl}^1 \to v'$. In layman terms, *fl* acts as an "electrical" switch: whenever the first bit in inp is 1, fl^1 enables the normal BP evaluation flow; whenever the first bit in inp is 0, fl^0 redirects the flow to the terminal node 1 – thus skipping the real function evaluation.

Definition 8 (Augmented branching programs for circuits in NC^1 with flare nodes). *Let* BP *be the branching program corresponding to some circuit* $\mathscr{C}_{nimv} \in \mathsf{NC}^1$ *that embeds nimv. Let* $\prec$ *denote a node ordering relation. Let* L_1, L_3 *denote lists of increasingly ordered vertices settled by* nimv *and auxiliary nodes. Let* L_2 *be an ordered list of nodes that are settled by inputs. Let* $L_1 \prec L_2 \prec L_3$ *such that the relation is applied vertex-wise. For any node* v *in* L_2 *such that* $v \to v'$ *and* $v' \notin L_2$ *introduce a node* fl^0 *such that* $v \to \mathit{fl}^0 \to 1$*. Introduce* $\mathit{fl}^1 \to v'$*. Let the node* fl^b *be triggered by the value* b *of the first input bit.*

Finally, the first input bit will be linked to a dummy node. Therefore, the arity of ADP is artificially increased by 1. When the ADP is evaluated such that the first, artificial, input bit is 0 the output is 1; when changing the first input bit to 1 we use the normal evaluation mode.

Related to the size, similarly to auxiliary nodes, it can be noted that adding flares preserves the polynomial size of the BP, the increase can be loosely upper bounded by twice the size of the ABP already augmented with auxiliary nodes.

A Puncturable PRFs with Evaluations in NC^1

In this part, we provide evidence that a particular version of the constrained PRF from [11] – namely the "toy" puncturable PRF informally introduced by Boneh, Kim and Montgomery in [8, Section 1] – admits an NC^1 circuit representation of the evaluation function. This informal scheme is chosen for space reasons, and also for simplicity (avoiding the usage of universal circuits in its description). The notations that are used in this part are as follows: $|\mathsf{inp}|$ stands for the length of the input string, λ stands for the security parameter, n and m stand for the dimensions of the matrix used in the construction, q stand for the LWE modulus.

<u>$\mathsf{pPRF.Setup}(1^\lambda, 1^{|\mathsf{inp}|})$:</u> given the unary description of the security parameter λ:

1. Sample acolumn vector: $\mathbf{s} \leftarrow_{\$} \mathbb{Z}_q^n$.
2. Sample $|\mathsf{inp}|$ matrices $\mathbf{B}_i$ of dimensions $n \times m$ uniformly at random over $\mathbb{Z}_q^{n\times m}$, for all $i \in [|\mathsf{inp}|]$. That is: $\mathbf{B}_i \leftarrow_{\$} \mathbb{Z}_q^{n\times m}$.
3. Sample 2 matrices $\mathbf{A}_0, \mathbf{A}_1$ as before: $(\mathbf{A}_0, \mathbf{A}_1) \leftarrow_{\$} \left(\mathbb{Z}_q^{n\times m}, \mathbb{Z}_q^{n\times m}\right)$.
4. Set as secret key: $\mathsf{k} \leftarrow \left(\mathbf{s},\ \mathbf{B}_1,\ \ldots,\ \mathbf{B}_{|\mathsf{inp}|},\ \mathbf{A}_0,\ \mathbf{A}_1\right)$.

<u>$\mathsf{pPRF.Eval}(\mathsf{k}, \mathsf{inp})$:</u> To evaluate input inp under pPRF key k, proceed as follows

1. Use the $\mathsf{PK}_{\mathsf{Eval}}$ evaluation algorithm from [11] (detailed below) in order to publicly compute a matrix $\mathbf{A}_{\mathsf{eq}}$.
2. Compute: $Y \leftarrow \mathbf{s}^\top \cdot \mathbf{A}_{\mathsf{eq}}$.
3. Return $\lfloor Y \rceil$, where $\lfloor \cdot \rceil$ is a rounding function: $\lfloor \cdot \rceil : \mathbb{Z}_q \to \mathbb{Z}_p$ that maps $x \to \lfloor x \cdot (p/q) \rceil$, i.e. the argument x is multiplied with p/q and the result is rounded (over reals).

<u>$\mathsf{pPRF.Puncture}(1^\lambda, \mathsf{k}, \mathsf{inp}^*)$:</u>

1. Return the punctured key for $\mathsf{inp}^* = (\mathsf{inp}_1^*, \ldots, \mathsf{inp}_{|\mathsf{inp}|}^*) \in \{0,1\}^{|\mathsf{inp}|}$ as

$$\mathsf{k}^* \leftarrow \left(\mathsf{inp}^*, \left\{\mathbf{s}^\top \cdot (\mathbf{A}_k + k \cdot \mathbf{G}) + \mathbf{e}_k\right\}_{k\in\{0,1\}}, \left\{\mathbf{s}^\top \cdot (\mathbf{B}_k + \mathsf{inp}_k^* \cdot \mathbf{G}) + \mathbf{e}_k^*\right\}_{k=1}^{|\mathsf{inp}^*|}\right) .$$

<u>$\mathsf{pPRF.PuncEval}(1^\lambda, dk^*, \mathsf{inp})$:</u> To evaluate in the punctured point:

1. Compute the encoding evaluation (detailed below) over the punctured key and obtain Y: $Y \leftarrow \mathbf{s}^\top \cdot (\mathbf{A}_{\mathsf{eq}} + \mathsf{eq}(\mathsf{inp}^*, \mathsf{inp}) \cdot \mathbf{G}) + \mathbf{e}'$.
2. Return $\lfloor Y \rceil$ where $\lfloor \cdot \rceil$ is the same rounding function used by the normal evaluation.

Observe that when $\mathsf{eq}(\mathsf{inp}^*, \mathsf{inp}) = 0$, the value Y computed in punctured evaluation is in fact $\mathbf{s}^\top \cdot \mathbf{A}_{\mathsf{eq}} + \mathbf{e}'$. The correctness and security are based on the constrained PRF scheme from [11], hence we ignore them herein. We focus on the runtime analysis of the punctured evaluation algorithm. In doing so, we need the public and the encoding evaluation algorithm.

A.1 The Encoding Evaluation Algorithm for the pPRF in [11]

Consider a circuit composed from the universal set of gates: AND and NOT.

AND Gates: let $g_{u,v,w}$ be and AND gate, where u and v denote the input wires while w denotes the output. Let $\mathbf{y}_u = \mathbf{s}^\top \cdot (\mathbf{A} + x_u \cdot \mathbf{G}) + \mathbf{u}$ and $\mathbf{y}_v = \mathbf{s}^\top \cdot (\mathbf{A} + x_v \cdot \mathbf{G}) + \mathbf{v}$ where x_u and x_v denote the value of wires u and v corresponding to same input. The evaluation over encodings computes:

$$\mathbf{y}_w \leftarrow x_u \cdot \mathbf{y}_v - \mathbf{y}_u \cdot \mathbf{G}^{-1}(\mathbf{A}_v) \ . \tag{5}$$

which will be a valid encoding corresponding to the value of w.

NOT Gates: we reuse similar notations for gates as per the previous case, with $g_{u,w}$ being a not gate and input wire is u, and $\mathbf{y}_0$ is an encoding corresponding to the value 0:

$$\mathbf{y}_w \leftarrow \mathbf{y}_0 - \mathbf{y}_u \ . \tag{6}$$

A.2 Punctured Evaluation's Parallel Complexity

Here we scrutinize the parallel efficiency of the gate evaluation corresponding to the equality function:

$$\mathsf{eq}(\mathsf{inp}^*, \mathsf{inp}) := \begin{cases} 1, \text{ if } \mathsf{inp} = \mathsf{inp}^* \\ 0, \text{ otherwise} \end{cases} \tag{7}$$

An unoptimized circuit that implements the eq function is built as follows:

1. use a gadget matrix that returns the boolean value of $\mathsf{inp}_i^* \stackrel{?}{=} \mathsf{inp}_i$ for some input position $i \in [|\mathsf{inp}|]$. This gadget matrix can be implemented as

$$\text{NOT}\left((\text{NOT}\left(\mathsf{inp}_i^* \text{AND} \mathsf{inp}_i\right)) \text{ AND } (\text{NOT}\left((\text{NOT } \mathsf{inp}_i^*)\text{AND}(\text{NOT } \mathsf{inp}_i)\right))\right) \tag{8}$$

   Thus the depth of this gadget is 5, and on each of the 5 levels further LWE-related operations are to be performed.
2. use a full-binary tree style of circuit consisting of AND gates that outputs $\bigwedge_{i=1}^{|\mathsf{inp}|}(\mathsf{inp}_i^* \stackrel{?}{=} \mathsf{inp}_i)$. Clearly, this circuit has $\lceil \log_2(|\mathsf{inp}|) \rceil$ levels.

Henceforth, the circuit that computes the evaluation (obtained by applying the construction in step 2 on top of the "gadget" circuit) has depth $\leq c \cdot \log_2(|\mathsf{inp}|)$ for some constant c. The matrix multiplication involved in the computation of an AND gate, the values of $\mathbf{G}^{-1}(\mathbf{A}_0)$ and $\mathbf{G}^{-1}(\mathbf{A}_1)$ can be pre-stored, the costly part being a vector $\times$ matrix multiplication. The inner, LWE-related computations within the punctured evaluation algorithm are in NC^1, as for other constructions using LWE tuples, (see for instance [2]). Further details on the complexity of circuits implementing addition/multiplication for elements in $\mathbb{F}_q$ are given in [23, Section 8]). Thus, we can assume that the there exists puncturable PRFs having their punctured evaluation circuit in NC^1 (as expected, also, by [25]).

B GKPVZ13's Encryption Procedure is in NC^1

In this section, we provide an informal argument for the existence of FE schemes having their encryption procedure in NC^1 (an assumption used in [25]). The notation used herein are independent from the ones used in other sections.

The FE Scheme from [17]**.** Goldwasser *et al.*'s proposal is to regard FE for circuits with a single-bit of output from the perspective of homomorphic operations. Their scheme's *encryption procedure* proceeds as follows: (1) Samples on the fly keys for an FHE scheme – namely $(\mathsf{hpk}, \mathsf{hsk})$ – and encrypts the input m bitwise; let Ψ stand for the FHE ciphertext. (2) Then, the scheme makes use of Yao's garbling protocol GS; this is employed to garble the circuit "$\mathsf{FHE.Dec}(\mathsf{hsk}, \cdot)$" and obtain two labels L_i^0, L_i^1 for each bit in the decomposition of Ψ; (3) Finally, the scheme encrypts Ψ, as well as hpk under a set of ABE public keys (in fact two-outcome ABEs are used). In some sense, Ψ corresponds to an attribute: if $\mathscr{C}_{f_i}(\Psi) = 0$ a label L_i^0 is revealed. Else, the label L_i^1 is returned.

For [17], a *functional key* for a circuit is nothing more than an ABE key issued for the "$\mathsf{FHE.Eval}$" circuit. The trick is that one decrypts an ABE ciphertext with an ABE key; this translates to applying $\mathsf{FHE.Eval}$ over an FHE ciphertext. Given the ABE ciphertext encrypts L_i^0, L_i^1, depending on the output value (a bit b), the label L_i^b is returned. After the labels are recovered, they can be used to feed the garbled circuit (included in the ciphertext); the decryptor evaluates and obtains (informally) $\mathsf{FHE.Dec}(f(\Psi))$, thus yielding the expected output in a functional manner. Therefore, it is natural to set the master keys of the FE scheme as only the ABEs' msk and mpk. The total number of ABE keys to be sampled is determined by the length of the FHE ciphertext.

B.1 Attribute-Based Encryption

When we consider a *key-policy* setting, a decryption key of an ABE must be generated for one Boolean predicate $P : \{0,1\}^\lambda \to \{0,1\}$. A ciphertext of an ABE in this setting is the encryption of a set of attributes α over $\{0,1\}^\lambda$ and of some plaintext $\mathsf{m} \in \{0,1\}^\gamma$. ABE's correctness specifies that having a decryption key enables to recover the plaintext as long as $P(\alpha) = 1$.

Instantiation of ABE. The seminal work of Gorbunov *et al.* [19] puts forward attribute-based encryption schemes for comprehensive classes of circuits. We review their construction, as it will serve in the circuit complexity analysis for this work. Our description is top-down: we describe the ABE scheme, and then review the TOR framework (their Two-to-One Recoding scheme).

Attribute-Based Encryption from General Circuits. A key-policy ABE is presented in [19]. The main idea consists in evaluating on the fly a given circuit. The bitstring representing the attributes – say α – is known *a priori*, as well as the topology of the circuit – say ϕ – to be evaluated.

For each bit α_i in α, there are two public keys associated – say $(\mathsf{mpk}_i^0, \mathsf{mpk}_i^1)$ – corresponding to 0 and 1. A vector $\mathbf{s} \in \mathbb{F}_q^m$ is sampled uniformly at random, and

$\mathsf{FE.Setup}(1^\lambda, n, \ell)$:
$\mathsf{msk} \leftarrow \emptyset$
$\mathsf{mpk} \leftarrow \emptyset$
for $i \leftarrow 1$ **to** ℓ:
  $(\mathsf{mpk}_i, \mathsf{msk}_i) \leftarrow\!\$\ \mathsf{ABE_2.Setup}(1^\lambda)$
  $\mathsf{mpk} \leftarrow \mathsf{mpk} \cup \mathsf{mpk}_i$
  $\mathsf{msk} \leftarrow \mathsf{msk} \cup \mathsf{msk}_i$
return $(\mathsf{msk}, \mathsf{mpk})$

$\mathsf{FE.Enc}(\mathsf{mpk}, \mathsf{m})$:
$(\mathsf{hpk}, \mathsf{hsk}) \leftarrow\!\$\ \mathsf{FHE.Setup}(1^\lambda)$
for $i \leftarrow 1$ **to** n:
  $\Psi_i \leftarrow\!\$\ \mathsf{FHE.Enc}(\mathsf{hpk}, \mathsf{m}_i)$
$\Psi \leftarrow (\Psi_1, \ldots, \Psi_n)$ // Note that $|\Psi| = \ell$
$(\Gamma, L_1^0, L_1^1, \ldots, L_\ell^0, L_\ell^1) \leftarrow\!\$$
  $\leftarrow\!\$\ \mathsf{GS.Garble}(\mathsf{FHE.Dec}(\mathsf{hsk}, \cdot))$
for $i \leftarrow 1$ **to** ℓ:
  $c_i \leftarrow\!\$\ \mathsf{ABE_2.Enc}(\mathsf{mpk}_i, (\mathsf{hpk}, \Psi), L_i^0, L_i^1)$
$\mathsf{CT} \leftarrow (\Gamma, c_1, \ldots, c_\ell)$
return CT

$\mathsf{FE.KGen}(\mathsf{msk}, f)$:
$\mathsf{sk}_f \leftarrow \emptyset$
for $i \leftarrow 1$ **to** ℓ:
  $\mathsf{sk}_i \leftarrow\!\$\ \mathsf{ABE_2.KGen}(\mathsf{msk}_i, \mathsf{FHE.Eval}_f^i)$
  $\mathsf{sk}_f \leftarrow \mathsf{sk}_f \cup \mathsf{sk}_i$
return sk_f

$\mathsf{FE.Dec}(\mathsf{sk}_f, \mathsf{CT})$:
$(\Gamma, c_1, \ldots, c_\ell) \leftarrow \mathsf{CT}$
for $i \leftarrow 1$ **to** ℓ:
  $L_i^{d_i} \leftarrow \mathsf{ABE_2.Dec}(\mathsf{sk}_i, c_i)$
return $\mathsf{GS.Eval}(\Gamma, L_1^{d_1}, \ldots, L_\ell^{d_\ell})$

Fig. 3. In this section, ℓ stands for the FHE's ciphertext's length, while $\mathsf{FHE.Eval}_f^i : \mathcal{K} \times \{0,1\}^{n \cdot \ell} \to \{0,1\}$ stands for a function that applies $\mathscr{C}_f$ on the encrypted input.

encoded under the $\mathsf{mpk}_i^{\alpha_i}$ as $\mathsf{mpk}_i^{\alpha_i} \cdot \mathbf{s} + \text{noise}$. Then, the circuit ϕ is evaluated on these encodings. The crux point consists of a **recoding** procedure, which ensures that at the next level, $\mathbf{s}$ is "recoded" under the next public key corresponding to the current gate. By keeping evaluating in such a way, the final output will be an encoding of $\mathbf{s}$ under a circuit-dependent key pk_{out}. The encoding of the form $\mathsf{pk}_{out} \cdot \mathbf{s} + \text{noise}$ is then used to recover the (symmetrically-)encrypted input X. We detail these procedures in what follows:

- $\mathsf{Setup}(1^\lambda)$: consists of ℓ pairs of public keys, where ℓ is the length of the supported attributes α: $\begin{pmatrix} \mathsf{mpk}_1^0 & \mathsf{mpk}_2^0 & \ldots & \mathsf{mpk}_\ell^0 \\ \mathsf{mpk}_1^1 & \mathsf{mpk}_2^1 & \ldots & \mathsf{mpk}_\ell^1 \end{pmatrix}$
  An additional key mpk_{out} is sampled. Concretely, each mpk_i^b corresponds to $\mathbf{A}_i^b \in \mathbb{Z}_q^{n \times m}$. The master secret key consists of $2 \cdot n$ trapdoor matrices, which are described in the TOR subsection (see below).
- $\mathsf{KeyGen}(\mathsf{msk}, \phi)$: considering the circuit representation of $\phi : \{0,1\}^n \to \{0,1\}$. Each wire in the circuit is associated with two public keys, corresponding to a 0 and a 1. For each gate $g_{u,v,w}$, a table consisting of 4 recoding keys are generated: $rk^w_{g(\alpha,\beta)}$ for $g^w_{\alpha,\beta}$ the value of the gate under inputs $\alpha, \beta \in \{0,1\}$. Based on the value of the gate applied on the inputs received from the attribute (which is known in plain) a recoding key is chosen. This recoding key is then used to recode the value of $\mathbf{s}$ under the new public key.
- $\mathsf{Enc}(\mathsf{mpk}, X, \alpha)$: encrypting X means sampling a random vector $\mathbf{s} \leftarrow\!\$\ \mathbb{F}_q^m$ and based on the decomposition of α, obtaining the encodings of $\mathbf{s}$ under $\mathsf{mpk}_i^{\alpha_i}$. Finally, the input X itself is encrypted – via a semantic secure symmetric scheme – under $\text{Encode}(\mathsf{mpk}_{out}, s)$, which acts as a key. Thus, the ciphertext consists of $\left(\alpha, \{\text{Encode}(\mathsf{mpk}_i^{\alpha_i} \cdot \mathbf{s} + e_i)\}_{i=1}^n, \mathsf{SE.Enc}(\text{Encode}(\mathsf{mpk}_{out}, s), X)\right)$.

- $\mathsf{Dec}(\mathsf{CT}, \mathsf{sk}_\phi)$: the decryption procedure evaluates the circuit given the encodings and according to the attributes, and recovers $\text{Encode}(\mathsf{pk}_{out}, s)$. This is then used to recover X.

Two-to-One Recodings. The beautiful idea in [19] stems in the Two-To-One Recoding mechanism. The crux point is to start with two LWE tuples of the form $\mathbf{A}_1 \cdot \mathbf{s} + \mathbf{e}_1$ and $\mathbf{A}_2 \cdot \mathbf{s} + \mathbf{e}_2$ and "recode" them under a new "target" matrix $\mathbf{A}_{tgt}$. The outcome is indeed a recoding of $\mathbf{s}$: $\mathbf{A}_{tgt} \cdot \mathbf{s} + \mathbf{e}_{tgt}$. In doing so, the recoding mechanism uses two matrices, $\mathbf{R}_1, \mathbf{R}_2$, such that $\mathbf{A}_1 \cdot \mathbf{R}_1 + \mathbf{A}_2 \cdot \mathbf{R}_2 = \mathbf{A}_{tgt}$.

Sampling $\mathbf{R}_1$ is done uniformly at random. $\mathbf{R}_2$ is sampled from an appropriate distribution, depending on a trapdoor matrix $\mathbf{T}$. We do not discuss the details of this scheme's correctness/security, as our interest is related to the efficiency of its encryption procedure.

Yao's Garbling Scheme [29]. Garbling schemes have been introduced by Yao [29]. A much appreciated way of garbling circuits is in fact the original proposal by Yao. He considers a family of circuits having k input wires and producing one bit. In this setting, circuit's secret key is regarded as two labels (L_i^0, L_i^1) for each input wire, where $i \in [k]$. The evaluation of the circuit at point x corresponds to an evaluation of $\mathsf{Eval}(\Gamma, (L_1^{x_1}, \dots, L_k^{x_k}))$, where x_i stands for the ith bit of x—thus the encoding $c = (L_1^{x_1}, \dots, L_k^{x_k})$. The garbled circuit Γ can be produced gate by gate, and the labels can be in fact symmetric keys.

B.2 Fully Homomorphic Encryption

Fully homomorphic encryption (FHE) has been described within the work of Rivest, Adleman and Dertouzos; it was an open problem until the breakthrough work of Gentry [14].

Instantiation of FHE using the GSW levelled FHE. For the sake of clarity we instantiate the FHE component used in [17] (see Fig. 3) using the GSW [15] fully homomorphic encryption scheme.

- $\mathsf{GSW.Setup}(1^\lambda, 1^d)$: Given the LWE parameters (q, n, χ), set $m := n \log(q)$. Let $N := (n+1) \cdot (\lfloor \log(q) \rfloor + 1)$. Sample $\mathbf{t} \leftarrow \mathbb{Z}_q^n$. Set $\mathsf{hsk} := \mathbf{s} \leftarrow (1, -\mathbf{t}_1, \dots, -\mathbf{t}_n) \in \mathbb{Z}_q^{n+1}$.
  Generate $\mathbf{B} \leftarrow_{\$} \mathbb{Z}_q^{m \times n}$ and $\mathbf{e_B} \leftarrow_{\chi} \chi^m$. Set $\mathbf{b} \leftarrow \mathbf{B} \cdot \mathbf{t} + \mathbf{e_B}$. Let $\mathbf{A}$ be defined as the $m \times (n+1)$ matrix having $\mathbf{B}$ in its last n columns, preceded by $\mathbf{b}$ as the first one. Set $\mathsf{hpk} \leftarrow \mathbf{A}$. Return $(\mathsf{hpk}, \mathsf{hsk})$.
- $\mathsf{GSW.Enc}(\mathsf{hpk}, \mu)$: to encrypt a bit μ, first sample $\mathbf{R} \leftarrow_{\$} \{0,1\}^{N \times m}$. Return as ciphertext: $\mathsf{CT} \leftarrow \mathsf{Flatten}\left(\mu \cdot \mathsf{I}_N + \mathsf{BitDecomp}(\mathbf{A} \cdot \mathbf{R})\right) \in \mathbb{Z}_q^{N \times N}$.
- $\mathsf{GSW.Dec}(\mathsf{CT}, \mathsf{hsk})$:
  Let $\mathbf{v} \leftarrow \mathsf{PowersOfTwo}(\mathbf{s})$. Find the index i such that $\mathbf{v}_i = 2^i \in (\frac{q}{4}; \frac{q}{2}]$. Compute $\mathbf{x}_i \leftarrow \mathsf{CT}_i \cdot \mathbf{v}$, with CT_i the ith row of CT. Return $\mu' \leftarrow \lfloor \frac{\mathbf{x}_i}{\mathbf{v}_i} \rceil$.

We do not discuss the circuit evaluation procedure, because it plays no role in FE's encryption procedure.

B.3 Parallel Complexity of [17]'s Encryption Procedure when Instantiated with GSW13 and GVW13

In this part, we provide an analysis of the parallel complexity of [17]'s encryption procedure when instantiated with GSW13 and GVW13. First, we look at the ciphertext structure in Fig. 3. It consists of two main types of elements: i) ABE ciphertexts and ii) a garbled circuit.

The ABE Ciphertext. We do not describe the two outcome ABE, but note it can be obtained generically from an ABE in the key-policy setting. The ciphertext structure is described above, and it consists itself of two parts:

1. **Index-Encodings:** According to our notations, α is an index. Based on the index's position α_i, one of the public key (matrices) is selected. Logically, this ciphertext component translates to:

$$\left(\mathbf{A}_i^0 \cdot \mathbf{s} + \mathbf{e}_i\right) + \alpha_i \cdot \left(\mathbf{A}_i^1 - \mathbf{A}_i^0\right) \cdot \mathbf{s} \tag{9}$$

   Here α_i is an index, but for [17], such indexes are generated through the hpk and the homomorphic ciphertext. Thus we complement Eq. (9) with two further subcases.
   - part of indexes will be the homomorphic public key, which consists of either i) the elements of $\mathbf{B}$ or ii) of a vector

$$\alpha_i \leftarrow (\mathbf{B} \cdot \mathbf{t} + \mathbf{e_B})_\theta \tag{10}$$

     where θ denotes a bit in the binary representation of the above quantity. When plugged in with Eq. (10), Eq. 9 becomes:

$$\left(\mathbf{A}_i^0 \cdot \mathbf{s} + \mathbf{e}_0\right) + (\mathbf{B} \cdot \mathbf{t} + \mathbf{e_B})_\theta \cdot \left(\mathbf{A}_i^1 - \mathbf{A}_i^0\right) \cdot \mathbf{s} \tag{11}$$

     The circuit to compute that quantity can be realized by several NC^1 circuits, the inner one outputting a bit in position θ, the outer one outputting one bit of ciphertext. As a consequence of [2], we assume that LWE-like tuples can be computed in NC^1. When plugged in with elements of $\mathbf{B}$ from case i), the equation is simpler, and we simply assume the circuit computing it has its depth lower than or equal to the previously mentioned circuit.
   - The second subcase is related to the usage of homomorphic ciphertexts as indexes for GVW13. The ciphertext of GSW13 has the following format:

$$\mathsf{Flatten}\left(\mathsf{inp}_\xi \cdot \mathsf{I}_N + \mathsf{BitDecomp}(\mathbf{A} \cdot \mathbf{R})\right) \tag{12}$$

     where inp_ξ is a real input for the FE schema and $\mathbf{R}$ is a random matrix. As for the previous case, a boolean circuit can compute Eq. (12) in logarithmic depth. The BitDecomp has essentially constant-depth, as it does rewiring. The matrix multiplication can be computed, element-wise in logarithmic depth (addition can be done in a tournament style, while element multiplication over $\mathbb{F}_q$ can also be performed in logarithmic time). The flattening part can be performed in $\log\log(q+1)+1$ [23].

Once Eq. (9) is fed with Eq. (12), the size of the circuit will still be logarithmic, as the outer circuit, computing the matrix sum can be highly parallelized.

2. **Label-Encodings:**
The second part of the GVW13 ciphertext is the encoding of the message itself. We analyse the format of these encodings, and also the message to be encoded (a label of a garbled circuit).
The encoding is done in two layers: first, a classical LWE tuple is obtained:

$$\mathbf{A}_{out} \cdot \mathbf{s} + \mathbf{e} \tag{13}$$

is obtained, which is then used to key a symmetric encryption scheme that will encode the input. We do not analyse the circuit depth of the SE, but we will assume it is in NC^1, and the Eq. (13) can be performed in NC^1, as we assume the existence of one-way functions in NC^1. Their composition is:

$$\mathsf{SE.Enc}((\mathbf{A}_{out} \cdot \mathbf{s} + \mathbf{e}), X) \tag{14}$$

Thus, the composition of these two families of circuits will be in NC^1, as long as obtaining X is in NC^1.
We turn to the problem of populating X. As we use Yao's garbling scheme, X will simply be itself a secret key of a symmetric scheme, used by a garbling table. Thus, generating X can be done by a low depth PRG in NC^1.

The Garbled Circuit. The final part of FE's ciphertext in [17] is the garbled circuit, which uses Yao's garbling. The garbled circuit can be obtained gate by gate. The circuit to be garbled is GSW13's decryption. This decryption procedure consists of an inner product, followed by a division with a predefined value (in fact a power of two), and by a rounding. The total circuit complexity is logarithmic (thus NC^1).

We now inspect the complexity of the circuit producing the garbling of the gates of FHE.Dec. It is clear that every gate garbling process can be parallelized: the structure of FHE's decryption circuit is fixed, enough labels must be sampled (by NC^1 circuits). For each wire in a gate, there must be one SE key generated. After that, producing one garbling table has the same depth as the encryption circuit together with the SE's key generation procedure. Given that these components are in NC^1, the complexity of the combined circuit is in NC^1.

References

1. Agrawal, S., Rosen, A.: Functional encryption for bounded collusions, revisited. In: Kalai, Y., Reyzin, L. (eds.) TCC 2017, Part I. LNCS, vol. 10677, pp. 173–205. Springer, Cham (2017). https://doi.org/10.1007/978-3-319-70500-2_7
2. Banerjee, A., Peikert, C., Rosen, A.: Pseudorandom functions and lattices. In: Pointcheval, D., Johansson, T. (eds.) EUROCRYPT 2012. LNCS, vol. 7237, pp. 719–737. Springer, Heidelberg (2012). https://doi.org/10.1007/978-3-642-29011-4_42

3. Barak, B., et al.: On the (im)possibility of obfuscating programs. In: Kilian, J. (ed.) CRYPTO 2001. LNCS, vol. 2139, pp. 1–18. Springer, Heidelberg (2001). https://doi.org/10.1007/3-540-44647-8_1
4. Barrington, D.A.: Bounded-width polynomial-size branching programs recognize exactly those languages in NC1. J. Comput. Syst. Sci. **38**(1), 150–164 (1989)
5. Barthel, J., Roşie, R.: NIKE from affine determinant programs. In: Huang, Q., Yu, Yu. (eds.) ProvSec 2021. LNCS, vol. 13059, pp. 98–115. Springer, Cham (2021). https://doi.org/10.1007/978-3-030-90402-9_6
6. Bartusek, J., Ishai, Y., Jain, A., Ma, F., Sahai, A., Zhandry, M.: Affine determinant programs: a framework for obfuscation and witness encryption. In: Vidick, T. (eds.) ITCS 2020, vol. 151, pp. 82:1–82:39. LIPIcs (2020)
7. Bollig, B.: Restricted nondeterministic read-once branching programs and an exponential lower bound for integer multiplication. RAIRO-Theor. Inf. Appl. **35**(2), 149–162 (2001)
8. Boneh, D., Kim, S., Montgomery, H.: Private puncturable PRFs from standard lattice assumptions. In: Coron, J.-S., Nielsen, J.B. (eds.) EUROCRYPT 2017, Part I. LNCS, vol. 10210, pp. 415–445. Springer, Cham (2017). https://doi.org/10.1007/978-3-319-56620-7_15
9. Boneh, D., Sahai, A., Waters, B.: Functional encryption: definitions and challenges. In: Ishai, Y. (ed.) TCC 2011. LNCS, vol. 6597, pp. 253–273. Springer, Heidelberg (2011). https://doi.org/10.1007/978-3-642-19571-6_16
10. Boneh, D., Zhandry, M.: Multiparty key exchange, efficient traitor tracing, and more from indistinguishability obfuscation. In: Garay, J.A., Gennaro, R. (eds.) CRYPTO 2014, Part I. LNCS, vol. 8616, pp. 480–499. Springer, Heidelberg (2014). https://doi.org/10.1007/978-3-662-44371-2_27
11. Brakerski, Z., Vaikuntanathan, V.: Constrained key-homomorphic PRFs from standard lattice assumptions. In: Dodis, Y., Nielsen, J.B. (eds.) TCC 2015, Part II. LNCS, vol. 9015, pp. 1–30. Springer, Heidelberg (2015). https://doi.org/10.1007/978-3-662-46497-7_1
12. Canetti, R., Chen, Y.: Constraint-hiding constrained PRFs for NC^1 from LWE. In: Coron, J.-S., Nielsen, J.B. (eds.) EUROCRYPT 2017, Part I. LNCS, vol. 10210, pp. 446–476. Springer, Cham (2017). https://doi.org/10.1007/978-3-319-56620-7_16
13. Garg, S., Gentry, C., Halevi, S.: Candidate multilinear maps from ideal lattices. In: Johansson, T., Nguyen, P.Q. (eds.) EUROCRYPT 2013. LNCS, vol. 7881, pp. 1–17. Springer, Heidelberg (2013). https://doi.org/10.1007/978-3-642-38348-9_1
14. Gentry, C.: Fully homomorphic encryption using ideal lattices. In: Mitzenmacher, M. (eds.) 41st ACM STOC, pp. 169–178. ACM Press (2009)
15. Gentry, C., Sahai, A., Waters, B.: Homomorphic encryption from learning with errors: conceptually-simpler, asymptotically-faster, attribute-based. In: Canetti, R., Garay, J.A. (eds.) CRYPTO 2013, Part I. LNCS, vol. 8042, pp. 75–92. Springer, Heidelberg (2013). https://doi.org/10.1007/978-3-642-40041-4_5
16. Goldwasser, S., et al.: Multi-input functional encryption. In: Nguyen, P.Q., Oswald, E. (eds.) EUROCRYPT 2014. LNCS, vol. 8441, pp. 578–602. Springer, Heidelberg (2014). https://doi.org/10.1007/978-3-642-55220-5_32
17. Goldwasser, S., Kalai, Y., Popa, R.A., Vaikuntanathan, V., Zeldovich, N.: Reusable garbled circuits and succinct functional encryption. In: Boneh, D., Roughgarden, T., Feigenbaum, J. (eds.) 45th ACM STOC, pp. 555–564. ACM Press (2013)
18. Goldwasser, S., Rothblum, G.N.: On best-possible obfuscation. In: Vadhan, S.P. (ed.) TCC 2007. LNCS, vol. 4392, pp. 194–213. Springer, Heidelberg (2007). https://doi.org/10.1007/978-3-540-70936-7_11

19. Gorbunov, S., Vaikuntanathan, V., Wee, H.: Attribute-based encryption for circuits. In: Boneh, D., Roughgarden, T., Feigenbaum, J. (eds.) 45th ACM STOC, pp. 545–554. ACM Press (2013)
20. Ishai, Y.: Secure computation and its diverse applications. In: Micciancio, D. (ed.) TCC 2010. LNCS, vol. 5978, pp. 90–90. Springer, Heidelberg (2010). https://doi.org/10.1007/978-3-642-11799-2_6
21. Ishai, Y., Kushilevitz, E.: Perfect constant-round secure computation via perfect randomizing polynomials. In: Widmayer, P., Eidenbenz, S., Triguero, F., Morales, R., Conejo, R., Hennessy, M. (eds.) ICALP 2002. LNCS, vol. 2380, pp. 244–256. Springer, Heidelberg (2002). https://doi.org/10.1007/3-540-45465-9_22
22. Jain, A., Lin, H., Sahai, A.: Indistinguishability obfuscation from well-founded assumptions. In: Khuller, S., Williams, V.V. (eds.) STOC 2021: 53rd Annual ACM SIGACT Symposium on Theory of Computing, Virtual Event, Italy, 21–25 June 2021, pp. 60–73. ACM (2021)
23. Jaques, S., Montgomery, H., Roy, A.: Time-release cryptography from minimal circuit assumptions. Cryptology ePrint Archive, Paper 2020/755 (2020). https://eprint.iacr.org/2020/755
24. Knuth, D.E.: The Art of Computer Programming, Volume 4, Fascicle 1: Bitwise Tricks and Techniques; Binary Decision Diagrams (2009)
25. Lin, H., Pass, R., Seth, K., Telang, S.: Indistinguishability obfuscation with non-trivial efficiency. In: Cheng, C.-M., Chung, K.-M., Persiano, G., Yang, B.-Y. (eds.) PKC 2016, Part II. LNCS, vol. 9615, pp. 447–462. Springer, Heidelberg (2016). https://doi.org/10.1007/978-3-662-49387-8_17
26. Regev, O.: On lattices, learning with errors, random linear codes, and cryptography. In: Gabow, H.N., Fagin, R. (eds.) 37th ACM STOC, pp. 84–93. ACM Press (2005)
27. Sahai, A., Waters, B.: How to use indistinguishability obfuscation: deniable encryption, and more. In: Shmoys, D.B. (ed.) 46th ACM STOC, pp. 475–484. ACM Press (2014)
28. Wegener, I.: Branching programs and binary decision diagrams: theory and applications. SIAM (2000)
29. Yao, A.C.-C.: How to generate and exchange secrets (extended abstract). In: 27th FOCS, pp. 162–167. IEEE Computer Society Press (1986)
30. Yao, L., Chen, Y., Yu, Y.: Cryptanalysis of candidate obfuscators for affine determinant programs. Cryptology ePrint Archive, Report 2021/1684 (2021). https://ia.cr/2021/1684

Correction to: Upper Bounds on the Number of Shuffles for Two-Helping-Card Multi-Input AND Protocols

Takuto Yoshida, Kodai Tanaka, Keisuke Nakabayashi, Eikoh Chida, and Takaaki Mizuki

Correction to:
Chapter 10 in: J. Deng et al. (Eds.): *Cryptology and Network Security*, LNCS 14342,
https://doi.org/10.1007/978-981-99-7563-1_10

In the original version there is a correction in the chapter title. "Multi-Input and Protocols" should be changed to "Multi-Input AND Protocols". This has been corrected.

The updated version of this chapter can be found at
https://doi.org/10.1007/978-981-99-7563-1_10

J. Deng et al. (Eds.): CANS 2023, LNCS 14342, p. C1, 2023.
https://doi.org/10.1007/978-981-99-7563-1_26

Author Index

J. Deng et al. (Eds.): CANS 2023, LNCS 14342, pp. 589–590, 2023.
https://doi.org/10.1007/978-981-99-7563-1

Printed in the United States
by Baker & Taylor Publisher Services